THOMAS PAKENHAM

The Scramble for Africa

1876–1912

ABACUS
History

An *Abacus* Book

First published in Great Britain in 1991 by
George Weidenfeld & Nicolson
This edition published in 1992 by Abacus
Reprinted 1992, 1993 (three times), 1994, 1995, 1996, 1997, 1998,
1999, 2001, 2002 (twice), 2003

A CIP catalogue record for this book
is available from the British Library.

ISBN 0 349 10449 2

Printed in England by Clays Ltd, St Ives plc

UK companies, institutions and other organisations wishing
to make bulk purchases of this or any other book
published by Time Warner should contact their local
bookshop or the special sales department at the address below.
Tel 020 7911 8000. Fax 020 7911 8100.

Abacus
An imprint of
Time Warner Books UK
Brettenham House
Lancaster Place
London WC2E 7EN

www.TimeWarnerBooks.co.uk

Contents

Illustrations

The pioneers relax after the Shona rebellion, July 1896 (From *Trooper Peter Halket of Mashonaland* by Olive Schreiner)

General Dabormida's Last Stand at Adowa, 1 March 1896 (*The Graphic: Mansell Collection*)

The wounded Dervish commander Mahmud during the Battle of Atbara, April 1898 (*Private collection*)

Marchand's black *tirailleurs* drive off the Dervish gunboats from Fashoda, August 1898 (*L'Illustration*)

Marchand rows across to confront Kitchener at Fashoda, 19 September 1898 (*Wingate Archive of Durham University*)

President Kruger and his advisers, 1899 (*Author's collection*)

The vanguard of Roberts's invasion force crossing the Zand River, 10 May 1900 (*F. Mackern. Author's collection*)

'Bulldog' Morel (*Anti-Slavery International*) and inset: Roger 'Tiger' Casement (*Kevin MacDonnell*)

Governor Leutwein and General von Trotha in Windhoek, July 1904 (From *South-West Africa under German Rule* by H. Bley)

The price of Congo rubber: severed hands (*Anti-Slavery International*) Hendrik Witbooi, killed in battle by the Germans (From *South-West Africa under German Rule* by H. Bley)

Cartoons and engravings

Maps

For Val

and in grateful memory of
Gervase Mathew and Asserate Kassa
who together introduced me to Africa

'All I can add in my solitude, is, may heaven's rich blessing come down on every one, American, English or Turk, who will help to heal this open sore of the world.'

David Livingstone's last words inlaid in brass on his tomb in Westminster Abbey

The
SCRAMBLE
for
AFRICA

Introduction

The Scramble for Africa bewildered everyone, from the humblest African peasant to the master statesmen of the age, Lord Salisbury and Prince Bismarck.

Ever since Roman times, Europe had been nibbling at the mysterious continent to the south. By the mid-1870s, much was still mysterious. It was known that Africa straddled the equator with uncanny precision. But no explorer had penetrated far along the dangerous latitude of zero towards the interior. No one knew which was Africa's greatest river or where it led. Europeans pictured most of the continent as 'vacant': legally *res nullius*, a no-man's-land. If there were states and rulers, they were African. If there were treasures they were buried in African soil. But beyond the trading posts on the coastal fringe, and strategically important colonies in Algeria and South Africa, Europe saw no reason to intervene.

Suddenly, in half a generation, the Scramble gave Europe virtually the whole continent: including thirty new colonies and protectorates, 10 million square miles of new territory and 110 million dazed new subjects, acquired by one method or another. Africa was sliced up like a cake, the pieces swallowed by five rival nations – Germany, Italy, Portugal, France and Britain (with Spain taking some scraps) – and Britain and France were at each other's throats. At the centre, exploiting the rivalry, stood one enigmatic individual and self-styled philanthropist, controlling the heart of the continent: Leopold II, King of the Belgians.

By the end of the century, the passions generated by the Scramble had helped to poison the political climate in Europe, brought Britain to the brink of a war with France, and precipitated a struggle with the Boers, the costliest, longest and bloodiest war since 1815 – and one of the most humiliating in British history. As for the pieces of the colonial cake, they have now become, ninety years later, for richer or for poorer (mainly for poorer) the forty-seven independent nations of Africa.

Why this undignified rush by the leaders of Europe to build empires in Africa? Anglo-French rivalry explains a great deal – but not enough. Historians are as puzzled now as the politicians were then. Scott Keltie wrote *The Partition of Africa* in 1893, before it reached its climax. He was sure that it was 'one of the most remarkable episodes in the history of the world', but confessed himself overwhelmed by the rush of 'jostling' events.

To these events historiography has added a pack of jostling theories. We have Eurocentric explanations, like John Hobson's (and later Lenin's) theory that surplus capital in Europe was the driving force behind expansion into Africa; Afrocentric explanations where the emphasis is placed on sub-imperialisms in

Africa itself; and combinations of the two, like the brilliant analysis of Professors Robinson and Gallagher, *Africa and the Victorians*. There are multi-volume histories of Africa like *The Cambridge History of Africa*, regional studies like John Hargreaves's studies of the partition of West Africa, and numerous specialist works dealing with the imperialisms of each individual European country. But there is no *general* explanation acceptable to historians – nor even agreement whether they should be expected to find one.

And, strange to say, no one since Scott Keltie has attempted to write a one-volume narrative of the Scramble, covering the whole continent and the race between all five European nations – and King Leopold.

In this book I have tried to fill this particular gap.

There are two strands in the story that I would like to emphasize, the motives and methods of the invaders.

In May 1873 David Livingstone, the celebrated missionary-explorer, died at Ilala, in the unknown heart of the continent, and his sun-dried body was brought home to be buried in Westminster Abbey. From his brass-plated tomb under the nave, Livingstone sounded a call for a worldwide crusade to open up Africa. A new slave trade, organized by Swahili and Arabs in East Africa, was eating out the heart of the continent. Livingstone's answer was the '3 CS': Commerce, Christianity and Civilization, a triple alliance of Mammon, God and social progress. Trade, not the gun, would liberate Africa.

The freelance promoters of the partition – the men who followed Livingstone out to Africa and scrambled greedily for their share – are now half-forgotten. In their day they were famous – and infamous – fêted as heroes, denounced as brutes or humbugs.

Each responded to Livingstone's call in his own fashion. But they all conceived of the crusade in terms of romantic nationalism. There were journalist-explorers like Henry Stanley, sailor-explorers like Pierre de Brazza, soldier-explorers like Frederick Lugard, pedagogue-explorers like Carl Peters, gold-and-diamond tycoons like Cecil Rhodes. Most of them were outsiders of one kind or another but no less ardent nationalists for that. To imperialism – a kind of 'race patriotism' – they brought a missionary zeal. Not only would they save Africa from itself. Africa would be the saving of their own countries.

At first European governments were reluctant to intervene. But to most people in their electorates, there seemed a real chance of missing something. Africa was a lottery and a winning ticket might earn glittering prizes.

There were dreams of El Dorado, of diamond mines and goldfields criss-crossing the Sahara. In Europe these were the drab years of the Great Depression and mounting stocks of unsold Manchester cotton, Lyons silk and Hamburg gin. Perhaps Africa was the answer to the merchants' prayers. There might be new markets out there in this African garden of Eden, and tropical groves where the golden fruit could be plucked by willing brown hands.

Or perhaps the lottery would pay best in terms of prestige. Overseas empire would soothe the *amour-propre* of the French army, humiliated by its collapse in the Franco-Prussian war. And it would no less bolster the pride of the political parvenus of Europe, Germany's Second Reich and a newly united Italy. Then there were the diplomatic advantages. Cards drawn in the jungle could be played out in the chancelleries of Europe. No harm for Bismarck to consolidate his own position by making mischief between France and Britain. And what about a place in the sun for emigrants – and a way to retain as citizens all those young sons of the Reich now taking the boat and vanishing without trace in America? Give it a whirl, the 'colonial whirl' (*Kolonialtummel*), in Bismarck's sardonic phrase.

In Britain, the Scramble was taken calmly – at first. Then there was growing resentment towards the intruders. Britain had pioneered the exploration and evangelization of Central Africa, and she felt a proprietary right to most of the continent. Besides, there was a vital interest at stake for Britain. As the only great maritime Empire, she needed to prevent her rivals obstructing the steamer routes to the East, via Suez and the Cape. That meant digging in at both ends of Africa.

And it was in Protestant Britain, where God and Mammon seemed made for each other, that Livingstone's words struck the deepest chord. The '3 cs' would redeem Africa.

That was not the way Africans perceived the Scramble. There was a fourth 'c' – conquest – and it gradually predominated. At first European expeditions were too weak to challenge African rulers. It was safer to use blank treaty forms, explained away by an empire-minded missionary, than to use live ammunition.

But paper imperialism soon proved inadequate. When effective occupation became necessary to establish a good title, conflict became inevitable. The African rulers best equipped to resist were understandably those who depended on violence themselves: African imperialists like King Cetshwayo of the Zulu, King Lobengula of the Ndebele, the Emperor Menelik of Abyssinia, the Mahdi in the Sudan, and Africa's twin white tribes, the Boers of the Transvaal and Boers of the Orange Free State.

Soon the Maxim gun – not trade or the cross – became the symbol of the age in Africa (though in practice the wretched thing jammed, and the magazine rifle did the job better). Most of the battles were cruelly one-sided (but not for the British against the Boers, or for the Italians against the Abyssinians). At Omdurman, British officers counted 10,000 Sudanese dead or dying in the sand. They made no effort to help the 15,000 wounded.

Atrocities were commonplace during the first phase of occupation by the Powers. When German brutality in South West Africa provoked a revolt by the Hereros, the German general, Lothar von Trotha, issued a *Vernichtungbefehl* ('extermination order') against the whole tribe, women and children included. About 20,000 of them were driven away from the wells to die in the Omaheke desert.

Europe had imposed its will on Africa at the point of a gun. It was a lesson that would be remembered, fifty years later, when Africa came to win its independence.

*　　*　　*

It is a pleasure to acknowledge the help I have received from numerous people in Britain, Europe and Africa, during the ten years I have spent working on this book.

I owe a deep debt to the following who have read all or part of the typescript, and given me advice and encouragement: Robin Denniston, Mark Girouard, Victoria Glendinning, John Hargreaves, Jeff Guy, Neil Parsons, Kenneth Rose, Anthony Sampson, Donald Simpson, and my mother, Elizabeth Longford.

Andrew Roberts was a mine of useful information.

I should like to record my thanks to Barbara Emerson for lending me some rare photo-copies, and to Bryan Maggs for letting me copy photographs from his collection.

Through the generosity of Raymond Carr and the Fellows of St Antony's I was given facilities at the college, for which I am most grateful.

I should like to thank the staff of the following institutions who have helped me in numerous ways. In these islands: Trinity College, Dublin, the National Library of Ireland, the National Library of Scotland, Rhodes House, the British Library, the London Library, the National Army Museum, the Public Record Office, the Royal Commonwealth Society, the Royal Geographical Society and the School of Oriental and African Studies. In Belgium: the Congo Museum, Tervuren and the Royal Archives in Brussels. In France: Archives Nationales, Section d'Outre-mer. In Africa: the libraries of the universities at Cape Town, Dar-es-Salaam, Ibadan, Nairobi and Kampala.

In the course of my research I visited twenty-two out of the forty-seven independent countries of Africa. To the following, under whose hospitable roofs I sheltered in Africa, I owe an especial debt: Jim and Barbara Bailey, Aelda and John Callinikos, Alexander and Sheila Camerer, Ewan and Sara Fergusson, John and Jean Johnson, John Laband, John and Elizabeth Leahy, April and Ian Percy, Mary-Anne and Tim Sheehy, Dick and Marina Viets, Frank and Christine Wisner.

Timothy and Patricia Daunt gave me inexhaustible hospitality in Europe and Turkey, and were, once again, an inspiration for my work.

Antonia and Harold Pinter gave me sanctuary in Corfu; and so did Jennie and Christopher Bland in the Dordogne, and Linda and Laurence Kelly in Cumbria.

I must thank two long-suffering friends, Heather Laughton and Janet Barton, for their amazing skill with word processors and typewriters; Dorothy Girouard performed wonders designing the lay-out. To Kevin MacDonnell once again I owe some splendid photographs and I should like to thank Richard Natkiel for his inexhaustible patience in drawing the maps.

Once again I owe an immense debt to my publishers, in London and New York, especially to Christopher and Gila Falkus, Amanda Harting and George Weidenfeld of Weidenfeld & Nicolson and Joe Fox of Random House.

Finally, I should like to thank my wife Valerie for sharing my ten-year trip down the rapids, modelling herself on Katharine Hepburn in *The African Queen*.

Note:
The term 'The Scramble for Africa' was apparently coined in 1884. Modern historians have not agreed exactly what period it should cover. I have used it to embrace the whole final hectic phase of the partition, beginning with a prelude in 1876 and ending in 1912.

PROLOGUE

The Crowning Achievement

Ilala, Central Africa
21 April–May 1873 and after

'I beg to direct your attention to Africa; I know that
in a few years I shall be cut off in that country, which
is now open: Do not let it be shut again! I go back
to Africa to try to make an open path for commerce
and Christianity; do you carry out the work which
I have begun. *I leave it with you!*'

David Livingstone,
Cambridge University address,
5 December 1857

At first no one, least of all Livingstone himself, realized he was dying. He
had been at death's door so often during the years of wandering with
Chuma, Susi and his other devoted African followers, many of whom were freed
slaves. Once, during a long tramp west of Lake Tanganyika, he had fallen ill
with pneumonia and had been carried for days in a litter, coughing and spitting
blood and only half-conscious, till they reached the lake where he was given
Arab medicine and nursed back to health by a party of Swahili traders who
befriended him.

But this week at the end of April 1873, in the great marsh to the south of
Lake Bangweolo, unable to eat, almost blind, and so faint he fell from his
donkey, Livingstone still kept the caravan turned westwards towards the head
waters of the rivers Lualaba and Luapula. It was there, close by, he was sure,
perhaps only a few miles away beyond these swamps, the glittering prize which
had baffled geographers and eluded 'Emperors, Kings and philosophers'[1] ever
since the time of Herodotus. It was the last great geographical mystery in Africa.
To solve it would be the crowning achievement of his life. He was searching
for the ancient 'fountains'[2] of Herodotus in which the Nile took its source.

Twenty years of tramping across Africa had made Livingstone the best-known
explorer alive. He was more: he was a missionary and philanthropist. Some
people called him a saint. His geographical discoveries – Lake Ngami in 1849,
the Victoria Falls in 1855, the central Zambezi valley leading across the continent
in 1853–6, Lake Nyasa in 1859, the river Lualaba in 1871 – his own discoveries
delighted and appalled him. For among the giant lakes and waterfalls, the
teeming populations where geographers had supposed all was desert, in that
Arcadia he had found the heart of darkness, a new outburst of the slave trade.
He called it the 'open sore of the world', and he believed he could find the

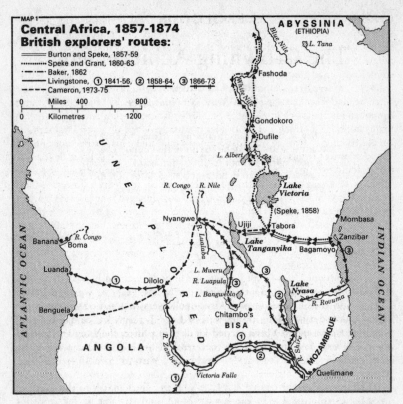

MAP 1
Central Africa, 1857-1874
British explorers' routes:
═══ Burton and Speke, 1857-59
········· Speke and Grant, 1860-63
·—·—· Baker, 1862
——— Livingstone, ① 1841-56, ② 1858-64, ③ 1866-73
– – – Cameron, 1873-75

| 0 | Miles | 400 | | 800 |
| 0 | Kilometres | | 1200 | |

ABYSSINIA
(ETHIOPIA)
Blue Nile
L. Tana
White Nile
Fashoda
Gondokoro
Dufile
L. Albert
R. Congo R. Nile
? ?
Nyangwe
R. Lualaba
Lake Victoria
(Speke, 1858)
Ujiji Tabora Mombasa
Lake Tanganyika Zanzibar
Bagamoyo
R. Congo
Banana Boma
Luanda
Dilolo L. Mweru
R. Luapula
L. Bangweolo
Chitambo's
BISA
Lake Nyasa
R. Rovuma
Benguela
ANGOLA
R. Zambezi
Victoria Falls
R. Shire
MOZAMBIQUE
Quelimane
ATLANTIC OCEAN
INDIAN OCEAN
UNEXPLORED

means to heal it by making an 'open path' from civilization. The Nile, bringing trade and Christianity 3,000 miles from the Mediterranean to the heart of Africa, would be the path – if only he could find it.

Perhaps Livingstone was grateful, during those wretched last days in the marsh, that he met no slave caravans, necks tied into wooden slave-sticks to prevent escape. He found the sight sickening. Yet often in the past slave caravans, flying the blood-red flag of the Sultan of Zanzibar, had brought relief for Livingstone: hot food and Arab medicine from the Swahili traders who owned the slaves. One bright sultry day in 1871, two years before, Livingstone had reached Nyangwe, a market town on the great river Lualaba when he was travelling under the protection of a Swahili called Dugumbe. Without warning, Dugumbe's men started firing volleys from their blunderbusses into the marketplace. Women screamed, trapped in the creek. Canoes were upset. Hundreds died, shot down or drowned by the current of the river, nearly a mile wide at Nyangwe. All along the river bank the Swahili set fire to the villages, shouting, laughing and beating their drums, and sending out canoes to catch slaves.

Livingstone counted the smoke rising in pillars from seventeen villages. He stood there aghast, not daring to use his own pistol on the murderers. It was like a day in hell, he said, that bright sultry day at Nyangwe, like 'the bottomless pit'.[3] He had still needed to beg the favours of those 'bloodhounds', to beg for enough cloth and gunpowder to continue his journey back to Lake Tanganyika.

In November 1871, a month after his return to Ujiji, his headquarters on the lake, he had been resupplied – 'found', if you like – by that brash young American journalist, Henry Morton Stanley, working for the *New York Herald*. Livingstone felt nothing but gratitude. It was the work of a good Samaritan. An old friend had warned him that Stanley would make his fortune out of him. 'If so,' replied Livingstone, 'he is heartily welcome, for it is a great deal more than I could ever make out of myself.'[4] Stanley's scoop was the answer to the rumours of Livingstone's death, spread by some of his own followers – men from Johanna in the Comoro Islands – who had deserted him in 1866. Stanley had brought Livingstone everything he needed and more: bales of cloth, boxes of beads, tin baths, huge kettles, cooking pots, medicines, ammunition, extra porters and, all important, letters from home. The two friends had finally parted more than a year before – in March 1872 – and no new supplies had reached Livingstone since August.

Now on 21 April, when Livingstone fell from his donkey, Chuma threw down his gun and ran forward to stop the caravan. They took him to a hut and built a *kitanda*, a litter made from a frame of wood, padded with grass and a blanket, and slung from a pole, with a second blanket to protect the Doctor from the sun. For several days they carried him, starting as soon as the dew was off the long grass and building a hut for him each night. Most of the villagers, terrified by slave raiders, fled at their approach. In one village, Livingstone, lying in the shade of the *kitanda,* managed to find a man to question about the source of the Nile – the fountains of Herodotus.

Did he know about a hill with four 'fountains' in which four rivers took their rise, two flowing north and two south?[5] No, said the man, we are not travellers here. And traders from Bisa who used to meet in Malenga's town had been swept off by the Mazitu (Ngoni), raiding for slaves; the survivors lived in the marshes.

Next day, at Kalunganjovu's town, the Chief himself, dressed like an Arab and wearing a red fez, met the *kitanda*. He presented them with a kid and three baskets of groundnuts. The caravan was paddled across a small river in dugout canoes belonging to the Chief. Livingstone was bleeding internally and could hardly speak for the pain in his back. Chuma gently lifted him into the largest canoe. The last hour's journey brought them to Chitambo's village, after splashing through marshes thick with papyrus and lotus plants, and through gaunt miambo woods, flooded by the river.

Only a few days before, Livingstone had been able to make light of these cheerless surroundings. 'A lion had wandered into this world of water,' he wrote in his diary, 'and roared night and morning as though very much disgusted: we could sympathize with him!'[6]

But now he was drowsy with the pain. They built him a large hut and filled it with the bales and boxes: bales of gaudy Mericani (American cloth), boxes of blue and red Venetian beads to exchange for food, and his own precious possessions – the damaged sextant and chronometer, the rifle for shooting game, the Bible and the rest – which had survived the last six years' wandering. One box they made into a table and on it they put the medicine chest. Livingstone's metal-backed notebook, for recording the day's log, remained unopened in a tin box. 'Nothing earthly will make me give up my work in despair,' he had written in the log on 25 March. 'I encourage myself in the Lord my God, and go forward.' He scrawled the final entry on Sunday, 27 April, when he could hardly see. 'Knocked up quite, and remain – recover – sent to buy milch goats. We are on the banks of R. Molilamo.'[7] Even now he did not think of turning back – or indeed of his approaching death.

That last day, 30 April, Chitambo paid him a courtesy call, but the Doctor asked him to come back next day, when he hoped to have more strength. He drifted into sleep. About 11 p.m. Susi was told to come to the hut. There were loud shouts in the distance. Susi heard the Doctor ask faintly, 'Are our men making that noise?' 'No,' replied Susi, 'the people are scaring away a buffalo from their *dura* [sorghum] fields.' Livingstone's mind wandered. 'Is this the Luapula?' Susi told him they were at Chitambo's. Then Livingstone, speaking this time in Swahili, asked:

> 'Siku ngapi kuenda Luapula'
> 'Na zani ziku tatu, Bwana'
> ('How many days is it to the Luapula?'
> 'I think it is three days, Master.')

Livingstone half sighed as if in great pain and then half sighed, half said, 'Oh dear, dear.'

An hour later Susi was called again to the hut. '*Bwana* wants you, Susi.' The Doctor told him to boil some water. Susi brought back the copper kettle full. Then he carried the medicine chest to the bed and held up the candle. With great difficulty the Doctor selected a bottle of calomel. 'All right. You can go out now.'

Before dawn Susi heard Majwara, the boy who slept at the door of the hut, call out, 'Come to *Bwana*, I'm afraid.'[8] The two men and other servants including Chuma and Matthew Wellington went to the hut. A candle was stuck by its own wax to the top of the box. Dr Livingstone was kneeling by the side of the bed, apparently in prayer, his body stretched forward, his head buried in his hands on the pillow. For a minute they watched him. He did not stir. Then Matthew went forward softly and put his hands to Livingstone's cheeks. His body was almost cold.

They covered him, and went out and sat by the fire. There was no moon. In a short time the cock crew.

*   *   *

Livingstone's lonely death might have been the crowning tragedy of his disastrous last expedition. But his last journey was not yet over – indeed, what became his most famous journey was only beginning. Susi and Chuma, who now found themselves in charge of the caravan, called the men together. There were about fifty, besides women and children. They were on their own, 1,500 miles from their homes in Zanzibar, at the unknown centre of the continent, lost in a wild country of warring tribes and slave raiders.

Chuma urged them not to bury the body, but to carry it back to Zanzibar. But they would have to conceal the plan from Chitambo. For, as they all knew, the local people would regard the death of a stranger with superstitious fear and the caravan would be asked to pay a crippling *hongo* (toll) which would mean their stock of trade goods would be exhausted long before they were safely home. How else could they show the Doctor's friends that he was really dead, that they had not, like the Johanna men six years earlier, deserted him? All the men agreed on this extraordinary plan, although they knew the safest course would be to bury the body secretly.

After the meeting Chuma went to Chitambo with a present of beads and cloth.

'Our master very sick. He does not like this old-smelling town and the rats. He wants [a hut] built outside.'

'I came yesterday but I could not see him. Can I see him today?'

'No. We shall cover him up in a cloth.'

'All right, let me know when I can see him, that I can tell my people to bring fowls to sell him.'[9]

Then he showed Chuma the place to build the new huts. It was nearby under the shade of a tall mvula tree. The men went off to chop wood.

Meanwhile, one of the Zanzibar men went back to Chitambo's to buy supplies and told the Chief that the Doctor was dead. Chitambo sent for Chuma.

'How can you hide his death? Do you think we want to eat him? Show me the man.'

'I cannot show him.'[10]

'Do not fear any longer. I too have travelled, and more than once have been to Bwani [the coast] before the country was destroyed by the Mazitu. I know that you have no bad motives in coming, and death often happens to travellers.'[11]

Next day Susi went to the Chief and admitted the truth. Chitambo said, 'All right. Now all my people shall mourn.'[12] He came, dressed in a broad red cloth and a cotton skirt, with his wives and his men who carried bows and arrows and spears. For two hours there was drumming and wailing, and Livingstone's men fired volley after volley from their guns over the body.

To prepare the corpse for the journey Susi and Chuma built a special hut without a roof. Then Farjala, who had been a doctor's servant at Zanzibar and seen him open up a body to find the cause of death, made a small cut in the chest. While the other servants screened the body, Farjala drew out the heart and intestines. These were buried in a tin box, twenty-five yards from the tall mvula tree, while Jacob Wainwright (one of the young African slaves liberated in India and taken to Nasik, near Bombay, to be educated by missionaries) read the burial service from Livingstone's prayer book. Then they covered his face with a cloth, rubbed the body inside and out with salt which they had bought in exchange for some beads, and anointed the mouth and parts of the hair with brandy from the medicine chest. Each day, for a fortnight, the poor emaciated corpse was exposed to the sun, and at night they lit a candle and sat watching to protect it from the hyenas. Each day Chitambo came to visit them. 'Why not bury him?' he asked. 'Oh no, very big man. Cannot bury him here.'[13]

At last the corpse was more or less cured. They wrapped it in a skin and, as they had no tools to make a coffin of planks, enclosed it in a cylinder of bark taken in one piece from a myonga tree. This was in turn wrapped in sailcloth, and the whole package was then fastened to a pole and painted with the tar intended for Livingstone's boat.

Before leaving Chitambo's, they put up a small memorial, in the shape of a couple of well-tarred wooden posts, and an inscription, cut by Jacob Wainwright, breast-high on the tall mvula tree, giving the date of Livingstone's death, '4 May' (they had miscounted the days; it was 1 May). They asked Chitambo to see that the ground was kept free of grass or else the mvula tree would be burnt in a bush fire. Then they gave the Chief a biscuit box and some newspapers, to prove to future travellers that a white man had passed there. Chitambo replied, 'But if the English come, let them come soon. For I fear that the Mazitu [Ngoni slave raiders] may come and then – if we have to leave this place – someone may cut the tree down for a canoe.'[14]

Five months later, in September 1873 at Tabora in the district of Unyanyembe, a letter in English was brought to the tent of the British officer, Lieutenant Verney Cameron, leading the latest search party sent out by the Royal Geographical Society from London. The letter was carried by Chuma and signed 'Jacob Wainwright, Dr. Livingstone Exped'. The caravan had heard reports that the search party had reached Tabora, led by Livingstone's son. (In fact, his son, Oswell, had returned to England and his nephew, Robert Moffat, had died of fever.) Jacob wrote, 'Your father died by disease beyond the country of Bisa, but we have carried the corpse with us, ten of our soldiers are lost and some have died. Our hunger presses us to ask you some clothes [cloth] to buy provisions.'[15]

At first Cameron could not grasp what the letter meant. Cameron himself had troubles enough. He was half-blind and one of his two English companions, Dr Dillon, was so deranged by fever that he blew out his brains a few weeks later. But Chuma was sent the supplies. A few days later the Doctor's body was carried into Tabora. Cameron tried to persuade the Africans to bury their master then and there. After all, Livingstone's wife had been buried where she

6

died, on the banks of the Zambezi. And Livingstone himself – though no one yet knew this – had written in his diary, in June 1868, that he should like to be buried in the 'still, still forest, with no hand ever to disturb my bones'. But Chuma, Susi and the others had set their hearts on carrying Livingstone home. So Cameron took some of Livingstone's navigational instruments for his own needs, including the damaged chronometer, and continued on his journey of exploration westwards. The cortège, joined by two of Cameron's companions, tramped on towards Bagamoyo and the sea.

On the first night a subterfuge was adopted. The corpse was repacked to look like an ordinary bale of cloth. Then a counterfeit corpse, made up of old grass, was carried back to Tabora and disposed of in a wood.

In April 1874, eleven months after his death, Livingstone's body finally reached England, to receive a hero's funeral in Westminster Abbey. From Zanzibar the body had arrived on a British ship, accompanied by Jacob Wainwright. It was Jacob, the humble African servant, who was given the place of honour as a pallbearer, alongside Stanley, Dr John Kirk, and Livingstone's other close friends and relations. In May, Chuma and Susi were brought over to England at the expense of the London Missionary Society. By then the British public had come to appreciate the astonishing character of what had occurred. Nothing about Africa had ever touched their imagination quite like this. The story illustrated not only Livingstone's extraordinary moral power. It showed that Africans too could display initiative and leadership. Black Africa had stretched out a hand to Britain. The response, it was agreed, must be swift and generous.

Only one man was missing from the triumphant funeral: twenty-eight-year-old Lieutenant Cameron, the man who had refitted the cortège at Tabora. After he had left his official task – to help rescue Livingstone – in the capable hands of Susi and Chuma, he had struck off on his own, hundreds of miles to the west, to try to finish Livingstone's final mission, exploring the mysterious river Lualaba.

On 2 November 1875, a year and a half after the funeral in Westminster Abbey, Cameron staggered down to a sandy beach near Benguela on the coast of Angola. He had failed to follow the Lualaba to the sea. Yet he was the first European ever to cross south Central Africa from east to west. And – even if he could not prove it yet – he believed he knew the answer to the last great mystery of African geography.

What he had discovered would have been a crushing blow to Livingstone. For all the evidence showed that the Lualaba *was* the Congo, not the Nile. Yet Cameron believed that this unknown source of the Congo was in fact the greatest of all Livingstone's discoveries. Four times the size of the Nile, when still 1,000 miles from the sea, the Congo would serve, far better than the Nile, as the open path to bring commerce and Christianity into the heart of Africa.

7

PART ONE
THE OPEN PATH

THE LION AND THE FOX.

BRITISH LION. "GOING TO HELP ME, ARE YOU? THANK YOU FOR NOTHING, MASTER FOX. I BEGAN THE WORK ALONE, AND I MEAN TO FINISH IT!!!"

CHAPTER 1

Leopold's Crusade

Brussels
7 January–15 September 1876

'The current is with us.'

Leopold II, King of the Belgians, at the Geographical
Conference in Brussels, 12 September 1876

'He [King Leopold] first explained his views to me
when I was his guest in Brussels some years ago ...
his designs are most philanthropic and are amongst
the few schemes of the kind ... free from any selfish
commercial or political object.'

Sir Bartle Frere, 1883

The Times was delivered at the palace of Laeken on 7 January 1876, as usual, in time for His Majesty's breakfast. Leopold II had been up since five. Normally he took a walk through the palace gardens, a tall bearded figure, tramping along the gravelled paths with a barely noticeable limp, or, if it was wet, inspecting the hothouses. He read *The Times* each day. It was the early edition, the one that caught the night mails to the Continent. His own copy was packed in a special cylindrical container, hurried by the South-Eastern Railway from Blackfriars to Dover, then by the steam ferry to Ostend, then thrown from the guard's van as the Brussels express clanged past the royal palace at Laeken where a footman was waiting to retrieve it. Leopold read the paper with the same earnestness he displayed when performing other royal tasks, brushing the front of his blue tunic with his right hand when something caught his eye.

That morning, 7 January, tucked away at the bottom of page six, was a brief note from *The Times*'s correspondent in Loanda, capital of the half-derelict Portuguese colony of Angola, dated nearly seven weeks earlier. Lieutenant Cameron, the British explorer, had reached the west coast after a three-year journey across Africa. He was too ill (half-dead from scurvy) to return to England before the spring. Meanwhile, he was sending some notes from his travels to be read at a meeting of the Royal Geographical Society on Monday next.

Four days later, under the heading 'African Exploration', *The Times* splashed Monday's meeting of the RGS across the first three columns of the home news page. The President, Sir Henry Rawlinson, called Cameron's journey 'one of the most arduous and successful journeys which have ever been performed into the interior of the African continent'. That seemed no exaggeration to those who read Cameron's own letters, given to the public at the meeting. Of course

Cameron was the first to point out there might be 'diplomatic difficulties' ahead, although no European power yet claimed the land either as a colony or a protectorate. This was because of the huge wealth at stake.

> The interior is mostly a magnificent and healthy country of unspeakable richness. I have a small specimen of good coal; other minerals such as gold, copper, iron and silver are abundant, and I am confident that with a wise and liberal (not lavish) expenditure of capital, one of the greatest systems of inland navigation in the world might be utilized, and from 30 months to 36 months begin to repay any enterprising capitalist that might take the matter in hand ...[1]

A country of 'unspeakable richness' waiting for an 'enterprising capitalist'. What were Leopold's own views about young Cameron and his sensational discoveries? Cameron's story certainly caught his eye. Within a few days he had promised the RGS that he would pay, if needed, the princely sum of 100,000 francs (£4,000) to cover the expenses Cameron had incurred on the journey.

In public, however, Leopold showed no flicker of interest. In the Senate he would stand like a Roman emperor, tall, bearded, his nose like the prow of a trireme. In his slow booming voice, he spoke the required generalities. He had learnt the craft of monarchy in a hard school. His father, Leopold I, was the son of an impoverished German princeling, the Duke of Saxe-Coburg-Gotha. He had had his eye on the good solid throne of England where he would have been consort, through his marriage to Princess Charlotte, George IV's heir presumptive. Charlotte had died in childbirth in 1817. In 1831 Leopold I had picked up a throne in Belgium – but a throne perched on a tightrope. Inside Belgium were two warring peoples, Flemish and Walloon, and two warring sects, Liberals and Catholics. Outside Belgium, hemming it in, were two warring Powers, France and Germany. The King of the Belgians was thus doubly vulnerable. His own survival depended on the goodwill of a bitterly divided people. Belgium's survival depended on the goodwill of two greedy neighbours. To preserve both throne and nation, the King must remain aloof from controversy. Aloofness seemed to come naturally to Leopold II. He seemed to have a natural coolness of heart – or at any rate a temperament chilled by the rebuffs of fortune. His father, Queen Victoria's 'dearest uncle', had shown scant affection for any of his three children. He found Leo gauche and self-willed. Leopold's gentle mother Louise, daughter of Louis-Philippe of France, was devoted to her children, though it was clear Leopold was not her favourite. She had died when Leopold was twelve. And his own son, on whom he doted, died tragically young, leaving Leopold without a direct male heir. At the funeral the King had, for once, lost control. To the alarm of onlookers, he broke down and sobbed aloud by the coffin.

Still, since his accession in 1865, he had hardly put a foot wrong in public. If he was known at all in the world outside Belgium it was as a model, if somewhat pedestrian, ruler. He was admirably free from those delusions of grandeur that so often seemed to fill the crowned heads of petty states.

To his own staff and the handful of politicians who dealt with him regularly, Leopold presented a more complicated character. No courtier could be more bland and charming than the King himself – when he chose. But on some subjects he was alarmingly obstinate – hardly rational, it seemed. He was haunted by the dream of carving out some piece of the unexplored world as an overseas empire for Belgium. '*Il faut à la Belgique une colonie*'[2] he had inscribed in 1861 on a paperweight made from a fragment of marble taken from the Parthenon, and pointedly presented, when he was heir apparent, to the then Minister of Finance, a well-known opponent of colonialism. He seemed obsessed by what he called the 'lesson of history'. It was colonies that gave modern states 'power and prosperity'. He cited examples from the Far East. A tropical colony of exploitation, such as the Dutch colony of Java, would pay hand over fist. It would also prove to the people of Belgium – '*petit pays, petits gens*' – that they were, despite themselves, an 'imperial people capable of dominating and civilizing others'.

At first, passionate words like these, spoken by Leopold, were not taken too seriously. His *chef du cabinet*, Jules Devaux, tried to laugh the matter off. These were the years when free trade was an article of faith for Belgium as well as Britain. Years before, his father, Leopold I, had toyed with the same idiotic idea: a royal colony. There was a hare-brained plan for investment at St Thomas de Guatemala. Some of the settlers died of fever and the old King had got his fingers burnt. The main promoter died in prison, a bankrupt, and his widow proved indiscreet. For the future, Leopold I had stayed out of colonial adventures and he, too, mocked his son's dreams of an empire in the East. It was one of Leo's '*enfantillages*', a childish fantasy, he told his secretary. The poor boy had spirit, certainly. But he had a lot to learn. He offended people by talking too much and asking too many tiresome questions. His taste for foreign travel amounted to a mania. He was supposed to have weak lungs and a lame leg. Under the pretext of a health cruise, Leo would set sail for months to the fever-ridden parts of the East. In 1854–5 he visited Egypt and the Near East; Egypt again in 1860, and again in 1862 when he showed his fascination with Lesseps's great plan to cut a canal through the isthmus of Suez. In 1864–5 he set off for India and China. '*Quel rage de voyager*,' grumbled the Belgian Ambassador at Rome. 'I'm beginning to think that our dear prince makes himself deliberately ill so that he can have an excuse to be off.' He added that the Belgians were 'displeased' with these endless tropical jaunts.[3] People noticed that the limp left Leo the moment he left Brussels. Why couldn't he endure the cold climate like everyone else?

After his father's death in 1865, Leopold II obstinately clung to the idea that they must be '*à l'affût*' ('on the lookout') for a colony. He claimed he owed it to his father's memory. In vain his advisers reminded him that his own government could have nothing to do with the scheme, as the Belgians were a business people, and colonies of exploitation and settlement – especially new ones in the tropics – were considered bad business. The King replied that he could afford the expense himself. In fact he was one of Europe's richest men, as he had inherited 15 million francs (£600,000) from his parents, which he soon increased by gambling with Suez Canal shares. He could afford it and he would rope in some bankers to form a financial syndicate. He asked an emissary to sound the Spanish Ambassador. The Spanish were said to be embarrassed for funds. Would they be interested in leasing the Philippines, at present run at a deficit? His syndicate would pay 10 million francs, half of it cash down, if they could exploit the islands. Inexplicably – so Leopold said – the Spanish were too proud even to discuss these overtures. The Spanish Ambassador explained that no minister could put such an offer to Parliament, no Parliament even discuss it; 'as for the Spanish King, if he took it up, it would be abdication, suicide ...' Equally irrationally, according to Leopold, the Portuguese government could not be induced to part with Angola or Mozambique, or with the island of Timor. Then his eye turned to the British.

In July 1875 he summoned the British Ambassador, Saville Lumley, to Brussels and disclosed his hand in a new project. Lumley, according to his own report to London, was somewhat shaken.

> What my country needs [the King began] is a safety valve for her surplus energies. Now the late King believed no better answer would be found than by establishing a Belgian colony – not only to develop our country's commercial interests, but to raise the morale of the army and create the merchant navy which we lack ...
>
> It's time [the King went on] that she [Belgium] takes her part in the great work of civilization, following in the footsteps, however modestly, of England ...
>
> I'm happy to offer my country a colony, covering the cost of establishment from my own private resources.
>
> The problem of where to site the colony is extremely difficult, but after reflection I believe that a site could be found in the island of New Guinea which is placed between Japan and Australia on a great commercial highway of the future ...
>
> I must confess my ignorance [replied Lumley] but I would be afraid that its climate might not favour Belgian colonists.
>
> Ah [said the King] I know my people are not as hardy and energetic as the English, but I think this great island ... [is] blessed in its fertility and nothing can exceed its beauty and the luxuriance of its vegetation.

Then explaining that the Belgian government had no part in the scheme at present, he solemnly put the question to Lumley, 'Does Her Majesty's government have any intentions with regard to this island? If so, I shall direct my search for a colony elsewhere.'[4]

In London Queen Victoria's ministers received the report of Leopold's solemn question and tapped their heads. The *Pall Mall Gazette* had recently described New Guinea as 'almost unexplored ... estimated to contain five million natives ... in the main ferocious cannibals'. How on earth, asked Lord Derby, the Foreign Secretary, were Belgian settlers to bring up their families among these people?' 'I cannot conceive any course of action with the prospect of so many drawbacks and offering so little in return.' He ridiculed Leopold's claim that an overseas colony would provide a safety valve for Belgium, diverting her people from their religious feuds. Besides, there would be diplomatic repercussions if they let Leopold try to colonize New Guinea. 'The Australian colonies have got it into their heads that New Guinea is a part of Australia. They mean to have it one day or other and would be mad with rage at the idea of seeing a foreign flag planted there.'[5]

Britain had no intention of planting the Union Jack among those five million ferocious cannibals at present. But Leopold must be 'discouraged', as Derby told Lumley. A few days later Lumley returned to the royal palace with this discouraging news, which delighted Leopold's long-suffering *chef du cabinet* Devaux.

Leopold's reactions to the rebuff were alarmingly resilient. 'The market is not encouraging, and I don't think it will help to insist,' he admitted to Lambermont, his Foreign Secretary, in August 1875. 'Neither the Spanish, nor the Portuguese, nor the Dutch' – and he might have added, nor the British – 'are disposed to sell [a colony]. I plan to make discreet inquiries if there's any thing to be done in Africa.'[6]

It was on 7 January 1876 that Leopold read that piece in *The Times*, describing Lieutenant Cameron's amazing discoveries in Central Africa, the land of 'un-speakable richness', only waiting for an 'enterprising capitalist'.

Might not Leopold, with his 15 million francs, play the part of the capitalist? But he did not want more rebuffs from those European dogs-in-the-manger, Disraeli and the rest. The trouble about Central Africa was that in some English people's eyes it had been pre-empted by Livingstone. In the previous year, 1875, a prefabricated steamboat, the *Ilala*, had chugged out into the waters of Lake Nyasa. It was the first permanent Anglican mission station, set up there in answer to Livingstone's solemn appeal from the grave. And the British public were beginning to feel proprietorial towards those parts of East and Central Africa where their explorers and missionaries had been the first to penetrate. At the same time the French government had encouraged their own explorers to push eastwards from their colony at Gabon into the unknown basin of the Congo. Officially, both governments, British and French, were reluctant to splash out taxpayers' money in expanding their African possessions. But this policy could change – indeed be reversed – in answer to Livingstone's call.

An idea began to take shape in Leopold's mind, as brilliant and devious as any from one of the masters of European diplomacy. He saw a way to make a strength out of Belgium's weakness and a way to exploit the crusading spirit of the British public for his own ends.

Six months later, in September 1876, about a dozen celebrated explorers began to arrive at Leopold's palace in Brussels for what was to be the first geographical conference on Central Africa. No one suspected how this modest conference would start to reshape the history of the continent as dramatically as the Suez Canal, opened seven years earlier. Naturally Jules Devaux ridiculed the whole business.

'I am caught up, despite myself,' he grumbled, 'in this damned African affair: a toy which it is true will do no harm to anyone, and delight the geographers, but makes us here all laugh.'[7]

*   *   *

Why was Leopold so keen to risk his family fortune, creating an African empire despite the giggles of his own staff? It was a question that must have interested a sharp mind like Jules Devaux's. The enterprise seemed utterly perverse, given the mountainous obstacles and the mouse likely to come out of them.

No continent was less inviting for European explorers. It was nearly 400 years since the smooth round profile of Africa had first decorated the charts of the Portuguese navigators. For most of that time the interior – with notable exceptions to north and south – had remained as mysterious as the surface of the moon. (In a way the moon's surface was less mysterious. Europeans could chart its mountains in safety with their telescopes.) South of the Mediterranean the coast of Africa became increasingly hostile. Harbours were rare. Even a sheltered anchorage was often hard to find behind the curtain of mangrove swamps and the surf crashing down on the coral reefs. It was true that from the time of the Greeks there had been tales of great rivers that led to the interior. The Nile apart, the great rivers seemed a mirage. The mouths of the Niger and Zambezi were a labyrinth of swamps and sandbars. The Congo was sealed by cataracts. Even the Nile eventually lost its way in a maze of papyrus. And along the valleys of the great rivers, hot and humid for most of the year, there flourished virulent strains of fever, malaria and sleeping sickness, dangerous for natives and generally fatal for intruders.

So for centuries Central Africa had resisted even the most timid kind of examination. The Enlightenment came, yet no European could answer the simplest questions. Were there boundless treasures in the interior, or was Africa the most barren continent in the world?

In the Middle Ages Africa had been the El Dorado, the gilded place. And not merely the gilded place of the imagination. To African wealth the great medieval city states of Europe – Genoa and Venice especially – owed much of their own. Two-thirds of the world's gold supply in the late Middle Ages came from West Africa. In the fourteenth century an African Croesus turned up at Cairo on his way to Mecca. He was Mansa Musa, King of Mali and a man to be reckoned with. He had crossed the desert with 500 slaves in his retinue and each carried a solid gold staff weighing four pounds. Europe welcomed that kind of exhibitionism. Kings and popes depended on gold for more than crowns and chalices. It was then, as now, the ultimate basis of foreign trade. Gold coins fed Europe's overland trade with the East. Plodding across the Sahara on the two-month passage to the Mediterranean came the camel caravans from Jenne and

Timbuctu. A year or two later the gold from their saddle-bags, minted in Europe, might have crossed Central Asia and been exchanged for silk in China or spices in the Moluccas. These were the golden threads that drew the unknown heart of Africa closer to Europe, and Europe closer to the unknown heart of Asia.

To tap this West African gold was one of the principal aims of the Portuguese navigators of the fifteenth century. No one knew where, beyond the Sahara, in what kingdoms of forest or swamp, the trickle of gold originated. But the Portuguese saw they could divert this trade from Italy to Portugal if they could find a direct seaway to and from West Africa. By the same token, they could grab the Indian spice trade and the Chinese silk trade if their seaway to Africa could be extended to the Indies. By the 1480s the first Portuguese ships were loading gold in the Senegal river and at El Mina in the Gulf of Guinea, gold apparently exported westwards and southwards from the unknown goldfields. Each year brought the Portuguese caravels further south, to the rainforests of the equator and the dry scrublands beyond. As Diego Cam and Bartholomeu Dias groped and fumbled their way along the coast, they set up tall stone crosses – *padrones* – to mark their progress. By 1497 Vasco da Gama had rounded the Cape and opened up the seaway to the Indies. The seaway supplanted the land route across Asia, and along the coast of Africa lay the main road of world trade.

No explorers have ever achieved such breathtaking success so fast and on such a scale as these daredevil Portuguese sailors of the late fifteenth and early sixteenth centuries. Indeed they were too successful, their explorations too far-flung. They founded a pair of African colonies – in Angola and Mozambique – and set up numerous trading posts in West Africa. But the trickle of African gold and the tusks of ivory and ostrich feathers could not compare with the flood of treasures from East and West. Columbus had made his first windfall on the islands of the New World five years before da Gama had found the route to the Indies. Soon the Spanish bullion ships were bringing crates of bullion from the tropical jungles of Chile and Mexico. Africa slipped back into the shadows, a steaming coastline, a confused line of coral reefs in the heat haze, a headland where an ominous stone cross guarded the way to the interior.

At the same moment a new kind of African export came on the market, which was even more important for world trade during the next 300 years than African gold had been in the Middle Ages. European investors plunged into cotton and sugar planting all over the New World. These plantations were unworkable without African slaves.

The West African slave trade – though hardly the line of business for the squeamish – paid Europe substantial profits from the beginning. Like the gold trade, it demanded no European interference in the mysterious affairs of the interior. Down to the steamy ports of the Slave Coast west of the river Niger came the lines of shuffling slaves, to be unshackled and graded, marketed, reshackled, loaded and despatched with minimum loss in transit (perhaps a third died) to the slave farms of Brazil, America and the West Indies. Africans needed no persuasion to enslave their fellows. Ten million black Africans are reckoned to have been exported like cattle on the hoof, or crates of chickens, during the three centuries after the Portuguese discoveries. It was the greatest migration ever recorded by Europeans, and the most terrible. Then Europe became conscience-stricken. First the slave trade, then slavery itself was banned by successive nations, led by Britain in 1807 and 1834 respectively. America reluctantly followed suit. With the rise and success of the anti-slavery movement came the discovery in the New World that sugar and cotton could, after all, be grown profitably without importing fresh slaves.

By the 1850s, west coast merchants had found acceptable alternatives to the forbidden market in slaves. It was all thanks to that genie of the brass boiler and black smokestack: steam. The steamboats' tall black smokestack was the symbol of the new Africa. The steam engine had not only revolutionized industrial production in Europe and, by means of railways, the transport of goods by land. It had revolutionized the transport of goods by sea. In the days of sail, only the most valuable, least bulky and least perishable goods could pay their transport costs. Now the great ports like Liverpool, ports that had grown fat on the barter of manufactured goods for slaves, could grow even fatter on the exchange of those same goods for tropical products: groundnuts, peanuts, palm oil. Here was the antidote for slavery, 'legitimate trade', a cure for the 'open sore' of Africa, applied miraculously by steam.

The steamboats, carrying Birmingham buttons and Manchester cottons to Africa in exchange for oil and nuts, also carried a new generation of explorers to try, with God's help, to open the interior. The most famous, and with good reason, was David Livingstone. As a doctor and scientist, he was the first explorer to show that quinine was the key to the locked interior. Before this discovery, the exploration of the Niger and Congo had proved suicidal. Malaria had destroyed all the recent expeditions to these rivers: Captain James Tuckey's to the Congo in 1816 and Richard Lander's to the Niger in 1832–4. Livingstone wandered for thirty years in South and Central Africa, succumbing to, but recovering from, numerous bouts of fever.

In 1858 he discovered the 350-mile-long Lake Nyasa. Here was a highway heaven-sent for steamboats, leading up the rivers Zambezi and Shire and into the heart of tropical Africa. In West Africa during the same period a naval surgeon, William Baikie, pioneered steam travel on the Niger. In 1854 he brought a steamer, the *Pleiad*, 300 miles up the river. For five years he successfully established himself at Lukoja, at the confluence of the Niger and Benue.

In East and Central Africa four other British explorers made the most dramatic discoveries of all. In 1857 Richard Burton and John Speke discovered Lake Tanganyika, and the next year Speke found Lake Victoria, which he guessed – quite correctly – was the main source of the White Nile. In 1860–3 Speke returned to explore Lake Victoria and the country around. His companion was James Grant. They descended to the Mediterranean via the Nile. On the way down they met Samuel Baker ascending. Soon Baker was to discover Lake Albert. The Nile system now seemed to most geographers more or less known.

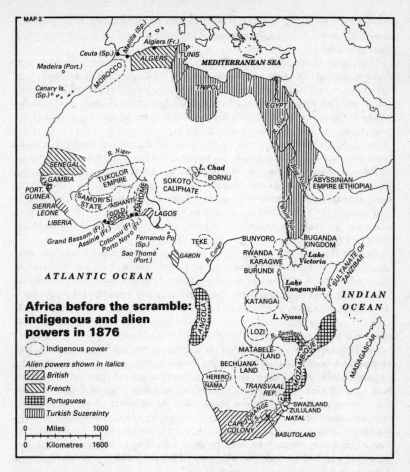

MAP 2

Africa before the scramble: indigenous and alien powers in 1876

◌ Indigenous power

Alien powers shown in italics

▨ British
▤ French
▦ Portuguese
▥ Turkish Suzerainty

The remaining great mystery in 1876 was the course – and identity – of the Lualaba, the enormous north-bound river discovered by Livingstone, far to the west of Lake Tanganyika. Cameron, as mentioned earlier, claimed the Lualaba turned to the west and became the Congo. Whether Cameron was right the world would soon know.

For Stanley, in 1875, had set out westwards from Lake Victoria to try and achieve what Cameron had failed to achieve: a direct descent by way of the Lualaba, all the way to the Atlantic.

One thing was clear – and to no one more than Leopold – that, together, quinine and the steamboat had changed everything. The blank spaces on the map of

Africa were shrinking fast. Soon the answers to the fundamental questions would be known. Was the interior full of boundless riches? Or was there nothing there to exploit?

Nothing at all, grumbled Jules Devaux and the rest of Leopold's entourage. Most of the world's experts appeared to agree, including the half-dozen famous explorers invited to Brussels that week in September 1876, except for Verney Cameron. The most distinguished of Leopold's guests was Grant, now a white-haired but spry veteran of fifty. In his travels along the whole course of the Nile with Speke, he had discovered no sign of great untapped wealth, except the ivory trade. But the great herds of elephants would not last long if the ivory trade was exploited systematically by hunters. The German explorers had come to the same depressing conclusions. In 1869–74, Gustav Nachtigal had explored the Sahara and the Sudanese province of Kordofan, west of the Nile. These were among the most barren places in the world. In 1865–7, Gerhard Rohlfs had crossed the Sahara and penetrated to Bornu and beyond. He saw no sign of riches – outside the region of the lower Niger, the centre of the booming palm oil trade.

Against this was the word of one young explorer, Verney Cameron, who talked of the 'unspeakable richness' of the Congo, although he had only skirted the southern border of the vast unknown basin. On one kind of trade, however, all the explorers did agree and their grim reports confirmed Livingstone's discoveries. The slave trade, snuffed out in West Africa, was alive and well in East Africa. Now organized by the Arab and Swahili people of the east, it was spreading like a cancer across the whole of Central Africa.

Livingstone's last journals, published in 1874, the year after he died, had etched these horrors on the mind of the British public.

Jules Devaux would have assumed that Livingstone was right, and that there was a crying need to open up Central Africa to Christianity and commerce as the way to extinguish this new slave trade in the heart of Africa. But the commercial prospects were extremely discouraging, of no interest to prudent investors. Only a reckless enthusiast – or a philanthropist – would want to hazard his money in this way. And the idea of the King turning philanthropist – Leopold, who had scoured the whole world for profitable investment – would have made Jules Devaux laugh once again.

About half-past six on the evening of 11 September 1876, the party of heavily bearded explorers and other international experts on geography, somewhat awkward in court dress, began to ascend the Staircase of Honour of the royal palace, Brussels. It was a brand new baroque double staircase of white marble, a whiff of Versailles to contrast with the plain palace buildings put up in the main square at Brussels by the Dutch governor thirty years before. At the head of the staircase the court was lined up to receive them. Together they filed into the throne room, lit by 7,000 candles, and bowed to their host, His Majesty King Leopold II.

The British delegates, hard-headed travellers, were bowled over by the King's hospitality. Sir Henry Rawlinson, the man who had deciphered the hieroglyphs at Persepolis, and one of the leaders of the RGS delegation, wrote to his wife that evening:

> I have a suite of magnificent apartments to myself – all crimson damask and gold. Everything is red, even the Ink and the Ammunition [the lavatory paper]![8]

Everyone was treated like a prince of the blood. Their host seemed to have thought of everything. A special mail steamer had collected them at Dover and spirited them across the Channel, mercifully flat, to Ostend. From there they were whisked in special state carriages to the railway terminus at Brussels, where the ADCs were waiting.

The King was in high humour. He had personally supervised every detail of the conference, down to the way the guests' names were spelt on the invitation cards ('*j' ignore si Backer* [Sir Samuel Baker] *s'écrit avec un CK ou avec un K seul*'), and the need for writing the appropriate initials, FRGS, FRS, KCB and so on after their names ('*il faut bien mettre toutes les lettres après ces noms*').[9]

At the end of May Leopold had made a flying visit to London and stayed at Claridges, supposedly incognito. He talked to Cameron (back in April from his travels), to Grant and other explorers, and took diplomatic soundings, as well as paying a courtesy visit to his cousin, Queen Victoria, at Balmoral. It turned out that Cameron, as Leopold had probably suspected, had tried to persuade the British government to extend a British protectorate over the part of the Congo that he had himself discovered. Cameron had already signed treaties with certain Congo chiefs. But Disraeli's government, Leopold was relieved to hear, would not consider a protectorate, and so would have nothing to do with Cameron's treaties.

The conference opened on 12 September in the theatrical splendour of the Great Gallery, modelled at the King's suggestion on the Tuileries. The King's speech of welcome was masterly. There was no hint of his own real feelings. He talked only of science and philanthropy:

> To open to civilization the only part of our globe where it has yet to penetrate, to pierce the darkness which envelops whole populations, it is, I dare to say, a crusade worthy of this century of progress.
>
> It appears to me that Belgium, a central and neutral state, should be territory well chosen for our meeting and it is that which has emboldened me to summon you today to my home in our little conference which I have the great satisfaction of opening today. Needless to say, in bringing you to Brussels I was in no way motivated by selfish designs. No, gentlemen, if Belgium is small, she is happy and satisfied with her lot. My only ambition is to serve her.[10]

The King then laid down an agenda for the conference, which included plans for publicizing the crusade and appealing for funds.

In due course the delegates divided up into separate groups – keeping the German delegates carefully separate from the French – to decide how best to co-ordinate the work of exploration. Next day the conference discussed the plans of the sub-committees: the location of 'stations' (depots) to be built across Central Africa between Loanda and Zanzibar. By the third day the conference had agreed on ways and means. The new international body would be called the International African Association. There would be a governing body called the International Commission, an international executive, and finally the various national committees for each country.

Everything had gone 'swimmingly', as Rawlinson observed.[11] 'The way the King presided over our deliberations was beyond description,' said Baron von Richtofen, leader of the German delegation. 'Never in any country at any time has hospitality so magnificently royal ever been dispensed ....'[12]

But would anything come of all this talk of an international crusade to open up Africa? Rawlinson, who had wondered whether his stomach could stand four consecutive days of banqueting, was somewhat cynical. 'I do not expect much from it, but on paper the arrangements look well.'[13] He was delighted, at any rate, to meet so many of his fellow explorers from other countries.

Would anything come out of it? No one knew. But all over Europe high-minded people, who read of this crusade in their newspapers, thought it a triumph for the King. A glittering new Leopold had suddenly emerged from the chrysalis. He had been thought dull, even boorish. Now they talked of the Leopold who was leading a modern crusade against the slave trade, the *beau sabreur*, a chivalric hero like Godfroid de Bouillon, whose statue decorated the main square in Brussels. In England, especially, people recognized that something important had happened. Here was a new answer to Livingstone's call from the grave to open up Africa. The King was prepared to spend his own money on this humanitarian task. Lesseps called it 'the greatest humanitarian work of this time'.[14]

Of course that was not the language of Jules Devaux and Leopold's staff – nor of Leopold to them. Lambermont had helped draft the crusading speech, but he remained sceptical like the others. They probably recognized the King's design. There was no hypocrisy in his appeal for international co-operation in exploring Central Africa. The cost of opening up the Dark Continent would be enormous. All the better if the public could be made enthusiastic contributors. For the time being the International African Association would be no sham. But it would remain under Leopold's control. The Secretary-General would be his own employee. He would remain the permanent president, however modestly he agreed only to serve for a year. Time enough before his real plans would emerge. What they were, how far they differed from an international crusade to suppress the slave trade, was made clear in a letter to the Belgian Ambassador in London a few months later:

I do not want to miss a good chance of getting us a slice of this magnificent African cake.[15]

Meanwhile Stanley was the one man whom Leopold needed in order to start the work of opening up the Congo. Stanley was leading an Anglo-American expedition which had set off three years before from Zanzibar. The last news received from him was sent in 1875 after he had circumnavigated Lake Victoria. It appeared that he was planning to return to Europe by a westward march across Africa. He was trying to achieve what Cameron had tried and failed to do: to follow the Lualaba all the way to the sea, and confirm it was really the Congo and not the Nile.

Without Stanley, Leopold could do nothing. But where in all that Dark Continent was Stanley now?

CHAPTER 2

Three Flags Across Africa

Central Africa and Europe
14 September 1876–June 1878

> 'Go back Wasambywe [Swahili] you are bad!
> Wasambywe are bad, bad, bad! The river is deep,
> Wasambywe ... You have not wings, Wasambywe.
> Go back, Wasambywe.'
>
> One of the Wenya boatmen addressing
> Stanley's expedition on the river
> Congo, 19 November 1876

September 14, 1876, the day that saw the end of the junketing at the royal palace in Brussels, also saw the start of the latest phase in Stanley's irresistible progress across Africa. He left Ruanda, a small village of conical huts on the western shore of Lake Tanganyika, marching towards the Lualaba – Livingstone's 'Great River'. They marched at a steady tramp, making more than nine miles a day along the winding paths through the high grass and the shrubby thorn trees. Most of the villagers fled at the sight of the expedition, what with its immense file of porters and soldiers, and the three flags carried at its head.

The first was familiar and ominous; the blood-red flag of the Sultan of Zanzibar. This was the assertion of the Sultan's power, a claim of Zanzibar over-rule carried in recent years to the heart of Africa by Swahili slave caravans. The second flag was new to the region; it was the Stars and Stripes. Stanley was an American journalist by profession; the *New York Herald* had commissioned the expedition.

The third flag was the most potent symbol of the future. Born in Britain, Stanley still yearned for recognition by the British public, and had enlisted a London paper, *The Daily Telegraph*, as a joint backer of the expedition.

Stanley was a short, stocky figure in white pith helmet and puggaree, grey tropical uniform, well-polished brown boots and gaiters. How different from Livingstone! For months at a time the old man had been more or less helpless, dependent on African charity.

Stanley travelled with what seemed like a well-equipped private army. After two years exploring, he still had 132 porters and soldiers (apart from the women and other camp followers) and 95 loads, including a collapsible boat, called the *Lady Alice*, carried in sections by twelve of the strongest men, and about ten loads of ammunition. Some of the bolder villagers were not too frightened to sell him food; goats, manioc, millet and so on. He paid them generously with cloth, glass beads, or the local currency, cowrie shells. There was something magical about Stanley as one of the local Waguhha tribesmen was quoted as saying that week, to Stanley's evident satisfaction. It was not only that he 'always goes covered with clothes, unlike all other people', and his feet were invisible inside those brown polished boots. What was he looking for? 'There is something very mysterious about him, perhaps wicked, perhaps he is a magician, at any rate it is better to leave him alone and not disturb him.'[1]

Two and a half years earlier Stanley's own spirit had taken fire, he said, when he had served as one of the eight pallbearers at Livingstone's funeral at Westminster Abbey. As the first handful of earth rattled on the coffin, Stanley took a private pledge: he would complete Livingstone's task – and more. 'If God willed it,' he later wrote, he would be 'the next martyr to geographical science, or if my life is spared, to clear up not only the secrets of the Great River throughout its course, but also all that remained problematical and incomplete of the discoveries of Burton and Speke, and Speke and Grant.'

Here was a geographical Labour of Hercules. Burton, Speke, Grant and Baker had failed to circumnavigate the three great equatorial lakes that had been their discoveries, Lakes Tanganyika, Victoria and Albert. The size and shape of all three lakes still baffled geographers. Greatest puzzle of all was Livingstone's 'Great River', the Lualaba. Was this the upper Congo, as Cameron now claimed (a claim supported by most armchair geographers)? Or was it the beginning of the Nile and the 'open path' from the Mediterranean to Central Africa, as Livingstone had hoped against hope? Stanley, the American journalist-explorer, had been commissioned to bring back the answers.

Stanley would also complete Livingstone's mission to 'open up Africa to Christianity'. The four months he had spent at Livingstone's side in Africa in 1871–2 had proved a revelation. Only once, before meeting Livingstone, had he met a man to whom he could expose his heart. Stanley was the illegitimate son of feckless Welsh-speaking parents, Elizabeth Parry and John Rollant (anglicized Rowlands). Baptized John Rowlands, he had been rejected by his parents and brought up in the local workhouse, St Asaph's, near Denby, run by a sadistic schoolmaster who might have served as the model for Squeers in *Nicholas Nickleby*. After thrashing his tormentor and leaving him like Squeers (according to Stanley's own account), stunned on the classroom floor, the boy had fled to his mother, who rejected him once again. At seventeen he had shipped to America, serving before the mast as a deckhand. In New Orleans he had the good fortune to be befriended and later adopted by a wealthy English cotton merchant called Henry Hope Stanley. It was this Stanley who gave the boy not only two of his own names, but the grooming which completed his education, and the love for which he had yearned so long. However, the idyll soon ended, for reasons that are not clear, in estrangement.[2] In due course, Stanley became the *New York Herald*'s model foreign correspondent: a cocky American manner concealing a bleeding Welsh heart within.

The months exploring Lake Tanganyika with Livingstone overwhelmed Stanley. He wept like a boy of eight, he said, when they parted. He had expected a crusty misanthrope. He found a man whose serenity transcended every frustration, a man so gentle and tender-hearted that he shrank from punishing his African servants when they had cheated him. Livingstone told Stanley that his own mission was not so much to preach the gospel to Africa. What could one or two men do in that respect? The first step was to preach to Europe what they must do about the horrors of the slave trade, to stop it once and for all. Later the regular missionaries would come, systematically organized, teaching the gospel, tribe by tribe, district by district. Stanley had pledged himself to Livingstone's service. He would be Livingstone's disciple and mouthpiece. That was the way he saw himself in his own serialized articles and in his book *How I Found Livingstone*. His writings touched the hearts of millions, on both sides of the Atlantic, who had never read a word of Livingstone's own writings.

Stanley had written solemnly in his private diary:

> May I be selected to succeed him in opening up Africa to the shining light of Christianity! My methods, however, will not be Livingstone's. Each man has his own way. His, I think, had its defects, though the old man, personally, has been almost Christ-like for goodness, patience, ... and self-sacrifice. The selfish and wooden-headed world requires mastering, as well as a loving charity.[3]

The 'mastering' on which Stanley himself relied in Africa came more from the Old Testament than the New: 'chastisement' of his enemies, he called it, and it soon made Stanley notorious.

The trouble was that in 1872 there had been many people who found the idea of Stanley as Livingstone's disciple too incongruous to stomach. They had greeted *How I Found Livingstone* with derision and disbelief. They did not merely doubt Stanley's motives: it was plain he had never met Livingstone; those letters were forgeries; the trip to Africa a stunt; the whole story a pack of lies.

To be called a forger and impostor dealt Stanley a wound that never fully healed. As he wrote years later: 'All the actions of my life, and I may say, of my thoughts, have been since 1872 coloured by [that] storm of abuse.'[4] He had good reasons to be touchy. He carried deep scars from his own childhood in the workhouse – the double stigma of pauperism and illegitimacy. He had tried to conceal them by assuming the identity of a full-blown American, sometimes bending, in trivial respects, the facts to fit his own story. (For example, he claimed to have served as an officer in the US navy, whereas he had really been a clerk.) His own sensitivity made him acutely insensitive to others.

The storm of misrepresentation that burst on his head after discovering Livingstone came from three sources: from rival muck-raking newspapers, jealous of the *New York Herald*'s amazing scoop; from eminent men of the Royal Geographical Society, humiliated by their own amateurish efforts to

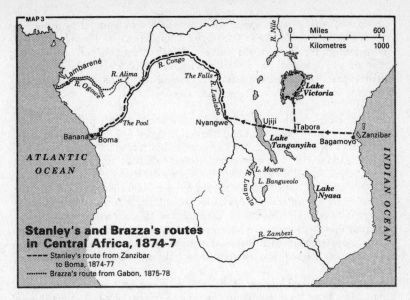

MAP 3

Stanley's and Brazza's routes
in Central Africa, 1874-7
---- Stanley's route from Zanzibar
to Boma, 1874-77
...... Brazza's route from Gabon, 1875-78

resupply Livingstone; and from personal friends of Dr Kirk (later Sir John), the British Agent at Zanzibar, whom Stanley had denounced for not giving prompter aid. Stanley had no talent for disarming this kind of enemy. He beat them to the ground or, as happened increasingly, he ignored them. As he said himself: 'So numerous were my enemies that my friends become dumb, and I had to resort to silence as a protection against outrage.'[5] Silence can be golden. It can sometimes be reckless too. It made him seem less vulnerable by concealing his acute sensitivity. It hardly served to defend his reputation the next time abuse came down on his head. And soon, like tropical rain, the abuse came pelting down once more.

The occasion was the first phase of this Anglo-American expedition to Central Africa: the circumnavigation of Lake Victoria and the exploration of Uganda. By Livingstone's standards, the long-term results of the mission in 1874-5 to the court of Mtesa, the Kabaka of Buganda (the dominant kingdom in Uganda), could have been judged a success. In 1862 Speke had visited the barbaric King. He returned with ghastly tales of human sacrifice: thirty brothers burnt alive by Mtesa to celebrate his own accession to the throne, others tortured and executed for the most trivial offences, such as speaking too loudly in the King's presence. But time seemed to have mellowed the tyrant. At any rate Mtesa welcomed Stanley in a more civilized way than any other African ruler. 'Thousands of men in line, hundreds of soldiers bearing guns. Chiefs to the number of a hundred and more, Mtesa sitting regally on a large chair covered with a cloth of gold.'[6] Although attracted by Islam, Mtesa expressed a keen interest in

Christianity, too. Mtesa's appeal for missionaries was reported by Stanley in letters addressed to *The Daily Telegraph* and the *New York Herald*, published in November 1875. Here was the most promising field for a mission, said Stanley, in all the pagan world. The appeal was heard. Indeed it marked the first step on the course that, in nineteen years, was to make Uganda a British protectorate. But meanwhile Stanley's other published accounts brought abuse raining down on him.

In April 1875, on his return from Mtesa's court, sailing in the *Lady Alice* down the western shore of Lake Victoria, Stanley had fallen foul of some tribesmen at a small island called Bumbireh Island. They had refused him food, threatened him with their spears and arrows, pulled his hair, as though it had been a wig, dragged the *Lady Alice* forcibly up the shore, and stolen her oars. Stanley extricated himself with difficulty from this encounter, killing fourteen of the enemy but suffering no casualties himself, not even a man wounded. In fact, he lost nothing but his dignity – and the oars. The oars were soon recovered, and four months later Stanley captured and chained up the petty chief of the island and offered him to his overlord in exchange for a suitable ransom. When this offer was refused, Stanley decided to make an example of the people of Bumbireh.

His own published account of the incident was vivid, too vivid for his own good. He wanted 'to punish Bumbireh with the power of a father punishing a stubborn and disobedient son'. The method he chose was to return to Bumbireh and empty box after box of Snider bullets into the ranks of the tribesmen while staying just out of range of their spears and arrows. He claimed to have shot down thirty-three men and wounded a hundred, many fatally. 'We had great cause to feel gratitude.' The 'victory' had put everyone into excellent heart. 'We made a brave show as we proceeded along the coast, the canoes thirty-seven in number containing 500 men [including native allies] paddling to the sound of sonorous drums and the cheering tones of the bugle, the English, American and Zanzibar flags flying gaily in union with a most animating scene.'[7]

A more subtle man than Stanley would have pretended that he had hated the business. Stanley seemed to have rather enjoyed it and – worse – enjoyed writing about it. If he had been, as he once was, a reporter describing a fight with Red Indians, his tone would have been more acceptable. In Africa the conventions were different.

Protests were made to the Royal Geographical Society and to the Foreign Office: such incidents disgraced the British flag Stanley boasted of carrying alongside the American one. Stanley's fellow explorers, like Baker, shook their heads. It was 'quite new' for simple explorers to go round 'plundering villages' and 'shooting natives'. 'Neither Speke, nor yourself,' Baker wrote to Grant, nor 'Livingstone nor myself ever presumed upon such acts, but suffered intrigue and delays with patience.'[8] Worst of all was Stanley's inability to keep his mouth shut. 'There is an amount of bad taste about him that is simply incurable.' If Stanley ever returned to England he would need friends. Why go out of his way to alienate people?

But would Stanley return? Stanley was himself far from certain of that in September 1876, despite his voyage in the *Lady Alice* around Lakes Victoria and Tanganyika, as he set off for the Lualaba to try to solve the last great mystery of African geography.

He reached the majestic Lualaba on 17 October. The sight filled him with 'secret rapture'. It was nearly a mile wide and pale grey, 'like the Mississippi, before the full-volumed Missouri pours its rusty brown waters into it'.[9] Ten days later he arrived at Nyangwe, a muddle of Arab houses and African huts and vegetable gardens, which served as the Swahili traders' main depot on the river, and the furthest point the Zanzibar flag had yet been carried west.

Nyangwe was also the furthest point down the Lualaba yet reached by any European. It was here, in the great market, on a bright sultry day in July 1871, that Livingstone had watched aghast as hundreds of defenceless African women were hunted down by slave traders led by Livingstone's own hosts, Dugumbe and Tagamoio. Those 'bloodhounds', as Livingstone called them, resented his interference and took care to see that he was forced to return to Ujiji, unable to buy or hire canoes for the journey down the Lualaba.

In 1874 Cameron, too, had found the bloodhounds blocking his path at Nyangwe. And there was another reason, Cameron was told, why Africans refused to sell him canoes to sail down the Lualaba. They were afraid he would open up the river to the slave trade. If he acted like the strangers who had gone before him, he could only prove a fresh oppressor to the natives, or open a new road for robbers and slave dealers. So Cameron had been forced to take a huge detour to the south-west, emerging in due course in Angola.

Although equipped with the *Lady Alice* and far better armed than either Cameron or Livingstone, Stanley recognized that success depended on winning the slave traders to his side. He met their leader, Hamed bin Muhammad (known as Tippu Tip), on the road to Nyangwe. Tippu Tip proved to be a tall, black-bearded half-caste in the prime of life, dressed in spotless white robes, with a scarlet fez, and a dagger at his waist. He was already famous as a warrior and slaver. Stanley was unprepared for his charm. At first Tippu Tip was hesitant to accept the enormous bait Stanley dangled in front of him: $5,000, for which he was to escort Stanley with 140 men armed with guns and spearmen to match.

If you Wasungu [white men] are desirous of throwing away your lives, it is no reason we Arabs should. We travel little by little to get ivory and slaves, and are years about it – it is now nine years since I left Zanzibar – but you white men only look for rivers and lakes and mountains, and you spend your lives for no reason, and to no purpose. Look at that old man who died in Bisa [Ilala]! What did he seek year after year, until he became so old that he could not travel? He had no money, for he never gave any of us anything, he bought no ivory or slaves, yet he travelled farther than any of us, and for what?[10]

The deal was finally struck on condition that Tippu Tip could return after going sixty days march beyond Nyangwe.

The combined caravan, 700-strong (including camp followers), wound out of Nyangwe on 5 November. The Swahili were conspicuous for their spotless white tunics and turbans and for their retinue of slaves, their necks tied in slave-sticks. Tippu Tip seemed a gentleman by comparison with bloodhounds like Dugumbe and Tagamoio. 'He has no feeling,' said Tippu Tip of Tagamoio. 'His heart is as big as the end of my little finger!' Still, business was business. 'Slaves cost nothing,' he told Stanley drily, 'they only have to be gathered.'[11] (Later he was to say, according to a traveller, when they saw a boatload of women and children swept over a waterfall and lost, 'What a pity! It was a fine canoe.')[12]

Soon after the caravan left Nyangwe, marching roughly parallel with the Lualaba, they saw ahead an ominous change in the scenery. Ever since they had left the coast, 900 miles to the east, the bush in all its shapes had been supreme: grassy downs dotted with the elegant plumes of acacia; stony gullies half choked with thorn; rolling valleys, crisp as parchment in the dry season and green as jade after the rains; and always beyond, the mysterious blue line on the horizon, half-mountain, half-cloud, which dominates the plains of Africa.

Now they saw ahead of them a black curving wall of rainforest which swallowed river and plain. Soon it was as dark as if they had entered a tunnel. Stanley could not see the words he had pencilled into his notebook. They had been in forest before, but never anything like this. Enormous mvula trees, the height and size of ships' masts, spiralled up from the tangle of bananas, palms and wild dates, which in turn were plaited together by a jungle growth of ferns, water-cane and spear-grass. The caravan had to burrow through the jungle like wild animals, crawling on hands and knees. Stanley, sweating heavily, handed his white pith helmet to his gunbearer. The brown soil, mulched with rotten leaves and decayed branches, steamed like a hothouse. And down every tree trunk poured streams of condensation. Soon the twisting path was churned up to a clay paste. To make matters worse, Tippu Tip's wild followers pushed ahead of Stanley's orderly caravan, causing endless delays.

Most disheartened of all were the twelve boatmen who carried the six sections of the *Lady Alice*. Men with axes had to cut a narrow path past fallen trees that blocked their way with mountains of twigs and branches. After the first day the boatmen were utterly exhausted. Although a dozen more men were sent to help them, they lagged hours behind the rest of the caravan, dragging the pieces of boat like blunt ploughs through the jungle, still slipping and struggling while the others ate and rested. Stanley was sorry for them, but did not dare show it. They might insist he return to Nyangwe, or burn his boat. After ten days Tippu Tip came to his tent and told Stanley the news he half expected. Food was short. The fetid air was killing his people. He could not continue. The contract was dissolved. It was a place only for 'vile pagans, monkeys, and wild beasts'.[13]

To turn back was unthinkable. Stanley was only prepared to compromise by turning north-east, away from the river, once he had established that the Lualaba was the Congo. That would take months. Equally unthinkable was to abandon the *Lady Alice*, the perfect vehicle to explore the river, and the talisman of the expedition.

It had been a closely guarded secret that Stanley had called his boat after the captivating young American, Alice Pike, with whom, in the weeks before he had left London, he had fallen head over heels in love. She was seventeen, with blue eyes and a veil of golden hair. Her father had been a poor Jewish immigrant who had distilled a fortune from whisky in Cincinatti and had now bobbed up, industrialist and patron of the arts, among the tycoons of Fifth Avenue, half-way between the Astors and the Vanderbilts. In New York the two lovers had signed a marriage pact: 'We solemnly pledge ourselves to be faithful to each other and to be married on the return of Henry Morton Stanley from Africa.'[14] And Alice had given him her photograph which he kept wrapped in silk in his breast pocket. Her dress was embroidered with flowers and she wore an ostrich feather in her hat. She had fixed the date for the wedding, 14 January 1877. That date was sadly premature, but it added misery to the delays, magnifying Stanley's impatience with his followers and drawing him like a spell onwards down the Congo (assuming the Lualaba *was* the Congo) to the Atlantic and Alice. 'You are my dream, my stay and my hope,' he had written to her in a last letter from Ujiji, 'and believe that I shall still cherish you in this light until I meet you, or death meets me.'[15]

It was her namesake, the *Lady Alice*, that now showed the way. Despite his misgivings about the cannibals said to inhabit the forest, Tippu Tip was persuaded to accept a new bargain. For $2,600 he agreed to continue for a further twenty marches. The caravan would split into two. Tippu Tip and the main party would march along the west bank of the river, where the jungle looked less dense and there was more prospect of food. Stanley would assemble the sections of the *Lady Alice* and, with as many canoes as could be found, sail down the Great River itself.

The river proved welcoming, a brown mirror on which the boat glided swiftly forward, impelled by the current between black walls of forest, a mile apart. The river people were less welcoming. There was no food to be bought. Panic had seized the local Wenya, who assumed Stanley's party had come to hunt slaves. Two of the Wenya, bolder than the rest, paddled across the river to meet them. One of them asked Stanley's interpreter who the strangers were.

'We are Warungwana.'
'Where from?'
'From Nyangwe.'
'Ah, you are Wasambywe [the uncircumcised, i.e. Swahili].'
'No, we have a white man with us ...'
'We do not want you to cross the river. Go back, Wasambywe; you are bad! Wasambywe are bad, bad, bad! The river is deep, Wasambywe ... You have not wings, Wasambywe. Go back, Wasambywe.'

Then the Wenya sang a wild war chant, '*Wooh-hu, ooh-hu-hu-hu*',[16] which was taken up and sent pealing across the river by hundreds of voices.

Eventually, Stanley persuaded some Wenya to help ferry the main party across to the west bank. He camped by the village and paid the people with beads. Next day they found the village deserted. The canoes were left at the landing place. Bananas and crimson palm nuts hung in clusters. Yet the people had fled into the jungle. It was the same at each village they passed. A small child, coming to fetch water at the river-bank, saw the *Lady Alice* approaching: 'Mama, the Wasambywe! The Wasambywe are coming!'[17] The market people screamed in terror as though they thought it was Tagamoio in person. Stanley saw the banana stalks shaken violently as if by the rush of a herd of buffalo. Then there was silence as the boat glided past the landing stage.

Rather than see his men starve, Stanley allowed them to help themselves to goat meat and manioc. But as the days passed the natives became more hostile. On 21 and 24 November there were skirmishes in which Stanley's captains were forced to shoot natives. Meanwhile the main party had lost their way in the jungle, and three of their men were cut off and shot down by arrows before Stanley found them. Morale fluctuated dangerously. Some days food was abundant. In the town of Ikondu – really a string of villages forming a street two miles long – they found wine pots hanging from palm trees, large melons in the gardens, plots of cassava and groundnuts, and waving fields of sugar cane. But the town was abandoned like the rest. All they heard were the eerie war-cries of the Wenya, '*Ooh-hu-hu-hu-hu*', echoing through the jungle, and the beat of drums, war-drums no doubt, carrying the news from village to village, 'The Wasambywe are coming.'

By mid-December a crisis was approaching. They were crippled by typhoid, dysentery, smallpox. Many of Tippu Tip's party had died, including three of the favourite girls from his harem; their bodies were rolled from the canoe which had served as a floating hospital. New tribes hemmed them in, blowing ivory war-horns, and shouting a new war-cry, '*Bo-bo-bo*', from the river-banks. On 19 December, at a village called Vinya-Njara, over 1,000 natives, most of them in canoes, tried to rush Stanley's camp. He had built three stockades and twin wooden towers, and cleared the grass to give a field of fire for Snider rifles. The attack was beaten off, with the loss to Stanley of four men killed and thirteen wounded. On the credit side were twenty-three captured canoes. But the battle proved the last straw for Tippu Tip.

He announced he was leaving. Although still short of twenty marches, Stanley paid him a draft on Zanzibar for $2,600, and loaded his party with presents: a donkey, a gold chain, a revolver, cloth, beads, wire.

On Christmas Day there were farewell games, including canoe races, and a hilarious three-hundred-yard sprint, Tippu Tip versus Frank Pocock, Stanley's only surviving white companion. Stanley offered a silver cup to the winner. Tippu Tip won by fifteen yards. It was misty on 28 December when the *Lady Alice* led out the flotilla of captured canoes. Tippu Tip and his Swahili in white robes lined the river-bank, singing a farewell like a lament. The sad notes hung on the air like a mist as the strong brown current carried the expedition away into the unknown.

Few of them, perhaps not even Stanley, would have continued if they had known what lay ahead.

For months they were to run the gauntlet from four different enemies: cannibals, disease, starvation and the river itself. At the Aruwimi river, 2,000 savages put out to attack them in a gigantic flotilla of war canoes. Each paddler stood erect, an ivory bangle on his arm and a parrot's feather in his hair, as he churned the river to foam with an ivory-handled paddle. Day after day the war cries, drums and horn-blowing merged with the ripping, crackling sound of Stanley's Sniders. Still more fearsome than the war-cries was the roar of the cataracts on the river. At a succession of seven huge falls, which he named after himself, Stanley was forced to cut a path through the jungle and the *Lady Alice* and the canoes were dragged overland. Even this was to be nothing compared with the next falls, 90 miles further west, which he named the Livingstone, thirty-two huge cataracts in succession. Many of his men were drowned. At the Isangila Falls, the *Lady Alice* had to be abandoned, left to rot in the sun, as the survivors struck out overland towards the sea, still sixty miles to the west.

All this was yet to come. As it was, when they left Tippu Tip in December 1876, most of Stanley's party were weeping, convinced that they would never see their homes in Zanzibar again. Uledi, the coxswain tried to sing, but his voice cracked, so that his friends did not know whether to laugh or to cry.

*   *   *

About 900 miles west of Stanley's position in early 1877, almost exactly along the line of the equator, a young French explorer, Pierre Savorgnan de Brazza, was struggling through the rainforest. It was this unknown young explorer who would soon represent the greatest rival to Stanley and his discoveries.

Brazza was at this time somewhere east of Lambaréné, on the unexplored upper reaches of the Ogowe. Most days he heard the tom-toms of the local tribes, and from the black walls of mangrove swamp would emerge men waving spears and beating drums. Some of these tribes, like the warlike Ossiebas, were cannibals. Occasionally there was trouble. The previous August Brazza had shot two men who tried to steal his canoe. Usually he was more patient. There were palavers between the white chief and the black chief, the exchange of gifts, chicken for cowrie, wrangles about more gifts. Days would be spent negotiating a passage for their canoes up the Ogowe. After squeezing Brazza for the last bead or cowrie shell, the chief would let him pass, warning him against the treachery of the neighbouring tribes. Then a few miles higher up the river the maddening process would have to be repeated over again.

Like Stanley, Brazza was an admirer of Livingstone and, though his men were reasonably well-armed, his style of travel was much nearer to Livingstone's. He could have forced the pace, shouldered his way through – at least through the more peaceful tribes. He resisted the temptation. He yearned to be first to find the source of the Ogowe. Here was a noble prize, the glory of colouring in a white space on the map, of giving his name to unknown rivers and animals, of pushing the French flag and French trade deeper into the interior – perhaps right up to the great equatorial lakes. But Brazza wanted to win confidence, inspire trust, even love. That was unusual for a European explorer. Still more unusual among explorers, apart from Livingstone, he felt a real liking for Africans.

People found Pierre de Brazza a strange kind of Frenchman. It could be questioned whether he was French at all. He spoke in a sing-song voice with a strong Italian accent. He had been brought up in Rome, the seventh son of an Italian nobleman from Udine, Count Ascanio Savorgnan di Brazza, who had influential connections in France and a cultivated mind, including a taste for romantic novelists such as Sir Walter Scott. From boyhood young Pietro (as he then was) was obsessed with exploration. With the encouragement of his father, his Jesuit schoolmasters in Rome and a family friend who happened to be a French admiral, he joined the French naval school at Brest. He won a commission as an ensign, and came to Africa. In 1871 the *Jeanne d'Arc*, one of the South Atlantic fleet, ferried reinforcements to Algeria where the tribesmen of the Kabyles had rebelled against French rule. He was shocked to see French troops shooting down the insurgents.

Transferred to the *Venus*, Brazza had his first taste of exploration. The ship often stopped at the small, poverty-stricken colony of Gabon, north of the Congo estuary. In 1874 Brazza tried his mettle on two trips up-country, travelling up the Gabon and Ogowe rivers and starting to learn the local languages. Then, by pulling strings, he got the French government to back his plan to explore the Ogowe to its source. The Minister of Marine to whom he applied was the same French admiral and family friend who had helped wangle him into the naval college.

Brazza was still barely recognized as a Frenchman (he was not naturalized until a month after he proposed the plan to the Minister of Marine). But with the help of friends in high places, including Jules Ferry and Leon Gambetta, he wheedled 10,000 francs out of the colonial treasury. The rest would have to come from Gabon and out of his own pocket. His rank was the lowest an officer could hold, 'auxiliary ensign'. He took three white companions: a sailor, Hamon; a scientist, Alfred Marche; and a burly young doctor, Noel Ballay. The rest of his team were black: ten *laptots*, hard-bitten sailors recruited by him in Senegal; some Gabonese guides and interpreters; and 120 boatmen with nine canoes, hired at Lambaréné, beyond which the rapids barred the way for steamers. He took the usual African trade goods, trinkets and artificial pearls, but added a bizarre collection of French fireworks to entertain the natives. When it suited him, Brazza was not averse to playing the fool.

At this time, 1875, Brazza was a coltish, awkward, taciturn boy of twenty-three, with a long aristocratic nose and large brown eyes. His resourcefulness did him credit and so did his idealism, naïve as it often was. At Lope he was awoken by the cries of a slave begging to be rescued from a cruel master. Brazza bought the slave for 400 francs; the going rate was a ten-centimetre string of beads. Of course he was then besieged by other slaves begging to be redeemed – no doubt prompted by their masters. So he hoisted a tricolour in his camp and told the astonished Africans that by touching the flag they could win their freedom, as France did not recognize slavery. The magic worked. But Brazza was saddened to find that most of the slaves wanted to return to the relations who had sold them originally.

For Brazza, as for most explorers, frustration was never in short supply. His own companions were a ready source, white as well as black. Fever lowered everyone's spirits. Marche, the scientist, became sulky and returned to the coast. They had pinned their hopes on following the Ogowe deep into Central Africa. In fact the Ogowe petered out a mere 200 miles above Lambaréné. Brazza pushed over the watershed of rugged hills, bought some fresh canoes and followed a sparkling new river called the Alima, down towards what the natives called mysteriously the 'big water'. It was here that, for the first and last time in his African travels, his unaggressive approach nearly cost Brazza his life.

This was the territory of the Apfourus, cannibals who had never before seen white people. Brazza met four or five of them and assured them of his excellent intentions, smoking his pipe and putting down his gun on the verandah of the hut while his interpreter talked to them in some unknown language. The first Apfouru village let their canoes pass. But that evening arrows came whistling across them from the river-bank. All night they heard the war-drums and cannibal threats of the Apfouru. At dawn they had to repulse an attack launched from thirty canoes. Brazza could not help admiring the reckless courage of these warriors. 'I shall always remember the man who was in the leading canoe, on which we concentrated our fire. He remained standing and waved his fetish over his head. He was spared the bullets that struck around him.'[18]

When their ammunition began to run low, Brazza decided to retreat. They abandoned their canoes and most of their baggage. Then they splashed through the swamps on the east bank of the river. The retreat became a rout. When the party regained the hills, they were suffering badly from leg ulcers and fever. Brazza had also received a painful shock. Why had pacific methods failed? Why had the Apfourus fought so ferociously to deny him a way through?

No doubt one reason was that Brazza had been too impatient to go forward and had failed to win the Apfourus' trust by palavers. It was not until after he had returned to Europe, in December 1878, that Brazza learned a second reason for the setback – and heard what he came to believe was the real significance of the episode. The Alima was one of the northern tributaries of the 'big water', the Congo itself. Down the Congo, a few months before his own disastrous expedition had come Stanley, crushing all who tried to oppose him. Brazza would later claim that the Apfouru had attacked him in retaliation for Stanley's brutal methods.

It was 5 August 1877, nearly a year since Stanley had vanished up the Lualaba, after sending his last reports to Europe and America. About half an hour after sunset two European merchants in the English factory at Boma, on the Congo estuary, were handed a strange-looking letter brought by four famished Swahili, dressed in rags. The elder merchant, a Portuguese called da Motta Veiga, put on his spectacles to read it.

Boma was not much of a place: a row of tall, box-like, tin-roofed houses lining the north bank of the huge yellow-brown estuary. Each house was protected by a white paling, like an outpost on the American frontier. Boma, too, was on the frontier – or beyond it. No European power had yet claimed the territory.

About eighteen white traders sweated it out here in the back of beyond, Dutch, French, Portuguese and English. They managed the half-dozen 'factories' (really trading posts) where the usual tawdry trade goods exported from Europe – cottons, pots and pans, gin and guns – could be bartered for African palm oil, groundnuts and ivory. There were no white women. No doubt some of the men followed the Portuguese habit of taking African mistresses. It was a humdrum life, apart from attacks of fever and occasional rows with the local Africans, firmly dealt with. (At the next trading settlement, Banana, at the mouth of the Congo, the European traders had tortured and killed forty Africans after one of their factories was burnt down.) What must have made Boma claustrophobic was that you could not move far inland. The African middlemen did a good job of bringing in the nuts and the ivory, and resented interference. The river was blocked by cataracts, and the country round Boma was bleak and stony, no place for walking. When Europeans did travel they travelled like chiefs, in white hammocks carried by eight strong bearers.

When the letter was handed to da Motta Veiga on 5 August 1877, he could not at first believe what he read. He questioned the Swahili. They confirmed the extraordinary story. The letter, headed 'Nsanda' (an impoverished village two days' journey up-country), was written in English:

To any gentleman who speaks English at Embomma [Boma].

Dear Sir,

I have arrived at this place from Zanzibar with 115 souls, men, women and children. We are now in a state of imminent starvation. We can buy nothing from the natives for they laugh at our kinds of cloth, beads and wire. There are no provisions in this country that may be purchased, except on market days, and starving people cannot afford to wait.

I do not know you; but I am told there is an Englishman at Embomma, and as you are a Christian and a gentleman, I beg you not to disregard my request . . . The supplies must arrive within two days, or I may have a fearful time of it among the dying. . . .

Yours sincerely,
H. M. Stanley, Commanding
Anglo-American Expedition for
Exploration of Africa.

PS: You may not know me by name; I therefore add, I am the person that discovered Livingstone in 1871....[19]

As soon as it was light, da Motta Veiga sent off a string of carriers with the answer to Stanley's cry for help: for the Swahili, sacks of rice, sweet potatoes, bundles of fish, tobacco, a barrel of rum, rolls of white and printed cotton cloth; for Stanley, loaves of wheat bread, two pots of butter, a packet of tea, sardines, salmon, a plum pudding, and bottles of pale ale, sherry, port and champagne.

Two days later, on 9 August, the good Samaritan and four other Europeans set off in their white hammocks to greet Stanley, as he was now reported to be close to Boma. They were in holiday clothes: white suits, jaunty straw hats, coloured neck-ties and patent-leather boots. Their path led up through the high grass, past grotesque baobab trees, towards the bare rocky ridge that dominates the estuary.

The meeting in that wilderness had something of the pathos and incongruity of the meeting between Stanley and Livingstone at Ujiji six years earlier. But this time it was Stanley who stared half-uncomprehending at the faces of his rescuers. How pale they seemed! Yet how well they carried themselves, these strange white men. Later he explained his feelings, proud and humble at the same time, as though he was part African himself.

> The words they uttered without gesture – they were perfectly intelligible. How strange! It was quite delightful to observe the slight nods of the head ... They were completely clothed ... and immaculately clean ... I did not dare to place myself upon equality with them yet; the calm blue and grey eyes rather awed me, and the immaculate purity of their clothes dazzled me.[20]

Of course Stanley was near collapse at the time. When his men began to sing a victory chant, he broke down and wept.

Da Motta Veiga put him in a hammock (despite his feeble protests that he was strong enough to walk) and they carried him in triumph to Boma. It was the 7,088th mile and the 999th day since Stanley had left Zanzibar. He had circled the Great Lakes and proved that the Lualaba *was* the Congo. He had completed all Livingstone's tasks, as he had promised himself – but at what cost, what suffering.

Stanley looked at the majestic brown river flowing past the tall square houses and the baobab trees. Its calmness seemed to him a kind of hypocrisy. It had robbed him of so many of his best men including Frank Pocock, the last survivor of his three white companions. Pocock had drowned on 3 June in one of the gigantic lower falls. At that time Stanley had been almost incoherent with grief, envying Pocock his death. ('Ah, Frank,' he wrote in his diary, 'You are happy, my friend. Out of this dreadful mess. Out of this pit of misery in which I am plunged neck deep.'[21]) Even now Stanley felt the hollowness of his triumph. He had sailed from Zanzibar with more than 250 men, women and children. Only 108 (including 13 women and 6 children) would now return safely to their homes. The rest had deserted or died: 14 drowned, 38 killed in battle, 62 dead of starvation, dysentery and so on. The thought made Stanley's throat burn and his eyes fill with tears. Often enough he had cursed them as no better than slaves. Now he came to think of them as heroes and martyrs.

He decided to postpone his own return to Europe so that he could take these shattered survivors home to Zanzibar. It was in Zanzibar that he received a private letter that must have given a still more hollow ring to his triumph. Alice Pike, 'the dream, the stay, and the hope' of his life, had jilted him and married an Ohio railroad millionaire ten months before he had set out down the Lualaba in the *Lady Alice*.

*   *   *

Meanwhile, in the palace grounds at Laeken, Leopold paced up and down the gravel walks, inspected the hothouses and scanned the columns of *The Times*, impatient to hear what had happened to Stanley. In June 1877 he had read the final despatch from Ujiji, sent the previous August. In September came the first ripple of news from the Congo: Stanley had cut his way through to Boma. Then, in mid-November, the full explosive story, confirming Leopold's brilliant hunch. Stanley had traced the Congo to the sea. And, like Cameron, he reported that Central Africa was a treasure house, a fountain of wealth waiting to be tapped.

On 17 November the King wrote excitedly to Solvyns, the Belgian Ambassador in London, to keep him '*au courant*'. As soon as Stanley had enjoyed his hero's welcome in London, they must seize the chance of bringing him over to Brussels. They would make him an offer. In due course Stanley might be the man to take over the Congo in the King's name, snatching it from under the noses of the English. Already Leopold was talking of his 'dream' of making the great traveller 'the Belgian Gordon Pasha'. Of course Solvyns was not to breathe a word of this to anyone in England.

> I'm sure if I quite openly charged Stanley with the task of taking possession in my name of some part of Africa, the English will stop me. If I ask their advice, they'll stop me just the same. So I think I'll just give Stanley some job of exploration which would offend no one, and will give us the bases and headquarters which we can take over later on ...[22]

For the time being, the King warned Solvyns, he must continue to use the International African Association to hide his own appetite for a slice of 'that magnificent African cake'. Already the King's own plans were growing like the orchids in the hothouses. The IAA could serve him in various ways. The national committees of the IAA, inspired by the King, had raised some useful funds. There were plans to send out various national expeditions to East Africa. Excellent. This would divert attention from the really appetizing parts of Africa, the immense Congo basin. At the same time, he would bend the IAA to his own will by making it delegate its executive powers to a committee which he personally controlled.

Predictably, the main opposition to the King's new ideas came from his own staff. Baron Greindl, the Belgian Secretary-General of the IAA, threatened to resign if the King acted so precipitately. Lambermont, the Belgian Foreign Secretary, warned Leopold what a bad name Stanley had made for himself in England by his rough behaviour to the Africans. To involve themselves with a man like this would compromise the IAA, international as it was, and dedicated to science and philanthropy. At least they should give Stanley the chance to clear himself of these charges with his forthcoming book. This would mean waiting till the following year.

Of course waiting was the last thing in Leopold's mind. He now decided that he must grab Stanley before the welcome that Stanley would receive in London went to his head. So off to Marseilles was sent Greindl, and another secret emissary, to intercept the great explorer and bring him back to Brussels. As for the idea that Stanley's rough methods would compromise them, Leopold thought it absurd. If anyone rejected Stanley for this reason, the more fool they. On 8 January 1878, the secret emissaries met Stanley at Marseilles railway station. His hair was grey and he seemed to have aged ten years since he was last in Europe. He politely rebuffed them, saying that he was too tired and ill to accompany them to Brussels at the moment.

In itself this might not have been too alarming for Leopold. But *The Times* soon confirmed the King's fears. In London Stanley had received a heady welcome. Up and down the country he went, appealing to businessmen and humanitarians alike. He re-named the Great River with the emotive name of his master, Livingstone. He repeated his own version of Livingstone's call. Central Africa was rich. It was Britain that must open it up to commerce and Christianity. Instead of the blood-red flag of the Arab slave traders, the Union Jack must fly over the Congo.

Yet by June 1878, Leopold was relieved to hear, Stanley had meekly accepted his invitation to Brussels.

Why had Stanley's appeal to Britain fallen on deaf ears – apart from a response to his call to send missionaries to Uganda? In 1878 the British public had little appetite for new colonies in tropical Africa. A year earlier, on 12 April 1877, Disraeli's government had made an unexpectedly bold move in South Africa, 2,000 miles south of the Congo. In one bite, Britain had annexed the Boer republic of the Transvaal. The chief motive was strategic: to protect the British base at the Cape. But already there were signs that Britain had bitten off more than she could chew.

CHAPTER 3

Two Steps Forward

Transvaal, Cape Town, Natal
12 April 1877–22 January 1879

'I am glad to know the Transvaal is English ground;
perhaps now there may be rest.'

Cetshwayo, King of the Zulus,
on hearing of the British annexation of the Transvaal

The British annexation of the Boer republic of the Transvaal passed off as quietly as a country wedding. It looked, at the beginning, as if the price would be as easy to pay.

It was 12 April 1877, four months before Stanley had struggled down to Boma. In Pretoria, capital of the Transvaal, the winter sun burnished the tin roof of the Dutch church and burnt the dusty grass brown where the oxen were tethered in Church Square. At about eleven o'clock the small group of British officials deputed by Sir Theophilus Shepstone, the British Special Commissioner, arrived to conduct the ceremony in Church Square. They stood in a line, seven English gentlemen incongruously dressed in tweed shooting jackets among the oxen and ox wagons, without an escort in a town full of colonial roughnecks and armed Boers. They were nervous and elated, still half fearing the worst.

'And whereas the ravaging of an adjoining friendly State by warlike savage tribes cannot for a moment be contemplated by Her Majesty's Government without the most earnest and painful solicitude....'

Melmoth Osborn, Secretary to the Mission, put on his spectacles and began to read the proclamation. His hands trembled violently and his voice faltered and died. Rider Haggard, Shepstone's twenty-year-old clerk, had to take back the printed text from him and continue the proclamation:

And whereas I have been satisfied by numerous addresses, ceremonials and letters ... that a large proportion of the inhabitants of the Transvaal see ... the ruined condition of the country and therefore earnestly desire the establishment within and over it of Her Majesty's authority and rule....[1]

There was polite cheering from the small crowd who were mainly English, like most business people in Pretoria. The seven British officials breathed a sigh of relief and prepared to return to the small house and garden where they had laagered with their horses. There were no flags, no bunting, not even a solitary Union Jack, or a note of 'God Save the Queen'. All that would come in a month or so, when the first British battalion arrived from Natal and marched into Pretoria.

The Transvaal had been formally, if provisionally, united to the British Empire. And it had proved, the British Treasury would be delighted to hear, a quiet wedding, costing almost nothing. Meanwhile a second ceremony, more like a funeral, took place at the side of Church Square, facing the government offices.

A small group of Boers – townspeople and bearded *takhars* (from the back-veld), some with rifles slung over their shoulders – listened as one of the Executive Council read out a solemn protest signed by Thomas Burgers, the Transvaal's mercurial state President. In 1852, by the Sand River Convention, the British government had pledged themselves to respect the independence of the Transvaal. Why should they now revoke their pledge? However, simply to avoid violence, the Transvaal government had agreed under protest to submit to the British. They advised the burghers to remain calm. They would be sending a deputation to London, led by Paul Kruger, the Vice-President, to try to reverse the annexation. In the meantime, strange to say, all the members of the Executive, except Kruger, had agreed to serve – and be paid by – the British.

The double ceremony, proclamation and protest, was the best compromise that could be agreed by Shepstone and Burgers, given the weakness of both their positions. Shepstone was supposed to rule the Transvaal, legally speaking, like a conquered country. But no conqueror had ever had to act more meekly to the enemy. He had ridden over the border from Natal with a staff of twelve, including a representative of the Standard Bank, and twenty-five mounted Natal police. The previous year the British had appointed him Special Commissioner to investigate the political and financial crisis in the Transvaal which seemed to threaten the security of the neighbouring British colonies, Natal and the Cape. He was something of a loner; an expert on the Zulus and other natives – he had thirty-two years' experience in the Natal government – but he knew little about the Boers. With unwonted daring, London had agreed to give him a free hand. If possible, Shepstone was to annex the Transvaal and administer it provisionally himself. But there was one condition: the annexation must be bloodless. According to the terms of his commission, he must win the agreement of the Volksraad (the Transvaal Parliament) or the majority of the white inhabitants – or at least 'a sufficient number'. It was vital that no blood was shed. For this was the first step in the British government's master plan for South Africa to persuade the Transvaal and the other Boer republic, the Orange Free State, to join the British Empire and federate with the two British colonies, the Cape and Natal.

With his twenty-five mounted policemen, Shepstone had come and seen and conquered. The political and financial crisis in the Transvaal was real enough. The white minority were split into three factions: Boers favouring the President, Thomas Burgers; Boers favouring the Vice-President, Paul Kruger; and newly arrived British, favouring imperial intervention. The result was that few taxes were being collected and the men who favoured Kruger had refused to support Burgers in the war against the Pedi chief, Sekhukhene, who controlled parts of the northern territory claimed by the Transvaal. So Burgers and his commandos had been repulsed by Sekhukhene. And the Treasury was empty, except for 12/6d. Apart from the cost of the war, there was a disastrous foreign loan for a proposed railway from Delagoa Bay in Mozambique to Pretoria. This project had collapsed, bringing the financial credit of the Transvaal to zero.

These were all deplorable facts cited by Shepstone in his proclamation. He added that Cetshwayo, king of the powerful Zulu nation, the Transvaal's hereditary enemy, had massed his Impis for invasion. So Shepstone, the Zulu expert, claimed. Only British intervention could save the Transvaal from a bloodbath that imperilled all South Africa.

This, then, was the case for annexation, made public in the proclamation, and agreed to by Shepstone's masters in London. It was one of the boldest strokes of imperial policy for many years. What made it still bolder, perhaps reckless, was Shepstone's own vulnerability. He must survive at first with only twenty-five policemen. It would take a full month before the first British battalion of troops arrived from Natal and marched into Pretoria.

To survive, Shepstone needed not only the acquiescence of the Transvaal Boers but of their fellow Boers in the Orange Free State and their Afrikaner kith and kin in Cape Colony.

And, of course, it was vital that the Zulus did not interfere. Shepstone had no worries about that. Ever since he had attended King Cetshwayo's coronation in 1873, Cetshwayo had called him 'father': 'Somsteu, the Father of Whiteness'. He knew how to handle the Zulus. Indeed, it was his power over the Zulus, the Zulu card by which he had taken over the Transvaal, that would remain the ace up his sleeve, ready for the next trick, too, if Shepstone had his way.

On 31 March 1877, twelve days before the annexation, the *Balmoral Castle*, newest and fastest of the Currie Line mailboats (the main lifeline with England in the absence of a cable link), dropped anchor in Cape Town harbour. Among the English passengers admiring the 'Table Cloth' – the fluffy white layer of cloud over Table Mountain – was Sir Bartle Frere, the new Governor and High Commissioner at the Cape, coming to claim his kingdom.

It had been a record passage – twenty-two days – but tedious nonetheless. At first Frere found life on shore equally uninspiring. Government House, with a Dutch gable on its barnlike façade, seemed a comedown after the palace he had used as Governor of Bombay. In his first report to London he had to confess he found the place 'sleepy and slipshod'. It would be difficult to imagine anything more 'dirty and unwholesome'[2] than Cape Town itself.

Then on 16 April, the editor of the *Cape Times* put an astonishing cable from Kimberley into Frere's hand. Four days earlier Shepstone had annexed the Transvaal. 'Good heavens,' was Frere's first thought according to his biographer. 'What will they say in London?'[3] But he decided that it was not for him to interfere. It would be like trying to tell a man shooting the rapids how to use the paddle. And anyway, why shouldn't London confirm the annexation? It was London's idea in the first place, this bold coup, exploiting the weakness of the

Transvaal to impose the annexation and then using the annexation as the first step in federating all South Africa under the British flag.

Perhaps Shepstone had been hasty. Time would show. But then hadn't Lord Carnarvon, the Colonial Secretary, been still more hasty the previous summer? On 20 September 1876 a message had reached the Colonial Office in London: the Transvaal Boers were '*in extremis*' and the British would be asked to intervene. For two years Carnarvon's ingenious plans for federation had been stubbornly resisted in Cape Colony. Now he saw a chance of a new start, by way of the Transvaal. Shepstone, the Zulu expert brought over to London for a conference on confederation that had failed, was hustled out on that Friday's mailboat. In his pocket was a secret commission to be the first British Governor of the Transvaal. There was no time to put the plan to the Cabinet. Carnarvon simply scribbled a note to Disraeli, the Prime Minister, saying that he wanted Shepstone to take over the Transvaal 'if the crisis on his arrival makes this in any way possible'. Back came Dizzy's characteristic reply (he was in the middle of an election banquet in Aylesbury), 'Do what you think wisest.'[4] Like most Englishmen, Disraeli found more rewarding things to worry about than Africa.

A month after Shepstone had been packed off on his daredevil mission, Frere found himself roped in by Carnarvon to go out to the Cape as Governor and High Commissioner. At first he had had misgivings. Frere was a gentle, unassuming man, an admirer of Livingstone. He knew his limitations. He had made his name as a pro-consul and humanitarian, a protégé of the royal family, with forty-one years' experience of Indian affairs (though he had been passed over for the viceroyship). He knew next to nothing about Africa. True, in 1873 he had led a successful mission to Zanzibar, which would have delighted Livingstone, to persuade the Sultan to ban the slave trade in his dominions. He had also guided the Prince of Wales on a visit to Egypt and the newly opened Suez Canal. But he had no experience of imposing his will on tetchy white colonials. Carnarvon reassured him. This would be no ordinary job. If all went well, he would be Governor-General of the new dominion of South Africa, a kind of African viceroy. He offered as bait (Frere made no secret that he was anxious about money) the unheard-of salary of £10,000 a year, double the ordinary Governor's.

Carnarvon made the job seem so rewarding, in every sense, that Frere's misgivings dissolved. He admired Carnarvon for his success as Colonial Secretary in uniting the Canadian states in a single dominion. He shared that faith in imperial unity. He also shared Carnarvon's faith in the 'forward' policy: pushing forward the frontiers of the Empire. At this date the word 'imperialist' was hardly coined. Frere, like Carnarvon, would have welcomed it. He was convinced of the need for South African confederation. British immigrants would pour into South Africa. So would British capital. Tariffs would fall like the walls of Jericho. There would be economies in everything from railways to prisons, which would gladden the heart of the Treasury, and there would be even-handed justice for all, including natives. No one needed to remind Frere

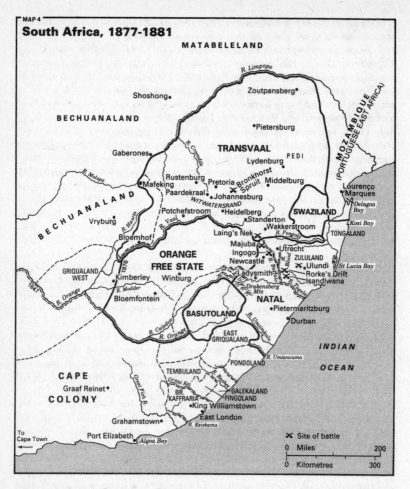

MAP 4

South Africa, 1877-1881

MATABELELAND

R. Limpopo

Shoshong

Zoutpansberg

BECHUANALAND

•Pietersburg

Gaberones

TRANSVAAL   PEDI

R. Crocodile

Lydenburg

Rustenburg Bronkhorst
Pretoria   Spruit Middelburg
Mafeking
Paardekraal   Johannesburg

R. Molopo

R. Marico

BECHUANALAND

Potchefstroom   Heidelberg

WITWATERSRAND

Vryburg

R. Harts

Bloemhof

R. Vaal

Standerton
Wakkerstroom

SWAZILAND

MOZAMBIQUE
(PORTUGUESE EAST AFRICA)

Lourenço
Marques

*Delagoa
Bay*

Laing's Nek

R. Pongola

TONGALAND

Kosi Bay

Majuba
Ingogo   •Utrecht
Newcastle   ZULULAND

ORANGE
FREE STATE

GRIQUALAND
WEST

1876

Kimberley   Winburg

1847

R. Orange

R. Modder

Bloemfontein

Ulundi   *St Lucia Bay*
Rorke's Drift
Isandlwana

Ladysmith

*Drakensberg
Mts*

NATAL

•Pietermaritzburg

BASUTOLAND

R. Caledon

R. Orange

EAST
GRIQUALAND

•Durban

R. Umzimkulu

INDIAN

OCEAN

PONDOLAND

R. Umtanvuma

CAPE

TEMBULAND

Great Kei

BR.
KAFFRARIA

GALEKALAND
FINGOLAND

Graaf Reinet•

COLONY

Great Fish R.

•King Williamstown

Grahamstown•

East London

R. Keiskama

To
Cape Town

Port Elizabeth•

Algoa Bay

✕ Site of battle

0   Miles   200

0   Kilometres   300

about the need to treat natives fairly but firmly; he had lived through the horrors of the Indian Mutiny and the reprisals after it.

Finally, Carnarvon revealed to Frere a heady vision of Britain's new empire expanding beyond South Africa. 'We cannot admit rivals to the East, or even the central parts of Africa: and I do not see why ... the Zambezi should be considered without the range of our colonization.'[5] Frere was swept off his feet. A new India was being created in Africa, a new age of empire-building was dawning. What a culmination to his own career it would be if the man who had been passed over for the Indian Viceroyship were to be chosen as the Clive of Africa.

A glance at the South African Blue Books brought Frere sharply back to earth. South Africa represented all that was worst about the British Empire. Take any one imperial problem: feuding between white communities, French and English, in Canada; bankruptcy among the mining industry in Australia; war between whites and Maoris in New Zealand; outrage and repression in Ireland. There were the same problems, only worse, in South Africa.

Yet Britain's interest as mother country seemed so simple. At Simonstown, a few miles south of Cape Town behind the fluffy white 'Table Cloth' was Britain's 'most important' naval base and coaling station in the whole world. This is what Lord Carnarvon had never shrunk from telling Disraeli and the Cabinet. To establish this base, Britain had grabbed the Cape temporarily from the Dutch East India Company during the French Revolutionary War, and made the occupation permanent after 1806. The Cape then guarded the only direct sea-lanes to India and beyond. In 1877, despite the opening of the Suez Canal in 1869, two-thirds of Britain's trade with India and the East still took the Cape route, and to guard it Britain needed not only a fortress-base – like Gibraltar – but a fortress-colony – like Canada – whose loyalty could be counted on, come hell or high water.

In fact, intermittent rebellion had proved a feature of the Cape from the days of the Dutch East India Company. Apart from the lush valleys around Cape Town, with their rolling wheatfields and neat, chequered vineyards, the land was half desert. At the heart of the colony was the great Karoo, too dry and stony for anything but sheep or cattle raising.

Despite the British takeover, many of the Dutch farmers remained poor and unassimilated. They called themselves Afrikaners (people of Africa) and their Dutch patois, Afrikaans. Many were trek-Boers, wandering pastoral farmers. History had given them three sources of strength: a passion for independence, a stern Calvinist morality and (though this often fluctuated) a collective sense of destiny. They were to prove formidable enemies to white and black alike.

In their conflicts with black people they were uniquely uncompromising. On the frontier they ruled by the whip and the gun. No matter that, in Cape Town, free-born Africans were equal before the law – on paper. The Boers on the frontier conceded no equality to Africans in Church or state. And the land seemed to be theirs for the taking, the land belonging to Africans who were still poorer, weaker and less united than the Boers. To work this land, like the settlers of the American South and the Caribbean, the Boers took Africans as slaves.

In 1834 the British Parliament decreed an end to slavery throughout the Empire. Compensation to slave-owners was slowly and clumsily paid. In 1835-6 about 6,000 Boers decided to leave Cape Colony in disgust. Off they trekked, with their flocks and about 6,000 African slaves and other dependants, across the Orange and Vaal rivers. Here they added to the chaos already created among African peoples by the Mfecane ('Crushing'), the destruction of weaker neighbours by King Shaka and the Zulus. Some of the trekkers were killed by Zulus led by Dingane, the successor of Shaka. Others were killed by the Ndebele led by Mzilikazi. Most survived, and went on to found miniature Boer republics in what became the Orange Free State, Natal and the Transvaal. This Great Trek was declared illegal by the British, but in practice ignored. Then Britain's 'forward' policy – imperial expansion – resumed. In 1842 Natal was taken over by the British in order to restore stability to the region; besides, there was a useful harbour at Durban. But vacillations at home then ended this phase of imperial expansion. The independence of the impoverished republics of the Transvaal and the Free State was guaranteed by the British in 1852 and 1854 respectively.

By the 1860s the old bitterness between British and Boers seemed to be passing. Then one day in 1867 an African shepherd picked up a strange glittering piece of rock from the veld. 'Gentlemen,' said the Colonial Secretary soon after in the Cape House of Assembly, 'on this rock the future success of South Africa will be built.'[6] He was absolutely correct. Diamonds were discovered, first in the river diggings in West Griqualand, close to the river Vaal, then at Colesberg kopje twenty miles away, a big pudding-shaped hill in what was soon to be christened Kimberley. Soon that big hill became the Big Hole, the largest man-made hole in the world. In five years the revenue of Cape Colony rose five times. The colony seemed set to exchange rags for riches. Tens of thousands of diggers scrambled for the blue mud of Kimberley, especially white Englishmen (like young Cecil Rhodes) and black Africans from all over South Africa. Of course Britain welcomed the treasure trove. It would relieve the hard-pressed British Treasury of one more overseas burden. Now, in 1872, Cape Colony was granted responsible government, making it fully self-governing like the Canadian federation, New Zealand or some of the Australian states.

Out of the Big Hole, however, came much that proved as hot to handle as if it had come from a volcano. For years there was an ugly wrangle about who owned West Griqualand where the diamonds were discovered. The Free State claimed it, but whatever their title – which of course paid scant heed to African ownership – they could not enforce it. The diggers invited the British to annex the place. The annexation was proclaimed in 1871 with the acquiescence, under protest, of the Free State. In due course, West Griqualand was attached to Cape Colony. And it seemed possible to silence Boer protests in the Free State – as later it seemed in the Transvaal – at a price. The Free State was eventually bought off with a lump sum of £90,000 in compensation.

Another explosive result of the diamond boom was that African wages rose to the roof, so it seemed to Europeans. Already white farmers and administrators found African labourers hard to recruit. Kimberley mines began to swallow labour on the scale of Britain's Black Country or the German Ruhr. Most miners were African, and paid a fraction of what white miners earned. Yet the shilling a day they were paid at the diggings seemed a fortune to them. They did not all spend it on beer or cheap spirits. Some of them used it to better themselves. After a few months they came back to the kraals, looking like white men, with breeches and shoes and – to protect themselves from attack – a breech-loading gun.

So these were the most disturbing features of the situation, to be faced by Frere when he arrived in South Africa: black labour was becoming rarer and costlier all over the British colonies; black wages were arming Africans with modern guns. Yet the old features of the situation remained as disturbing as ever.

First, although the more disaffected Boers had shaken off the dust of Cape Colony, other Afrikaners still made up two-thirds of the white population. Indeed, Afrikaners still outnumbered the British by three to two in the two British colonies of Cape Colony and Natal, and two Boer republics taken together. So there could be no real parallel between federating South Africa and federating Canada. In Canada the French were outnumbered two to one by the British. Second, all the whites in turn were greatly outnumbered by the Africans, especially in Natal and the Transvaal, where the ratio was at least ten blacks for every white man. It was in these two states that panicky talk of 'black peril' found most listeners, and white people relied on 'firmness' to keep Africans in their places.

Moreover, bordering Natal and the Transvaal was an African kingdom, Zululand, controlled by a powerful African ruler, King Cetshwayo. To many Natalians, Zululand itself, with its 30,000 disciplined and (supposedly) celibate warriors, seemed like a stabbing spear directed at their throats. Yet Cetshwayo had taken great care to reassure Shepstone that he would not move outside his borders – and had specifically welcomed the British annexation of the Transvaal as it would protect him from the Boers. In fact, he had skilfully wooed the British to defend himself from Boer encroachments throughout the twenty years since the Zulu civil war which had thrust him into power.

Frere's more immediate source of anxiety, which soon brought him near to despair, were the squabbles among the white minorities in the British colonies under his care, and their jealousy of imperial authorities, including himself. How to persuade Boers and British to federate under the British flag when the only thing they seemed to share was a reckless disregard for justice and prudence in handling the natives?

A frightening example of this disregard was presented by the recent Langalibalele affair whose echoes still reverberated from the Cape to Whitehall and Westminster. Langalibalele was the Chief of the seven-thousand-strong Hlubi people, refugees from Zululand settled by Shepstone twenty years before in a Natal reserve – 90,000 acres of green foothills under the shadow of the often snow-capped Drakensberg range. The Hlubi had prospered, doubly discomforting their white neighbours. Using modern ploughs they grew enough mealies to sell the surplus, under-cutting white farmers. They had no need themselves to take the low wages offered by white farms. Those who wanted cash went off to work in the mines of Kimberley, and returned from there in ever-increasing numbers, armed with guns.

In 1873 Langalibalele, like other chiefs, was summoned by a magistrate to register his people's firearms. The Chief tried to prevaricate. He was told to report to the colonial capital, Pietermaritzburg, to appear before Shepstone.

Langalibalele panicked. He knew of the case where John Shepstone, Theophilus's brother, had concealed his weapons, and thirty Africans had been killed when coming unarmed to a peaceful meeting. He was too frightened to leave his tribe and report to Shepstone. That October a mixed force – 200 Natal volunteers, 200 British regulars and 5,000 African levies – closed in on the Hlubi reserve. Shepstone sent an African messenger with a final warning. He returned to Shepstone claiming (falsely as it turned out) that he had been stripped and humiliated by the Chief. Langalibalele himself, with the men of the tribe, retreated towards the Drakensberg passes leading to Basutoland. The women, children and old men were left to fend for themselves in the caves of the foothills.

When news of what followed was eventually published, it raised a storm of protest among liberals in England. At first, it was the pursuers who suffered disaster. Maps read like fiction. The British regulars and colonial volunteers blundered around in the mists of the Drakensberg passes. The commander of the British regulars, Major Anthony Durnford, RE, slithered down a rocky slope with his horse and was badly injured. At the summit of the pass they met some Hlubi stragglers and a skirmish ensued. Three of the colonists and two African retainers were shot. Durnford was assegaied through the left arm but fought with courage, as did some Basutos loyal to the colonists. Most of the volunteers fled in terror back to the valley below.

Humiliated, but still hungry for the Hlubi lands, the colonists worked off their feelings on the Hlubi old men and other non-combatants. Women and children were smoked out of the caves. The colonists looted and burnt the kraals, carrying off all the cattle and grain. Several Hlubi stragglers were hunted down and shot. The colonists gloated about their 'strong hand' in putting down the 'rebellion'.[7] They not only took the entire Hlubi reserve for themselves, but went one better. They hunted down and shot several hundred of the neighbouring tribe, the Putini, who had no connection with Langalibalele, then took their lands too. Thousands of women and children from both tribes were marched down to Pietermaritzburg to be handed over to the settlers as 'apprentices', hardly better than slaves. The Lieutenant-Governor of Natal, an elderly colonial servant called Sir Benjamin Pine, then absolved the settlers from all atrocities committed during the affair by passing a formal act of indemnity.

Langalibalele himself surrendered with his tribesmen after being rounded up by the Basutos. He was prosecuted for high treason, in a trial that later became famous for its irregularities, sentenced to life banishment, and incarcerated on Robben Island, near Cape Town. The tribe was broken up, the men forced, like the women, to work for Natal farmers.

Such was the serial story of the civilizing mission of Britain's settlers in Natal, unfolding during 1874 and 1875. That it came to light at all was due almost entirely to the courage of one Englishman, irrepressible John Colenso, the 'heretical' Bishop of Natal. Colenso had scandalized fellow Christians in England in the 1860s by his assertion that the Bible (especially Genesis) was not to be taken literally. He had been inspired, by talking to some of his Zulu parishioners, to look more closely at these things. He tried to make a bridge between the new discoveries of Darwin and the accepted beliefs of Christianity. He was abused and ridiculed by English Christians from Arnold to Disraeli and the Archbishop of Canterbury. In South Africa, in 1863, he was formally tried for heresy in the cathedral at Cape Town, then deposed and excommunicated by the Archbishop. He appealed to the Privy Council and the Privy Council upheld his tenure as Bishop of Natal, though it could not save him from the deluge of ridicule.

Now Colenso, a decade later, risked a lynching to expose what he proved were a series of atrocities against the Hlubi and Putini. He took his documents to London and showed them to Lord Carnarvon, and Carnarvon reluctantly agreed he was right. Pine was sacked. The Putini were to be compensated. Langalibalele and his people were to be released. It was Colenso's triumph. Yet the cost was immense.

Colenso's closest family friend was Theophilus Shepstone, the Secretary for Native Affairs in Natal. Colenso had always regarded Shepstone as a champion of African rights. Shoulder to shoulder, the two men had fought to protect the African reserves in Natal from the hands of land-hungry white settlers. Now, in taking statements from African witnesses, Colenso realized he had been 'humbugged'.[8] Shepstone's behaviour was as arbitrary as any African chief's; he was a bully and a liar. In the Langalibalele affair he had condoned the atrocities and was hand in glove with the settlers. The revelation stunned Colenso. Then he decided it was to be 'war to the knife'.[9] And perhaps he already guessed where Armageddon lay: in Zululand, the private reserve, so it seemed, of the Shepstone family. Was Cetshwayo to be treated like Langalibalele, to be hunted out of his kingdom on the pretext of defying the white man?

One other Englishman rallied to help Colenso in the crisis, Anthony Durnford RE, now a colonel. Four years after being assegaied by Langalibalele's men in the Drakensberg, he still carried his left arm in a sling. But he was chivalrous and admired the courage of his African adversaries. He also admired the bishop's daughter, Fanny, and she fell deeply in love with him, although he had an estranged wife in England. Together they campaigned to help restore the Putini to their rights. Despite official discouragement, Durnford employed the men on public works so they could earn enough to buy new land for the tribe.

Meanwhile, Sir Bartle Frere had decided to come to Natal to see these problems for himself, on his way to confer with Shepstone in the Transvaal. Instead he was caught up by events in the eastern Cape, still more tangled and dangerous than the Langalibalele affair.

At this time the stony ravines of the Kei river marked the eastern boundary of Cape Colony. On the near side, in the Ciskei, lived relatively prosperous African peoples, Ngquika-Xhosa and Fingos (Mfengu). Beyond the Kei, in Transkei, under British supervision though not formally annexed, were the impoverished Gcaleka-Xhosa, led by a chief called Kreli Sarhili. They were the

Fingos' former masters and once owned the land the British had given to the Fingos in return for support in fighting on the frontier. In August 1877 a drunken brawl exploded into a new war. First the Gcalekas attacked the hated Fingos. Then they marched, armed with modern guns, against the nearest British police post inside the colony. They had not, however, mastered the use of their new weapons. The attack was beaten off by police and volunteers. The Gcalekas were then hunted back into the Transkei, as far as the Bashee river. Within a few months, 700 of them were dead, twenty chiefs killed and 13,000 head of cattle – the tribe's main wealth – captured by the colonial forces. It seemed punishment enough for Kreli's foolish 'invasion'.

However, despite the warning of the general in charge of the British regulars, some of the drifts (fords) in the Transkei were left unguarded. Back came some Gcalekas, across the Kei river and into the colony where they stirred up the Ngquikas led by their Chief Sandile. For seven months Frere was stuck in the British barracks at King Williamstown, in the centre of the disturbed area, trying to gain control of his own colonial ministers and their men. It was their weakness, he believed, that was responsible for the rising in Transkei and now this rebellion in the colony. From his experience of Indian affairs, he believed they should have annexed the Transkei long ago. It was 'wicked folly' to try these experiments with Kreli as an 'almost independent chief'. They should 'do their best' for them by ruling them at least as well as they had ruled the Fingos.[10] Towards the Ngquika, too, policy had been pusillanimous. Instead of supporting and supervising the natives, giving them confidence in British justice, they had encouraged Sandile's idea that he was a paramount chief with power to decide peace or war, and with the right to object to having colonial police within his territory.

Now that rebellion had broken out, the Cape government's policy had swung from reckless weakness to reckless violence. Columns of smoke drifted across the wooded hills beside the Kei. Local volunteers were burning kraals and looting cattle wholesale. What especially sickened Frere was that many wretched Ngquikas caught up in the rebellion were being executed without trial as 'rebels'. True, the chiefs might be guilty and deserve punishment; the common herd only needed to be disarmed and taught their duty to obey the law. It was a duty, Frere told his ministers stiffly, that many white men had yet to learn.

Colonials did not take kindly to being lectured by the Governor on how to treat 'kaffirs'. They were in an ugly mood, even the best of them. Molteno, the Cape's Prime Minister, Afrikaner-backed, insisted that the colonial forces should be free to hunt the rebels independently of imperial control. So Frere took the bold step of dismissing the Cape ministry and appointing a new Prime Minister, Gordon Sprigg, ready and able to form a new government.

Meanwhile, two new battalions of British regulars had been rushed to South Africa to bring to heel both the rebellious Africans and defiant colonials. A new British general, Lt-General Frederick Thesiger, took over the command. Soon the crude violence of the colonials – cattle-lifting, burning kraals and shooting 'kaffirs' – was exchanged for a regular military campaign. Fortunately for the British, the Africans continued to believe in mass attacks in the open, presenting perfect targets for Armstrong 12-pounders and Martini-Henry rifles. Sandile was killed, Kreli driven into exile. By April 1878 the rebellion was fizzling out and Frere felt it safe to return to Cape Town, after seven months sleeping rough at King Williamstown.

Soon the Transkei was to be annexed and Pondoland, too. Britain was taking over the whole strategic seaboard from the Cape to Natal. Naturally Frere found this excellent, if overdue. But how to apply the same sensible forward policy towards the white communities? The momentum to confederation had ended – if it had ever begun. That was the depressing news he heard on his return to the Cape.

Another blow had fallen. Lord Carnarvon, the Colonial Secretary on whom Frere relied to push his policy in Disraeli's Cabinet, had impetuously resigned on 25 January. The issue was Eastern policy, not Africa. Frere felt the loss keenly. The new Colonial Secretary was young, inexperienced Sir Michael Hicks Beach, whom he hardly knew, though he could count on a free hand.

Frere's job remained the same: somehow to nurse confederation along. In England, the Colonial Office had industriously produced a South Africa Bill, the constitutional mould in which to cast the great new united dominion. In South Africa the only unity seemed to be forged by Afrikaners in Cape Colony and Boers in the Transvaal and Free State against the *rooineks*, the English. Ever since Shepstone's annexation of the Transvaal, the opinion of the Boer majority seemed to be turning more sour. There was a substantial majority, according to a petition, against annexation. Two delegations had been sent to England, both led by Paul Kruger, to try to persuade the British government to restore the country's independence. Kruger was politely rebuffed, after being shown the artillery base at Woolwich, with a hint of what to expect if the Boers ever gave trouble. Trouble he gave in plenty when he sailed back to South Africa, stirring up both Free State Boers and Afrikaners in the Cape against either annexation or confederation.

Frere was delighted at having an empire-minded colonist like Gordon Sprigg at his side as Prime Minister of the Cape. But Sprigg could do nothing to advance confederation an inch when challenged by Molteno, now leader of the Opposition and backed by most Afrikaners in the colony. And Frere found that the colonists in Natal, though predominantly British, were cautious towards confederation, as they feared absorption by their powerful white neighbours.

The key, then, remained the Transvaal, the only state directly controlled by the imperial government. But why had Shepstone failed to convince Kruger and his Transvaal Boers to acquiesce in annexation – and so confederation? The question puzzled Frere. The imperial government had made a £100,000 grant to rescue the Transvaal from bankruptcy. But there were signs that Shepstone had fudged the books. Proper accounts were not being kept. The fellow wouldn't have lasted long in India! By the summer of 1878 Frere had come to the conclusion that poor old Shepstone was a liability, and must be replaced – a conclusion in which London regretfully concurred.

Then in July 1878, all these setbacks were followed by news from Natal which fell on Frere like a thunderbolt. The news concerned Cetshwayo and the Zulus.

Much as Frere deplored Shepstone's fumbling in the Transvaal, he recognized that on one subject – the Zulus – Shepstone was the expert. Here he put himself in Shepstone's hands. But after twenty years as Cetshwayo's acknowledged champion, as Somsteu, the father of whiteness, Shepstone had shamelessly changed sides. Perhaps this volte-face was inevitable, once he had taken over the Transvaal. The Transvaal Boers were natural enemies of the Zulus, and how better to woo the Boers than to take their side against their enemy? It was a new way of playing the Zulu card, the ace up Shepstone's sleeve.

In October 1877 Shepstone had gone to the border between the Transvaal and Zululand at Blood river and sent an ominous message to Cetshwayo. The burning issue that had long divided Zulus from Boers was the ownership of a large strip of land on the north-western boundary of Zululand. The Boers claimed it. It had been ceded to various Boer immigrants, they said, and they could prove proper title. Shepstone had always disputed this. One of his aims was to acquire this strip for Natal, as a corridor to the north for the use of imported African labourers. In fact, Cetshwayo's father, Mpande, had offered the strip to Natal to provide security for his people against Boer encroachment. Now Shepstone warned Cetshwayo that he must acknowledge Boer rights. Back came the gibe from Cetshwayo's messengers. They had called him 'father' and he had deserted them. He was a cheat and a fraud. Shepstone was left gasping on the river-bank.

The wound to Shepstone's pride suppurated. He wrote a furious report to London, which Frere had read. Cetshwayo must go. Unless his anachronistic regime was removed, there was no hope for progress in South Africa.

> Cetewayo [sic] is the secret hope of every ... independent chief hundreds of miles from him, who feels the desire that his colour shall prevail.... The sooner the root of the evil ... which I consider to be the Zulu power and military organisation, is dealt with, the easier our task will be.[11]

Shepstone had then orchestrated a press campaign against Cetshwayo: with garbled reports from disgruntled border farmers, traders in whisky and guns and – most virulent – Protestant missionaries. The latter had made only a handful of converts, and most of these were people who had fallen foul of the regime. Mutual resentment had developed between the King and the missionaries. One of them in particular fed Shepstone with especially appetizing lies, Robert Robertson, once a disciple of Colenso's, who had turned against everything he had believed in and succumbed to the lure of whisky and the pretty Zulu girls on his mission (he claimed he had been corrupted by Cetshwayo and his satanical followers).

These were the tales against Cetshwayo confirmed by Shepstone. The idea of ideological threat from the Zulus did not strike Frere as absurd. In the Cape rebellion had spread like a bushfire from tribe to tribe, just as it had spread in India during the Mutiny. Of course Shepstone must be right. Cetshwayo was a bloodthirsty tyrant and would have to go. Britain must control all South Africa from sea to sea.

To Frere the King seemed an ignorant savage. Yet the King had certainly responded with maddening skill to the challenge thrown down by Shepstone at the Blood river meeting the previous October. Cetshwayo had sent messages to Bishop Colenso and the Governor of Natal, Bulwer, asking for advice. Bulwer arranged that a Commission of Inquiry should be appointed to hear the evidence on the disputed strip of territory lying between the Transvaal and Zululand. Cetshwayo was delighted. Again and again he had begged the British (through Shepstone) to arbitrate on this issue.

Frere gave his agreement with misgivings. But Shepstone had assured him that he had now seen with his own eyes the evidence which would prove the Boers had full title. And two of his family were going to smooth things along: his brother John, as one of the 'impartial' commissioners, and his son Henriques, as one of the Transvaal delegates. So Frere was assured that Cetshwayo would lose the Award. Probably he hoped that Cetshwayo would then lose his head, too, and precipitate a crisis which could only be resolved by war.

Was Frere, the gentle evangelical, the admirer of Livingstone, champion of the oppressed, reconciled to the need to fight the Zulus? Certainly not to attack them – at first. But in July 1878, when the thunderbolt fell, he had suddenly reversed his strategy.

The thunderbolt was the Award made by the commissioners. This incongruous trio – a lawyer called Gallwey, John Shepstone and Colonel Durnford – had been camping for weeks at Rorke's Drift on the Buffalo river, taking evidence from Zulu warriors and Transvaalers. Incredibly, the Boers – through the agency of the two Shepstones – had failed to produce any documentary proof of the Transvaal title. On the contrary, all the evidence went to confirm the Zulus' title. The Boers had bullied and wheedled and encroached – as they had encroached on tribal lands all over South Africa – but here they had not even made a nominal payment to local chiefs. The Zulu monarchy was too strong for that. Cetshwayo and his father, Mpande, had contested the claim from the beginning. So the commissioners gave the Award to Cetshwayo on the main issue, the ownership of the disputed strip of territory.

It might have been welcomed as the happy ending to a long wrangle which had imperilled the peace of the region for twenty years. To Frere it was a death blow to his grand design. What a way to win friends in the Transvaal and support for annexation! And what a duffer he had been to listen to Shepstone. All over South Africa people would be talking of Downing Street and the negrophiles. The Award was a monstrosity. Frere kept it secret from the public, half-secret in fact from London, in the wild hope of persuading the commissioners to change their minds.

In September he sailed back to the Cape. Like a plant, war needs warmth and time to ripen. Fortunately, it seemed to him, his hands were free, as there was no cable link with London. Frere began to drop hints in that direction, to warm the blood of the Colonial Office without frightening them. He needed reinforcements (though he could make do without them). Frere also dropped hints to the editors in Natal that a crisis was coming. The Natal press needed no encouragement.

> We have been all our lifetime subject to bondage, our colonists may well say, by reason of this black shadow [the Zulus] across the Tugela.... Such a nation must of necessity form a constant menace to the peaceable European community beyond their borders. Civilisation cannot co-exist with such a condition of things upon its outskirts.[12]

As late as November, when writing to London, Frere still presented himself as a man who was trying to make a diplomatic settlement and keep the peace. But he now drafted a crisp ultimatum to Cetshwayo, taking care not to warn London of its terms. The missionaries must be restored (they had never actually been expelled); the King must accept a British Resident (in effect, Zululand would be made a protectorate). He must abolish the military system – the bachelor-age regiments – in fact, destroy the foundation of his own state. Failure to comply with these terms within thirty days would force the British to invade. And there was no fear of the King complying. Frere meant the ultimatum to make war certain. Now was the time.

On the morning of 11 December 1878, close to where the river Tugela meets the sea, the King's messengers should be finally told the commissioners' decision on the boundary dispute. That afternoon, as they were digesting the good news, they would be handed the ultimatum like a poisoned cup.

Colonel Anthony Durnford was in his element, wearing a bush hat and on active service again, though his left arm still hung limp on his saddle. He had no difficulty in riding his charger, Chieftain, with reins dangling, though the horse was too wild to let anyone else on his back. The rumours of war had hardened to a certainty. By late December 1878 Durnford expected to be one of the British commanders invading Zululand. It was the chance he had longed for, strange to say, considering that he, like his friends the Colensos, was convinced the war was both unjust and unnecessary.

Durnford explained himself like this: 'I am not of course a negrophilist, and as a soldier I should delight in the war; but as a man I condemn it.'[13] As a commissioner in the boundary dispute, he had certainly done his bit to 'play fair', as he put it.[14] For weeks he had dug in his toes and blocked Frere's attempt to try to tamper with the Award. He was supported by Bulwer, the humane Governor of Natal, who had opposed Frere's belligerence as long as he could. Then Durnford the soldier took over from Durnford the man of peace.

He had escorted Shepstone to Cetshwayo's formal coronation in 1873, so he knew the Zulus better than most British commanders. He warned his men there would be some kind of scrap, 'the Zulus will charge home'. Yet he shared – or so he told his mother, perhaps to reassure her – the idea that the invasion would be a kind of 'military promenade'.[15] How to expect anything else in a contest of artillery and modern rifles against an enemy armed largely with spears?

Frere's thirty-day ultimatum expired on 11 January 1879. Next day the British C-in-C, Lt-General Lord Chelmsford (General Thesiger had inherited this title early in the year), launched a three-pronged invasion with 7,000 British troops. Durnford was attached to No. 3 Column, the headquarter column, under Chelmsford's direct command at the centre. On 18 January Chelmsford took two regular battalions – the 1st/24th and 2nd/24th – and was ferried across the border, the river Buffalo at Rorke's Drift, then vanished up into the stony hills of Zululand. To Durnford's chagrin, he was put in charge of the base camp at Rorke's Drift. He was in charge of a large native contingent, including some of the unfortunate Hlubi and Putini tribesmen he had rescued after the Langalibalele affair. He wrote to his mother on 21 January that it was wet and miserable. 'I am "down" because I am "left behind", but we shall see.'[16]

Chelmsford himself was in high spirits, supremely confident. He pitched camp on a grassy *nek* under a strange-looking outcrop of rock, twelve miles inside Zululand. No trenches were dug nor any attempt made to fortify the camp. After all, in this one column he had ample men to thrash the Zulus: 2,000 imperial redcoats, 1,000 colonial volunteers and 1,000 natives, with six field-guns to match. He brushed aside warnings from a Boer veteran J. J. Uys, who told him to remember the fate of the voortrekkers (the Boer pioneers) killed by the Zulus. 'Trek into Zululand with two laagers close to each other. Place your spies far out, and form your wagons into a wagon laager.'[17] Chelmsford smiled. That was forty years ago. The British had the most modern army in the world.

The morning sun threw long shadows on that strange-looking outcrop of rock about 200 feet high, shaped something like a crouching lion, or sphinx. The Zulus called it Isandlwana, meaning 'the Little House' or 'Cow's Stomach'. It was a name that would soon echo round the world.

At his tin-roofed house, Bishopstowe, 150 miles to the south-west, Bishop Colenso waited with his family. Especially anxious was his favourite daughter, Fanny, who had lost her heart to Durnford. Until late December they had all hoped Frere's belligerence was a bluff. An invasion scare might force Cetshwayo to modernize his state and open it to civilization – something that Colenso, like all missionaries, felt was long overdue. In November, when Frere came to Natal, he called on Colenso in person and the bishop was touched by the honour. Surely it was a good omen too for the High Commissioner to visit the bishop, boycotted by his parishioners because he championed the Zulus. Then, at the end, Colenso saw it was hopeless. All Frere wanted from him – and got – was his silence. He had been 'humbugged' once again.

*   *   *

At Ulundi, in the great circle of beehive huts that formed the royal capital, 150 miles to the east, King Cetshwayo waited with his wives. To the end he too had hoped for peace. But the ultimatum, as Frere saw, gave him no such choice. To accept those terms would have been to abdicate as king.

What Cetshwayo felt about Frere is not recorded, but two years earlier he had told Robertson, that wreck of a missionary, what he felt about Shepstone:

> I love the English. I am not Mpande's son. I am the child of Queen Victoria. But I am also a king in my own country and must be treated as such. Somsteu must speak gently to me. I shall not hear dictation ... I shall perish first.[18]

So he had called his age-regiments, and given them their orders. No doubt they accepted them, like the soldiers of any country, with mixed feelings. Yet they knew they would be fighting to defend their independence. Besides, by custom the younger warriors needed a war before they were allowed to marry. This would be the first war of Cetshwayo's reign, the first 'washing of the spears'.

Shepstone had annexed the Boers as the first step in the making of a great new British dominion. But the second step was not to be confederation; it was to be the invasion of Zululand. Now the British – and in due course the Zulus – would have to pay the price in blood, treasure and humiliation.

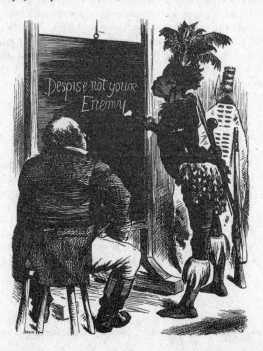

CHAPTER 4

The Crouching Lion

London, Zululand, London
November 1878 – 22 January 1879

'How very amusing! Actually attacking our camp! Most amusing.'
Lt-Col Crealock to Major Clery, 22 January 1879.

The prospect of a Zulu war lowered Disraeli's spirits. He blamed Frere, Shepstone, and especially their old Chief, 'Twitters' – Disraeli's nickname for Lord Carnarvon, the former Colonial Secretary.

His own health seemed to be failing; at any rate it was too fickle for a Prime Minister's. In June 1878, in the great palace in Berlin, he had somehow risen to the occasion. He towered over the Congress, attended by the greatest men in Europe. '*Der alte Jude, das ist der Mann*' ('the old Jew, that's the man'), growled Bismarck. Then came the reaction. He spent September living like a recluse at Hughenden, his romantically gabled, red brick, neo-Tudor manor house, where he could survey his peacocks under the shadow of the great beech woods of the Chilterns. It was here that he had first set himself up as a landed gentleman thirty years before. This was the outwork from which he had assailed Society.

Bronchitis and gout now assailed him in turn. Any change in his routine – leaving his library to drive out in the carriage to return the visits of neighbours – would bring on a new fit of coughing. In November 1878 he was back fighting for breath in 10 Downing Street, where the fog made the windows as opaque as the minds of some of his Cabinet colleagues.

He would not forgive Twitters (though Twitters had resigned from the Cabinet the previous January) for the blunder of the impending Zulu war. Not that he doubted the outcome, any more than anyone else in London. It would be a walkover. But what a time to choose. Peace in Europe was as fragile as his own health, despite his triumph at the Congress of Berlin, thwarting the Russians' attempts to seal their recent victory over the Turks by new territorial gains in Europe. And outside Europe, the Cabinet had already one unpopular war on their hands: an invasion of Afghanistan. This was being forced on them by a headstrong Viceroy, Lord Lytton, who claimed it was the only way to protect India from the Russian bear hug.

Frere and Shepstone now seemed to be playing the same tricks as Lytton with still less excuse.

... if anything annoys me more than another [Disraeli wrote in September to his intimate friend, Lady Bradford], it is our Cape affairs, where every day brings forward a new blunder of Twitters'. The man he swore by was Sir T. Shepstone, whom he looked upon as heaven-born for the object in view. We sent him out entirely for Twitters' sake, and he has managed to quarrel with Eng., Dutch, and Zulus – and now he is obliged to be recalled but not before he has brought on, I fear, a new war. Froude [Carnarvon's tactless adviser on federation] was bad enough and has cost us a million; this will be worse. So much for Twitters.[1]

Disraeli realized that the recall of Shepstone might please the Boers and help reconcile them to the annexation of the Transvaal, but it could hardly prevent a war with the Zulus. It was Frere who was trying to provoke this war, Frere who had the bit between his teeth. How to stop the runaway? In October the Cabinet had sent him a polite reproof by way of the new Colonial Secretary, Sir Michael Hicks Beach. Frere must show a 'spirit of compromise' and 'for-bearance' towards Cetshwayo and the Zulus. As for the reinforcements he claimed to need, the request was rebuffed. The Cabinet had decided that with a trade recession at home, an African war was worse than a luxury they could not afford. It would be 'a serious evil'.[2]

If it was fair for Disraeli to blame Twitters for the Zulu business, he must blame himself for appointing Twitters Colonial Secretary four years before. Perhaps he had only now begun to grasp that implicit in Carnarvon's own policy for confederation was a radical plan for expanding the Empire: by eliminating the independent African kingdoms, and pushing the frontier 1,000 miles north to the Zambezi. Disraeli and his other colleagues saw absolutely no need for a forward policy of this kind in Africa. No British interests, strategic or commercial, seemed threatened in Africa by other European Powers. The matter had not come to a head in Carnarvon's own time at the Colonial Office since he had resigned on quite a different issue. But Carnarvon's policy continued, whipped to a gallop by Frere.

In November Hicks Beach confessed that to control Frere was beyond him:

I cannot really control him without a telegraph. (I don't know that I could with one.) I feel it is as likely as not that he is at war with the Zulus at the present moment; and if his forces should prove inadequate, or the Transvaal Boers should take the opportunity to rise, he will be in a great difficulty, and we shall be blamed for not supporting him.[3]

Hicks Beach then persuaded the Cabinet to accept a compromise, which no one who knew Frere could have expected to work. The belligerent proconsul would get his reinforcements after all, but they were to be used strictly for defensive purposes. It was a final shake of the reins to the runaway horse.

Disraeli continued to grumble about Frere and Twitters. But at least the war in Afghanistan was going better than Lytton deserved.

Meanwhile, on 11 November, Disraeli took his carriage to the Guildhall to speak at the Lord Mayor's Banquet. That morning the task had seemed beyond him, so frail was his voice, yet by evening people found it powerful and clear.

A thousand guests rose to their feet, waving their handkerchiefs and napkins in delight. The peroration caught the mood of the moment, pride in his own diplomatic triumph at Berlin. Who dared to say England's power was on the wane? Yet the appeal was to old-fashioned patriotism, not to a new imperialism, meaning imperial expansion. Dizzy's eyes remained fixed on the Eastern question, and beyond, to those fastnesses of Central Asia, where Russia was supposed to be preparing to swoop down on India.

A new empire in Africa? The idea was absurd.

There was, of course, one man above all who believed in extending Britain's empire in Africa, Henry Morton Stanley. He had reached London ten months earlier, in late January 1878, and had been fêted everywhere. His discovery of the Congo was hailed as the most important geographical discovery ever made in Africa. Old Africa hands like Baker and Grant made full amends for having doubted him. He was the lion at every society dinner, the protégé of royalty. The Prince of Wales presided when he addressed the Royal Geographical Society in St James's Hall.

There was still one stain on his reputation: he had not behaved like a gentleman towards the natives. But even this stain began to fade in light of all his achievements, and his apparent admiration for Britain and her Empire.

Stanley, however, remained puzzled and angry at his reception. He took as an affront the sight of some empty seats in the great meeting in St James's Hall. He was convinced that no one – the politicians, editors, philanthropists and financiers he met every night at dinner – really took him seriously. He wrote later, 'I do not understand Englishmen at all. Either they suspect me of some self-interest, or they do not believe me. My reward has been to be called a mere penny-a-liner. For the relief of Livingstone I was called an impostor ... for trying to kindle them to action I am called ... a hare-brained fellow totally unused to business.'[4]

What drove him to despair was his failure to convince anyone that Britain should take over the Congo, whose immense wealth was going begging.

In Marseilles, after landing in January 1878, he had rebuffed Leopold's overtures and brushed aside a royal invitation to Brussels, because all his hopes were centred on taking the Congo for Britain. But he had reached London at the worst possible moment. It was the week in January when a Cabinet crisis, brought on by the Turkish defeat in the war in the Balkans, finally came to the boil. Carnarvon, the only politician who might have understood what he was saying, resigned as Colonial Secretary. The mood in Britain remained sceptical towards new colonial ventures, a mood shared by businessmen as well as politicians. The City had got its fingers badly burnt in the current Egyptian crisis: the bankruptcy of the Khedive, brought on by reckless borrowing – and the banks' reckless lending – in Europe. The trade recession at home meant that everyone had to tighten his belt. Tropical ventures were notoriously speculative. A new African colony would take years to pay its way. Meanwhile the taxpayer would have to grind his teeth and pay up. Anyway, at a time when trade was comparatively free, when most of the world's export markets were Britain's oyster, why on earth did Britain need new colonies?

As for the missionary lobby, they were fully stretched sending out missions to Nyasaland and to Uganda. The Congo would have to wait.

In the spring of 1878 Stanley had thrown himself into the job of working up his Congo diaries for publication. He called the book *Through the Dark Continent,* and pounded out the two volumes at the characteristic rate of fourteen pages a day. By June he had begun to wonder why he had rebuffed that royal invitation to Brussels. Solvyns, the Belgian Ambassador, obliged with a new one. On 11 June King Leopold received him in the royal palace. Stanley was bowled over by the pomp and glitter, but the King said little or nothing. He was sizing him up. Stanley went on to Paris, where he was fêted even more rapturously than in London. In August he began detailed discussions with Leopold's confidants. They took back to their master Stanley's estimate of the cost of opening up the Congo. Still not committed, Stanley returned to London to make a last effort to stir British public opinion. He stumped up and down the country, giving thirty lectures. But his plans for the Congo were greeted with indifference or suspicion.

Late in the autumn of 1878 Stanley had formally committed himself to Leopold: to serve King Leopold II in Africa for a term of five years. The plans were vague, and he was warned to keep things secret as long as possible. If Disraeli or other members of the British government happened to enquire, he was to tell them that the project was a 'very simple and modest one'. Three hospitals and scientific stations between Boma and Stanley Pool, a transport plan to link the upper and lower Congo: this was at present all his 'philanthropical and scientific' mission[5] amounted to, and it was part of Leopold's crusade to open up Africa under the auspices of the International African Association. That much Stanley could tell Disraeli.

Stanley was at first unsure what to believe himself. He found the attempts at secrecy somewhat absurd. A large map of the Congo, with his intended stations marked in red, was hanging in the offices of the King's organization, the *Comité des Etudes du Haut Congo,* in Brussels. The secret plans were open to the public. 'The Belgians', he noted, 'are a peculiarly innocent people. Innocent in the sense of not being suspicious of other people's penetrative power.'

On 10 February 1879, after completing plans for the new expedition, Stanley left Brussels to return to the Congo, travelling under the absurd alias of 'M. Henri'. He, at least, was no innocent. Indeed, he was beginning to see things clearly. 'The King is a clever statesman. He is supremely clever, but I have not had thirty opportunities of conversing with him without penetrating his motives ... under the guise of an International Association he hopes to make a Belgian dependency of the Congo basin.'[6]

Stanley's bitterness left him as he realized the scale of the task with which he was entrusted.

Disraeli and the British government had not bothered to enquire about Stanley's

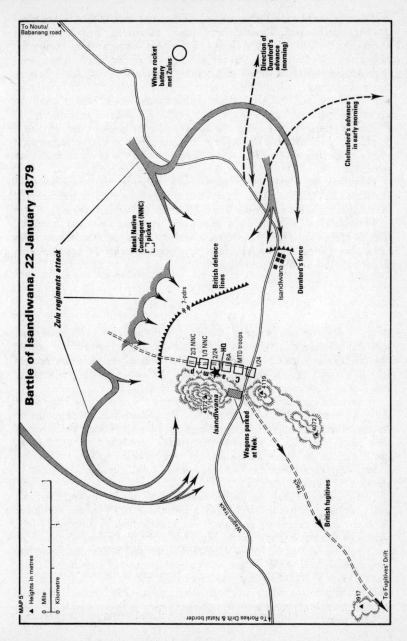

Battle of Isandlwana, 22 January 1879

To Noutu/Babanang road

Where rocket battery met Zulus

Direction of Durnford's advance (morning)

Chelmsford's advance in early morning

Natal Native Contingent (NNC) picket

Zulu regiments attack

British defence lines

7-pdrs

Isandlwana

Durnford's force

2/3 NNC 1/3 NNC 2/24 HQ RA MTD troops 1/24

4372

Isandlwana

4119

4072

Wagons parked at Nek

British fugitives

To R.D. track

Wagon track

3917

To Fugitives' Drift

To Rorkes Drift & Natal border

MAP 5
▲ Heights in metres
0   Mile
0   Kilometre

involvement with Leopold. One reason was that the Foreign Office had received a confidential report about Stanley which confirmed Whitehall's worst suspicions. Dr John Kirk, the Consul at Zanzibar, denounced by Stanley for failing to supply Livingstone, was the author of the report, based on interviews with Africans who had served with Stanley. They made wild claims: Stanley had kicked a man to death, kept a black mistress, captured Africans and sold them as slaves, and attacked villages without provocation. Kirk believed the claims, and reported Stanley's expedition had been a 'disgrace to humanity'.

The FO agreed that his behaviour had been 'to say the least discreditable'.[7] In plain English, the man was a rotter, the last person to choose to entrust a plan for opening up Africa in the unlikely event of the government's being interested.

That week the Cabinet was complacently waiting to hear the news from Zululand. Sir Michael Hicks Beach had suddenly become optimistic. The reinforcements had now reached Frere. Hicks Beach reassured Disraeli, 'There is, I hope, a good prospect, in this case, of the war being short and successful, like the Afghan campaign.'[8] Resentment against Frere's high-handedness began to evaporate. After all, he was the man on the spot. Even his reckless ultimatum might be 'a thoroughly successful stroke'.

*   *   *

At 1.30 a.m. on the morning of 22 January 1879, the night before the new moon, with Isandlwana a dim silhouette against the sky, Major Francis Clery pushed open the flap of Lord Chelmsford's tent. Clery was a genial and bewhiskered Irishman, staff officer to the central column. He brought an urgent message pencilled across a crumpled sheet torn from a notebook.

The general's tent was in the upper camp at the top of the slope, close under the rocky outcrop, Isandlwana, shaped like a crouching lion, or the sphinx on the regimental cap badge of the 24th Regiment. Most of the men had retired to their tents, or lay round the campfires, spread over half a mile of hillside, chatting about the march into Zululand. It was proving a walkover, a letdown in fact, after all the tales they had heard of the Zulus. Pity the niggers had no stomach for a scrap.

Two days earlier they had pitched camp here at Isandlwana and gazed out over the plain, 300 feet below. It seemed quite deserted. There was no sign of life in the kraals thrown up like molehills across the folds of the plain. To the south-east you could make out the old track of the traders' ox wagons. This cut a pale line across the rolling green downs, dipping briefly into the gullies before vanishing over the skyline, still forty miles short of Ulundi and Cetshwayo's great kraal. Westward, the same track led to the Natal border at Rorke's Drift, twelve miles away. Badly waterlogged, it had been scraped brown by the hundred-odd commissariat ox wagons, now unloaded beside the rows of white tents.

Clery woke the general, then lay face down close beside the camp bed and read him the message. Major Dartnell, sent to reconnoitre the track ahead with the Natal Mounted Police, the Volunteers and the Natal Native Contingent, reported some of the enemy marked down in the ravines to the left. To attack them in the morning he needed a couple of companies of white troops. Chelmsford did not hesitate long. His plan of campaign was simple. With his three small columns he was to sweep the Zulus back towards Cetshwayo's kraal at Ulundi. The central column, to which he had attached himself, would go directly by the old traders' track. He had only one fear, apart from the difficulties of taking ox wagons along waterlogged tracks: the Zulus might break into small parties and escape him. This was one of the trying features of native wars, as he had found to his cost in the campaign against Kreli and Sandile the previous year.

The campaign would probably be dull but not dangerous. There was no fear – this was an article of faith with Chelmsford and the HQ staff – that the Zulus were the kind of enemy who might mount a serious attack. What chance had savages armed with assegais and blunderbusses to get within half a mile of several thousand British troops, including mounted men and a battery of modern artillery? So nothing had been done, either back at the depot at Rorke's Drift, or out here on the hillside at Isandlwana, to dig trenches or build any kind of defences to protect the camp. Why, as Chelmsford himself had said, 'it would take a week'[9] – a ridiculous hold-up. Nor had he any qualms about dividing his forces still further, as he now explained to Clery.

Chelmsford would send most of the column to assist Dartnell. 'Order the 2nd Battalion 24th Regiment, four guns and all the mounted troops to get ready to start at day-break.' He would bring up Durnford's reserve force. 'Order up Colonel Durnford with the troops he has to reinforce the camp.'[10] Next to the general's tent were the tents of the HQ staff, including that of Colonel Crealock, the military secretary whom Clery had fallen out with. Unfortunately Crealock overheard, and asked the general who was to give Durnford the order. Was it to be Clery, the staff officer to the central column? 'No, let you do it.'[11] Crealock wrote out the order, but there was characteristic confusion. Crealock did not tell Durnford clearly who was to command the camp, or whether he had been summoned to reinforce it or to support Chelmsford's advance.

No reveille was sounded, as Clery did not wish to rouse the whole camp, or to warn the enemy. In the pitch darkness he quietly woke each of the commanders and gave them their instructions. Before it was light, the general had dressed and left his tent. Then it struck Clery that no orders had been given to Colonel Pulleine, the CO of the 1st/24th, the infantry left behind to guard the camp. On his own initiative Clery wrote out orders which he sent round by his batman. Pulleine was to be in command of the camp in the general's absence. He was to act 'strictly on the defensive'.[12] Clery thought so little of the dangers that he had misgivings about telling this to Pulleine. Suppose parties of Zulus came in reach of the camp and Pulleine failed to attack them? The blame would rest on Clery. On the other hand Clery, who had been a Professor of Tactics at

Sandhurst, knew that on paper, at any rate, the Zulus had been given a great opportunity.

With Chelmsford at the head, the HQ staff, Clery and the main part of the column clattered off south-east, as soon as it was light enough to see the track. There were six companies of the 2nd/24th (the seventh Company had been left behind to guard Rorke's Drift), four out of six guns, and all the mounted infantry. Meanwhile, a young transport officer, Lieutenant Horace Smith-Dorrien, had ridden off down the track in the darkness, carrying Crealock's confusing message to Durnford.

The track to Rorke's Drift continued for four or five miles north-westwards along the flanks of the stony hills before swinging sharp left down to the river. As Smith-Dorrien rode along that morning, he passed close to the kraal of Sihayo, a Zulu chief. The huts were now burnt and abandoned. There had been skirmishing in the place the week before, leaving a few Zulu dead, and 400 cattle had been looted by the British. Smith-Dorrien rode down to the river. Unknown to him, the abyss yawned at his feet – an abyss that concealed the main Zulu army.

Hidden in the ravines to the east of the track, huddled together like an enormous swarm of bees, silent and motionless, without lights and without fires, lay 20,000 of Cetshwayo's picked warriors. The King's plan was as simple as Chelmsford's, but better concealed. He had mustered about 30,000 men at Ulundi and addressed them with these words:

I am sending you out against the whites, who have invaded Zululand and driven away our cattle. You are to go against the column at Rorke's Drift, and drive it back into Natal. . . . You will attack by daylight, as there are enough of you to 'eat it up', and you will march slowly so as not to tire yourselves.[13]

The Zulus had strict orders not to cross the border into Natal. They had marched from Ulundi on 17 January, and on 21 January reached the valley east of Isandlwana where they now lay concealed. There was a superstition that Zulus should not fight when the moon was 'dead', so it was planned to postpone the attack till the morning of 23 January, the day of the new moon. Meanwhile they lay hidden beyond the lip of the plateau. As well as their short stabbing spears and long black and white cowhide shields, many of them carried modern Martini-Henry rifles. These weapons, bought from the traders, were as untried as the army itself, for it was twenty years since a Zulu army had last taken the field – during the Zulu civil war – and no one present had ever fought against a white man.

At Rorke's Drift, Colonel Durnford received the message brought by Smith-Dorrien soon after 5.0 a.m. He conferred with his political agent, George Shepstone, son of Sir Theophilus and (despite Durnford's disapproval of his father's policies) a devoted admirer of Durnford's. 'Ah, just what I had expected,' Durnford replied. 'We are to go on at once. The general has gone out to attack an Impi.'[14] His own force was too small to be much support, only a rocket battery and a corps of 300 mounted natives from Natal and Basutoland. But these were Hlubis and other natives whom Durnford had trained himself. They served him with a touching devotion. By 10.30 a.m. Durnford, riding his charger Chieftain, reached Isandlwana, and there met Colonel Pulleine, the CO of the 1st/24th. But who was in command at the camp itself? And what was Durnford's role? The orders sent by Crealock left these questions open. Pulleine explained bluntly, 'I am sorry you have come, as you are senior to me, and will of course take command.' Durnford demurred. 'I'm not going to interfere with you. I'm not going to remain in camp.'[15] The divided command certainly weakened the garrison further. Not that either Pulleine or Durnford – or for that matter, George Shepstone – had any inkling of the danger. All that was known was that small parties of Zulus had been seen hovering about the plateau to the north-east, a position that Chelmsford had failed to reconnoitre the previous day. At 8.0 a.m. Pulleine had sent a message to the general reporting these movements. The latest reports from Pulleine's scouts spoke of the Zulus retreating, in fact withdrawing to the south-east, towards Chelmsford and the main column.

In the months ahead, during the endless wrangles about how the catastrophe could have been avoided, it was recognized that the arrival of Durnford was the critical moment. If Durnford and Pulleine had both realized their desperate situation and immediately planned a defence, if they had chosen the best line within or beside the camp and set about fortifying it, if shelter trenches had been dug and stones hurriedly piled up to add to the defence lines, if the wagons had been moved to form a wagon laager, if the tents had been struck to clear a field of fire – in short, if a defence had been prepared, not according to the ideas of Chelmsford or any of the HQ staff or even Clery, but according to the advice of the Boers – then perhaps there still would have been a chance.

As it was, Durnford believed the threat, if it existed, was to Chelmsford and the main column. Soon after 11.0 a.m. he took George Shepstone with his faithful corps of natives and the rocket battery and cantered off on Chieftain to intercept the Zulus, his withered left arm flapping from the saddle bow.

Lord Chelmsford was having a trying morning, which put him out of temper with his own and the column's staff. He found Dartnell, the colonial who had bivouacked with his mounted men ten miles away at the south-east end of the plain. But he did not find the Zulus whom Dartnell had claimed were marked down in ravines to the left. Most of them had slipped away. There was a small 'bag', only eighty of the enemy. Clery noted how overwork and the absence of a proper HQ staff had made the general surprisingly touchy. He could not endure this new setback. 'Beyond killing a certain number of these fellows, we were going through our morning's work for nothing.'[16]

At about 9.30 a.m. Clery was shown the important message brought by a galloper from Pulleine: 'Report just come in that the Zulus are advancing in force from left front of camp. 8.05 a.m.' Clery showed it to the general. 'What is to be done on this report?' 'There's nothing to be done on that.'[17] Clery bit his lip and left. In fact, Chelmsford sent back to Pulleine one weak battalion of Natal natives under Commandant Browne. He also told two officers to climb a neighbouring hill and have a look at the camp through their telescopes. They stayed there till eleven o'clock, and reported nothing unusual. Meanwhile, Chelmsford decided the troops should bivouac for a second night out in the plain. He told Captain Gardner to ride back and ask Pulleine for the tents and other gear to be sent forward in the wagons.

The day wore on, as frustrating as before. Clery, the Professor of Tactics, could not shake off the feeling that Chelmsford was taking unnecessary risks. Why had he divided his force? Why not withdraw to the camp, now that Pulleine reported the Zulus advancing 'in force'? But the general discouraged any advice of that kind.

Out of sight, and nearer the camp than Clery, rode Colonel Harness, the cheerful, plodding CO of the artillery battery, who had been told to take four of his six field-guns and follow Chelmsford. Some time before one o'clock, he and his gunners were astonished to hear the rumble of field-guns from the direction of the camp. They saw the splash of shells bursting against the plateau to the north-east. They must be the two guns left with Pulleine. Harness decided to investigate. Soon a galloper appeared. He brought a desperate message from Commandant Browne, the man whom Chelmsford had sent back to the camp earlier that morning. The message ran, 'For God's sake, come back. The camp is surrounded.'[18] Harness needed no urging. With the four guns he spurred off back along the track. But he had been spotted by Chelmsford's senior ADC, who reported Harness to his chief. Within minutes Harness was recalled and told to pay no attention to Browne's hysterical message.

Chelmsford held grimly to his own opinion that the camp could not be in any danger. After all, there were 1,000 riflemen and two guns there to defend it. He brushed aside the continuous rumours of fighting at the camp. About 12.15 p.m. some Zulu prisoners were questioned by his interpreter. They said that a great Impi, upwards of 20,000 men, was expected from Ulundi that day. The news did not alarm Chelmsford. The more concentrated the enemy, the quicker he could end the campaign. But just then there came the rumble of field-guns to the north. 'Do you hear that?' exclaimed the Zulu prisoners. 'There is fighting going on at the camp.'[19] An hour later a native came galloping down from the ridge. He said he had actually seen the smoke of battle at Isandlwana. Chelmsford and his staff humoured the man by riding up to the ridge themselves. They levelled their fieldglasses on that strange-shaped hill ten miles away. The sun shone serenely down on the neat rows of white tents below the crag. There were men moving between them. Nothing odd in that. Crealock turned to Clery. 'How very amusing! Actually attacking our camp! Most amusing.'[20]

From the shocked survivors one can piece together something of that terrible day.

A Zulu Impi was supposed to attack like a charging buffalo, with the chest and loins held back and the horns stretched forward to encircle the victims. It was more like a great river in spate, a river that first quietly flooded its banks, and then smashed down into the valley below, tossing aside trees and houses like a tidal wave.

At first Colonel Durnford seemed to his men to be exhilarated by the danger. The sight was awe-inspiring. The green plateau turned black with men as the Impi flooded over the rim. Durnford sent the rocket battery to the left while he cantered forward to stem the advance on the right. The rocket battery was quickly swamped and Durnford himself thrown back with the survivors to a gully half a mile east of the camp. George Shepstone galloped off to warn Pulleine of the danger. Durnford told his men to dig in. One of his Basutos, called Jabez, later described the scene:

> At last we came to a bad stony place and a little stream quite close to the camp. Here we made a long stand, firing incessantly. The Colonel rode up and down our line continually, encouraging us all – talking and even laughing with us – 'Fire, my boys!' 'Well done, my boys!' he cried. Some of us did not like his exposing himself so much, and wanted him to keep behind. But he laughed at us, and said, 'All right, nonsense.' He was very calm and cheerful. There were not many of us, but because of the way in which we were handled by our leader we were enough to stop the Zulus on that side for a long time ... But at last our cartridges were nearly done.[21]

As Durnford's small mounted force was driven slowly back up the hill, Pulleine's five infantry companies, two teams of field-guns and half-armed native infantry tried to stem the onrush of thousands of Zulus into the other side of the camp. At first there was no panic. These companies of the 1st/24th had been seasoned in the war against Kreli and Sandile. They knew what never failed to break up a native attack: case shot from artillery and concentrated volley fire from Martini-Henrys.

But there were 20,000 Zulus, and they did not behave like Gcalekas. The centre swamped the forward defence lines. The wings flooded down into the camp. As the range narrowed, the guns switched from shrapnel to case shot. Still the Zulus surged forward, firing rifles and muskets, waving their spears, shrieking war-cries, and humming like a gigantic swarm of bees. Terrified out of their wits, the native infantry broke and fled.

Suddenly the solid world of Aldershot, of disciplined movement, of whistles blowing and men moving by numbers, collapsed into horror. The men tried to fall back on the camp but it was full of smoke and awash with Zulus. It was every man for himself. Many natives had already fled down the rocky track towards the river. Soon the track was blocked by panic-stricken men, many of them wounded, screaming for help. The infantry had no chance. Some of the 24th were rallied by their officers. Small groups stood fighting back to back until their ammunition ran out. Others tried to burst their way through the mob of Zulus, but were overtaken on the track. The gunners were trapped in a gully and the guns were overturned. Pulleine withdrew to his tent, it was said, to write a final note to Chelmsford. Durnford, too, spurned the idea of escape. He seems to have turned Chieftain loose, Chieftain the faithful charger that would let no one else on his back. Then he took up his stand on the *nek*, close under the crag itself. George Shepstone, who had a good horse too and might have saved himself, turned back to join him.

Only a handful of white men lived to describe the massacre. One of them was Horace Smith-Dorrien, the young transport officer who had ridden down to Rorke's Drift and back early that morning.

Before we knew where we were, they came right into the camp, assegaing everyone right and left. Everybody then who had a horse turned to fly. The enemy were going at a kind of very fast half-walk and half-run. On looking round we saw we were completely surrounded and the road to Rorke's Drift was cut off. The place where they seemed thinnest was where we all made for. Everybody went pell-mell over ground covered with huge boulders and rocks until we got to a deep spruit or gulley. How the horses got over I have no idea. I was riding a broken-kneed old crock which did not belong to me, and which I expected to go on its head every minute. We had to go bang through them at the spruit. Lots of our men were killed there. I had lots of marvellous escapes, and was firing away at them with my revolver as I galloped along. The ground there down to the river was so broken that the Zulus went as fast as the horses, and kept killing all the way. There were very few white men; they were nearly all mounted niggers of ours flying. This lasted till we came to a kind of precipice down to the River Buffalo.

I jumped off and led my horse down. There was a poor fellow of the mounted infantry [a private] struck through the arm, who said as I passed that if I could bind up his arm and stop the bleeding he would be all right. I accordingly took out my handkerchief and tied up his arm. Just as I had done it Major Smith of the Artillery came down by me, wounded, saying 'For God's sake get on, man, the Zulus are on top of us.' I had done all I could for the wounded man and so turned to jump on my horse. Just as I was doing so, the horse went with a bound to the bottom of the precipice, being struck by an assegai. I gave up all hope, as the Zulus were all round me, finishing off the wounded, the man I had helped and Major Smith among the number. However with the strong hope that everyone clings to that some accident would turn up, I rushed off on foot and plunged into the river, which was little better than a roaring torrent.

I was being carried down the stream at a tremendous pace, when a loose horse came by and I got hold of his tail and he landed me safely on the other bank.[22]

The Zulus kept firing from the east bank, killing the men beside him. Smith-Dorrien was too exhausted to mount. His boots were full of water. The Zulus chased him for three miles beyond the river. He staggered on and somehow reached Helpmekaar, ten miles inside Natal, that night. He found he was one of only five imperial officers to survive the massacre. In all, only thirty white men had escaped out of the 800 who had cheerfully breakfasted in the camp that morning.

By three o'clock Lord Chelmsford realized that the main Zulu army had slipped through his fingers. Riding at the head he led the column slowly back towards the camp. He was tired and irritated. A hard day's work and nothing to show for it. About five o'clock he met Lonsdale, the commandant of one of the native battalions. Lonsdale had had a bad fall the previous day and was suffering from concussion, but he was an eye-witness of what had happened in the camp.

His pony was badly knocked up. He had lost touch with his men after chasing a mounted Zulu. Then he had ridden absent-mindedly back along the track about three o'clock. He came to the camp and some careless native sentry had fired at him. He was dazed and exhausted. The camp was full of redcoats. Then it dawned on him. Those red coats covered black bodies. There was not a white man to be seen. The Zulus were looting the camp. He turned his pony's head and somehow whipped it into a gallop, bullets whistling around him.

Clery saw Chelmsford's face. Even Clery, who had had his premonitions, was dumbfounded. Many officers at first refused to believe the news. Chelmsford pulled himself together. As Clery later said, 'He was all there – never apparently flunked.'[23] There was only one thing for it.

Chelmsford formed up the six companies of the 2nd/24th and addressed them: 'Men, the enemy have taken our camp. Many of our friends must have lost their lives in defending it. There is nothing left for us now but to fight our way through – and mind, we must fight hard. For we will have to fight for our lives. I know you and I know I can depend on you.'[24]

It was pitch black when the column tramped back up the slope towards the crag silhouetted on the summit. There were scattered watch fires, and an ominous glow down by the mission station at Rorke's Drift. Chelmsford was afraid of a trap. The wagons appeared to have been drawn across the *nek* to bar their progress. Someone was sure he saw movements; others thought they heard hoarse cries and the rattle of assegais on shields.

Chelmsford ordered the artillery to fire four rounds of shrapnel at the wagons. The deafening blast echoed and re-echoed up the valley, and far across the plateau (as far as the men of Colonel Evelyn Wood's column at their camp fires twenty-five miles away to the north). Then the sound died away. Chelmsford ordered a party to seize the stony hill opposite the crag. They signalled their success by a cheer. When they reached the wagons they found them deserted. The Zulus had withdrawn as silently as they had come. The guns had been firing into the empty night.

The column were ordered to lie on their arms, in case of attack. There can have been few more macabre nights ever spent by a British column. They were bivouacking on the spot where the fighting had been thickest. Now they stumbled over bodies wherever they tried to find a place to lie. Chelmsford paced up and down, telling the men not to sleep. Some no doubt succeeded despite him.

Others lay there, as in a nightmare, alongside the comrades they had left that morning.

Before it was light, Chelmsford ordered the column to retreat to Rorke's Drift, where they might have to cut their way through the main Zulu force. He was too worried to allow his men to bury their comrades. Even the sight of the bodies might be too much for them. One of the civilians, Charles Norris-Newman, a reporter from the *Standard*, got up an hour before dawn to take a quiet look around and see if he could recognize any of the dead. What he saw turned his stomach. Many of the men had been stripped of their red coats and were naked or half-naked. In almost every case the bodies had been mutilated by the Zulus, with the ritual slash across the abdomen. They lay in clusters, shot and stabbed, twisted into every kind of position, mixed with broken bags of tea and sugar from the wagons, waste paper, dead horses and oxen.

Few of the dead could be recognized. Someone spotted a gold watch on a body identified as an engineer officer's by the scarlet waistcoat. Months later the watch was identified by Bishop Colenso as Durnford's. It had stopped at 3.40 p.m. He had fought to the bitter end, nearly four hours after the attack began. George Shepstone had died beside him.

Chelmsford's shattered column tramped down to the Buffalo in fear of an ambush. When they reached Rorke's Drift they found the mission station was still burning. But the garrison, and the passage across the Buffalo, was safe. One company of the 2nd/24th, even more outnumbered than the men at Isandlwana, had driven off a huge Impi of Zulus. They had survived by a simple expedient: a hurriedly improvised defence line of biscuit tins and stone walls.

*   *   *

The disaster of Isandlwana sent a shock wave across Natal and the Cape before reaching England. Chelmsford and his staff turned up breathless at Pietermaritzburg, having left the remains of the force to their own devices. The general was 'awfully cut up', according to Crealock. The HQ staff were afraid he might break down altogether. All over Natal, as far south as Durban, men built laagers and braced themselves for a Zulu invasion. In fact, the Impis held firm to the King's instructions not to cross the border.

In London, an hour after midnight on the morning of 12 February, a telegram was brought to Hicks Beach's house in Portman Square. What it said was so astounding that it might have been a hoax. Half Lord Chelmsford's central column had been massacred by the Zulus at a place called Isandlwana. Lord Chelmsford and the survivors had fled back into Natal. It proved to be the most humiliating British military defeat since the start of the century. The Zulus had killed 858 white men (including 52 officers) and 471 black troops (including non-combatants). The Cabinet were aghast. Disraeli saw correctly that it was a mortal blow to his government. 'I am greatly stricken,' he wrote, 'everybody was congratulating me on being the most fortunate of Ministers, when there comes this terrible disaster!'[25] It would change everything, he told the Queen, humiliating Britain in the eyes of other Powers, sapping her influence, bleeding the revenue white. The Zulus would be conquered in due course; that was a foregone conclusion. But the price would be paid by Disraeli's government. Isandlwana would precipitate Gladstone and the Liberals back into power.

Twitters and Frere and Shepstone had dreamt of a new British Empire stretching from the Cape to the Zambezi. That dream had died on the battlefield of Isandlwana. Yet the past could be no more easily buried than the bleached bodies lying out there on the hillside.

Soon it would be up to Gladstone to take charge of Africa and face a series of new challenges. The bungled forward policy of Carnarvon, Frere and Shepstone had set in motion forces that could not be reversed. An aggressive new nationalism was being forged by the Boers of the Transvaal. Moreover France, jealous of Britain's pretensions, had her eye on a new African empire for herself.

Still, in 1879, neither Boer nationalism nor French imperialism seemed an immediate threat to Britain.

It was to a crisis in Egypt that British eyes now turned. There was a strange incident, a kind of abortive mutiny, in the streets of Cairo, which seemed to play into the hands of Ismael Pasha, the Khedive (Turkish Viceroy), who dreamt of founding a great Egyptian empire in Central Africa and had pawned his country to pay for it.

CHAPTER 5

Ismael's Dream of Empire

Egypt and the Sudan
18 February 1879–June 1880

'For a foreign Power to take this country [Sudan]
would be most easy. The mass are far from
fanatical. They would rejoice in a good government,
let its religion be what it might. ... It is the
[Egyptian] government that needs civilising far more
than the people.'

Colonel Charles Gordon, Governor of Equatoria,
in his letter home, 11 April 1876

The strange incident in Cairo – it hardly deserved the name of riot, let alone a real mutiny – occurred a few minutes after noon on 18 February 1879.

A broad, tree-lined street, incongruously straight, like all of Cairo's new Parisian-style boulevards, connected the Khedive's vast rococo palace at Abdin with the sober Malieh, the Ministry of Finance. Down this handsome boulevard, in opposite directions, came two covered carriages without an escort. In the first rode the President of the Council (in effect the Prime Minister), an Armenian Christian, Nubar Pasha; in the second the Minister of Finance, an English taxation expert, Rivers Wilson.

Suddenly Wilson heard shouts and saw some men armed with pistols and swords rush forward and grab hold of the heads of the horses pulling Nubar's carriage. Wilson gallantly got out to try to help Nubar, striking out with his cane. He was mobbed, pulled by the beard, kicked and hustled into Nubar's carriage. Nubar, too, was jostled, his fez knocked sideways, his cravat torn, and his coat covered in dust. Then the two men – politically the most powerful in the country, not even excepting the Khedive – were taken by the mob to the Malieh. There the leaders forced their way into Wilson's office on the upper floor, with shouts of 'Death to the dogs of Christians!'[1]

Nubar and Wilson were shocked to find that the men were officers of the Egyptian army. They included a colonel called Arabi, recruited from the fellahin, the common people. They said they and their families were starving. They were protesting against the decision to put them on half-pay a couple of weeks before, without their arrears being settled.

Meanwhile, Consul-General Vivian, the British diplomatic representative in Cairo, had heard of the incident and galloped off to warn the Khedive. His Highness the Khedive, Ismael Pasha, a graduate of the French officers' cadet school at St Cyr, was not lacking in courage – not lacking, at any rate, in theatrical talent. Without waiting for his escort, he drove with Vivian to the Ministry, which they found besieged by the officers. The mob respectfully made way for the Khedive's carriage and cheered His Highness loudly. It was common knowledge that Ismael detested Nubar Pasha – and the feeling was reciprocated. After Ismael had assured himself of Nubar's safety, he turned to the rioters and ordered them to leave, promising that he would settle their just demands. 'If you are my officers you are bound by your oaths to obey me; if you refuse I will have you swept away.'[2] He harangued them from the windows (speaking in Turkish, his own first language, rather than Arabic).

By this time his bodyguard had galloped up and taken its stand in front of the mob. When the officers refused to disperse he ordered the troops to fire in the air. In the confusion that followed several men were injured, including the Khedive's chamberlain, standing at His Highness's side, who received a sabre thrust on his arm. Someone else was shot in the foot. Then the riot subsided, like a small dust storm. It had lasted barely half an hour.

Next day Cairo was buzzing with the story that the Khedive had stage-managed the whole affair. He was certainly pleased with the outcome. The foreign consuls – British, French, German, Italian – trooped into the Abdin Palace to congratulate him on his manly bearing during the crisis. He thanked them in French with his usual delicacy, but beneath the soft words, there was no mistaking his desperation. He could no longer tolerate the humiliating role of constitutional monarch imposed on him by international agreement in 1878. As Khedive, nominally viceroy of the Sultan of Turkey, he was responsible for the safety of the state, yet he had been stripped of all political power. His ministers did not even consult him. The officers' 'mutiny' – '*une grande effervescence*'[3] as he called it in a report to the Sultan – had brought matters to a head. The officers must be paid in full. But first he dismissed the hated Nubar Pasha as President of the Council and installed his own easy-going son, Tewfik, instead.

On 8 April Ismael took his defiance of the Powers a step further.

The dream of his life was to rule the richest empire in Africa, an empire the length of the Nile, 3,000 miles from the Mediterranean to the equator. He wanted to rule like a modern pharaoh. Yet he was hemmed in on every side: badgered by the decrepit Turkish Sultan, his nominal sovereign; bullied by the Great Powers who grew fat on the success of the Suez Canal; bled white by every money-lender in Europe, to whom he had pawned his country to pay for that same empire.

There was one last chance. Ismael decided to cancel the informal agreement, made in 1878, by which two European ministers – one French, the other English – dominated the Cabinet. On 8 April he sacked Rivers Wilson and his French counterpart. He would reserve the Egyptian government for Egyptians, provided they were men he could trust to do exactly as he said.

It was a desperate gamble, this coup against the Powers. Yet it was in the buccaneering spirit of the two men he most admired, the conquering heroes of modern Egypt, his grandfather, Muhammad Ali Pasha, and the Emperor Napoleon Bonaparte.

To talk of buccaneering might seem absurd when one actually met the Khedive. Behind the grandiose façade of the Abdin Palace was a modest set of private apartments, decorated with humdrum furniture, like the rooms of a French provincial hotel. It was here that Ismael worked for eight, ten, twelve hours a day, slaving away at his desk like a bureaucrat, the tedium only relieved by visits and interviews.

Foreign visitors were unprepared for the experience. There he sat, His Highness Ismael Pasha, small, plump and cheerful, ready with a dazzling smile for each visitor. There was no swagger, no trace of fanaticism, nothing alarmingly oriental. He could laugh at himself and make the dullest visitor feel suddenly important. It was hard to believe that this was the man who dreamt of ruling half Africa, and now dared the current allies – but traditional rivals – Britain and France, to depose him if they could.

The rivalry between the two Powers in Egypt went back to the days of Ismael's hero, Napoleon. On 1 July 1798 Napoleon had landed near Alexandria, marched up the Nile and smashed the army of the military élite that ruled Egypt – the Mameluke beys – at the Battle of the Pyramids. He had claimed that his plan was to liberate Egypt and restore the power of the Turkish Sultan, usurped by the Mameluke beys. But by October 1801 the fleeting French occupation had ended in fiasco, and in due course their enemies, the British, handed Egypt to its overlord, the Sultan in Constantinople.

Yet, as the years went by, French influence intensified. The rulers of modern Egypt had a hunger for French ideas which only grew sharper with time. With Napoleon's blue-jacketed *cuirassiers* had marched an army of *savants*: 165 scholars, scientists and men of letters. Their work took root, even among the dust and chaos of the French retreat. Muhammad Ali, an Albanian adventurer, seized power and forced the Sultan to recognize his authority as pasha. For nearly half a century – from 1805 to 1848 – he bestrode Egypt, and the country which he admired above all was France. His style, it must be said, remained oriental. Revenue was not raised; it was beaten out of the fellahin, the peasant cultivators, with a buffalo-hide whip called a courbash. He betrayed and crushed the *ulama*, the Islamic notables who had helped him to the throne. The Mameluke chiefs continued to defy him, so one evening in March 1811 he honoured them with a grand banquet in the Citadel at Cairo, a banquet brought to a sudden close by the ceremonial massacre of all the guests. Later he took *ulama* estates, and pocketed the entire land revenue of the country.

Yet Muhammad Ali was a great reformer as well as a great tyrant. His wild armies of fellahin and slaves were soon disciplined and modernized under the eye of French instructors. He sent his favourites to be trained in Paris. Others were taught in the new French *lycées* that now sprouted among the palm trees. Canals multiplied, dividing the Delta like graph paper. The revenue rose like the Nile in August. Egypt seemed set for industrial revolution – ready to build a Manchester beside the sphinx, though the muscle power of slaves was hardly a match for the coal-and-steam power of western Europe.

Abroad, Muhammad Ali's success was equally Napoleonic, and more short-lived. To capture black slaves for his army he sent an expedition southward, beyond the cataracts, and conquered the Sudan as far as the junction of the Blue and White Niles, where he founded Khartoum in 1823. Earlier he had crushed a Wahhabi revolt in the Hejaz and seized Central Arabia in the name of his overlord, the Sultan. From 1831 to 1833 he successfully challenged the Sultan and took the rich province of Syria for himself. By the end of the decade, the Sultan trembled at the thought of his vassal.

Then Britain, France and the other Powers decided Muhammad Ali threatened their diplomatic equations. They needed Constantinople, rickety as it was, for a buttress against Russia. Muhammad Ali was put in his place – which was in Africa. When he died, senile and friendless, in 1849, a year after abdicating, his dreams of conquest had evaporated except for the slaving empire in the empty wastes of the Sudan. His sons and successors, Abbas (1848–54) and Said (1854–63), added little to Egypt's power or prestige. Abbas tried, as far as he dared, which was not far, to encourage European investment, especially British investment in railways. Said, who favoured the French, was much more daring than Abbas. He gave Ferdinand de Lesseps the momentous concession for the Suez Canal. However, by the time he died, the French-built canal was only half-way through the sands of the isthmus.

It was Ismael who squared the Sultan, completed the canal in 1869, and made it the dazzling symbol of the new Egypt, not just a cut through the isthmus but a link between continents. 'We are not now a country of Africa,' he said proudly, 'but a country of Europe.'[4] Implicit in everything Ismael did was the idea of partnership with Europe.

Muhammad Ali had failed because in the last resort he did not understand the role allotted him by the Powers. He was a great reformer and a great warrior, but no diplomat. By contrast his grandson Ismael had studied diplomacy with the passion of a scholar. He was also a master of public relations. The moment a ship touched at Alexandria, the passenger list would be telegraphed to the Abdin Palace, a hundred miles away in Cairo. Then back would come the invitation to be the Khedive's guest: Would Colonel This or Lady Sarah That, or the representative of the *Daily World* or the *Weekly Globe*, pay His Highness the compliment of accepting his hospitality? Then money would be spent like water, with all bills to the palace. And in due course the fortunate traveller would find himself being ushered into the small room on the first floor with the modest gilt table and the damask-covered sofa, and treated to a display of flattery so subtle and delightful that it sapped all resistance.

Of course it was a gamble, Ismael was the first to tell his visitors, to try to turn this ancient land, the land of the pharaohs, into a progressive modern state within one man's lifetime. But what else did His Excellency advise? Had he seen the new sugar mills at Rhoda? Had he inspected the new docks at Alexandria? Would he like to visit the model farm at Heliopolis? All these projects cost

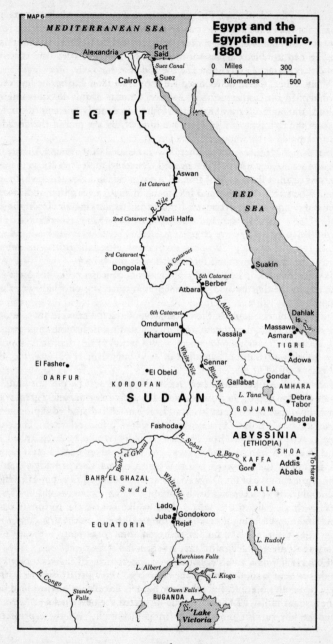

MAP 6

MEDITERRANEAN SEA

Egypt and the Egyptian empire, 1880

Miles 0 — 300
Kilometres 0 — 500

Alexandria
Port Said
Suez Canal
Cairo
Suez

E G Y P T

Aswan
1st Cataract
R. Nile

RED SEA

2nd Cataract Wadi Halfa
3rd Cataract
Dongola
4th Cataract
5th Cataract Berber
Atbara
Suakin

6th Cataract
Omdurman
Khartoum
Kassala
R. Atbara
Dahlak Is.
Massawa
Asmara
T I G R E
Adowa

El Fasher
D A R F U R
KORDOFAN
•El Obeid
Sennar
Gallabat
Gondar
AMHARA
L. Tana
Debra Tabor
G O J J A M
Magdala

S U D A N
Blue Nile
White Nile

Fashoda
R. Sobat
ABYSSINIA
(ETHIOPIA)
R. Baro
S H O A
KAFFA
Gore
Addis Ababa
→ To Harar

Bahr el Ghazal
BAHR EL GHAZAL
Sudd
White Nile
G A L L A

Lado
Gondokoro
Juba
Rejaf
EQUATORIA

L. Rudolf

Murchison Falls
R. Congo
L. Albert
L. Kioga
Stanley Falls
Owen Falls
BUGANDA
Lake Victoria

76

money, in fact millions in foreign currency. Fortunately the economy of the country was as strong as the broad backs of the fellahin. During his reign the tonnage of cotton exports had risen three and a half times and the government's revenue had doubled. Compared with most oriental rulers, Ismael seemed a paragon, a perfect collaborator for the Powers of Africa.

In one respect the Khedive had gone one better than any of the Great Powers. He extended his empire into the heart of Central Africa. Neither Britain nor France was in any hurry to meet that call from Livingstone's grave to open up the country to legitimate trade as a means of ending the slave trade. In 1876 King Leopold of the Belgians had taken up the challenge. Under the aegis of his International African Association he had launched his own crusade. But a decade earlier the Khedive had begun to push his own empire southwards towards the equator, to Uganda's Lake Victoria, and Lake Tana, the sources of the two Niles. In 1869 he commissioned Sir Samuel Baker, the British explorer who had discovered Lake Albert, to establish a province in the far south called Equatoria. At the same time he sent expeditions to conquer the eastern and northern borderland of Abyssinia. And he leased from the Sultan two strategic ports on the Red Sea – Suakin and Massawa – claiming that he would use them to stop the slave trade between the Sudan and Arabia.

Was Ismael, who owned thousands of slaves himself, and ruled a great Muslim state where the use of slaves was taken for granted, really planning to end the trade in slaves? At this question Ismael would put his hand on his heart and protest. Did he look like a humbug? Slavery and the slave trade were utterly different. He pointed to Baker, his proconsul in his new African empire. Could anyone doubt Baker's commitment to rid Africa of this scourge? Why, it was even whispered (and no doubt Ismael's eyes twinkled as he said this) that Sir Samuel Baker had first set eyes on Florence, his beautiful Hungarian wife, in a Turkish slave market, and had rescued her by buying her as his own slave.

When Baker retired from the Khedive's service in 1873, Ismael chose Colonel Charles Gordon as the new Governor of Equatoria, and gave him the same dual mandate: to push the Egyptian empire to the Great Lakes and the heart of Central Africa, and to crush the slave trade. And who could doubt 'Chinese' Gordon's own dedication to this noble enterprise? Gordon was a *beau sabreur*, the darling of the British public for his exploits in rescuing the Emperor of China, a soldier-saint in the making, the stuff of legends. No better man could be found to take up Livingstone's call.

Where Ismael's choice of European collaborators was less inspired was in the men he had chosen to advise him on finance. Ismael, so understanding in many ways, was a simpleton when it came to money. The rake's progress began as soon as he came to the viceroy's throne. Indeed the first steps down that slippery path had been taken by his easy-going predecessor, Said. The terms for building the Suez Canal, imposed on Said by Lesseps and his brother financiers, fell little short of exploitation. Egypt lost the transit trade across the isthmus, yet Said had to provide free of charge to the company a ninety-nine-year lease of the canal and large areas of agricultural land beside it. He also had to use the *corvée* (forced labour) to do much of the work. All he was to get in return – before the ninety-nine-year lease expired – was a dividend on the capital he had invested, like foreign shareholders, in the canal company.

Understandably Ismael insisted on renegotiating these terms, but Nubar Pasha, who acted for him, struck such a wretchedly bad bargain that Ismael ended by paying over £4 million in compensation to the company. This money could only come from international loans, floated at ruinous rates of interest, and a ruinous sinking fund. And soon each loan was lost in an ocean of new borrowing. This was not simply due to extravagance, or even megalomania. Ismael's grandiose new public works – harbours, railways, irrigation canals, sugar factories – were often surprisingly well designed and operated. The economy, based on an export trade ranging from cotton to mummy-bones (for fertilizer), was perfectly sound. But the cotton price was unexciting after the collapse of the brief 1864–5 boom, caused by the blockade of the Southern states in the American Civil War. Egypt's revenue had only doubled during Ismael's reign. During the same period the national debt had risen to £90 million, and most of this reckless borrowing had simply been spent paying foreigners the exorbitant interest on earlier loans. Where would it end? To the tune of Verdi's *Aida* – commissioned for the opening of the Suez Canal – the country was marching grandly into bankruptcy.

In 1875 Ismael could only keep the wolf from the door by selling to the British government his last big asset, his £4 million holding in the Suez Canal shares. Next year the wolf was back at the door and he was technically bankrupt. He defaulted on the interest on foreign loans. The European Powers then established the Caisse de la Dette Publique, an international commission to protect the foreign bond-holders who had made fortunes lending money to Ismael at extortionate rates of interest. France and Britain put in their own bailiffs in the shape of the twin controllers of the Egyptian revenue and expenditure, a system known as 'dual control'. In 1878 the Powers made Ismael swallow his pride still more and accept the role of constitutional monarch. The new ministry of August 1878 was dominated by Nubar Pasha and Rivers Wilson.

So the moment had come for Ismael's double gamble of 1879: first to stage-manage (or at least to exploit) the officers' revolt in February, and then on 8 April to sack Rivers Wilson and his French counterpart, and spring a coup against the Powers in alliance with the disgruntled officer class. It was an incongruous alliance, since this new Egyptian middle class had a long tradition of resentment towards the Turkish élite, represented by Ismael, which was no less explosive than their feelings towards Armenian Christians like Nubar, or Europeans like Rivers Wilson. But then beggars, even when they are Khedives, cannot be choosers. It was to be Ismael's final, disastrous throw.

Meanwhile soon after dawn on the morning of 20 February 1879 the Governor-General of the Sudan, seconded to the Khedive's service, Colonel Charles Gordon, CB, put on his shirt and trousers and went down to his office, the *divan*, in the white-walled palace at Khartoum. He worked in his shirt sleeves, a short, slight, sunburnt Englishman, with eyes like sapphires. He hated pomposity and he hated this palace. It was a gaunt, lonely barracks, despite its beautiful situation. Out of the louvred windows, beyond the speckled shade of the date palms, he could see the shimmer of the Blue Nile, half a mile above that sandy beach, where the White Nile joined forces with the Blue, poised for the last, great, looping 1,800-mile-long journey through the desert to the sea. But that morning when Gordon reached the *divan*, his Sudanese secretary, Berzati Bey, greeted him with a grin, a splash of ivory across his shiny black face. A telegram had just come in from His Highness in Cairo. The officers' revolt had occurred two days earlier. Gordon's *bête noire*, Nubar Pasha, had been dismissed. In fact, it was the first step towards the Khedive's coup against the Powers that would take place in April.

Gordon could not make it out. HH had dismissed Nubar? This was the day he had expected the sack himself for defying HH's order to return to Cairo.

Then the news was confirmed. HH, freed (so it appeared to Gordon) from the baleful influence of Nubar Pasha, conceded Gordon everything. He could postpone his return to Cairo. Indeed, he could set off for the provinces of Kordofan and Darfur, 1,000 miles to the south-west, to put down a revolt by the slave raiders. Gordon was off before the Khedive could change his mind, off on a four-month jolting march by camel across that terrible wilderness, thirty miles a day, jolting like a sack of rice across a sandy plain covered with dried yellow grass and scrub by trees, starting two hours before dawn, and only resting during the heat of the day. Gordon shrank from the ordeal, yet submitted. It was God's will. 'He knows what is best for a poor worm like me.'[5] It was the last chance to deal a death blow to the slave trade.

As Gordon jolted along on the camel, so violently that sometimes he felt his liver and lungs would be permanently displaced, his thoughts swung back to Ismael – surprisingly mellow. 'He is the perfect type of his people,' he told his family, 'thoroughly consistent to all their principles – a splendid leopard! Look at the numberless cages out of which he has broken his way, when it seemed impossible for him to do so.' There was a streak of hero-worship in Gordon that responded to Ismael. He also had a puritanical dislike of the European community in Cairo and Alexandria ('in morality they differ very little from Asiatics') and deplored the way that Britain and France had taken their side against Ismael. 'Let us keep clear of interfering with their [Egypt's] internal affairs; let us leave reforms to them and their peoples.'[6]

Yet to say that Gordon admired or disliked anyone was to say very little. He changed his opinions more frequently than his clothes. One day Ismael would be a splendid leopard. The next day he would be weak and evasive. Often Gordon's frustrations in the Sudan seemed to drive him close to madness. The people were irredeemable, Arabs and blacks alike. For days he would shut himself up, talking to no one, longing for death. Once when he was quite alone in his vast palace, he fell ill and wandered through the huge, empty rooms delirious from fever, answering imaginary petitions that sent him wild, as the same conundrums were presented over and over again.

Then the mood would swing round from near despair to near mania, as swiftly as a change of wind. Gordon would leap on his camel and ride forty miles at a stretch as though the camel had wings, forgetting the jolting march and the escort of flies, revelling in the silent, cushion-like tread of the great beast, exulting in the pure air, and lonely grandeur of the desert. It was these wild moods that made him a legend – was he a *djinn* or an Old Testament prophet? – a legend he gladly exploited. He was 'fire', he boasted. He came on his people 'like a thunderbolt'.[7]

Two years before he had had to face another revolt by the slavers in Darfur. He flew there at the speed of the telegraph, so it seemed to one Arab chief. In his own account he compared his advance to the biblical Jehu's. A few specks had been sighted in the vast plain. Then he burst upon them, a wild figure dressed in a marshal's uniform. 'It is fearful to see the Governor-General arrayed in gold clothes flying along like a madman' (so he wrote to his family) 'with only a guide as if he was pursued. The headman had not time to gather himself together before the enemy was on him. Some of the guards were down at a well drinking; it was no use; before they'd got halfway to their arms, the goal was won ... the Gordons and the camels are of the same race – let them take an idea into their heads and nothing will take it out.'[8]

Then the reaction would come and he would feel the hopelessness of his mission. Suppose he did crush the slave trade and open up the Sudan to civilization? Would the Khedive and Egypt use his own conquests wisely? A fierce doubt seized him, like the pain at his chest after a close call in battle. Would the Sudan be better *uncivilized*? It was at moments like this that Gordon's faith in God was stretched like a rope in a gale. The rope held – 'God is the sole ruler, and I try to walk sincerely before Him ...'[9] – but sometimes he compared his life to a kind of crucifixion.

Gordon's walks before God in the Sudan had begun five years before, after Nubar Pasha had met him by chance in Constantinople and persuaded him to take over the governorship of Equatoria. Nubar gave him a free hand and told him the task was two-fold, to open up the country and end the slave trade. Did this mean extending the frontier of the Egyptian Empire to include Uganda, which was dominated by Buganda, apparently one of the most powerful, most populous and (above all) richest kingdoms in Africa? Nubar hoped so, but if King Mtesa of Buganda proved shy at present, Gordon was at least to open up the Nile as the main channel for civilizing Central Africa. This meant establishing a line of fortified stations, and then a line of trading steamers, from Khartoum to Lake Victoria. Once trade began to flow down the river, the effects would be miraculous. The province would be rich. The naked blacks, now living in misery on the banks of the Nile, prey to the slave raiders, would soon be as well off as the fellahin in Egypt, and the slavers would give up slaving and turn to legitimate trade. It was, Nubar explained, just as had been predicted by that great compatriot of Gordon's, David Livingstone.

Gordon listened to Nubar and was filled with foreboding. Suppose the whole expedition was a 'sham, to catch the attention of the English people'?[10] He decided that Ismael was acting in good faith, but Egypt was full of rottenness. He felt 'like Moses who despised the riches of Egypt'. He would not 'bow to Haman'.[11]

Gordon reached Gondokoro, the capital of Equatoria (a few miles from the modern town of Juba), after weeks of steaming against the current from Khartoum. They steamed night and day, passing herds of elephant and hippos, silver-sided in the moonlight. They found the great Sudd – the hundred-mile-long papyrus swamp – providentially 'open'; the current had cut a channel through it. They only halted to collect wood for the engine. Gondokoro was a wretched little station, a mere collection of huts beside the oily brown waters of the Nile. Baker had settled for this swampy site because it was the end of the line from Khartoum. Beyond, the cataracts made the river unnavigable. But Gondokoro was a graveyard. Most of Gordon's followers fell sick with fever; many died. And the natives hated the soldiers, who looted their cattle. It was dangerous to travel far from the station. Gordon chose two healthier sites nearby, at Lado and Rejaf, and gradually won the natives' confidence. Then he began to push further stations up-river, his black soldiers hauling his 108-ton steamer, the *Khedive*, over the cataracts as the rain pelted down.

After eighteen months of driving his men like a madman ('it is the hunting season with me for the hunter and with nearly everyone else for the hunted'),[12] Gordon had met his match in the Nile. A hundred miles to the south, the mysterious, oily brown river vanished into a rocky gorge at Dufile which no steamer could pass in any season. There was nothing for it but to strip down the *Khedive* and re-assemble it the other side of the cataract. From there the steamer chugged on to Lake Albert. But two more great falls blocked the way into Lake Victoria. As Stanley had already grasped (and King Leopold would eventually realize) the Nile was only a back road to Central Africa. Equatoria itself was 'just a wretched marsh'.

Equally unpromising were the chiefs of Bunyoro and Mtesa, the King of Buganda. Gordon sent 160 soldiers to Mengo, Mtesa's capital, to form a garrison and establish a kind of protectorate over Buganda. Mtesa captured them. With difficulty they were extricated. In 1876 Gordon threw in his hand as Governor and returned dispirited to Cairo. He had honoured his bargain with the Khedive by setting up that line of posts as far as Lake Victoria, but in the great task God had given him – to improve the life of the wretched blacks and to crush the slave trade – he had achieved almost nothing.

Gordon yearned to leave the Khedive's service. He was more than ever convinced that Egyptians were not the stuff for empire-building. Many in high places in Cairo – Nubar, for instance – had proved so half-hearted that the whole expedition to the Lakes must have been a sham, a blind to curry favour with the Powers (especially Britain) by showing how hard Cairo was working to end the slave trade. Others – no doubt including the notoriously corrupt Minister of Finance, Ismael Pasha Sadyk – had real hopes of exploiting the wealth of Equatoria and Buganda, but could they be trusted? 'What right have I to coax the natives to be quiet, for them to fall into the hands of a rapacious pasha after my departure? What right have I to ... delude Mtesa with security, to be eventually swallowed up?'[13] By 1876 he could answer his own question in the voice of Bunyan's Christian. 'Comfort-of-Body – a very strong gentleman – says, "You are well; you have done enough; go home ..." Mr Reason says, "What is the use of opening more country to such a government? There's more now under their power than they will ever manage." '[14] Now Gordon understood why God had decided to frustrate his attempt to take Buganda. Egypt could not be trusted.

In his own mind Gordon usually absolved Ismael from the corruption and injustice perpetrated in his name, but in November 1876 he had a chilling experience, suggesting that he knew the Khedive less well than he imagined. It was part of the secret of HH's flattery that he played the role of a delightfully civilized European surrounded by Orientals. 'Of course we Europeans,' he would begin, offering his guest the very latest delicacy from Paris.

Gordon had no interest in the delicacies, but he had swallowed the flattery. Then, in the autumn of 1876, he had seen from the deck of his steamer as he approached Cairo another side of HH, a chilling oriental side. A *diabeyah* (sailing boat) came upstream, with all the windows nailed up and soldiers posted around it at the door of the cabin. People hardly dared to whisper what had happened. But apparently the man inside the *diabeyah* was the infamous Minister of Finance, Ismael Pasha Sadyk. Gordon knew he was notorious for creaming off money for himself from the Khedive's foreign loans. But he hardly deserved this fate. Ismael had dismissed him, then sent him up-river nailed in this boat without food or servants. Sadyk, according to official reports, died at Wadi Halfa. But others claimed he was already dead before the boat left Cairo, strangled on the Khedive's orders, others that he had been dumped in the Nile – 'sacked' in the original oriental sense of the word. Gordon reached Cairo in December 1876, shocked and angry. 'What an affair! Everyone speaks in bated breath of it. I have (DV) ... made up my mind to serve HH no longer.'[15]

Gordon had changed his mind, of course, and by March 1879, had already served the Khedive a further two years. He had changed his mind because HH, God bless him, had overruled Gordon's enemies at Cairo – men like Nubar Pasha – and promoted him to the rank of Governor-General of the whole Sudan. Gordon had insisted on this promotion as the only way of cutting the slave trade at its root. There were few slave caravans, it had turned out, passing through Equatoria. The slave traders' main hunting ground was in Bahr al-Ghazal among the pagan peoples of the south-west. The wretched slaves were brought eastwards through the deserts of Darfur and Kordofan before being ferried across the Red Sea and passing into the harems of Arabia and beyond.

The final showdown with these slavers, Gordon knew, had long been delayed by Ismael's own equivocal policy. The undisputed king of the slave trade was a Sudanese official, Zebehr Pasha. He had gambled on being made Governor of the province of Darfur, but overplayed his hand. He sailed down to Cairo to press his claims on the Khedive, who put him under house arrest. Then Zebehr instigated a revolt among the slavers of Bahr al-Ghazal, led by his twenty-year-old son, Suleiman. The revolt spread to Darfur and Kordofan, where the Sudanese had ample reason to resent Egyptian over-rule. Zebehr coolly offered to pacify these districts by going there himself, indeed he offered £25,000 a year for the privilege. Equally coolly, shortly before his own downfall, Nubar had proposed to accept Zebehr's offer – a proposal furiously rebuffed by Gordon.

So this was how Gordon came to be jolting on a camel through that terrible wilderness of dried yellow grass and scrub trees in March 1879, planning a death blow to the slavers.

The main campaign against Zebehr's son, Suleiman, Gordon delegated to Romolo Gessi, a young Italian interpreter he had first met in the Crimea. Gessi was a man who represented the buccaneering side of Gordon's own character. Gordon described him as 'a cool, most determined man. Born genius for practical ingenuity and mechanics. Ought to have been born in 1560 not 1832. Same disposition as Francis Drake.'[16] And Gessi took a leaf out of Gordon's own Chinese book by the brilliance of his irregular warfare. He had less than a thousand Egyptians and Sudanese, some of whom deserted. He was out-numbered ten to one and was so short of ammunition that his men had to collect spent bullets after a battle. After ferocious fighting he wore Suleiman down, rescuing 10,000 slaves taken by Suleiman from the villages among the swamps. The slaves were mainly women and children. Those that could be identified were sent back to their families. '*Quant à la population,*' he wrote to Gordon, '*elle est au paroxysme du contentement.*'[17] By May, Suleiman's robber army of 10,000 had been reduced to a few hundred fugitives, with Gessi in hot pursuit. He had shot down hundreds of the slavers. Others were left to villagers to finish off with their spears. Even the women were killed, for fear that their breed would survive.

Gordon received Gessi's enthusiastic reports with mixed feelings. He felt no compunction himself towards the slavers, and Gessi had his full permission to shoot Suleiman if he was captured. (Gessi cheerfully did so in July.) As Gordon himself rode on through Kordofan and Darfur, he rode in the tracks left by the poor slaves. Everywhere there were skulls, children's skulls grinning from the sand beside the wells, so that even fresh water (at least to Gordon) tasted horrible. Egypt had a lot to answer for.

These atrocities had been going on for years. But his own attempts to deal with the slave caravans in the district left him sickened. Many caravans eluded him, forcing the slaves to go days without water, leaving stragglers dead in the sand. He rescued about 2,000 slaves, many no more than skeletons. He could hardly return these to their homes, hundreds of miles away in the swamps, so he had to hand them over to new masters. The desert seemed to be full of strings of slaves, women and young children, driven in every direction. Gordon's impotence made him despair. No man could put an end to this horrible traffic without ending the institution of slavery itself, but it was the staff of life in the Sudan and Egypt.

As he plodded back towards the Nile on 27 May, half-dead from fever, Gordon decided once again to throw in his hand. 'I shall write no more letters to the Khedive about the misery of these lands ... I know he has not time even to think of them.' To serve the Sudan was impossible while the Sudan was governed by a callous and corrupt country like Egypt. But the present system could hardly continue long. The Khedive's day of reckoning was approaching. Gordon added prophetically, 'In fact one almost doubts if he is still Khedive.'[18]

In mid June, 2,000 miles away in Cairo, among the rosewater and the French mirrors of the Abdin Palace, Ismael was run to ground by his creditors. He played his final scene with dignity, even pathos. The Powers had taken two months to summon the strength to deal with his forlorn hope, his coup of 8 April. Heading the pack were the French bond-holders and their sympathetic government. The British were anxious to keep in step, though Disraeli was sensitive to the Liberals' jibe, 'moneybags'. Bismarck (kept up to the mark by his banker, Bleichroder, according to gossip) insisted on fair play for the bond-holders. The Italians were thought to be intriguing with the Turkish Sultan at Constantinople, the Sublime Porte. Then everyone fell into line, including the Sultan, no stranger to bankruptcy himself. In fact it was only the mercy of Allah that he was not in the Khedive's slippers. He owed over £100 million to the same bond-holders. He would have liked to replace Ismael with Ismael's uncle, Halil Pasha, who lived in Constantinople, but he was desperately anxious to do whatever was asked of him, provided he was allowed to depose the Khedive himself. The Powers decided Tewfik, Ismael's easygoing son, would make an excellent Khedive. The Porte was allowed to draft the fatal telegram.

Ismael kept cool and kept busy. When advised to abdicate by all the representatives of the Powers, he said it was up to the Sultan. Perhaps he dreamt even then of a vast new foreign loan by which he would bribe the Sultan to save him. (The actual bribe he sent was quite inadequate.) At the same time he had gathered his faithful harem and selected his favourite wives and mistresses. He also took all their jewellery and stripped the diamonds and other stones for easy removal. Then he began to pack up his treasures from the Abdin and other palaces: Coptic plate, Aubusson carpets, the silver sconces from the walls, twenty-two of the best dinner services. Everything went smoothly, except that the rejected ladies from the harem ran amok and smashed mirrors and furniture to the tune of £8,000.

Early on the morning of 26 June, a strange telegram was delivered to the office of the Master of Ceremonies at the Abdin Palace. It was addressed in Turkish to 'Ismael Pasha, ex-Khedive of Egypt'. In the East the messenger with bad news fares badly. No one would take the telegram upstairs to His Highness.

Eventually Nubar's successor as Prime Minister, Sherif Pasha, screwed himself up to the task.

Ismael read the telegram, his political death sentence, without blinking. Tewfik was sent for, the son Ismael had always somewhat disliked. He kissed his son on both cheeks, then continued efficiently packing up his treasures.

That afternoon the people of Cairo were astonished to hear the guns thundering a royal salute from the Citadel. The Powers sent their representatives to welcome Tewfik as the new Khedive. Four days later a long luggage train steamed out of Cairo station, stuffed with treasures. Ismael and his family followed in a special. Next day his yacht, the *Mahroussa*, rounded the great mole at Alexandria and sailed for Naples, saluted by the ships in the harbour. For a gambler who had lost every game, he had not done badly; apart from the treasures, the Powers paid him a 'competency', later valued at £2 million.

When Gordon reached Cairo on 23 August, he was upset to hear how his friend Ismael had been hustled off his throne. But he found Tewfik friendly, especially when Gordon told him that he himself had resigned. Before returning to England, he agreed to try and patch up diplomatic relations with Egypt's awkward southern neighbour, the Emperor Yohannes of Abyssinia. He set off next month by mule on that difficult mission.

By 1880, a new spirit of nationalism was stirring in Cairo which would soon cause far more anxiety in the chancelleries of Europe than Ismael's spendthrift ways. Colonel Arabi and the other Egyptian officers who had rioted in February had learnt their strength. Next time they would do more than pull the beards and knock the fezes off Nubar and Rivers Wilson. Egypt, looted by Ismael, humiliated by the Powers, would stand on its own feet.

But in London no one had yet heard of Arabi. Egypt slipped from the mind. In December 1880 British eyes suddenly focused on a crisis in Britain's newest colony, the Transvaal, at the other end of Africa.

CHAPTER 6

One Step Backward

South Africa and London
16 December 1880–3 August 1881

'[the Boers] . . . have all the cunning and cruelty of
the Kaffir without his courage or honesty . . . they
could not stand up against our troops for an hour.'

Sir Garnet Wolseley (British High Commissioner) to Sir
Michael Hicks Beach, October 1879

It was 16 December 1880, Dingane's Day, the Day of the Covenant, the anniversary of the Boer victory over Dingane and the Zulus in 1838. Within a few days a great convulsion was to sweep the Transvaal. Yet outwardly little seemed to have changed in the capital, Pretoria.

Three and a half years earlier, Shepstone's proclamation of annexation had been read out in Church Square, Pretoria. The capital still looked like a *dorp*, a Boer village, although most of the white population were British. Oxen would still graze on the spare brown grass below the battered gables of the Dutch Reformed Church. Hundreds of covered wagons outspanned there when it was time for *Nachmaal* (Communion). But today the place was half deserted.

There were few signs of British rule, apart from the coconut matting where some people played cricket in the square, the Union Jack flapping on the pole beside the tin-roofed government building, and the single battalion of redcoats in the thatched-roof barracks beside the convent. But there was one vital innovation, a small telegraph office, the end of a line of posts marching beside the cart track across the rolling veld to the blue hills of Natal, and so (by way of Durban and the submarine cable route via Aden) connecting Britain's newest Crown Colony with London. This telegraph line had been a rushed job, and so had cost a fortune, £30,000, about a fifth of the territory's budget for the year. But it would come in useful, the imperial authorities agreed, in case there was a 'row', meaning a war, with the Boers.

Not that anything of the kind was forecast by anyone in government buildings the week before Christmas, high summer in the Transvaal and the season for lawn tennis. The Administrator, Colonel Sir Owen Lanyon, was a tall, swarthy Irishman, 'Long John' to the Boers, 'Billy' to the British community, the shop-keepers, businessmen, surveyors and their families. Lanyon had taken over the Transvaal from Shepstone in 1879, and now ruled the territory under the eye of the new High Commissioner for south-eastern Africa, Major-General Sir George Colley, who was based in Natal. Both Lanyon and Colley had come to a simple conclusion about the Boers: their talk of fighting to restore their beloved republic was simply Boer 'brag'.

A mass meeting of armed Boers was planned for Paardekraal ('Horsekraal'), near Rustenburg, on 8 December. Let them brag away. As Lanyon told Colley before applying for leave in October:

> Some of the good folk here are beginning to cry out 'Wolf, wolf' about the coming mass meeting, but they have done so on every similar occasion. I don't feel any anxiety about it, and if the people will only let them alone, they [the Boers] will do nothing. Several have come to me and said ... 'Oh, you must put your foot down!' Nothing would play their game better than if we made any martyrs. ...[1]

After the convulsion it would be convenient to dismiss Lanyon and Colley as perfect idiots. How could they have missed those tremors, signs of the great earthquake about to engulf them?

Yet Sir Garnet Wolseley, Colley's patron and predecessor as High Commissioner in the Transvaal, reckoned the brightest general in the whole army ('our only soldier', Disraeli called him, without much exaggeration), was *the* expert on Africa, and he, too, had missed the telltale signs.

Perhaps Wolseley was too self-intoxicated, too much of a prodigy, to notice much around him. Certainly he had viewed his appointment in South Africa in 1879 with distaste; a distraction from his life's task of modernizing the British army. From the moment he had joined the army as a slight, almost girlish young ensign in the 1850s, he had been swept along by what he called 'a mad and manly fury' to give Britain the most efficient army in the world. How else could she protect herself, how retain – or, better still, extend – her far-flung empire? In that sacred cause he had not spared himself, or the readers of his numerous writings. As every British schoolboy knew, he had been half-blinded in the Burma War, and nearly blown to pieces by a shell in the Crimea. But reckless daring was no rarity among young officers. More unusually, Wolseley was an intellectual. And what was exceptional – almost suicidal – about him was his attack on the British military establishment, the Horse Guards.

Behind those walls the promotion of every officer was decided, and the Horse Guards were part of the pickings of court and society, epitomized by the bloated form of the Commander-in-Chief, the Queen's cousin, the Duke of Cambridge. Wolseley found him a disgusting anachronism – the Royal George, alias the Great German Sausage. As one of the protégés of the War Minister, Cardwell, Wolseley had set about Pall Mall with his sword, chopping out the dead wood, cutting out commissions by purchase and every kind of unprofessional behaviour, cleaning up Cardwell's new short service army so that it was 'all Sir Garnet', as the wits called it. In 1879 he was impatient to do the same for the British army in India, but the appointment in South Africa stood in the way.

The appointment gave Wolseley two hats: a proconsul's black top hat and a general's white helmet. Both hats were picked up, so to speak, on the battlefield of Isandlwana. Disraeli and his Cabinet had resisted the temptation to sack Sir Bartle Frere after this disaster. Instead they humiliated him, by giving his most demanding role to Wolseley, the role of High Commissioner responsible for Zululand and the Transvaal. They left Frere as Governor and High Commissioner at the Cape, in the forlorn hope that he might still be able to negotiate confederation. At the same time Wolseley was told to take over the army from Lord Chelmsford as Commander-in-Chief in South Africa. He arrived a fortnight too late.

To Wolseley's chagrin, victory for that poor 'noodle' Chelmsford had supervened. In principle Wolseley warmly approved of Frere's plan to add Zululand to the British Empire. But Frere's plan had a fatal flaw: using Chelmsford. To Wolseley the battle of Isandlwana represented all that was most preposterous about the unreformed British army. The general had divided his forces and left the camp wide open to Zulu attack. Unfortunately the same general, Chelmsford, stumbled his way to victory despite himself. With large reinforcements (which brought the costs of the war to over £1.3 million), Chelmsford had crushed Cetshwayo's warriors at the battle of Ulundi on 4 July 1879. All Wolseley was left with was the fag-end of the campaign, the unglamorous job of hunting down the 'obese' king, as Wolseley called him.

He wasted no time. Cetshwayo was packed off on a mule wagon, bound for prison in Cape Town. Then Wolseley, giving himself no proper time for consultation, imposed a settlement in Zululand. He would have liked to annex the territory outright, but Disraeli's Cabinet, reluctant imperialists at the best of times, had learnt their lessons with Frere and forbade Wolseley to extend the Empire and its expenses. So Zululand was made nominally free – sliced up into thirteen independent miniature states, each to be ruled by a separate chief in conflict with his neighbours. It was divide-and-rule with a vengeance. And predictably, Wolseley's impatience made the settlement doomed. (Zululand was formally annexed by Britain.)

After carving up Zululand, Wolseley, still wearing the proconsular hat, rode off impatiently to settle the hash of the Transvaal. Before he even reached Pretoria, he made it clear that he was having no nonsense with Boer talk of restoring the old republic. Two miles from the town, he met a deputation of Boers who had ridden out to welcome him. 'As long as the sun', he said, pointing to the sun over Observation Hill, 'shines over South Africa, the British flag will fly over Pretoria.'² The rebuff was all the more wounding to the Boers as they realized the British flag was not, after all, going to fly over Zululand.

That Wolseley was out of sympathy with the Boers was only to be expected. The struggle to succeed, the ten years of war against the Horse Guards, had scarred and mutilated him as cruelly as the swords and shells of the enemy. He came from an Anglo-Irish family fallen on hard times. He combined an acid wit with a set of extravagant English prejudices. According to his private campaign journals, where he safely let off steam, he disliked most of the human race. Who dared to call himself an English gentleman? Not 'Sir Hitch-Bitch' (Hicks Beach) or 'Sir Bottle Beer' (Bartle Frere). Not Gladstone and 'those vestrymen' (the

Radicals), nor Parnell and his murderous Home Rulers ('I should like to hang one of them myself'), nor British colonials, Jews and businessmen of all kinds. As for the Boers, they were 'the only white race that has been steadily going backwards to barbarism ... [and is] now in many respects below the black man'. So why pay any attention to their claims to be able to govern themselves? 'Wherever I go,' he wrote, 'I hear the same thing, that the anti-English feeling grows stronger every day all over South Africa.' Yet that was not to imagine that they would risk their necks to regain their independence. 'I believe the Transvaal Boer to be a coward pure and simple, who will swagger & talk big when he knows he can do so with impunity, but the moment he is collared, he collapses.'[3]

A month after arriving in Pretoria, Wolseley had marched out again up the road to the east, a long, dusty ride across the veld, almost featureless except for occasional clumps of thorn scrub. If he had arrived in South Africa too late to crush the Zulus in battle, at least he could settle with Sekhukhene, the 'robber chief' of the Pedi, in his mountain lair near Lydenburg. It was Sekhukhene who had proved too hard a nut for President Burgers and his commandos to crack in 1876–7. Indeed, Sekhukhene's defiance had been Burgers's downfall – and Shepstone's opportunity. In his proclamation of 1877 Shepstone had explained that only by British intervention would the Transvaal be saved from its enemies. Now Wolseley was impatient to redeem this promise. How he revelled in cutting through Gordian knots. The Boers would be glad to see their old enemy humbled and his own troops would benefit from the exercise. The Treasury would grumble at the expense, but then stationing troops there to keep an eye on Sekhukhene had already cost a pretty penny. And he could warn those skinflints in the Treasury that, until Sekhukhene bit the dust, the natives would no more pay taxes to the British than they had to the Boers.

Cocky as he was, Wolseley seemed to be right. The campaign proved a model: as short and sweet (for Wolseley) as Chelmsford's had been ponderous and costly in blood and treasure. Sekhukhene's Pedi warriors conveniently gathered for a last stand on a kopje above their 'town', a miserable collection of huts. The kopje was stormed on the morning of 28 November 1879, the attack led by a few companies of redcoats supported by Krupp field-guns. The brunt of the fighting was borne by some wild native allies of the Boers ('a dreadful lot' according to Wolseley),[4] 8,000 Swazis, mainly armed with assegais.

It was all over in a few hours: the town a blackened ruin, the cattle driven off by the Swazis, while the ground shook as the neighbouring caves, refuge of the survivors, were methodically blown up with gun cotton. Sekhukhene could count himself lucky to be taken alive and packed off to join Cetshwayo in prison at Cape Town.

Wolseley's small war had cost only about £100,000, less than a tenth of the Zulu war, and achieved more. For his firm handling of the Pedi had a salutary effect on the natives everywhere, Wolseley noted with satisfaction. Now the Transvaal natives were reported eager to pay the hut tax; £30,000 was expected in taxes in 1880, more than was forthcoming from the Boers.

If only the Boers had learnt their lesson too. Wolseley found he earned no thanks from them for destroying their traditional enemies. On the contrary, when he marched back to Pretoria in December 1879, the Boers proved as intransigent as ever. Indeed, by removing their enemies he seemed to have put new heart into them. Lanyon had made no progress in the trial of strength with their leaders. The delegations, led by Paul Kruger, had already gone to London to try to persuade Disraeli to reverse the annexation. Shepstone, they claimed, had annexed them under false pretences. They backed this claim with a petition for a restoration of the republic signed by 6,591 burghers. A mere 587 British loyalists in the Transvaal signed a counter-petition. The more extreme Boers refused to pay their taxes, and threatened to boycott British shopkeepers. Even the more moderate asked why Britain did not honour the promises given in Shepstone's annexation to give them self-government under the British flag. Indeed, apart from the crushing of Sekhukhene and Cetshwayo, it could well be asked what advantage the British flag had brought them. The Transvaal Treasury was still in deficit and the British Treasury's tight-fisted grant of £100,000 had been quickly swallowed up paying for official salaries and the new telegraph. The absence of development in the country – no civil hospital, no bridges, no metalled roads – only fed the grievances against Britain.

To this Wolseley's reply was uncompromising: pay your taxes, prove your loyalty, and one day you will have full self-government like the Cape Afrikaners. Meanwhile, direct rule – Crown Colony government – was all that could be safely allowed. On 10 May 1880 he opened a new legislative council in Pretoria, in which the British community was represented by selected members. Kruger and the Boers were left out in the cold.

On 10 December 1879 several thousand armed Boers had gone into laager in Wonderfontein, near Potchestroom. They renewed their call for independence and threatened to use their rifles to get it. Wolseley's reply was to arrest two of the Boer leaders, Bok and Pretorius, for high treason, although he did not choose to press the charges. He had called their bluff – so he believed. 'Poor silly creatures, they go on playing at soldiers & blustering, knowing in their hearts they would bolt at the sight of the first troop of our Dragoons.'[5]

Wolseley recommended to London that the British garrison in the Transvaal and Natal could be safely reduced from six to four battalions. Then Major-General Colley sailed from India to relieve him and he left Pretoria for home in April 1880. As he galloped impatiently down the rutted track towards Natal, covering 200 miles in less than three days, he prayed he would never have to return. He had one regret. If the Boers had only shown fight, instead of funk, he would have put an end to their nonsense once and for all.

After Wolseley had gone, Colley and Lanyon remained polite but firm. By November 1880 the trial of strength had reached a new stage. Burghers must pay their taxes or the law must take its course. A farmer called Bezuidenhout owed a tax bill of £27-10s. The name was potent in Afrikaner folk memory. In 1816 another farmer called Bezuidenhout had been one of those hanged from a beam at Slachters Nek in the Cape, convicted of rebellion against the Crown, and a martyr for the volk, or so it seemed to the men of the Great Trek twenty years later.

The sheriff's men seized Bezuidenhout's farm wagons to pay for his taxes, but the attempt ended in fiasco when armed Boers, led by a firebrand called Piet Cronje, restored the wagons to their owner.

Then in December 1880 Lanyon learnt of the mass meeting of armed Boers at Paardekraal near Rustenburg. He decided to take only one precautionary step: to send a spy to report proceedings. For his part, Colley, 200 miles away in Natal but kept informed by telegraph, had already decided to draw in some of the outlying garrisons. Word was sent to Lydenburg that the two companies of the 80th stationed there should march back to Pretoria. But Lanyon claimed he felt no anxiety. Those 'good folk' were just 'crying wolf'.[6]

Lanyon had forgotten the point of the story. Those who cried wolf were not listened to. They were right in the end: the wolf ate them.

The spy sent by Lanyon to report on the banned meeting at Paardekraal on 8 December was confronted by an astonishing sight. The burghers of the Transvaal were thought to total a mere 8,000. More than half that number – perhaps more than 5,000 armed men – were gathered on the stony hillside. Some had brought their families, as though they were going to *Nachmaal*, after jolting across the veld for days in their covered wagons. Others had ridden up on horseback, just as they would for a hunting expedition, a black servant at their side, a blanket and rifle on the saddle-bow and strips of biltong (dried buck) tied to the harness. They hobbled their horses, and waited for their leaders to decide when the hunt would begin.

Edward Jorissen, the State Attorney of the old republic, rode up on 9 December and was greeted by Kruger with the words: '*Het is klaar*' ('It is ready').[7] Jorissen was one of the new breed of foreign experts, imported from Holland by President Burgers. A clergyman turned lawyer, he had quickly become Kruger's closest political adviser. Together they had been chosen by the Volksraad to go on the mission to London in 1877, the first of the two abortive missions to reverse the annexation. They presented a striking contrast, those two men: Jorissen, an urban intellectual, tall, spare, diffident, humourless; Kruger, a prodigy from the veld, half-man, half-lion, with a mane of black hair, shoulders broad enough to lift a loaded cart, and a massive frame under the ill-fitting black Dopper jacket he habitually wore. Together the two men paced up and down the hillside, as though they were alone, while the moon rose and the camp fires glowed like the lights of a city.

The die was cast, both men agreed. Piet Cronje had forced their hand in November when he seized Bezuidenhout's wagon from the bailiffs and defied the British to arrest him. This was the turning point. The people – the volk – were united at last. If they did not strike now, they might as well give up all idea of restoring the republic.

Why had it taken nearly four years to unite the volk against the British? No one could answer that question better than Kruger. It had taken nearly forty years – all his political life – to unite the volk behind him. Sometimes their quarrels had brought him near despair. He had even contemplated joining a new trek beyond the borders of the Transvaal. Anarchy and disorder seemed as natural to the nomadic Boers of that frontier community as law and order were to the Boers of the Free State, and their brother Afrikaners at the Cape. It was the crippling disunity, the utter collapse of President Burgers's government, that had led directly to the British annexation, but now, thanks be to the Lord, the British in their folly had given the long-despaired unity back to the volk.

Kruger could play the clown. He could also play the biblical prophet. He was a voortrekker, one of the pioneers, as rough-hewn as the new state they had carved out of the wilderness. When he was ten he had followed his parents on the Great Trek out of Cape Colony to search for the Promised Land beyond the Orange and the Vaal rivers. With his own eyes he had witnessed – as he never failed to repeat – the birthpangs of the republic: the laager of a few dozen Boer wagons drawn into a square for defence, the wheels of the centre wagons chained together, the gaps stuffed with brushwood except for the loopholes; the war chant of the Ndebele, the frenzied drumming on their shields; then thousands of warriors in full warpaint throwing themselves forwards against the wagons; the screams of the wounded; the hiss of assegais; the smoke of the flintlocks – and the Lord, bless the Lord, he had given the volk a great victory.

Kruger boasted that his only education came from the Good Book and the gun. He found both equally serviceable as weapons. Before he was fifteen he had shot his first lion. Before he was eighteen he was a field-cornet, a local official. At twenty-eight he was commandant-general. When the quarrels of the volk broke into civil war, it was Kruger who bombarded the rebels, then acted as mediator. His main support came from the backveld, the home of the poorest and most conservative Boers. He wore the short black jacket of the Doppers, the ultra-Calvinist sect that had broken away from the Dutch Reformed Church.

Yet like a born hunter Kruger could be patient, and thought nothing of having to retreat when stalking a dangerous enemy. He had collaborated with President Burgers and temporized with him. Burgers was an *ex*-clergyman from the Cape, so advanced in his theology that Kruger hardly rated him a Christian. Burgers had equally advanced ideas about modernizing the Transvaal. Kruger saw that Burgers was going too far and too fast for the volk. By a mixture of luck and cunning, he thwarted Burgers. The crisis that followed, the double fiasco of the Delagoa railway project and the Pedi war, suited him perfectly. Then came the disaster he had failed to anticipate: Shepstone's intervention.

To unite the volk against Britain demanded more than luck and cunning; it needed all Kruger's moral muscle. The danger was a premature revolt. He had to calm the hotheads. At the same time he had to win over the waverers. In fact he gathered larger numbers at each of the mass meetings – one at Doornfontein in 1878 and two at Wonderfontein in 1879. Till 1880 he had hoped the British would recognize they had been misled by Shepstone and Frere and voluntarily restore the republic. Then, one day in June 1880, a blow fell which made Kruger realize that war was more or less inevitable.

Kruger had been sent down to Cape Town by the National Committee of burghers to lobby against Frere's latest plan to push federation through the Cape Parliament. This was not difficult. The Afrikaners at the Cape comprised the majority of the white voters at the Cape. 'Do not wash your hands in the blood of your brothers,'[8] said Kruger. The Afrikaners had no intention of doing so. Once they realized the Boers were trying to reverse the annexation, their sympathies were entirely on their side. They were also hostile to the idea of federation with Natal (the feeling was reciprocated). In July 1880 Frere had the final humiliation of seeing his federal plan collapse without a vote in the Cape Parliament. In August he was recalled to London, a casualty of Shepstone's impatience and his own ignorance. His policy was in ruins, ahead was chaos, but still Frere talked of the coming federation.

Meanwhile the blow had fallen that made Kruger and the others turn secretly to oiling their rifles and their ammunition. In April, Gladstone had succeeded Disraeli as Britain's Prime Minister. In his election campaign the previous autumn he had hinted that he would restore the independence of the Transvaal. At least he had thundered against the annexation in the speeches at Midlothian: he had called it 'insane' and 'despotic'[9] and declared that the new colony could only be held down by force of arms. Gladstone's right-hand man, the Whig leader, Lord Hartington, had gone even further. He had said, in the House of Commons, that a false sense of dignity should not stand in the way of restoring the Transvaal's independence, and like Gladstone's, his speech was widely publicized in South Africa.

However, when Kruger read the text of the Queen's Speech of the new Liberal government there was an ominous reference to self-government, not independence. Earlier, on 10 May, Kruger wrote officially to Gladstone. Did he intend to repeal the annexation? Gladstone's reply reached him in June while he was still in Cape Town. It was so bland, so uncompromising, that it might have been drafted by Disraeli: he could not advise Her Majesty to abandon her suzerainty over the Transvaal.

At Paardekraal, that Saturday, 10 December 1880, the solemn decision was taken by the Boers to hoist the Vierkleur, the national flag, and restore the republic. There was no need to count votes. The meeting unanimously agreed that the old government and the old Volksraad of 1877 should resume their function. Technically a triumvirate would be in charge: the Vice-President, Paul Kruger; an ageing ex-President, Marthinus Pretorius (son of the founder of the state, Pretorius, after whom the capital was named); and the inexperienced new commandant-general, Piet Joubert. Kruger, of course, towered over the other two men. It was he and Jorissen who now hammered out the plans for war as they paced up and down on the hillside.

They must draft a proclamation to give legitimacy to the restored government. It would also be a declaration of independence and an ultimatum to the

British. This must be taken to Potchefstroom, south of Paardekraal, printed and distributed. The new Boer government would make its quarters at Heidelberg, sixty miles south of Pretoria, a central rallying point and far enough from the nearest British troops. The plan of campaign was simple and daring. They would send small parties of burghers to besiege Pretoria and the other towns where there were British garrisons. Meanwhile the main army under General Joubert would converge on Natal and prevent General Colley from marching north with reinforcements.

Could such a plan succeed? Would the same men who had fled from the assegais and flintlocks of the Pedi and left President Burgers in the lurch in 1876 now risk their lives against professional British troops? Only once before had they fought redcoats – at the battle of Boomplaats in 1848. They had received a severe drubbing then; how could they fare better today?

The Boers of the Transvaal were still untrained, with not even a token regular army, or any professional soldiers to lead them. Their rifles were excellent, it was true – single-shot, sporting rifles, Martini-Henrys and Westley-Richards, quite as good as any the British could bring against them. But they were short of ammunition, with hardly fifteen rounds a man, and had no artillery of any kind.

They had just two advantages. First, by raising the whole burgher force of perhaps 7,000 men, they would outnumber Colley's forces in the Transvaal and Natal by about three to one. (But by every steamer the British would pour reinforcements into South Africa, so they must strike fast.) Second, though they knew nothing of European warfare, the burghers were experts in war on the veld. With their rifles they had hacked a state out of a wilderness, hunting down Africans as they hunted game. Now they would hunt *rooineks*, the British, the same way – with the help of God and the Martini-Henry.

Meanwhile the burghers observed the Sabbath at Paardekraal. Jorissen said later that he would have needed the pencil of a Rembrandt to record that scene – the patriarchs with flowing beards seated on the stony hillside. He and other leaders had pitched their tents on a small terrace at the top of the plateau. Below them, packed together as though in an amphitheatre, were thousands of burghers, a few sitting on camp stools, but mostly stretched on the ground. Everyone looked intently up at the preacher. He had taken a small table as his pulpit, on which he put a Bible. There was a prayer and a hymn. Then in a voice trembling with emotion, the preacher read an appeal from the National Committee asking the clergy to support the volk in the impending struggle. 'You have called me. Here I am. I shall go with you and stand with you.'[10]

On 15 December the great meeting broke up, and the burghers divided according to the plan of campaign. Piet Cronje, the firebrand who had lit the fuse of the revolution by seizing Bezuidenhout's wagon, rode off to Potchefstroom to see that the proclamation was printed. Kruger, Jorissen and the leaders trekked to Heidelberg. It was there the republic would be solemnly proclaimed on 16 December, Dingane's Day, the Day of the Covenant.

But first they performed a ceremony that would be remembered even more vividly than the proclamation itself, for it symbolized the new unity of the volk. Before he left, each man picked up a stone from the hillside. The stones were heaped into a cairn, close to where the pulpit had stood, a monument of 5,000 lives pledged to the restored republic. Then the Vierkleur – orange, red, white and blue – was hoisted on a bamboo pole above the cairn.

The column of redcoats, two dust-stained companies of the 94th regiment, totalling nine officers and 248 men, plodded along the rutted wagon track from Lydenburg south-westward to Pretoria, hampered by their train of 34 baggage wagons and cursing the frequent thunderstorms. They had marched on 5 December. By 20 December, they had covered barely 130 miles, but in two days they would be in Pretoria. Already the landscape was softening. The harsh flat veld of the eastern Transvaal, as dry and boring as an army biscuit, was merging into a country of green valleys and thorn trees. At the head of the column, to keep up the men's spirits, marched the regimental band, playing 'God Save the Queen'.

In front of everyone rode the CO, Colonel Anstruther, and the baggage conductor, named Egerton. It was about 1.0 p.m. The two men were going to select a camp site a mile or so ahead at Bronkhorst Spruit (Watercress Ditch). Then Anstruther heard the music stop. He turned around on his horse. A party of about 150 armed Boers had ridden up among the thorn trees on the left side of the track. One of them emerged under a white flag with a note for Anstruther in English. The Boer commandant informed him that the republic had been proclaimed at Heidelberg four days before, and an ultimatum given to the British. He must halt where he was; otherwise the Boers could not be answerable for the consequences.

Anstruther replied that his orders were to go to Pretoria, and to Pretoria he would go. He galloped back to join the column, shouting to his men to extend into skirmishing order.

The next scene burst on the British with the force of a nightmare.

A storm of bullets caught the bandsmen as they dropped their drums and bugles and scrambled to get their rifles out of the wagons. It swept through the soldiers beginning to line out in the grass, smashing through the wagons behind them, and driving the wounded oxen berserk. The soldiers tried to return fire as they had been taught, firing in regular volleys. But the Boers had vanished into the smoke, hidden behind the trees and rocks. Others fanned out to encircle the column, picking off the leading oxen of each wagon and killing the African drivers.

For a few minutes the column endured the nightmare. The officers, armed only with swords and revolvers, stood up in the skirmishing line to encourage their men. It was brave but suicidal. At length Anstruther gave the order to the bugler to cease fire. The track looked like a butcher's yard. Five of the nine officers were dead or mortally wounded, including Anstruther, with five bullets in his legs. Someone raised a white flag. A third of the men were dead, another third were wounded, mostly severely. Wounded oxen caught up in the traces plunged about, dragging the broken wagons among the dead and dying.

As the white flag went up, Boers in bush hats galloped down from all sides. They grabbed the men's rifles, pulled off their white helmets and made them squat like Africans. Their leader, Commandant Frans Joubert, shook Anstruther's hand and said he was sorry to see he was hurt. Joubert dealt equally humanely with the other wounded. They were left a doctor and a fatigue party to look after them; a messenger was sent to Pretoria to fetch extra help. Then the Boers herded up their unwounded prisoners and marched them towards Heidelberg along with the much-needed loot: all the carts, horses and wagons, including three vital wagonloads of Martini-Henrys and ammunition.

The war of independence had begun well enough, thanks be to the Lord. In just over ten minutes the Boers had annihilated an eighth of all the British troops in the Transvaal.

*　　*　　*

At first no one in London was unduly alarmed to read of the Boers' declaration of independence. It was the week before Christmas, the wettest in living memory, people said (as they did most years). People swam in the Serpentine alongside the ducks, and fished beside the barges on the Thames where the towpaths were flooded for miles up the river. Nothing – certainly not a proclamation on the veld, 6,000 miles away – could spoil the holiday spirit. At Crystal Palace there was the daring new Black and White Minstrel Show. People crowded the zoo to see the latest imperial acquisitions: a tame jaguar presented by Lady Florence Dixie and a man-eating tiger, on loan from the recently-sacked Indian Viceroy, Lord Lytton.

As for the Transvaal, neither the Colonial Office experts nor *The Times* leader writer knew what to make of the affair. Durban reported that the Boers had cut the telegraph line west of Standerton, so the cables were brief and confused. Major-General Sir George Colley's official telegram, sent from his HQ in Natal on 19 December, reached London on the 20th, and *The Times* published it the next day. He reported 'No collision or violence'.[11] Indeed, who would have expected any? For months everyone had been assured by Lanyon and Colley that things were on the mend.

Before Christmas Gladstone and his Cabinet steamed majestically out of London by train, bound for the country. Most of this Liberal Cabinet came from the Whig nobility, with great country estates to match. Guns were oiled, keepers given a final briefing, house parties welcomed to the great *battus*. In these circles a good Christmas included a record bag of pheasants, a record run with the hounds. Lord Hartington, Secretary of State for India, held court at his father's ducal estate at Chatsworth; Lord Kimberley, Secretary for the Colonies, at Kimberley; the Duke of Argyll, Lord Privy Seal, at Inverary; Lord Spencer, Lord President of the Council, at Althorp; Lord Granville, Foreign

Secretary, at Walmer, and so on. Only two Radicals had seats in the Cabinet: John Bright, Chancellor of the Duchy of Lancaster, and Joseph Chamberlain, President of the Board of Trade. Their homes were in Rochdale and Birmingham, the great industrial cities which had made them rich. Gladstone himself was a merchant's son from Liverpool, but his wife came from the landed aristocracy and had brought the Hawarden estate into his family. Gladstone was too high-minded for field sports, unless you included his well-advertised custom of chopping up oak trees. This Christmas he spent quietly at Hawarden, reading the lesson in the parish church and studying in his library, his 'Temple of Peace'. It was a short respite from the succession of crises that had shaken his Cabinet, blowing him off course as though they were tropical storms: Afghanistan, Ireland, the Queen herself.

On Christmas Day the news of the Bronkhorst Spruit disaster was cabled to the duty officer in the Colonial Office, and repeated to Lord Kimberley, Gladstone, the Cabinet and the Queen. No one was more incredulous than Kimberley, the Colonial Secretary. He could only blame himself for being fooled by Lanyon and Colley. Now he had to warn his chief that the news was 'serious' because a 'first success is bound to give a great impetus to the rebellion'.[12] He hesitated to ask for reinforcements since Gladstone's distaste for military spending was notorious, but Colley insisted he needed one extra regiment. (Why only *one*, people would soon ask.)

The Queen took the news as well as could be expected. She was spending Christmas quietly with Princess Louise and Prince Leopold at Osborne, on the Isle of Wight, as usual. Nothing that had occurred since Gladstone took over the government had changed her views about that abominable man. His scurrilous attacks on Disraeli and his unctuous manner to her both made him personally unfit to hold office. In vain she had tried to spike his guns before he became PM, by begging in turn each of the Whig leaders, Hartington and Granville, to take the job. Now she wrote, perhaps with a touch of *schadenfreude*, 'The Boers are a dangerous foe, and we shall have to support Sir G. Colley strongly.'[13]

At Hawarden Gladstone grudgingly gave his assent. Mercifully he was still spared from acknowledging his own part in provoking the Boer rebellion. Later he would recognize – dimly at least – that this was his own great blunder. In Opposition he had led the Boers to believe that independence was theirs for the asking. In government he gave them nothing but a slap in the face: independence was not negotiable.

Why had Gladstone, as quick as an eagle to pounce on the moral failings of others, failed to honour his own promises? Why had this champion of oppressed nationalities across the globe stood idly by and let the Transvaal drift to disaster? It was to his own great credit that he had detected from London what the men on the spot – Wolseley, Colley and Lanyon – had failed to recognize. The Boer resentment at being ruled by the British was a passionate grievance about a vital principle. Difficulties in the Transvaal could not be brushed under the carpet by writing off Kruger and the leaders as a handful of irreconcilables. Yet to brush them aside was precisely the policy of the Colonial Office, supported by the new Liberal Minister for the Colonies, Lord Kimberley. Despite Frere's sacking, the CO officials still hankered to find some way of federating the Transvaal and Cape Colony. Against his better judgement, perhaps, Gladstone acquiesced. In May he had formally committed his government to stay in the Transvaal. The truth was the Transvaal had slipped from his thoughts. He was up to his neck in what he called the Irish 'soup', and the brew was 'thickening' – and poisoning everything. Civil war threatened, both in Ireland and in the Cabinet.

A land war was raging in Ireland, only 50 miles from the shores of Britain. By every post there were reports of fresh agrarian outrages: houses burnt, cattle killed or hamstrung, landlords shot or hacked to pieces. Almost worse than the actual outrages was the breakdown of law and order. This was caused by the virulent campaign against landlords organized by the Irish Land League, who got their way by intimidation of witnesses and the threat of violence. The police and the courts confessed themselves helpless to deal with the conspiracy.

To cap it all, the explosive grievances of the land had been successfully merged with the great question of Home Rule, that is, Irish self-government. Charles Stewart Parnell, the arrogant new leader of the sixty Irish MPs in Westminster, had been elected President of the Land League. He now boasted he would obstruct all parliamentary business unless the League's demands were met in full. He meant to get his way, so the Liberals thought, by fair means or foul.

How was Gladstone to deal with Parnell without destroying his own party in the process? The Whig landowners in his Cabinet identified themselves as closely with the rights of landlords as the Radicals did with the rights of the tenants. And each faction threatened to resign unless they got their way.

On 29 December, Gladstone steamed back to Downing Street to prepare for a vital Cabinet meeting next day. It was his birthday, his seventy-first, and his private secretaries had presented the great man with a 'Gladstone Bag', the kind of squashy black bag he had made famous, capacious enough to be a conjuror's. Eddy Hamilton, his thirty-three-year-old protégé and junior secretary, noticed how astonishingly fit and well Gladstone looked. For a man of seventy-one, he was a prodigy; despite his white hair, his shoulders were like an athlete's, his eyes like an eagle's. Today he wore what his wife called his gravest 'official' look. As Hamilton noted in his diary: 'He has the whole weight of Ireland on his shoulders, and in the Cabinet he stands between the two fires of the right and the left wing.'[14]

At the Cabinet meeting next day the Grand Old Man pulled a new trick out of his conjuror's bag. To reassure the Whigs, he agreed to suspend Habeas Corpus. This would give the government power to arrest the known trouble-makers without the need to bring evidence against them in court. To reassure the Radicals, Gladstone threw all his energy into brewing up a new kind of land reform (a 'double x' brew, he called it)[15] to be embodied in a new Land Bill.

A further comfort for the Radicals was the formal decision to withdraw from

Afghanistan. This was a reversal of Disraeli's forward policy of previous years, but the great Whig landowners approved. They had no more love for expensive imperialist adventures than the rest of the party. If only the same could have been said about the Queen, who was still at Osborne. On 4 January 1881 she saw the text of the Queen's Speech to be spoken at the opening of Parliament on the 6th. There was a paragraph announcing her intention to withdraw the last of the troops from Afghanistan: 'It is not my intention that the occupation of Candahar shall be permanently maintained.'[16] Lords Granville and Hartington took train and ship to Osborne to receive the royal assent. At first the Queen refused point-blank. She said she had never been so treated since she came to the throne. After a day-long siege, the ministers were told she was 'highly displeased' by the way they had behaved, but she surrendered with bad grace.

'Poor woman!' as Gladstone said (according to Eddy Hamilton). 'It was certainly rather hard that She should be made to express satisfaction at the withdrawal from a place to which only a few months ago she had by her late Ministers been made to attach so much importance.'[17]

In all the fuss about the Queen, and the search for a way to prevent the Liberals tearing themselves to pieces over Ireland, Gladstone had made an omission that passed unnoticed. The Cabinet met. Parliament reassembled. The Queen's Speech was read and debated. Not a word was spoken about the Transvaal.

By the end of February this omission would seem all the more astonishing. By now it was the coldest winter within living memory, people said (and this time they were right). The Thames froze. Skaters competed with the ducks on the Serpentine. Snow drifts were piled high in Downing Street. The Prime Minister's head was bandaged after a fall in the snow when visiting the Prince of Wales at Marlborough House, and the bad news from the Transvaal had at last displaced the bad news from Ireland. General Colley, reinforced by that single regiment, had fought two more engagements with the Boers, at Laing's Nek on 28 January, and Ingogo on 7 February. In each he had been repulsed with heavy loss by a small force.

At the same time the new Governor of Cape Colony, Sir Hercules Robinson, reported to London a most ominous widening of the crisis. The Boers in the Orange Free State were flocking to join their brothers in the Transvaal. The Afrikaners in Cape Colony, far more numerous than either, were tempted to follow. This despatch from the Cape did not convince the senior experts at the Colonial Office, but it had a decisive effect on the Colonial Secretary, Lord Kimberley. Suddenly he reversed his policy and proposed negotiating peace with the Boers. Kimberley turned to Gladstone. He had said all along that Disraeli's annexation was a deplorable blunder. Better surely to negotiate – even after three defeats – than to turn the whole of South Africa into another Ireland. Their own mistake, as Eddy Hamilton had to admit, was the failure to send out commissioners to negotiate the Transvaal's independence last April, as soon as the Liberals had come to power. But that would have meant sacking Frere and

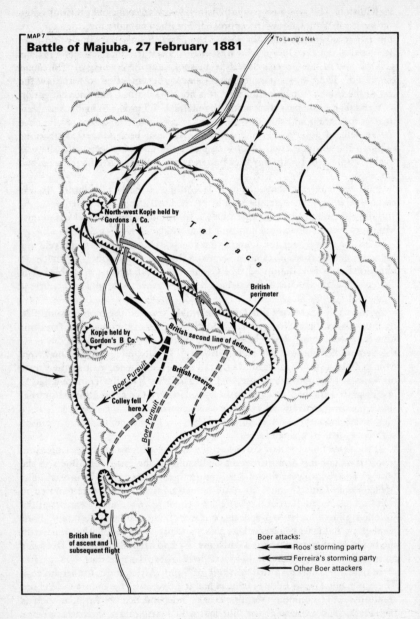

MAP 7

Battle of Majuba, 27 February 1881

To Laing's Nek

T e r r a c e

North-west Kopje held by
Gordons A Co.

British
perimeter

British second line of defence

Kopje held by
Gordon's B Co.

Boer Pursuit

British reserves

Colley fell
here X

Boer Pursuit

British line
of ascent and
subsequent flight

Boer attacks:
Roos' storming party
Ferreira's storming party
Other Boer attackers

cancelling the annexation forthwith, which would have brought the full weight of the Queen's displeasure down on Gladstone's head.

Gladstone was never one to shrink from that if his conscience insisted – and the party would swallow it. In fact, handing back the Transvaal to the Boers would be welcomed by the Radicals as patriotic and honourable. The Whigs would acquiesce. The Queen would be frantic and the jingoes would howl. Let them!

On 16 February Colley was told to offer Kruger an armistice and an invitation to peace negotiations. Provided they would accept British suzerainty (in effect supervision of foreign relations), independence was now theirs for the asking, without further need for shooting.

* * *

The Queen was displeased. The Tories were suspicious. But there was nothing that either could do for the moment to stop Gladstone making a humiliating peace ('peace under defeat') with the Boer rebels. Out on the veld, on the windy hillsides of Natal, facing the Boers' entrenched position at Laing's Nek, Sir George Colley had more freedom. The talk of peace appalled him. He wanted another chance to wipe the slate clean. He must not only redeem himself; he must redeem the honour of the army. No sacrifice could be too great for that.

Colley did not disobey the Cabinet's orders to try to make an armistice. He did not need to. His instructions in Kimberley's cable of 16 February were just vague enough to be misinterpreted. 'Inform Kruger that, if Boers will desist from armed opposition, we shall be quite ready to appoint Commissions with extensive powers ... Add that, if this proposal is accepted you are authorised to agree to suspension of hostilities.'[18] He cabled back for clarification. Did Kimberley really mean that he was to leave the Boers in possession of Laing's Nek (just inside Natal) while the British garrisons in the Transvaal were still under siege? 'Yes,' cabled Kimberley. 'If the arrangement proceeds', he was *not* to try to occupy Laing's Nek, nor to relieve the garrisons in the Transvaal. He was merely to ensure that they were free to provision themselves. The crucial condition then was 'if the arrangement proceeds', meaning if Kruger accepted the armistice. To discover this, Colley must fix a 'reasonable time' within which Kruger must reply.[19]

What was a 'reasonable time'? Forty-eight hours, said Colley – without informing London. He was specifically warned by the Boers that it would take at least six days to get a reply from Kruger, who was at Heidelberg. (In fact, he was at Rustenberg and it took twelve days.) Forty-eight hours, repeated Colley. A most reasonable time, if the aim was to sabotage the armistice.

A plan for a dazzling feat of arms had suddenly entered Colley's fevered brain. On the far west of the enemy's trench line at Laing's Nek was a 2,000-foot-high table mountain, Majuba, commanding the country for miles around. Seize it by a *coup de main*, as Wolfe had seized the Heights of Abraham before

Quebec, and the Boers would be forced to evacuate Laing's Nek and slink back across the border into the Transvaal. Victory would depend on speed and secrecy. It might also be bloodless. The natives claimed that the Boers had not fortified the mountain and would therefore be unable to contest the attack.

Colley hurriedly put together a scratch body of 600 men. There were three companies of the 92nd Highlanders who had landed at Durban only a fortnight before. The column would take three days' rations and all their equipment, including spades and shovels. They would march at 10.30 p.m. to dig in on the evening of Sunday 26 February, the day after the forty-eight hours expired. Only a couple of staff officers would be trusted with the secret of their destination. The first the men would know of it was when they began to climb the mountain itself.

A night ascent of a mountain demands good guides, good nerves and a fair slice of luck. Colley rejoiced in all three. The African guides lost their way for only a moment, then found the sheep track that led to the summit. The men groped and stumbled over the rocks, panting under the weight of their rifles and greatcoats, tins of bully beef and pouches of spare ammunition. A halt was called every few hundred yards. The steepest part, near the top, could only be negotiated on hands and knees. But the ascent passed unchallenged. (In fact the Boer picket deputed to watch the kop that night had lost its own way in the darkness.) At about 4.0 a.m. Colley himself led the long file of encumbered men on to the flat summit. The men flopped down on the grass to recover their breath. Colley looked over the lip of the plateau. Less than a mile away and 2,000 feet below them, lanterns flickered among the Boers' wagon laagers. The enemy slept, unaware of their presence.

As dawn flooded the plain with light, exposing the Boer trenches like the trenches on a sand table, an overpowering sense of relief took hold of Colley. The strain of the last few weeks, the bitterness of his own defeats, suddenly evaporated. Colley had always had the knack of looking cool in a crisis. Now he unburdened himself to Stewart, his chief staff officer, unable to keep his elation to himself. 'We could stay here forever,'[20] he told Stewart. There was no need to dig trenches on the summit, he told Major Fraser, his second-in-command. The men were fagged out. No need to disturb them; the position was already impregnable.

He formed half the men in reserve at the centre and told the others to line the edge of the plateau. Otherwise he made no preparations. The enemy were already on the run. That was the meaning of what he saw in the valley below: Boers scurrying to and fro like ants, horses saddled, wagons on the move. He telegraphed a jaunty cable back to the camp, for relaying to London. His men were equally lighthearted. They made no effort to keep their presence concealed. Some of the Highlanders stood shaking their fists at the enemy. One of the officers even loosed off some rounds at a Boer far below, until Colley gave orders to stop the firing.

The Boers could hardly miss the Highlanders on the skyline. The sight filled the laager with panic. A young officer, an assistant field-cornet called Stephanus Roos, described the moment. 'Everybody & everything was in confusion. I felt in my heart we are lost if we do not drive the English off the kop at once, but give them time to fortify themselves and bring up guns. There was no time or opportunity to call a council of war. I caught hold of my horse & raced in to the foot of the mountain. Here and there I saw single men ... also galloping up ... I shouted & waved my hat to collect them all under the rocks.'[21]

Commandant General Piet Joubert had set up his outposts as usual and was quietly working in his tent, writing a letter to President Brand, of the Free State, about the peace overtures. Suddenly he heard cries of 'Up saddle! Up saddle!' and realized that the British were on the kop. Joubert felt bitter and angry. He had been put off his guard by the peace offer. In due course he would write to protest to Brand. But now, as he said, 'Everything was lost to us' if the British kept hold of the kop. He shouted at the faint-hearts who were talking of retreat, 'Now you're going to fetch them.' Then he told one of his best men, Fighting-General Nicolas Smit, to take charge of operations, as though they would be simple enough, like the mountain fighting in the endless wars with the natives. Smit delivered a brief, passionate speech to the burghers calling for volunteers. 'Those who are not cowards must follow us.'[22]

Up on the first rocky terrace, in the shadow of the mountain itself, Roos and his men had already dismounted and knee-haltered their ponies in the shelter of the gully. The burghers looked more like a hunting party than a body of soldiers. Officers and men were dressed alike in their everyday clothes: baggy corduroys, bulging waistcoats and floppy brimmed hats. Some were fat, whiskered old men, others young boys hardly more than thirteen or fourteen. Everyone had a modern rifle, a single shot breech-loader, and everyone was draped with cartridge belts, except for these who had an African groom to carry the rifle and spare ammunition.

On the terrace Roos found another officer, Commandant Joachim Ferreira, and the two men called on the burghers to swear to be true, as they had sworn the solemn covenant two months earlier at Paardekraal. The men took the pledge: 'We will follow you & we shall take the kop or fall.' Roos said, 'Our God will help us & we shall take the kop, because there is nothing else to be done.'[23] Then they agreed to divide into two parties, Ferreira's to storm the small kopje that commanded the north-west corner of the main kop, Roos to attack the summit ridge itself by climbing up directly, terrace to terrace.

They had chosen to use exactly the same rough and ready tactics against the British as they would have used against natives holding a kop. The men below each party would give covering fire for their comrades to creep forward by rushes, and each storming party would provide flanking fire to support the other. The tactics worked perfectly. It was hard, slow work climbing up on their stomachs over the tussocks of grass and loose rocks, with volleys of British bullets spattering overhead. But the furious barrage from below protected them, making the British keep their heads down, as if the Boers had cover from artillery. After three or four hours, about midday, Roos and his men had crawled up to within a few feet of the summit ridge, separated from the enemy only by the width of a large boulder. He raised his head, and ducked back, terrified. The kop was alive with *rooibaatje*, redcoats.

Roos was a brave man and a pious one. He hoped that the dear Lord would forgive him for just one lie. He rose again from behind the boulder and waved his hat, shouting 'Come on now, you chaps! Come quickly! The English are flying.'[24]

While the Boers had crawled on their stomachs up the mountain, the British lay flat on their backs on the summit. That was how many spent the morning. The smooth grassy plateau sloped inwards from the rim of boulders down to a small line of rocks and a hollow at the centre. The African bearers dug two wells there and pitched a hospital tent. After breakfast the men lay down. The sun was hot, they were fagged out, and the general had given no orders. The barrage of rifle shots fired from below did not worry them, even when ricochets smacked the air overhead. On the contrary, the barrage seemed to confirm the Boers' impotence.

Out on the rim of the plateau, the bullets sounded and felt different. Lieutenant Ian Hamilton had seen the Boers and guessed their plan. He was the bumptious young subaltern in charge of A Company of the Gordon Highlanders (the 92nd). Through his glasses he had watched large parties of Boers (in fact Roos's and Ferreira's men) gallop forward across a mealie field to the ravine where they left their ponies. Then he saw them rush forward across twenty yards of open ground, ten or fifteen men at a time, covered by men in the rear, before all disappeared from view below. He decided he ought to report the matter to the general. Ducking to avoid the bullets, he ran back to the centre. Everybody there seemed very comfortable, Hamilton said later, 'eating, sleeping or smoking'.[25] Colley thanked Hamilton, who returned to his post. The process continued: 100, 200, 350, 400 Boers had got underneath them and were advancing unseen up the mountain. Four times Hamilton reported the news to Colley. He asked for reinforcements, but received only five men and an officer. Finally he was told the general was asleep.

About 100 yards to the left of the place where Hamilton lay in the grass was a small kopje, projecting from the main plateau and unoccupied by his scanty force. To the left of this kopje lay the other company of the Highlanders, B Company, under the charge of Lieutenant Hector MacDonald. Soon after midday Hamilton was astounded to hear a crashing volley of rifle fire and saw bullets rip up the ground for sixty yards to the left of him. The Boers – in fact Ferreira's men – had seized the small kopje. Two or three poor fellows were killed at once; the others fled. Reserves were brought up by the officers, Highlanders with fixed bayonets and Blue Jackets with cutlasses. They looked startled and worried – as well they might. Again came that terrible volley from the kopje. About sixteen men of the reserve were knocked over and the rest fled. Before Hamilton had got over his astonishment a line of Boers charged out of the smoke, firing snap-shots from the shoulder. There was nothing for it.

Hamilton ran for his life back to the small line of rocks in the hollow at the centre. Behind him most of his own company and almost all MacDonald's company lay dead or wounded, except for a few lucky ones taken by the enemy.

Colley, out of sight in the hollows, did not have long to ponder the significance of the crashing volley at such close range. The reserves came rushing back over the ridge, beaten and panicky. The three units were now hopelessly confused, Highlanders mixed up with the 58th, the 58th with Blue Jackets, so that it was hard for the officers to make the men stand. 'Rally on the right! Rally on the right!' Somehow a new firing line was established close to where Colley stood, behind a small line of rocks. Only thirty yards away in the smoke lay the Boers, firing away at point-blank range, visible only from the points of their muzzles. The noise was appalling. You had to shout, said Thomas Carter of the *Natal Times*, to make yourself heard above the infernal din. Officers bellowed 'Now, my lads, wait till they show up; fire low, fire low!' Then cries of 'Deploy! Deploy!'[26] But no one wanted to leave the shelter of the rocks. Gradually the Boers were pushing round the rim of the plateau, as Colley's men on the flanks melted away from their posts, making the excuse they had been told to fetch ammunition. Some returned when ordered, others did not. For about ten minutes the men in the centre stuck to their firing line. Ian Hamilton, who had recovered his breath, asked Colley to let them make a bayonet charge, adding that he hoped it was not presumptuous of him to ask. 'No presumption, Mr Hamilton,' came the cool reply, 'but we will wait until the Boers advance on us, then give them a volley and charge.'[27]

They were Colley's last recorded words, for his own men would not wait. That thin red line behind the rocks – a jumble of Highlanders, 58th and Blue Jackets, confused, ill-led, ill-protected – had finally had enough. Carter heard a 'sudden piercing cry of terror' behind him. The line wavered. In vain the officers pleaded and threatened: 'What the devil are you doing? Come back, come back.'[28] Before Carter could rise to his feet, a wave of fugitives broke over his head, as panic-stricken men tried to flee back towards the path they had climbed early that morning. They were followed by the officers, Hamilton included, who was running for dear life despite a crippling wound in his wrist.

There was no last stand at Majuba. Soldiers were shot down like bolting rabbits. Only one man stood at his post, to die as the Romans died, with his face to the enemy, General Colley. He had much to answer for. On his own authority he had rejected the armistice, tried a reckless coup at Majuba, then failed to dig in on the summit. Now he atoned as far as any man could. When last seen alive Colley was walking slowly towards the enemy, carrying his revolver. Roos, leading the charge of the Boers, noticed the solitary figure, but did not know who he was. A moment later Colley fell, a Boer bullet in the centre of his forehead.

* * *

The news of Majuba, cabled to London early next day, Monday 28 February, sent a shudder of humiliation through England, worse than the feeling after Isandlwana. Gladstone slumped in bed when he was told. For a moment he seemed beaten. He was assailed on all three sides, denounced for weakness by Radicals, Whigs and Tories.

Chamberlain, Bright and the other Radicals accused Kimberley of bungling the peace negotiations, and threatened to resign unless Kimberley was sacked. For them, the disaster proved a handy pretext for 'dishing the Whigs'.

The Queen and the Tories united in denouncing the policy of weakness that led to this ignominious fiasco. The shame of Majuba went even deeper than Isandlwana. The Boers took men alive (56 at Majuba, apart from the 132 wounded, and 96 dead); the Zulus only left dead heroes. Isandlwana had also been redeemed by the heroic stand at Rorke's Drift. Finally, the Zulus had been taught their lesson at Ulundi. So the Tories were adamant. It was a question of who was master. As *The Times* put it: 'Unless we are prepared to retire from South Africa immediately and unconditionally' (unthinkable of course) 'we must restore our authority where it has been defied.'[29]

The Whigs felt the same emotional needs: to redeem the shame of defeat and vindicate British authority. Even Kimberley began to lose faith in his own beliefs, and to abandon the peace policy.

No one felt more humiliated than Wolseley. Colley was his own protégé, second-in-command of the Wolseley ring. And at the root of Colley's failures was Wolseley's own conviction that the Boers would not fight. To cap it all, the government chose Wolseley's hated rival – Sir Fred Roberts, hero of the march to Candahar – to lead the 10,000 extra troops now sent out to crush the Boers if peace hopes faded.

But Wolseley was soon reconciled to being passed over for this particular command, for Gladstone now pulled a new trick out of his conjuror's bag. He out-manoeuvred the Radicals by his mastery of the Whigs. The Cabinet was shown the cables to and from South Africa, and heard about Colley's 'reasonable time'. In fact Kruger accepted the armistice on 4 March, so Majuba need never have been fought. The Cabinet also saw the ominous messages from the Governor of Cape Colony. It had been hard to make peace before Majuba. It was harder now, yet peace was more urgent than ever. Otherwise Cape Colony might dissolve into civil war and the whole of South Africa would be lost to the British.

On 23 March provisional peace terms were signed by both Boer and British delegates at O'Neill's farm, where the wounded had been brought after Majuba. The war was over. The British soldiers besieged in Pretoria and the other garrison towns were free to leave when they chose. By 3 August the relations between the Transvaal and Britain were formally defined in the Convention of Pretoria. It seemed the best compromise in the circumstances. The Transvaal was a republic once more. Independence was restored, but not complete independence. Britain would maintain 'suzerainty', enshrined in a series of clauses giving her the right to interfere, especially in foreign relations.

Perhaps this was the measure of Gladstone's conjuring trick – which would have astonished no one more than Gladstone. Behind that tactical retreat, hasty and humiliating, the way was being secured for a strategic advance far to the north of the Transvaal.

CHAPTER 7

Saving the Bey

Paris and Tunis
23 March–November 1881

> 'We have our backs to the wall and Europe is
> watching us to judge if we are still something...'
>
> *Le Marquis de Noailles* (French Ambassador at Berlin) to
> Saint-Hilaire (the French Foreign Minister), 26 January
> 1881

The Director of Political Affairs at the Quai d'Orsay (the French Foreign Office) was an urbane aristocrat; tall, domeheaded, forty-six-year-old Baron Alphonse de Courcel. An admirer of the current Prime Minister, Jules Ferry, Courcel was the senior diplomat charged with putting teeth into French foreign policy. But what hope of that was there, wondered Courcel. Public opinion was as virile as a wet sponge and politicians of all parties quivered at the thought of the coming elections.

He crossed the narrow cobbled strip of the rue de l'Université that separated his own office at the Ministry from the grandiose apartments of the President of the Chamber, Léon Gambetta. It was only seven in the morning, a clear, cold morning, as he recalled twenty years later. The street was still deserted, though sunshine lit up the mansard roofs and ponderous cornices under the chimney stacks. His heart thumped at his rib cage. He had screwed himself up to go and see Gambetta, to clasp the knees of that 'monster', as he called the powerful head of the Union Républicaine, and Jules Ferry's rival, in the forlorn hope of persuading him to help make Jules Ferry's government reverse its policy on Tunisia.[1]

This was the last chance, he was sure. Tunisia was the strategic key to Algeria, France's principal colony. It was also the key to regenerating France. Either they seized their chance, adopted a forward policy in foreign affairs, meaning a policy of colonial expansion, and took up their secret option for protecting Algeria by occupying Tunisia. Or else they must resign themselves to being the laughing stock of Europe, toothless and impotent, while Italy snatched Tunisia from under their noses.

It was three years since the Congress of Berlin when Bismarck and Salisbury had offered Tunisia to France as a makeweight in the new balance of power they had imposed on the Mediterranean and the East. 'Do what you like there [Tunisia],' Lord Salisbury, Britain's Foreign Secretary, had generously told Waddington, his French opposite number, according to the latter's official report. 'You will be obliged to take it. You cannot leave Carthage in the hands of the barbarians.'[2] Later Lord Salisbury had his doubts about Waddington's 'vivacious' version of his remarks. He told Disraeli, 'He makes me talk of Tunis and Carthage as if they had been my own personal property, and I was making him a liberal wedding present.' But Salisbury agreed the 'general tenor' was quite accurate.[3] Britain was committed not to intervene – if France wanted to take Tunisia. However, for fear of giving offence, this agreement was kept secret. Tunisia was, at least nominally, subject to the suzerainty of Turkey. At Berlin, Salisbury – and Disraeli – reversed the traditional British policy of trying to shore up the crumbling Turkish Empire. They forced Turkey to disgorge Cyprus for use as a British *place des armes*, a new Gibraltar in the East, guarding Suez and the Straits. To placate the French, Turkey would also have to yield Tunisia to France. This was the secret agreement to which Germany, France and Britain had all been committed. But it was a double humiliation: for Turkey whose empire was being parcelled out by her friends; and for France, as men like Courcel believed, for not having the guts to take up her option and grab Tunisia.

What was France frightened of? Come empire, come republic, the people of France were shy of imperialism. They had learnt their lesson from the years of trouble in Algeria, ever since they had taken Algiers in 1830, and from recent disasters in Mexico. All the same, it was unfortunate that it was Bismarck, not Salisbury, who had initiated the plan to give away Tunis. He had originally encouraged Disraeli to take Egypt instead of Cyprus, and to the French he offered Syria – or Tunisia. The Tunisian 'pear', said the great man smacking his lips, was ripe 'to be plucked'.[4] But the French politicians of the Third Republic trembled. They remembered the fall of Paris in 1871 as though it had been the fall of Troy. '*Et dona ferentes*' ('even bearing gifts'), Bismarck and his crew frightened them out of their wits. A whole decade after defeat by the Germans at Sedan and the resulting loss of Alsace-Lorraine, the French were still licking their wounds. To many patriotic Frenchmen, monarchists on the Right, republicans on the Left, the idea of overseas expansion was simply a trap. They suspected Bismarck of setting a snare to divert their minds from the real task, *revanche*: beating the Germans and winning back Alsace-Lorraine.

To this Bismarck's reply was disarming indeed. It was absurd to talk of hidden motives or to call him a Machiavelli. He made no secret that he wanted the French to stop mourning for the lost provinces. That could only end in a new Franco-Prussian war and a new defeat by Germany, which had by now far out-stripped France in both population and industrial power. France must steel herself to forget Sedan, forget Metz and Strasbourg. A reconciliation was a vital interest for France, as well as for Germany – and for the peace of Europe. What the French needed, asserted Bismarck, was a healthy new outlet for their energies – meaning one where there was no possibility of a clash with Germany. The Germans had never seen the point of colonial expansion, so why did the French not pluck that Tunisian pear? Why not soothe their *amour propre* in building a vast new empire, a new French civilization on the foundations originally laid by those unspeakable Turks?

High-ranking and high-minded civil servants like Courcel needed no prompting from Bismarck. By 1881 heady talk of a great new French Empire beyond the Sahara was already to be heard in the corridors of the Quai d'Orsay and the Ministry of Marine in Paris (which also covered the colonies), of which no word had yet reached the public in France, let alone the world at large. It would be hard to exaggerate the importance of this subtle change in the French official mind. Britain was the greatest naval and colonial power on earth, the foremost exporter of manufactured goods. After the defeat of the French in 1815 she had had no rival in Africa beyond the borders of the Mediterranean for over sixty years. But by 1881 two rivals were stealthily preparing a challenge. The first was Leopold, still disguised as an international philanthropist. The second was France, outwardly Britain's closest ally, but inspired by motives that still puzzle many historians.

Why did the Quai choose this moment to challenge the British in Africa? It is a question that takes us to the heart of the puzzle that dominates the history of the next two decades in Africa. Informal empire – meaning invisible empire, the effortless way that Britain had been able to exploit Africa without bothering to govern it – still seemed to have many years to run. Britain was *the* Paramount Power, the imperial top dog, with exclusive rights to most of Africa. Out of the blue was to come this challenge from the pack.

In Leopold's case there was no mystery about his motive and timing. He wanted to make a fortune and in 1876 he had turned to Africa almost by accident, inspired by Cameron's talk of an El Dorado. In the case of France, the motives were complicated and the timing hard to explain. But two opposing forces can be identified: both powering French nationalism and propelling France into a forward policy. One was hatred of Germany, dating from 1870–1; the other was envy and suspicion of Britain, dating from the Napoleonic wars and largely confined to members of the French navy. Together these two very different kinds of phobia drove the French forward, like the twin cylinders of a reciprocating steam engine whose pistons, despite occasional back-firing, advance alternately.

It was the naval anglophobia that seemed to diplomats like Salisbury most mysterious and unnatural. After all, hatred of the Germans should have locked the French in the arms of the British. Yet French sailors had long memories and scores to wipe off the slate. Nelson had destroyed their navy and they had lost to Britain the only good naval base in the Indian Ocean, the Île de France, now Mauritius. This had created a permanent anti-British reflex among French naval officers in the same way as Moltke's destruction of the French army and the loss of Alsace-Lorraine had created Germanophobia among her army and the people at large. Anglophobia was at the root of the forward policy which was coming to dominate French colonial planning. The colony had been founded as a French trading post in the seventeenth century and remained the centre of French power in West Africa. There were two colonial ports – St Louis and

Dakar – and a thin chain of trading posts stretching 300 miles up the Senegal river.

In 1879, the Governor of Senegal, Brière de l'Isle, had begun a thrust eastwards. Brière de l'Isle began to push further up the river, egged on by the Minister of Marine, who controlled the colonies, Admiral Jauréguiberry. There was talk in French colonial circles of building a trans-Sahara railway to link Algeria with Senegal by way of Timbuctu and the western Sudan. This megalomaniac project was officially taken up by Jauréguiberry's ally, Freycinet, then French Minister of Public Works. It soon came to grief when Colonel Flatters and his mission to the southern Sahara were squashed flat by the Tuaregs in 1881. South of Senegal were French outposts in the Gulf of Guinea, including a treaty-port at Cotonou on the coast of Dahomey and commercial settlements on the Ivory Coast. In both areas, French authorities and businessmen were deeply suspicious of their British neighbours in Sierra Leone, the Gold Coast and the Oil Rivers (modern Nigeria).

Until the late 1870s the Quai d'Orsay had deplored this rivalry as strongly as any Englishman. The French Minister of Foreign Affairs from 1877 to 1879 was William Waddington, himself half English and an admirer of Lord Salisbury ever since he had had been an undergraduate at Cambridge. But after Waddington had gone, the Quai found it harder to counter the anti-British arguments of the Ministry of Marine run by Admiral Jauréguiberry and his successor.

There would appear to be two main reasons for the Quai's new attitude to Britain, each somewhat paradoxical. First, Lord Carnarvon, Frere and Shepstone had inaugurated a forward policy in southern Africa which had set the French trembling. It seemed, even before the annexation of the Transvaal in 1877 and the invasion of Zululand in 1879, that the British were becoming more enterprising and aggressive. In southern Africa the Anglo-Saxons seemed determined to convert nebulous paramountcy into a formal empire from the Cape to the Limpopo. Where would it end? The French did not need a spy in the Colonial Office to sniff out the intoxicating dream that had inspired Lord Carnarvon, Frere and the senior advisers at the Colonial Office, the dream of painting red the whole continent, except Senegal and Algeria. As far as the French were concerned, this dream was now official British policy. From now on there was nothing that Salisbury or Hicks Beach, Carnarvon's successor, could do or say, fully to reassure them. 'We have rivals, implacable rivals, who constantly oppose the influence which we already exert,' wrote Jauréguiberry. 'They strive to frustrate us in every possible way.'[5] Ironically, the Quai was coming round to this suspicious view of British intentions just when Salisbury thought he had laid the ghost of the forward policy.

Equally ironically, the appearance in April 1880 of Gladstone's government, committed to turn its face against imperialist ventures, had strengthened the hand of men like Jauréguiberry. It was partly because the French anglophobes were even quicker than the British Tories to write off Gladstone as a hypocrite, and the Quai found Lord Granville, Gladstone's Foreign Secretary, much less sympathetic than Lord Salisbury. More important, the British defeat at Majuba in February 1881 was interpreted as a sign that the British army had become hopelessly degenerate, coming as it did after the disaster at Isandlwana. Had Gladstone decided to redeem these humiliations by sending a proper army to teach the Boers a lesson, he would have earned respect on the Continent. As it was, by their hasty retreat after Majuba, the British army were thought to have shown that their famous paramountcy was based on brag. Their much-vaunted navy seemed a paper tiger too. For years the British navy, the mainstay of imperial defence, had had little real work, except fighting the odd slave trader. So this was the moment, as one of Jauréguiberry's cronies put it, to 'reassert our rights ... while Britain is engaged in so many disastrous wars all over the world'.[6]

Alphonse de Courcel, the urbane director of political affairs at the Quai, did not express his opinions so crudely. He recognized Gladstone's difficulties. But in this Tunisian affair, at least, he saw no reason to expect unpleasant complications with England. A French naval base in Tunisia would balance Italian power in the north. Gladstone would feel bound by the commitment made at Berlin, which was one of the main reasons for choosing Tunisia as the starting point for an active forward policy. The French Ambassadors to Germany and Italy welcomed the plan. After a decade of drift they would at last go forward.

If only Courcel could have persuaded Jules Ferry and the Cabinet too. Barthélemy Saint-Hilaire, the Foreign Minister, put it to the Cabinet, but only he and the two service ministers voted for the proposals. The diplomatic arguments were compelling but the timing was impossible. 'An expedition to Tunis in election year?' Jules Ferry said to Saint-Hilaire after the Cabinet meeting was over. He passed his arm round his colleague's shoulder. 'My dear Saint-Hilaire, you're not thinking!'[7]

Meanwhile, alarming news arrived from Tunis, sent by Théodore Roustan, the energetic, swarthy French Consul at Tunis charged with smoothing the path of his compatriots. Formerly Roustan had found it easy to manipulate the Bey of Tunis, Muhammad es-Sadok. The old man was as soft as camembert, far more interested in a pretty face at court – a boy's face – than in the intrigues of the European powers. Roustan had spent time and money on the current favourite, a twenty-seven-year-old Adonis of Jewish extraction, Mustapha ben Ismael, whom the Bey had made Prime Minister. Unfortunately, at the end of 1880 Mustapha had turned against Roustan. A huge coastal estate called the Enfida, which Mustapha coveted, was snatched up under his nose by a French bank. In vain Roustan called on the other influential servants of the Bey, especially General Mussali, an Egyptian Catholic, whose beautiful Genoese wife was publicly acknowledged as Roustan's mistress. Mustapha was implacable. He wanted the Enfida and he would move heaven or hell to get it. He had the Bey's heart in his pocket. The Bey now began to reject France's overtures in favour of Italy's.

Italy's man in Tunisia was Licurgo Maccio, the Italian Consul, in every respect as energetic as his French opposite number. The Italians in Tunisia were strong in numbers, weak in money bags. They regarded the country, only ninety miles from Sicily, as a natural outlet for their ambitions. The rivalry had split European society in Tunis, and its Levantine hangers-on, into two furious cliques, each centred on a salon. Maccio hurled his thunderbolts from the salon of Signora Traverso, sister-in-law of the beautiful Madame Mussali and Maccio's own mistress. Roustan hurled them back from the Mussalis'. In this operatic war of the two Consuls and their mistresses it was easy to forget that the stakes were so high. Who was to take over the economy, and in due course the government, of Tunisia – France or Italy?

When Mustapha had been his ally Roustan had won the race for financial concessions hands down. First the French built the telegraph to Algeria. Then they won a lucrative contract from the Bey to build the main railway to Algeria. This line was now under construction. The Italians had to be content with buying from the English, at great cost, a small debt-ridden railway leading from Tunis no further than the suburbs. The French had then won two other big concessions – a contract to build a port and another for new railways to Bizerta and the south. But after Mustapha turned against Roustan, everything went the way of the Italians. All the French contracts were left in the air.

Mustapha hatched a plot to capture the Enfida estate by embroiling the English. He put up a straw man, a Maltese Jew called Levy, who possessed English nationality and claimed a pre-emptive right, as a neighbouring land-owner, to buy the Enfida. Mustapha's crony in this intrigue was a fast-moving young English lawyer named Alexander Broadley who had left India in a hurry to avoid landing in gaol. Now he doubled as lawyer for Mustapha and as political adviser to the Bey, as well as acting as special correspondent of *The Times* and the *Daily Telegraph*.

Roustan was being tormented by the Enfida affair in late January when Courcel persuaded Saint-Hilaire to put the case for French intervention to Jules Ferry and the Cabinet. As mentioned, the Cabinet rejected the idea out of hand. Then they tried a foolish compromise: bullying the Tunisian court, which had to settle the Enfida affair, by sending a French battleship, the *Friedland*, to demonstrate in Tunisian waters. This was too much even for Gladstone's Cabinet. It brought a British battleship, the *Thunderer*, steaming down on the leader of the French. Both ships then sheepishly withdrew. But the Enfida affair, still unresolved, left a sour taste in everyone's mouth – except Broadley's – and made the British appear to support the Italians. Roustan felt humiliated and threatened to resign. Even the Tunisians now despised the French; they had fallen '*jusqu'au fond du fossé*' ('to the bottom of the ditch'). The only hope he saw was that the humiliation itself would soon force the French, willynilly, to adopt a 'virile resolution'.[8]

Roustan's *cri de coeur* to Courcel struck home. What added to his frustration was that Italy still had its hands tied and at present would have to acquiesce in French intervention – but not for long. The simple fact was that the current Italian government, led by Cairoli, was going broke. An enormous Italian government loan, 650 million francs, was being placed on the Paris Bourse. Once they had the money, the Italians could afford to be more aggressive.

As for Germany, Bismarck was clearly losing patience. He told the German Ambassador in January that first Waddington's 'puritanism' and then Freycinet's 'torpor' had let slip a great opportunity. One fine day they would wake up and find a cordon of Italian troops on the border with Algeria.[9]

It was to avoid this disaster that at 7.0 a.m. on 23 March 1881 Courcel swallowed his pride and went to beg the support of Gambetta, head of the ever more powerful Union Républicaine, Ferry's likely successor and a master of low intrigue, detested by high-minded republicans like Courcel and his chief.

Precisely what passed between the two men is not recorded. But if Courcel's hand clasped the monster's knees, his words went straight to Gambetta's heart. Perhaps he quoted the despairing letter written by the French Ambassador in Berlin to the French Foreign Minister a few weeks earlier:

You say that you'd like to wait until the elections are over and do it then ... What folly and what blindness! In ten months you'll be faced with a secret alliance conclusively organised against us, and you will have to back down once again, because it won't any more be a question, as it is now, of a military promenade – we'll have a European war on our hands if we want to save our Algerian colony. Ah, my dear Minister, you're a good patriot. And so's M. Gambetta. See him, talk with him, and save our country from the new humiliation, the new '*amoindrissement*', that threatens. . . . We have our backs to the wall and Europe is watching us to judge if we are still something; one act of firmness, of energetic will, without serious danger, without bloodshed, and we'll resume our place in the good opinion of other nations; a new proof of our feebleness and we'll succeed in being relegated to the level of Spain.[10]

As Courcel spoke, he saw Gambetta's craggy features relax. Hostility vanished, as did his usual air of reserve. At length his finer feelings got the better of him, or so Courcel later told the story: 'His ardent patriotism, his love of action, his wide-ranging intelligence, his idealism, all the generosity of his nature, with the satisfaction of escaping, if only for a few moments, from the sordid parliamentary intrigues which were his bitter daily fare.'[11] When Courcel left a couple of hours later, he knew that his appeal to Gambetta's patriotism had struck home. One should add, though Courcel did not tell this part of the story, that Courcel's words had also appealed to Gambetta's pocket. A spider's web of financial intrigue surrounded the great republican. With a successful French takeover of Tunisia, his cronies – international bankers like Erlanger and Rothschild – stood to make millions out of the boom in Tunisian government stocks.

With Gambetta heart, soul and pocket behind Courcel's scheme for taking Tunisia, Ferry's and the government's opposition quickly crumbled. An ingenious plot was hatched in the Quai d'Orsay with Roustan. The key to success would be speed and firepower: a thrust across the Algerian border of two columns – say 30,000 men – followed by a naval landing at Bizerta. To avoid bloodshed, as well as complications in the French Parliament, this invasion would claim to be acting in support of the Bey. It would be easy to disguise it as a punitive expedition to help the Bey to deal with the Kroumirs, the Berber hill tribes on the eastern borders of Algeria who could be relied on to give trouble whenever required or not.

The Kroumirs did not fail to oblige. On 4 April, ten days after Courcel went to see Gambetta, Ferry reported a serious frontier incident with the Kroumirs. Three days later the Chamber of Deputies voted five million francs for punitive raids. Conscripts were packed off in thousands from Toulon bound for Algeria. On 25 April, less than five weeks after that cold, clear morning when Courcel had crossed the cobbled strip of the rue de l'Université, two French columns under Generals Bréart and Forgemol crossed the hills of the Algerian frontier with tricolours flying. They paid no attention to the Kroumirs. Anyway the Kroumirs had vanished. Each column marched straight down the dusty road to Tunis.

In Paris, Saint-Hilaire explained airily: 'We are not at war with the Bey, and we do not wish to be at war with the Bey ... it is as allies that we plan to enter and operate on Tunisian territory and put down the disorders.' [12]

*   *   *

About two miles from the western gate of Tunis itself, across the shimmering Manouba plain towards the violet hills, rose the grim walls of the half-ruined Bardo, for hundreds of years the official abode of the Beys of Tunis. Beside its outer ditch was a modern, four-storeyed, lime-washed palace built of stucco in the Italian style. It was the Kasr-es-Said ('Abode of Felicity'), half-hidden in a great bower of roses, jasmine and orange trees. In this delightful spot the Bey, Muhammad es-Sadok, had made his own home as soon as it became vacant. (The original owner, one of his more enterprising ministers, had been strangled for plotting with the Bey's brother.)

That morning, 23 April, there was no outward sign of the crisis as Alexander Broadley, Tunis correspondent of *The Times*, rode down the avenue of palm trees and pepper trees towards the Kasr-es-Said. It was still early but already the stucco façade quivered in the blinding sunlight. Above the flat roof floated the symbol of the Bey's authority, the two-bladed golden sword of the Hassanite dynasty emblazoned on a green, red and orange banner. Outside the Turkish band played as usual. Inside the palace, Broadley found a motley crowd of officials talking in whispers of intervention by the Powers. 'Is there any news from the frontier? What do the latest newspapers say? Have the English fleet come? Are the Italian troops already at Palermo?' [13]

Muhammad es-Sadok himself received Broadley, taking him by the hand and sitting him down in a salon furnished in faded yellow damask. The old man was grey-bearded and red-faced, dressed in a black frock coat and red trousers, with a pasha's sword and Turkish insignia. He did not look like the Bey of Tunis as described in the French press, a weak, corrupt, effeminate Oriental. He had kept his dignity, even if half-dead with worry.

'You have come lately from England, do Englishmen believe in the Khamirs [Kroumirs]?'

'I'm afraid they know very little about them. But the English press has unanimously deprecated the expedition.' [14]

Muhammad es-Sadok said he knew this and was grateful. He then gave Broadley a solemn message for England and the rest of Europe. For 200 years the Beys of Tunis had done whatever was asked of them by the English. His cousin Ahmed had been the first Muslim sovereign to abolish slavery. He himself had promoted English commercial interests in every way he could. He had no quarrel with the French. He had been pleased to allow them to build a railway and a telegraph. But for thirteen months the French Consul, Roustan, had made his life a misery by trying to bully him into accepting a French protectorate. To accept suzerainty was, of course, out of the question. The Bey pointed to his jewelled Turkish sword and the Order of Osmanlie in diamonds. He was a Turkish pasha, a vassal of the Sublime Porte, bound by a firman (the Sultan's edict), and by treaties confirmed by the Powers. As for the Kroumirs and the claims of these disorders, let any fair-minded person judge for himself. But he and his people were too weak to make armed resistance against the French. All he could do was protest. He would leave his fate 'to the justice of Europe'. [15]

Two days later, on 25 April, at noon, a messenger galloped towards the Bardo with the dreaded news and an hour later all Tunis learnt that the French columns had crossed the border. Protests were despatched to the Powers, drafted with the joint help of Alexander Broadley and the Italian Consul, Maccio. The cable to the British government had to be sent by an Italian steamer, which crossed the straits to Sicily that night, since the French had jammed the ordinary telegraph. It was a *cri de coeur*. 'We appeal to our august ally, Her Majesty, the Queen of Great Britain, as well as to all the Governments, signatories of the Treaty of Berlin. ... In our hour of dire distress we implore the Great Powers to interpose their friendly offices on our behalf.' [16]

But the days passed and from the Great Powers there came nothing but silence, a mocking silence from lips sealed, unknown to the Bey, three years before in Berlin.

Meanwhile, at the Bey's suggestion, an English friend of Broadley's, a business-man called Perkins, was sent off to the camp of the Bey's brother, Ali Bey, which was close to the border, to act as an impartial witness to how the French dealt with the Kroumirs.

After a tiresome two-day journey, first by the French railway, then on horseback, Perkins rode up to Ali Bey's camp at Sidi Salah on the night of 24 April. The scenery was operatic: rocky gorges covered with cork trees and umbrella pines. Still more operatic was the scene next morning as Ali's army advanced towards the French. As heir presumptive to his brother, Ali Bey had drafted a 'regular' force of several thousand men resplendent in European uniforms: coats, trousers and boots, topped with red Tunisian caps. Most of them found the boots and trousers superfluous, and trudged along bare-legged and bare-footed. Ali Bey himself rode at their head in a gilded carriage drawn by four mules, followed by an enormous train of his personal baggage packed in wooden trunks, covered with brown leather and studded with brass nails. The baggage was followed by an equally cumbersome retinue: the *imam* (chaplain), the coffee-maker, the gun-bearer, the sword-bearer, the water-bearer and the buffoon.

Ali Bey received Perkins with the utmost cordiality, but confessed he was somewhat out of touch. Could Perkins elucidate the latest developments at court? He was afraid there was 'double play going on at the Bardo'. His own role, as he saw it, was to soothe the ruffled feelings at the border, so from time to time he halted and sat in his great tent to receive the homage of the Kroumirs. Hundreds of these fearsome tribesmen then approached, armed to the teeth. Each man waved a rusty flintlock, seven foot long, and wore a pair of huge pistols in his belt, with two or three knives of different sizes; legs bare, with a broad girdle and pouch round his waist to hold spare powder and bullets. Inside the tent they filed in front of Ali, running in a circle and calling out '*Ya Sidna*' ('Oh, our master') before discharging their flintlocks accurately in front of their overlord, and then to everyone's relief leaving the tent.[17]

Perkins was favourably surprised by their discipline. So, it seemed, was Ali who told Perkins that the dispute with the French could now be settled. It had all begun in an absurd dispute over a cow, part-owned by a Tunisian, part by an Algerian. But next day a message arrived from the French general, which threw the whole camp into visible dismay. General Forgemol informed His Excellency that it would be superfluous to repeat details of the complaints against the Kroumirs. The general had orders to punish these tribesmen and punish them he would.

The same day the French crossed the border, and brushed aside the Kroumirs who tried to defend their cornfields and stock. Over 200 were killed or wounded. The rest melted away into the stony hills and forests of cork trees. Under orders not to engage the French, Ali Bey sent a dignified letter of protest. He would no longer believe that the French only wished to settle a border dispute. In fact he did not know what to believe. The French assured him they had come '*in accord*' with his brother, Muhammad es-Sadok. He heard that the French had bombarded the frontier port of Tabarca, over which the Bey's flag was flying. Now they were advancing rapidly along the coast. To make Ali's position worse, his own men began to accuse him of betraying them to the French. Perkins saw that Ali was equally afraid of his own men, the Kroumirs and the French. He could only swallow his pride and beat a retreat.

At 2.0 a.m. on 28 April tents were struck and Ali Bey in his gilded carriage drawn by four mules, the train of brass-studded brown leather trunks, the gunbearer, the sword-bearer, the buffoon, Perkins and all the other players in this opéra bouffe began the long jolting journey back to the Bardo, creeping away from Ali's infuriated army under cover of darkness.

Back in the 'Abode of Felicity', the role thrust on Ali's brother, the Bey, was equally frustrating, if less operatic. Every day the French advance continued. They took Bizerta. They killed some tribesmen and their families at Shelkhia. There was no more pretence of punishing the Kroumirs. Broadley and other advisers drafted heart-rending appeals to Britain and the other Powers, to be rushed across the straits by special steamer. But the Powers were deaf. From the Bey's overlord, the Sultan of Turkey, came reassurance and promises of help, elegant but empty phrases. Muhammad es-Sadok began understandably to feel betrayed. He had taken a bold stand against the French because the Italian Consul, Maccio, had egged him on. Now the Italians, like the other Powers, left him to his fate. Perhaps Muhammad es-Sadok already recognized that one of his own family had turned traitor. Ali Bey was loyal, but the French Consul, Roustan, had succeeded in persuading their other brother, Taib, to accept a French protectorate. Taib would be installed as Bey in Tunis if Muhammad es-Sadok wanted to go down fighting.

Perhaps a jihad (a holy war) could have been declared against the infidel, a fundamentalist uprising igniting the explosive xenophobia that lurked just below the surface of the Muslim world. But Muhammad es-Sadok was an old man who valued his comforts – and was a Turk, not an Arab. Like Ismael Pasha in Egypt, he was a practised gambler, but no fanatic. When he held no court cards he could only throw in his hand and trust to the goodness of Allah – and of his enemies.

That final moment came at five o'clock on the evening of 12 May, in the third week after the French had launched their invasion.

Early that morning the advance guard of General Bréart's column had been crossing the line of hills at the edge of the Manouba plain. By noon it was raining in torrents. The column pitched tents and occupied the cavalry barracks beside the Kasr-es-Din. They appeared to have trained artillery on the palace itself. The Bey bravely refused the troops an interview. His morale was stiffened by a cable from the Sultan at the Sublime Porte: 'On no account sign any convention with France ... say that you will submit the matter to us.'[18] But a few minutes after this cable had been decoded, about four o'clock, Roustan rode up to see the Bey, followed by the general and his suite, wet through, but armed with swords and revolvers. The party was shown up to the salon on the first floor furnished with faded yellow damask, where Broadley had been received three weeks earlier. General Bréart wasted no time with oriental compliments or comments on the weather. He took out of his pocket a draft ten-point treaty, copied that morning in the French chancellery in Tunis, and handed it to the Bey. But the treaty was written in French and the Bey could not grasp a word. He asked for a written translation in Arabic, and was given the gist. A permanent French resident and French army would help to cement 'the ancient relations of friendship and good neighbourliness'. Tunisia was to be a French protectorate in all but name.

'At any rate you will grant me twenty-four hours for consideration?' asked the Bey.

'Certainly not. I expect an answer before eight o'clock tonight, and shall remain here till I get one,' Bréart replied.

After Bréart had retired from the salon, Roustan reminded the old man that he had always done his best for him. He had warned him it would come to this. Taib Bey, his brother, was much more helpful. 'Your Highness has nothing to do but to sign, and if you decline it does not matter, for there is another who will.' Muhammad es-Sadok wavered. 'Sign' said his ministers (after a friendly warning to Mustapha, the handsome Prime Minister, that he would otherwise be court-martialled and shot as a subject of the French Republic). 'Sign' said the chief eunuch, despatched with this message from the ladies of the harem, understandably terrified by the glimpse through the lattice windows of the French artillery trained on the palace. At about five o'clock the old man's courage failed. He put his signature to that document he could not read, writing his name in trembling Arabic characters.

Outside the Kasr-es-Din rumours of the treaty spread rapidly among the sullen population. A deputation led by a scent-seller approached Mustapha. What had been agreed? The Prime Minister replied wittily, 'The Khamirs [sic] having beaten the French, the latter have taken refuge under the shadow of the palace walls, and we are giving them bread until they go back to their own country.'[19]

But for Muhammad es-Sadok the comedy was over. The humiliation was too much. When he was alone he broke down and wept like a man bereaved.

*   *   *

At first Ferry's *fait accompli* seemed to have achieved everything at a bargain price. The campaign had been a walkover, a military promenade. But at the Quai d'Orsay the victory celebrations were short-lived. The complications with the Powers were more damaging and their ill-effects more lasting than Courcel had forecast.

Only the anglophobes were satisfied to observe the bad grace with which Gladstone took the news of the French triumph. He looked down his nose, and made it clear he did not approve of the invasion. The British public were unsympathetic. They had read Broadley's spirited articles in *The Times* and the *Telegraph* and were at first still unaware of the Berlin agreement. The French were derided for pretending to be the Bey's allies while stealing his throne. The Tories' champion, *The Times*, took the lofty view that only two arguments could justify imperialism of this kind: strategic necessity or the declared wishes of the inhabitants themselves. Neither argument applied in this case.

In Italy the government's impotence so infuriated its supporters that Cairoli and his Cabinet were swept from power. Feeling ran high in both Italy and France. Heads were broken in Marseilles and reprisals taken against French property and Frenchmen all over Italy.

Still, passionate nationalists and promoters of the forward policy, like Courcel, would not have grumbled too much about foreign reactions if the French public had taken the correct patriotic attitude. As it was, the original misgivings of Ferry were entirely justified by events. After the Treaty of Bardo, as it was called (the surrender at Kasr-es-Said would have been more accurate), there came a brief, joyless honeymoon. Muhammad es-Sadok swallowed his pride and decorated General Bréart and Théodore Roustan with the Grand Cordon of the Nichan. Mustapha ben Ismael repressed his lust for the Enfida and sailed for France where he received a fifteen-gun salute and all the honours of a state visit, including the Cross of the Legion of Honour. All senior Tunisian officials were confirmed in their posts, except the President of the Municipality, who was replaced by the Bey's buffoon. And Roustan, the Bey's new master, styled the French Resident, anticipated no further trouble from the effeminate old man.

Roustan was right about that. The trouble, when it came at the end of June, came from the Arabs in the centre and south of the country, furious with the way a Turkish bey had betrayed their independence. The southern towns of Sfax and Gabes rebelled. Tens of thousands of nomadic tribesmen joined the fray. Ferry hoped to minimize the political damage by putting down the revolt before the Chamber of Deputies reassembled. Sfax was bombarded by a naval squadron and was successfully stormed by marines on 26 July.

But the days of the military promenade were over. The campaign became ugly and protracted. Reinforcements were rushed from France and Algeria. Several thousand French soldiers died of typhoid and other avoidable diseases. The campaign spread misery over southern Tunisia. A hundred thousand nomadic tribesmen fled with their families over the border to Tripoli, claiming protection from the Ottoman authorities. By November, when the Chamber of Deputies reassembled, Bismarck's Tunisian pear had proved a dud avocado.

A torrent of mud greeted Ferry's claim that France had reached the moment of truth. Either she must expand overseas, he said, carving out a new empire rich with opportunities for trade and commerce, and guarded by new overseas bases, or else she must go down the road to decadence. These were the colours of Courcel and the Quai d'Orsay that Ferry had now nailed to his own mast. But the Chamber of Deputies would have none of it. It did not annul the Treaty of Bardo, but Ferry was hooted out of the Chamber, his place as Prime Minister taken over by that 'monster', the man whom the Quai had the least reason to trust, Léon Gambetta.

At the time it appeared that the forward policy of the Quai d'Orsay, so diffidently adopted by the politicians, had bogged down in the mud thrown at Ferry. In the spring the absence of an enemy (what on earth had happened to those Kroumirs?) had made the French look ridiculous; by the autumn they

looked like burglars and bullies. The Opposition press reiterated the charge that
the whole affair had been engineered to make money for Gambetta and his
Jewish backers.

In fact, Bismarck's pear had changed everything. With an opéra bouffe
overture, a new colonial era had begun. The prelude was nearly over. A new
phase of partition was beginning and the race for Africa was only a year ahead.
Only one thing prevented this: the forty-year *entente* between Britain and France.
It was to be Gladstone, the leading anti-imperialist of his era, who snapped the
link and inadvertently started the race, while up to his neck in the sands of
Egypt.

CHAPTER 8

Saving the Khedive

London and Egypt
31 December 1881–October 1882

> 'Our first sight in Egypt, be it by larceny or be it by
> pre-emption, will be the almost certain egg of a
> North African empire that will grow and grow until
> ... we finally join hands across the Equator with
> Natal and Cape Town.'
>
> *W. E. Gladstone* in
> *The Nineteenth Century*, August 1877

The black year of 1881 was over at last, thank heavens, thought Eddy Hamilton, Gladstone's devoted young private secretary. 'Internal affairs' (meaning Britain's futile attempt to rule Ireland) had brought the Great Man 'a perfect sea of troubles',[1] Hamilton wrote in his diary on the last day of the year. The state of Ireland was as deplorable on 31 December as it had been on the previous 1 January. How would it end? Gladstone had tried coercion and he had tried conciliation. Neither firmness nor fairness seemed to bring peace any closer.

It was a mercy that 'over-sea', as Gladstone called foreign affairs, better fortune had attended the government. Britain's relations with the Powers in Europe, including France, were unruffled. True, that strange Tunisian business had soured the diplomatic climate for a few weeks in April and May. Granville, the Foreign Secretary, had even tried to pull some strings in Europe to stop France misbehaving in Tunisia. Gladstone deplored the business even more strongly than Granville. But Granville's plan for intervention was quite impractical, as Gladstone and the rest of the Cabinet pointed out to him. To stop the French needed help from Bismarck. Bismarck was egging on the French. Moreover, Gladstone could not repudiate the secret agreement at Berlin because he wished to keep Cyprus, the *quid pro quo* for Tunisia.

By now the dust had settled in Tunisia. Gladstone looked back on the affair as an absurd aberration by the French. Why had they fallen for Bismarck's malevolent game? It was a threat to international order, a disturbance of the equilibrium. Gladstone regarded the whole affair as an anachronism, a return to the bad old days of brag and grab. He was sickened by the humbug of a punitive expedition: invasion disguised as friendly intervention. Thank heavens he had managed to extricate Britain from similar adventures, precipitated by the Tories' reckless forward policy in Afghanistan and the Transvaal. The PM recoiled at the thought of the 'blood guiltiness'[2] of imperialism.

Gladstone would have been appalled if he could have looked only a few months into the future. The year 1882 was to be even blacker for him than the black year of 1881.

Personal tragedy awaited him in Ireland. Within seven months his own government would be the invaders of Egypt. All the most deplorable features of the French invasion of Tunisia – the humbug and the blood guiltiness – and more – would his own Liberal government repeat on a larger scale. Worst of all, just as he had predicted in 1877, this Egyptian adventure was to be the 'egg' of a new British Empire in Africa and of a new kind of aggressive imperialism that would change the whole course of history.

By the end of 1881 the state of Egypt seemed better than for a long time and no one in England dreamt of the impending collision. 'Dual control', the system by which Britain and France, in concert with the other Powers, managed Egyptian affairs, was labouring to restore the country to solvency. The foreign bond-holders were happy – perhaps too happy. Their enormous loans to Ismael, in the days when he was dreaming of a great African empire, had incurred the extortionate rates of interest appropriate when a speculator is heading for a crash. Then the Powers had stepped in, deposed Ismael and rescued Egypt – and the bond-holders. But the interest remained extortionate. The real sufferers were the fellahin, the Egyptian peasants, who paid the interest with or without the encouragement of the courbash, a buffalo-hide whip. It was an aspect of dual control that gave the Liberals a sore conscience, and the Tories too. However, the French insisted. The French changed their own government with bewildering frequency, but remained consistently faithful to the interests of French bond-holders. British governments, much less vulnerable to financial pressure groups, and proud of their humanitarian tradition in Africa, felt helpless to lower the interest much. Keeping the French sweet remained a priority, even when their government was headed by Gambetta, notorious for his financial intrigues.

In December 1881 there was only a small cloud on the Egyptian horizon, and it was hard to make out what it portended. Was it the shape of a fellahin's hand, or merely the tarboosh of some disgruntled colonel? Eddy Hamilton was a personal friend of the dashing young English diplomat-turned-explorer, Wilfred Blunt, who claimed to know the answer. On 9 September there had been some kind of coup by Arabi and his fellow colonels in the Egyptian army. That Christmas Blunt wrote a masterly report on the affair which Hamilton passed to his chief. It was all the more significant because Blunt was the man employed by the British agent, Sir Edward Malet, to sound out Egyptian public opinion. He reported that Arabi's coup had not merely been an affair of disgruntled officers, like their 'mutiny' in Cairo in 1879, but something much more exciting – a patriotic movement, a movement of 'national regeneration', aiming to achieve by a peaceful revolution what natural justice demanded: 'Egypt for the Egyptians.'[3] Hamilton was impressed. His chief shuddered.

In principle Gladstone was all for small nationalities struggling to be free. It was one of the themes in his Midlothian speeches that had set the hearts of his supporters ablaze. But in Egypt they had trouble enough already without Egyptian patriotism: a rickety system of dual control, with the French breathing down British necks and the bond-holders baying for their interest; nominal Turkish suzerainty, with a new Sultan, Abdul Hamid, no less erratic than his predecessors; and built-in confusion which the new Khedive, Tewfik, seemed determined to make the most of for his own ends.

Blunt's report made no dent in Gladstone's determination not to intervene. Gladstone and Granville saw no choice but to maintain the *status quo* – that is to do what the French asked for the time being. They would, of course, extricate themselves from dual control as soon as possible. It would be much more appropriate if the Canal – the only *real* British interest – could be placed under wider international control.

Yet already, unrecognized by Gladstone, the new French Prime Minister, Gambetta, had committed him to a reckless move forward. By 30 December 1881 Gambetta had drafted a strong note to be presented to the Khedive, signed by both France and Britain. This reached the Kasr-el-Nil Palace on 8 January 1882. It was intended to calm the situation by strengthening the Khedive's hand, and thus the hands of his manipulators, Britain and France. Its effect was exactly the reverse.

*   *   *

Wilfred Blunt, the tall, Byronic, young English explorer who had thrown up a career in diplomacy to devote his life to the cause of Islam and the Arabs, had pitched his tents outside Cairo in the autumn of 1881, a few weeks after Arabi's coup of 9 September.

At first Blunt had been suspicious. An officers' coup was hardly the stuff for creating a parliamentary democracy on English lines. But when he met Arabi in mid-December he had been swept off his feet. Arabi received him in his modest rented house near the Abdin barracks. The doorway and passage were blocked with supplicants. Arabi was the idol of Egypt, 'El Wahid', the Only One. At first Blunt wondered where his magnetism lay. He looked only too like a fellah: tall, heavy-limbed, slow-moving, dull-eyed, with a dreamy look on his plain features. This was the type of man that the Egyptian ruling class – Turks and Circassians – had exploited for centuries, a man who would work without pay or complaint, a poor, faithful, plodding beast of the Nile. But when Arabi smiled it was as though the sun had suddenly illuminated a dull landscape. One saw the 'kindly and large intelligence within'. Even his boorish looks were part of his secret. They enabled the masses to identify with him: El Wahid, the only one of them who had ever risen to power, out-manoeuvring the Turks and Europeans.

On his part Arabi was delighted to meet a rich, cultivated, enthusiastic Englishman like Blunt, equally at home with the classical Arabic of the desert and the rustic patois of the Nile. He was especially impressed to hear of Blunt's family connection with Byron, his wife's grandfather. Not that Arabi claimed to have read a line of Byron's poetry, but he held him in high esteem for his 'work for liberty',[4] fighting to liberate the Greeks from Turkish rule. Blunt offered to do as much for Egypt if it came to a war. Meanwhile, he claimed to have the ear of Mr Gladstone, the friend of liberty, and a man, he assured Arabi, who was to be trusted completely.

Arabi explained the background to his own coup, a great deal more complicated than it had seemed in London. At one level it was like the coup against Nubar Pasha and Rivers Wilson two years earlier. Common to both affairs were the grievances of Egyptian officers. They were under-paid and under-privileged compared with the Turkish and Circassian officers, a pampered and corrupt élite. Arabi and his fellows were determined to take over control of the army for themselves. Matters had come to a head on 9 September, when they were warned that the Prime Minister, a Turk called Riaz Pasha, was planning to send them into exile.

But Arabi was not merely a spokesman for disgruntled officers. Behind him stood the Egypt-for-the-Egyptians movement, comprising the whole spectrum of constitutional reformers in Egypt. They ranged from a few enlightened Turks like the ex-Prime Minister, Sherif Pasha, and the ex-Minister of War, Mahmud Bey Sami, to most of the country's intellectuals and journalists. The great majority were fellahin by origin. What united them was a determination to break the power of the Turkish oligarchy. They were not, at least at first, anti-Western. Indeed, they admired Western institutions and planned to set up a Western-style democracy with an elected Parliament and with the Khedive playing the role of constitutional monarch. However, they had become increasingly suspicious of the French and British since the invasion of Tunis. That Christian act of aggression had sent a shudder through the Muslim world.

There seemed an alarmingly close parallel between the situations of Tunis and Egypt. The crumbling of Turkish power exposed all her vassal states to the appetites of the two predatory Powers. Of course a python takes time to swallow its victims. First came the foreign bankers eager to lend at extortionate rates; then the financial controllers to see that the interest was paid; then thousands of foreign advisers taking their cut. Finally, when the country was bankrupt and helpless, it was time for the foreign troops to 'rescue' the ruler from his 'rebellious' people. One last gulp, and the country had gone.

Where did the Egyptian ruler, the Khedive, stand in all this? It was a question that puzzled Arabi and the reformers as much as anyone. Till September, Tewfik had faithfully played the role designed for him by the two Powers: a constitutional monarch, meaning a rubber Khedive, whose ministers always bent to the will of the Powers. But even Tewfik had his pride. Could this be exploited by the reformers? Did he dream of being like Ismael? There was some evidence of this. At any rate, it appeared that he was partly in collusion with the plotters on 9 September, when Arabi launched his coup, just as Ismael had been partly in collusion with the army plotters who had ousted Nubar and Wilson two years before.

The coup itself had therefore been even more theatrical than it seemed. It was not so much a coup against Tewfik, as was claimed in London and Paris, as one against the corrupt Turkish oligarchy exploited by the Powers. Nor had Tewfik really played quite the craven role on 9 September that his British advisers attributed to him.

Their story was as follows. That morning Arabi had ridden up with a drawn sword to the front of the Abdin Palace, sealing off the main entrance with his infantry, while artillery blocked the western gate. Enter the Khedive, trembling, assisted by his British advisers, Charles Cookson (acting consul in Malet's absence) and Auckland Colvin, the Financial Controller. 'What on earth do I do?' poor Tewfik had whispered to Colvin. 'Tell him to dismount,' Colvin replied.[5] Arabi put up his sword and dismounted. At that moment, so Colvin later insisted, Tewfik had Arabi in his power. Mehemet Ali, Tewfik's great-grandfather, would not have hesitated. He would have shot Arabi with his pistol and put an end to the nonsense there and then. Instead Tewfik parleyed and was lost. Arabi had been able to dictate terms: the reactionary, Riaz Pasha, was to go; the reformer, Sherif Pasha, was to replace him as Prime Minister; Arabi was to be Minister of War; the army was to be increased in size to 18,000 men, there was to be a new constitution and a new Parliament. Collapse of the craven Khedive. Victory for the mutineers. This was the legend spread by Colvin and Cookson in the British government's Blue Books describing the affair.

In fact, according to Arabi, the Khedive was as delighted with the immediate outcome of the coup as his father had been with the earlier one. But neither Tewfik nor Arabi had anticipated its disastrous effect on relations with the Powers. Auckland Colvin, an Anglo-Indian firebrand, was irreconcilable, though he lay low for the time being. He was all the more influential because he had somehow won the ear of the chief Liberal newspaper, the *Pall Mall Gazette*, edited by John Morley. On the other hand, Malet, the British Consul, was puzzled but sympathetic, as he knew that Gladstone was anxious not to alienate the reformers. It was thus that young Wilfred Blunt found himself thrust to the centre of the stage, the intermediary whom both protagonists, Malet and Arabi, counted on to help prevent the disaster of foreign intervention.

On 8 January the menacing Joint Note, drafted by Gambetta, reached Cairo. Malet showed it to Blunt. He was aghast. 'They will take it as a declaration of war.' The note assured the Khedive that Britain and France were united in their resolve to guard against all causes of complaint, internal or external, which might threaten the *status quo*. Before the French invasion of Tunis, this might have sounded innocuous enough. Now it had the effect of a dam burst.

Blunt was sent by Malet to explain to Arabi that intervention was the last thing in the world London wanted. (This was true enough, though Colvin privately admitted that he was trying to force a show-down.) Blunt found Arabi alone in his official room in the Kasr-el-Nil palace. His face was like a thundercloud. There was a peculiar gleam in his eye when Blunt asked him what he made of the Joint Note.

'Tell me, rather,' he asked Blunt, 'how you understand it?' Blunt gave him a disingenuous message from Malet. The Note was supposed to reassure the nationalists that no one would interfere with the new role of the Khedive as constitutional monarch.

'Sir Edward must really think us children who do not understand words,' replied Arabi. 'In the first place,' he went on, 'it is the language of menace. There is no clerk in this office who would use such words with such a meaning.' As to the unity of French and English policy, this meant that, just as France had invaded Tunis, so England would invade Egypt. 'Let them come,' he said, 'every man and child in Egypt will fight them. It is contrary to our principles to strike the first blow, but we shall know how to return it.'[6]

Blunt retired crestfallen. He knew he had been sent on a fool's errand.

The political crisis developed with alarming speed. A flood of national sentiment poured through Cairo, confirming the alliance between Arabi and the civilian nationalists and leaving the Khedive high and dry, the puppet of the two Powers. In early February nationalists issued a direct challenge to the Powers. By now half the state's total budget of nine million pounds was already pledged to the foreign bond-holders, to pay the interest on Ismael's mountainous foreign debts. Although bitterly resented by the nationalists, they were resigned to this arrangement. However, they insisted on principle that the Council of Notables – the newly convened Parliament – should be allowed to vote on the rest of the budget. As a first instalment of reform they recommended raising expenditure on the army to allow widespread promotion to fellah officers, as well as the increase of total numbers to 18,000. The Financial Controllers – Colvin and his French counterpart – rejected these ideas out of hand. They controlled the budget and it was indivisible. Such an increase in military spending, they claimed, threatened the interests of the bond-holders. The two Powers told the Khedive to instruct his ministers not to allow the change in the law. But the Khedive was helpless. Sherif Pasha resigned as Prime Minister and was replaced by a supporter of Arabi's. Arabi himself moved to the centre of the stage as Minister of War, and the real ruler of Egypt. A collision seemed inevitable: on one side the Powers, supporting the old system of informal empire and the new interests of the bond-holders; on the other, Arabi and his movement, flexing the muscles of an ancient land, once the giant of Africa.

*   *   *

Meanwhile in Paris the new government of Léon Gambetta was involved in a double contrast: to beg or bully both the French Parliament and the British Government into taking a tough line in Egypt. Gambetta was equally the *bête noire* of the far Left and the far Right, and by common consent a prodigy, a man who defied all the rules. His looks and his origins were mysterious. You could see he came from the south, with his plump, fleshy features, high colour and exuberant greying hair. It was whispered – incorrectly – that he was a Jew. What was true was that his financial associates were Jewish, and that his secret mistress, Léonie Léon, was half-Jewish, half-mulatto. His father had been a humble Italian grocer, his mother a Gascon; born in Cahors, he had not been naturalized till he was over twenty. This was the man who had come to represent militant French patriotism incarnate.

At thirty-two he had risen – literally – to instant fame during the 'hours of misfortune'[7] (his euphemism for the worst part of the Franco-Prussian war). He had been appointed Minister of the Interior and had escaped from the besieged city of Paris by balloon. In September 1870 he was virtual dictator, and directed the war from the provinces. He improvised new armies, planned to relieve the capital, and finally proposed war to the knife when Paris had capitulated.

Gambetta's ally in this reckless enterprise was Freycinet, and no two men could have presented a greater contrast. Freycinet was an engineer and bureaucrat, tall and thin, and seemingly so dry and characterless that he was dubbed the 'white mouse'. Gambetta was all wit and warmth, a creature of impulse, as plump and supple as a dolphin, a master improviser and opportunist, consistent only in his devotion to his adopted country and to his own star. The two men remained friends and allies in the tempestuous decade after the war. Freycinet became Prime Minister and, in 1879, Foreign Minister, emerging as the main architect of the policy of colonial expansion.

At first Gambetta was passionately against expansion. As the head of the noisiest republican group in the Chamber of Deputies, he was the embodiment of the spirit of *revanche*; nothing must be allowed to weaken the French will to wrest back from Prussia the provinces of Alsace and Lorraine. However, by 1881, when Freycinet had been succeeded as Prime Minister by Ferry, Gambetta had seen the light. He adopted colonialism with all the zeal of the convert. Colonial expansion would propel France back to greatness. It was not yet time for the day of reckoning with Prussia. As President of the Chamber from 1879 to 1881, he was master of '*pouvoir occulte*', the political backstairs. It was in this spirit that he had agreed to help Courcel, the ambitious Director of Political Affairs at the Quai d'Orsay, in March 1881 when Courcel had proposed the takeover of Tunis. Now, in 1882, as Prime Minister, he decided to make his name with a policy of 'vigour'. In Egypt the French must insist on absolute equality with the British, insist that both governments keep the reins in their own hands, and prevent the British making any concessions to Arabi and his friends.

To a burning nationalist like Gambetta, this policy of sticking up for France and prodding Britain was long overdue. '*Dual* control' sounded fine. In practice the British now had the upper hand, politically and commercially. The financial crisis of 1878 had given Rivers Wilson the plum job, Minister of Finance, in Nubar Pasha's government. His French counterpart, Blignières, was left to swallow his pride as Minister of Public Works. Naturally Rivers Wilson fed the best jobs to his fellow countrymen. By July 1879 they were in clover: railways,

posts and telegraphs, ports, lighthouses, customs, even the Khedive's sec-
retariat – every single department went to an Englishman. All the French got
were left-overs, the Bulgah Museum and the Khedival Library.

It was much the same wretched story with trade and finance. French bond-
holders never stopped belly-aching while British investors licked their lips and
bought more Egyptian bonds. As for trade, the British had grabbed 70 per cent
of the Egyptian trade by 1881, and French trade was flat. Foreign imports had
leapt, yet French business had flopped so badly that the French colony in Cairo
and Alexandria was dwindling away. Only in one respect could the French
claim to be ahead, in culture and the 'civilizing mission'; French was still the
first language after Arabic and the French educational system still dominated
schools and colleges. Yet even in culture the Anglo-Saxons were creeping up.
Since 1881 English had been recognized as the official language of the law courts
and the administration, breaking a lucrative French monopoly.

To reverse these trends and restore true parity with the British was already
beyond Gambetta's power, his own advisers in Paris and Cairo believed. But he
insisted the attempt must be made. The first step was the Joint Note handed to
the Khedive on 8 January 1882, the one drafted by Gambetta himself in menacing
language.

When it failed to bluff the National Party into submission – when they called
the bluff and all Egypt rallied behind Arabi – it only stiffened Gambetta's resolve.
He refused to allow Gladstone and Granville to mollify the National Party in
any way. On the contrary, he seemed determined to force a crisis. (In London
Gladstone was disappointed by the discovery that 'popular principles' – that is,
democracy – counted so little with Gambetta. How sad that the great Republican
lacked any of the 'spirit of a true Liberal'.[8]) Gambetta paid no more attention
to Gladstone's delicate feelings than to Arabi's. He instructed the French Consul-
General in Cairo to report on the feasibility of sending French warships to give
a show of strength at Alexandria, and arranged for an expeditionary force of
6,000 French marines to be prepared at Toulon. By the end of January he seemed
set on a collision course. He decided on a naval demonstration. If this final bluff
failed, he would probably send in French troops. But would Gladstone and the
British agree on a joint landing, and was the real aim, as Bismarck hinted, to
make France, not Britain, the dominant partner? Nothing was clear except that
Gambetta seemed hell-bent on risking a double collision: breaking the peace in
Egypt and breaking the *entente* with Britain.

It was at this moment that the daredevil in Gambetta took full possession.
Two collisions were not enough. He decided on a collision with the French
Chamber, too.

For years he had campaigned for reforming the electoral system by making
fewer and larger multi-member constituencies. It was an issue that in 1881 cut
across groups and parties. Widen the constituency, said Gambetta, and you will
raise the intellectual level of the deputies, and give France a truly national policy.
In 1881 the Chamber of Deputies voted for the change and the Senate rebuffed
it, so the issue was unresolved. In January Gambetta decided to gamble every-

thing on the issue. He was warned that this was suicidal. He replied that if he won, he would have the Chamber 'in his grasp'. If he lost, well, he had 'fought the good fight', as he told his mistress, Léonie Léon.[9]

In fact, Gambetta's recklessness was partly the result of his bizarre private life. Recently he had begged Léonie to marry him. It was time for some domestic comfort. Indeed, he was as emotionally dependent on Léonie as he was high-handed and insensitive to others. Still she refused, jealous of his success, awash with self-pity, a hypochondriac, terrified of publicity. No doubt Léonie encouraged the wild gamble on electoral reform. And Gambetta must have known that by losing the vote he was more likely to win Léonie. As he wrote to her, 'Ah! How impatient I am to be done with this interrupted life, spent in running after one another, never able to enjoy my Mignonne's presence without thinking that in a few minutes I am going to lose her.'[10]

By the time he wrote these words, Gambetta had won his freedom, and persuaded Léonie to marry him – so it seemed. On 26 January electoral reform was voted out, Left, Right, and Centre: the majority against him was 268 to 218. He immediately resigned and his former ally, Freycinet, the so-called 'white mouse', stepped forward to form a new government. His plans were as colourless as his personality. He decided not to risk a tough line with the Egyptian nationalists, given the ugly mood of the French Chamber. So the initiative slipped back to London, much to the relief of Gladstone's anxious and distracted Cabinet.

*   *   *

However, one of Gambetta's ideas had not been allowed to lapse: the proposal for the naval demonstration. This did not seem too bad a compromise. Gladstone was hemmed in on every side. The mayhem in Ireland was threatening to spread to his Cabinet. The Radicals renounced coercion and autocracy, the Whigs concession and conciliation. At least in Egypt they might be able to find something negative to share: the traditional Liberal taboo against an aggressive foreign policy and the neighbourly policy of avoiding a row with the French. So Gladstone proposed a plan for a new exercise of bluff by the two Powers, the naval demonstration. If that failed to convince the National Party of the danger of tampering with dual control, then the problem of Egypt would have to be internationalized.

One solution was that the Turks should be persuaded by the Powers to send troops to support the Khedive against the nationalists. It was a 'hateful'[11] thought, Granville admitted, to invite into Egypt the 'unspeakable Turk' fresh from those ghastly atrocities against the Bulgarians. All that could be said was that the Sultan, Abdul Hamid, was legally the Khedive's overlord. It seemed the least bad way of avoiding direct intervention by France and Britain together – or, worse still, of Britain being forced to go it alone.

There was only one flaw in this sheepish plan for Turkish intervention: the

French would not hear of it. They were still smarting at the rash of tribal risings that had broken out in 1881 in southern Tunis and Algeria itself. They attributed this defiance of their authority to a pan-Islamic movement, directed, they claimed, by the Sultan at Constantinople. Arabi's revolt was only another symptom of this Muslim plague, nationalism. Therefore getting Abdul Hamid to do their own dirty work was out of the question; if anyone was to occupy Egypt it must be Britain and France, marching shoulder to shoulder. So nothing was done for the moment. In Egypt, Arabi's power, and the power of the nationalists, stealthily accumulated like water behind the walls of a great dam.

Meanwhile Ireland was the battlefield for Gladstone's Cabinet. In May the PM had sent his own nephew, Lord Frederick Cavendish, as a reforming Irish Chief Secretary. A few days later Gladstone heard that Lord Frederick had been stabbed to death in Phoenix Park, Dublin, by Fenians armed with surgical knives. The Phoenix Park murders sent Gladstone reeling and left the Cabinet still more divided.

But in Egypt the French were prepared to compromise. Freycinet proposed they go ahead with a naval demonstration, followed by Turkish intervention if all else failed. The Turkish troops would be under Anglo-French control. That was the plan, agreed to by both governments. Accordingly, Germany and the other Powers were formally told in mid-May that an Anglo-French fleet was on the high seas, steaming towards Alexandria. They would strengthen the Khedive's authority and safeguard law and order.

In fact the joint fleet, like the Joint Note, had exactly the opposite effect. The sight of the ironclads – two French and two British – anchored in the outer harbour at Alexandria made the nationalists' blood race. They knew what it meant. In Tunis the arrival of the French fleet had been the prelude to invasion. Arabi stood defiant, all Egypt behind him. From the Liberals' point of view everything now depended on Turkish intervention.

On 25 May it was reported that Tewfik had nerved himself to dismiss Arabi and his ministers – relying on his own masters. But the previous day Granville had received alarming news. Freycinet was getting cold feet. Terrified of the anti-Turkish mood in the French Chamber, he refused to call in the help of the Sultan. Tewfik was left in the lurch. By 30 May Arabi and the ministers had called Tewfik's bluff. They were back in the saddle, and Cairo felt like a powder keg.

The first explosion occurred on 10 June. In full view of the joint fleet, mobs went on the rampage in Alexandria, killing fifty Europeans or European-protected people, wounding many more, including the British Consul, and making a bonfire of millions of pounds of Egyptian property.

The Alexandria 'massacres' shocked London, inured to bad news from Ireland. The Cabinet was now split on Egypt, too. Lord Hartington, Secretary of State for India, led a revolt by the Whigs. He mocked French bad faith and Granville's gullibility. Sarcastically he congratulated the Foreign Secretary on settling the problem: 'At least I suppose it is settled, as there has been no Cabinet. . . . But I am rather anxious to know how it has been settled. Has Arabi

Pasha given in, or has M. de Freycinet been persuaded to get out of bed?"[12]

Hartington and the Whigs were now converted to a forward policy. Like Salisbury and the Tories, they were against intervention when it could be avoided. But not when a vital strategic interest was threatened, as in Egypt. Gladstone and Granville had failed because they had sentimental general ideas about the concept of Europe and the rights of oppressed nationalities. They had tried appeasement: kotowing to the slippery French, the unspeakable Turks, the murderous fellahin. Now they must steel themselves to defend the Empire. On 18 June Hartington defiantly suggested that Britain should send in its own troops if all else failed. If nothing was done, the Whigs would resign.

Naturally the idea of going it alone was deplored by Gladstone and Granville, still playing for time and pinning their hopes on Turkish intervention. A conference of the Powers had been arranged at Constantinople in June. Nothing could be decided until its outcome was known, but the Cabinet was daily growing more confused and its leaders more isolated.

The Whigs, whose tough policy for Ireland infuriated the Radicals, made common cause with them on the need for intervention in Egypt, but the two factions disagreed on what to do next. The Whigs saw Egypt in narrow Palmerstonian terms: a gunboat or two, the landing of some redcoats, the authority of the friendly ruler restored, a whiff of grapeshot or perhaps only the threat of it, and all could go on as before. This was not the view of the Radicals led by Joe Chamberlain. They agreed that Arabi must be suppressed. It was assumed, quite wrongly, that he was in some way responsible for the massacres. He had thrown off the mask and no one would trust his professions that he respected the rights of the bond-holders and therefore of dual control. He was no national leader, merely a 'military adventurer'. The true spirit of Egyptian nationalism, the nucleus of a really national and patriotic party, was there in the Chamber of Notables (actually a group of conservative landowners). Thus intervening in Egypt was not only to protect the Canal but to save the new national movement from the grip of military dictatorship.

The confusion in the Cabinet aptly reflected the confusion in Egypt itself, as it was reported to London. It was far from clear who was in control of events, Arabi or the mob. And if it was Arabi, what were his intentions? Did his takeover threaten the Suez Canal? In early July the commander of the British fleet at Alexandria, Admiral Seymour, requested permission from the Cabinet to bring matters to a head. He claimed that Arabi's men were working on shore batteries that threatened the safety of his ships. Could he send them an ultimatum that either they stop work on the batteries or he would bombard them with his naval guns? Freycinet was asked how he felt about this violent proposal. He replied by withdrawing his ships to Port Said. So Britain stood alone – and so did Gladstone in the Cabinet.

Just as the Egyptian crisis neared its climax, the Irish crisis, too, threatened to blow up like a volcano, showering Westminster with fragments of the Liberal Party. Outwardly Gladstone remained as calm as if nothing had happened, noted Eddy Hamilton on 9 July. Yet that first week of July was one of the most agonizing in the PM's long political life. In Ireland, a deal with Irish nationalist MPs – the Parnellites – seemed to be on the point of collapse. Parnell and others, arrested for supposed complicity in the land war, had been released from prison on condition they collaborated with the government. The Whigs loathed this deal almost as much as the Tories. The Radicals insisted, and Gladstone had pushed ahead. But when a clause in a Crime Prevention Bill was put to the vote in the House, Gladstone found the government defeated; the Parnellites had broken their pledge to support it, and twenty Whigs had repudiated Gladstone.

The chief was on the verge of resignation. There was talk of Hartington trying to form a Whig Ministry, but how would he buy the Radical support? It was assumed the Tories would take over. In the midst of the confusion, the Cabinet had to decide whether to allow Admiral Seymour to send his ultimatum. Whigs and Radicals joined hands on the warpath: let Seymour blaze away. They were all for the final step of sending redcoats in to replace Arabi with someone more understanding. Granville and the moderates still shrank from this step. They accepted the case for Seymour's ultimatum, but were still hoping to avoid a war. A few shell bursts and the threat of an expedition might be enough to topple Arabi.

Gladstone alone – except for John Bright – was against the Admiral's ultimatum. After all, as Bright put it with blinding simplicity, Britain's only interest was to defend the Canal. 'If the attack on the port endangers the Canal, the attack should not be made.'[13] But Ireland had now brought Gladstone to the end of his tether. He told Granville he saw no need for the ultimatum, 'But I am willing to defer to your decision and judgements.'[14] In effect, he had sacrificed Egypt and his own Liberal principles in order to prevent the Cabinet breaking up.

Two days later, Seymour's ultimatum expired and the shore batteries at Alexandria disappeared in spouts of smoke and flame. So did many handsome public buildings on the seafront. The destruction of the city was completed when Arabi withdrew his troops into the delta. Two nights of looting and killing by a mob then supervened.

The Cabinet now took the final step. There were reports that Arabi intended to destroy the Canal as a reprisal for the attack on Alexandria. He was proclaiming a Holy War. (In fact, Arabi had behaved with what was to prove fatal restraint.) The Liberals had no difficulty in persuading the Tories that troops must be sent to Egypt forthwith. On 27 July the House, by an overwhelming majority, voted the credit to pay for the expedition. It was to cost £2.3 million, which would raise income tax by a penny – that is, by nearly 10 per cent. Sir Garnet Wolseley woud lead the force of 15,000 British troops from Malta and Cyprus, and 10,000 British troops from India.

Only one fear haunted the planners. What part, if any, would the Sultan or the White Mouse have in the expedition? Neither was expected to add anything to the efficiency of the British force. Fortunately the Sultan, still negotiating with Arabi, proved incapable of making a decision in time. As for Freycinet, for once he threw caution to the winds and staked everything on trying to get the French Chamber to vote money for French participation in protecting the Canal. He was dealt an overwhelming defeat in the Chamber, a defeat to which Gambetta, who had a score to settle with his old ally, contributed all he could.

Now it was up to General Wolseley. He arrived at Alexandria on 16 August. Could his new model army, humiliated by Zulus and Boers, for once win a battle in Africa?

*   *   *

By 12 September Wolseley was ready to advance from Ismailia. Beside him, a circle of swords and white helmets, rode most of the 'Ashanti Ring' (alias 'Wolseley's Gang'): Colonel Redvers Buller, Colonel William Butler, Major J. F. Maurice and the rest of the HQ staff. All of them would win fame – or notoriety – in the years ahead. Yet it is odd how few of these men, in the front line of the new imperialism, were to style themselves imperialists.

Their chief was one – and proud of it. Wolseley, Irish Protestant by origin, boasted that he was a jingo. He yearned for a forward policy in Africa as well as in Afghanistan. He despised Gladstone and the Radicals as much for their funk in colonial policy – the white feather after Majuba – as he despised the Tories for trying to block army reform at home. By contrast Buller, the West Country landowner, was a Whig of the old school. He admired Wolseley's professionalism, but the general's aggressive patriotism must have grated on him. Restoring independence to the Boers seemed as sensible to him as it did to men like Gladstone or Granville. And Butler went further still. He was an Irish Catholic and an Irish Nationalist, a Home Ruler and an admirer of Parnell. He had to admit, somewhat ruefully, that he had not come to Egypt to fight for a particularly noble cause. This was a financiers' war, a war for the bond-holders. However, as he wrote later, the modern soldier had to be content with the best cause he could get. Better not to look the gift horse – this particular war – too closely in the mouth.

One link of the magic circle was missing, the most brilliant man of all and Wolseley's favourite, Colley. Poor fellow, he had paid the price of his brilliance at Majuba. Wolseley himself usually mixed audacity with caution. In strategic terms he had now decided to take as few risks as possible. The previous year Colley had rashly tried to launch a campaign against 2,000 Boer invaders with a mere 1,200 British regulars. For this Egyptian expedition Wolseley had insisted on a British force of 25,000 in all, virtually a whole army corps, mostly veterans, well led and armed with the latest artillery. The official strength of the Egyptian army was only 18,000. Even that figure exaggerated Arabi's strength. Although Arabi had conscripted thousands of extra troops in the last months, much of his army consisted of old men or raw recruits. Only the regiments who had fought in the Sudan or Abyssinia knew anything about war.

Wolseley was equally cautious in choosing his line of advance. He had plumped for the longest and safest route, the Canal. And here fortune favoured the cautious. Lesseps, head of the Suez Canal Company, and passionate to protect his brainchild from violation, had explained to Arabi that the Powers intended to respect the neutrality of the Canal in the event of war. Of course Wolseley had no such intention; on the contrary, his plan was to advance on Cairo by the easiest route, by the hard crunchy sand of the eastern desert. The easiest way to do this was to seize the Canal at both ends, Port Said and Suez, then sail in as far as Ismailia, roughly its mid-point. Ismailia would serve as the main port and base camp for the invasion force. From here it would be a mere hundred-mile dash across the open desert to Cairo, borrowing Lesseps's excellent Ismailia railway to bring up supplies, and his admirable Sweet Water Canal to water the thirsty troops and horses.

These were the sensible plans, complete with a precise timetable, drawn up by Wolseley in the War Office back in July, and no British campaign had ever gone more smoothly. Before seizing the Canal, Wolseley made a naval feint at Aboukir, but it was hardly worth the trouble. Arabi had been fooled by Lesseps and had left the Canal and its cities undefended. There had been only one change of plan. Owing to what Wolseley called the 'criminal'[15] stupidity of Admiral Seymour, Alexandria had been bombarded and taken over by the Blue Jackets. This allowed Arabi to concentrate most of his force in the south, while Wolseley had to divide his own invasion force and station one brigade uselessly in Alexandria. He gave the brigade to one of the Ring who was getting above himself, Sir Evelyn Wood. (Wood could do with a spell cooling his heels in the Med. He was beginning to 'think himself Napoleon', said the chief acidly.)

By 12 September Wolseley was ready to advance from Ismailia, days ahead of his own timetable. There were a few skirmishes along the railway line, and then one hard nut to crack, Arabi's fortified camp at Tel el-Kebir, sixty miles from Cairo. By now Arabi had concentrated most of his army there. So much the better; Wolseley had set his heart on crushing Arabi and his army with a single knock-down blow before making the dash for Cairo. This would end the campaign at a stroke – and prove England was still a power to be reckoned with. As Wolseley put it, scribbling to his wife from his tent as the regimental band hammered out a romantic Irish air to the fly-ridden desert: 'I do so long for a complete victory that may make the world feel that England has yet something left in her, and that her soldiers have still strength and courage notwithstanding the ... spirit-crushing influence of radicalism.'[16]

But how to crack that hard nut, Tel el-Kebir? In the cool darkness before dawn on the previous day, Wolseley had ridden out to show his eighteen generals his secret plan for an attack just before dawn. This was as novel, tactically, and as daring as the strategy was conventional.

A night march, with an attack just before the first gleam of dawn, can be as full of surprises for the attackers as the defenders. A trivial error of a few minutes or a few hundred yards, a chance collision with the enemy's scouts – can lead to disaster. Darkness can turn the best-trained troops into panicky fools. Wolseley put his faith in the steadiness of his own men. It was a gamble, but consider the advantages. First, the all-important gift of surprise. Second, darkness would shield the attackers from rifle and artillery fire up to the moment they stormed the ramparts. Third, darkness would also shield the men from the paralysing heat of the desert. Finally, if the cavalry were to make that dash for Cairo after the battle, they would have plenty of daylight. This cavalry dash was perhaps the only way to save the capital, for Arabi was reported to have promised to burn Cairo if he lost Tel el-Kebir.

Everything depended on surprise. Would they in fact catch Arabi napping? When Wolseley took his eighteen generals to study the four-mile-long ramparts of the fort that morning, he first peered at his watch. Splashes of dawn marked the sky behind the ramparts. It was only now that the enemy's vedettes were leaving the gates to go out on patrol. 'Note the time,' observed Wolseley. It was 5.45 a.m. 'Our attack must be delivered before this hour ... otherwise those vedettes will detect our presence.'[17] The attack was fixed for 5.0 a.m., with Lieutenant Rawson to navigate the army by the stars. To ensure surprise the plan was kept secret from most of the army until the final moment.

That afternoon the men were marched out of camp, leaving the fires burning. No bugles were sounded and they were given strange orders: march in silence, and no smoking. They plodded along under the weight of their gear, Martini-Henry rifle and bayonet, a hundred rounds of ammunition in pouches, water bottle in haversack, all of them adding an extra white diagonal stripe to their scarlet serge uniforms and the tunics of the Highland regiments. By 11.0 p.m. they had found the bivouac at the 'Ninth Hill', a heap of sand and stones about a mile north of the railway.

Then the formation was set for the attack: two divisions, each of two infantry brigades, separated by the forty-two guns of the field artillery, attacking over a front of four miles, with the cavalry division and horse artillery on the far right. An Indian brigade and a naval brigade were to follow along the wadi in which lay the railway and the Canal. They had orders to keep well behind in case they should alert the enemy by colliding with dogs, geese or camels.

At first the advance went smoothly enough. One soldier had brought a bottle of rum and had emptied the bottle. Butler heard his weird drunken laughter echoing in the darkness. He was quickly subdued by his friends. Then about 3.30 a.m. came a brief halt and an incident in the Highland Brigade that, ludicrous as it later seemed, brought them close to disaster.

The Highland Brigade was the leading brigade of the division on the left, and its line was formed of four battalions in half columns. The order to halt was passed in a low voice from battalion to battalion and company to company, and took time to reach the flanks. So the flank battalions, the Cameronians and the Black Watch, lost direction. When the brigade halted, the straight line had curved inwards to form a crescent. When the brigade advanced again, the two flank battalions were about to march into each other when their Brigadier, Major-General Alison, gave the order to halt. Wolseley himself, his nerves taut as a ship's cable, grasped the danger. Butler, carefully counting each step, rode forward to investigate. It took Lieutenant Rawson and the staff half an hour to sort out the confusion, then the march resumed.

They had marched another mile when a second, even stranger, incident occurred. A shaft of pale sky, shaped like a sheaf of corn, appeared in the east directly over the enemy camp. If this was the first light of dawn, the attack was too late. In fact, the sheaf of corn was a comet, the Great Comet of 1882, and the attack was perfectly timed. The Highland Brigade was now only a few hundred yards from the ramparts. The next moment Wolseley and his staff heard a single shot away to their right front, followed by two or three more shots, and then what Colonel William Butler described as a 'thunderous roll of musketry' and the crash of heavy guns, as the long dim line of ramparts exploded with fire from end to end.[18]

The battle of Tel el-Kebir is sometimes called a 'soldiers' battle', meaning that there were no tactics to speak of, just the crunch of steel on flesh, as the two armies collided. For Arabi's men, those that survived, it was not an experience to forget. They had manned the ramparts all night, thousands of well disciplined fellahin in white uniforms and red tarbooshes, lying there with their rifles ready. But no one had dreamt of an attack launched out of the darkness: of kilted figures swarming over the parapets, stabbing and hacking with their bayonets as though they were savages; of shell bursts smashing through the lines like water spouts, and bodies gashed and broken by shrapnel; of the cavalry riding down fugitives, slashing at them with heavy steel sabres, like reapers in a cornfield. The battle lasted a little more than half an hour, according to Wolseley's staff, then in Colonel Buller's words to his wife, 'I can pass over what followed.'[19] In fact, when the battle was over, the massacre began.

It is Colonel William Butler, Irish Nationalist and mercenary, who has left us the sharpest images of the battle and its aftermath. Wolseley and his staff moved forward a few minutes after the Egyptian line broke and fled. It was just after 5.45 a.m. and the sun had already clipped the horizon. The grey gravelley desert in front of the ramparts was dotted with wounded, mostly Highland Light Infantry who had been caught in that first wild fusillade from the Egyptian line. Ahead of them the British field-guns had broken a hole in the ramparts and followed the infantry into the camp. Inside, the desert was littered with dead Egyptians, dead horses and dead camels. Beyond, where the desert sloped to the railway and Canal, the wreck of Arabi's army was strewn in all directions. 'Down the slopes, through the camps,' wrote Butler, 'over the railway and across the Canal, the white-clad fugitives were flying south and west in dots, in dozens in hundreds.'[20]

At 6.20 a.m. Wolseley and his staff reached the bridge over the Canal and Wolseley gave the orders to the cavalry: gallop for Cairo. Arabi, one of the first to flee from the camp, had an hour's start. Wolseley wrote a triumphant telegram to the War Office. He had every right to boast. Like his hero, Caesar, he came, saw and conquered – all in the space of thirty-five minutes.

Meanwhile, Butler and other officers were trying to stop the shooting of the wounded. 'The seamy side of a battle was here painfully apparent: anything seemed good enough to let off a rifle at. Dead and wounded men, horses and camels, were on all sides.' Some British officers carried water to the Egyptian wounded, but the men were not feeling particularly chivalrous towards the enemy. 'I heard an officer ask a man who was filling his canteen at the canal to give a drink of water to a gasping Egyptian cavalry soldier who was lying supporting himself against the abuttment of the bridge. "I wadna wet his lips," was the indignant reply.'[21] Other British soldiers set off to loot and plunder, as soldiers usually do after a battle, beating up villagers in the wadi if they tried to resist.

Butler grabbed some breakfast at a lock-keeper's hut, then mounted a fresh horse and rode back slowly under the flaming sun to inspect the battlefield. *Vae victis*: woe to the conquered. Of wounded very few were to be seen. 'Too many successive waves of armed men had crossed this portion of the field.' He felt sympathy, even admiration, for the defeated.

Not a moment was given them to awake, form up, prepare, or move into position. The assault fell upon them as a thunderbolt might fall upon a man asleep. The leaders in whom they could trust, were, like themselves, fellaheen; few among them knew anything of war, its arts, manoeuvres, or necessities; they were betrayed on every side, yet they fought stoutly wherever ten or twenty or fifty of them could get together in the works ... the heaps of dead lying with and across their rifles facing the upcoming sun bore eloquent testimony to that final resolve of those poor fellows.[22]

Two days later Wolseley and his staff steamed into Cairo in a train driven by Sir Redvers Buller. They were greeted on the platform by some understandably anxious-looking pashas. It might have been a routine visit. Without a shot, Cairo had surrendered the previous day to a small force of cavalry. So had Arabi and the other revolutionary leaders. Wolseley could not have dreamt of a more decisive victory. He had not only knocked out the Egyptian army. He had knocked down the National Party's coalition like a house of cards.

For the next few days Wolseley and his staff lorded it like pashas in the Abdin Palace. 'What a change,' wrote Wolseley to his wife that first day in Cairo, 'in forty-eight hours!! from the squalor and misery of the desert, with all its filth and flies, to the cool luxury of this spacious palace. Yesterday living on filth, today having iced champagne.'[23] Honours were showered on him by telegraph, including a hysterical letter from Gladstone offering him a barony. It should have been a viscountcy, grumbled Wolseley, when he heard that Admiral Seymour was to get a barony, too. 'Seymour destroyed Alexandria. I saved Cairo.' He blamed the Queen for doing him down. 'I suppose the Queen as usual is against my having any reward.' But even Wolseley had to admit he was now in the best of spirits. He felt as 'fit as a sandboy'.[24] On 25 September, Cairo was en fête for the return of the Khedive. Tewfik drove through the city amid obsequious cheers. Cringing pashas and quaking notables made their peace with Tewfik and his advisers. Sherif Pasha was reappointed Prime Minister. All traces of the revolution seemed to have vanished like a mirage – except the dead buried in large mounds in the desert above the Canal at Tel el-Kebir, and Arabi himself, with a couple of others, a state prisoner in the Citadel. (About Arabi, at least, Wolseley cheerfully concurred with the Queen. The man must be hanged as a traitor.)

A month after replacing Tewfik on his throne, at a cost of £2.3 million to the British taxpayer, Sir Garnet Wolseley was welcomed back in London at Charing Cross by a vast cheering crowd, including the Prime Minister, who was swept off his feet in the throng. A few days more and the Queen received him at Balmoral, where they got on famously. In fact the two old adversaries found they had common enemies in Gladstone and the hated Radicals.

Gladstone's hysterical relief at Wolseley's success soon evaporated. He had bought some time. That was all it amounted to. The inner strains in his Cabinet had not been removed. Ireland still threatened to tear the party in two. And in Egypt there was to be trouble enough in store, trouble that would soon destroy the country's confidence in the party.

This Egyptian adventure had been forced on Gladstone by an unholy alliance of Whigs and Radicals. He had compromised his principles and outraged his instincts, but he had submitted. Now he planned to withdraw from Egypt, just as he had withdrawn from the Transvaal, the moment it was safe. This would certainly be supported by the Radicals, but it might easily be contested by the Whigs. Gladstone said that he longed to resign as leader. But that, too, must wait till he had squared the Whigs and safely extricated Britain from Egypt by restoring the *status quo* as it had existed before Arabi – but without any power for the French.

But would Gladstone be able to extricate Britain from Egypt – and from the Egyptian empire in the Sudan, now threatened by a self-styled redeemer, the Mahdi? In thirty years, when the Scramble was complete, historians would look back on the British invasion of Egypt as the turning point.

The prelude was over. Britain had bungled its forward policy in South Africa, first advancing, then being forced to retreat. But Britain's rivals, seizing their opportunity, had begun to move forward. France had snatched Tunis from under the nose of Italy. Already a race had begun in the Congo between Pierre de Brazza, brandishing the tricolour, and Henry Stanley, acting for King Leopold, the self-styled philanthropist.

Now the relations between France and Britain, governed by an *entente* for the last forty years, were to be poisoned by the British occupation of Egypt.

How this would give a dangerous new dynamic to the partition, exploited both by King Leopold and the German Chancellor, Prince Bismarck, the bewildering years ahead would reveal.

PART TWO
THE RACE BEGINS

THE "IRREPRESSIBLE" TOURIST.

B-sm-rck. "H'M!—HA!—WHERE SHALL I GO NEXT?"

CHAPTER 9

The Race for the Pool

Europe and Central Africa
30 May 1882–April 1883 and before

> *Brazza:* White men have two hands. The stronger
> hand is the hand of war. The other hand is the hand
> of trade. Which hand do the Abanhos want?
> *Abanhos* (all together): Trade

From Brazza's diary, September 1881

Four and a half months earlier, at the end of May 1882, when Arabi was still sweeping all before him in Egypt, a small British cargo boat had steamed up the Irish Channel, rounded Holyhead, and passed through the lock gates into the British and African Steamship Company's capacious dock at Liverpool. She was the *Corisco*, one of thirty-six British ships on the regular West Coast service. Months before she had steamed off for Gabon, carrying the usual cargo of British exports – Birmingham kettles, obsolete rifles, black powder and cotton bales from Manchester. Now she steamed back with a return cargo of pungent tropical goods – barrels of palm oil, bales of gum and rubber, tusks of ivory. There was nothing about her to attract attention. Her arrival rated only a line in the shipping columns of *The Times*.

Among her passengers were two bearded French explorers and the usual crop of old Africa hands down on their luck. The elder of the two explorers spoke French with a strong Italian accent. He was tall and romantic-looking, but suffering from malaria. In fact he was only thirty, but seemed prematurely aged.

It was Brazza, hollow-cheeked and wild-eyed after two and a half years of tramping through the bush of Gabon and the northern Congo. Perhaps he told his strange story to the other passengers and they took pity on him. (Poor fellow. Not the first, nor the last either, to go round the bend in West Africa.) He claimed to be a French naval lieutenant and the leader of an official French expedition to explore the river Congo, especially the Pool which was the gateway to the navigable upper reaches of the river. He had made a treaty with an African king called Makoko, who claimed control of the Pool. So the treaty gave France the gateway to the heart of Africa, and to tens of thousands of square miles of fertile soil only waiting for peaceful exploitation. Now he was on the way back to Paris to see that France ratified the Makoko treaty. That was his story.

But Brazza's blue ensign's uniform was in rags. Neither he nor his companion had a penny to their names. After the *Corisco* docked, they went to the French

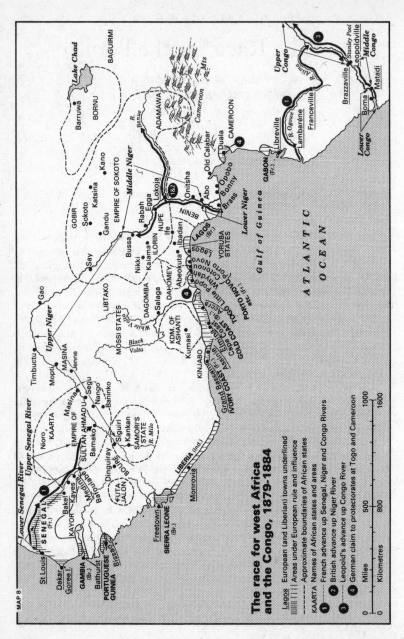

The race for west Africa and the Congo, 1879-1884

MAP 8

Lagos European (and Liberian) towns underlined

||||| Areas under European rule and influence

------ Approximate boundaries of African states

KAARTA Names of African states and areas

(1) French advance up Senegal, Niger and Congo Rivers

(2) British advance up Niger River

(3) Leopold's advance up Congo River

(4) German claim to protectorates at Togo and Cameroon

Miles   0   500   1000

Kilometres 0   800   1600

Consul to ask for assistance. 'Brazza and mechanic Michaud arrived from Gabon without any resources,' cabled the Consul to the Minister of Marine in Paris. 'Should I pay their fare?' Back came the answer, like a bucket of seawater in the face, 'Urgent you pay fare to repatriate Brazza in the cheapest possible way.'[1]

It was the treatment that Brazza had come to expect from Admiral Jean Jauréguiberry, the French Minister of Marine, despite all his efforts, in the last three years, to woo him. No one had proved keener than Jauréguiberry to promote French empire-building in West Africa and Senegal. Like many officers of the French navy, he was an ardent anglophobe, a self-made man from Bayonne, an ex-governor of Senegal and a patriot of the most bellicose kind. He was understandably suspicious of Brazza. More government money for Gabon and the Congo could mean less government money for West Africa and Senegal. And he resented Brazza's string-pulling. Who was this Italian aristocrat? He had been jumped into the French navy and pushed forward over the heads of young Frenchmen, simply because he had friends in high places, like Ferdinand de Lesseps, Jules Ferry and Admiral Montaignac, Jauréguiberry's predecessor as Minister of Marine. It was in 1875 that Montaignac had given Brazza the official backing of his ministry for the first major expedition, the one to explore the upper Ogowe in Gabon. In 1879 Jauréguiberry had done his best to wash his hands of Brazza. All he agreed was to give him leave to go exploring, to pay his passage money and to lend him sixteen Senegalese *laptots* (sailors) to accompany him on his new expedition to the Congo.

At this point Brazza's old patron, Admiral Montaignac, had once again come to the rescue. Montaignac was a keen geographer, a member of the Société Géographique de Paris, the SGP. Recently he and other members of this society had answered King Leopold's stirring call for an international crusade to open up Africa to civilization. As leaders of the SGP they were now formally constituted as the French National Committee of Leopold's International African Association (IAA). Moreover, Jules Ferry, as Minister of Public Instruction, had promised 100,000 francs (£4,000) of French government money for the private ventures of this new French committee. As a result of Montaignac's lobbying, it was agreed that Brazza's expedition should get half of this small subsidy. Brazza would set up one of the two stations for the French committee, linking the upper Ogowe in Gabon with the upper Congo. It was on the lower Congo that Stanley, commissioned by Leopold and the main IAA in Brussels, had already started work earlier that year, 1879.

One might have imagined that there would be co-operation between the two expeditions. After all, they were both trying to open up the same river and were both sponsored by the same association, the IAA. On the contrary, each of the two expeditions was kept as secret as possible from the other. The more that Brazza, Montaignac and his other backers on the French committee of the IAA learnt about Leopold and the main committee, the more they had begun to wonder. Stanley had left Europe in February 1879 under the alias of 'M. Henri'.

Then it began to emerge – perhaps blurted out by one of Leopold's French supporters like the chairman, Lesseps – that the philanthropic IAA was being replaced by a mysterious new organization called the Comité d'Études du Haut Congo (CEHC). This seemed to be a purely commercial organization designed to exploit the wealth of the Congo for its investors, a group of international businessmen, including French, Dutch and English. Still stranger, it turned out that in November 1879 all these investors were returned their money except for the investors from Belgium, believed to be acting for the King. If this were true, Stanley was no longer engaged on a great international crusade; he was founding a colony of exploitation for the King and his associates. Brazza's mind jumped to the obvious conclusion. Call it the IAA or the CEHC – what did it matter? Wasn't the whole business a sham? If the main IAA was to be a front for King Leopold and the Belgians, why should the French committee not be a front for the French?

At that time the French committee did not know what to think, their loyalties were so divided. Imagine the dilemma of the chairman, Ferdinand de Lesseps. How to serve four masters at the same time: Leopold, France, God and Mammon? Brazza felt no such division in his loyalty. He was heart and soul behind his adopted country. He made a renewed appeal to Jauréguiberry, brazenly offering to steal a march on Stanley and the Belgians. He could 'plant the French flag at Stanley Pool' (the economic key to the upper Congo because it was at the end of the cataracts and the beginning of the navigable river system) 'before the Belgians do the same'.[2] Stanley himself was laboriously hacking and blasting his way from the Congo estuary to the Pool, bypassing the series of cataracts which blocked the final 200 miles of the lower river. Brazza asked for a commission to forestall Stanley by taking a short cut to the Pool by way of Gabon and the upper Ogowe. He would then claim the territory for France. The commission could be kept secret and would only take effect if Brazza arrived first. If he did not, his expedition could be made to look like a simple piece of geographical exploration for the French committee.

Admiral Jauréguiberry turned down these reckless political ideas with ill-concealed distaste. The young lieutenant seemed to have forgotten that he was employed on a private mission. But the irrepressible Brazza had a better hearing from Léon Gambetta and Jules Ferry, soon to emerge as France's leading champion of colonial expansion. In August a vote for the credit of 100,000 francs sailed through both Chamber of Deputies and Senate without a murmur. Ferry was careful not to breathe a word about Brazza's political aims. All he told the Chamber was about the civilizing mission that the French committee of the IAA had so generously undertaken. He was politician enough to know that to mention colonial expansion in 1879 would have killed any hope of getting a single franc. It was up to Brazza to do the rest. He could still win the race for the Pool, though he would start four months behind Stanley.

By August 1880 Brazza had crossed the watershed and was approaching the upper Congo, after passing his first station on the Ogowe (later called Franceville). He had no means of knowing who was winning the race. In fact Stanley's expedition was still stuck in the lower river, struggling like a hippopotamus among the cataracts. By 15 August 1880 he had only reached a point 25 miles above Vivi, 200 miles short of his goal.

That same night Brazza saw his first sight of an unknown river, the 'Olumo'. He had tramped for days through a forest, in country so parched that his men were dying of thirst. For some reason the local chief had tried to block their path. In a pantomime of crazy laughter – and the part came naturally to Brazza, half-mad with thirst and fever – Brazza drove him out of the way with a stick. 'Fool, fool! Trying to fight the white man.'[3] After midnight they saw an immense river ahead, stretched out like a sheet in the moonlight beyond the forest. Brazza threw himself down by the river bank and drank and drank before falling asleep. The 'Olumo' was in fact the Congo, but it was several days before Brazza realized he had won the race with Stanley.

Less than a fortnight later Brazza opened the crucial negotiations with the local Teke chief living above the Pool at the head of the cataracts, King Makoko. Once Makoko's ancestors had been the overlords of the whole region, and his name was still one to conjure with because of the influence he exercised over the local chiefs. Brazza was advised by his guides to approach this great man in his best suit of clothes. So Brazza exchanged his dirty khaki for his ensign's uniform, tattered blue serge, with gold braid. The Senegalese *laptots* discarded their rags for French sailors' blue uniforms. Brazza recorded the solemn scene in his diary:

Preceded by a bugler and a French flag, I arrived at the village. . . . We stopped in front of the door of the chief's compound. . . . An iron bell hangs on a pole inside the gate. They strike it to announce someone's arrival. . . .

At last, preceded by his wives, Makoko arrives. He and his senior wife wear large copper necklaces. . . . He himself wears a big cloth robe, large bracelets on his feet and arms, a woollen hat woven in the style of a tapestry and fixed to his head with an iron pin to which two very long feathers [were] attached. . . .

Chief Makoko sits on a great carpet four metres wide, in blue and red squares on which there is a travelling rug decorated with a lion. . . . Then the men who brought me go and kneel in front of him. . . .

The medicine man [then] gets up and kneels in front of me, holding his spear and his sword . . . after that he lays his hands on mine as a mark of respect.

Then I let the chief know that I am a chief in my own country, and that when two chiefs meet, they shake hands. . . . Then I go and shake his hand, and then I sit down beside him on a bale.[4]

For the next twenty-five days Brazza's starving men were entertained in royal style by King Makoko. They gorged themselves on maize and pistachio nuts, drank themselves silly on beer made from manioc and wine from palms. The negotiations, too, went swimmingly. Makoko, like most up-country chiefs, had a strong motive for making a deal with Europeans. Little, if anything, was produced up at the Pool; trade was the basis of local wealth and local power. France could give him the key to the new trade being opened up with the coast. He arranged for Brazza to have a site for a French station at Ncuna (the future Brazzaville) on the north bank of the Pool. The ground really belonged to some minor chiefs of the Abanhos under Makoko's authority. They were pleased to welcome their new neighbour after Brazza performed one of his usual pantomime turns. Brazza jumped up, cartridges in his right hand, trade cloth in his left, and said to the chiefs, 'White men have two hands. The stronger hand is the hand of war. The other hand is the hand of trade. Which hand do the Abanhos want?' 'Trade,' they all cried. Then Brazza threw the cartridges in a hole, planted a tree on top, and said, 'May there never be war again until this tree bears a crop of cartridges.'[5]

Meanwhile, on 10 September, Makoko had solemnly put his mark to a political treaty of the highest importance. It gave Brazza everything – that is, everything required to thwart Stanley. Makoko ceded his inheritance rights as overlord to France, and placed himself under the protection of the French flag. It had cost Brazza nothing, apart from his presents to Makoko: a few trivial trade goods (two pieces of cloth, and a few beads, Stanley claimed later). Brazza pocketed the precious treaty, along with a proclamation confirming the agreement of the local chiefs – in effect the title deeds of a new French Congo, if only the French government would be persuaded to ratify the treaty – and hastily made the preparations to return to the coast. But how was he to defend this new protectorate from Stanley in the meantime? Everything depended on the Senagalese *laptots* whom Brazza left behind. He chose the most resourceful of them, a tall, cheery fellow called Malamine, a Karama, promoted him to sergeant and put him in charge of the station until he returned. 'I can't give you any money or supplies,' he told Malamine. 'You have your men, your hands and your firearms. Just play it by ear, but don't abandon your post.'[6]

Finally he gave Malamine a copy of the Makoko treaty to show any white man who asked awkward questions about French sovereignty. Makoko and his subordinate chiefs were warned that the only white men to be allowed access to the territory in future were the Falla, the French. Any friend of Brazza's would be easy to recognize: he would carry a cock's feather in his hat.

After warning Malamine, once again, not to desert his post, Brazza tramped off down-river along the rocky north bank, heading towards Boma and the coast. Soon his small party vanished beyond the spray of the first of the thirty-two cataracts of the middle Congo.

On Sunday 7 November 1880 an excited young African servant called Lutete Kuna burst into Stanley's camp at Ngoma Point below the falls at Isangila and handed him a small crumpled piece of paper. Stanley could just make out the words, 'Le Comte Savorgnan de Brazza, *Enseigne de Vaisseau*'. It was a 'Francess' [Frenchman], added Lutete. 'He kept firing at the trees with a gun that shoots many times. Now, Bula Matari, tell me why do white men shoot at trees. Is it to kill the bad spirit?'[7]

'Bula Matari' was the nickname given Stanley by the natives, and a well-earned compliment. It meant 'Breaker of Rocks', the magic worker who smashes all obstacles lying in his path.

Since his arrival at Boma fifteen months before, Stanley had suffered a series of crushing blows. In Brussels the King made the job sound like a picnic. He was to build three stations and a road from the lowest cataract to the Pool – not too difficult for a few thousand men of the right kind. As it was, Stanley had only 215 men, black and white. They included 68 dependable men from Zanzibar, and one of their leaders was Susi, Livingstone's headman. But it took months to build the first station at Vivi, below the lowest of the falls. Then the two small steamers, *Royal* and *En Avant*, had to be stripped down and man-handled on wagons up a new road towards the Pool. Sometimes the road itself had to be hacked and blasted out of the rocks at a rate of less than 100 yards a day.

All the time an endless flow of advice came from the King in Brussels, relayed via Colonel Strauch, the Secretary of the mysterious Comite d'Etudes du Haut Congo. Stanley found this the most frustrating part of the whole business. 'It is indispensable', wrote the King, 'that our stations should be model stations ... and if [they] are to represent the cause of civilization worthily, we must have first-rate people in charge of them.'[8] It was easy for the King to talk. Stanley had no man he could trust to put in charge of Vivi, and no one to leave with the road-building party while he pressed ahead to the Pool. Some of his best men died of fever. The Belgians whom Leopold sent him were seconded from the Belgian army cartographic service. They did not die, but perhaps Stanley wished they would. Their fecklessness drove him wild. Lieutenant Harou let discipline slip so far that his men burnt down their huts after an orgy of palm wine. Lieutenant Braconnier drove the wagons so recklessly that he was nearly crushed by the boiler of the *En Avant*.

Meanwhile, Leopold pestered Stanley with warnings that Brazza was going to steal a march on him unless he hurried. The King's secret agents on the French committee had sent him a copy of Brazza's letters to Jauréguiberry of early 1880, promising to forestall Stanley. Stanley's reply was characteristically blunt. He refused to be hustled: 'I am not a party in a race for Stanley Pool.' But if the King wanted him to go faster, he must send more men and supplies. 'Double our power ... and we will double our speed; treble the working power, and our progress will be three times quicker. With sufficient men we could be at Stanley Pool within one month.'[9]

By 7 November, the day when Brazza reached Stanley's camp, Stanley had only completed one station, Vivi, and built about forty miles of roadway. Ahead were still bigger obstacles, a great triangle of rocks in the canyon below the Isangila Falls, and Ngoma mountain, 1,500 feet high, a wall of quartz and sandstone sweeping down sheer to the river.

Brazza was utterly exhausted when he arrived, but wary. He told Stanley he had set up a small guard post at Ncuna (the Pool), manned by three negroes, including Sergeant Malamine. He said nothing about the Makoko treaty in his pocket. He needled his host with a forecast that it would take Stanley six months to pass Ngoma mountain with his wagons. Stanley kept his temper. Perhaps he was reassured. He had never understood why the King had made such a fuss about Brazza. It was only a couple of years since he had first heard the fellow's name.

And how these excitable Latins did exaggerate difficulties. Six months to pass Ngoma mountain? It took Stanley only a month to hack his way through, scooping out thousands of tons of rock with dynamite. The second station, built at Isangila, was completed by February 1881. Despite further deaths from fever, morale rose. The smaller steamer, the *Royal*, was reassembled and ferried the sections of the *En Avant* and other supplies over the next ninety miles, which proved to be navigable.

In late February, four months after Brazza had passed down-river, Stanley made an unpleasant discovery. Two English Baptist missionaries, Crudington and Bentley, had boldly pushed ahead from their base in Angola along the north bank of the river, hoping to set up a mission post at the Pool. They reported to Stanley that they had been welcomed there by one of the chiefs at Ntamo on the south bank, a man called Ngaliema, whom Stanley had made a blood brother when he discovered the Pool in 1877. But the other chiefs threatened them with guns. Apparently Malamine had warned them not to help these white men who wore no cock's feathers. Bentley and Crudington were forced to beat a retreat.

Then in May Stanley was knocked flat by a bout of malaria that everyone, including Stanley, thought would kill him. He gathered his men round his bed to say goodbye. 'Tell the King', he murmured, 'that my strength has played me false, and that I am sorry not to have been able to carry out to a finish the mission he entrusted to me.'[10] But he recovered. The third station, Manyanga, was finished and the final assault began. Like Brazza, Stanley recognized that the key to the Congo was the Pool, that great lake which formed the gateway to 5,000 miles of navigable waterway. Who controlled the Pool? Leaving the road-builders and the wagon caravan about fifty miles behind, Stanley set out first to negotiate with the chiefs of the north bank. At the post at Ncuna (the future Brazzaville) he found a tricolour flying over the French station, just as Brazza had told him.

At first all went well. Malamine proved to be a tall, bronzed Senegalese about thirty years old. With his delicate features and slender build, he appeared part Berber, part Arab. He was politeness itself. Flanked by two other Senegalese sailors, he showed Stanley the Makoko treaty and invited him to their 'station'. Stanley was impressed, though not by the station, which was just a wretched hut, or by any French amenities. Malamine's sergeant's uniform was only worn on special occasions; normally he dressed in scanty African rags, with his hair plaited, Teke-style, like the ribs of a melon. What struck Stanley was Malamine's intelligence, air of command and refinement, as though he were a real Frenchman. Malamine said, according to a French missionary, 'in all seriousness that, being the only white man there, he was glad to see others arrive to keep him company'.[11] Stanley could see that Brazza had trained him well to act 'tactfully and subtly on his master's instructions'.[12]

It took a few days before it was clear that these instructions were to run Stanley out of Stanley Pool. While reassuring Stanley that he would do everything to accommodate him, Malamine spread the word that the white man was to be refused all supplies. Suddenly all markets were closed against Stanley and his men. The local chiefs gave them the same warning as had been given to the English Baptist missionaries the year before: leave here or starve here. Meekly, he withdrew to Ntamo on the south bank, where it turned out that there was one chief rich enough and powerful enough to resist the spell of Malamine.

He was Ngaliema, created Stanley's blood brother in 1877. When the two met again on 2 August 1881 Ngaliema's eyes sparkled and his mouth watered. He was a rich Teke ivory broker, a man who in the space of a few years had created a slave army of 150 muskets, and a store of ivory and other trade goods worth £3,000. He dressed like a dandy, in silks of yellow, blue and crimson. He did not need to be told he had Stanley, politically speaking, over a barrel. The gifts he claimed were a king's ransom: a black Newfoundland dog called Flora, two donkeys, a large mirror, a gold embroidered coat, jewellery, glass clasps, long brass chains, a figured tablecloth, fifteen more lengths of cloth and a japanned tin box with a Chubb lock.

Four years earlier, when he was battering his way down-river, Stanley would never have dreamt of conceding to such outrageous demands. More likely he would have given the Chief what Stanley cheerfully called 'a bellyful of lead'. But empire-building demanded more subtle methods than exploration. This time a peaceful conquest was imperative, so Stanley meekly handed over the presents – and more beside. But nothing would assuage Ngaliema's appetite for fine silks and velvets. Stanley soon realized that he was himself too poor in trade goods to buy a concession from such a rich and ambitious chief. There was nothing for it but to send one of his officers, a Belgian called Valke, all the way back to Loanda to buy £500 worth of silks and velvets. Meanwhile, eleven of the Zanzibaris, led by Susi – Livingstone's Susi – would stay with Ngaliema at Ntamo to keep him happy. Stanley himself returned to bring up the road-building party, slowly blasting their way forward to the Pool, dragging a long line of wagons after them, including those with the precious sections of the paddle steamer, En Avant.

By November 1881, when the road was nearly complete and the whole caravan was already in sight of the Pool, Susi and the other ten Zanzibaris re-appeared in Stanley's camp, driving two donkeys. Ngaliema had expelled them, returned all the presents and joined the general boycott. The Pool was closed to them after all. It turned out that the boycott had been engineered by Malamine, playing on the fears of the local Kongo traders, who were naturally alarmed at the prospect of losing their lucrative monopoly for carrying ivory to the coast.

Stanley responded with a practical joke worthy of Brazza. When Ngaliema was reported to be on the warpath with 200 men in full warpaint, Stanley told his own men to hide in various huts and wagons, and to remain there till summoned by gong.

Ngaliema found the camp almost deserted. Stanley was reading a book without concern. Ngaliema asked to see the latest presents and passed his hand lovingly over red baize, bright handkerchiefs, tin boxes and iron trunks. Then he saw Stanley's Chinese gong.

'What is this?'

'It is a fetish,' said Stanley solemnly.

'Bula Matari, strike this; let me hear this.'

'Oh, Ngalyema, I dare not strike it; it is the war fetish.'

'No, no. Beat it, Bula Matari, that I may hear the sound.'

'I dare not, Ngalyema. It is the signal for war. It is the fetish that calls up armed men; it would be too bad.'

'No, no, no! I tell you to strike it. Strike it, Bula Matari.' He stamped on the ground with childish impatience.

With all his force, Stanley struck the gong a series of resounding blows. Then out of the earth and down from the sky – so it seemed to Ngaliema's terrified braves – came a stream of demon warriors. Ngaliema's men threw down their muskets and ran back to their village screaming in terror. Ngaliema was left clinging to Stanley's waist, while the Zanzibaris lunged at him waving their rifles and screaming.

'Save me, Bula Matari; do not let them hurt me. I did not mean anything.'

'Hold hard, Ngalyema,' [Stanley cried,] 'keep fast hold of me, I will defend you, never fear.'[13]

The pantomime ended with friendship fully restored and the story of Ngaliema's humiliation spread Stanley's name for miles across the south bank of the Pool. Within a few months the fourth and biggest station was rising there: wooden huts, villas, storehouses, gardens and a harbour. It was to be the capital of the new colony, Leopoldville. Meanwhile Ngaliema remained an erratic ally, but the other chiefs welcomed the prospect of trading directly with white men. The *En Avant* was sent speeding up-river and reported ivory in abundance. Best of all, by the summer of 1882 the natives reported that Sergeant Malamine, recalled to Gabon, had given up his lonely vigil on the north bank. Patience seemed to have won the game for Stanley. Despite all Leopold's nagging, he had scooped the Pool.

It was the recall of Malamine that still haunted Brazza when he reached Liverpool on board the *Corisco* at the end of May 1882. It was the culmination of a series of setbacks. His own scheme to put steamboats on the upper Ogowe had collapsed because the boats proved defective. His friend, Lieutenant Ballay, had to return to Europe for replacements. The other officer who had joined him was Lieutenant Mizon, chosen by the French Committee as his successor. The two men fell out. In April 1882, when the funds were exhausted, Mizon ordered

Malamine to return, an order Malamine had disobeyed as long as he could.

The previous year, in April 1881, Brazza had written a *cri de coeur* to the French Committee. He had sacrificed himself to carry out the plans agreed to with them, but they had failed to use their influence to support him with the French government. He reiterated all his achievements: he had discovered a treasure house of ivory and rubber, a country of unbelievable wealth ripe for exploitation; he had hoisted the French flag at two new stations, at Franceville in Upper Gabon and at Ncuna on the Congo; he had broken the monopoly of the local traders and opened the upper Ogowe to French trade; he had pacified the warlike natives and erased the unhappy memories left by the belligerent Stanley; his flag of peace was 'planted where Stanley had fought'. He was half-dead from dysentery and terrible leg ulcers, but he refused to accept defeat. 'I will go on as long as my strength supports me. If I fall, it will be never to rise again.'[14]

Now, on 2 June 1882, Brazza was repatriated to Paris like a down-and-out. One can understand his sense of betrayal. Then, that afternoon at the Gare du Nord, he realized that his *cri de coeur* had been answered after all.

A delegation from the SGP – the same men who were the leaders of the French Committee – were waiting to greet him with flags and bunting. Montaignac, his patron, was there. So was Lesseps, who made a speech on the platform. The young explorer was the hero of the hour. He had upheld France's honour in a distant land. He was then rushed to a public meeting of the SGP already in progress. The members rose to salute him as though he were David Livingstone back from the grave.

What had turned the SGP and the French Committee so decisively in his favour? The *cri de coeur* of April 1881, and subsequent letters, had certainly struck a receptive chord. In fact this was the year when one section of French public opinion had begun to warm to the idea of empire-building. The success of the colonial lobby had also provoked a reaction. Ferry's government had collapsed in November 1881, deflated by the military débâcle in southern Tunisia. Gambetta had plumped for a forward policy in Egypt, only to lose the vote on electoral reform in January 1882. Freycinet was already shrinking from the thought of intervention against Arabi. The trouble with ambitious forward policies in the Mediterranean was that they were always fraught with inter-national complications. And the *revanchistes* could claim that such adventures would weaken the capacity of the French home army for dealing with Germany in the final struggle to recover the lost provinces. The beauty of hoisting the tricolour in Central Africa was that it would be cheap and easy and threatened no important vested interests. In fact it risked almost nothing – except the lives of heroes like Brazza.

This was the argument already planted among journalists and politicians by the SGP and the French Committee. Hence the ground was prepared for a campaign to persuade the government to ratify the Makoko treaty. Back in the salons of Paris, Brazza could now pursue the campaign in person with the theatrical gifts he had shown among the savages of the Congo. His romantic mixture of bad French and good looks, heightened by his sufferings, made him perfect for the part. He pressed the case for ratification with the three usual justifications of empire-builders: humanitarian, economic, and political. All three gave him the opportunity to have a kick at Stanley.

First Brazza exulted in the peaceful nature of his mission. He had come, like Livingstone, to redeem Central Africa, to save it from slavery by introducing legitimate trade. Everywhere the natives grasped at the tricolour. Here was their chance to find the French equivalent to Livingstone's '3 cs': French Catholicism, French civilization and French commerce (not free trade, of course, but trade only with France). By contrast Brazza blackened Stanley's character as that of an irredeemable man of violence. Stanley boasted that during his journey of 1876–7 he had hurled himself down the Congo like a hurricane, shooting down terrified natives left and right. No wonder they had turned against him on his second journey to the Pool.

Brazza applied his rhetoric to economic arguments. What treasures were going begging in the Congo. 'Without a blow', France could acquire an immense territory full of resources crying out for exploitation. The natives were born traders: friendly, industrious, intelligent. The place was a cornucopia, a feast of tropical riches: palm nuts, ivory, rubber, maize, copper and lead. To open up this commercial paradise, he had discovered a short cut to link the Congo with Gabon. (On his way back from the Congo he had found that the Kwilu-Niari route in Gabon, though hardly a short cut, was less arduous than the way by the upper Ogowe.) By contrast, poor Stanley had wasted millions of francs belonging to Leopold's mysterious International Association trying to build a route through the impossible terrain of the lower Congo.

The third theme, the political one, was naturally the most provocative, and here Brazza had little need to exaggerate. In August 1882 he sent a full report to his old enemy in the Ministry of Marine, Admiral Jauréguiberry. He had made a treaty with Makoko on the north bank of the Pool, a king 'whose power was still great, and whose influence, of a religious character',[15] stretched further still. But on the other side of the Pool the flag of the IAA flew over Leopoldville, Stanley's fourth station. Unless the French government acted swiftly to ratify the treaty, France would lose all access to the wealth of the Congo. Leopold claimed that his work in Africa was international and philanthropic, but already his agents had signed treaties with natives on the lower Congo at Vivi that gave him exclusive commercial rights to exploit the produce of that area. Soon the King's agents would be establishing a monopoly over the whole Pool. (This was true enough. The threat from Leopold was serious.)

Brazza ended his appeal to Admiral Jauréguiberry with a dig at the British designed to appeal to the well-known anglophobia of the Ministry of Marine. The Portuguese claim to the Congo was ridiculous, but the British were now staking a claim through the agency of the Baptist missionaries in the area. At present Britain had no real commercial interests to defend, Brazza claimed – a surprising statement in view of the British factories on the lower Congo. But all this would change once the wealth of the Congo was recognized. If the French government was to ratify the Makoko treaty, it was now or never.

Back came an astonishing reply from Admiral Jauréguiberry. At least he did not reject these arguments and he conceded that to ratify the treaty might bring 'favourable results'.[16] But to found a colony in the Congo would impose an extra financial burden on the Ministry of Marine whose resources were already stretched tight by the expansion in Senegal and the upper Niger. This was not a matter for his department; it must go to the political director at the Quai d'Orsay. Predictably, Courcel proved still more in favour. He noted that the response by the French press to Brazza's campaign was enthusiastic. Stanley's efforts and Britain's pretensions to snatch this prize from France were a sure sign of its potential. He recommended that the issue be put before the Cabinet.

Meanwhile, a honeyed invitation from the palace in Brussels had reached Brazza. It must have provoked a wry smile. Months earlier, back in Gabon, at the time of Malamine's recall, he had had a letter from a well-wisher in Brussels. Leopold, he learnt, was gloating over his discomfiture. 'M. de Brazza will have to look sharp,' the King was quoted as saying. 'He'll never get his treaty ratified. They are playing with the Congo like a toy. M. de Brazza would better employ his time if he came and joined us.'[17]

Brazza agreed to go to Brussels. But what could the King have to offer, now that everything seemed to be going Brazza's way?

Leopold had been studying the moves of his rivals with his usual assiduity. On 30 May 1882, the day the *Corisco* was reported in the shipping columns of *The Times* to have docked in Liverpool, the King suggested that he would invite Brazza to Brussels. No doubt Lesseps, or one of his other supporters on the French Committee, had tipped him off. Why then the three months' delay in bringing him to Brussels? Probably the plan was to let Brazza enjoy his triumph for a bit. It would soon prove hollow. Like Stanley, on his return to England in 1878, Brazza would realize that he was crying for the moon if he expected his countrymen to let him found a colony in the Congo.

That year, 1882, the news from the Congo seemed better to Leopold with each month that passed. The *En Avant* was afloat on the upper Congo and the endless wrangling with Stanley was over. It was high time. For three years the King had been putting his private fortune – perhaps 3 million francs (£120,000) of it had been swallowed up already – into a venture that his own staff still thought laughable. What had he to show for his money? The terrible 200 miles of wagon road were finished at last, and so were the four first stations: the port for ocean-going ships at Vivi, the port for steamers at Stanley Pool, and the two intermediate stations on the middle Congo. In April Stanley wrote to say that he was off at last on the *En Avant* to start the real work of carving out a great trading empire on the upper Congo. It was here, on the 5,000 miles of navigable rivers, that the profits would be made. In April, the first two tusks of ivory had been bartered for silk and brass rods at the Pool. Stanley had forecast a net return of £28 a pair: nearly a 50 per cent profit after paying the exorbitant cost of porterage from the Pool down the middle Congo. In due course they would build a railway here, then the profits up-river should rise dramatically. The cost of buying ivory would fall, the deeper they drove into elephant country. Already Stanley promised he could make the Congo pay if only he was given enough porters, silk bales and brass rods to buy the ivory.

On the political front, Stanley's news was equally heartening. In May he reported Malamine's recall and the collapse of the French threat at the Pool. He had signed a treaty with a chief called Gobila, giving Leopold's CEHC exclusive rights from the Pool for 100 miles along the south bank of the river, eastwards as far as the river Kwango. This treaty was made in the nick of time, as the French marine sent to recall Malamine had tried to interfere. He was rebuffed by Gobila. 'No, I have made brotherhood with Bula Matari. I have given him all I have.'[18]

Stanley was now steaming further up-river, with clear instructions to pre-empt Brazza by signing exclusive treaties with every chief along the banks the whole 1,000 miles to Stanley Falls. He expected to be up-river till December, provided his health could stand it.

But later that summer a strange mood seemed to come over the French public. Leopold gradually realized that Brazza was still more of a threat in Paris than he had been at the Pool. His name was on every lip, the gentle Latin explorer, loved by the natives, the man who had humbled that Anglo-Saxon brute, Henry Stanley. Leopold decided to try to neutralize his rival by buying him for his own side.

What was his price? 'We will do well,' he told Colonel Strauch in early September, a couple of days before Brazza was due at the palace, 'to consult Brazza on the best way to invite French capital to participate in our work and take whatever part in it they would like. This will be the way of leading up to an invitation to Brazza to become interested in our enterprises and direct some of them.'[19]

It would have been difficult to have chosen a worse bait to ensnare the ardent young patriot. Brazza was welcomed at the palace on 12 September, but the gilded furniture, the red carpets and royal flattery left him unmoved. Leopold could do nothing with him. The talk of the fat profits to be made out of the Congo only confirmed Brazza's conviction that the international crusade of the IAA was a gigantic sham. Later Brazza wrote sarcastically:

> Without a doubt the King was completely disinterested. He gave his millions solely with the aim of civilizing the savage tribes. However I believe there was a political idea beneath the humanitarian sentiments of the King of the Belgians. I was far from blaming him for this, but it did not stop me having my own political ideas as well. And mine were very simple. If there was advantage to be gained from the Congo, I would prefer that it was the French flag, not the Belgian 'international flag', that floated over this splendid African territory.[20]

After Brazza had departed, Leopold made a desperate appeal to his old French ally, Lesseps. He felt betrayed by the French Committee of the IAA (though, contrary to later claims, he had never contributed a sou to their funds). He begged Lesseps to realize that ratifying the Makoko treaty would lead to a general scramble for territory, each country trying to impose a monopoly on 'the traffic that is now open to all'. To introduce European quarrels into Africa would be the ruin of everyone's efforts. He would very much like to offer a helping hand to young M. de Brazza, whose work, *comme explorateur*, he so admired. But there would be one condition: Brazza must confine himself to work for 'commerce, civilization and progress'.[21]

On whose side was Ferdinand de Lesseps? It was several weeks before Leopold received the bleak reply that the French Committee was handing over its stations to France, as the French Cabinet was now expected to recommend the Makoko treaty for ratification. What Lesseps did not reveal was that he and his committee had lobbied furiously for ratification.

Already, by the first week of October 1882, anxiety in the royal palace in Brussels was turning to panic. 'I am also certain that the Paris Cabinet will, in the end, ratify ... Brazza has very cleverly taken hold of the national fibre, all the press is for him.' When the two men had met face to face, Leopold must have finally realized he had met his match. The young explorer's appetites extended far beyond the frontiers of the northern Congo. Brazza's dream, Leopold wrote that week, 'is not only to see the treaty ratified, but after that to take the whole Congo basin for France.'[22] For a moment Leopold lost his head. He asked Henry Solvyns, Belgian Ambassador in London, to approach the British Foreign Office and try to induce Gladstone to send a warship to the Congo estuary to frighten off the French. 'A very small ship could suffice to foil Brazza's plans.'[23]

Naturally Solvyns rejected this idiotic idea as politely as he could. If he had acted on it, he confessed to Baron Lambermont, 'I would have deserved to be recalled immediately.' His own advice was simple enough, though he was probably too sensible to waste it on the King. Throw in the sponge. Brazza had won the game. To continue with Stanley as agent and Brazza as adversary would be 'pure foolishness'.[24] He should not try to compete with Brazza. But if he insisted, he should set up a trading company in the Congo under the French flag.

The *French* flag, Leopold would have retorted, the flag of the country which did not even pretend to accept free trade and shunned international competition like the plague? He gathered his wits. What about a personal appeal to the head of the French government? By October the Egyptian crisis had precipitated the fall of Freycinet's government. His successor was Duclerc, known to be anxious to avoid foreign complications of any kind. Leopold sent his closest financial associate, Léon Lambert, the Belgian banker, to try to talk sense into Duclerc. The Congo must be kept open to all trading nations or it would let loose an ugly scramble for territory. Duclerc was a keen businessman, a director of a French company struggling with the British for supremacy in Nigeria. Surely he would want to avoid a similar imbroglio over the Congo. But Lambert came back from Paris empty-handed.

It was at this point, beset on every side, that Leopold heard of a new and completely unexpected source of danger. Stanley, weakened after another attack of malaria, had suddenly abandoned the Congo to recuperate in Europe. He could hardly have chosen a more fatal moment. 'What can be done to make Stanley keep quiet?' asked Leopold wretchedly. Perhaps this terrible illness was only a 'pretext'. 'Is he not coming back to Europe to frustrate M. de Brazza's efforts for the annexation of the Congo to France?'[25] But there was no stopping Bula Matari, the Breaker of the Rocks, the bull in the china shop, from breaking crockery in Paris.

And break it he did. Aghast, the King read in the French newspapers of the appalling scene in Paris on 19 October 1882 when Stanley had battled with Brazza for the Congo like a prize-fighter, smashing the gentlemanly façade of the IAA that Leopold had laboured so long to create.

The fight formed a fitting climax to Brazza's theatrical campaign to persuade his adopted country to accept the Congo. It was a stroke of luck that he exploited with his usual flair, but he had another of still greater importance, in the week preceding.

On 14 September the Paris newspapers reported Wolseley's shocking defeat of Colonel Arabi at Tel el-Kebir on the previous day. It was shocking because it confirmed what the French professional class had only dimly foreseen: they, too, had suffered a humiliating defeat in Egypt. Gladstone had proposed to Freycinet that together they attack Arabi. Freycinet had dithered, then suggested a passive kind of intervention, simply to defend the Canal. Even that chicken-hearted proposal had been too much for the nerves of the Chamber of Deputies, so Freycinet lost the vote for the necessary funds and was replaced by Duclerc, who was anxious to please everyone. But now the French public felt increasingly bitter and humiliated. Ever since Ismael's bankruptcy in 1876, Egypt had been a veiled protectorate, half-French, half-English, administered by dual control. Now, as the smoke of Tel el-Kebir evaporated, it began to look as if dual control had been blown to smithereens. The British were in possession and could henceforth control Egypt unaided.

France had been beaten: by October that was the unanimous verdict of the French press. Worse, she had made a fool of herself. So there was a new psychological motive for expansion overseas. It was there that France would redeem herself – and at a paltry financial cost. Otherwise she would sink to the level of a third-rate power like Italy. It was this new spur to wounded pride that pricked Brazza's campaign that autumn into a gallop. Stanley, though working for Leopold, was the stereotype of the overbearing Ango-Saxon; Brazza, despite his halting French, served as the symbol of all that was most chivalrous in France.

The collision between the two men took place in the Continental Hotel on 19 October. Stanley was the guest of the Paris branch of the Stanley Club (his French fan club). There is a story that the two men had met accidentally on the boulevards that morning. 'Brazza, I'm going to kill you tonight,'[26] said Stanley.

Brazza decided there and then to attend, and spent the afternoon drinking black coffee and chain-smoking cigarettes while he learnt by heart a speech someone had translated for him into English.

In his own speech, so violent and clumsy that people thought he was drunk, Stanley only showed how deeply Brazza's press campaign had got under his skin. He ridiculed this 'Italian gentleman's pretensions' as an explorer.

> When I met M. de Brazza, in 1880, on the Congo, about forty miles from our lower station, I had not the least idea that I was about to entertain one who would shortly exercise so much power over us. A shoeless, poorly dressed person, remarkable only for a faded uniform, frock coat and a high topee, was not as yourselves might imagine an imposing figure or one likely to inspire a thought that he was some illustrious person in disguise.

All this 'shoeless' explorer had achieved was to explore 160 miles of new ground between Gabon and the Congo.

Then Stanley mocked Brazza's claims as a humanitarian, a new Livingstone. The French press called him an 'apostle of liberty' who had dealt 'a death blow to slavery in West Africa'. Negroes were said to have come running in great numbers asking him for freedom and welcoming him as the great liberator. 'You will admit that this is most astounding news, and I have been blaming myself greatly ever since that I was so blind as not to perceive in the strange guest I entertained in my tent the sublime virtues described.'

In fact, Stanley snarled, Brazza was not only a charlatan but a liar and a cheat into the bargain – as well as a traitor to his own employers, the IAA. He had tried to swindle Makoko out of his territory in exchange for a French flag, two pieces of cloth and a few beads. Was it conceivable that Makoko had really sold his territory for this price? Of course he had given Brazza no political rights at all; merely a commercial agreement for the north bank, similar to his own agreement on the south bank, to build a station at the Pool. How could Brazza claim this area for France and hand out tricolours to the natives like sweets to children? His actual employers were the French Committee of the International African Association. Half his funds came from Belgium, owing to the extraordinary generosity of the King of the Belgians. He had no moral right to hand over his stations to France. His claim to be a French patriot was a sham, like everything else about him. 'The French flag was evidently used as a cloak to cover a scandalous disregard of moral obligations.'[27] In short, this impudent young Italian was only out to make mischief – or to make money for himself out of the unfortunate natives of the Congo.

By contrast, Stanley showed no false modesty about his own achievements in this international crusade. He ended with a bombastic peroration: a curse on Brazza's head for threatening to ruin the great work.

> As yet the Congo basin is a blank, a fruitless waste, a desolate and unproductive area. ... It has been our purpose to fill this blank with life, to redeem this waste, to plant and sow that the dark man may gather, to vivify the wide,

wild lands so long forgotten by Europe. But cursed be he or they who, animated by causeless jealousy and a spirit of mischief, will compel us to fire our station, destroy our work so conspicuously begun, and abandon Africa to its pristine helplessness and savagery.

It was at this moment, that Brazza, with his usual sense of theatre, pushed his way into the room and asked to be allowed to speak. His good humour was like a rapier against a knuckleduster, a boyish charm against Stanley's clumsy diatribe.

First Brazza delivered the prepared speech in English he had learnt by heart. He had heard that Stanley was to be honoured, and he wished people to know that he regarded Stanley not as an antagonist, but as a fellow labourer in the field. They represented different interests, but their common efforts converged to work for the same end, progress in Africa. He raised his glass. 'Gentlemen, I am a Frenchman and an officer of the Marine. I drink to the civilization of Africa by the simultaneous efforts of all nations, *each under its own flag*.'[28] There was loud applause; then the cheers turned to gasps when Brazza went up to Stanley and said he had heard that he had been attacked that evening. All he wished to offer in reply was this: he reached forward and histrionically shook Stanley's hand.

Next day Brazza's supporters must have been in ecstasy. The Paris newspapers denounced Stanley with still more venom than before. He had called their hero a '*va nu-pieds*', a barefoot tramp. He had mocked the French flag and Brazza, the illustrious patriot, had turned the other cheek.

The passing of the bill to ratify the Makoko treaty became a foregone conclusion.

This was the crisis facing Leopold as he looked aghast at the French newspapers on 20 October. He was helpless to stop France snatching the northern part of the Congo from under his nose. Unless he acted swiftly, the tricolour would soon be flying over the whole Congo basin, with his own steamers barred from the river. Suddenly a dazzling new idea entered his head. The way to fight the tricolour was with a flag of his own. His interests could no longer be protected by those happy fictions, the International African Association or the Comité d'Études du Haut Congo. The Congo must become a real colony, a fully-fledged state.

But wasn't this – as Brazza assumed – part of Leopold's grand design from the very beginning? *Il faut à la Belgique une colonie* were the burning words he had had engraved on that marble chip of the Parthenon presented, as a coal of fire, to Frère-Orban, the Belgian Finance Minister nearly twenty years before. The King's grand design had matured since then, yet it was still essentially simple: not a political idea but one for making money. Leopold planned to reap a vast fortune out of a trading monopoly in what was politically a blank on the map, an African no-man's-land. He had not seen any need to go to all the trouble and expense of filling that blank.

His dazzling new idea was only for the ears of the handful of intimates – men like Solvyns and Strauch and Jules Devaux – who could hardly conceal their scepticism. There was no need for poor blundering Stanley to know. He still believed he was employed by that happy fiction, the Comité d'Études, which had in fact been defunct for more than a year. Leopold decided to create a new front called the International Association of the Congo. It would be in this diplomatic dress that he would found the Congo Free State.

Leopold never forgot that he was Coburg. It was more his style to wear a crown as head of state, than a top hat in a City boardroom. Under the new plan the fronts would be discarded and reveal him as absolute ruler of a sovereign state, *le roi souverain* whose selfless aim was to bring civilization to Africa. He would thus not only shake off the French challenge, but would liberate himself from the taint of money bags and the odium of a commercial monopoly. His volte-face had a touch of genius. The Free State would encourage business but not do business itself. This bait for private investors – free trade, on paper at least – would be a trump card to win the British and damn the French.

But how to complete the volte-face without anyone noticing? The previous year Stanley had been told to sign up all the chiefs from Vivi to Stanley Falls in order to pre-empt the French. Treaties had now been signed at Isangila (8 May), Manyanga (13 August), Ngombi (24 September), Leopoldville (12 October), and so on. But although Leopold had talked vaguely of the Comité's 'suzerainty' these treaties had been designed to confer only exclusive commercial rights. New treaties would have to be drafted by Stanley, conferring exclusive *political* rights, while all the damning traces of the commercial monopolies would have to be expunged.

The King was now ready to receive Stanley and tell him the little he needed to know. Stanley arrived at the royal palace in late October, still smarting after his humiliation in Paris and sick and tired of the Congo. To his astonishment, Strauch warned him that he would be held to his original five-year contract, which still had two years to run. Impossible, said Stanley. His doctors had warned him that to stay longer in that climate would be suicide. In fact he had determined to throw in his hand.

The King's first words were, 'Surely, Mr Stanley, you cannot think of leaving me now, just when I most need you.'[29] Those were his only words of reproach. He said nothing about the appalling indiscretions at the Continental Hotel. Leopold was at his silkiest, soothing and calming the explorer. He was kingly, paternal, intimate, inspiring Stanley's devotion by speaking to him as a friend. Stanley wavered and was lost. How could he let his benefactor down? The King was nobly prepared to subsidize from his own fortune, to the tune of £60,000 a year, the dream of Stanley's life, to civilize the whole heart of Africa.

The two men worked together like brothers. There would be more Zanzibaris, more silk and velvet trade goods, more of everything that Stanley required to buy ivory. He would return to Africa immediately and steal a march on Brazza. He would found new stations on the upper Congo. Everywhere he would sign new treaties with the chiefs (for which the text would be supplied from Brussels).

And, of course, he would display great tact towards his rivals. Remember, the King said, that 'the French government shows very friendly feelings towards our Association'.[30]

Friendly or not, Stanley was told to keep his plans secret from the French when he returned to Africa. He travelled under a new alias and on 14 December, before it was known he had even left Europe, he was back at the mouth of the Congo, four months ahead of Brazza.

In Paris, on 18 November, Duclerc was happy to submit the Makoko treaty to the Chamber of Deputies for ratification. It passed without dissent. Duclerc's government rose in public estimation. Brazza was the most famous Frenchman of his generation. He had outflanked all his enemies, including Jauréguiberry and the Ministry of Marine. Paris took him especially to its heart. When Léon Gambetta died of blood poisoning in December after accidentally wounding himself while cleaning his revolver, it was Brazza who was chosen to accompany the cortège of the national hero.

In April 1883 he was back in Gabon with the government's commission to extend French sovereignty far and wide in the Congo. He had been voted 1,275,000 francs by Parliament, ten times as much as he had had on his previous journey. Now he rivalled Stanley in means as well as in ambition. He had a staff of 88 white men, 291 Senegalese *laptots*, 400–500 boatmen and 350 tons of goods to supply his needs. No one could now call him a *va nu-pieds*, a barefoot tramp in a battered old topee. Still only thirty-one, he had the rank of colonial governor.

Stanley had found the Congo. Leopold had backed him. Brazza had raced Stanley. The rivalry caught the imagination of the French public, still reeling after the fiasco in Egypt. In this strange sequence, fraught with accidents, later historians would discern the start of the Scramble.

But at the time no one in Europe could have guessed that a race for a whole continent had begun. In Gladstone's England the forward policy was thought to have failed in southern Africa and was still officially out of fashion, despite the temporary occupation of Egypt. In Bismarck's Germany the stirrings of the colonial movement passed unnoticed. Only in France had patriotism touched hands with colonialism, and even there, the movement was somewhat frivolous. Could anyone find the Congo on the map?

To Admiral Jauréguiberry, grinding his teeth at the Ministry of Marine as he had to prepared those 350 tons of stores for that young puppy, M. de Brazza, the Congo was an irrelevance, an absurdity. Jauréguiberry was passionate that France should become a great African power. But the priority was for the mastery of the western Sudan. It was there, in the barren lands 2,000 miles north-west of the Congo, that the advance of the French army had already begun, despite frequent discouragements from the French public and their representatives.

Still, if the public was now serious, it was in this direction that they should now look. It was here he believed that the real El Dorado lay, along 1,500 miles of the river Niger, soon to be conquered either by France or her traditional enemy, Britain.

CHAPTER 10

Head in the Clouds

The Upper Niger and France
1 February–July 1883

'With plenty of prudence combined with plenty of
audacity, I am convinced that we can achieve the
complete destruction of the detestable [Tukolor]
empire.... Any other policy in my opinion, would
be feeble and inept; it could only serve British
interests.'

Col. Borgnis-Desbordes to the French authorities,
9 April 1881

While Brazza was still drinking champagne in Paris, a battle-hardened
French column, a chiaroscuro of white officers on horseback, white
soldiers on mules, black Spahis on horseback, and bare-footed black *tirailleurs*,
was plodding eastwards along the caravan track over the bleached, rocky
uplands beyond the upper Senegal river, 2,000 miles from the Congo.

It was the third season they had been plodding along this desolate track to
reach the great river beyond the watershed, the Niger itself. They marched in a
grey-brown cloud of dust and sand, driven straight into their eyes by the
hamattan, the harsh, dry, east wind that blows from the Sahara for most of the
dry season from December to April. After crossing a final ridge on 1 February
1883 they found their reward at last at Bamako: the Niger, no mirage, but a
shining ribbon of water. Some hundreds of miles from its source, it was already
half a mile wide, a great brown python of a river, coiling and squirming as it
descended from the wooded hills to the burning plain.

The leader of the column wore the blue uniform, leather gaiters, white
breeches and white tropical helmet of a lieutenant-colonel in the French colonial
artillery, the Artillerie de Marine. He was Lieutenant-Colonel Gustave Borgnis-
Desbordes, a tough customer (so everyone, black and white, agreed), a man
known for his silences. When he did speak, you did not quickly forget. Out of
that cold, impassive face came a glance as sharp as a sabre, followed by a short,
clanging word of command. But on 7 February, a week after they had first
pitched their camp at Bamako, Desbordes decided for once to indulge himself:
he would make a speech. His friend, Captain Louis Archinard, would fire an
eleven-gun salute. They would hoist the tricolour for the first time and lay the
first stone of the first French fort on the upper Niger, the foundation stone of
a vast new French empire in the western Sudan. After their three-year struggle
against enemies at home and abroad, it was time for a celebration.

Desbordes drew up the column outside the village of Bamako, a collection of perhaps a hundred mud huts, built far enough from the river-bank to be safe from the annual flood. The natives, two or three hundred half-naked Bambaras, came out to stare in amazement. The column might have been on parade back in Saint-Louis in Senegal: two companies of white colonial infantry, black Spahis mounted on chargers, wearing red cloaks and turbans and carrying sabres, black *tirailleurs* in baggy trousers with their new Gras rifles at the ready, muleteers and donkey-men in the blue and white cloaks they kept for special occasions. Captain Archinard loaded the field-guns with blanks, and an elegant French tricolour, presented by a Parisienne admirer to one of the French officers, was attached to the halyard of the flagpole. Then Desbordes spoke:

When I took the upper Senegal command, in November, I addressed you with something like these words: 'We're not in the Sudan to talk, but to act. We've got to go to the Niger, and we shall go there.' Well, we're *there*.

He began to explain their civilizing mission:

You all know in what state we began our occupation of the Sudan. In 1880 we lacked everything, except the driving force and dedication of the Governor [of Senegal], Brière de L'Isle. I can say that we were troubled with ominous warnings from every side....[1]

Were our own ancestors, the Gauls, any more savage, more primitive, more pig-headed or more ignorant than these Malinkas and Bambaras through the midst of whom we have passed? To be sure the latter won't become traders at the first invitation. They won't get an instant grasp of railway trains, steamboats, the telegraph, exchange rates....[2]

Then Desbordes reminded them how often in the last three years they had been told that they had their feet in the mud and their heads in the clouds. Well, the mud was Senegal, and the clouds were Bamako.

And I thought on my part ... that this person who was so tall and whose feet and hands were so far apart – this person could be the French Republic, and it struck me that she'd have no trouble in knowing how to get herself out of the mud in her way and out of the clouds that obscured her view.[3]

Desbordes reached his peroration:

I wanted you to hear these words at Bamako, at the most dangerous moment, perhaps, of our campaign, for the storm growls all round us. This does not stop us looking at things calmly and with sang-froid.

Then Desbordes laid the first stone of the new fort. What a modest ceremony, he thought. He had only a few coins in a jam jar – and a piece of paper with a few names, like those of the President of the Republic and the Minister of Marine – to bury for posterity in the foundations. The small tricolour flapped in the wind. The artillery crashed out eleven times. The sound 'won't reach beyond the mountains at our feet', said Desbordes to his men, 'but the echo ... will be heard well beyond Senegal.'[4]

It was in November 1880 that Desbordes had been chosen for this newly-created independent command by Colonel Brière de L'Isle, Governor of Senegal, and given the labour of Hercules of joining the upper Senegal river and the upper Niger river with a triple link – a chain of forts, a telegraph and a railway line. By this means he was to start to exploit the legendary wealth of Segu, Timbuctu and the unknown land further down the Niger – 'a new India' according to its promoters.

The dream of a new India on the banks of the Niger was a legacy from the days of Louis Faidherbe, the masterful Governor of Senegal, who served there from 1854 to 1861 and from 1863 to 1865. Faidherbe was energetic and despised weakness, especially if shown by politicians in Paris. He had been trained in the hard school of the Algerian campaigns of the 1840s, when 200,000 French troops were needed to crush the fanatical Islamic revolt led by Abd el Kader. His idea of imperialism was a soldier's, not a diplomat's, or a businessman's. Military security took priority over trade, and the best form of defence was to advance. Yet he was also a passionate Africanist, a man free from the anti-Muslim prejudices of the day.

His plan of advance sounded straightforward. Throw up a chain of French forts across the bleak watershed between the upper Senegal river and the upper Niger. Build a port at Bamako on the Niger. Then sail down the river to Segu, Timbuctu, and the El Dorado in the middle and lower Niger.

The chief obstacle to a French advance in the 1850s and 1860s (as it would remain in the 1880s) was the rival empire of the Tukolors, an Islamic empire carved out of the wilderness by the genius of a Muslim holy man, Al Haj Umar. It was Umar who led his people, the Tukolors of Futa Toro, to leave their homeland on the south side of the Senegal river and wage a ten-year jihad (holy war) against the pagans to the east. Born in 1797, he had made the pilgrimage to Mecca and been appointed the Khalifa (representative) of a religious fraternity. In 1852 he launched his jihad against the spirit-worshipping peoples to the east. Thousands of *talibés* (religious students) rallied to Umar's standard. Umar provided them with modern rifles, bought from European traders, as well as with primitive muskets using locally-made black powder. Soon he controlled the most powerful army in the region. Fired with zeal for the Muslim *sharia* (the rules of Koranic law), or zeal for booty, or both, they swooped down on Kaarta, to the east. Soon the conquered land was being parcelled out among his disciples. Woe to the uncircumcised! Mosques were built, Koranic law strictly enforced, the people of Kaarta forcibly converted, enslaved or killed.

But Faidherbe, too, was advancing east – and not afraid to provoke Umar. He persuaded one of Umar's enemies to let him build a French fort at Médine, a strategic outpost 300 miles up the Senegal river. The fort served both to rally opposition against Umar, and to establish the first base on the way to the Niger. Umar took the bait, and besieged it in 1857 with an army of 20,000 *talibés* armed with swords and muskets, and with their eyes set on paradise. But to capture the fort was beyond their power, and the huge losses they suffered dealt a damaging blow to Umar's prestige. He withdrew eastwards, leaving the whole of Senegal to the French.

In his jihad against the Bambara people of Beledegu and Segu he was more successful. Finally, in 1861, with nearly 30,000 men, he invaded Masina, a Muslim sultanate of the Fulas, hundreds of miles to the east. At first God seemed to bless – or pardon – this unprovoked attack on fellow Muslims, whose hospitality Umar had cheerfully exploited earlier. He gave Masina to one of his nephews to rule, and claimed tribute from Timbuctu. But by now Umar had overreached himself. In 1863, Masina rebelled, followed by Segu. Umar was cut off and killed during the siege of Hamdallahi, the capital of Masina.

Earlier that year, during his second term as governor, Faidherbe had sent an emissary to sign a peace treaty with Umar and the Tukolors. Peace was in the French interest, he believed, until it was time for the final reckoning with the Tukolors. His emissary was a courageous twenty-six-year-old naval lieutenant, Eugène Mage. Faidherbe made Umar a generous offer: in return for being allowed to lease the land to build a chain of forts and trading posts across the watershed, they would promise to recognize Umar's conquests further east and supply him with cannons and rifles.

However, by the time Lieutenant Mage reached Segu, Umar himself had been killed by the rebels at Hamdallahi. Masina and Timbuctu were lost, the whole empire was crumbling. At Segu, the new sultan, Umar's son Ahmadu, was pinned down by a revolt of the Bambaras. Still, Ahmadu drove a hard bargain with Lieutenant Mage. All he would offer was a peace treaty and commercial agreement provided the French supplied him with artillery. He refused him a lease for forts and trading posts – the main purpose of the mission.

Meanwhile Faidherbe had returned to Paris, and Paris lost all interest in the supposed El Dorado on the Niger. The disasters of the Franco-Prussian war supervened. There was no spare cash in France for colonial adventures in Africa. Senegal had to pay its own way. By 1874 the value of its main export trade – groundnuts and gum – had been reduced 30 per cent by a worldwide glut. It was not until the late 1870s that Paris once again began to cast its eyes towards the Niger.

The first scheme sounded like the title of a novel by Jules Verne: 'Trans-Sahara', a railway direct from the Mediterranean to the Niger across 1,500 miles of burning sand. In the Chamber of Deputies this amazing plan was taken as seriously as if it were a plan for a line through the Paris suburbs. Charles de Freycinet, then Minister of Public Works, fell for it. So did Gambetta's closest confidants, Paul Bert and Maurice Rouvier. The Trans-Sahara, one of its sponsors earnestly claimed, would create 'a vast colonial empire ... a French India rivalling its British counterpart in wealth and prosperity; to open up unlimited markets for trade and industry, [and] to give free rein to our civilizing impulses.'[5] Rouvier gloated over the riches of the western Sudan: 'There lie vast regions watered by great rivers and great lakes, regions of unbelievable fertility inhabited by 200 million people. Shall not these regions provide unlimited opportunities for our trade?'[6] Before the end of 1879 the Chamber voted 800,000 francs (£32,000) for preliminary surveys of the route. But within two years the scheme was abandoned; for the survey team, led by Colonel Flatters, had been massacred by some nomadic Tuareg.

It was more sensible, if less heroic, to advance on the Niger from the west, by way of Senegal, as Faidherbe had proposed. In 1880, Faidherbe's plan was revived by Admiral Jean Jauréguiberry, the Minister of Marine. As a young captain he had served as Governor of Senegal in the interval between Faidherbe's two terms of office. He proved equally energetic, but tactless. Even Faidherbe was shocked by his clumsy policy of alienating white traders and burning native villages in Futa Toro. Time had not added polish to Jauréguiberry's political style. In the Chamber he was still uncouth, but he at least knew what he wanted: political control over the whole of the western Sudan in order to tap the wealth of this 'new India'.

At the Ministry of Marine in the Rue Royale, the officials produced estimates for a Senegal-Niger railway: 45 million francs for the railway between the two rivers, 82 million francs for the forts to protect the line – a total of 120 million francs (£4.8 million) if the line was built the whole way from the Atlantic. These estimates would soon prove absurdly low, but already they terrified the Chamber of Deputies. In February 1880, Jauréguiberry asked for 9 million as a first instalment. All he could squeeze out of Parliament was 1.3 million francs, voted in July, after a wretchedly long delay. Jauréguiberry had to warn the Governor of Senegal that peaceful railway building was the priority; on no account must the budget be exceeded. Then he himself retired – for the time being – from the Ministry of Marine in the Rue Royale.

In the Governor's Mansion at Saint-Louis, Senegal, Colonel Brière de L'Isle turned a deaf ear to the warning. He was a fire-eater of the Algerian military school: more intolerant and insubordinate than either Jauréguiberry or Faidherbe. He specialized in the use of the *fait accompli*. His reply to protests from Paris was always the same. Only by the course he had adopted was it possible to safeguard the security of the colony. In 1877 he had pushed a French column into Futa Toro, and bullied the natives into accepting a French protectorate. Next year he attacked a fortress, Sabouciré, in upper Senegal. Paris swallowed its fears for the budget, and accepted the new expansionism.

However, by 1881, Admiral Jauréguiberry's successor at the Rue Royale, Admiral Cloué, decided that Colonel Brière de L'Isle had got too big for his boots. Brière refused to accept the decision that peaceful railway building must take priority. He had ordered the commander of upper Senegal, Colonel Borgnis-Desbordes, to make a punitive expedition towards the Niger and impose a protectorate on Bamako. Brière had disobeyed orders. He was recalled to Paris under a cloud.

The news of Brière's downfall did not disturb Colonel Desbordes; on the contrary, it helped to free his hands, for Brière was the one man who might have controlled him. Brière's successors, try as they might to please Admiral Cloué in Paris, were quite unable to look after themselves. In the rainy season epidemics of typhoid and yellow fever descended on lower Senegal. They killed

Brière's first successor within four months. The second found the chaos created by the epidemics too much for him and was sacked after abandoning all hope for the great new railway.

The railway building had become a farce. Millions of francs had already been spent, and not a metre of track was yet laid. By 1882 all the estimates had proved absurd. Yet by now the Ministry of Marine had spent too much public money to cut its losses. The Ministry applied to the Chamber for a new credit of 7.5 million francs, to which the deputies gloomily assented. More important still, in the spring of 1882, Admiral Jauréguiberry returned as Minister of Marine, determined to make at long last a pounce on the Niger.

That summer of 1882, when Colonel Desbordes returned to Paris on leave, he paid a call on Jauréguiberry in the Rue Royale.

The two men were soon agreed. The last years of campaigning in upper Senegal had been intensely frustrating for both. Every year at the close of the rainy season the French column had sailed up the Senegal river and advanced towards the Niger. Every year they had been beaten back by a combination of typhoid and yellow fever in Senegal, a shortage of supplies, and faint hearts back in Paris. Two stone and mud forts had been built by Desbordes along the route between the rivers, at Badumbe and Kita. That was about all there was to show for all the blood and treasure expended.

Desbordes warned his chief that none of their imperialist rivals in West Africa had been idle during these years: not Ahmadu, the Sultan, fighting to retain the Tukolor empire inherited from his father, Umar, the great Khalifa; not Samori, the upstart from the mountains of Guinea, carving a new empire of his own south of the Niger, financed by sales of gold and slaves; not the perfidious British, pushing forward from their strategic bases in Sierra Leone and Gambia. With Samori and the British, conflict might not be inevitable, provided the French moved fast enough. But with Ahmadu, Sultan of the Tukolors, some kind of collision could hardly be avoided. For it was on Ahmadu's empire that the French now had designs.

Two years earlier, Desbordes had looked on with distaste when his superiors sent out a peace-making mission to Segu, the Tukolor capital. The mission had been led by a rival of his, thirty-one-year-old Captain Joseph Simon Gallieni. Years later Gallieni would be recognized as a master of colonial diplomacy. But at this time he was almost as bellicose as Desbordes. He tried not so secretly to encourage the local Bambara tribesmen to rebel against their Tukolor overlords, while he also professed peace and friendship with Ahmadu. But Ahmadu had been told by his spies of French encouragement to the rebellious Bambaras. For ten months, in fear of his life, Gallieni was forced to cool his heels (or rather boil his head) in a mud hut at Nango, twenty-five miles from Segu. During this trying time, he became convinced that the British were preparing to negotiate a treaty with Ahmadu, and he was determined to forestall them. In due course he wheedled a treaty out of Ahmadu, signed in November 1880, which stipulated that Ahmadu should accept a French protectorate and concede France exclusive commercial and navigation rights on the Niger. In return, the French promised not to construct fortified posts on the Sultan's territory, and never to invade the Tukolor empire. They would also pay generously for their new rights: four mountain guns, with full accessories, 1,000 rifles and 4,000 cartridges, as well as an annual rent of 10,000 francs, with 200 flintlocks, 200 cannon balls and 200 barrels of gunpowder.

Naturally Gallieni had no intention of carrying out his part of the bargain. Nor, it appeared, had Ahmadu. The cunning Sultan had eluded the crucial commitment giving the French a protectorate by dropping it from the Arabic version of the treaty. Anyway, Gallieni had conceded too much, so Paris refused to ratify the Treaty of Nango. Instead there was an uneasy truce, contrasted, on the French side, by a bloody encounter with Samori in February 1882.

Gallieni's rebuff pleased Desbordes, as did the uneasy truce. But would Paris give him the completely free hand he needed? That day in the summer of 1882 when he left Jauréguiberry's office in the Rue Royale, a daring new plan had begun to take shape. He would be allowed to advance on Bamako during the next campaigning season. Once astride the Niger, he would reassemble the gunboats brought overland from the upper Senegal river. Then the small column could resume its advance towards the Sultan's capital – and to Timbuctu beyond.

There was only one obvious danger in this plan. What were their opponents' own designs? If Ahmadu set his mind to it, his enormous Tukolor army, ill-armed though it was, could squash the French like a kola nut.

*   *   *

Ahmed ibn Umar, Amir Al-Muminin (Commander of the Faithful), known to the French as Sultan Ahmadu, lived in a modest two-storey stone and mud palace at Segu in a style that befitted his means. Unlike those once great Islamic rulers of Africa, the Bey of Tunis and the Khedive of Egypt, he had not pledged his kingdom to foreign bankers. It was already vulnerable enough. His capital at Segu looked imposing: a walled city fully three miles around, astride the south bank of the Niger about 150 miles east of Bamako. Yet at the first whiff of European artillery those twelve-foot-high stone and mud walls would prove little better than cardboard.

The place had originated as the fortress of the king of the local Bambaras, captured by Umar in 1861. Ahmadu rebuilt Segu as a typical Tukolor fortress. Down came the temple of the Bambaras, polluted by heathen practices, to make way for a mosque, while a minaret replaced the trees hung with fetishes. Opposite the mosque, where the faithful were called to prayer, Ahmadu built the central arsenal and treasury for his empire. It was also big enough to hold all the loot of twenty years of warfare: 800 wives and perhaps as many horses, both decorated in the finery of a Moroccan or Turkish court, finery that had been carried on camels across the Sahara, to be exchanged for the gold or slaves of the Sudan.

In his own modest apartments, Ahmadu received visitors, according to the account left by Lieutenant Mage, sitting on the ground with nothing but a goatskin under him, surrounded by a wild-looking pack of slaves armed with guns. He was now forty-eight though people thought him younger.

His face is delicate [Mage had written in 1864], his expression calm, and he has an intelligent air. He stammers a little in speaking but he speaks softly and gently. He has large eyes, a good profile, and finely cut nostrils. His forehead is broad and high. His worst feature is his mouth, as his lips protrude. This and his receding chin give him a negroid look. The colour of his skin resembles that of bronze.[7]

Ahmadu wore a blue cotton cap that might have been made in Rouen or Strasbourg and a loose-fitting robe of the same material. He held a set of Muslim prayer beads in one hand and fingered them during the conversation. Behind him on the goatskin lay a book written in Arabic, his sandals and his sword.

He had spent the last twenty years trying to put the pieces of his father's empire back together again. Sometimes he had used the traditional methods of African warfare; whole towns had been put to the sword or their peoples enslaved. But his armies were far weaker than his father's. Anyway, the weapon he preferred was diplomacy, at which he excelled. The two central provinces, Kaarta and Segu, were safely brought to heel despite attempts at rebellion led by some of Ahmadu's half-brothers. Masina was beyond his control, ruled by Umar's nephew as an independent state. The southern province of Dinguiray was virtually independent, too, ruled by one of Ahmadu's brothers. The Bambaras of Beledegu were only partly subdued. Most of what Ahmadu still held he governed as a loose federation, but he governed it well by the standards of the age.

The insoluble problem was how to deal with the French. For twenty years there had been an uneasy truce between the two empires. Then Desbordes had begun his advance towards the Niger, expelling the Tukolors from the western part of Ahmadu's empire. Could the peace survive this latest provocation, the pounce on Bamako?

Many of Ahmadu's warriors could not conceal their frustration at his inaction. The most militant were the ones the French had expelled from a Tukolor fort at Murgula, which was a potential threat to their own fort at Kita. These Murgula refugees fled to one of Ahmadu's brothers, Muhammad Muntaga, the Governor of Nioro in Kaarta, where they stirred up hatred of the French. A message was sent to Desbordes, a letter with a bite like a snake's:

From Muhammad Muntaga, son of the Believer, the great sheik Umar, for whom God opened all countries and ordained the conversion of all men, Umar who fought a holy war in God's name, according to the laws of God and nothing more. To the uncircumcised, son of the uncircumcised, Colonel Desbordes, may God confound and bring ruin on your friends. . . . No one is more of a malefactor, no one more of a traitor, no one more wicked than you.

You say that you only wish to open up a road for trade. This is false and contrary to sense and reason. Your desire is to destroy the country, to close the trade routes and make war on Believers ...

Muntaga ended:

The day when we meet, the birds of the air will not need to look elsewhere for their food.[8]

Two years earlier, when Gallieni had been at Nango, negotiating the treaty, the news of Desbordes's advance to Kita and a provocative attack on Goubanko had reached Ahmadu at Segu. There had been great excitement in the capital. Feeling ran high against whites, who were said to 'dream of nothing less than conquering the Tukolor empire'. Ahmadu had remained grim and silent, while his advisers were called for consultation. The hotheads were for violence. Ahmadu shared their mistrust of the French, but refused to be provoked. His sombre closing words were quoted to Gallieni as follows: 'Despite everything, I should still like to finish my business with the captain [Gallieni]. But as I say, I have no confidence ... I shall wait, and if the French want to make war on me, God will uphold me against them.'[9]

Now, in 1883, Ahmadu still shrank from war with the French. His hold on his sprawling empire was far too precarious. His own people were split into factions. His immediate aim was to crush the dissident Bambaras, who menaced the southern and western provinces. Meanwhile he would continue to try to negotiate an arms deal with the French. But if he could not buy guns, he could at least buy time. Perhaps a collision with the French could be postponed for many years yet. In the interval the newcomers would have other enemies to contend with.

Ahmadu felt too weak to strike. But the French were weaker still, their numbers drained by fever and dysentery, their supply lines to Senegal stretched to breaking point. Why not snip these supply lines and crush Bamako before the fort was complete?

The French had rebuffed Ahmadu's treaty, so why not then join hands with the African enemies of the French, especially with that rising star in the south, the warlord Samori? Together the two armies, Tukolor and Samorian, could crush the Europeans. In the bitter years ahead this was the strategy that Ahmadu would reluctantly adopt. But in 1883 he still shrank from such a humiliation, such defilement. His only initiative was a polite boycott of trade with the French. He ignored the upstart Samori. Ahmadu was the son of Al Haj Umar. Who was Samori's father? A fetish-worshipper, a beer drinker, an uncircumcised evildoer, like the French.

A few miles south of Bamako, where a small tributary joined the tree-fringed banks of the great river, lay a small village called Weyanko. It looked as wretched as any other Bambara village: a collection of rectangular mud huts protected against attack from their neighbours by a crumbling *tata*, an outer defence wall built of mud, and surrounded by scattered fields of millet and gardens of fruit and vegetables. It was here, as menacing as a cloud of locusts, that several thousand musketeers of Samori's northern army, commanded by Samori's brother, Fabou, suddenly descended on the last day of March 1883.

The villagers did not wait to test the good nature of Fabou's men. They fled in terror. The first that Desbordes heard of the approach of Samori's men was when his scouts reported that the Bambaras had abandoned their villages in the valley. Rumours multiplied. It was said that one party of Fabou's men were advancing along the south bank of the river. His main party threatened Bamako directly while a third detachment had apparently headed up into the hills to cut their supply lines. This was on the caravan track linking Bamako with Kita, more than ten days' journey across the rugged country to the west. The district around Bamako was so poor that the garrison needed almost daily supplies of slaughter cattle, as well as new horses to replace the frequent casualties. But already the new telegraph link had gone dead, presumably cut by Fabou's men. It was said that there was panic among the villages all along the track.

On 31 March Desbordes took the gamble of sending a tiny column to try to re-open the line. They were a half-company of *tirailleurs*, white soldiers on mules, and twelve Spahis, all under the command of Captain Pietri. As they vanished into the hills, a chill descended on Borgnis-Desbordes's right-hand man, Captain Louis Archinard. He was normally self-confident and even arrogant, but now that Pietri had gone, they had less than 300 men left capable of bearing arms. Recent losses from disease had been sickening; that very day, he had buried four white soldiers who had died of a pernicious fever.

'One wouldn't need many days like that,' Archinard wrote in his diary. 'The colonel thought we should be attacked by Samori's warriors tonight; we had to stay on alert all night. There's a time when it's no longer possible to take one's boots off at night and when one must go to sleep with a revolver in one's hand. It's being continually on the alert which begins to be disagreeable.' Archinard gathered that Samori was expected to attack their position from two sides. 'That would be clever enough, but it has been very imprudent to let us build the fort, which is now nearly complete in all essentials.'[10] However, the panic in the neighbourhood slowed up the construction. It depended largely on forced labour by the Bambaras who had now fled. The colonel had told Archinard to close the gaps in the outer wall at all costs, and this was soon done.

Just after midnight on 1 April they had what Archinard called '*un poisson d'avril sérieux*'[11] ('a real April fool') when a Spahi from the main guard galloped up to the gate, shouting that he had seen a large number of the enemy pass by one of the forward posts. In a moment the bugles sounded the alert and the whole garrison turned out, including the artillery with two fieldpieces. A few rifle shots rang out somewhere in the darkness – and that was all. After several hours everyone returned sheepishly to bed.

It turned out next morning that the Spahi had been right. Fabou's large column had arrived by forced marches at Weyanko. His infantry refused to attack. But some of his cavalry had galloped up to the wall of Bamako in the darkness and sabred one of the herdsmen. They were trying to grab some slaughter-cattle and some women slaves belonging to the *tirailleurs* when the garrison had frightened them off with those rifle shots Archinard had heard.

Desbordes decided to launch a frontal attack before Fabou's men recovered their balance. He was in no position to resist a regular siege, what with a half-finished fort, the rainy season impending, and a garrison half-crippled by disease. But first he arranged a military ceremony to impress the people of Bamako. The leader of the local Moorish traders, Karamoko Bile, had proved welcoming. The same could hardly be said for his two brothers, Tiekoro and Sidikoro. Desbordes believed they were in league with Samori's men. Already he held them prisoner in the fort as hostages for the good behaviour of the village. Now, before the column marched out against Fabou, Desbordes had the two unfortunate traders taken out and shot by firing squad.

The column of 242 men was protected by a machine gun and two pieces of artillery. They cheerfully marched out to attack Fabou's camp in the cool of dawn on 2 April. A few hours later, in the crushing heat of midday, the survivors staggered back again.

The white soldiers were so exhausted that they had to cling to the tails of their mules to stand up. Some of them were wounded. Others were carried on stretchers. Everything had gone wrong. Fabou's men had repulsed the frontal assault on their camp with fanatical courage. Worse, they had fought with skill and intelligence. At one point it looked as though the whole French column would be overwhelmed. Ammunition was running low. The rifles were too hot to hold. There was no doctor, only one veterinary surgeon to look after all the wounded. The last boxes of cartridges were handed out, and Europeans were advised (according to one eyewitness) to keep the last round for themselves. Then a square was formed and the survivors staggered back to the fort, deadbeat and demoralized.

In the next few days morale sank even lower. Nothing had been heard from Captain Pietri. The telegraph was still dead and men continued to die of disease. As Archinard put it, '*Nous étions tous très inquiets.*'[12] In three years Desbordes had come to think himself invincible, which made this dangerous repulse all the more inexplicable. Who were these half-armed black soldiers who could withstand the fire of machine gun and artillery without flinching? Who, indeed, was Samori, the great warlord from the Milo, who had trained these pagans to fight with even more desperate courage than the soldiers of a Muslim jihad, only a swordthrust away from paradise?

*   *   *

High up in the wooded flank of the Guinea Highlands, a land of icy streams and alpine pastures, rises the stripling Niger, and its affluents, the Dion, the Sankarani and the Milo. Southward, beyond the rocky watershed, the mountain streams have bored their way down the cliffs and are lost in the vast stifling rainforest that blocks off the Highlands from the Gulf of Guinea. But on this northern flank each river has carved out a delightful valley of its own, and the most delightful of all is the Milo valley, an African garden of Eden.

It was here, in the district of Konya, that the kola trade had flourished since the Middle Ages, providing its own bonanza. The kola nut was grown in the clearings of the forest, marketed in the valley and then carried laboriously across the wilderness for hundreds of miles to the mud villages and mud cities of the Sudan and beyond. The nut, one of the few stimulants allowed by Islam, was served as a luxury thoughout Islamic Africa, and the Middle East. To organize this demanding trade came the Dyula, Muslim immigrants from the coast. The Dyula metropolis was Kankan, a teeming village of mud huts on the banks of the river Milo.

The lines of trade pushed out and became more sophisticated. The arterial trade routes designed for the delicate and perishable kola nut – fair markets, dry storehouses, trustworthy guards, able porters – could also supply delicate girl slaves from the forests. In return back came ingots of salt from the Sahara and the luxuries of North Africa that the caravans had brought from still further away: fine cloth from Morocco, pottery from Tunis, horses from Arabia.

The eighteenth century saw a kind of Dyula revolution. The slave gangs now plodded south through the forests to the slave ports of Guinea and Sierra Leone. From there they were packed off to the plantations of the New World. Back through the forest tramped porters with luxuries from the Old World on their heads: Spanish knives, British kettles, French cloth and, above all, obsolete firearms of every kind. Guns and gunpowder were soon to be as essential as a staple food. Starved of guns, a chief and his people would soon find themselves snapped up by the Dyula to become a line of merchandise plodding down to the slave ports.

A greater Dyula revolution was yet to come, and it was Samori, the warlord from the Milo, who reaped its harvest. The revolution began in the 1830s when a holy man from Kankan called Mori-Ule Sise left Kankan and proclaimed a jihad against the local pagans living between Konya and Toro. At first the merchants of Kankan kept their distance. The inspiration for the jihad came from the Muslim city of Masina in the north, where the Fulanis had proclaimed a jihad in 1818. The Dyulas traded with these Fulani cattle-breeders and despised them. But the Fulani idea of a centralized kingdom suited the purpose of Mori-Ule Sise. He needed an army to pursue the jihad and a capital city in which to concentrate it. He found both at a place called Moriuledugu, humble enough, yet the first centralized kingdom that the region had ever seen. Though Mori-Ule Sise soon fell by the wayside, hacked to death by rivals, his sons pushed on with the jihad. By 1860 they were the masters of upper Konya and the Milo valley. Then they met their match in Samori. In alliance with the local pagans, Samori recaptured the Milo in the 1860s and soon his Malinke empire reached from Futa Jallon to the goldfields of Bure. By 1880 he had crushed the Sise and stormed the gates of Kankan, which he now transformed as the centre of the Dyula network.

Unlike the founders of most great empires, Samori came from humdrum peasant stock. His family was from the Ture tribe, once Muslim traders, who had reverted to paganism and to farming the land. Samori preferred trading and the rule of Islam to herding cattle and worshipping spirits. And he identified with the Dyula. In 1853, when he was about twenty-three, his mother had the misfortune to be captured by the rapacious Sise. For Samori it was no misfortune. He spent five years at Moriuledugu learning from his mother's captors how to rule a state in peace and war, and how to profit from the Sise's mistakes.

Two innovations explain his own success, unparalleled by any ruler between the Niger and the mountains. Both exemplify how Samori had understood how to adapt the Dyula revolution and bend it to his own purposes. First, there was astonishing religious tolerance throughout his empire. The conventional jihad, offering pagans the choice of conversion or death, was not only expensive in human flesh. Where pagans were in the great majority, it was also dangerously ineffective. This was the mistake made by both Mori-Ule and the Tukolors. These black Islamic empires spread a creed of resentment among their subjects, like the Bambara, nominally subject to Islam, but hardly bothering to conceal their contempt for their shaven-headed, water-drinking masters. Samori was no fanatic in religion, but he respected its political use. To his spirit-worshipping subjects he had the magic of the 'Faama', the pagan overlord. To his Muslim subjects, he had the magnetism of the 'Almami', the man who leads the prayers in the mosque. And to everyone, pagans and Muslims alike, he offered the same inspiring materialism, the message of all sensible imperialists: his empire would bring peace and peace would bring prosperity. Along those arteries of trade developed by the Dyula would pour a flood of gold, slaves and kola nuts, the lifeblood of the empire.

The second innovation was the military system. Samori was a military organizer of genius. With his new model army of infantry that soon grew to be over 30,000 strong, he conquered and then ruled his empire. He had borrowed the idea of a centralized army from the Sise, as he borrowed the idea of a centralized kingdom. Then he transformed it by building a new system of loyalties focused on himself. Traditionally, African warlords recruited their soldiers from prisoners-of-war or conscripts, grouping them according to age and locality. Each group would already be set in its own particular loyalties. Samori was determined to break the mould, so he created each regiment from the mixed clay of randomly selected recruits. Each regiment thus developed a new kind of *esprit de corps*, focused on Samori, and was in turn grouped in an army commanded by one of Samori's most trusted warriors. Each army was allocated to one of the five provinces into which the empire was divided. At the centre was the headquarters district, the Forobah (the Great Field) which Samori reserved for himself. From the Forobah he operated a system of secret agents that let him keep everything under his thumb. It was from here, too, that he controlled the supply of modern rifles in which he took such personal pride. He trained his village blacksmiths to copy the latest French rifles, realizing that their superior firepower would be decisive. Yet his men, often armed with modern rifles and always superbly disciplined, were understandably not trained in the techniques of modern warfare. Samori was an organizer and strategist of genius, but he knew nothing yet of the best tactics for fighting Europeans.

How then to retain, let alone expand, his new empire, faced by the relentless advance of the French? It was a similar problem to Ahmadu's, to which Samori had no better answer. He felt no more inclination to make an alliance with the Tukolors than they with him. All he could do at present was to build up his own strength and try to prevent a confrontation with the French – though that might be unavoidable in due course. Already he had had one brush with the French in 1882, when a raiding party led by Desbordes had attacked a town called Keniera, recently captured by Samori. This experience taught him that he did not yet know how best to fight Europeans, so he had warned his generals to play safe. The current orders for his northern commander, Fabou, were to capture Bamako from the Bambaras and make it his strategic base. But this did not mean attacking Desbordes. On the contrary, Samori predicted that to attack the French on the Niger would invite disaster.

Ten days passed, and Samori's prediction was precisely fulfilled. Desbordes knew he had to strike fast to save his weakened garrison. On 12 April he found a flaw in Fabou's defence line – an undefended gap at the back of the stone wall – and he struck. A column of 200 *tirailleurs* and colonial infantry charged through the gap and swept down into the camp. The rout was total. Fabou's men fled across the Niger, leaving tons of grain and several hundred pounds of homemade gunpowder to be dragged back in triumph by Desbordes's men. Fabou's camp, built of thatched huts, made a fine bonfire.

Desbordes breathed again. It turned out that Pietri, too, had behaved like a hero. He had re-opened the supply line after trouncing the enemy and recapturing the lost slaughter oxen, as well as rounding up Fabou's cattle and sheep. By the end of April Desbordes felt it was safe to return to Senegal, leaving a garrison of only 155 men to finish and guard the fort. Before he marched off, he arranged a victory dance for the black *tirailleurs*. '*Un grand tam-tam*,' Archinard observed sardonically, in which Titi, the half-naked chief of Bamako, 'led the ball' while the new chief of the Moorish traders, Karamoko Bile, 'was in attendance, carrying lightly the duty of mourning his two executed brothers'.[13]

*   *   *

When the news was cabled to Paris everyone praised the heroism of Desbordes and his tiny column. Jules Ferry, more enthusiastic about the empire than ever, despite his rebuff after the Tunis débâcle of 1881, had become President of the Council (Prime Minister) once again in early 1883. He hailed the capture of Bamako as a triumph by 'these heroic sons of France ... who astonish us by their courage, by their daring and by the range of their abilities'.

In fact Ferry risked nothing by supporting Desbordes's aggressive empire-building in the western Sudan. Unlike Tunis or the Far East, the Sudan was politically safe ground. In the Chamber of Deputies the idea of colonialism was usually blackened on two counts: these adventures weakened France's metropolitan army and therefore postponed the great day of reckoning when the Lost Provinces would be recovered; or else they were tainted with *affairisme* and the grubby financial speculations of which Gambetta had often been accused. The Sudan was clean on both counts. Its garrison never exceeded 4,000 men. These heroic sons of France were drawn only from the despised marine corps reserved for service in the unhealthy colonies. And no one had yet found enough wealth there to dream of *affairisme*.

Safe, too, was the reputation in Paris of these French conquistadors in the Sudan. No matter that Desbordes had disobeyed orders in his eagerness to serve the flag and promote his own military career. The *fait accompli* had proved as irresistible in the Sudan as in Algeria. He had completed the first part of Faidherbe's grand design: to build a chain of forts linking the Senegal and the Niger and to establish a base on the river itself. No left-wing deputy in the Chamber would now dare to try to make the French army disgorge this new empire on the Niger. Retreat was unthinkable. Apart from the dishonour to the flag, there was the supposed risk to the security of Senegal. Any show of weakness, it was claimed, and the whole of French West Africa could collapse like a house of cards. Even Ferry's most bitter enemies, like Clemenceau, had to acquiesce in this triumph of the new colonialism.

No one recognized his own achievements more clearly than Desbordes himself. In May he sailed back down the Senegal river to Saint-Louis and found the acting Governor, Le Boucher, less than sympathetic to the heroes of Bamako. There was the usual epidemic in Saint-Louis, typhoid – serious enough to have polished off Le Boucher's predecessor, Servatius. Desbordes was disgusted to find his men in quarantine on a nearby island. He protested violently to Jauréguiberry and seized on the pretext to resign his command. As he expected, Jauréguiberry refused to accept the resignation. Le Boucher was reprimanded, Desbordes ordered back to Paris to serve as a Sudanese expert in the Ministry of Marine.

Desbordes's return to Paris coincided, as he probably anticipated, with a depressing new swing of the pendulum. Jauréguiberry, the red-hot expansionist, was replaced by a cooler and more level-headed Minister of Marine. There was a feeling in the Chamber of Deputies that Jauréguiberry had lost control. At the same session in July, Ferry had to sing the praises of Desbordes. There was general censure of the disastrous finances of the Sudan. The Trans-Sudan railway had made its promoters a laughing stock. The estimated cost had now doubled, 60 million francs had already been spent, and only a few kilometres of track had been laid. The Chamber of Deputies grudgingly approved a further 4 million francs. But the future of the railway was now in doubt, and on the railway depended any prospect of moving beyond Bamako.

As Desbordes climbed the stairs to his new office in the Rue Royale, it must have been obvious to him that the rush to the Niger had ended as suddenly as it had begun. For the moment the initiative was passing to France's enemies,

Ahmadu and Samori. Perhaps they were too weak to seize their chance – Desbordes certainly thought so – but the French public was losing interest in the Niger. The next phase would be an anti-climax: consolidation. This was to be expected for one very simple reason. The Trans-Sudan railway had captured the imagination of the public because it would be a train ticket to El Dorado. But was there gold – indeed, was there anything at all in those barren hills? Nothing that the army had discovered on the upper Niger – the wretched mud huts at Bamako, the starving cattle, the stony soil, the savage population – offered the least encouragement to businessmen. The French public were now determined to leave the upper Niger to the men who valued it so highly, the heroes of the marine corps. But they were in no hurry to spend a single franc acquiring any more of this blighted region.

Even in the Ministry of Marine there was growing scepticism about prospects on the upper Niger. The eyes of Jauréguiberry's successors were turning to a more plausible El Dorado 1,500 miles away, the lower end of the same river. It was here, where the spoils of trade were so much richer, in the creeks and swamps of the delta, among the oil-palm groves, that a real contest loomed between the two chief rivals for supremacy in Africa. The British, that nation of shopkeepers, had a head start. The French, their heads in the clouds, had lost time in the western Sudan. Was it already too late to catch up? It was, after all, in the lower Niger that was centred the second part of Faidherbe's dream of a new India.

CHAPTER 11

Hewett Shows the Flag

London and West Africa
January 1883 – 19 July 1884 and before

> 'We your servants have *join* together and thoughts
> its better to write you a nice loving letter ... We
> *wish* to have your laws in our towns. We want to
> have every *fashion* altered, also we will be according
> to your Consul's word.'
>
> Petition for a British protectorate sent to Queen Victoria
> by King Acqua, Prince Dido etc., Cameroon river, 1880

Brazza, the darling of France, had new designs on the Congo. Desbordes and his heroes were about to steam down the upper Niger, brandishing the tricolour. Neither piece of African news, reprinted in small print in the English newspapers that month, January 1883, caused much stir in the British Cabinet. They had anxieties near home.

Gladstone, the Liberal Party made flesh, was in failing health. Now seventy-four, he was fretful and depressed and complained he could not sleep. In the worst of times – in May 1882 when Lord Frederick had been murdered, or in July when they had waited breathless to hear the news of Arabi's latest act of defiance – even then Gladstone had prided himself on his mastery of seven or eight hours sleep at a stretch. These nights he could barely manage four. The Queen pestered him about Sir Charles Dilke, Granville's deputy at the Foreign Office. She loathed Dilke. The man was untrustworthy, unfit for the Cabinet; a secret republican, she was convinced. Did she indeed trust her own Prime Minister, who had now given half a century of public service? Gladstone pleaded that he was quite 'overdone' by such 'personal questions'. His friends were afraid he might now carry out his long-matured threat of resigning.

Could one attribute Gladstone's strangely deflated state to a reaction, perhaps even a crisis of conscience, after the conquest of Egypt? The enormity of that step was only now beginning to be grasped by anyone, Liberal or Tory, English or French. Lord Dufferin, the masterful British Ambassador to the Sultan, had just delivered a report on Egypt which made grim reading. They must abolish dual control: the partnership with the French was unworkable. To knock Egypt into shape meant turning the country inside out, and Britain must act alone. Taxation, justice, agriculture, everything was in a deplorable state. To clean up the Augean stables would take at least five years; meanwhile, part of the British army would have to stay in occupation. So the Liberals would be trapped in Egypt. This was a new kind of informal empire, invisible no more. To all appearances they would be rulers of the country they had conquered. They would rule it nakedly as though it was a new province of the British Empire, a western province of India – naked, that is, apart from a fig leaf in the shape of the Khedive's throne.

Gladstone loathed the thought of this bondage in Egypt, and no one ever derived less pleasure from being called a hypocrite. He had a clear conscience about the invasion. He was no imperialist and he had not added an acre of Egypt to the Empire. The intervention had been forced upon Britain by the failure of the other Powers, especially France, to take their responsibilities seriously. Someone had to rescue the Egyptians (and the bond-holders) from the chaos. If he abandoned them, the chaos would be worse than before. That was Gladstone's lofty pledge. But it would appear somewhat less lofty if he now threw in the sponge and resigned as Prime Minister.

The prospect made the Cabinet tremble, and none more than the Grand Old Man's chief rivals for the succession: the favourite, Lord Hartington, Leader in the Commons; the dark horse, Lord Granville, Foreign Secretary, Leader in the Lords and Gladstone's deputy in the Cabinet. There was small hope that either man – Hartington or Granville – could hold the Liberal Party together for a single day.

In early January 1883 Lord Granville was relieved to hear that Gladstone had agreed to take a winter holiday at Cannes in the south of France. Granville would hold the fort while he was out of the country. The arrangements suited all the Liberals. For the time being there was little to fight about; only a bill for local government in London. Of course none of the tormenting wrangles over Ireland was really settled. But at least the Cabinet had a breathing space. Europe was at peace, though the press in both Germany and France were absurdly violent about England. The worst legacy of the Egyptian invasion had been the way it had aroused the jealousy of the French public and was beginning to poison Britain's diplomatic relations with France's leaders. In Germany, on the other hand, Bismarck could be relied on to ridicule the anglophobia of his people, and remain staunch, in his cynical way, to Britain. After all, it was Bismarck who had generously proposed, back in 1878, that Britain should take Egypt as her own little plum, while France popped Tunis, 'the ripe pear', into her mouth.

Lord Granville was, it must be said, more diplomatist than statesman. He was a typical Whig: charming, handsome, polished and modest – with good reason – about his creative abilities. For inspiration he drew on Gladstone's bubbling spring of ideas. When that spring failed, as it had failed in both Egypt and South Africa, it was usually because it had been pumped dry by Ireland. Africa, too, had failed to cast its spell over Gladstone. It was the repellent continent, a pestilential swamp devoid of lofty endeavour, a place of moral contamination where white men were soon reduced to the level of savages. Nothing had ever really flourished there, except the sickening trade in which Gladstone's merchant forebears had made the family fortune. The slave trade. Gladstone must have shuddered at the thought.

Granville enjoyed the moral security of a man descended from generations of high-minded English landowners, but he too cared little for Africa, least of all for its most pestilential part, the west coast from Gambia to the Congo. British interests there had never been strategically significant; they were mere traders' interests. Granville's lip curled. As far as possible he left these commercial questions to the officials at the FO and to his radical-minded deputy, Charles Dilke. After all, Dilke's family had made their fortune in trade. But on West Africa Dilke had made a nuisance of himself. He had sided with Edward Hewett, the impetuous British Consul. Hewitt had sent an absurd despatch the previous year urging that Britain should impose a formal protectorate over the whole district of the Oil Rivers. This was the coastal strip named after the palm-oil it produced, running 300 miles eastwards from Lagos to the Niger delta and Calabar, all the way to Cameroon. (With Lagos added, it covered the whole coast of modern Nigeria.) Granville found it hard to see the point. Did Britain not already control the Oil Rivers as far as she needed? Was informal empire not enough?

The conventional wisdom at this period was that the British flag was a handicap to British trade. At any rate, it could only follow trade after several generations, when life was complicated enough to demand formal sovereignty and business was big enough to carry the costs. In the meantime, traders kept life simple and business blossomed in the political void. This was the secret and invisible empire, the network of trade supported by the network of informal power that British consuls and British gunboats extended around the coasts of Africa, invisible as an electrical field.

Kimberley, the Colonial Secretary, agreed with Granville, and tried to veto Hewett's scheme. Dilke was stalled. All he could do was to ask Hewett to report back to the FO about the situation in Cameroon and spell out the case, if case there was, for a formal protectorate.

The letter that started the trouble was a 'loving letter' from some Cameroon chiefs ('kings' and 'princes') appealing to Queen Victoria. They begged the Queen to take over Cameroon. The letter had arrived three years before and the FO had left it, with characteristic detachment, unanswered. It was followed by a similar appeal from 'King' Acqua and 'King' Bell to Gladstone, which suffered a similar fate. The text of the letter to the Queen carried the authentic tang of the Oil Rivers:

Cameroon River

Acqua Town

Dearest Madam,

We your *servants* have *join* together and thoughts its better to write you a nice *loving* letter which will tell you about all our *wishes*. We *wish* to have your laws in our towns. We want to have every *fashion* altered, also we will do according to your Consul's *word*. Plenty wars here in our country. Plenty murder and plenty idol worshippers. Perhaps these *lines* of our writing will *look* to you as an *idle* tale.

We have *spoken* to the English consul plenty times about having an English *government* here. We never have answer from you, so we wish to write you *ourselves*.

When we heard about Calabar River, how they have all English *laws* in their towns, and how they have put away all their *superstitions*, oh, we shall be very glad to be like Calabar now.

> We are, etc.
> King Acqua
> Prince Dido Acqua
> Prince Black
> Prince Jo Garner
> etc.[1]

These were the kings and princes, notorious slave-owners and no doubt sodden with Oil Rivers gin, whom Hewett and Dilke were proposing should be given an honoured place in the British Empire.

On 18 January 1883, the day after Gladstone's train steamed out of Charing Cross Station carrying the chief on the first leg of his journey to Cannes, a delegation of frock-coated businessmen presented themselves at the Italianate front door of the Foreign Office in Whitehall. They had come to see the Foreign Secretary. They were the directors of the National Africa Company and were led by an elderly peer who happened to be Granville's old Liberal crony, Lord Aberdare.

Perhaps Aberdare pointed out to the others the glowing frescoes that decorated the double staircase which beckoned (as it still beckons today) up to the Foreign Secretary's magnificent room overlooking St James's Park. The frescoes showed Britannia welcoming the gifts of the sea traders. What could be more appropriate for their mission that day? Aberdare and the delegation were sea traders too and they had come to put a plan to Granville that sounded innocuous enough, but was actually even more ambitious than Hewett's scheme. If it succeeded, it would give Britain political control over a great slice of the Niger and central Sudan, whose population comprised about a sixth of the whole continent.

It was no coincidence that Lord Aberdare was a pillar of state, a former Home Secretary of Gladstone's and a former political ally of Granville's. This was why he had been chosen as a front for the National Africa Company. The real leader of the delegation was the company's aggressive and eccentric managing director, forty-three-year-old George Goldie Taubman. Goldie, as he would soon be known (after discarding the inappropriate German part of his surname) came from a family which had been landed gentry on the Isle of Man for generations. The Goldie Taubmans had made their pile in the eighteenth century smuggling trade, but then settled down as conventional squires, landlords and magnates. The eldest son presided over the island from a baronial hall modestly called The Nunnery, whose lawns swept down to the sea. From here he dominated the island's Parliament, the House of Keys, as though it were part of his family estate. The youngest sons were sent out to fight and die in the wars of the Peninsula and Crimea. George Goldie was the fourth son, headstrong and brilliant, as clever and perhaps even more reckless than any of his ancestors in the smuggling trade.

At first it seemed likely that Goldie would come, sooner rather than later, to a bad end. He joined the army, as was expected of him. But he was a human powder magazine (in his own words). He was blind drunk when he passed into the Sappers at Woolwich. After two years he inherited a fortune from a relation, threw up his commission, bolted to Cairo, met a beautiful Egyptian and vanished with her into the wilds of the Sudanese desert. Stories of this part of his life read like a cheap novel. Goldie himself called this strange episode his 'Garden of Allah'. For three years he revelled in his freedom. Perhaps his life was dissipated, but he was not idle. His beautiful mistress taught him colloquial Arabic and they conversed with pilgrims on their way from the Niger to Mecca. Occasionally they rode their camels to Suakin, on the Red Sea, where Goldie would collect a parcel of books sent out from England. He devoured Henry Barth's five-volume masterpiece, *Travels and Discoveries in North and Central Africa*. Slowly an extraordinary idea began to form in his mind.

There was a unity about the vast Sudanic heart of Africa, stretching from the Niger to the Nile, and it was not just the unity of the void. South of the Sahara, the Niger had irrigated a series of ancient civilizations, and Islam had enriched them. It was here, between the Sahara and the sea, between Niger and Nile, that Goldie's El Dorado lay. He would redeem himself by building a vast commercial empire there – under the British flag.

The scheme had the megalomaniac ring of King Leopold's still secret plan for exploiting the Congo. In fact it sounded still more ludicrous. For one thing, unlike the King of the Belgians, Goldie was not one of the richest men in Europe. He was a ne'er-do-well and a misfit who knew nothing about business. For another, this was the heyday of free trade and of Britain's invisible empire. Why on earth should British traders wish to start waving the British flag?

Goldie paid no attention to the conventional wisdom. And he did nothing, it must be said, to detract from his reputation as a rotter. He was bored by the Garden of Allah and by his delightful Egyptian companion, so he abandoned them. He had no sooner returned to The Nunnery in the Isle of Man than he fell head over heels in love with the family governess. He persuaded the poor girl, Matilda Elliot, to elope with him to Paris where they began a stormy affair. Then the love nest snapped shut like a trap. It was August 1870. Bismarck lunged at the French capital with his armies. Paris was besieged. Goldie and the governess endured all the agonies of love on an empty stomach. When they emerged next year, even Goldie had to face responsibility. The pair were married quietly in St Marylebone, London, and Goldie was not to be a particularly faithful husband.

It seemed like a moral tale. Poor George! Look at that bungled career, that unfortunate marriage, the blighted life of a young man from whom so much had been expected.

George was saved, paradoxically enough, by a near bankruptcy in the family. His eldest brother, John, had made a respectable marriage to a sensible girl called Amelia. Her father, Captain Grove-Ross, was secretary of a small London company, Holland and Jacques, which had begun trading for palm oil on the Niger in 1869. By 1875 this admirable firm was in deep water, and sinking fast. Grove-Ross sent an SOS to his son-in-law. The Taubman family rallied round, and bought the assets of Holland and Jacques for a relatively small sum. George, the black sheep, was given the chance to prove himself by saving Amelia's papa. He fancied himself as an expert on the Sudan, so why not go out to the Niger to see for himself what had gone wrong?

Goldie's first plan was predictably wild. He and a younger brother, Alexander, would take a boat up the Niger and follow the caravan track of the Hausa pilgrims in the general direction of Mecca (and the Garden of Allah) – that is, right across the Sudan to the Nile. This plan collapsed when Alexander nearly died in Nupe, not far beyond the rainforests of the Niger. But Goldie had seen enough to confirm his diagnosis of what was wrong with the Niger trade. The disease was competition: too many traders chasing too little palm oil. Only a monopoly could restore the Niger trade to health. On his return he pushed through a drastic scheme to knock together the heads of the four competing English companies. The Taubman family refloated Holland and Jacques as the Central African Trading Company. By 1879 Goldie had amalgamated his own firm with all three of its rivals, including the much bigger firms of Miller Brothers of Glasgow and the West Africa Company of Manchester. The interests of all four firms were pooled in a new United Africa Company, soon changed to the National Africa Company.

One might well ask how Goldie pulled off this coup, when he was a novice in business and had no cash to buy out his rivals. The answer lay partly in Goldie's explosive powers of persuasion. Hard-bitten Glasgow traders trembled when they saw the flash of his bright metallic eyes and felt his wit scorch them like the wind from a blast furnace. But logic was also on his side. The Niger firms were immeasurably stronger now that they could agree to keep down the price they were paying for oil. The chief danger to profits was by paying too high a price to the African producers and middlemen. Money from palm oil seemed like money for jam. The Industrial Revolution had created a double appetite for vegetable oil in Europe: to make lubricants to keep the wheels of the new factories turning; and to make soap to keep the new generation of factory workers clean. But Europe was not prepared to pay fancy prices. There were other sources of supply as well as West Africa. The world price fell steadily as tonnage soared. By ending competition among the English and Scottish traders, Goldie saved the Niger from pricing itself out of the world market.

There remained the threat of competition from Africans. A web of sophisticated black middlemen had once controlled the entire trade of the west coast, ferrying the oil in their canoes along the maze of creeks, taking it from the oil belt in the north of the delta down to the British merchants trading close to the open sea. In parts of the delta and in the other muddy rivers along the coast to the east, all the way to the mountains of Cameroon, these African middlemen had managed to retain a monopoly of the intermediate trade, secured by commercial treaties with the British traders.

But in the main course of the Niger, the four competing British firms had brushed aside what they denounced as an African Mafia. In the rainy season the river was navigable to steamboats all the 300 miles up to the rapids at Bussa. Up the river went the companies' steamboats, the black smoke from the funnels blending with the black mud of the mangrove swamps, until they emerged triumphant in the groves of oil-palms beyond. Here the native chiefs were only too anxious to co-operate. When the African middlemen struck back and sent one of Holland and Jacques's steamboats to the bottom, the traders called in British gunboats to punish the natives. But burning villages and sinking canoes was crude and not particularly effective. There was an obvious lesson, as Goldie saw. The days of unofficial empire were over. It was hopeless to try to do business where they could not impose real law and order by taking direct political control.

Still more alarming, from Goldie's point of view, was the threat of competition from a new source, two large French trading companies. Most alarming of all was the recent news that the French government had openly thrown its weight behind these traders. Would France now annex the middle and lower Niger and try to create there a monopoly for French trade, as she was already doing in Senegal and on the upper course of the same river? It was in order to prevent this disaster – that is to confirm a British monopoly and exclude a French one – that Lord Aberdare and the five directors had presented themselves at the Italianate door of the Foreign Office on 18 January 1883 to see the Foreign Secretary.

No one seems to have kept formal minutes of the meeting, but the arguments can be pieced together from the letters and notes of the principals. Granville was flanked by his advisers, including the Assistant Under-Secretary, Villiers Lister, and the FO's African expert, Percy Anderson. No doubt Goldie did most of the talking; he was irrepressible. Aberdare simply introduced the delegation. Granville was told that the African Company had no wish for 'exclusive advantages' to monopolize the trade of the Niger. What was meant by this was that the NAC believed that free trade would offer them an honest monopoly by allowing them to undercut all competition. By contrast the protectionist French would impose an unfair monopoly by blocking competition with tariffs. Relations with Africans were 'most amicable', the delegation continued, except for a few 'barbarous natives on the Delta'. The danger was the new French designs on the Niger.

The French as you are aware are pushing on, with some vigour, in Railway communication between the Senegal and Sego [sic] and the upper Niger.

Should they succeed in doing so they would probably obtain the monopoly of the traffic above Timbuctoo. To this, however objectionable in principle, we do not object – the District seems beyond the reach, for many a long year, of English commercial enterprise.

Nor do we wish to imitate them on the Lower Niger. We are perfectly willing to encounter all fair competition. But we have reason for fearing ... that the French government may induce some native rulers on the *Middle Niger* to give them the monopoly of the traffic, and to impose heavy duties on British goods – so as to prevent the natural upward extension of British traffic.[2]

It was James Hutton, a cotton trader, Liberal MP and the NAC's most experienced director (he was President of the Manchester Chamber of Commerce), who explained the reason for these fears. Hutton also had an alarming new story to tell about Brazza, whom he had recently met in Paris. The young explorer had told him that originally he had been instructed by the French government to go to the Niger and make treaties giving France a protectorate there. Then he heard about Stanley's plans and was sent off to the Congo instead. This was actually just a piece of Brazza's blarney, but the Whitehall officials took the point. Brazza had shown how to be a hero, French-style, by giving France a slice of Africa. Other would-be heroes would follow in his trail, and make treaties with the Niger chiefs; and these treaties might be ratified. So how could Britain stop France from grabbing the lower Niger? Only by annexing it as a British colony, or at least declaring it a protectorate? Either method would slam the door on the French. But they would have to convince the Cabinet, and Gladstone, who talked as though free trade was part of the moral law and annexations were the temptations of the devil.

Goldie had his own dramatic plan which he did not yet care to let Aberdare reveal to the British government. The National African Company would take over the whole of the lower and middle Niger and govern it themselves under a royal charter, as their own private colony. What Aberdare told the British government was much more innocuous. Goldie had apparently heard through the grapevine that Whitehall favoured a comprehensive settlement with France to slice up West Africa into British and French spheres of power and influence. Aberdare now tried to persuade Granville to make a Niger deal along these lines. The French would promise not to attempt a political takeover anywhere on the Niger south of, say, Timbuctu; in turn the British would agree to give France a free hand in the upper Niger. Perhaps a deal could be made involving a swap of the French settlements scattered along the west coast for the British colony of Gambia. But whether the French took the Gambia bait or not, a simple bargain made sense: west of an agreed line the Niger should be French, east of the line the Niger should be British – that is if the British government would bother to take up the option.

Nothing was revealed of Goldie's own political designs for the Niger, and of the great highway leading to his El Dorado in the central Sudan. Nor was there

any thought of trouble from Germany. In January 1883 no one dreamt that
Bismarck would try to grab a slice of Britain's unofficial empire.

In the next few days, Granville's cautious advisers at the FO digested Goldie's
plan. Despite themselves, they were impressed. It saved British trade on the Niger
from being stifled by the French. It asked nothing of the British government. Lord
Lyons, the British Ambassador in France, was expected to sound the Quai
d'Orsay. Meanwhile, the file was passed to the Colonial Office. They had
notoriously little appetite for increasing their own responsibilities, but with
Gambia thrown in (or more accurately, Gambia thrown out), would the co
take the bait?

In 1882 it had been Lord Kimberley, as Colonial Secretary, who had turned
down flat the ambitious scheme of Consul Hewett for accepting the appeal of
King Acqua to Queen Victoria and taking formal control of the whole coast
from Lagos to Cameroon. Kimberley had written pungently, 'The coast is
pestilential, the natives numerous and unmanageable.' The new Colonial Secretary was Lord Derby, the great Lancashire magnate, ex-Foreign Secretary and
refugee from the Tory Cabinet, from which he had resigned with 'Twitters'
(Carnarvon) in a mysterious fit of conscience five years earlier. His conscience
showed no sign of troubling him as Colonial Secretary. He seemed so supine
that his absence would hardly have been noticed. The Colonial Office's affairs
were left in the hands of two languid civil servants: Robin Herbert, the Permanent Under-Secretary, and Robert Meade, the Assistant Under-Secretary.
The two men read Goldie's plan and they too were impressed. They were
worried at the thought of the French trying Brazza tactics on the Niger, but
they felt helpless to act.

It must be emphasized that there were three British empires supposed to be
ruled from Whitehall. India belonged to the India Office. The colonies, white,
brown and black, belonged to the Colonial Office. Protectorates, official and
unofficial (like Egypt), and the whole invisible empire of trade, all belonged to
the Foreign Office. So the Colonial Office was perfectly happy to acquiesce in
Goldie's scheme. He had asked nothing of them at all.

However, as Meade pointed out to Herbert, if the deal with France was made
by surrendering Gambia, that too would suit the Colonial Office. Meade had a
Gladstonian horror of new colonies. They always lost money – at any rate at
the beginning. But if money could be saved by extending the frontiers of old
colonies – that was quite different. The French settlements on the west coast
drove a fatal wedge between the British ones. Not one of these was really safe
(from the risk of the Colonial Office having to bail them out). They did not
control enough of their hinterland or seaboards. This in turn meant they could
not levy enough taxes to pay for their running costs. But a Gambia swap would
change everything. Gambia was a liability: fever-ridden, impoverished, boxed
in by Senegal. Give it to the French and let Senegal swallow it. In return let the
whole west coast be British to exploit when it suited them: the Ivory Coast, the

Gold Coast, Togoland, Dahomey, Lagos, the Niger and Cameroon (King Bell and King Acqua included).

Herbert disputed the point with Meade. Parliament would never agree to surrender Gambia. But he was prepared to acquiesce in Goldie's plan, and the point soon became academic. In early March 1883 came a devastating reply from Lyons, the British Ambassador in Paris. Gladstone had just decided to abolish dual control in Egypt. This had put the French in such an ugly frame of mind that it would be useless to talk of any new arrangement with them. Since March the new Prime Minister had been Jules Ferry, who could be counted on to play up to the new jingoist mood of the French. It was as though the Nile had burst its banks and flooded the desert all the way to the Niger.

To add to the difficulties the Congo, too, suddenly threatened to overflow into the Niger. In trying to protect British commercial interests on the Congo, the Foreign Office had had the bold idea of doing a deal with Portugal. This put the French in a still uglier frame of mind. It was even feared they might take reprisals against the British on the Niger.

It was not Leopold's designs on the Congo that drove the cautious experts of the FO to take this initiative. Leopold was a philanthropist, so he said. His real motives might be somewhat less high-minded, and the FO, after Stanley had let the cat half out of the bag, had a shrewd idea what they were. But they saw no danger of the King trying to interfere with British trade on the Congo, either at the mouth of the river or up-country. In fact, a rumour had just reached their ears in February 1883 that the King's Congo interests would be taken over by a British company. This was 'not unlikely', according to Villiers Lister, the Assistant Under-Secretary. The FO had always assumed that the King's childish escapade into the Congo would run into the sand.

The man who worried the FO, as he worried the CO, was Leopold's rival, Brazza. In November 1882 the British had been badly rattled by his success in persuading the French government to ratify his treaty with King Makoko. Were the French now planning a political takeover of the whole enormous Congo basin? If so, French tariffs would soon extinguish free trade, meaning British trade supremacy. These had already hampered them in Gabon, the base of Brazza's operations. So the FO made a bold attempt to stymie Brazza. Within a fortnight of the French decree ratifying the Makoko treaty, Britain began wooing Portugal. The British government would formally recognize Portuguese sovereignty over both banks of the lower Congo.

Setting Portugal against France – that was a rusty weapon to use, and it crumpled in the hands of the FO. Influential Liberals denounced their own government in the House of Commons.

In the first place, it was an absurdity to accept Portugal's claim after more than fifty years of strenuously repudiating it. Ever since 1810 there had been bitter disputes between Britain and Portugal over the slave trade. Until mid-century, Portugal had claimed the right to export slaves from the part of the West African coast under her own sovereignty – this included both sides of the

Congo estuary as far north as Cabinda. Britain had disputed both the moral right to export slaves and the territorial sovereignty.

In the second place, how could Portugal be trusted to respect free trade? The British government rightly perceived that French tariffs would kill off British trade with the Congo, but they were now planning a treaty with a country whose colonial tariffs were even more discriminatory than France's. Dilke desperately cited the safeguards. Under the terms of the proposed treaty, Portugal would have to agree to three conditions: a maximum tariff, most-favoured-nation status for Britain, and an Anglo-Portuguese commission to control traffic on the lower Congo.

The proposed treaty soon stirred up a hornet's nest. In England it was denounced by the very traders whose interests it was supposed to protect. It also brought down the wrath of the Anti-Slavery Society and the Baptist missionaries, neither of whom placed any confidence in the Portuguese, judging them by their disgraceful behaviour in Angola. (Both campaigns – free traders and do-gooders – were secretly orchestrated by King Leopold.) Still more momentous, Britain's reckless deal with Portugal drove France to fish around for new allies. (It was Bismarck who came up in the net, to the consternation of the British. But this is to anticipate.)

In the spring of 1883 the Nile and the Congo had only just begun to overflow into the Niger. Neither Hewett's plan nor Goldie's had got off the ground and no one in either the Foreign Office or the Colonial Office seemed to think there was much urgency to do anything about them. Then in April the French made two moves forward that suddenly convinced the FO that a French takeover of the whole west coast was 'no longer a contingency' but 'imminent'.

First, as a result of a treaty between the French republic and King Tofa of Porto Novo, the French naval commander on the west coast had hoisted the tricolour at that town and re-established a French protectorate there that had been abandoned for twenty years owing to the savage practices of King Tofa's father, and the difficulty of defending Porto Novo. This and other treaties with local kings gave the French control of the main coastline of Dahomey, to within fifty miles of Lagos at the western end of the same lagoon. Second, the French sent a gunboat, the *Voltigeur*, to cruise along the Niger delta and the Oil Rivers. In April the ship's captain tried to make a commercial treaty with King Pepple at Bonny and later the same month he bobbed up in Cameroon. For the time being the French overtures had been rebuffed. But the Admiralty reported that King Acqua and King Bell of Cameroon might sign the treaty with the French. They had lost patience after three years without an answer to that appeal to Queen Victoria.

These reports roused even the Colonial Secretary from his slumbers. Re-establishing the protectorate at Porto Novo was an example, said Lord Derby, of French 'aggression'.[3] Action was urgent. But what kind of action would be effective? As the anxious memoranda flew between the great departments of state, it became apparent even to Whitehall that an undignified race, a scramble for West Africa, was now in progress, parallel to the scramble for the Congo.

Here, too, Britain seemed to have all the advantages. She had been first to explore the Niger's secrets, first to tap its hidden oil, first to rule it unofficially. Would Britain now try to regularize the union with a formal contract for a protectorate? Apart from Dilke, Gladstone's colleagues still shrank from formal union and visible empire, as though the proposal were somehow indecent.

Goldie had got nowhere in Whitehall. Was it all bluff, this invisible empire, a bluff that France could be ill-mannered enough to call?

*   *   *

Everything now depended on Edward Hewett, the masterful British Consul and unofficial ruler of the Niger. One of his bases was at Bonny where he enjoyed the picturesque title of Her Majesty's Consul for the Bights of Benin and Biafra. There was little else on the west coast to enjoy, but Hewett did not grumble. He was an ex-officer of the militia, something of an explorer and a convivial fellow except when he was prostrate with fever, as he was much of the time.

Bonny was the place where the mail steamers dumped their loads of Manchester cottons and crates of obsolete rifles, among the walls of dark green mangrove, mud flats and white factories of the traders. People said Bonny was a nice place once you got used to it – if you lived that long. But nobody talked of love at first sight. 'Good heavens! What an awful accident. We've gone and picked up the Styx',[4] Mary Kingsley was to remark in the 1890s, as the steamer slipped in across the foam of the sandbar, gleaming and wicked against Breaker Island. There was nothing but dripping walls of rotten mangrove and reeking mud, apart from the half-submerged black ribs of old hulks (once used as trading stations), like the skeletons of unclean beasts poisoned by Bonny water. During the 'wet' – the dismal months from May to September – there were only two sounds, the crying of the curlews and the dull roar of the rain. Sometimes it rained for six weeks at a stretch, coming down like a water spout.

The same old coaster who claimed that Bonny was a nice place when you got used to it, would go on to describe the last epidemic of yellow fever, when nine out of eleven white residents died in ten days. During one funeral two junior clerks who had been drinking fell into the grave before the coffin, which was lowered on top of them, and all three had to be pulled out again. 'Barely necessary though, was it?' someone would say, 'for those two had to have a grave of their own before next sundown.'[5]

If Bonny was nothing more than a mangrove swamp, so was the rest of the coastal strip of Consul Hewett's unofficial empire, a dark green line of swamps from Lagos to the Rio del Rey. It was thought to be the largest coastal swamp in the world. Mary Kingsley saw that it had beauty of a kind. In *Travels in West Africa* she compared its gloomy grandeur to that of the Himalayas. But at first the sameness was crushing. It seemed to be a landscape without landmarks. Every steaming inlet, every reeking tidal creek, every rotten mudflat looked the same for hundreds of miles, as though cast from the same mould.

To find a way up the Niger was like exploring a hundred miles of green sponge. It turned out that the delta had twenty-three real mouths and numerous false ones. No wonder that explorers had taken longer to find the exit from the Niger than the source of the Nile. Later, slave-runners had played hide-and-seek with the navy for years in those pestilential creeks, too shallow at low tide for anything but a dug-out canoe.

Hewett had returned in the rainy season of 1882 despite warnings from his doctor that his health would not stand it. The immediate problem was to settle the endless trade disputes with Africans, and restore order where it had been disturbed. Still more important, he had to report back to the FO to explain why Britain must take formal control over the whole coast from Lagos to Cameroon.

Informal empire was not enough. That was the long and the short of it. He was expected to impose law and order, but he did not have the means to do so. Formal empire was essential for two reasons: to break the power of the African middlemen who made it impossible for Europeans to trade safely and profitably on the Oil Rivers – and to keep out the French.

Hewett found that while he had been away things had gone to the devil in many parts of the Niger. On the coast the chief troublemaker was King Ja-Ja of Opobo. Most African traders acquiesced in Hewett's overall authority. Some even welcomed it. Unfortunately Ja-Ja rejected it as a matter of principle. Ever since Hewett had arrived in 1880, Ja-Ja had been a thorn in his side. Ja-Ja had outmanœuvred Hewett with the same maddening finesse he displayed towards all his opponents, black and white. Now Hewett had finally lost patience with this upstart.

Years before, Ja-Ja had been brought to Bonny as a humble Ibo slave. He was tall and handsome and proved a genius at trading. After most of the slaves were liberated, he led one faction of them in a revolt against George Pepple, the King of Bonny. He was beaten by the leader of a rival faction of ex-slaves and fled with his people to the safety of a neighbouring creek, Opobo. He was finished – so it appeared. Within a few years he emerged as the king of the biggest black trading empire on the coast. He sold 8,000 tons of palm oil a year to the white traders at Opobo and he imposed a ruthless monopoly on the black producers in the oil-palm forest inland. Anyone attempting to touch this monopoly, black or white, ended with their canoes smashed and their bodies floating in the creek.

Hewett had to investigate a recent dispute between Ja-Ja and the people of Qua Ibo. Ja-Ja's business methods horrified him. Ja-Ja's men had taken a hundred prisoners from Qua Ibo back to Opobo. A few were said to be still alive. Most had been tortured and killed. Some had been eaten. When Hewett protested, Ja-Ja laughed in his face. He had made it worth the while of the Liverpool traders to support him through thick and thin. Then Ja-Ja wrote Granville a courtly letter (no doubt drafted by one of the traders), apologizing for 'troubling him again on native affairs'. He admitted dealing firmly with Qua Ibo, but was it 'the wish of Her Britannic Majesty's government thus to extend protection to every little African village who aspired to independence, and in so doing to murder the emissaries of their rightful sovereign'.[6] Hewett failed to persuade London that Ja-Ja must be deposed. Instead the Liverpool traders lobbied Granville to give Hewett the sack.

Up the Niger itself, away from the pernicious influence of middlemen like Ja-Ja, trade was in better shape. In Hewett's eyes a monopoly, when exercised by Goldie's National African Company, became a healthy instrument of British policy. In the bad years before Goldie had taken over, British gunboats had to make punitive expeditions up the Niger every rainy season as soon as the river rose. These gunboats left a trail of havoc in the towns that gave trouble to white traders; everything was methodically burnt (after the British trade goods had been first moved to safety) and the bodies of women and children left in the charred ruins. Nowadays there were fewer of these unpleasant episodes. However, the NAC had no police or army – or indeed authority – to keep order. After his return from England in the summer of 1882, Hewett got an SOS from the NAC's manager, David McIntosh. There had been trouble from the Patanis 120 miles up the river. Presumably they resented the company's monopoly. They had looted the factory at Asaba, after killing the manager and four of his men. Unless these Patanis were taught a lesson, the company might as well pack its bags and leave the Niger.

Hewett's punitive expedition in the autumn of 1882 was not particularly violent by the standards of the time or place. But Hewett could cite the attacks on company property, as he cited King Ja-Ja's atrocities, to show that informal empire was not enough. On 14 November he boarded HMS *Flirt*, which left the main channel and headed up one of the branches of the river leading through dense palm forests. A day's steaming brought them to Asaba. Someone fired a blunderbuss at them from the river-bank. Hewett ordered the town to be destroyed by shell-fire and rockets. During the night they heard war chants and the sound of tom-toms. It appeared that an attack by canoes was imminent. The Gatling guns fired into the darkness and the noise ceased. Next day another town, Abari, was destroyed by shell-fire after the people had refused to give up any offenders. To make the destruction more complete, some Blue Jackets landed and burnt all the huts in the neighbourhood. A third town, Torofani, was left in smoking ruins and the inhabitants killed or expelled. None of the men who had attacked the factory at Asaba was handed over to justice. But Hewett sailed back to Bonny, pleased that he had taught the Patanis a useful lesson. The right of the British to 'trade in a peaceful manner'[7] had been vindicated at low cost: two sailors grazed by slugs. But punitive expeditions were no substitute for real authority. This was the first reason why Britain must take over the Oil Rivers.

The second reason was to keep out the French. Hewett had found the tricolour spreading like a rash far up the Niger and its tributaries. In 1880 there had not been a single French trading post from Brass to Nupe. By 1882 the tricolour had penetrated further up the Benue than the Union Jack. The first French company bold enough to challenge the British on the Niger was a subsidiary of Desprez and Huchet, the powerful Paris firm. This subsidiary was called the Compagnie Française de l'Afrique Equatoriale, the brainchild of an ex-officer of *tirailleurs*, the Comte de Semellé. The poor man had died of west coast fever in 1880, but the directors then persuaded another colonial army officer, Captain Mattei, to take on this dangerous post. As an encouragement, the French government made Mattei its consular agent. In 1882 a second French firm, the Senegal Company, owned by the politically well-connected Marseilles firm of Werminck added its support. There was now a total of thirty-three French factories on the river, designed as a direct challenge to their British counterparts. Soon the French might outnumber the British. Even without French tariffs, this reckless competition would cripple the NAC. But if the French government annexed the lower Niger as seemed to be imminent, they would impose tariffs against British goods. Then the NAC would sink like a stone. Commercially, as well as politically, the Niger would be a French river from its source to the Gulf of Guinea.

This was the alarming lesson that Hewett took back with him when he sailed home in April 1883. He added confirmation of his own claim that the Niger chiefs would be only too glad to be incorporated in a British protectorate. He even brought back an appeal for protection, signed by three chiefs of Akassa, where the NAC had its headquarters. And he had at long last paid a flying visit to Cameroon to see King Acqua and King Bell. Hewett was most impressed; the place was full of commercial promise. Despite the failure of Queen Victoria to answer their 'loving letter', King Acqua and King Bell still seemed desperate to join the Empire.

*   *   *

Commandant Antoine Mattei, Agent-General of the CFAO and Consular Agent of the French Republic, did not return to the mouth of the Niger from Paris until 3 April 1883. While he had been away, the French government had sent the *Voltigeur* on the cruise that had so alarmed the Foreign Office in London. In fact the *Voltigeur* had achieved nothing except to stiffen opposition. In Bonny the French were laughed at. In Cameroon only a disreputable chief called King Pass-All was prepared to sign on the dotted line.

The moment Mattei returned he decided to attack. He had brought draft treaty forms. He would sign up Brass, the site of his own HQ, at the central mouth of the Niger, and the thorn in the side of Goldie's company. When Mattei had been made agent-general by Desprez, he was told that his mission was *'plus patriotique que commerciale'*. Yet Mattei himself was not an anglophobe like so many officers of the French Marines who had served in Algeria and Senegal. He was a Frenchman from Corsica, an excitable man with a heavy jowl and a great bushy moustache, intensely patriotic, yet fascinated by the British. How strange they seemed to him, those gloomy, tongue-tied British army officers bound for Ashanti, whom he had met on the boat out from Liverpool. As his nephew said, they might have been made of polished marble. But how he envied them the steamers of the two great British shipping lines, based in Liverpool, that dominated the West African run. Why on earth couldn't patriotic French shipowners start a West African line of their own?

'*Allez, voyez, faites comme les anglais.*'[8] Those had been his original instructions from the Ministry of Foreign Affairs in Paris: act like the British. How he longed to! But there were handicaps of every kind. Not least was the deadly climate. He lost seven of his young, patriotic companions, including the brave young nephew who had come out to serve as his secretary. The terrible British, who were seeking in these regions a new India to add to their empire, suffered heartbreaks too, but at least they could always rely completely on the support of their government. It was this 'blind' confidence in his government that was the British businessman's greatest asset, according to Mattei – a view that would have brought a cynical laugh from Goldie.

Mattei had chosen Brass as the Achilles heel of the NAC on the Niger. Brass's black middlemen had been slowly starved out by the British firms on the delta above them. Once they had exported 5,000 tons of palm oil through their port. Now they were lucky to export 1,500. They had appealed to Whitehall for fair play: 'We have no land where we can grow plantains or yams; if we cannot trade we must starve.'[9] As rivals of the Niger Company, the Liverpool traders backed them. But Whitehall turned a deaf ear. In desperation they had bought arms from the Liverpool traders and taken reprisals against the ships of the firms which had stolen their markets. It was they, or their African allies, who had sent the Holland and Jacques steamer to the bottom. In turn, British gunboats took violent reprisals against Brass, burning towns and villages along the river.

On 9 August 1883 Mattei offered to rescue Brass by taking it under his wing. He showed the chiefs the terms of the protectorate, which excluded any further treaty with any rivals. They agreed to sign, but next day he returned to find they had gone back on their word. It turned out that British solidarity had been too strong for him. Even the Liverpool traders, sworn enemies of Goldie's monopoly higher up the river, closed ranks to keep the French out.

The rebuff jolted Mattei. He gamely set off northward hoping to get his own back. He stocked up the company's steamer, the *Nupe*, with the usual European offerings for sale – powder, guns, gin, rum, iron bars and so on – and steamed up the Niger, beyond the limits of the palm forest, then headed eastwards up the Benue, higher than any European explorer had ever been, except for the intrepid William Baikie who had pioneered trade there thirty years earlier. He was now on the south-east fringe of the Islamic states that owed allegiance, at least in theory, to the great Sultan of Sokoto. A month later, Mattei was steaming north up the Niger itself into the rich Islamic kingdom of Nupe, after which his steamer had been named. Already the NAC depended on Nupe for about a third of its total Niger trade: roughly £50,000 from ivory and £50,000 from shea butter (a kind of margarine). Goldie had made no secret of his conviction that it was in these rich populous Sudanic states of the Sokoto empire, north of the Niger and Benue – Nupe, Gando, Adamawa, Sokoto itself – that his El Dorado lay.

Mattei shared Goldie's golden dream. The western Sudan was a world away from the putrid swamps of the delta: a limitless savannah of dry heat and great dazzling skies. The people up here were comparatively civilized. Mattei felt repelled by that fetid coast; by the yellow mud of the Niger that polluted the water ten miles out to sea, by the degraded pagan rites and fetishes. To an officer who had served with the *tirailleurs* in Algeria, the Sudan was more like home. There was a unity about Islam under the skin, a sense of values shared with Europe. You saw this in the disciplined lines of white turbans bowing to Mecca; in the respect for lawyers and scholars (and for bankers and letters of credit); in the power, however precarious, of one throne backed by the fear of one god.

In Nupe, it must be said, the power of the Emir's throne seemed to be unusually precarious. But this proved to Mattei's advantage. In 1882 he had arrived there to find the Emir paralysed by a rebellion of Niger boatmen. The Emir's cavalry and guns, sold to him by the NAC, were cut off on the west side of the river and he himself was stuck in his palace at Bida to the east. Mattei insisted on sending his own steamer to assist the NAC's improvised gunboat, which was steaming to the rescue. Mattei's intervention not only had helped break the rebellion, it broke the NAC's monopoly in Nupe. The grateful Emir granted Mattei sites for factories alongside his rivals. By 1883 French competition threatened to make Nupe as unprofitable for Goldie as the rest of the Niger.

Leaving the tricolour flapping in the clear air of Chonga, the finest factory yet to be established, Mattei steamed back into the murk of the palm forest, and the putrid mangrove swamps of Brass. Despite his successes in the north, he was becoming discouraged. How right Desprez had been to call this mission '*plus patriotique que commercial*'. He was making no money for his firm, the Compagnie Française de l'Afrique Equatoriale, by challenging the British monopoly. Surely the next step must be political: direct support from the French government. It struck Mattei as strange that he, the consular-agent, never received any instructions from the Ministry of Marine or the Ministry of Foreign Affairs. He had been humiliated by the French government's refusal to send fitting presents to the Emir of Nupe. All he had been given for this purpose was a tenth of the sum available to Consul Hewett. Moreover, the French navy seemed to have forgotten him.

To add to Mattei's troubles, the rainy season of 1883 proved shortlived, and the level of the Niger fell overnight. As a result, two of his newest steamers, the *Nupe* and the *Moleki*, were stranded up-river, where they would have to remain, high and dry, until the following June. Worse, the property of his firm, the CFAE, was overtaken by a series of mysterious accidents. One of the steamers, the *Adamawa*, was sunk after a collision and a factory at Loko was burnt down with the loss of 70,000 francs of trade goods.

In December Mattei embarked once more by a British steamer bound for Liverpool. He was sick and utterly demoralized. Patriotism would not suffice. He decided to resign from the company.

Meanwhile, Gladstone's Cabinet had been finally forced to turn its gaze towards the repellent west coast of Africa. For a year and a half Hewett's voice had been ridiculed in Whitehall when he advocated an Oil Rivers protectorate. In June 1883 he found an ally in the man who, for the next decade, would do more than anyone else to see that Britain got her rightful share in the Scramble for Africa. This was Percy Anderson, head of the newly-created African Department in the Foreign Office, and brilliant (in a blinkered kind of way). Hewett reported back to the office at the beginning of June. A week later Anderson sounded a trumpet call for action which must have been designed to rattle the windows in Whitehall and send the CO's eyeglasses flying.

He had talked to Hewett, he said, who confirmed that a protectorate under one flag or another was inevitable. Unless the chiefs of the Oil Rivers were given British protection, for which they were prepared, they would 'unquestionably put themselves in the hands of the French'. Anderson went on:

> How can we doubt that the French will take them? If there is one thing clearer than another, it seems to be that the French have a settled policy in Africa, both on the East and the West coast and that that policy is antagonistic to us. The progress of this policy is sometimes sluggish, sometimes feverish, but it never ceases. ... Railways are being pushed in Senegal from Saint-Louis to the Upper Niger. Connection is being established with the Soudan, and a push is being made towards Timbuctoo. New stations have recently been established at Grand Bassam, and Assinie [on the Ivory Coast]. M. de Brazza is on the Congo ... from Porto Novo the trade of Lagos is attacked; the French official agent is at work above the delta of the Niger, while the captain of the 'Voltigeur' is trying to induce the natives of the mouths of that river to accept his Treaties. If he succeeds in this, the final step will have been taken, and British trade will have no chance of existence except at the mercy of French officials.
>
> Action seems to be forced on us, and if this is so, we are fairly forced into a corner as to the direction of it. Only one course seems possible; that is, to take on ourselves the Protectorates of the native States at the mouth of the Oil Rivers, and on the adjoining coast.

Only by putting out both hands to grab these protectorates could Britain avoid 'an unseemly and dangerous race with the French'[10] – in short, a Scramble. If this was done, the French would have to give up their intrigues; they would have to negotiate. Then, and only then, would it make sense to talk about exchanging Gambia, which was the real objective of French policy. They could be made to pay a lot for it: Gabon, the lower Niger, the Gold Coast and the Ivory Coast. These would be cheap at the price.

'Action seems to be forced on us ... we are fairly in a corner.' Lord Derby and his staff at the CO received Anderson's trumpet call with studied distaste. The FO could declare protectorates – that was up to them – but the CO could take no responsibility. Months passed. The FO changed tactics. By October 1883 Granville was suggesting that a more suitable solution might be to make the

Oil Rivers a *colony*, and thus it would be directly governed by Britain and the responsibility of the CO, not the FO. The new tactics flushed out Derby at last. Crown colony or protectorate? Derby agreed that the wrangle could only be resolved by Gladstone and his Cabinet, and it was presented to them on 22 November.

Gladstone looked at the murky waters of the Niger with as much distaste as Derby. His own thoughts were far away. After his return from his winter holiday in Cannes, he had flung himself into the parliamentary fray with his old pugnacity. Egypt continued to be the government's bed of nails. The French were furious about a British plan to build a second Suez Canal and the plan collapsed. There was a debate on Egypt in June during which Gladstone was outraged by the sneers of the Tories. How dare they suggest that the Liberals had gone into Egypt to usurp the place of the Khedive's government? They had gone there only to reinstate it. As for Gladstone's own colleagues, they had stuck together surprisingly well, except that Lord Rosebery, over-sensitive to criticism, insisted on resigning and Joe Chamberlain, insensitive as always, made a speech at Birmingham which the Queen called 'dangerous and improper'.[11] Without Cabinet approval, he forecast universal household suffrage and payment for Members of Parliament. Gladstone had to apologize to the Queen in order to rescue Chamberlain from his folly.

But how to rescue the Oil Rivers from the French? The Cabinet naturally plumped for the cheapest possible answer. This brought them straight back to Hewett's and Anderson's plan. A paper protectorate, with virtually no administration, would cost nothing compared with a real colony – at least in the early years. So protectorate it must be. But even the trifling cost of the protectorate – salaries of two or three vice-consuls, say £5,000 a year plus their expenses – was too heavy a burden for the British taxpayer. Someone else must pay. The Cabinet was adamant. It was left to the FO to decide where to send the bill.

That a French coup in the Oil Rivers was imminent had been recognized for months. But even now, after the government had steeled itself to make a decision, the FO was still in a corner. The problem was how to find that trifling sum of £5,000 a year to pay for the new protectorate. As the FO understood the rules, taxes could not be raised on exports from a protectorate, as opposed to a colony, for a protectorate was, at least on paper, foreign territory. Would British traders volunteer to pay? Could they be trusted to keep a secret? The FO was alarmed that their plans would leak out and precipitate the French coup. Then someone – Granville perhaps – had a brain-wave. Of course there *was* one man he could vouch for among the traders, his old friend Aberdare. Aberdare could sound out all the other traders – in complete confidence. The Niger trade was worth £300,000 a year. Why should it be a problem for the traders to cough up the missing £5,000?

Time was more precious than money. If Goldie had been a simple-minded British patriot trying to colour the map red, as some of his later admirers took him for, now was the moment to show it. But he had his own ideas, as mentioned earlier, not for a protectorate run by the FO, but for one administered under royal charter by the NAC. In short, he would rule the Niger himself. This revolutionary plan still had to be kept secret from the Foreign Office, but Goldie was still trying to torpedo an ordinary protectorate. No, the traders would not pay a penny of that £5,000 a year, though the NAC would supply an unpaid vice-consul in the shape of their own agent-general, David McIntosh. This was Aberdare's resolute reply to his old friend Granville. He did not feel free to add that he had consulted no other traders. He spoke only for Goldie and the NAC.

Back in their corner once more, the FO dismally cast about for economies. They were forced to accept McIntosh as vice-consul which might save about £1,500 a year. The balance would have to be raised by closing consulates all over the world. Valparaiso, Honolulu – the axe rose and fell. Like an impoverished landlord forced to reduce his list of charities, the representatives of the richest trading country in the world slowly performed this painful exercise. At last it was done. On 16 May 1884 Consul Hewett, loaded with blank treaty forms and rum for King Acqua and King Bell, was free to set sail for the Oil Rivers coast.

The Cabinet's interest in the Niger had long since ebbed away. In May 1884 it was the Congo that was in full spate along Downing Street. After more than a year's shilly-shallying, hoping to get better terms from the French, the Portuguese had finally signed the Congo treaty with Britain. This acknowledged Portugal's right to sovereignty over the lower Congo as far as Matadi and the first rapids. It was thus supposed to protect British trade by blocking Brazza's advance to the sea.

But the French made a hullabaloo, threatening to take reprisals in Egypt, which was still bankrupt, despite the British occupation. Britain needed the other European Powers' agreement to raise loans for Egypt, or she would have to subsidize Egypt all by herself. Jules Ferry persuaded Bismarck to join sides with France against Britain. That killed the Anglo-Portuguese treaty stone dead.

It was fortunate for Britain – so Gladstone's Cabinet could reflect – that Bismarck had never shown the slightest appetite for colonies in Africa or anywhere else. He ridiculed the very idea.

After Hewett had sailed, Percy Anderson, his principal supporter, ought to have been forgiven for a moment's self-congratulation. He had stopped the rot. The old, informal British Empire was doomed. It had taken exactly two and a half years to rouse the Cabinet and Whitehall to recognize this simple truth. Hewett's mission would inaugurate a new formal empire. The Gambia swap would follow and then Britain would take over the whole west coast from Senegal to the Congo. Prompt action would prevent that 'unseemly and dangerous race with the French'.

Poor Anderson. If only it had been as simple as that.

*   *   *

Hewett's ship, the *Benguela*, dawdled along the steamy little west coast ports and did not anchor in the harbour at Benin till 18 June 1884. Thereafter Hewett lost no time in arranging palavers to make a chain of treaties, working his way west from Opobo and then sailing east to Cameroon. Thus he planned to keep the pleasantest part of his mission till the end. No doubt Kings Acqua and Bell had been counting the days till his return. In Cameroon there were green hills above the river and a delicious breeze from a 13,000-foot-high mountain. Hewett intended to build a sanitorium there and perhaps to make it his own headquarters.

In early July he embarked on HMS *Flirt*. The FO had given him blank treaty forms, each consisting of the same eight articles. Articles I and II gave Britain political rights to a protectorate. Article VI gave her the right to free trade, ending the middlemen's monopoly. There was no problem about the first two articles, but there were no takers for Article VI at any of the ports of the delta. Nonetheless, Hewett hoisted the Union Jack, distributed presents and obtained a series of treaties at numerous ports along the Niger coast. These treaties, however little they were understood by the men who put their marks on the blank treaty forms, were to be of vital importance. They would serve as the title deeds of Britain's future colony of Nigeria.

On 15 July Hewett was still engaged in palaver with the chiefs at Benin when a British naval officer brought him alarming news of a foreign gunboat in Cameroon. There was a report that those on board were negotiating a treaty with King Acqua and King Bell; however, the Kings had agreed to give Hewett a week to make a counter offer. Hewett dropped everything. On the afternoon of 19 July, HMS *Flirt* steamed into the harbour at Bell Town.

Hewett peered through the heat haze and then rubbed his eyes. Three foreign flags were flying from flagstaffs among the mangrove swamps. But they were not the red, white and blue of the tricolour. They carried the black cross of the Kaiser's Germany.

Five days earlier the famous German explorer, Dr Gustav Nachtigal, now Imperial Consul-General for the west coast of Africa, had been rowed ashore from the gunboat *Möwe* by a party of German Blue Jackets. He informed the astounded British traders that he was taking possession of Cameroon in the name of the German emperor.

Bismarck had stolen a march on everyone. Nothing could now stop that 'unseemly and dangerous race'. The most feverish phase of the Scramble had begun.

CHAPTER 12

Why Bismarck Changed his Mind

Germany, Africa and London
19 May 1884 – November 1884

'[I look] with satisfaction, sympathy and joy upon
the extension of Germany in these desert places of
the earth.'

The British Prime Minister, W. E. *Gladstone*, 1 September
1884

It was not only Hewett who was astonished. Bismarck's own advisers reeled.
Two months earlier, on 19 May 1884, the Imperial Chancellor, Prince
Bismarck, had cabled secret orders to Nachtigal in Lisbon that startled even
Bismarck's inner circle at the German Foreign Office. Nachtigal was to hoist
the German flag at Cameroon – and more. His mission was to seize two other
protectorates as well: at Little Popo (Togoland) and Angra Pequena (south-west
Africa). Together they would give Germany an African colonial empire five
times the size of the Reich. The Chancellor had always ridiculed colonies as a
liability for Germany. What on earth had possessed him to change his mind
now?

That astonishing cipher cable to Nachtigal had been despatched from 76
Wilhelmstrasse, the headquarters of the Foreign Ministry in Berlin, next to
which Bismarck had his own quarters. This was a modest, single-storeyed house,
with a small garden at the back, out of character and scale, one might have
thought, with his own demonic spirit. But Bismarck had no desire to live like a
prince in Berlin. He despised the place for its pettiness and snobbery. Berlin was
the great gossip factory. His heart was in his magnificent country estates;
Friedrichsruh, in the rich, clayey, wheat-bearing land near Hamburg; and
Varzin, in the sandy beech and oak forests of Pomerania. Both were the spoils
of war, paid for by his admirers – Varzin for cutting down Austria in 1866,
Friedrichsruh for crushing France in 1870–1.

Bismarck was now sixty-nine and time had treated him far better than he
seemed to deserve.

As a young man he had looked like a parody of a hero from one of his
favourite English authors, Scott or Byron, hell-bent on destroying himself with
drink or horses. He was a young giant with black hair, a pale face and a wasp
waist. That was still Disraeli's romantic description of him after the two men
met in 1862. By 1878, when Bismarck presided over the Congress of Berlin, he
had come to look like an 'ogre' (Disraeli's phrase to Queen Victoria): a red-

faced, bald, full-bearded, eighteen-stone ogre whose appetite for power was as repellent as his appetite for the shrimps and cherries he munched as he talked.

Now, in May 1884, Bismarck had shaved off the beard, lost four stone in weight and looked ten years younger. The Princess, his long-suffering wife, and his brash young Jewish doctor, Dr Schweninger, had bullied him into a diet; not even one bottle of Rhenish wine a day. The Chancellor, his nerves flayed bare by years of asthma, neuralgia and self-indulgence, meekly obeyed.

Dr Schweninger's diet did not cure his foul temper or his reckless language. When it suited him, his tongue could be as sweet as an angel's. At other times it could be as rough as a hacksaw. No one was safe – not even his royal master, Kaiser Wilhelm I or the Empress or his royal masters-to-be, the Crown Prince and the Crown Princess (especially if there was a journalist present who could be trusted to be indiscreet). Or rather, only one man was safe. Bismarck was never disloyal to Herbert, the clever, loutish, favourite son whom he used as his international errand boy and was apparently grooming as his successor.

It was bad luck on Herbert to have inherited most of his father's worst qualities – his violence, arrogance and vanity – without any of his genius. But he had served his father faithfully enough. Only once had he tried to challenge his wishes. Herbert wanted to marry a young divorcée, Princess Carolath, connected by birth and marriage to some of his father's oldest enemies. The Chancellor exploded in tears, threatened to cut Herbert out of his will, threatened to kill himself. Herbert gave way. But the experience left a deep wound that perhaps explained some of the harshness of the young man's character.

When in a state of nervous collapse, as he often was before Dr Schweninger's miraculous cure, Bismarck talked of resigning and retiring to his beloved beech forests at Varzin, much as Gladstone talked of retiring to his beloved beech woods at Hawarden. Then his spirits bounded up again. He was as indispensable to the new Reich as he had been to the old Prussia (as indispensable, he might have said, as Gladstone was to the new Liberals).

In thirty years Bismarck's magic wand had turned Prussia, one of many German kingdoms, into what was militarily the most powerful empire in the world. At the heart of the Reich was a single gargantuan ego. The unification of Germany, the promotion of the King to Kaiser, the constitution of the new Reich – all had been designed to facilitate the Chancellor's own power. The Reichstag, the lower House of Deputies, was not a sovereign Parliament. The Kaiser was sovereign. It was only to the Kaiser that the Chancellor answered; only the Kaiser who could dismiss him at will.

That was the constitutional theory, but in practice, Bismarck lorded it over both the eighty-four-year-old Kaiser and his subjects, cajoling or browbeating as he thought fit. He made no secret of the contempt he felt for democracy. Sometimes, it is true, he would put in an appearance at the Reichstag and address the awed members in a thin, reedy voice, but his purpose seemed more to sneer at his adversaries than explain himself to the people. He found committees too tedious to attend.

So people were astonished when they heard in mid-June 1884 that Bismarck planned to appear before the Budget Committee of the Reichstag to explain the volte-face in his foreign policy, the decision to give Germany an empire in Africa.

The Bismarckian 'system', which he had made famous, was exclusively concerned with Europe. 'Here is Russia and here is France,' he later told a startled German explorer, 'with Germany in the middle. That is my map of Africa.'[1] Germany was in the middle, the most vulnerable state in Europe. The map explained everything. He had humbled three of Prussia's rivals: Denmark, Austria and France. But 'genius is knowing where to stop', in Goethe's famous phrase. To try to humble the most dangerous neighbour of all, Russia, would have been to go the way of Napoleon. So Bismarck had spun a magic net, a mesh of overlapping (and often conflicting) treaties to save Germany from the other Powers and the other Powers from themselves.

In 1879 he had cast the net over Austria. The aim of the Austro-German alliance was to calm the Austrians by assuring them of their safety against Russian attack. Bluntly, it was an anti-Russian alliance. Two years later he cajoled Russia and dragged Austria into another treaty: the League of the Three Emperors. The target here was Britain, Russia's traditional rival in the Mediterranean and Asia. Then Bismarck added a third strand to the magic net. He brought Austria's rival, Italy, into an alliance, the Triple Alliance, with Austria and Germany. Now that he had successfully cast a spell over these aggressive spirits, he turned to the area where he needed his most potent magic, reconciliation with France. After the French humiliation in Egypt which poisoned Anglo-French relations, 1884 seemed the moment to encourage the French to move in the direction of Germany. To be ready to bind up France's wounds, like the victor in a duel helping his fallen enemy – this was obviously the right stance for Germany, the new leader of Europe. It had been Bismarck's own policy ever since he had inflicted those wounds in 1871. Giving the French a stake in Africa – Tunis, the 'ripe pear' – was supposed to take their mind off Alsace-Lorraine.

But what was giving Germany a stake in Africa supposed to achieve? That was the puzzle for Bismarck's senior officials, such as the warm-hearted Secretary of the Foreign Ministry, Count Hatzfeldt, or the Senior Councillor, and master of the spider's web, Baron Holstein, a brilliant and dangerous young bachelor, the protégé and personal friend of the Bismarcks ever since he had served with Bismarck in the embassy at St Petersburg twenty-four years before.

The day that Holstein learnt of Bismarck's volte-face was 5 May, only a fortnight before the cipher telegram to Nachtigal. He puzzled over it in his diary. No one knew better than Holstein how the chief had always ridiculed the idea of involving the state in colonies. 'So long as I'm Chancellor,' Bismarck had told him recently, 'we shan't pursue a colonial policy.'[2] He had repeated the same solemn vow to other officials and in the Reichstag he had always rubbed the deputies' noses in it. For four different reasons colonies would be an absurd liability for the Reich.

First, would new colonies pay their own way? It was unfair to ask the taxpayer to foot the bill. Second, was public opinion ready for them? And even if they were politically acceptable, how well would the rigid German bureaucracy cope with easy-going life in the tropics? Third, how could the German navy defend such colonies? It was diminutive, smaller than Italy's. Colonies would make the Reich strategically vulnerable. Fourth, what about the damage to his own diplomacy? Whether established for prestige or profit, colonies would produce complications with the Powers.

Those were the old objections. Holstein recognized that most of them had now been overtaken by events. Take the last two: the difficulties of defence and the threat to Bismarck's own diplomacy. The Congress of Berlin and the network of alliances that followed had made the idea of war implausible, if not impossible. In the relaxed atmosphere of 1884, no one would object to Germany stealing a march on Little Popo or Angra Pequena – 'one or two islands', as Holstein put it, or 'barren tracts of land'. As for France, she would surely welcome these coups provided they involved no territory she coveted and they looked like a slap in the face for Britain.

Stealing a march on Britain, in particular, would serve the Chancellor's purposes in both foreign diplomacy and domestic intrigue. It would promote an *entente* with Britain's new adversary, France. It would also spike the guns of the only German whose career prospects seemed to threaten Bismarck's, the Crown Prince. Kaiser Wilhelm I was eighty-seven and the fifty-two-year-old Crown Prince, Friedrich, might become Kaiser at any moment. As an admirer of English liberal ideas, he favoured the Liberals in the Reichstag. Bismarck thought him a poor creature, completely under the thumb of his English wife, Bismarck's *bête noire*, who loathed Bismarck quite as cordially as did her mother, Queen Victoria. So the new colonies would put a new weapon in Bismarck's hand for a colonial dispute with Britain would create a wave of anglophobia. This would put the future Kaiserin, and hence the future Kaiser, in Bismarck's power. (It was this cynical political explanation for his colonial policy – to 'drive a wedge between the Crown Prince and England' – that Bismarck was himself to give to the Tsar that autumn. '*Voilà qui est intelligent*,'[3] was the anti-British Tsar's awestruck reply.)

No doubt Bismarck saw that this weapon would come in handy. But did it wholly explain Bismarck's volte-face? Holstein thought not. The key, he thought, lay in the third of Bismarck's original objections to colonies: that the public were not yet ready. The opposite was now true. In the Reichstag the Deputies were crying aloud for them. The newspapers reported that a 'real fever' for colonies had gripped the German public. Only a few years earlier, a group of enthusiasts had founded the 'Deutsche Kolonial Verein' (German Colonial Union). The membership was still only a few thousand, but the ideas that they promoted spread like the germs of an epidemic. There was little serious analysis of the economic advantages of an overseas empire, although for ten years a worldwide depression had blighted the Ruhr, inducing Bismarck to abandon free trade, English-style, in favour of a low tariff wall. Colonies might come in handy if those walls grew higher. But the appeal of the colonial craze was to the heart, not the head. Many Germans had read – and believed – the wild claims of English and French explorers. Central Africa was an El Dorado 'waiting for enterprising capitalists'. Stanley and Brazza were racing for it. The spoils were unknown, but prestige as well as profit would be one of them. Why should Germany, the most powerful nation in Europe, be left out? From this confusion of ideas was born the colonizing mania. There was a scramble for colonies. The door was closing. Unless they grabbed something now, the chance would be lost forever. This was the 'door-closing-panic', the *Torschlusspanik*, that seized the German electorate in the spring of 1884 and began to make the Scramble a reality.

According to Holstein, Bismarck was cynically exploiting this panic in the electorate. Holstein believed he understood the way the Chancellor's mind worked. The colonial policy was 'simply an election stunt'. Indeed, Bismarck's own words could be cited: 'All this colonial business is a sham [*Schwindel*], but we need it for elections.'[4] In the autumn there was to be a Reichstag election and Bismarck blurted out these words to one of the Prussian ministers. Of course this explanation did not exclude a connection between colonies and the succession. To woo the German voters with colonies was one way in which Bismarck could brace himself for the coming struggle with the Crown Prince and his maddening English wife.

Was Holstein's explanation too simple – and too cynical? To claim that he could read the small print of Bismarck's mind would be rash for any historian today, but recent research has shown that Bismarck had revised his ideas on his first objection, too: that colonies would be a commercial liability. The colonial policy was not a mere *Schwindel*. Bismarck seems to have believed in it more than Holstein guessed, or than he himself was later prepared to admit.

The story behind that astonishing cable to Nachtigal, sent on 19 May, can be untangled in the German archives. It began with a letter sent to Bismarck thirteen months earlier on 8 April by the leading colonial enthusiast in the Foreign Office. 'Beware France and Britain,' warned Heinrich von Kusserow, the Privy Councillor in the legal-commercial department. He reported that France and Britain were planning to share out the whole West African coast between them and had agreed not to levy custom duties on each other's nationals. Woe betide German traders! Absurdly, Kusserow had misread the French text of an Anglo-French agreement on Sierra Leone published the previous month, in March 1883. It was a false alarm. (The agreement was about protection of life and property, not trade). But Kusserow's grim forecast coincided with another from a weightier source, Adolph Woermann, head of Woermann's of Hamburg, one of the biggest German firms trading in Africa. In March Woermann warned the Chancellor that the Scramble had begun: the Portuguese were sealing off the Congo; the French were pushing out from Gabon; a British consul (Hewett) was reported to be planning to annex Cameroon, the coast where German firms had their main bases. All this could be ruinous for German trade. Woermann was a vocal colonialist. He claimed there was only one way for Germany to counter the threat of France, England and Portugal stealing her trade: she must annex some territory and build up a naval base to protect her commercial interests.

Bismarck was not going to be hustled by one Hamburg trader. But he was impressed enough to call for a full report from the ports most involved in African trade: Hamburg, Bremen and Lubeck. The replies were surprising. For years these rich Baltic ports involved in Africa had, like their British counterparts, extolled the blessings of free trade. Now Hamburg swung round to Woermann's line and so did Bremen. The Hamburg Chamber of Commerce (Vice-President, Adolph Woermann) begged Bismarck to base a naval squadron in the area and annex Cameroon in the name of the Kaiser. There was not a moment to lose. If Germany hesitated, other powers would step in and steal the 'inexhaustible' markets of the interior. Here was the first whiff of *Torschlusspanik* from the Baltic. Only Lubeck kept calm; the city reported that Africa did not interest them enough to deserve a reply.

The Chancellor, too, kept calm. But by August 1883 his policy, under the influence of Kusserow and Woermann, was imperceptibly changing. Earlier in the year Bismarck had rebuffed the request of an obscure Bremen tobacco merchant, Adolf Lüderitz, who had graduated to the African guano trade. The man wanted the 'protection' of the flag of the German empire for his small trading post at Angra Pequena, a barren harbour on the Skeleton Coast of south-west Africa – in modern Namibia – between Cape Colony and Angola. All he had meant by protection was the usual consular help given to Germans abroad, and the odd visit by a German warship. In February 1883 even that had been more than Bismarck had been prepared to allow. Instead he had sent a despatch to London on 4 February inviting the British government to take over the job. Germany, he said, had no interest in 'overseas projects'[5] and would be only too happy to see Britain extend its protection to German settlers in those regions.

Now in August 1883, Bismarck instructed the German Consul in Cape Town to give the usual consular help to Lüderitz and arranged for this generous move to be publicized. The public liked it. Gathering confidence, Bismarck decided to go one better. His precise intentions have baffled historians – as they no doubt baffled the German Foreign Office. But it appears that at this stage he had no plans to take Angra Pequena for the Reich. Lüderitz would be safe if Germany underwrote his independence, free from British interference. All he needed was to prevent encroachments by the British. That autumn Bismarck sent an increasingly forceful series of despatches to London, designed to force Britain to admit it had no claim. Would Her Majesty's government please confirm that they had no title to sovereignty over Angra Pequena and the neighbourhood? Bismarck's desire to save Lüderitz from the British was not, however, matched by a desire to save Woermann and the Hamburg lobby. It was assumed in Berlin that Consul Hewett had returned to London to arrange for British annexations of Cameroon, and perhaps other parts of the west coast. Bismarck did nothing to forestall Hewett. On the contrary, in December 1883, he told Hamburg that a commissioner would be sent to negotiate commercial treaties with independent chiefs. But the Reich could take no colonies. It was not in its interests.

By March 1884 there was still no reply from London disclaiming sovereignty over Angra Pequena. Bismarck's impatience boiled over. This was intolerable: *Deutschfeindlichkeit* – hostility to Germany – and bad faith.. He thought he knew why they had not replied; he had provoked Britain's appetite and they were trying to steal Angra Pequena. As his indignation mounted, so did pressure from the Baltic business lobby. They denounced the reported British plans to annex Togo, where there were important German trading posts. In February, news of the Anglo-Portuguese agreement on the Congo had caused a howl of protest. Then in March Lüderitz returned from South Africa with a story of a preposterous new claim by the British. They had found a long-forgotten document *proving* title to Angra Pequena.

Bismarck trembled on the brink. Colonies might be essential to protect business interests from the rapacious British and French. But would they really *work*? Could the Reich really administer them? It was at this crucial moment that Heinrich von Kusserow, the Foreign Office expert and colonial enthusiast, the man who had misread the Anglo-French treaty and wrote absurdly long-winded reports, stepped forward and resolved Bismarck's final objections.

Why should the Reich have to administer or pay for new German colonies? The British had developed their great empire in India on the charter company system, and recently revived it for North Borneo. (Goldie's plans for a charter were of course unknown to him.) The beauty of the system was that it would demand so little from the Reich. It would be up to Lüderitz to govern the territory under imperial charter. All this was suggested in Kusserow's crucial memorandum of 8 April. Years later Bismarck was to confess: 'Von Kusserow dragged me into the colonial whirl (*Kolonialtummel*).'[6] On the same day there was a dramatic cable from Lüderitz's agents in South Africa. The government at Cape Colony was apparently poised to annex Angra Pequena. Bismarck's mind was made up. He told Kusserow, 'Now let us act.'[7]

Freed from anxieties about the cost and difficulty of administering Angra Pequena – one of the most inhospitable tracts of land in the world – Bismarck's mind raced. He had rescued Lüderitz. He would do the same for Woermann and the other west coast traders. A cable was sent to stop Nachtigal at Madeira, on his passage south, while new instructions were prepared. By 19 May all was ready for the secret cable ordering Nachtigal to hoist the German flag over Togo and Cameroon, as well as claiming Angra Pequena. This would take him at least until early July. Meanwhile, what was to prevent the British from claiming these choice territories for themselves? There was a choice of gambles: Bismarck could put his cards on the table, and trust the British to respect his right to an African empire. Or he could deceive them about his intentions.

It was natural that Bismarck, who trusted no one, except perhaps his wife and his son Herbert, should assume the worst of the British. *Realpolitik* was not a parlour game. To practise, but never to admit, deceit was part of the rules. The diplomatic ruse he adopted was simple. On 24 April he told the German

Consul in London to inform Her Majesty's government that Angra Pequena was 'under the protection of the empire'.[8] This was for the record, but it was cryptic enough not to alert the British to the new policy, just as Bismarck intended. The same deception was practised on the British Ambassador in Berlin, Lord Ampthill, and on the German Ambassador in London, Count Münster. Both were left completely in the dark about Nachtigal's new instructions. London was to continue to believe that Nachtigal was merely being sent to 'inquire about German commerce'.[9] Münster's role in the deception was to assure the British that they need not pay much attention to Angra Pequena; Bismarck had no intention of founding a colonial empire. Meanwhile the gunboat *Möwe* (which aptly enough means '*Gull*') would be steaming south towards the West African coast carrying Dr Nachtigal with his precious load of flags and proclamations.

Bismarck's strategy assumed that this new Scramble had too great a momentum to be halted. The Germans would win it, stealing a march on Consul Hewett in West Africa and on the Cape government at Angra Pequena. He was all the more frustrated when he heard in late May that the British Colonial Secretary, Lord Derby, had told a delegation from the Cape that Britain had a 'sort of general right to exclude foreign powers'[10] from the coast of south-west Africa. According to Derby, the British government had twice invited the government of the Cape to annex the area. In early June Bismarck heard from the German Consul in Cape Town that the Cape government had now agreed to take over the territory as far as their existing outpost at Walvis Bay, far to the north of Angra Pequena. Bismarck's frustration turned to rage. He was being forced to put his own cards on the table prematurely. Dr Nachtigal and the *Möwe* were still a month away from the west coast. All he could do now was to spin out the diplomatic moves to give Nachtigal the best possible chance in the race. Count Münster was still to be left in the dark. In mid-June Bismarck sent his aggressive son Herbert on a special mission to London to warn Gladstone to keep his hands off Angra Pequena, now definitely earmarked as a German possession.

In mid-June, after Herbert had taken the train to London, Bismarck felt confident enough to flatter the Reichstag by revealing his own volte-face. The Reichstag was stunned and delighted. He still kept secret Nachtigal's actual mission. All he said was that it was their duty to found a colonial empire in Africa. He cited the old objections and explained why they no longer applied. The overseas empire would not consist of state-run colonies, but would be based on the British charter company system. It would mean making protectorates of territories already established by German traders, at Angra Pequena and any other place. The Chancellor ended with a hint of menace well calculated to bring the Deputies to their feet. He could not agree that Britain, or British colonial governments like the Cape, had any right to block German claims, except by proving that the territories already belonged to them. 'If the question were asked what means the Empire had to afford effective protection to German enterprises in distant parts, the first consideration would be the influence of the

Empire, and the wish and interests of other Powers to remain on friendly relations.'[11]

Decoded, this meant that if Britain gave trouble, Germany would not hesitate to join hands with France and hit Britain where it would hurt most: in her underbelly, Egypt.

Count Herbert von Bismarck steamed into London on 13 June 1884. The next day he was conducted up the great staircase at the Foreign Office, past Britannia and the sea traders, to see Lord Granville in that splendid room overlooking St James's Park. Judging from his own reports to Berlin, Herbert enjoyed the talks, which gave him ample opportunity to display his gift for calculated rudeness. His father, the Reich Chancellor, had been insulted by the delay in answering his request. The Cape government was trying to annex south-west Africa behind his back and the British Colonial Secretary was secretly egging it on. This was the main burden of his bluster, which he managed to spin out until 19 June.

What must have astonished Herbert was that the British took all this like lambs. There was no need to bludgeon Granville with the threat of reprisals in Egypt. The Foreign Secretary begged for mercy: 'It is very hard for me, as I have so much to do, that I cannot go into detail on these colonial questions.... Besides this, a part of the Parliamentary business falls on me as leader of the Upper House in this difficult time. On top of this I have to conduct the awkward Egyptian negotiations.' Granville blamed himself and he blamed Lord Derby. The whole Angra Pequena business had been a terrible 'mess'[12] on their part, but an honest mess. They would never have dreamt of trying to act behind the Chancellor's back. It had simply never occurred to them that Bismarck was interested in colonies. On the contrary, they believed, up to the last moment, that all the Germans required was that the British should take responsibility for protecting Germans.

The abject confession was true. Misled by Ampthill and Count Münster, the British Foreign Office had been completely gulled by Bismarck. His volte-face had escaped their notice up to that week.

Two days later Gladstone and the Cabinet confirmed Granville's surrender. Dilke wrote later that Bismarck had been 'very rude to Lord Granville about Angra Pequena, which was mentioned to the Cabinet, which would do nothing'.[13] In fact the British were too vulnerable in Egypt to deny Bismarck anything so worthless as Angra Pequena. A cable was sent to Cape Town to warn the colonial government and Granville withdrew the invitation to extend the Cape's responsibility north towards Angola. But surrender was not so simple. By early July it became clear that Derby was deeper in the mess than ever, trapped between rival claimants for the coast – Bismarck and the Cape government.

How had Derby and the CO got themselves into this mess? And why had the Cape ministry stayed lukewarm for so long and then suddenly turned into red-hot imperialists?

Early in 1884 Lord Derby had infuriated Bismarck by failing to disclaim

British sovereignty at Angra Pequena. Instead, on 3 February, he had invited the Cape government to take over south-west Africa. His own performance had been quite as feeble as Granville's, even if his misconceptions were not quite as profound. He shared Granville's illusion that what Germany really wanted was for Britain to give protection to Lüderitz. That had been Bismarck's original request of 4 February 1883, the one which specifically stated Germany herself had no interest in colonial projects. However, Derby and his advisers at the Colonial Office were anxious not to give Bismarck any excuse for changing his mind. Unlike the FO, the CO did not regard the coast round Angra Pequena as worthless. It was too close to the Cape frontier for comfort. There would be complications with the natives if it passed into the wrong hands. Besides, there was a powerful business lobby at Cape Town, led by a Cape trading firm, De Pass, Spence & Company, who claimed to have invested £300,000 in the area. Public opinion at the Cape had for long favoured taking it over. Moreover, in 1877 the Cape Parliament had formally asked London, when they agreed to take over the settlement at Walvis Bay, to include the whole coast from the Orange river northwards. But at that time London had refused. Now, alarmed by Bismarck's questions about title, Derby decided that the time was right. He cabled the Cape on 3 February to invite them to annex the coast as far as Walvis Bay.

Incredibly, the only answer to the cable was the cryptic: 'Ministers ask matter to be kept open, pending Cabinet meeting here. Premier away.'[14] The ministers had already written once again to the CO, asking for Britain to annex the coast, but as they had no wish to accept financial responsibility themselves, they let the matter drift. (According to a famous story, the vital cable was forgotten in the Prime Minister's pocket.) Lord Derby dawdled until May, then he repeated the cable of 3 February. Was the Cape prepared to pay for the annexation? This was a hint that if they refused then Germany might take it over. There was no answer, this time because the Cape government had fallen. So matters drifted until Herbert Bismarck bullied the British Cabinet into surrender.

In the Cape, however, as Derby learnt to his dismay, there was now a new ministry, led by what he called a 'chauvinist', John X. Merriman. In fact Merriman was a colonial nationalist, and was angry and humiliated at the way his country was being sacrificed by the imperial government. A double colonial interest was at stake: the right to protect Cape traders and Cape frontiers. On 9 July Derby received an alarming cable from Merriman. What steps were being taken to protect their interests? Caught between two fires, Derby and the Colonial Office launched a reckless attempt at compromise. On 14 July Derby cabled back to Merriman. Provided it would foot the bill, the Cape had permission to annex all the coast *north* of the Lüderitz concession – that is, from Walvis Bay to the border of Angola. But the Cape went one better – or worse. On 17 July the government cabled to London that it had annexed the whole coast from the Orange river northwards, including Angra Pequena.

It was Derby's final bungled attempt to get something from the months of procrastination and confusion. All he achieved was to give Bismarck a real grievance, and to provoke him to play his Egyptian card.

In early July, Bismarck returned to Varzin, his princely estate in Pomerania, delighted by the brusque way Herbert had dealt with Granville. 'Right,' he wrote in the margin of his son's report to Berlin in which Herbert quoted his blunt words to Granville: 'My government would decline to give an answer in a matter that is of no concern to you.'[15] That was the point. The British had no right to question him about his plans for south-west Africa. He would take as much as suited him when it suited him without asking anyone's permission. Very soon now would come the report of Nachtigal's successful mission.

In high summer Varzin was a paradise after the frustrations of Berlin, the weeks wasted with dealing with Liberals in the Reichstag and the intrigues of their allies, the Crown Prince and Crown Princess. At Varzin he worked incessantly but lived like a recluse. For days he saw no one except his own family and the trumpet-sounding postillion who rode from Schlawe, the nearest point on the railway, carrying boxes of cipher telegrams and other secret papers from Berlin. The black line of the forest, beech and oak, an endless horizon which most people would have found claustrophobic, brought balm to his frayed nerves. These aristocrats of the forest were his to exploit as he wanted, to axe when he chose.

Bismarck's mood changed abruptly in the third week of July when he read the preposterous cable from the Cape. The authorities there claimed to have annexed the whole coast north of the Orange river, *including* Angra Pequena. They had asked for it now.

He cabled to the Foreign Ministry to arrange for Germany to join France in making it hot for the English in Egypt. The occasion was the London conference of the Great Powers, called by Britain, and supposed to help her rescue Egypt from a new bout of bankruptcy. The British reckoned that Egypt needed a new loan of £8 million, roughly half of which would go to compensate foreigners for their losses in the British bombardment of Alexandria in 1882 and the disastrous riots that followed. Britain was prepared to put up the loan provided she got preferential treatment in interest and repayment. This meant changing the Law of Liquidation, the international agreement of 1880, at the expense of the foreign bond-holders, many of whom were French. In June Ferry's government had seemed prepared to co-operate. They made it clear that it was reconciled to British supremacy in Egypt for the next few years and to the end of dual control. But at the second meeting of the conference, on 22 July, it was obvious that the gap between Britain and France was the width of the Channel. The French wanted to restore some of the power of the old Caisse de la Dette, whose commissioners for debt included Frenchmen. And they saw no reason to give preferential treatment to the new British loan. In late July Britain looked desperately to Germany to help her out of this hole; otherwise British taxpayers might have to bail out Egypt. This was the moment when Bismarck decided to play his Egyptian card.

It was as effective – and as humiliating for the British – as Bismarck could have hoped in his most bloody-minded mood. The German delegate was Count Münster, the Ambassador to London who had unwittingly deceived Granville about Bismarck's policy. Now the unfortunate man had to punish Britain by sabotaging the conference. He did so with a red herring in the form of Egypt's sanitation, an absurd irrelevancy with which to involve the conference. By 2 August, the conference had collapsed amid recriminations between Britain and France.

Towards Bismarck, however, Granville was humility itself. Once again, he mumbled, he must apologize. There had been an absurd muddle; the wires had become crossed between the Foreign Office and the Colonial Office. Neither he nor Derby had any idea that Germany intended further annexation. But nothing suited Britain better than to have a colonial neighbour like Germany. Of course the Cape authorities would be told that London could not ratify their own claims. Granville was only rescued from his embarrassment in mid-August when the news that Bismarck had so long awaited at last reached Europe.

Togo and Cameroon had been formally declared German protectorates by Dr Nachtigal in July. On 7 August the captain of the *Elizabeth* had annexed Angra Pequena. It only remained to complete the annexation of the whole coast of south-west Africa in the name of the Kaiser. This was formally proclaimed by the captain of the German gunboat *Wolf* at the end of August.

Bismarck, his good humour restored, now prepared to earn the first dividend from his colonial policy in the shape of a *rapprochement* with France. The current French Ambassador in Berlin was Baron de Courcel, the man who had persuaded Gambetta three years earlier to support intervention in Tunis. In August Bismarck invited him to stay at Varzin to concert policy on two African issues where their countries' interests seemed to coincide: keeping the Niger and the Congo open to international trade, and upholding the bond-holders' rights in Egypt.

Courcel was understandably nervous about bearding the great man in his lair. Before he left Britain, he consulted Bismarck's clever protégé, Holstein. Never interrupt the Chancellor, was Holstein's warning. Courcel then admitted that France had 'lost its equilibrium'[16] and that his own government believed Germany could help restore it. Holstein liked his candour. Of course Bismarck's plan was disequilibrium. Holstein hoped that Bismarck would do his best to embroil France and Britain, for which Africa offered splendid opportunities, but he was beginning to lose confidence in the Chancellor's gift for blood and iron. The chief problem was Herbert von Bismarck. He was more of a bully than ever in home affairs, but he was beginning to turn soft in foreign policy. He had enjoyed his visit to London, where he had received nothing but flattery from all Count Münster's English friends, despite his appalling manners. Holstein was afraid that Herbert would be a bad influence on his father, anxious to let the English off the hook, which meant withholding full support for the French. If only the conference on Egypt had ended with a really decisive slap in the face for the British.

However, when Courcel reached Varzin on 27 August, the Chancellor swept him off his feet. 'The Englishman is like the dog in the fable', were his words to a young German diplomat that summer, and perhaps he said the same to Courcel. 'The dog who cannot bear that another dog should have a few bones, although the overfed brute is sitting below a bowl full to the brim.'[17] Together, France and Germany could make that selfish brute disgorge. On Egypt he was evasive. But as regards West Africa – the Congo and the Niger – he proposed to organize an international conference in Berlin. He gave a firm commitment to support French claims against British ones. How firm? Courcel returned to Berlin and confessed to Holstein that he was 'under Bismarck's spell'.[18] Still, Holstein wondered when Courcel's chief, Jules Ferry, would wake up to the fact that the Chancellor had fooled them.

Meanwhile Bismarck, the lion-tamer of Europe, was back in the ring, cracking his whip with his usual zest. In September he left Varzin, with Herbert and his other son, Bill, to escort the Kaiser to the ceremonial embrace of the three emperors in a railway hut at Skierniewice, a small town just across the Russian border. This imperial meeting was the annual symbol of the Pax Bismarck. Everything depended on the continued embrace of this strange trio: the erratic young Tsar, Alexander III, Franz Josef, the veteran Emperor of Austria, and the frail old Kaiser, Wilhelm I. Bismarck exulted in his own creation. While the Reich had Russia as an ally, war with any other Great Power was unthinkable. But that was no reason why he should not enjoy himself grabbing a slice of the African cake on the cheap by playing off France against England.

After putting the Emperors through their hoops at Skierniewice, and before playing host to the West African conference in Berlin, Bismarck had first to deal with the tiresome Reichstag. The election was held on 28 October. Here his new colonial policy was supposed to earn its second dividend. Certainly the voters gave short shrift to the New Liberals, the Party favoured by the Crown Prince and Crown Princess. In alliance with other Liberals, they had held 117 seats in the old Reichstag. Now they had only 67. The parties which normally supported the Chancellor – Conservatives, Imperialists, and National Liberals – had originally held 119 seats. Now they mustered 157. So far so good. Unfortunately, the Socialists had added even more dramatically to their seats, which rose from 10 to 24. Other groups hostile to the Chancellor maintained their vote. So the new Reichstag would still be a thorn in Bismarck's flesh, hurting his pride and cutting down his budgets whenever they chose. Obviously the new surge of German imperialism did not extend to the urban working class. What they cared about was curing the Great Depression, meaning more jobs, better pay, better conditions of work. They were sceptical about this El Dorado in Africa, these dazzling new markets in the deserts of the Skeleton Coast and the malarial swamps of Togo or Cameroon.

Worse still, when Bismarck started to talk of the cost to the government of the three new protectorates, he found that the colonial traders' lobby suddenly fell silent. That autumn he held a conference at Friedrichsruh near Hamburg, attended by Adolph Woermann. Naturally he looked to Woermann as the Reich's agent in Cameroon. Woermann's fleet of ships was at his disposal, as were his warehouses and staff. It was these men who had paved the way – with generous bribes of rum and credit – for the hoisting of the German flag. In the summer of 1884 Woermann's Duala agent had negotiated the preliminary treaties with King Acqua and King Bell, dramatically confirmed on 14 July by Dr Nachtigal. Now Bismarck looked to Woermann for the next step: to run the protectorate under imperial charter. Woermann politely refused, as did the partners in the other German firms involved. They were businessmen, not colonial administrators. The cost of accepting a charter would be too high for any German firm, however patriotic. After all, this was not India or the East. It was poverty-stricken Africa.

Bismarck began to realize how hollow was Kusserow's claim, which he himself had echoed in the Reichstag in June, that there was no need for expensive state-run colonies, *Reichkolonie*. Togo, Cameroon and south-west Africa would be protectorates only in name. The Reich, not the traders, would have to carry the burden. Therefore the Reichstag would hold the purse-strings, as they did for all budgets. Far from smoothing his path in the Reichstag, colonies would put a new obstacle in his way. This was the merry prospect for his final years as Reich Chancellor.

It was Kusserow who had led him on this 'colonial whirl'. He had already been removed from his post directing colonial policy, apparently suffering from a swollen head. Soon he was sent in disgrace to a minor post in The Hague. Bismarck did not easily forget Kusserow. He had achieved more than most: he had fooled Bismarck.

'I incline to suppose', wrote Gladstone on 5 September 1884, 'that [Bismarck's] conduct in the conference [on Egypt] was a return slap for Angra Pequena.'[19] It had taken Gladstone a whole month to grasp this obvious fact. It was quite an eye-opener. He had always distrusted Bismarck, and he knew the feeling was reciprocated. But he had relied on Germany to continue to defend him from the French as the British reeled from crisis to crisis in Egypt.

It was the bondage in Egypt which had occupied Gladstone's thoughts for the last few months, to the exclusion of almost everything else. Egypt had re-opened the cracks in the Liberal Party, burst them like the seams of a sinking ship. Now Egypt left Britain naked in Europe.

Meanwhile, 1,000 miles up the Nile from Cairo, a new Islamic jihad had swept through the desert like a plague.

It was in 1881 that Muhammad Ahmad, the son of an obscure boat-builder from Dongola in the northern Sudan calling himself the Mahdi (the Expected One or Redeemer), had first hoisted the black flag of revolt against the Khedive. By November 1883 the whole of the Sudan was at his feet. On 5 November the last fighting force of the Khedive's original army – 10,000 Egyptian soldiers, many of them survivors from Tel el-Kebir – were massacred with their British commander, Hicks Pasha, at the Battle of El Obeid in Kordofan (Shaykan). The British government was relying on Sir Evelyn Baring, their agent at Cairo, to rebuild authority – and solvency – for the Khedive. This was the only way back to the security of invisible empire and Britain's own formal withdrawal. Baring had told the Khedive to wash his hands of his empire in the Sudan and to evacuate the surviving Egyptian garrisons. The Khedive's ministry chose to resign rather than accept this instruction. Still bankrupt, the Khedive was reduced to the level of Baring's lapdog. As for the Egyptian garrisons, the British Cabinet had arranged for an efficient Englishman to evacuate them. Their choice was that wayward hero, 'inspired and mad'[20] (according to Gladstone), General Charles Gordon.

How to rescue Gordon now baffled and divided the Cabinet. He was trapped in Khartoum, or perhaps he was free (that was his brother's conviction) but turning a Nelson eye to his orders and refusing to budge. No one could say. It was months since the last messenger had slipped back through the desert to bring word to Baring, the British Agent and the Khedive's master, in Cairo.

The newspapers were baying for a Gordon relief expedition. Gladstone described Gordon in Parliament as having 'hallucinations'. In August 1884 he reluctantly agreed to a provisional rescue plan, making Wolseley the leader. 'Too late' was already the catch-phrase of erratic Tories like Lord Randolph Churchill. The Cabinet dithered, beset on all sides and from within.

'Too late' was again the cry when the astonishing news from the Oil Rivers reached Europe, and 'Too Late Hewett' became the soubriquet for the unfortunate Consul. The Cabinet was not amused to find that Dr Nachtigal – and Bismarck – had won the race to annex Cameroon by five days. Radicals like Chamberlain and Dilke agreed it was preposterous. 'The Cameroons!' Chamberlain told Dilke in September. 'It is enough to make one sick. As you say, we decided to assume the protectorate eighteen months ago, and I thought it was all settled. If the Board of Trade or Local Government Board managed their business after the fashion of the Foreign Office and Colonial Office, you and I would deserve to be hung.'[21] Soon he discovered that Bismarck, not content with grabbing three African colonies, wanted to steal a slice of New Guinea from under the nose of the Australian government. 'I don't care a damn about New Guinea,' wrote Chamberlain that winter, 'and I am not afraid of German colonisation, but I don't like being cheeked by Bismarck.'[22]

Even some of the old-fashioned Whigs in the Cabinet felt humiliated by the way Britain had surrendered to Bismarck's bullying at Angra Pequena. They had not lifted a finger, said Lord Selborne gloomily, in the hope of avoiding a breach with Germany 'that would make our chances of honourable extrication from the Egyptian difficulty even less than they are'. Granville blamed Derby for the muddle, and Derby blamed Bismarck for 'sharp practice' in deliberately misleading them.[23]

But Gladstone felt no shame about trying to soothe Bismarck. They owed him an apology for the dawdling over Angra Pequena. And what was wrong with giving a good neighbour like Germany a slice of Africa or New Guinea?

Unlike the pushful Radicals and their allies on the Right, he had stayed true to the old Liberal faith. Imperialism was immoral, a form of wrongdoing. Unless there was a strategic necessity, why extend the formal British Empire when most of the world was open to British trade? Reluctantly, Gladstone had agreed to protect British trade interests against a French tariff by declaring the Oil Rivers a British protectorate. Now he could say, as on 1 September at Midlothian, that he looked 'with satisfaction, sympathy and joy upon the extension of Germany in these desert places of the earth'.[24]

It was not hypocrisy, though Gladstone was somewhat sceptical about Bismarck's belated conversion to the utility of these desert places. The Chancellor was 'reluctantly working [in German colonization] for election purposes'. Gladstone was also well aware that a kind word from himself might not go down particularly well with Bismarck. 'I am not sure that my words, if they meet the eye of the mighty man, will please him, as he probably likes to have something to strike at.'[25]

To appease Bismarck, at any rate, was Cabinet policy up to a point, provided that there was no strategic objection. Had the limit now been reached? In these tormenting weeks when the future of Egypt and Gordon seized the headlines, the forward group in the Cabinet stealthily launched plans to block further German expansion in both south-western and south-eastern Africa.

Earlier that year, President Kruger had taken ship to London to renegotiate the Convention of Pretoria, signed after the Transvaal War of 1880–1. Under this convention, the Transvaal (South African Republic) had reluctantly agreed to accept qualified independence. There was to be British 'suzerainty', whatever that meant, and various specific limitations, including one protecting the rights of the natives, and another precluding the Boers' right to make treaties with foreign powers. In 1884 Kruger successfully negotiated a new convention with the Colonial Secretary, Lord Derby, and this became known as the Convention of London. It pleased both sides. Kruger wangled more independence, suzerainty vanished from the text, and so did the crucial clause protecting natives' rights. There was no change in the clause precluding foreign treaties.

What the British gained was an agreement defining the western border of the Transvaal, the border with Bechuanaland. This was a sandy waste to the north-west of Cape Colony, the home of various impoverished Seswana-speaking tribes, under chiefs Montshiwa and Mankurwane. In recent years this native sanctuary had been invaded by wagon-loads of Boer freebooters trekking from the Transvaal. The government of Cape Colony was anxious to stop this encroachment and the Colonial Office backed them. Their motive was not so much to protect the natives, though this idea appealed to the missionaries, but to foil Cape freebooters who wanted to keep open their own line of expansion, via the road to the north, to that supposed El Dorado, the land of King Lobengula, across the river Limpopo.

Now into this three-cornered struggle for land – Boers against natives, Cape interests against both – came a fourth contender, the German colony in south-west Africa. Where was the link? Lüderitz's concession at Angra Pequena gave him a border only twenty miles inland, but both the Cape government and the imperial government now decided it was too big a strategic risk to give the

Germans a chance of meddling with Bechuanaland. Bismarck had given a hero's welcome to Kruger when the President turned up in Berlin in the spring of 1884 before taking the boat home. What was to stop the Germans using Bechuanaland as a bridge with those dangerous republicans in the Transvaal? The forward group, led by Hartington and Chamberlain, pushed this strategic argument strongly in the Cabinet. Britain must take Bechuanaland either as a protectorate or absorb it into Cape Colony. The Colonial Office was sure that it would be plain sailing – there was no risk of fighting the Boers or offending the Afrikaners in the Cape – now that the Transvaal's frontier was defined. Reluctantly, Gladstone agreed in November to authorize 4,000 Cape irregulars, led by a British commander, Colonel Charles Warren, to do the job. He did it without firing a shot. In England few people noticed, though it marked the first attempt to stand up to Bismarck's bullying and to steal a march on Germany.

A second equally successful, equally unnoticed, British advance was made by seizing the harbour at St Lucia on the east coast. Here the strategic arguments for intervention were stronger still. St Lucia was a harbour that Germany could seize and hold as a gateway for the hostile Transvaal. This could not be allowed. Yet in December Derby confessed that he found it all somewhat absurd, this new competition to seize obscure corners of the globe:

> I agree with you that there is something absurd in the sudden Scramble for colonies, and I am as little disposed to join in as you can be; but there is a difference between wanting new acquisitions and keeping what we have; and both Natal and the Cape Colony would be endangered, as well as inconvenienced, if any foreign power chose to claim possession of the coast between the two, which is virtually ours now, but not ours by any formal tie that other nations are bound to recognize. . . .[26]

The sudden 'Scramble'. This was the ironic new word for the race for colonies, as undignified as a scramble for pennies, forced upon Britain by her rivals. Belatedly the Cabinet was coming to see that the days of invisible empire were ending. Yet to jump for pennies like children! The sense of absurdity was shared by the British public. Even the Tory press welcomed the Germans at Angra Pequena, if only they could find out where it was. At this stage there was no call for new colonies, no fever for empire, as in Bismarck's Germany or even Brazza's France. Britain shared in the white dominions and had gathered a great empire without any apparent need for imperialism. How strange this ironic detachment would seem within a few years.

Meanwhile the scene was set for two pieces of theatre that would, in different ways, alter the Scramble out of recognition. Bismarck was to hold an international conference in Berlin, and with French help he was expected to try to prise the oil-rich Niger from British hands. At the same time Wolseley was struggling up the cataracts of the Nile towards Khartoum, to save Gordon – and the nation's honour – from defilement by the Mahdi.

CHAPTER 13

Too Late?

The Sudan
26 September 1884–26 January 1885

'In the name of God the merciful and compassionate
... Those who believed in us as the Mahdi, and
surrendered, have been delivered, and those who did
not were destroyed...'

Muhammad Ahmad, the Mahdi, to Gordon Pasha of
Khartoum, 22 October 1884

'From the top of the Serail', wrote Gordon on 26 September 1884, jotting it down in his journal with the innocence and vulnerability of a small boy writing home to his mother, 'one commands views all round for miles.' He would stand there on the flat roof of the palace at Khartoum in full view of the Mahdi's gunners, a small, lonely figure with a telescope, searching the heat haze in either direction, searching for the smoke of a steamer. From the north, the British relief expedition – if it existed – would cut its way up the Nile, recapturing Berber, then push on past Metemma to smash the Mahdi's outer lines at Halfaya. From the south-east, Gordon's own steamers would come down the Blue Nile, bringing desperately needed grain from Sennar. This food convoy would have to run the gauntlet of the Dervishes (the European name for the Mahdists) camped along the river-bank – only the vanguard of the Mahdi's army, but already tens of thousands strong.

That afternoon at four o'clock a line of wood-smoke notched the desert to the south-east. 'Steamers from Senaar in sight. Now we shall be all together, thank God.' With his heart in his mouth, Gordon focused his telescope on the three small paddle steamers, as frail as Thames penny steamboats. 'The Arabs fired from guns and rifles with fury – we could see that from the roof. All the steamers have got small-pox from bullet marks!'[1] All three docked safely, though several of the crew were killed (including a boy) and there were seven shell holes in the steel plates, some wide enough for a man's hand and shoulders. The *Bordein* was hit by a shell within a foot of the water-line, and might have been sunk if one of the crew hadn't remembered to put aside bits of old tents ready to stuff into the shot holes. Gordon regarded the escape as providential, a sign that God's hand was stretched over them. 'If we could believe it, we are as safe in the fiercest battle as in a drawing room in London.'[2] The grain, too, was providential. In July Gordon had forecast that they had grain enough to last four months, that is, till mid-November. Now they had an extra 2,000 *ardebs* (about 10,000 bushels), enough to keep the garrison till mid-December before starvation made them 'throw up the sponge'.[3]

Today was the 198th day of the siege. On 18 January 1884 Gordon had blithely taken the eight o'clock boat train from Charing Cross, after Lord Granville had bidden him God-speed on the platform and Lord Wolseley had to lend him some spare cash for the journey. On 18 February, the Governor-General's yacht, the *Tewfikieh*, had steamed up to Khartoum and received a rapturous welcome. Gordon Pasha had come home, Gordon, their own Mahdi, the deliverer of the Sudan. Three weeks later, on 12 March, before he had any chance of evacuating the garrison, the siege had begun. A force of 4,000 Dervishes swooped down on Halfaya, nine miles down-river, and hacked the copper wire from the telegraph poles. The line to the north – to Metemma, Berber and Cairo, 1,000 miles beyond the cataracts – was as silent as the desert. From that day Gordon had been cut off from the world like a man locked in gaol. The echoes he received from outside were as confused as those they heard in Cairo and London: telegrams and notes, copied on small scraps of paper and smuggled in and out by runners at great risk to themselves, often out of sequence and sometimes impossible to decipher.

There had been enough barriers to understanding before the siege began. In Cairo, in late January, Baring, the British agent and the Khedive's master, had given Gordon his official instructions; and though the two men were utterly out of sympathy, Gordon took the instructions as literally as if God had given them. To evacuate the Egyptian soldiers, their Egyptian officials and their families at Khartoum (as well as the surviving garrisons elsewhere in the Sudan), was the sacred mission with which he had been entrusted, sealed by a firman from the Khedive, as instructed by Baring, who was in turn authorized by Gladstone and his Cabinet.

But *how* was Gordon to extricate the garrisons? He had brought one British soldier, Lieutenant-Colonel J. D. Stewart. Baring gave him none, nor did he at first ask for any. Was he supposed to charm the garrisons out of the Sudan by magic, the *baraka* of the great pasha, whose feet the Sudanese kissed at Khartoum, crying 'Sultan' and 'Father'. Gordon had strange ideas, but he did not over-estimate the power of his own magic. In those three weeks before the gates of the gaol clanged shut, he had sent increasingly desperate appeals down the line to Baring. To evacuate Khartoum and the other garrisons, both Baring and Gladstone agreed, could not mean a simple policy of 'skidaddle' or 'rat'. For practical as well as moral reasons, they simply could not run away, with the devil to the hindmost. Gordon must hand over the reins to some nominated successor. Thus it came down to a double task: to evacuate *and* to impose some form of self-government in the Sudan that was powerful enough to resist the political tide of Mahdism.

Gordon's first choice of a successor at Khartoum seemed bizarre. He chose Zebehr Pasha, the great Sudanese slave dealer who had once ruled the Bahr al-Ghazal as his private slave empire. It was Suleiman, his son and heir, who had been captured and executed by Gessi with Gordon's approval in July 1879, after

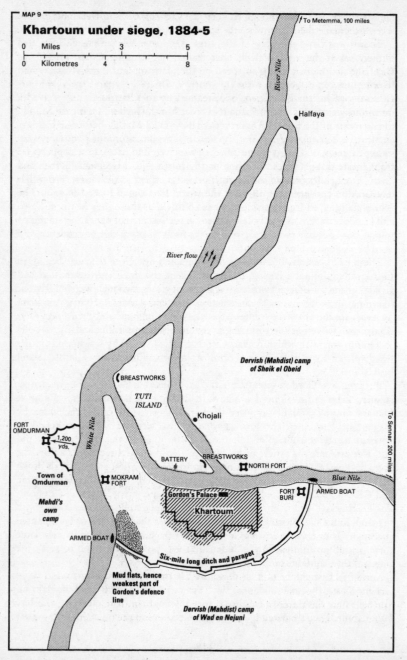

MAP 9

Khartoum under siege, 1884-5

0	Miles		3		5
0	Kilometres		4		8

To Metemma, 100 miles

River Nile

● Halfaya

River flow

Dervish (Mahdist) camp of Sheik el Obeid

⟩ BREASTWORKS

TUTI ISLAND

● Khojali

FORT OMDURMAN

White Nile

←→ 1,200 yds.

Town of Omdurman

BATTERY

BREASTWORKS

NORTH FORT

Mahdi's own camp

⊠ MOKRAM FORT

To Sennar, 200 miles

Blue Nile

Gordon's Palace ▬

FORT BURI ⊠

ARMED BOAT

Khartoum

ARMED BOAT

Six-mile long ditch and parapet

Mud flats, hence weakest part of Gordon's defence line

Dervish (Mahdist) camp of Wad en Nejuni

Suleiman had led the slave dealers' revolt against Gordon. Zebehr himself had been sentenced to death by Gordon, but the sentence had not been upheld by the authorities in Cairo. He had made his peace and now lived there in comfortable retirement. It was reported that Zebehr had not forgotten how Gordon had treated Suleiman; yet this was the man, with a blood-feud against him, whom Gordon wished to take with him to Khartoum to install as his successor.

Baring was at first surprised by the choice, but then he saw the point and recommended it. No one else knew the ropes in the Sudan as well, or had half the prestige of Zebehr; and years in Cairo had taught him how to behave. At any rate, a hefty subsidy from the Egyptian government (Zebehr would have to draw £300,000 a year from the Khedive's bankrupt treasury to out-Mahdi the Mahdi) would depend on his behaving himself. This was Gordon's ingenious plan. The British government turned it down flat. For Gordon, the hero of the anti-slavery crusade, to appoint a notorious slave dealer as his successor was too provoking. Parliament would never stand it.

What *was* the alternative to Zebehr – apart from the Mahdi? Gordon's suggestions became more desperate. Would the Sultan of Turkey take over the job? Would the British send Muslim troops from India? Would the British make a diversion by sending men across the Red Sea to Berber? All these ideas were rejected by London. So Gordon returned to the case for Zebehr. 'If you do not send Zebehr, you have no chance of getting the garrisons away.'[4] This was Gordon's grim forecast of 8 March, four days before the telegraph went silent. Once again the proposal was turned down in London by the Cabinet. Once again they were terrified of the high-mindedness of their own supporters. (Significantly, Gladstone was more optimistic. He agreed that to send Zebehr was a *pis aller* and thought he could have persuaded the public, but Gladstone was away ill when the Cabinet met.)

Before Gordon could be told of the Cabinet's final rebuff, the wire was cut and the siege had begun. Now he expected the worst. 'We are always *just* too late,'[5] he wrote to Lord Dufferin. To his eldest sister, Augusta, who had acted like a mother to him (it was for her he was making those boyish jottings in his journal) he wrote:

> This may be the last letter I send you, for the tribes have risen between this and Berber, and will try to cut our *route*. They will not fight us directly, but will starve us out ... What I have to do is to submit my will to His, *even* however bitter may be the events which happen to me.[6]

The mood was prophetic, though it was too soon for farewells. When the siege began, Khartoum had a population of 34,000, of whom about 8,000 were soldiers of one kind or another. It was reckoned there was food for six months, until September. From the start Gordon was determined to make an active defence. For that to succeed everything depended on the mobility and firepower of his strange fleet of paddle steamers.

Until June the waters gradually receded. Even then the converging Blue and White Niles gave Khartoum an impregnable moat on the northern and western sides, provided that the steamers remained masters of the rivers. Six miles of ditch-and-parapet, laboriously dug across the desert to the south, joined the two Niles and completed the triangle of defence. Across the water, Gordon set up two outposts: the fort at Omdurman on the west bank of the White Nile, with a line of fortifications down to the river, and the North Fort on the north bank of the Blue Nile immediately facing Khartoum. At low water, there were sandbanks below the fort at Omdurman, a dangerous chink in that small garrison's armour; the Blue Nile was also too shallow for steamers, so Gordon had to content himself with small raids on the surrounding country. Sometimes these succeeded in grabbing a few hundred extra bushels of local grain. But once they were beaten back with heavy losses, attributed by Gordon's Sudanese to the treachery of two local pashas. (Despite his own misgivings, Gordon had them both executed.)

By July the waters began to lap over the sandbanks as the two Niles advanced once again in defence of Khartoum. Gordon was grateful for the chance of putting his grand fleet on the offensive. It was a strange-looking collection. All eight boats had been built to be as slow and placid as donkeys. There was one Khedival yacht, the *Tewfikieh*, and seven tubby wood-burning paddle steamers. Some had been dragged over the cataracts in the time of Ismael's father, Said Pasha; others were rusty hulks from the time of Sir Samuel Baker, others again dated from 1877 when Gordon himself had brought them in sections on camel back across the Nubian desert. From these incongruous materials Gordon improvised what he called 'a cavalry' and mobile artillery. Their guns were fitted in wooden turrets at bow and amidships, their decks were protected by steel boiler plates, bolted to wooden stanchions and loop-holed for rifles. How their ancient engines hissed and wheezed! Gordon took a boyish pride in their exploits. The commander was Muhammad Ali Pasha. On 12 August a group of four steamers carried 600 of Muhammad Ali's men against Gereif, one of the besiegers' forts on the Blue Nile, in support of a party of irregulars riding along the river-bank. They brought back to Khartoum 3,000 bushels of grain and 1,000 rifles. The next raid took them up to Abu Haraz, and two steamers went on to Sennar, 160 miles up the Blue Nile. This expedition brought back 9,000 bushels of grain. By the end of the month they seemed to have raised the siege. The country was clear of Dervishes for the moment and the local people seemed to be wavering. Gordon felt strong enough to recapture Berber, the key to re-opening communications with Egypt. But first he sent his victorious army and four steamers to attack El Ilafun, once again giving the command to Muhammad Ali Pasha. The district was wooded and rich in grain, oil and coffee. Like his neighbours, the local Chief, Sheikh Obeid, had sided with the Dervishes, but he was known for his unusual sanctity and the prestige this gave him, second only to the Mahdi's in this district.

The attack on El Ilafun, a village on the river-bank, went off exactly as planned and one steamer returned to Khartoum loaded with booty. Then victory went to Muhammad Ali's head. He asked Gordon for permission to leave the steamers and pursue the enemy to a second El Ilafun, a village fifteen miles inland, the birthplace of the Sheikh. Gordon had misgivings. It was deep in the woods, ideal for an ambush. (Many Egyptian soldiers had been cut off there during the original conquest of the Sudan.) Then he acquiesced after agreeing to send some irregular cavalry to meet Muhammad.

They could not find him and next day the steamers returned with news that sent a shudder of grief throughout Khartoum. Muhammad Ali's force had been hemmed in and cut down in the forest – 1,000 of Gordon's best soldiers, led by his best general – after being betrayed by a guide. The tale of this disaster was uncannily like the tale of Hicks Pasha's disaster at El Obeid the previous November. The pendulum swung back. Now the offensive was firmly in the hands of the Mahdi again.

Of course Gordon himself did not flinch at the news. None of the Mahdi's men was more resigned to the will of God than Gordon. 'I thank God for all things,' he told a deputation of Egyptian officers. 'I am sure that the days of these men were fulfilled.' Yet he also reproached himself. 'I felt sorry when I heard the account of the fight ... that the arrow did not return to his master.'[7] How was he to proceed now? The Nile was close to the peak of the flood; soon it would be ebbing away. Its fall promised new delays for Wolseley's relief expedition trying to manhandle the heavy boats up the cataracts, new dangers for Khartoum as the ebbing waters exposed the frail line of parapets. Gordon decided to encourage his two British companions, Colonel Stewart and young Frank Power, *The Times* correspondent and British Consul, to make good their own escape down the Nile.

At first Stewart protested that it would be shabby to leave his chief. Gordon explained he had a mission for him of the utmost importance. Stewart knew everything, and his word would be accepted better than Gordon's own. It was the only way to bring home the real situation of the garrison and to 'shame'[8] the British government into action. He hardly knew which of his own brief messages, taken by runners, had reached their destination. All that was clear was that both Baring in Cairo and Gladstone's Cabinet in London had completely misunderstood him.

They sent him idiotic messages asking if 'there is any danger at Khartoum'. They had got it into their heads that he was recklessly trying to involve Britain in a war with the Mahdi. As if he had any choice! At times he let off steam by poking fun at his political masters, like a cheeky schoolboy writing about his headmaster. At other times he bitterly reproached them:

How many times have we written asking for reinforcements [he wrote to Baring], calling your serious attention to the Sudan!

While you are eating and drinking and resting on good beds, we and those with us, both soldiers and servants, are watching by night and day, endeavouring to quell the movements of this false Mahdi....

The reason why I have now sent Colonel Stewart is because you have been silent all this while and neglected us, and lost time without doing any good.[9]

On the night of 9 September, less than a week after the disaster to Muhammad Ali's force, the small paddle steamer *Abbas* slipped away down-river from Khartoum, carrying Stewart and Power, some Greek refugees and the French Consul. Gordon had arranged an escort of two larger steamers, the *Safia* and *Mansura*, which should help them run the gauntlet of the Arabs at Berber. He had also put a mounted gun and fifty soldiers in the *Abbas* and had equipped her with special wooden buffers, a foot below the water-line, to protect her against hidden rocks. In case of emergency, Stewart had a pair of sailing boats in tow. Gordon warned the colonel to trust nobody. The one thing that gave him misgivings was Stewart's over-confident and trustful nature. (Very different from himself, he noted. He was 'made up' of suspicion.)[10] So he warned Stewart never to anchor close to the bank and to cut firewood only in isolated spots. He gave Stewart a mass of confidential papers to confirm the predicament of the garrison, including the Foreign Office cipher. In effect, Stewart was sent as a human SOS – to plead for help in words that Gordon would have been too proud to speak himself. The garrison's plight was desperate. By mid-November all their food would be gone. The relief column must come like the wind, otherwise (as Gordon said with a stiff upper lip) the 'game is up, and Rule Britannia'.[11]

On 26 September, the three other steamers, including the *Bordein*, sent up the Blue Nile to Sennar for grain, returned in triumph. Now they had food till mid-December. Once again the pendulum swung back towards hope. Gordon pictured Stewart and Power, safely at Debba by the 28th, already 250 miles north of Khartoum. He was assured they had safely passed Berber. Other encouraging messages began to filter through to him. A small party led by a young major in Arab dress, Herbert Kitchener, had reached Debba after a dangerous ride on camels across the desert. In a short note from Kitchener he heard the first definite news of Wolseley's relief expedition. By mid-October Gordon was calculating on relief within a month. He was convinced that even a couple of hundred British redcoats on board his steamers would be enough to break the siege. Three steamers – the *Safia*, *Mansura* and *Tel el-Houreen* – had been sent down to Metemma ready to bring the troops up. He expected his friend Stewart to return at their head.

Gordon's spirits rose like the Nile and flooded his journal with comic asides. He pictured Wolseley's men wobbling on their camels.

'See-saw, see-saw, why it is enough to kill a fellow. I can't keep my eyes open. I would give a shilling to have an hour's sleep! Yes, of course, *you* say it is close at hand, *you black devil*.' ... 'Hi! Stop! Catch hold of the brute ... Can't you stop the brute (noise of a body falling); well there is an end of it. I will walk *now* sooner than embark again on the ship of the desert.' ... Walks half a mile, boots full of sand.

Then he lampooned the senior officers:

Chermside to Kitchener: Any news of *him*? [Gordon]
Kitchener to Chermside: Nothing particular; two or three more men down.
Steamers at Matemma. Abuse as usual of Intelligence Department. Mahdi
doing much better: *he* [Gordon] finds it more difficult to get his letters
through, and will have time to get over *his* liver complaint and injustices.
Stewart says it was perfect pandemonium to be boxed up with him when in
his tantrums. [To Gordon] *I hope you are well. Let me know if I can do
anything for you . . . .*
Kitchener to Chermside: Hurrah! Capital news! The Mahdi has *him* [Gordon]
on the hip! He has gone to Omdurman. Bottled *him* up now! We will have
no more impertinent remarks about the Intelligence Department. Dongola
illuminated! Regular feast of lanterns! Wish you were here, old fellow; hope
you are well! Can I, etc. etc.[12]

Gordon began to prepare to move out of the palace, to make room for his
rescuers. The place was empty since Stewart had left. He had found himself a
new companion, the kind that a prisoner finds in his cell. 'A mouse has taken
Stewart's place at table,' he wrote in his journal on 12 October. 'She (judging
from her swelled-out appearance) comes up and eats out of my plate without
fear.'[13] He tried to make friends with an ill-tempered turkey-cock, rocking him
to and fro till he slept. When the bird woke, it flew at him.

As for the Mahdi, Gordon still did not despair of lulling him to sleep as well.
Gordon had no clear idea where he was. Then on 9 October a boy came in,
claiming he had left the Mahdi's camp four days earlier. The Mahdi had reached
the White Nile about a hundred miles south of Khartoum and was marching
towards the city along the west bank with about 4,000 men and all his European
prisoners, including some Greek nuns. He would cross the river dry-foot by a
miracle. That was his boast. The news raised Gordon's spirits further. He liked
the absurdity of the Mahdi being escorted by nuns. Besides, from the very
beginning he had longed to meet his enemy face to face.

It was Gordon's style, a feat only he would have attempted, to ride out into
the desert, alone among those fanatical warriors, a small figure in a tarboosh
with the bright blue eyes of a prophet, trusting in God's will. Originally London
had forbidden the meeting, but now the Mahdi was coming to Khartoum – and
so were Wolseley's men. The coincidence struck Gordon with the force of
revelation. Perhaps he would meet the Mahdi only in this final battle – 'Armageddon' he called it. The thought gave him neither pain nor pleasure. All he
wanted, he said wearily (and he was surely honest with himself), was to evacuate
the garrisons and get out of this wretched country without sacrificing his own
or his country's honour.

Gordon stared out from the roof of the palace towards the featureless west
bank of the White Nile where the Mahdi's troops would soon be encamped.
The waters were just beginning to recede. His spirits fell, too. One of the
troubles with the siege was that Gordon admired his enemies too much for his
own good. Though he believed the Mahdi to be a false prophet and hated his

cruelty, his own God took much the same puritan form as the Mahdi's. Both men loved the clean wind from the desert. 'I would sooner live like a Dervish with the Mahdi, than go out to dinner every night in London,' Gordon wrote in the journal. 'I hope, if any general comes to Kartoum, he will not ask me to dinner.'[14] He was only half-joking. As for the Mahdi's tattered followers, they were just the kind of army Gordon would have loved to lead. 'I wish I commanded the Arabs (speaking professionally)'[15] was the way he put it in his journal. He instinctively identified with the oppressed blacks, the have-nots of the Sudan, rather than with the effete pashas and men of property inside Khartoum. He was even afraid that the have-nots among his own garrison wanted to join the Mahdi. 'Oh! Our government, our government! What has it not to answer for? Not to *me*, but to these poor people. I declare if I thought the town wished the Mahdi, I would give it up: so much do I respect free will.'[16]

A week after Gordon wrote this, on 22 October, a courtly letter in Arabic was brought to his lines, embossed with a large red seal and inscribed with the name of the Mahdi. Even when translated, Gordon could hardly make head or tail of it.

> In the name of God the merciful and compassionate [it began solemnly] praise be to God, the bountiful Ruler, and blessing on our Lord Mahomed, with peace.
>
> From the servant who trusts in God – Mahomed the son of Abdallah.
>
> To Gordon Pasha of Kartoum: make God guide him into the path of virtue, amen!
>
> Know that your small steamer, named *Abbas* – which you sent with the intention of forwarding your news to Cairo, by way of Dongola, the persons sent being your representative, Stewart Pasha and the two Consuls, French and English, with other persons have been captured by the will of God.
>
> Those who believed in us as the Mahdi, and surrendered, have been delivered; and those who did not were destroyed – as your representative aforenamed, with the Consuls and the rest – whose souls God has condemned to fire and eternal misery.[17]

Stewart and Power were dead, and the cipher messages captured. That was Gordon's first terrible thought. Then his head cleared. It must be a mistake.

The letter quoted confidential papers taken in the *Abbas*. But those papers had never been in the *Abbas*. Anyway, the news from two other steamers confirmed that the *Abbas* had got safely down. Gordon breathed again, put the matter out of his head and began to play the fool in his journal. 'I must say I hate our diplomatists,' he wrote cheerfully that day. 'I think with few exceptions they are arrant humbugs and I expect they know it.' Then he drew a ludicrous sketch of Baring, sporting a monocle, like an illustration for a Nonsense poem by Edward Lear. It was inscribed: 'B...G' with the text: 'Most serious! Is it not! He calls us humbugs! *Arrant humbugs!*'[18] Characteristically, Gordon sent instalments of this amazing journal down-river in the *Bordein* for Wolseley and Baring to see for themselves.

Would Baring appreciate the joke? Perhaps Gordon would never know. Perhaps it even occurred to Gordon that the journals would be read by the Mahdi instead. Would *he* appreciate the joke? That, too, was a mystery, for no European had yet met the Mahdi since his rise to power and returned to tell the tale.

There was one European who was determined to accomplish this feat. His name was Rudolf Slatin, a dashing, blue-eyed, thirty-one-year-old Austrian soldier of fortune whom Gordon had appointed Governor of the westernmost province, Darfur. He had surrendered when his province was over-run the year before. Many prisoners were tortured and killed, but the Mahdi took a liking to Slatin. The young man claimed to be a believer (he had already converted to Islam because his own soldiers had believed their defeats were due to having a Christian as leader). Slatin had now exchanged the white uniform and scarlet tarboosh of a bey for the patched *jibbah* (smock) of the Dervish. Outwardly he was now a pious Muslim, Abdul Kadir, one of the Mahdi's most devoted servants. It was all a sham. Slatin was waiting his chance to escape. As the Mahdi's vast army approached Khartoum, creeping forward 'like a great tortoise'[19] in Slatin's own phrase, he decided to seize his chance.

Six days before the Mahdi had written that letter to Gordon claiming that Stewart was dead and the *Abbas* captured, Slatin was summoned into the Mahdi's presence. It was the evening of 14 October, and the army was now only a day's journey from Khartoum. Sitting on a sheepskin rug, the Mahdi received Slatin with a smile. He was a strikingly handsome man, Muhammad Ahmad, the Deliverer and Expected One: tall, broad-shouldered, of light brown colour, with a black beard and sparkling eyes. His features were smooth and regular apart from three tribal scars on each cheek. He wore a quilted *jibbah* with Dervish patches stitched on, but carefully washed and scented with musk and rosewater. His voice was eloquent. But it was his smile which gave an impression of good humour and piety together, exposing his white teeth and the gap between his two front ones, the gap which is taken as a sign of good luck in the Sudan.

In the year since his surrender, Slatin had lived in the household of the Khalifa, the Mahdi's deputy, and had learnt much about the extraordinary power the Mahdi exercised over his followers. He had appeared from nowhere. In fact, Muhammad Ahmad was the son of an obscure boat-builder from Dongola claiming, on no particular authority, to be descended from the Prophet. When he was still young, his family moved near Khartoum and then, in search of good timber for boat building, to Abba Island on the White Nile. Young Muhammad Ahmad became the devoted adherent of a Sufi sheikh, Muhammad Sharif, head of a celebrated mystical order. Soon he became known for the extreme asceticism of his life and broke with his own master, who permitted music and dancing at a family celebration – an abomination, according to Muhammad Ahmad. He set up on his own, and the local tribesmen flocked to see this hermit of Abba Island. Even Gordon's paddle steamers, bound for Equatoria 500 miles to the south, had slackened speed to show respect as they passed the island. To Europeans he seemed harmless, if a little cracked. He spoke only of the vanities of this world and the greatness of Allah. No one could have guessed how quickly he would prove his point.

Muhammad Ahmad's chance came in 1881, with expectations of a Mahdi already in the air. The people of the Sudan had had their fill of Egypt. The 'Turks' from the north would stop at nothing to enrich themselves. Government by Egypt was government by robbery. Of course this was what the Sudan had suffered ever since Muhammad Ali had carved a state from this vast tribal wilderness in the 1820s. Ismael Pasha's attempted reforms in the 1870s had added to the sense of outrage. Most Sudanese were shocked by Egypt's attempt to stop the slave trade from the south. Slaves were the natural basis of the Sudan's wealth, the cornerstone of trade, of work at home and work in the fields. How could Ismael claim authority to denounce an institution that was accepted by the Koran?

The truth was that Ismael's high-minded European advisers had launched him on his crusade against slavery, but they had not bothered to work out how, or at what cost, this great reform could be achieved. Ismael had turned to two Christians he could trust to be incorruptible: Baker and Gordon. To improvise an administration, they had brought in adventurers like Romolo Gessi and Rudolf Slatin. Gordon claimed to have won the war against Suleiman and the slavers. But was it not only a battle? And what was the cost in alienating the people?

The moment Gordon had left the Sudan in 1879, most of the country rose to greet the Mahdi, the Expected Deliverer, to reverse Gordon's reforms. Like the leaders of the jihads of Islam, the Mahdi could unite all the disaffected under a single revolutionary banner. His sacred mission was to restore the golden age of the Prophet Muhammad. He would expel 'Turks' and Christians, abolish the hated poll tax imposed from Cairo, restore respect for the great, and have mercy on the humble. These were the burning words he preached, the text of his jihad, which he carried across the Sudan like a flaming sword. People said that the angels helped him to victory. At the battle of El Obeid (Shaykan) in November 1883 he had destroyed an army of 10,000 Egyptians, led by Hicks Pasha, almost without loss to his men. After capturing El Obeid, the capital of Kordofan, he seemed invincible. The humble hermit of Abba Island had become the hero of a national revolution that would sweep the Sudan bare of corruption. The Mahdi even claimed he would soon carry his fiery message to other corrupt Islamic states – to Cairo, Mecca and beyond.

These were the claims, advanced with such chilling spiritual fervour, that Slatin heard (no doubt from the lips of the Mahdi himself) in the great camp outside Khartoum. It was news that would hardly reassure Gordon, but Slatin was anxious to help his old chief, as well as himself, and believed he could do so. Gordon had certainly under-estimated his opponent by under-estimating the spiritual fervour of the jihad, but Slatin himself did not think the Mahdi invincible.

First, the Mahdi's character seemed to be changing, softened and corrupted by power. He still posed as an ascetic and wept like a child at the feast of Bairan when he read the prayers to the faithful. But his intimates knew that most of this was a sham. When captured slave girls were distributed after a battle, the Mahdi had first pick and he always chose the prettiest. Second, the great emirs were quarrelling among themselves and seemed to have lost their appetite for battle. No one was anxious to assault Khartoum, although the place was known to be full of loot. Some disaffected sheikhs would even have liked to join Gordon, if they could have done so without abandoning their wives and families.

This was the reassurance that Slatin yearned to take to Gordon. With energy and perseverance Khartoum could hold out for months. Knowing the Mahdi's intentions, Slatin would surely be a godsend to the defence. And perhaps he also envisaged an adventurous trip down-river in one of Gordon's steamers, to link up with the relief expedition, known to be marching south. But first he had to make good his escape to Khartoum. It was the Mahdi himself who now seemed to offer him the opportunity.

When the Mahdi called Slatin to his tent on 14 October, he told him that he must persuade Gordon to surrender. 'Tell him that I am the true Mahdi, and that he ought to surrender with his garrison, and thus save himself and his soul. Tell him, also, that if he refuses to obey, we shall every one of us fight against him. Say that you yourself will fight against him with your own hands.'[20] Slatin replied that the words would have no effect; Gordon would not believe them. It would be better if he wrote to Gordon offering to act as the intermediary to arrange the surrender. The Mahdi agreed.

That night Slatin wrote to Gordon in German, explaining his plan to escape, on the pretext of arranging the surrender. He asked Gordon's complicity in the subterfuge. A fifteen-year-old boy took the letter to Gordon's lines. He returned with the bleak news that the Pasha had no answer to make. In desperation Slatin wrote again. He had a non-committal reply from the Austrian Consul (who must have translated the letter for Gordon), but once more Gordon rebuffed him.

Ironically, this did not save Slatin from being suspected of trying to escape. That night he was seized and disarmed by the Khalifa's men. Heavy iron rings were hammered round his neck and legs, secured by a long chain. Two days later, the great war-drum sounded the advance. The tents were struck, the camels were loaded, and the Mahdi's army lumbered forward, throwing up an immense cloud of dust. In its midst rode Slatin, astride a donkey and supported by men on either side, since the chains were so heavy that he would have overbalanced. That afternoon they halted on rising ground and Slatin could see the palm trees of Khartoum where he so longed to be. Why had Gordon rebuffed him?

From the roof of the palace Gordon continued to stare into the heat haze, looking down the great river, counting the days before Wolseley could reach him. He expected the *Bordein* and the other steamers to return with the vanguard – and no doubt Stewart too – by about 10 November.

Poor Slatin. It was true, it would have been a godsend to have him in Khartoum. 'What one has felt so much here', Gordon wrote in his journal, 'is the want of men like Gessi ... or Slatin.'[21] But he had no choice but to reject Slatin's plan. It was against the stern code of honour that gave consistency to Gordon's own wayward character to allow Slatin to escape by breaking his parole. This 'should be as sacred when given to the Mahdi as to any other power'. Perhaps in his heart Gordon had not fully forgiven Slatin for abandoning Christianity and conforming to Islam. The fellow was no 'Spartan', not the stuff that martyrs were made of. Still, he would like to help him. 'If he gets away I shall take him to the Congo with me, [King Leopold had invited Gordon to take over the Congo from Stanley] he will want some *quarantine*; one feels sorry for him.'[22]

Early in November Gordon checked the food supplies and was furious to find that a quarter of the biscuit supply – 252,750 lbs – could not be accounted for. It turned out to have been stolen the year before. He still reckoned he would have to 'throw up the sponge' in mid-December unless Wolseley reached them. The thought made him 'rabid'. 'I should be an angel (which I am not, needless to say) if I was not rabid with Her Majesty's Government; but I hope I may be quiet on the subject of this Soudan and Cairo business, with its indecision; but to lose all my beautiful black soldiers is enough to make me angry with those who have the direction of our future.'[23]

Then, about four o'clock on the afternoon of 3 November, a wisp of blue wood-smoke was spotted on the horizon. It was the *Bordein* steering back from Metemma. Ceremonial salutes were fired, and Egyptian flags run up on the forts and steamers. People rushed down to the quay to be the first to touch hands with their rescuers.

No Englishman stepped ashore from the *Bordein*. Nor were there any sacks of grain for the garrison. Instead there were two official communications: a ciphered telegram from Lord Wolseley and a short letter from Major Kitchener. The telegram he could not read, as Stewart had taken the cipher. The letter informed him that the *Abbas* had been captured and its occupants were believed dead. So the Mahdi had told the truth. Stewart and Power were dead and his own SOS had never been received.

Had Gordon been able to read Wolseley's telegram, sent on 20 September from Cairo, it would have made him even more 'rabid'. Wolseley had totally failed to grasp the desperate state of the garrison. He had cabled, 'We hear that siege has been raised; is this true? If so, what would be the use of sending British troops to Khartoum?'[24] In fact, Wolseley had halted for a month at Dongola, 300 miles to the north, and was not planning to begin his advance until December.

A week later the Mahdi's personal troops launched an assault on the small outpost across the river, attacking with a pluck that Gordon had to admire. It was still dark when the attack was launched. With difficulty it was beaten back.

One tumbles at 3.0 a.m. into a troubled sleep; a drum beats – tup! tup! tup!
It comes into a dream, but after a few moments one becomes more awake,
and it is revealed to the brain that *one is in Kartoum*. The next query is where
is this tup, tupping going on. A hope arises it will die away. No, it goes on,
and increases in intensity ... At last, it is no use, up one must get, and go on
to the roof of the palace; then telegrams, orders, swearing and cursing goes
on till about 9.0 a.m.[25]

Meanwhile, in desperation, Gordon had written to Wolseley explaining that the
besiegers had tightened their hold on the city and repeating once again that he
had only forty days' food supplies: 'after that it will be difficult'. But this official
phrase, in the convention of the stiff upper lip, might have been misunderstood
by Wolseley. So he wrapped up the latest instalment of the journal – written
from the heart, as he swung between hope and despair, with all its boyish
candour, the lampoons on Chermside and Kitchener, and the caricature of
Baring – and sent it off in the *Bordein* for Wolseley to read. 'Six weeks
consumption!! And then the sponge must be thrown up.' Now Wolseley could
not say he had not been warned. And let him ponder this: 'It is, of course, on
the cards that Khartoum is taken under the nose of the expeditionary force,
which will be *just too late*.'[26]

'See-saw. See-saw.' It was quite as comic as Gordon had imagined. Wolseley's
relief expedition of 10,000 men was to be led by a flying column, a picked force
of 1,600 officers and men with 2,500 camels, ready if necessary to dash across
the desert ahead of the river column. Here was the flower of the British army
led by the flower of London society – including eleven peers or peers' sons –
precariously mounted on camels. By mid-November they were plodding along
the banks of the Nile, strung out in groups of 150, all the 240 miles from Aswan
to Wadi Halfa.

What confirmed the air of a charade was the outlandish uniform of the new
Camel Corps, a hybrid of the seventeenth century and a circus: red jumpers,
breeches and bandoliers, sun goggles and white helmets. 'Fancy a Life Guardsman clothed like a scarecrow and with blue goggles on, mounted on a camel,
over which he has little control. What a picture!'[27] was Wolseley's comment.
The camels, too, were a strange collection, raked up at the last minute from as
far away as Aden, beasts of all colours and sizes, from the great brown baggagers,
each as large as a rhinoceros, to the elegant fawn-coloured racing camels from
Arabia. The men found that mounting a frisky camel was exciting work, and
they often came a cropper. Wolseley himself fell off, painfully hard, on a piece
of gravelly sand, in front of his army. He hated camels. 'They are so stupid;
they begin to howl the moment you put a saddle on them and they smell
abominably ...'[28]

Wolseley was thoroughly out of humour with everything. Gordon was his
hero, the only hero he said he had ever known personally. To rescue him was
a sacred mission. Otherwise he would never have embarked on this desert

venture. He loathed the policy of abandoning the Sudan to the enemy. It was against all his principles as a leader of the forward policy. He was furious with Gladstone's government. How he loathed those 'vestrymen' who had made a fool of England and destroyed her prospects – including his own. Gone were the golden years when he had carried all before him on the battlefields of Africa and in Whitehall. At Tel el-Kebir in September 1882 his star had reached its zenith. That campaign glittered like a sword blade. How could he recapture the speed and power with which within twenty-six days of his landings at Ismailia he had decapitated Arabi's rebellion and made his own triumphant entry to Cairo?

He had started three months too late. That was his overwhelming handicap as he saw it, and this could hardly be challenged. It was in April that he had first proposed to Lord Hartington, the Minister of War, a controversial plan for rescuing Gordon and the garrison. There were strong arguments against this plan. The obvious way to Khartoum was by way of the Red Sea port of Suakin, across 250 miles of desert to Berber, and then along an easy stretch of the Nile, a further 200 miles to Khartoum. Wolseley scoffed at this route. There would not be enough water and the country was hostile. It was 'infinitely preferable' to take his 10,000 men alongside the Nile, all the way from the port of Alexandria, using the railway for the first 220 miles (to Asyut), steamers and barges for the next 540 miles (to Wadi Halfa), and then a fleet of small boats for the final 860 miles.

Four months had been lost in delays before Gladstone would agree to sanction the expedition. So the case against the Nile route was now much stronger. Indeed, the Suakin route seemed better to all the most knowledgeable authorities at home and in Egypt. The Suakin–Berber route was a quarter of the distance – 450 miles from a supply base, compared with 1,620 miles. True, 500 miles of the Nile's second loop could be avoided by a 180-mile short cut across the desert from Korti to Metemma. But if this short cut was necessary, why not use the short cut from Suakin? Speed was the essence of this expedition. To manhandle boats across the series of cataracts above Wadi Halfa would occupy months – and might not be practical at all.

Wolseley had replied stubbornly that he had dragged small boats up Canadian rapids, one of them taller than Niagara, in the Red river expedition of 1870, and that he would drag small boats up the Nile. He summoned to his aid the magic circle of his protégés – the Wolseley Ring – who had shared with him those deeds of daring on the Red river. They reported that 'the Nile will be found the easiest, the safest and immensely the cheapest line of advance to adopt'.[29] Finally Hartington was convinced. Wolseley and his Ring were despatched in August to go by the Nile route, in case Gordon could not free himself. Wolseley himself thought there was 'a great hope' that the Mahdi's men would lose heart before the army approached Khartoum.

Easiest, safest, cheapest? All this might be true. But was it the quickest? It was this question that Wolseley, intent on recapturing his youthful exploits in the Red river, had not faced. At his own most optimistic forecast, the first boats would not reach Khartoum till four months *after* the city's supplies must have run out. So the situation of the garrison would surely be desperate. Or, put it another way, one route offered a forlorn hope, the other no hope at all. Were Wolseley and the Ring trusting their own powers to work a miracle?

The truth about Wolseley was more prosaic. Gordon was only in real danger if the Mahdi was a real enemy, and Wolseley despised the Mahdi almost as much as he despised Mr Gladstone. The rebels would lose heart long before his own army reached Khartoum.

It was now 17 November, and all Wolseley's forecasts of progress had proved recklessly optimistic. He was back at Wadi Halfa, still 860 miles by water from Khartoum, on the wrong side of the worst rapids in the whole river. He now forecast that the army could not be concentrated at Debba till 7 January, at the earliest. Therefore the river column could not reach Khartoum for months after that date. So he was glad of the Camel Corps, the small, eccentric flying column that had been thrown in as an afterthought in September, in case it was needed.

Why was the river expedition weeks behind schedule? Wolseley had ridden back to Dongola to find out, and characteristically blamed everyone in the Ring but himself. His Chief of Staff, Colonel Sir Redvers Buller, he found, had failed to check that coal supplies were properly arranged with Thomas Cook's local agent. For want of coal the steamers between Aswan and Wadi Halfa had been held up for twelve days. He decided that Brackenbury would do better. But Brackenbury had 'Greek blood in him'[30] and so could not be trusted. Butler was becoming an impossible man, too. He had no gift for business. As for Sir Evelyn Wood, Wolseley concluded that he was 'a very second-rate general and an unpatriotic and selfish public servant'. What Wolseley could not forget or forgive was Wood's 'ignominious' peace with the Boers after Majuba. He blamed Wood for deciding 'to make an end to the war, *coûte que coûte*',[31] before Roberts could arrive to supersede him.

The truth which Wolseley did not dare admit to himself was that he had made a second error imperilling the expedition. Not only had he chosen the wrong route, but the wrong means of transport. One of the disadvantages of the Nile route was the great numbers of camels required. Wolseley's reply was that a specially designed flotilla of small boats could do the job better. The boats were indeed designed and built in record time, but they had to be sent all the way from England, with a motley collection of Red river boatmen – *voyageurs* – brought all the way from Canada. Then there were delays which no one had forecast. The boats' gear was lost or damaged; the boats themselves needed repairs and they were too small for their loads. When Wolseley returned to Wadi Halfa in mid-November, the first boat of this immense flotilla had only just been tried in the rapids above the town. Meanwhile, instead of buying camels on a large scale, a task which could have begun in August, Wolseley had given orders for only 4,000 – not even enough for the small flying column. This was to prove his third crucial error.

There was a fourth, compounding all the others, and Wolseley committed it that day, 17 November, as he stood fuming at Wadi Halfa. A field telegram was put into his hand, sent from Debba, the forward post then held by the army, and signed by Kitchener. The text was a desperate message from Gordon dated only thirteen days earlier. Here at last was an answer to the question of how long Gordon could last out. Gordon repeated what he had said before. His food had nearly gone. 'We can hold out forty days with ease; after that it will be difficult.'[32]

A general must be judged not only by the soundness of his strategy, but by the speed with which he abandons it when proved wrong. Wolseley had grossly under-estimated the Mahdi. So now was the time to give absolute priority to that afterthought, the flying column. Forty days from 4 November. No, that was impossible. But if the flying column was hustled to the front at the expense of the river column, precious days would be gained. Wolseley did nothing of the sort. The flying column continued its leisurely progress along the Nile. Wolseley cabled the text of Gordon's letter to Hartington, and explained that this did not alter anything. The flying column would not leave the river at Korti for the dash across the desert till the beginning of January. Wolseley was understandably full of anxieties, but anxiety that he might be too late to save Gordon does not appear to have been one of them. Contempt for the Mahdi and blind faith in Gordon, the miracle worker, had replaced all rational considerations. As one of his staff put it to a journalist in camp: 'If Gordon says he can hold out for six weeks, he can do so for six months.'

The flying column hung around Korti, near Debba, for three weeks after the main army had begun to collect there for the advance by river. Nothing Wolseley did suggested a sense of urgency. The shortage of camels – and Wolseley's insistence that everyone should be able to ride – meant the flying column lost ten days while they established a post in the desert, and then returned for more supplies. On 2 January Wolseley received a final desperate scrap from Gordon, a smuggled piece of paper the size of a postage stamp with the words, 'Kartoum all right, 14.12.84, C. G. Gordon.'[33] The messenger brought a confused verbal account. Fighting was going on night and day. To most people it would have been clear that the fall of Khartoum was imminent, but this was not Wolseley's view. He cabled London that he was proceeding to send the desert column to Metemma as arranged, and they could 'communicate with Gordon by steamer, learn exact position and if he is *in extremis* before infantry arrive by river, to push forward by camel corps to help him at all hazards'. In other words, he was not yet sending a rescue party. He was sending the flying column to Metemma and then making a reconnaissance by steamer to learn Gordon's 'exact position'.[34]

These were, indeed, the orders Wolseley gave his subordinates. Sir Herbert Stewart would take the flying column to Metemma and wait there. Sir Charles Wilson, the Chief of Intelligence, would proceed to Khartoum in one of Gordon's steamers. He was not, it must be repeated, sent to rescue Gordon; he was only to give him a letter, march some British troops especially dressed in red uniforms through the city 'to show the people that British troops were near at hand',[35] and then steam back to Metemma, leaving Gordon in Khartoum. Wolseley added, 'it is always possible' that the Mahdi would abandon the siege at the mere sight of the terrifying redcoats.

Inspired by this cheerful forecast, Stewart and Wilson, with a division of the naval brigade, a squadron of hussars, some mounted infantry, half a battery of artillery and the 1,600 men and 2,500 camels of the Camel Corps, lumbered off into the desert on 8 January 1885. The men were in high spirits at beginning, at last, the real business of the campaign. Their strange uniforms looked stranger still after two months' plodding along the Nile. Most were in tatters. But they were hardened camel riders. Some of the officers rode horses and Lord Charles Beresford had brought a white pony. The advance seemed a walk-over. The desert was flat and gravelly, an easy march even without camels, the days hot with a pleasant breeze, the nights lit by a moon and brilliant stars, and deliciously cool.

After four days the column reached Jakdul, the oasis where Stewart had established his supply post a fortnight earlier. Now the desert was covered with *savas* grass and mimosa. By the 18th they were approaching Abu Klea, the final oasis before Metemma, but it became clear that the extra ten days lost in the double journey to Jakdul had alerted the enemy. A large force – some said as many as 10,000 – was waiting for them astride the track to Abu Klea. That night they heard the sound of war-drums beating from an unseen camp. In the darkness, shots flew over their heads, ricocheting off the rocks with an eerie wail. But most men were too exhausted to keep awake. Next day the storm broke with terrifying violence.

Stewart had divided his small force into two: one to defend the camp, dug in behind a thorn-and-stone *zeriba*, the other to advance in a moving square. The square was thus a kind of moving fortress of dismounted cavalrymen, horses, camels and sailors. To use the square in this way demanded training and experience that the cavalry and sailors lacked. Nor was anyone prepared for the ferocious courage of the enemy.

At about ten o'clock the square moved slowly forward, with ammunition camels in the centre, while skirmishers and outriders (hussars and mounted infantry) protected the flanks. The enemy's sharp-shooters harried the square, as they had harried the *zeriba* the previous night. Then the square halted at the top of a stony ridge a few hundred yards from the caravan trail. There, half-hidden in a ravine, were the black and green flags of several thousand Arabs.

It was now, unfortunately for the square, that the British changed formation. The order was given by Colonel Fred Burnaby, a six-foot four inch guardee, balloonist, self-publicist and London clubman, who had come out as a freelance, an eccentric whom Wolseley, somewhat frivolously, had made second in command. Burnaby decided it was time to bring out the Gardner gun manned by Beresford and the sailors. So he told the Blue Jackets to bring the gun down from the rear face of the square to the left corner facing the enemy. Meanwhile the camels of the heavy regiment, carrying the ammunition and stretchers, had lagged behind, and their drivers were trying to flog them into closing up. The result was a mêlée of roaring camels and swearing sailors, some of whom became separated from their gun. Above the din, Burnaby shouted to the cavalry to wheel out from the square to let the sailors re-form. He himself rode out from the square, a gigantic figure in a blue cavalry uniform, riding on a borrowed pony.

By itself Burnaby's error might not have been too serious, but Stewart, too, had under-estimated the enemy. His own skirmishers were still outside the square, hundreds of yards away. Seeing their chance, the Arabs charged in five columns at a quick, even pace.

Men in the square could not help admiring the regular order, so unexpected in a mass of natives. They all wore the Mahdi's uniform, the patched *jibbah*. Each column was led by an emir or sheikh on horseback, carrying a flag and accompanied by attendants. As they bounded forward, their banners fluttered in the winter sun and their low, murmuring war-cry sounded like rushing water. Stewart's skirmishers ran for their lives, though their comrades bellowed at them from the square to lie flat, so that their comrades could fire over them.

All the skirmishers safely reached the square, except one who was hacked to death. Meanwhile those inside the square could not fire, and when they did many of the rifles jammed. It was this disaster, and the gap in the rear – the mêlée of the Heavy Brigade, the sailors and the Gardner gun – which gave the Arabs their reward. Suddenly the wall of Martini-Henrys at the left rear dissolved, and a torrent of Arabs carrying six-foot-long spears surged through the breach, like water smashing through a dam.

Colonel Sir Charles Wilson, the third in command, was standing close to the tail of Stewart's horse, near the front ranks, at the moment when the square broke. He had been watching the Dervish charge with mixed feelings: pity that they would all be shot down within a few minutes, and admiration for their coolness. It seemed impossible that men in such close formation could charge across a bare slope, straight up to the muzzles of the Martini-Henrys. Then, about eighty yards from the line, a huge pile of dead began to block the advance. To his astonishment Wilson saw the Dervish columns wheel, as though on parade, and swing towards the rear. He had just time to think, 'By jove, they will be into the square,'[36] when he saw a fine old sheikh on horseback, carrying a banner in one hand and a prayerbook in the other, ride into the centre of the square behind the camels. One moment he was chanting from the prayerbook. Then he had planted his banner and was shot, bringing it down in his fall.

There was a moment of wild confusion. The front ranks of the Guards turned to fire backwards into the square, killing some British officers, as well as Dervishes. Wilson saw Stewart's horse shot from under him, and Stewart at the mercy of three Arabs who had ducked under the camels' bellies and run forward to spear him. Wilson shot one with his revolver; the others were killed by the mounted infantry officers at his side. Further back, behind a heaving wall of camels, the Guards and the naval brigade fought for their lives.

It was another of those 'soldiers' battles': hand against hand, spear against bayonet, each man hacking and cutting like a butcher. For five minutes there was pandemonium. But the outer ranks of the broken square had closed, sealing in the attackers, and the wall of dead camels prevented them advancing beyond the centre. The bloody business was soon over. It only remained to try to help the British casualties and finish off the Arab wounded.

Wilson, a sensitive man, was surprised to find how quickly his feelings were blunted by the horrors. A Dervish shook himself from the pile of dead, jumped up and charged at an officer waving a spear. The officer seized the spear with his left hand, and with his right hand ran his sword through the man's body. Neither man could move. And there they stood, like a pair of gladiators on a fresco, till someone ran up and shot the Dervish.

Something like hysteria seized the ordinary soldiers after the fight was over. The officers could do nothing with them until they were marched fifty yards on, and re-formed in a new square. The novelty of the experience had indeed been unnerving.

In that five minutes, sixty-five men of the British force were killed and sixty-one wounded, mostly from the heavy camel regiment. Outside the square lay the huge form of Fred Burnaby, dying from a spear wound. Two officers of the Naval Brigade died beside the Gardner gun, which had jammed at the tenth round. Charlie Beresford had an amazing escape. The Dervish charge knocked him down. He lay there stunned, under a heap of bodies, till he managed to scramble back to safety.

Most of the British dead were buried in a long trench a little below the ridge. About 800 Dervishes lay beside their crumpled black and green banners, the mounds of dead marking the accuracy of the charge and the butchery in the square. Others lay scattered in the *savas* grass for miles beyond the battlefield. No doubt many of the wounded lay there for days. A few lucky ones were given food and water by some women who came out from Metemma.

Meanwhile, Stewart marched the square two miles forward, captured the wells at Abu Klea, and sent waterskins back for the wounded and the reserves left in the *zeriba*. But his path to the Nile at Metemma was still barred. Despite a night march through a tangle of rocks and scrub, where the guides lost their way and a hundred loaded camels vanished like ghosts, the column was unable to reach the river before daylight.

A second battle followed at Abu Kru, a few miles from Metemma. Stewart himself was mortally wounded while recklessly exposing himself to fire. Perhaps the Dervishes could have annihilated the whole column if they had pinned the square down with rifle fire in the open plain till the men collapsed from thirst. But the Dervishes' courage was their undoing. They charged the square with the same disciplined fervour as their comrades had shown at Abu Klea. The square held firm. The skirmishers had been withdrawn in good time and the cavalry had learnt how to stand and shoot like infantry. The Dervishes never got close enough to use their spears. Another great mound of dead soon marked the battlefield, with patched *jibbahs* and prayer beads among the crumpled banners and broken spears.

Wilson, now leader of the expedition, re-formed the column after the exhausted men flung themselves down on the banks of the Nile near Metemma. Morale was still precarious. Wolseley had told them to capture the small town of Metemma and send a party on to Khartoum in Gordon's steamers. No one had prepared them for the experience of meeting 10,000 fanatical warriors out in the desert. They had lost a tenth of their number in killed and wounded. The attack on Metemma proved abortive, as the shells from their screw gun passed through the mud huts without damaging them. Wilson, a sapper, not a fighting general, wondered how to summon reinforcements. If only there had been a field telegraph, or some quick way of communicating with Wolseley back at Korti.

During the abortive attack on Metemma, Wilson was told that several paddle steamers flying the large red flag of the Khedive were coming down-river. They proved to be the expected steamers, three of them sent down by Gordon to meet the rescue expedition the previous autumn. The fourth, the *Bordein*, had only left Khartoum on 14 December, carrying Gordon's latest letters and the sixth volume of his journals. Wilson read these carefully, as well he might.

The journals concluded with the prophetic words: 'NOW MARK THIS – if the Expeditionary Force, and I ask for no more than 200 men, does not come in ten days, *the town may fall*; and I have done my best for the honour of our country. Good bye.'[37] From his private letters it was clear that Gordon expected the worst. The town would fall soon after their food ran out in mid-December. It was now 19 January. There was just a chance, one might have thought, if Wilson took the fastest steamers, loaded them with food and his toughest fighting men, that Gordon could still be rescued.

But that was not what Wilson thought. He stuck to Wolseley's orders. His first priority was the safety of his own force. Of course Gordon would hold out. A few days' extra delay could make no difference. Wilson steamed up and down the river, confirming that no Dervishes threatened the camp. He carefully overhauled the ships' engines. After three days' delay the *Bordein* and the *Talahawiyeh* steamed majestically towards Khartoum with twenty red-coated soldiers, all that could be spared from the Sussex Regiment. (Their own red coats had been lost or looted, but some were borrowed from other regiments.)

The black crews of Gordon's steamers were in high spirits as the two boats surged forward against the current. For many of them Khartoum was home. Wilson lay awake that night, unable to sleep, burdened by one anxiety. How was he to break the bad news to Gordon that he could not now be relieved till Wolseley's Nile column arrived in March? Meanwhile his own orders were not even to leave Gordon the twenty redcoats he had brought to terrify the Mahdi.

Four nights after Wilson set off, two hours before dawn on 26 January, the Mahdi gave the word, and his army brushed through Gordon's defence lines and burst into Khartoum.

CHAPTER 14

Welcome to a Philanthropist

Berlin, Brussels and London
15 November 1884–27 February 1885

> 'Leopold II ... has knit adventurers, traders and
> missionaries of many races into one band of men,
> under the most illustrious of modern travellers
> [H. M. Stanley] to carry into the interior of Africa
> new ideas of law, order, humanity, and protection
> of the natives.'
>
> The *Daily Telegraph*, 22 October 1884

The West Africa Conference began on Saturday, 15 November 1884. Winter had come early to Berlin; snow fell every night that week, in a rococo blizzard which decorated the grey fluted pilasters and coarse yellow bricks of Bismarck's house at No 77 Wilhelmstrasse, and then reverted to slush each day when the delegates alighted from their carriages.

On Saturday afternoon, just before two o'clock, the nineteen plenipotentiaries, with fifteen assistants, representing fourteen great and lesser Powers, climbed the stairs to the large music room and took their seats at the horseshoe table ready for the inaugural session. The plenipotentiaries wore the glittering court dress of the diplomatic corps. Their host, Prince Bismarck, sat there, stomach to the table, face to the open end of the horseshoe, as he had sat there on that summer day six years earlier to welcome his guests to Berlin for the celebrated Congress. The music room was arranged in much the same way as before. It was a tall, white, vaulted hall, running the whole width of the building, more or less undecorated except for some grey marble pillars, red damask curtains and a single enormous chandelier suspended from the ceiling.

But this was only a conference. At the Congress six years earlier, Berlin had been flattered to welcome the giants of the age. Then it had been Disraeli who sat on Bismarck's right, and beyond him Lord Salisbury, Britain's Foreign Secretary; on Bismarck's left had been Gorchakov and Schuvalov to speak for Russia, Andrassy for Austria, Waddington and de Vallier for France. All six of the great Powers – three empires, two kingdoms and a republic – had sent their leading statesmen to the horseshoe table. Now the Great Powers had been invited to send only their local ambassadors, relative pygmies, who already lived within carriage distance of the Wilhelmstrasse.

Those giants in Berlin in 1878 had been playing for the highest stakes. It was grand strategy then. When the Russians grabbed slices of the Ottoman Empire

Bismarck had seized the chance to offer titbits (Tunis and Cyprus) to Britain and France. Together the Powers had created a new balance in the East. Today at Berlin there was no sign of this great game. There was only a diplomatic mess to be cleared up after the collapse of the British attempt to give the mouth of the Congo to Portugal. This in turn had been caused by the undignified rush for slices of the African cake, which might prove dangerously heavy on the stomach. No wonder people poked fun at the Scramble and wondered what Bismarck expected to get out of the conference. Was it simply a free trade conference to safeguard German traders in the Congo – and the Niger? Or was there a great game after all – to carve up the whole African continent? What were Bismarck's motives in calling the conference?

It was an intriguing puzzle, but of no great concern to most of the fourteen delegations. The majority must have felt bemused to find themselves at the horseshoe table. There would be no titbits for onlookers like them. Their countries had no appetite for colonies, no stake in Africa, and little hope of expanding trade, welcome as it would have been during the present industrial depression. The list of onlookers included three great Powers – Russia, Austro-Hungary and the United States – and a number of small ones, Denmark, Sweden, Norway, Holland, Belgium, and so on. On the other hand there were two Great Powers who had every reason to get the wind up. Britain, with her large formal African Empire and even larger informal empire, was intensely vulnerable to Bismarck's designs. Was she now going to lose more of her informal empire – the Niger and East Africa – as she had lost Cameroon, Togo and Angra Pequena? France, too, though Germany's ally, was also vulnerable to Bismarck's declared aim of enforcing rules to liberate trade. For France was the world's leading protectionist. Then there was Portugal, half-senile and three-quarters bankrupt, hoarding her ancient possessions in Africa, Angola and Mozambique, more out of pride than of any hope of profit. She was a protectionist, too. Did Bismarck aim to break her traders' monopoly? Finally, more vulnerable than any foreign state, was Leopold's International Association of the Congo – the name to which Leopold had changed the CEHC. This state-to-be had not even been invited to the conference. Did Bismarck intend to steal the Congo from Leopold?

A popular theory, advanced by *The Times*'s masterful correspondent in Paris, Henri Blowitz, was that Britain would come off worst at the conference. Bismarck aimed to complete the rupture of relations between Britain and France caused by the Egyptian affair, and to expose Britain's helplessness to withstand the united will of the new allies, Germany and France. Blowitz's theories about Bismarck had to be taken with a pinch of salt, as the two men loathed each other. (Blowitz would never forgive the Chancellor, gossips claimed, for only giving him a third-class decoration after the Congress in Berlin in 1878.) But in this case Blowitz's theory seemed to coincide with the French government's. Their Ambassador to Berlin, Baron de Courcel, was the man who had been to Varzin last August and returned full of confidence in Bismarck's goodwill. He now expected Bismarck to smash Britain's maritime ascendancy just as he had smashed France's military and political ascendancy fifteen years before. 'Indications tend to prove', he reported secretly to Paris, 'that he is preparing a fundamental attack on English power, calculated to reach its vital parts, and to ruin England to the advantage of Germany's industrial and commercial greatness.'[1]

'Calculated to reach its vital parts'. What did Courcel mean by this ominous phrase? Presumably he was referring to the Niger and the rest of Britain's vast informal empire on the west and east coasts of Africa. How could Britain deal with this threat if Bismarck was backed by Jules Ferry, the French Prime Minister?

The official head of the British delegation in Berlin was Sir Edward Malet, the former Ambassador in Cairo who had just taken over as Ambassador in Berlin after the sudden death of the venerable Lord Ampthill. But Malet was quite out of his depth, as he was the first to admit, and the real leader of the delegation was the masterful head of the Africa desk in the Foreign Office, Percy Anderson, sent to provide expert assistance. It was Anderson whose brilliant memorandum on the French 'settled policy' of antagonism to Britain had persuaded Gladstone to back Consul Hewett's plan to take over the lower Niger and the Oil Rivers. Now he had helped determine Malet's official instructions from the Foreign Office: to concede nothing to France, the real enemy, and to give Bismarck everything he wanted, except in one district in which Britain had a vital commercial interest, the Niger. As Anderson put it, 'We must take our seat as *the Niger Power*.'[2] But the Foreign Office was prepared for the worst. With Bismarck and Ferry in such an aggressive mood, the West Africa Conference in Berlin might go the same way as that humiliating London conference on Egyptian finance which had collapsed in August. As the Permanent Under-Secretary put it, 'The Conference *may* end in smoke.'[3]

At two o'clock on 15 November Bismarck rose to welcome the delegates with a short speech in French. He looked magnificent in his scarlet court dress, as fit as a guardsman, sleeker and younger than ever. Yet he seemed curiously uncertain of what he had to say. He began with a pious declaration that took them back to the '3 CS' – commerce, Christianity, civilization – and the ideals of Livingstone. The aim of the conference was to promote the civilization of the African natives by opening the interior of the continent to commerce. He then defined three limited goals: free trade for the Congo, free navigation on the Niger, and agreement on the formalities for future annexations of territory – meaning a set of rules acceptable to all countries. But much the most important point he made was a negative one: the conference would not concern itself with sovereignty. In short, it might decide on the rules for the Scramble but it would not debate the lines of the carve-up itself. Then after further nods to the cause of peace and humanity, the Iron Chancellor sat down.

All over Europe, in the corridors of power, officials reacted to Bismarck's speech with mild astonishment. It appeared that the conference, as one Foreign Office official minuted in London, was to do nothing more than 'register a few platitudes about freedom of commerce and navigation'.[4] Was there nothing to hope – or fear – from Berlin but a blizzard of platitudes and a howling anti-climax?

The Times was delivered at Laeken on Monday, 17 November in the usual royal style, thrown from the Brussels train in a special container and then brought by a footman to the palace in time for His Majesty's breakfast at 6.0 a.m. Leopold looked pale, people noticed, but was in good spirits. The raw north-easter that pelted Berlin with snow had smeared the Low Countries with a dismal fog. It was cheerless in the park at Laeken. On wet days like this Leopold took his early morning stroll in the enormous heated greenhouses, treasure houses of tropical plants, with a gold star on the top of the Congo glasshouse to symbolize his own dreams for the Congo.

That morning the piece by Henri Blowitz about the current West Africa Conference dominated the third column of the foreign page of *The Times*. There was no mention of King Leopold and his own plans to exploit the Congo, or of the conspicuous absence of a representative from the International Association at the horseshoe table. No doubt Leopold breathed a sigh of relief. To be conspicuous might ruin everything at this delicate moment, the climax of his six-year struggle to found an empire in the Congo. It was this that made Stanley such a dangerous partner in the venture. Publicity, Stanley's meat and drink, rarely failed to land him in the soup. But Leopold had a part for Stanley to play, as he had for the Great Powers themselves, especially the United States, France, Germany and Britain. In his breath-taking self-confidence he trusted that he, not Bismarck, would pull the strings at Berlin.

To make these puppets dance to his own tune at Berlin without leaving the royal palace at Laeken, Leopold needed not only the majestic self-assurance of a Coburg, but a cat-like flair for intrigue. He would pursue regular diplomacy with the help of his own loyal staff at the palace, the employees he had hired for the International Association, and the Belgian government's own diplomats. But some of the most delicate missions he had entrusted to a spider's web of brilliant amateurs. Flattery was the coin in which he paid these men, and in some cases the prospect of business if the great enterprise succeeded. There were three men in particular to whom he directed the royal smile, and who served as intermediaries with foreign governments and foreign vested interests: an American, a Scotsman and an Englishman. All were hard-headed businessmen, yet they were swept off their feet at the honour of serving His Majesty in his great philanthropic enterprise. Did they really believe these claims of the disinterestedness of their royal patron? The King's real motives were known to few men at this date, and no one would have been more shocked to learn them than some of his closest collaborators.

The American was a 61-year-old aristocrat from Connecticut (his mother's family were Founding Fathers of the state), a free-wheeling ex-diplomat who had been sent by Abraham Lincoln as US Ambassador to Belgium, a financier who had then plunged into citrus growing and property development in Florida. He was styled 'General' Henry S. Sanford, though he was not and never had been a soldier. The military title was a reward for his generosity in the Civil War, when he presented a battery of field-guns to the First Minnesota Regiment. A still more important task he performed for the Union side during the war was to organize the American secret service in Brussels, buying Belgian guns and raising money. In the process he had acquired a network of contacts at the Belgian court and a deep feeling of hero-worship for Leopold.

The Scotsman came from a humble home in Campbeltown, Argyllshire. One of his associates described him as a 'leetle, dapper, upright man, with an aquiline nose, side whiskers ... and a strutting manner'.[5] His name was Mackinnon and he had started his career as a grocer's clerk. Forty years later he was a merchant prince, the head of the British India Steamship Navigation Company, one of the world's great shipping lines. His links with Sanford dated from the 1870s when he, too, dabbled in Florida real estate. His admiration for Leopold was already well-rooted in 1876 when he had been one of the British delegates to the Geographical Conference in Brussels. Leopold's clarion call for a crusade in Central Africa in the spirit of Livingstone coincided exactly with Mackinnon's own ideas; and it was perhaps Sir John Kirk, British Agent at Zanzibar and one of Livingstone's old lieutenants, who helped bring the two men together. Kirk saw in Mackinnon the kind of high-minded trader and shipping magnate who would destroy the slave trade by opening up Africa to legitimate commerce, and both men saw in Leopold one of the great philanthropists of the era. Mackinnon, it must be said, was not expecting to lose money by his association with the King. He had invested money in the Comité d'Études, and after Leopold had bought out foreign investors, he expected to have a cut in the lucrative railway syndicate for the middle Congo, soon to be launched.

The Englishman had inherited a small family business involved in trade with West Africa, and had built up a fortune from cotton in Manchester. He was James Hutton, one of Goldie's partners in the National Africa Company and President of the Manchester Chamber of Commerce. His admiration for Leopold, like Mackinnon's, was based on the highest principles, recognition of Leopold's crusade in the spirit of Livingstone. But he, too, expected a dividend from his principles. Like Mackinnon, he had been bought out of the Comité d'Études with the expectation of soon receiving a fat slice of the middle Congo railway.

That year, 1884, Leopold had set himself and his collaborators, official and unofficial, two delicate tasks. First, they must gently pull the carpet from under the Portuguese, whose treaty with Britain threatened to block the mouth of the Congo. Second, they must cajole the Powers to recognize the blue flag of the International Association of the Congo – a blue standard with a single golden star borrowed from the old kingdom of Congo in Angola – as the flag of a sovereign state. The two tasks fitted together. Already, in the previous November, Leopold had sent General Sanford speeding across the Atlantic with honeyed words for President Arthur and the American government. Sanford carried a personal letter to the President which he had translated from the King's own courtly French. The blue flag with the golden star 'now floats over seventeen stations, many territories, seven steamers engaged in the civilizing work of the Association, and over a population of many millions'. Would the United States welcome this as a friendly flag? Leopold assured the United States that there would be complete freedom from duties on all American goods exported to the Congo.

The King also gave Sanford a set of confidential instructions in his own hand which emphasized his own lofty motives. The President was to be assured that the constitution of this Free State, or States, would be modelled on that of the United States of America and other civilized countries. At present the Association – in other words, the King – was subsidizing the Congo and had provided its chief executive, in the shape of Stanley, the great American explorer. But soon the Free State or Free States would belong to the whole civilized world:

> As soon as the development of the resources of the Free States [the United States of the Congo] permits it, the Association will end its tutelage and dissolve itself. Its goal will be attained, its mission complete, when it has established in the Congo basin an independent political organization capable of working without subsidies, and assured of the unchecked expansion of commerce and of civilization, and the abolition of the slave trade....
>
> But if they ask: but how, without customs duties, can the Free States pay for their running costs, one should reply: the philanthropic International Association of the Congo is in the course of endowing them ('en train de les doter').[6]

Two days after disembarking at New York, Sanford was shaking the hand of President Arthur at the White House. Six days later, on 4 December 1883, there appeared in the President's Message to Congress a paragraph which looked uncommonly like one of the drafts brought by Sanford from Brussels: 'The objects of the society are philanthropic. It does not aim at permanent political control, but seeks the neutrality of the valley. The United States cannot be indifferent to this work, nor to the interests of their citizens involved in it.' The paragraph ended with an oblique threat to protectionists such as Portugal and France. 'It may become advisable for us to co-operate with other commercial Powers: protecting the rights of trade and residence in the Kongo [sic] valley free from interference or political control of any one nation.'

So far so good. The poor innocent President had been easily fooled. In Brussels the King sent a reply to Sanford's jubilant cables: 'Enchanted with Emile'[7] (the codename for President Arthur). Leopold could assume the next step would be formal American recognition of the Free State flag. Meanwhile, he threw his hidden resources into the struggle to prevent Portugal from blocking the Congo. The Anglo-Portuguese treaty had been signed on 26 February 1884. At first Leopold had been appalled. Then, to his relief, the other Powers began to grumble and soon the grumble became a roar of protest. Leopold realized how he could make this treaty his salvation. Suddenly he was being courted by the man who represented a much bigger threat to his grand design than any Portuguese: Jules Ferry, the French colonial enthusiast who had by now succeeded as both Prime Minister and Foreign Minister.

Characteristically, Leopold chose not to approach Ferry through any of the normal channels provided by the Belgian Foreign Ministry. His secret intermediary was an English picture dealer, Arthur Stevens, brother of two of the Impressionists, himself well-known and respected in both the *haut monde* and *demi-monde* of Parisian society. Stevens had begun talks with Ferry in November 1883 and at first reported that the French would not consider recognizing the sovereignty of the International Association. But – for a price – the French would agree to 'respect' the possessions of the Association. It turned out that the price was quite reasonable. Ferry agreed that Leopold's motives were just what he professed – philanthropic and disinterested. That was the trouble. With the Association run by such an innocent, unworldly man (a 'dreamer'[8] was the word Ferry used to describe the King when writing to Courcel), it was obvious that both Leopold and the Association would go bust. It was equally obvious to the French who would pick up the pieces: the perfidious English. Already the place was swarming with Englishmen. Stanley was, of course, English at heart, under the disguise of an American explorer. It was all – so men like Brazza and Ferry were convinced – part of the English master plan for Africa. The English had planned a takeover of the Congo, to add to Niger and Nile, using the Belgians as their dupe.

So Ferry's price for 'respecting' the Congo was that Leopold must make a formal promise not to 'sell its possessions to any power'[9] – which meant not to sell them to Britain. There was one further condition: Leopold must agree to sack Stanley from the post of chief executive. The French would never forgive him for the language (*'va nu-pieds*, he goes barefoot') he had used about their hero, Brazza.

Leopold must have smiled at the violence of Ferry's reaction. Normally his own policy was to soothe and calm his excitable neighbours, to work like a masseur rubbing oil into their aching nerves. How could they feel threatened by him and his poor weak International Association, dedicated as it was solely to the cause of progress, a kind of 'Society of the Red Cross'[10] (his own words in one anonymous article to a newspaper)?

However, the previous autumn, in 1883, a personal letter from Stanley had been published in *The Times* in which the explorer had reverted to his old dream that Britain should declare a protectorate over the Congo. Naturally the King rapped his employee's knuckles for this idiotic suggestion. Strauch was told to tell Stanley, 'the King begs him earnestly not to write that again to anyone'.[11] Yet privately Leopold admitted to Strauch, the man to whom he revealed more of his grand design than anyone else, that he was rather pleased with Stanley's tactlessness. For once it could be used to good purpose, like a little jolt of electricity to the nerves. 'It is my judgement', he told Strauch, 'that we should not try to make a correction. It does no harm for Paris to fear that a British protectorate could be established in the Congo.'[12] In short, the King realized that a little anglophobia might help concentrate Ferry's mind.

That is why Leopold must have smiled to himself when he received Ferry's demand in 1884, sent by way of Stevens, that he should promise not to sell the Congo. He was delighted to make the promise, since he had no intention of selling the Congo to anyone, least of all to Britain. Why should he want to sell the Congo when he knew perfectly well that it was one of the richest spots on earth? Then, on the spur of the moment, an idea came to Leopold, as dazzling in its own way as the plan conceived the previous year of creating his own sovereign state. Why not offer the French a *right of pre-emption*, a first option on the Congo if Leopold ever should decide to sell?

Ferry fell for this bait like a hungry pike. He was sure he had outwitted Britain, Portugal *and* Belgium. In fact, the deal horrified Leopold's own advisers in the Belgian Foreign Ministry, who understandably saw Belgium as the natural heir to the Congo state. Within a few days all details were settled with the Quai d'Orsay. On 23 April 1884 the International Association gave the formal promise demanded, plus the right of pre-emption. In return the French government on the same day signed a pre-emption treaty by which they agreed to respect the blue flag with the golden star and not to interfere with the exercise of its rights. This was a giant step for Leopold, his main rival's recognition of the sovereignty of the state. But there were still bigger obstacles ahead, including the need to induce France to agree on frontiers encompassing one-tenth of the whole of tropical Africa – claimed by the voracious new state.

Meanwhile, Leopold was charmed to receive more jubilant cables from Sanford in Washington. As expected, the Senate had been as easily hoodwinked as President Arthur. Putting slavery in its place went down well with black voters, and everyone liked the idea of increased American exports to Africa. Besides, they were flattered by the tall story that the constitution of the Congo would be modelled on that of the United States, and reassured by the King's modest plan to retire from his great philanthrophic venture as soon as the state could pay for itself. On 10 April 1884 the Senate voted confidentially in favour of recognition. On 22 April this decision was embodied in a formal letter from the Secretary of State, 'recognising the flag of the International African Association [he meant the International Association of the Congo] as the flag of a friendly government'.[13]

With these innocent new allies in the bag, the King now renewed his efforts to wring recognition from Britain and Germany, and smash the Anglo-Portuguese treaty. It was here that the pre-emption treaty with France proved a godsend. France had signed it for fear that the Congo would be sold to England. Suddenly the other industrial Powers realized the danger. If Leopold failed to make a go of the Congo – and at this moment no one doubted he would fail – then France, the arch-protectionist, would take over a million and a half square miles of Central Africa, stretching from Gabon to the Great Lakes. This was unthinkable. At a stroke Leopold had created new allies of France's rivals, anxious to believe what he said, and to help him to succeed. Like a masterstroke at chess, he had revolutionized the game by appearing to sacrifice a piece.

At first, it must be said, Leopold's masterstroke earned him no applause in

Britain. The Foreign Office complained that the pre-emption treaty was a 'shabby and mischievous trick'.[14] *The Times* grumbled that it was duplicity to offer an option to France that would make nonsense of Leopold's claims to be opening up Africa in the interests of all countries.

Leopold's British sympathizers were able to play a crucial part in soothing the Foreign Office and British public opinion. In fact, Mackinnon happened to have lent a large sum of money to one of the MPs at the Foreign Office, to save him from bankruptcy. This was Austin Lee, Private Secretary to Lord Granville. Lee kept Mackinnon supplied with confidential information. But even without Lee's help, he had easy access to all the officials at the FO. He lobbied tirelessly to explain the International Association's good intentions. So did James Hutton, representing Manchester's trading interests. So did the Baptist missionaries such as Howard Bentley, the pioneer missionary of the Congo. Gradually it became apparent that, as regards the Anglo-Portuguese treaty, they were pushing at an open door. The Foreign Office was beginning to recognize, as mentioned earlier, that this treaty was impractical for the simple reason that France and Germany vetoed it. Unratified by the British Parliament, it was dead by June.

With the hateful treaty out of the way, Leopold intensified his campaign for British recognition. The emphasis was to be on free trade plus the '3 CS'. Strauch came over to London in July and was helped by Mackinnon to meet the leaders of the anti-slavery movement and other humanitarians. Stanley arrived in August and was invited to Walmer Castle to see Lord Granville. The tale he told was not so high-flown as the one Sanford had given President Arthur, but it stressed that the work of the International Association was 'non-commercial'. The state would be subsidized by £50,000 a year from Leopold's own pocket. In September and October Stanley addressed enthusiastic meetings of the Chambers of Commerce of London and Manchester. How neatly they fitted together, Christianity, Civilization and Commerce in the Congo. Stanley estimated that if every negro in the Congo bought one Sunday dress and four everyday dresses, it would require 3,840 million yards of Manchester cotton, worth £16 million – and this did not include the cloth for winding sheets. A press campaign was orchestrated by Mackinnon and the public was bombarded with optimistic articles on the Congo. By October the Foreign Office had been besieged for months by Leopold's emissaries. Led by James Hutton, the Manchester Chamber of Commerce petitioned for recognition of the new state; so did John Bright in Parliament. Yet the Foreign Office still held out. Now the Berlin Conference was only a month away. What had gone wrong with Leopold's well-laid plans?

Probably Leopold was himself warned by Mackinnon, who was in turn tipped off by Austin Lee. The Assistant Under-Secretary at the FO, Thomas Villiers Lister, pointed to the secret text of some of the treaties signed by the Congo chiefs – copies of which had reached the FO – giving the International Association an exclusive commercial monopoly. These proceedings, said Lister, were 'absurdly irregular'. In effect, Lister was claiming to have unmasked the King. All that talk about free trade and the '3 CS' was nonsense. The King had hoodwinked President Arthur and Jules Ferry. He had spent a fortune himself.

His aim was simply to make money, to create a gigantic trading monopoly behind a smokescreen of philanthropy and altruism. In short, the King was a humbug and the International Association a sham. To recognize the new state would be to help create an enemy to free trade in the Congo far more dangerous than Portugal – perhaps even worse than France. Lister's advice to Granville was not to let Britain, or any other government that valued free trade, recognize this 'absurdly irregular'[15] state.

The King was deeply hurt by such evidence of mistrust. How could he prove his good faith to Granville and sceptics like Lister? Already he was feeling his way in a new direction, and before the conference opened he had found the key to a new door. It was Bismarck who put it in his hand.

As soon as Bismarck had read the pre-emption treaty with France and realized that France wanted to take over the Congo, he decided, despite the brand-new *entente* with France, that a French takeover must be prevented. In June 1884 he approached Leopold with an offer of recognition, subject to two conditions. First, Leopold must guarantee absolutely free trade for all German nationals in the whole Congo basin. Second, if he sold the territory to anyone – meaning to France – under the pre-emption treaty, he must arrange for the newcomer to give the same guarantee. Leopold baulked at the second condition, which provoked an outburst from Bismarck which would have made the royal ears tingle if they had heard it:

> His Majesty displays the naive and pretentious egoism of an Italian who finds it natural that much is done for his *beaux yeux* without anything being asked in return.[16]

Leopold's instincts saved him in time. He ate humble pie. Suddenly Bismarck became the gracious patron, the godfather to the whole enterprise. What kind of frontiers did Leopold envisage? The Chancellor looked at Leopold's map giving him the whole core of the continent, and agreed that this made excellent sense. Of course, Bismarck was cynical about the Congo, as he was about all foreign affairs. He admitted as much to Baron de Courcel when the French Ambassador came to see him in Varzin in August. He did not expect that the new state 'would succeed in establishing itself very seriously'. But it would be 'always useful for diverting troublesome rivalries ... that we could handle less easily ourselves'.[17]

On 8 November 1884, a week before the conference opened in Berlin, Bismarck had secretly granted formal recognition to the new state. Now Leopold counted on the Chancellor to complete the task. Somehow Britain must be induced to grant recognition too, and Britain and France and Portugal must be induced to accept those amazing frontiers that gave Leopold the lion's share of Central Africa.

By the third week of the conference the British delegation was relieved to find Blowitz's forecast absurdly wide of the mark. Bismarck was courtesy itself. He seemed to have no plans to steal any more of Britain's informal empire – not at this conference, at any rate. But was he prepared to help the French try to steal the lower Niger from the British? It was hard to tell.

Bismarck did regard this conference on West Africa as a conference on free trade. At least that seemed clear. In principle, he wanted to guarantee free trade for German traders in as wide an area of the Congo basin as possible. In practice this meant that all the Powers, especially Britain, should recognize the sovereignty of the International Association as the best guarantor of free trade. On 19 November he formally asked Sir Edward Malet, the British Ambassador, to help the Association 'in its endeavour to become a state'.[18] The cards were down on the horseshoe table: British recognition for Leopold was the price Britain must pay for German support; otherwise France might be let loose in the lower Niger.

The British had come to the conference armed with Anderson's plan to butter up Bismarck in order to fight off the French challenge for the Niger. Anderson was quite prepared to pay Bismarck's price, though he cheerfully admitted Bismarck had been hoodwinked by Leopold. Back in London Anderson's fellow mandarins at the Foreign Office were less cheerful; at least some of them still had their scruples about what they called 'complete surrender' to Bismarck. Lister, the Assistant-Secretary and Anderson's immediate superior, led the counter-attack. Leopold was the last man who could be trusted to guarantee international free trade. They knew from the copies of the Free State treaties that the King's aim was a commercial monopoly, pure and simple. But Malet reported from Berlin that Bismarck had warned him that unless Britain recognized the Association there would be an 'unfriendly attitude of Germany on matters of the greatest importance'.[19] This cut Granville like a whip. It was not just a question of defending the Niger. Bismarck was threatening to intervene again on the side of the French in Egypt.

The dithering ended. Granville blocked his ears to Lister's protests and passed the recommendation to Gladstone's Cabinet. On the next day, 2 December, the crucial cable was sent to Malet at Berlin. To placate Bismarck, the British government would recognize Leopold. This was embodied in a formal treaty between Britain and the International Association, signed on 16 December, and in the weeks that ensued Britain's lead was followed by a series of almost identical treaties with the other Powers: with Italy on the 19th, with Austro-Hungary on the 24th, with the Netherlands on the 27th.

Meanwhile, Leopold was watching every nuance from his palace in Brussels, as though he were riding on a cloud high above Berlin. He did not let victory go to his head. This struggle for recognition by the Powers was only one battle. The next step in the campaign was to reconcile the Powers to his remarkable appetite for territory. The main danger was that France and Portugal would try to swallow the whole west coast between themselves, and so seal off the Congo from the Atlantic. It would 'strangle the Association at birth',[20] in the words of one of the King's staff. Leopold relied on Bismarck to save him from this fate. Strictly speaking, this was not a matter for the conference at all. The French had insisted that sovereignty would not be discussed at Berlin. They wanted to isolate Leopold and deal with him alone in Paris. But Bismarck made his own rules as he went along. Informal negotiations about sovereignty were in fact discussed in parallel to the formal negotiations at the horseshoe table, and Bismarck recommended that the French should give Leopold the whole vast slice of Africa that he hungered for.

To the French delegation, led by Baron de Courcel, this was too much to endure. They had been led up the garden path at this wretched conference. A demon of mischief had seized their wayward ally, the Chancellor. Courcel and Ferry had planned a conference that summer of 1884 in the flush of the honeymoon with Germany. It was to be a double coup: to force their way into the lower Niger by humbling the English and internationalizing the river, and to assert their power by confirming their right to the north bank of the Congo by virtue of Brazza's sublime discoveries. Instead, they had been put on the defensive from the first day of the conference. Bismarck had devoted himself to supporting their antagonists. Courcel lost his temper during one session in early December – it was about the case for neutralizing the Congo in the event of war – and shouted across the hall at the German and British delegates: '*Nous prenez-vous pour des brigands?*'[21] With the single exception of France's protectionist ally, Portugal, all the other Powers at the conference took their cue from Bismarck, and he seemed besotted with pushing the claims of Leopold. By mid-December Leopold's impudent territorial claims were on the table and there seemed to the French no way of reconciling either their own demands or those of their ally, Portugal.

By virtue of her fifteenth-century explorers, Portugal claimed both banks of the lower Congo as far east as Vivi, the final port before the cataracts seal the river. Leopold claimed Nokki, further downstream, insisting that otherwise he would be sealed off from the sea. He was exaggerating. But certainly without Vivi there was no way of joining a railway from the Pool to a deep-water port on the Atlantic.

France's case was different. To steal a march on Stanley, Brazza had made his treaty with King Makoko in 1880. Now France claimed both banks of the upper Congo at the Pool. This meant they claimed Leopoldville, the future capital of the Association, as well as their own capital at Brazzaville. Leopold contested both claims, as he refused to recognize Makoko's right to either territory. The King went further. To steal a march on Brazza, Stanley had built stations on the Kwilu-Niari, the river system between Gabon and the Congo. Leopold was generously prepared to offer to sell this territory to France for the sum of five million francs. Otherwise he would be forced to prevent the French from developing the Congo using their base in Gabon. The idea drove Courcel wild.

Courcel wrote to Paris to brief the Prime Minister, Ferry, who told him to give Bismarck a solemn warning: either Germany must agree not to interfere any more on Leopold's side, or the French would not only sabotage the conference, they would demolish the whole *entente*. Perhaps Ferry was not bluffing.

At any rate, Bismarck was not prepared to put him to the test and Courcel was reassured. As for Bismarck, when the British Ambassador, Sir Edward Malet, met him on 17 December, he seemed chastened. He hummed and hawed; to Malet's amazement he said he could do no more for Leopold. The King's claims were really too extravagant. It would be better if Leopold fought his own battles alone with Ferry.

Bismarck was as good as his word. The territorial negotiations were now transferred to Paris and the Berlin Conference adjourned until Ferry saw a chance of squeezing an agreement out of Leopold.

On the morning of 31 December 1884 Leopold's two official representatives were shown into Ferry's Cabinet room in the Quai d'Orsay. They were M. Eugene Pirmez, a Belgian liberal politician, and Emile Banning, one of Leopold's special delegates to the conference at Berlin. The interview began badly, though it had its comic side. Pirmez had prepared a long biting memorandum (a 'masterpiece of irony' according to his companion) which ridiculed Brazza's claim that King Makoko's empire extended to both sides of the Pool. It was strange that this vast empire should have escaped the attention of so many distinguished Frenchmen in their own account of the region. Pirmez and Banning were determined to put this biting memorandum into Ferry's hands. But Ferry was equally determined not to be bitten. He blocked his ears when Pirmez threatened to read some extracts aloud, for fear that they could then be published in an official diplomatic report. But it was clear to the Belgians that this preposterous claim to the left bank of the Pool was only a bargaining counter. The French would surrender it in exchange for the Kwilu-Niari. That would be no exchange, the Belgians replied. That would be a surrender. They then put forward a claim for financial compensation of five million francs. Impossible, said Ferry. We could not dream of such a figure. He had to think of the 'budgetary situation' and the 'spirit' of the French Chamber. The compensation he could offer was of quite a different kind: recognition for a private association and support in dealing with the claims of Portugal. Ferry ended the interview on a note of quiet menace. The King should remember that he would not be able to 'deal with the Portuguese without using us as intermediaries'.[22]

When negotiations were resumed two days later Pirmez and Banning were astonished to find a deal within their grasp. There were two stumbling blocks. First, where would the boundary be between French territory and the Association on the north bank? The French wanted the whole north bank of the middle Congo, all the way from Brazzaville down to Vivi. The Belgians offered a point midway, at the village of Manyanga. Second, how to find an alternative to the five-million-franc compensation for the Kwilu-Niari. Ferry could only offer a pittance – 300,000 francs – all that could be raked up from the Treasury without putting the issue to a vote in the Chamber. Then Pirmez tried a new tactic: what about a lottery in France in order to raise funds for the Association? It was one of the King's wild ideas and neither Pirmez nor Banning thought it had the faintest hope of success. But Ferry seized on it immediately. The lottery could have a capital of twenty million francs. In this case he would accept Manyanga as the border. The Belgians hurried off by train to Brussels with this thrilling news for Leopold. Would His Majesty now go ahead with the deal – and snap up Ferry's generous offer to act as honest broker with Portugal?

Had Banning seen the faces of the Portuguese delegation in Paris waiting to be ushered in to Ferry's Cabinet room that same day, he might have been less hopeful. When he rejoined the Belgian delegation in Berlin a few days later, it turned out that honest broker was hardly the term for Ferry. The Portuguese had no intention of allowing the Association to take the whole right bank of the Congo as far as Nokki, the best place for a deep-water port. And the French backed them. Instead of attempting to persuade the Portuguese to compromise, Ferry informed the unfortunate Pirmez in Paris on about 8 January 1885 that 'nous sommes sous engagement'[23] with Portugal, and could offer no better terms. A stormy interview followed on the 12th which was reported to Berlin by Colonel Strauch. It was said that Ferry had offered the Portuguese both banks of the river. Why Ferry had acted in this treacherous way was not clear to Leopold's men in Paris, or to Leopold himself in Brussels. The beauty of the pre-emption treaty was that it gave the French, as Leopold's heirs, a motive to take the toughest possible line. Instead Ferry complained to Bismarck that Leopold was 'intransigent' about Portugal. Ferry must have taken leave of his senses. But if he was trying to rattle Leopold, he did not succeed. There was deadlock in Paris. Then, tacitly confessing that he was beaten, Ferry handed the ball back to the Iron Chancellor in Berlin.

Bismarck was blowing off steam like a train kept too long in a siding. For the whole of January 1885 the conference had been held up by these wretched territorial negotiations. At one point he had been heard to mutter that the Belgians and the Portuguese should have been locked up together in a room all night, like a British jury. That would soon have produced an agreement. He now took the lead in inducing the French to sign a formal treaty with the Association on the lines agreed to a month earlier and this was signed on 5 February.

Bismarck now had to bully the Portuguese into a compromise. His task was made easier by Leopold's own nimble footwork. In Paris the King's men had been unbending to Portugal. Now Leopold offered some nice little plums on both left and right banks of the Congo. The Portuguese could have Nokki after all, provided he could take Vivi, and they could keep an enclave at Cabinda, north of the river. A bargain was struck on these lines.

There was one more idiotic hold-up before the conference could get back to business. The Portuguese delegate, an experienced diplomat called M. Penfiel, accepted the new deal in principle, provided that Germany, France and Britain recommended it firmly enough to his government. A triple note was duly despatched to Lisbon. The reply brought Bismarck's boiler close to explosion. Lisbon replied with a slap in the face. Portugal must have the port of Banana on the north bank and the port of Vivi on the south bank. In other words, Leopold's new state must be strangled at birth. At the same time there were ugly stories afloat that a gunboat had had the effrontery to plant the Portuguese flag at Banana, so that Portugal was now the Power actually in possession of the mouth of the Congo. (The rumours were true about the attempt to plant the flag, but it had been uprooted from a mudbank by a quick-thinking British naval commander.)

The next day a deeply embarrassed M. Penfiel explained to Bismarck and Malet that the slap in the face from his government was not a slap in the face at all, but a cry for help. His government needed something stronger than the triple note in order to cover its flanks from opposition in the Cortes (Parliament): an ultimatum to Portugal would do the trick. He offered to draft it for Bismarck. The Chancellor was not amused by the farce, but the same day the ultimatum was sent and accepted. By 15 February the two months of labour pains were finally over. Leopold's baby had been safely delivered at Berlin, giving the Association full access to the Atlantic, including excellent ports at Banana and Vivi on the north bank of the Congo.

Compared with the drama of the informal negotiations, when the future of Central Africa hung in the balance, the second formal phase of the conference was as grey as the February weather, and a good deal drier.

The third specific goal of the conference was finally reached. This was the question of 'effective occupation': how to set rules for the acquisition of new territory? Like the other two specific goals – free navigation of the Niger and Congo, and free trade in the Congo – this was originally conceived by France and Germany as a way of cutting Britain down to size. She was the greatest colonial Power in the world and the greatest dog in the manger. She not only governed colonies which she had formally annexed. Some parts of the world she exploited by a system of informal empire, others she controlled by a system of protectorates. Could she be made to disgorge this kind of paper empire – at least the part she was not prepared to govern?

This was the ugly question facing the English delegation when discussions started. But like the other threats to Britain, to press it home demanded a real sympathy – and common interest – between France and Germany. In this case the French interest was much more like the British. Each wanted to be left a free hand to deal with the vast possessions they had already claimed. Germany was isolated. At this date Bismarck still believed that charter companies, not the Reich, would be responsible for governing Germany's African colonies. Hence agreement on the third goal ended as toothless as the other agreements in the formal proceedings.

The conference decided that the rules of effective occupation of new territory – meaning the necessity to govern it – should apply only to the coasts, where there was almost no new territory to be occupied. Then, after a brisk fight with Bismarck, the British persuaded him and the other delegates that the rules of effective occupation should exclude protectorates, the main method of occupation adopted by the British. (Though often they were indistinguishable in practice from colonies).

The signing of the General Act of Berlin on 26 February 1885 must have brought a general sigh of relief from the assembled delegates. Bismarck gave the concluding speech. They were in 'complete accord' about 'all points of the programme'. They had secured free access to the interior of Africa for all nations, and freedom of trade in the whole basin of the Congo (and in a region beyond the Congo named the 'conventional basin'). They had also shown 'much careful solicitude' for the moral and physical welfare of the native races, and the Chancellor cherished the hope that this principle would 'bear fruit'[24] and help introduce the populations to the advantages of civilization.

At least the conference was over – and amicably so. But what exactly had been achieved? There were thirty-eight clauses to the General Act, all as hollow as the pillars in the great saloon. In the years ahead people would come to believe that this Act had had a decisive effect. It was Berlin that precipitated the Scramble. It was Berlin that set the rules of the game. It was Berlin that carved up Africa. So the myths would run.

It was really the other way round. The Scramble had precipitated Berlin. The race to grab a slice of the African cake had started long before the first day of the conference. And none of the thirty-eight clauses of the General Act had any teeth. It had set no rules for dividing, let alone eating, the cake.

In one sense, however, the Berlin Conference marked a turning point in the history of Africa and Europe. There was something that came to be called 'the spirit of Berlin'. For the first time great men like Bismarck had linked their names at an international conference to Livingstone's lofty ideals: to introduce the '3 cs' – commerce, Christianity, civilization – into the dark places of Africa. It is easy today to dismiss this talk as rhetoric. Of course the main policy of the Powers was directed to strategic and economic objectives such as protecting old markets or exploiting new ones. But the Berlin brand of philanthropy was not entirely hollow. At any rate, a commitment had been made which would not be forgotten by the humanitarians, when Leopold's true character became known.

Meanwhile a huge stride had been taken in the Scramble – not in the formal conference of Berlin, but in the informal negotiations. Germany and Britain had given away to Leopold most of the Congo basin, meaning most of Central Africa, a million square miles of jungle and bush. The main object was to keep this enormous prize out of the hands of France. But with the land went the responsibility of acting in the spirit of Livingstone. In effect the self-styled philanthropic King had been chosen to act in Africa as a trustee for the whole of Europe. It was a responsibility he was only too delighted to assume, with assurances that his whole fortune was at the service of mankind. Thus it was Leopold's professed idealism, not Bismarck's *Realpolitik*, that dominated the final session of the conference. With the signing of the treaty with Portugal the last obstacle to Leopold's taking his seat among the Powers was removed. Not that the King was prepared to step out of the shadows in Brussels and join the throng in the Wilhelmstrasse. He relied on his network of agents among the different delegations: Sanford and Stanley with the Americans, Mackinnon with the British, Banning and Lambermont with the Belgians. No doubt they led the applause when it was announced by Bismarck that Colonel Strauch, President of the International Association, had formally signed notice of his adhesion to the General Act of Berlin. Bismarck himself paid a fulsome tribute to Leopold. The new Congo was one of 'the chief protectors' of the work in view. He trusted that the 'noble aspirations of its illustrious founder'[25] might be fulfilled.

The next day Percy Anderson took the train back across the frozen fields of northern Europe and caught the boat for England. He was satisfied with the conference. They had beaten off the French threat to the Niger. That was all that really mattered. It had proved a victory for British commonsense. Did he have any qualms about the prize given to Leopold? Anderson prided himself on his realism. When referring to the International Association, he did not talk of the noble aspirations of its illustrious founder. But he relied on Bismarck, Leopold's patron, to keep the King up to the mark.

That week the London papers offered their congratulations for British statesmanship. *The Standard* welcomed the vast market for British goods that would be shortly opened in the Congo Free State: 'cotton goods, blankets, crockery, muskets, gun powder, hardware of all kinds, and cheap finery of every description'.[26] The *Leeds Mercury* toasted good King Leopold, that 'noble-minded Sovereign who had the wisdom and courage to begin the enterprise of the Congo which would be the bright centre to the new Federation of Freedom and Peace'.[27]

But when Anderson reached the classical portico of the Foreign Office in Whitehall he must have been in no mood to celebrate. Terrible news had just arrived from Africa that made the success in Berlin seem hollow indeed. A great disaster had overtaken the British in the Sudan. Khartoum had fallen on 26 January – by treachery, it was claimed. No one knew Gordon's fate, but the worst was feared.

Now the whole of the government's policy in Egypt and the Sudan was back in the melting pot. Lord Salisbury and the Opposition in Parliament saw their chance to bring Gladstone down. So did the French, more anglophobic than ever after their humiliation in Berlin.

PART THREE
RIGHTS OF CONQUEST

The Rhodes Colossus

CHAPTER 15

Gordon's Head

England, Egypt, Sudan and elsewhere
5 February 1885–8 June 1885

'All my visions of fighting ... outside of *Khartoum*
and of my riding into that city the same evening and
of congratulating my old friend Gordon upon his
heroic and magnificent defence ... all, all dashed to
the ground.'

Lord Wolseley, diary, 17 February 1885

At about 1.15 a.m. on the morning of Thursday, 5 February a carriage clattered down South Audley Street and turned the corner into Tilney Street, Mayfair. Then someone knocked urgently at the first house, the home of Regy Brett, the elegant, pushy, young private secretary of the War Minister, Lord Hartington. It was Sir Robert Thompson, the Permanent Secretary at the War Office. The older man must have been fuddled with sleep. Half an hour earlier he himself had been roused by a special messenger with a slip of paper, marked 'Secret', but put into an open envelope; a scribble from the War Office cipher clerk. It proved to be the first sentence of a secret cable sent by Wolseley four hours earlier from Korti, 1,400 miles up the Nile. 'Khartoum is reported to have fallen on the 26th.'[1] Just that sentence, like the blow of a hammer – and not a word about Gordon.

Brett and Thompson drove across Piccadilly to the ramshackle collection of old buildings that comprised the War Office in Pall Mall. Gaslights were blazing as other senior officials drove up, and a crowd, no doubt tipsy as well as curious, gathered in the street. The two men laboriously deciphered the rest of the cable. Wolseley was asking urgently for instructions. But he added nothing about Gordon's fate. Either he was dead or, perhaps worse, a prisoner of the Mahdi. Brett was horrified – and astounded. Like everyone in the War Office, from the messengers to his own chief, Hartington, he had had complete confidence in Wolseley's ability to rescue Gordon. Now Wolseley had failed – without any explanation. And there was a further horror to face: Gladstone's government would presumably throw in the sponge and evacuate the whole Sudan.

But where *was* the government? Parliament was in recess till 19 February. Characteristically, most of the great Whigs seemed to have gone to earth on their great estates, leaving the middle-class Radicals, like Dilke and Chamberlain, to govern the Empire from London. Brett spent the rest of the night trying to hunt down the Cabinet. At 2.30 a.m. he bounded into Eddy Hamilton's bedroom at

10 Downing Street, where Eddy was peacefully asleep after an 'important dinner' at the Empire Club, a dinner to discuss the Birmingham Choir. Eddy had been left in London while the PM and Hartington took a holiday at Holker Hall in Lancashire as guests of Hartington's father, the old Duke of Devonshire. Cipher telegrams were sent to Holker at once to recall them, and another to the Queen at Osborne. At about 3.0 a.m., Dilke and Brett went to knock up Lord Granville in his echoing London house in Mayfair. They kicked their heels for half an hour in the hall before the valet told them that his master was at Walmer in Kent. (It turned out that he was in the house all the time.) So it was impossible to think about arranging a Cabinet meeting that morning to answer Wolseley's question about what to do next.

At the beleaguered War Office, Sir Robert Thompson, alarmed that the Cabinet should be the last to know of the disaster, struggled to put a lid on the news, and failed. The special messenger had had the brains to read that slip of paper in the open envelope. He sold the news to a news agency. A special late edition of the *Daily Telegraph* printed the scoop at 8.0 a.m., and out it went, clicking across the telegraph wires to every corner of the world. By midday, the War Office was forced to publish the full text of Wolseley's telegram. At first people everywhere were incredulous.

And what had happened to Gordon? The uncertainty added to the sensation. In Downing Street, Eddy Hamilton was still vainly trying to get word from Holker. 'The blackest day since the horrible Phoenix Park murders,' he wrote in his diary. He added: 'Execrations are already being plentifully poured out on the head of the Government to the tune of "Too late!"'[2]

If Holker, up in Lancashire, was still silent, Osborne, on the Isle of Wight, was only too vocal. The Queen took the news, brought to Osborne by cipher cable, even worse than might have been anticipated. Lady Ponsonby, wife of the Queen's private secretary, Sir Harry Ponsonby, was sitting after breakfast in the drawing room of their cottage in the royal grounds when she was amazed to see a figure in black enter unannounced and unattended. 'Khartoum has fallen. Gordon is dead,'[3] said the figure in sepulchral tones. It was Her Majesty herself, stricken as though she had just been bereaved once again. In her own journal that day the Queen wrote: 'Dreadful news after breakfast. Khartoum fallen, Gordon's fate uncertain! All greatly distressed. It is too fearful. The government is alone to blame, by refusing to send the expedition till it was too late. Telegraphed *en clair* to Mr Gladstone, Lord Granville and Lord Hartington expressing how dreadfully shocked I was at the news....'[4]

That telegram was to be famous, not only for *not* being in cipher, like other confidential telegrams to her ministers, but because of its amazing grammar. 'These news from Khartoum are frightful, and to think that all this might have been prevented and many precious lives saved by earlier action is too frightful.'[5] Ponsonby's own indignation did not calm the Queen one bit. She told him that he was 'not half indignant enough'.[6] He was packed off to London to tell the Cabinet that HM insisted on a tough line in the Sudan. They must discover

Gordon's fate and they must teach the Mahdi a lesson. If 'we simply turn *straight back again*', then 'our power in the East will be *ruined*, and we shall *never* be able to hold up our heads again!'[7]

After Ponsonby had taken the ferry to the mainland, the Queen continued to bombard him with messages for Gladstone, as her heart flushed with rage at the way she had been treated by him. How she longed for the day when that deluded old man would go:

> She *meant* that Mr G should remember what SHE suffers when the British name is humiliated ... & he can go away and resign but she MUST REMAIN and she has suffered so cruelly from humiliation & annoyance from the present Govt. *since* the unlucky day when Mr Gladstone came in – that she was boiling over with the indignation & horror which *everyone* in this country felt and feels! Mr G *never* minds loss of life etc. and wraps himself up in his own *incomprehensible delusions and illusions....*
>
> In the Queen's heart (& that of many others she knows) she holds *Mr Gladstone responsible* by imprudence, neglect, violent language for the lives of many 1000ds tho' unwittingly. ... Look at our relations abroad! No one trusts or relies on us & from '74 to '80, especially the lst three or four years ... England stood very high....
>
> Sir Henry must speak very seriously to Ld Hartington as to eventualities but without making him *think* that he *is certain* to be Mr Gladstone's successor.[8]

Meanwhile, on 5 February, the cipher telegram from Eddy Hamilton sat on a tray in the servants' hall at Holker because the valet had received no instructions to wake his lordship in the state bedroom before midday. Hartington was enjoying his holiday even more than usual. His father, the Duke of Devonshire, was a widower and something of a recluse. When he did emerge, he would organize prayer meetings or go for carriage drives. But the rest of the house party were in high spirits. Apart from the Prime Minister, the house party included Gladstone's wife and his daughter, Lucy. The only absentee was Louise, the fascinating Duchess of Manchester (*née* Gräfin Alten) and Hartington's 'intimate friend',[9] in the coy phrase of his official biographer, for more than thirty years. As everyone who was anyone knew, Louise Manchester and Harty-Tarty were lovers. But there were times when it was impossible for even such a domestic couple to be together. He was a man of stolid, aristocratic good sense, and the poor old Duke of Manchester had no reason to be difficult. So there was no ripple of scandal to disturb his commanding position in the Liberal Party. He remained the most eligible bachelor in the kingdom. Now fifty-one, he was heir apparent to the Duke of Devonshire, with four stately homes and a rent roll of £180,000 a year (the second highest in the peerage), besides being heir apparent to Gladstone and the Liberal Party.

The week before, Hartington had met Gladstone by accident in the train from Liverpool and invited him to be his guest at Holker. It was an odd invitation to make to an invalid, for Holker was a huge, draughty Jacobean palace on the lip of the moors. Gladstone had been in such poor health at the beginning of January that he had had to leave Downing Street and retire to Hawarden. It was a recurrence of his old trouble, insomnia, brought on, it was thought, by the Egyptian crisis and its deplorable effect on Britain's relations with France. At first Gladstone's friends thought the great man might have to retire to the Mediterranean, as he had in January 1883. But he found he was sleeping more soundly the moment he reached Hawarden. The Cabinet was left in Hartington's firm hands. Gladstone read the telegrams but did not interfere much, except for occasional raps on the knuckles of his colleagues, such as the time he told them that the 'Egyptian flood' was upon them, like 'the sea upon the host of Pharaoh', who had 'just as much business to pursue the Israelites as we had to meddle in Egypt'.[10]

At Holker, the Prime Minister seemed to be once again in the pink. He braved the weather to go rambling in the park. He even broke with habit and set off, gun in hand, to flush the Duke's pheasants out of the shrubberies. Every morning he bounced into Hartington's dressing-room and then they spent hours closeted together, going over the telegrams. This was much more congenial for both men than the squabbling and back-biting of the Cabinet in Downing Street. Never before had Hartington felt so close to the Prime Minister, not even during the awful days when his brother, Frederick Cavendish, the new Irish Chief Secretary, had been hacked to death in Phoenix Park. There was every reason for Hartington to keep close to the leader. Now was the golden moment, as he saw it, for Gladstone to take his long overdue reward: to retire and let Hartington be Prime Minister.

The PM, too, seemed to sense that his time was up. As Hartington wrote cheerfully to Louise on 3 February, Gladstone was 'really looking forward to his retirement soon'.[11]

But could the great man be trusted to go of his own accord? In January 1883, on the last occasion when Gladstone was ill and had threatened to retire, Hartington had been terrified that he was serious. Hartington was then quite unprepared to take over as leader. If Gladstone had gone, so would the Liberal Party, smashed in pieces: Radicals against Whigs, and both against the Gladstonian rump. Now everything had been reversed; today the danger was that Gladstone was not serious enough. Chamberlain and Dilke, the leading Radicals, were prepared to make a pact with the Whigs. The Radicals yearned for high office and the Whigs needed their skill in managing the electorate. The pact had been made during those last weeks while Gladstone was away at Hawarden. Not to put too fine a point on it, Radicals and Whigs had together plotted a coup. It was Gladstone's presence that now seemed to be an obstacle to party unity. A majority of his own Cabinet had lost patience with him and hoped he would hand over to Hartington of his own accord. Otherwise he would have to be pushed.

This was the situation at about midday on 5 February at Holker, when Hartington came sleepily down to breakfast, no doubt looking for kidneys and bacon, but instead was given Hamilton's cipher telegram announcing the fall of Khartoum. The news had arrived at a moment when Gladstone seemed to be like one of his own oak trees at Hawarden, severed with his axe. By a miracle the giant stood. The gentlest push, and it would come crashing to the ground.

Gladstone's real situation, and the real miracle, were entirely different.

He knew nothing about the plot against him and when he read Eddy Hamilton's telegram all thought of resignation left him. He felt younger and fitter than he had for a long time. He must return to London to take a firm grip on the Cabinet in this hour of national humiliation. His coolness and decisiveness astonished everyone. It was as though he were a young man again. True, he was furious about the Queen's telegram *en clair* ('These news from Khartoum are frightful ... and to think that all this might have been prevented ...'), which reached him at Cartmel Railway Station on his way back to London that afternoon. Obviously it had been read by all the telegraphists along the line. But Gladstone kept his temper, and sent back in cipher what Eddy Hamilton called a 'dignified'[12] reply. It was certainly not calculated to calm the Queen, however, as Gladstone assured Her Majesty that if the government had erred, it was not in delaying the relief, but in ever agreeing to send it. Then he rallied the Cabinet to face the question of whether to tell Wolseley to advance or retreat, and how to cope with the expected onslaught in Parliament.

One might have imagined that, as young Regy Brett had been appalled to think, Gladstone's policy would now be to throw in the sponge and evacuate the Sudan. That would have been consistent with his long crusade against aggressive imperialism, his original desire not to meddle in Egypt, his desperate attempts not to be dragged into the Sudan, and his genuine resolve to evacuate not only the Sudan but Egypt too, as soon as the right safeguards could be negotiated. The Cabinet gathered at midday on 7 February. But far from advocating retreat, Gladstone sounded the bugle for the advance.

His volte-face was astounding. He brushed aside the difficulties. If Gordon was in the Mahdi's hands and alive, then Wolseley would have to smash the Mahdi to free him; if Gordon was dead, then he must be avenged. Either way, Wolseley would have to take terrifying risks and extend the Sudan campaign into the following autumn. There would be a vast expenditure of treasure and blood − all without any material compensation. Eddy Hamilton was thunderstruck when he heard of this volte-face and ventured to tell the chief that 'this is a large order of things'. The great man admitted as much, but said the stakes were high. They concerned the very survival of Britain's empire in India. (He did not mention the survival of his own Cabinet.) The Cabinet's decision, the PM told Hamilton (in what would today be called the domino theory), had been 'determined by the regard which they felt bound to have for the effect which the triumph of the Mahdi would have on our Mahometan subjects'.[13] On 9 February the Cabinet voted with alacrity to spend £2.75 million on reinforcements for Wolseley. Eddy Hamilton was still appalled. What had come over Gladstone, who had always valued thrift as much as he loathed imperialism? Hamilton predicted that when the Sudan bill came to be paid, 'there would be a pretty general singing out to the tune of "Oh! My!" [14]

On 11 February a new shock wave hit England, severe, though more or less expected. The newspaper correspondents in the Sudan reported that Gordon was believed to have been killed in the assault on Khartoum of 26 January. In London the news was confirmed on 13 February. Gloom and rage knew no bounds. Unfortunately for Gladstone, he chose to go to a theatre with Lady Dalhousie on the night of the 11th. How foolish, thought Eddy Hamilton, and warned the chief that this would 'upset people'. But Gladstone insisted on going and so brought down a torrent of abuse on his head. 'Is it conceivable', shrieked *The World,* 'that the Prime Minister, responsible for all the horrors of such a war, could be so heartless?' [15] A blizzard of anonymous letters rattled the window panes in Downing Street. The famous acronym GOM ('Grand Old Man') became 'Gordon's Old Murderer'.

Gladstone withstood the tempest with astonishing calm. It was due no doubt to his having a 'clear conscience', was Hamilton's comment, and no doubt it was this that maddened his enemies. The mind of London society was 'poisoned by hatred towards Mr G. Had Lord Beaconsfield [Disraeli] been in office now, we should hear of nothing but the prowess of our troops, the glory of our arms and the splendid upholding of our prestige.' [16] Though he did his best to exonerate the chief, Hamilton had to admit that the Cabinet's policy in Egypt and the Sudan had been a disaster. 'Facts and events ... have been too strong for the Government', he wrote grimly, when asked to prepare a brief on the Gordon case. What worried him most was that this disaster would precipitate – or at least coincide with – Gladstone's long overdue retirement. 'To think that so great a career should close in such troublous times is like a perpetual nightmare.' [17]

However, each day that passed brought new evidence of the Prime Minister's vitality. Abuse of the government simply rallied the Cabinet and united the party behind him. That enigmatic young Whig, Lord Rosebery, consented at long last to join the Cabinet. At a time of national disaster, he said, all Liberals must sink their differences. The opposite happened to Gladstone's friends who had plotted to depose him, Harcourt and Hartington included. They sank their agreements and resumed their differences. So the great coup against Gladstone fizzled out like a candle in the rain, without his ever having noticed it.

In Parliament Gladstone's speech defending the fiasco in the Sudan was one of the most eloquent of his career. Of course he defended the indefensible. 'Too late' – that had been the dismal chant of 1884. Now it was re-echoed in Gordon's tragic *cri de cœur* from the pages of his journal, two words presenting the whole pith of the case against the government. Gladstone bore a personal responsibility. He had obstructed Hartington until he had threatened, in July 1884, to resign. It was because of Gladstone's refusal to face the reality of Gordon's plight that the relief expedition had set off at least two months too late. Wolseley had then compounded the error by perversely choosing the long route by river. Fortunately for Gladstone, no one in London yet knew the full facts. Gordon's journal was still unpublished in Wolseley's tent. Instead, Gladstone was able to exploit a wild story that Khartoum had fallen through treachery, and from this to argue that the treachery could have happened at any time, so that the two months' delay was irrelevant.

Far from destroying the government, the fall of Khartoum gave it a new appetite for power. Conversely, it broke the nerve of the Tory Opposition, led by Sir Stafford Northcote. It was true that in the Lords the leader was Lord Salisbury, who had plenty of fighting spirit and did not flinch from pressing home the charges of incompetence against Gladstone's government. But Salisbury's acid wit could not conceal the confusion in his own party. The young hopefuls of Disraeli's day were now an old guard, gouty and down in the mouth. They seemed years older than Gladstone. Most of them were ill or on holiday in the south of France when the Khartoum crisis blew up. Apart from Salisbury, the most active member of the Opposition was erratic young Randolph Churchill, a thorn in his own party's flesh. (Perhaps it was a blessing that he was away shooting tigers in India.) At any rate, Salisbury could make little dent on Gladstone's majority. Nor could Gladstone's lieutenant, John Morley, who deplored Gladstone's volte-face. The government beat down both censure motions without difficulty.

* * *

At Korti, 1,400 miles up the Nile, his nerves stretched as taut as the single line of copper wire connecting him with the outside world, General Lord Wolseley read the cipher message from Hartington, telling him of Gladstone's volte-face, and Wolseley gasped. He was to advance after all. The fall of Khartoum, of which he had learnt four days earlier, was a blow to his pride like the kick of a camel. He had been haunted by thoughts of disaster to the relief force – strings of boats sunk in the Nile, whole batteries wandering like lost sheep in the desert. He had never dreamt that his hero, Gordon, might run out of food and succumb to the Mahdi.

> ... and in myself [he wrote in his diary on 17 February] I feel obliged to retreat! What a horrible word! ... and to retreat before a rabble such as that the Mahdi commands! It is a heavy blow to sustain, a heavy punishment to have inflicted on me.[18]

Yet there were worse blows, worse punishments, than to be told to retreat. It soon dawned on Wolseley that advancing was one of them. His loathing for Gladstone and his government grew like a fever. At first he had hoped that the news of the disaster would dispose of that 'imbecile' Gladstone. 'If anything can kill old Gladstone this news ought to, for he cannot, self-illusionist though he be, disguise from himself the fact that he's directly responsible for the fate of Khartoum.' At any rate, Wolseley was glad to feel that his own mission would be cancelled once it was clear that Gordon was dead. He was astounded by Gladstone's decision to smash the Mahdi. The more he considered it, the more awkward he found his own position. He believed the army should evacuate not only the Sudan but Egypt. Of course, 'simply as a soldier', he longed for the scrap. But what kind of a scrap would it be?

> I believe the approaching Soudan war [he wrote in his diary on 24 February] to be a hideous mistake, the outcome of Mr Gladstone's foolish policy in Egypt. . . . The civilian gentlemen who rule from Downing Street are prepared to rush into any war when by doing so they can retain office, and they do it with a light heart on account of their ignorance, but any soldier who knows our Army as I do can only view a serious war with dread, and this war in the Soudan is likely to be the most serious war we have undertaken since the idiotic Cabinet of 1854 declared war against Russia.[19]

Personally Wolseley thought that the Cape of Good Hope was more important strategically than the Suez Canal, and so the Canal could be controlled well enough from a base on Cyprus. That is why Britain should 'clear out of the Sudan and Egypt as soon as we can'. Instead he was being ordered to advance for an endless war in the unknown. His heart sank at the difficulties. 'If the Mahdi be wise he will retreat before we can tackle him seriously: we shall have spent ten millions & done nothing and when we begin to withdraw we shall very likely to have a pack of yelping curs at our heels taking long shots at our retreating troops.'[20] Of course the campaign would be all right if the British army was put on a professional footing. No chance of that! For one thing, there was the commander-in-chief, the Duke of Cambridge, 'with his great square fat bottom to his fire in the Horse Guards',[21] telling him that one man was as good as another, and blocking all promotion by merit. Then there were the Radicals, determined to reduce Britain to the level of a second-rate Power. Did they dare to put the army on a proper footing? 'Mr Chamberlain and all other screwmakers and carpet-makers from Birmingham will never consent to that.'[22]

By 25 February, when Wolseley read a Reuter's cable about Gladstone's eloquent defence of his policy in the Commons, he could not control his rage. '. . . a vote of confidence!! Was there ever such brazen impudence! In the history of England of my day, this loss of time by an ignorant Minister is more certain to leave its mark upon our Army, our resources and our national debt than any event . . . since I have been a soldier.' On the same day Wolseley read the last of poor Gordon's journals, brought back by Colonel Sir Charles Wilson, and his mood became calmer. He found the journals of his hero 'intensely interesting', as well he might; 'if God ever granted the gift of inspiration in our day to men', he knew no one better suited for this commission than Gordon. Up to the last moment Gordon had complete faith in God's purpose. Wolseley reflected, 'This is a lesson to me, when I say trust in God and feel He will not forsake me in my difficulties. My faith tells me this, but so it seems to have told Gordon & yet he died just as safety was almost secured to him.'[23] How inscrutable were His ways.

The full story of the last weeks of Gordon's life will never be known. The final volume of journals ended on 14 December, six weeks before the fall of Khartoum.

All that Wolseley could learn came from hearsay. However, Colonel Wilson had now returned to Wolseley's camp at Korti after his perilous trip to Khartoum and back. According to Wolseley, Wilson's nerve had completely failed him. Wolseley interrogated the man closely, although he confessed that 'he gives one the blues to look at him and he is enough to demoralise any little army he is associated with'. He wished he could send Wilson home at once. What on earth had come over him? 'I can understand a man in a responsible position like myself breaking down.' But why should a subordinate whose only stake was his own wretched skin? It was 'beyond all comprehension'.[24] In fact, Wilson had been entrusted with the most dangerous mission in the entire war and had only escaped by a miracle.

Years later survivors of the siege gave various kaleidoscopic accounts of Gordon's end. Food had run out completely by the middle of January. The garrison at Omdurman had surrendered. In Khartoum the garrison ate donkeys, dogs, rats and gum. The pith of palm trees was handed out instead of rations. Dysentery compounded the starvation. Many of the soldiers were too weak to stand at their posts. Gordon was everywhere: checking and re-checking the fortifications, visiting the sick, an indomitable spirit among the despairing garrison.

On 20 January a spy from Omdurman brought the intoxicating news of General Stewart's victory at Abu Klea. But that oasis was more than a hundred miles to the north. Despair returned. Years later the men who were with the Mahdi – including his young Austrian prisoner, Rudolf Slatin – explained the sequel.

After they heard the news of Abu Klea, the Mahdi and almost all his Emirs were at first for throwing up the siege and retreating to El Obeid. Then it became clear that Stewart's small British force was no threat to their army. In the meantime Khartoum was theirs for the taking. There was no need of traitors within the garrison. Famine, disease and the fall of the Nile had done the work for them. On the south-west corner of the six miles of defences, the White Nile had exposed a long muddy ridge, and the garrison was too weak to extend its line. It was here the Mahdi decided to strike. He slipped across the river at twilight on 25 January. He gave each of the Emirs his orders; victory would be theirs in the name of God and the Prophet. The next morning, about two hours before dawn, when the moon had already set behind the palace, tens of thousands of the Mahdi's wild soldiers splashed across the muddy ridge and fell on the garrison.

Exactly how Gordon died remains uncertain. He had scorned to fortify the palace and make it a last redoubt. If the townspeople were to die, he would die with them. According to a story told later by a merchant, Bordeini Bey, he came out on the steps of the palace wearing his white uniform, his left hand on his sword hilt, and peered into the darkness. All around he must have heard the ghastly sounds of the massacre. Gordon did not raise his sword as the first Dervish charged up the stairs. A long spear caught him in the chest. He pitched forward on his face. It was still an hour before dawn.

Later the same day they brought a bundle to the Mahdi's camp at Omdurman. Across the river in Khartoum the frenzy of rape and massacre continued. Slatin could hear the noise from his tent. Then they unwrapped the bundle and proudly exposed the contents, a human head. The blue eyes were half open and the hair was quite white. 'Is not this', they cried exultantly, 'the head of your uncle, the unbeliever?' Slatin recognized with horror that the head was Gordon's. 'What of it?' he managed to reply. 'A brave soldier, who fell at his post. Happy is he to have fallen. His sufferings are over.'[25]

None of this was known to Colonel Wilson's party in Gordon's old paddle steamers, the *Talahawiyeh* and *Bordein*, as they fought their way up-river to Khartoum on 28 January. Wilson's orders from Wolseley were not to try to rescue Gordon, or even to bring him food or ammunition. He was merely to make a reconnaissance, with twenty men of the Sussex Regiment in red coats to frighten the Mahdi. Wilson knew that his unpleasant task was to tell Gordon that it would take two months before rescue could reach him.

What happened to Wilson was a great deal more unpleasant. As they approached Khartoum, the two paddle steamers had to run the gauntlet of half a dozen field-guns, and of thousands of rifles fired by tribesmen from the river-bank. The bullets smashed like a tropical storm against the steel plates bolted on the ships' sides, but both steamers continued. Then Wilson saw through the battle smoke Gordon's palace towering above the palm trees. At first he could not believe it: the Khedive's red flag was no longer flying. No steamer came to meet them. The message was unmistakable. The city had fallen. Massed on the sand spits were thousands of warriors waving banners. The rifle-fire and shell-fire intensified. The two steamers fought their way back through a tempest of bullets. Later, both steamers were wrecked at the cataracts, and some of the Sudanese crew deserted to the Mahdi. When Wilson and the survivors staggered into the British camp near Metemma on 4 February, Wilson must have been grey with exhaustion and shock. This should have been no surprise to anyone – except to Wolseley.

Back at Korti, everything was at last becoming clear to Wolseley. Two men, two duffers, had cheated him of a well-deserved success. Gladstone was the first. With his party of idiotic vestrymen – not to speak of those screw-makers like Chamberlain – he had lost the vital two months. Despite that, there had still been time to save Gordon. (In his own mind Wolseley ignored most of the facts, especially his own choice of the wrong route, the failure to buy enough camels, and his own fatuous orders about the soldiers in red coats. In any case it was hardly likely that Gordon would have agreed to save his own skin by returning with Wilson and abandoning the garrison.)

Wilson was the second duffer. Wilson could have saved Gordon. If only he had not lost those three vital days between 21 and 24 January dithering at Metemma: 'he must never again be employed on active service ... He could have reached Khartoum quite easily on the 25th Janry & had he done so,

Gordon would still – in all human probability – be still alive. Great God, it is too dreadful to dwell on the hairbreadth by which we failed to save Gordon and *Khartoum*.'[26]

Wolseley's sense that he was an injured man did not, however, prevent him from acting prudently in his own difficulties. In mid-February the situation was changing rapidly. He was committed by the government to advancing to 'smash up' the Mahdi. Large reinforcements under General Graham were now to be landed at the Red Sea port of Suakin. These could be used to attack the Mahdi's forces to the east of the Nile and, after subduing them, join in a converging movement on Berber. Meanwhile, the hot season was approaching. On 20 February Wolseley ordered his two main columns to make a tactical retreat to Korti. Neither column had been making much progress. The desert column, now led by Colonel Redvers Buller, was in a shattered condition because most of its camels had collapsed or died. The original commander, General Stewart, had been mortally wounded on 19 February and the force had suffered seriously at the battles of Abu Klea and Abu Kru. The Nile column, too, had lost its commander, General Earle, killed in its first fight, and had only advanced fifty miles up-river in a fortnight. At that rate it would be two months, well into the hot season, before they reached Berber. So the advance had to be postponed, worse luck, until the autumn.

Outwardly Wolseley was in his element, as cocky and belligerent as ever. He sang and whistled ostentatiously in his tent. In fact, his morale was swinging like a pendulum, the swings duly recorded in his private journal. The tactical retreat made him feel 'broken-hearted'. The men would feel all down on their luck, with hard fighting behind them, all to no purpose. As the sun became hotter and the camp filled with the smell of dead camels, he began to dread the onset of the summer. The dust and the flies and the scorpions would make life wretched for an army pegged down in its tents. He longed for autumn and the autumn campaign.

Under the spur of humiliation, his old belligerence revived. All the humiliations he had suffered, including the retreat, would be paid off with interest when he settled the score with the Mahdi. The plan to push on to Khartoum, from which he had shrunk in February, now began to grip his imagination. He fixed 15 September as the day he would move forward. On 11 March he cabled 'poor, old and palsied' Lord Granville, asking for formal permission to call himself Governor-General of the Sudan. He would go ahead and do so unless they forbade him. 'I think this tone & style of language will make Old Pussycat "Sit-Up": I don't suppose his diplomatic ears ever heard such dictation ... but then he has not had to deal much with soldiers before.'[27]

By mid-March, however, there was a new source of anxiety. Telegrams from London reported that Russia had designs on Afghanistan, so threatening India. Suppose Gladstone lost his nerve and countermanded the autumn campaign? On 13 March Wolseley heard ominous news from Hartington: he was not to be made Governor-General and Hartington talked of taking Graham's force away from Suakin and sending it on to India. Three days later there was a private telegram from a friend in the War Office: he must brave himself for a new volte-face by the government. Wolseley was ready to believe anything of such a set of charlatans, yet when the blow fell it was bitter enough.

Hartington cabled him on 14 April saying that 'Imperial interests' might necessitate withdrawing from the Sudan. This was followed by a private letter saying that the government 'were determined to get out of the Soudan campaign & were casting about for some good excuse to do so'.[28] In short, come war or come peace with Russia, it was the end of the campaign against the Mahdi. 'Of all the miserably foolish policies this is the worst,' was Wolseley's comment. It was a 'cruel absurdity' not to decide this after the fall of Khartoum. 'What a set of men to serve.'[29]

Back in Cairo a few weeks later, Wolseley asked himself this riddle. Why did God choose to deprive England of his own friend, Herbert Stewart, mortally wounded two days after Abu Klea, and 'leave us, that hoary bearded old sinful & untruthful humbug, Mr Gladstone'? God, he decided, 'has some good reason for humbling us', and Mr Gladstone 'is the fiend selected for this awful work ...'.[30]

*   *   *

The Queen left Osborne for Windsor Castle at the end of February, just in time to bid farewell to her precious Grenadier Guards, about to sail for the Sudan. She was still almost hysterical with grief about Gordon. 'Mr Gladstone and the government *have* – the Queen *feels it dreadfully* – Gordon's innocent, noble, heroic blood on their consciences. ... It is all this that has made the Queen *ill*.'[31] In early March she guessed, from the decision not to make Wolseley Governor-General, that Gladstone's Cabinet was having second thoughts about the Sudan. 'It is this hopeless way of going on which would make me hail a change of government. Otherwise if they *will* but be *firm, honest* and *not* so miserably undecided ... I don't care if they remain in. But I have *no* confidence left, and lose all heart, all hope! Why cling to office when they are so discredited at home and abroad? It is so humiliating and dreadful for me.'[32]

In April she was on holiday at Aix-les-Bains when she heard that the government was evacuating the Sudan. She wrote to Gladstone to tell him that 'After the loss of all the blood and treasure' it was 'painful in the extreme'[33] to hear this. Over the next month she kept up a running fight with the Cabinet, trying to persuade them of what 'is right and what is due to the honour of England'. On 17 May she launched a last emotional appeal to Gladstone's heir apparent, Lord Hartington. She was amazed, she said, that he had submitted to reverse his own policy: 'to see for the second time our troops recalled and retreating before savages – probably and *most probably* only to have to send them out again in a little while – is to make us the laughing-stock of the world!' She ended with a broad hint that Gladstone should go: '*she* cannot resign, if matters go ill, and her heart bleeds to see such short-sighted humiliating policy pursued.'[34]

It might seem odd that a Cabinet, which fought like Kilkenny cats on every other issue, and apparently contemplated suicide for the sake of Ireland, could cordially unite on the Sudan. Yet even Hartington had to admit that Wolseley's forward policy was impractical for two reasons.

First, the Russian threat was not a mere pretext, as Wolseley wanted to believe. From the end of March, when the Afghan crisis blew up, until the first week of May, war with Russia seemed a distinct possibility. How could Britain fight a war in Central Asia with half the army (and the best half at that) stuck in the wastes of the Sudan? War on two fronts would be absurd for an army as small as the British army. Then it turned out that the Afghan crisis was a tragicomic mistake. The Russians had killed some Afghan tribesmen at Pendjeh, close to the frontier, but had no intention of marching on Herat. Nevertheless, the war scare had sent a shudder through British India.

The second and more compelling reason was that public opinion, among Tories as well as Liberals, had lost its appetite for a war to avenge Gordon. The spasm of horror at his heroic death had been succeeded by a cool look at the difficulties. When Gladstone announced in April that the government needed an extra £11.5 million to cover the military and naval expenditure in the Sudan and India, excluding the cost of the advance to Khartoum, the public lost its stomach for the forward policy. As it was, the government was planning to raise income tax from sixpence to sevenpence in the pound, and (worse luck for Liberal brewing interests) to put heavy duties on beer. What chance had Wolseley, for all the blood and treasure he was allowed to spend, of hunting down the Mahdi in the infinite wastes of the Sudan? Through March and April the news from the Sudan was hardly encouraging. Wolseley's own two columns had been forced back to Korti. General Graham's men were still boxed in at Suakin, losing men, yet unable to get to grips with Osman Digna, the Mahdi's elusive general on the Red Sea coast.

By 22 May, when Gladstone left London for a fortnight's holiday at Hawarden, the Liberals' horizon seemed less murky than it had for months. Gladstone was prepared to admit to Hartington that the government had made two errors in 1884 – for both of which, he made bold to say, Hartington was primarily responsible. The first was to send troops out to Suakin on the coast of the Sudan: the second was to send Gordon to Khartoum. But both errors he thought 'pardonable' since they had been approved by the whole country. Now that the evacuation of the Sudan was also approved and safely underway, the priorities abroad were to make sure that the Russians behaved themselves on the Afghan border, and to persuade France and Germany to stop playing the fool with Egyptian finance. At home, Ireland was the great bed of nails for the government, but fortunately the bed was shared by both parties. The Tories were bemused by Lord Randolph Churchill (now returned from his tiger shoot in India) and Ireland divided them as cruelly as it did the Liberals. There was little doubt the Liberals would win the next general election, not least because by the autumn there would be a new democratic register, based on universal household suffrage, which would allow the labouring poor to rescue the Liberals.

But who would lead the Party? In January, both Whigs and Radicals had hatched a plot to get rid of the Grand Old Man, and give his place to Hartington. Now they were begging him not to carry out his threat to resign. He had handled the Sudan crisis with a masterly opportunism, advancing and retreating with all his old genius. He was the only man who could keep the party from being destroyed by Ireland. Whigs and Radicals had swallowed their pride to stay in his government. Would he desert them on the eve of the election?

Up at Hawarden Gladstone was as frisky as a colt. Ten days earlier he had insisted that he was going to resign. It was only a question of choosing the moment. This week? Next week? Now, when he saw the sacrifices they had made to keep him, he agreed to stay for a while longer. He was disappointed, of course – but not as disappointed as Eddy Hamilton expected. He would submit. It was God's will.

Perhaps as the sun flashed on his axe, when he felled one of the giant oaks in Hawarden forest, the PM thought of those lines from his hero, Tennyson, writing of Ulysses:

> We are not now that strength which in old days
> Moved earth and heaven; that which we are, we are.

'Allah is great, and his servant is Muhammad.' In the Sudan, Muhammad Ahmad, the Mahdi, found even less difficulty in submitting to God's will than Gladstone. On the day after the fall of Khartoum he crossed over from Omdurman to inspect the fruits of victory, accompanied by his chief deputy, the Khalifa Abdallahi. The two men gave no sign of emotion.

At least 4,000 people out of the 30,000 civilians and 6,000 soldiers of the doomed garrison had been massacred the previous morning. The bodies of men hacked to death and then ritually decapitated lay in every part of the city. Efforts continued, by dint of the courbash (the buffalo-hide whip), and still more drastic methods, to persuade the survivors to point out where they had hidden their gold and silver. The Mahdi ordered his men to stop further killing and not to damage the buildings, which would be needed for God's work. All loot was supposed to be handed over to the Mahdist treasury and reserved for the needy. The wives and daughters of the townsmen were distributed as slaves, the youngest and choicest naturally set aside for the Mahdi and the Khalifa.

The Mahdi made it known that he regretted Gordon's death. His orders had been to spare the Pasha so that he could be converted, like other Christians, to the true faith. But he pardoned the man who claimed to have killed Gordon, and took no steps to prevent the desecration of his corpse. The previous day the headless body, stripped of the white uniform, had been left in the palace garden, hacked about by each passing tribesman. Now it was thrown down a well. As for the head, it was placed in the fork of a tree and pelted with stones till no one could have recognized it.

The repulse of Wilson's paddle steamers, *Bordein* and *Talahawiyeh,* two days after the fall of Khartoum, set the seal on the Mahdi's triumph. The unbelievers had fled. This was the news that he announced to the faithful in the mosque. He added a picturesque revelation, received from the Prophet, that Allah had seen fit to puncture their water-skins, so the crews had died of thirst in the desert. This story seemed to be confirmed a few weeks later when the *Bordein*, captured by his men, steamed back to Khartoum. If the Prophet himself had come back to earth, chastising the unbelievers with a flaming sword, the Mahdi's soldiers – the *Ansar* (helpers) – could hardly have been more dazzled. It was the completeness of their victory that made people gasp, and conquered the secret doubts of even the most sceptical.

The Mahdi showed no surprise. As he had foretold, the unbelievers had been put to flight. By the will of God, the *Ansar* had captured the capital of the Sudan, with its arsenal full of guns and gunpowder, almost without loss. They had now taken control of almost all the Egyptian Sudan, except for the southernmost province, Equatoria, where Emin Pasha (alias the German doctor Eduard Schnitzer, converted to Islam) still retained his garrisons, protected by the vast swamps of the Sudd. It was time to pursue the second part of the Mahdi's programme, the holy war, the jihad, to be carried throughout the unreformed Muslim world and beyond.

The natural target for the jihad was Egypt. As the oppressors of the Sudan and collaborators with unbelievers, the Khedive and the other 'Turks' were doubly obnoxious. In due course the Mahdi drafted a letter to Tewfik as 'Governor of Egypt', warning him of his perilous spiritual position. He recounted his own divine mission and the dazzling victories assured to the party of God. His destiny was to rule the world. Tewfik was advised to join in the jihad and to co-operate against the unbelievers. Otherwise the Mahdi would invade Egypt. In fact neither of the two northern armies – on the Nile and on the Red Sea – was yet strong enough for such a campaign. Disease, desertion and shortage of money had crippled the Mahdi's army in those sandy wastes. For the moment all that could be done was to hustle Wolseley's columns back down the Nile towards the border with Egypt, and to drive Graham's force back across the desert to Suakin.

More vulnerable targets were the Egyptian garrisons that still held out on the borders of Abyssinia and in the huge ramshackle Christian empire that lay beyond. Soon after the fall of Khartoum, the Mahdi wrote a letter to the Negus (Emperor) Yohannes of Ethiopia, offering him peace. He reminded him that twelve hundred years earlier the Ethiopians had welcomed Abu Bakr, the Khalifa (successor) of the Prophet; the Negus of Ethiopia, he claimed, had been converted to Islam. He recommended that Yohannes now follow the same course, by adopting the *jibbah* of the faithful. Otherwise his territory, too, would be invaded. Already the Mahdi's army was besieging the Egyptian garrisons at Sennar and Kassala. The next step would be to repossess the whole crescent of territory running from the Blue Nile to Massawa on the Red Sea in the Abyssinian foothills, which Egypt had captured and added to the Sudan. But from

Yohannes there came no echo of the time of Abu Bakr, only an ominous silence from the great mountain fastness beyond the foothills.

Despite epidemics of typhus, dysentery and smallpox, which carried off thousands of prisoners (a judgment on them, no doubt), life in the twin oases of Khartoum and Omdurman had certain compensations. Of course there was no relaxation of the strict rules of Muslim law, the *sharia*. Smoking was forbidden on pain of a flogging (eighty strokes); so were other traditional pleasures like alcohol (a hundred strokes) and dancing; and bad language was punished by eighty lashes for each loose word. Khartoum was now thoroughly purified. In Gordon's palace, every taint of corruption was soon washed away, like the bloodstains on the palace staircase. It was here, behind the carved wooden shutters, that Khalifa Abdallahi kept his harem of fair-skinned girls taken after the sacking of the city. The two other Emirs took the next best accommodation for their harems: Khalifa Sherif the Catholic mission, and Khalifa Ali the house of a rich merchant. The luxurious homes of Greeks and Copts fell to the lot of the ordinary soldiers. No doubt they found the furniture useful for firewood, and gold brocade made good patches for their *jibbahs*.

From his modest house across the river, beside the great mosque at Omdurman, the Mahdi continued to announce to the world his universal mission. He was the Elect of God, come to cleanse the world of its sins. Outwardly his own style of life continued simply enough. He still wore his patched *jibbah* when he climbed the pulpit to preach in the mosque. His detractors, European prisoners like Rudolf Slatin, and a priest called Father Joseph Ohrwalder, naturally claimed that this was a sham. The example he set to his intimates was in debauchery. Slatin had now been released from his chains and appointed servant to the Khalifa Abdallahi. One day in June he heard from his master that the Mahdi was ill. At first no one paid much attention; had not the Mahdi himself assured them over and over again that his own life was to be an exact parallel of the Prophet's, ending with the conquest of Mecca, Medina and Jerusalem? Then the faithful were told the Mahdi needed their prayers. He was stricken with typhus.

A few days later, on 22 June, the Khalifa Abdallahi announced God's will to a stunned congregation in the mosque. Crying hysterically he climbed the Mahdi's own pulpit. According to Slatin, who was present, he shouted:

> Friends of the Mahdi! God's will cannot be changed. The Mahdi has left us, and has entered into heaven, where everlasting joys await him. ... The good things of this life are not lasting. Seize, therefore, with both hands the good fortune which is yours of having been the friends and adherents of the Mahdi, and never deviate in the slightest degree from the path he has shown you. You are friends of the Mahdi, and I am his Khalifa. Swear that you will be faithful to me.[35]

Tens of thousands of men swore their loyalty to Khalifa Abdallahi as the Mahdi's successor.

Of the three Khalifas, he came from the humblest background, with the fewest supporters among the Emirs. Yet he had the strongest claim. Two years earlier the Mahdi had made him the senior Khalifa, comparing him to Abu Bakr, who had served the Prophet. The two other Khalifas – Ali, representing the Mahdi's original disciples, and Sherif, representing the Mahdi's own family – had been kept in second place. Their own armies, the *Ansar* of the Red Flag and Green Flag respectively, were scattered in various provinces. As commander-in-chief, Abdallahi had kept his own men of the Black Flag strategically placed at Omdurman. So for the moment his claim to the succession could not be contested, though enemies he had in plenty, both inside and outside the Sudan.

* * *

Within a few months of the fall of Khartoum a great change had come over the whole vast region stretching from the upper Nile and the Red Sea to beyond the equator. By chance the death of the Mahdi coincided with a four-cornered scramble for the spoils of the Egyptian empire in the south. As the Mahdi's men advanced east and the British retreated north, two other European powers, Italy and France, were coming to compete with Ethiopia for supremacy. Further, in East Africa, beyond the equator, there was another scramble in the making: Germany was pushing inland, hungry for the possessions claimed by Zanzibar, the languid Oriental sultanate over which Britain had for two decades exercised informal empire.

To cap it all, a change was coming over the way the English regarded their empire, in a way that no one could have anticipated. Gladstone's government had fallen. On 8 June, a fortnight before the Mahdi's death, the Liberal government had been beaten in a vote on the budget amendment to stop the proposed extra penny on beer. In itself the issue was trivial, but Gladstone's Cabinet, weakened by squabbles of every kind, snatched at the opportunity to resign. They would return refreshed. In the meantime the Tories, weakened by Lord Randolph Churchill, would find the taste of power bitter indeed.

The new Prime Minister had other ideas. It was Lord Salisbury, a reluctant imperialist, yet the man who, in the long run, was to do more than any other Englishman of this period to expand the British Empire in Africa.

CHAPTER 16
The Sultan's Flag

England, Zanzibar and East Africa
8 June–December 1885

'I got tired of belonging to the pariahs and wished
to belong to the master race.'

Carl Peters

To say that the new Prime Minister was unenthusiastic about the Empire was to say very little. Robert Cecil, third Marquess of Salisbury, shrank from the display of emotion in any shape. Enthusiasm set his teeth on edge. As alien to him as incense and candles – or confidence in democracy – it was part of that heresy he called 'optimism'.

Salisbury had been brought up at Hatfield, the great Renaissance palace near London. He was the second son, a grave, lonely, motherless boy among the dazzling pictures by Jannsen and Geeraghts in the dusty corridors and state rooms. At Eton he had been tormented by bullies. He took refuge at Hatfield. It was the home of his family, the Cecils, who had governed England for Queen Elizabeth and then rested on their laurels for 300 years. Had it not been for his family, he would probably have been a scientist or an inventor; he built a laboratory under the main gallery. As it was, his father gave him a seat in Parliament when he was hardly more than a boy. He took his own right of leadership for granted. It was a duty and he asked no thanks in return.

Sometimes Salisbury talked like a cynic, and found a sardonic pleasure in exposing the pretensions of politics, mocking the jingoes for their arrogance, ridiculing the 'swagger' of imperialism as much as he mocked the Radicals for their humbug. His scepticism and pessimism were real enough. No Prime Minister could have been less convinced of England's divine mission to rule the world. In that first week of June 1885, he shrank from taking power himself. At the best of times he found it painful and embarrassing; at this moment the prospect for a Tory government was, in his own words, 'intolerable'.[1]

The trouble was that Gladstone's outgoing government had passed a reform bill giving the vote to every male householder in town and country. A general election could not be held till November when the new electoral register would be ready. Till then the Tory government would be stuck on a bed of nails, immobilized in a permanent minority, unable to pass the laws they wanted, yet perhaps incurring the odium of a Coercion Bill for Ireland. Meanwhile the Liberals would take a breather. At the general election a wave of two million new working-class voters would presumably propel them back into power.

Why had Salisbury, the man of no illusions, blundered on to this bed of nails at Westminster? Who had persuaded him to take office?

It was on 8 June that Gladstone's government had evaporated without warning. Some of his more sensitive Liberal supporters, anxious not to offend the powerful beer and liquor lobby, had refused to swallow the Budget's proposed new taxes on beer and spirits. Gladstone and his Cabinet gratefully seized on the chance to resign and the Queen was equally grateful to accept. Of course she scolded Gladstone when he refused to come up to Balmoral to explain his resignation to her in person. It was too inconsiderate of him to expect *her* to come down to Windsor that odious Ascot Week, when the town was full of rowdy race-goers. 'The Queen is a lady nearer 70 than 60,' she told Gladstone, himself nearer eighty than seventy, 'whose health and strength have been most severely taxed during the 48 years of her arduous reign, and ... she is quite unable to rush about as a younger person and a man could do.'[2]

In the event, it was Lord Salisbury, a stripling of fifty-five, who did the rushing about. He had decided to refuse office for the Tory Party, but was at least prepared to brave the journey to Balmoral to explain this to the Queen. Characteristically, he travelled alone and incognito. He took a first-class sleeper on the Highland Express, then slipped into a third-class carriage soon after it was daylight, amused to find that the journalists who boarded the train at each small Scottish station were completely thrown off the scent. He shrank from the press as a well-bred man would shrink from a boor. Fortunately for his peace of mind, at this point the British public hardly knew his face, though he had already served thirty-two years in politics, including a couple of years as Disraeli's Foreign Secretary. Soon his features were to be as famous as Gladstone's, to which they presented a delightful contrast for cartoonists: Gladstone, the king of birds, eagle-eyed, claws and beak ready to snap; Salisbury, king of the beasts, lion-headed with a great shaggy mane of a beard, yet a lion who often seemed to inhabit some world of his own.

At Balmoral the Queen played on the loyalty owed by all her subjects. She also appealed to a side of Salisbury that the public could not have guessed, the boyish chivalry he felt for her as a woman. She knew that he dreaded taking office to face this moribund but hostile Parliament where he would have responsibility without power, like a man trying to drive a coach with both hands tied behind his back. How much worse was it for her! She felt personally responsible – it was absurd but true – for the bungled affairs of her Empire. Salisbury did not need to be told of the Queen's longing to be rid of Gladstone and the Radicals, but he was astonished by other confidences she imparted.

Foreign affairs were his special study, and he shared her own deep suspicion of Russia and its erratic Tsar. Now he heard from the Queen's lips (confirmed later from confidential documents) that the row with Russia about the Pendjeh incident was by no means settled. Turkey was expected to join a pro-German and anti-British alliance and seal off the Straits at Constantinople. Moreover, Bismarck had been irritated by Lord Derby's ineptitude about Angra Pequena. Now Bismarck seemed determined to combine with France in sabotaging British control of Egypt. (So this was the Liberals' precious 'Concert' of Europe, Salisbury commented ruefully a few days later. 'They have succeeded in uniting the continent of Europe – against England.')[3] In short, the old Queen turned to Salisbury with the desperation of a maiden looking for a knight errant. Her once great Empire was beset by enemies at home and abroad. How could he abandon her at a time like this? Salisbury found the Queen irresistible, though he made a proviso that the Liberal majority must promise to play fair in Parliament.

Despite a heat wave and those awful crowds of race-goers, the Queen did have to drag herself down to Windsor before some kind of deal could be hammered out with Gladstone. Salisbury, too, had a task he loathed: deciding how to place his pushy colleagues in the Cabinet. Other men's appetite for office never failed to astonish and disgust him. The public took him for a cynic. Whenever he formed a ministry, he said, the Tories' club, the Carlton, was 'like the Zoological Gardens at feeding time'. In fact Salisbury's cynicism concealed a dangerous innocence about human nature. On this occasion he was shocked to find that Randolph Churchill refused to serve if Northcote were to be Leader in the Commons. Salisbury had to sacrifice his old friend Northcote, despatching him to the Lords as Lord Iddesleigh, before Randolph sulkily accepted the India Office.

At long last, on 24 June, the incoming and outgoing Cabinets took trains from Paddington Station, both bound for Windsor to perform the ritual kissing of hands and the exchange of seals of office. According to *The Times*, the two special trains steamed past each other in opposite directions a few hundred yards outside Windsor station. It must have been a fine sight, a gift for a cartoonist, the Up Train and the Down Train: Gladstone, Chamberlain, Granville and Co. returning to London in high spirits after handing in their seals; Salisbury gloomily resigned to office; a dozen Liberal top hats ironically raised behind one tall smokestack, a dozen Tory top hats huddled behind the other tall smokestack. But Salisbury's misgivings had begun to evaporate like the steam from the boiler. The rest of the Cabinet, even the impetuous Lord Randolph Churchill, drove meekly back to the station after they had kissed hands and taken the seals surrendered by Gladstone. Salisbury stayed on for a long time, talking to the Queen.

The short dumpy Queen and the tall, shambling Prime Minister were as far apart in temperament as in appearance. She was the prisoner, he the master of the emotions. Yet they were a fine match in other ways, better balanced than the Queen and a charmer like Melbourne, or a showman like Disraeli. A romantic patriotism, a simple faith in God, disillusionment with democracy: they had plenty in common. They also had a respect for each other's eccentricities. The Queen's neurotic fear of crowds, her refusal to wear anything grander than a bonnet on state occasions, even her infuriating habit of dragging her ministers up to Balmoral were all perfectly acceptable to Salisbury. Her keen interest in foreign affairs astonished him. He was to be his own Foreign Secretary. The post was of critical importance and he could not entrust it to any of his colleagues. The Queen seemed delighted with this arrangement. It was unchivalrous of him to say so, but he confessed that when he talked to the Queen about foreign affairs, it was like talking to a man.

As Leader of the Opposition in the Lords, Salisbury had repeatedly rapped the Liberals' knuckles during the last five years for 'vacillation and inconsistency' in Africa. He had mocked them for fighting the Boers in the Transvaal and then, after a deplorable defeat, handing the country back to them. He had mocked them for failing to intervene in Egypt until Arabi had set the place alight. Above all, he had mocked them for 'scuttling out'[4] of the Sudan. The delay in sending help to Gordon was the culminating folly. This was all common ground with the Queen, and perhaps with a majority of her subjects. His own party's policy, he no doubt assured her, would be both resolute, consistent and prudent.

But how could this prudent policy be pursued among the dangerous rivalries of 1885? The next day Salisbury moved his own headquarters, not to Downing Street (which was given to Lord Iddesleigh, the new First Lord of the Treasury), but to his old berth in the Foreign Office. It was here, up the magnificent staircase, past the picture of Britannia and the sea traders, in the great room overlooking St James's Park, that he had presided in 1880 before handing the post over to Lord Granville. How different it all seemed now, in 1885, when Salisbury was briefed by the courtly, monocled officials of the Foreign Office. Five years before one hardly heard Africa mentioned. Now there was a rush to slice up the whole continent like a cake, and no sooner had some kind of order been established in the share-out of one part of Africa than the unseemly Scramble burst out in another.

The man in the Foreign Office charged with ensuring that Britain got the best slices of the cake was the recently knighted head of the African department, Sir Percy Anderson. Salisbury knew him and liked him. They shared many of the same prejudices, among them a distaste for the African continent in general and for the kind of British businessmen ('buccaneers', Salisbury called them) who made fortunes there. In this both men were typical of the British landed and professional classes of the period.

Where Anderson was unusual was in being one of the first to recognize that Britain's cheap and simple exercise of power without responsibility – informal empire – was doomed in Africa. In 1883 he had backed Consul Hewett's plan, as mentioned earlier, for making a protectorate of the Niger and Oil Rivers. The plan had been adopted by Lord Granville and Gladstone's Cabinet, despite themselves. In Cameroon the same initiative had been thwarted by Bismarck. But in the Niger and the rest of Oil Rivers, Anderson's policy, with the help of George Goldie, had carried all before it. Second only to Leopold, Anderson was the main victor at the West Africa Conference in Berlin.

In June 1885, Anderson's monocle was focused on the opposite side of Africa, the East African coast between the Horn and the Portuguese colony of Mozambique. This was the focus of a new Scramble, for a supposed new El Dorado. The problem was a diplomatic puzzle of the first order. It raised the central question. If the Scramble could not be avoided, what were the priorities

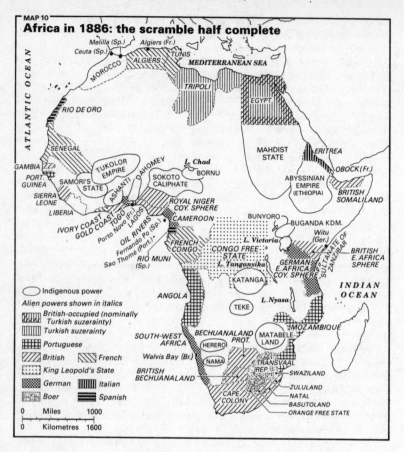

MAP 10

Africa in 1886: the scramble half complete

Indigenous power

Alien powers shown in italics

▨▨▨ British-occupied (nominally Turkish suzerainty)

‖‖‖ Turkish suzerainty

▦▦▦ Portuguese

▨▨▨ British   ◹◹◹ French

⋮⋮⋮ King Leopold's State

▨▨▨ German   ‖‖‖ Italian

▨▨▨ Boer   ▬▬▬ Spanish

0 Miles 1000

0 Kilometres 1600

in Africa for British interests and which British interests were expendable?

Anderson's starting point, like everyone's in the FO and Parliament, Tory as well as Liberal, was Britain's bondage in Egypt. Ever since the French had realized that the British were not going to restore dual control there, Egypt had served as a ball and chain on every step in British strategy, diplomatic or military. Yet Egypt had to be kept in safe hands, whatever the cost. Ever since 1869, when the opening of the Canal put Egypt on the main shipping lane to India and the Far East, the country's security had been one of Britain's most vital strategic interests. When could she restore Egyptian independence – subject to British supervision? So confused was the international situation that this happy day seemed as far off as ever. British control of the country was still crippled by France's childish determination to sabotage any arrangements to put Egyptian finance on a sound footing. There were two unpleasant consequences.

First, Britain was dependent on Germany as honest broker in the negotiations over finance. This meant humouring Bismarck in other parts of the world, satisfying his new appetite for colonies with the least possible sacrifice to British interests. Second, Egypt's own crumbling empire had to be sacrificed in the drive for economy. Seen from Whitehall, Ismael's dream of a great tropical empire spread from the highlands of Ethiopia to the source of the White Nile was an absurdity. So the FO had advised Granville to make a clean break. The Khedive must bite the bullet and evacuate all his garrisons south of Wadi Halfa, in the Sudan and beyond. This might have been done with dignity but for the Mahdi's revolt. Now it must be done despite it. Having failed to save Gordon, Wolseley was retreating miserably northwards. Only four Egyptian garrisons in the Sudan south of Wadi Halfa had survived the convulsion: one at Suakin on the Red Sea; two on the borders of Ethiopia, at Metema (Gallabat) and Senhit (Keren); and Emin Pasha's posts in Equatoria, far to the south. Three of these had now been evacuated by sea: the one at Suakin rescued by the Martini-Henrys of General Graham's expeditionary force, the two on the borders of Ethiopia by the muskets and spears of their former enemy, the Emperor Yohannes. As for Emin Pasha, no one knew whether his gallant band was still holding out beyond the Sudd, or had been murdered or enslaved months before.

It was only beyond the Sudan, outside the reach of the Mahdi, that an evacuation could be conducted with dignity. In fact it had precipitated a new kind of Scramble. To the south and east of the Sudan, the Khedive Ismael had daringly built two outposts of his Egyptian empire. One was at Massawa, where the gorges of the Abyssinian plateau swept down to a sun-bleached port on the Red Sea; the other was at Harar, a walled city famous for xenophobia, astride the dry, scrubby hills facing the deserts of Somaliland. Neither place had generated enough trade to make it economically self-sufficient. So by direction of the British both had been quietly abandoned in 1884–5.

The barracks at Massawa were empty only a few days. Yohannes had obliged the British by rescuing the garrisons at Metema and Senhit, not only because he wanted to take over the towns himself; he also wanted the port of Massawa. At long last the Ethiopian empire would have an outlet to the Red Sea, lost to the Turks 250 years before. But in February 1885 Italy snapped it up – by a secret agreement with the British. The FO was happy to oblige this rival of France; for the French had recently established a foothold at Obock (Djibouti) in Somaliland. For her part, Italy was looking for compensation after her humiliation over Tunis. Massawa would make the starting point for a Red Sea colony, the future colony of Eritrea.

As for Harar, it was too poor and too isolated to interest any of the Great Powers for the time being. Rejected by these lions, it passed to a hungry jackal, Menelik, King of Shoa in southern Ethiopia, and Yohannes's main rival for control of Ethiopia. The British were content with a nibble at Berbera on the north side of the Horn, while to the south, the Italians took another bite at what was to become Italian Somaliland.

The only loser in this arrangement was the Emperor Yohannes. Understandably he felt let down by the British. The Italians he regarded with suspicion. Otherwise this half-hearted Scramble for the poverty-stricken coast of the Red Sea and the deserts of Somaliland passed off without much unpleasantness.

The real test was to be the partition of East Africa, and here Sir Percy Anderson and his colleagues at the Foreign Office confessed themselves at a loss how best to safeguard British interests. For the last nine months British plans for East Africa had swung between two extremes: backing the Sultan of Zanzibar, who laid claim to an enormous empire on the mainland which stretched more than 600 miles from Somaliland to Mozambique, or creating a new British protectorate at the expense of the Sultan, by disputing his claim and dismembering his empire.

At least one thing was clear to the frock-coated experts puzzling over trade figures and caravan maps at the Foreign Office. In East Africa, even more than in the Niger delta in West Africa, there were vital British interests at stake. The island of Zanzibar had become the most prosperous port between Durban and the Suez Canal. Its imports and exports combined were believed to total £2 million. Most of its imports were manufactured goods from Britain or India, and its trade was largely in the hands of British Indians. The luxuriant plantations on Zanzibar itself and on the neighbouring island of Pemba produced most of the world's supply of cloves. But its principal wealth came from the entrepôt trade with the mainland. All along the coast of the mainland local harbours connected the web of caravan routes to and from the interior with the great central market in Zanzibar. Down to the coast came the strings of porters carrying on their heads the tusks of ivory, bales of rubber and hides and other merchandise. Up country they returned, carrying bales of Manchester or Bombay cloth, Birmingham brass and Sheffield knives.

Best of all, and a source of pride to Bible-reading Englishmen, was the boom in legitimate trade. Twenty years earlier Zanzibar had been notorious for the slave trade, but in 1873 the British had forced the Sultan to close the slave markets, both on the islands and on the mainland. Slavery itself was still legal in the Sultan's empire; indeed the clove plantations depended on slave labour. This abuse was expected to be abolished as soon as it could be done without ruining the plantation owners. Meanwhile, Zanzibar was the base for the anti-slavery patrols of the British navy.

By 1884 it seemed clear that the mainland would soon be opened up by a new explosion of trade. Ever since the great journeys of exploration by Livingstone, Speke and Stanley, it had been known that tracts of country around Lake Victoria, and between there and Lake Tanganyika, were blessed with rich soil and a luxuriant climate. Here was a new India in Central Africa, it was claimed, a garden of Eden, bursting with tropical crops of every kind. But how to reach that garden and open it up to Europe for legitimate trade?

Livingstone had lost his life in the quest for an opening. Stanley had found the Congo, but the Congo was still remote. And who could honestly say that low-lying region was suitable for European settlement? With the blessings of soil and climate went a particularly nasty crop of tropical diseases, especially malaria. To colonize and rear families safely in Africa, Europeans needed a temperate climate like Algeria's or that of the South African veld.

The latest generation of explorers, British, French and German, had recently discovered two regions with just such a climate, both near Zanzibar. The first was the small plateau around the snow-capped peak of Mount Kilimanjaro, just to the north of the main caravan route to Ujiji and Lake Tanganyika. The second was the much larger area of highlands around the snowy heights of Mount Kenya. The first, though smaller, seemed more tempting for colonists. Not only was it near an existing caravan route, but the natives were apparently friendly, even anxious to help Europeans. By contrast, the ferocious Masai tribesmen, who grazed their vast herds of cattle in the Kenya highlands, had a complete disregard for the rights of strangers.

It was crucial to the British, in autumn 1884, to forestall a foreign power from grabbing this juicy plum below the snows of Kilimanjaro. It was now or never. Parties of French and German explorers were reported to be sniffing around Kilimanjaro. A German colony would doubtless rob Zanzibar of one of its best harbours on the mainland. It would also break Zanzibar's monopoly of the caravan trade with the Great Lakes, the main source of wealth. But a French colony would be even worse, a disaster not only to Zanzibar but to Britain. No doubt the French would play the dog-in-the-manger, as they had in Senegal and other parts of West Africa, abolishing free trade and stifling British enterprise with their colonial bureaucracy. The French could also establish a naval base, threatening the sea-lanes to India and the East, almost as if they controlled the Suez Canal. There was nothing for it, said the FO in September 1884, but to make a British protectorate of Kilimanjaro, served by a port on the mainland. All they needed was to take up the offer of a bumptious twenty-six-year-old British explorer called Harry Johnston, now encamped at Chagga close to the mountain. He would sign a treaty of protection with the local chief, 'King' Mandara.

Up went this uncharacteristically daring plan of action to Granville's desk, and from there it was passed to the Cabinet. A cable was sent to Sir John Kirk, the British agent in Zanzibar, telling him to report on the scheme immediately by telegraph 'as French and Germans are believed to have designs of annexation'.[5]

Strange to say, a majority of the Liberal Cabinet favoured this move forward. This was the moment when they had just been made fools of by Bismarck and the press was full of the fiasco at Angra Pequena. So it was tit for tat: Kilimanjaro in return for Cameroon and Angra Pequena. But on the road to annexing Kilimanjaro lay two insuperable obstacles. Sir John Kirk, the British Agent, was determined to frustrate any step that would weaken the authority of the Sultan, an authority he had spent the last twenty years helping to create. He recommended extending the Sultan's empire so that it would include the Kilimanjaro district. Granville and most of the Cabinet agreed. Then Gladstone found out what was going on and torpedoed Kirk's plan. He failed to see the point of doing anything with that 'mountain country behind Zanzibar with the unrememberable name'.[6]

Gladstone's torpedo struck in December 1884. On 3 March 1885, a few days after Bismarck had steered the Berlin West Africa Conference to a polite conclusion, the German Chancellor launched his own torpedo at the British Cabinet. The official gazette in Berlin revealed that a *schützbrief*, an imperial charter, had just been granted to a 'German colonisation company' to establish a protectorate in East Africa. Without a word of warning, Bismarck had grabbed a fourth slice of Africa for his colonial empire. The borders were left vague. All that was clear was that they included central regions under the Sultan's flag – Usagara, Ungulu, Uzigua and Ukami – on the main caravan route to the Lakes, yet claimed by the Germans to be outside the dominions of the Sultan of Zanzibar.

It turned out that this scheme was the work of a young adventurer called Carl Peters, the moving spirit behind the Company for German Colonization. He and three other young Germans were said to have disguised themselves as deck passengers on a boat to Zanzibar. They had spent only a few weeks in the region, and their 'treaties' with native chiefs were even more suspect than others of their kind. However, Bismarck stood four-square behind them, so the Foreign Office recognized the *fait accompli*. It was vital to humour Bismarck – to feed the monster, and perhaps choke him with dry crusts of Africa. Starve Bismarck, and Britain might lose control of Egypt.

As for Kilimanjaro, Anderson still had vague hopes that Johnston's plan for a British colony there could be adopted. A group of British businessmen in Manchester and Liverpool had been alerted to the threat to British markets, egged on by the more forward-looking officials of the Foreign Office. The most ardent promoter was Kirk's senior assistant at Zanzibar, Frederick Holmwood, who had himself produced a wild scheme for a railway to Kilimanjaro, starting from the coast at Mombasa, north of the region claimed by Germany. The railway would run smack across the plains controlled by the fearsome Masai. Holmwood assured his colleagues that the Masai, once offered a good price for hides, would prove friendly enough.

The capitalists in Britain, however, did not seem too keen to risk their own skins – or their money – in the region. The leaders of the group were Sir William Mackinnon and James Hutton, King Leopold's ablest partisans in Britain. At this period both men had their heads full to the brim with the Congo. They were trying to set up a syndicate to help Leopold build the vital railway to bypass the cataracts of the Congo. Kilimanjaro seemed unappetizing. Before they put a penny into that railway, they insisted on large concessions from the Sultan, along with a guarantee from the British government, neither of which was likely to be forthcoming.

Anderson was not surprised by the inertia of the Manchester capitalists. If they complained about the threat to their overseas markets, they could only blame themselves for their lack of enterprise. 'Manchester will not advance a sixpence unless the money is safe,' Anderson wrote in April 1885. By June he predicted that Carl Peters and his sham treaties would have a clear field – unless the British government was prepared to subsidize the railway to Kilimanjaro. This wild hope did not then enter the heads of the men in the Foreign Office.

So by the time Salisbury replaced Granville at the Foreign Office in June 1885, no one had much confidence in forestalling Germany either by backing the Sultan or by creating a new British colony. Bismarck seemed destined to swallow most of East Africa unless Salisbury felt strongly against it – or the Sultan managed to stop him.

* * *

The British agency and consulate in Zanzibar was a large, yellow, flat-roofed building just to the east of the Sultan's palace and within reach of the spray from the harbour. In summer, when the monsoon blew from the south-west, it brought the whiff of cloves and of dried shark from the dhows as well as the stench of offal from the sandy beach. The British Agent was inured to the smells. He studied the latest telegrams from London, aghast that his life's work was being cast away to appease Bismarck.

It was nineteen years since Zanzibar had first thrown its strange spell on the British Agent and Consul-General, Sir John Kirk. Out of a sapphire sea rose a coral island of incandescent green, studded with groves of coconut and mango, and orchards of cloves, the palm forest decked with pink convolvulus, a thin line of creamy surf beating languidly on the milk-white sand. Approaching across the shimmering lagoon, one saw a city that might have been summoned by Aladdin's lamp, its arches and colonnades, towers and turrets, flags and flagpoles, refracted upwards in the frenzy of a mirage.

But there was little sign of magic once ashore. Lining the seafront, like four barrack blocks, were the consulates of four Powers: Britain, France, the US and Germany, the four national flags flapping sternly at their masts. Beside them stood the Sultan's palace with his blood-red flag on a high pole.

The palace was an unpretentious affair of white-washed stucco. Beside it, guarded by a rusty cannon and half in ruins, stood the fort built by his father, Sultan Sayid. There was a large, solemn mission house built by the new Universities Mission for Central Africa. Otherwise there seemed nothing to the town, only a handful of mosques with short, stubby minarets and a maze of narrow lanes lined with tall, stone buildings, each with a finely carved wooden doorway. Apart from the doors, the houses were as plain as warehouses, which many of them were. They belonged to the richer Arabs and to the Swahili who owned most of the plantations, or to the leaders of the 4,000 British Indian merchants who controlled most of the trade. Beyond this Oriental city was a vast African shanty town where tens of thousands of slaves and ex-slaves lived in indescribable squalor.

In short, the city was closer in spirit to Liverpool than to Venice, and no one had bothered to enrich it with anything beautiful except the doorways. Perhaps it was the languor of the climate, the soft, insidious wind that blew from the palm forest heavy with spice – and heavy with fever too. Anyway, most white men went there seized by the single, simple idea of making their fortunes. If they were lucky, they did so. If they were luckier still, they left before malaria killed them.

Sir John Kirk had led a charmed life in a climate so deadly that most of his predecessors had died at their post or left it doomed men. Kirk seemed to have earned his good fortune. He was a tall, taciturn Scot, the last of Livingstone's lieutenants in the field. If anyone had inherited the mantle of Livingstone, it was not Stanley (as Stanley liked to claim) but Sir John Kirk. In 1858, at the age of twenty-six, he had joined the great explorer as doctor and botanist on the government-backed Zambezi expedition. For the next six years he had tramped and splashed his way across eastern Central Africa, on foot or by dug-out canoe, patient and indefatigable, a godsend for Livingstone. It was dangerous, disheartening work with few great discoveries – once they had found the Shire Highlands and Lake Nyasa – to compensate for the frustrations. One of Kirk's own discoveries was that his hero, judged as a leader of Europeans, seemed to have feet of clay. When things went wrong, Livingstone could be alarmingly harsh and tactless. And go wrong they did – from the beginning to the end of the trip.

In Central Africa the slave trade was the Fourth Horseman, riding behind War, Famine and Plague. All across the Shire Highlands, Kirk and Livingstone saw villages burnt and abandoned in the slave hunt, fugitives cowering in the bush, corpses bobbing in the river. But what could they do to help? Kirk could not even keep his own companions or Livingstone's wife Mary from dying of fever. There was fighting with natives, and Kirk, for the first and last time in his life, had to kill a man in self-defence. Twice he nearly died himself, once when his canoe overturned in the rapids of Cabora Bassa (he lost all eight volumes of his botanical sketches), and once after running out of water.

When he returned to England in 1863, sick and exhausted, one would have thought he would have shaken the dust of Africa off his feet forever. But he had been bitten by something even more potent than the bite of malaria – by one simple idea, which was Livingstone's too. Philanthropy would never end the slave trade. It needed all the '3 Cs' together: commerce, Christianity, civilization. Based on Zanzibar, Kirk was determined to put this into practice.

So he returned there, first as doctor and Vice-Consul at the British consulate, then as the British Agent and Consul himself, and slowly and patiently carried out his plan for the great crusade.

Officially Kirk was a diplomat with a double function: as Agent the adviser of the Sultan, and as Consul the champion of British subjects. He was accredited to the court of an independent Arab monarch, His Highness Sayid Barghash-bin-Sayid, Sultan of Zanzibar. In practice, the influence of the British Agent was so powerful that he exercised a kind of indirect rule. For eighty years Britain had exercised an unofficial protectorate over the possessions of Sultan Sayid and his successors, Arab princes from Muscat and Oman, who had settled in Zanzibar. The British shielded each Sultan from his enemies, European or Arab. But if the Sultan was bold enough to defy the British Agent on a matter of British interest, then woe betide the Sultan. Intervention was the last resort in the days of informal empire. It meant using the iron fist of the British navy. Much better to keep it concealed in the velvet glove. Kirk himself had never had to use force, though once or twice he had to speak very plainly to make sure that Barghash knew where he stood and who his real friends were.

Originally the Sultan had been as wild as a young horse and his own worst enemy. Before Kirk's time he had been reckless enough to listen to the French, and had tried to grab the throne from his invalid brother, Majid, in the confusion after the death of their father, the great Sultan Sayid, in 1856. The rebellion had been put down with the help of Consul Rigby and a detachment of British Marines. This was lucky for Barghash. If Majid had captured him, he would no doubt have ended up with his throat cut. As it was, he had to agree to leave Zanzibar 'forever' and to confess in full durbar (court) that he would 'never again listen to the advice of the French ... nor of anyone except the British government'.[7]

Exile in Bombay had had its compensations. The British generously gave him a house and a carriage and an allowance of 12,000 rupees (£1,200 a year sterling). After cooling his heels for two years, in 1861 he was allowed back to Zanzibar. By the time Kirk came on the scene in 1866, he seemed a reformed character. Kirk found him 'a man of energy, determination and intelligence'.[8] Then came a double blow – a devastating epidemic of cholera and a typhoon that tore up most of the trees in the island. These were followed by a trial of strength.

The trial came predictably enough, when the British Parliament finally lost patience and decided to abolish the sea-borne slave trade. Over the years there had been attempts at compromise. In 1845 Sultan Sayid had agreed to reduce the slave trade to his own basic needs and to forbid slave ships from sailing except between Zanzibar and his other possessions on the mainland and the other islands. This left two slave trades in operation: the legal trade with the empire of Zanzibar and the illegal trade between the empire, South Arabia and the Gulf. To separate the two was an impossible job for the British navy. When it was obvious that both trades were increasing, the British forced Sultan Majid to proclaim a ban on all slave-running during the months of the south-west monsoon, the wind which carried the slave dhows back to Arabia. Even then the slave-runners were too much for the British navy. In the three years from 1867 to 1869, it was reckoned that 2,645 smuggled slaves were rescued, while 37,000 others were spirited off to Arabia and beyond.

In 1873 Parliament lost patience and sent off Sir Bartle Frere on his mission to impose Parliament's will on the recalcitrant Sultan. The Sultan defied Frere. Encouraged by dreams of French assistance, he refused to sign the treaty. The wealth of Zanzibar depended on cloves, and cloves depended on slaves. Without them Zanzibar would be ruined.

It was Kirk, after Frere's departure, who succeeded in explaining to Barghash the plain fact that he had no choice. On 3 June 1873 Kirk went alone to the palace. There he explained how in 1870 Paris had been besieged and forced to surrender. Then he read Barghash and his four councillors part of a telegram he had just received from the British government. Unless Barghash signed Frere's treaty, the British navy would blockade Zanzibar. Earlier that morning the four councillors had agreed on a policy of defiance. Now Barghash again asked their advice. 'Shall I give him [Kirk] the word we agreed upon this morning?' 'No, no!' came the whispered answer. Kirk patiently explained that it was futile to hope for French intervention. 'I have not come to discuss, but to dictate!'[9] He had spoken for the last time. To reject what he said would mean war. Two days later Kirk was able to report to London that Barghash had signed Frere's treaty and had closed the great slave market on the same day. It was the triumph of the velvet glove.

Whatever he felt, Barghash accepted defeat with a good grace and Kirk noticed no sign of resentment. In the years that followed, he came to think of himself as the Sultan's friend, not merely his adviser. Certainly Barghash had honoured his part of the bargain. He closed the slave markets up and down the mainland, and imprisoned anyone who tried to defy him.

At first, it is true, the new treaty seemed self-defeating. A gruesome land trade sprang up along the routes from the southern port of Kilwa to the Somali ports in the north. By 1875 it was reckoned that about 12,000 slaves were being marched along this terrible route, leaving a trail of dead and dying in the bush. But Barghash needed no prompting from Kirk. He stamped out this land trade by a new proclamation.

As the slave trade withered, legitimate trade rose to take its place. Within a decade of Livingstone's death, Kirk could report that Kilwa, once the worst slave port on the coast, had grown fat on the rubber trade. Europe's appetite for African exports like rubber and gum copal (used for making varnish), coupled with the boom in ivory, must have exceeded Kirk's most optimistic forecasts. Since his accession, Barghash's tax revenue had risen to £300,000 a year. By any standard he was a rich man. He indulged himself in a few personal luxuries – a coach road and a telephone line between two of his palaces. But unlike the Khedive or the Bey of Tunis, he kept out of the hands of the money-lenders.

By 1885, there remained for Kirk only the final step of outlawing slavery itself from the Sultan's empire, as it has been outlawed in 1834 from the British Empire.

Kirk seems to have committed little to paper on how he intended to achieve this. One obvious way was to make the whole of the Sultan's empire an official British protectorate. Kirk knew that London was not yet ready for this. By 1884 he had become alarmed at the encroachments by French and German explorers. Then in September 1884 he heard news that amazed him: the Foreign Office had decided to forestall Germany or France. Nothing could be better. But why must they destroy the Sultan's empire in the process? Johnston's proposal for a colony at Kilimanjaro could only undermine the Sultan's growing power on the mainland which Kirk had striven so long to create.

The main argument for making the Sultan's empire a formal British protectorate was that it would be the quickest and safest way to extend the power of the Sultan from Zanzibar to the Great Lakes. At present, Barghash had only created a skeleton of a state beyond the coastal ports of Dar-es-Salaam, Mombasa and Lamu. Kirk had encouraged him to hire a motley collection of Indian and Zanzibari mercenaries, led by a British officer called General Lloyd Matthews. So far they had built two small forts to defend the caravan road that carried the ivory trade. Beyond the forts, the Sultan's red flag flew at the caravan towns of Tabora and Ujiji. But the whole state was run on a shoe-string. Barghash seemed to have no interest in his empire on the mainland except to suck it dry of revenue. Instead, he had been persuaded by some Frenchmen to invest a large sum of money in a steamship line of his own. Once again the moral was obvious: the British must take over.

> I do wish he would give up his ships [Kirk wrote to a friend]. They are ruining him and keeping him from paying attention to the government of his own country. The coast is quite neglected and not a dollar expended on the smallest improvements. How easy it would be to govern this country and make it rich but how uphill work it is to influence a native ruler pulled by all interested consuls and traders. This ought to be a British protectorate and let the French do the same in Madagascar...[10]

The French were doing the same in Madagascar. And now it seemed that the Germans would take Zanzibar. The recognition that the new Foreign Secretary, Lord Salisbury, might stand idly by while Germany took the *whole* of the Sultan's empire – islands and mainland combined – gave Kirk a sense of hopelessness. Then in June 1885 came that extraordinary cable announcing that the German Emperor had declared a protectorate over the part of the mainland where the Sultan exercised most authority, because it was on the caravan route to the Lakes. In reply the Sultan sent a formal protest to the German Emperor. He also despatched two expeditions to the mainland, both led by General Matthews. The first was to subdue one of his rebellious Governors, the Governor of Witu, who was known to be intriguing with the Germans. The second was to assert his authority in the district of Kilimanjaro. What did the British Agent advise?

Kirk could offer the Sultan no advice. The new Foreign Secretary had sent no instructions about his new policy – if he had one. Kirk watched helplessly as the Sultan turned to other advisers in the European community. Perhaps Barghash would make his peace with Germany; this might be where his interests lay, and the only way to keep his empire intact. Kirk himself sent Salisbury a cable which at least made plain where his own heart lay: 'German pretensions will not bear examination for a moment if judged by any rule of truth or justice.'[11] This despatch received no direct answer. Instead, Salisbury simply warned Kirk to co-operate with Germany in everything. And he should not allow 'any communications of a hostile tone to be addressed to German agents ... by Zanzibar authorities'.[12]

Kirk felt the humiliation like a wound. For nineteen years he had patiently worked to save East and Central Africa from itself. The empire of Zanzibar in its present form was largely his own creation. Of course his first loyalty was to Britain and the British crusade against slavery. But he had given his word to Barghash. Stamp out the slave trade – against all the instincts and the traditions of his people. In return, Kirk would make him rich and protect him from aggression by foreign powers.

Now Salisbury seemed to be asking Kirk to betray everything he stood for. He was to hand over the empire he had built to a pack of 'unscrupulous German rogues'.[13]

*   *   *

Kirk was hardly being fair to the complexity of Carl Peters's character. As the leader of the Company for German Colonization, he was certainly an odd fish to find creating a new German empire in the wild places of Africa. At first sight he looked more like a schoolboy – or a young professor. He was frail and short-sighted, with pince-nez covering his large, pale blue eyes, a waxed moustache and thin brown hair parted in the centre. A photograph taken in 1884, shortly before sailing for Africa, shows him and his two frock-coated companions like the Three Musketeers of a college play: Dr Carl Peters (the doctorate was for his brilliant metaphysical dissertation, 'Willenswelt und Weltwille'), his college friend, handsome blond Carl Jühlke, and the dashing aristocrat, Graf Joachim von Pfeil.

None of them had any experience of exploring Africa. Peters had been brought up in a country vicarage, far from the centres of power and knew almost nothing of the world except from his voracious reading. A visit to England in 1882 had made him green with envy. 'I got tired of being accounted among the pariahs,' he wrote later, 'and wished to belong to the master race.'[14] But his first great feat ended in farce. Twice he tried to swim the English Channel, and was dragged half crying from the icy waters. He returned to Germany and founded the GDK (Company for German Colonization) recruiting its members from the same class as his own: obscure provincial doctors and professors, patriotic, yet outsiders in the new Reich, men who wanted a place in the sun.

Peters's plans to conquer East Africa seemed as half-baked as those to conquer the English Channel. The GDK was better at raising hopes than raising money, so he started out with no proper financial backing. It was for this reason that he and his two companions, Jühlke and Pfeil, had travelled as deck passengers to Zanzibar, not (as Kirk imagined) to fool the British. It also explained the near collapse of the expedition when they reached East Africa. They had only thirty-six porters to carry all the supplies for the expedition and half a dozen personal servants, including the interpreters. This was an even smaller party than most of Livingstone's expeditions and a fraction of the size of any of Stanley's. Within five weeks they began to run out of food which meant that everything had to be done at whirlwind speed. A speech of welcome by the chief's hut, tents pitched, treaty forms handed over for signature, flags hoisted, hands shaken, drums beaten, the birth of a new German province – all in the space of a few hours, before the exhausted empire-builders had to rush on to the hut of the next impoverished African chief.

Judged as a piece of theatre, it would have been hard to beat Peters's whirlwind campaign. All over Africa, in these heady years of the Scramble, the blank treaty form and the national flag had become part of the explorers' stock in trade, like their barter goods of Venetian beads and their bales of American cloth. Stanley had signed up chiefs by the score; so had his successors in the Congo. On the Niger and Oil Rivers Consul Hewett had hundreds of 'treaties' to his credit; and Dr Nachtigal had sped impatiently through Togo and Cameroon.

Behind this orgy of treaty-making was the authority of some of the world's most powerful governments. What distinguished Carl Peters – like Brazza – was his own astonishing cheek. When Peters reached Zanzibar Berlin had warned him by cable that his treaties would not be recognized. Peters turned a Nelson eye to the cable, took a dhow to the mainland, then raced off cheerfully to found a new German empire.

Later, he liked to relate the breathtaking Gothic tale of how close he came to disaster. After signing a treaty with the 'Sultan' of Usabara (actually a local chief) and hoisting the black cross of Germany, he decided that they were now so short of food that he would have to make a forced march back to the coast. Jühlke accompanied him to collect further supplies while Pfeil and some of the Africans stayed to begin the work of building a headquarters for the new colony. Both Peters and Jühlke were so ill that they had to be carried in hammocks, their heads exposed to the sun, their bodies lacerated by thorns and attacked by bloodthirsty insects. Each morning before dawn, with drawn revolvers, the Germans had to force their porters to begin work. For much of the time Peters was delirious with fever and tormented by wild dreams. He now depended for food on his Arab interpreter, Ramasan, who fortunately managed to buy some cabbage and turnips at a village beside the caravan track. On 14 December 1884 they had reached a place called Ukari, and Peters felt near the end of his tether:

That evening I had a pulse rate of 140, and I saw that I might die that night. I now made arrangements for this eventuality. I forbade Jühlke, who was sadly and anxiously holding my hand, to bury my body in Ukari. He was to make a dash, without stopping, down to the coast. If he, too, died, Ramasan was to take the treaties down with him.

Somehow they kept going, 'gloomy, downcast, almost apathetic towards each other'.[15] On 17 December, soon after sunset, Peters staggered into the mission church run by a German order of monks at the palm-fringed town of Bagamoyo, on the coast opposite Zanzibar.

From the porch beckoned the cross of Christ: a symbol that we were back in the cultural world of Europe. And as we entered the building, then suddenly the brightly-lit Gothic windows blazed out to meet us, and out boomed the thunder of the organ! I cannot describe the impression this made on me; but I am not ashamed to say that I broke down in convulsive sobs and all the tensions of the last weeks dissolved in a stream of tears.[16]

Back in Berlin on 5 February 1885, shortly before the successful conclusion of the West Africa Conference, Peters waited on tenterhooks to see how Bismarck would take this story. It was pitched at the right level – convulsive sobs and all – to appeal to the romantic streak in the great man. However, Peters had been warned by Kusserow, Bismarck's soon-to-be-deposed expert on colonial affairs, to expect a rebuff from the chief. For one thing, the German election was now over, and the honeymoon with France as well. Mischief apart, Bismarck no longer had reason to pick a quarrel with England. Indeed, ever since November when he had squeezed that major concession out of England at the conference – recognition of Leopold's flag in the Congo – he had every reason to accommodate the English. To this, coached by Kusserow, Peters had his answer. He would appeal to Bismarck's well-known appetite for a bargain. Backed by the right sort of German capitalists, the new protectorate in East Africa would not cost the Germany Treasury a single mark. Diplomatically, too, like Tunis, it was one of those ripe 'pears' that costs nothing to pick. What with the Mahdi descending on Khartoum and the Russians lunging on Afghanistan, England was in no position to tell Germany to keep out of her orchard. Of course nothing could be done, Kusserow had to admit, if the Chancellor had no more stomach for colonies. Peters agreed. Nothing, except – and here was the temptation, a cock to crow for him as for his sacred namesake – to offer his new colony to King Leopold.

In the event, Peters had no temptation to resist. Bismarck was impressed by his story. The charter for his East African protectorate, given him in the name of the Emperor, was signed in Berlin on 17 February 1885 and kept secret till after the end of the West Africa Conference. As mentioned earlier, it covered four undefined regions opposite Zanzibar. For Peters, of course, this was only a beginning. He could see clearly enough that the whole empire of Zanzibar – islands and mainland as far as Lake Tanganyika – was now fair game for the Scramble. Why should Germany not grab the lot? And why not take all East Africa up to Lake Nyasa as well? Kusserow and other supporters at the German Foreign Office urged him to be sensible. There were certain awkward facts. His own company, the GDK, was virtually broke; and the British seemed determined to press the Sultan's claims in order to strengthen their own grip on the region.

Peters's reply was to create facts of his own that would force a showdown with both the Sultan and his backers. He recruited a handful of daredevils to join Jühlke and Pfeil in order to push out the frontiers of the new colony as fast as possible: army officers, an architect, a horticultural engineer and other technical experts. To each party he had given the same provocative orders: let the mark of the expedition be '*schnelles, kühnes, rucksichtloses*' ('fast, daring, and ruthless').[17] Take new territory by agreement with the Sultan in Zanzibar – if he agrees. If not, grab it. Then hoist the German flag and proclaim the Emperor's charter.

Peters's provocative orders seemed to work well enough. By July he received cables from Zanzibar to say that his men had extended the frontier for hundreds of miles on either side of the original four districts: as far as the Rufiji river south of Dar-es-Salaam, and as far as Witu, on the coast near Lamu, to the north. The latter acquisition was all the easier because Simba, the 'Lion of Witu', had for some years defied the authority of the Sultan of Zanzibar.

The Sultan reacted exactly as might have been expected. He sent his protest to the German Emperor that arrived in Berlin in May. Then he launched the two counter-expeditions, under General Matthews, to Kilimanjaro and Witu. No doubt Peters had calculated that, with any luck, there would soon be some ugly clash between the Sultan's sizeable army and the heroic little band of German explorers. In the hullabaloo in Berlin that would follow, Bismarck would have no choice but to take some very firm measures indeed – fast and daring, and ruthless towards the British.

What Peters had in mind emerged when he was called to the Chancellor's office at the end of May. 'It was an astonishing sensation', wrote Peters later, 'to feel those great penetrating eyes of the Iron Chancellor turned on me. His gaze seemed to plumb the depths of my soul and read my innermost thoughts.'[18] He was told to help Kusserow draft a reply to the Sultan's protest. Before he left the room, the Chancellor tossed him a question: 'What can we do then against Zanzibar?' Peters explained that the Sultan's palace faced a shimmering lagoon where warships of the Imperial German fleet could anchor whenever they chose. The Sultan could hardly be keen to have his home brought crashing down about his ears.

Bismarck nodded. The reply to Barghash's protest proved to be an ultimatum. Either he must withdraw his 'unseemly' protest and recognize the Emperor's authority or he must face the consequences.

On 7 August the people of Zanzibar were astounded to see a squadron of five German warships, including the *Stosch, Gneisenau* and *Prinz Adalbert*, steam into the lagoon and run out their guns opposite the Sultan's palace. They were still more amazed to learn the identity of one of the passengers.

Twelve years before, one of the Sultan's sisters had had a reckless love affair with a German trader called Reute. She became pregnant. Under Islamic law, both lovers were liable to be stoned to death, but they were lucky. A chivalrous British officer spirited the Princess away to Aden and she married her lover before the baby was born. At the time, the affair had threatened to cause an international incident. It soon blew over. The Sultan simply forbade his sister ever again to set foot in his kingdom.

Now it turned out that the German squadron had brought the Princess (alias Frau Emily Reute) back to challenge her brother's authority. Perhaps it was simply a crude attempt to bait the Sultan. He might lose his head and try to seize – and punish – his sister. But others ascribed a more subtle intention to the Germans. The British Vice-Consul, Kirk's assistant, was convinced that the Germans planned to replace the Sultan with his young half-German nephew, Emily Reute's twelve-year-old son.

*   *   *

At the Foreign Office in London the mood in August 1885 was calmer than in Kirk's agency facing the lagoon in Zanzibar. In the two months since he had taken over the Foreign Office from Granville, Salisbury had brought his cool, sardonic mind to bear on the antics of Carl Peters. Perhaps Gladstone would let this adventurer walk off with the whole mainland of East Africa. That was not Salisbury's intention. Nor was it the advice of the African expert at the Foreign Office, Sir Percy Anderson. Carl Peters had effectively forced them to adopt a forward policy. What a relief it must have been for Anderson, after all those years of muddle under Granville, to have a chief who, once his scepticism was overcome, gave him unequivocal support.

Anderson explained to Salisbury that Kirk's ideas were impractical. Salisbury agreed. The two men then settled on a plan to cut short Carl Peters's antics. They would partition the mainland between Britain and Germany. The lines of the two 'spheres of interest' (the stage before formal protectorates) would be drawn by a joint boundary commission already offered by Germany. This was the answer to the diplomatic puzzle of how to identify priorities and decide what was expendable. It was the Sultan who was expendable. Even inside this new German 'sphere' – south of the new boundary line – Anderson was convinced that neither British humanitarian nor British trading interests would suffer. If the protectorate prospered, it would help open up the interior to the '3 Cs', as Livingstone had hoped; the Germans would put down the slave trade. At the same time it would open up the country to British goods, as the Germans could be relied on to respect the rights of free trade, now confirmed in the region by the Berlin Act. If the present protectorate failed (which was more likely than not, given Carl Peters's half-baked ideas), then no harm would be done. Either way, Anderson was disputing Kirk's claim that this new arrangement would damage the interests of the British Indian traders who controlled all the trade between the mainland and Zanzibar itself. The only loser would be the Sultan.

But the main thrust of Anderson's argument was that traders from Britain, not traders from India, should be surging forward to open up East Africa. There would be a new British colony or protectorate there, once the boundary commission had reported to London and Berlin. This colony cried out for the resources and daring of some great British capitalist, a man eager to do there what Sir George Goldie was doing on the Niger. Weak-kneed as he was, Sir William Mackinnon seemed the only great capitalist available, so Mackinnon

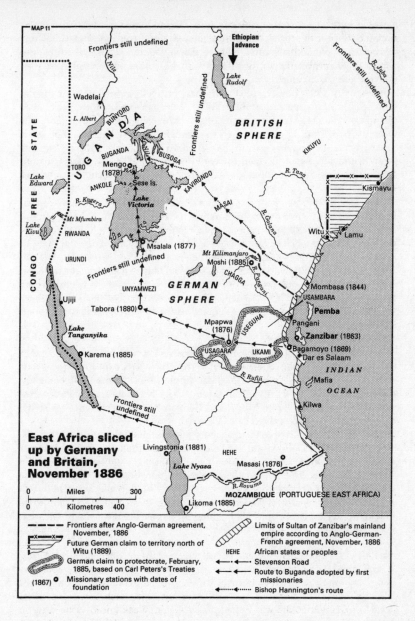

MAP 11

Ethiopian advance

Frontiers still undefined

R. Nile

Frontiers still undefined

R. Juba

Frontiers still undefined

Lake Rudolf

BRITISH SPHERE

KIKUYU

Wadelai

L. Albert

BUNYORO

U G A N D A

BUSOGA

R. Tana

X—X—X—X

Kismayu

TORO

BUGANDA

Mengo (1878)

Sese is.

KAVIRONDO

MASAI

R. Galana

Witu

Lamu

Lake Edward

ANKOLE

Lake Victoria

Mt Mfumbira

RWANDA

R. Kagera

Lake Kivu

URUNDI

Msalala (1877)

Frontiers still undefined

Mt Kilimanjaro

Moshi (1885)

CHAGGA

R. Pangani

Mombasa (1844)

USAMBARA

CONGO FREE STATE

UNYAMWEZI

GERMAN SPHERE

Pemba

Ujiji

Tabora (1880)

Mpapwa (1876)

USEGUHA

Pangani

Zanzibar (1863)

Lake Tanganyika

USAGARA

UKAMI

Bagamoyo (1869)

Dar es Salaam

Karema (1885)

R. Rufiji

INDIAN OCEAN

Mafia

Frontiers still undefined

Kilwa

East Africa sliced up by Germany and Britain, November 1886

Livingstonia (1881)

HEHE

Masasi (1876)

0 — Miles — 300

0 — Kilometres — 400

Lake Nyasa

R. Rovuma

MOZAMBIQUE (PORTUGUESE EAST AFRICA)

Likoma (1885)

– – – Frontiers after Anglo-German agreement, November, 1886

x—x—x Future German claim to territory north of Witu (1889)

German claim to protectorate, February, 1885, based on Carl Peters's Treaties

(1867) ⊙ Missionary stations with dates of foundation

Limits of Sultan of Zanzibar's mainland empire according to Anglo-German-French agreement, November, 1886

HEHE African states or peoples

◄·–·◄ Stevenson Road

◄—◄ Route to Buganda adopted by first missionaries

◄········ Bishop Hannington's route

it would have to be. In due course a new charter company could be created, similar to the one in process of negotiation by Goldie. From a port at Mombasa, this company would reach out a hand to that El Dorado in Central Africa, the garden of Eden by Lake Victoria. This was the golden future that Anderson sketched out for his chief.

By January 1886, however, Salisbury had gratefully retired at least for the time being, to his country seat at Hatfield. As he had expected, the November election on the new register of voters had restored the Liberals to office, and Queen Victoria had to resign herself to another dose of Gladstone. But when Salisbury handed back his seals to the Queen, he could at any rate take modest pride in the success of his own forward policy in Africa, in contrast to the Liberals' backwards-and-forwards-and-backwards policies that had preceded it.

As Anderson forecast, Kirk was prepared to swallow his pride when ordered. For twenty years he had promised to defend the integrity of the Sultan's empire. In August 1885, he had to explain to the Sultan that half a loaf – half a promise – was better than none. The Sultan signed a letter meekly accepting the German protectorate over part of his empire on the mainland.

For several days Emily Reute could be seen walking up and down the seafront, escorted by German officers. No response came from behind the white shutters in the Sultan's palace. On 24 September, the *Stosch, Gneisenau* and *Prinz Adalbert* hoisted anchor in the lagoon, and vanished into the heat haze beyond the mango trees.

In the short run, Salisbury seemed to have struck a sensible balance, neither risking a collision with Germany – and disastrous repercussions in Egypt – nor submitting to Bismarck's bullying. That autumn of 1885 the joint boundary commission began its work amicably enough. By November 1886, East Africa was to be partitioned into a British and German 'sphere of influence', with the frontier running westwards to Lake Victoria.

But it would soon emerge that Salisbury had been misled by Anderson in one vital respect: Carl Peters could not be dismissed as a buffoon. In his character there was a *rücklosigkeit*, a passion to succeed at all costs, regardless of who stood in his path. That would soon make him notorious. He was hardly the man to help serve Livingstone's great crusade in East Africa. Nor were British trading interests as safe as Anderson supposed. It was Peters's ambition to be first in the race for that tropical El Dorado, the garden of Eden by Lake Victoria.

CHAPTER 17

Cries from the Heart

East Africa and England
25 September 1885–December 1886

'When you see running water you may expect more
to follow ... Better stop it at source.'

Advice to Mwanga, King of Buganda, September 1885

On 25 September 1885 a thirty-six-year-old Scottish missionary presented himself at the tiger-grass gate of the great royal Bugandan enclosure at Mengo. He was short and slight, with a neat brown beard and a pair of sharp blue eyes under his Austrian felt hat; his hands were stained with oil and grease. He was Alexander Mackay, the chief representative of the Church Missionary Society's most daring venture in Africa, the Buganda mission. This was based in a two-storeyed wooden house at Natete, about three miles north-west of the palace, on the edge of the Bugandan capital of Mengo, which straddled for miles the green lumpy hills immediately north of Lake Victoria.

A few days earlier, Mackay and his two fellow missionaries had read alarming news in the mail brought across the lake by the *Mirembe* ('Peace'), the wooden sailing boat he had assembled and built himself. Mackay decided he must be the first to break the news to the young, unpredictable King. Now a series of tiger-grass gates were opened in turn, as scarlet-robed pageboys led him deeper into the great hive of Mengo, past courtyard after courtyard of royal storerooms, audience chambers, parade grounds and execution grounds, till they reached the thatched palace of King Mwanga, the great Kabaka himself.

The mail had included a telegram, dated 17 June, which claimed that the German fleet had been ordered to threaten Zanzibar. A Beluchi trader brought still more alarming news: the Germans had 'eaten'[1] part of the mainland and demanded the port of Bagamoyo from Sayid Barghash. He had refused, so the Germans had declared war. Mackay realized the effect this news would have on the Sultan's jittery subjects who had settled in Buganda, the half-caste Arabs and Swahili who had made Mwanga's barbaric court their base for the caravan trade between Buganda and their original homes on the coast and at Zanzibar. They would now have a new reason to vilify the European mission.

It was ten years since Mackay had first read Stanley's challenge to Christendom, sent from the suffering heart of Africa and published in the *Daily Telegraph*. The King of Buganda, Stanley had said, invited a Christian mission to his court. It was now seven years since Mackay had struggled up the fearful, fever-ridden, eight-hundred-mile caravan track from the coast to the Great Lake in 1878, eager to be the first to sow the good seed in this fertile red soil.

Ever since his arrival, the Arabs had been a thorn in his flesh, for he threatened their most lucrative trade, imported guns and gunpowder in exchange for slaves from Buganda's neighbours in the region, Uganda. For years the Arabs had tried to blacken his name in the eyes of Buganda and its rulers. They had warned King Mtesa, Mwanga's father and predecessor, that the *Bazungu*, the Europeans, had come to eat the country. 'Let the *Bazungu* alone,' came Mtesa's reply. They 'will not begin at the interior to eat the land; when I see them beginning at the coast, then I shall believe'.[2] Now, with the Germans nibbling at the east coast, with the Belgians pushing up from the west, with Emin Pasha perhaps about to come down from the Sudan, and with a wild, weak young Kabaka on the throne of Buganda, there would be no restraining the Arabs. Suspicion among the Baganda (people of Buganda) at Mwanga's court would turn to panic. They knew these *Bazungu*. They were all the same. They had come to eat the King's land.

To make matters worse, Mackay's mail from Zanzibar also included an enthusiastic letter from his Church Missionary Society superior, James Hannington, the first missionary bishop of East Equatorial Africa, and a keen explorer. Hannington proposed to visit the CMS mission in Buganda by striking out to the north-east from Mombasa and taking a short cut through Masai country, and then Busoga. To go that way at any time, Mackay knew, was reckless. At a time like this, with the Scramble surging forward, it was madness. Busoga was called the 'back door' to Buganda, a door kept firmly locked, as it exposed the kingdom on its vulnerable flank. No white man would be allowed to come that way, even supposing that the ferocious Masai let him pass. So Mackay sent an urgent warning to his bishop: avoid Busoga like the plague. Take the conventional southern route by way of Tabora, or panic could grip Buganda, threatening death not only to himself but to the mission at Mengo and its black converts.

How was Mackay to calm the fears of the wayward young Kabaka? Mwanga was only twenty, a large, oafish-looking young man, who laughed too easily and had frequent fits of temper, provoked by smoking hashish. He had inherited none of the acumen and elegance of his remarkable father, Mtesa. Mackay had known him since he was a child and regarded him as dangerously weak and self-indulgent. After his audience that day, 25 September, Mackay scribbled down the tense words of their dialogue:

> 'Will Burghash fight?'
> 'You are king and can best decide the matter.'
> 'I believe he will come to terms without fighting.'
> 'We think you have judged rightly.'

At this, one of Mwanga's ministers disagreed. He was Kibare, who had acted as regent while the Kabaka was away on a provincial tour. He thought Barghash would fight after all:

'What are these Badushi [Germans]? Are they *Bazungu*?'

'Yes, they are *Bazungu*, a very powerful nation. They fought the French not long ago, and beat them, even capturing their king.'

'Which is the stronger, the English or the Germans?'

'The Germans are the stronger, especially by land. The English could not beat them if they went to war.'

'If the English beat them, Burghash need not try.'[3]

Mackay then explained that the Askopu (the bishop) threatened no one. He was an Englishman, not a German, and was coming as 'a chief, not of this world's goods, but of religion'. Mackay asked permission to send the mission's sailing boat, the *Mirembe*, to intercept the bishop at Kavirondo, on the east side of the lake, before he could reach Busoga. Permission was granted and the Kabaka ordered a cow to be given to Mackay as a mark of respect.

The next day Mackay was alarmed to hear through his young Ganda converts that the weak young King had changed his mind. He called a council of ministers. 'All seemed to be of one mind,' Mackay reported later, 'that white men were all one and that we and the bishop were only the forerunners of war. We were only waiting for our head man to come, when we would commence to eat the country.'

One of the chiefs then suggested that they should go and fight the bishop, another that they should kill all the white men. 'When you see running water you may expect more to follow . . . Better stop it at the source.'[4] Everyone agreed that the bishop ought not to be allowed to come to Busoga through the 'back door'. Mwanga trimmed and temporized, finally deciding that the mission boat could collect the bishop at Kavirondo and take him away to the CMS mission station at Msalala, on the south side of the lake, beyond the borders of Buganda, to await the Kabaka's instructions.

It was in a swampy creek at Kagei, near Msalala, that Mackay's fellow CMS missionaries had made their first base eight years earlier, in 1877, when they struggled up from the coast carrying a prefabricated boat called the *Daisy*. Mackay himself had had to retire to Zanzibar, crippled with malaria. When he returned in 1878, one of his companions had died, two had been killed when caught up in a tribal war, and the rest had been invalided home. So he was the only one of the pioneers left to sail the *Daisy* across the vast fickle lake (as stormy, he thought, as the Sea of Galilee) and reach the promised land of Buganda.

What he found there had filled Mackay with a strong mixture of excitement and loathing. Physically Buganda was indeed a kind of paradise, just as Speke, Grant and Stanley had described it. 'The climate is delightful,' wrote Mackay, 'like an ever-English summer.' Food grew so easily in these green, lumpy hills that there seemed no work need be done in the fields. When he felt hungry a man simply cut down a bunch of green plantains or a handful of bananas. Cotton, coffee and tobacco all grew as strong as weeds. Mackay found the ordinary people as delightful as their climate: 'not savages nor even barbarians', but 'far in advance of any race I'd met with or even heard of in Central Africa ... exceedingly neat-handed'.[5]

Mackay rejoiced to be able to sow the good seed in these hearts. His style was a great deal more practical than Livingstone's; he was a missionary, not an explorer. He had taken to heart Stanley's advice that it was not enough to teach God's words. To save Africa, a man must teach God's work too, curing diseases, building houses, showing people how to plough and harvest – in short, turning one's hand to anything, like a sailor.

Mackay was a professional engineer, trained at Edinburgh University and in Germany, and he had a rare gift for improvisation. He designed the mission house at Natete, the only two-storey building in the country. He built a printing press for publishing copies of the Sermon on the Mount and the Gospel of St Luke, which he had translated into Luganda. He installed a forge, a lathe and a miraculous pump that projected water twenty feet into the air. People cried out in astonishment, *'MKay lubare! MKay lubare dala!'* ('Mackay is the great spirit! Mackay is truly the great spirit!'). Mackay explained that he was only a man like themselves and that the pump was no miracle, but only a copper tube that drank water like an elephant's trunk. Converts flocked to his thatched chapel to be baptized, shouting to each other: 'Oh the *Bazungu*, the *Bazungu*! They are the men; they can do everything; the Arabs and the Wangwana [coastal men] don't know anything at all.... But oh, Mackay is clever, clever; the king will get them to carry him here to see this wonderful thing.'[6]

However, Mackay had often found his reception cool enough when he approached the royal enclosure of Mtesa and his court. Part of the trouble was that he was by origin a Calvinist of the Free Church, not broad-church Anglican, like the other two CMS missionaries, Robert Ashe and Philip O'Flaherty. He could not compromise with what he took to be the devil's work. And the devil seemed to have been as active in this region as the local snakes and pythons. Cruelty, slavery, polygamy, witchcraft – there was no end to the loathsome evils that Mackay felt called upon to denounce in public. Naturally this made him powerful enemies.

Witchcraft apart, he found the Muslims as guilty as the pagans. Indeed, these half-breed Arabs had brought a new vice into the country that so revolted Mackay that he could not bear to speak its name, and this unmentionable sin infected the court. (It was sodomy.) His intolerance had thus united his enemies, and even alienated some of the men – fellow Europeans – who should have been his natural allies.

In 1879, a year after Mackay founded the English Protestant mission, there arrived at Mengo three White Fathers, recruited by the leading Catholic crusader in Africa, Cardinal Lavigerie. Their leader was *Père* Lourdel. He had been sent to plant a rival Catholic mission in the same rich, red soil. The irony was devastating to Mackay. Here they were at one of a handful of English missions in the whole continent – outside the lines of stations between here and Zanzibar, there were only three other CMS missions in Africa – and now the French insisted on competing. Not that he had any objection to Frenchmen as such, but Mackay, the Scottish Calvinist, had a personal horror of 'Romanists' which his English colleagues must have found embarrassing:

> Oh that foul leaven of thine which is hypocrisy! [he wrote on his way down to the Mediterranean] 'what is Italy today but what thy corrupt teaching for centuries has made it? What is Spain? What is Ireland? Even in Malta thy vileness is everywhere conspicuous. Beggary, ignorance, blackguardism, crime – these are the characteristic marks, with filth and poverty, too.
>
> We go to plant churches of the living God in Central Africa, but we go sowing the good seed, knowing only too well that thy hand will soon come and sow tares among the wheat. The good meal will soon be leavened by thy stealthy hand, till the whole be one vile mass corrupted by thy Mary worship and thy mass worship.[7]

Small wonder then, that Mackay could barely restrain his sneers when competing to save souls with the White Fathers led by *Père* Lourdel.

Of all the two million Bugandan souls to be saved, the greatest prize was obviously the soul of the Kabaka. He was the only man who could serve as the African Constantine: a Christian Kabaka for a Christian state. From the first, King Mtesa had responded to Mackay's overtures with tantalizing ambiguity. He allowed Mackay to proselytize in the centre of the royal enclosure, preaching one Sunday on the theme of the Prodigal Son to the whole court, with the Katikiro (Mtesa's Prime Minister) translating from Swahili to Luganda. No one tried to stop the royal pages from becoming 'readers' – that is, learning to read Christ's word in his church. But Mtesa could not summon the courage – so it seemed at first to Mackay – to do more than toy with the word of God. He wanted to be Christian, Muslim and pagan all at once, as though Christianity was just another kind of witchcraft and the Good Book simply a new *jembe*, an idol (as most people said at court), or a new charm that was worth putting to the test.

Mackay put his trust in God, but could not hide his disappointment. At Christmas 1879 a famous *lubare*, a witch doctor, was invited to try out his spells in front of the Kabaka. Mackay heard the terrible drumming and the shrieks of the women as the loathsome wizard passed by. He felt Mtesa's soul slipping from his grasp. Then a few days later his hopes revived. Someone said that Mtesa had asked the chiefs, 'Are you not going on with reading? You are only living for this world and trying to amass riches. You had better prepare for the world to come.' At the year's end Mackay wrote cheerfully in his journal, 'The old serpent has tried again to bruise the heel of the seed of promise, but the head of the enemy will soon be destroyed by the power of the Lord our Righteousness.'[8]

The truth was, though Mackay was the last to see it, that he and the King were at cross-purposes. Mackay believed he had received an invitation from the King, by way of Stanley, 'to come and stop with him, and teach his people the knowledge of God'. No, said the King; you were invited to teach us 'how to make powder and guns'.[9] This was a chasm that Mackay's faith in God could not bridge. The Katikiro, the Prime Minister, put it still more strongly: they wanted the Bazungu to bring them 'guns innumerable as grass.'[10] Mackay replied that he had never refused to help them with any practical job and showed his oil-stained hands to prove it. But he would have to return to England if he was not allowed to teach the word of God. He was sharply reminded that he did not have permission to leave the Kabaka's court.

In effect a prisoner, Mackay had still greater disappointments to suffer at the hands of the man he had once admired. Mtesa had a loathsome, incurable disease, and was advised by the witch doctors to resume the practice of *kiwendo* – human sacrifice – to propitiate the gods. Victims taken at random, unsuspecting peasants bringing in plantains to sell in the capital, were bundled off and held in slave-sticks for the night, then publicly butchered in the morning. Sometimes 2,000 people were killed in a single day. Mackay was aghast as he heard the drums of the executioners and the agonizing cries of the men being speared or roasted alive. 'All this merely to gratify the bloodthirstiness of this monster ... this murderous maniac,' he wrote in his journal, 'called by good people in England ... the *humane* king of Uganda [Buganda]'.[11] Now he felt he knew the real Kabaka at last. 'Mtesa is a pagan – a heathen – out and out. All the faculties of lying, low cunning, hatred, pride and conceit, jealousy, cruelty ... combined with extreme vanity ... concentrated in him. All is *self, self, self*. Uganda exists for him alone.'[12]

In 1884 Mtesa died and was succeeded by Mwanga. Once again Mackay's hopes revived. Here was a weak pagan soul who might be recast in God's melting pot. But disillusionment with Mwanga proved even more rapid and painful than with Mtesa. In January 1885 he arrested Mackay and his companions, shortly before they were to board the *Eleanor* for a trip on the lake. They were hustled back under guard to their HQ near Mengo. Mackay was baffled by the incident, as both the King and the Katikiro had authorized the trip. But to have offended the King, whatever the reason, proved to have ghastly consequences. Three of the young boys who worked for the mission, one of them a handsome ten-year-old called Lengalama, were arrested and taken away to a swamp near the town. Despite Mackay's desperate efforts to rescue them, they were slowly burnt alive on a kind of spit, after their arms had first been hacked off by the official executioner. Later Mackay bravely reproached Mwanga with the murders and Mwanga shrugged them off. Apparently the Katikiro had ordered them, jealous of the Mission's ownership of such handsome slaves. But it was well known that the Kabaka had connived in the murders.

Throughout that year, 1885, relations with the Kabaka fluctuated dangerously, and the fate of the mission seemed precarious. At first their friends could only visit them at night because guards were set on their house. Then the guards were removed and 'readers' flocked back to collect the printed sheets issued from Mackay's press. Converts included several wayward princesses, sisters of Mwanga, who were not known for their chastity, a boy admiral called Gabunga, and a chief called Sebwato. There were stories of plots and rebellions. In June

Mwanga appeared anxious to placate the missionaries, and was especially good-humoured when Robert Ashe, one of Mackay's CMS brethren, agreed to take off his clothes and go for a swim in the muddy royal pond behind the royal palace. The King was amazed to find that Ashe could really swim, just as he claimed. (Swimming was considered a miraculous feat in Buganda.) However, in August Mwanga fell into a rage with Mackay when the royal flagstaff, being raised by Mackay's rope, but contrary to Mackay's advice, crashed to the ground and killed a man.

The stage was now set for that enthusiast, Bishop Hannington, to pass through the Masai and emerge from the bush to the east of the lake. After Mackay's audience on 25 September, the King had agreed to allow the *Mirembe* to sail to Kavirondo to intercept the bishop and take him back to Msalala to await instructions. By October, however, there was renewed confusion about what the King had agreed. Then, with a fearful suddenness, the blow fell on Mackay and the other missionaries.

It was just after dawn on Sunday, 25 October, and Mackay was holding a service in the newly-built thatched chapel at Natete. One of their young Christian lads, a royal page, brought the news that the two *Bazungu* along with twenty Wangwana porters from the coast (actually fifty) had been arrested in Busoga.

Another page reported that the *Bazungu* had been put in the stocks by the local chief. The taller of the two *Bazungu* had lost a thumb. Ashe said at once, 'It is the bishop.' He knew that Hannington had lost a thumb years before in a shooting accident. The boy added that the Kabaka and his ministers had already decided to kill the whole party.

Mackay at once dismissed the congregation for their own safety, and he and Ashe hurried off to the palace to try and plead with Mwanga. As they entered the great gate, one of the pages whispered, '*Bagenze kubatta*' ('They have gone to kill them').[13] The Kabaka refused them an audience. The next day, 26 October, they tried again, and were told that they could leave a letter to be translated by the French missionaries. Mackay then had to swallow his pride and beg Father Lourdel to intercede. Lourdel did his best, and the Kabaka promised to send a messenger to arrange for the bishop to be spared. The bishop was to be refused entry. But days passed and Mackay was told by the pages not to believe that he had been spared. The second messenger had been sent to confirm, not to countermand, the orders to kill the bishop.

That same Monday, 26 October 1885, was the fifth day Hannington had spent in prison in Busoga. At first he had been dazed by the shock, and broke down and wept on his bed. He had been half dragged, half carried by men he took to be robbers, his clothes torn to shreds, expecting death at every moment, singing 'Safe in the arms of Jesus' and laughing aloud at the very agony of the situation. Then he was dumped in a verminous black hole of a hut that belonged to the local chief, a man called Lubwa.

After two days the bishop's conditions slightly improved. He was allowed to pitch his tent in the courtyard, and to send a message to Mackay explaining his predicament. The Chief gave him back his Bible, his sketchbook and the small travelling diary, with which he 'amused himself', as he put it. When the Chief's wives came to inspect him, he felt like a 'caged lion in a zoo'. Nothing could rob him of his sense of the absurd – nor, despite his experiences, his hope and trust that he would be allowed to proceed:

> October 26. Limbs and bruises and stiffness better, but I am heavy and sleepy. Was not inclined to get up as usual, and if I mistake not, signs of fever creep over me. Mackay should get my letter today, and sufficient time has passed for the chief to receive an answer to his first message sent before I was seized, the nature of which I know not, probably – White man is stopping here. Shall I send him on? Waiting your Majesty's pleasure. If they do not guess who it is, they will very likely, African fashion, talk about it two or three days first of all, and then send a message back leisurely with Mwanga's permission for me to advance.
>
> About thirty-three more of the chief's wives came and disported themselves with gazing at the prisoner. I was very poorly and utterly disinclined to pay any attention to them, and said in English, 'O ladies, if you knew how ill I feel, you would go.' When my food arrived in the middle of the day I was unable to eat. The first time, I think, since leaving the coast . . .[14]

Three months earlier, Hannington had jauntily led his party of 200 Wangwana porters, a Goan cook and a black deacon, out of the fetid, palm-fringed coast. On their heads the porters carried enough trade goods for six months or more – twenty-four bales of cloth, five loads of wire and twenty-one boxes of beads – as well as the bishop's cot, bath and other luggage.

To look at, Hannington seemed the archetype of the muscular Christian: a tall, lithe, bearded, square-jawed, grey-eyed, passionate Englishman, carrying Bible and elephant gun in the service of the Lord. All his life he had found danger irresistible. His father was a businessman who had retired early and amused himself with yachting. Before Hannington was seven he was an experienced sailor. As a boy he was known for his madcap courage when he rode at fences, and for the reckless skill of his canoeing. As an Oxford undergraduate and theological student, he had fought bare-fisted in the riots between Town and Gown.

Later Hannington threw himself with the same pugnacious enthusiasm into the battle to convert the heathen. One of his closest friends, and his biographer, a clergyman called E. C. Dawson (they had rowed together in St Mary's Hall Eight at Oxford), described Hannington's gusto for African travel: 'Arms swinging, eyes ever on the alert to notice anything new or remarkable – now a snatch of song, again a shout of encouragement – a leap upon some rare flower or insect – the very life and soul of his company; while ever and anon his emphatic voice would be raised in the notes of some old familiar tune, and the wilderness would ring to the sound of a Christian hymn.'[15]

At first there were the troubles that beset every European traveller. Some porters threatened to desert. Others threw themselves down, half-dead with thirst, and had to be driven to the nearest wells. Much of the country they passed through had been depopulated by famine. But Hannington had brought along a newly-ordained black deacon, an ex-slave called William Jones, who worked wonders with the porters. Hannington was full of praise for his clever young companion, and Jones hero-worshipped the bishop. Both men were delighted with the expedition's progress in the first weeks.

Everything pointed to the advantages of the new northern route that they had chosen to pioneer. First, it was north of the boundary expected to divide the German and British 'spheres' in East Africa. Second, it linked the newest mission stations, the ones the bishop had personally set up at Taita and at Moshi, on the flanks of Kilimanjaro, to Mackay's mission in Uganda. Third, it was much shorter and apparently healthier – except for the Masai, who roamed over these dusty plains, raiding caravans and preying on the local tribes like a pack of hungry leopards.

There was only one explorer who had tried this northern route before them. This was Joseph Thomson, a young Scottish explorer sent out by the Royal Geographical Society in 1883. He had made no attempt to enter Buganda, having found the Masai alarming enough. Because of the Masai, Thomson had advised Hannington not to attempt the journey by this route.

Unfortunately, Mackay's latest letter, the one that warned him not to go north because Busoga was the locked 'back door', had never reached Hannington. It was equally unfortunate that the experts in Zanzibar disagreed with Thomson, and were quite unaware of the dangers of trying to enter Busoga. In fact, no one in Zanzibar had the faintest idea that Germany's bullying of the Sultan had sent a wave of panic all the way to the Great Lake, threatening the lives of the missionaries there. Sir John Kirk, the best-informed man in the whole region, favoured Hannington taking the northern route. So did the church authorities, who shared the bishop's ultimate hope of evangelizing the Masai and Kikuyu.

By 18 August 1885, Hannington had reached the edge of the cool green forests where the Kikuyu had their fastness. At first it was impossible to buy food from the terrified natives, so much had they been ill-used by Swahili slave-hunters. But the bishop persevered, boldly waving his umbrella. After a fortnight of frustration and anger, the caravan was stocked up enough to move on.

An alarming encounter with the Masai followed in early September. The bishop's party had failed to build a strong palisade to defend the camp. When they invited the Masai women to bring goods for sale, the Masai menfolk joined them. They were El Moran, young warriors smeared in red mud, carrying huge spears and singing war songs. To allow the bishop's party to pass, they insisted on an enormous *hongo* (toll): forty coils of iron wire, six pieces of calico and forty strings of blue and white beads. After fruitless argument, the bishop had to give them what they demanded. All day the Reverend Jones watched aghast as fresh bands of warriors poured into the camp like hungry wolves. Even the bishop seemed puzzled and confused. 'His tent was stormed by Masai elders,' wrote Jones later, 'who seated themselves on everything. The boys did not know what to do. Nobody dared to tell a Masai to move.... [The bishop's] tent was filled. The chair, the cot, the wash tub, bags, biscuit boxes – all held Masai.' Apart from pilfering anything they could find, the warriors coated the tent with red mud and oil, and ran their filthy fingers over the bishop's hair and beard, murmuring *'Lumuruo kitó!'* ('a very great old man').[16] Nothing, it seemed, would save the caravan from a riot, perhaps even a massacre. But the bishop's good nature and absolute fearlessness had a magical effect on the warriors. By sunset they had all melted away, without a life lost.

By mid-October the caravan had safely passed through Masai country and was approaching the Great Lake. Even now disaster might have been avoided. If Hannington had waited at Kavirondo for Mackay's boat, *Mirembe*, he would probably have avoided arrest. As it was, he left most of the caravan there, putting it under Jones's orders. He was too impatient – too trusting – to wait himself. With a handful of porters, he pushed on to Busoga.

Now, in late October, a prisoner, without any idea why he was being held, Hannington sketched his prison in his sketchbook, read Psalm XXVII ('I had fainted, unless I had believed to see the goodness of the Lord in the land of the living') and tried unsuccessfully to bring himself once again to face being inspected by the Chief's wives.

October 27. Only a few ladies came to see the wild beast today. I felt so low and wretched that I retired within my den, whither they, some of them, followed me; but as it was too dark to see me, and I refused to speak, they soon left.

October 28. Evening; fever passed away.... Word came that Mwanga had sent three soldiers, but what news they bring they will not yet let me know.

October 29. A hyena howled near me last night, smelling a sick man, but I hope it is not to have me yet.[17]

Perhaps the ink was still wet on the page that morning when the bishop received welcome news. He was to leave his prison at last. They took him through the forest to rejoin the porters of his caravan.

The shock of that meeting must have been terrible. The porters were indeed there, but naked and bound in the clearing, like sheep in a pen. The soldiers stood ready with their spears. As they tore the clothes from his back, the bishop managed to shout, 'Tell the King that I am about to die for his people, that I have bought the road to Buganda with my life.'[18] He knelt in prayer. Then a signal gun was fired. With a wild shout the soldiers leapt on the bishop, leapt on the trembling porters, hacking and spearing till the gap in the forest was choked with dead.

It was months before Jones's caravan crept back to the coast. They had waited till December at Kavirondo, hoping against hope that the story of the murders was false. Of the fifty porters, four had returned in safety. At first they were thought to be deserters, but local reports confirmed what they said. Mwanga had ordered the bishop's death.

Jones set off for the coast, carrying a blue pennant (blue is the African colour for mourning) on which ICHABOD was printed in white letters. By the time they staggered down to the coast, the porters were half-naked or dressed in skins. Jones himself was crippled by dysentery and dazed by the disaster. When his battered white helmet appeared in Rabai, he could only repeat wretchedly to his weeping friends, 'It is of the bishop I most think now.'

At first, Hannington's friends were incredulous. For the bishop to die as a result of his contempt of danger did not seem improbable. But to be murdered in cold blood by an African king – there was no precedent for a tragedy of this kind. Casualties in the mission field were heavy, but they were almost always the result of malaria or dysentery. The death of two CMS missionaries, companions of Mackay, killed in tribal fighting in 1878, had been unfortunate exceptions. Now the question echoed and re-echoed around Zanzibar, and was repeated in the cables and letters to England: whatever had possessed Mwanga? Why had he chosen to defy the British with this bloodthirsty act?

Meanwhile, all the missionaries under the shadow of the great straw palace at Mengo – French as well as British – heard the news of the murders and lived in daily fear for their own lives and the lives of the faithful.

Père Lourdel, who was far more tactful than Mackay in handling the Kabaka, was secretly warned that Mackay and the other two Englishmen would be murdered, too. After warning them, he boldly went to the palace to ask Mwanga whether his own life was at stake. The King reassured him, then mournfully added, 'I am the last King of Buganda. The white men will take my country after my death. While I am alive, I know how to stop them. But, after me, there will be an end to the line of the black kings of Buganda.'[19]

At first the King seemed anxious to make up to the French. He was suffering from a minor infection of the eyes and Lourdel was invited to treat him with opium pills. On his second visit to the palace, he found the King all smiles. The King called him 'my father', and made him promise never to leave Buganda. Then he took the priest's hat, put it on his own head, and burst out laughing when he saw how he looked in the mirror. But the next day the King felt sick. Lourdel found the Katikiro in tears, the King himself weeping and groaning, 'like a lost child'.[20] He recovered, but the story went round the court that the white man had tried to poison the Kabaka in revenge for the bishop's murder.

Soon after, *Père* Lourdel was horrified to hear that the chief of the royal pages, a devoted young Catholic called Joseph Mkasa, had been handed over to the executioners. His crimes were that he had fallen foul of the Katikiro for trying to stop fetish worship at court, and he had tried to save Hannington by warning Mackay of the plan to kill the bishop. A few days earlier he had boldly asked the Kabaka, 'Why have you started killing the white men? Mtesa, your father, never killed one of them.' Mkasa was taken away, bound with cords, and slowly burnt alive on a spit. The other pages ran to Lourdel, begging to be baptized before they, too, were treated the same way. Lourdel baptized 134 in all. But he could only teach catechism in secret. He believed that the King, weak though he was, trusted him. But the Katikiro, despite his excellent manners, and his spotless Arab robes, was a 'wild beast' who longed to kill all Christians and drive the white men from the country.

Mackay was told by the Beluchi about the murder of Hannington and all the brethren. On 31 October, he wrote in his journal, 'O night of sorrow! What an unheard of deed of blood!' But why commit this terrible crime? It would have been easy for Mwanga to have ordered the defenceless bishop and his party to be turned back at the frontier. 'Surely if they fear invasion, they must see that by such an act they give the imaginary invaders a *capital* excuse for coming in force ... God knows the cause, and He alone knows what the consequences will be.'[21]

How could they now save themselves from this bloodthirsty monster? Lourdel was not the only person to warn Mackay of the dangers. Several Christians, including one of the Catholic princesses, told him that he should make a gesture of friendship to Mwanga, or it would be thought he was plotting revenge. So Mackay and Ashe had to humiliate themselves by writing to the Kabaka, pleading friendship, and sending bales of presents to both him and the Katikiro.

The sight of these presents only drove Mwanga into a violent passion. Let the *Bazungu* explain themselves! Mackay and Ashe went up to the palace without expecting to return alive. Lourdel interceded for them (though Mackay suspected Lourdel was longing to get rid of the Protestant heretics). Why had they sent the presents? Mackay replied that he only wanted to hear news of their friends in Busoga. Mwanga began to abuse the two men, calling them '*bagwagwa*', low savages. He would kill anyone, even a chief, who came near the mission. As for the *Bazungu*, they would be put in the stocks. Let word of that reach the coast and he would challenge England and all Europe to come and rescue them. What could the white men do to him? How could they come into his country unless they flew in the air?

When the storm had blown itself out, Mackay and Ashe returned to their daily tasks of translating the Gospel of St Matthew into Luganda, printing copies on their press, making a loom and a kind of spinning jenny, and baptizing their lads in secret. Such was the fear of persecution that none of the Baganda dared come to the chapel except at midnight. But the missionaries tried to act as though things were normal. One day Ashe went up to the palace and had an interview with Pokino, the senior minister and formerly a diligent 'reader' at the mission. Ashe boldly warned him that it was vain to profess to fear God and yet carry out robbery and murder. Pokino replied that the Baduchi, the Germans, were people who knew God, yet they came to annex land not their own. 'Do not even English make gunpowder and cannon? Do they do so for the love of God?'[22] Ashe could not find a suitable reply.

Mackay wondered whether they should try to escape by canoe, but after weeks of fearing he would be murdered, he decided to trust to God and stick to his post. He believed Mwanga could not make up his mind whether to defy

Preceding page: 'Brought by faithful hands over land and sea'. Jacob Wainright arriving at Southampton with Dr Livingstone's coffin and trunks, 16 April 1874, on the way to Livingstone's funeral in Westminster Abbey

Above: Susi (centre) and Chuma (right), dressed in blue reefer jackets given them by British admirers, show Livingstone's diaries to his children and to Horace Waller (far right), at Newstead Abbey, June 1874

Opposite: To launch his African crusade, King Leopold presented this gilt-framed portrait of himself to his guests in Brussels, 12-14 September 1876

OFFERT
PAR LE ROI
A
SIR HARRY
VERNEY BART

SOUVENIR
DE LA
CONFÉRENCE GÉOGRAPHIQUE
DE BRUXELLES
12-14 SEPT
1876

(*Top left*): 'Twitters', Lord Carnarvon,
the Colonial Secretary with a
master-plan for Africa. (*Top right*):
Sir Bartle Frere, High Commissioner
at the Cape. He was surprised to hear
of the annexation of the Transvaal.
(*Bottom left*): Paul Kruger, leader of the
Boers who defied the British.
(*Bottom right*): Piet Joubert, Boer
commander in chief at Majuba

Opposite: Cetshwayo, King of the Zulus,
in exile after the Battle of Ulundi in 1879

Opposite: A day to remember: Majuba Hill, 27 February 1881

Above: Hoisting the tricolour at Tunis, May 1881. (*Inset*): The unfortunate Bey, Muhammad-es-Sadok

Following page: Alexandria after the naval bombardment, July 1882: Arabi's smashed guns and dead gunners. (*Inset*): Arabi awaiting trial

First page of section: Brazza, entertained at the court of King Makoko, before signing the treaty, 10 September 1880

Opposite: Congo rivals in 1882: Brazza (*top left*), with Jules Ferry (*top right*), versus Stanley (*bottom left*), with King Leopold (*bottom right*)

Above: Ivory traders at Zanzibar in the 1880s. The slave trade suited the ivory trade and both made the fortune of Tippu Tib (*inset*)

Niger rivals in 1883: Sultan Ahmadu (*right*)
and Colonel Borgnis-Desbordes (*below*)

Opposite: Empire-builders of the 1880
George Goldie (*top left*),
Charles Gordon (*centre left*)
and Carl Peters (*bottom left*).
Reluctant imperialists:
Lord Granville (*top right*),
Gladstone (*centre right*)
and Prince Bismarck (*bottom right*)

Lord Wolseley, en route for the Sudan to rescue Gordon, August 1884

Opposite: Wilson's two steamers try to break through to Khartoum, 28 January 1885

A present for Slatin (left), 26 January 1885

the world and kill them, or to hold them as hostages to protect himself from European intervention.

In the long run European intervention seemed the only solution to Mackay. He assumed that the Germans would gradually push up from the coast and eventually make Buganda part of the German Reich. He had no objection. Two years as an engineering student in Berlin had given him great respect for the German people, or at least for the sober, God-fearing Protestants he had met. Or perhaps Buganda would fall to another Power – to Leopold's men, now exploring its western borders, or to the British, ultimately responsible for the Egyptian province of Equatoria. In his heart Mackay had begun to believe that best of all would be a takeover by Britain, the 'one Power which is able to respect the cause of liberty and good government'.[23] Gordon had been one of Mackay's heroes, and he was full of admiration for the way the last of Gordon's band, Emin Pasha, was still apparently holding out in his province of Equatoria. Perhaps Emin would be able to assimilate the two regions, Equatoria and Buganda. Unfortunately, he was afraid that this new British protectorate, once created, would be scuttled by Gladstone if he returned to power. Perhaps Europe should set up Emin as the Governor of a 'Free State' of East Africa and the southern Sudan, on the same idealistic lines as the Congo Free State. However, it was several years since letters had been received from the gallant Emin. Perhaps he had already succumbed to the Mahdi.

In February 1886, however, news arrived from the north which gave Mackay new hope for his secret plan to persuade Emin to help redeem Buganda. A long-lost Russian explorer, Dr Junker, sent word from the neighbouring country of Bunyoro that, a few months earlier, he had left Emin alive and well and holding his own in his province. Mackay arranged safe conduct for the Russian as far as Buganda, a difficult task as war had just broken out between that kingdom and Bunyoro. But it seemed to Mackay that Mwanga and his ministers were anxious to help Dr Junker, 'to make up in a measure for the murder of Bishop Hannington and all his people'.[24]

In general, he thought, the King was torn between greed to possess what the white man could bring him and fear of the retribution he so richly deserved. Printing and selling pamphlets of the Gospel went on as before, though more in secret than otherwise. 'The stone rolling noiselessly,'[25] was the way Mackay described it. In March 1886 the missionaries seemed to be returning to favour. At least Philip O'Flaherty, who had been seriously ill, was allowed to leave for Europe, and Mackay was given 10,000 cowries and told he was Mwanga's 'favourite'.

Then, one evening that month, when Mackay and Ashe were at prayers, there was a strange glow in the sky to the south-east. The boys came in shouting, 'Kibuya kiyide!' ('The palace is burning'), followed by 'Mizingu' ('Guns') and 'Bamasa' ('They're fighting').[26] There were dull explosions like the reports of small cannon. It turned out that the Kabaka kept his gunpowder in a straw hut where a fire had been left burning. The royal pages had left their posts in the hut to say their prayers in secret. While they were away, a spark had caught on a cobweb in the straw roof. Soon the whole building was ablaze, and the kegs of gunpowder began to explode. In the high wind the fire soon spread to the rest of the royal enclosure and destroyed most of the King's precious possessions.

Mwanga heard the explosions and ran out waving a naked sword, convinced that rebels had attacked the palace. *Père* Lourdel found him running for his life. When the Katikiro gave him sanctuary, the latter's store house was struck by lightning. None of this, of course, sweetened Mwanga's temper. He claimed he had been bewitched by the *Bazungu*. Others told Mackay that the *Bazungu* had set fire to the palace 'so that the king might have no powder to face the white enemy' whom the *Bazungu* 'were bringing to eat the country'.[27]

A week or two later the army returned to the capital from the campaign in Bunyoro, the kingdom of their neighbour and rival, Kabarega. Ashe was assured that they had burnt Kabarega's capital, but it turned out that the Baganda had been badly beaten, their commander-in-chief killed, and many with him. There were rumours that Dr Junker was dead, too. By mid-May there were ominous signs of a new explosion of rage against the white men and their alien god.

Then, just as the volcano burst, Dr Junker, the long-lost Russian explorer and Emin's emissary, strode into the two-storeyed mission house at Natete. Mackay gave him a passionate appeal for help, to be sent to London. 'Can nothing be done to waken our Christian land from its lethargy regarding the suffering and dreadful wrongs endured by our helpless fellow-Christians in Africa? Will you all allow them to continue to be murdered and tortured and hunted for their lives, for decades of years, merely because ... it will cost a little diplomacy, a little effort, and perhaps a little expense to secure to them the bare rights due to humanity?'[28] By mid-July Dr Junker somehow had managed to slip way across the lake and join a caravan for the coast. He was now the bearer of a double SOS: from Emin, stuck at Wadelai in Equatoria, and threatened by the Mahdi, and from Mackay and the other Europeans, stuck at Mengo and threatened by Mwanga.

*　　　*　　　*

The first news of Junker's double SOS was cabled to the Foreign Office in London on 23 September 1886:

> News from Uganda, 12 July ... Missionaries in extreme danger; [Junker] urgently requests our demanding from king their being allowed to withdraw. Emin at Wadelai holds province, but urgently needs ammunition and stores. Objects, if he can avoid it, deserting the 4,000 loyal Egyptian subjects there. No time to be lost if assistance decided on.[29]

This cable was sent by Frederick Holmwood, acting Consul at Zanzibar, in the absence of Sir John Kirk. Holmwood then put foward a scheme for double relief. If the government agreed to relieve Emin, thus avoiding another disaster like the fall of Khartoum, 'this would be a good opportunity for dealing at the same time with Uganda, the infamous conduct of whose King has for many years been prejudicial to the development of the interior.... Were Uganda freed from this tyrant, [Emin's] Equatorial Province would be within eight weeks post of Zanzibar and a safe depot ... for the retention of the upper Nile....'[30] In short, Holmwood was proposing a military expedition to carve out a huge new protectorate straddling East and Central Africa.

Holmwood's ideas were received with gasps at the Foreign Office. The African experts were amazed to hear that Emin was still alive and well – and no less amazed by this sudden proposal to extend the British Empire 800 miles from the Indian Ocean to the upper Nile. Was it either desirable or practicable? 'Madness', was the general view, shared by Lord Wolseley, when asked if Holmwood's 'five hundred seasoned Egyptian troops' would provide the 'overwhelming force'[31] capable of dealing with King Mwanga. By mid-October 1886, Holmwood's double relief scheme, annotated with sarcastic comments from the mandarins in the Foreign Office and War Office, was ready to be forwarded to the Prime Minister, Lord Salisbury, for the expected *coup de grâce*.

That week Lord Salisbury was visiting the Queen at Balmoral and he had things other than Africa on his mind. The last twelve months had brought a dramatic ebb and flow in his own fortunes. The year 1886 was proving to be the year when a tidal wave from Ireland swamped British politics and split the Liberal party in two. As we have seen, the general election of 1885 had brought down Salisbury's caretaker administration. He had resigned in January and Gladstone had resumed office. But Parnell and the Irish Nationalists, baying for Home Rule, held the balance in Parliament. To give them what they demanded and rid himself of the anti-Home Rulers in his own party, now became Gladstone's daring objective. However, Gladstone had miscalculated. Most of the Whigs, led by Lord Hartington, and some of the Radicals, led by Joe Chamberlain, defied the Liberal whip. When the vote on the Home Rule Bill was taken on 7 June 1886, ninety-three Liberals voted against the government. The government was in a minority of thirty. Parliament was dissolved and the general election of June–July gave the Conservatives an overall majority of forty. On 28 July 1886, six months after he had returned his seals to the Queen, Lord Salisbury took the train back to Windsor to kiss hands as Prime Minister once again.

In the interval nothing had occurred to excite Salisbury's appetite for risking taxpayers' money in Africa. But he had a high opinion of Sir Percy Anderson, the FO's chief African expert.

At first Anderson was unenthusiastic about Holmwood's scheme. In mid-October he explained that double relief – of both Emin Pasha and the missionaries – was impractical. Instead, the Foreign Office tried a half-hearted attempt at diplomacy. A letter was sent to King Mwanga asking him to have the grace to let the missionaries withdraw. Unfortunately, the despatch of the letter was entrusted to the leader of the Arab slave traders, who was Mackay's *bête noire* and notoriously anti-British. As regards Emin, however, Anderson warned the Prime Minister that there 'may be a strong feeling in favour of saving this able and gallant man [Emin] and the last of the Egyptian garrisons'.[32] Salisbury was not impressed. The government could not risk anyone's life in trying to rescue Emin; they might have to 'rescue or avenge him'. Salisbury concluded briskly: 'I think the Germans should be placed in possession of our information. It is really their business, if Emin is a German.'[33]

The idea of offering Emin to the Germans – and giving them Central Africa on a plate – appalled one of Anderson's senior colleagues, Sir John Kirk, recalled to London for consultations with the Foreign Office.

In the last eighteen months, Kirk had run an emotional steeplechase: from despair, that his life's work was being cast away, to relief that so much could still be saved. Now they must seize their chance. The situation had changed again in the last few days. For one thing, the FO had just heard from Mackay that Emin did not want to be rescued. He wanted to be resupplied so that he could establish Equatoria as a British protectorate. The second development was the new Anglo-German boundary agreement for East Africa. This was signed that week, on 30 October, and was, Kirk apparently recognized, the best that could be hoped for. The British generously allowed the Germans to grab the whole southern half of the Sultan's empire on the mainland, from the 'river Umba Wanga' to the Portuguese border. The British grabbed for themselves the northern half as far as Somaliland. Inland, the new boundary went slicing across Masai country to the eastern shore of Lake Victoria. On paper it looked a fair split – if the Sultan's interests were ignored. In practice the British had given themselves the better port (Mombasa rather than Dar-es-Salaam) and the larger area of fertile and healthy highlands (centred on Mount Kenya rather than on Kilimanjaro). But the most interesting question was not covered by the agreement at all. Who was to have that delectable plum, Uganda? Kirk was terrified that Uganda would be the next prize of that 'unscrupulous adventurer',[34] Carl Peters.

Ten days after the Prime Minister had rejected the idea of a government-sponsored expedition to relieve Emin, on 30 October, Kirk wrote to his friend, the Scottish tycoon Mackinnon, hinting that he should take up the idea himself. In fact, Kirk hoped for a great deal more. For a year Mackinnon had been flirting with the idea of a business concession around Kilimanjaro. Now he should exploit the new boundary agreement and use Emin's 'well governed and quiet' province as the heart of a new British East Africa. Kirk wrote:

> We have Mombasa under the Sultan and a free run inland to the lake [Victoria].... We have the best of any line for rail if ever one is made. We also have the Equatorial Province, now held by the brave Emin Bey, well-governed and quiet to this day.... This is the outline of the scheme and you will see we have an opening as good as any.[35]

Within a week, Kirk was advising Mackinnon who to choose to lead the Emin Pasha relief expedition. It was Stanley. Mackinnon warmed to the idea. So did Percy Anderson, who agreed to try to persuade Lord Salisbury to look favourably on Mackinnon's plan.

Meanwhile, knowing nothing of this private scheme, the humanitarian lobby was straining every nerve to persuade the government to save Emin. The moving spirit was R. W. Felkin, an Edinburgh doctor who had met Emin on his way up the Nile to Uganda in 1878. He wrote letters to *The Scotsman* and stirred up the Scottish Geographical Society. He was assisted by Charles Allen, of the Anti-Slavery Society, and other enthusiasts. They painted a picture of Emin which the Victorian public found irresistible, if somewhat confusing. His past might be 'mysterious' and his character 'enigmatic', but he was the 'noblest' of Gordon's lieutenants. 'Having betrayed the master', wrote one correspondent, 'we might well exert ourselves a little to deliver his man.'

But was this a mission to rescue him – or resupply him? At first the public assumed that, like Gordon, he needed rescue. Then his own published letters proved that all he needed was more supplies and ammunition. His own wish was to be left 'to plant a broad area of civilization in the very heart of Africa'.[36] It was claimed that he had accumulated a huge store of ivory to pay for it.

Within three weeks Mackinnon's scheme was ready to be put to the government. Stanley was delighted to lead the expedition, provided Leopold would release him. But who was to provide the £20,000–30,000 required? Fortunately, Sir Evelyn Baring – effectively British ruler of Egypt – was approached by Schweinfurth, the famous German explorer, who suggested that the Egyptian government put up £10,000 for a German expedition to relieve Emin. Baring agreed to put up the money if it allowed his government to wash their hands of Emin. Baring's offer reached Mackinnon's ears. If he could get this £10,000 Egyptian subsidy for a British expedition, he and his friends agreed to put up the rest. Anderson strongly recommended that the British Cabinet accept. Of course the project was for much more than the relief of Emin. Mackinnon and his friends planned to make treaties with the natives and to found a 'large trading colony', based on Mombasa, stretching all the way to the upper Nile. In due course it would be established by a royal charter. So much was clear. But what part would Emin himself play? Was he to be rescued or reinforced? What was Stanley's role? And how could his obligations to his current employer, King Leopold, be reconciled with Mackinnon's grandiose scheme to extend the British Empire?

None of these thorny questions had been resolved on 3 December 1886, when Lord Salisbury and his Cabinet accepted Anderson's recommendation and gave Mackinnon the go-ahead. They felt it did not concern them. After all, as Anderson said, Stanley would go 'as a private agent of a private Company'. It was nothing like sending Gordon to Khartoum. If Stanley failed to relieve Emin, the British government would not have lost a penny. It was the Egyptian government who would be out of pocket. If Stanley died, there would be 'no more obligation on the British government to avenge him than there is to avenge Bishop Hannington'.[37]

Only one important change was made to the plan for the expedition. As conceived originally by Mackay, adopted by Holmwood and then by Kirk, it was a scheme to open up Central Africa from Mombasa to the upper Nile by way of Uganda. Emin's difficulty was Britain's opportunity. So was Mackay's difficulty. One of the main objects would be the relief of the British missionaries from the tyranny of King Mwanga and the opening up of Uganda to the '3 cs'.

However, it now turned out that Stanley was not prepared to lead the expedition if it was to take the regular Arab trading route from the east coast by way of Uganda. Stanley wanted to break new ground. His employer was King Leopold. The King insisted that it would be a great sacrifice to release Stanley at all. He could only permit it if Stanley took the longer route from the west coast, by way of the Congo. Perhaps he could return by way of East Africa. Mackinnon had no choice but to agree. Leopold had his own reasons, of course, and they would soon become clear.

Within three weeks of the Cabinet go-ahead on 3 December, Stanley had cut short his lecture tour in the United States, rushed back across the Atlantic, consulted the King in Brussels, and started to organize the expedition in London. Another three weeks and he was at Cairo, concerting plans with Baring, on his way to hire porters in Zanzibar. Everyone who met Stanley was swept off their feet by the speed and self-confidence of the great explorer. The change of route attracted little adverse comment, except from Sir John Kirk, who protested in private to Mackinnon. The delay might well give Germany the chance of reaching Uganda first.

It would soon turn out that from every point of view – except Leopold's – the change of route was a change for the worse. No one had ever tried it. It would take months longer to struggle through the Congo rainforests than to stride across the open plains of the east. It would also do nothing to help Mackinnon establish his colony in East Africa and to take Uganda for Britain. As for Mackay and the missionaries, were they to be left forever to the tender mercies of King Mwanga?

That autumn, 1886, the missionary press published a series of astonishing letters from Mackay and Ashe about events in Uganda. In May the long-expected storm had burst over their heads. The origin lay in the 'splendid disobedience' of a young page who had defied the 'negro Nero' and refused to be made the victim of an 'unmentionable abomination'.[38] The lad was a Christian and his disobedience was only punished by beating. But the incident and the refusal of the other pages to be defiled by the King, seemed to have finally unhinged Mwanga. On 25 May, in a paroxysm of rage, he had ordered all Christian 'readers' at court to be seized. Some were castrated, others hacked to death, their bodies left to the vultures. On 3 June, one large group – eleven Protestants and thirteen Catholics – was taken and burnt on a funeral pyre at Namgongo. What was most astonishing about these terrible events, astonishing even to the executioners, was that the young boys died singing and praising the white man's God. Many had been offered freedom if they abjured Christianity. They chose martyrdom.

Livingstone had hardly made a convert in twenty years of wandering through Central Africa. Mackay had made hundreds. Now they were dying for their faith like the early Christians.

But Mackay was still an obscure Scottish missionary. His passionate letters –

desperate appeals to save his converts from persecution – went unreported in the London press. All eyes were now turned towards the swamps of Equatoria where the heroic Emin, Gordon reborn, was said to have built a citadel of freedom and justice.

There were two great anxieties. The British public wondered whether Stanley, whose services had generously been loaned by that philanthropist, the King of the Belgians, would reach Equatoria in time. Or would Emin, too, fall victim to the Mahdi?

Kirk and his friends wondered who would reach Uganda first, Stanley or Carl Peters.

CHAPTER 18

Dr Emin, I Presume?

Brussels, Congo, Equatoria and German East Africa
29 December 1886–January 1890

'It was rather harrowing to read, day by day, in the
British Press that one of Gordon's officers, at the head
of a little army, was in danger of . . . sharing the
remorseless fate which had overtaken the . . . chief
and his garrison at Khartoum.'

Stanley describing his motives for setting out to rescue
Emin Pasha in 1887

Before he left for Africa in late January 1887, Stanley paid two fleeting visits
to Brussels to see his employer, Leopold. The first took place on 29 December
1886, and Stanley found it 'harrowing'.

He strode into the King's room at the palace, unable to conceal his 'hot anger'
at the 'tricks'[1] the King had played on him. For eighteen months he had been
kicking his heels in London, expecting a summons to return to the Congo. In
the last year, his relations with Brussels had become increasingly strained. In
1884–5 he had spent his leave writing a thousand-page history of his labours on
behalf of King Leopold, *The Congo and the Founding of the Free State*. It took
him eighty-nine days to complete this enormous work.

He was not amused when one of the King's secretaries returned the proofs
with a line through some of the more interesting passages, including sharp
words against Belgian officers and certain sovereign governments. These would
only re-open old wounds, the secretary said: 'His Majesty wishes that your book
should be pleasant to all nations.' It turned out not so much pleasant as dull,
the only dull book Stanley ever wrote.

In June 1885 Stanley's leave expired and he was ready to start for Africa at
a moment's notice. His Congo equipment – £500 worth of kit, tent and instruments – stood packed in trunks and boxes in his rooms in New Bond Street.
He had brought a donkey from Cairo and a servant from Zanzibar. But all that
came from Brussels was a series of evasive letters from royal secretaries, and
reports in the press that he had fallen from the King's favour. Finally, he wrote
direct to the King, asking if these reports were true. What had he done to
displease His Majesty?

The King's answer, by way of the Count de Borchgrave, was flattering but
evasive. Stanley should pay no attention to newspapers. 'Just now we find that
[our] interest undoubtedly demands your presence in Europe. We are daily and

actively busy with great difficulties.... We do not, however, lose heart and have firm hope of arriving at a successful result, but when? It would be more than rash to attempt to fix a day.'[2] In September 1885 Stanley was told that the Congo State government was inviting offers for a concession to build the long-awaited and vital railway from the lower Congo to Stanley Pool, to bypass the cataracts. He jumped at the chance of involving a syndicate of English financiers; especially his own friends and the King's admirers, William Mackinnon and James Hutton. But once again he found himself trapped like a fly in a web. Was he to return to the Congo as its Director-General, a position he had been promised as long ago as 1878? Or had he lost the King's confidence? Until the syndicate knew the answer, they would not put up a penny for the vital railway.

Back came an answer from Brussels, as soft as velvet. Perusal of Stanley's letter had produced an impression, 'all the more painful on His Majesty',[3] since he had intended to inform Mr Stanley that he would shortly be invested with the Order of Leopold. His ten-year contract with the King, due to expire in 1888, would be extended for another three years, with a further option until 1895 – provided that Stanley undertook not to publish a word about the Congo without express permission from His Majesty. Stanley, Mackinnon and the other members of the syndicate were all delighted with the new arrangements. They raised £400,000 and had worked away for eight months when suddenly, without warning or explanation, negotiations were broken off. It turned out that the railway concession was to go to a Belgian company. Once again Stanley felt the King's 'cold disapproving silence'[4] settle round him like a fog.

By December 1886, when Stanley received permission to make a short lecture tour in the United States, he could no longer conceal his bitterness towards his employer. What had he done to deserve being kept like a puppet on a string?

There was another and more personal reason for Stanley's bitterness, which had nothing to do with Leopold. One of the mixed blessings of his new life had been the opportunity to enter London Society. Naturally, Stanley was lionized as the greatest African explorer of his age. But in the presence of women he felt absurdly shy and awkward. He longed for marriage, but where would he find the woman he could trust enough to give her his heart? It was ten years since he had been jilted by Alice Pike and still he felt the sting of that wound.

Then, in the summer of 1885, he had been taken to a party given by a thirty-four-year-old Society hostess and amateur painter called Dorothy Tennant. Everyone in London knew Dolly, especially the rich and the famous. She was a tall, gushing, pre-Raphaelite beauty, a column of silk and lace crowned with auburn hair, scented with nectar and ambrosia. She had been the model for Millais's famous picture of a girl writing a letter to reject her suitor, the picture entitled 'No'.

Dolly had swept Stanley off his feet and he found himself courting her like a boy of twenty. He wrote her long, stilted letters from a holiday in Italy. He wished she had been there with him at Pompeii because 'interchange of sentiments regarding the awful calamity would have seemed to have increased one's pleasure and interest in the scene'. They cruised round the Scottish Isles together on William Mackinnon's splendid yacht. Despite the incessant rain, Dolly was in the highest spirits and Stanley's heart pounded like a steam engine. A fortnight later he sent, by special messenger, a formal proposal of marriage. He threw himself at her feet, 'poor, helpless, trembling [so he said in the letter] ... only rich in love of you, filled with admiration for your royal beauty'.[5] Back came the reply of Millais's model, an emphatic 'No!'

The rebuff cut Stanley to the quick. He believed she despised him for his 'base origins' – the bastard from St Asaph's workhouse. 'I have been living in a fool's paradise,' he burst out to William Mackinnon. 'That woman entrapped me with her gush, and her fulsome adulations, her knick-knacks enscribed with a "Remember Me", her sweet scented notes....'[6] She had been toying with him – like Leopold.

Now, when Stanley strode into the King's palace in December 1886, immediately after his return from America, his anger burst like a shell. Why had Leopold treated him like this? 'Well, Mr Stanley,' said the King, smiling apologetically – so benevolent, so fatherly, that Stanley almost felt his anger evaporate and his old hero-worship return, at least while he was in the King's presence:

> I confess it has been hard on you but it could not be helped.... *Haute politique* ... to which we must all bend ... I was as anxious to send you to the Congo as you were to go, but the existence of the State was at Stake....

Stanley, great explorer as he was, had never explored the King's mind very far. He found this talk of *haute politique* 'very mysterious'. Then it came to him; the King must be referring to 'some threat made by the French government, who did not desire my presence on the Congo'.[7] No matter, they could not stop his new mission. But what did the King hope to gain from the new expedition? This became clearer when Stanley made a second visit to the palace, which took place in January 1887. The King insisted on his taking the Congo route to relieve Emin, despite the extra distance. That suited Stanley, who longed to pioneer a new trail across the north-east Congo. The King also gave Stanley two diplomatic tasks to tax his subtlety to the utmost.

The first was to negotiate a deal with Tippu Tip, the Zanzibar ivory merchant and slave trader who had organized Stanley's first expedition to the Congo in 1876. Tippu Tip was now the uncrowned king of the Arabs in Central Africa. He had exploited Stanley's discoveries to build up a great commercial empire, exporting ivory and slaves, and importing cloth and beads into the vast unexplored regions east of Stanley Falls. Relations between the Congo State and these Arabs had taken an ugly turn in 1886. Rashid, Tippu Tip's headstrong young nephew, had attacked the station at Stanley Falls, trying to get his hands on some slave girl who had taken refuge there. He seized control of the Falls after its terrified occupants, including the slave girl, burnt the station and fled.

Leopold recognized that, in the long run, war between the Arabs and the Congo State was inevitable; they were competing for control of the same part of Central Africa, from which was extracted most of the world's supply of ivory, on which the Congo depended for its main income. But the Congo State was not yet rich enough to afford a sizeable war, so someone must patch up a peace. Stanley agreed to try and suggested officially appointing Tippu Tip Governor of the Falls. The boldness of this idea astonished even Leopold. After all, Tippu Tip was a notorious slave dealer, and the political success of the Congo State was built on its reputation for philanthropy. But Stanley persuaded the King that Tippu Tip would behave himself. With a good salary, he would be as good – as gold. The patch-up was essential to Stanley as well as Leopold, for Tippu Tip's control of the porters in the north-east Congo could make or break Stanley's expedition.

Stanley's other diplomatic task was still more delicate. He was to try to persuade Emin Pasha to throw in his lot – and his province of Equatoria – with the Congo Free State. The King was well aware that Stanley, his own employee, also owed loyalty to Mackinnon and his English friends who were putting up half the cost of this new expedition. In fact, Mackinnon was now negotiating with the British government for a royal charter for a protectorate to occupy the new British sphere in East Africa. It did not escape Leopold that Mackinnon might also be fishing for Emin. Equatoria would be a fine catch to add to the new East African protectorate. So it was one more gamble. Could Stanley be trusted to grab Emin for the Congo, and keep him away from Mackinnon?

After Stanley had left, the King resumed his long, lonely walks around the ever-increasing number of glass houses at the royal palace – the Winter Garden, the White Staircase and the Congo greenhouse with the star of the Free State crowning its five domes – an immense corridor of glass which would soon run for a kilometre across the park at Laeken. Over the years he had acquired the finest collection of tropical plants in Europe. How subtle and delicate was their foliage, and how crude by comparison was Stanley, the Breaker of Rocks. The King must have smiled at Stanley's naive questions.

Couldn't Stanley see how close he had come to upsetting the whole Congo apple cart? The French would never forgive the way Stanley had treated Brazza. Nor would the Belgian officers he had ridiculed in his official reports to Brussels. No doubt the King prided himself on his insight into Stanley's character and capacity for hero-worship. A lesser man, a less patient player at this great game, the Scramble for Africa, would have dismissed Stanley, but Leopold had kept him in reserve till exactly the moment when he would prove most useful. And here was the slot, exactly. Mackinnon and his friends (as well as the unfortunate Egyptian taxpayers) would invest in Stanley. Leopold would earn the dividend. Stanley would cut his way through the Congo–Nile watershed, hacking his way through the rainforests till he burst out into the rich green valleys of the equatorial Nile.

The Nile. The very name set Leopold's imagination on fire. It was there, on the river of the Pharaohs, among the pyramids, that he had spent his honeymoon, notebook in hand, asking technical questions about colonial development. A colony on the Nile would be a 'gold mine'.[8] He had said that in 1854, long before Ismael Pasha had indulged his wild dreams of empire. Now Stanley and Emin would go one better and join the Congo to the Nile. That was Leopold's plan – to push his empire right up to the banks of the Nile, and perhaps snatch the whole Sudan from the Dervishes.

The senior members of Leopold's own staff must have shuddered at this talk of the Nile. If the King had already digested the Congo, the plan to take a gulp at the Nile would have looked reckless enough. As matters stood, His Majesty seemed to have the appetite of a greedy child. For the Congo itself had stuck in his gullet. That bonanza of palm oil and ivory, forecast by Cameron and Stanley, had been conspicuously absent. The ivory from Congo elephants went to the Arabs trading with Zanzibar in the east. The Congolese on the upper Congo were too primitive to develop a palm oil trade. As a result the expenditure of the Congo Free State exceeded its income by about ten to one: about two million francs (£80,000) in the first years, soon rising to three million francs (£120,000), and still ten times the income.

Even a great colonial power like Britain would have flinched from this kind of deficit. Indeed, it was the common belief that developing the Congo would not prove a commercial proposition that had given Leopold such a name for philanthropy and restrained his competitors. As a private citizen, philanthropic or not, the King would find it hard to bear the humiliation of bankruptcy. He desperately needed to float loans for development, not only to pay the salaries of his fever-stricken officials, but for roads, hospitals, steamers, harbours, store houses, and all the infrastructure of a new state. But he had still to persuade the Belgian government to advance any money. Despite the King's diplomatic triumph at Berlin in 1884–5, the newly created Congo Free State seemed close to bankruptcy. Stanley had warned everyone from the start that success depended on building a railway to bypass the cataracts. This would slash the costs of both imports and exports and divert the ivory trade away from the Arabs trading with Zanzibar to the Congo's own harbours on the west coast. But so far all Leopold had decided was – to the disappointment of Mackinnon and his friends – that he would give the railway concession to a Belgian company. No one had surveyed the route, let alone raised the money.

Yet that year, 1887, fortune smiled once again on the King's gambles. In February came news from Zanzibar that Stanley had driven a suitably hard bargain with Tippu Tip. He had persuaded the trader to take the post of Governor of Stanley Falls at the salary of a mere £30 a month. In return Tippu Tip formally agreed to give up slave trading, at least below the Falls, and concentrate on 'legitimate private trade' – that is, trading in ivory, cloth, guns, gunpowder. Tippu Tip also promised to supply Stanley with extra porters – Manyema from the Falls district – to carry cases of ammunition to Emin, although the number of porters was not specified. Finally Stanley had persuaded Tippu Tip, with his retinue of ninety-six followers, including his wives and concubines, to brave the ocean and accompany Stanley's party by sea, around the Cape from Zanzibar to the Congo. Thus the new Governor would be in place at Stanley Falls in time to help the great expedition strike out overland through the rainforest.

This was followed by equally encouraging news about the Congo railway.

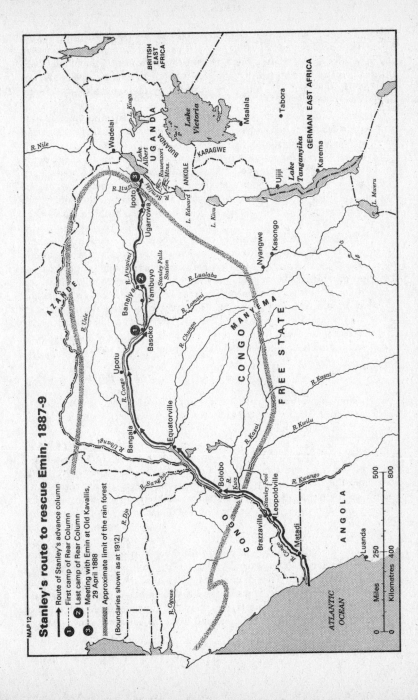

MAP 12

Stanley's route to rescue Emin, 1887-9

➡ Route of Stanley's advance column
① First camp of Rear Column
② Last camp of Rear Column
③ Meeting with Emin at Old Kavallis,
  29 April 1888

⋯⋯ Approximate limit of the rain forest

(Boundaries shown as at 1912)

One of Leopold's junior staff, a thirty-seven-year-old equerry called Captain Albert Thys, was commissioned to survey the railway route past the cataracts, and in May he sailed for the Congo. Despite the fearsome terrain and its fever-stricken climate, he reported that the idea was practicable. By 1888 Thys was back in Brussels, and had started to raise the 25 million francs (£1 million sterling) to build the railway.

However, Leopold's astonishing luck now seemed to evaporate. By the summer of 1888 it was becoming clear in Europe that some kind of disaster had overtaken Stanley's expedition.

News was sketchy, but it was known that on 15 June 1887 his advance column had been dropped by a motley collection of steamers at Yambuya Rapids, 1,000 miles up-river from Stanley Pool. Carrying a steel boat in sections, the advance column had then set off on the 500-mile tramp towards Lake Albert and Equatoria, leaving a second column to bring up the rear with the bulk of the ammunition for Emin.

A year passed, with not a whisper of news about Stanley reaching Europe. Then, in May 1888, a telegram arrived at Mackinnon's London headquarters, addressed to him as chairman of the Emin Pasha Relief Committee. It was from the officer in charge of the rear column, Major Edmund Barttelot, who had been stranded for months at Yambuya. The rear column had suffered appalling casualties from disease and starvation. Now they were asking for instructions. Worse, they believed Stanley was dead. He and the advance column had marched off into the steaming forest the previous June – and vanished. The Ituri rainforest had closed behind them like water closing over the head of a swimmer.

*   *   *

Five hundred miles to the east, on the other side of that vast morass of jungle and forest, Stanley and the survivors of his advance column were slowly recovering from a terrifying ordeal.

They had zigzagged for 160 days through the forest without having seen, as Stanley said, a green field the size of a cottage floor. The only variety was in the height of the trees and the depth of the gloom that hung over everything. Sometimes they followed twisting paths between villages, or the rough trails gouged out by elephants. Often they had to hack out a path with billhooks, dragging the sections of the boat through the tangle of creepers, slipping and sliding through the jungle and the hundreds of brown streams that cut their own way through the forest. They had started 390 strong, most of them well-armed and well-fed, including Stanley, four other European officers – Capt. Robert Nelson, Lieut. Grant Stairs, Dr Thomas Parke and Mounteney Jephson – and a European servant. They carried a Maxim gun to impress the natives. But with every mile the strength of the column was weakened and dissipated. Disease hung over them like a fog: malaria, dysentery and gangrenous ulcers the size of mushrooms that cut flesh to the bone and filled the camp with the stench of rotting flesh.

But starvation was the worst enemy. To buy food of any kind – manioc or plantain or sweet-corn – was usually impossible. They had no cloth to spare for barter, and in any case the natives assumed the worst of them. Stanley's men had to fight them for food, raiding and burning villages along the way, and shooting the natives who tried to resist, as though they themselves were a gang of marauding slave traders. Indeed, it was the Arab raiders they met who identified, as a matter of course, with Stanley's expedition, giving them food and looking after their sick.

On 5 December 1887 the advance column finally broke out of this region of horrors, exhausted and starving, and came to a fertile plateau, high above Lake Albert. But when they reached the south-west corner of the lake, they could find no trace of Emin. Then, on 18 April 1888, came news that brought the Zanzibari porters crowding round Stanley's hut, excitedly shouting *'Burruwah, burruwah'* ('The letter, the letter').[9]

It was a letter from Emin Pasha, dated three weeks earlier, the first con-firmation that he was still holding out against the Mahdists' attack. For a man cut off so long from the world, Emin seemed in surprisingly good shape. He cheerfully offered to fetch Stanley's exhausted party and take them by steamer to his base at Tunguru at the northern end of Lake Albert. 'Be pleased, if this reaches you, to *rest where you are*, and to inform me by letter, or by one of your people, of your wishes. I could easily come ... and my steamer and boats would bring you here.'[10]

Stanley's reply was to send one of his young lieutenants, twenty-eight-year-old Mounteney Jephson, to bring Emin to their aid. The humiliating truth was that he had little to offer Emin in return, only thirteen boxes of ammunition, and little prospect of helping him return to civilization. Most of the loads of ammunition for Emin were stranded at Yambuya. To be rescued by Emin – the man they had themselves travelled 5,000 miles to rescue from the Mahdists – seemed ludicrous. How had Stanley, the most successful explorer of his gener-ation, got himself into this disastrous position?

From the beginning, this expedition had been the most ambitious and ill-organized of Stanley's whole career – a catalogue of confusion, mishaps and mistakes, some of which (much as Stanley hated to admit it) were of his own making.

His first blunder had been to agree to the King's plan for the expedition to take the difficult route through the unexplored forests of the Congo instead of one of the open routes by way of the east coast. The King had promised him a great 'flotilla' of steamers to carry the party as far as Yambuya, where the rapids began, leaving a 'few hundred miles' to be covered on foot or by collapsible boat. But that great flotilla existed only in the King's imagination. Stanley had ruefully discovered what the approaching bankruptcy of the Congo meant in practice. Leopoldville, once the proud capital of the state he had founded, was by 1887 a mere collection of tumble-down huts, and the great harbour at the Pool was overgrown with weeds. So the 'flotilla' consisted of only one large steamer, the *Stanley*, a whale boat and a small steamer, the *En Avant* (without paddles or engine). True, Stanley had managed to commandeer from English and American missionaries two other steamers, the *Peace* and the *Henry Reed*. But there was still not nearly room enough on board for the whole party of 800 men and 1,000 loads. After leaving the advance party at Yambuya, the steamers had returned to Leopoldville for the second load of men and supplies. In the meantime, it was hoped, Tippu Tip would have recruited 600 extra porters at the Falls. So Stanley was faced with a difficult choice. The expedition was divided and it was also short of porters, as a result of his own and Leopold's over-confidence. But should Stanley reunite them as soon as possible by waiting at Yambuya for the rear column – with four officers including Barttelot and a young naturalist, James Jameson – to catch up? Or should he press on with the advance column, taking the best of the porters and the supplies essential for mobility, leaving the rear column – and most of Emin's ammunition – stranded at Yambuya?

With hindsight it appears obvious that Stanley was too impatient. He should have waited at Yambuya. He was not General Wolseley marching up the Nile to rescue Gordon. He was an explorer taking ammunition to resupply Emin, who was not *in extremis* – or rather, there was no reason to think he was. And it was rash to entrust the safety of the rear column to the goodwill of Tippu Tip. Those 600 extra porters were a forlorn hope. As Stanley well knew when he persuaded Tippu Tip to serve as Governor of Stanley Falls, the authorities of the Congo Free State recognized that war with the Arabs was inevitable, but hoped to postpone it for the time being. How much could be expected of Tippu Tip, alienated from his fellow Arabs and yet not trusted by the State authorities?

The authorities had not even kept their part of the bargain with Tippu Tip. In Zanzibar he had promised to provide 'a number of able-bodied men'[11] as porters, recruiting them from the district around the Falls. They were to be armed with their own guns, but the Congo Free State was pledged to supply caps and ammunition. A whole year had passed, leaving the rear column stranded at Yambuya, and still the Congo authorities had not honoured this pledge – nor even bothered to send food to the famished men at Yambuya.

These were the blunders – some the result of Stanley's impatience, others of Leopold's illusions about the Congo, and of the incapacity of the Congo authorities – that had brought the expedition to the edge of disaster. Now they were to be rescued by Emin, Stanley had to face yet another illusion – concerning the character of Emin himself.

Among the few crates of stores the expedition had brought the beleaguered Governor was a box containing a suit of new clothes tailored in London. It was designed for a robust man of about six foot. This was Emin as he had been imagined: tall, masterful, decisive, the last of Gordon's noble lieutenants. The Emin who greeted them, as he was rowed ashore from his steamer on Lake Albert, could hardly have been more different. He was six inches shorter, absurdly short-sighted, with a dark grizzled beard and a pair of spectacles that made him look like an Italian or Spanish professor.

In contrast to Stanley's half-naked followers, Emin and his officers were dressed spotlessly in Egyptian style, with white cotton drill suits and neat red fezzes. There was no sign that they needed help of any kind – except for the ammunition, most of which Stanley had left behind. They had two fine steamers, the *Khedive* and the *Nyanza*, that were beautifully maintained, with fresh white paint and well-polished brasswork, proud relics of the days when Sir Samuel Baker had governed the Sudan. The steamers, brought above the rapids by Gordon, were still the key to the administration of this far-flung province. The *Khedive* could make six knots, so it took Emin less than a week to cover half the province – that is, from Nsabe, at the south end of Lake Albert, to Dufile, at the head of the Fola rapids. Altogether there were eight stations still apparently occupied by Emin's troops. To the north of Dufile the position seemed more confused. The Mahdists, in two of Gordon's other old steamers, were advancing up the river. Apparently Emin could not count on the loyalty of his own troops, most of whom were Sudanese.

Materially, Emin was much better off than anyone had imagined. On the other hand, Stanley was shocked by Emin's character. He seemed as evasive as any Oriental, a man who could not make up his mind about anything.

As Emin wriggled under Stanley's questioning, Stanley struggled to nail him down. With the Mahdists advancing from the north, would it not now be sensible for Emin to bend to necessity and withdraw from Equatoria? In Stanley's view, this course had much to recommend it. His nose for a scoop told him that this was the right way to handle a story – to rescue the Pasha just as his enemies were closing in. It was also the advice of the Egyptian government, which was paying half the cost of the expedition. The Khedive had given Stanley a letter to hand Emin, telling him that he and his men were free to stay in Equatoria, but that they did so at their own risk. If they did not seize this chance of withdrawal, the Egyptian government would wash their hands of them.

But Stanley was not free to press this solution on Emin beyond a certain point. He had also to serve two other masters – Mackinnon and Leopold – and to put to Emin their proposals which, he admitted, were 'somewhat conflicting'.

Stanley began by putting Leopold's case. He explained that the King was interested in adding this territory to the Congo and was prepared to employ Emin as the governor of Equatoria at a salary of £1,500 a year. If the province could supply sufficient ivory and other produce, the King could supply £10,000–12,000 for the cost of administration. Emin must also do his best to 'keep open communications'[12] between the Nile and the Congo. That was the proposal, fairly put to Emin, according to Stanley's published account. Emin, however, had a different story. He blurted out later that Stanley had advised him 'instantly to refuse it'.[13] Then Stanley put the case for what he believed would best suit Mackinnon. Emin should take his garrison to the north-east shore of Lake Victoria and take service under the British flag in the new British protectorate of East Africa.

If Emin's version is correct – and he had no reason to lie – Stanley had broken faith with Leopold in order to serve Mackinnon. Why the betrayal? No doubt Leopold's icy silences still rankled. He could not forget the humiliation of being treated like a kept woman, of kicking his heels in London while the foreign press mocked him to his face. But Stanley also had practical reasons for shifting his allegiance to Mackinnon. On his recent trip up the Congo he had seen how near to collapse was the great shambling giant of a state he had founded. It also seemed, in that terrible 160-day march through the Ituri rainforest, absurd to talk of 'keeping open' communications with the Nile.

In contrast, it was in Emin's own interest, as well as Mackinnon's, for the garrison to withdraw to Lake Victoria. Once there, they could be resupplied from Zanzibar. There was another reason, romantic and sentimental perhaps, for Stanley to throw in his lot with Mackinnon. Outwardly Stanley was toughened steel, a ruthless, cynical self-made man of the world. Inside there was a bleeding English heart. His first plan for the Congo – to give it to England – had been rebuffed by his ex-countrymen. Despite this, and his American citizenship, he still longed to be recognized as a patriot. Here was a second chance. He would use Emin to help Mackinnon found a great new colony in East Africa.

As far as Stanley could grasp, Emin seemed attracted by the idea of a tactical retreat, but he would not commit himself until he had sounded out the men in his northern stations. So in May 1888 Stanley and his porters marched out of Emin's camp, having agreed to send his own boat specialist, Mounteney Jephson, to accompany Emin on the voyage to the northern stations. In the meantime he would himself take on the unenviable task of marching back westwards through the rainforest towards Yambuya in order to rescue the rear column. When he returned with it – at best, by about December – Emin would have made a final decision whether to leave or stay. In either case, Stanley's caravan could march back to the east coast by way of Lake Victoria and the borders of Uganda, taking care to give a wide berth to that terror of the missionaries, King Mwanga.

Mounteney Jephson revelled in the cool breeze on his cheek as the *Khedive* steamed rapidly northwards up the blue waters of Lake Albert and into the brown, reedy waters of the Nile. What a relief it was to exchange Stanley's company for Emin's. Jephson was a clergyman's son, trained in the merchant navy, yet something of an aesthete: small and delicate, almost effeminate in appearance, with a scientist's eye for rare plants and butterflies along the trail. He could be hot-tempered when provoked. There had been an appalling row during the trip up the Congo, when Stanley had lost his head and screamed abuse at Jephson and his friend Stairs in front of their own Zanzibaris, telling them to tie up their masters to trees and then insisting that both men were dismissed from the expedition. The row had been patched up, but the wounds had left scars.

Jephson admired what he called the 'European' side of Stanley's character, 'the wonderful powers of resource, the indomitable energy and strength of mind, the dogged determination to carry through to a successful issue all he had taken in hand. . . .' He loathed what he called the 'Arab' side of Stanley, the 'falseness and double-dealing . . . the meanness, brutality and greediness . . .'. There were times when he confided to his diary that Stanley was a monster. 'I do not suppose a more impatient, a more ungentle, a more untruthful man than Stanley could exist. He is most violent in his words and actions, the slightest little thing is sufficient to work him into a frenzy of rage.'

What a contrast between the two leaders. With Stanley, things were done by 'brute force only'.[14] With Emin, 'it is wonderful to hear with what love and affection his own people speak of him, and how they all look up to him and revere him'. Emin put his hand on Jephson's shoulder and talked to him like a father. Jephson dashed off with a butterfly net to capture new specimens for Emin's famous scientific collection destined for the British Museum. It was delightful to serve such a famous collector. 'His face quite lights up with pleasure if one brings him some beetle or bug of an uncommon species!'[15] For his part, Jephson was able to boast of one remarkable geographical discovery he had made. A month earlier he and Dr Parke had discovered an enormous, snow-covered mountain range – the 16,000-foot Ruwenzori mountains, just to the south of Lake Albert. At first Stanley had 'pooh-poohed' the discovery, then characteristically claimed that he had been the first to make it. Emin must have been astonished. He had lived for years in the region, but had never noticed the mountains when the weather was clear, presumably because of his crippling short sight.

For days the idyll continued as the *Khedive* steamed northwards, carrying the enthusiastic young Englishman in a tattered English topee and the bespectacled German scholar, dressed in white robes and red fez. At each station the troops would parade in their white uniforms, with red-coated trumpeters to play the Khedival hymn, a kind of Egyptian national anthem. Jephson would make a speech to the assembled garrison in Swahili, and letters from the Khedive would be read aloud in Arabic. There would be three cheers for the Khedive and cries of 'We will follow our Pasha!'[16]

But gradually it began to dawn on Jephson that these demonstrations of loyalty signified very little. As Emin had warned Stanley, most of the men in the garrisons had taken wives in Equatoria and few of them wished to leave the province for an unknown future in Egypt. Perhaps they would follow the Pasha, perhaps they would not. It depended on which way he tried to lead them.

Emin's own intentions seemed more and more obscure to Jephson the further north they travelled. The *Khedive* was left at Dufile, above the Fola rapids. On 16 July they set off on the seventy-five-mile overland journey to Rejaf, the largest and northernmost of the stations along the river-bank. Emin rode on a donkey, while Jephson preferred to walk. Beside them the Nile, only a hundred yards wide, foamed and tumbled into a narrow red gorge. At one moment an immense herd of two or three hundred elephants appeared, moving parallel through the plain, only a few hundred yards to their left. To Jephson the sight of the huge black bodies and the long white tusks was 'perfectly overpowering'. He was entranced with the scenery, which struck him as 'perfectly beautiful' and 'of a wild parklike description'.[17]

At the first three stations they were received as cordially as before, but at the fourth they heard confirmation of the rumours about the mutiny of the 1st

Battalion based at Rejaf. Emin decided that it was too dangerous to proceed. He ordered the 1st Battalion to come south and make its submission. If it continued to defy him, he would evacuate the loyal stations and follow Stanley. Rejaf would be left to its fate.

The situation remained confused. By early August 1888, Emin had started to evacuate the northern stations that were still loyal: Muggi and Labore. Meanwhile the mutiny had spread southward to Dufile. When Emin and Jephson retreated there on 20 August, they found no soldiers drawn up ready to salute them, only a crowd of onlookers, curious to see what would happen to the Pasha and his friend. Both men were promptly put under house arrest. In due course the mutineers marched down from Rejaf and were received with flags flying and trumpets playing. With great courage, Jephson reproached them for their ill-treatment of Emin, who had looked after them like a father for thirteen years. In turn they reproached their father for threatening to desert them. One of the common soldiers explained how they felt. They knew very well the Khedive's letter was a forgery. 'If it had come from *Effendina* [the Khedive], he would have *commanded* us to come, not have told us we might do as we pleased.'[18] They also knew that there was only one road to Egypt and that it led by the Nile and Khartoum. 'If the Khedive really wanted the people to come, let him send up his steamers and we will go down to Khartoum.'

Were there ever such idiots as these people, wrote Jephson, 'always harping on Khartoum'? In early September he managed to persuade the mutineers to take him to Lake Albert in the *Khedive* so that they could discuss the situation with Stanley. Meanwhile, Emin remained shut up in the governor's house at Dufile. Jephson's heart went out to him, 'with all those semi-savages ... thinking only of what fresh concessions they can wring out of him'.[19] He was coming to despise the Sudanese more and more. Emin had sacrificed himself for these treacherous people, 'throwing away every opportunity of leaving the country and returning to a more congenial life, where he could indulge in the luxury of ... conversing with clever and scientific people'. Were the Sudanese worth saving? 'Are not such men as Gordon and Emin too good for such a useless sacrifice?' However, Jephson was prepared to sacrifice himself for Emin. 'If I left, it would savour too strongly of what Gordon called "ratting out".'

Within a fortnight Jephson was back with Emin shut up in the governor's house at Dufile. All attempts to locate Stanley had failed, and the mutineers had taken over the ammunition brought for Emin. There followed a meeting of the mutineers' council, to which delegates were invited from all over Equatoria. Despite Jephson's eloquent pleading, the council decided to depose the Pasha and send him under arrest to Rejaf. This decision was a shattering blow for both Emin and Jephson. 'If he is taken away to Rejaf,' wrote Jephson, 'I'm afraid Stanley will never be able to extricate him from the country. In case he goes to Rejaf I will go with him, if I am allowed to by the rebels, for I cannot desert him.'[20] He feared that the poor man might be driven to take his own life in the hope that this would induce the rebels to release his daughter, Farida, at present a prisoner with him.

Help now came from the most unlikely quarter, the north. On 15 October 1888 a soldier arrived with the news that three of Gordon's old steamers had just reached Lado, fifteen miles north of Rejaf. They were the *Talahawiyeh*, *Safia* and *Muhammad Ali*. At first the simple people imagined that this was the long-awaited rescue party sent by the Khedive. Then, a couple of days later, Jephson saw three strange-looking emissaries march into Dufile. 'Their white coats are all patched over with black, green and red patches. They all have big rosaries, and a large many-coloured shawl wound round their heads. Each carrying a long sword and three spears. When asked what they came for, they said they came to conduct us by the true path to Heaven and to teach us to pray, as they, the true believers, the true Mussulmen.'[21] Of course the steamers from Khartoum had brought reinforcements to the Dervishes, the Mahdist troops, and soon panic-stricken refugees filled Dufile. Rejaf was stormed by the Dervishes. The result was, predictably, a rally in favour of the Pasha.

One faction wished to reinstate Emin; Jephson did not doubt that. If Emin had been a more masterful character, he would have had the mutineers in his grasp. As usual he dithered, and refused to resume the governorship. He was equally reluctant to abandon his people and retreat to Lake Albert. He was only prepared to retreat as far as Wadelai. The weeks passed as the war in the north ebbed to and fro. Dufile fell to the Mahdist troops – and was then recaptured by the mutineers, who tortured the Dervish emissaries, clubbed them to death, and threw their bodies to the crocodiles. Jephson was sickened – and utterly confused.

Week by week his hero-worship for Emin had been eroded by events. He felt vaguely cheated. Everyone in England had been misled about Emin's situation; both by Robert Felkin, the missionary, and by Junker, the explorer. In reality he did not need to be saved from his enemies but from himself. He had not the strength of character to govern Africans. If only Stanley would return. 'One quite longed to have Stanley here for a few days to reduce the whole people to a state of order ... by his firmness.'[22]

On 7 November 1888 Jephson wrote an SOS to Stanley, to which Emin added a note. It was the kind of desperate plea for help that might have been written from Khartoum four years earlier. 'We are like rats in a trap; they will neither let us act nor retire, and I fear unless you come very soon you will be too late, and our fate will be like that of the rest of the garrisons of the Soudan.'[23]

Yet even if offered the chance of leaving Equatoria, Jephson had no idea whether Emin would agree to take it. He believed that Emin hardly knew himself, so rapidly did he swing from one opinion to another. At times he seemed perfectly sensible; at others, he was a prisoner of his own quixotic idea of honour. His people had betrayed him, but he could not bear it to be said that he had betrayed his people. It needed a man like Stanley to knock some sense into him. But where *was* Stanley? How could a man with 200 porters simply vanish from the face of the earth?

On 17 August, nearly three months earlier, Stanley had been asking precisely the same question about Major Barttelot, James Jameson, and the rear column. His own party was in canoes, approaching Banalya, on the Ituri river, still about ninety miles above Yambuya, when they noticed that a stockade had been built and a red Egyptian flag hoisted above the village. Stanley sprang to his feet and cried (so he said later), 'The Major, boys! Pull away bravely.' They saw a great number of strangers in white robes. 'Whose men are you?' 'We are Stanley's men,' was the reassuring answer in mainland Swahili. They had been sent by Tippu Tip.

Closer to the river-bank, they spotted an Englishman, who proved to be William Bonny, the doctor's assistant hired for the expedition. Stanley pressed Bonny's hand.

'Well, Bonny, how are you? Where is the Major? Sick, I suppose?'
'The Major is dead, sir.'
'Dead? Good God! How dead? Fever?'
'No, sir, he was shot.'
'By whom?'
'By the Manyema – Tippu Tip's people.'
'Good heavens! Well, where is Jameson?'[24]

It turned out that Jameson had gone (he was actually dying of fever that very day at Bangala, hundreds of miles down-river). The other two officers had retired. The rear column was a wreck. Of all the setbacks in Stanley's long career as an explorer, this was the worst. Words failed him – choked him.

It was the most 'deplorable story', he later wrote, 'one of the most remarkable series of derangements that an organized body of men could possibly be plunged into.'[25] At the time he was stupefied by the horror of what he saw and heard. He had left 133 men at Yambuya, with Barttelot and Jameson and their servants, when he had set out the previous June. In August the steamer *Stanley* had made its second journey with men and loads. By then the rear column numbered 271, roughly a third of the expedition, with most of the stores for Emin. There were now only sixty with the column who seemed likely to live. A hundred had died at Yambuya, mostly from starvation, ten men more on the march to Banalya, and forty-five were now on the point of death. The whole camp had the stench of a charnel house.

Stanley was at his worst as he blamed everyone but himself for this disaster. He wrote a furious letter to Jameson (who was dead by this time): 'I cannot make out why the Major, you, Troup, and Ward have been so *demented* ... all of you seem to have acted like madmen.'[26]

The charge was a wild one, even if Major Barttelot had become slightly unhinged by depression and fever. One morning the Manyema carriers, sent at long last by Tippu Tip, had been celebrating a festival. Barttelot was woken by the noise of a woman singing, drum beats and joy-shots fired in the air. He got up in a rage, buckled on his revolver, and was about to strike the woman, when he was shot just below the heart by her husband (who was later executed for murder).

In due course, Stanley was to blame his officers for disobeying his orders to follow him, conveniently forgetting his orders were to wait at Yambuya until the extra carriers were supplied by Tippu Tip. He also accused Tippu Tip of defaulting on the agreement to provide the carriers. In fact, both the officers and Tippu Tip had done their best. As mentioned earlier, the roots of the disaster lay in King Leopold's mistaken choice of the Congo route – for political reasons – and of Stanley's reckless impatience to push ahead, as though Emin were Gordon besieged by the Mahdi.

But Stanley, as well as the rear column, paid the price of these mistakes. Violent recriminations broke out in England. Stanley lashed out in all directions (even playing up the story that Jameson had paid for a girl to be eaten by cannibals so that he could make a drawing of the scene). People shook their heads. Stanley was no gentleman. Ever since that affair when he had shot down the natives at Bumbireh Island in 1875, it had been clear that the fellow did not know how to behave.

Meanwhile, Stanley's talent as a Breaker of Rocks – smashing his way past every obstacle – was to be tested a third time in the swamps of the Ituri. Leading the shattered survivors of the rear column, he marched back the way he had come. The five-hundred-mile journey to Lake Albert became a nightmare. At one point the whole column was on the point of starvation. Stanley sent out a foraging party. A week passed without their return. In the camp, twenty men died of starvation. Stanley later told Parke that he had set out to look for them 'bringing his revolver and a full dose of poison to destroy himself with, in case he could not find them'.[27] He had never been in such a state of despair on any African expedition.

Somehow plantains were found and the expedition staggered on. By 19 December they had reached the banana and corn plantations of Fort Bodo; by 11 January 1889 they had broken out of the terrible gloom of the forest at last, into the open skies of the grassland; by 16 January they were on the high plateau and only a few hours' march from the lake. But on that day, at about 5.0 p.m., Stanley received a new blow like the kick of a horse to his spine.

Two Wahuma messengers arrived with Jephson's SOS, written on 7 November, to which notes and postscripts had been added by him and Emin: they were free, yet prisoners. Stanley was incredulous. He could understand the mutiny by Emin's men, and the attack by the Mahdists, and the anarchy and confusion that had spread across the whole northern part of Equatoria. But he could not understand how it was that Jephson, his most energetic officer, had been robbed of all power of decision, and infected with Emin's fatal fascination for the Sudan, the disease that had destroyed Gordon.

The next day Stanley had recovered sufficiently to write a cold, gruff letter for both Emin and Jephson. He had now brought the second instalment of supplies, another sixty-three cases of Remington ammunition and twenty-six cases of gunpowder. He had kept his word and Emin must now make up his mind once and for all. 'Will you stay here, or accompany me?'[28] If he heard no more, he would leave in twenty days.

To Jephson Stanley added an emotional postscript; almost like one penned by a lover:

> I read your letters half-a-dozen times, & my opinion of you varies with each reading. Sometimes I fancy you are half Mahdist or Arabist, then Eminist.
>
> Don't you be perverse, but obey – and let my order to you be as a frontlet between the eyes, & all, with God's gracious help, will end well....
>
> I could save a dozen Pashas if they were willing to be saved. I would go on my knees & implore the Pasha to be sensible in his own case.... Be kind & good to him for many virtues, but do not you be drawn into that fatal fascination Soudan territory seems to have for all Europeans of late years....
>
> Come, I am ready to lend all my strength and wit to assist him. But this time there must be no hesitation – but a positive Yea or Nay, and home we go.[29]

To Stanley's ill-concealed relief, Jephson obeyed. On 7 February 1889 the young man returned, somewhat sheepishly, to the fold he had left nine months earlier. Stanley received him with a smile; he was forgiven. A week later Emin himself arrived at the camp, bringing his daughter Farida and eight of his trusted officers. The Zanzibaris gave him a rapturous reception, shouting at the tops of their voices. Jephson felt he would like to have 'hugged the dear old Pasha, I was so pleased at getting him once more amongst us'. Emin begged for more time to collect his men from the various stations and Stanley relented by giving him until April.

In the event, the expedition did not set off southwards till 8 May, as Stanley was struck down by a dangerous attack of gastritis. Emin only managed to persuade a miserable rabble to follow him: 190 men (mostly Egyptians), and 380 women and children, many of whom were obviously too weak to survive the journey. Stanley's own force was now reduced by death and desertion to 350, a third of its original size; and the Maxim gun was rusty and battered. To procure extra porters for the refugees' baggage, Stanley took the drastic step of raiding and enslaving neighbouring tribesmen. Jephson was sickened by the barbarous way the natives, mostly women and children, were dragged from their homes. 'Orders are however orders & we must obey them in spite of the heartrending scenes & shameless brutality we see in these raids.'[30]

Equally upsetting to Jephson was the sudden change that came over the dear old Pasha, once he had joined their camp. All his nobility seemed to have evaporated. Here was the man who was supposed to be a champion of the anti-slavery movement, a second Gordon, and yet they heard nothing from his tents but the shrieks of girls and women being beaten. Emin became petulant and spiteful to his rescuers – and he tried to blame Stanley's officers for these raids which were so repugnant to them. Apparently he believed the malicious stories circulating in the camp, and brooded over them, then sent offensive messages to Stanley by way of Jephson. Jephson confided his disgust to his diary. There was a furious row during which Emin shouted to Stanley, 'I think you had better leave me here, I wish you had never come to help me.' Stanley rejoined, 'You are a most thankless & ungrateful man.'[31] Of course Jephson sided with his chief. He felt he had been 'duped' by Emin and the others. They were 'utterly unworthy' of help.

By mid-May 1889, the long ragged column of soldiers, porters, slaves and Egyptian refugees uncoiled across the grassy plateau south-east of Lake Albert. Slowly the huge, spiky snow peaks of the Ruwenzori mountains – soon to be christened the Stanley Range – began to emerge from the mist. Despite all the unpleasantness, Stanley was not unduly upset by Emin's ill-humour. Perhaps his own feeling was a sense of relief.

It was true that he had failed his own employer, King Leopold. He had also failed in the main task for which Mackinnon had commissioned the expedition; to expand the British Empire. They had been told that Emin was a great pro-consul, a man who had created an oasis of civilization in the wilderness and to resupply his 2,000 well-disciplined troops with ammunition was all that was needed. Then Emin would add the plum of Equatoria to Mackinnon's East African colony. Instead they had achieved the opposite. Their arrival had precipitated Emin's downfall, causing a mutiny which had exposed the province to the onslaught of the Madhists.

Viewed as a humanitarian venture, Stanley's expedition had been equally futile. It had cost the lives of more than half the expedition and of hundreds of the Africans they had met on the journey. What had been achieved in return? Emin was being rescued more or less against his will. 'We are bringing a lot of useless, rotten Egyptian clerks, Jews, Greeks and Turks out of the interior,' said Stanley's officers bitterly, 'people who don't so much as thank us for doing so.'[32]

But if Stanley had failed as an imperialist and as a humanitarian, he had not failed as a journalist. He knew his public. He had found Emin, and he was bringing him home. That was even more than he had done for Livingstone. It was the biggest story of his career.

On 4 December 1889, seven months and 1,100 miles from Lake Albert, after a grim struggle through unexplored country round Lake Edward, past the border-land of Buganda, down to the main caravan track south of Lake Victoria and so to the coast – the expedition staggered triumphantly into Bagamoyo. Clean white uniforms had been sent ahead to replace the ragged uniforms of Stanley and his officers. On the previous evening the surviving Zanzibaris had gone wild, shrieking like madmen in the moonlight. Faintly sounding across the thirty-mile-strait came the boom of the evening gun at Zanzibar, the sound of home. Now the expedition was reunited with the Indian Ocean itself, bluer than any African lake, lapping at the familiar sandy beach.

But Bagamoyo itself was hardly recognizable. A neat German colonial town had sprung up among the mud huts and sprawling coconut palms, a town *en fête* to greet them. Palm branches decorated the new houses along the streets, two-storey houses with tin roofs. The German Commissioner for East Africa,

Major von Wissman, rode with Stanley and Emin into the town. A triumphal salute crashed out from the guns of the battery at the fort, echoing across the water to the German warships anchored offshore.

There followed a banquet in the German officers' mess, a long two-storeyed building with a balcony on the first floor, decorated with palm branches and the German eagle. It seemed an astonishingly happy ending to a story of so many trials and disasters. Wissman's chef had worked wonders with local delicacies and champagne flowed like a fountain. Emin was in such high spirits that he was hardly recognizable. To be fêted by his compatriots had transformed him, and he was overwhelmed by a cable of congratulation from Kaiser Wilhelm II, the new German Emperor. He made a speech in his deep, resonant voice, expressing thanks both to the generous people of England and to the Emperor of Germany. Afterwards, he went around the tables, chatting and joking with Dr Parke and the others. From below the balcony came the sound of wild cheers and the beat of drums as the Zanzibari celebrated their homecoming.

Stanley was talking to Wissman about the latest troubles, a revolt by the Arabs, when suddenly a servant boy whispered in his ear that the Pasha had 'fallen down'. It turned out that, peering short-sightedly into the darkness, Emin had fallen from the balcony, crashed through the roof and dropped fourteen feet into the street. He had been rushed unconscious to the hospital, suffering from a suspected fracture of the skull. In fact he was only concussed, but had to spend several weeks in the German hospital at Bagamayo.

This new mishap was only the first of a series of shocks that were to greet Stanley at his moment of triumph. A great change had come over the way Europe regarded imperialism in Africa during the three years that he had been absent. A sudden new Scramble for territory had begun. Partly it was Stanley's own doing. His aim had been to make the search for Emin, like the search for Livingstone, seem to direct a spotlight into the darkness. By now he was only one of a number of European explorers competing for the attention of the public as they raced with their country's flag to the remotest corners of Central Africa.

Mackinnon had despaired of Stanley's helping him to grab new territory between Mombasa and Equatoria. In 1889 he had launched a new expedition in that direction, led by a hunter called Jackson. At the same time Carl Peters, the founder of German East Africa, was on the same track. In 1889 he left the coast with a caravan, heading west. A scramble for Uganda seemed inevitable.

After a few days' rest at Zanzibar, Stanley took ship for Cairo, where he was to write in a mere fifty days a 900-page account of his travels. Emin remained behind in the hospital at Bagamayo and rebuffed Stanley's repeated enquiries about his intentions. Then news came which Stanley had half expected, yet was still hardly able to comprehend, so far did it reduce his achievements to absurdity. Emin sent a message resigning his commission in the Khedive's service; he had decided to join Wissman and take service with his own compatriots. Under the aegis of the new German Emperor, he would return as soon as possible to his old province.

Hundreds of men dead, thousands of pounds spent – the three most wretched years of his life. All that Stanley seemed to have done was to give Emin – and Equatoria – to the Germans on a plate.

CHAPTER 19

Salisbury's Bargain

England, German East Africa and Germany
June 1888–July 1890

> *'L'appétit vient en mangeant.'*
>
> *Lord Salisbury* explaining his African policy to the French
> ambassador in London

It was in the early summer of 1888 – while Stanley was still struggling with the cannibals of the Ituri rainforest – that Lord Salisbury had started to develop a discreet new appetite for Africa. Hitherto his interest in Africa had been largely negative, a policy of calculated concession, a retreat – orderly and dignified perhaps, but no less a retreat – in the face of Bismarck's bullying. Now he decided to give the signal for the advance.

Of course this was only for the small band of the initiated. In public Salisbury remained as alien to enthusiasm as ever. Scepticism about imperial adventures suited the Tories' traditional distaste for government spending and helped to unite them with the Liberal Unionists, the Whigs and Radicals who had left the Liberal Party in 1886; their support was indispensable if the Tories were to stay in power. It also suited Salisbury's own style: the Olympian detachment expressed in his sardonic wit, in his high-domed forehead and short, iron-grey beard, in his long, black, old-fashioned trousers with baggy knees.

No one was more surprised at his chief's secret encouragement than Harry Johnston, Vice-Consul in the Niger delta, and the youngest and most bumptious of the new generation of empire-builders. Back on leave in late June 1888, he was suddenly summoned to that awesome room overlooking St James's Park, Salisbury's command post in the Foreign Office.

For the Foreign Secretary to summon a mere vice-consul, this seemed startling indeed. (Poor Clement Hill, chief clerk in the African department, could not conceal his jealousy. 'I have been in the Foreign Office since 1871 ... and – will you believe me? Lord S. has never once asked to see me and wouldn't know me if we met in the street.'[1]) Salisbury invited Johnston to explain his policy in the Niger delta. Why had he deposed and banished King Ja-Ja, the famous African middleman? The Irish members of the Commons had taken up Ja-Ja's case. Salisbury reluctantly condoned by Johnston's explanation, though later Salisbury released Ja-Ja, for Ja-Ja's crime was simply to challenge the monopoly of the Royal Niger Company. At least Johnston said later that in African affairs he felt he was 'talking to an equal'. The interview was followed by a still more startling invitation. If Johnston cared to catch the train leaving St Pancras at

4.0 p.m. (travelling in the reserved saloon carriage), he could spend the Saturday-to-Monday with the great man and his house party at Hatfield.

Oh, the agonies, Johnston blurted out later (in *The Gay-Dombeys*, an auto-biographical novel, and his autobiography, *The Story of My Life*), oh, the delicious agonies of that first weekend in high society. Johnston had strong views on how to slice up the African cake. He was also a precocious young man of the world: explorer, diplomatist, writer, botanist, ornithologist, zoologist, painter and ethnologist. But he was unmistakably middle-class, an old boy of Stockwell Grammar School. Aged thirty, he looked like a child, a strange *enfant terrible* of five foot three inches, with a voice that hardly seemed to have broken. No wonder he felt out of his depth at first, more at home among the cannibals of West Africa than in the rarefied air of the reserved saloon carriage from St Pancras, where his fellow travellers' raised eye-glasses were more alarming than blowpipes. But once the landau reached Hatfield, he was taken under the wing of 'Pooey', Lady Salisbury's plump, elderly sister, and soon he was playing charades as though born to the purple. He acted a Moorish slave dealer in charge of a crew of large, unwieldy female slaves. Later he played a piece of a whale. Lady Gwendolen Cecil, the Prime Minister's unmarried daughter and future biographer, wore a huge moustache and played Lord Randolph Churchill trying to seduce the ladies of Johnston's harem. Pooey's blood-curdling screams delighted everyone. When he took his candle up to bed that night Johnston could claim blood brotherhood in a new and powerful tribe.

The next day after lunch the chief himself invited Johnston to accompany him for a walk down the great avenue of beeches that led towards the village. Salisbury was in high spirits and told some excellent stories, according to *The Gay-Dombeys*, about Disraeli and peacocks:

And now [said Lord Wiltshire, alias Lord Salisbury] that I am tolerably out of hearing of my excellent tenantry ... now let us settle the fate of the Niger. It is, I may observe, a curious anomaly that the future weal or woe of millions of black and brown people ... is being determined in a Hertfordshire beech avenue in latitude 51° something, North, where there hasn't been a ghost of a palm for – what shall we say? You evolutionists are so liberal in this – two million years. I suppose it is all due in some way to the Glacial periods which made us what we are, able to lay down the law to the coloured peoples who kept snug in the tropics while we were battling against the cold. And now to business. We've settled – more or less – our frontiers with the Cameroons, and as regards the French.[2]

In Johnston's whimsical novel, Lord Wiltshire went on to settle the fate of Africa with young Eustace in a Hertfordshire beech avenue in latitude 51° something, North. In Johnston's autobiography Lord Salisbury did precisely the same with young Harry. He 'unrolled his plans' for extending the Empire, generously allotting so much for the French, the Germans and Portuguese. Then they turned back down the avenue, past a young Cecil treating the ladies to a demonstration of how to play the new game of golf, and Johnston 'had a sort of feeling' that the eye of the great man rested for a moment on himself. 'What a pity it is no one could put the whole African question lucidly before the public; in some newspaper article, I mean,'[3] said Lord Salisbury as they tramped back to the house.

A few weeks later, on 22 August 1888, Clement Hill, the chief clerk in the African department of the Foreign Office, was outraged to open *The Times* and read an article entitled 'By An African Explorer'. Someone had leaked Lord Salisbury's secrets. 'Did *you* write this?' he asked Johnston. 'Yes. And I think I may say Lord Salisbury knew of my doing so and did not disapprove.' 'Well: all I can say is, it is a very extraordinary proceeding.'[4]

Extraordinary the ideas certainly were, in every sense. Inspired by Salisbury, *The Times* piece is the clearest sketch we have of Salisbury's positive ideas for Africa. There were two globe-rocking proposals that neatly coincided. The first would soon be famous as 'Cape-to-Cairo': a plan to bridge the 3,000-mile gap between British South Africa and British-controlled Egypt. This would mean taking the Sudan, Equatoria ('Emin's territory', Johnston called it), a corridor west of German East Africa, and then the whole 'vacant' area north of the Transvaal, including 'Zambezia', and the African territories sandwiched between Angola and Mozambique. The second was 'Cairo-to-Old-Calabar' or 'Niger-to-the-Nile':[5] to bridge the gap between North and West Africa by way of Lake Chad, and then to push westwards, up to the line of the upper Niger, nearly to Senegal, taking Dahomey and the Ivory Coast from the French in exchange for Gambia.

How much of this visionary plan was Salisbury's own, how much merely that of his bumptious young Vice-Consul? It is clear from the sheaf of letters that passed between the two men in the next few weeks that Salisbury was genuinely intrigued by the logic of consolidating all British interests in a 'new India' in West Africa. But as a politician he was pessimistic about the chances of success in exchanging territory. In 1876 Lord Carnarvon had proposed to cede Gambia to the French, but it had proved too much for Parliament to stomach. There would be even more parliamentary opposition now, with the Conservatives dependent on the favours of the Liberal Unionists, and the Irish Party hell-bent on obstruction.

On the other hand, the much more radical 'Cape-to-Cairo' idea was not as vulnerable in Parliament, simply because it did not involve an exchange of territory. The plan had far more to commend it in Lord Salisbury's eyes as well. Above all, it fitted his overriding diplomatic aims in Africa. They must protect the Empire by protecting Egypt, which meant extending the Empire 2,000 miles south of the Mediterranean, to the head-waters of the Nile.

Paradoxically, it was Salisbury's rebuff over Egypt in 1887 that explained his growing appetite for Africa in 1888. Until then, he had shared Gladstone's original assumption that the British occupation of Egypt was a temporary expedient. Wolseley and the British army had purged the country of Arabi; in due course Tewfik and the Egyptian ruling class, prodded by Baring, would pull themselves together and resume self-government; British *influence* must be kept predominant, but they must evacuate the troops there as soon as was practical. That was the objective common to most politicians, except for the jingo minority on the right wing of the Tory Party.

By 1887 the Egyptian entanglement was getting worse and Salisbury found British imperialism there 'very inconvenient and somewhat humiliating'.[6] The right of the French to block Egyptian finance still threatened to sabotage the government. Worse, out of spite over Egypt, the French were trying to make it hot for British interests the world over. This in turn gave Bismarck the power of blackmail. He threatened to patch up relations with France and attack Britain in Egypt – unless he was paid his price, which was to force Britain into a 'downright quarrel' with France.

Salisbury loathed being dependent on a man like Bismarck. He also shrank from the crudity of those English jingoes who wanted to keep Egypt simply for the sake of acquiring territory and painting the map red. 'I heartily wish we had never gone into Egypt. Had we not done so, we could snap out fingers at all the world. But the national, or acquisitional feeling has been aroused; it has tasted the fleshpots and it will not let them go ...'.[7] His own plan for extricating himself from Egypt had been cleverly devised to satisfy the French and Germans without falling foul of the English jingoes.

Early in 1887 Sir Henry Drummond Wolff had been sent to negotiate an agreement with Sultan Abdul Hamid at Constantinople, the nominal suzerain (overlord) of Egypt. Britain would agree to withdraw her troops from the country in five years, subject to two main conditions. First, the withdrawal would be postponed if there were internal or external threats to Egypt. Second, if either kind of threat developed later, Britain would reserve the right of re-entry. These terms were predictably welcomed by the Central Powers, Germany, Austria and Italy. Equally predictably, Sultan Abdul Hamid dithered. Salisbury told a Cabinet colleague to control his impatience; to catch a Turk was like fishing for salmon. 'The length of time during which you must play your fish depends on *his* choice, not on yours.'[8] But at long last, Abdul Hamid came flapping into Salisbury's net. If the British agreed to withdraw in three years instead of five, he would put his name to the agreement.

Baring was far from happy with these concessions. As Salisbury himself admitted it would take fifteen years to complete the job of cleaning up Egypt. But Salisbury was prepared to sacrifice 'Egyptian interests' in order to get his hands free of this entanglement. The agreement was signed by the Sultan on 22 May 1887.

Then suddenly a huge hole appeared in Salisbury's salmon net. The French public had succumbed to the rhetoric of an ultra-patriotic War Minister, General Boulanger, and the resulting fever of Boulangism produced a serious attack of anglophobia. France joined with Russia and fired a torpedo smack into the great *seraglio*. They told Abdul Hamid he was abrogating the Treaty of Berlin and signing away the Ottoman empire. If he insisted on ratifying the agreement, they would be forced to invade his territory themselves, the Russians marching into Armenia, the French into Syria. Abdul Hamid was regarded by Lord

Salisbury as 'sickly, sensual' and 'fickle'. He was hardly the man to stand up to such threats. The agreement vanished as suddenly as an unwelcome guest, put in a sack and dropped into the Bosphorus.

If this diplomatic bullying by France and Russia was supposed to frighten Salisbury into surrendering the right of re-entry, it had precisely the opposite effect. 'France is, and must always remain, England's greatest danger,'[9] wrote Salisbury to the Queen. That summer a Cabinet committee reported that the British fleet was too weak to hold its own in the Eastern Mediterranean if the French and Russian iron-clads made a combined attack on them. So it was goodbye to British supremacy at the Straits of Constantinople. This made Salisbury all the more anxious to dig in his toes at the Delta of Egypt.

It was Baring who now put the lid on any further talk of withdrawal. By 1887 he had extracted enough taxes from the unfortunate fellahin to bring the embarrassing series of deficits to an end, deficits which had made British rule so vulnerable to French vetoes and German blackmail. On the other hand, there had been next to no agricultural reform. The price of efficient tax-gathering – in the interest of foreign bond-holders – had thus destroyed any confidence between rulers and ruled. The Pasha class, who collected the taxes, could not survive without British bayonets to protect them. Baring viewed his own collaborators with unconcealed contempt. The Khedive's men were a shifty pack of Orientals, Armenians and Turks, incapable of honest rule and utterly out of sympathy with the Egyptian fellahin. Take away the hand from the puppet and the Khedive could lose his throne tomorrow. Such a despicable governing class posed a double threat to stability. There would come a new Colonel Arabi, beating the nationalist drum. And a jealous European Power such as France would be anxious to exploit the trouble.

There was another reason why Salisbury was persuaded of the unfortunate necessity of keeping Egypt permanently under his thumb. In 1888 a great change had come over the strategic map of north-east Africa. For three years after the killing of Gordon, the capture of Khartoum and the death of the Mahdi, the Khalifa had been busy strengthening his personal power and eliminating that of his rivals among the faithful. Now he was at last ready to carry the black flag of the jihad against the infidel. The British had kept only one of the old garrison towns of the Sudan, at Suakin on the Red Sea. This was to be the first target. Egypt itself was the second. A large Dervish army was being prepared for a direct march on Cairo down the Nile, brushing aside the garrison at Wadi Halfa. The third target was the Christian empire of King Yohannes of Abyssinia.

External aggression of this kind would have certainly made British withdrawal from Cairo impossible, even if Abdul Hamid had plucked up the courage to sign Drummond Wolff's agreement. But it was not the strength of the Khalifa that seemed the worst threat to Egypt. His weakness was still more alarming. If the Khalifa's power collapsed, the vacuum might be filled by France or Italy, each of whom had acquired territory east of Khartoum: the French on the Red Sea at Obock, the Italians on the Red Sea at Massawa, below the mountain fastness of Abyssinia. Moreover it was Baring's *idée fixe* that it would be fatal to allow any European power except Britain to control the basin of the upper Nile. The reason for this belief may seem bizarre today. But in the 1880s it was believed by otherwise sober men that a European power on the upper Nile could divert the Nile away from Egypt and so destroy the country's economy. (In fact the water levels made the idea preposterous.)

Hence, by the summer of 1888 Salisbury and the FO had a completely new strategic imperative. There were two very different conditions for preserving imperial supremacy over the Eastern Mediterranean, the Canal and the sea-lanes to the east. The first was negative: not to disturb Baring and the British army from sitting pretty at Cairo. They would keep the Khedive dancing to their tune, that strange dance of the 'veiled' protectorate in which a flimsy piece of Khedival silk concealed naked English power. The second was extremely positive: to reach out a hand to the equator, grabbing all the territories of the White Nile as far as its source in Lake Victoria – pushing 1,400 miles from the Egyptian frontier to Uganda by way of the Sudan and Equatoria.

As if this was not ambitious enough, in 1888 Salisbury recognized another strategic imperative, symmetrical with the first, on the other side of the same axis. They must also reach out a hand to the equator from the south, since imperial supremacy over the Cape, like imperial supremacy over the Canal, was vital to the protection of the sea-lanes to the east. This was why Simonstown was the largest British naval base outside Britain. But imperial power in southern Africa was under permanent threat. The danger was not only the inherited hostility of the Boers in the Transvaal and Orange Free State, but the doubtful loyalty of the British in Natal and the Cape. In 1888 some of these colonials from the Cape, led by an erratic young diamond magnate called Cecil Rhodes, were pressing the British government for permission to push the power of Cape Colony far to the north. They would thus outflank both the Orange Free State and the Transvaal. Rhodes's territorial ambitions seemed more than a little wild to the Foreign Office. But it did make political sense to push British power north, right up to Lake Nyasa, where the Scottish missions were hampered by the Portuguese and beleaguered by Arab slavers.

In any case there were two overwhelming attractions about Rhodes's scheme. First, he claimed to be 'good for a million'. The Rothschilds backed him and he asked nothing from the British taxpayer. All he wanted was a royal charter for a new company, the British South Africa Company, which would administer 'Zambezia', a vast El Dorado (Rhodes hoped), between Central Africa and the Transvaal. Second, his scheme complemented that of William Mackinnon, who had now applied for a charter for British East Africa. This would take the British 'sphere' in East Africa, including Uganda and Equatoria, to Lake Nyasa and the south, linked by a corridor behind German East Africa.

In short, the Cape-to-Cairo idea was not simply a pipedream of young Harry Johnston. By 1888 it was seriously entertained by Salisbury as a way of meeting Britain's strategic imperatives at the Canal and at the Cape.

It meant thrusting from three directions, up the Nile from Cairo, across to the Nile from East Africa, and up to the Lakes from the Cape. Of course, other

European Powers would try to frustrate these thrusts. But the main obstacles anticipated by Salisbury were not diplomatic. In Cairo they had to work through a protectorate which was a sham, but its deficits had been real enough, and there was no question of re-conquering the Sudan until the Egyptian taxpayer could afford the burden. As for Rhodes and Mackinnon, it was questionable whether they had the capacity – the steel in the character and the gold in the bank – to found great empires.

It was a paradox, perhaps the central paradox of British imperialism, that the British taxpayer was too absent-minded to pay for the expansion of the empire. So the government of the day (Tory or Liberal) left it to a handful of rich amateurs in whom they had singularly little confidence.

Lord Salisbury knew of nothing to recommend Rhodes except his money. He had long experience of Mackinnon, and it had made him deeply suspicious of the man. Yet he advised the Queen to sign the royal charter giving political responsibilities and commercial rights to the new Imperial British East Africa Company. It was thus, on 3 September 1888, that the sixty-five-year-old Scottish shipping magnate came into his vast and unexplored kingdom.

To call Mackinnon an amateur might seen to be stretching the word. Fifty years of hard work, thrift and professionalism had propelled him forward to the tune of 1,000 cash registers. He was Sam Smiles, Scotch Presbyterian style. Truly God's goodness and mercy had followed him – so he was reminded – from the village grocer's shop in Campbelton, near the Mull of Kintyre, to the general store on the Ganges, from the trading firm in Calcutta to the chairmanship of one of the world's great shipping lines. Money had brought him the power to be generous and hospitable. He loved to play host to the famous, taking King Leopold to shoot grouse on his moor in Scotland and the Duke of Sutherland to go cruising on board his private steam yacht, *Cornelia*.

Yet something of the richness of life still seemed to elude him. It was more than a longing for public recognition; it was the need to reconcile his own intense old-fashioned Christianity with the aggressive capitalism and aggressive nationalism of the new age. In Livingstone's call to open up Africa he thought he had found the answer. People described him as a canny Scot. But there was another Mackinnon besides – an idealist and a romantic, struggling to escape from behind the cash register. With Africa he had to suffer the pain of an intermittent and unrequited love affair.

What must have made the pain worse was that he knew Lord Salisbury misunderstood his motives. Salisbury saw his ambivalence and took it for weakness. Of course those experts at the FO had no idea of the risks of putting money into unexplored territory, and as a businessman, Mackinnon shrank from the risks. A simple canny Scot would never have become involved.

Mackinnon's love affair with Africa went back a decade, to 1878, when Kirk had first encouraged him to take up Livingstone's burden and try to open up the whole coast of East Africa. Mackinnon had approached Sultan Barghash of Zanzibar for a concession and asked the British government for its blessing, but

Salisbury, at the time Disraeli's Foreign Secretary, soon lost confidence in him and secretly warned Barghash against going ahead. The German eruption ended that option on the mainland for good.

Then in 1886 Mackinnon had boldly embarked on the Emin Pasha relief expedition. The plan, as described earlier, was not simply a mission of mercy to rescue Emin. Mackinnon had decided to invest £10,000 of his own (and his friends') money as a first step in bringing the '3 cs' to the new British 'sphere' of East Africa, north of the line of partition. Stanley was to be the first administrator. On his way to the coast he would sign treaties with the local chiefs west of Lake Victoria. The new British company would build its headquarters at Mombasa, and start to exploit the Great Lakes, using Birmingham brass rods and rolls of Manchester cotton to destroy the slave trade, as soon as Stanley emerged from the interior.

When Stanley did not emerge from the interior, and the half-starved men of his rear column reported him dead, Mackinnon must have been tempted to throw in the sponge. Yet he stuck to his own timetable, just as Stanley had stuck to his. On 24 May 1887 Sultan Barghash signed a concession formally giving Mackinnon's East Africa Association (a group of businessmen and humanitarians formed three years before) the right to administer the east coast ports north of the partition line for a term of fifty years. In return they would pay him an annual fee based on Customs House revenue, plus 50 per cent. As for the interior which he had claimed to control, Barghash now agreed to do his best to persuade the local chiefs in the British sphere to sign treaties, transferring their sovereignty to Mackinnon's Association. Early in 1888 Mackinnon launched with a splash the public company, the Imperial British East Africa Company, which would take over the concession.

Its capital was to be £1 million, of which the first instalment came to £200,000. Within two months the issue was a sell-out. This was no surprise when one considered the list of directors. 'Good names and good subscriptions,'[10] said Percy Anderson, somewhat grudgingly. The directors came from the cream of British humanitarians: Thomas Fowell Buxton, leader of the struggle against slavery; William Burdett-Coutts, stripling husband of the philanthropic Baroness; Alexander Bruce, Livingstone's brother-in-law and a partner in an Edinburgh brewery. Then there were the high-minded businessmen who formed Mackinnon's 'clan', including James Hutton, the Manchester cotton magnate; Henry Younger, Bruce's partner in the brewery, and George Mackenzie, a director of Mackinnon's shipping company. The other directors included a brace of famous generals – Sir Donald Stewart, former C-in-C in India, and Sir Arnold Kemball, now in business with the Duke of Sutherland – and the two most distinguished East African hands, Sir Lewis Pelly and Sir John Kirk. Who could resist such a roll-call of the great and good in the age of steam-power and Bible-power?

If there was one man who was the driving wheel behind Mackinnon's dream, and the steel bed-plate of common sense within, that man was Sir John Kirk. It was three years since Gladstone and the Foreign Office had allowed that 'unscrupulous adventurer'[11] Carl Peters to cripple Kirk's life's work. He had dreamt of extending British control over the whole of East Africa on the principles sketched out by his first employer, David Livingstone. In July 1887 he had retired from the foreign service, unable to stomach the weakness of the FO's policy. He was fifty-seven, his constitution still tough as a piece of mangrove wood, despite more than twenty years in the fetid climate of Zanzibar. He took his wife and four daughters to live in a small gabled house near Sevenoaks, less than an hour's ride by train through the London suburbs and over the North Downs. The landscape was cool chalk and clay – chalk downs naked except for a crest of beech woods, waterlogged in winter, with turret-like oast-houses for drying hops – very different from the pungent world of Zanzibar. But though Kirk felt glad to be home and sickened by the FO's appeasement of the Germans, he remained true to his own – and Livingstone's – vision. In Mackinnon he saw the only hope of rescuing something from the ruin.

The main question, even before obtaining the charter, was how to proceed: whether to work cautiously inland from Mombasa, or to stake everything on the race for territory in Uganda and Equatoria before it fell to the Germans.

If Kirk had trusted Salisbury, he would have recommended caution. As he told Mackinnon in January 1888, 'The danger is getting drawn into expensive schemes ... my doctrine always has been that no philanthropic scheme can do good in Africa or to ourselves unless it has in it the elements of commercial success.'[12] And it made no commercial sense to spend several hundred thousand pounds pushing into Uganda – or worse still, Equatoria – before building a profitable base on the coast. But Kirk was haunted by the thought that Salisbury was planning a new betrayal of British interests in East Africa. When he went to the Foreign Office to pick the brains of his old colleagues – men like Villiers Lister, who shared his Livingstonian ideals – he found them as baffled as he was. What was the chief up to? They confessed they did not know. Salisbury kept his cards so close to his chest.

Unfortunately East Africa was still wide open to Germany, despite the agreement in 1886 to divide it into British and German 'spheres'. First, the line of partition that ran north-west, skirting Kilimanjaro, ended at the north-east corner of Lake Victoria. So Uganda and Equatoria were not included in either sphere. Second, the agreement defined the Witu 'sultanate' (a barren strip of coast between the Tana and Juba rivers) as a German protectorate. Witu, its harbour blocked by sand-bars, was an absurdity in itself, but its strength was that it might allow the Germans to claim a hinterland *behind* the British sphere. This was the nightmare that sat on Kirk's chest: the Germans could strangle the British sphere with a pincer movement north and south. Without access to the riches of the 'new India', those bumper crops astride Lake Victoria and the Nile, Mombasa might be more barren than Witu.

In the summer of 1888 Kirk and Mackinnon heard the news they dreaded. A group of German colonialists had commissioned Carl Peters to lead a new expedition beyond the German sphere. Outwardly it was another mercy mission to rescue Emin Pasha, but no one believed this. Privately Peters admitted that his object was to found a new colony and, if possible, to induce Emin to bring Equatoria into the Kaiser's new empire in Africa. Would Salisbury step in to block Peters? Mackinnon wrote to the Foreign Office and was told not to be alarmed. It was the usual German bluff; the odds were that Peters would never leave Germany. Anyway, it was a purely 'private' affair. The German Foreign Office had assured Salisbury that Peters would be given no official encouragement. This did not reassure Kirk or Mackinnon. And Harry Johnston threatened to put the blame, somewhat unfairly, on poor Mackinnon. 'If you let the Germans get to Emin Pasha first, I shall never forgive you.'[13]

Nonetheless there was also reassuring news for Kirk in August 1888. Through the grapevine he heard that Salisbury had approved – grudgingly no doubt – the royal charter. So, without even waiting for the Queen's signature, the Imperial British East Africa Company (IBEAC) began to stretch out its hands to its vast paper empire in Africa.

George Mackenzie was chosen to go out to Mombasa to start the caravans rolling. He was an expert on eastern transport, an energetic director of the British India Steam Navigation Company and Mackinnon's right-hand man. After thrashing out the details with Kirk, he sailed for Mombasa. In September 1888 he set up the company headquarters close to the Arab fort, and founded his empire with a roadway and a line of telegraph posts. If the local natives were puzzled by these proceedings, Mackenzie was tactful and efficient. It was conspicuous that he flew the red flag of the Sultan of Zanzibar. He was also conspicuously generous with the Company's funds.

By early October he had arranged for a large caravan to proceed up-country, led by a man called Swayne, a British artillery officer intoxicated with the joys of killing elephants. Unfortunately this made him impractical as an empire-builder and he was quickly replaced by a more sensible pioneer, Frederick Jackson. But were Jackson's instructions practical? He was to buy for the Company safe passage from the Masai. This assumed a sense of enlightened self-interest on the part of the tribe that no explorer had yet observed. He was then to press on to the Nile and link up with Emin at Wadelai. But what could be assumed about that bastion of civilization? In the eighteen months since Stanley had disappeared into the Congo rainforest, not a whisper had been heard from Emin. Yet Jackson was not instructed to bring him arms; he was told to exploit Emin's great wealth in ivory by establishing a caravan link between Wadelai and Mombasa.

As 1888 passed into 1889, that rosy picture of Emin's province began to fade. Stanley, broken by fever, sent a message from somewhere west of Lake Victoria. Emin's men had mutinied. The Mahdists had invaded. Probably Stanley would return with Emin's survivors. That was all Kirk could assume. So where did this leave the tropical treasure-house by the lakes? If the company had stuck to Kirk's original plan of advance, feeling its way slowly inland from Mombasa, the £200,000 it had raised might have sufficed for a time. As it was, Kirk now saw only the dangers of being cautious. Jackson was told to push on towards

Lake Victoria. There were protests from some of the Company's more sober directors. The Company had a bumper harvest of debt and it would be years before there was a prospect of income from trade. This was not philanthropy, plus or even minus 5 per cent, but the way to bankruptcy. Mackinnon consulted Kirk, who had the bit between his teeth. Lord Salisbury was not to be trusted; he would let Carl Peters take Uganda, the pearl of East Africa, unless Jackson got there first.

Meanwhile, south of the river Umba, the straggling line of palm and scrub that marked the frontier between the two spheres, the Germans under Carl Peters had begun to move forward. So reckless were their own proceedings that Mackinnon's Company soon faced a completely new danger. In September 1888 some Swahili and Arabs on the coast, slavers turned rubber and ivory traders, had rebelled against the German protectorate. Soon it was feared the Arabs would unite and sweep the Europeans on both sides of the river Umba into the Indian Ocean.

*   *   *

The leader of this first uprising against German imperialism in Africa was a hot-headed Swahili sugar-plantation owner called Abushiri ibn Salim al-Harthi. He was short and muscular, with the piercing dark eyes of his Galla mother, and the manner (so one of the Germans said) of a 'springing panther'. For a century the intrigues of his clan, the al-Harthi, had defied the Sultans of Zanzibar, and he knew that he risked losing his head if he turned up in Zanzibar. At Pangani, in September 1888, Abushiri raised a wave of revolt against the Sultan's persecutors.

The immediate cause of the rebellion was the high-handed action of Emil von Zalewski, a young German agent who had come to be known in Swahili as 'Nyundo' ('the hammer').[14] Pangani was only thirty miles from Zanzibar and was the largest port on the coast after Bagamoyo. It was an Arab boom town of white washed stone houses and narrow streets, crowned with a stubby minaret and sheltered by opulent sugar and tobacco plantations beside a beach of pearly sand. One day early in August 1888 Zalewski sailed unexpectedly into the harbour. He wasted no time on courtesies. The Wali was the principal dignitary of the town. Zalewski told the Wali that he intended to employ him, as he was taking over the administration. The Wali should report to him four times a day for his instructions.

The German East Africa Company founded by Carl Peters had far less cash than Mackinnon's. It needed to make money, not enemies. In May 1887, Carl Peters had despatched Captain Laver as the company's representative at Dar-es-Salaam, the Sultan's newly built port in the German sphere, with only seven German companions and a bodyguard of twelve Arabs provided by the Sultan. At first Laver had tried to win the Arabs' allegiance with soft words and small presents. He also gave the Muslim town two sets of Christian missionaries, one

Lutheran and the other Benedictine. Then in April 1888 the Sultan agreed to lease the whole administration of the southern coastal strip to the German Company. In return, they must pay him a percentage and take care to act in his name and under his flag. The Sultan's Wali, Suleiman ibn Nasr, was asked to tour the coast to proclaim these new arrangements.

But the Germans did not adopt the style of tenants; they swaggered around like conquerors. At Tanga people were outraged by the sight of some dogs owned by the Germans being allowed into the mosque during Ramadan. At Bagamoyo, Dar-es-Salaam and Kilwa the Company raised its own flag and insulted the Sultan's. Up and down the coast there were stories of humiliation for the red flag of Zanzibar. The Swahili men of property, used to the lax and corrupt administration of the Sultan, were now asked for prompt payment of new taxes – a head tax, a burial tax, an inheritance tax. Worst of all, everyone must register his property and failure to show proper title would result in confiscation.

Fear and resentment spread from the coast like a wind from the sea. The pagan tribes of the interior saw that they would lose their power to levy *hongo*, the toll on the ivory caravans. A chief from Usambara sent 6,000 armed men down to Pangani, declaring that they would 'fight to the last man' rather than become slaves of the Germans.

As this tidal wave began to gather strength all along the coast, Emil Zalewski saw no reason to compromise. Far from acting in the name of the Sultan, if there was further trouble, he threatened to bombard the coast and send the Sultan himself 'to Germany in chains'.[15] When the Wali at Pangani refused to co-operate, Zalewski signalled a nearby German warship. A party of 100 marines came splashing through the surf, arrested the Sultan's officer and then invaded the Wali's harem, smashing the furniture. The Wali fled. Next day the marines appeared and cut down the pole carrying the Sultan's flag. Then they sailed back to Zanzibar, leaving Zalewski with a small garrison.

There was an ominous lull. People waited to see if the Sultan would take his revenge. Zalewski called for the Sultan to send troops to confirm his authority, but when they disembarked they refused to arrest the notables who defied Zalewski. In early September 1888 Abushiri emerged as the leader of the militant faction among the notables. They dug trenches and fortified houses which commanded the harbour. Meanwhile, the town was filled by wild tribesmen from up-country, demanding that the Germans should be strangled or beheaded. To save their lives, the more conservative notables locked Zalewski and his comrades into the German agency, and a guard was put on the house. When the Germans in Zanzibar sent a representative to help them, Abushiri's men drove them off with gunfire.

To break the stalemate, the German Consul persuaded the Sultan to send over General Lloyd Matthews, the British expatriate who commanded his army. Matthews succeeded in rescuing Zalewski and the garrison, but otherwise failed to mediate. Refugees streaming into the town from the north reported that the Germans had bombarded Tanga, the nearest town to the frontier with the

British 'sphere'. On the night of 21 September, Abushiri called a meeting at his sugar plantation and persuaded the people to defy the Sultan's wishes. He planned to raise all the coastal towns against the Germans. The Sultan's generals sailed back to Zanzibar.

By now the various factions amounted to a wild army of 20,000 men, some armed with modern rifles, others with swords, spears, bows and arrows. Apart from the hatred of the Germans, there was nothing to give them solidarity. Muslims and pagans, slave dealers and slaves, they could have no political objective in common – not even agreement to restore the power of Seyid Khalifa. Abushiri himself admitted his aim was to build his own empire as an independent warlord. Nationalist sentiment, in the modern sense, was completely lacking. But for the moment the wave of hatred and hysteria was enough to hold the rickety alliance of factions together.

Up and down the coast the German agents were hunted down like rats. One was shot, another committed suicide. Most managed to flee by dhow. By the end of September the whole coast was evacuated, except for outposts at Dar-es-Salaam and Bagamoyo which could be supported by German warships. But there were still many Europeans at risk – mostly isolated groups of missionaries – and thousands of British Indians, who managed the trade with the interior. Towards both these vulnerable groups Abushiri and his followers acted with commendable restraint. Abushiri made it clear that his quarrel was only with the German invaders. He bravely intervened to protect the missionaries in danger. Some, it is true, were captured and ransomed for hard cash. Abushiri was desperately short of funds to buy food and ammunition, and was anxious to prevent his hungry followers from looting. By November 1888, two months after expelling the Germans, Abushiri's revolt was beginning to lose its way.

It was almost impossible to control 10,000 wild Africans who charged around the town, fantastically dressed in captured uniforms, firing rifles and chanting 'Death to all Europeans'. It was equally hard to reconcile the growing split between the conservative Swahili traders, anxious to restore the Sultan's authority, and people like Abushiri himself, who felt that the Sultan had betrayed their trust and sold them to the Germans. So he decided to march south and open a new front. He exchanged the wild tribesmen for a picked force of 2,000 men, mostly Arab and Swahili, and collected three captured cannons. By early December he had reached Bagamoyo and started digging siege trenches to cut off the Germans from the harbour where several warships were still anchored.

Meanwhile, Dar-es-Salaam, the only other outpost still held by the Germans, was besieged by 1,000 men under a Swahili notable called Suleiman ibn-Sef. What political motives impelled Suleiman remain obscure. Apparently he was furious that the Germans had confiscated the slaves from his sugar plantations and set them to work at the German missions. In January 1889 he took his revenge. His men destroyed the mission station, killed three missionaries, and made prisoners of four others. But the Company's own station proved too tough a nut to crack. At Bagamoyo Abushiri, too, was unable to prevail against superior firepower and discipline. In April 1889 he reconciled himself to a truce with the German admiral. Then in May he decided to try another assault on the German HQ at Bagamoyo, despite the stone walls, barbed wire fences and bright lights guarding the perimeter. He called in the services of a well-known astrologer and poet, Hemedi bin Abdullah, who duly predicted that the infidel planned a counter-attack. This would be a disaster for the faithful: 'War and death of many men and much looting and destruction of persons.'[16] Abushiri was incredulous. An army of fifty Germans against 10,000 men! Allah, the Great and Merciful, had weighted the scales against the infidel.

*   *   *

But the astrologer was right. By May 1889 Bismarck had intervened against Allah with enough weight to bring down the scales the other way with a bang. He had done a deal with Lord Salisbury. The governments agreed on a joint naval blockade of the coast to prevent the import of guns and ammunition. The aim was supposed to be humanitarian, to block the Arab slave trade. The real target was Abushiri. Bismarck had sent out a distinguished German explorer, Major von Wissman, with orders to take with him enough German officers and African mercenaries to make short work of the rebels. The Reichstag had voted two million marks to equip Wissman's expedition, so success was a foregone conclusion. So was the cancellation of the German East Africa Company's *schutzbrief*, their imperial charter to govern the country. The Company's high-handedness had provoked the rebellion and their resources had proved too feeble to repress it. Once pacified by Wissman, German East Africa would have to be governed directly as an imperial colony.

As for Carl Peters, who had founded German East Africa, Bismarck dismissed him as a mere 'freebooter'. Bismarck shared Salisbury's distaste for this kind of flag-waving, buccaneering patriot. By now he had decided that the coastal blockade should apply to Peters as well as to Abushiri. Far from being given official encouragement, he was not supposed to set foot on German territory. That was part of the agreement with Salisbury. Not that Peters was a great one for obeying official instructions; and Bismarck was opportunist enough to see that Peters might still prove a useful secret weapon, when the time came to bring Salisbury to the negotiating table for the final partition of East Africa.

At seventy-four, Bismarck still seemed indestructible physically and politically. In February 1887 he had helped the conservative *Kartel* – the Centre Party and the National Liberals – to flatten his enemies, the Liberal Opposition. The Chancellor had conjured up the bogey of a war with France, exploiting the ludicrous belligerence of the French War Minister, General Boulanger. The *Kartel* was swept back to power on a wave of patriotic fervour. Of course Boulanger was a paper tiger and Bismarck knew it. What he wanted was to beat down the Liberals and their patron, the Crown Prince, before the latter succeeded as Kaiser. But it was soon apparent that Bismarck had been flogging a dying horse. On 9 March 1888, Kaiser Wilhelm I finally expired, but by then the

Crown Prince was already speechless with terminal cancer of the throat. Death released him from the throne after ninety-nine days. So by 15 June 1888, Bismarck had a second new master, the son of the Crown Prince and Crown Princess, twenty-nine-year-old Kaiser Wilhelm II, notorious for his erratic temper, brashness and a tendency to over-rate his own abilities.

It was these defects in Wilhelm's character that Bismarck had cultivated to turn him against his parents. Not that Wilhelm needed much turning. He had always sided with the Bismarck family against his parents, who he felt neglected him. Herbert von Bismarck was his boon companion. They would stay up all night drinking brandy and Herbert came to think of himself as Wilhelm's most trusted adviser. As for the Chancellor, he paid no more attention to the brash young Kaiser than he had to the Kaiser's ninety-year-old grandfather. Herbert could handle him; that was the Chancellor's fond belief. He left Berlin for his country estate soon after Wilhelm's accession, and did not return until January 1889.

When the new Kaiser tried to interfere, Bismarck did not pretend to listen. Polonius-like, he lectured him on politics. His Majesty should try to learn from Bismarck's example; at present His Majesty's views were more than a little immature. The new Kaiser might be erratic, but he now kept one aim constantly in mind. He had conceived a great loathing for both the Bismarcks and one day, sooner rather than later, he would like to send both of them packing.

Neither of the Bismarcks had any inkling of this. Without giving a thought for his new master's views, the Chancellor continued to pursue his foreign policy which had worked so brilliantly since the 1860s – protecting Germany's European supremacy by stirring up trouble between her enemies.

It was here that Bismarck's *Kolonialtummel*, this absurd 'colonial whirl', could make sense. The best justification for Germany's four colonies was that, because Britain coveted the same territory, they would cause trouble for Britain. For a negligible investment by the Reich, Bismarck had obtained a useful diplomatic return. Perhaps now was the time to draw some extra dividends, either by an alliance with England, or by using the colonies to extract some appetizing plum in Europe.

On 11 January 1889, Bismarck wrote to Count Hatzfeld, the German Ambassador in London, with a dramatic proposal for Salisbury: a defensive alliance against France. He accompanied this with cordial protestations in the Reichstag by himself and Herbert to the effect that British friendship was worth more to Germany than the whole of East Africa. Salisbury did not take the bait. General Boulanger's antics were now ending, and in any case British interests in Egypt demanded German support, rather than a formal alliance. So Bismarck swung round to the idea of a swap: German territory in Africa in exchange for British territory in Europe.

The European plum on which he had set his heart was the island of Heligoland. It might seen a strange choice, a few square miles of naked red sandstone, complete with a few hundred impoverished fishermen, exposed to the North Sea forty miles west of Cuxhaven. Ever since the English had seized it from the

Danes in 1807 they had found the place useless. But to Germany, and in particular to the German navy, its possession would prove 'invaluable',[17] as Herbert put it.

Suppose war broke out between Germany and France and the French navy were able to use it as a coaling station? They could thus seal off the entrance to three great estuaries, including the Elbe leading to Hamburg, as well as blocking the new Kiel canal. Once in German hands, Heligoland could be developed as a major naval base, comparable to the British bases at Malta, Gibraltar and the Cape. All the authorities in Berlin agreed on this – Bismarck and the new Kaiser, the German Foreign Office and the German Admiralty. The danger was that Lord Salisbury would get wind of the plan and raise the ante. So when Herbert was sent on a mission to London in 1889, it was agreed that they should not show 'excessive eagerness'[18] after Joseph Chamberlain suggested a swap of Heligoland for south-west Africa, the latter to be added to Cape Colony.

In June 1889, Count Hatzfeld went to see Salisbury and played the poker game as Bismarck had instructed. Frankly, he could not say whether Heligoland would be of any *positive* use to Germany. But it would certainly damage England's relations with Germany – perhaps beyond repair – if French warships ran for cover there during a Franco-German war. Salisbury took the point, to Berlin's delight, but declared he too could not see 'any real advantage' in the Germans' taking Heligoland. It would cost millions to make anything of the place, and he understood that it had been badly undermined by the sea. On the other hand, he told Hatzfeld, 'with a smile' (so Hatzfeld reported confidentially to Berlin), that he 'had no great enthusiasm'[19] for helping Cape Colony take over south-west Africa. The colony was more or less independent and Britain would get no thanks for any sacrifice she made on its behalf.

By the summer of 1889, Bismarck felt he should leave the Heligoland plum to 'ripen' a little. Meanwhile the news from East Africa was confused. In May the new imperial commissioner, Major von Wissman, had achieved a success against Abushiri, but the rebel leader was still on the loose. At the same time, despite the attempts of both the British and German authorities to stop Carl Peters landing in East Africa, that adventurer had somehow broken the blockade, and was now carrying the black, white and red German flag westwards in the direction of Uganda and Equatoria.

* * *

If Bismarck expected Peters to brush aside all the obstacles Berlin had set in his path, his confidence was not misplaced. Peters landed in Zanzibar in June 1889 to find that Mackinnon's shipping line had handed over his arms and ammunition to the British navy, commanded by Admiral Fremantle. Fremantle told him bluntly, '*C'est la guerre*.'[20] If he didn't like it, why not cable Berlin? The German Consul refused to help him recruit porters and the German Foreign Office refused him any form of mediation or support against the British. Peters paid no more attention than in 1884 when he had been told by cable from Berlin not to grab any territory on the mainland. He simply hired a small steamboat, flying British colours, from an Indian shipping firm and seized at gunpoint a couple of dhows from the Arabs, who at first thought he was British. Then he ran his men and contraband ashore on a deserted beach near Lamu. Before Admiral Fremantle woke up to the trick, Peters had slipped through his fingers and was marching through the heat-haze up the straggling line of trees marking the river Tana.

To pull off this trick, however, cost Peters most of his vital equipment. In Berlin he had planned a full-scale expedition: 100 Somali soliders and 600 porters, the soldiers equipped with modern rifles, the porters carrying the usual trade goods, as well as extra rifles and supplies for Emin. But he had landed on the beach with only sixty porters and twenty-seven soldiers. He had no trade goods of any kind, no rolls of American-made cloth, or boxes of British-made wire, or bottles of German-made gin, nothing at all to buy safe passage through the territory of the ferocious Masai who straddled the barren steppes leading to Lake Victoria. This meant abandoning all pretence of bringing supplies to relieve Emin. It also meant that Peters's tiny force would probably have to fight its way to the lake.

And fight it did. Peters had been trained as an academic and looked the part, with his lean figure, floppy-brimmed hat and dark, shiny spectacles. Yet of all the conquistadores carving up Africa during the Scramble, he was certainly the most pugnacious, the one who openly confessed to the 'intoxication'[21] of killing Africans. On 6 October 1889 he burst without warning into the kraal of some Galla tribesmen with whom he had previously signed a solemn treaty of peace and friendship. In the *mêlée* he killed a sultan and six of his leading men. In November he pushed up into the Wadsagga country, his line of march marked by blackened villages and dead warriors. His policy was a deliberate departure from the diplomacy adopted by previous white travellers. People must understand that '*c'est la guerre*'.

Perhaps this policy of terror was inevitable, given Peters's tiny force and the fact that he had no goods to trade for peace. But he would probably have adopted it anyway. In December he struggled out of the upper Tana valley on to the cool, green, transparent ramparts of the Kikuyu. This was literally a land of milk and honey, overlooked by the seven-crowned snow peak of Mount Kenya which lifted his heart above 'the petty cares and thoughts of everyday life'. Then fifteen Kikuyu tribesmen, newly hired as carriers, 'impudently'[22] tried to abscond with their advance payment. Peters ordered them to be shot as a warning to others.

By 20 December 1889 the expedition had passed the wall of primeval thickets protecting the Kikuyu from tens of thousands of Masai warriors. The main challenge followed. Peters was well aware of the Masais' reputation among European explorers. Even the best-equipped expeditions either had to avoid the route or submit to humiliating exactions. Instead he decided to humiliate the Masai. The only thing that 'would make an impression on these wild sons of the steppe was a bullet from a repeater. . . .'[23] On the pretext that the Masai had refused to supply him with a guide, he launched a dawn raid on their camp at Elbejet, killing seven of its defenders and driving off 2,000 cattle. The Masai counter-attacked with arrows and spears, and lost thirty-three more men, compared with Peters's seven casualties. For the next few days Peters's tiny column was hunted by a howling pack of Masai. But his guns made him invincible. In early January Peters began to descend to Lake Baringo, leaving the Masai to bury their dead. By late January he had marched to Kavirondo, and by February crossed Busoga, the gateway to Buganda, the place where Bishop Hannington had paid the price for his foolhardiness (according to Peters) and had been murdered five years before.

Painful news now reached Peters that at first he refused to believe. He learnt that a year earlier, in 1888 – before he had even landed on the beach near Lamu – Emin had abandoned Equatoria and begun the retreat to the coast with Peters's rival, Stanley. The two expeditions had missed each other by six months and several hundred miles. This news was confirmed by a letter written by Stanley on 4 September 1888, when he was staying with Mackay, the Scottish missionary, at Makolo on the southern shore of Lake Victoria. Stanley's letter was actually addressed to Jackson, the pioneering representative of the IBEAC whom Mackinnon had told to send a caravan into Kavirondo, and if possible to link up with Stanley. But Peters felt no more compunction about opening his rivals' letters than he did about shooting down Africans.

Peters's first reaction to Stanley's letter was to cry like child. So all his labours were in vain! He felt utterly forlorn (so he said), 'repudiated' by his own fatherland, which had failed to prevent Stanley from snatching Emin. As the night wind swept through the rustling banana groves above his tent, he relieved his 'passionate distress' with 'an outburst of convulsive sobbing'. The next day he felt more like himself. The game was not lost after all.

From various sources came reports that the previous summer King Mwanga had tried in vain to persuade Stanley to help restore him to the throne of Buganda from which he had been recently expelled by the Arab party. Stanley had felt his forces were too weak to accept the invitation. Now Mwanga was appealing to Jackson for help. But Jackson, too, felt that he had not strength enough to intervene in the civil war in Buganda. A few weeks before Peters marched into Kavirondo, Jackson had marched out of it for a spell of elephant hunting. Since then Mwanga's fortunes had taken a turn for the better. With the help of the Catholic and Protestant parties, he had established his ascendancy on the lake. And he was now offering a great political concession to the IBEAC. If Jackson helped him back to the throne, he would give the British a protectorate.

So Peters steeled himself to snatch a new prize. 'Up then and away.'[24] With only sixty men, he would advance where Stanley had feared to tread with a thousand. He would go to the rescue of King Mwanga and try to establish a German protectorate over Buganda.

*   *   *

353

Early in 1890, unaware of Carl Peters's extraordinary plan for grabbing Uganda, Lord Salisbury confidently began to resume negotiations for a general settlement with Germany. He took his time. Mackinnon was an alarmist. Salisbury relied on Bismarck's prudence and on his unconditional assurance in June 1889 that Uganda and Equatoria lay beyond the German sphere.

In the past year fortune had certainly seemed to favour the new axis, 'Cape-to-Cairo'. In April 1889 Cecil Rhodes and other South African diamond magnates had formally applied for a royal charter covering 'Zambezia' to be conferred on the syndicate which would in due course become the British South Africa Company, the future Chartered Company. Rhodes's resources made Mackinnon look like a country grocer. The financial assets controlled by him and his friends were estimated at £13 million, and the political assets included the bedrock of the City, Society and Parliament. Despite his own misgivings about Rhodes's erratic character ('Who *is* Mr Rhodes?' Harry Johnston quoted Lord Salisbury as asking. 'Rather a pro-Boer MP in South Africa, I fancy'.)[25] Salisbury was prepared to accept Rhodes's cash. There was no alternative.

His Chancellor of the Exchequer was Goschen, an ex-Liberal who had set his face against imperial expansion. The Treasury – and the British taxpayer – were determined not to fork out the millions needed to extend British supremacy over southern Africa. It was all very well to say (as the anti-slavery lobby did) that Rhodes was a share-pusher and a buccaneer, not a man to be trusted in anything, least of all in respecting Africans' rights. But without Rhodes's intervention, this strategically vital region would pass to the Boers, the Germans or the Portuguese – none of them particularly tender-hearted towards Africans. Safeguards for the natives would have to be built into the charter. After weeks of wrangling over the small print, Salisbury recommended the Queen to assent. She duly signed Rhodes's charter on 29 October 1889. Now it was up to Rhodes and his partners to put flesh on their paper empire.

As well as generously helping himself to a huge colony in southern Africa, Rhodes also agreed to support a small imperial takeover: of Nyasaland in Central Africa. It was Livingstone's old hunting ground, on the west side of Lake Nyasa, where the Scottish missions and some Bible-minded Scottish businessmen of the African Lakes Company had created a tenuous foothold. It was a foothold that in 1888 they looked likely to lose, squeezed out by two sets of enemies: Arab slavers from the east coast and Portuguese empire-builders from Mozambique.

Then, in January 1889, Salisbury had appointed Harry Johnston to be HM Consul at Mozambique with the princely salary of £800 a year. It sounded rather a come-down for the bumptious young man who had enjoyed the Prime Minister's special patronage; but Salisbury had a delicate and dangerous role for Johnston. He was to explore the disputed area north of the Zambezi, plying the local chiefs with lavish presents and blank treaty forms. When the time came to negotiate with the Portuguese, the Scottish missions could claim that local treaties gave them the right to British protection. Johnston was delighted to oblige. The problem was, 'as usual', persuading the Treasury. Goschen turned down the idea of any extra expense – especially the lavish presents for the chiefs.

It was Cecil Rhodes who broke the impasse. He met Johnston over oysters and soup at a friend's house in May 1889, shortly before Johnston was due to set sail. They talked Cape-to-Cairo the whole evening, and continued for the rest of the night in Rhodes's suite at the Westminster Palace Hotel. In the morning Rhodes wrote out Johnston a cheque for £2,000 to cover the expense of the treaty-making. After confirming that the cheque did not bounce – and rushing off to the Army & Navy Stores to buy the presents for the chiefs – Johnston brought the news to Lord Salisbury, who welcomed Rhodes's offer, provided he did not claim Nyasaland for the Charter Company. From that moment Johnston felt assured of success. Years later he regarded it as the turning point in his own life, although Nyasaland was not formally proclaimed a British protectorate until 1891.

In March 1890 Salisbury's leisurely plan for a general settlement with Bismarck received an unexpected jolt. Bismarck vanished from the scene, his thirty-year reign ended at a stroke by the young Kaiser. The colossus who had created the German Reich was forced to sign a humiliating letter of resignation and retire to Varzin. (Bismarck had tried to sabotage an international labour conference which the Kaiser was sponsoring. But the Kaiser's coup could have come at any time.) Georg von Kaprivi, Bismarck's successor, professed his government's friendship for England. So did Marschall, the new head of the German Foreign Office. It was the new Chancellor's master who inspired Salisbury with understandable distrust. How would the Kaiser react to the flag-waving of the German colonial lobby? The previous summer Bismarck had been denounced in the conservative press as being too soft on the British. Now the Kaiser might choose to play the colonial card with a vengeance.

On 30 April 1890 Percy Anderson left for Berlin to take up the negotiations in detail. As the cables hummed between Berlin and London, there seemed to be nothing to support Salisbury's original confidence. Uganda (and by extension, Equatoria) remained the great 'stumbling block'.[26] In November 1886 Salisbury had conceded British recognition of the German protectorate over the impoverished sultanate of Witu and the barren coast between the Tana and Juba rivers. He had *not* conceded the Germans' claim to any of the huge hinterland to the west of that region. It was this claim for the hinterland that terrified Mackinnon. If successful, it would prove fatal to the Imperial British East Africa Company's claim to Uganda and Equatoria, encircled by Germans from north and south. Robbed of their best territory, the Company might have to give up the fight. Now, in May 1890, the Foreign Office in Berlin reneged on Bismarck's assurance that Uganda and Equatoria were beyond the German sphere. At the same time two reports arrived from East Africa that appeared to confirm Mackinnon's worst fears.

The first concerned Emin. As described earlier, Stanley's heroic expedition to rescue him had ended in farce and confusion. Emin had fallen from the balcony in Bagamoyo. Then he rebuffed his British rescuers and joined the German imperial service under the command of Wissman. Now he was rumoured to have left Bagamoyo, on 26 April, heading for his old province, Equatoria. (The rumour was correct. Wissman had urged him to extend the German sphere wherever possible.)

The second report concerned Carl Peters. By May 1890 it was becoming clear in London that the German Emin Pasha relief expedition had achieved a great deal more than its British counterpart. In fact Peters appeared to have won the game.

Peters had signed an agreement with Mwanga giving Germany a protectorate over Uganda. He had achieved this with the support of the French Catholic missionaries who had helped to put Mwanga back on his throne. Mackinnon's emissary, Jackson, had arrived too late. That was the amazing news from East Africa. Would the Kaiser exploit it by making Peters's protectorate official? Indeed he might, unless agreement could be reached. So Salisbury was warned by Marschall at the end of May.

Already Stanley's noisy claims about six treaties he claimed to have made west of Lake Victoria, and equally noisy denunciations by the Germans, had stirred both colonial lobbies and created a hullabaloo in the press of both countries. Mackinnon was pleased to use Stanley's flair for publicity, and the Scottish missions joined in the campaign. They were terrified that the Germans planned to grab Nyasaland, the territory west of Lake Nyasa. They were not reassured by the news that Salisbury had already sent out a thirty-one-year-old consul, Harry Johnston, to Mozambique, his luggage full of presents and blank treaty forms for the chiefs.

Salisbury had no need to be overawed by the wrath of the Scottish kirks, any more than by Stanley's bellowing or Mackinnon's bleating. On the contrary, it had been his aim for some time – certainly since that weekend with Johnston at Hatfield – to make the British public face reality. If they felt like taking a huge new slice of Africa, they must pay for the privilege. In this case the proposed cost was modest. To be precise, it would cost Britain one island, roughly three miles around, a barren, red, sandstone rock covered with seagull droppings, forty miles out in the North Sea.

There are times when a master in diplomacy can wave a barren island like a magic wand. On 13 May 1890 Salisbury saw Count Hatzfeld at the Foreign Office. He offered Heligoland – just that and no more. In return, would the German government agree to concede the 'sum of his wishes'?[27] Salisbury listed four giant demands: a British protectorate over Zanzibar; cession of the German protectorate of Witu and all territory north of the Tana; access from Uganda to Lake Tanganyika; and the lion's share of the land west of Lake Nyasa. Together this would satisfy all Britain's interlocking interests, humanitarian, commercial and strategic. Would the Kaiser make impossible counter-demands?

The Kaiser accepted the swap with hardly a murmur. By 29 May Hatzfeld had been told by Berlin that Heligoland was 'of supreme importance'.[28] Without it the Kiel Canal was useless. Heligoland must be acquired, whatever it cost in Africa. But Hatzfeld could not resist teasing one or two concessions out of

Salisbury. The British agreed that the newly-extended frontier between the spheres should run along the parallel of one degree south, until it met the Congo frontier. This would have blocked the 'All-Red' route from Lake Tanganyika to Uganda. But Salisbury had made a deal with King Leopold by which Mackinnon's Company was to be ceded a corridor behind the German sphere.

By July 1890 Salisbury's magic wand seemed to have given everyone the best of all worlds. The Kaiser had chosen to play the naval, not the colonial card. His decision made him a hero in Germany and helped popularize his naval programme. Mackinnon and the Scottish churches were squared, and so were the Liberals who backed them in Parliament. Queen Victoria gave Salisbury a *mauvais quart d'heure*. She grumbled, 'Giving up what one has is always a bad thing.'[29] It was pointed out to Her Majesty that she was gaining as well as losing: three new protectorates (Zanzibar, Uganda and Equatoria) covering at least 100,000 square miles of Africa, in exchange for three square miles of Europe. In July, before Parliament broke up for the summer recess, there was a desultory debate in the Lords. In general people welcomed the sensible compromise between two great Powers that had better things to do than squabble about paper claims to Africa.

A month later Salisbury took a step to end the estrangement between Britain and France that had begun with the British occupation of Egypt eight years earlier. On 5 August he signed an agreement with the French giving them a 'sphere of influence' covering nearly a quarter of the continent, including several million square miles of the Sahara – 'what agriculturalists would call very "light" land',[30] as he wittily described it in the Lords when asked why he had been so generous.

CHAPTER 20

An Insubordinate Army

Paris and the Western Sudan
12 August 1890–November 1893

'An irresistible movement is bearing the great nations
of Europe towards the conquest of fresh territories.
It is like a huge steeplechase into the unknown ...
whole continents are being annexed ... especially
that huge black continent so full of fierce mysteries
and vague hopes ...'

Jules Ferry, 1890

In his office at the War Ministry in the Rue de Dominique, Charles de Freycinet, the pale, thin, veteran statesman known as the 'White Mouse', read on 12 August Lord Salisbury's *bon mot* about the Sahara being 'very "light" land' and he was not amused. In March 1890 he had wearily taken over the helm of the French government for the fourth time, combining the portfolio of War Minister with the role of *Président du Conseil*. But if he was irritated by Lord Salisbury's quaint sense of humour, he made no protest. Only a gentle rap on the knuckles was administered by William Waddington, Freycinet's half-English Ambassador in London. 'No doubt the Sahara is not a garden [but] you might well have left us to find it out.'[1]

What was important to Freycinet was that the Anglo-French agreement, signed by Waddington and Salisbury on 5 August 1890, was generally welcomed in France. The minority who did oppose his government now blamed Freycinet for giving too much to the English, not, as before, for trying to take too much for themselves.

The pendulum had swung back towards colonialism during the last five years, despite the political confusion in France. A whiff of colonial fever, a panicky fear that the door was closing (what the Germans called *Torschlusspanik*) had infected the French public, spread by the publicity for the Scramble involving the other Powers.

In the 1880s colonialism had been the downfall of France's leading statesmen. After the Tunisian débâcle in 1881, and again in 1885 after the setback in Indo-China, Freycinet's hero, Jules Ferry, had been hounded from office. So had Freycinet himself (and, indirectly, Gambetta, another of his heroes) as a result of the fiasco in Egypt in 1882. It was the anti-colonialists of the Left and Right who had combined against the government, mocking them for their aggressive imperialism. Now, when the Anglo-French agreement came under fire from the

Left and the Right again, the government was denounced for not being imperialist enough. They had allowed the English to have their own way in Egypt and to take all the plums in Africa, giving the French the left-overs – Salisbury's 'very "light"' land. No doubt Freycinet saw the irony of this sudden conversion, but it was no bad thing to hear his enemies bang the imperialist drum.

The general welcome in Paris for the Anglo-French agreement of 5 August contrasted with the general sense of outrage at the Anglo-German agreement signed a month earlier. Had Salisbury forgotten the formal agreement of Britain and France in 1862 to guarantee Zanzibar's independence? But the new deal signed with Salisbury on 5 August was much more than a compensation for English tactlessness. It gave France a free hand in Madagascar. It also removed two serious obstacles from Freycinet's diplomatic path: first, the threat of Britain's blocking French expansion into the Sahara and beyond, to link up all the far-flung French possessions in Africa; second the danger of obscure colonial disputes in Africa causing friction – or even war – between France and her nearest neighbour in Europe.

Freycinet's own dismissal in 1882, after the fiasco in Egypt, had taught him a lesson. It confirmed his distaste for the reckless opportunism of his fellow politicians. His own instincts were alien from those of most of his contemporaries, especially his heroes. He was self-effacing, unaggressive and unemotional to a fault. His nickname, 'White Mouse', was an exaggeration; grey was his predominant colour. He stood for the virtues that appealed to civil servants and school masters: industry, logic and prudence. Yet inside Freycinet's calm, bleak shell – better suited, people said, to a notary for widowed ladies than to a man who was to be the Third Republic made flesh – there was a romantic struggling to get out. He had a secret passion for steel and steam. This was the age of Jules Verne, of the technocrat as national hero, of oriental fantasies fulfilled by steam, of the coast-to-coast railway and the transcontinental canal. In 1879 Freycinet had summoned the genie from the lamp, by appointing a Trans-Sahara Commission to report on the feasibility of a railway to carry the riches of the Sudan across the burning wastes of the Sahara all the way to the Mediterranean. The genie refused to produce the railway. Now, in 1890, with public opinion having swung back towards colonialism, he summoned the genie again by reappointing the Trans-Sahara Commission. Was the dream at last technically and financially feasible now that England had given France the diplomatic go-ahead?

Perhaps the Trans-Sahara was still only a dream. But the grand design for French Africa seemed to Freycinet practical enough, if pursued in a prudent way. To redeem France's humiliations in Europe by acquiring a great overseas empire, and to develop new overseas markets for France, were the twin aims common to all French colonialists. Where Freycinet and his conservative Foreign Minister, Alexandre Ribot, differed from many of their countrymen was in their anxiety to avoid friction with the other Powers. Britain, pushing west up the Niger, had been the strategic obstacle to France's expansion. But now Salisbury had signed an outline agreement giving France a 'sphere of influence' over nearly a quarter of the continent, that is, most of the north-west quadrant from the Mediterranean to the Gulf of Guinea. The British were to keep three isolated footholds in West Africa – Gambia, Sierra Leone and the Gold Coast – and one important commercial colony, Nigeria. No doubt Morocco would soon give up the struggle to maintain its independence. And then the Sahara would serve as the bridge for all eight French territories: Morocco, Algeria and Tunisia, Senegal, Guinea, Gabon, the Niger and the French Congo. So France would then have the lion's share of the continent, judged by territory, exceeding even the British share.

Very light land would make a very fine bridge. Freycinet could be forgiven for an uncharacteristic bit of swagger when he contemplated the new agreement of 5 August.

He had inherited none of Lord Salisbury's advantages: a stable system of government (when would the next scandal pull the carpet from under his own ministry?); a united people (the French army, so busy fighting itself, needed no foreign enemies); and commercial enterprise in Africa (why could France not produce a Sir George Goldie of its own?). Yet the agreement with Salisbury was a bargain. As the Quai d'Orsay put it in their official report:

> Without much effort, without any real sacrifice, without the expense of exploration ... without a single treaty ... we have secured the recognition by Britain, the only Power whose rivalry we need fear, ... that Algeria and Senegal will in the near future form a single domain ... We have joined to the Senegal 2,500 kilometres of the Niger which thus becomes, for most of its course, a French river.... Today the government can proclaim to the nation that this vast African empire is no longer a dream, a distant ideal ... but a reality.[2]

This 'reality' was in the future. What the deal gave France was the opportunity to absorb the new empire in its own good time, according to a commercially viable plan, without being hustled by England. In short, it removed a great chunk of Africa from the Scramble.

But, imperialism is not conducted on Cartesian lines. Although Freycinet had got a good bargain from Salisbury, he was no match for one empire-builder who worked away both inside and outside his own government – Eugène Etienne, the hustler from Algeria.

As Under-Secretary for the Colonial Department (except for one short gap) since 1887, Eugène Etienne had struggled to free his hands from the control of both the Quai d'Orsay and the Ministry of Marine. Now his department in the Rue Royale had been put under the Ministry of Commerce. But he was more like a minister on his own account, for he attended Cabinet meetings and held office, like other ministers, by presidential decree. With the Quai d'Orsay his relations remained bellicose. It was partly a matter of personality. Etienne was a flamboyant colonialist, an Algerian *colon*, the son of a French officer who had taken part in the original conquest. In the Chamber of Deputies he represented the vociferous *pieds noirs* (poor immigrants) of Oran. He despised Ribot, the Foreign Minister, who was a conservative. No doubt he thought him even more of a wet blanket than Freycinet. Not that Etienne disapproved of Waddington's new deal with Salisbury – as far as it went. But was old Ribot the man to wrap himself in the tricolour, and take possession of this glittering new prize? It was a role Etienne claimed for himself.

In February 1890 he had struck the first blow, as the champion of the colonial lobby, by secretly authorizing Colonel Louis Archinard, the fire-eater in charge of the French garrison in the western Sudan, to march down the Niger and seize the Tukolor capital of Segu. This not only violated the peace treaty with Ahmadu, the Tukolor Sultan, but the policy of the government – and especially that of the Quai d'Orsay. Several years before, the Quai had decided, because of the alarming cost of the victories, to postpone any advance up the Niger. That May, in 1890, Ribot and the other officials of the Quai d'Orsay were astonished to read in the Paris newspapers that Archinard had captured Segu. Why had they not been consulted? Etienne's reply was a calculated insult. He had no need to explain himself; the Cabinet had been informed, and the newspapers were perfectly accurate. Of course the capture of Segu was popular in the press. Freycinet made no attempt to slap Etienne down.

Etienne had had another chance of baiting the Quai d'Orsay when he addressed the Chamber on 10 May on the subject of Dahomey. The Cabinet had agreed to defend their coastal protectorate of Porto Novo, a protectorate on the Slave Coast re-established in 1883, at the risk of war with the neighbouring King of Dahomey. Etienne then announced his own African policy, which was to grab most of north-west Africa:

> If you drop a perpendicular from the frontier of Tunis, through Lake Chad to the Congo, you could say that the greater part of the territories bounded by this line and the sea ... are French, or destined to be included in France's sphere of influence. We have there a vast domain which it is for us to colonize and make fruitful....[3]

The idea was so extravagant that some deputies of the Right burst into laughter.

However, Etienne was explaining that France now had the chance to make Lake Chad the hub of a vast new empire, with its spokes radiating to the French possessions in all directions. In private he was already prepared to make his own play for Lake Chad from each direction, wresting it from the grasp of Goldie's Niger Company, whether the Quai approved or not. To do so he plotted a *fait accompli* with the secret help of the hard-line colonialists, led by a journalist known as 'Harry Alis' (Henri-Hippolyte Percher was his real name). Alis and his friends had set up a commercial company, the Syndicat français du Haute-Benito, and an offshoot, the Compagnie française de l'Afrique centrale. Already they had sent a private expedition to Chad, led by Paul Crampel, who was moving up from the French Congo in the south-east. They now proposed two further attacks on Chad: one from the west, from the upper Niger, led by Commandant Monteil; the other from the south, from the lower (that is, British)

Niger, led by Lieutenant Mizon. The British would be told that Mizon was an explorer engaged in purely scientific and commercial work. In fact, Mizon's job, like Crampel's and Monteil's, was purely political: to sign treaties with the natives in order to force Ribot's hand when France next negotiated frontiers with England and Germany. Etienne was invited to give covert support (including 50,000 francs) to these operations, which could always be officially disavowed if their cover was blown.

Etienne was delighted to oblige. He arranged for the Cabinet to sanction both missions, taking care that the Quai d'Orsay and the Cabinet knew as little about the real purpose of Mizon's trip as the officials of Goldie's Niger Company. Apart from these secret agreements, he continued to bully the Quai d'Orsay, demanding a forward policy all along the steaming coast from Senegal to the Niger delta. The Anglo-French agreement of 5 August 1890 now gave the go-ahead to link the three French footholds – on the Guinea coast, the Ivory Coast and the Slave Coast – with the upper Niger and the interior of the Sudan. (Of course it also implicitly sealed off the three British footholds of Gambia, Sierra Leone and the Gold Coast.)

Where was to be the main line of the French advance from the sea? It had always been assumed that Senegal was the gateway to the Niger, but epidemics of yellow fever haunted Senegal and the cost of a Senegal–Niger railway defied belief. Now Captain Louis-Gustave Binger's recent explorations in the interior of the Ivory Coast seemed to suggest that in the open bush to the east of the mountains of Samori's empire lay the key to commercializing the Niger. Certainly Etienne believed that Binger's explorations had changed everything. He stamped on the British proposal, in 1889, that the Ivory Coast, French Guinea and the Slave Coast should all be swapped for the Gambia, so that the French could unite both parts of Senegal. It was the Ivory Coast, not Senegal, that was the true ladder to the Sudan and Etienne sent his West African trouble-shooter, Jean Bayol, to secure its frontiers in discussions with the British. He had already insisted that Binger's treaties in the interior be formally notified to the Powers.

Everything was now ready for exploiting that cornucopia of tropical goods and tropical gold awaiting discovery in the upper Niger. About its existence, Etienne, like all the civilian colonialists, had little doubt; the question was simply how to exploit it. To put it bluntly, was it now time for traders to take over from soldiers?

The previous year, 1889, Etienne had set up a departmental commission and thrown the book at them. Must they still send out military columns every year? Were there too many expensive forts? Need this disastrous Senegal–Niger railway be extended further, or should they start again from the south? Above all, was the foothold on the Niger at Bamako sufficient? Or did they need to smash the Tukolor empire, then push on east to Timbuctu before they could start to make the Sudan pay?

The Commission's replies were sobering. To make the Sudan viable, 'The period of military conquest must now be considered as closed.'[4] Fewer European troops were needed, many forts could be evacuated or reduced to storage depots; the disastrous railway must be stopped in its tracks and redesigned as a narrow-gauge line. Only two concessions were made to the notoriously headstrong French marine infantry in the Sudan. First, an extra battalion of *tirailleurs* should be raised. Second, the commanding officer should be independent of the civilian Governor of Senegal, making him in law what he was already in practice, the independent military Governor of the Sudan. These proposals were all the more remarkable because Colonel Joseph Gallieni, the ambitious commander in the Sudan during 1887–8, had signed the Commission's report.

In fact, those two years of campaigning had changed Gallieni out of recognition. As a young officer he had hungered for military success, measured in territory captured and Africans slaughtered. Now he measured it by the standards of peace. As he told Etienne, 'A campaign like that waged by my predecessor [Desbordes] would be absolutely fatal for the Sudan . . . .'[5] His aim was to avoid fighting and advance trade. He had still to crush one adversary, Al Haj Mahmadu Lamine, a fire-raising *marabout* (holy man) on the upper Senegal, whose jihad threatened his lines of communication. But after burning Lamine's fortress and driving him into British territory at Gambia, Gallieni pursued his first season's march to the Niger without firing a shot. Next season he killed the *marabout*, which ended the revolt, and then devoted himself to encouraging trade. Mud villages, burnt by the French in previous seasons, were rebuilt by Gallieni and monthly fairs were organized.

As for the two rival imperialists to the east and south – Ahmadu, Sultan of the Tukolors, and Samori, the great Malinke warlord – towards them Gallieni had been careful to keep a dignified reserve. In his heart he felt they were doomed and that their empires would, in due course, fall into the hands of the French. Meanwhile, the solemn treaties signed with Ahmadu and Samori did not stop him doing his best to hasten the process. Gallieni had used secret agents to urge the Bambaras to resist their Tukolor overlords, and had given arms to encourage Tieba, the King of Sikasso, to resist Samori – a gift which was so effective that Samori's army never recovered from their repulse when besieging his capital.

Etienne, at any rate, was convinced, like Gallieni and the Commission, of the overriding need for peace in the Sudan. Why then had he given permission in February 1890 for Gallieni's successor, Commandant Louis Archinard, to push down the Niger to Segu and capture Ahmadu's capital? It would seem that this decision was made against Etienne's better judgement. Archinard claimed, quite incorrectly, that Ahmadu threatened to break the peace. But perhaps Etienne's decision was also a product of his feud with the Quai d'Orsay, affording a temptation to bait Ribot that he could not resist. If so, it proved a boomerang. Etienne would rue the day when he gave Archinard his head.

* * *

Archinard, a protégé of both Gallieni and Gallieni's predecessor, Desbordes, had an unusual style for a soldier. He was short and slim, wore his brown hair in a fringe and his moustache neatly clipped, and spoke slowly without raising his voice or repeating himself. At first sight, he might have been taken for the chaplain, rather than the commander. But there was something compelling about Archinard. His face remained impassive even in the heat of battle, apart from a discreet smile he sometimes allowed himself when pleased. Normally his calm, golden brown eyes remained half hidden by a pair of steel spectacles. Archinard was a man of steel will and intense but limited vision.

Two years earlier, before Gallieni was converted to the need for peace, he had sent his protégé a word of warning: 'Don't pay any more attention to the missives of M. Billecoq & Co. [Mr Soft-Hat & Co., i.e. Etienne] than you think necessary ... Everything I accomplished during these two campaigns was done in spite of the ministry ....'[6] Of course Archinard agreed. He despised civilians and their claptrap about the civilizing mission. What he wanted was military victory for the French army, and professional advancement for himself.

To deceive Paris by claiming Ahmadu was about to attack, and to deceive Ahmadu by posing as a peace-maker: neither *ruse de guerre* cost Archinard much sleep. In January 1890 he wrote to the Sultan, promising to keep the peace, provided the Sultan did the same. Six months earlier, he had sent off a young lieutenant called Jean-Baptiste Marchand (a name that would be famous before the decade was out), with instructions to reconnoitre Segu without arousing the Tukolors' suspicions. Ahmadu himself was away at Nioro, in northern Kaarta, and had made his son, Madani, Governor of Segu till he returned. So Marchand took the gunboat *Mage* 150 miles down the Niger and steamed past the city, taking notes from the deck like a tourist.

In November 1889 Marchand reported that Segu was *'très fort'*.[7] The immensely thick oval walls of the *tata*, nearly two miles in circumference, were built of mud, not stone. This was the difficulty. Once breached, mud walls would collapse and provide new cover for the defenders. Within the walls there were a network of redoubts and a strong point, Madani's headquarters. In short, if the defenders decided to defend it, Segu would be a tough nut to crack.

Archinard did not share this view; and Archinard was proved right.

At half-past five on the morning of 6 April 1890, Archinard concealed his impatience at the late arrival of his Bambara allies, led by Mari-Diara, and their fleet of dug-outs. Across the Niger, the French column caught its first glimpse of the city of Segu, silent in the orange glow of dawn. Its huge *tata* of mud walls, and five great gateways, dominated the south bank like a mirage. The Niger, bloated and yellow with recent rains, filled the deep channel, 1,000 metres wide, winding through the sandy plain.

As Archinard suspected, the river was impossible to ford. So he had to wait till his motley force – 103 French officers and men, 4 native officers and 635 Senegalese *tirailleurs* and Spahis, supported by 3,000 wild Bambara auxiliaries and their even wilder camp followers – could be ferried across in dug-outs to a landing place below the city. The mountain guns followed. Then the commander gave the order to open fire. Two huge 95-millimetre siege guns, dragged up to the sand dunes of the north bank, began to hack out a breach in the riverside wall close to the Governor's house. The small mountain guns on the south bank poured hundreds of shells into the maze of alleyways. Not a shot came in reply.

At about half-past twelve Archinard learnt from some villagers that the Tukolors had fled. There was no need to charge through the great jagged breach made by the two 95-millimetre guns; Archinard's men marched in by the main gate. They found disappointingly little loot, apart from the Sultan's wives abandoned in the harem and a battered hoard of old coins and jewellery hidden in the treasury. The famous treasure of Segu, rumoured to be worth over 20 million francs, proved to be worth, at most, a tenth of this; and Ahmadu had taken (or spent) most of it, leaving only 250,000 francs (£10,000) in Segu.

Archinard had never been much interested in money, so he soon got over the disappointment. His aim was to smash the Islamic empire of the Tukolors and to turn the pagan Bambaras, their unfortunate victims, into loyal subjects of France. The first task proved easier than the second. Madani had fled. Other Tukolors sent a deputation, begging protection from the Bambaras. Archinard gave them five days to leave for their homeland, Futa in Senegal, from which their fathers had come over thirty years earlier. Then he chose a new Fama (King) for Segu, Mari-Diara, the son of the last Bambara ruler. On 11 April he sent one column towards Bamako, including the Sultan's wives, riding on oxen, and a mass of Tukolor refugees. He himself took the guns and a small column towards Kaarta to attack the Tukolor fortress of Oussébougou. This he captured on 27 April after a surprisingly stiff fight, in which he lost three Europeans and thirteen Senegalese, apart from the casualties among his Bambara allies. But soon Archinard was wearing that discreet smile again.

In late May Ahmadu was stung into trying to cut the strategic railway intended to link the Senegal river to the Niger, and in June he attacked Kale and Kayes. All three attacks were beaten off, and Archinard claimed he had proved his point: Ahmadu could never be trusted. Now the French had a pretext to invade Kaarta and seize Koniakary.

The next season, 1890–1, as soon as the rains made the Senegal river navigable, Archinard returned to attack Ahmadu at Nioro, in northern Kaarta, on the edge of the Sahara. Ahmadu had been joined by his son Madani and his force appeared formidable: 10,000 warriors, according to one account that reached Archinard. For his part, the commander could only put a column of 1,700 men into the field, less than 200 of them Europeans. But Archinard's men were Spahis and *tirailleurs*, well-trained and armed with magazine rifles. Once again they brought along the 95-millimetre siege guns that had struck terror into the garrison at Segu. Once again the Tukolors made no attempt to withstand a siege. After a brief struggle outside the town on 1 January 1891, Ahmadu and a picked band of followers abandoned Nioro and fled eastwards across the desert to Masina, beyond Segu, the last redoubt of the Tukolor empire. Three thousand of his best troops were killed or captured. Archinard lost only five men killed and fifty-three wounded. As he had anticipated, the second campaign, like the first, was a walk-over.

Meanwhile, there was trouble with the Bambaras. Mari-Diara, the proud descendant of the Bambara kings of Segu, had never inspired much confidence in Archinard after he had kept him waiting for half an hour before the assault on the city. Mari-Diara and his advisers seemed to be more interested in loot than good government. Nonetheless, he had been appointed Fama under the eye of Captain Underberg, the French Resident, and a small garrison of *tirailleurs*. Two months later the captain was told that the Fama was plotting to make the *tirailleurs* drunk and escape south to Nango. The Fama and his advisers were speedily despatched by firing squad and a rival claimant called Bodian was appointed in his place.

This incident occurred in June 1890. The following February, the Bambaras revolted in Baninko, to the south of Segu, and for a time things looked unpleasant. It turned out that Mari-Diara's three brothers had stirred up the revolt, which soon spread to Segu. Bodian, the new Fama, was away on campaign with the French. But Archinard persuaded 2,000 of the Tukolor warriors, who had surrendered, to enlist against their traditional enemy, the Bambaras. With these high-spirited allies (who brought 5,000 slaves and other camp followers) Archinard led his small column rapidly south, leaving behind the two siege guns, which he imagined would be unnecessary. On 18 February he crossed the Niger at Nyamina, swimming the horses and cattle across, while the rest were ferried over in dug-outs. On 24 February they reached a mud-walled village called Diéna, the centre of the revolt. After a seven-hour bombardment from light artillery, the rebels still had plenty of fight left in them. Archinard gave the Tukolors the honour of going first into the two breaches, north and west, but they were driven back in confusion. The bugle sounded for the Senegalese *tirailleurs* to carry forward the tricolour. But the flag soon vanished in the confusion of hand-to-hand fighting among the ruins of the village. The French had to hunt out the Bambara street by street and lane by lane – bayonets and rifles against muzzle-loaders and poisoned arrows – until the enemy fled across the plain, hacked and skewered by a pursuing pack of Spahis.

Archinard had to admit that the Bambaras fought with stubborn courage. His own victory, he realized, had been dearly bought because there were no siege guns to smash open the defences. He had suffered several hundred casualties: sixteen European officers wounded, eleven natives dead, ninety-three wounded, as well as an unknown number of casualties among his Tukolor allies. He remarked sourly to the Governor of the Senegal that he had not been given the means to do the job properly. Yet Archinard remained as confident as ever. 'Today the situation is restored,' he wrote two days after storming Diéna. 'We are masters everywhere, and those who wanted to attack us are now wondering how to defend themselves.'[8]

With the Tukolors routed and the Bambaras brought to heel, Archinard now judged it time to deal with Samori, the most formidable African power in the western Sudan, and the main threat to his advance – apart from those duffers, M. Billecoq & Co., in the Rue Royale at Paris.

At first the incumbent in the Rue Royale, Eugène Etienne, was delighted with the success of Gallieni's protégé. The conquest of Segu, the invasion of Kaarta, the capture of Nioro and the expulsion of Ahmadu had ended the tyranny of the Tukolors with surgical efficiency. It was the Bambara revolt that began to puzzle and disturb him. The French should have been received as liberators. Why did the Bambaras fight them with such ferocity? Public opinion, he told Archinard, needed to be reassured that the Sudan would not be plunged into permanent warfare.

Etienne was still more disturbed when he learnt about Samori. Archinard reported that Samori, the *imam*, was intriguing with the British in Sierra Leone and buying modern magazine rifles. (Both reports were true.) From this, Archinard concluded that a campaign must be launched to crush him as soon as possible. He followed this up with claims that Samori was hand-in-glove with Ahmadu and (somewhat inconsistently) had fomented the Bambara revolt. But Etienne refused to be persuaded to break with Samori. On the contrary, he sent strict instructions to Archinard *not* to attack. He was despatching Captain Péroz to negotiate a new treaty as soon as possible.

No one ever claimed that Etienne's face remained – like Archinard's – impassive in the heat of battle. Etienne must have turned purple when he next heard from the upper Niger. Defying Paris, Archinard had marched off and captured Kan-kan, south of the river, Samori's headquarters. Etienne called it 'an absolute violation of instructions',⁹ and issued a fierce reprimand. Archinard proved indifferent. When he was accused of failing to report to his superiors, he replied airily that he never bothered to report minor incidents. What could Etienne do to halt this runaway horse?

The dismal truth was that, once begun, the war against Samori had to be continued. The new French garrison at Kan-kan could not be pulled back or abandoned for fear of the damage to French prestige throughout the Sudan. This was the view of the Governor of Senegal, de Lamothe, much as he deplored Archinard's disobedience of orders. Even sacking Archinard proved beyond Etienne's power. Archinard went down with blackwater fever and was invalided home, a hero of the Sudan, and promoted colonel, presumably on the recommendation of his pugnacious old chief, Desbordes, now a general. At least Etienne felt he would be able to keep a tight rein on Archinard's successor, his friend Gustave Humbert.

That, too, proved a forlorn hope. Commandant Humbert defied Paris with a brutal frankness that made even Archinard 'tremble', he confessed later, for his friend's career. The cost of holding the Sudan exceeded the estimates by over a million francs. The political costs were even higher. Etienne was forced to promise not to authorize further expeditions without approval of the Chamber. But it made no difference what Etienne promised. Humbert was in command.

Worst of all, Humbert proved much less effective fighting Samori than in defying the Colonial Department in the Rue Royale. Archinard had recklessly under-estimated the difficulties of the war he had launched. Humbert's advance soon became bogged down in the wooded valleys south of Kan-kan. These setbacks were as bad for French prestige as the Governor had feared. Once again Segu rose in rebellion.

Back in Senegal, yellow fever raged. Forced to retreat, Humbert suffered from tantrums, denouncing the Governor and Etienne for letting him down. He threw up his command: 'I was wrong to expose myself to disaster and dishonour ... I was lucky to escape ... I shall leave here ... to sacrifice my position and my life in order to make the truth known.'[10] He then turned on his friend Archinard, as the main cause of the disaster; why on earth had he failed to consolidate his conquests after defeating Ahmadu? This was fair enough. However, there was another reason why Humbert failed to subdue Samori. He was fighting a man of genius.

The country to the south of Kan-kan, with its Arcadian valleys along the river Milo and rugged mountains above, is ideal for guerrilla warfare. From this green fastness, 250 miles from the sea, Samori preyed upon the *tirailleurs*. He would have been flattered to hear Humbert's verdict on his method of warfare: 'Samori's troops fight exactly like Europeans ... with less discipline perhaps, but with much greater determination.'[11] Samori had learnt that large-scale encounters were too costly in either attack or defence, because the French were armed with artillery and magazine rifles.

From the mid-1880s Samori had been buying Gras rifles for his warriors, importing them from arms dealers in Freetown, Sierra Leone, with the connivance of British officials. To pay for them, he sent pack mules loaded with gold and ivory back over the mountains. He also paid, indirectly, in slaves: rebels or men captured in war, whom he sold to the wild tribes of the eastern plains in exchange for horses. He could never get enough modern rifles, even though his village blacksmiths had been trained to produce their own efficient copies of the Gras repeater. Nor did he ever succeed in training his men to use their rifles as the Europeans did. Disciplined though they were, his warriors were too excited to co-ordinate their fire – or even to fire straight – unlike the Africans trained by the French. It was this handicap, together with his lack of artillery and the decline in the number of his troops, that forced Samori to concentrate on guerrilla war.

At its peak Samori's army had numbered at least 30,000 men, all armed with guns of various kinds. That was before the disastrous siege of Sikasso in 1887, and the wave of uprisings that had followed. In 1886 the treaty with the French had looked like a diplomatic coup for Samori. In fact Gallieni, as mentioned earlier, had secretly armed one of Samori's rivals, Tieba, the Fama of Sikasso. In the eighteen-month-long siege of his town, Samori had lost his best generals and the flower of his army. Anarchy then spread across most of his empire. Undaunted, Samori re-conquered these provinces and re-opened the strategic road to Freetown. By 1890 he was back in the market, buying British rifles, ready to face what he knew to be the final showdown with the French.

For Samori had no illusions about the treaty he had signed with Gallieni. It gave him only a breathing space, as the French had no intention of sharing the spoils of the Sudan with any rival imperialist, white or black.

When Archinard broke the treaty and seized Kan-kan in early April 1891, Samori retreated and regrouped. He fought a series of delaying actions as Humbert's column plodded up the valley of the Milo. Tactically, he showed an agility no European commander could match. At first there was a stalemate. The French column halted under the mountains. As Humbert began to run out of supplies, Samori adopted scorched-earth tactics, and the stalemate became a retreat. Yet even now, when Humbert was writing despairing letters home, Samori knew that he had lost the war.

Humbert had left behind small garrisons in hastily built forts at Bisanduga and Kérwané. It would be months before help could reach them. But Samori had no artillery – or men who could aim their rifles – and he found it impossible to crush these frail garrisons.

In February 1892 he came to a daring, perhaps reckless decision. He would abandon his whole empire to the French – the green fastness of Konya, the heartland of his trading empire, as well as the sandy plains south of the Niger. He would take his people and carve out a new military empire, unclaimed by rivals, among the wild pagans north of the Ivory Coast.

*   *   *

Back in Paris, Commandant Humbert found everyone at sixes and sevens. The Ministry, unable to cope with his tantrums, wanted to replace him with Gallieni. The generals refused. Gallieni was now openly denouncing Archinard, who replied that his old friend was a 'scoundrel'.[12] The generals in Paris, Brière and Desbordes, both arch-expansionists, took Archinard's side. He was appointed to replace Humbert so that he could prove the falseness of Humbert's accusations against him.

So once again, the Under-Secretary of the Colonial Department found himself tied to this runaway horse, while promising the Chamber of Deputies that he would authorize no further advance.

By the summer of 1892, when Archinard returned to the Sudan, Freycinet's government had expired and Etienne had been cast out of the Rue Royale. His unfortunate successor, Emile Jamais, was a well-meaning nonentity. Jamais had appointed Archinard military governor of the Sudan, and had forbidden him to lead expeditions in the field, or to allow his commanders to launch new operations. Archinard snapped his fingers. He sent Commandant Combes to pursue part of Samori's army across the frontiers of Sierra Leone – British territory – nearly causing a diplomatic crisis. In March 1893 he sent a new column another 150 miles down the Niger and led it in person. His pretext was that Ahmadu had now displaced his brother, Muniru, as Sultan of Masina, but it was a slap in the face for Paris just the same. In turn, Archinard captured the cities of Masina beyond Segu – Jenne and Mopti and Bandiagara – and installed Aquibou, another of Ahmadu's brothers, as Sultan, while Ahmadu himself fled eastwards down the river to Timbuctu and beyond.

When the triumphant Commandant-Supérieur returned to Paris in the summer of 1893 he found the Colonial Department even less welcoming than on his previous return. Jamais had resigned. The new Under-Secretary installed at the Pavillon de Flore (the Colonial Department's grand new home adjoining the Louvre) was Théophile Delcassé, a rising star of the young colonialists and a persistent critic, as *rapporteur* of the colonial budget, of Archinard's unauthorized campaign. For support in the Chamber, Delcassé could now count on the newly formed Groupe Coloniale de la Chambre, a pressure group of ninety colonialist deputies drawn from all sides of the Chamber, including Etienne, who had a personal score to settle with the Commander. Common to all of them was the conviction that imperialism was about trade, not conquest. None of them could find a good word to say for Archinard and what he stood for. The Sudan credits voted by the Chamber spoke for themselves: in 1891, 3,890,000 francs; in 1892, 5,200,000 francs; in 1893, a projected 8,000,000 francs. And what had the military achieved with their unnecessary wars of conquest? Trade was at a standstill. No progress had been made in opening the great east-west trade route to Chad and beyond. Military conquest was the antithesis of true colonial expansion, which was advanced by diplomatic missions and commercial treaties, not 95-millimetre siege guns.

Worst of all in the eyes of humanitarians (though the French Chamber had no equivalent to the English humanitarian lobby) was the fact that Archinard was quite happy with African methods of government, making a mockery of his mission to civilize. He installed client kings, like Aquibou, who grew fat, like their predecessors, on the trade in slaves and other loot. Archinard made no effort to stop these *razzias*, raids for slaves. *Le Siècle*, the main colonialist newspaper, denounced him for running the Sudan as 'a slave bazaar'.[13] This seemed mere rhetoric – yet the prospect of plunder was indeed the main reason why Senegalese enlisted as *tirailleurs*. Female prisoners were rationed out to them after battle, to be used as concubines (under the euphemism of '*épouses libres*'). When the enemy's slaves were freed it was only to be forced to serve as porters or conscripted as *tirailleurs*. In general the slave trade flourished under the walls of the new French forts just as it had flourished under the town-walls of Ahmadu and Samori. It paid better than any other business, and Archinard gave it his blessing by taking the traditional 10 per cent tax.

The loathing that many deputies felt for the military gave Delcassé the courage to strike. In November 1893 he dismissed Archinard without warning and appointed a civilian Governor of the Sudan. 'The era of conquest is definitely closed,'[14] he reported. Yet within weeks the irrepressible marine infantry were advancing once again, their eyes firmly set on Timbuctu, which was captured in 1893.

But this lay in the future. We must turn back three years, to 27 June 1890, when Cecil Rhodes's pioneer column splashed across the Motlousi river and set out to occupy and develop his vast new empire in the territory to which he would give his name.

CECIL JOHN RHODES

CHAPTER 21

A New Rand?

Mashonaland and Matabeleland (Rhodesia), Cape Colony, the
Transvaal and England
27 June 1890–December 1892 and before

'I am tired of this mapping out of Africa at Berlin;
without occupation, without development ... the gist
of the South African Question lies in the extension
of the Cape Colony to the Zambesi.'

Cecil Rhodes in the Cape House of Assembly, 1888

It was just over fifty years since the *voortrekkers*, the Boer pioneers of the
Great Trek, had shaken the dust of Cape Colony off their feet. In their canvas-
covered wagons, followed by their cattle, sheep and African servants, they had
splashed across the drifts of the Orange and Vaal rivers to carve out an empire
in the 'empty' veld to the north. On 27 June 1890, it was the turn for a Great
Trek, British-style, out-Boering the Boers – a leap out of Cape Colony, clean
over the Boer republics, past Matabeleland into Mashonaland. It was here that
Cecil Rhodes would use his pioneers to create his own kingdom, 'Rhodesia', in
the still 'emptier' land between the Limpopo and the Zambezi, 300 miles to the
north of the Transvaal.

To compare the two treks might seem absurd. They were as different as
biltong (dried meat) from roast beef. Of course there were the same discomforts
that attended any South African trek in the dry season: dust everywhere,
enclosing everyone like a cloud, from the African *voorloper* at the front of the
first covered wagon to the men bringing up the rear; and the constant bang of
the springless tyres of the wagon wheels grinding over the ruts in the veld and
jamming in the stony streambeds. But the Boers had gone over the frontier as
fugitives without a flag, defying the British authorities to stop them. In contrast,
Cecil Rhodes's pioneers carried two Union Jacks; both the Cape government's
and the imperial government's. Their mission was confirmed by the royal charter
for Rhodes's company, and London had cabled the go-ahead.

The Boers had migrated in families, like flocks of birds, each family and clan
grouping and regrouping under different leadership. Rhodes's pioneers had not
a woman among them. They were a single invading column, an assegai made
in Britain, paid for by Rhodes's new Charter Company and honed by military
discipline.

That at any rate was the theory. But Rhodes himself was not with the column
on the Bechuanaland border at the Motloutsi. He had been forced by a political

The pioneers' push into Mashonaland, June-September 1890

→ Route of Rhodes's Pioneer Column
■-■-■► Missionaries' and traders' route to King's Kraal at Bulawayo
==== Track to Mashonaland via Bulawayo

Miles 0 — 200
Kilometres 0 — 300

BAROTSELAND

Victoria Falls

Death of Shangani Patrol in 1893 ✗

MATABELELAND

BECHUANALAND PROTECTORATE

Shiloh
Bulawayo
Thabas Induna
Matopo

Mangwe

Tati R. Shashi

Motloutsi Tuli

Palapye Elebi

Shoshong

To Mafeking & Kimberley

R. Zambezi Zumbo

Tete

R. Hunyani

R. Umfuli R. Mazoe

Mt Hampden Salisbury

Hartley Hill MASHONALAND

R. Shangani R. Gwelo R. Umniati Fort Charter

R. Bemzesi Forest

Gwelo Iron Mine Hill

Hills

Belingwe Fort Victoria Providential Pass GREAT ZIMBABWE RUINS

R. Umzingwani R. Lundi

R. Nuanetsi R. Sabi

Boer Trek ZOUTPANSBERG

R. Limpopo or Crocodile

TRANSVAAL REPUBLIC

MOZAMBIQUE

To Beira, 150 miles

MAP 13

crisis at the Cape – which resulted in his taking over as Prime Minister – to stay behind at De Beers in Kimberley, his own financial and political power base 200 miles further south. Even if his restless spirit was everywhere, a great deal had to be done in a hurry and a great deal left to luck.

The column at the Motloutsi was a strange makeshift, judged by military standards. The 200 raw recruits had come by train to Kimberley and then ridden up to this dusty camp in the bleached dry end of the Bechuanaland protectorate. They were young, would-be farmers and prospectors, with new rifles and brown corduroy trousers and 'digger' hats. To escort them were 500 men of the newly formed Charter Company (British South Africa Company) police with a naval searchlight powered by steam; and to help cut the road were 350 Ngwato labourers and 2,000 oxen pulling 117 ox-wagons, with hundreds of other Africans to do the menial tasks. The Pioneers were supposed to represent an élite of a kind. Rhodes had promised £87,000 to a young Cape adventurer,

Frank Johnson, to organize the expedition, and to choose the 200 pioneers in the Cape, to be picked as carefully as Noah picked animals for the Ark. For reasons of Cape politics, the pioneer column must have Afrikaners as well as British. In practice it had something of everything: not only farmers, but doctors, engineers, cricketers, parsons, butchers, bakers, unemployed miners, army deserters, even a Jesuit priest. This was hardly the way to choose men, either as settlers or as a fighting force.

Equally bizarre was Rhodes's choice of leaders. To push a fighting force across hostile, unexplored country demands leadership of a high order and a clear chain of command. Rhodes had made sure there were enough leaders with overlapping functions to provide plenty of confusion.

There was an experienced British regular officer, Lieutenant-Colonel E. G. Pennefather, of the 6th Dragoon Guards, chosen by the Government of the Cape to command the column. But there was a natural conflict of interest between Pennefather and the twenty-three-year-old contractor, Frank Johnson, who would be bankrupted by any serious delays. There was also a special emissary sent by Rhodes, Dr Leander Starr Jameson, or Dr Jim as the Press called him, the excitable young doctor from Kimberley who carried Rhodes's own power of attorney as managing director of De Beers. Finally, there was Frederick Selous, a strong, silent big-game hunter turned folk hero, whose recent bestseller, *A Hunter's Wanderings in Africa*, had made him a legend in Britain and America. Selous was to show the expedition the way – if he could find it. They were to cut a path for their carts along an old hunting track into Mashonaland, skirting Matabeleland and the Ndebele warriors of King Lobengula. Selous was uncommunicative about the route. If all went well, they would be beyond Matabeleland as far north-east as Mount Hampden, wherever that was, before the rains broke.

On 24 June, when the column had concentrated at the Motloutsi, a brass hat from the Cape, Major-General Paul Methuen, gave them a certificate of efficiency. This formal blessing of the imperial government, arranged by Rhodes, was the final piece of swagger. If the officers had misgivings about the route, the general's inspection cannot have done much to dispel them:

Lord Methuen: Gentlemen, have you got maps?
The officers: Yes, sir.
Lord Methuen: And pencils?
The officers: Yes, sir.
Lord Methuen: Well, gentlemen, your destiny is Mount Hampden. You go to a place called Siboutsi. I do not know whether Siboutsi is a man or a mountain. Mr Selous, I understand, is of the opinion that it is a man; but we will pass that by. Then you get to Mount Hampden. Mr Selous is of the opinion that Mount Hampden is placed ten miles too far to the west. You'd better correct that: but perhaps, on second thoughts, better not. Because you might possibly be placing it ten miles too far to the east. Now good morning, gentlemen.[1]

What were the aims of the 200 pioneers as they splashed across the Motloutsi on 27 June and vanished into the dust clouds that enwrapped them like a smoke screen? For some it was enough to be part of an adventure organized by South Africa's leading British colonial, Cecil Rhodes, the Colossus. Others were, no doubt, attracted by the lure of the 3,000-acre farms to be given away free to each Pioneer in return for cutting the road to Mount Hampden. (No mention was made of the present occupiers of the land, the Shona, whom Lobengula and the Ndebele claimed as their vassals.)

But the main attraction was obviously gold – the fifteen gold claims to be given free to each pioneer. Mashonaland was believed to be the biblical land of Ophir. There had been gold mines there in the time of the kings of Monomatapa, the African rulers who had traded in gold with the Portuguese who settled on the littoral of Mozambique during the sixteenth and seventeenth centuries. For unknown reasons, that mysterious African kingdom had collapsed. Nothing was now left of Monomatapa, except some grandiose ruins called Zimbabwes dotted about the bush and the auriferous quartz from the abandoned gold-mines. In 1867 these quartz seams were discovered and reported to be sensationally rich by a German schoolmaster turned explorer, Carl Mauch. So it was gold that would power the Charter Company's new colony in Zambezia (soon to be re-named Rhodesia), just as gold had already transformed the economic and political power of the Transvaal since the discovery of the Rand in 1886. It was this simple idea of a new and bigger Rand, an idea as dazzling, creative and destructive as the African sun, that lay behind all Rhodes's tortuous manœuvring of the last four years.

In 1886, when the first sample of gold-bearing conglomerate from the Rand was brought in a stagecoach to Kimberley, Rhodes's meteoric business career was approaching its apparent apogee. As managing director and one of the largest shareholders of De Beers, one of the four main diamond companies at Kimberley, he had just announced to the world what seemed an impossible dream: a plan to grab for De Beers – and himself – a monopoly of the entire diamond industry.

Already Cecil Rhodes was well known in Kimberley for the way he combined boyish dreams of power with precocious expertise in business. He had arrived there in 1871, the first year of the great diamond rush that was to propel the torpid agricultural communities of the Cape into the world of industrial finance and *Realpolitik*. Rhodes was then a shy, solemn, delicate-looking, fair-haired, gangling boy of eighteen, the third son of an obscure but affluent Hertfordshire vicar. After an illness he was supposed to convalesce quietly in South Africa with his older brother, Herbert. But it turned out that Herbert had staked a diamond claim on Colesberg Kopje, the barren hill that soon became famous as the richest hole in the world; and Herbert had not the stamina for business. He became a wanderer and died eight years later when an exploding keg of rum set fire to his hut in Nyasaland. It was Cecil who, despite attacks of poor health apparently caused by a congenital heart defect, soon dominated the mining camp at Kimberley, where the diggers were as tough and as wild as any in the west of America.

How did young Cecil achieve personal mastery over such men? He seemed so naive and so vulnerable; in cricketing flannels, reddened with the dust of the veld, his hands in his pockets, his legs twisted together, he would sit on a bucket dreaming for hours, looking down into the depths of a mine. He was certainly an eloquent talker, when he felt like it, with a flair for attracting allies and 'squaring' enemies (as he called it) that amounted to a kind of genius. But what was special about Cecil Rhodes, what gave him charisma, was not merely the exercise of these skills, which served him so well in business and politics. It was his pride in what he called his 'big ideas',[2] his sense of being born for greatness, of serving great ideals. However extravagant or contradictory they seemed – at one time he was a pro-Boer sneering at the 'imperial factor',[3] at another he was planning to make the whole world subject to the Anglo-Saxon race – South Africa hungered for leadership and many people began to look on Rhodes as their man of destiny.

The source of Rhodes's boyish dreams of power, so strange to encounter in the leader of a colonial mining community, was an intermittent eight-year undergraduate course at Oriel College, Oxford, which he alternated with his business career in Kimberley. He dawdled over his Pass degree in Latin and Ancient History, subjects for which he had painfully little aptitude. The letters he sent back to his business partners in Kimberley, who were manning the mine pumps during his absence, incongruously mixed solemn advice, like the cost of pumping 5,000 gallons of water to a head of 250 feet, or the best type of ice-making machine for the mines, with a high-spirited account of the 'tremendous skirmishes'[4] he had had with his dons, and how he had been nearly caught going to the Epsom races.

No doubt, in contrast with later generations of overseas scholars who perpetuated his name, Rhodes was more interested in impressing his fellows by playing hard at polo and riding to hounds with the Drag than by working to impress the dons. Yet none of his biographers has fully explained why he felt the need for this double life – why a man for whom minutes seemed to be worth millions in South Africa should idle away the months at Oxford. It is enough to say that in some respects Rhodes never grew up. The Oxford of the 1870s, effete as it seemed, put its print on him and strengthened his somewhat confused sense of destiny. He would be the new Midas. He would use his power to transform the world. But what precisely did he have in mind?

It was when Rhodes made a Confession of Faith and drew up his Last Will and Testament in 1877 that the laughable quality of his biggest ideas became apparent to the few who knew him intimately. He left his fortune in trust to Sidney Shippard, the attorney-general at the diamond fields, and to Lord Carnarvon, the Secretary of State for the Colonies, who were to form a 'Secret Society' composed of dedicated fanatics and modelled on the Jesuits. The true aim of this Secret Society was to be 'the extension of British rule throughout the world, the perfecting of a system of emigration from the United Kingdom

... especially the occupation of the whole continent of Africa, the Holy Land, the valley of the Euphrates, the Islands of Cyprus and Candia [Crete], the whole of South America.... The ultimate recovery of the United States as an integral part of the British Empire ... then finally the foundation of so great a power to hereafter render wars impossible and promote the best interests of humanity'.[5]

Fortunately for Rhodes's reputation as a politician, this imperialist fantasy was not made public till after his death. His political reputation in South Africa was based on his stance as a no-nonsense colonial, the man who could square the Afrikaner Bond (Union), and reconcile them with the English, by standing up to 'Grandmama',[6] as he called the home government. This anti-imperialism was not a pose or simply a tactic. There was a consistency about Rhodes's political speeches in the 1880s which showed he had as sound a nose for the political realities of the Cape as he did for the great pipe of diamonds at Kimberley on which everything depended.

There were two inescapable facts of life in Cape Colony. First, the majority of the whites were Afrikaners and eighty years of British rule had given them no sentimental attachment to the British flag. But they did recognize the usefulness of the British connection protecting them from other predatory Powers. Second, the minority who were English by origin and did have a sentimental attachment combined it with a virulent colonial nationalism, fed by the grant of self-government in 1872. They shared the Afrikaners' passion for independence and resentment of the least interference by Downing Street, especially if Downing Street tried to protect African rights. So it was Rhodes's longterm aim to unite the two white communities at the Cape at the expense of Grandmama – and the Africans.

Rhodes went further. Already by the late 1880s two things pointed to the eventual union of the self-governing states of South Africa. These were the need for a common native policy (meaning the need for black labour and white supremacy), and the need for a common railway-and-customs policy (meaning the need to prevent the Cape from being squeezed out of the lucrative Transvaal markets). Rhodes promised the voters that the Cape would be the dominant state in this new dominion and the dominion would naturally be under the British flag. But how could the Cape's leadership be restored just when the gold discoveries of the Rand seemed to be tilting the balance of power towards the Transvaal? It was here that Rhodes offered what he called his 'key' – the El Dorado north of the Limpopo.

He had first focused the attention of the Cape on the north soon after becoming a member for Barkly West, near Kimberley, in the Cape Parliament. He was a poor speaker who fidgeted like a child, wore eccentrically shabby clothes and had a habit of breaking into falsetto laughter. But he quietly made a name for himself as a man of unusual conviction.

The first step, Rhodes insisted, was to secure Bechuanaland for the Cape. This was the corridor running north from the diamond fields in the Cape along the western borders of the Free State and the Transvaal. It was through Bechuanaland that the great missionaries Moffat and Livingstone had pushed northwards into Central Africa, and possession of this Missionaries Road in the wilderness was essential if in due course the Cape was to expand into the rich, cool plateaux of Matabeleland, Mashonaland and beyond. Rhodes put this strategic imperative to the Cape House of Assembly on 16 August 1883:

> You are dealing with a question upon the proper treatment of which depends the whole future of this Colony. I look upon this Bechuanaland territory as the Suez Canal of the trade of this country, the key of its road to the interior. The question before us is this: whether the Colony is to be confined within its present borders, or whether it is to become the dominant State in South Africa, and spread its civilisation over the interior.[7]

To Rhodes's chagrin, the Prime Minister of the Cape, Thomas Scanlen, was not interested in the forward policy. Bechuanaland was mostly desert, with squabbling native chiefs, expendable. He would do nothing to stop the Transvaal taking it. At this time the Cape's Treasury was crippled by a recent war with Basutoland and a £14 million railway debt. It could not afford a penny to expand its frontiers. Already freebooters from the Transvaal were trekking across into Bechuanaland. In due course their unofficial 'republics', called Goshen and Stellaland, would be adopted by the Transvaal. In desperation Rhodes turned to London.

He was full of misgivings about involving Grandmama. For one thing it might upset the Cape Afrikaners, who sympathized with the Transvaal's expansionist policy. For another, there would be protests from the missionary lobby about the land taken by the Boer freebooters. Rhodes had no interest in saving African land from being stolen by Europeans, whether Boer or British. What he did insist upon was that the new settlers should acknowledge the Union Jack of the Cape. In the event, Grandmama – in the form of Gladstone's easy-going Colonial Secretary, Lord Derby – was as deaf to Rhodes's appeals as Scanlen. The Liberals were still licking their wounds after Majuba and shrank from any form of forward policy as if it were the work of the devil.

The next year, however, 1884, was the year of the great volte-face in the colonial policy of Gladstone's government. Already Rhodes had thoroughly put the wind up the British High Commissioner at the Cape, Sir Hercules Robinson. Ever since Majuba and the defeat of Carnarvon's plan for federation, British paramountcy in South Africa had depended on the dominance of the Cape. Now this dominance was threatened by the expanionist aims of the Transvaal. Rhodes's arguments, polished up by Robinson, began to be taken seriously by the mandarins at the Colonial Office. London would try to help the Cape secure Bechuanaland, even if it would be hard to snatch it from under the nose of the Transvaal without offending the Cape Afrikaners.

Fortunately, Kruger and the other Transvaal delegates sailed into London in February 1884 in just the mood for compromise. They had come to re-negotiate the Pretoria Convention which had sealed the peace after Majuba. Under the new Convention of London Kruger won almost complete independence in internal affairs. Lord Derby agreed to abandon the British pledge to protect the

Africans in the Transvaal and give up the imperial veto on legislation which affected them. On his part, Derby persuaded Kruger to accept a western boundary *excluding* Bechuanaland. To reassure the humanitarians, London appointed a well-known missionary, John Mackenzie, to sort out the mess in the unofficial republics in preparation for the handover of Bechuanaland to the Cape.

In August 1884 Mackenzie was sacked for being too well disposed to the Africans. Rhodes was appointed instead, by his friend, the High Commissioner. He squared the Boer freebooters of Stellaland by promising to confirm the titles of land they had taken from the natives. But even this offer did not win over the stubborn Boers of Goshen. It turned out that Kruger was behind them; he had double-crossed Rhodes by issuing a provisional order annexing Goshen to the Transvaal.

Had it not been for one extraordinary change in the strategic map, Gladstone's government would almost certainly have surrendered to Kruger's *fait accompli*. But in August 1884 Bismarck made his astonishing lunge at Angra Pequena. Now Rhodes's arguments had an irresistible momentum. The Cape had a new German colony on its north-west border. If the Transvaal was allowed to take Bechuanaland, it could join hands with Germany and snap its fingers at British paramountcy. So, as we saw earlier, Gladstone's Cabinet plucked up the courage to defy Kruger.

They sent Sir Charles Warren and a military force to impose law and order. Warren's intervention cost the imperial government £1.5 million, and the Transvaal Boers proved the least of his problems. Warren tried to rescue the Africans from their predatory white neighbours, but Rhodes had no intention of letting Grandmama – and the missionary lobby supported by Warren – take direct control of Bechuanaland. It should belong to the Cape; and the freebooters must be allowed to keep their land if they accepted the British flag. He set about making Warren's life unendurable, denouncing 'the imperial factor' as violently as any of his Afrikaner constituents. He was not pro-Boer; he was simply a realist. The only way to check the expansion of the Boer republics was to 'enclose them by the Cape Colony'[8] – in other words, by Cape imperialism. The metropolitan variety would never stand the expense.

Gladstone's government found itself trapped. Rhodes had exploited the hornet's nest stirred up by Warren. The Liberals were indeed shocked by the thought of a large new colony, cut off from the sea and too poor to be self-supporting. But the missionary lobby at Westminster was in full cry. In 1885 a compromise was reached. Northern Bechuanaland, the land of King Khama of the Ngwato, was, by agreement with Khama, made a protectorate and rescued both from the Transvaal and the Cape. Southern Bechuanaland, including the unofficial republics, was made a Crown Colony, to be absorbed in due course into the Cape. (The unfortunate descendants have been paying the price as the Tswana of Bophutatswana, the South African 'homeland', as distinct from the Tswana of independent Botswana.)

On balance, Rhodes was the victor. At least he had taken the first vital step towards building an empire in the north. At no cost to himself, he had his 'Suez

Canal' between the Transvaal and the Kalahari desert, and had saved the road to the north. But who would finance the much more expensive second step of advancing into that mysterious El Dorado in Mashonaland?

It was in 1886 that providence seemed to take a hand and Rhodes found himself, like Midas, turning everything to gold – or to diamonds.

These years between 1886 and 1890 were the most astonishing of Rhodes's astonishing life. It was as though he had been given the magical power to live four careers simultaneously and they were all telescoped into those four years. In Kimberley he was the Great Amalgamator, the Bismarck of the diamond mines. In Johannesburg astride the Rand gold-mines, he was a pioneer of goldbugs and Randlords. At the Cape he was the august Prime Minister of Cape Colony, trusted by both Afrikaners and the English-speaking community. Across the Limpopo he was to be a new kind of colonial imperialist, outflanking all rivals, Boers, Germans and Portuguese, as he pushed up into Mashonaland and the north.

Of course Rhodes's personal magic, which cast a spell on so many of his contemporaries, and now seems somewhat flat, depended on the largely invisible help of assistants. By far the most important of these was Alfred Beit, the son of a Hamburg businessman of Jewish origin, himself born a Lutheran, and a financier and diamond expert of genius. It would be hard to imagine anyone more different in either character or appearance from Rhodes. With his heavy jowl, aquiline nose and high forehead Rhodes looked like a Roman emperor. Beit was as small and round as a gnome. He was also painfully shy and liked publicity as much as a bat likes sunshine. But he was dazzled by Rhodes's talk of 'big ideas', and realized that they shared the same dream of amalgamating the diamond mines. Without Beit's financial skills, Rhodes's big talk might have been merely absurd.

Second came Charles Rudd, a cheerful and industrious Old Harrovian who had come to the veld, like Rhodes, in search of health, and had found a fortune there as well. Rudd was no genius, but he was completely trustworthy, which was more than could be said for many of the 'koppie-wallopers' who bought diamonds legally or illegally at Kimberley. It was Rudd who kept Rhodes's business going while Rhodes was gallivanting around Oxford. Rudd always had his feet on the ground, whether running a mine or mopping up rival diamond claims in Kimberley.

Rhodes's third partner might have seemed especially incongruous: Jan Hofmeyr, the leading Afrikaner politician of his day. At first Hofmeyr had been put off by Rhodes's style in the Cape Parliament, his buffoonery. He suspected him of jingoism. Then Hofmeyr, like Beit, suddenly realized that they shared a dream and must join forces. Hofmeyr's dream was to amalgamate South Africa into a single nation. He saw no reason why Afrikaners should not belong to the British Empire, provided that they were given a dominion with virtual independence in home affairs, like the French in Canada. Hofmeyr knew it would be years before the Boers of the Transvaal and Orange Free State would be mature enough to accept federation or union; meanwhile he found Rhodes perfectly sound as a political ally, a man without any dangerous liberal principles. Hofmeyr stood for old-fashioned tariffs to help prop up Cape agriculture, and for a new 'firmness' in native policy. This meant cutting back the growing African electorate in the colony so as to protect white supremacy. To pass racist laws in a colour-blind constitution needs a certain ingenuity. Hofmeyr had plenty. With Rhodes's enthusiastic support he achieved his objective in 1887 by changing the property qualifications of Africans who owned communal land. A quarter of the black and brown electorate were successfully disfranchised.

In 1886, when Rhodes made his second astonishing fortune, his share of the Transvaal gold rush, Beit was not his partner there. Rhodes did not come off best in the Scramble for the Rand, alias Witwatersrand, the Ridge of White Waters, where the mine chimneys from gold-bearing territory began to blacken the veld. Rhodes's own expert from Kimberley, a celebrated American geologist called Gardner Williams, was out of his depth in the Rand. Williams turned up his nose at the confused 'banket' reef (named after a Boer kind of sticky sweet), far more fragmented and far deeper running than conventional gold-bearing quartz. Beit had his own partnership with a fellow German, Julius Wernher. Rhodes left most of the buying to Rudd, and Rudd was cautious. He turned down one farm for £20,000 which was later sold for £20 million. Based on the stake in the Rand, taken by his joint venture with Rudd – Goldfields Ltd – Rhodes's share proved smaller than those of four other Randlords, Alfred Beit, Julius Wernher, Barney Barnato and J.B. Robinson. On the other hand, Rhodes's share of Goldfields Ltd was still a fortune and he arranged for the company to pay him a third of its profits, irrespective of his shareholding.

Then in 1888 Alfred Beit, Rhodes's rival on the Rand, helped him stage the long-awaited coup at Kimberley against Barney Barnato. It was Barnato's Central Mining Company that controlled the best diamond mine of all and blocked an amalgamation of the mines and the control of the market. Barnato was a Jew from London's East End slums, accused of illicit diamond-buying, an ex-showman and prizefighter, not a man to inspire confidence in the City of London or the bourses of Europe. With the help of the firm of Rothschild and other European bankers, Rhodes and Beit first out-manœuvred and then bought out Barnato. Their new company, De Beers Consolidated, soon established a virtual monopoly of the South African diamond industry which provided the world with 90 per cent of the annual diamond sales. The new company also gave Rhodes a special opportunity for empire-building since its unusual trust deed officially empowered it to use its profits for buying land and building an empire.

By 1888, flush with gold and diamonds, Rhodes and his associates were almost ready to move into Mashonaland. Originally he had planned the advance as a piece of official imperialism. But bitter experience in Bechuanaland had taught him to steer clear of both governments. The home government in London, whether Tory or Liberal, was too responsive to the bleeding hearts of the missionary lobby. The Cape government, whether British or Afrikaner dominated, was too concerned about bleeding the local Treasury. It was best for Rhodes and his fellow tycoons to go it alone. Constitutionally they would take the same trail that Goldie had blazed in West Africa, and Mackinnon was about to use in East Africa. They would use the mechanism of a British public company empowered by royal charter to conquer, govern and develop the territory in the name of the Queen. But before applying for a charter from the Queen in London, they needed to wheedle some kind of concession out of King Lobengula, the Ndebele King who claimed sovereignty over neighbouring Mashonaland, conquered by the Ndebele when his father, Mzilikazi, led his people north to escape the spears of Shaka Zulu and the guns of the voortrekkers.

The story of Rhodes's concession is tortuous and not particularly edifying. Lobengula was illiterate but highly intelligent. Like the victim of a Greek tragedy, he found himself caught in the toils. For years he had been besieged by concession hunters of various nationalities, including Boers. He recognized that his kingdom, blessed with a soil and climate superior to that of any of the other South African states, would be the next target for European expansion. Only its remoteness had saved it so far. By 1888 the telegraphs and railways advancing to Kimberley and Johannesburg pointed menacingly across the Limpopo. Lobengula had one of the most powerful armies of any African kingdom, perhaps 15,000 Ndebele and Shona warriors, organized in Impis like their Zulu cousins, and subject to the same ferocious discipline. Their weapon, too, was the assegai, the short stabbing spear which had punctured the Queen's redcoats at Isandlwana. But Lobengula had no illusions about his chance of defending his kingdom by force of arms, although some of his *indunas* (chiefs) and most of the young braves were anxious to wash their spears in European blood.

Lobengula had understood the lesson that the defeat of the Zulus at the battle of Ulundi in 1879 held for them all. No African army, however brave or well-disciplined, could survive long against Europeans armed with modern rifles, machine guns and artillery. Where were Cetshwayo and his boastful Impis now? The best way to defend his people was by diplomacy, either playing off one set of Europeans against another, or by taking his cue from his enemy and rival, Khama, King of the Ngwato, who had placed his country under British protection in 1885. But how to proceed?

There was no shortage of advice in his kraal from Europeans, a riff-raff of traders, hunters and gold prospectors. They squabbled among themselves, and Lobengula very sensibly trusted none of them. His *indunas*, too, were bitterly divided. Should they try to strike a bargain with the English? In that case, which Englishmen could be trusted to keep their word? Lobengula favoured closer relations with the imperial government, perhaps a formal protectorate. But nothing had been settled beyond a negative agreement called the Moffat Treaty, after John Moffat, the British government's emissary, who had negotiated it in February 1888, at Rhodes's suggestion, in order to block the overtures of the Boers. Under this treaty Lobengula undertook not to give away his territories 'without the previous knowledge and sanction'[9] of the British High Commissioner. This was the unresolved situation in September 1888 when

Rhodes's delegation, led by Charles Rudd, rode into Lobengula's capital at Bulawayo.

As a pastoral people, living mainly by cattle-rearing and cattle-raiding, the Ndebele, like the Zulus (and unlike the gold-exporting builders of Zimbabwe, the Shona), had never concerned themselves with architecture. Lobengula's capital was a large oval circle of mud huts, plastered with cow dung, at the centre of a grassy plain dotted with mimosa trees. Twelve miles away to the south the horizon was sealed off by the great granite wall of the Matopos; otherwise it was an open and largely empty landscape. Inside the oval circle of mud huts the visitor was taken to a second circle, the royal enclosure. Here the King had made his palace out of a trader's covered wagon, his throne out of a packing case that had once stored tins of condensed milk.

It was easy to mock the King behind his back as 'an old savage' or a 'shifty customer'[10] in the words of Rhodes's men. No one mocked Lobengula to his face. He was nearly six foot tall and at least twenty stone, naked except for a small loin cloth, and bare-headed except for a Zulu ring. Etiquette at his court was demanding. Visitors of every nationality had to crawl on all fours into the royal presence, then squat in the dust, without a chance of sitting on a chair or getting out of the sun, during endless palavers with the King.

No wonder Rudd and the others were impatient to get their concession in the bag and be off. They were an oddly chosen trio. Charles Rudd was an expert in sorting out mining claims, but knew little or nothing about African rulers. This deficiency was supposed to be supplied by F. R. Thompson, an explorer who spoke Sethuana, which was understood by Lobengula. Unfortunately Thompson had an aversion to the Ndebele. As a boy he had seen his father murdered by some Ndebele rebels in front of his eyes (they forced a ramrod down his throat). The third member of the delegation was more bizarre: a soft-living Fellow of All Souls College, called Rochfort Maguire, a man with whom Rhodes had hob-nobbed at Oxford and had persuaded (much against his instincts) to exchange the fleshpots of All Souls for life on the veld as the legal expert of the delegation.

Left to themselves this odd trio would have made little headway with Lobengula, and there were other concession hunters, representing various interests, who might have snatched the prize from them. But Rudd held a trump card in the shape of the British official, Sir Sidney Shippard, Deputy-Commissioner for Bechuanaland, who now appeared on a visit. Like Sir Hercules Robinson, his boss at the Cape, Sir Sidney believed heart and soul in Rhodes's personal brand of imperialism (a belief that was to be rewarded in both cases, when the men left the colonial service, by substantial gifts of shares, as well as directorships of Rhodes's companies).

Shippard's timely visit was no coincidence. He had come to play a double role: in private advising Rudd on tactics, in public reassuring Lobengula that Rhodes had the blessing of the imperial government, and that to grant him a concession was the best way out of the mess. Rhodes's monopoly would keep out the Boers and also put an end to the pestering by the Boers and other concession hunters.

At first Lobengula was full of misgivings. He must have known that the Swazi ruler, King Mbandzeni, to whom he was related, had lost most of his land by inadvertently granting concessions to Europeans. Rudd asked only for a monopoly of *mining* rights, but obviously they wanted land to farm and develop. Lobengula refused to grant anything of the kind. With the help of Shippard and a missionary called C. D. Helm his misgivings were overcome. The written concession to Rudd conceded no land rights, only 'complete and exclusive charge over all metals and minerals situated in my Kingdom, principalities and dominions, together with full power to do all things that they [the concessionaries] may deem necessary to win and procure the same'. In case this polished text, drafted by Rochfort Maguire, was a little hard for Lobengula to follow, the missionary Helm then insisted that the trio gave an oral explanation of the nature of the agreement. Helm's motives are obscure. Perhaps he was only trying to be fair to the King. But this oral explanation included a promise that finally persuaded Lobengula that Rudd and his friends could be trusted. According to Helm, the promise was that

> ... they would not bring more than ten white men to work in his country, that they would not dig anywhere near towns, etc., and that they and their people would abide by the laws of his country and in fact be as his people.[11]

Poor innocent Lobengula. If he had asked for this promise to be made in writing – or, better still, included in the text of the concession – how different might have been the course of his country's history. But he trusted Helm.

And Helm, in turn, apparently believed what he was told by Rudd; he must have been even more innocent than Lobengula. At any rate, with the assistance of Helm and Shippard, the bargain was finally struck. The price for buying a monopoly of mining rights was not excessive under the circumstances: £100 a month, 1,000 Martini-Henry breech-loading rifles, 100,000 rounds of ammunition and a gunboat on the Zambezi. At noon on 30 October both parties signed the concession, Lobengula putting his cross and using the elephant seal made for him in Europe.

Within a few hours, Charles Rudd set off on a wild ride for Kimberley, which nearly ended in his losing the precious document and dying of thirst, so desperate was he to reach Rhodes before the King realized he had been duped.

*　　*　　*

If Rhodes felt queasy about the means he had used to extract this concession from Lobengula, he certainly did not show it. What were a few white lies to the 'old savage' when so much was at stake? It was a small price, compared with having to fight for the country – or see it pass to the Boers. No doubt this was the general view of Rhodes and his partners. Even Sir Sidney Shippard, who was supposed to be impartial, felt that the cruelties inflicted by Lobengula and his Ndebele on their African neighbours put them beyond the moral pale. If he had had his own way, he confessed on his return from this mission, the Ndebele would be wiped out to a man, 'cut down by our rifles and machine guns like a cornfield by a reaping machine'.[12] The only question was which group of Europeans were to take over from Lobengula.

To out-manœuvre Lobengula had cost Rhodes little, except lies – and the promise of a few hundred pounds of cash and equipment. Far more expensive was the task of out-manœuvring other Europeans who had designs on Lobengula's country. For the next nine months, from the autumn of 1888 to the summer of 1889, Rhodes strained every nerve to buy out or buy off his rivals. The most formidable was a London syndicate headed by an adventurous peer, Lord Gifford, and a well-known stockbroker, George Cawston. Their company had sent an agent to Lobengula's court, Lieutenant Maund, who had arrived directly after Rudd. They already owned mining rights in Bechuanaland, granted by Chief Khama. They could count on even more influential backers in the City and Parliament than Rhodes and his buccaneering friends from the Cape. At this time little was known in London about Rhodes – and what there was hardly redounded to his credit. Lord Salisbury's own comment: 'Rather a pro-Boer MP in South Africa, I fancy', summed up the general attitude. Rhodes's antics as a colonial nationalist at the Cape – his obstruction of General Warren, the imperial peacemaker sent out to protect the Africans from the Boers, his denunciation of the missionary John Mackenzie, Livingstone's heir – had left a sour taste in people's mouths in England. Besides, as noted by Edward Fairfield, one of the world-weary Colonial Office staff, Rhodes was 'not to be regarded as a serious person'. His eldest brother had been to Eton and Rhodes himself had hunted with the Drag hounds at Oxford. But there was a code of decent behaviour which the man took pleasure in flouting. He was, Fairfield noted, 'grotesque, impulsive, schoolboyish, humorous and almost clownish'.[13] In short, the fellow was no gentleman.

Rhodes returned to England in the spring of 1889 determined to get a royal charter. Without one the Rudd concession was useless. He had already agreed, at the suggestion of the Colonial Office, to try to make a deal with Gifford, Cawston and his associates, but unfortunately these rivals had already done him serious damage. In November Lieutenant Maund, their agent at Lobengula's court who had arrived too late to get the concession himself, spilt the beans to the old savage. Rudd had duped him, Lobengula was told, and the King sent Maund with two aged *indunas* to London to protest to the Queen. The news of this deputation's impending arrival focused more opposition on the so-called Rudd Concession. There were protests not only from the missionary lobby, but from British businessmen who resented the idea of a Cape monopoly in a region where they would have liked to see free trade. The Colonial Office became thoroughly confused. Edward Fairfield disapproved in principle of a royal charter for Mashonaland and Matabeleland. 'Something is to be got which will look well enough to invite fools to subscribe to. Such a Chartered Company would never really pay. It would simply sow the seeds of a heap of political trouble and then the promoters would shuffle out of it, and leave us to take up the work of preserving the peace.'[14]

With the arrival of Maund and the deputation from Lobengula, the Colonial Secretary, Lord Knutsford, decided he could not support Rhodes's claim, disavowed by Lobengula. On 27 March 1889 he gave the two elderly *indunas* a letter in what he took to be the correct Ndebele idiom: 'A king gives a stranger an ox, not his whole herd of cattle, otherwise what would other strangers have to eat.'[15] Gifford and Cawston – Maund's own employers – were now negotiating with Rhodes; they were appalled. Soon after, Rhodes received a second, equally unexpected blow. Sir Hercules Robinson, High Commissioner at the Cape, who believed in Rhodes heart and soul (and pocket), was reported to have made a public speech at Cape Town denouncing 'the amateur meddling of . . . ill-advised persons in London which would turn many a colonist from an imperialist into a republican'.[16] It was Robinson who was ill-advised. His frankness caused uproar at Westminster and forced his resignation from the post of High Commissioner.

These setbacks did not unduly dismay Rhodes when he reached London. He believed that everyone had a price and that he could well afford to pay it. Gifford and Cawston were bought off by being given a large block of shares in a new company called the Central Search Company. Other rivals, men with the flimsiest claims, who had vowed to expose the fraud against Lobengula, were dealt with in an equally generous way. Hercules Robinson himself was rewarded with several thousand shares in Central Search.

By the autumn of 1889 the Colonial Secretary had swung back to supporting Rhodes. Now that he had some respectable supporters, influential in the City and the Court, the man's oddities could hardly prove an obstacle to granting a royal charter. The seal was set on the newly-created company, called the British South Africa Company, when two leading dukes, the Tory Duke of Abercorn and the Liberal Duke of Fife, agreed to serve as chairman and vice-chairman respectively. The third pillar of the establishment to join the board was Albert Grey, a member of the South African committee in the House, a supporter of John Mackenzie and a champion of African rights. By the time the royal charter was granted on 29 October 1889, there were no further sneers about the credentials of Rhodes and his associates. On the contrary, people were as impressed by his ideals as they were by the great civilizing mission of King Leopold in the Congo. Some of these new admirers, notably Verschoyle of the *Fortnightly Review* and Scott Keltie, of the Royal Geographical Society, had been secretly put on Rhodes's payroll. Others, like Sir Charles Dilke, the disgraced ex-minister, now devoting himself to good causes, had been privately offered the chance to buy the shares at par, less than the public would pay when they came on the market.

But there were others, colonial enthusiasts like W. T. Stead and Flora Shaw (the future Lady Lugard) who had no private financial inducement to sing Rhodes's praises. They were bewitched by the vision of a far-flung empire, perhaps stretching all the way from the Cape to Cairo, which the great man expounded in his halting sentences and squeaky voice. The new royal charter set no limit on the northern expansion of the Charter Company. Nor did the trust deeds of Rhodes's two highly profitable South African companies, De Beers and Goldfields, which he would use to finance the Charter Company.

It will be recalled that a slice of territory north of the Zambezi, beside Lake Nyasa, was occupied by a British company of a different kind, the African Lakes Company, founded by Scottish philanthropists eager to carry the '3 cs' into the heart of Central Africa. But by 1889 Livingstone's dream had turned sour indeed. The small band of traders and missionaries were in a desperate plight, close to bankruptcy, hemmed in by the Portuguese to the south and by Arab slavers to the east. By now Rhodes seemed the answer to their prayer. With the approval of Lord Salisbury and the Foreign Office, the Lakes Company appealed to the Charter Company for help. No one could be more welcoming than Rhodes. He was delighted to join forces. The Charter Company would pay a subsidy for the Lakes region – £9,000 a year – and would throw its weight behind the campaign to stamp out the slave and liquor trades.

At the same time Rhodes and his associates made no secret of their aim to incorporate into their empire the vast region directly between the Zambezi and the Congo – that is, Barotseland and the territory to the east. The timing was perfect. Lewanika, the Lozi chief, had appealed for protection against his enemies, the Ndebele. He was impressed by the way the Great Queen had protected his neighbour in Bechuanaland, Khama, chief of the Ngwato. If the British did not intervene, clearly the Portuguese would expand into this unclaimed territory linking Mozambique and Angola. Rhodes was delighted to rescue Lewanika and to block the Portuguese. The Foreign Office warmly approved. That summer of 1889, when Rhodes began to echo Harry Johnston's talk of the 'All-Red'[17] route from Cape to Cairo – that is, the Chartered empire joining hands with Mackinnon's empire in Uganda and the upper Nile – it seemed more than a pipedream.

Salisbury, the missionaries in Nyasaland and Harry Johnston each had their own brand of imperialism, but they all looked to Rhodes as the answer to their prayer. He, of course, generously offered to throw the wealth of Kimberley and the Rand behind the 'All-Red' crusade to save Africa from itself.

*   *   *

At Bulawayo in the great kraal of Lobengula the name of Rhodes and his associates excited only feelings of distrust that summer. Month by month the opposition to the Rudd Concession from the riff-raff of white men and the respected *indunas* had been gaining ground. The King had sold his country for a few hundred pounds. But by the time Maund returned from London with the two elderly envoys, he and his employers had changed sides. They no longer denounced the Rudd Concession as an empty sham. It was the rock on which their claim to the Charter was built. Unfortunately, the letter to Lobengula brought back from London by Maund and the *indunas* told a different story: 'A king gives a stranger an ox, not his whole herd of cattle.'

On 6 August 1889 this warning was translated for the benefit of the King. At first reassured and flattered, he dictated a reply on 10 August which made clear his own complete agreement. He did not believe in monopolies for mining or land settlement. 'The white people are troubling me much about gold. If the Queen hears that I have given away the whole country, it is not so.'[18] (This letter was tactfully held up in Bechuanaland for several weeks by Rhodes's admirer, Sir Sidney Shippard, and so arrived in London too late to swing the Privy Council against granting the charter.) A second warning letter, from the Aborigines Protection Society in London, advised Lobengula 'to be wary and firm' in resisting the concession hunters.

By the end of August the mood at the King's kraal was charged with menace. One of the elderly envoys, Mshete, had celebrated his return with a long spree on African beer. He claimed he had been told by Queen Victoria that Lobengula should allow no white men to dig for gold except for him and his servants. The storm rose, and the King had to bend. Most of the *indunas* and virtually all the warriors were now violently opposed to concessions for foreigners. To extricate himself Lobengula decided to make a scapegoat of his principal *induna*, Lotshe, the man who had taken a fancy to Thompson, the Sethuana-speaking member of Rudd's delegation, and backed the Rudd Concession. On 10 September Thompson was riding back to Bulawayo when he heard the grim news that Lotshe and all his clan, perhaps 300 people, had been executed, beaten to death by the royal executioners. Someone added meaningfully, 'The killing of yesterday is not over.'[19]

For months, Thompson had felt he was camping on a powder keg. Now he could take no more. He grabbed a horse and rode hell for leather towards Bechuanaland. He was found, half-dead with thirst, and given mealies by some friendly Makalaka north of Shoshong. He had buried the crucial document – the concession signed by Lobengula – in a melon gourd. Later, it took all Rhodes's mesmeric power to persuade the poor fool to return to Bulawayo and behave as if nothing had happened. But back Thompson went in October, escorted by Dr Jameson, Rhodes's closest confidant. Their task was to square the white riff-raff, as well as to reassure the King. Thompson unearthed the document from the melon gourd. It was all a pack of lies, what their enemies said about the concession. All they wanted was to dig for gold, just ten men at a time. They wanted no land. Of course they had no designs on the King's country. Both Jameson and Thompson repeated this lesson. Soon there was a chorus of white riff-raff, well-oiled by several thousand pounds from Rhodes, happy to echo Thompson's words and eat their own.

Lobengula did not yet know that the Queen, after warning him against giving away his country, had done precisely that herself by granting the royal charter. But he was not so much of a fool as to be confused by the white riff-raff and their volte-face. 'Tomoson [sic] has rubbed fat on your mouths,' he said with a smile. 'All you white men are liars. Tomoson, you have lied least.'[20]

By November 1889 Moffat felt brave enough to break the news to the King that the Queen had signed the charter a month earlier. This was followed by a second letter from Her Majesty's Colonial Secretary in London, brought to Bulawayo by a special delegation of five officers and men of the Royal Life Guards. Lobengula was impressed by their red coats and shiny breast-plates, not by what they brought. He told them that 'the Queen's letters had been dictated by Rhodes, [and] that she, the Queen, must not write any letters like that one to him again'.[21] Moffat did not dare admit that he was now the official representative at Bulawayo, appointed by the Queen but paid by the Chartered Company.

As the trekking season approached, Dr Jameson redoubled his efforts to win the King's confidence. The King suffered from gout and Jameson administered injections of morphine. In return, Lobengula gave grudging permission for miners to dig a new road to the east of Bulawayo, but he remained understandably suspicious. To demonstrate his repudiation of the charter, he still refused to accept delivery of the 1,000 Martini rifles that had been brought in wagons months earlier. In April 1896 Selous, the famous hunter hired by Rhodes to act as pathfinder, arrived in Bulawayo. By now Lobengula had changed his mind about the road to be taken by the pioneers; they must take the usual road by way of Bulawayo. Then Jameson, the charmer, returned, the only man who dared to laugh in the King's presence, and the man who carried morphine in his bag. He found the King understandably agitated. The best he could get out of him was the admission that he had never refused the pioneers permission to enter the country (or as he put it, 'never refused the road to him and his Impi'.)[22]

After Jameson had gone, Lobengula twisted and turned. He saw no escape. He could easily wipe out a small column like Jameson's. But he knew Cetshwayo's fate. The Europeans were irresistible. His only tactic was to buy time. The young warriors were mad for action. He told them they would have the white men soon, but that they must be patient, go home and wait for orders. In June, when he heard that the pioneer column had reached the border, he sent a message to its commander. 'Why are so many warriors at Motloutsi? Has the King committed any fault, or has any white man been killed, or have the white men lost anything that they're looking for?' A fortnight later there was a last futile appeal to Jameson's honour. 'How is it that the doctor agreed at Bulawayo to dig only at a place pointed out by the King?'[23]

The march of the Pioneer Column was an anti-climax, judged by the standards of colonial adventure. The members of the expedition did not complain. It was a miracle everything had gone so smoothly, considering the leaders and the makeshift way the column had been organized.

From the first, Rhodes had recognized that the priority was speed. Everything must be sacrificed to this – even common sense and diplomacy. The Company must go into Mashonaland that season or they might be forestalled by the Boers or Portuguese. Originally Rhodes had arranged to throw off the mask there and then, and launch a cold-blooded attack on Lobengula. Astonishingly, his advisers agreed – Jameson, Moffat, even Helm, the missionary who tried to be fair. Rhodes was right, said Jameson. 'We will never be able to work peaceably alongside the natives and the sooner the brush is over, the better.' Selous agreed it was 'now or never'.[24] A secret contract was signed in December 1889 with young Frank Johnson. For £150,000 and about 100,000 acres of land he undertook to raise a force of 500 colonials, crush the Ndebele army of 10–15,000 warriors and hand over Lobengula, dead or alive. Fortunately perhaps for all, one of the conspirators blurted out the plan when he was drunk and the news prematurely reached the ears of the new High Commissioner, Sir Henry Loch. He summoned Rhodes, who put the blame on Johnson and lied his own way out of the scrape.

In the event, Rhodes found a way of pleasing everyone except Lobengula. He adopted Selous's plan of taking a route east of Bulawayo and so avoiding trouble from the Ndebele. Lord Knutsford warmed to this idea and the imperial government threw its diplomatic weight behind the Company. Kruger was persuaded to prohibit a Boer trek that was in the offing. (In return, he was offered a deal on Swaziland.) This removed the last main obstacle. Of course everything depended on Knutsford's believing, contrary to all the evidence, that Lobengula had authorized the invasion of Mashonaland, and that the Company was happy to respect the Rudd Concession, which gave them mining rights, not rights of settlement. If they could believe that in England, they could believe anything.

At Tuli, in early July 1890, the column built a fort, and then the advance began in earnest. Two wagon roads had to be hacked out of the bush by the Ngwato labourers. Down this double track the column rode and marched, apprehensive and sweating in the winter sun. Every night they hobbled the horses and drew together to form a square wagon *laager*, protected by the naval searchlight powered by a steam engine. Charges of dynamite were planted and exploded outside the *laager* as a warning to the Ndebele. In fact, Lobengula sent only patrols to shadow the column but did not otherwise interfere. On 1 August they halted at Lundi, south of the main range that separates the bush veld from the high plateau of Mashonaland. Selous climbed up through the bush to explore and saw with relief the open veld. He had hit upon a pass, to be called Providential Pass, up the main range.

As they drove deeper into Mashonaland, fears of attack began to evaporate. By 6 August the column had resumed its advance. By the 14th it was astride the main plateau, on the site of what was to become the second fort, Fort Victoria, close to the mysterious granite walls of great Zimbabwe. The invaders played rugby and paid a visit to the ruins, disappointed only by their failure to find gold. On 12 September they reached their final destination, close to Mount Hampden, now christened Fort Salisbury after the Prime Minister. The next day they paraded in full dress and the Union Jack was hoisted up the straightest tree that could be found. Two seven-pounders fired a twenty-one-gun salute and a prayer was said by the police chaplain, Canon Balfour. Then as a formal piece of swagger of no legal validity, but to celebrate the way they had fooled

Lobengula, the Company patriotically annexed Mashonaland to the British Empire. (This was to be celebrated as Pioneers' Day for the next ninety years.) After three cheers for the Queen, the men were dismissed, and within a few days the column was disbanded. Frank Johnson was duly paid off with his promised £87,000, and the pioneers scattered to stake out their claims for gold and farms.

Thanks to Lobengula's cool nerves and his skilful control of his people, the conquest had been a walk-over. In one bound Rhodes's buccaneers had won the race with the Transvaal and had pushed the frontiers of colony and empire 300 miles nearer the equator. Of course success had depended on more than one African king's restraint. It was won by co-operation between old rivals: colonial cash and initiative, imperial caution and diplomacy. Without Grandmama, the pioneers would probably have been annihilated. Without the pioneers, Grandmama would have watched helplessly as Kruger took over from Lobengula.

Lobengula had been fooled into surrendering Mashonaland without a blow. That was the exultant message of the three cheers from Salisbury. Now it remained for the Chartered Company to honour its promises to the people who mattered: the investors who had subscribed £1 million to the new company, the home government, and the various other empire-minded people who had backed the venture, ranging from colonial Afrikaners to British missionaries.

But where was that second Rand on which everything depended? By the end of its first dry season in the new territory, the Chartered Company was no nearer answering that question, and an unpleasant thought began to assail many of the 1,000-odd white immigrants: had they too been fooled?

That year, 1890, the summer rains were implacable, as though summoned by Lobengula (it proved to be a record rainfall of fifty-four inches in Salisbury), and Selous's dusty wagon tracks were soon rivers of mud. By Christmas the pioneers were locked into the country. Colonel Pennefather had gone south on leave and was believed to have died. (A nasal colonial voice, shouting 'delayed, delayed' across the roaring river Shashi at Tuli, was interpreted as saying 'died'.) The pioneers lived like Africans in huts of mud and grass. No new supplies – no axes, no spades, no salt, no sugar, no candles – could reach them until the end of the rains. Boots rotted like paper. Malaria spread rapidly. There were few medical comforts and no hospital.

The men cheered up at the beginning of the dry season. The first women arrived – nuns for a hospital, and recruits for the red-light district. But there were still no reports of gold discoveries, nothing to confirm the value of those fifteen claims with which each member of the column had been paid.

It was not until August 1891 that a director of the Chartered Company first splashed across the Limpopo into the country. He was Alfred Beit, the shrewdest and richest of the diamond-and-gold magnates. It needed no great talent to see that the Company was going broke. Later that year Rhodes himself took the thorny way up from Beira. Half the million pounds raised by the subscribers had already been spent: £87,000 for Johnson, £200,000 for police pay, £70,000 for buying out rival concessions, £50,000 for the telegraph line, and so on. To make matters worse, by December 1891 Rhodes's murky arrangement with Central Search was brought to light. The Chartered shareholders – and the British government – realized that they too had been fooled. They did not own the Rudd Concession after all; it belonged to Central Search, which was still controlled by Rhodes and his inner ring. So the impoverished Chartered Company now had to buy the Rudd Concession from Central Search in exchange for a million shares in Chartered.

Rhodes decided to bluff things out. After all, the press knew the dazzling wealth of Mashonaland, especially the papers whose editors were on his pay roll. Rhodes's concession to panicky shareholders was to make a reckless economy in police pay. By Christmas 1892 he had reduced the number of police in Rhodesia from 650 to 150. There were protests from the pioneers. Rhodes explained that, as warriors, the Ndebele were over-rated. As for the Shona, they welcomed the white invaders as a shield against raids from the Ndebele.

Both assumptions, it proved within a short time, were equally fatuous. But at this period the question in Europe was simply how long Rhodes's bluster would sustain him before the government of his colony was officially declared bankrupt.

CHAPTER 22

Msiri's Mocking Smile

Brussels and Katanga
19 April 1890–October 1892

> 'I am master here and while I'm alive the kingdom
> of Garanganja [Katanga] shall have no other master
> than me.'
>
> *Msiri* to the British missionaries at Bunkeya, 1890

It was Saturday, 19 April 1890, two months before Rhodes's pioneers splashed across the Motloutsi river, and a brisk easterly strummed the leafless elms in the park of the royal palace at Brussels. A few miles away, at the palace of Laeken, the scent of tropical orchids hung heavily on the still air of the huge, bulbous glasshouses.

Leopold liked to spend the weekend quietly at Laeken. There he could devote himself to *The Times* with undivided attention, like a monk reading his breviary. Today he was not amused by what he read. The three-year saga of Stanley's latest expedition to Central Africa had ended in farce. Emin was to have been the second Gordon, the last defender of civilization against the Mahdi; and Leopold had counted on Emin for his next leap forward all the way to the banks of the Nile – if only Stanley could persuade him to work for the Congo rather than for Mackinnon and British East Africa. But Emin had no sooner reached safety in December 1889 than he had fallen on his head. Now he had decided to work for the Germans. The King fingered his beard with his left hand, a nervous habit he had developed, a kind of tic. He was not going to reproach Stanley for his failure. The Emin relief expedition had opened up the game, turned up new cards on the table. Though Stanley had failed to use Emin, the King might still be able to use Emin's followers left behind in Equatoria; and he could use Stanley.

That Saturday, 19 April, the Belgian public were waiting to greet Stanley on his return from Africa. There would be a hero's welcome for him now in Brussels, and later in London. (In Paris, by contrast, they had just given him an icy reception, for they had not forgotten his remarks about Brazza, the *va nu-pieds*.) That Saturday afternoon the King sent a special train to meet Stanley's party at the French frontier. When the special steamed into the Gare du Midi in Brussels the explorer was welcomed by a guard of honour, and then whisked into the King's carriage, driving through streets lined with crowds shouting 'Viva', straight to the royal palace. There he was given the scarlet and gilt 'imperial' apartments, normally reserved for kings and emperors. His Majesty would welcome him on his own return from Laeken.

Stanley had been warned by letter that the King had an 'important under-taking'[1] for him, and wondered what to make of this. He was happy to let his extraordinary new popularity rub off on the King. But he felt dazed and numb, after the strains of the last three years: the disaster to the rear column, the three terrible marches through the rainforest, the mutiny of Emin's men. (He ought to have carried a piece of paper around his forehead, he confessed later, with a warning to the public: 'Ladies and gentlemen, I have been in Darkest Africa for three continuous years, living among savages, and I fear something of their spirit clings to me.'[2]) To relieve his emotions he had holed up in Cairo and written the half million words of his latest bestseller in a demonic eighty-five days.

Now, in Brussels Stanley blinked at the crowds like a man trying to rouse himself from a dream. When he had last been there, in 1887, it had been the fashion to talk of the King's African schemes as 'madness'. Today there seemed no stopping the enthusiasm for them. The explorer was mobbed at a series of receptions held in his honour, including a lavish one at the Belgian Bourse, hung with pictures of the Congo. Medals studded his chest like a pin cushion: gold and silver medals from Brussels and Antwerp, the Order of Leopold and the newly created Grand Cross of the Congo and more. The King basked in Stanley's reflected glory, an irony that Stanley found irresistible. He could no longer bear the King a grudge for the shabby way he had treated him.

Every morning between 10.30 and 12.0 the two men conferred in the King's private room on the first floor of the royal palace. Everything in the room was just as Stanley remembered it: the writing paper, ink and pencils and paper knife laid out on the marble table, the King sitting with his back to the window, the better to cross-examine his visitor. Only the two men themselves had changed. The King's fine brown beard had turned grey from ear to ear, and Stanley's hair, iron-grey when he had last sat in that chair, was now as white as the ivory paper knife.

First they talked of the astonishing change in public opinion about Central Africa. Leopold said he owed it to Stanley and the excitement that his great discoveries had generated in the newspapers. These had helped float the Belgian company for building the railway to Stanley Pool, the railway to bypass the cataracts. Its shares had now been well subscribed by the public and the dream would soon be a reality. In the meanwhile, the King begged Stanley's advice on three delicate subjects: suppressing the Arab slave trade centres at Stanley Falls; extending the frontier with Mackinnon and the Imperial British East Africa Company eastwards to Lake Albert; and extending his power to the north-east by establishing a post somewhere on the frontier with French territory.

Stanley was prepared to help in the negotiations with Mackinnon. As for the French frontier, he warned Leopold against squandering resources trying to conquer new territory. A wild goose chase to the north-east could cost £80,000. Almost every penny was needed for the railway to Stanley Pool. Stanley was prepared to accept one other high priority by ending all collaboration with the

Arab slavers in the heart of the eastern Congo. He had not forgotten what he called the treachery of Tippu Tip in failing to supply the rear column with porters. Only a military expedition of 2,000 men could break the power of these 'pirates' and their state within a state. Stanley recommended the cannibals of the Manyema as excellent fighting men for the purpose. But what was the 'great undertaking' for which the King had brought Stanley to Brussels?

'Have you guessed?' asked Leopold one morning with a gleam in his eye.

'No, sire,' replied Stanley, 'I thought perhaps you meant the suppression of the slave raids.'

'My mission is a still greater one. It is one which will draw the attention of the whole world.'

The King waved his arms theatrically and spoke with exaggerated emphasis. 'Try now and think what it is.' Stanley shook his head. The King continued to wave his arms up and down, and now he was smiling broadly.

'Well, I have revolved the idea a long time in my mind, and I have kept the mission as a *bonne-bouche* for *you*, because there is only one *Stanley* – the *Great Explorer* – the *Founder of the Congo State*. Now what do you say to the taking of Khartoum? There, that is your mission.'[3]

On 26 April 1890, Stanley exchanged the cheering crowds of Brussels for the cheering crowds of London. He was still dazed by Leopold's *bonne-bouche* for him to take 20,000 Congolese cannibals and smash the Mahdists. No wonder the King had originally been written off as a madman. The scheme was preposterous from start to finish. First, it would take at least four years to discipline an army of Congolese savages and in that time most of their European officers would have died of fever. Then think what the British and French would make of Leopold's plan to conquer the Sudan! Stanley shuddered at the diplomatic implications. But he soon had other and more attractive things to consider than Leopold's crackpot schemes.

Fortune smiled on Stanley with the force of the African sun at midday. Down the cheering streets he rode, from Charing Cross Station to Piccadilly, the most admired explorer of the age, double gold medallist of the Royal Geographical Society (the men who had once called him an impostor), guest of Queen Victoria and friend of the Prince of Wales. And in the heart of London he made one more extraordinary new discovery.

He had thought his heart was numb. Now he found he was in love once again. Within three weeks he was engaged to marry the woman who had earlier mocked his feelings: handsome, sparkling Dolly Tennant, the Society hostess and painter. Marriage put a happy end to Stanley's wandering, even if the Furies still hovered close. That autumn of 1890 controversy over the fate of the rear column exploded in the world's press and continued to haunt Stanley till the day of his death in 1904.

In the meanwhile, Leopold did not allow Stanley's practical objections to put him off his own dreams of conquering the Nile. He did not live by the ordinary rules; no visionary did. He had made a practice of achieving the impossible by snatching most of Central Africa from under the noses of the greatest Powers in Europe. As the weeks passed, schemes for expeditions to the Nile began to crowd his mind, more far-flung though less fantastic than the plan for sending cannibals to Khartoum. But the priorities, he had to agree with Stanley, were first to finance the Congo Free State within its existing boundaries; and second to put an end to his own collaboration with the Arab slave traders which made a mockery of his claim to have brought civilization to the Congo. The two were interlocking, and the key to both, Leopold saw, lay in the anti-slave trade conference to be held in Brussels that spring of 1890.

Two years earlier, in July 1888, an eccentric prince of the Church, Cardinal Lavigerie, had launched an international crusade against the slave trade from the pulpit of the church of Saint Sulpice in Paris. Charles Lavigerie was an African missionary, Archbishop of Algiers and Primate of Africa, the founder of the African missionary order of White Fathers (the French priests who had clashed with Mackay in Buganda). He was also a Basque and a firebrand. In his sermon at Saint Sulpice he described the horrors of the slave trade like scenes from hell: villages surrounded and burnt; people fleeing in terror, men captured and yoked together by the slave hunters; the bleached bones on the route to the coast; and the women and children penned like cattle in the slave markets. His facts were based on the twenty-year-old reports of British explorers like Livingstone, Cameron and Stanley. What shocked his French audience was Lavigerie's claim that the hellish trade was still alive and flourishing in East and Central Africa. It was now depopulating the continent, he said, at the rate of 400,000 human beings a year.

Lavigerie's sermon sent a shudder through Europe. In London he was welcomed by the Anti-Slavery Society and in return he paid emotional tribute to Livingstone. He pleaded for funds to allow 500 volunteers – a new order of chivalry – to go out and combat the great evil. In Belgium he reminded his audience of the parable of the wheat and the tares, casting Leopold as the good sower and Islam as the enemy. The people of Belgium, indifferent to the Congo, were the sleeping servants. 'It was while you were sleeping that the enemy came. Barbarity, the foe of all that is good, did its work, and the tares which it sowed and the evil which threatens to invade everything, is slavery.'[4]

Leopold found Lavigerie's ideas utopian and his praise embarrassing. It sounded fine to be cast in the role of the good sower. What he feared was a crusade by the Great Powers effective enough to investigate his own rule – or lack of it – in the Congo. He was alarmed by reports of the money that the Cardinal had succeeded in raising. He would try to 'absorb it', he decided, by proposing that the Cardinal put a steamer on Lake Tanganyika, otherwise it would 'leave the Cardinal with the temptation of disposing of the money in other directions'.[5] As usual, the King was aiming not to ward off a threat so much as to turn it to his advantage.

Leopold's opportunity came the next year, in November 1889, after Lord Salisbury had proposed that he convene an anti-slave-trade conference at Brussels. For some time the officials at the Foreign Office had been anxious to stiffen their own measures at sea against the slave runners. Salisbury was also keen to respond to the outcry in Britain at the horrors so eloquently described by Lavigerie; and Bismarck, still in office at this date, was keen to help Salisbury. Since the Abushiri revolt in East Africa, the German Chancellor had noticed that the best way to get the Reichstag to pay for a colonial war was to call it a war against the slave trade. High-minded motives were also claimed by the other thirteen Powers which had signed the Berlin Act of 1885, the Act that included a resolution to 'help in suppressing slavery' – whatever that meant. (This clause was called 'sadly milk and watery' by the British.)

By now anti-slavery committees had sprung up in France, Belgium, Holland, Italy and Spain. Despite the incongruous attendance of Turkey, where slavery (though not the slave trade) was a legal institution, the Brussels conference launched by Leopold in November 1889 was welcomed by the whole civilized world. It was a milestone, *The Times* explained, in international co-operation. The Belgian delegate, the Prince de Chinay, put it more elegantly. Never before had all the Great Powers come together so single-mindedly set on so generous, pure and disinterested a purpose to save the 'oppressed and decimated' races of Africa and end the monstrous trade in human flesh.

How Leopold must have enjoyed those adjectives. Single-minded he was; generous, perhaps; but certainly not disinterested. His own aim was to use the conference to save the Congo – and himself – from bankruptcy.

In the last few years the Congo Free State had sucked the King's own huge fortune almost dry. For one man, even one of the richest in Europe, to try to finance the development of an enormous state, to build roads and bridges, harbours, railways, cities, and pay the costs of law and order was quixotically generous, no doubt, in the eyes of the King's bankers. By 1890 twelve years after the King had first commissioned Stanley to open up the Congo, the bankers were losing patience. The Congo State was overspending its income by nearly three million francs (£120,000) a year. The state's whole income was less than the proceeds from one small factory in Europe, about 300,000 francs (£12,000) a year, which came from the 15 per cent duty on the existing exports of ivory, rubber, palm oil and the like. Simply to finance this huge deficit without squandering money on new conquests, Leopold needed to raise a mountain of new cash, either as taxes or loans. New taxes meant import duties. But here the Berlin conference had set an obstacle in his path as menacing as the cataracts below Stanley Pool by guaranteeing free trade for the whole 'conventional' basin of the Congo. This was the most famous clause in the General Act of 1885. It did not affect Leopold's right to tax his own exports, but it meant that Europe was free to send its manufactured goods to the Congo and that Leopold was banned from taxing them.

Leopold had turned in desperation, like the Khedive and the Bey of Tunis before him, to the money-lenders of Europe. First he tried the great Bleichroder,

Bismarck's banker, and Charles de Rothschild, his own friend. It was an embarrassment for these unfortunate men of affairs to explain to His Majesty that he was no longer a banking proposition. Then Leopold went to the European market and tried to raise a huge 150-million-franc (£6 million) interest-free loan based on a lottery (like premium bonds today). The first tranche of 10 million francs (£400,000) had to be discounted at 83 per cent of par, despite Leopold's desperate attempts to hold the price at 92. Then the second tranche, 60 million francs (£240,000), flopped disastrously. Less than half were taken by the public. Fortunately for Leopold, these rebuffs did not affect the 25-million-franc (£1 million) project for building the vital railway to Stanley Pool.

In 1889 the Compagnie du Chemin de Fer had been successfully floated in Belgium with the help of a 10-million-franc loan (£400,000) from the Belgian government. However, the railway was not due to be completed until 1894 (and was not complete till 1898). Meanwhile the Congo Free State continued to plunge deeper into debt, dragging the King down with it, to the alarm of the court and his own family. It was from this chasm that Leopold sought to extricate himself, like Houdini, in May 1890.

By now the anti-slavery conference had been plodding away for six months. Sir John Kirk, the retired Consul from Zanzibar and the most knowledgeable and idealistic of the British delegates, was exhausted by the long hours and the wrangling. Humbug seemed to him the main theme of the conference – except for the part played by Leopold's delegates. 'I don't believe there is a single power but ourselves and Belgium that cares about the S[lave] T[rade] – it is all private ends they look to; and Germany is the worst of the lot, for all her cant in the Reichstag.'[6] Kirk felt a rapport for few of the delegates, except for the Belgian president of the conference, Baron Lambermont, and Emile Banning, the King's faithful adviser on colonial affairs. What the conference showed was that the slave dhows could go on running circles round the British navy in the creeks and inlets of the Red Sea. The place to tackle the problem was at its sources. This means (as Kirk put it) not just a great crusade, but establishing 'good government'.

It was on 10 May, a fortnight after Stanley's welcome in Brussels, that the King intervened with an electrifying offer. Through the Belgian Minister for Foreign Affairs, Leopold declared that the Congo Free State would throw all its energies behind the noble crusade against the slave trade. But the Congo needed the means. The free trade clause in the Berlin General Act should now be revised by the fifteen signatories, allowing him to finance his crusade against the slavers with a 10 per cent duty on all goods from abroad.

Two of the delegates – those from America and Holland – were flabbergasted. The 'conventional' basin of the Congo extended from the west coast of Africa to Zanzibar. Therefore it would be a tax on their country's traders over a huge region and would give Leopold a monopoly of the Congo trade. They protested that the free trade clause was the crucial clause in the Berlin Act. The leading American delegate, General Sanford, felt betrayed by Leopold; it was he who had persuaded the American government to take the lead in recognizing the

Congo State in 1884 and to sign the Berlin Act (though the US had never ratified it). Sanford claimed that recognition had depended on the pledge of full free trade.

But the American and Dutch opposition strengthened, if anything, Leopold's claim to be acting in the interests of humanity. His lofty aims and meagre resources excited general sympathy. As Kirk said, 'I will do all I can to fight for the poor man. I think he deserves well of us all . . . .'[7]

On 2 July a new General Act was put on the table at Brussels. It ran to a hundred articles, most of which had either been emasculated in committee or would prove ineffectual in practice. All except the Dutch were prepared to sign. Far more significant was the separate declaration which conceded the crucial 10 per cent duty on imports. All except the Dutch and Americans signed this declaration. Soon Leopold was able to call their bluff too; both conceded the import duty.

Leopold's success on the diplomatic stage was rewarded within a matter of days by an equally dramatic success in the Belgian Parliament. A year earlier the King had made a secret offer to Beernaert, the Prime Minister, that in the fullness of time Belgium could take over the Congo State. He would gladly leave it to the nation in his will. In return, he would like to borrow the tidy sum of 25 million francs (£1 million), interest free, to finance the development of the country. In August 1889 this had seemed like crying for the moon. By July 1890 it looked like practical politics. The Cardinal's crusade, Stanley's encomium, the King's triumph at the anti-slavery conference – everything favoured it.

On 3 July 1890, Beernaert put the motion in the chamber: to advance a 25-million franc loan to the King, giving Belgium the right to take over the Congo after ten years. A few days later Beernaert published the King's will, and with it a royal letter stressing the sacrifices the King had made in order to found this colony for his people. The motion was passed with hardly a murmur against it. For the moment the King's money troubles were over. Yet he remained vulnerable, despite the interest-free loan. This would buy a little time. That was all. The railway would not be finished for years – eight years, as it turned out. Meanwhile the Congo would need every penny it could squeeze out of the ivory trade, the rubber trade, or anything else that could be made to pay.

Most gamblers threatened with bankruptcy and then bailed out by their friends would feel constrained to take the next few steps with caution. No such thought occurred to Leopold. Within weeks of receiving the promise of the 25-million-franc loan he decided to send out a whole series of expeditions in order to expand the area controlled by the Congo State. The first was to explore the remote south-eastern plateau of Katanga, claimed to be within the frontiers of Leopold's empire. Ever since Livingstone's time, the wealth of Katanga had been spoken of with awe. A month's journey to the west of Kazembe, so Livingstone had been told, lay the great mines where people smelted the metal into bars of solid copper, as heavy as a man could lift. Cameron had heard the same story, and had seen men and women wearing the copper crosses used for money in Katanga, and had heard that gold could be extracted from the copper which the Portuguese refined at Benguela. The Africans did not value it, as they preferred 'red copper to the white'.[8]

In 1883, the first intrepid explorers, two Germans called Paul Reichard and Richard Böhm, had penetrated through Angola to this mysterious land, and found it uninviting. There was indeed an export trade in copper, ivory, salt and slaves, and a healthy market for European guns and powder. But these imported guns – like the slaves for export, and everything else in Katanga – were held tight in the iron fist of an African warlord called Msiri. It was Msiri's way of impressing his European visitors to show them the varied collection of human skulls hanging on the trees outside his hut 'like hats on pegs'. The German explorers did not prolong their stay in Katanga. They were followed by some intrepid British missionaries, Plymouth Brethren, who had established a precarious foothold at Bunkeya, Msiri's barbaric capital. Of course their task was to save souls, not to involve themselves in politics.

For two reasons Leopold decided in 1890 to make a quick grab at Msiri's empire. The first was to exploit the gold reefs he expected to find there. A gold strike would confound the scoffers and catapult the Congo back into solvency. The omens looked right; after all, vast gold reefs had been found in the Transvaal. The second reason was to pre-empt a grab for Katanga being planned by Cecil Rhodes and the Chartered Company.

From his careful study of *The Times*, Leopold knew that Frederick Arnot, the first English missionary to return home from Katanga, had publicly recommended the country to the attention of British philanthropists. Here was the place to harvest souls, he claimed – a healthy plateau above the swamps, a haven of peace and order under the benevolent eye of its ruler, Msiri ('a thorough gentleman')[9] and, incidentally, immense copper deposits. This challenge did not only catch the eye of philanthropists. In 1889 Rhodes commissioned Joseph Thomson, the explorer of Masailand, to try to push the Chartered Company's frontiers northwards to include Katanga. It was a threat that Leopold had to take very seriously. Katanga lay within the borders claimed by the Congo State since 1885 – a claim acquiesced in by the British and other European governments. But in the intervening years since the Berlin Act, Leopold had not lifted a finger to establish effective occupation. Technically, it was true, the Berlin Act only demanded effective occupation on the *coast*. In practice it had a broader scope – or so the British public believed. At any rate, in 1889 *The Times* suggested that Katanga, at present a no-man's-land in Central Africa, was ripe for takeover by Cecil Rhodes's new Chartered Company. Leopold wrote to the Foreign Office to protest at the idea, but was fobbed off by a letter from Anderson, friendly, and conceding nothing.

By August 1890, Leopold decided he could no longer trust Salisbury to back his claim against Rhodes's unless he hoisted the blue flag of the Free State in Katanga. To increase his chances of success, he mounted no less than four separate expeditions, the first led by a Congo State agent, the others by agents of the new commercial companies he had set up in the Congo to help finance

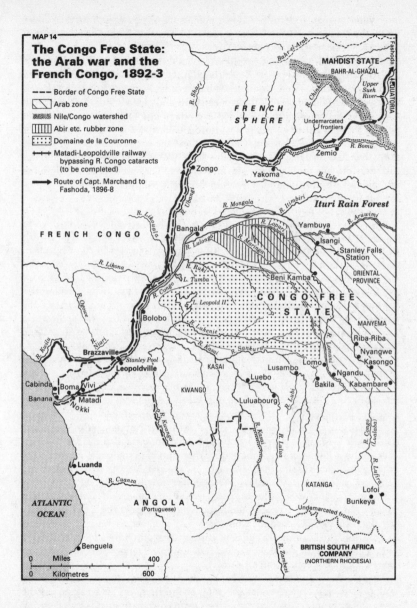

MAP 14

The Congo Free State: the Arab war and the French Congo, 1892-3

- - - - Border of Congo Free State
- Arab zone
- Nile/Congo watershed
- Abir etc. rubber zone
- Domaine de la Couronne
- ┼━┼━ Matadi-Leopoldville railway bypassing R. Congo cataracts (to be completed)
- ➤ Route of Capt. Marchand to Fashoda, 1896-8

MAHDIST STATE
BAHR-AL-GHAZAL

Upper Sueh River

EQUATORIA

Fashoda

R. Shari

F R E N C H
S P H E R E

R. Chinko

Undemarcated frontiers

R. Bomu

Zemio

R. Uele

Yakoma

R. Ubangi

Zongo

R. Likouala

R. Mongala

R. Itimbiri

R. Aruwimi

Ituri Rain Forest

Bangala

R. Lulongo

R. Lopori

R. Maringa

Yambuya

Isangi

Stanley Falls Station

FRENCH CONGO

R. Likona

R. Ruki

L. Tumba

R. Congo

Beni Kamba

C O N G O   F R E E
S T A T E

ORIENTAL PROVINCE

R. Ogoue

L. Leopold II

R. Lomami

MANYEMA

Bolobo

R. Lukenie

Riba-Riba

R. Kouilu

R. Niari

R. Kasai

R. Sankuru

Lusambo

Lomo

Ngandu

Nyangwe

Kasongo

Brazzaville

Stanley Pool

Leopoldville

KASAI

Luebo

R. Lubi

Bakila

Kabambare

Cabinda

Boma Vivi

KWANGO

Luluabourg

R. Lulua

R. Congo (Lualaba)

Banana

Matadi

Nokki

R. Kwango

R. Kasai

R. Lufira

Luanda

R. Cuanza

KATANGA

Lofoi

Bunkeya

ATLANTIC
OCEAN

A N G O L A
(Portuguese)

Undemarcated frontiers

BRITISH SOUTH AFRICA
COMPANY
(NORTHERN RHODESIA)

R. Zambezi

Benguela

| 0 | Miles | 400 |
| 0 | Kilometres | 600 |

development. It was the third of these, led by Stanley's ex-lieutenant, William Grant Stairs, newly returned from the expedition to relieve Emin, that was to push home the attack with a pugnacity worthy of his old chief.

This race for Katanga did not divert Leopold from the side of the Scramble that had come more and more to obsess him, the race for the Nile.

When Stanley had proceeded to London in April 1890 after a hero's welcome in Brussels, he had followed the King's instructions to negotiate with Mackinnon new borders between the Congo State and the Imperial British East Africa Company. Leopold had chosen the time well. Bismarck had just been sacked by the Kaiser and Germany, under new management, was about to try to strike a bargain with Britain to settle all those tiresome disputes in Africa. No one knew if the negotiations would succeed. At this critical time the King flattered Mackinnon with the offer of a 'treaty' for exchanging sovereign rights between the Congo and Mackinnon's company.

At present, the north-east boundary of the Congo was a clumsy affair of two straight lines, the 4th parallel and the 13th meridian, which fenced it off from the Nile watershed. What about some adjustments to the fence? The British could push up to the snow peaks of Ruwenzori, discovered by Stanley's men, if this took their fancy. More important, Leopold was delighted to give them a corridor running between German East Africa and the eastern boundary of the Congo, all the way from Lake Tanganyika to Uganda. This corridor was the missing link in Cecil Rhodes's 'All-Red' Cape-to-Cairo route. In return, the Congo State would be allowed to push on to the Nile, with a swoop down to Lake Albert, then a leap to Lado, 200 miles up the west bank of the Nile in Equatoria, now controlled by the Mahdists.

On 18 May, bemused by Leopold's flattery, Mackinnon submitted this strange draft to Salisbury. Three days later Salisbury wrote to the King to say the Foreign Office had 'no objections'[10] to the arrangements which His Majesty had concluded with Mackinnon's company. When Leopold arrived in London for a flying visit a few days later Salisbury repeated this assurance.

But Salisbury was dissembling. This was the critical moment of the poker game with Germany. He needed to calm Mackinnon and the Cape-to-Cairo enthusiasts, who might wreck the game if they started to shout about the missing corridor which Salisbury had decided was expendable. As it happened, the Germans objected to a British corridor, either through their own territory or the Congo's, and soon Salisbury was reassuring them that the Mackinnon 'treaty' was not to be taken too seriously; a mere company could not give away sovereign rights. The corridor would never be occupied. It was a very curious idea, he told the Lords on 10 July – as curious, he might have added, as the idea of Leopold defeating the Mahdists and setting himself up on the Nile. (Salisbury had never taken Leopold too seriously.)

Leopold was not worried by what Salisbury thought. He was used to being under-rated; in fact he encouraged it, by laying stress on his weakness as the poor philanthropist at the mercy of the Great Powers. In great secrecy during the summer of 1890 he organized a large expedition to advance over the Congo watershed. The leader was a thirty-seven-year-old veteran of the Congo, Captain van Kerckhoven. On 3 October 1890 van Kerckhoven sailed from Flessinghe, bound for Boma. His instructions were to take 500 Free State soldiers with 14 officers and advance into Equatoria. There he should find the mutineers from Emin's beleaguered garrisons, explain that the British had ceded this region to the Congo and enlist the men in Leopold's service. With these unlikely recruits Leopold planned to defeat the Mahdists and at last stretch out a hand to the Nile.

✻   ✻   ✻

As the rival expeditions, two from the Chartered Company and four from the Congo Free State, converged on Katanga, the missionaries there found their self-imposed vow of neutrality subjected to increasing strain.

By November 1890 it was already five years since Fred Arnot had set up the Garenganze Evangelical Mission in a humble wooden hut, 'Mountain View', at Bunkeya, Msiri's capital. From a low hill it commanded the bare sandy plain and the distant blue wall of the mountains, beyond which was Chitambo's village, where Livingstone died. Arnot was a Scot who consciously set out to walk in the footsteps of Livingstone. He and the gallant brethren who came out to join him longed to help the multitude of poor benighted souls in this corner of the Dark Continent. Strange to say, five years had not brought a single heart to be reborn in Christ at Msiri's court. Yet Bunkeya seemed ideal for spreading the news of God's word. This dry, sandy plain, dotted with park-like mimosa trees and abounding with zebra and lion, was as healthy a place as you could find in Central Africa. It was close to the flat backbone of the continent, the imperceptible watershed where during the rainy season the headwaters of the Congo merged with those of the Zambezi. Bunkeya was also a magnet for trade from every direction: Africans from Tanganyika came to buy iron for hoes; Arabs from Uganda to buy copper and salt; half-castes from the west coast to sell Msiri his supplies of guns and powder in exchange for the latest crop of slaves and ivory.

When Brother Arnot had told the people in London's Exeter Hall that Msiri was a 'thorough gentlemen' it was, it must be said, a manner of speaking. He found the man a paradox. Msiri looked the part of a venerable chief: white-bearded, six foot and fourteen stone, wearing two yards of dirty calico, day in, day out. Yet there was a rigorous side to his character which shocked Arnot. His cruelty to his own subjects, the cutting off of a hand or a foot or an ear for the most trivial reasons – and his covetousness towards his neighbours whom he caught and enslaved – could not be condoned. On the other hand, for good motives or bad, Msiri befriended the missionaries. He listened politely, even when they reproached him for his injustices, and he showed an 'uncommonly kind heart'[11] in his concern for their welfare. He laughed with them like an old friend. '*Kapoli vali okufa*' ('no more death'),[12] he said teasingly when he saw their large stock of medicines. In short, he welcomed them as his guests and played the cheerful host to the white men as successfully as he played the cruel tyrant to his own people.

In 1888 Arnot had set off on a long, dangerous 1,000-mile march down to the west coast on his way home for a rest in England, and by mid-November 1890 his replacements at Bunkeya found that relations with Msiri were becoming soured.

At its zenith, the empire of this merchant prince and warlord had covered a region the size of Great Britain, stretching from the Lualaba river eastward to the Luapula and back along the Congo-Zambezi watershed. Now the old man was running out of gunpowder, and his subjects, especially the Basanga tribe, were becoming rebellious. He was impatient with the neutrality of the missionaries. Why had they come if they refused to help him buy powder? (It was the same question that Mwanga had put to Mackay, the Scottish missionary in Uganda.) On their part, the new set of Scottish and English brethren were temperamentally less able to tolerate the sight of those white skulls outside Msiri's palace.

Of all this hardy band of British evangelists, isolated in this no-man's-land hundreds of miles beyond the writ of the European Powers, the most outspoken was a blue-eyed, brown-bearded Scottish boy of nineteen, Dan Crawford. His father, the master of a Clyde schooner plying the coastal trade, had died of consumption when Dan was four. Dan, too, caught consumption when working as a painter's book-keeper at Greenock, and he was given a year to live. But at sixteen he became a born-again Christian. Soon he heard the call, from the lips of Fred Arnot, to bring God's word to the tribes beyond the Lualaba, the people that Livingstone, even while he was dying, had dreamed of reaching. In 1889, before he was nineteen, Dan Crawford had set off from Benguela on the 1,000-mile long pilgrimage through warring tribes. He took only one bundle for himself: bedding, a spare coat, an Ulster, three pieces of underclothes, a pair of slippers, a cake of soap, a cheap rifle and as much tea as you could carry in two hands. His biographer records that he bubbled over with joy, as he rode a donkey up the stony track from the coast, singing God's word at the top of his voice.

When he saw the white skulls of Msiri's palisade Crawford's first prayer was that 'God in His Sovereign Grace may be pleased to save Mushidi [Msiri]'. He also prayed for what he called 'holy grit', in order to bear witness boldly to the tyrant without 'tact or diplomacy'. His own view of Msiri was more straightforward than Arnot's. The Chief's redeeming features, his generosity and good humour, seemed to Crawford merely a snare. 'To characterise Mushidi's mode of government as *rigorous* is altogether to choose the wrong word. It is *murderous!*' Crawford believed the system was on the point of collapse. 'The great marvel to me is that the kingdom of Mushidi – which is nothing other than a monster system of slavery – has been kept together for so long.'[13]

That same month, November 1890, the first of the rival expeditions reached Bunkeya. It was led by Alfred Sharpe, the second emissary paid for by Cecil

Preceding page: Mengo, capital
of Buganda, the largest kingdom
in central Africa. King Mtesa (*inset*),
claimed British missionaries
were welcome

King Mwanga (*top left*), Mtesa's
erratic successor. Mackay (*centre left*),
the missionary who sent the SOS
to England. Emin Pasha (*right*),
last of Gordon's heroic lieutenants

The pushy new imperialists of the 1890s:
Joe Chamberlain (*top left*), Cecil Rhodes
(*top right*), Alfred Milner (*centre left*),
Fred Lugard (*centre right*). Lord Salisbury
(*below*), tried to go his own pace

Following pages: (*Left*): Rhodes's
pioneers invade Mashonaland,
July 1890. Dr Jameson (seated left).
Frederick Selous (seated at rear),
Alexander Colquhoun (seated right).
(*Right*): The pioneers relax after
the Shona rebellion, July 1896

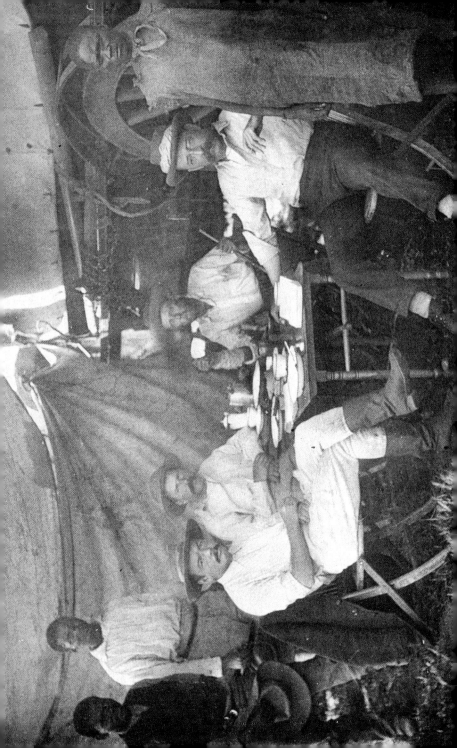

Preceding pages: General Dabormida's Last Stand at Adowa, 1 March 1896. Emperor Menelik (*inset*), who used the Scramble to double the size of Ethiopia

Above: The wounded Dervish commander, Mahmud, in blood-stained jibbah (centre), after being dragged out by Kitchener's black soldiers during the Battle of Atbara, 8 April 1898.

Preceding page: Marchand's black *tirailleurs* drive off the Dervish gunboats from Fashoda, August 1898

Above: Was it to be war? Marchand, with tricolour, rows across to confront Kitchener (right), in the gunboat *Dal* at Fashoda, 19 September 1898

Opposite: President Kruger and his advisers, 1899

Preceding page: The vanguard of Robert's invasion force – 43,000 strong in all – crossing the Zand River, 10 May 1900

Liberating the Congo: 'Bulldog' Morel and (*inset*), Roger 'Tiger' Casement

Following page: Pacifying German South-West Africa: Governer Leutwein (centre), and his heavy-handed successor (extreme right), General von Troth, in Windhoek, July 1904

Above: Hendrik Witbooi, eighty-year-old leader of the Nama rebels, killed in battle by the Germans

Following page: The price of Congo rubber: severed hands

Rhodes. (Joseph Thomson, the first emissary, had already been driven back by smallpox and famine.) Sharpe was a professional big-game hunter, recruited by Harry Johnston as a vice-consul for Nyasaland, given a hundred pounds worth of presents and deputed to go to Msiri. Unfortunately, he had been persuaded to leave most of his caravan the other side of Luapula, and arrived with an unimpressive escort and an even poorer set of presents than he had started with. Worse, there was a prophecy that the man who had come to 'eat' gold and destroy Msiri's kingdom would come from the east. Sharpe had come from the east. With great difficulty, the missionaries persuaded Msiri to ignore the prophecy and grant Sharpe an audience. He was received with scant civility. What could he offer besides mere rolls of calico? Was this all his Queen could afford? And where were the kegs of powder to help Msiri destroy his enemies?

If Crawford had handled the negotiations, Sharpe might have received a better hearing. Crawford might have refused to give any advice to Msiri, and taken a neutral stance, which would have helped Sharpe. But Crawford was the youngest and most recent recruit to the mission. It was Swan, an older man, who acted as interpreter and intermediary between Sharpe and the Chief; and Swan shared Arnot's admiration for the generous side of Msiri's character. Quixotically, he took it upon himself to frustrate Rhodes's and Johnston's plan. Sharpe suggested that Msiri should simply be told that the British wanted to be friends, and then be asked to put his mark on the treaty, making his territory a British protectorate. Swan insisted that the treaty be translated in full to Msiri – who flew into a rage and refused to sign. Msiri said he had been warned by Arnot 'to have nothing to do with anyone who wanted him to sign papers, and that it meant giving away his country'. Sharpe was not told how narrowly he had escaped with his life. He returned to Harry Johnston grumbling that 'these missionaries do a great deal of harm when they take upon themselves to advise native chiefs'.[14]

Five months later, in April 1891, the first of Leopold's expeditions tramped into Bunkeya. This was the one led by Paul le Marinel, a Congo Free State commander from Lusambo, on the Sankuru, one of the Congo tributaries 400 miles to the north-west. It was a lavish 300-man expedition; many of the soldiers were recruits from British West Africa, armed with breech-loaders, and the porters carried bales of expensive velvet and many kegs of gunpowder. After the velvet had been presented, Msiri told le Marinel that he 'liked white men very much'.[15] He gave the Belgians permission to build a small Free State post two days' journey from Bunkeya in a pleasant site beside the river Lofoi, facing the mountain wall beyond. But he refused to accept the blue flag of the Congo Free State. The British missionaries were at first impressed by the 'judicious' behaviour of the Belgians who settled down peacefully, though soon Msiri was pestering them for presents of gunpowder and alcohol, demands which they found it impolitic to refuse.

In the meanwhile, the coming of European soldiers encouraged his African enemies, the rebel Basanga. Their attacks became increasingly bold, and soon threatened Msiri's rule in his own capital. Huts were mysteriously set on fire in the middle of night, attacks were made on the villages which supplied the capital with food, and raiders set upon men hoeing the sorghum fields. Refugees began to stream out of Bunkeya. Then, flush with gunpowder given him by the Belgians, Msiri counter-attacked against the palisaded villages of the Basanga. But it was clear that his power was waning. Determined to preserve their neutrality, the missionaries retired to the Free State post on the Lofoi. But this created new problems. Previously, many local people had been prepared to attend the Sunday gospel readings. Now they fled from the missionaries, alarmed by the sight of the Free State soldiers' breech-loaders, and the Sunday gospel readings went unattended.

As the crisis deepened, threatening the whole region with famine, the second Belgian expedition, 300 soldiers with porters and camp followers led by Alexandre Delcommune, staggered into Bunkeya. For days the Belgians had been dreaming of succulent rice dishes and of bathing in the sparkling waters of the local river. They found Bunkeya to be just another mud-walled village, beside three bare hills, set in a bleak monotonous plain. The sparkling water proved to be a large muddy pool left behind after the rainy season. Four days later Msiri consented to give an audience to Delcommune in the palace compound surrounded by skulls. This compound enclosed six Portuguese-style houses that Msiri had built, sleeping in them at random to avoid assassination. The Belgian officers were entertained with native beer, which tasted delicious once it was strained, and an exhibition of erotic dancing, in which Msiri himself (somewhat ludicrously) tried to take part. Then the Belgian officers and their black troops gave an impressive display of drill, bugle calls and volley firing. When Delcommune explained his mission, the old man scowled, 'more like a chimpanzee than a human', said Delcommune. In vain the Belgians pressed the advantages of accepting the protection of the Free State.

At present you are frightened of everything; you make a secret of where you sleep; you're afraid someone is going to poison you or otherwise kill you. . . . You have neither peace nor tranquillity. To change all that, all you have to do is accept the protection of Boula-Matari [Stanley's name had become a synonym for the State], to fly the [blue] flag with the star at each of your villages, and then things will calm down and peace and plenty will return to your country.[16]

The old man's reply was brutally direct. He knew the British wanted him to accept their protection. He had refused it. He gave Bula Matari the same answer. 'I am master here and while I am alive the kingdom of Garanganja [Katanga] shall have no other master but me.'

Msiri became still angrier when he heard that Delcommune was planning to march south into the region controlled by the Basanga rebels. The crisis impelled him to reverse his policy towards the British, or at any rate, to play off the British against the Belgians. He summoned Dan Crawford and dictated a letter to Alfred Sharpe. He had been hasty in sending him away; why did he not return to discuss that paper proposing friendship between the two countries?

Meanwhile, the third and best-equipped Belgian expedition – 336 men led by Captain Grant Stairs and financed by the Katanga Company by arrangement with Leopold – had left Bagamoyo. Stairs was burning to be the first to run up the blue flag at Bunkeya and stop Rhodes 'jumping' the Free State's claim to Katanga.

It was a cosmopolitan team. Stairs was now twenty-seven, a fair-haired delicate-looking young British officer of Canadian origin who had become Stanley's favourite on the Emin relief expedition. He was accompanied by two other British volunteers, Joseph Moloney, a London doctor and bon vivant, and a soldier called Robinson, a Grenadier Guardsman turned carpenter. Despite endless squabbles with their Belgian and French colleagues – a Free State officer, Captain Bodson, and a big-game hunter, well known in the Rockies, the Marquis de Bonchamps – the British members of the team were quite as keen to win the race against Rhodes as the others were. Adventure, sport and glory were the lure, according to Dr Moloney. (On the other hand, he was doubtful whether the Belgians had it in them to make serious colonists and administrators.) As for Stairs, he was risking his life by coming out once more to win laurels in Africa. Dr Moloney was shocked to find that his leader's left lung was damaged and that his whole constitution was still weak from malaria.

Bagamoyo, they found, was a squalid and depressing little port battered down under night curfew as a result of the Abushiri rebellion. The Germans talked little but ivory, and ruled the town, wrote Moloney approvingly, 'with a rod of iron'. Two of its more exotic inhabitants caught his eye and ear. These were Farida, the dark, handsome, eight-year-old daughter of Emin Pasha by an Abyssinian woman, left there with a nurse when her father marched off with the Germans back towards his old province. Farida was 'very self-possessed' and wore an English sailor hat 'at a becoming angle'. There was also the famous Charlie Stokes, ivory trader and gunrunner, who had once been a lay missionary and had then gone native and married the daughter of a Wanyamwesi chief. Stokes had dined well. He woke up the party, shouting strange oaths in an Irish brogue, and kicking on the door 'undecided between pugilism and excessive affection',[17] dragged Stairs out of bed to shake him by the hand, then tried to make off with the Marquis's boots in the confusion.

Despite the collapsible steel boats carried in sections on the porters' heads, the men tramped rapidly westwards, swinging their arms rhythmically, averaging eight or ten miles a day, a record for the period. Moloney was appalled by the monotony of the diet, endless mealie and goat, as well as by the absence of lions to bag. They passed several large German caravans bound for the coast loaded with hundreds of tusks of ivory. Otherwise they encountered little of interest except for meeting the notorious slave trader, Tippu Tip. The old man, tall, bland and grey-bearded, was on the way to Zanzibar to defend a legal action brought against him by Stanley for Tippu Tip's alleged failure to supply the rear column with porters. The charge did not seem to worry him. (Stanley lost the case.) With an air of 'disinterested regret' he addressed Stairs's party. 'How it was, he could not say, but the great white chief [Stanley] had acquired an indifferent reputation throughout Central Africa. His shortcomings on the score of veracity were notorious.... In fact Mr Stanley's unpopularity would endanger his life were he to return to the Congo; and even at Zanzibar he might run some risk of assassination.'[18] Stairs and his fellows could hardly restrain their laughter until Tippu Tip had turned his back.

The march brought them by the main caravan road to Tabora, and by October 1891 they had gained the eastern shore of Lake Tanganyika. They crossed in hired dhows (it was easier than using the collapsible boats) but some of the dhows leaked so badly that they nearly sank. On the west bank flew the flag of the Congo Free State and here they heard news which gave a new momentum to the march. Two Englishmen had reached Bunkeya. This was not true, but the truth was alarming enough. As they stumbled towards the Lualaba, Stairs was handed a letter sent by Msiri weeks before. It was the letter addressed to Alfred Sharpe inviting him to return to Bunkeya. Stairs felt no more compunction in reading Sharpe's mail than Carl Peters had felt in reading Jackson's in Uganda. He promptly wrote Msiri a letter, making 'salaams' to him and telling him that he had come across the sea expressly to visit him; he signed it 'Stairs, the Englishman'.[19] It was sent ahead by way of Massoudi, a co-operative chief, escorted by four Zanzibari soldiers and enough porters to carry a large present of cloth.

On 19 November the expedition crossed the Lualaba in the steel boats and a fleet of dug-out canoes. By now they were covering fourteen miles a day, an astonishing speed for a large caravan. As they approached Bunkeya they saw ominous signs. The sorghum had been burnt in the fields. Most villages were deserted. Meat could not be bought for love or money and grain cost a famine price. The further west they went, the worse the effects of the war, but hunger acted as a spur to the men.

They were met by Massoudi and his escort returning from Bunkeya. He brought back two messages, both in the handwriting of the missionary, Dan Crawford. The first was only a scrap of paper, an official reply dictated by Msiri. He said he was overjoyed at the white men's coming. They should receive the greeting of brothers. The second message was a long gloomy letter from the missionary giving 'a full account of the King's oppression, and the ruin caused thereby'. 'Well,' remarked Stairs, as decisive as ever. 'I'll soon put a stop to Mr Msiri's little game.'[20]

Crawford, the pacifist, waited anxiously at Bunkeya. He was afraid for Msiri's soul if there should be a violent collision. It would have been better for Msiri if God's witnesses had never come than that, having come, he should have closed his eyes against the light. Msiri's own mood oscillated between good humour and blind rage. Stairs had signed his letter 'the Englishman'. That made Msiri's heart 'white' towards the newcomers, he cheerfully told Crawford. He shouted to his followers, 'They are English, they are English, do you hear, sons of dust? ... And we know the English to be true people.'[21]

Then Msiri harangued his remaining men for days, boasting of the great victories he would win, the great feats of arms he would perform once he got the powder – for the Englishmen, of course, were bringing him powder. During these harangues he would turn scornfully to the missionaries who had refused him what he had asked for, and bellow defiance at the Belgians too. Yes, he knew why the Belgians came – to eat his country. One day the missionaries brought new presents, including a musical box and 150 yards of cloth. The cloth was treated like an insult. Msiri's face became as 'wild and wicked' as the Devil himself. Why did they still not give him powder? Crawford thought he might pay the price with his own head. But these storms quickly blew themselves out, and the Chief would soon send him an apologetic message, begging his 'friend' to come and visit him again.

At long last, on 14 December, Crawford saw the 300-strong travel-stained caravan of Zanzibaris march across the blackened fields to the capital with drums beating and flags flying. He was told by Msiri to show the Englishmen the camping ground; then he was free to return to the new mission post on the Lufira. Stairs had his own interpreter so Msiri had no further desire for Crawford's services. Nothing suited the missionary better.

Stairs was pleased to have the missionaries out of the way. In his view it was a mistake to send people like that to this barbarous place. He blamed them for their weakness in indulging the tyrant so long, in allowing him to call them his 'white slaves', and in letting him think that all whites were like them. If it came to 'decisive action'[22] – meaning a fight – he wanted them safely out of Msiri's clutches.

At their first palaver, Stairs found that his host's beaming smile rapidly faded. Msiri tried to play Stairs off against the Belgian officer stationed at Lofoi, Lieutenant Legat. Stairs pretended to agree that Legat must go. He also offered to give Msiri any amount of powder to use against the Basanga rebels – provided that Msiri agreed to hoist the flag of Bula Matari. Msiri offered to hoist the Ingleza (English) flag, but not the Belgian. Caught on the raw, Stairs let fly at the Chief, telling him his 'monstrous cruelties' could no longer be tolerated. But Msiri still refused to accept the blue flag, and Stairs had got nothing out of the stormy interview.

Two days later Stairs tried again to bully the old man into submission. They spent four hours wrangling. Msiri offered to make him a blood brother and to hoist the flag next day. Stairs would have none of this; the flag must go up at once. Finally, he grabbed a pole from Msiri's palisade and climbed a hill above the town. Defying Msiri to stop him, he himself attached the blue flag to the pole. Msiri did nothing either to prevent or acknowledge the act of defiance. Disappointed, the officers returned to the camping ground. That night they half-expected an attack from Msiri's warriors, but nothing occurred. In the morning Stairs sent four successive messages, offering to accept blood brotherhood. Each time came the same answer: the King sleeps.

In fact Msiri did not sleep that night in any of his houses in Bunkeya. He had fled in terror to Munema, the village of his half-caste wife, Maria, half an hour from the capital. Stairs decided the 'poor comedy'[23] had gone on long enough. Msiri would have to be placed under arrest, even if it meant war. After all,

Katanga was already the territory of the Free State, according to international agreeement. He sent off 115 Zanzibaris with breech-loading rifles, led by Captain Bodson, to put Msiri in irons. Then, after sending a message to the missionaries to tell them to take refuge in the Free State post, Stairs and Moloney watched Msiri's village anxiously through their binoculars.

It will never be known exactly what happened in the dusty square outside Msiri's hut. But this was certainly a foolhardy way of trying to arrest the King. Bodson and a dozen Zanzibaris, including one called Hamadi, were led there by a guide, while Bonchamps and the rest remained out of sight beyond the *boma* surrounding the labyrinth of huts. According to Hamadi, they were faced by 300 hostile warriors, most of them armed with guns. Bodson told Msiri to follow him back to 'the great white chief in the camp and no evil shall happen to your person'. Msiri said nothing, but ground his teeth in rage. Then he grabbed the sword, given him three days before by Stairs, and made a lunge at Bodson. Bodson fired his revolver twice at the King. All hell broke loose in the village.

About midday, Moloney heard the firing and saw through his binoculars the soldiers 'peppering the village'. So Msiri was 'showing his teeth'.[24] Moloney was not prepared for the scene he found when he marched breathlessly up to the village square. The place was in pandemonium. In front of the hut, Msiri lay on his back, dead. Bodson was *in extremis*, shot through the stomach. Hamadi and another of the Askaris were writhing in pain, shot in the thigh and ankle respectively. The victorious Zanzibaris had lost all control, hunting down chickens, goats and women like madmen. Moloney set about him with a large stick. Then he fetched porters to carry the three injured men back to Bunkeya, with eight extra men to carry the corpse of Msiri, whose face, Moloney noticed, wore 'a mocking smile'.[25]

Bodson died at eight o'clock that evening. He whispered to Moloney, 'Doctor, I don't mind dying, now that I've killed Msiri.' He told Stairs, 'Thank God, my death will not be in vain. I've delivered Africa from one of her most detestable tyrants.'[26]

At first that seemed to be the reaction of Africans, too. No one was bold enough to avenge the old man. On the contrary, most of his supporters seemed glad to see the last of him, shovelled into the royal burial plot after a wild night of drumming and beer drinking. Stairs divided Msiri's kingdom swiftly and cleanly: the land around Bunkeya for the King's adopted son, Makanda; two villages for Makanda's uncles; the rest to be restored to the Basanga. To enforce the new settlement, and to give permanence to the Free State's sovereignty symbolized by the blue flag, Stairs then built a large, hexagonal wood-and-mud fort in the middle of the capital, taking most of the materials from Msiri's abandoned palace. It was there that Stairs celebrated Christmas 1891 with a plum pudding especially reserved for the occasion.

But as the weeks passed, Moloney found it hard to forget that mocking smile of Msiri's. The famine intensified, killing not only the natives, but seventy-three of the Zanzibaris in Stairs's column. Ninety others vanished into the wilderness, looking for food. Worse, all the European members of the party except Moloney fell seriously ill. Then, providentially, in late January 1892, the fourth expedition sent by Leopold – three hundred well-fed men led by Captain Bia – tramped into the capital after a seventy-two-day march from one of the southern tributaries of the Congo. Stairs was now persuaded to hand over the fort to Captain Bia, and make for the coast with the survivors of his column. He set off on 4 February, carried in a hammock, too ill to be able to follow much of what happened around him.

*   *   *

It was late July 1892 before news of the fate of Stairs's expedition reached Leopold in Brussels. Stairs had died of haematuric fever within sound of the sea at Chinde. Bia had died too; but not before he had prospected in southern Katanga for precious minerals. First reports were not encouraging. He had found no sign of any gold at all. Copper there was, in enormous quantities, but in 1891 copper was not a valuable commodity. It was probably not worth building a railway to the middle of Africa to carry copper from Katanga to the sea.

Leopold took the news from Katanga with his usual calm. He accepted that there had to be setbacks and sacrifices. If the Congo was like a battlefield, his own fortune was one of the casualties. What was important to Leopold was that he had won – and Cecil Rhodes had lost – the race for Katanga. In the meanwhile, gold or no gold, he was planning a new stratagem for exploiting the Congo, which caused a crisis of conscience among his advisers and risked the loss of his oldest supporter, Emile Banning.

It was under the flag of free trade that Leopold had won the Congo at Berlin in 1885. It had still been his flag – plus 10 per cent for import duty – at Brussels in 1890. Literally, this meant that traders of every nation were free to compete in the Congo. It meant competition between the international companies trading there, companies in which Leopold could make a substantial private investment. In September 1891 Leopold suddenly reversed his policy. He had issued a secret decree ordering the authorities in two remote districts, Aruwimini and Ubangi-Uele, to secure all the ivory they could on behalf of the state. This was followed by successive orders banning natives from hunting elephants or harvesting wild rubber unless they sold it to the state. When the news leaked out, the meaning was unmistakable: the Free State was becoming a state monopoly. Coupled with the decree came a new interpretation of who *owned* the Congo. All land belonged to the state except that actually occupied or cultivated by the natives, and the price of its two most valuable products – ivory and rubber – was to be decided by the only buyer.

Naturally this revelation shocked many of Leopold's collaborators; it was as though Leopold had lowered the blue flag and hoisted the skull-and-crossbones. The Belgian companies he had helped to create, especially those in the northern region, lobbied against the new policy. The Governor-General, Camille Jansen, resigned. Baron Lambermont protested; there was talk of resignation by the entire Cabinet of M. Beernaert. Emile Banning wrote a memorandum in which he could not conceal his sense of moral outrage:

> The doctrine of state ownership of land ... is the exact opposite of the regime [of free trade]. The doctrine should not be allowed to prevail, either against the natural rights of the indigenous population, which it would in effect dispossess, nor against the rights of the Powers, as laid down in the Berlin Act.[27]

Leopold paid not the slightest attention to this warning. M. Banning's memorandum was 'interesting apart from his false conclusions'. For thirty years he had depended on Banning as his most experienced and loyal adviser on colonial affairs. Now Leopold cut Banning dead in public and jeered at his stammer behind his back.

But the commercial companies were not so easy to humiliate. In October 1892 the King had to offer a compromise. The Congo was divided into three zones: the *domaine privé* north of the equator, for the exclusive use of the state; the middle zone, open to traders; and the south and east, including Katanga and the Arab-controlled regions, still in process of assimilation. The compromise worked, or at least Beernaert's government acquiesced. In fact, it was largely a sham. Most of the rubber and ivory producing regions were grabbed by the state. Parts of the 'open' zone were parcelled out to concessionary companies and several of these, including one called Abir, were simply fronts for the King. These were the companies which within ten years would give the King fame and fortune, and make him infamous too, for the methods he used to extort work from the natives.

No one could have guessed this in October 1892. At that period the Congo deficit was still running deep and strong, like the Congo river. Next year it ran stronger still.

Reports began to reach Brussels that van Kerckhoven was dead and his expedition to the Nile threatened with disaster. As Stanley had forecast, the job was far beyond Leopold's resources.

Worse, despite Leopold's explicit orders to keep the peace with the Arabs, there was a report of a general Arab rising. A trader called Hodister and his colleagues on the upper Congo had acted provocatively. In May they had apparently been murdered by the local Arab chief, Nserera. Now there was the threat of a full-scale war breaking out between the Free State and the Arabs, with both armies eagerly supported by cannibals.

CHAPTER 23

The Flag Follows the Cross

Uganda, Paris and London
25 December 1891–November 1892

'The English have come ... they have built a fort,
they eat my land, and yet they have given me nothing
at all.'

King Mwanga, after Lugard's arrival in Buganda, 1890

On Christmas Day 1891, when Stairs was celebrating the fall of Msiri with plum pudding and champagne at Bunkeya, a British officer in a mud-stained khaki jacket, pith helmet and broken leather boots was tramping painfully back towards his HQ at Kampala, a hilltop opposite Mengo, the capital of Buganda, 900 miles to the north. The officer was a short, wiry, masterful austere thirty-three-year-old: Captain Frederick Lugard DSO, the Resident and chief representative of the Imperial British East Africa Company in Buganda.

Of all the freelance imperialists who promoted the Scramble, Lugard was to prove the most tenacious and, ultimately, the most successful. In the next forty years no other proconsul would put such a powerful moral stamp on the character of European rule in Africa. Significantly, both his parents were missionaries, and his hero was David Livingstone. Yet he had sailed for Africa more to cast away his life than to build an empire.

As a brave, priggish young officer of the East Norfolk Regiment, based on Lucknow in India, he had lost his heart to a beautiful divorcée called 'Clytie' (her full name is not known). In 1887, when campaigning in Burma, he received a telegram to say that Clytie was close to death after overturning her carriage at Lucknow. He rushed back to India only to find she had sailed for England. He sailed for England and found her – it would seem – in bed with one of her admirers. The shock unhinged Lugard. He lost his faith in God, threw up his career and then took a boat as a deck passenger down the Red Sea, hoping to die in a noble cause. The British consul at Zanzibar told him that the British missionaries of the African Lakes Company based in Nyasaland were beleaguered by the local Arab slavers and needed a knight errant to organize their defence. Lugard obliged – and was dangerously wounded in both arms when leading a reckless charge against the Arab slavers' stockade at Karonga. After his recovery, he returned to England a convert to the case for the British government to intervene in Africa. Imperialism was the only antidote to the East African slave trade. When the British government gave a royal charter to Mackinnon's Imperial British East Africa Company, it was Lugard who was chosen to open up Uganda. His injuries healed slowly; both the wounds to his body inflicted by the Arab slavers and the wound to his heart inflicted by Clytie.

Now, on Christmas Day 1891, the Company's tattered flag – a rising sun supported by a Union Jack – flew at the head of his huge, sprawling caravan of Sudanese, Swahili and Baganda. About 100 men were armed with rifles, and there was a battered Maxim gun – the same battered Maxim gun that Stanley had dragged across Africa on the Emin relief expedition. Now, almost within sight of the lumpy green hills of the capital, Lugard was handed the long-awaited mail bag from England.

For a whole year he had been out of touch with his employer, Mackinnon. His original instructions had been notably vague. He was to take 300 men and a Maxim, and march 800 miles through the wilderness to the capital of Buganda. There he was to impress the Kabaka 'with his power'.

The Kabaka was Mackay's adversary, Mwanga, the erratic tyrant whose murder of Bishop Hannington and massacre of Christian converts in 1885–6 had horrified Europe. Lugard was to induce him to sign a treaty that would regularize the Company's delicate position in the country. (Lord Salisbury had won a British 'sphere' in Uganda by the Anglo-German agreement of July 1890, but no one had explained this to Mwanga, its absolute ruler.) Lugard was also to impress with his 'power' the two political factions, Protestant and Catholic, created by rival European missionaries. They had beaten the third faction, the Muslims, in a civil war, and were now at each other's throats. Lugard was to be 'perfectly impartial' while obtaining 'control of all white affairs',[1] whatever that meant. But one thing was perfectly clear: it was Lugard's job, by fair means or foul, to impose a protectorate on Buganda and its vassal states in the rest of Uganda.

In the event, Lugard had done prodigies for his employers. Then he opened the mail bag, and was hit by what he called a 'thunderbolt'. The Company had run out of money; he was to abandon Uganda and retire to the coast as 'speedily as possible'.[2]

From his first day in Buganda, a year earlier, Lugard had been committed to a permanent British occupation. This was why he had to show the Baganda who was master. As he put it in his diary, he had not 'come here to trifle and fool, and mean to go thro' with my work [in] spite of Mwanga'. Etiquette demanded that visitors wait at the frontier, then seek royal permission for each stage of the advance, but Lugard and his Maxim made brutally straight for the capital. He arrived on 18 December 1890, and was instructed to camp in a damp hollow below the royal palace of Mengo. He promptly pitched his tent on a hilltop at Kampala, a commanding hilltop opposite the palace. Next day he put on 'court' dress – an old pyjama jacket with brass buttons added – and marched across the valley to the palace, through crowds of sightseers swarming like 'the bees inside a hive'.[3]

There he had his first audience with the King. Flute players welcomed him in the grass-strewn durbar hut, choked with hundreds of excited Baganda nobles, who were dressed in long white cotton robes and armed with muzzle-loaders. Lugard brought his own chair and calmly sat down to read his letters of introduction, to be translated into Swahili and Luganda for the King and the court. Then he shook the King's hand. He was not impressed by Mwanga's habit of giggling, and of caressing his pages in public. He had 'good features', but his face showed irresolution and 'a good deal of sensuality'. Before taking his leave, Lugard explained he had brought a 'treaty of friendship',[4] and he advised the King and chiefs to sign it.

Lugard let the young man wriggle for a few days. Then, on 26 December 1890, he returned to the durbar hut, threatening to use the Maxim if the Kabaka refused to sign the treaty. Mwanga put a mark, more like a blot than a cross, on the document. This was followed by the crosses of the Protestant Katikiro (Prime Minister), Apolo Kagwa; the Catholic Kimbugwe (Second Minister), and other great chiefs. They had all 'consented',[5] so these marks said.

What did Mwanga make of Lugard? He was, understandably, in a state of shock.

At the age of eighteen he had inherited, from his father Mtesa, the largest and richest kingdom of Central Africa, where the Kabaka was traditionally free to torture or kill his subjects at his own whim. In practice, absolute power had brought him nothing but absolute torment. In the last seven years the power of the Bugandan throne had been battered and broken, then patched up again, in the course of a four-sided revolution. Paganism – with witchcraft, polygamy and hashish – was the traditional prop of Bugandan society, of its autocratic monarchy and its courtly rituals. The first to knock away this prop were the Muslims attracted by Mtesa, Arab and Swahili merchants, buying slaves and ivory in exchange for guns and gunpowder. Then came the Christian missionaries attracted by Stanley: the English (and Scottish) Protestants of the CMS and the French White Fathers sent by Cardinal Lavigerie. It would have taxed Solomon to satisfy all four groups in this struggle for temporal and religious ascendancy: the pagan traditionalists who smoked hashish or bang (the Wa-Bangi), the Muslims, the Protestant – i.e. pro-English – faction called the Wa-Ingleza, and the Catholic – i.e. pro-French – faction, the Wa-Fransa.

In 1886 Mwanga had swung to the side of the Muslims. To please them he had murdered Hannington and burnt alive the young Catholic and Protestant pages at the court. In September 1888, when the Muslims threatened him, he swung to the pagans, the Wa-Bangi. They agreed to expel the leaders of all the 'new' religions and maroon them on an island in the lake where they would die of starvation. The Wa-Bangi's crazy plot ended with Mwanga's deposition and a short-lived alliance between the Muslims and the two Christian factions. Within a few weeks civil war broke out. The Muslims seized power and replaced Mwanga with his brother. The missionaries were expelled and Mwanga fled to the south of the lake. Then, using the guns and boat supplied by Charlie Stokes – the ex-CMS lay missionary who had gone native and become an arms dealer – Mwanga had been restored to the island of Bulingugwe a few miles across the lake from Mengo. It was from this island base that Mwanga had been restored as Kabaka in 1889, after the Christians had driven out the Muslims with appalling slaughter. It was then on 25 February 1890, that Carl Peters, dressed in scarlet court dress, entered the durbar hut at Mengo and quickly persuaded Mwanga to sign a treaty with the German East Africa Company.

The new treaty extorted by Lugard on 26 December 1890 had marked the failure of that last desperate attempt to play off the Germans against the English. It was also much more demanding than Peters's treaty of friendship. It did not simply interfere with the Kabaka's right to control foreign affairs, to make treaties or make war as he pleased; it abolished his independence in home affairs, too. Significantly, some of the conditions were the direct result of the anti-slavery conference concluded in Brussels only five months earlier. Slave trading and slave raiding were prohibited. The arms trade was to be controlled by the Company as a representative of the 'protecting' Power. Foreign traders and missionaries were to be free to settle in the country. Free trade and freedom of conscience were to be guaranteed. As for the government of the country, the Kabaka had signed away control of his own revenues ('The revenues of the country shall be collected and the customs and taxes shall be assessed by a Committee or Board of Finance'). No longer did he command his own army ('The King, assisted by the Company, shall form a standing army, which the officers of the Company will endeavour to organize and drill like a native regiment in India'). Nor could he decide his own policy (The Resident's 'consent shall be obtained ... in all grave and serious affairs and matters connected with the state').[6]

No wonder Mwanga had tried desperately to avoid signing away these rights. This white man had not even brought him a set of presents. (These were to follow in the next caravan.) 'The English have come,' said Mwanga acidly, 'they have built a fort, they eat my land, and yet they have given me nothing at all. They have made me sign a treaty, they curtail my power and I get nothing at all from them in return.'[7] Walker, the CMS missionary who was understandably impressed by Lugard, was struck by the loathing Mwanga felt for the English. So were the French priests who were becoming a thorn in Lugard's side. 'What a humiliation', wrote one of their biographers, 'for the proud Mwanga to put all the thousands of subjects and of people from his vassal states under the protection of a simple commercial company!'[8]

In the first days Lugard had been delighted by the way he had knocked the stuffing out of Mwanga. A few weeks in the fifty-yard-square camp on Kampala Hill soon taught him how precarious was his own situation. Out of the 300 men in his caravan, only 100 looked capable of using a rifle, and they were a wild bunch of natives – Sudanese, Swahili and Baganda. Stanley's battered Maxim gun could not be expected to fire more than a few seconds without jamming. Food was dangerously short. Bananas there were in plenty, but no spare grain and little meat in the capital or the surrounding countryside. Worse, there was no faction in the kingdom that he could trust. Lugard found the place as friendly as a 'hornet's nest'.

Most hostile, of course, were the Catholics, the Wa-Fransa, now led by the bewildered Mwanga. For advice they turned to the White Fathers. Lugard longed to persuade these excitable Frenchmen of the necessity for all Europeans to stand together, but the Frenchmen were patriots and imperialists like himself. They could not reconcile themselves to conceding power in so promising a field for their country's work. Even now France might take over Buganda from the British; after all, Lugard only represented a British company believed to be rapidly approaching bankruptcy. So Lugard's efforts to pacify the Wa-Fransa were thwarted by the priests. Both factions, Wa-Fransa and Wa-Ingleza, had originally agreed to share the great offices of state, and the fat income that went with them. But in early 1891, with Mwanga at their head, the Wa-Fransa were gaining in numbers. They would never agree to a standstill on the division of offices if the French priests could prevent it. What about the control of the Sese islands, rich in food and the main naval base, with its fleet of canoes, if there was to be a war on the lake? At present these strategic islands were the King's special preserve. Should they be partitioned between the two factions? Not if the priests could prevent it.

Since they had infuriated the Wa-Fransa and their French advisers, one might have thought that Lugard would have warmed the hearts of the Wa-Ingleza and the English missionaries. In practice he made stern efforts, as instructed by his employers, to stand aloof from both factions. It was, he believed, the only hope of avoiding a civil war. Predictably, the price was to alienate the Wa-Ingleza who felt betrayed by their natural protector. Even his compatriots, who at first found Lugard 'a quiet and patient man', soon came to distrust what they called his 'strange ignorance'[9] of the real situation – meaning their own political power – and were soon denouncing his perverse efforts to see both sides of the question and work through the King. By the end of January 1891 the hornet's nest was looking more like a volcano. The Wa-Ingleza, weaker in numbers, guns and powder, were so alarmed that it looked as if they might have to abandon their homes and flee to Busoga, leaving the Muslims to deal with the Wa-Fransa.

At this dangerous moment Lugard had received a crucial helping hand from his employers on the coast: seventy-five Sudanese and a hundred Swahilis, with a second Maxim gun and porters to match, commanded by an experienced British gunner, Captain W. H. Williams. In a sense, Captain Williams was *too* experienced; he was senior to Lugard by a few weeks. After some embarrassment, he agreed to swallow his pride and serve as second-in-command. The reinforcements transformed Lugard's position – although the second Maxim gun jammed, like the first, when he demonstrated it. The most immediate threat, as it turned out, came from that incongruous white trader, Charlie Stokes, who owned a steamer based on the southern side of the lake, the shore controlled by the Germans.

Stokes arrived at Mengo on 5 February 1891, an indignant Irishman dressed in Muslim robes, protesting his innocence of arms smuggling. He swore he hadn't an ounce of powder with him. Lugard gave him a candle-lit dinner in his camp and calmed him. No doubt he told Stokes about the provisions of the

Brussels conference. What he wanted was an assurance that Stokes would not sell guns or powder to Mwanga or either of the two factions. There were already 2,000 or 3,000 muzzle-loading guns in the country; any more guns would make war virtually inevitable.

Stokes explained he could make £1,440 for every load of powder sold. But he was fed up with the heavy-handedness of the Germans (though they paid him £1,000 a year to organize supplies), and would prefer to come north and work with the British Company. Would Lugard buy his current stock, which incidentally included fifty loads of powder and 250 guns, worth £5,000? Lugard bought some cloth and proposed that he develop the ivory trade in Buganda. Stokes asked Lugard to give him a chance and not put too great a temptation in a poor man's way. Would he agree to *store* the powder for him at Kampala to keep him from selling it to Mwanga? Lugard could hardly believe his ears. Of course he was delighted to oblige.

For the next two months Lugard dug himself in at Kampala, making the camp a regular fortress, and excavating a large magazine for Stokes's powder kegs. Morale was kept up with a heavy hand. The flogging parade was a regular affair, and one would-be deserter who deserved to be shot, Lugard felt, was let off with 100 lashes ('He did not get it half hot enough to please me. However this is only the first instalment, and he shall have a real good flogging next time.')[10] Often there were hysterical rows between the factions and sometimes men were killed.

On 19 February Lugard was told by the King that war was imminent. At first he paid little attention, as he had heard the same story so often before. Then the Wa-Fransa were seen taking up battle positions on the King's hill. Lugard marched up with the Sudanese, appealed to their chiefs, and threatened to open fire with the Maxim. That afternoon he had much the same difficulty with the Wa-Ingleza. The next day the Wa-Fransa were on the warpath again, rushing about waving a huge French tricolour. It needed all Lugard's moral strength and the sight of the Maxim to calm the hysterical mob. He found himself exhausted by these war scares. 'So the game goes on,' he wrote a week later, 'and each day seems to bring news which must lead to war; each day we manage to stave it off – but how long will this last?'[11]

At the end of March 1891 a second reinforcement reached Kampala, a poor, broken-down caravan led by an illiterate Maltese called Martin. The majority of the men were unarmed, and anyway '*quite* unfit',[12] Lugard noted, to hold a rifle. Fortunately they had brought some useful trade goods – cloth and so on – and also Lugard's long-delayed presents for the King. Best of all, they had brought back the two envoys Mwanga had sent down to the coast with Jackson the previous year, the Catholic and Protestant sent to check the British claims that Uganda was in their 'sphere'. Lugard was relieved to find that the Wa-Fransa accepted the envoys' report philosophically, and the presents to the King, including rolls of chintz furnishings, caused a sensation. Lugard was assured that Mwanga, too, had come to terms with the new protectorate. He had got over his hatred of the 'Kapelli' (Captain), as he called Lugard; he knew he was there to uphold his honour and state, not to oust him. So Lugard was assured by one of the leading Protestants, and he let himself believe it. For his part, he certainly wished to humour the King and give him his head as far as possible – provided he did what Lugard told him.

A heaven-sent opportunity to please the King and both the Wa-Ingleza and Wa-Fransa was now there to be seized. The defeated Muslims had found refuge with Kabarega, the King of the Bunyoro, Buganda's neighbour and hereditary enemy. Recently the Bunyoro had taken advantage of the confusion at Mengo to raid the border province of Singo. Lugard agreed to join a military expedition to put down these Muslim rebels and their champions in Bunyoro. It was a daring decision: to leave a junior officer to guard his base at Kampala while he plunged into the unknown, taking sides in a war between two African armies. It was still more daring, and perhaps reckless, to extend this expedition hundreds of miles to the Ruwenzori, to march across the vassal states of Ankole and Toro to Kavalli, Emin's old HQ on the upper Nile.

This was Lugard's amazing plan in the spring of 1891. For the war against the Muslims he could make a case, though a stronger one could be made for imposing peace on the Christian factions at Mengo. As for a flag-waving expedition to the Ruwenzori, there were treaties to be made with the vassal states. But to leave the protectorate and trek to the southern Sudan, all the way to Kavalli – could this really be justified?

Lugard's first aim was to enlist Emin's old troops for service in Uganda – the men of the Sudanese garrison who had been unable or unwilling to leave with Stanley and Emin in 1888 and whom Emin was even now rumoured to be trying to recruit for German service. His second aim was so wild and fanciful that it seems no more than a boyish dream. Once in possession of Emin's troops and steamers, he hoped to steam down the Nile, crush the Mahdists and avenge Gordon by re-capturing Khartoum from the south.

It was this absurd dream that had dissolved in the light of reality. In other respects Lugard had accomplished prodigies. On 7 May 1891 he had brought the Maxim to the help of the Christians during the battle against the Muslims inside Bunyoro. The Muslims fled, leaving about 300 dead on the battlefield. Lugard then wanted to take the wild mob of Christian Baganda to help him dispose of King Kabarega. It turned out that the road was impassable because of the rains, so Lugard left Williams to march back with the victorious Christians to Mengo, while he set off westwards to Ankole. There he confirmed the Company's protectorate by sealing a pact of blood with the envoys of the local ruler, King Ntare. He also built a fort for the King of Toro and promised to protect him from aggression by King Kabarega of Bunyoro. Meanwhile there was a rumour that Emin had stolen a march on Lugard and led some of his old troops from Kavalli back into German territory. This took Lugard on a wild goose chase to the further side of the snow-capped Ruwenzori.

By 7 September he had at last crossed into Equatoria and reached Kavalli. There he found a sight that moved him greatly: two regiments of Sudanese, about 600 armed men, the last survivors from Emin's garrison, and still loyal to the Khedive, their master.

Thank God, he told them, he had been able to come in time to rescue them. The Sudanese formed a hollow square and presented arms, each regiment marching past with its French-style band of drums and bugles at its head. 'It was a sight to touch a man's heart', Lugard wrote that night in his diary. 'To see this noble remnant who were fanatical in their loyalty to their flag and their Khedive, scarred and wounded, many prematurely grey, clad in skins, and deserted here in the heart of Africa – and I *do* thank God (as I said in my speech) that it has fallen to my lot to come to their relief, as well as that I have been able to secure so fine a body of men for the Company's service.'[13]

But as soon as they turned back eastwards, Lugard's feelings cooled towards this fine body of men. It was many years since they had been properly disciplined. Lugard thought he could trust their commander, Selim Bey ('a huge man, some six ft. 2 in., and very stout',[14] with the shiny black skin of the true Sudanese). He gave Selim orders against looting and making slaves of local women. The Sudanese frequently chose not to obey orders. For the rest of the journey back to Buganda Lugard found himself caught up in a grim struggle against the depredations of his own men. He blamed Stanley – and Emin – for the irresponsible way they had allowed their men to rob the peasants of the countries they passed through. Now his own men were earning the same reputation.

They were like a swarm of locusts on the march. Not only did they grab grain and chickens (which Lugard allowed, for no one would sell them food), but they stole cattle and made slaves of the local women to add to the enormous retinue of porters, wives, concubines and children forced to accompany them. Lugard was appalled to find that the caravan totalled over 8,000 people. The best he could arrange was to build a series of forts along the Bunyoro border, then to detach most of the Sudanese and camp followers to garrison them. But he knew that the moment his back was turned the Sudanese would resume their looting and slaving.

So it was with only about 100 Sudanese from Kavalli and their commander, Selim Bey, together with his own original force and his porters that Lugard was approaching Kampala on Christmas Day 1891, when he received that thunderbolt from the mailbag: abandon Uganda and retire to the coast.

This peremptory order was explained by George Mackenzie, the Company's harassed managing director, in a private letter dated 10 August 1891. Mackenzie thanked Lugard for his 'very excellent work'. He would be flattered to know that copies of his 'interesting' report had been circulated to the Foreign Office, War Office and Cabinet. However, the Company's position was 'so entirely changed' that there was no help for it but to retrench and retire. The 'critical position' in which this might leave the British CMS missionaries had 'not been overlooked'. But 'whatever the result', Lugard must withdraw as 'speedily as possible', exercising his own discretion on how best to do this while inflicting the least possible damage to the 'general interests of the country and the Church

Missionary Society in particular'.[15] Mackenzie added that the Foreign Office concurred.

The reason was simple: the Company was going bankrupt. In Uganda alone it was spending £40,000 a year 'without a penny of return'. What about borrowing more money from the public? Unfortunately the City of London was in the throes of one of the most severe crises it had ever known. The crash had brought down the great firm of Baring Brothers and other banks were tottering.

Any hope of rescuing the Company from disaster depended on building an immensely expensive railway 800 miles from Mombasa to Lake Victoria in order to open up Uganda to trade. Ever since the Brussels anti-slavery conference, which committed Britain to try to cut the east coast slave trade at its roots, the directors had pinned their faith on Lord Salisbury's government agreeing to guarantee the cost of the railway. Such a guarantee might have induced the public to back the scheme, but the anti-imperialist wing of the Liberals had given the plan such a pasting in Parliament during July 1891 that Salisbury was forced to shelve the railway guarantee and substitute for it a mere railway survey. It was this rebuff that had precipitated the Company's decision to abandon Uganda.

The railway survey remained a gleam of hope, along with some advice from Mackenzie to Lugard. He should keep the Germans out of Uganda; he should try to get Mwanga to extend the current treaty to one in perpetuity; and he should impress on Mwanga and his people that the withdrawal was 'of a temporary nature' – as indeed it was. The moment the funds allowed it, Lugard would be back to 'resume' his good work.

'*Resuming*' his work. How the underlinings striated Lugard's diary as he rejected this preposterous idea. He had devoted two and a half years of his life to making a British protectorate in East Africa. Now all his toil was to be 'merely waste – and worse'. The collapse would be '*terrible* in its results'. First, the Ingleza would leave Buganda '*for certain*', and the British missionaries would follow, which meant the 'annihilation' of the Uganda mission. Second, the Muslims would swoop down and 'mop up' the Fransa. Third, he would have broken the word he had given the King of Toro that the British would stay to protect him. The result, would be a 'general massacre' by King Kabarega of Bunyoro. Fourth, evacuation would be a blow to British prestige that 'can *never* be recovered'.[16]

'Well if it is to be done, there is a cruel, cruel wrong to be done. Hundreds – nay thousands – of lives will be sacrificed, and the blood must lie at someone's door.' Lugard had an agonizing struggle with his conscience. Should he defy the order to scuttle? Must he throw up his career and devote his life to saving these people? He decided that there was a loophole in his instructions from London. He could leave one 'volunteer' behind to act as Resident at Mwanga's court. The idea was 'madness'. 'A volunteer for what? – to stay in Uganda without position, authority, regard for personal safety, with no power to face anarchy. Would you find a volunteer to go and hang himself? – it is pure madness.'[17] But it might be possible to station this volunteer in Toro, supported by the Sudanese rescued from Kavalli, men who could live off the land and demand no wages.

Back in Kampala, Lugard found that little had changed for the better in the eight months he had been away. His correspondence overwhelmed him; he had an official report to write and 140 private letters to answer. Meanwhile, he decided not to breathe a word about evacuation to anyone, except his second-in-command, Captain Williams.

Williams, too, was astounded at the news. 'He exclaimed it simply *could not be done*,' wrote Lugard later. How could he ever hold up his head as a gentleman if he were involved in so grave a breach of faith? But how to defy the evacuation order if they had no money to pay their men? Williams proposed a way out of the dilemma. He had a little money of his own. He would give every penny he had in the world sooner than break faith with the people he had pledged to protect. Lugard accepted the 'noble and unselfish' offer. 'It was worth the anxiety and responsibility of that time to prove a man of such mettle as this!'[18] Together, two Arthurian knights in the quest for a tropical Grail, they would save England's name from dishonour, and Uganda's people from a bloodbath.

But before this romantic pledge could be consummated, a telegram arrived from London, carried by a new supply caravan. It was a reprieve; enough funds had been raised in the autumn of 1891 by the CMS and other humanitarians in London for the Company to postpone evacuation for a year, till the end of 1892. Lugard handed the telegram to Williams and they shook hands over it like a couple of schoolboys. 'It *was* a great relief.'[19] But of course the reprieve did not alter the furious rivalry between the Wa-Ingleza and the Wa-Fransa, and between the two embattled camps of missionaries, the CMS at Namirembe and the White Fathers at Rubaga. If anything, the rivalry had become more bitter, and Mwanga's own behaviour still more erratic than before.

On Lugard's return to Kampala he had found an '*enormous*' home-made flag, two lances and a shield on a red ground, flying over Mwanga's capital. It dwarfed the Union Jack and there was no hope of persuading Mwanga to take it down. Lugard regarded it as a provocation, an assertion of independence. On the other hand, Mwanga assured Williams, who had gone to see him secretly late at night, that he was 'thoroughly one'[20] with the British and threatened to leave the Wa-Fransa. Lugard called in the Sekibobo, the chief at the head of the Wa-Fransa, and gave him a friendly word of advice. The situation was impossible. The country was English by treaty. The King flew a flag of his own. Every day there were evictions and outrages between the two factions. It was time to stop all this; the King and the Wa-Fransa should 'declare for England, and take the flag, and let those who wished read what religion they liked'.[21]

Lugard's friendly words did not calm the storm. Indeed it was all too clear that a cyclone was on its way. He warned the Ingleza to call in their fighting men from the provinces where some had gone to fight the Muslims and others to fight the Wa-Bangi, the hashish-smoking robbers who had joined forces with the pagans.

Friday, 22 January 1892 should have been a day of celebration. It was Lugard's thirty-fourth birthday. But soon after breakfast some Ingleza chiefs rushed up the hill to Kampala in a state of hysteria. One of the Fransa sub-chiefs had wantonly murdered an Ingleza in the streets of Mengo and his body had been left lying in the sun. Lugard marched across the valley to Mengo to demand an explanation from the King. He was kept waiting for half an hour, sitting outside the audience chamber in the hot sun as though he was a beggar. He was not in the best of tempers when he was finally shown into the King's presence. He found only the Fransa chiefs, who were in high spirits, giggling and laughing like children. Obviously they had come to some sort of arrangement with the King.

Lugard told Mwanga bluntly that the murderer must be shot. Anyone who had provoked the murderer should be thoroughly flogged. That was the only way to avoid plunging the country in civil war. Mwanga took this piece of advice with feline politeness. He asked Lugard to wait to hear the Fransa sub-chief's story. But Lugard was not in the mood to wait. He stumped off, leaving his Somali interpreter to follow him back with the news. It turned out that Mwanga took the view that the killing was in self-defence. The Fransa had been provoked by the Ingleza, who had followed him into his enclosure while trying to recover a stolen gun. According to Buganda custom, the attacker was let off scot-free. Naturally, Lugard protested furiously.

If Lugard had had fewer letters to write and had not been kept waiting in the sun, he might have found it easier to come to some accommodation with Mwanga. Certainly the King had always been terrified of the prospect of war. The Wa-Fransa, on the other hand, seemed to be spoiling for a fight and the White Fathers, so it was reported to Lugard, were egging them on. The priests told their flock that Lugard and his men were only a trading company and 'could be driven out with sticks'.[22] The leader of the White Fathers was a French bishop, Mgr Jean-Joseph Hirth. He had arrived in Buganda at the same time as Lugard, and from the first took a strong line against the men he called 'the heretics'. In July he had warned Williams that if the Protestants triumphed it would be 'through *violence*'.[23] This was the lesson, he claimed, of the history of Protestant and Catholic rivalry in heathen lands.

On Saturday 23 January Lugard wrote to Hirth, imploring him to step in and calm the Fransa. 'Can you, Monseignor, use your influence to save so terrible a blow to the country as must be produced by war – a war which we have now with the utmost difficulty succeeded in averting for over a year?'[24] Hirth would do nothing. He refused even to come over to Kampala for discussions, on the grounds that he had his Sunday duties to fulfil next day. He explained that he supported the King's decision to liberate the Fransa sub-chief, and warned Lugard not to support the 'unjust pretensions'[25] of the Protestants. He hinted – significantly, in the light of what followed – that public opinion in Europe was watching each step that was taken in the struggle.

Everything now depended on whether Mwanga would climb down. Lugard sent his trusted interpreter, Dualla, back to the audience chamber with a blunt letter to be read in public to the King. The murderer must be handed over. It was justice, or war – as simple as that. If Lugard was losing patience, Dualla noticed that a new self-confidence had taken possession of the King. Instead of his usual terror at the word 'war', he seemed relaxed. The Fransa chiefs giggled hysterically.

Mwanga replied, 'All right. I have made my decision and won't alter it. If the Captain wants war, it is his matter....' To Dualla's amazement, the Fransa chiefs then began to insult Lugard openly. 'If he sends Askari to help the Protestants they will be killed to a man and if there is a war we shall take Kampala, and all the goods, and not only that, but all the Europeans will lose their lives.'[26]

This extraordinary scene in the audience chamber, duly reported by Dualla, convinced Lugard that the Fransa were about to launch an attack. Already war drums were beating in the Fransa camp. The previous evening Lugard had taken the plunge, and begun to distribute arms and powder from his magazine. About forty muzzle-loaders were handed out to the Ingleza, and a keg of powder. Despite these arms – which belonged to Stokes – the Ingleza faction was much the weaker. Many of their best men were still away fighting the Muslims and Wa-Bangi. As for his own garrison, Lugard had his original 100 fighting men and about 200 of Selim's Sudanese, who were armed with modern Snider rifles and the two battered Maxim guns. But Lugard realized that he could never withstand a siege at Kampala. Apart from the porters, there were about 1,000 women and children dependent on the garrison. The whole hillside was alive with their ramshackle huts, and there was no hope that they could all be squeezed inside the camp, let alone the fort, only fifty-foot square.

Kampala was the smallest of the four lumpy green hills at the capital. It faced the other three across a valley roughly a mile wide. To the south was the hill of Mengo, the royal town itself, where the King's huge red flag dominated the banana plantations, the palace enclosure and the compounds of the various chiefs. To the south-west was Rubaga, where the White Fathers had just completed a spectacular cathedral built in the native style, a towering affair of poles and reeds. To the west, at Namirembe, the CMS were building a church to rival this.

Lugard was up early on the morning of Sunday, 24 January; he had not dared take his clothes off since the crisis had blown up. Through his binoculars he could see that the Fransa were collecting in front of Rubaga and Mengo. A messenger arrived from the palace. His Majesty begged the captain to stop the war. Not unless he sends me the murderer, came Lugard's stern reply – not until he makes the Fransa apologize for their public insult. Lugard then sent down arms to the Ingleza, including the rest of Stokes's 500 muzzle-loaders and some extra Sniders. He had already offered sanctuary to both sets of missionaries. The sound of stray shots now floated across the valley. Through his binoculars he watched the Ingleza take their stand about half a mile away from the Fransa, stretching in a long line all the way from Kampala and Namirembe. Even now he clung to the idea that Mwanga might give way. But his patience was finally exhausted. And if it came to war, he believed he had no choice but to fight on the side of the Ingleza.

Negotiations were still in progress when the firing became more general. Soon a strange new sound could be heard, louder than the war-drums and the war-cries, more terrifying than the rattle of the Sniders and the crash of the muzzle-loaders. It was the heavy, intermittent beat of the Maxim. Lugard's most costly victory, the battle of Mengo, had begun.

*   *   *

It was late May before the first detailed account of the battle reached Europe. It took the form of a *cri de coeur* sent by Bishop Hirth to his superior in Algiers. The long, passionate letter, headed 'Bukoba', in German territory, on 10 February, was passed on to the French government, and so shocked them that Ribot, the Foreign Minister, protested to the British Ambassador at Paris, Lord Dufferin, on 25 May. A week later, Hirth's atrocity story exploded in a Catholic paper published in London:

> A terrible drama has just been enacted in Uganda. The Catholics who have long been persecuted, have been foully betrayed, and driven out with their king, Mwanga, at their head, accompanied by their bishop and 17 missionaries. This is the work of the Protestants, supported by the agents of the English Company. In place of the fair Catholic kingdom of Mwanga, the domination of the Crescent has sprung up, which the English themselves have had to call in to find a king to give the conquered country to. This is one of the most shameful pages in the civilisation of the Dark Continent.[27]

The letter went on to denounce Lugard in person for the systematic abuse of his position. From the first, Hirth reported, he had undermined Mwanga's authority, because Mwanga had sided with the Catholics. In January, replenished with arms and ammunition, he had decided on a showdown. This had precipitated the battle of Mengo and the victory of the Protestants, which would have been impossible without the help of the Sudanese Muslim troops and the Maxim gun. The great cathedral at Rubaga, the headquarters of the bishop's mission, had been left a smoking ruin. Hirth and his missionaries had narrowly escaped with their lives ('we regret one thing – not to have been held worthy of martyrdom').

But Lugard's blackest deeds had been committed on 30 January, a week after the battle of Mengo. When Mwanga and the Catholics had been driven from the capital, the King had taken refuge in his old sanctuary on the lake, the island of Bulingugwe, a few miles from Mengo and a few hundred yards from the shore. There, in front of the bishop's eyes, Lugard's Maxim turned victory into massacre:

It was two o'clock in the afternoon. On the road I saw fifteen boats rapidly approach the island. All of a sudden the bullets began to rain upon the royal hut, making a terrible noise in the copse that surrounded us; it was the Maxim *mitrailleuse*, which joined its fire to that of the boats loaded with soldiers. The King seized me by the hand and dragged me away; if we were not riddled it was the Lord who shielded us. A crowd of women and children fled with us. How many fell! We had soon gained the other shore of the island; the bullets could no longer reach us. But what a sight! Just a few canoes, and a crowd of 3,000 or 4,000 throwing themselves into the water to cling to them; it was heart-breaking. What shrieks! What a fusillade! What deaths by drowning![28]

As this atrocity story echoed across France and Germany, giving this obscure tribal feud in Africa the character of an international incident, the great Cardinal Lavigerie raised himself from his death-bed to denounce the massacre to the Pope. The French government pressed for an official inquiry into the mal-treatment of French subjects. The same day that Lord Dufferin was summoned to see M. Ribot, Lord Salisbury received an unwelcome call from M. Wadding-ton, the French Ambassador in London. He detailed the losses inflicted on the French mission: one cathedral, sixty chapels, twelve schools, and 50,000 Cath-olics said to have been sold into slavery. Naturally this did not shake Salisbury's calm. No whisper had yet been heard from Lugard, to confirm or deny the charges, nor a word from the CMS missionaries.

In fact, ever since rumours of a massacre had reached Paris in April, the Foreign Office had been trying to discover what on earth was going on. Gerald Portal, the Consul General at Zanzibar, had heard the same rumours and confessed privately that the Company might be to blame. However, by mid-June Portal was still in the dark, and still baffled. 'It is an extraordinary thing,' he told Sir Percy Anderson, 'that we don't get a word either from Williams himself or from Lugard.'[29]

The French and Germans did not find the silence extraordinary. They found it incredible. Both governments continued to press for an end to the cover-up. So did the Irish members in the British Commons. The atrocity story came in handy to them, and their Catholic supporters, for baiting Salisbury's govern-ment. More moderate were the anti-imperialist Liberals, such as Gladstone, who had opposed the Ugandan railway. He denounced Lugard's forward policy but admired Lugard 'as a brave man, an able man, and an upright man'.[30] Those were Gladstone's generous words in March of that year. Now that tempers were rising, and the French were impugning him as a liar and a murderer, Lugard's honour attracted still more patriotic Englishmen to defend it. Most of the British press took his innocence for granted. As for Lord Salisbury, he expressed complete confidence in his proconsul. 'All his reports breathe a spirit of the utmost impartiality and loyalty....'[31]

However, a testimonial from Lord Salisbury was not to be relevant much longer. By-elections had gnawed away at the government's majority until governing was impossible. The Parliament of 1886 was formally dissolved on 28 June 1892. In those final weeks Salisbury took two different steps to sort out the mess in Uganda. The first appeared like a step back; he formally accepted the plan of Mackinnon's IBEA Company to evacuate Uganda by the end of the year. After his experience in the Uganda railway debate the previous summer, he felt that his Party was too weak, the country too divided, and the Company itself too inefficient to make it worth urging Mackinnon not to throw in the sponge.

The second step was directed at the hullabaloo in France and on the Continent. On 24 June, still without a word from Lugard, the government announced that it would commission an 'impartial report' on the troubles in Uganda. Instructions were telegraphed to a young British engineer officer, Captain James MacDonald, who had already left Mombasa to conduct the railway survey. He was to draw up a report gathered from 'reliable sources', which would explain the 'causes of the outbreak and the action of the British officials'.[32]

Unruffled by optimism about the outcome, Salisbury handed over the seals of office to the Queen and retired to the 'Chalet Cecil' at Dieppe. It would take more than recriminations over Uganda to keep him from his summer holiday on the French side of the Channel.

*   *   *

Soon after two o'clock on 15 August 1892, under a summer sky as blue as the Mediterranean, Gladstone, eighty-two-year-old Prime Minister designate, embarked at Portsmouth on the *Alberta* ferry amid an explosion of good-humoured clapping. At Cowes, on the Isle of Wight, a small crowd greeted him with hisses as well as cheering. Then he took a carriage to Osborne, to kiss the Queen's small, frigid hands for the fourth (and presumably final) time.

That afternoon Gladstone found the Queen's coldness so 'menacing'[33] that at his first audience he clean forgot to kiss hands and had to return that evening for a second opportunity. The audience, he grimly told Algy West, his new chief-of-staff, was 'such as took place between Marie Antoinette and her executioner'.[34] The Queen was hardly more flattering about 'that dangerous old fanatic' (her phrase to her private secretary, Sir Henry Ponsonby). She found him 'greatly altered'. He was not only 'much aged and walking rather bent with a stick', but his face had shrunk, and he was 'deadly pale with a weird look in his eye, and a feeble expression in his mouth'. But the decline of her enemy gave her no comfort. It was into the trembling hands of this 'old, wild and incomprehensible'[35] man that she had to entrust the sacred interests of the country and her vast empire.

She was much relieved to learn that, for reasons she could not fathom, Lord Rosebery had consented to serve in that 'iniquitous government'. If there was anything she could share with Gladstone, it was a desire for the success of his dazzling but enigmatic protégé. Fortune had showered its favours on the 5th Earl of Rosebery, not only in the Derby winners he had led back in triumph to the royal enclosure, but in the £2 million dowry his wife had brought him (she was Hannah Rothschild, heiress of Mentmore and its treasures), and in the Liberal throne that beckoned him as Gladstone's heir apparent.

Yet Rosebery seemed oddly miscast as a politician. He always held himself aloof from his fellow men, and seemed more suited by temperament to be an artist than a politician. Since Hartington and the other Whigs had seceded to form the Liberal Unionists, Rosebery appeared more isolated than ever, baffling his friends with his black silences. When he spoke, his views on foreign affairs seemed to coincide almost exactly with those of Tory imperialists like Lord Salisbury. But the anti-imperialist Liberals, so ready to squabble about most things, agreed that the government needed Rosebery if the government was to survive. Without Rosebery it would never achieve credibility with the public.

After the July election, Gladstone had invited Rosebery to be Foreign Secretary. He refused. He was crippled by insomnia. Anyway, he loathed politics. Power meant nothing to him. (In private he told his friends he thought Gladstone was finished. He had no wish for a berth on the sinking ship.) His friends reported that he was still in a state of shock after the tragic death, two years before, of the wife who understood better than anyone his strange, self-tormenting nature. He resisted every appeal – from old school friends like Eddy Hamilton, and from his political rivals like Harcourt. Then, worn down by still more weighty intercession, including an approach from the Prince of Wales (acting for the Queen) as well as a sixteen-page letter from George Buckle, editor of *The Times*, Achilles left his lordly tent at Mentmore and reluctantly returned to the struggle.

His abortive campaign against taking office had at least won him one concession he valued. He could insist on being given a free hand to follow Salisbury's policy at the FO – or he would throw up the job. A collision between Rosebery and the anti-imperialists seemed inevitable. As Harcourt acidly observed to him, 'Without you the government would have been simply ridiculous; now it is only impossible.'[36]

On 19 August, Gladstone celebrated his electoral victory with a formal meeting of the new Cabinet at 1 Carlton Gardens, the sumptuous white stucco house overlooking the Mall lent him by an admirer. Presumably because of his deafness, he announced that he would sit by Rosebery at a small table apart from the others. He too was deeply relieved to have dragged Rosebery back from the abyss. Yet despite this, and a working majority of forty in the House of Commons, victory tasted bitter enough to the new government. It had failed to win an overall majority. To govern, it needed the support of the Irish Party. And if Parnell's disgrace and death in 1891 had broken his party into two warring factions, this did not make them easier allies for the Liberals. Even if a new Irish Home Rule Bill passed the Commons, which was doubtful, it was doomed to fail in the Lords – as it was to fail in 1893. But at least Ireland would take the Party's mind off its self-inflicted wounds, the collision of principles and personalities that gave each Cabinet meeting the gory air of a prizefight.

Uganda, it turned out, was to be the occasion for the first fight in this series.

In August the French returned to the attack on the Foreign Office. Waddington, the French Ambassador, greeted Rosebery with a colourful list of grievances, amplifying the earlier accusations of the 'atrocities' committed by Lugard against the French missionaries and their converts.

In fact no French missionary had been injured. Later Lugard was to claim – convincingly – that he had taken no part in atrocities. One Maxim had jammed each time it was fired more than a few rounds. The other Maxim had broken completely. Less easy was it for him to avoid responsibility for precipitating the civil war. His defence: he had only joined the Protestant side to protect his position at Kampala.

Rosebery then commissioned an 'impartial' précis on Uganda from Sir Percy Anderson. This had to deal with more than Lugard and his Maxim gun. Predictably, Anderson took a strong line about the strategic threat from France. At present the Company was due to evacuate the country on 31 December 1892. Should this decision be reversed? If the Company left Uganda, the French would fill the void, take over the headwaters of the Nile – and threaten Britain's hold on Egypt. Before circulating the memorandum to his colleagues, Rosebery decided that it would serve as his own manifesto. He stiffened Anderson's text with three pugnacious pages of his own.

The government should let Mackinnon throw in the sponge, then annex Uganda themselves. The railway should be constructed after all. After taking over Uganda, they should push up into the Sudan in order to parry an expected French move from the Congo.

Rosebery sent off this provocative memo, still disguised as a Foreign Office paper, to his colleagues in the Cabinet, most of whom were scattered to the four winds in pursuit of belated summer holidays. For good reasons he attached copies of the latest telegrams from Sir Gerald Portal, the newly knighted British Consul General at Zanzibar. Portal had just discovered the reason for Lugard's silence. He was on his way home, and when the two men met, Lugard had briefed him on the precarious balance of power in Uganda. Portal advised Rosebery to give Lugard an interview, so Rosebery cabled for Lugard to come to London at once. And Portal did not mince his words: evacuation 'must *inevitably* result in a massacre of Christians such as the history of this century cannot show'.[37]

The scattered Cabinet found that the news from Rosebery did not add to the enjoyment of their holidays. 'I have read Sir P. Anderson's paper with care,' wrote Gladstone to Harcourt, 'I thought it was a pleading from a missionary society or from the Company, or should have thought so, but for the date from the FO.' Gladstone did not 'know who Sir G. Portal is', but found his warnings of massacre 'astonishing'.[38] Harcourt, the new Chancellor of the Exchequer, was more blunt; he found Anderson's memo pitched 'in the highest Jingo tune'. It was preposterous to talk of holding on to Uganda:

Cui bono? Is it *trade*? There is no traffic. Is it *religion*? The Catholics and Protestants ... are occupied in nothing but cutting each other's throats.... Is it *slavery*? There is no evidence that there is any slave question in this region....

I see nothing but endless expense, trouble and disaster in prospect if we allow ourselves to *drift* into any sort of responsibility for this business....[39]

As these letters ricocheted back and forth between Gladstone, Harcourt and Rosebery, the three men found it increasingly hard to keep their tempers. Gladstone told Algy West that he was shocked that Rosebery had succumbed to the FO's 'Jingoism'.[40] There was no Uganda question as far as he was concerned. Harcourt denounced Lugard as a man 'so swollen with his own importance ... that he has quite lost his head, as his letters sufficiently show'. Campbell-Bannerman, the new War Minister, went further: 'The general opinion of Lugard', he told Harcourt, 'is that he is a lunatic, aiming at being a second Gordon – just what we thought.'[41] By this time Lugard was steaming back to London. Clearly the ghost of General Gordon had begun to haunt both sides of the dispute in the Cabinet. Rosebery told Algy West that his insomnia had returned and that if the disaster at Khartoum was repeated in Uganda, he would never sleep again. The Queen did not help. 'The fate of Gordon', she cried like Cassandra, 'is not, and will not be, forgotten in Europe!'[42] On the other hand, Gladstone warned Rosebery that he must understand the anxieties of men who had 'gone through, like Harcourt and some of us, the terrible and instructive experience of the Gordon mission'.[43]

Of course the 'terrible experience' was not the government's inability to prevent the fall of Khartoum. It was the *responsibility* for that disaster which had cut into Gladstone's soul. By the same token he and Harcourt were now determined to avoid letting Lugard make himself a new Gordon with the help of his Sudanese troops – 'Emin's ruffians', as Gladstone called them.

By late September, Rosebery was pressing for the crisis to be settled in the Cabinet and Gladstone agreed, 'with pain'. It was the *first* time, he said, in his Cabinet experience of twenty-two or twenty-three years, that he had known the Foreign Secretary and Prime Minister to go to a Cabinet on an issue of foreign policy before resolving their own differences. Still, he knew whose side the Cabinet would take. Almost every senior minister was alarmed by the thought of annexation: the new no-nonsense generation of Centre Liberals which included young Henry Asquith, the Home Secretary, as well as veteran Little Englanders such as John Morley, the Irish Chief Secretary. On his part, Rosebery boasted that the whole Cabinet was against him, but was damned if he would stay if they tried to over-rule him. Gladstone then told Algy West he would 'sooner die than submit to a military occupation [of Uganda]'.[44]

Expecting the worst, the Cabinet met on Thursday, 28 September. Nothing happened; or rather, there was deadlock. Gladstone and Rosebery denounced each other's policies with growing excitement. No one could calm the pugilists.

The root of Gladstone's bitterness went deep, to Egypt, the source of that humiliating defeat inflicted on him ten years earlier by Hartington and the Whigs. Small wonder that Gladstone – or Harcourt or Morley – did not appreciate the FO line about keeping Uganda in order to save Egypt. They longed to escape from Egypt. Uganda was simply an equatorial red herring and the talk of slave trade a typical piece of jingo humbug. Their own aim was to patch up some kind of agreement with the French that would get them off the Egyptian hook. Their instincts were to trust French democracy and break their humiliating dependence on the Germans. But for ten years, Britain – some foolish Liberals included – had been hoodwinked by Anderson and the FO into baiting the French and grovelling in front of the loathsome Bismarck.

The morning after the Cabinet meeting, Algy West walked across to see his chief at Carlton Gardens, determined to try to postpone the disaster. West admired Rosebery, though he blamed Rosebery's neurotic sensitivity for adding to his chief's burdens. Why not buy time by paying the Company to delay its departure? As it happened, Harcourt was already working on such a plan, which would give a three-month extension of the Company's rule. Gladstone snatched at this compromise.

When the Cabinet met that afternoon, they were bewildered to learn of the reprieve. Portal cabled from Mombasa to say that the Company would accept the three months' extension. So Rosebery, who had expected to be out of office by luncheon, found himself happily signing his own reprieve in a memo for the Cabinet. What Rosebery did not tell the Cabinet, but wrote in great confidence to the Queen, was that he believed that 'delay is favourable to his [own] policy'[45] – in effect, that his enemies had played into his hands.

Like most of the new generation of imperialists, Liberal or Tory, Rosebery was not too proud to pull strings in the press. No doubt he told the editors, as confidentially as he told the Queen, that when the public realized the importance of the issues involved, they would back him. At any rate George Buckle, the editor of *The Times* and his close friend, obliged with a thunder of assent. Public opinion would have the chance of 'declaring itself in ways more impressive to the tremulous politician than the most convincing argument'.[46] In varying degrees, support came from all the other national newspapers, except for the *Manchester Guardian* and the *Daily News*, both of which were vigorous opponents of a forward policy. To orchestrate this press campaign, Rosebery could not of course act in the open. His main weapon was Lugard himself, summoned to London at the speed of the fastest steamer.

Lugard arrived on 3 October, just in time for the start of Rosebery's campaign. (Harcourt's sour comment was, 'Lugard, I observe, has come here. I hope however we shall have the firmness to shut out the blast.')[47] As Marjorie Perham, Lugard's official biographer, has pointed out, a lesser man would have given priority to saving his own good name, now challenged by Captain MacDonald's investigation into the 'atrocities'. But Lugard plunged straight into the campaign to save Uganda. First he fired off an eloquent two-and-a-half-column letter to *The Times*. Britain, he wrote, needed new tropical markets to exploit. Why reject the riches of Uganda: the coffee, wheat, cotton and gum? Britain also needed security for Egypt, and Egypt needed security for Uganda and the sources of the Nile. What would happen if these fell into the hands of France or

Germany? British honour, too, was at risk. He had pledged the Company to protect the natives – and the Company was pledged to act in Britain's name. Finally, how could the missionaries be abandoned to their fate? How could Uganda be left to a civil war which the Muslim slave traders were bound to win? (Tactfully, Lugard made no reference to his own war with the French missionaries. He referred to them merely as fellow sufferers along with the CMS missionaries.)

It was a week when most of the best-known African experts invited themselves to address the public in the press. 'Save Uganda' trumpeted Stanley, Jephson, Horace Waller (Livingstone's ally) and Lord Grey. But Lugard was the lion everyone wanted to hear roar. He found himself invited everywhere, by the Prince of Wales and the Duke of Cambridge, lionized by Society hostesses from Mayfair to Belgravia. He made a delightfully civilized hero. Stanley had always brought a whiff of the saloon bar to the drawing room; he was so pugnacious and *touchy* – a good man in Africa no doubt, but a dangerous ally in Europe (as Leopold had found to his cost). Lugard was the very type of the chivalrous Englishman, an African knight errant in a shabby khaki jacket, wild-eyed and haggard from his ordeal in desert and jungle, yet absurdly modest about his own achievements.

As well as orchestrating his own 'Save Uganda' campaign from the FO, Rosebery encouraged two other campaigns in parallel. The first was run by Mackinnon's Imperial British East Africa Company, working through the great Chambers of Commerce, the second by the CMS, working through other humanitarian groups. Lugard strained every nerve to help. In November he began a barnstorming tour of the great manufacturing towns – Manchester, Birmingham, Glasgow, Newcastle and Liverpool – and also spoke to packed meetings in London, Edinburgh, Cambridge and Norwich. All these efforts were reported in the press, usually with enthusiasm. Perhaps, as his biographer has suggested, Lugard disappointed his audiences. His style was like a civil servant's and he took great pains to avoid political controversy. No one would have guessed that this small, quiet man had ever fired a shot in anger. The truth was that Lugard was preaching largely to the converted. Yet there was something about him – perhaps the dangerous-looking brown eyes – that compelled attention and inspired people. At any rate, his audiences obediently reported to the government that the country was solidly behind Rosebery.

The country? The 174 petitions which flooded in to the FO in November and December came from every hill and dale, but they were not equally representative of political opinion. It was noticed that not a single Liberal or Radical Society had sent a petition. The Chambers of Commerce were not particularly impressed by the economic prospects of Uganda. The fact was that the movement inspired by Rosebery was primarily drawn from the anti-slavery lobby and other humanitarian groups. This robbed it of a political cutting edge, and made it easy for Harcourt to dismiss the whole movement as artificially puffed up – 'The whole force of Jingoism at the bellows'.[48] How could Rosebery convince his sceptical colleagues?

Rosebery had to convince the Cabinet of only one thing, and that was that when he talked of resigning, he meant it. As Lugard steamed up and down the country, confronting the cheering crowds, Rosebery grimly threw down the challenge to Gladstone and his other colleagues. Either they agreed to save Uganda or he would abandon ship – which would promptly sink. He said it twice, on 7 November and 11 November. By the end of the month he had bullied his colleagues into submission, just as they had bullied him so successfully that summer.

The Uganda crisis was ended on 23 November by what looked like a compromise. The Cabinet agreed that an Imperial Commissioner should be sent out to 'inquire and report' on what to do about Uganda. That sounded non-committal. But the Commissioner chosen was Sir Gerald Portal, Salisbury's protégé, well-known to be an ardent imperialist determined to keep Uganda. By accepting Portal, the Cabinet effectively threw in the sponge and let Rosebery have his own way. Rosebery made sure that Portal knew what to report. He sent him instructions that were kept secret from the Cabinet, telling him it was mainly a matter 'of form' that he should only go out to inquire and report. His real job was to take over the country from the IBEA Company and administer it for the Crown. That was what 'public sentiment here will expect and support'.[49]

By surrendering to Rosebery, Gladstone had surrendered to the FO and its 'jingoism', meaning the strategic imperatives of Sir Percy Anderson – his determination to keep the Nile sources out of French or German hands. The Prime Minister was eighty-two, his body crumbling like his Cabinet, yet he was still haunted by the dream of bringing Home Rule to Ireland. If he found any comfort in this wretched Uganda business it was that Portal was Salisbury's Commissioner in Zanzibar, so he could blame Salisbury for Portal. Otherwise, all he could truthfully say was that he had sacrificed Uganda and the Nile in the best interests of Ireland.

Lugard's barn-storming tour was abruptly called off after Rosebery's victory in the Cabinet. All 174 petitions might have been drafted by him. Their dominant themes were the threat to the lives of the Christian missionaries, the need to maintain the suppression of the slave trade, and the damage to Britain's honour if the country reneged on her pledges. It was an old familiar crusade, the one for which Livingstone and Gordon and Bishop Hannington had died – the crusade against the Muslim slave traders.

Meanwhile, as the rising sun of the IBEA Company's flag was replaced by Sir Gerald Portal's Union Jack in Uganda, and Britain proclaimed a formal protectorate over the region, a new threat to European rule had erupted in the country to the west. After years of uneasy peace, Arab slavers had crossed the Lomami river, determined to drive King Leopold out of the Congo.

CHAPTER 24

An Ivory War

The Congo and Brussels
August 1892–Summer 1894

> '... a large shining map of Africa marked with all
> the colours of a rainbow. There was a vast amount
> of red – good to see at any time, because one knows
> that some real work is done in there, a deuce of a
> lot of blue, a little green, smears of orange, and, on
> the East Coast, a purple patch, to show where the
> [Germans] .... drink the jolly lager-beer. However,
> I wasn't going into any of these. I was going into
> the yellow. Dead in the centre. And the river was·
> there – fascinating – deadly – like a snake.'

Marlow signs up with the Congo Free State, in *The Heart
of Darkness* by Joseph Conrad, 1902

Leopold was displeased to read, in August 1892, of the murder of Arthur Hodister and other commercial agents at some obscure place called Riba-Riba on the river Lualaba. There were also alarming stories in the press about a general Arab rising in this region, Manyema, the Arab zone between Stanley Falls and Lake Tanganyika, the frontier of German East Africa. Leopold consulted his main adviser on the Congo, Edmond Van Eetvelde, the Free State's Secretary-General in Brussels. The King was told that, 'as usual',[1] the local agent, Tobback, had been exaggerating. There was no danger from the majority of Arab chiefs, for they owed loyalty to Tippu Tip and Tippu Tip wanted peace. As for Hodister's death (if he was dead, and the rumours were only based on the word of a slave), the fellow had, in a manner of speaking, brought it on himself.

For the last ten years Arthur Hodister's charismatic reputation had spread from the heart of darkness to the heart of Brussels. He was a brilliant ivory trader, and an eccentric. He did not bully or beat the stuff out of the natives, like most of the international riff-raff employed as traders on the Congo. He charmed the ivory out of them. Without a single black soldier to protect him, he had pushed deep into the dangerous elephant country beyond the river Lomami. There he held court, bewitching his listeners with his fluent Swahili, white-robed and turbaned like an Arab, and attended by elegant slaves. Up and down the foaming rapids of the Lualaba, from the Falls to Kasongo, he rode in a canoe, honoured by the great Arab chiefs as a guest. To the simple Africans, his white skin and neat black beard gave him the air of a god.

Even to Europeans Hodister seemed inspired, for he came to preach a doctrine of commercial progress with all the zeal of a missionary. Yet jealous rivals said there was a taint, a whiff of corruption about him. Perhaps his sympathies were too wide; perhaps he had attended more African ceremonies than was good for him, though he professed himself as horrified as any European by human sacrifice and cannibalism. At any rate, he had made enemies as well as admirers. Joseph Conrad, who spent disillusioning months as a steamer captain on the Congo in 1890, used the tales about Hodister for elements of his portrait of Kurtz, the lost soul in *The Heart of Darkness*.

Of course Leopold was not interested in the personal oddities of a commercial agent in the upper Congo. Ivory was at this time the main source of wealth in the region, and Leopold's preoccupation. What had irritated the Congo Free State authorities about Hodister was that he had persuaded his employers – the newly-formed Compagnie de Katanga, run by Captain Thys, Leopold's old collaborator – to adopt a new forward policy in the hunt for ivory. Trust the Arabs and open up Manyema, said Hodister. It was commerce, not conquest, that would civilize the region and help its peaceful assimilation into the Congo State. So Leopold had come to regard Hodister and his employers as rivals of the Free State government. When the time was ripe the State would exploit the commercial opportunities of Manyema for itself. Meanwhile, it was the State's policy not to risk its *entente* with the Arabs by pushing soldiers beyond the Lomami. Still, Leopold was not prepared to let Hodister steal a march on him. It was decided to send a State agent, the deputy agent at the Falls, Lieutenant Michiels, to join Hodister's caravan. He would keep an eye on the fellow, and compete with him by buying ivory for the Free State direct from the Arabs.

Early in 1892 Hodister's well-equipped trading caravan – eighteen white agents with hundreds of unarmed followers – steamed up the Congo as far as Isangi, and there divided in two, to collect ivory. The first party, including Michiels, continued as far as Stanley Falls, then pushed on by canoe southwards up the Lualaba towards Riba-Riba and Nyangwe. The second, led by Hodister, steamed parallel to them along the Lomami, 200 miles to the west. After reaching Beni Kamba, Hodister continued on horseback, since the Lomami was blocked by rapids. He was now near the limit of the great rainforest. Further south the country was half-unexplored: high grass and thorns, mixed with forest, true elephant country. It was between here and Nyangwe that Tippu Tip's rival, Mohara, had carved out a prosperous little kingdom.

To complicate Hodister's mission and increase the risks of a showdown with the Arabs on the Lualaba, Captain Guillaume Van Kerckhoven had left Leopoldville in February 1891 to penetrate the no-man's-land north of the Aruwimini, an even richer source of ivory. Van Kerckhoven, it will be recalled, was the thirty-seven-year-old Belgian officer commissioned by Leopold to hack his way through the north-east corner of the great Ituri rainforest that had tormented Stanley in 1887–9, cross the Congo-Nile watershed, and carry the blue and gold flag of the Free State all the way to Equatoria. Now, in August 1892, the British were thought likely to abandon Uganda. So Leopold was all the more anxious to get his hands on Emin's old base at Wadelai, sign up any Sudanese survivors from Emin's garrison, then march down the Nile towards Khartoum. (This was the mission that the King had first offered Stanley, who called it preposterous.)

At first Van Kerckhoven had confounded the croakers. Leopold had lavished rifles on him. He had fourteen white officers and NCOs and 600 African soldiers. This was three times the firepower given to Stairs to subdue Msiri, or to Stanley to rescue Emin. Ostensibly, this army was needed for the crusade against Arab slave traders. In reality, Van Kerckhoven's instructions were more mundane: he was told to grab all the ivory he could find. North of the river Aruwimini he need not bother to pay for it. He was to take it from the Arabs, if necessary by force; they had no business to be north of Manyema.

Kerckhoven obediently hacked his way through the Uele rainforest and out into the elephant country beyond, grabbing ivory, and shooting Arab traders when they tried to stop him. After one clash, on 24 October 1891, he captured 800 tusks of ivory. A few days later, he took more ivory and made the Arabs pay a heavy price for their rashness in trying to stop him. According to a Belgian missionary priest, the Arabs lost 1,800 men in the battle.

In Europe, no one wept over the death of Arab slave traders, helpless to resist modern weapons (though most of the men Van Kerckhoven shot down were probably slaves themselves). What caused irritation at the Quai d'Orsay and hullabaloo in the French press was that Van Kerckhoven was apparently hacking his way along the Uele in territory claimed by France. (The north-east frontier of the Free State had not yet been demarcated.) There was another row in the autumn of 1892 when the British Foreign Office heard that Kerckhoven had crossed the Congo-Nile watershed and had supposedly reached Equatoria. In fact, Van Kerckhoven's luck had finally run out. He was dead – accidentally shot by his gun carrier on 4 October of that year, when almost in sight of the Nile. The diplomatic shock waves from his expedition were to be felt in Europe for the next two years. But it was the Arabs of Manyema who reacted first and reacted most violently.

Nicholas Tobback, the Free State agent at the Falls, had only fifty men to defend him. When he reported new threats, his reports were dismissed in Brussels. He was exaggerating, 'as usual'. But Van Kerckhoven had been taking ivory not only from bands of stray Arabs – or from Tippu Tip's rival, Mohara. The bulk of the ivory belonged to Tippu Tip's own clan, which was naturally outraged at this treatment by the state with which they had loyally collaborated. Sefu, Tippu Tip's son, demanded compensation. So did Rashid, his nephew, who had taken over as Governor of the Falls when Tippu Tip had retired to Zanzibar in 1890. Both Sefu and Rashid claimed huge losses in men killed and ivory stolen. They made common cause with Mohara, who claimed he had lost one and a half million francs worth of ivory. How could they now repay the money advanced by the European commercial companies?

Tobback's deputy, Lieutenant Michiels, warned Hodister in April that the

Arabs were in an ugly mood. In March Mohara had rebuffed Michiels when he tried to establish a government post at Riba-Riba. His people told Michiels that now they knew why the State wished to establish itself at Riba-Riba. It was to fight them, just as 'Boula-Matende' (the African nickname for Van Kerckhoven) had done, shooting their agents and taking their ivory. Mohara was blunter still. He wanted no white men at Riba-Riba, neither state agents nor commercial agents.

A further complication in this delicate and confused situation was the presence of two defenceless envoys of the Free State – Lieutenant Lippens and Sergeant de Bruyne, residents at the court of Sefu in Kasango. Both men were sick and demoralized – and hostages in the heart of the Arab zone. If the Arabs rose, Lippens and de Bruyne would be the first to pay the price.

But Leopold was assured that there was no danger of this. By September the crisis, viewed from Brussels, seemed to be passing. Tippu Tip was to be paid a fee to return from Zanzibar and mediate among his followers. Van Eetvelde suggested that a sum of 25,000 francs (£1,000) would cover his fee, plus expenses. The King thought this excessive, and suggested paying Tippu Tip 30,000 francs in all. The main point was to ensure that Tippu Tip would prevent his followers from making common cause with Mohara. Perhaps they would even hand over that villain to justice.

Otherwise Leopold's policy in the autumn of 1892 remained the same as it had been in the spring, before the wretched Hodister affair. In due course they would have to take firm measures against the Arabs of Manyema. But just now, all his strength was needed for pushing out the frontiers, for snatching the upper Nile from under the noses of the French, and whisking away Katanga before it fell to Cecil Rhodes. So the government of the Congo repeated its warnings to its garrison commanders west of Manyema. They were to stick to the defensive and take no risks. Above all, they were not to cross the Lomami river and risk provoking a general war with the Arabs which the State was quite unready to fight.

* * *

The garrison commander at Lusambo who received this fresh warning was thirty-year-old Commandant Francis Dhanis, who was supposed to rule the vast region between Kasai and Katanga with a few hundred black regulars. It was the building of his small stockaded fort at Lusambo in 1890 that marked Leopold's decision to block the Arabs from advancing west of the Lomami. Lusambo would be resupplied directly from Leopoldville, 700 miles to the west, by steamers using the Sankuru, Kasai and Congo rivers. That was how it looked on the map. In practice, Leopold's state was so overstretched that no steamer would reach Lusambo for months at a time. There was no telegraph. So an energetic young commandant like Dhanis was left very much to his own devices, expected to press-gang local troops, commandeer food, and even buy slaves to make into soldiers. Dhanis found the independence exhilarating.

He was all the more shaken by the double blow that struck him on 8 October. The first was the news of the murder of Hodister and his companions. The second was the order to take no action against the Arabs, above all not to compromise the *entente* by crossing the Lomami. Instead, he was to go south and explore Katanga.

In a couple of years his compatriots would be fêting Dhanis as a national hero. But at this time he had made no mark outside the obscure circle of Belgian officers who had volunteered, as patriots, or adventurers, or both, to serve their King in the Congo. Dhanis's style was cool to a fault. He had the exaggerated reserve of an Englishman and people thought him arrogant. Actually, he was a modest man, though intensely ambitious. He had been born in London, the son of a Belgian Consul who had married an Irishwoman (and all his life he spoke French with a slight English accent). In the Congo he seemed to prefer soft words to warfare. He had talked the province of Kwango into submission, subduing the whole province, eight times the size of Belgium, with only eighty soldiers and 150 porters. But now, after hearing of Hodister's death, he lost patience. 'Instead of waiting for the enemy, and being overwhelmed, we should try the offensive!'[2]

The news about Hodister's mission was indeed enough to turn a stomach hardened by years in the Congo. On 9 May Mohara's representative at Riba-Riba, Nserara, had an altercation with Noblesse, Hodister's agent, and Michiels, the State agent. Despite Mohara's ban, Noblesse was determined to build a station there. Michiels tried to hoist the Free State flag. He warned Nserara that he could call on thousands of soldiers if he wished. 'Go and get your thousand guns then,' was Nserara's reply. 'We shall kill you and plant that flag above your heads.'[3]

What he did was considerably worse. The next day Noblesse was tied to a sugar-cane crusher outside Nserara's hut and slowly flogged to death. Then his body was cut up and given to the natives to eat. Michiels escaped, but was captured after a fortnight's wandering in the bush. Then he, too, was tied to the sugar-cane crusher, flogged to death and eaten.

Meanwhile, Hodister and his three companions – an agent, a doctor and a cook – were blithely riding across the bush between the Lomami and the Lualaba. On 15 May they met a threatening band of Arabs. Apparently Hodister dismounted to parley – optimistic to the end. At least he died quickly. He was shot or speared with his companions, and the four heads were sent to Nserara. Their bodies were eaten. Then the same fate was dealt out to the last of Hodister's agents in the field, Pierret, at his base in Lomo, on the upper Lomami. The survivors fled down the Lualaba in a nightmare flight back towards the Falls, losing two more men from fever. Another agent went mad and drowned himself. By the end of May, nothing was left of Hodister's expedition but his prancing Arab horse and some scattered human bones.

This was the story whose gruesome details had filtered through to the Falls and now haunted Dhanis. How to take the offensive against these murderers?

It would be months before reinforcements reached him, even supposing that headquarters at Boma countermanded its orders not to attack. In fact, Dhanis had already made his own arrangements by stitching together a strange alliance of three powerful chiefs west of the Lomami: the dashing young Batetela warlord, Gongo Lutete, and two of his ex-vassals and rivals, Lupungu and Mpania Mutombo. Gongo had carved out an empire on the marshy banks of the Lomami, based at Ngandu, a stockaded town of between 10,000 and 15,000 people, defended by six loop-holed gateways. Like most of their neighbours, these Batetela were inveterate cannibals. According to the count of Dhanis's medical officer, Captain Hinde, at least 2,000 polished human skulls formed a solid white pavement in front of each loop-holed gateway. Human skulls crowned every post in the stockade.

Yet Gongo himself seemed almost civilized. He was an athletic man of about five foot nine inches, with a brown skin, luminous brown eyes with long lashes, a small mouth with thin lips, a short straight nose and (his most striking characteristic) long, supple, restless hands, always opening and shutting. He could play the dignified chief. But on the warpath he was a different person. His orders hissed out like bullets from a Maxim and he would lead his warriors at a run for hours at a time.

When a child Gongo had been reared as a slave by the Arabs, and taken by Tippu Tip. Impressed by his exploits in battle, Tippu Tip gave him back his freedom. Then for several years he served as Tippu's lieutenant in the upper Lomami, hunting slaves and ivory, like others loyal to the Arabs, with a pack of obedient cannibals. (Troublemakers were distributed as rations.) When Sefu succeeded him as Tippu Tip's lieutenant, Gongo felt strong enough to hunt slaves and ivory on his own account. But in April 1892 Dhanis beat him in battle, then won over his vassal chiefs. By September Gongo had agreed to risk everything by joining his army to the Free State's.

With 10,000 of these wild allies – half of them armed with spears, half with muzzle-loaders – Dhanis felt a match for the Arabs.

At Kasongo, the sprawling Arab town in a valley near the Lualaba, where Sefu had his base, what happened next was a matter of life and death for the two Belgian officers, Lippens and de Bruyne, left in Sefu's power.

Kasongo was 100 miles east of the Lomami and over 200 miles south-east of Lusambo. It would take a messenger over a month to reach Commandant Dhanis. On 6 October Lippens wrote a long, passionate SOS.

Before the murder of Hodister and the others, his position had been difficult enough. He had been given a cool, high, square-topped Arab house, a house full of slaves. He had nothing to do all day but lie on the verandah in his white turban and white robes, while the slaves brought him rice on copper dishes and served him coffee out of cups of silver filigree. He was cheered when de Bruyne joined him. Yet he still felt wretchedly homesick and ill. For fourteen months he had suffered from dysentery, pneumonia and hepatitis. At first, Sefu and his clan had treated him with studied politeness. But he had known, even then, that he was a hostage. '*Méfie-toi de tous ces gens, mon cher*,' he had written to Tobback, the State agent at the Falls, in November 1891. 'Don't be fooled by their air of submission, for it's false, utterly false. They're wolves in sheep's clothing ... I repeat, don't trust them and keep your eyes open, for they are planning to play us dirty tricks....'[4]

After the news of Van Kerckhoven's raids and the resulting murder of Hodister and the others, the atmosphere at Kasongo changed dramatically. Sefu and the Arabs did not conceal their blind hatred of all white men, including the State's envoys. Lippens's house was burnt, his goods stolen, his servants killed, and he himself held under house arrest, unable to communicate with de Bruyne. They were treated 'like slaves', so Lippens said. His fear of Sefu reached the point of hysteria. The man was a 'veritable tiger'.[5] At any moment he might pounce. Already he mercilessly taunted his victims, reminded them that they were hostages for the behaviour of Dhanis. He encouraged Lippens to send his SOS, which carried an ultimatum from Sefu.

The letter to Dhanis confirmed that Mohara had not yet won over Sefu. This remained Mohara's aim, and all the Arabs at Kasongo were at heart his supporters. What held Sefu back was the treaty with the Free State, arranged by his father, Tippu Tip, who feared for his assets in Zanzibar. But Mohara's cause was gaining ground. He had a much larger army than Sefu, 12,000 men, well armed and experienced. This was the situation when Gongo Lutete joined the Free State. By arranging this, Dhanis had put himself in the wrong and placed the two envoys at Kasongo in mortal danger. Gongo, the ex-slave of Tippu Tip's, was still a vassal of Sefu's. By making a rebel of him, Dhanis had freed Sefu from any scruples about breaking the treaty. In effect, Dhanis had already broken it.

But there was still a way of stopping Sefu joining Mohara, and forming an invincible army of 15,000 men with guns. Gongo should be handed over to Sefu in exchange for peace. That was Lippens's advice on 6 October, encouraged by Sefu. Soon afterwards de Bruyne was led away under escort, heading for the Lomami, a hundred miles away, carrying the SOS himself, with its last bitter *cri de coeur*: 'There's only one thing, that's to have an understanding with Sefu. It's hard, but it's necessary; to do anything else would be criminal and madness.'[6]

It is conceivable that if Lippens's SOS had been sent direct to Dhanis in October, Dhanis might have considered some kind of parley with Sefu. But Lippens's SOS was not to reach Dhanis for many weeks. Probably the delay made no difference, for de Bruyne sent two appeals of his own to Dhanis, warning him that Sefu, with 10,000 men, was advancing on the Lomami and begging Dhanis to come to terms. In a second letter, which reached Dhanis on 11 October at Bakila, de Bruyne pleaded with Dhanis to let the officer in charge of a forward patrol, Lieutenant Scheerlinck, come and meet Sefu across the Lomami:

Our life is in your hands, our safety will depend on what follows. First, if you continue to refuse to come to Ikere [east of the Lomami] they will begin to kill us without pity. Second, they will cross the Lomami, attack and exterminate your weak expedition. Third, they will invade the camp, turn south, and this will be a terrible disaster for the State.[7]

Dhanis was only three days' march from the Lomami when he read these words. By 15 November he could have been talking to de Bruyne – and Sefu. His own officer, Scheerlinck, had promised Sefu an immediate answer. Dhanis gave no answer to anyone. He halted at Kolomini, then continued slowly towards the Lomami.

Why did Dhanis, the patriot, show such a stony heart towards his beleaguered friends? One can surmise his reasons. He knew little about the Arab zone, and did not recognize that he had put himself in the wrong by persuading Gongo, Sefu's vassal, to change sides. He expected to be attacked – in which case he would soon take the offensive. At any rate, he was not going to be blackmailed into surrendering Gongo. Lippens and de Bruyne were soldiers. They should know the harsh code of their profession. How Dhanis himself interpreted that code was explained by one of his men. 'He told us ... he had no intention of returning alive from the campaign if it were unsuccessful, and that if any of us were unfortunate enough to be taken prisoners by the enemy, he would consider us as dead, and would not risk a man to save us.'[8]

On 20 November Dhanis finally reached the Lomami, after a five days' halt at Kolomini, long enough for events to gather a momentum of their own.

Meanwhile, Lieutenant Jean-Désiré Scheerlinck and Captain Sidney Hinde, the column's British Medical Officer, had waited in vain to hear from Dhanis. In the absence of orders, they did not dare parley with Sefu. Besides, they suspected he was plotting to capture them or murder them. As Scheerlinck put it in his reply to the Arabs, Sefu shouldn't think that 'we would let our throats be cut as though we were sheep'.[9] On the other hand, they were prepared to go to the rendezvous at the Lomami to try to rescue de Bruyne. Later Hinde wrote a dramatic account of what followed.

The Lomami at Goi Moyassa was 200 yards wide, brown and fast-running, yet safe enough for a swimmer. At 8.30 that morning, before the sun had burnt off the morning mist, two parties approached the grassy river-banks from the plantations on either side. To the west bank came Hinde and Scheerlinck with about fifty black soldiers, including the best shots in the force. Opposite them they recognized Sergeant de Bruyne. A yard behind him walked the leader of the Arabs, and fifteen yards further back marched another forty men, leaving the main body a quarter of a mile in the rear.

'Can you swim?' [shouted Hinde across the river]
'Yes.'
'Does anyone on your side understand French?'
'No.'

Hinde told his men in French to select their targets, but to leave the Chief for him.

'I've got picked shots hidden in the grass and I can save you. Jump in the river!'

There was a silence for about half a minute, an unbearable silence, then de Bruyne spoke.

'No, thank you. I cannot abandon Lippens.'[10]

Scheerlinck, too, tried to persuade de Bruyne, but received the same reply: his chief was ill and he could not leave him. However, he begged Scheerlinck to make terms with Sefu, who was still anxious for peace.

At about ten o'clock, Scheerlinck saw de Bruyne led back by his captors from the river to start the long, painful march back to Kasongo. The brave fellow had a 'heavy heart', so Scheerlinck reported to Dhanis. Perhaps he already knew the ghastly fate that awaited him after he reached Lippens, though he would hardly have guessed that, half a century later, he would still be famous in Belgium for his heroism.

Sefu, rebuffed once more by Dhanis, launched the war four days later.

It will never be known how far the Arabs intended to carry their offensive. At the time, Dhanis's officers talked as though it were Sefu's plan to invade the Free State and take all the country as far as Leopoldville, 700 miles to the west. But no evidence of this has ever been found on Sefu's side. To mount a large-scale co-ordinated attack was quite beyond his power. He had 10,000 soldiers, but few of them had modern rifles. His army had no artillery, no steamers and no technical training – or even discipline – of any sort. Most of his men were raw cannibals, slaves or dependants of the local warlords, armed with spears or muzzle-loaders. They could be recklessly brave in attack, but once checked, they would turn and run for their lives. Worst of all, Sefu had no means of co-ordinating his offensive with that of other distant Arab chiefs, even those within his own 'clan', who owed allegiance to Tippu Tip. His closest neighbour was the formidable Mohara, the rival from whom he still wanted to keep his distance.

The result was that Sefu's advance across the Lomami, a few miles above Ngandu, on the night of 19 November, seemed curiously weak and hesitant. It took two days for several thousand men to paddle across the river in canoes and build a stockaded fort on the west bank. With little difficulty they drove in the outposts of Gongo Lutete. But on 22 November there was a tornado of wind and rain that flattened the makeshift bamboo shelters and soaked the powder of the muzzle-loaders. Sefu returned to the tents on the east side of the river to wait until the storm should subside.

Meanwhile, Gongo had sent a warning to Lieutenant Michaux, the corpulent but energetic young officer Dhanis had sent to patrol the river-bank, and Michaux had made a forced march for twelve hours to reinforce Gongo and try to block the Arabs' advance. Michaux got no sleep on the night of the tornado.

Next morning Gongo told him his men could not attack Sefu because their muzzle-loaders were soaked. This was a 'flash of light' for Michaux. He realized that Sefu's men would have the same problem; but rain would have had no effect on the modern rifles of his own regulars. He gave the order to storm the fort immediately.

Sefu's fort took the form of two irregularly-shaped stockades built in a clearing just beside the river. It was a typical Arab makeshift boma, a tough nut to crack if the defenders' guns worked, but otherwise as weak as a toy fort. There were no deep trenches or stone walls, and the lines of stockade were made from freshly cut saplings. Michaux sent Gongo and his horde of spearmen to guard the flanks in order to stop the Arabs breaking back through the dense forests at either side. Then he directed his 150 black regulars – mainly West Africans – to make a frontal assault on the stockade, the rear lines to give covering fire to the storming party led by two black NCOs, Sergeant Frees and Corporal Benga.

The Arabs, stupefied by the storm, made no defence. It was, Michaux wrote later in his diary, 'as though destiny wished to punish the Arabs for all their past crimes'.[11] The two NCOs smashed their way through the feeble stockade, and the rest of the regulars stormed through the gap after them. They found the outer stockade deserted. 'To the Lomami', shouted Michaux, and led the attack with fifteen men. It was their fifteen rifles (if Michaux is to be believed) that drove several thousand of their panic-stricken opponents to throw themselves into the Lomami, which was running like a mill stream towards the nearby rapids. Then the rest of the 150 regulars poured mazagine fire into the struggling mass. It was 'grandiose and demoniacal', wrote Michaux later:

> The Lomami in spate drew thousands of men towards the rapids, men dressed in fantastic clothes, terror drove them mad, paralysed their movements; the mass prevented them swimming, and in the spasms of despair, they tried in vain to keep themselves afloat above the dead bodies of their companions . . . Satan himself would have been frightened, for I doubt whether a Demon Sabbath ever approached this vengeance by Christians.[12]

The next day Dhanis arrived hot foot, followed by the main column. Hearing that Michaux had suffered a reverse, he had marched half the night through the forest to bring help. What he found left him more than satisfied. 'A thousand dead, more than a thousand prisoners, a thousand guns captured and as many lost in the river! I lost two men.'[13] So he wrote home a few days later with pardonable swagger. Hinde put the enemy's loss much higher. He counted 600 dead on the battlefield, and reckoned 2–3,000 others had been killed or drowned in the river. The enemy had dropped thirty rifles in their panic, along with 2,000 muzzle-loaders, and quantities of black powder.

Sefu himself escaped, but his power was broken, his son dead and many of his senior chiefs shot down or drowned. Best of all, Dhanis took Sefu's invasion to be the pretext he needed for his own offensive. He had no intention of asking Boma, the State HQ, for permission to advance, and waiting several months for the answer. On 26 November he sent the advance guard, including Hinde, across the Lomami by canoe.

It was Dhanis's Rubicon. What could now stop his march on Rome – Mohara's capital, Nyangwe, on the Lualaba? Michaux had shown the crushing power of the repeating rifle in the hands of a few disciplined West African troops led by Europeans. Yet this would be no walk-over, Dhanis recognized. 'The war which has started will be cruel, with few prisoners taken on either side.' Dhanis was gripped by the spirit of the jihad; Hodister and his companions had been hacked to death, and eaten by cannibals. 'Our enemies are implacable, ferocious, treacherous, torture their prisoners ...'.[14]

What hope could there be for poor Lippens and de Bruyne when the news of the massacre at the Lomami reached Kasongo? It was to be months before Dhanis learnt the answer to that grim question. It turned out that on about 1 December some of the retreating Arabs brought back a false report of the death of Sefu, confusing him with a dead chief of similar name. Twelve men went to Lippens's house, and sent word they had news of a big battle. They stabbed Lippens on the verandah. De Bruyne was at his writing desk when the assassins came for him. His body was hacked into small strips. The hands and feet of both men were sent to Mohara at Nyangwe. When Sefu returned to Kasongo, he was shocked by the murders and gave orders for the mutilated remains to be collected and buried in a grave outside Lippens's house.

Such was the fate of the two Europeans who had struggled hardest for peace. A few weeks earlier, at Kinena, nearly 300 miles away in the rainforest north-east of Nyangwe, the uprising had claimed a third European victim, in the shape of a man, the most enigmatic of all explorers of Africa, whose fame seemed to have dissolved into farce and ignominy – Emin Pasha.

After his reluctant return with Stanley to Bagamoyo in December 1889, and his unfortunate fall from the balcony on to his head, Emin had been flattered to accept the invitation to change sides and join the Germans. In April 1890 he had set off back the way he had come, at the head of a large German expedition, intending to try and grab Uganda – perhaps even Equatoria. Nothing was achieved. The Anglo-German agreement of July 1890 made a mockery of his empire-building – just as it killed off Carl Peters's treaty with King Mwanga. After a frustrating year, Emin kicked over the traces and set off on an un-authorized expedition of his own. He tried to recruit his old Sudanese soldiers, the men he had left behind on the shores of Lake Albert. But here, too, he failed. The Sudanese, led by Selim Bey, indignantly explained they were still the Khedive's men. (So it was Lugard, not Emin, who, as we saw, managed to recruit them under his flag.) To cap it all, Emin's caravan was then ravaged by smallpox and he had to send most of the survivors back to Lake Victoria.

After this, Emin decided to throw in his lot with a caravan of Arab ivory hunters and strike out to the west for the 'hinterland of the Cameroons' – a mysterious goal, somewhere beyond the great rainforest, on the far side of Africa. For a young man in perfect health protected by soldiers, this would have been a recklessly dangerous mission. Emin was fifty-two, almost defenceless, in wretched health, and three-quarters blind. The Arabs he trusted were the men whom the Belgians had driven to the edge of war.

Two years later, shortly before the Belgians hanged him for murder, an Arab called Ismaeli told the following story to an American officer who was interrogating him.

The Pasha was sitting on the verandah, writing at his table, surrounded by specimens of birds and insects he had collected in the forests. He was in high spirits, laughing. He had just read the letter from Kibongo, a powerful chief on the Lualaba, giving him permission to proceed. His host, the local chief, suggested that the Pasha send his men to gather bananas and manioc in the nearby plantations, leaving their guns behind on the verandah.

Tell your men to get all they wish; and I hope that you won't think of paying for them, as it is my present to you and is in return for the many little things you have given me and my women since you have been my guest.

For some time after Emin's soldiers had left for the plantations, the local chief chatted with Emin. Then he gave a signal. Ismaeli and another man pinioned Emin by the arms.

'Pasha, you have got to die.'

Emin turned and shouted testily, 'What do you mean? Is this a joke?' As he struggled to reach his revolver, five men held him down in his chair. He told the Chief it was a ridiculous mistake. He had had a letter that morning from Kibongo. It was there on the table, the letter giving him safe conduct.

'Pasha, you read Arabic, don't you?'
'Yes.'
'Then read this.'

The Chief produced a second letter from Kibongo. Emin was so blind that the Chief had to hold it close to his eyes. He read the letter, and drew a long breath.

Well, you may kill me. But don't think that I am the only white man in the country. There are many others who will be willing to avenge my death: and let me tell you that in less than two years from now there won't be an Arab left in the entire country held by your people.[15]

Emin showed no sign of fear for himself, but trembled when he spoke of his new daughter, born to a Sudanese woman who was with the caravan. At a sign from the Chief, the Pasha was lifted out of the chair and thrown on his back. One man held each leg, Ismaeli his head. Emin made no effort at resistance. His head was drawn back until the skin was tight and, with one movement of the knife, another Arab cut his throat. The blood spurted over them and in seconds the Pasha was dead.

Later that day Emin's body, headless and naked, was thrown into the bush. His head was carefully packed and sent off to Kibongo at the Lualaba, together with his trunks and boxes, and the meticulous journals he had kept right up to the end. His men were all made slaves. But his daughter, a child of two, was placed in the care of Kibongo.

Meanwhile, Dhanis's force, swollen by the slaves captured from Sefu, was converging in two columns on Mohara's capital of Nyangwe.

Nothing illustrates the abject deficiencies of the Arab armies better than Mohara's own preparations for defence. The long-range repeating rifle gave the Europeans an overwhelming advantage in fire power. Their alliance with Gongo Lutete nullified the Arabs' advantage in numbers. There remained only one way to fight them: first to combine with the other Arabs, and second to fight a war of attrition. But Mohara, though famous for his military exploits, had no special insight into tactics or strategy. He was neither the leader of a jihad state, like the Mahdi, nor a natural warrior like Samori. The Swahili Arabs had grown fat in the clove plantations of the east coast, and showed their genius in trade, not war. Most of the battles they had fought were simply *razzias*, slave raids against defenceless Africans. Faced with an enemy who had sharper teeth than themselves, wolves went like sheep to the slaughter.

On 9 January 1893 Mohara was killed in confused fighting that hardly deserved the name of a battle. Dhanis, expecting reinforcements from the west, found himself caught between Mohara's army and a new army brought up by Sefu, who had hurried back from Kasongo. But in the high grass and *cassada* fields the two Arab rivals were unable to join hands, and Dhanis's *tirailleurs* were mistaken by Mohara's men for Sefu's. Later, after hearing Mohara's fate ('We ate him the day before yesterday,'[16] said Gongo's men), Sefu fled once again. Nyangwe now lay wide open. A fortnight later, Dhanis's all-conquering invasion force – 400 regulars under six white officers, together with 10,000 of Gongo's cannibals, including the captured slaves – burst out of the forest and reached the muddy river-bank opposite Nyangwe, causing a sensation in the elegant white-washed streets of the city.

It was the 1,000-yard-wide, brown, swirling water of the Lualaba, not the Arabs, that blocked any further advance. For weeks the invaders kicked their heels on the west bank, taking potshots at Arab cattle, while odd pieces of iron or copper, fired from Arab muzzle-loaders, came wailing back over their heads. After another victorious skirmish with Sefu, Dhanis persuaded the Wageni – the local boatmen who controlled all transport on the river – to interest themselves in the possibility of looting Nyangwe. On 4 March they produced 100 canoes and, yelling like demons, ferried the whole column across the river. The city fell almost without a shot.

Five days later, after Sefu had asked for a truce and many of Mohara's men had handed over their arms, there was a rumour of treachery, and a sudden wild outburst of firing. It is not clear why – or who began it. Michaux was later convinced that it was Gongo's cannibals who, for their own good reasons, spread the rumour. The result, according to one Belgian, resembled the St Bartholomew's Day Massacre. A thousand Arabs and their followers were shot down in a few hours, and Dhanis's men, too, lost heavily, when many were killed by Gongo's troops, inadvertently firing on their own side. The next day Dhanis told his troops to burn the town in order to prevent further trouble and then throw the dead bodies into the Lualaba. But of dead bodies there was no trace. Their African allies had eaten them, discarding only the heads.

Of course Dhanis did not emphasize the embarrassing appetites of his allies when he wrote his official reports about his crusade against the Arab slavers. At first his own officers were incredulous. After one early skirmish Hinde noticed that the bodies of both the killed and wounded had vanished. He refused to believe that those cheerful allies, the 'Friendlies', had cut them up for food. When fighting broke out again Hinde saw the Friendlies, who were dancing ahead, drop their loot on the road and run; the loot included human arms, legs and heads. Other officers, fresh from Europe, were aghast, but soon even the oddest practices of this war began to seem natural to the conquerers.

'Happily Gongo's men', a young officer wrote home, referring to the massacre at Nyangwe, 'ate them up [in a few hours]. It's horrible but exceedingly useful and hygienic ... I should have been horrified at the idea in Europe! But it seems quite natural to me here. Don't show this letter to anyone indiscreet.'[17] Michaux himself assured a newcomer that cannibalism was 'horrible, but still, for the moment, we have to pretend not to see it'. In fact, he was 'already blasé,'[18] quite resigned to it.

It was Gongo Lutete himself who felt most sickened by the habits of his people, who ate their own dead – or wounded – as well as the enemy's. He had become as fastidious as the Arabs who had brought him up. After the massacre at Nyangwe he hid himself in his quarters, appalled by the sight of thousands of men smoking human hands and human chops on their camp fires, enough to feed his army for many days.

All this time, Dhanis had been fighting in the teeth of the orders from head-quarters at Boma to stay on the defensive. However, in March 1893 he learnt that his immediate superior, Inspector Fivé, approved of his initiative. In early April there arrived the first practical result of Fivé's support; Commandant Gillian marched into his camp, followed by a caravan of ammunition and reinforcements from Lusambo. Dhanis was now ready to storm Kasongo, Sefu's formidable capital, two days further up the Lualaba. Kasongo was a walled city of some 50,000 souls, with towers and battlements, set in orchards of orange and pomegranate and plantations of rice and sugar cane. But Sefu made no serious attempt to defend it. Dhanis's men rushed the city on 22 April, amid scenes of frightful confusion. One band of panic-stricken refugees begged the Wageni to ferry them across the river, but the Wageni threw them overboard or made them slaves, as the fancy took them.

At Nyangwe the Arabs had at least had time to evacuate their homes. Here at Kasongo the attack was so sudden that the victors found themselves in possession of unheard-of luxuries.

... even the common soldiers [wrote Dr Hinde later] slept on silk and satin mattresses, in carved beds with silk and mosquito curtains. The room I took possession of was eighty feet long and fifteen feet wide, with a door leading into an orange garden, beyond which was a view extending over five miles .... Here we found many European luxuries, the use of which we had almost forgotten: candles, sugar, matches, silver and glass goblets and decanters were in profusion. We also took about twenty-five tons of ivory; ten or eleven tons of powder; millions of caps; cartridges for every kind of rifle, gun and revolver perhaps ever made; some shells; and a German flag, taken by the Arabs in German East Africa.[19]

After his whirlwind campaign, Dhanis needed time to consolidate. Thousands of slaves were looking for new masters. ('Sheep without a shepherd', Hinde called them.) Dhanis set slaves to work in the maize fields and orchards and soon they were supplying the whole army with food. Meanwhile the government of Boma had finally accepted this *fait accompli*, and reinforcements were steaming in from the west and north. The brunt of the new fighting was carried by other commanders: Commandant Chaltin, who recaptured Riba-Riba and rescued Tobback, still besieged at the Falls; Commandant Ponthier and Commandant Lothaire, who took Kirundu and the large towns to the east. By September 1893 they had sealed their victories by linking up with Dhanis at Kasongo.

Yet in that same month an unforeseen disaster occurred at Ngandu. Gongo Lutete, the local warlord whose change of loyalties had precipitated the war with Sefu, had served Dhanis faithfully throughout the campaign. Without his man-eating warriors, victory would have been impossible. Even now it was Gongo's cannibals who managed the crucial supply line leading to Lusambo and the west. Not a case of food, not a load of champagne, not a rifle had ever been lost. But Gongo's fidelity to his new masters, and a more relaxed attitude to discipline, had encouraged his rivals. He was accused of plotting to murder Dhanis, court-martialled by three young officers led by Lieutenant Scheerlinck, and sentenced to be shot.

When Dhanis heard this story he knew it was absurd. Why on earth should their faithful ally choose the moment of victory to betray them? But Dhanis was at Nyangwe, six days' journey by forced marches from Ngandu. He ordered Hinde to march off to try and save Gongo, but the doctor arrived two days too late.

The proud African Chief had hanged himself in his cell to avoid execution. He was discovered, cut down, resuscitated, marched out, and shot by firing squad.

It was without a doubt the greatest error committed on the part of the State in the entire war. Already the drums were carrying the fatal message from village to village. Gongo, the great Chief, had been murdered by his white allies. People heard the drums and answered the challenge. The transport agents Gongo had billeted in the villages were killed and eaten. Anarchy spread like a fever.

In a few weeks this was contained. What was worse was the outrage felt by the Batetela, Dhanis's most courageous auxiliaries. Many defected, and their absence aggravated his difficulties in the final phase of the war. Others seemed to remain loyal, but could not forget or forgive what the white men had done to their Chief.

It was their pent-up feelings that finally exploded in the great Batetela mutiny of 1897, the bloody uprising that would nearly cost Dhanis his life, and was to cripple King Leopold just when he thought the Nile was in his grasp.

* * *

Of course all this lay in the future. By the spring of 1894 Leopold was waiting to welcome Dhanis back in triumph, and give him a barony as a reward for his brilliant act of disobedience. The great Arab chiefs had been killed, captured or driven out of the Congo. All that was left was to mop up: to collect up the Arabs' ill-gotten gains – hundreds of tons of ivory and tens of thousands of slaves – and put them to the service of the State; and to hang the murderers of Hodister, Emin, Lippens and de Bruyne. This work would soon be accomplished.

The conquest of the Arabs did not, however, divert Leopold from his main strategic aim, the conquest of the Nile. In March 1894 he received an astonishing offer from the new British Prime Minister, Lord Rosebery, that seemed to give him the key to the southern Sudan.

It was certainly odd that Lord Rosebery, the Liberal imperialist who had insisted on the strategic necessity of defending the upper Nile, should offer it to Leopold. But then Rosebery, like Sir Percy Anderson and Lord Salisbury – his twin mentors – had consistently under-rated Leopold as a rival.

In the autumn of 1892 one of the few issues that had united most of Gladstone's crumbling Cabinet was their dislike for Lugard's forward policy and a yearning to abandon Uganda. They also yearned to abandon Egypt – and without Egypt there was no strategic reason to hold Uganda and the upper Nile. But Rosebery, the Foreign Secretary, had dug in his toes. As it will be recalled, he had won a reprieve for Lugard's policy by persuading his colleagues to agree to send out a keen young imperialist, Sir Gerald Portal, to report on Uganda's future. By December 1893, when Portal finally reported, echoing many of Lugard's arguments but putting the main emphasis on the strategic imperative, the retention of Uganda was a foregone conclusion.

Despite his jingoism, Rosebery was the only man who could hold the crumbling Cabinet together, the man tipped to succeed Gladstone. Whereas Portal recommended only 'some form of British preponderance'[20] in Uganda, Rosebery went further: the way to block the French advance on the Nile was to make Uganda a British colony. In March 1894 Gladstone finally succumbed to the thoughts of peace at Hawarden and retired. To the Queen's delight, Rosebery brushed aside Harcourt and became Prime Minister.

One of Rosebery's first proposals to Parliament was to declare Uganda a protectorate. The move was denounced by his fellow Liberals, but backed by Lord Salisbury and the Tories. But how could the French be prevented from sending men across from the Ubangi to the southern Sudan which was apparently their plan? An expedition had already been sent off, led by Monteil. Rosebery's first idea had been to use the German colony of Cameroon to block the French, by encouraging the Germans to extend their frontier up to the Nile watershed, but this would not have sealed off the frontier completely. In any case, the plan miscarried. In February 1894 the Germans handed over a crucial strip of territory to the French. In desperation, Rosebery turned to Leopold, who was also threatening the Nile. Would His Majesty be interested in a lease of the southern-most of Egypt's old Sudanese provinces, Equatoria and the Bahr al-Ghazal?

Of course this would mean accepting Egyptian – that is, British – sovereignty. But the lease would give him a hand-hold on the Nile at little cost, and put a stopper on the French. In return, was Leopold prepared to lease the British the corridor west of German East Africa connecting Uganda with Lake Tanganyika? This was the missing link in the 'All-Red' route, Rhodes's wild dream of a Cape-to-Cairo railway.

Leopold wasted no time in snapping up the offer and cheerfully accepting its conditions. The truth was that his claims to the Nile were a sham. After Van Kerckhoven had been killed by his gunbearer in October 1892, the expedition had staggered on towards the river, but it was too weak and its supply lines too stretched to maintain itself against the Mahdists. The survivors staggered back towards the Congo. Leopold had fooled the British Foreign Office by arranging for false reports of the expedition's success to be leaked to the Belgian press, and Rosebery had taken the threat from Leopold seriously enough to try to use the King to block the French.

At this point Leopold overplayed his hand. A secret treaty with the British was signed on 12 April 1894. Four days later the King was negotiating with the French to settle the Ubangi frontier, that long-disputed north-eastern boundary of the Congo. The French offer was dependent on their getting access to the Nile via the Bahr al-Ghazal. Leopold tried to conceal his treaty with the British, but the truth leaked out. Outraged, the civil servant leading the French delegation, Gabriel Hanotaux, broke off negotiations and threatened to unleash a French press campaign that could knock Leopold off his throne.

At first, this threat from a civil servant seemed absurd, and in May the French government itself collapsed. Unfortunately for Leopold, the Foreign Minister chosen for the new government turned out to be Gabriel Hanotaux. He relentlessly baited Leopold, denounced the Anglo-Congolese treaty, whose details were made public on 12 May. Then the Germans joined in the game, claiming that the British corridor between Uganda and Lake Tanganyika would block the back door of German East Africa. Leopold offered to scrap the corridor and Rosebery (who had never seen much point in Rhodes's scheme) was prepared to agree. But by now the French and the Germans had Leopold on the run. The French wanted the whole of Bahr al-Ghazal for themselves, and told Leopold to disgorge it. All they would let him keep was a life interest in part of Equatoria, the Lado enclave. This was a small, muddy triangle along the Nile as far north as Lado, a chain of desolate mud forts, where Emin's Sudanese had fought and mutinied while trying to resist the advancing tide of Mahdists.

Leopold appealed for help to Rosebery, and for once Rosebery let his Cabinet colleagues over-rule him. To risk war with France over Leopold was an absurdity. It would be better to try to stop these endless wrangles with France. Rosebery agreed. To defend Egypt, he would defend the Nile from the Mediterranean to Lake Victoria; that was to be the backbone of British Africa, the irreducible minimum. There was plenty of surplus fat in other parts of Africa, especially in the west. Leopold, it was now recognized, had outlived his usefulness. No one in the Foreign Office had particularly liked his style: the bullying and whining and wheedling. No one trusted Leopold. To sacrifice him was the work of a moment.

Leopold was forced to disgorge all his Nile territory, except the Lado enclave. Once again Britain had backed down when faced with the incongruous alliance of France and Germany. And a new force in European politics had emerged, Gabriel Hanotaux, eager to divert to safe channels the sudden upsurge of colonial fever which the outrageous Anglo-Congolese agreement had precipitated in France.

CHAPTER 25

Blank Treaty Forms on the Niger

Paris, London and West Africa
5 September 1894–January 1897

> '[We] are now *very sorry indeed*, particularly in the
> *killing* and *eating* of the parts of its employees.'
>
> *King Koko* and chiefs of the Brassmen to the Prince of
> Wales, 1895

On 5 September 1894 Gabriel Hanotaux welcomed the British *chargé d'affaires*, Constantine Phipps, to his sumptuous room on the first floor of the Quai d'Orsay. He was eager to bring some order into this dangerous *course de clocher* (steeplechase) – the new French name for the Scramble. Hanotaux had seemed an odd choice for Foreign Minister when Dupuy gave him the post during a reshuffle at the end of May. He was a backroom boy of forty-one. For thirteen years he had worked away, buried among the files at the Quai d'Orsay, a bespectacled figure with a neatly trimmed beard, dressed in black, nicknamed 'the Professor'.[1] He had been an archivist and historian until Gambetta, captivated by an historical piece he had written for *Le Temps*, had persuaded him to join his staff at the Quai. In due course he had become Director of Consular and Commercial Affairs. In that dusty world Hanotaux seemed a delightful companion and dazzling conversationalist, and somehow he still found time for writing history. In 1893 he published the first part of a two-volume biography of his hero, the master diplomat, Cardinal Richelieu, a work which would be acclaimed by the Académie française. He also found time (though this was at first discreetly managed) to keep as his mistress the beautiful and unpredictable actress, Valentine Verlaine.

Politically, Hanotaux was a moderate Republican, like Dupuy and his colleagues in the Cabinet, and a pragmatist, yet mildly infected, nonetheless, with Gambetta's and Ferry's enthusiasm for colonies. As a diplomatist, his style was firm but cautious. The moment was a dangerous one. Freycinet's policy of 'Franco-Russe' – the *entente* with Russia – had not smoothed Anglo-French relations. On the contrary, Russia had an interest in perpetuating the estrangement between Britain and France caused by the British occupation of Egypt. Hanotaux believed in the Franco-Russe. But he also believed in an 'amicable settlement'[2] with Britain in order to protect France against the Triple Alliance (Germany, Italy and Austria). To achieve this there might have to be sacrifices in Africa. Would the *enragés* of the Colonial Party in the Chamber and the ardent new Minister for the Colonies, Théophile Delcassé, have the good sense to make these sacrifices?

There were two tiresome matters urgently needing an 'amicable settlement' in Africa. The first was to partition West Africa, fixing northern boundaries for the three isolated British territories – Sierra Leone, the Gold Coast and the Niger Company's sphere – bordering the Niger and the western Sudan. The second was to decide who was to control the vast deserts of the upper Nile and the eastern Sudan now occupied by the fanatical followers of the Mahdi.

It was to decide the first of these – by allotting the main 'spheres of influence' – that the Anglo-French Agreement had been signed by Salisbury and Waddington in London on 5 August 1890. This agreement established the principle that the 'very "light" land' of the Sahara should be French and so should a huge slice of hinterland to the south of the desert, including the upper Niger as far as Say. But no northern boundary had been subsequently fixed for any of the three British territories, Sierra Leone, Gold Coast or the Niger territories, although these boundaries were supposed to be established by commissioners. Poor little Gambia, as slim as a tapeworm, was the only British colony in West Africa with agreed frontiers.

By 1894 the dangers were obvious. At any moment there might be a violent collision between rival parties carrying blank treaty forms: British soldiers pushing north towards the upper and middle Niger, and French soldiers pushing south and east towards the sea and the lower Niger. In the case of Nigeria, it was true, the British Foreign Office claimed that the 1890 declaration had already defined the northern frontier in principle. This was according to the clause that defined the southern limit of French Mediterranean possessions as the line drawn from Say to Barruwa on Lake Chad, a line curving north to include 'all that fairly belongs to the kingdom of Sokoto'.[3] But in February 1894, just before Hanotaux became Foreign Minister, the Quai d'Orsay produced the ingenious claim that the southern limit of the French possessions was not after all the same as the northern limit of Nigeria. The agreement only referred to *Mediterranean* possessions. So the country to the south of the line was still no-man's-land, and a prize for French explorers, if they could get there first.

It is not clear whether Hanotaux himself approved of this argument. Probably he had some sympathy with the British Foreign Office, which called it 'preposterous'.[4] Certainly he disapproved of the provocative policies of the Department of the Colonies at the Rue Royale under Etienne and his successors. As described already (see Chapter 20), Etienne had pulled the wool over the eyes of both the French Cabinet and the Quai d'Orsay when he announced three 'scientific' expeditions to Lake Chad in 1890. These were actually treaty-making missions. But none of them achieved much besides humiliating the Quai d'Orsay and infuriating the British. Crampel, who had set off from Gabon, was killed by some aggressive natives. It was Mizon who caused the ugliest row; indeed the Mizon affair was one of the ugliest little episodes in the Scramble, although at times it seemed destined to finish in nothing worse than a farce.

Mizon was the pushy young army officer who had nearly lost Brazza his colony in 1883 by ordering Sergeant Malamine, the Senegalese NCO left by Brazza at the Pool, to abandon his post and go home. Seven years later he was hired by the mysterious Syndicat français du Haut Benito to extend the French empire. The driving force was Harry Alis, the leading propagandist of the French colonial movement, who had persuaded Etienne to give his blessing to Mizon's expedition to Bornu and Lake Chad. Mizon was to steam up the lower Niger and then turn north-eastwards up the Benue to Bornu and Adamawa, territory claimed by both the British and the Germans (who were advancing on Bornu from Cameroon). Mizon's instructions for the Benue were kept secret, but the British knew that he might try to make treaties both inside and outside the British sphere. Both threats naturally alarmed Goldie, the London-based manager of the Niger Company, who coveted even more territory than he claimed. When Mizon's wood-burning steam launch was reported by telegraph to have reached the mouth of the Niger in October 1890, Goldie tried to bar its passage, and the Quai d'Orsay protested to London. The Quai insisted Mizon's well-armed expedition was purely 'scientific and commercial', which would give him right of free passage according to the Berlin General Act of 1885. (By contrast, Goldie had the right under the Berlin Act to bar a military or political expedition.)

The Foreign Office supported Mizon against Goldie. Then Goldie tried to bar Mizon's passage with a different argument, quite as bogus as Mizon's claims to be a scientist. The Berlin Act said nothing about *landing* rights and without landing rights, the right to gather food and fuel, nobody in a wood-burning steamer could proceed. The Foreign Office over-ruled Goldie once again. Mizon would achieve nothing; let him pass.

Back in Paris in the summer of 1892, Mizon claimed to have founded a new protectorate at Adamawa. He was greeted at the Gare d'Orléans like a conquering hero. The colonial movement seized on him as a symbol of the new French empire in Africa. Prince d'Arenberg, President of the Comité de l'Afrique française, spoke at the banquet in Mizon's honour, hailing him as a new Brazza, and contrasting him with that crude Anglo-Saxon, Stanley, now a candidate for the British House of Commons.

> If our compatriot Mizon were to take it into his head to present himself as a candidate – for Adamawa [the Prince added smiling], one would not have to ask him, as they asked Stanley, 'How many niggers have you killed in Africa?'[5]

Mizon's appeal was irresistible to women. He was the hero of the Paris salons, the man who had beaten the British at their own game, a courtly knight, complete with a beautiful black princess, N'Sabou, whom he had saved from some African dragon.

Etienne and Delcassé hurried to accept Mizon's discoveries in the name of the Republic. They were indeed important. Mizon had learnt that the huge 'sphere' claimed by Goldie's Niger Company covered a much wider area than the territory over which the Company could claim treaties with the local emirs. As for Adamawa, the new protectorate Mizon claimed was partly inside and partly outside the sphere claimed by the Niger Company.

Mizon had the colonial movement solidly behind him – that is, the Comité de l'Afrique française, the ninety deputies of the Colonial Party in the Chamber, and the Colonial Department. No time was lost in arranging for his return to develop Adamawa, and a chartered company was floated to exploit his rights there.

Mizon was given a hundred Senegalese soldiers and two steamboats, each armed with quick-firers. Of course it was still only a 'scientific and commercial' expedition. Once again, when Mizon was reported at the mouth of the Niger, Goldie tried to bar his passage, but was again over-ruled by the Foreign Office, after protests from the Quai d'Orsay. Mizon was a gentleman, and must be given every possible assistance.

Mizon's true character began to emerge in May 1893, when the expedition's doctor, a Frenchman called Henri Ward, let the cat out of the bag in an article in the radical paper, *L'Intransigeant*, on his return to Paris.

The protectorate in Adamawa was a fiction. Far from signing a treaty with Mizon, the Emir had warned him not to return. How then was he to carry out his mission? Mizon had deliberately run his steamers aground in the Benue, knowing that they could not be refloated till the following summer. Then, taking the ship's guns, he set off to ingratiate himself with another Emir, the ruler of Muri, 150 miles *within* the borders of the Niger Company's sphere. This Emir was displeased with Goldie's company because it refused to help him raise revenue in the traditional Islamic way – by a *razzia* for pagan slaves. Mizon had no such scruples. On Christmas Day, of all days, he had personally directed an attack on a pagan village, Kwana, firing thirty rounds from his ships' guns against the mud walls. Then his Senegalese *tirailleurs* stormed in through the breach and sacked the town. Fifty of the townspeople were killed and 100 wounded. The rest of the 2,000 inhabitants fled to the hills, but were soon rounded up and sold into slavery. The delighted Emir offered Mizon the pick of his slaves, but Mizon only accepted two young girls for his Arab servant, Hamed, and a child of eight or nine for the amusement of his beloved N'Sabou, the so-called Black Princess. (She was the niece of a Niger Company pilot; he had bought her as a slave three years earlier.)

This was Ward's lurid exposé in *L'Intransigeant*, later confirmed by two other members of the party. Mizon had murdered or enslaved 2,000 British protected subjects, and Ward quoted the proud words of Prince d'Arenberg at the Mizon banquet: 'One would not have to ask him, as they asked Stanley, "How many niggers have you killed in Africa?"' As Ward put it, 'One may ask him that now.'[6]

The French government did its best to hush up the Mizon affair, and newspapers were asked not to publish Ward's allegations. (In London, Goldie was delighted to arrange for them to be reprinted in *The Times*.) After months of confusion, Mizon was recalled. He first claimed that the orders of recall were forgeries made by the Niger Company. Meanwhile, there was a farcical duel between Ward and the editor of the incongruously named *La Libre Parole*, in which Ward got a bullet in the knee. Matters were not helped by the revelation that Mizon had left his beloved N'Sabou in the care of the Catholic fathers at Onitsha. A few weeks later she gave birth to a boy, remarkably light in complexion.

The Quai d'Orsay groaned at this wretched Mizon affair. A bungler was bad enough, but a slave raider – it was 'outrageous',[7] one of his French colleagues told Phipps at the British Embassy. The storm blew itself out later in 1893 when Goldie made a deal with the Germans to secure his eastern frontier. This split Adamawa between Britain and Germany. The deal also secured Bornu, and deprived the French Colonial Department of further temptations to nibble at Goldie's eastern frontier up to its northernmost corner, where it petered out in the mysterious waters of Lake Chad.

Early in 1894 the French government were reconciled to this Anglo-German deal after the Germans gave them access to a navigable tributary of the Benue – much to Goldie's rage. Had the Colonial Department learnt its lesson? There seemed no reason to think so. Indeed, what alarmed Hanotaux was the madcap plan that it had concocted for sending an expedition hundreds of miles beyond the watershed to challenge the British at Fashoda on the upper Nile. It was this plan which Hanotaux feared – prophetically – could bring Britain and France to the brink of war.

Théophile Delcassé had first taken over the Colonial Department when it was made an independent department of state in the reshuffle of January 1893. He was a *méridionale*, from Ariège in the South of France, where men had the reputation for red blood and recklessness. In April 1893 he privately decided to send Parfait-Louis Monteil on a mission to Fashoda. Monteil was the well-known explorer who had been despatched by Etienne to steal a march on the British by attacking Lake Chad from the west. He had achieved little, except an extended tour of the 'light land' of the Sahara, ending his journey at Tripoli.

Why send Monteil to Fashoda? Delcassé, it seems, was swept off his feet by a lecture, given in January 1893, by a French hydrologist called Victor Prompt, proposing an enormous dam in the swamp at Fashoda, 500 miles south of Khartoum on the upper Nile. The dam would be the key to Egypt. Whoever controlled it would be the master of the Nile, able to flood Egypt or deny it water at will. Amazingly, prudent statesmen – in England as well as France – believed it was practical. If it was, those billions of tons of water could 're-open the Egyptian question',[8] as Delcassé put it, with a vengeance.

Understandably, Monteil was reluctant to accept the honour of conquering Fashoda. Delcassé had to drag him off to the Elysée Palace, where the President, Sadi Carnot (by profession an engineer), handed him a lithograph of Prompt's lecture and solemnly told him, '*Il faut occuper Fashoda.*' Monteil saluted. 'You are the head of the army, the head of the navy. Give me an order; I will obey.'[9] Preparations were hurried forward. His expedition would leave from Brazzaville. The stores were sent ahead. But Monteil dragged his feet, complaining that the northern boundary of the Congo State must be settled with

King Leopold before it would be safe for him to advance. (In fact, Leopold was manipulating Monteil through his secret agents in France, men like Harry Alis of the Comité de l'Afrique française.) A whole year passed after the stores had left for Brazzaville, and Delcassé had started to look for a replacement for Monteil. At long last, on 16 July 1894, the reluctant explorer sailed for Africa.

But by May 1894 Leopold's provocative treaty with Britain had changed everything. The upsurge of anglophobia focused attention on the upper Nile once again, making what had been an obscure question of boundaries seem like a question of national honour. As Etienne put it in the great debate in the Chamber on 7 June, 'Gentlemen, so it's the Egyptian question which now opens in front of us!'[10] Control of the upper Nile meant control of Egypt, and the French public turned again to denouncing perfidious Albion. The English would not make good their promise to evacuate Egypt. Hanotaux tried to calm the hysteria by announcing the Monteil mission as though it was to be a coup against Britain. In fact this was the last thing he wanted; he had allowed Monteil to delay his departure till July in order to subvert Delcassé's instructions. Now he expressly forbade Monteil to go to Fashoda. He was not even to leave the Congo; Hanotaux made him promise this on his word of honour. 'No troops, not even one soldier'[11] were to set foot in the Nile Valley. A month later, after Leopold's climb-down and the collapse of the Anglo-Congolese Treaty, Delcassé impulsively recalled Monteil, who had just landed at Loango. Hanotaux was not consulted and the decision displeased him. To bait the British was madness. But to keep Monteil up his sleeve on the Congo border might have helped the coming negotiations go with a swing.

Now flattering Phipps, now threatening him, Hanotaux played cat-and-mouse when the Anglo-French negotiations began on 5 September 1894. But a cat needs plenty of room to manoeuvre, and public opinion in both countries was becoming dangerously rigid.

Hanotaux let Phipps make the running at first, and Phipps asked the French to make two major concessions. They should accept the British claim over the entire upper Nile, up to the Congo watershed, on the understanding that occupation by the British did not mean that the Sudan ceased to be – at least on paper – part of the Egyptian empire. In other words, the British needed the Sudan as long as they needed Egypt. Second, the French must honour the declaration of 1890, as the British understood it. The Say-Barruwa line *was* to be the northern frontier of the Niger Company's sphere, securing Bornu and Sokoto, after adjustments.

In return, Phipps offered France some 'compensation' in West Africa. The British would cede enough of Borgu, in the western part of the Niger Company's sphere, to give Dahomey a wide corridor to the upper Niger hinterland; and there would be 'a favourable rectification'[12] of the frontier in Sierra Leone. Moreover, £10,000 would be paid to the French White Fathers in Uganda to settle their claims for damages inflicted by Lugard's Maxim gun and the Wa-Ingleza during that unfortunate civil war.

Hanotaux was prepared to listen to the Niger part of the proposal. As for the Nile, he needed a real bill of fare to offer Delcassé and the greedy colonialists, not this handful of crumbs. What if the British agreed to accept that the upper Nile stay *Egyptian*, and that both Britain and France promise to keep out, until the Egyptians had expelled the Mahdists and resumed occupation? In short, the British sphere would be bounded by Uganda, the French sphere by the Congo, and the upper Nile would continue, for the moment, to be no-man's-land.

Phipps fell for this suggestion, innocent that he was, and reported it to London on 6 October, as an 'indication'[13] of the settlement. Sir Percy Anderson had been keeping an eagle eye on the telegrams, and like an eagle he pounced. He was displeased with Phipps. To be blunt, the man had been made a fool of. The French were offering a sham concession in agreeing to stay out of the upper Nile; their 'pretensions' there were 'extravagant'.[14] They had no troops who could beat the Mahdists and take over the Sudan. If they showed their noses there, the British would expel them. For this non-concession the British were supposed to give up half Borgu and stay out of the Sudan. It was Anderson at his most jingoistic, speaking more like a politician than a civil servant. He turned down Hanotaux's proposal flat.

Perhaps if Lord Salisbury had been in power, he would have cut Anderson down to size and stretched out a hand to Hanotaux. There was a bargain to be struck, it would seem, but on the Niger only, not the Niger *and* Nile. The mistake was surely to allow those two waters – already muddy and turbulent – to become further confused. The middle Niger did not yet arouse violent emotion, nor was it yet a matter of national prestige. Border adjustments could be made by Goldie's company on no-nonsense commercial grounds; the French could concede the area around Sokoto in the north in exchange for British concessions in Borgu to the west. But nothing could now be done about the upper Nile – at any rate not till tempers cooled.

The French public looked on Egypt with the passion of a jilted lover, or a man cheated of a family heirloom. To gain redress was a matter of honour, cost what it might. The British, too, had come to see their prestige as dangerously vulnerable in Egypt – and, because of the Nile threat, in the Sudan as well. It was not just a triple calculation of strategy – protecting the Sudan which protected Egypt which in turn protected the Canal and the sea-lanes to India and the East. Gordon's lonely death had added passion and pride to the equation. Soon British soldiers would have to show the French exactly who was the Power in possession. Meanwhile the Foreign Office would offer nothing but recriminations. Poor Phipps was punished for the failure of the talks by being packed off as Minister to Brazil.

*   *   *

With the collapse of the Paris talks, the Scramble passed into a new and dangerous phase. In the middle Niger there was one immediate result. Back to the centre of the stage came a thirty-six-year-old veteran of African warfare – and conflict with France – Captain Fred Lugard.

Late that July of 1894 Lugard suddenly vanished from his chambers in London. On 28 August he reappeared at Akassa, the Niger Company's main port in the mangrove swamps of the Niger delta, bent on a secret mission for Sir George Goldie's Niger Company. Goldie had put no confidence in the ability of the Foreign Office to square the French, either on the Niger or the Nile. Instead, he had two alternative plans for Lugard. The first was to secure treaties in Borgu, the forbidding bushland to the north-west of the Company's sphere. The second was to push out the Niger Company's frontier beyond Lake Chad towards the Nile itself.

The choice of Lugard was not expected to please the French. It was two years since the story of Lugard and his Maxim gun had first exploded in the French newspapers – the gun with which he had terrified Monsignor Hirth and the French White Fathers, and shot down their converts in Uganda. It was also a calculated risk to employ a man who had shown such a flair for publicity in the cause of imperial expansion and the defence of his own good name.

But Goldie prided himself on the secrecy of his operations, and asked Lugard to pledge himself not to breathe a word about his exploits on the Niger without the Company's permission, for five years after he had left its service. Everything depended on speed as well as discretion. The French government was reported to have sent out a large expedition from Dahomey, under Captain Henri Decoeur. Now there was to be a *course de clocher*, a steeplechase indeed: Lugard versus Decoeur, the French government versus the Niger Company, each racing into the unexplored bush of Borgu.

Lugard had accepted Goldie's offer with a heavy heart. It was not so much the hardship and danger that he shrank from; no contemporary could have had fewer illusions about Africa and its murderous climate. Nor did he find it in the least romantic to contemplate warfare, that is, killing men, for its own sake. (He attributed this lack of martial ardour to what he called his *'woman's* character'.[15]) But he yearned to be back in Uganda. He had seemed to find his destiny there with his 'own child',[16] as Goldie himself had phrased it. In 1892 and 1893, Lugard had tasted the sweetness of a double victory over his enemies, in the fight to clear his name in England and in the fight to retain Uganda for the Empire. But by 1894, the victory had turned sour. He put out feelers, on the collapse of the Imperial British East Africa Company, hoping to be sent back to govern the protectorate he had created in Uganda. The idea was rebuffed by both Rosebery and Percy Anderson, Lugard's admirers in the Foreign Office. Making Lugard the first Governor would look too much like baiting the French. They had nothing against Goldie using his services in the Niger for the race against the French. That was up to Goldie. The FO would not take a view either way.

In the event, what had persuaded Lugard to sign up with the Niger Company was the character of Goldie himself. Superficially the two men could hardly have had less in common. Lugard was the Victorian gentleman, stern, silent, high-minded, modest, even priggish, sensitive, jilted by his first love, Clytie, with that wound still only half-healed after years of torment. Goldie was a throwback from the Regency, pleasure-loving, Byronic, buccaneering, a man who took pride in his own egotism, and snapped his fingers at the conventions of Society. Yet their ambitions could run in harness. Both men were romantic imperialists, zealots of the same exacting faith. Goldie (like Cecil Rhodes) could charm the birds from the trees when it suited him; and Lugard found Goldie's appeal as a patriot as irresistible as so many women (including Flora Shaw, the future Lady Lugard) found Goldie's appeal as a man.

By 30 August, Lugard had cast anchor and was steaming up the Niger in the wood-burning ship, *Nupe*, bound for Borgu. He had not received the agreed telegram in code from Goldie ('Kuka') which would have meant he was to head for Lake Chad and the Nile. He had not expected to. Yet he was half hoping to be sent on that madcap adventure, which might mean racing Monteil to the Nile. Those boyish dreams of conquering the Mahdists recurred to him. ('Possibly Zobeir himself [the slave-dealing Governor of Gordon's day, Zebehr Pasha] would be sent to join me, and if I saw my way to conquer the Sudan – Mahdi [sic] included – I could do it.')[17] Lugard supposed, correctly, that he would only have been sent to Lake Chad if relations with France had already broken down, and this was not yet the case. His main target was to be the city of Nikki in western Borgu. Nikki was perhaps the capital of the whole region; nobody could say. At any rate, it dominated the western borders of the Company's sphere, closest to Dahomey. Lugard's job was to sign a treaty with its ruler, whoever he was, as well as with the other rulers of this mysterious region west of Bussa, before Captain Decoeur stole a march on him.

After Nikki, Lugard was to pay the French in their own coin and try to cut off Dahomey from its hinterland. He was to push westwards into Mossi, the unclaimed hill country between the great bend of the Niger and the Gold Coast. His expedition would consist of several hundred porters, carrying sumptuous presents of cloth, and would be accompanied by about forty Hausa soldiers. Force should be used only as a last resort; indeed, Goldie stressed that 'diplomacy and not conquest is *the* object of your expedition . . . the exercise of force cannot further your objects, but must on the contrary prevent them being attained.'[18]

As he steamed up the Niger, Lugard shook off the low spirits that had dogged him since landing in this foetid world of mangrove swamps, whose roots assumed fantastic shapes ten feet out of the water. He was astonished by the breadth and depth of the Niger, so different from the meagre rivers of East Africa. Despite the torrential rain, he found the panorama of the forest 'exquisite', a dense wall of rainforest painted various tints of green, splashed with a scarlet flowering tree, reminding him of an English hawthorn. Ferns and orchids abounded, and mahogany trees lined the banks. This excellent timber was already being cut down and exported by the Niger Company. It was a 'great pity'[19] they did not have elephants to assist in this work. He sent the Company some useful hints on the training and diet of elephants in the teak country of upper Burma.

Excited as he was by the economic potential, obviously much greater than East Africa's, Lugard found himself less impressed by the administrators of the Royal Niger Company. So far they had done little for the Africans; indeed, by driving their African rivals, the Brassmen, out of business, they had condemned them to starvation and misery. Some of these impoverished natives were still cannibals, he was told. He was shocked by the rawness of nature all around him, 'Women bathing close alongside the steamer *absolutely* naked and soaping themselves on the banks with no attempt at all to screen themselves in the water.'[20] Lugard modestly bathed behind a canvas screen on the foredeck of the *Nupe*. There were tales of loose morals among the administrators themselves, not to mention the account he was given of that French bounder, Lieutenant Mizon, who had seduced the so-called Princess N'Sabou, the eleven-year-old niece of one of the Niger Company's pilots. ('*Ex uno disce omnia*'[21] – how typically French – was Lugard's comment.)

The truth was that the Niger Company made only a pretence of governing territories under its royal charter. It was a trading company, more or less confined to the steamy banks of the river. Here it had built half a dozen tin-roofed trading stations, guarded by native constabulary and Hausa soldiers. These were soldiers only in name. When Lugard began to organize the 320-strong caravan at the Company's HQ in the north, Jebba, he found the forty Hausas hardly knew how to fire a Snider. Fortunately their services were not, at first, likely to be in demand.

On 8 September 1894 while this large caravan was still being assembled, Lugard took a flying column and set off on a 100-mile dash to Bussa, marching overland as the river was in spate. He marched at a furious pace. 'I rather overdid it – am not sure if I was not spitting blood … and was played out.' At Bussa he found that diplomatic etiquette strained his patience to breaking-point. He was kept waiting for half an hour in the sun by the self-styled 'king' and had to wear a ridiculous kind of court dress. 'I brought the scarlet coat emblazoned with gold lace and stars and foolery, but I wrapped it up in a towel and only put it on at the door. I detest this mummery, it is more irksome to me to dress myself up like a Punch and Judy show than to visit a dentist. The King of all the Bussas turned out to be a specially dirty and mean-looking savage surrounded by … crowds of naked girls and semi-nude women.'

Days were lost in wrangling, and nothing was gained by the visit, except the promise of some letters of introduction (in exchange for guns, powder and salt) and confirmation of the weakness of Bussa. It was only one small state in a Borgu federation; so the Company's existing treaty with Bussa could confer no general sovereignty over the whole of Borgu. Back Lugard dashed by canoe to Jebba, wondering if he could stand a life of such indignities in the service of the Company. It was not his style, eating dirt before a petty chief. He was used to 'ruling and asserting himself'. A man used to '*trading*, arguing and haggling'[22] might do the job better.

It was 27 September before Lugard marched off with the caravan bound for Nikki. But the rainy season had not yet ended, and the men had to lie wet through all night. Almost everything else that could be wrong was wrong with this west coast caravan. There were no Askari to act as NCOs (as there would have been in East Africa), only two headmen; and both the young Europeans supposed to help him went down with malaria; anyway they were useless. The Nupe, Hausa and Yoruba porters fought each other over their ill-packed loads. Somehow Lugard licked the chaotic caravan into shape without having to flog any of the porters. On 11 October he tramped into Kishi, the last Yoruba town before the border with Borgu. From here onwards, he had been warned, he must expect attacks from Borgu marauders. But the ruler of Kiama, one of the most influential Borgu 'kings', gave him a surprising welcome.

The man came to Lugard's tent late at night, dressed in pyjamas and escorted by two naked girls, one of whom carried his sword. He told Lugard that now he had set eyes on him, he would be his lifelong friend. To show his confidence, he would sleep in Lugard's tent. As for the blank treaty, he was delighted to sign it and commit Kiama to the protection of the British Empire. In return Lugard gave him some yellow and red plush and a credit for salt at Jebba. The King gave him an introduction to his brother king at Nikki, but warned Lugard against his fellow countrymen in Borgu. They were extremely treacherous, he said. It would be madness to allow them into his camp or go to meet them alone and unarmed.

With the Kiama treaty in his baggage, Lugard pushed on to Nikki through high, green grass and torrential rain that put out the camp fires night after night. The whole country seemed a malarial swamp. On 30 October he was met by a messenger from the King of Nikki, forbidding the white men to proceed. His medicine men had warned him that if White Men came to Nikki, the King would die. Lugard replied that Nikki was not the only place in Africa. If the King did not send for him within two days, he would march in another direction and the loss would be the King's. The bluff apparently succeeded. On 5 November, just over three months since he left his London club, Lugard pitched camp on a rocky spur outside the walls of Nikki.

The next day Lugard met the *liman* (*imam*), the King's right-hand man, who said he had been told by the King to negotiate on his behalf, because the King had a superstitious dread of meeting a white man face to face. Lugard's interpreter, a black from Sierra Leone called Joseph, *was* allowed to meet the King, who was old and blind, and confirmed that the *liman* was his proxy. On 10 November 1894 the *liman* signed the FO's printed treaty form, the King's name now inserted in manuscript: 'I, Lafia, also called Absalamu, son of Wurukura, King of Nikki and of all Borgu country ...' The treaty did not specifically transfer sovereignty to the Company. But it did give the Company control over foreigners in Nikki and, in effect, over Nikki's external affairs. (It was, of course, an exaggeration to claim it covered 'all Borgu country' as well as Nikki.) According to these title deeds, the Company would open the country to trade and give Nikki help against its enemies 'as far as practicable'. The King and *liman* were also given 'donations'[23] by the Company to the value of £11.

Two days later, bidden a fond farewell by his new African friends, Lugard marched back in heavy fog towards Yoruba territory, the precious Nikki treaty in his baggage.

Decoeur and the French had lost the race, he cheerfully cabled to Goldie when he reached Akassa, near Brass, on 21 January 1895. 'Treaty Nikki covers all Borgu ...'.[24] Two days later came a somewhat mysterious question from Goldie. 'If Lugard Akassa, where is expedition? What date treaty? French say theirs is dated November 26.'[25] Lugard explained that he had now returned, and that his treaty was dated 10 November. Back came Goldie's terse: 'Bravo Lugard.' Lugard was over the moon – *excessively* pleased',[26] he wrote in his diary. But nothing in West Africa was simple. The next day the Niger Company's station at Akassa was sacked and burnt by the Brassmen. And, far from admitting defeat, the French were pushing on beyond Nikki to the Niger itself.

*　　　*　　　*

The revolt of the Brassmen temporarily overshadowed even the advance of the French. In London, it sent the Niger Company's officials reeling. 'We always looked on Akassa as being as safe as Piccadilly,'[27] Goldie told the Foreign Office. (Lugard, who may have owed his life to his dislike of the foetid heat of Akassa and his decision to go up-country three days earlier, was equally astonished.)

It turned out that the rising had been led by the King of Brass himself – Koko, a lapsed Christian who had exchanged his European suit for the loin cloth, holy water and monkey skulls of West African *ju-ju*. On 29 January 1895, in the fog before dawn, he and 1,000 warriors paddled out of the creeks of Nembe, the capital of Brass, daubed with chalk and armed with Enfield rifles. Swiftly they slipped through the mangrove swamps and glided into the Company's harbour at Akassa. Still unobserved, they raced to the two-storey house of Captain Morgan, the local police captain, and fired a volley into the wooden building. Morgan and four other white men – including two French naval officers – were well armed and made a desperate stand. But they were only saved by the providential arrival of the mail steamer, *Bathurst*, which drew the attention of the attackers and allowed the white men to escape by launch.

Meanwhile, the Brassmen wreaked vengeance on the Company's boatyard and engineering workshops, and massacred the Kru-boys who worked for the Company. About seventy-five natives were shot or hacked to death in their shanties; others were trussed up and taken off in the war canoes. Later that morning the defenceless British Vice-Consul at Brass was astounded to see canoe-loads of prisoners brought back to the town, with drums beating and flags flying. The majority were then cooked and eaten during an orgy of human sacrifice presided over by the local fetish priest.

About twenty-five prisoners were spared. One ex-Christian (educated, by coincidence, in Goldie's Isle of Man) was seen 'jumping about quite naked, painted white, with pieces of human flesh hanging to him'.[28] But other Christians held fast to their faith. They refused to murder, let alone eat, their own prisoners, as the fetish priest insisted. The twenty-five prisoners were handed over instead to the British consulate. Whether Christian, lapsed Christian or animist, the insurgents agreed not to interfere with the consulate itself. Their quarrel was with the Niger Company, not with the Queen. 'The Company is not the Queen's man,' King Koko and his chiefs wrote to the Vice-Consul; 'if we Brass people die through hunger, we had rather go to them and die on their *sords* [sic].'[29]

Die on their *sords*? What had precipitated this act of despair?

In London, reading the cables of the disaster, Goldie assumed that loot was the main motive. So the 4,000-odd Brassmen in Nembe deserved exemplary punishment, and Goldie proposed that the royal navy should 'exterminate Nembe'.[30] This proposal did not appeal to the Liberals in Parliament. Privately, Major Claude MacDonald reported that it was the 'Company's practice' which had provoked the rebellion. MacDonald was the British Commissioner and Consul-General for the Niger Coast Protectorate, which included the coastal territory of the Niger Company. So damaging were the charges that Rosebery's Foreign Secretary, Lord Kimberley, sent Sir John Kirk, the retired African expert, to investigate. In the meantime, the Royal Navy had made a half-hearted expedition to punish the Brassmen and lost five officers in the process.

It was August before Kirk returned with a judicious report on the rising. In the meantime the Liberals in Parliament, the Liberal press and the humanitarians in general gave an ear, at long last, to the poignant grievances of the Brassmen. King Koko and his chiefs wrote to the Prince of Wales, begging to be forgiven for their attack on the Company. They were 'now *very sorry indeed, particularly in the killing and eating* of parts of its employees'. They assured the Prince that in future, 'We now throw ourselves entirely at the mercy of the *good old Queen*, knowing her to be a most kind *tender-hearted* and sympathetic *old mother*.'[31]

Goldie's prose was no match for King Koko's. In fact the case against the Company was unanswerable. Before the Niger Company's arrival at Akassa, Brass had been the Venice of the Niger delta, its fleets of canoes ubiquitous, its merchant princes courted by the Liverpool traders. They were the master middlemen of both the palm oil and the liquor trades. Goldie had put an end to all that. In defiance of its own royal charter, the Niger Company had proceeded to smash all competition, European and African. At first the Liverpool traders made an alliance with the Brassmen and promised that the Queen would redress their grievances. In 1893 Goldie bought out the Liverpool traders, and was able to seal off the Brassmen from the wealth of the Niger. Henceforth there was no opening for the Brassmen except by smuggling, which the Niger Company took violent means to suppress. By the end of 1894, trade had been stifled. The people of Brass were starving, and a raging plague of smallpox precipitated claims by the fetish priests that only human sacrifice would end it. All this and more, including the rape by a Company clerk of a respectable African woman, drove the people of Brass to their doomed rebellion in January 1895.

Kirk's report tactfully avoided blaming either the Company or the Brassmen. But he did conclude that the current system was impossible and that the

Company's monopoly should be broken. Could this reform be achieved without breaking the Niger Company, too? Kirk thought so. However, before Kirk had even returned from Akassa, the Liberal government of Lord Rosebery had succumbed to its own internal strains. Lord Salisbury embarked on his third ministry in June 1895. To avoid alienating Goldie – needed to keep out the French – Kirk's report was rejected and the Brassmen were left to starve.

Almost at the same moment in January 1895, when news of the Brass rebellion reached London, came the equally astonishing news of the French advance towards the Niger. It turned out that Delcassé, Minister for the Colonies, had launched four French expeditions smack into the sphere claimed by the Company: three of them overland from the newly conquered colony of Dahomey and the fourth up the muddy Niger itself.

What distinguished them from Lugard's was that they were official military expeditions with the weight of a powerful government behind them. Their leaders were not, like Lugard, merely 'pegging out claims'[32] for the future (in Rosebery's phrase), by persuading some obscure African ruler to put his cross on a printed treaty form. They had enough soldiers to build forts and actually occupy the land they claimed. It was this that posed the greatest threat to Goldie's claims for his sphere. Contrary to popular belief, the General Act at Berlin had only specified 'effective occupation' as one of the rules of the game during the Scramble in the case of *coastal* colonies. But there was no doubt that even a token occupation made a paper claim much more impressive at the negotiating table, and might call Goldie's bluff in his claim to Bornu and Nupe. This, in turn, would give the French traders what they most needed – access to the lower Niger, navigable below the rapids of Bussa.

Encouraged by these instructions, Decoeur had marched into Nikki on 16 November 1894, five days after Lugard had marched out. Decoeur proved a timid explorer, forever expecting disaster, but he was blessed with a hundred tough *tirailleurs* from Senegal, as well as a mountain of supplies. Faced with Decoeur's rifles, the King of Nikki soon forgot his superstitious dread of white men. On 26 November he signed a treaty giving the French an exclusive protectorate.

Decoeur's cautious thrust was followed by a lunge forward by the energetic new Governor of Dahomey, Victor Ballot. He was not content with merely following in Decoeur's footsteps and obtaining formal repudiation of Lugard's treaty. (The King of Nikki now claimed that this was a fraud committed by the *liman*, who had wanted the English presents for himself.) Ballot struck out east for the Niger and established a series of stations, where he posted soldiers, and also began to survey the river for nagivation. Late in February 1895 the third expedition, led by Captain Georges Toutée, reached the river Nupe and built 'Fort d'Arenberg', called after the patron of the French Colonial Party. To bait Goldie, a garrison was left there, flying the tricolour. Toutée then continued Ballot's work of surveying the river up to the Bussa rapids, establishing posts and signing rival treaties with Goldie's trading partners.

Meanwhile, in December 1894, the French had sent a naval gunboat, the *Ardent*, to show the flag on the river itself. Its captain soon came to grief, stuck on a sandbank a hundred miles from the sea. (Two of its officers came to Akassa. They were the Frenchmen who narrowly escaped death at the hands of the Brassmen.) The captain refused to acknowledge the authority of the Niger Company over ships in the river. He declared it was international water, as free as La Manche, the so-called 'English' Channel.

The Niger Company's scanty constabulary, tied down in the delta by the Brassmen's rebellion, had no way of ejecting the French. In the House of Commons the news provoked an outburst. To challenge the British claims in this way was an impertinence. But Rosebery had no chance of persuading his warring colleagues to agree on a counter-attack. All he could do was bluster. He instructed Sir Edward Grey, Under-Secretary of State for Foreign Affairs, to show exemplary firmness in the Commons debate of 28 March 1895. The government came under fire from the Tories, who linked the *fait accompli* in West Africa with the threat to the Sudan. The French had shown their contempt for ordinary diplomatic rules on the Niger, so what was to stop them sending an expedition to the upper Nile to grab Fashoda in order to force concessions from Britain?

To this Sir Edward Grey made a reply that had not been cleared with Rosebery, but was to echo like a roll of distant thunder around Europe, and came to be called the 'Grey Declaration'.[33] He had no reason to believe that the French had any such plan, because to send 'a French expedition under secret instructions, right from the other side of Africa, into a territory over which our claims have been known for so long ... would be an *unfriendly act*, [Grey emphasized these words] and would be so viewed by England.'

Grey's '*fameuse manifestation*' caused as much hullabaloo in Paris as the news from the Niger had caused in London, and the matter was of much greater strategic importance. Here was England threatening war, it was said (though that had not been Grey's intention), over her claim to the whole Nile valley. This was a far more unfriendly act, said Courcel, the French Ambassador, than to send a 'wandering column of explorers' to Fashoda. Courcel's chief, Hanotaux, however, was more anxious than ever to arrange a *rapprochement* with England. The dividends from the *entente* with Russia were proving elusive to France, although exploited by Germany. Outside the Nile and the Niger, the interests of France and England could be fairly easily reconciled. Even in Africa, when public opinion was not involved matters could be arranged. For example, the Italians wanted to use Zeila, the British port in Somaliland, for their advance into Ethiopia. When the French, allies of the Ethiopians, protested, the British refused to let Zeila be used by the Italians.

The collapse of Lord Rosebery's government in June 1895, and the triumphant return of Lord Salisbury as Prime Minister and Foreign Secretary, gave Hanotaux a new opportunity for peace-making. He found the Foreign Office anxious to play down Grey's thunderbolt. They had now swung round to the idea of a separate deal on the Niger. Although Hanotaux refused to withdraw his country's claim to Borgu – he backed Decoeur's and Ballot's story that Lugard's treaty of Nikki was a fraud – he sent out no fresh expeditions. Nor did he choose to make difficulties about the naval gunboat, *Ardent*, stranded on a sandbank in the lower Niger. When the river rose in August, the *Ardent* was recalled, and the captain got a flea in his ear from the Quai d'Orsay for his pains. In return, the British refused to help Samori, who wanted guns to fight the French.

Hanotaux had precious little time to work on his *rapprochement* with England after Salisbury's return to power, though he had the Nile-Niger talks back on the agenda. His principal success was a deal about Siam negotiated that summer. Then, in November 1895, Ribot's ministry was replaced by that of Léon Bourgeois, and Hanotaux resigned rather than be contaminated by the Left. The new Minister of Foreign Affairs was a distinguished chemist called Marcellin Berthelot, more anglophile than Hanotaux, but an innocent in politics. He proved easy meat for the colonial enthusiasts at the Quai and the Pavillon de Flore – the new home of the Colonial Ministry, next to the Louvre. His officials recommended the new mission proposed by thirty-one-year-old Jean-Baptiste Marchand in succession to the cancelled mission of Monteil's. Marchand's scheme looked harmless; 200 men would march across into the Bahr al-Ghazal in order to give France the right to attend a conference on the Nile valley, whenever it should be held. Put like that, the Marchand mission sounded positively dull.

Marchand's own memorandum about his mission was more fanciful. The expedition would make an '*entente*' with the Mahdists, the fanatical horde who enslaved or killed all Europeans they encountered. In respect of the sovereignty of the Khedive of Egypt, this would be a strictly civilian expedition. They would fly no flag and make no treaties. Only if he encountered another foreign mission would Marchand hoist the tricolour. But there could be no risk of conflict; the two missions would salute each other with 'all urbanity and correctness that could be desired'.[34] On 30 November Berthelot signed a secret letter of approval and there the matter stood.

Unknown to Berthelot, the officials at the Quai and the Pavillon de Flore had a hidden agenda for Marchand's mission, precisely the sort of plan denounced in Grey's '*fameuse manifestation*'. Marchand *would* fly the tricolour throughout. It *was* to be a military expedition to grab Fashoda. But even the officials at the Quai can have had no inkling of how, within three years, Marchand and his 200 men would bring France and England to the brink of war.

*   *   *

Since returning to Downing Street in July, Lord Salisbury had given the highest priority to a *rapprochement* with France. Of course he knew nothing of Marchand's madcap scheme to grab Fashoda. He recognized that negotiations over

Egypt were doomed for the time being, as French public opinion was too inflamed to see straight. The important thing in the Sudan was to let sleeping dogs lie. For both Britain and France, Egypt was emotional dynamite. The least dangerous policy was to leave those deserts in the hand of the common enemy, the Mahdists, for as long as possible. In West Africa, on the other hand, he could hope to make progress by sacrificing some of Goldie's claims for Bornu. Unlike Rosebery, he was prepared to separate the two issues, Niger and Nile, along the lines proposed by the hapless Phipps in 1894.

However, in the autumn of 1895, a new danger loomed out of the heat haze of East Africa to threaten the *rapprochement* with France. This was Britain's anxiety to help Italy against the common enemy, the Mahdists, and against France's ally, Ethiopia.

For years Britain had done its best to save Italy, the weakest member of the Triple Alliance, from itself. Francesco Crispi's attempt to carve Italy a colony in East Africa had seemed to Lord Salisbury a mistake from the beginning. Massawa, that malarial outpost on the Red Sea, had been abandoned by the Egyptians in 1885. It proved a graveyard for the Italians. At the time it had seemed likely that the survivors would be driven into the sea by the Emperor Yohannes. They were saved from this fate in 1889 when Yohannes was killed at the battle of Gallabat (Metema) by the Mahdists, who invaded Abyssinia from the west.

In 1889 Crispi had authorized the Treaty of Wichale with the King of Shoa, Menelik II, and recognized in him Yohannes's successor as King of Kings. According to the Italian version, the treaty gave Italy a protectorate over Ethiopia. Britain recognized this protectorate – or at any rate the 'sphere'. Crispi used it to build up the impoverished colony of Eritrea: a hand-hold on the green rim of the plateau, as well as a foothold on the deserts of the Red Sea. The hand-hold was precarious, for the Mahdists were massing behind Kassala. But Menelik disputed the protectorate and insisted on his independence; egged on by the French and Russians, he had imported a huge stock of modern rifles and artillery. There were now only two formidable African powers left unconquered in the Scramble. Here they stood, the Sudan and Ethiopia, threatening to choke the life out of Italy's new-born colony.

That year, 1895, Crispi decided to risk a trial of strength with Menelik. The gamble began to fail almost immediately. Crispi asked Salisbury to lease him Zeila, in British Somaliland, as a base to block the import of arms from neighbouring French Somaliland. The request had already been refused by the Liberal Foreign Secretary, Lord Kimberley. Salisbury agreed to give Crispi the lease. Berthelot protested. The Foreign Office was warned that this would be the end of the Niger negotiations. Salisbury told the Italians they would have to settle things with the French. And that was that.

However, Salisbury did not turn Crispi down outright when he asked for help against the Dervishes. In January 1896 he was told that Kassala, captured by the Italians in 1894, was under threat of counter-attack. Would the British care to create a diversion? If so, would they send the troops to Suakin on the

Red Sea, or else advance 200 miles up the Nile to Dongola? Cromer favoured the Suakin diversion, the generals at the War Office the Dongola advance. Salisbury decided that for the time being it would be safer to do nothing.

To advance up the Nile towards Dongola was a momentous step. This was the first milestone on the way to reconquer the Sudan, liberate Khartoum, avenge Gordon and secure the whole vast basin of the White Nile, running from the rim of the Congo to the blue mountains of Abyssinia. Ever since the 1880s this had been part of Salisbury's plan for imperial defence. But he wanted to advance from the opposite direction: *down* the Nile, not up the Nile. Within a few years he planned to have built the 800-mile railway from Mombasa to Lake Victoria. The cost would be ruinous, but the advance of British troops from Uganda would at last become practicable.

In early March 1896 Salisbury received dramatic news that stirred him to action. The Italians had been repulsed in Ethiopia and might be driven into the sea. To save the survivors from the Dervishes was now pressing. The advance to Dongola would 'kill two birds with one stone' – that is, save Italy *and* 'plant the foot of Egypt rather further up the Nile'.[35]

Somewhat hesitantly – for they were still haunted by the ghost of General Gordon – Salisbury's Cabinet authorized General Kitchener to advance to Dongola, beyond the third cataract.

In Paris, outrage at the news of the British advance played straight into the hands of the hard-line colonialists at the Quai and the Pavillon de Flore. Berthelot's olive branch withered and he was forced to resign. The Niger negotiations were broken off. Most important, Léon Bourgeois, Berthelot's successor, ordered Marchand to make all speed to launch his secret expedition to the swamps of the White Nile.

The race to Fashoda had begun.

But what were the tangled events in the land of the Blue Nile which had fired the starting pistol?

CHAPTER 26

A Lion's Share

Eritrea, Italy and Ethiopia
26 September 1895–January 1897

'I have no intention of being an indifferent looker-
on if the distant Powers have the idea of dividing
up Africa, for Ethiopia has been for more than
fourteen centuries an island of Christians in the
middle of the sea of pagans ...'

The *Emperor Menelik*'s address to the European Powers,
10 April 1891

Six months earlier, on 26 September 1895, a steamer from Aden had landed at Massawa with the Governor of Eritrea, General Oreste Baratieri, impatient to get to grips with the enemy.

Massawa was the capital of Eritrea, Italy's only overseas colony, but not much of a town – an irregular line of wooden huts, white-washed barracks, a Turkish fort, a Governor's palace, a mosque crowned with two minarets and the tall flagstaff flying the black and red striped Italian flag. The attraction of Massawa lay in its harbour, formed by two pale pink coral islands linked to each other and the mainland by a causeway. Here was a harbour that was both deep and secure, one of the best in the Red Sea. Trains from the harbour clattered across a causeway to the mainland. However, the railway line evaporated after five miles. Outside the town there was nothing but finely scalloped beaches strewn with mother-of-pearl, and the shimmering glare of the desert.

Now General Baratieri took the train for five miles, then mounted his mule and rode off along the sandy track to rejoin his army at Adigrat, 150 miles to the south; beyond the lip of the 8,000-foot escarpment, the cool, green, Ethiopian plateau beckoned through the blur of heat.

Twenty-eight years before, in 1867, gouging out that sandy track, had come 5,000 British and Indian redcoats, complete with artillery and a troop of long-suffering Indian elephants. This was General Napier's expedition to bring the Ethiopian Emperor Theodore to heel. Napier marched 350 miles to Magdala to rescue the British Consul and assorted missionaries, held hostage on a mountain top by the manic-depressive monarch. The expedition cost the British (and Indian) taxpayer nearly £9 million. But Disraeli's government had no plans for a new African colony. Theodore shot himself with a revolver sent him by Queen Victoria. Napier marched back to the shimmering coast, leaving the local warlords – King Menelik of Shoa and Ras (Prince) Kassa of Tigre – to scramble for the imperial throne among themselves.

To a romantic like Baratieri, Napier's self-denial must have seemed folly or humbug. The Scotsman had turned his back on a colonial paradise. Up on the high plateau, only two days' mule ride from the Red Sea, the air felt like champagne on an empty stomach. Spring seemed to linger there for most of the year – a Mediterranean spring, only twelve degrees from the equator – and the chocolate-coloured soil was as rich as a garden's. In July and August the heavens opened. Then the emerald grass was splashed with alpine wildflowers, there was the tang of wood-smoke and the music of mountain streams. No one had yet tried to estimate how many square miles of wheat and olives could flourish in this fertile wilderness. In the decade since the Italians had been hacking out a foothold in southern Eritrea, on the northern lip of the Ethiopian plateau, they had more pressing matters to consider.

In February 1885, a fortnight before Britain learnt the news of Gordon's death, a British captain had run down the Egyptian flag at Massawa and evacuated its garrison. There was little trade at Massawa, apart from the export of mother-of-pearl. The port needed a subsidy of £20,000 a year to survive. Gladstone was up to his neck in the Sudan and determined to be rid of all the profitless leftovers of Ismael's disastrous African empire. But it was important to stop France, Britain's arch-rival in the Red Sea and the Nile, from getting her hands on Massawa. A secret deal had been made with Italy for her to take over the port. Italy had little money to spare for colonial adventures, so might be expected to behave with restraint. The arrangement did not, however, seem so gentlemanly to the Ethiopian emperor, Yohannes.

As Ras Kassa of Tigre, the northern province of the plateau, and the principal collaborator with Napier against Theodore, he had been given Napier's surplus arms, ammunition and stores, worth half a million pounds. Not surprisingly, he won the race to be Theodore's successor, and was duly crowned emperor at Axum in 1872. Yohannes had two consuming ambitions: to unify the Christian empire, splintered by civil war for most of the previous two centuries, and to extend its frontiers to the deserts beyond the eastern escarpment which had passed into hostile Muslim hands more than 300 years earlier. Crucial to both ambitions was the possession of Massawa. It was the nearest port on the Red Sea; without it Yohannes could not hope to build up a modern army against his rivals. But Massawa, Tigre's gateway to Europe, was in the hands of the Khedive, Ismael Pasha, his enemy, who banned the import of arms.

In November 1875, and in March 1876, Yohannes defended the highlands of Tigre against successive invasions by Ismael Pasha's army from the sea. The second of these invading forces numbered 12,000 Egyptians, armed with the latest rifles and artillery and officered by expatriate mercenaries, including some talented Americans. Yohannes's warriors fought with obsolete guns, swords and spears, but they outnumbered the infidel by at least ten to one. Of the 6,000 Egyptians who took part in the battle of Gura, only about 2,000 returned to the coast. The rest were killed in battle, died of wounds, or were massacred as prisoners.

In 1884 Yohannes signed the Treaty of Adowa with Ismael Pasha's successors, the British. He agreed to help them against their new common enemy – the Mahdi – by giving safe conduct to the Egyptian garrisons marooned on the Sudanese frontier. Yohannes also agreed to prohibit the slave trade in all markets of the empire. In return, the British promised to let him have Bogos, the lowland province north of Tigre, and assured him of 'British protection'[1] to secure free transit through Massawa of all merchandise, including modern arms. Nothing was said about who was to control Massawa itself. But Yohannes assumed that it was he who would reclaim Ethiopia's ancient inheritance, the Red Sea pearl stolen by the Turks in the sixteenth century.

In the event, the Italians had snatched Massawa from under the Emperor's nose, then marched up that sandy track towards the plateau. At first Yohannes thrashed them as soundly as he had thrashed the Egyptians. About 500 Italians were ambushed at Dogali in January 1887, of whom about 100 survived. But Yohannes, still relying on muzzle-loaders, swords and spears, was soon threatened by war on three sides. In the north-west, the Khalifa had sent an army of Dervishes to raid the highlands. They defeated Yohannes's vassal, the king of Gojjam, and sacked the holy city of Gondar. At Massawa the Italians had established a bridgehead which they could maintain from the sea; and the rich southern highlands were controlled by a reluctant vassal and dynastic rival, King Menelik of Shoa, who let the Italians court him in order to arm himself against Yohannes.

Which of the three wars to fight first? Yohannes took a combined force of 100,000 warriors, some from the loyal provinces of Begemdir and Tigre, and others from less dependable Wollo, and led them down to the desert to fight the infidel. At the battle of Gallabat (Metema), on 9 March 1889, he was mortally wounded, just when victory was in his grasp. The combined army disintegrated and the dead Emperor was brought face to face with the Khalifa: a severed head to be whirled round on a pole. King Menelik of Shoa did not long mourn his fate. Within a matter of weeks he had declared himself Emperor.

For the next few years the courting of Menelik seemed the masterstroke of Italian imperialism. Menelik had himself crowned near his tent at Entotto, on the southern lip of the high plateau. Taking the romantic name of Addis Ababa (New Flower), this sprawling Shoan camp site became his permanent capital. Tigre, five hundred miles away, was enemy country controlled by Mangasha, Yohannes's natural son, who claimed, with good reason, to be Yohannes's heir. Menelik had no compunction in dividing Tigre with the Italians.

By the Treaty of Wichale, signed by Menelik on 2 May 1889, the new Emperor agreed to give Italy a small slice of the Christian high plateau – as far south as Asmara – and also the Muslim lowlands of Bogos to the north. In return, the Italians promised to feed, if not satisfy, Menelik's hunger for modern rifles. Already a shipment of 5,000 rifles had reached Addis Ababa, with ammunition carefully chosen not to fit them. More was to follow, bought by a two-million-lire loan (£80,000) guaranteed by the Italian government. Confident that Menelik was now their dependant, the Italians soon pushed south to the river Mareb, fifty miles beyond Asmara and the line agreed in the Treaty of Wichale. Menelik protested. Nothing daunted, the Italians notified the Powers, according to the requirements of the Berlin Act, that Italy claimed the whole Ethiopian empire as an Italian protectorate.

The Italians supported this astonishing claim by citing Article 17 of the Treaty of Wichale, which specified that 'the Emperor consents to use the Italian government for all the business he does with all the other Powers or Governments'. This was the Italian version. No one was more amazed than Menelik. It turned out that the Italian negotiator had deliberately left Menelik an Amharic version with a different meaning: 'The Emperor has the option to communicate with the help of the Italian government for all matters that he wants with the Kings of Europe.'² Of course Menelik refused to accept the *fait accompli*, protesting to the Powers that the Italians were trying to cheat him of his country. In 1893 the Italians tried to pacify him with two million cartridges, bought with the loan they had guaranteed. Menelik took the cartridges, but refused to accept the Italian interpretation of the treaty. He announced that the Treaty of Wichale was dead. The Italian Prime Minister, Crispi, was content to press his shaky claims in Europe for a protectorate, which were accepted by all the Powers except three: Turkey, humiliated by the way Italy had snatched Massawa, and two pushy newcomers to the region, Russia and France.

How easy, General Baratieri must have reflected in 1895, his task would have been if Russia and France had been on the same side in this affair as Italy. As it was, the cooler Menelik's relations became with Italy, the warmer they became with Russia and France, who supplied him with arms by way of French Somaliland. To blockade Ethiopia was thus as impractical as to make her a compliant ally. But Menelik's empire was already threatened by rivals in every direction. So Italy's main interest was to build up a buffer state in Tigre, the province controlled by Menelik's principal rival, Yohannes's twenty-seven-year-old heir, Ras Mangasha.

Crispi's strategy, in theory, was to shore up Mangasha against Menelik, just as Menelik had been shored up against Yohannes. But in practice Baratieri had little to offer Mangasha. The boy was brave but callow, and attracted no support outside his feudal territory. The Italians had already cut his patrimony in half, and what remained of Tigre was in ruins, devastated by war and famine. In fact, Baratieri offered Mangasha nothing but promises. In June 1894 Mangasha despaired of Italy's help and rode south to Shoa, to eat his pride and make his peace with Menelik. Other feudal chiefs followed suit. Baratieri shrugged his shoulders. Ethiopia's ancient empire might be at last united under the King of Kings, but could hardly hope to withstand the advance of a modern army.

The first trial of strength was made by Baratieri himself at the end of 1894, and the result was all that he could wish for. One of Italy's allies in Eritrea, an erratic chief called Bahta Hagos, had been intriguing with Mangasha and Menelik. Recklessly he declared he was liberating the province from alien rule.

Baratieri killed Hagos and stamped out this revolt. Then, with 4,000 native troops, he pursued Mangasha south across the *de facto* frontier line into central Tigre. The battles were indecisive, but the invasion had succeeded and was hailed as a triumph in Eritrea. Mangasha pulled back his large but ill-armed forces, leaving Adigrat, Adowa, Makalle and most of the province in Baratieri's hands. In July 1895 Baratieri sailed back to Italy to persuade Crispi's Cabinet that he needed money for reinforcements. There he was given an ovation in Parliament, welcomed as Italy's greatest living soldier and embraced by the President as the true disciple of Garibaldi.

Even more heartening for Baratieri, was that Crispi's Cabinet, despite the financial crisis, reluctantly agreed to increase the subsidy for Eritrea from 9 million lire (£360,000) to 13 million lire (£520,000). The Italian public, cool enough towards a colony beside the Red Sea, now seemed to have taken fire from Baratieri's conquests on the plateau. At any rate, there was talk of sending out colonists to this alpine paradise as soon as the fighting was over. Baratieri himself promised that he would bring Menelik back in a cage.

This was the background to Baratieri's landing at Massawa on 26 September 1895, hungry to return to his army at Adigrat. The general was a romantic imperialist, a writer and politician as well as a soldier. His military ideas seemed simple enough.

In early October he had only 9,000 men to put into the field to defend the southern border of Eritrea. Apart from the officers, and a white battalion of *Chasseurs* (cavalry), all these were Eritrean natives, the Askari. But they were brave, seasoned and disciplined fighters, armed with the latest magazine rifles and backed with modern artillery.

At first Baratieri believed he was not strong enough to hold Tigre against an invasion force from the south, assuming that Menelik was able to support Mangasha in mounting a counter-attack. However, there was no sign of that in October 1895. On the contrary, by 9 October, Mangasha had fled in panic after a brush with Baratieri's vanguard. So Baratieri pushed his columns forward into southern Tigre. He now planned to fortify three strategic strongpoints in the province: Makalle, as the first redoubt, and Adigrat and Adowa as the natural line of defence. Together they commanded the two roads to the north. From Adigrat, the town of Adowa was invisible, twenty miles to the west, beyond a line of fantastic peaks, shaped like towers and turrets. Baratieri had been determined to occupy the town earlier that year, but had been over-ruled by Crispi's government on the grounds of economy. Now he was confident he had a second chance.

For the time being, Baratieri put more faith in the weakness of the enemy than in his own strength. Diplomatically, Menelik could trust no one: not the Muslim Sultan of Aussa in the eastern desert, nor the Dervishes in the west, nor the great feudal *rases* (princes) at home. Then there was Menelik's problem of transport and supply. As a commander, Baratieri knew the difficulties of supplying even a modest field force 150 miles from its base. Menelik would have to transport his feudal armies 500 miles across the tangled gorges of the high plateau, and supply them with food in Tigre, ravaged by war and famine. Baratieri dismissed the idea of Menelik being able to put more than 30,000 men on the Tigrean border, and doubted whether there would be a war at all; in November he cabled to Rome to say that he was not sure whether Menelik would advance. The sultanate of Aussa was on the verge of revolt. The imperial army was crippled by desertions. Menelik himself was believed to have been struck by lightning.

The truth was much more extraordinary. Under the shadow of those fantastic peaks at Adowa, Italy was shortly to endure the bloodiest defeat ever endured by a colonial power in Africa.

On 17 September 1895, nine days before Baratieri landed at Massawa, boasting that he would bring back Menelik in a cage, the war-drums were beating in the palace compound at Addis Ababa 500 miles to the south. The criers summoned the people to hear the words of *Jan Hoi*, meaning His Majesty, Menelik II, the King of Kings. It was a few days before the feast of Maskal, the Finding of the Cross. The laborious sowing of the *teff* crop (a kind of grain) was nearly finished and the tableland of Shoa, flatter and greener than the stony uplands to the north, sparkled with spring flowers.

A European traveller could ride into Addis Ababa, the 'New Flower' founded by Menelik, without realizing he had arrived. There were no streets and only a handful of stone buildings. The capital had sprung into life ten years earlier from the sprawling camp sites of Menelik's *rases*. It was now like 100 African villages thrown together: 10,000 mud huts sprawling below the southern rim of the Shoan tableland in a green valley dotted with flowering mimosa trees and gashed with rust-red streams. The heart of the capital was a great open bazaar swarming with white-cloaked traders and their donkeys. There were no public buildings other than five conical, thatched churches – Raphael, Mary, Trinity, Oriel and St George – modern reminders that Ethiopia had been a Christian kingdom since the fourth century. There was also the *Adderach*, a huge, gabled banqueting hall, and a group of incongruously Indian pavilions, designed by a Swiss engineer. These formed Menelik's palace in the heart of the imperial compound, guarded by a pair of mangy lions in a cage, symbols of the Emperor's biblical style as Lion of Judah.

Menelik himself was the most striking monument in the city. He rode barefoot on a mule with a scarlet saddlecloth, while a servant held each stirrup and a boy ran beside him carrying a golden parasol over His Majesty's hat. The hat itself was an ordinary grey felt wide-awake with a floppy brim. The Emperor had dark, pock-marked skin with markedly semitic features, a high forehead and a well-cut nose. His lips, however, were unusually thick (perhaps inherited from his mother, a humble serving woman seduced by his father). When he spoke, his face glowed with intelligence and good humour. When a European visitor explained some astounding invention, like plumbing or electric light, he could hardly contain his curiosity. Modern firearms, in particular, excited him.

Yet he owed his empire to his genius for diplomatic manoeuvre; people said he had no stomach for warfare.

'Assemble the army, beat the drum.'[3] A slow drum roll prefaced each solemn reading of the *Ketit*, the order for mobilization. It was couched in the rhetoric of a crusade, an appeal to the instincts of Christian nationalism more than fifteen hundred years old. Now, at last, it seemed clear that the Emperor intended to fight. The years of prevarication with the Italians were over, and his people would put their trust in their ancient faith and their new European rifles. The Italians would be driven back into the sea like all previous invaders – like Ismael Pasha's Egyptians, twenty years earlier, like Mahomed Gragn's Somalis of the sixteenth century. They were all 'infidels'.

> God, in his bounty, has struck down my enemies and enlarged my empire and preserved me to this day. I have reigned by the grace of God. As we must all die some time, I will not be afflicted if I die ... Enemies have come who would ruin our country and change our religion. They have passed beyond the sea which God gave us as our frontier ... These enemies have advanced, burrowing into the country like moles. With God's help I will get rid of them.[4]

As the messengers galloped away down the network of dusty caravan tracks and the war-drums echoed the proclamation in every thatched village, a wave of excitement gripped the capital. The palace servants made ready the *Adderach*, the great banqueting hall where 2,000 warriors could sit down to unleavened bread and raw meat. These feasts confirmed the loyalty of each provincial army. No army's loyalty was more crucial than that of Ras Makonnen, the Emperor's first cousin, the Governor of the province of Harar, the rich province which linked Shoa with the southern routes to the desert and the Red Sea ports south of Massawa. It was along this precarious lifeline to Harar that had come every rifle and box of ammunition bought from the French arms dealers at Jibouti and the British dealers at Zeila. The Emperor's war chest now numbered over 70,000 modern rifles and some assorted artillery, for the use of which some Russian adventurers had tried to train Ethiopian gunners.

A week later Ras Makonnen and the army from Harar obediently surged into the capital. Soon the city of mud huts became a city of tents. The sun was obscured by the dust of thousands of slaughter cattle, the moon by the smoke of thousands of camp fires. Apart from their incongruously modern rifles, the army of Menelik looked medieval, like the army of the Priest King whom Europe had christened Prester John. The leaders wore scarlet and gold brocade, and head-dresses of lion mane. Retainers carried swords, buffalo-hide shields and bread baskets. Priests displayed processional crosses under a canopy of striped umbrellas. Everyone – *rases*, priests, common soldiers, whether riding or walking – travelled barefoot. The heavy work was done by women and slaves. At night the camp was like a carnival, and the song composers were already celebrating Menelik's victory: 'You, base city of Rome: Menelik, saviour of the world, will not leave even one of your seed to bear your name.'[5]

On 11 October, the Shoan contingent, about 50,000 strong, set off, with

Menelik and Empress Taitu riding in the centre. Every night the pitching of the scarlet royal tent was a signal for the whole army to halt. It took eighteen days to reach Woro Illu, 100 miles to the north, as they had to cross numerous streams and rivers. Here the Emperor waited to allow other provincial armies to join him. There were surprisingly few defections. When they left Woro Illu the army totalled nearly 70,000, not counting a vast number of camp followers. Menelik's chief anxiety was not the loyalty of his troops but the difficulties of supplying them with meat and grain.

The mobilization had been perhaps too successful. Menelik knew that, after the battle at Dogali, Yohannes had advanced with 100,000 men to attack the Italians in Eritrea, but had been forced to retreat by the failure of his commissariat. Was this to be Menelik's fate, too? Every step that his army marched towards Tigre brought him closer to a region of stony canyons, ravaged by drought and cattle sickness, as well as exhausted by war.

Menelik sent Ras Makonnen ahead of the army to join hands with Ras Mangasha. As his trusted cousin, Makonnen was authorized to open negotiations with Baratieri. Of course it was merely a device to buy time. He was determined to fight. Yet, despite the proud words of his proclamation, Menelik did not intend to try to get rid of the Italians; all he wanted was to push them back into Eritrea. This he was sure he could achieve, if God in his bounty granted him food for his army.

Baratieri's good humour received a violent jolt early in December. Up to this date he still only half-believed in the possibility of a collision with Menelik. He had heard that desertion was crippling the Ethiopian armies, and that the threat of a flank attack from the Muslims of Aussa preyed on the Emperor's mind. No more than 30,000 men could be expected to mount a counter-attack, and this, Baratieri assured his masters in Rome, was nothing to fear.

Now he was astonished to hear that he had greatly under-estimated Menelik's forces. The vanguard *alone* numbered about 30,000 men, and it had swamped his own forward positions in Tigre. First it annihilated Major Toselli and 2,000 Eritrean Askari, cut off on the mountain of Amba Alagi. Then it laid siege to the 1,200-strong garrison holed up in the fort of Makalle. Baratieri could do nothing for these unfortunates. He pulled back to Adigrat, his base close to the Eritrean frontier, while reinforcements of white troops were rushed from Italy to Massawa.

By late January 1896 the threat to Baratieri seemed to have receded again. After a forty-five-day siege, Menelik released the garrison of Makalle under flag of truce and expressed himself anxious for peace. Meanwhile, Baratieri's first reinforcements had marched up from Massawa. Even the cloud of defeat over Amba Alagi had a silver lining. Crispi's shocked Cabinet agreed to advance a further 20 million lire (£800,000) to ensure the disaster was avenged.

Baratieri spent February warily eyeing his opponent through a telescope across the wild mountains of Tigre. Peace negotiations were abortive; Crispi's government still insisted on a protectorate. Politically, they needed a victory more than peace. Baratieri wondered how that victory was to be achieved. To attack would be exceedingly dangerous, given Menelik's force now outnumbered his own by five or six to one. The Italians had a strong defence line in the stony ridge south of Adigrat, but unfortunately Menelik refused to knock his head against it, and had moved to outflank Baratieri by taking Adowa, in the strategic valley west of Adigrat. Baratieri dug a second defence line at Sauria, halfway towards Adowa, but there was still no sign that Menelik would oblige him by taking the offensive.

By the end of the month, Baratieri was more puzzled than ever. He had now a field force of roughly 20,000 men, supported by fifty-six guns, and his supply line was only 110 miles long, taking the shortest track from Massawa. (By comparison, Menelik's two supply lines from Shoa were 500 miles long, and the eastern one crossed Wollo, hostile country.) Yet Baratieri was absurdly short of camels, mules and donkeys, and the narrow, stony, twisting track from Massawa broke the hearts of his supply officers. In late February it was reckoned that there was only ten days' food for the 20,000 men at Sauria. After 2 March Baratieri would have to pack his bags and retreat – unless there was a battle first.

As a student of war, Baratieri knew the textbooks well enough. He was outnumbered at least five to one by a well-armed enemy known for its bravery in battle. His correct strategy was to continue the Fabian policy of patience. Within a matter of days Menelik's Shoans would have eaten Tigre bare, and be forced to retreat. All Baratieri needed was the strength of character to march back into Eritrea and let Menelik destroy himself.

Unfortunately for Baratieri, his chief did not see the situation in the same light as the writers of military textbooks. Crispi wished to have Menelik humbled on the battlefield. Honour demanded it and so did the Italian electorate. It was the only way to settle the score after Amba Alagi. It would bring Menelik to heel and force him to submit to a protectorate. In fact Crispi had already lost patience with Baratieri, goading him with a telegram that later became famous. 'This is a military pthisis [T.B.] not a war.' (So ran the cable Crispi sent on 25 February.) 'Small skirmishes in which we are always facing the enemy with inferior numbers ... There is no fundamental plan in this campaign ... We are ready for any sacrifice in order to save the honour of the army and the prestige of the monarchy.'[6]

The first sacrifice was Baratieri himself, whom the Italian Cabinet secretly agreed to sack the same day. His successor, General Baldissera, would put teeth into the attack. He sailed for Massawa, under an assumed name, before February was out.

Spurred on by Crispi's insulting telegram but without an inkling of his own sacking, Baratieri called his four brigadiers to an informal council of war on the evening of 28 February. He put to them the naked choice – advance or retreat – and seemed to favour a retreat. 'Retire? Never!'[7] cried General Dabormida, Commander of the Second Infantry Brigade. In Italy the government would prefer to lose 2,000 or 3,000 men rather than sacrifice their honour. Retreat would also be bad for their own soldiers' morale. Dabormida's confidence was shared by General Albertone, Commander of the Native Brigade, who added that two of Menelik's *rases* were reluctant to fight. The other two brigadiers concurred.

'The Council is full of spirit,' Baratieri commented drily. 'The enemy is brave and despises death. How is the morale of our soldiers?' 'Excellent,'[8] replied all four brigadiers in unison.

The next day was 29 February, for it was a Leap Year. Baratieri's guardian angel finally took flight. Baratieri decided to advance on Adowa. His plan must have seemed cautious enough to those, like his commanders and most of his soldiers, who still thought that one Italian (or Askari) was more than a match for six wild Africans. The brigades were to march forward under cover of darkness. Each would follow a different track towards the line of fantastic peaks nine miles west of Sauria. By daybreak they would be holding a defence line on the far side of the peaks. Menelik might then be provoked into a costly attack on the Italian line, his warriors charging over open ground towards mass batteries of artillery. Or he might sit tight, in which case he would lose face; or his starving army might panic at the sight of the Italians, and turn tail, in which case Adowa would fall to Baratieri without a shot.

These were the three possibilities optimistically envisaged by Baratieri. But a night advance along narrow tracks over unknown mountainous ground, dotted with mimosa scrub, strewn with huge boulders and torn with ravines, is always a perilous undertaking. There was a fourth possibility, too awful for Baratieri to contemplate, and it was this that occurred. Two of the brigades lost their way in the confusion, and never formed a line of defence. On the morning of 1 March, the two leading brigades, Albertone's and Dabormida's, a whole mountain apart, blundered separately into the arms of the enemy.

It was soon after the eleventh hour on the night of the Feast of St George, according to Menelik's chronicler (about 5.30 a.m. on the morning of Monday, 1 March), when a horseman galloped up to Menelik's red tent and begged the attendants to wake *Jan Hoi*, His Majesty. Why did he come so late in the night? The horseman, Kineasmatch Tadesse, blurted out his extraordinary message. '*The Ferangi*', the foreigners. Beyond the church of Abba Garima. Coming in huge numbers to surprise the camps.

That Monday was the day fixed to strike these camps, so desperate was the situation. Food had virtually run out. Blocking the tracks between the tents were the bodies of horses and mules that had died of disease and starvation. The previous week the chiefs had proposed that the army should make a desperate attempt to storm the enemy's lines at Sauria. Menelik had agreed, then revoked the plan. Ras Mangasha reminded him that this was how *his* father, the Emperor Yohannes, Menelik's enemy, had cast away his life, storming the forts of the Dervishes at Gallabat. Moreover those forts had been made of wood, not with stone, like the forts of the Italians. Menelik's advance was doomed to retreat – unless the Italians attacked. No one supposed this likely.

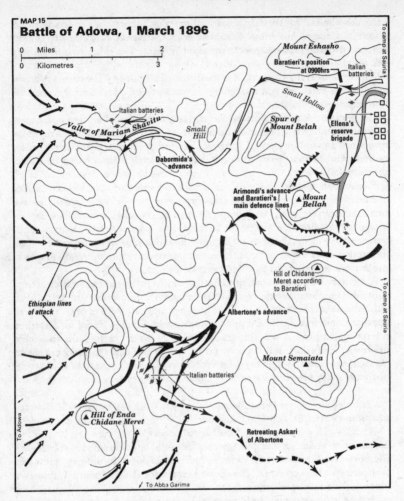

MAP 15
Battle of Adowa, 1 March 1896

0   Miles   1   2
0   Kilometres   3

To camp at Sauria

Mount Eshasho

Baratieri's position
at 0900hrs   Italian
batteries

Small Hollow

Italian batteries

Valley of Mariam Shavitu

*Small
Hill*

*Spur of
Mount Belah*

Ellena's
reserve
brigade

Dabormida's
advance

Arimondi's advance
and Baratieri's
main defence lines

*Mount
Bellah*

Hill of Chidane
Meret according
to Baratieri

Ethiopian lines
of attack

Albertone's advance

Mount Semaiata

To camp at Sauria

Italian batteries

To Adowa

*Hill of Enda
Chidane Meret*

Retreating Askari
of Albertone

To Abba Garima

'Until the enemy comes to attack me in my camp, and I hear the fusillade and
I see them with my eyes, not until then shall I send out my army in order of
battle.'[9] This had been the warning of the Emperor. Now it seemed like the
voice of a prophet.

When Menelik heard the rumble of guns and saw the smoke from the rifles,
he told his servants to prepare for battle. He rode off towards the church at
Abba Garima, dressed in a white *shamma* (a cloak), like a common soldier's.

That day the *Liq-Mekonas*, a high official of the court, rode to battle in the scarlet brocade of the Emperor. (This was a traditional ruse to protect the Emperor.) Beside Menelik stood the archbishop, Abuna Matthew, dressed in silk vestments as though attending a service. There were also some priests from the cathedral of Axum, who had actually come to complain about the requisitioning of their food supplies, displaying a banner with the picture of Mariam, Our Lady. Beside the priests were the ladies of the court, including the formidable Empress Taitu. She carried a black umbrella, a symbol of mourning, and dismounted to kneel in prayer on the bare ground, a large stone on her back, to indicate submission to God's will. A thin cloud of incense drifted overhead as the priest chanted aloud, accompanied by the boy trumpeters from the cathedral.

Five miles to the east, near the church of Enda Chidane Meret (Covenant of Mercy), the air was thick with black powder. The smoke was for the two combatants, in the words of the royal chronicler, 'like the shade that a tree gives to a man that shelters under its branches'.[10] There was little else than smoke to shelter under. With wild battle cries, the barefoot Ethiopians stormed across the stony hillside, waving spears and firing their rifles wildly, while General Albertone's Askaris, also barefoot, replied with regular volleys.

At first the Ethiopians made little impression on the well-disciplined Askari. Menelik's gunners did not have the skill to deploy their French artillery in these tangled valleys. Two batteries of Italian mountain guns beat down the line of attackers time and again. Bullets cut through the shields of buffalo hide and splashed against the rocks like torrential rain. But Menelik's men continued to run from the nearest camp towards the sound of the guns, 'as monkeys do when they see a haystack'[11] (in the quaint words of the chronicler). Soon Albertone's Native Brigade was outnumbered by ten or fifteen to one. The Askari knew the way they would be treated if taken alive, and many fought like heroes. Others lost heart and began to make off back down the valley to the east, ignoring the shouts and curses of their officers.

In most battles there comes a crucial moment when the scales waver. Here it happened at about 9.0 a.m. For more than three hours the mountain guns of Albertone's brigade had torn holes in the lines of barefoot warriors. Menelik, with Taitu and the court at Abba Garima, was too far away to see the smashed limbs and headless bodies. But from the line of wounded men struggling back across the valley, it must have been obvious that the Ethiopians were taking fearful losses. Three separate armies had made every effort to dislodge the Italians, each led by rulers who at some time had represented a dangerous challenge to his power: Ras Makonnen of Harar, Tekla Haimanot of Gojjam and Ras Michael of Wollo. No doubt Menelik was proud to see them take such a share in the battle. He still kept his main Shoan army in reserve.

It was the Empress Taitu who seized the initiative, striding forward (according to Menelik's chronicler) under the shelter of the black umbrella, leading the ladies of the court. 'Courage!' she cried. 'Victory is ours! Strike!'[12] Her own bodyguard then directed their fire on the enemy. This operatic intervention apparently persuaded Menelik. It was then that he committed his reserve of 25,000 Shoans, waving spears, firing rifles and screaming war-cries. Albertone's brigade vanished in the smoke, like a ship struck by a tidal wave. When the smoke cleared, Albertone's brigade had foundered.

For two hours since dawn, General Baratieri had been pestering his brigadiers on the right, a professorial figure peering at the sketch map through his pince-nez. The brigades on his right were late getting into position. He was mildly surprised by the disappearance of Albertone on the left. He had pointed out the hill his brigade was to occupy, when the brigadiers were given their orders the previous afternoon. It was 'Chidane Meret' – there it was, marked on the sketch map, towards the southern end of the line of tangled peaks, between Mount Belah and Mount Semaiata. For some reason Albertone had advanced nearer the enemy.

At 6.15 a.m. Baratieri sent off two messengers to find Albertone's position. Half an hour later he decided to push Dabormida forward to occupy the forward spur of Mount Belah, the mountain which his brigade was supposed to be holding. Dabormida could set up his guns on that spur to cover his own advance and (in the words quoted later by Baratieri) 'join hands as quickly as possible' [13] with Albertone. Of course this assumed that Albertone was a mere half mile beyond his allotted position.

It was 8.30 a.m. before the truth dawned on Baratieri. He climbed Mount Eshasho and saw wisps of smoke far away to the east. Albertone had occupied quite a different Chidane Meret – *Enda* Chidane Meret. He was *four miles* beyond his allotted place, astride a second line of mountains, the one that commanded Adowa itself.

Victory had not already slipped beyond Baratieri's grasp. He had over-whelming advantage in weight of guns, and in strength of discipline. Provided he re-formed his defence line, he might have dealt a bloody repulse to Menelik's wild army, thrown off balance by their forward rush, and defeat might have been avoided.

For an hour Baratieri dithered. He saw the first broken Askari from Albertone's brigade straggling back across the valley south of his own position. He also received two notes from Albertone, the second of which was timed 8.15 a.m., telling him the enemy were in great numbers and 'reinforcements will be well received'.[14] If he intended to pull back Albertone before he was overwhelmed, it was now or never. But Baratieri relied on Dabormida to retrieve the situation by stretching out to reach Albertone. Perhaps he was out of reach. But Dabormida did not even stretch a hand in his direction. For reasons that have never been explained, Dabormida swung far away to the right, heading straight for the enemy's camp at Mariam Shavita.

He might as well have thrown himself into a nest of giant ants. Dabormida's blunder compounded Albertone's, turning defeat into disaster and disaster into catastrophe.

Meanwhile, Baratieri was like a man who has lost both his left hand and his right hand without realizing it. He still imagined Dabormida had dug in with his guns on the spur of Mount Belah. He fussed over his third brigade, Arimondi's, which he put at the centre of the original defence line, leaving the fourth brigade in reserve. He was shocked to see the fugitives from Albertone's brigade still pouring along the valley to the right. Well, he would deal with those cowards when the battle was over. Then, about 10.30 a.m., reality began to intrude with the force of a nightmare.

Thousands of screaming Shoans swamped the spur of Mount Belah ahead of Baratieri. He tried to drive them off with two companies of *Bersaglieri*, élite riflemen. The sacrifice was in vain. The Shoans held the spur and began to outflank Arimondi's brigade on Mount Belah itself. A native battalion on the Italians' left then lost its nerve and stampeded. At about midday Baratieri ordered the buglers to sound the retreat in the centre, supported by Dabormida's brigade. He still imagined Dabormida to be in touch on the right. In fact, the screaming hordes of Shoans who had captured the spur were the men who had earlier forced a wedge between the two Italian brigades, until Albertone was crushed and Dabormida cut off.

To conduct an orderly retreat needs efficient staff officers, as well as a rearguard brave enough to cover it. Neither was apparent in the confusion. Baratieri's defence line on Mount Belah had been washed away by wave after wave of Shoans. Almost at once the retreat became a rout. Baratieri himself later described his own futile attempts to rally men stupefied by exhaustion and thirst:

> In the midst of this turmoil I was retiring ... surrounded by a few groups of brave men who were still kept in hand by their officers ... I noticed a walled-in enclosure, perhaps the ancient cemetery of a ruined church. I endeavoured to renew some kind of resistance in order to protect the retreat – and I collected Alpini, Bersaglieri and other white soldiers with officers among them ... '*Viva l'Italia*,' I called out, grasping my revolver; and this shout was repeated by perhaps a hundred mouths, parched with thirst and blood-stained! But on the inside, the wall did not permit us to fire, because it was higher than the shoulders of a man. An instant later the Amhara gained a position overlooking the spur; and every moment the confusion kept increasing owing to the waves of men swept by the hail of bullets, the sight of the dead and the dying – while my heart was being torn in two, as I despaired of ever being able to give an order or of getting it carried out.[15]

While Baratieri was waving his revolver and shouting '*Viva l'Italia!*', Dabormida still waited for orders in the narrow valley he had conquered that morning. No doubt if engineers had set up a heliograph, the brigade might have been recalled in time to help extricate the centre brigade. Dabormida was as ignorant of his own predicament as of the rest of the army's. In fact, he was surrounded.

About 2.0 p.m. he began to take stock. His men had fought for four hours to conquer this narrow valley of Mariam Shavita, suffering losses, especially among the officers, who rashly disdained to take cover. Now the surrounding hills bristled with Shoans. Despite thirst and exhaustion, for the men had been on their feet since the previous day, the brigade was still full of fight. But where were their comrades? 'It is a serious thing, a serious thing,' Dabormida murmured, pacing up and down near the sycamore tree in the centre of the valley. 'No message, no order, no reinforcement – nothing,' he told his brigade staff. Headquarters 'seems to have vanished'.[16] Towards 3.0 p.m. he decided to retire by a track to the north.

In contrast to the humiliating rout of the centre brigades under the eye of Baratieri, Dabormida's retirement was a model of a fighting retreat. Their losses were heavy; the Shoans charged forward like madmen, hacking with their swords and spears at the wounded left in the trenches. But each battalion obeyed orders. The rearguard companies were sacrificed for the sake of their comrades. Most of the gunners died bravely, defending their guns.

No one knows for certain how Dabormida met his death. It appears that he was wounded but dragged himself as far as a village called Adi Shum Wahena where an old woman saw him ('a chief, a great man, with the spectacles and the watch and the golden stars; he asked me for water and said he was the general').[17] His body was found months later, in the dust among the thousands of obedient dead that defended every rock and boulder on the long line of retreat.

*   *   *

Seldom has a telegram caused more of a sensation than the incoherent one published by the government in Rome on 4 March 1896. It was from Baratieri, the country's most successful general, and he appeared to be half-demented. He described his soldiers fleeing from the battlefield 'as if mad', and throwing down their rifles 'to avoid emasculation'.[18]

However, the completeness of the disaster was soon confirmed by the butcher's bill: 4,133 Italians were dead and missing, about 2,000 captured out of 10,596 in the original force; still more were wounded; and a further 4,000 Askari killed or captured out of 7,100. Baratieri himself was made a scapegoat. He was tried before a court in Asmara, the capital of Eritrea, for his 'inexcusable' plan of attack, and for the cowardly way it was claimed he had abandoned his men and fled the field. Sensibly, he was acquitted on both criminal charges, though the judge decided he was 'entirely unfitted' for his command.[19]

A similar verdict of unfitness was soon passed by the Italian people on Crispi's ministry. There were street riots in most Italian cities. Crispi was hounded from office within a fortnight of the news of the disaster. The new Prime Minister, the Marquis di Rudini, was voted a much larger sum by Parliament, 140 million lire (£5.6 million), to secure peace, than Crispi had been given for his disastrous war. The proviso was that there must be no more colonial adventures.

Two thousand miles away in Eritrea, General Baldissera, the Governor appointed in February to replace Baratieri and put teeth into the attack, docked at Massawa on 5 March, in time to pick up the pieces. It was quite a task. All over the southern borders of Eritrea were the shattered remnants of the army corps – demoralized, exhausted, half-naked and in many cases wounded. Most had passed through a second nightmare in the days after the battle when, without guides or food, they had to run the gauntlet of the Tigrean peasantry, who gave no quarter to the fugitives. Baldissera's first job was to gather together these remnants and organize them into four battalions capable of defending Eritrea. His second was to extricate the small garrison cut off at Adigrat; the third to retrieve the garrison besieged by 5,000 Dervishes at Kassala. The fourth – and on this all the others depended – was to open negotiations with Menelik to discuss terms of peace, including the release of the 4,000 prisoners taken at Adowa.

Menelik seemed in no mood for peace, however, during Baldissera's first days in Eritrea. On 12 March the Shoans were reported ready to cross the river and occupy the colony's southern borderland. When Baldissera sent an envoy, Major Saba, under flag of truce, Menelik had him arrested. But less than three weeks after his arrival, Baldissera heard news that must have made him gasp with relief. The whole menacing army – Shoans, Gojjamis, Hararis, everyone except the Tigreans – were hurrying back the way they had come, taking the Italian prisoners with them back to Shoa. Why had Menelik thrown away the initiative just when he had a chance of driving the Italians into the sea?

The price of victory had been excruciating. That was the first and simplest explanation. On the evening of the battle the Empress is said to have wept over the Ethiopian dead, 'her face,' according to the chronicler, 'usually so luminous, now dark with tears.'[20] The Ethiopians had lost about 7,000 dead and 10,000 wounded, many of them crippled for life. These were far higher casualties than those suffered when Yohannes was killed by the Dervishes at Gallabat.

No wonder Menelik was told, when he enquired if they could advance into Serae (in Eritrea), that this was impractical. It was not only that the rivers were dry and food unobtainable; the men had simply had enough fighting. Soon the Small Rains would be on them. It was time to return home, to plough and to sow.

The march back to Addis Ababa took the main contingent, including the Emperor and Empress, two months. Even for the Shoans it proved an ordeal. Grain and cattle had to be taken by force from local farmers, while the Muslims in Wollo harried the flanks of the army. Mules and donkeys were rarer than gold. Relief was the keynote of the victory parade when Menelik finally reached the capital, to be honoured with a triumphant salute from the field-guns captured at Adowa.

For the 1,900 Italian prisoners, some of whom were seriously wounded, the 500-mile journey to Addis Ababa proved still more of an ordeal. The men stumbled after their captors, half-starved, their boots worn out, their clothes in rags, while the rain poured down. The diplomatic climate, however, was changing for the better. Menelik was determined to use his victory to cement a permanent peace.

On 23 August 1896 the Italian envoy, Count Nerazzi, was told that Menelik had only two pre-conditions: the abolition of the Treaty of Wichale, and recognition of Ethiopia's unqualified independence. Astonishingly he was only asking for the restoration of the status quo. The government of di Rudini hastened to oblige. Within two months a peace treaty was signed in Addis Ababa confirming the boundary of Eritrea as the line of the river Mareb. There followed a convention for the repatriation of the Italian prisoners. After payment of an indemnity of ten million lire (£400,000), all 1,705 Italian survivors were sent down to Harar on their way to the coast. About 200 of the wounded had died of the effects of their terrible march. Perhaps about the same number of Askari prisoners, who had had their right hands and left feet ritually lopped off after Adowa, had died of the effects of this ghastly operation.

Once the Italian prisoners had returned home, to be welcomed coolly by the new government, and warned not to speak to journalists, Italy and Ethiopia resumed normal commercial relations. (It was only in the Italian army that Adowa was to leave, for the next forty years, a deep scar of humiliation.) Menelik then turned to the other Powers to confirm his diplomatic triumph. The French had contributed the arms essential to his victory, the British had given moral support to his enemies. Menelik drove an equally shrewd bargain with each. From the French he took a large part of French Somaliland in exchange for secretly promising his unconditional support for their scheme to take over the upper Nile. From the British he obtained a large part of British Somaliland and the right of duty-free imports through Zeila in exchange for help against the Mahdists. At the same time he promised the Mahdists in the Sudan a mutual commercial pact. (All three promises were, of course, incompatible. Menelik was keeping his options open to see which of the Powers would win the Scramble for the upper Nile.)

The next year, 1897, Menelik sent out his Shoan armies on a new war of conquest against the Kaffa of the south-west and the Galla of the southern borderland. These unfortunate neighbours, who had only a few hundred muzzle-loaders between them, were no match for Menelik's warriors armed with magazine rifles. Tens of thousands of blacks were killed, or sold into slavery. Their cattle and gold were looted, their land parcelled among Shoans. Soon Menelik's empire was double the size of Yohannes's empire at its peak. It was imperial expansion and *Realpolitik*, African-style, and it brought greater rewards than any European war in Africa. With the gold looted in Kaffa and the south, Menelik was able to re-equip his army, start the process of modernizing his ancient state, and thus extend the dominance of Shoa far into the twentieth century.

CHAPTER 27

Rhodes, Raiders and Rebels

Birmingham, Rhodesia and the Transvaal
August 1895–1897

'You have said that it is me that is killing you: now
here are your masters coming ... You will have to
pull and shove wagons; but under me you never did
this kind of thing.'

King Lobengula's last speech to his people, 1896

It was August 1895, one of the golden Augusts of the century, and the English Midlands glowed like the South African veld. Near Birmingham the green fields had turned the colour of old gold. As for the copper spires on the Town Hall, the sun had burnished them with the force of the nearby steel company's blast furnaces. A few miles away, in his private paradise, Highbury, Joseph Chamberlain, screw manufacturer turned imperial statesman, sat on the well-watered lawn and basked in his sudden stroke of fortune. He still looked the self-made man of the *Punch* cartoons, his steel eye-glass fixed imperiously in the right eye, a home-grown orchid sprouting from his button-hole. But there beside his deck chair was a new government despatch box, marked 'co', bringing a flash of royal scarlet to the green lawn.

That spring, disgust for politics had nearly choked Chamberlain. He had had half a mind to throw in the sponge and give up his career. He was fifty-nine. For nine years he and Hartington had led the Liberal Unionists on the back benches of Commons and Lords, and had led them into the wilderness. Before 1886 he had every hope of succeeding Gladstone as leader of the Liberals. The split over Home Rule had destroyed that hope for ever. By April 1895 his position seemed as blighted as the garden at Highbury, where the hothouses had been cracked by frost and the camellias blackened by a winter of extraordinary severity. He was compared unfavourably with Judas by some friends who had stayed true to Gladstone's old party (though he retained the loyalty of Harcourt); and he was still a dangerous Radical in the eyes of many of the Tories with whom he had to rub shoulders on the back benches.

Then, in June 1895, the Liberal government led by Gladstone's successor, Lord Rosebery, had vanished in a small puff of smoke. (Rosebery's government was demolished by an amendment about the shortage of cordite.) Lord Salisbury sardonically resumed the helm. But this time the Liberal Unionists were welcomed in a coalition, and Chamberlain was offered almost any post he cared to name. The Treasury, the Foreign Office, the Home Office – the whole field was open to him. He chose the Colonies. For a month the coalition soldiered on without a parliamentary majority. Then came the General Election of that golden summer in which the leaderless Liberals were chased from the field, leaving the coalition with a stunning majority of 152.

Why had 'Pushful Joe', as the papers called Chamberlain, picked such a dim berth as the Colonies? It was a question that puzzled experts at Westminster, not least the Prime Minister and his nephew, Arthur Balfour, now Leader of the Commons and heir presumptive of the Tory Party. To think of Chamberlain following in the footsteps of poor, cracked Lord Carnarvon ('Twitters'), or of nonentities like Lord Knutsford ('Peter Woggie'). Salisbury had always imagined that Joe was only a 'theoretic imperialist'.[1] But it was one thing to make vague appeals for imperial unity, and quite another to run a poverty-stricken department of state notorious for bungling – trapped as it was between the global diplomacy of the Foreign Office and the narrow, penny-pinching politics of the Treasury.

The first cause of the Colonial Office's weakness was that imperial expansion was largely the responsibility of the Foreign Office. The second, the meanness of the Treasury, takes us back to the central paradox of the Scramble. There was little imperialism, meaning popular enthusiasm for expanding the Empire, behind Britain's huge new stake in Africa. That was the strange fact.

In other countries the reverse had been true. Colonial fever had swept Germany in 1884, readily exploited by Bismarck, when it suited his electoral calculations, as an opportunity to grab four African colonies. Brazza's discoveries in the Congo had sent a thrill through French society, which in turn the French colonial army was able to exploit. But in Britain, the country with far the biggest commercial and strategic stake in Africa, the public's appetite for Africa had been sluggish – at least until the 1890s. Apart from the strategic race for the Nile, the running had been left to individuals: enterprising capitalists such as Cecil Rhodes and George Goldie, humanitarians such as Lugard and Mackinnon, eccentric naturalists such as Harry Johnston. It was these men who had prodded the Foreign Office into keeping up with their rivals. Since the start of the Scramble, two million square miles had thus been added to the British Empire in Africa: in Mackinnon's East Africa, Lugard's Uganda, Goldie's Niger territories, Rhodes's Matabeleland and Mashonaland, Johnston's Nyasaland, as well as in Lord Cromer's (Sir Evelyn Baring's) 'veiled protectorate' imposed on Egypt.

But the race was by no means won. The final phase, the triple race for the Nile, the Niger and the South African veld, was about to begin. This was why Chamberlain had chosen the Colonies. It needed a strong hand. He would push aside the timid diplomats of the Foreign Office and make the CO champion Britain's part in this triple race. His ambition was to make imperialism a popular crusade, and to use the same crusade to try to promote imperial unity.

'Imperialism' in 1895 was an elastic term, with two quite distinct meanings, corresponding to the two kinds of British Empire. When a Colonial Secretary spoke of 'imperial unity' and 'imperial federation',[2] he was not talking of the

Crown Colonies and the black-and-brown empire he ruled. He referred to that other empire for which he had responsibility: Canada and the other white, self-governing colonies, New Zealand, Australia, Natal and the Cape, all of which would soon follow Canada's lead in taking the name of dominions. Chamberlain's plan was to persuade these more or less fully-fledged nations to draw closer to the mother country for mutual advantages of trade and defence.

Chamberlain's ultimate dream was to put all the white peoples of the Empire in the melting pot and forge a single imperial federation. The first step was to forge individual federations in Australia and South Africa, cast in the mould of the great Canadian federation already set up at Ottawa. In Australia, Canberra would soon take its place as capital of the new federation. But in South Africa everything was confused by the differences of race. For one thing, the region straddled both British Empires – white and black-and-brown. For another, two of the states, the Transvaal and the Orange Free State, were Boer republics – outside the British Empire. Already the attempt to annex and federate the Transvaal had stirred up a hornet's nest among the Boers, as Frere and Carnarvon had discovered to their cost in the 1870s. It would be a brave Colonial Secretary who would wish to re-open that question in a hurry.

In August 1895 Chamberlain left his beloved Highbury to take over the CO in earnest. That dingy Italianate pile, hemmed in by the luxurious Foreign Office and the India Office, was still lit by gas and candles. No one could doubt which was the Cinderella of Whitehall. Chamberlain transformed the building – so we are told by one of his admirers. With a wave of his wand he replaced candles by electric light. It was a 'total transformation; the sleeping city awakened by a touch'.[3] Then the Master (as he became known) removed himself for a seven-week family holiday in the Pyrenees. It was not till the end of October that he returned to the office, which had been redecorated with the latest maps. He felt years younger. His wife marvelled at the way he warmed to success. Even the Liberals had a good word for him. In the *Daily Chronicle*, Massingham forecast that his management of the colonial empire would be 'perhaps the most interesting experiment in administration which has ever been tried in this country'.[4] Chamberlain ruefully told his wife in mid-November that a 'smash must come'.[5] All this praise, after the years of abuse, was too good to be true.

Within six weeks the smash did come, a kick in the stomach straight from the South African veld. On 29 December 1895, Dr Jameson, the administrator of Rhodesia, took the bit between his teeth and he set off from British territory to invade the Transvaal with a column of 500 Rhodesian troopers. Chamberlain's world was never to be the same again.

The following night was the night of the annual servants' ball at Highbury. Chamberlain was about to dress for dinner when he received a secret telegram from the CO warning him of Jameson's invasion of the Transvaal from British territory. The telegram astounded him. Clenching his fists he said, 'If this succeeds it will ruin me. I'm going up to London to crush it.'[6] Then he telegraphed back to London, 'Leave no stone unturned to prevent mischief.'[7] It was a cold starlit night. He caught the London train at 12.50 a.m. and reached his home in Prince's Gardens before 4.0 a.m. That day he repudiated the Raid with a series of thunderbolts from the CO. But nothing could stop Jameson until his battered column raised the white flag to Kruger's burghers at Doornkop, near Johannesburg, three days later. By then blood had been spilt on both sides and the Raid had become an international incident.

On 3 January 1896 Kaiser Wilhelm sent a telegram from Berlin to congratulate Kruger on beating the British invaders. Britain claimed paramountcy over the Transvaal according to the London Convention, so the Kaiser's telegram caused a violent outcry in the British press and raised an overwhelming question that would soon have to be answered. Should Britain join one of the European alliances?

The next few months saw Chamberlain fighting for his political life. It emerged that Cecil Rhodes was the leader of this half-baked scheme to pursue the federation of South Africa by a short cut – that is, by forcibly taking over the Transvaal. Rhodes's fellow conspirators included the two richest gold magnates of the Rand, Alfred Beit and Julius Wernher. They had financed a rising by the British Uitlanders in Johannesburg, the British immigrants denied a vote by President Kruger for the very good reason that they were now believed to outnumber the Boers. The Johannesburg rising had gone off like a scene from *opéra bouffe*. It was a fiasco. But that was not what worried Chamberlain. Rhodes and the conspirators had also arranged to launch Jameson's raid from Bechuanaland in support of the rising.

Later that year Rhodes made the astounding claim that Chamberlain was a party to the conspiracy.

This riddle is still unresolved after nearly a century of mud-slinging, but its genesis lay in the uneasy partnership between Cecil Rhodes, the colonial buccaneer, and 'Grandmama' – alias the imperial government – in the years before the Raid. The absence of a firm hand from Downing Street not only explains the fiasco of the plot for revolution and the disaster of the Raid. It also explains no less than three wars in Rhodesia: the first a buccaneering war of conquest before the Raid, the second and third a pair of disastrous African rebellions which the Raid itself precipitated.

* * *

For five years Cecil Rhodes had championed South Africa, the independent Colossus with three heads. He was Prime Minister and diamond magnate of Cape Colony. He was one of the great gold magnates of the Boer republic of the Transvaal. He was the man who had persuaded the Queen to give him a royal charter and had founded a new British colony, north of the Transvaal, in his own name.

To federate these three states, and indeed all South Africa, under the British flag, was an aim he shared with the Colonial Office and almost all British politicians at Westminster, Liberal as well as Liberal Unionist and Tory. Of course Rhodes wanted a federation that he could control. But what chance was there of achieving it, given the coldness of the Cape, the hostility of the Transvaal and the near bankruptcy of Rhodesia?

In 1890 the new colony was piling up debts at terrifying speed. Much of the £1 million raised by Chartered Company shares had been spent by the end of the first year, swallowed up in the grim months after the invasion of Mashonaland. There was small chance of making the country pay, either in developing farms or gold-mines, until a railway was built. Rhodes was the first to see the political danger this presented. His personal fortune was about £2 million in 1895 and was already pledged in the Cape or the Transvaal. So were the fortunes of his principal allies, Alfred Beit and Julius Wernher, who were far richer gold magnates than he. This meant that most of the funds for developing Rhodesia had to be borrowed on the London market, or had to come, with unwelcome strings attached, from Downing Street. Worse still, if Rhodes, like Sir William Mackinnon in East Africa, could not raise the capital for his private empire, the Charter would evaporate, and Downing Street would have to intervene to prevent Kruger and the Transvaal Boers from taking over the state. That would spell the end of the Charter Colony of Rhodesia, and mean the birth of a new Crown Colony called 'Zambezia', or something similar.

Ever since Rhodes's pioneers had invaded Mashonaland in 1890, Rhodes's single overriding priority was to cut costs to the bone while pushing on with the railway. The bill for the mounted police alone had been running at £150,000 a year. Rhodes saved £100,000 a year by cutting the police force from 650 to 150. He eased out the first resident commissioner of the colony, a former Indian official called Colquhoun who was too bureaucratic for a frontier community. His replacement, Rhodes's crony from Kimberley, Dr Jameson, knew how to cut corners and was perfectly in sympathy with Rhodes's rough and ready ideas – or so Rhodes had believed. Then, in July 1893, Jameson suddenly astonished Rhodes with a plan for a full-scale war. He proposed a buccaneering raid on their neighbour, King Lobengula, to grab his kingdom, Matabeleland. What on earth made Jameson propose this extraordinary gamble?

Cutting costs meant keeping the peace with Lobengula. And Lobengula himself had given every sign that this suited his own policy, despite his difficulties in keeping a leash on his bloodthirsty regiments ever since Rhodes had obtained the Rudd concession and occupied Lobengula's dependency, Mashonaland, in 1890. It was sixty years since the Ndebele had last washed their spears in the blood of a white enemy: the Boer trekkers who had driven them from the Transvaal when the Ndebele pushed north from Zululand. The younger generation of Ndebele warriors was confident that it could 'make breakfast' on the white intruders. Lobengula knew otherwise. He had watched the defeat and humiliation of Cetshwayo and his Zulus, the Ndebele's kith and kin, and he had done his best to temporize with the intruders.

From Rhodes's point of view the ambiguous peace had worked well enough. The King claimed to have cancelled the Rudd concession for Mashonaland which he said (understandably) had been obtained by deceit, and in any case was only a mining concession and did not confer land rights. In protest against the charter, the King had for long refused to accept the 1,000 rifles delivered by Rhodes according to the terms of the Rudd concession. On the other hand, Lobengula was prepared to let Rhodes pay him a monthly rent for occupying Mashonaland. He also did his best to prevent a collision between the settlers in Mashonaland and his own warriors, accustomed to raid there for cattle and slaves. He indulged the regiments with alternative bloody pastimes, such as letting them raid Lewanika's territory north of the Zambezi, where they hacked and tortured without interference, and letting them murder one of his own most loyal (and sensible) advisers, Mhlaba, who had been 'smelt out' for witchcraft. Probably the real reason why Mhlaba was stabbed to death, with all his family, was that Mhlaba counselled peace.

In July 1893, however, Lobengula made a fatal error of judgement. Some Shona tribesmen had stolen cattle close to the border. He sent a large raiding party to punish the thieves, who lived on the outskirts of Fort Victoria. Theoretically, Lobengula had retained the right to punish his subjects in Mashonaland as well as in Matabeleland. But it was rash to send raiders across the border into the heart of the white men's territory. Worse still, the raiders disobeyed the King's commands to respect the white men's property.

The result was an old-fashioned massacre under the walls of Fort Victoria: perhaps 400 wretched Shona tribesmen hacked to death by the Ndebele raiders, houseboys murdered in white homes, women and children dragged off as slaves, others fleeing for refuge into the fort itself and the raiders claiming they should be handed over for execution. The damage to white property was incidental – the theft of a few cattle and horses. The raid was only an incident to the settlers, yet it left behind a fever of shock and outrage. The black wave of barbarism was lapping against the walls of their new citadel; how dare anyone now speak of peace with Lobengula?

Jameson caught the fever quicker than anyone. He had spotted an irresistible short cut to what Rhodes called 'All-Red: my dream'. The King had played into their hands. The Ndebele could be crushed once and for all. Within days of the 'Victoria incident' he had planned his full-scale war of conquest.

At first, Rhodes was shaken by Jameson's cockiness. How could they risk such a gamble at this moment of approaching bankruptcy? He sent a stern warning by the new telegraph line: 'Read Luke XIV:31.' With the help of the telegraph clerk, who had a Bible, Jameson read, 'Or what king going to make war against another king, sitteth not down first, and consulteth whether he be able with ten thousand to meet him that cometh against him with twenty thousand?'[8] Jameson claimed he only needed 1,000 men against Lobengula's hordes. Had he forgotten Isandlwana? No, but the British army's mistake had been to use infantry against Zulus. The Boers knew better. Mounted columns, using a wagon laager at night, was the only way. A three-pronged attack on Bulawayo – from Salisbury, Victoria and Tuli – would do the trick. All Jameson asked of Rhodes was to provide the money. 'You have got to get the money,'[9] he expostulated during a long 'debate' by telegraph.

In the event, Rhodes agreed to take the gamble. Perhaps he saw that the finances of Mashonaland were so disastrous that only a wild gamble could save them. At any rate, he agreed to sell £50,000 worth of his own Chartered Company shares in order to pay for Jameson's war. The main cost was for 1,000 horses that had to be raked up from the Transvaal. Recruits were also winkled out from there (despite a thunderbolt from Kruger to ban enlistment). These recruits and the white volunteers from Mashonaland were all to be paid by results – in land and cattle looted from the enemy. Later, when someone let the cat out of the bag, there was outrage in the Liberal English newspapers. But in South Africa, white settlers had never been particularly squeamish about the way they fought 'Kaffirs'. To pay for wars in loot was the normal African code. In the settlers' view, Matabeleland was stolen property anyway – land the Ndebele stole from the Shona.

After choosing to back Jameson's gamble, Rhodes's main problem, in the summer of 1893, was to convince the imperial authorities that he had no choice, and that war was unavoidable. Fortunately for him, the High Commissioner at the Cape, Sir Henry Loch, did not know how to restrain Rhodes and ended by abetting him. Loch was instructed by the Colonial Secretary in London (then Lord Ripon) to prevent 'any offensive movement'[10] by the Chartered Company and to warn Rhodes that an attempt to implicate the imperial government in his quarrel with Lobengula might prove fatal to his Charter. But Loch hoped to exploit the invasion himself, in order to cut Rhodes down to size. If there was to be an invasion, imperial troops should be first into Bulawayo.

The result was that Loch became the dupe of Rhodes and the Company. He transmitted false information to London reporting that Lobengula's raiders had deliberately fired on white men during the Victoria incident. The truth was the reverse. After Jameson's arrival at Victoria, the raiders had been driven back by force of arms. About a dozen had been shot by Jameson's men without attempting to return fire.

More important still, Loch allowed himself to be persuaded that Lobengula had mobilized his army and was preparing to invade white territory. In fact, the Ndebele army was crippled by smallpox. No doubt this helped the unfortunate King, desperate to prevent hostilities, to restrain his young warriors from further raids across the border. He sent off an experienced envoy, Mshete, to carry a letter to the Queen. Loch took the letter from him and reported that there was no point in negotiations, since Lobengula insisted on his right to raid the Shona.

By then Loch had decided to launch his own invasion with imperial troops, a column of 225 Bechuanaland Border Police supported by nearly 2,000 Bechuana natives, led by Chief Khama himself. The invasion now became a race between rival armies: the High Commissioner's (or Grandmama's) representing London and imperial control, and Jameson's representing the buccaneering spirit of Rhodes, the Charter and colonial nationalism. To the victor would go the privilege of dictating terms to the Ndebele.

Rarely in history has a gamble paid off as neatly as Jameson's war on the Ndebele. His invasion force was even smaller than the pioneer column of 1890: less than 700 white volunteers, their supplies carried in 31 lumbering ox wagons attended by 300 native 'boys'. But they were heavily armed. They had two seven-pounder field-guns and a number of machine guns, including five Maxims. In mid-October 1893 the Salisbury column splashed across the Umniati river, the effective border between Mashonaland and Matabeleland. The Salisbury column soon joined hands with the Victoria column; there was nothing to oppose them as they clattered along through the dry bush. For this they had the smallpox epidemic – and Lobengula's doomed peace efforts – to thank. It was not until 25 October that the Ndebele tried to wash their spears.

About 6,000 warriors launched a courageous night attack against the columns laagered by the Shangani river. The attack was beaten off at a cost of one white trooper and one Cape Coloured killed, with six white men wounded. The Ndebele were cut down by hundreds. (About fifty unfortunate Shona refugees were also killed, stabbed by the Ndebele or caught in the crossfire.)

A week later, when the columns were only twenty miles from Bulawayo, the Ndebele launched a second courageous attack, but it cost the columns no more effort to repel it. Jameson's men lost four dead and seven wounded, compared with nearly 1,000 Ndebele casualties. On 4 November, just over a month after setting out, the ox wagons clattered into Bulawayo. The Company's flag – a Union Jack with a Rhodesian lion across the middle – was hoisted on a makeshift flagpole, while a pipe major of the Scots Guards saluted the cheering troopers with a victory air. Lobengula and the whole population had fled, leaving the town burnt and abandoned, except for two white traders playing poker on the roof of the store.

The cheering soon had to stop. Jameson made a futile effort to capture the King, the King made a futile effort to buy off his pursuers by sending a bag of 1,000 gold sovereigns and a note, 'Take this and go back. I am conquered.'[11] The sovereigns were promptly pocketed by two white batmen, who hid the message. On 3 December, the forward patrol of the pursuing force came up with the wagons left by Lobengula, only a few hours before, on the banks of the river Shangani. Next day this Shangani patrol, thirty-four men led by Major Allan Wilson, paid the price for a reckless blunder. Wilson decided all the stuffing had been knocked out of the enemy. He would make a dash and grab the King. His patrol was surrounded and the men were stabbed to death, with their backs to a tree, fighting to the last round.

Lobengula rode away to the north, protected by the remnants of his Impis. His last bitter speech to his people has been preserved: 'You have said that it is me that is killing you: now here are your masters coming ... You will have to pull and shove wagons; but under me you never did this kind of thing ... Now you be joyful because here are your future rulers ... the white people are coming now. I didn't want to fight with them ... O, I am remembering the words of Lotsche ...'.[12] At least Lobengula was spared the humiliation of being hunted down like Cetshwayo. He died like a king, taking poison with his chief counsellor when he heard that the last of his Impis had surrendered. His servants buried him sitting in a cave, wrapped in the skin of a black ox, his chief counsellor buried at his feet, along with his remaining possessions.

Despite the King's unavoidable absence from the victory parade, and despite Wilson's reckless blunder on the Shangani, Rhodes was well pleased. At modest cost – about fifty white lives and £50,000 – Jameson had swept a dangerous neighbour from the map, doubled the size of Rhodesia, and perhaps rescued the Charter Company from bankruptcy. He had also beaten the imperial authorities. For the High Commissioner's own troops – the Bechuanaland Border Police – lumbered into Bulawayo ten days too late. This was partly because Loch had forgotten to tell them to hurry, partly because Jameson's men delayed them – on Jameson's orders. In January 1894 Rhodes left Salisbury to return in triumph to Cape Town. He was determined not to let Grandmama interfere with his final solution for the Ndebele.

Rhodes had an influential stake in the Cape Town press and could square most of the correspondents who served the London newspapers. Back from England came the news that the invasion was generally welcomed. As Rhodes had hoped, Grandmama was philosophic about losing the race for Bulawayo; at least, the Colonial Office made no serious attempt to interfere with his rough and ready way of settling Matabeleland. The official accounts of the Victoria incident convinced most people that the war had been unavoidable. The missionary lobby in England welcomed the chance of proselytizing. Only a small section of the Radical press – in particular Henry Labouchère's *Truth* – saw through Rhodes's mask. Labouchère denounced the war as a crime and accused Rhodes (with good reason) of backing Jameson's gamble in order to save Mashonaland from bankruptcy.

Even the worst disaster of the war, the massacre of the Shangani Patrol, was soon turned to Rhodes's advantage. In colonial South Africa it came to be regarded as a glorious defeat in the best British tradition. All over England, too, people thrilled to read of the little band of brave men singing 'God Save the Queen' when their last round was fired, until one by one they died.

Within two years – by March 1896 – Rhodesia would be the scene of the first African war of independence precipitated by the Scramble, and Rhodes's settlement would be recognized to be full of fatal blunders, recognized even by Rhodes himself. But in the euphoria after the capture of Bulawayo, neither Jameson nor Rhodes nor any of their cronies had any insight into the feelings of the African population. What delighted them was that the royal charter now covered the whole country, in practice, as well as on paper. Of course the legal title to Mashonaland was extremely shaky. Originally it had been a mining concession to Rudd (later repudiated by the King), followed by a land concession to Edward Lippert (which years later the British Privy Council would declare void). By contrast, the title for Matabeleland was based on conquest. This meant, according to European ideas of war, that everything that had belonged to the defeated government now belonged to the Company. Since Lobengula had been nominally all-powerful, almost everything of value in the country – land, cattle and other possessions – could technically be treated as loot.

To share out this loot between the white volunteers and the Company was the first act of the new government in 1894. Under the Victoria Agreement, each volunteer was entitled to 6,000 acres of captured land. Rhodes did not bother to decide where it would be prudent to locate these farms; there was simply a scramble for the best land. Within twelve months, 10,000 square miles of the rich red soil, virtually all the high veld within eighty miles of Bulawayo, had been pegged out as European farms. When the Ndebele villagers returned, dazed after their defeat, they found themselves either dispossessed or treated as tenants of the white settlers. The land was taken, and most of the villages burnt, on the simple technicality that it had been the King's land, though very little of it had been directly controlled by Lobengula.

It was the same with the cattle, and here confusion about ownership played into the hands of the Company. Under the old regime, privately-owned cattle were essential for *lobola*, the dowry system by which marriage was legalized. On the other hand, few individuals, not even the King's *indunas*, dared claim more than 100 cattle for themselves. To do so would have been imprudent, an invitation to be hacked to death after being 'smelt out' for witchcraft. But the King farmed out vast herds of cattle to his subjects, granting them the right of using the milk. Only in a technical sense were they the King's cattle. Now the bulk of these vast herds suddenly began to be confiscated from the Ndebele. Some were looted by the Company directly; others were taken by the white volunteers, who were permitted to seize them as spoils of war, provided they handed over half of them to the Company. Others again were stolen (or repossessed) by the Ndebele's ex-subjects, Shona or Amaholi, and driven off to Mashonaland. Thousands more were stolen by white cattle rustlers from the Transvaal. By the time the official commission appointed to count the cattle made its report in the autumn of 1895, it was decided that *all* confiscated cattle would be treated as having belonged to the King. Probably 200,000 had already been seized. The Company then decided that a further 33,000 out of 74,000 were needed for redistribution as loot. No wonder the Ndebele began to doubt whether they would end up with any animals at all.

Land and cattle – these were the central props of the Ndebele's cattle-ranching society, the main sources of wealth and prestige. To kick away these props, as the Company did, completely disoriented the Ndebele. Their third support was the tribesman's own pride in his membership of a warrior caste, a black aristocracy. This prop, too, was now kicked into the dust by the Company in its haste to hammer assegais into ploughshares. They forced the Ndebele to labour for the white man.

There was plenty to do. Within six months of the invasion, the bumptious white capital of Bulawayo had bounced into life, soon eclipsing Salisbury and the other Mashonaland townships. Three miles from the blackened ruins of Lobengula's kraal it rose, a colonial parody of a British suburb, red brick and gabled with tree-lined streets 120-foot wide, broad enough (according to legend) for Rhodes to turn a full span of oxen. Its amenities included banks, hotels, golf club, turf club, cricket club, roller-skating rink and a hall for amateur theatricals. However, there was also something of Dodge City, and the restless frontier world of hard liquor and six-shooters. When Jameson inaugurated the town in June 1894, he stood on a box opposite the uncompleted Maxim Hotel and announced impatiently, 'It is my job ... to declare the town open, gentlemen. I don't think we want any talk about it. I make the declaration now. There is plenty of whisky and soda inside, so come in.'[13]

For the majority of these newcomers, 'home' meant Britain, not South Africa. According to a census taken in Bulawayo in 1895, 1,017 out of the 1,537 white inhabitants were born in the United Kingdom, compared with only 299 born in South Africa. (The balance were mainly Germans and Americans.) But in their sense of superiority to Africans, the British showed no significant difference from other white colonials. The first axiom of white South African society, whether British or Boer, was that all the menial work was to be done by the black. Who was to dig the drains, as prescribed by the Bulawayo Sanitary Board? Who was to cut the wood and bake the bricks for the new 'stands' of houses rising opposite Market Square? The appetite for cheap African labour was as insatiable in the new towns as it was in the new farms and mines. But the ten shillings a month was no great attraction for the men of Lobengula's regiments. These aristocrats had no tradition of manual work. In the past it had been done for them by the Amaholi, their own slaves, or by Kalanga and Shona. So the Company sent native police, armed with *jambok* and rifle, to force the young men to work.

Of all the grievances that were gathering strength, the one of forced labour was felt most bitterly. To lose land and cattle was at least in the tradition of conquest which the Ndebele understood. But to be flogged by a servant of the white men, and then forced to work like their own Amaholi dogs was unbearable for a nation of masters like the Ndebele. Back in Mashonaland, even the men whom the whites had liberated from these masters saw no reason to be grateful. Paradoxically the invasion of their overlords had added to the burdens of the Shona. Nothing illustrates better the insensitivity of Rhodes and his Company. For three generations the Shona had been cursed by the raids of the Ndebele. Now that curse had been lifted, yet white task-masters proved still more exacting than black ones.

Many of the Shonas' prized cattle were confiscated by the Company's police. Sometimes there was a pretext that cattle had been driven across from Matabeleland after capture (or repossession) by the Shona. But often the confiscation was nothing better than official theft. At the same time the Company was able to start taxing the Shona as their *own* subjects, now that Lobengula, who had claimed this right for himself, had been removed from the scene. So the Company was authorized by the Colonial Office to charge ten shillings a year for each hut in Mashonaland, the tax to take effect from September 1894 and to be paid in cash, or in grain or stock if this was impossible.

The hut tax was a respectable weapon of colonial government in places like

Natal and Zululand, especially favoured by the authorities because it killed two birds with one stone. It brought African shillings to the revenue, and it brought African sinews to the labour market, for it forced the natives to work in order to pay the tax. But in Mashonaland the hut tax was collected in characteristically rough and ready style. At first it was technically illegal, for it began months before the official date of September 1894, and tax collectors were amateurs who acted like bandits. When a regular white staff was appointed, assisted by native police, the abuses were not checked. Indeed, even if humanely collected, the hut tax would still have seemed a kind of punishment to the long-suffering Shona. They had a choice – between losing their herds or losing their menfolk, between confiscation and forced labour. But they had done nothing to deserve this punishment not yet imposed on their former oppressors, the Ndebele.

Land, cattle, forced labour, hut tax: here were combustible gases unnoticed by the new settlers in both Matabeleland and Mashonaland. If the whites were planning to produce an explosion, they could not, as a modern historian put it, 'have worked more effectively'.[14] Yet the fuse was still missing. It was supplied by three apocalyptic disasters that now threatened the lives of both Ndebele and Shona.

The first was a plague of locusts. In 1890, the year of the pioneers, the locusts too made their first appearance. Each year they returned, till by 1895 they swarmed, forming enormous clouds that darkened the horizon and blotted out the sun. The second was a drought that had begun early in 1894, after Jameson's invasion of Matabeleland. In many districts little rain had fallen for two years, and the crops had blackened and died. The third and most terrifying disaster was rinderpest. No one had any experience of this malignant cattle disease which apparently crossed the Zambezi into northern Matabeleland early in 1896. (It had broken out in Somaliland in 1889 and swept through Uganda and Barotseland like a forest fire, before being checked by the Zambezi.) By March 1896 it was heading for Bulawayo, killing the transport oxen dead in their tracks and leaving a trail of stinking carcasses along every road. The authorities panicked.

Uninfected cattle were herded into kraals, then destroyed in a futile attempt to stop the epidemic. Within two years the epidemic – and its mishandling – killed about 2.5 million cattle south of the Zambezi, that is, the majority of the cattle in southern Africa. The effect on the black people of Rhodesia can be imagined. Thousands of cattle that had escaped being looted were now taken and slaughtered by the Company. The disease was ready to take the rest.

It was no coincidence, thought superstitious Africans, that locusts, drought and the mysterious cattle plague all followed the white man's flag. Here was the fuse for the explosion. Yet the match that lit the fuse was an event that hardly seemed connected, Dr Jameson's reckless ride into the Transvaal.

The fiasco of the Raid sent a shudder through the new Rhodesia. Rhodes had organized it, most of the participants were Rhodesian police and its leader was Jameson, the administrator of Rhodesia. On 2 January 1896 the Raiders raised the white flag at Doornkop. Then they were hauled off to Pretoria prison.

Salisbury happened to be cut off from the world during those crucial days by a break in the telegraph line. When the line was repaired on 3 January, a sheaf of Reuter news telegrams were read out to a merry group of Rhodesians celebrating the New Year. One of the group later described the electric effect:

The impetuous start of the police from Pitsani; their forced march through the Transvaal; their hopeless battle against superior odds at Krugersdorp, and then the final paralysing account of their surrender of Doornkop. Good heavens! Jameson, Willoughby, White – all our police officers, prisoners, at the mercy of Kruger! ... Deeply and bitterly we cursed the treachery of the Committee [of would-be revolutionaries] at Johannesburg. With dreadful misgivings we wondered whether the Doctor and other gallant leaders had been shot as conspirators. Our dinner party was forgotten.[15]

What was also forgotten in all the excitement was how vulnerable Rhodes had left his colony by taking the Rhodesian police for the Raid. There were now only forty-eight policemen left in Rhodesia, and this had not escaped the sharp ears of the Ndebele. Jameson, their conqueror, was defeated and a prisoner; Rhodes, the white chief, was being attacked on every side, and Matabeleland itself was now a prize for re-taking.

By mid-March 1896 the rinderpest was advancing on Bulawayo so rapidly that the authorities were afraid of famine, for there would be no oxen to transport grain. Frederick Selous, the celebrated hunter now employed as the agent for a 200,000-acre land-and-gold company at nearby Essexvale, was one of the official inspectors appointed to stop the spread of the disease. On Monday 23 March he rode to Dawson's store at the ford of the Umzingwani, twenty-five miles south-east of Bulawayo, where he was told the news of a fracas nearby; two native policemen had been set upon and shot by Ndebele on the night of 20 March.

Selous was not alarmed. He had hunted for twenty years in the wilds, and knew the Ndebele as well as any European. His instincts told him that the Ndebele were reconciled to the Company's rule, though he knew there were prophecies of a coming disaster for the white man, purporting to come from a 'Mlimo', a god who spoke from a cave in the Matopo Hills. He had also noticed that one of Lobengula's old *indunas*, a 'gentle-mannered savage'[16] called Umlugulu, had taken a close interest in the fate of Jameson, repeatedly questioning Selous about the Raid and its repercussions. But who cared what Mlimo said or Umlugulu thought? The point was that the mass of the people were perfectly submissive, despite their losses of land and cattle. This was not only what Selous had seen for himself; it was confirmed by others who knew the country, including the veteran missionary, Charles Helm, who had persuaded Lobengula to grant the Rudd concession seven years earlier.

When he returned to his thatched homestead at Essexvale the next day, 24 March, Selous found everything as usual. Some friendly Ndebele, from a village which had formerly been a military kraal, came over to borrow axes – apparently to strengthen their cattle fences. His young English wife, new to Africa, lent them the tools, and they chatted about the shooting of the two policemen nearby. His wife told Selous to tell the men that it was folly, for the white men would punish them. The villagers laughed. 'How can the white men punish them? Where are the white police? There are none left in this country.'[17]

Later that day Selous and his wife heard an ominous story of the killing of a native commissioner on the other side of the Malungwani Hills, his throat cut by one of his own men. Selous stayed up that night, his gun and cartridge belt beside him.

In the morning it seemed quiet, until one of his natives reported a group of Ndebele had driven twenty or thirty of the Company's cattle from a nearby kraal, threatening to kill anyone who stopped them. The men were armed with guns or assegais, and they wore white ox tails round their left arms and necks, meaning that they were on the warpath. A second, larger group of cattle was driven off. Something serious was afoot. Yet even now Selous had no real appreciation of the danger.

Before dark he rode into Bulawayo, meaning to take his wife to safety before returning with an armed posse to recover the stolen cattle. In the capital he found a scene of confusion. It appeared that a general insurrection had begun. In fact that week, all over the country, about 200 Europeans and at least as many black servants were hacked to death with spears, knives and axes. By 30 March, not a white man, woman, or child was left alive in the outlying districts of Matabeleland.

The survivors, about 2,000 Europeans with several thousand loyal blacks, built sand-bagged laagers in the four main towns: Bulawayo, Gwelo, Bellingwe and Mangwe. The Ndebele had failed to cut the telegraph lines; in due course relief could be expected from outside. But the details of the atrocities against women and children left the Europeans aghast. When Selous had ridden into Bulawayo he had felt a certain chivalry towards the insurgents. If they wanted to try to recover their country, 'why shouldn't they try', if they thought 'the game worth the candle'. Now he had heard of women and children hacked to death by their household servants. To kill them like that was a kind of 'sacrilege'.[18] Rage seized him. He wanted to kill the murderers with his own hands, to shoot them down like dogs. What had possessed these docile black subjects to turn and rend their masters?

Even now, a century later, the origins of this great revolt – the first nationwide war of independence in any of the new colonies created during the Scramble – are contested by historians. It is not clear how large a role the oracular cult of 'Mlimo' (or the Shona cult of 'Mwari') played in instigating the revolt. Perhaps the priests of Mwari fomented the rebellion for their own reasons and made a 'marriage of convenience'[19] with the secular chiefs. Or perhaps the oracular priest most influential in the revolt, Mkwati, was important only because one of his wives was the daughter of Uwini, the secular leader in the Gwelo district.

What is clear is that the primary role fell to Lobengula's *indunas*, the great men of the old regime. They could represent the grievances of both the Ndebele aristocracy, and many of the Amaholi who had been absorbed by them. Their objective was brutally simple: to get the Company off their backs by massacring all whites – men, women and children.

For a few days success seemed to be within their grasp. Their military organization was intact, and they still had 2,000 Martini-Henry rifles, hidden since Jameson's invasion. The white community had had no warning of the rising and were virtually undefended, once Jameson rode off with the police. But success needed more than modern rifles, it needed some plan of campaign. Apparently the explosion had been planned for the night of 29 March, the night of a ceremony called the Big Dance, and of the full moon. For some reason it went off at half-cock a week early. Worse, from the insurgents' point of view, there was too much reliance on the power of Mlimo or Mwari to turn the white man's bullets to water and too little thought of strategy.

There was no attempt by the Ndebele to co-ordinate the rising with their Shona neighbours, presumably because of the long history of mutual antagonism; no plan to go straight for the centre of white power, Bulawayo, while the town was still defenceless; above all, no attempt to ambush coaches and wagons on the road from Bechuanaland and the Cape, along which food could be transported and, in due course, imperial troops, sent to the rescue by the white Queen.

For all these reasons, the initiative slipped from the scattered armies of Ndebele after the first week of the rising. During April, the 600 armed white volunteers in Bulawayo, outnumbered by perhaps fifteen to one, gradually gained confidence. In action they fought as mounted riflemen and this gave them far more mobility than their enemies, despite their own desperate shortage of horses. They could also shoot straighter and had plenty of ammunition. In April they won a series of small tactical successes, driving the Ndebele temporarily back across the Umguza river into the bush. Fighting was merciless on both sides. The volunteers lost about twenty killed and fifty wounded. No white man survived capture by the Ndebele. On their part the volunteers were eager to avenge the murders of women and children. When the enemy turned to flee, they shot them down in hundreds. They took few prisoners and usually executed them after interrogation. This grim policy seemed to work.

By the end of April, the rebels' confidence in Mlimo was ebbing. Now they were mainly on the defensive. On 11 May the volunteers were strong enough to push a column of 300 men eastwards to join hands with the 600 fellow Rhodesians, including Cecil Rhodes himself, who comprised the relief column marching from Salisbury. The combined force rode triumphantly into Bulawayo at the end of May.

At first it appeared that imperial reinforcements would only be an embarrassment, and an extra expense which the Company could ill afford. The Company had tried to raise its own amateur force in the Cape. The British government had intervened, insisting that a local imperial officer, Major Herbert Plumer, take temporary charge of the Matabeleland Relief Force. Plumer's column – 700 white volunteers raised in Mafeking (including about 200 of Jameson's Raiders who had now been shipped back to South Africa), plus 200 blacks from the Transvaal and the Cape – did not reach Bulawayo until the end of May, beaten to the post by Rhodes's relief column from Salisbury. A week later, the first imperial officers arrived from Britain: Colonel Robert Baden-Powell and General Sir Frederick Carrington, a veteran of small wars in Africa, who took supreme command. Baden-Powell was terrified he was too late for the 'fun'.[20]

He need not have worried. By mid-June a new disaster hit Rhodesia. Encouraged by the initial successes of their ex-masters, and the departure of Rhodes and the Salisbury relief column, the downtrodden Shona rose in revolt, adopting the same grim methods as the Ndebele. Again the whites had no inkling of danger. Over 100 men, women and children were murdered in outlying parts of Mashonaland. The insurrection was spread by spirit mediums, who promised the Shona immunity from white bullets. But unlike the Ndebele and the Zulus, the Shona were not a centralized monarchy with a warrior caste and a ferocious talent for offensive war. Mashonaland was split into numerous small clans used to feuding against each other. Soon the rising lost its momentum. The Salisbury relief column hurried back to Salisbury. More imperial officers arrived from England, complete with a column of British regulars and mounted infantry rushed up with Portuguese help from the port of Beira.

*   *   *

Meanwhile, in London, damning new stories about Chamberlain's collusion in the Raid continued to reach the press, which his Liberal ex-colleagues, such as Harcourt, generously refused to believe. It was decided to make Harcourt chairman of an all-party committee of inquiry, on which the Colonial Secretary would serve – and to which he would also give evidence. By comparison with the Raid, the rebellions in Rhodesia now rated little space in the press.

The big questions were these. Was Chamberlain guilty of collusion with Rhodes – as Rhodes's and Jameson's supporters claimed? Would Chamberlain now be forced to resign, bringing Salisbury and the Unionists down with him? Or if he was innocent, would he turn on his accusers and cancel Rhodes's charter, aborting colonial Rhodesia and creating a new 'imperial' colony of 'Zambezia'? Or was there a third possibility – that Chamberlain was at least technically guilty so that Rhodes would be able to square him? In other words, would there be a real inquiry or a cover-up?

The all-party inquiry occupied months of 1897 and was nicknamed, with good reason, 'the Lying-in-State at Westminster'. The Liberal Members were convinced that they could trust Chamberlain's word when he put his hand on his heart and swore he had absolutely no idea of Rhodes's plan for the Raid.

In fact, Chamberlain had been sufficiently guilty of collusion to have decided in 1896 to make a deal with Rhodes. Chamberlain agreed to shield Rhodes and not to cancel the Charter, or even to reform the Chartered Company, apart from making Rhodes resign as Managing Director. Rhodes agreed to shield Chamberlain by not producing the 'missing telegrams' to the Inquiry. (These were the seven telegrams sent to South Africa by Rhodes's agents in 1895 that documented the role of Chamberlain and the CO in the planning of the fatuous revolution and the reckless Raid.)

The charges against Chamberlain by his enemies were – and remain – serious. He was accused of collusion in a criminal plan to use Rhodesian police – that is, British troops from the Crown Colony – to overthrow a neighbouring friendly state, the Transvaal. Jameson was sent to prison for making the attempt. Now it was the job of the Colonial Secretary to be well briefed about plots by British subjects. The government might have to send troops to Johannesburg in due course to sort out the mess. A contingency plan had already been secretly agreed by Chamberlain's Liberal predecessor, Lord Ripon, that had been arranged by the then High Commissioner, Sir Henry Loch. But it was one thing to be ready to intervene *after* law and order had broken down in a spontaneous rising of oppressed British subjects, and quite another to promote a conspiracy and help arrange for Rhodesian troops to be sent in *simultaneously* with the rising. This was the charge against Chamberlain, and the seven 'missing telegrams' would seem to confirm it.

Only one of these telegrams has been published in full, but the contents of the others have come to light, amplified by private evidence from the CO. It appears that Chamberlain had agreed to provide the base for the Raiders in the Bechuanaland protectorate, knowing 'unofficially' what purpose Jameson intended it for. (Missing telegram dated 13 August 1895: 'Chamberlain will do anything to assist ... provided he officially does not know of your plan.')[21] Second, he had interfered in the timing of the revolution and the raid designed to support it. (Missing telegram dated 7 November 1895: 'Secretary of State says you must allow decent interval and delay fireworks for a fortnight.')[22]

Such was the evidence suppressed by Rhodes to spare Chamberlain's blushes. In public, Chamberlain gave a eulogy of Rhodes's high sense of honour. In private, he said that he was being 'blackmailed' by Rhodes and his gang. The imperial statesman had been outmanoeuvred by the colonial buccaneer. Chamberlain's bold plan for an imperial federation in South Africa would have to be postponed for years. President Kruger and the Boers could now deal with the Uitlanders as they chose. They were now backed by the Afrikaners at the Cape, aghast at Rhodes's attempt at a shotgun marriage. In Rhodesia, Rhodes was still in complete control, though he had resigned from the Chartered Company's board. His Company would continue to treat its black subjects hardly better than beasts of burden, safe from interference by Grandmama.

Thanks to the deal with Rhodes, and the naivety of his ex-colleagues like Harcourt, Chamberlain had saved his own bacon at the Inquiry. He had lost the race for the veld, at least for the moment. Now he turned to the two other parts of the Scramble: the race for the Niger and the Nile.

CHAPTER 28

Calling Hanotaux's Bluff

London, Paris and West Africa
1 January 1896–14 June 1898

'We ought – even at the cost of war – to keep the
hinterland of the Gold Coast, Lagos and the Niger
territories ... I do not think we ought to yield a jot
of threats.'

Joseph Chamberlain, the British Colonial Secretary,
September/December 1897

Meanwhile Chamberlain's discomfiture had not unduly disturbed his chief,
Lord Salisbury, presiding at either of his Downing Street offices, the
Foreign Secretary's or the Prime Minister's.

Lord Salisbury had anxieties of his own. He was on holiday on New Year's
Day 1896, when the windows of Hatfield were first rattled by the news of the
Raid. There followed that wild telegram from Kaiser Wilhelm II to President
Kruger, congratulating him on defeating the English raiders. The telegram,
which made the Raid an international incident, was well received in most parts
of the Continent and provoked a corresponding howl of rage from the English
press, followed by a *cri de coeur* from Balmoral. How dare William interfere
in the Transvaal, which was subject to *her* suzerainty? The Queen was eager to
hear the advice of her Prime Minister. She was already distraught at the news
that fever had struck down poor 'Liko', her son-in-law, Prince Henry, now
serving on a British punitive expedition in Ashanti. But how to deal with this
'outrageous' insult from her grandson, the German Emperor?

She had already sent William a sharp note to tell him what a 'painful
impression' the telegram to Kruger had made in England. Back came the sheepish
reply to his 'dear Grandmama'; he had meant no harm. He had acted only in
the interests of 'peace' – and of German financiers in the Transvaal. The Queen
sent Lord Salisbury copies of what she called 'this lame and illogical'[1] reply.
The Prime Minister replied soothingly that the German Emperor now saw the
error of his ways and to avoid further unpleasantness, Her Majesty should
'accept all his explanations without enquiring too narrowly into the truth of
them'.[2]

Less easy to answer was a second *cri de coeur* from the Queen, one that went
to the core of Salisbury's foreign policy. How were they to respond to the
dangerous new world of the 1890s? As she put it, 'affairs are so different from
what they so used to be'.[3] The advent of the global telegraph, mass-circulation

newspapers and household suffrage seemed to have ended the age of gentlemen. International statesmen echoed the malevolent tone of the popular press. Fists were shaken at Britain by President Grover Cleveland of America (denouncing Britain for refusing arbitration in the Venezuela/British Guiana frontier dispute), by France (in a state of chronic indignation at Britain's occupation of Egypt), and by Russia (threatening India and egging on the French to take more active measures against England's intransigence in Egypt). Was it not time to abandon Britain's traditional foreign policy of isolation – 'splendid isolation'[4] as it was called by Chamberlain in a speech on 21 January, borrowing the phrase from a Canadian politician – in favour of joining some kind of alliance?

Salisbury respectfully pointed out to the Queen that this was indeed the purpose of the Kaiser's belligerent telegram. For months Wilhelm had been trying to 'frighten England into joining the Triple Alliance' (the one originally forged by Bismarck to tie up Austria and Italy and play them off against Russia). But this would involve a military commitment which Her Majesty would find impossible 'because the English people would never consent to go to war for a cause in which England was not manifestly interested'. Isolation, Salisbury agreed, had its dangers, and what could be more absurd than to call isolation, in the new catchphrase, 'splendid'? But would it not be still more dangerous to be 'dragged into wars which do not concern us'?[5]

Salisbury's own policy, which had been the policy of the Foreign Office ever since he was a child, was to preserve the balance of Europe without succumbing to the embrace of any other Power. But the Foreign Secretary now had to keep his own balance while engaged in a kind of top-hatted, frock-coated dance, leaning first to one Power, then to another. No one knew the steps of this intricate dance better than Lord Salisbury, and he had no intention of letting the Kaiser's boorish telegram force him to change. On the contrary, it would teach the Kaiser a lesson to see England leaning a bit closer to France. He mischievously let drop the hint to the Germans that he was toying with a plan to evacuate Egypt, and take the first step towards an *entente cordiale* with the French.

In fact, this was the very last thing Salisbury was planning. There could be no warmth between France and England while England insisted on staying in Egypt. And stay she must; that was agreed by every British politician, Liberal, Liberal Unionist and Tory – except a few left-overs from the old Gladstonian rump and the Irish party. England should go further, and – in due course – re-conquer the Sudan. This was a most positive part of Salisbury's global strategy. To safeguard Egypt, the whole upper Nile valley must be safeguarded in turn. He knew this would displease the French and perhaps even start a 'row' (the current euphemism for war) between England and France. They would have to cross that bridge when they came to it.

But in January 1896 it seemed premature to talk of reconquering the Sudan. A series of electric storms flickered on the horizon, in the Dardanelles, in India, in China. This was hardly the time to go cap-in-hand to the House of Commons trying to raise money for an African war. As for tapping the generosity of the

Caisse (in effect, the Egyptian taxpayer), the idea would be turned down flat by the other Powers.

Fortunately, there did not seem any hurry to deal with the Sudan, even though British intelligence expected French military expeditions to the upper Nile from both sides of Africa – from French Somaliland on the Red Sea, and from the French Congo on the Atlantic. It was claimed that each group planned to advance to Fashoda, north of the great Sudd (the 100-mile long barrier of swamp), in order to link together the two parts of the French African empire. But for months nothing had been heard of either expedition. Perhaps they had fallen victim to the Mahdists, now in decline, who were unwittingly playing a useful role. For a decade they had kept out the French, and kept the place warm for the British. In a couple of years the Uganda railway would be running, and British troops would be able to advance to Fashoda from Uganda.

One mysterious feature of the situation was the role played by Leopold, the King of the Belgians. In December 1895 Lord Salisbury revealed to the Queen's Private Secretary the proposals made to him by the King, in all seriousness: England was to help Leopold extend the Congo State all the way to Khartoum. Salisbury had done his best to avoid listening to this nonsense. Britain apart, the King's own ministers were apparently dead against it. But the King insisted on elaborating his plan. The British should leave Egypt and

> ... as the price of that policy and the favour we should thereby win from France, we should be able, without spending a shilling or losing a man, to annex China to the Indian Empire ... [but] we were first to persuade the Khedive to give a concession of the valley of the Nile from Khartoum upwards 'to some person who was *au courant* of the affairs of Africa'.[6]

Leopold was too modest to mention who that person was.

Salisbury recognized that the King was up to 'some mischief'.[7] As he was believed to be nearly bankrupt, Salisbury supposed that he was trying to sell a reversion of the Congo to France, and wanted to sweeten the sale by including some rights in the Nile valley. But as usual the King had to be humoured, or he might be driven into the arms of the French. The Queen's comment was blunter. Poor Leopold! He must have taken leave of his senses.

Meanwhile, until the Uganda railway was ready, the policy for the upper Nile was to let sleeping dogs lie. It was a 'waiting game', as Salisbury himself called it. And, if an *entente cordiale* was impossible, why not at least a *détente* with the French?

So by mid-January 1896 the Queen had the answer to her second *cri de coeur*. Britain would have to remain isolated, perhaps dangerously isolated. But it was the Cabinet's wish 'in the present state of things to settle as many questions with France as possible'.[8] First on the list was the share-out of great slices of West Africa, on which subject there had been no progress since the Anglo-French Agreement of 1890. In January 1896 the Anglo-French talks on West Africa were resumed. To Salisbury there now seemed a real chance of clearing these tiresome disputes from the scene – provided he could counter the objections of the Cabinet member most closely concerned, Joseph Chamberlain, the Colonial Secretary.

In dealing with Chamberlain, the Prime Minister often found his store of patience dangerously depleted. It was partly Chamberlain's style. The aggressive, not to say jingo tone, so valuable to the Unionists at the last election, grated on a patrician like Lord Salisbury, trained to conceal his own ambitions behind a cynical detachment. But there were also differences of principle. Salisbury's strength in negotiation was that his over-riding concern in foreign affairs was strategic. On other issues he was a pragmatist. He was delighted to be generous in West Africa – to give away territory in Lagos, the Gold Coast, or even in Goldie's 'sphere' on the Niger – if it would help him tighten his grip on the Nile. Chamberlain, an ex-businessman, had taken up the opposite cause, the defence of the West African lobby. For years this small band of British officials and merchants, braving death in the malarial swamps of Lagos and the Gold Coast, had sent querulous reports to Whitehall begging for imperial grants and loans. Their predicament was indeed serious.

Ever since 1870 the price of wild palm oil, the staple export, had melted away, owing to a glut on the world market. The only hope of balancing the colony's books was to develop other staple exports. Progress had been made in growing crops like cotton, coffee and indigo, for which there was a healthy market in Europe. But this was scientific agriculture. It needed more resources than the Stone Age canoes and slimy jungle tracks which carried the trade in wild palm oil. It needed Steam Age development – harbours, roads, railways and the education to show Africans how to use them. Most important of all, new exports depended on securing the hinterland for trade. At present the bush country behind the coastal swamps was subject to a double threat: from paralysis due to tribal warfare and encroachment by French empire-builders from adjoining colonies. This was the SOS from the traders in the Crown Colonies of the Gold Coast and Lagos, and Chamberlain had pledged himself to be their champion.

In November 1895 he warned his Cabinet colleagues that private enterprise was inadequate for opening up Britain's vast 'undeveloped estates'.[9] The state must lead the way with money and troops. Then, without consulting the Prime Minister, he announced the punitive expedition to Ashanti, the hinterland north of the Gold Coast (the expedition which later cost the life of Prince Henry).

It seemed fortunate for the unity of the Cabinet that the Jameson Raid swept across Chamberlain's desk a fortnight before the start of the Anglo-French talks on West Africa. Chamberlain would have no time to promote the West African lobby when he was fighting for his own political life. But as it happened, the Anglo-French talks had only just got under way when a storm from the wilds of East Africa brought them to an abrupt conclusion.

The storm was that bloody defeat inflicted by the Emperor Menelik on General Baratieri's 20,000 soldiers at Adowa. The news of the Italian disaster on 1 March reached Europe two days later. Within ten days Salisbury, as already mentioned, had decided to save Italy and 'plant the foot of Egypt further up the Nile'.[10]

He would abandon the waiting game and take the first step towards reconquering the Sudan. Here was a diplomatic opportunity that might never come again. The Italians were begging the British to help their isolated garrison at Kassala and were furious with the Germans for leaving them in the lurch. Moreover, to save the Triple Alliance, of which Italy was the weakest member, the Kaiser was now desperate to patch up his quarrel with Salisbury. Late on the evening of 3 March, he called on the British Embassy in Berlin himself and explained how France was the villain of the piece for it had backed Menelik with French rifles. Now there was a plot between France and Russia to strip England of its Empire. So England must save the Italians at Kassala.

Salisbury politely agreed to co-operate by creating a diversion. He would order the Sirdar of the Egyptian army, Sir Herbert Kitchener, to make a cautious advance up the Nile beyond the Egyptian border at Wadi Halfa. He would not have to ask the House of Commons for a penny; the Egyptian taxpayer would oblige, for a majority of the Caisse (the International Debt Commission) would be in favour now that Germany, Italy and Austria were backing Britain.

So it all turned out. Despite the misgivings of many of Salisbury's Cabinet, including Chamberlain – who felt that for once the Prime Minister was being a little impetuous – Kitchener's army was ordered to advance as far as Dongola, 200 miles up the Nile into the Sudan, retracing the steps of Gordon's last journey, and of Wolseley's inglorious withdrawal.

Talk of taking Khartoum and avenging Gordon was still premature. There was no money in the Egyptian Treasury to pay for the advance beyond Dongola. The advance from the south – Uganda – was still the only practical way to re-conquer the Sudan. But the Uganda railway would not be ready for several years. Meanwhile, 'we must trust to our luck', as Salisbury told Queen Victoria, that the French did not get to Fashoda before them.

By May 1896 the Niger talks had broken down. The news that the English were invading the Sudan sealed their fate. As the fumbling French ministry of Léon Bourgeois was replaced by that of the protectionist leader, Jules Méline, the brief spell of *détente* was replaced by bitter recriminations.

*   *   *

Gabriel Hanotaux, diplomatist and man of letters, a silk stock knotted jauntily at his wing collar, returned to the Quai d'Orsay in April for a third term as Minister for Foreign Affairs. After six months out of office, he was hungry for power and the freedom to exercise it. If only he could be a fixture at the Quai, with a real chance to make consistent foreign policy like his hero, Cardinal Richelieu. But in the politics of the Third Republic, now dominated by the second outbreak of the Dreyfus Affair, no one was indispensable, least of all an ex-civil servant like himself, a man without political supporters. And Hanotaux found that his policy was continually being undermined by the fire-eaters at the Ministry of the Colonies.

The more Hanotaux looked at Captain Marchand's secret instructions, drafted by the Ministry of the Colonies at the Pavillon de Flore in February, the less he liked them.

This was a time, he recognized, of rising anglophobia among the French public. The Jameson Raid added its poison to the atmosphere, as did the British invasion of the Sudan. Already there were painful differences with England in most other parts of the globe – from Nigeria to Siam, from the Congo to Abyssinia and the upper Nile. But it was Egypt – so rich with associations from France's noblest epoch, Napoleon's – that presented the most explosive problem for diplomacy. Hanotaux felt that he had to advance over ground which was 'burning and crumbling and mined'.[11] It was at this dangerous moment that his colleagues at the Ministry of Colonies were recklessly provoking England.

The hidden agenda for Marchand's mission, already mentioned, illustrated the ministry's own irresponsibility. In September 1895, as Foreign Minister in Ribot's government, Hanotaux had interviewed Captain Marchand at the Quai. Hanotaux had not committed himself, though the plan seemed relatively harmless; the captain was to advance no further than the Bahr al-Ghazal and carefully to avoid provoking the English by raising the tricolour or claiming any territory for France. The point of the mission was only to give France the right to attend a conference on the Nile valley whenever that should be. If Marchand met the English, the two missions would salute each other with 'all urbanity and correctness'.[12] This plan had been drafted by Marchand and duly authorized by Hanotaux's successor at the Quai, Marcellin Berthelot, in November 1895. However, Berthelot was a simple-minded chemist and was hoodwinked by the Ministry of Colonies. The instructions drafted by them in February, unknown to Berthelot, were far more extreme: to advance beyond the Sudd to Fashoda itself. In fact the advance was to be a 'raid' on Fashoda (that English word, inauspicious as it was, had been borrowed by the fire-eaters in the Ministry of Colonies). Marchand was also to make 'serious alliances', claiming territory from those local chiefs who would give France 'indisputable title'.[13] With these provocative orders, Marchand's advance guard had sailed for Africa a few days before Hanotaux returned to the Quai and discovered the Ministry of Colonies plan.

To conceal the plan would have created a political storm and might have been the end of Hanotaux. He did what he could to cut the new Minister of Colonies, André Lebon, down to size. He diluted the orders and tried to take out their sting. The new orders, signed in June 1896, made no mention of Fashoda, or of claiming any territory. All they said was that Marchand should 'strictly maintain'[14] current policy, whatever that meant.

Perhaps Hanotaux hoped Marchand would never reach the Nile. After all, there were hundreds of miles of unexplored bush in the watershed between Congo and Nile. If he did struggle over the watershed, and avoided being killed by the Dervishes, he would fortunately be too weak to do much harm. To save food – and also to avoid provoking the Dervishes – Marchand had applied for only 200 men, mostly Senegalese soldiers and boatmen. He could hardly do much damage to Anglo-French relations with a wretched expedition like that – provided he obeyed orders. Hanotaux was almost reconciled to the idea. Years later he was supposed to have told Marchand that he was to be a 'pistol shot on the Nile'.[15] But his actual policy was only to establish a French presence in the Bahr al-Ghazal, to give a gentle pinprick to that distant part of Egypt's underbelly.

In general, Hanotaux pinned his faith on using the new international alignments of the Powers to squeeze concessions out of England. The Franco-Russian alliance should have been the jewel in his crown. But despite the high hopes raised by Lobanov, Russia's anglophobic Foreign Minister, no concerted plan emerged from the talks at St Petersburg. The best that Hanotaux could do was to work with the Russians to sabotage a half-million-pound loan from the Egyptian Caisse to pay for Kitchener's advance to Dongola. The French claimed (and the international courts eventually confirmed they were right) that the Caisse needed a unanimous decision, not simply the majority formed by the English, Germans and the other two members of the Triple Alliance, Austria and Italy, to sanction this large sum. In due course, the British taxpayer had to put up the money after all. But Hanotaux failed to persuade Lobanov of the urgency of joint action in the Red Sea; and Germany rebuffed Russian efforts at co-operation.

In October the Tsar visited Paris and this seemed to offer Hanotaux his chance. The Russians duly agreed that the two countries would 'together make very serious efforts to join up with Menelik'.[16] In practice, however, the efforts were anything but serious. What shocked Hanotaux was the discovery that the Minister of Colonies, André Lebon, had seized on the supposed Russian support to put extra teeth into the Marchand expedition. All Hanotaux had agreed was for Léonce Lagarde, the Colonial Governor of French Somaliland, to discuss border problems with Menelik's right-hand man, Ras Makonnen of Ḥarar. But it later emerged that the Ministry for Colonies had issued its own orders. Lagarde was to push on with the Franco-Ethiopian railway, a crack-brained scheme to link the White Nile with the Red Sea by way of the mountain fastness of Ethiopia. More relevant, Lagarde was to help launch two French expeditions to the White Nile from the Red Sea. According to their orders, it was essential that these should arrive in time to join hands with Marchand at Fashoda. The Ministry of Colonies had also secretly told Lagarde to persuade Menelik to push his army right down to the east bank of the White Nile, which he could claim as a border with the new French 'possessions' on the west bank. Lagarde was pleased to oblige. Without sanction of Hanotaux or the Cabinet, he signed an agreement with Menelik to share out part of the Egyptian Sudan. The Emperor promised to give every support to the two French expeditions. In return, France recognized that the empire of Ethiopia had moved hundreds of miles west – right up to the banks of the White Nile.

In March 1897 the plan was put to the Cabinet. Hanotaux was no Richelieu;

he swallowed his pride and weakly accepted the Cabinet's ruling that this astonishing new plan must go ahead. Three French expeditions would converge at Fashoda – Marchand's, Clochette's and Bonvalot's – and at their side would be the wild, invincible army of Menelik.

No wonder André Lebon's views on foreign affairs seemed as crude to Hanotaux as Chamberlain's seemed to Salisbury. Both Ministers of Colonies belonged to the aggressive new school of imperialism that had pushed its way to the surface in the final feverish stages of the Scramble. National prestige was identified with the size of an empire, so painting the map red or blue had now become an end in itself, irrespective of the productive capacity of the land or its strategic value. To the old school, it might seem an irrational throw-back to the time when only land had conferred prestige, and all the richest and most powerful men in the Western world were owners of great estates. But politically it made sense in the 1890s. The new mass electorates welcomed each colonial acquisition with a bourgeois pride, and did not bother to ask whether it would bring either commercial profit or strategic advantage.

Lebon himself believed that there was money as well as prestige to be got from West Africa. His hero was Gambetta. Lebon, too, had shadowy links with overseas business – for example, he was soon to become a director of the railway at Dahomey. But his political concern was expansion, irrespective of cost or profit. The most important prize was the upper Nile. By taking Fashoda, France could take all the Bahr al-Ghazal, and so drive a wedge of French territory between Egypt and Uganda, a wedge that would cripple the 'Anglo-Saxons' at a stroke. It would be the end of their arrogant north-south axis, Cecil Rhodes's dream of an 'All-Red' route from Cape-to-Cairo. Instead, it could join the Red Sea to the French Congo and beyond by using the railway through Ethiopia yet to be built, and would provide the missing link to a magnificent French empire, running east-west across the whole width of the continent.

In parallel with the three French columns fired like torpedoes towards Fashoda, Lebon fired off salvoes in West Africa. A powerful new French base there was Dahomey, acquired after the conquest of King Behanzin in 1892. Lebon's aim was a *fait accompli* in West Africa as in the Sudan. He would force the British to accept French territorial gains by right of occupation, rather than by right of treaty. It will be recalled that 'effective occupation' – away from the coast – was *not* one of the requirements of the Berlin Act of 1885. But would the British dare argue against it? After all, conventional diplomacy had failed to settle matters. It was now six years since Salisbury had hatched the Anglo-French agreement and still the Niger talks had come to nothing.

There remained three overwhelming questions in the Niger territory and the country to the west. First, who was to take the neighbouring hinterlands of the Ivory Coast and the Gold Coast, those vast, tangled half-unexplored hills between the rainforests of the Atlantic and the semi-deserts of the upper Niger? Second, would the French strike east from Dahomey and snatch Borgu, the western part of Nigeria claimed by Goldie and the Niger Company, but not included in the Anglo-French agreement? Third, would even the Anglo-French agreement itself be respected by the French; or would they try to swoop down from the north and cut the Say-Barruwa line drawn to protect Sokoto and Goldie's northern frontier?

The race for the hinterlands of the Ivory Coast and the Gold Coast was confused and slow-moving. As we shall see, the British expedition to Ashanti was successful, as far as it went. But Ashanti only extended a couple of hundred miles from the coast, and British control remained nominal. Further north, the rainforest gave place to the wooded mountains of Upper Volta. It was there, to the north-west, that Samori, the great Dyula warlord expelled by the French from the western Sudan, had made his lair, carving out a vast new empire in the northern hinterland of the Ivory Coast and Gold Coast. No doubt Lebon recognized that Samori would welcome a British protectorate; nothing would please him better than to be protected by the British against the French, and allowed to buy the modern rifles he so desperately needed. But Lebon was pleased to find that the British resisted the temptation. The reason was obvious; those tangled hills were too poor to support legitimate trade. Samori's main export was a thin, shackled line of slaves. The British left Samori to Lebon. (By September 1898, Samori's new empire succumbed to a French invasion, and Africa's most formidable guerrilla leader was shipped off to die in exile in Gabon, a few months after Lebon himself had fallen from grace.)

The race for the Niger, by contrast, was soon to be one of the most celebrated episodes of the 'steeplechase'. Lebon organized an attack on Goldie's empire from west, north-west and north. Effective occupation now proved a most effective test of sovereignty, for the French could show that many of Goldie's claims to control the area were a sham. A French officer, Lieutenant Hourst, took a boat down the Niger from the desert of Timbuctu, all the way to the Bussa rapids, and then travelled down to Leaba, without finding a trace of British influence. Other expeditions set out from the rainforests of Dahomey, some to the north to link up with the Sudan, others to push into Borgu.

By February 1897 a French officer, Lieutenant Bretonnet, had established a post at Bussa, where the English had treaty rights. To the north another officer, Lieutenant Cazemajou, signed a treaty with the Emir of Argungu, east of the Niger. Both initiatives were acts of defiance directed at Britain. Bussa provided a test case for effective occupation; Argungu apparently threatened the agreement of 1890, as the Emir was alleged to be a dependant of the Khalifate of Sokoto. (The Khalifa himself did not waste time on legal arguments. He had Cazemajon murdered.) But meanwhile Lebon neither endorsed nor disowned the high-handed behaviour of his officers. The new French claims would come in handy when the two countries got down to the Niger talks once again.

* * *

In London, Joe Chamberlain was prepared to meet Lebon's challenge head on. If the French could play at effective occupation, so could the British.

He had already anticipated the French challenge in the southern part of the hinterland of the Gold Coast. It was there, into the pestilential forest of Ashanti, that he had despatched a British column in the dry season of 1895–6. The column marched triumphantly into the capital, Kumasi, without firing a shot. They found some skulls and other traces of human sacrifice, a convenient discovery since their official object was to end the bloodthirsty reign of King Prempeh. But the main aim of the expedition was not humanitarian; Chamberlain wanted to confirm British supremacy over Ashanti and pre-empt French encroachments. King Prempeh and his principal chiefs were packed off in exile to Sierra Leone, and his people fined a war indemnity of 50,000 ounces in gold. Then the column marched back to the coast, leaving a British Resident in a newly-built fort. The British garrison might be nominal, and the Ashanti symbol of power – the Golden Stool – was left in the hands of the Ashanti. But the French challenge had been answered, and the base secured for future expansion.

However, when Chamberlain turned his mind from the Gold Coast to the Niger, imperial intervention of this decisive kind was out of the question. The British government had farmed out the country to Goldie's Niger Company, and soon the recriminations between Chamberlain and Goldie were even more violent than those between Chamberlain and the French.

The root of the problem was that Goldie's company had been chartered to act as a government, and told to guard a large empire in the interests of Britain. This was an undefined 'sphere' which ran hundreds of miles behind the commercial frontier based on river trade. But in reality the Company was only a trading company. It did not have the cash to fight wars or occupy unprofitable territory – effectively or ineffectively – and could defend itself only with paper claims. In 1894–5, Goldie had hired Lugard, as mentioned earlier, to defend Borgu by making treaties with the ruler of Nikki and other towns. Lugard had done wonders, given his small expedition. But he had not had the means to leave behind at Nikki even the smallest Company outpost. So the moment he marched back towards the Niger, the French marched in from Dahomey, first Decoeur, then Ballot, the Governor of Dahomey. They formally disputed Lugard's treaties, installed military posts, and penetrated up to Bussa itself. After the collapse of the Anglo-French talks in the spring of 1896, the situation was critical.

If Goldie had been able to concentrate all his strength against the French in Borgu, he might have been able to counter these encroachments. But he was engaged on too many fronts, defending the heart of the Company's sphere as well as its far-flung frontiers. French *tirailleurs* were sniffing at the shadowy frontier of Sokoto. There were also the rebel Brassmen of the Niger delta, the men who had been driven to desperation by the Company's trade monopoly in 1895, and burnt Akassa to the ground. There were more *tirailleurs* defying the Company's treaty with Bussa, and two Islamic warrior states, Nupe and its neighbour Ilorin, challenging Goldie's authority on the middle Niger. Finally, there was Ilorin's long-standing enemy and the Niger Company's sternest critic, Governor Carter, the British Governor of Lagos.

As a firm expansionist Governor Carter had the ear of the Colonial Secretary. A few months before Chamberlain took over the Colonial Office, Carter had pressed for permission to 'destroy the headquarters of this band of robbers'[17] at Ilorin. In 1895 and 1896 he repeated the request, and proposed annexing Ilorin to Lagos.

Carter was not simply a reckless empire-builder. Ilorin and its more powerful ally, Nupe, were militant Islamic states, carved out of Hausaland by Fulani nobles in the 1820s during the great jihad. In the 1880s no one had tried to stop them raiding for slaves among the Yoruba in Ibadan, across the northern part of the Lagos protectorate. Now Carter had pushed Lagos forward into its own hinterland, cutting roads through the bush and building forts in order to boost trade – and revenue. If Goldie was too weak to control these robbers at Ilorin, then Lagos would do the job. Early in 1896, the Emir of Ilorin provocatively attacked an outpost of the Lagos police. Chamberlain gave Goldie little time to react. If he could not deal with Ilorin 'at once',[18] then Carter should do it and charge the bill to Goldie.

It would have been odd if a man as proud and pugnacious as Goldie had lost the initiative with Chamberlain. He postponed the invasion till the autumn of 1896, when the Niger would rise and the Company's stern-wheelers could safely get over the sandbanks of the middle Niger. He also made a more belligerent plan of campaign than envisaged by Lagos. To attack Nupe, not Ilorin, would be his first objective. Nupe, straddling the Niger, had snubbed Goldie recently by capturing forty-five of the Company's policemen, led by two British officers. (The men were released, but not their modern rifles.) Well, he would smash Nupe and then strike at Ilorin.

Some adventurous British regulars joined the Company's army, seconded from their regiments. But only 30 white officers, 513 African soldiers and 900 porters marched from the Company's base at Lokoja on 6 January 1897. The Nupe forces, Fulani cavalry armed with firelocks, swords and spears, were expected to outnumber them by at least ten to one. Tactically, Goldie pinned his faith, like Lugard before him, on the magazine rifle, the Maxim gun, and the advance made in the form of a square. He would also exploit the strategic weakness of Nupe. Its forces were bisected by the Niger, and the boatmen who owned the only canoes were in a state of rebellion.

Goldie led his men in person against each of the Emir of Nupe's armies in turn. The western army, commanded by the *Markum* (deputy), Mohamedu, dispersed up-river, and the Company's steamers stopped stragglers crossing to help the Emir. The eastern army, under the Emir's own control, formed up for battle in front of the walled city of Bida. On 26 January, Goldie's small army was attacked by successive cavalry charges made by thousands of white-robed Fulani. But the Company's square was never broken. The enemy's cavalry were cut down in swathes. The next day Goldie brought up a twelve-pounder Whitworth gun under the shelter of the square, and shelled Bida from a few hundred yards. The crippled army of the Emir withdrew as the city caught fire.

Goldie had lost eight dead and nine wounded. In due course he signed a treaty with the *Markum*. The Emir was deposed, and the *Markum* succeeded him. Goldie was still too weak to impose direct administration, but he initiated a form of indirect rule that would later become the pattern for northern Nigeria. The new Emir would govern Nupe, but 'conform to such directions ... as the representatives of the Company may give him from time to time'.[19]

Three weeks later, on 16 February 1897, Goldie repeated his winning throw. He launched his small column against the mud brick walls of the city of Ilorin. Try as they would to break the British square, the Ilorin cavalry were broken in their turn. Shelled from close range, the city was soon ablaze from end to end. But when the fires subsided Goldie was lenient enough with the Emir of Ilorin. He was restored to the throne, on condition that he sign a new treaty, like the treaty with Bida, in which he agreed to conform to the Company's directions issued 'from time to time'.[20] Slave-raiding must cease, the border with Lagos must be respected, and all trading stocks of gin and rum must be destroyed. Otherwise, matters were left much as they were, with slavery still the bedrock of life within the emirates.

North of Nupe and Ilorin, however, things had changed disastrously for Goldie. This was the result of his own success. For Goldie's new militancy had alarmed Hanotaux, even though Lord Salisbury reassured him that Goldie had pledged himself not to take his column further up-river. For once Lord Salisbury played straight into the hands of his enemies. The French were indeed reassured – and grabbed Bussa, north of Ilorin, the strategic key to the middle Niger. In March 1897 Goldie marched to his northern outpost, Fort Goldie, without his column, as he had reluctantly promised the Foreign Office. He had already heard that a foreign expedition had hoisted a strange flag and threatened to burn the King's house at Bussa if the King failed to submit. Now Goldie received a letter headed '*Résidence de Bussa*', informing him that a certain Lieutenant Bretonnet had taken possession of the town 'in the name of the French Republic'. Bretonnet claimed to 'occupy effectively the territory of Bussa'.[21] Goldie was helpless without his column. All he could do was bite his lip and repeat that Bussa was within the Company's sphere, and that the matter must now be referred to the British and French governments.

* * *

The news that the French had hoisted the tricolour at Bussa reached London in April 1897 and thrust this obscure mud-walled town on the banks of the Niger to the centre of international politics. Bussa was a strategic post on the river immediately below the rapids, giving the French access to the whole middle and lower Niger. There was no dispute about title, as Goldie's treaty with the King was impossible to fault on paper. The point was that the French were there on the ground. The French had called the British bluff. Or would it be the other way round? At any rate, Bussa was the test case for the proposed new rules of the Scramble – effective occupation.

Meanwhile, Salisbury was still struggling to get talks on the Niger re-started. In March he paid a secret visit to Hanotaux to suggest submitting these 'petty disputes'[22] to international arbitration. The suggestion fell flat. In April, May and. June the Foreign Office protested politely; had Lieutenant Bretonnet exceeded his instructions? Hanotaux, now committed to the forward policy by Méline's Cabinet, refused to back down.

If West Africa had been the only bone of contention, Salisbury's job might have been easier. It would also have been less urgent. The upper Nile question touched far more tender nerves, and was still unresolved – indeed, a collision there was growing more and more likely. Not that British intelligence had been able to find out much about any of the three shadowy French expeditions. All that was known was that the French were trying to converge on Fashoda westwards from Ethiopia and eastwards from the Congo. There was also a report that Leopold had sent a huge expedition northwards from the Lado enclave, which had been leased from Britain, in order to beat both Britain and France in the race for Fashoda.

By August 1897 Salisbury at last heard some good news. Kitchener's army, partly staffed by British officers but financed by the Egyptian taxpayer, was steaming forward across the desert south of Dongola as fast as the tracks of its railway could be laid. On 31 August Kitchener captured the town of Berber, only 200 miles north of Khartoum. Was Kitchener's army the broom to sweep the French – and Leopold too – out of the Sudan? But Fashoda was 600 miles south of Khartoum, and the Mahdists still showed plenty of fight; so Salisbury was still content that the British advance on Fashoda would come from the south, from Uganda. Unfortunately, his own political protégé, the Uganda railway, was still stuck in the lion-infested plain, hardly eighty miles from the Indian Ocean. So Salisbury ordered Major James MacDonald, the commanding officer in Uganda, who had succeeded Lugard in 1893, to push on to Fashoda with a small column. MacDonald was expected to arrive there in the summer of 1898, and then there would be a 'row'.

In his sombre moments, Salisbury was already anticipating a war with France for possession of Fashoda and the upper Nile, economically a worthless swamp, but the strategic key – so he believed – to Egypt.

Month by month, Salisbury was more anxious to settle those wretched disputes about the Niger and West Africa. Then, in October 1897, the French agreed to resume the talks in earnest. Salisbury leant over backwards to be conciliatory. He was delighted to buy strategic security on the Nile in exchange for some of the Niger Company's 'light land'. He offered Hanotaux a 130-mile-long corridor linking Dahomey with a station on the Niger below Bussa. He was supported by the old guard in the Cabinet, including Hicks Beach, the Chancellor, and Goschen, the First Lord of the Admiralty. But there was one smooth piece of rock blocking all progress on the Niger – Chamberlain.

The Colonial Secretary rejected all attempts to barter away the hinterlands in West Africa to prevent a war over the Nile. The Gold Coast and Nigeria must not be 'strangled' by the French. In December 1897 he protested to Salisbury that they should not 'yield a jot to threats'.[23] Privately he warned Selborne, the Under-Secretary at the Colonies and Salisbury's nephew by marriage, that the Prime Minister was 'prepared to give away everything and get nothing'.[24] They must do things Chamberlain's way, or he would resign. Salisbury was helpless. Without Chamberlain, the hero of the new imperialism, the government might as well throw in the sponge.

With the Niger blocked once more, the Nile was running in spate. By the beginning of 1898 Salisbury heard that Major James MacDonald's advance on Fashoda from the south had collapsed in confusion. His Sudanese soldiers – Emin's fickle old soldiers with whom Lugard had garrisoned Uganda – had suddenly mutinied and killed their British officers. The shifty ex-Kabaka, Mwanga, then launched a revolt in Bunyoro, joining hands with his former enemy, King Kabarega. Mutiny and rebellion in Uganda extinguished all hope of MacDonald's arrival at Fashoda during that year, so Salisbury and the Cabinet had suddenly to reverse their own plans.

After all, the British advance on Fashoda must come from the north and from Kitchener's army. But were his Egyptian troops men enough to capture Khartoum, smash the Dervishes and avenge Gordon? Not according to Kitchener and Cromer. To do that, Kitchener's army would need some expensive stiffening – a couple of brigades of British troops, which would cost the British taxpayer at least £1 million. With misgivings, Salisbury put the case to his colleagues. By January 1898 it was agreed that there was no alternative to sending British brigades to assist the Egyptians. Of course this would madden the French, and Sir Edward Monson, the British Ambassador in Paris, gave a solemn warning to the Cabinet: in the present extraordinary atmosphere – with France tearing itself apart in the second agonizing phase of the Dreyfus Affair – France might seek relief by rushing into a war with England.

Nonsense, said Chamberlain. The French had fooled Monson, Lord Salisbury and most of the Cabinet. They were bluffing on both Nile and Niger. He would now call their bluff on both rivers by outplaying them at their own game of effective occupation.

But worse than the chicken-heartedness of his colleagues was the truculence of Sir George Goldie, which tormented Chamberlain from May 1897 to February 1898. The root of the trouble was that by now Chamberlain had decided to buy out the Niger Company, as the only way to end the protests against the Company from every quarter: protests from Lagos for Goldie's failure to govern; protests against his illegal monopoly from well-fed Liverpool merchants as well as from the starving Brassmen; not to speak of the aggressive French government. But the buy-out would take time and in the meanwhile it was Goldie's job as head of the Niger Company and a patriotic imperialist to collaborate with the Colonial Office in fighting off the French challenge.

When the two men met in May 1897, Goldie shrugged his shoulders. He had heard the rumour that the government was going to revoke his charter. Well, let them deal with the French themselves. He would give them nothing – not a crane on the docks, not a paddle steamer on the river. At first Chamberlain tried to ignore Goldie's defiance. He ordered the Governor of Lagos to prepare to cross the frontier and occupy parts of the Company's sphere in Borgu in order to block the French encroachments from Dahomey. The Admiralty would support him with two gunboats on the Niger and the Niger Company would, he hoped, supply river transport.

In fact, the Niger Company would do nothing of the sort. In July 1897 Goldie made that maddeningly clear. Chamberlain must first make up his mind about the future of the Company. If the Charter was to be revoked, then let the deed be done quickly, with fair compensation. Goldie then proposed a wild scheme of his own. If the British navy would blockade Dahomey, he would lead 1,000 African troops against Bussa, as soon as the dry season began, and annihilate the French garrison. He then rounded on the government for failing to support him against the French, and accused Chamberlain of proposing foolish concessions – the corridor to the Niger – which would result in the Fulani being corrupted by a flood of cheap gin and firearms. It would be better to surrender territory beyond the river, northern Bornu and Sokoto. To give up Bussa would be the most fatal blunder since Majuba.

At this Chamberlain (a member, in his Liberal days, of Gladstone's Cabinet which had handed back the Transvaal to the Boers after Majuba) began to steam like a Birmingham boiler. To be accused of failing to defend the Empire was too much.

> I should like to tell him that the British government does not ... agree that he is to take all the profits and that we are to spend hundreds of thousands or possibly millions in securing his claim against the French ...
> If this is his view, our best course will be to expropriate him at once, lock, stock and barrel – paying the capital value of his property but allowing nothing for goodwill or future profits ...[25]

The trouble was that 'at once' was a phrase that meant nothing in the dusty corridors of the Treasury. It took Chamberlain till February 1898 before he could persuade Hicks Beach, the Chancellor, and his officials that they must guarantee to pay the Niger Company fair compensation. Then, and only then, would Goldie give grudging agreement to help the 3,000-strong imperial force, the WAFFs (the West African Frontier Force) that Chamberlain was organizing to beat the French at their own game. Their commander was not, after all, to be the Governor of Lagos. For this pugnacious scheme, Chamberlain had chosen that Nigerian expert, Major Fred Lugard. Of course, this was bound to provoke the French even further; it was Lugard and his Maxim gun who had driven the French out of Uganda. But Chamberlain wanted to show the French he meant business. (Besides, unlike Chamberlain, Lugard hero-worshipped Goldie, a failing that would do him no harm with the Niger Company.) In February,

Lugard sailed again for the Niger, with orders to make life in Borgu as difficult for the French as he could.

Meanwhile, the Niger talks in Paris surged forward to a climax. In theory they were conducted by the British Ambassador, Sir Edward Monson, on the instructions of the Foreign Secretary, Lord Salisbury. In practice, the main instructions were drafted by Chamberlain. He had shouldered Salisbury aside, determined to call the French bluff. If Hanotaux would never risk a war for Bussa, the same could not be said of Chamberlain.

* * *

When Lugard accepted Chamberlain's new commission, he did so with a heavy heart. 'The task before me', he wrote in his diary for 23 October 1897, 'is one from which I shrink and which I detest.'[26] He had thrown up a very lucrative freelance job – leading an expedition into the Kalahari desert for a British exploration company – in order to return to government service. But his heart was in Uganda, in the green hills of East Africa, not in the swamps of West Africa. He was sickened to hear of the mutiny in Uganda, caused, he did not doubt, by the harsh policy of his successor and rival, Major James MacDonald. Unfortunately, East Africa was controlled by the Foreign Office, who had found Lugard too independent-minded for their taste.

As for West Africa, Lugard had grave misgivings about Chamberlain's plan for calling the French bluff. His own proposal, coinciding with Goldie's, was for political concessions. Why not buy off the French with a large slice of territory north of the river, the still unconquered empire of Sokoto? Chamberlain turned this down flat. Lugard must out-play the French at their own game, adopting tactics derided by Lugard as the 'chessboard policy'.[27]

He was supposed to infiltrate in and behind the French posts in Borgu, flying the Union Jack alongside the tricolour, so that for every town and village supposed to be French, there would be another town and village they could show to be British. In short, it was a plan to make a farce of effective occupation – without starting a war. But would it work? For four months, from November 1897 to March 1898, Lugard wrangled with Chamberlain, trying to convince him that his plan was folly. Suppose the French were *not* bluffing? Or if they were, and were prepared to play fair (which Lugard doubted) it would be almost impossible to restrain the African troops employed on both sides. One shot fired by mistake could set the whole of Borgu alight. Chamberlain would not budge, and the eye behind the eye-glass became dangerously bright. This was the policy, and Lugard could take it or leave it.

Humiliated, Lugard wrote out a letter of resignation. Then Goldie, his hero, begged him not to be such a fool. Goldie would 'work the press and Parliament'[28] against Chamberlain's chessboard policy. But Lugard must not dream of resigning. He was indispensable; the Empire – and the Niger Company – depended on him. Like many other masterful men – and women – Lugard found Goldie's flattery irresistible.

By 6 April 1898 Lugard was steaming up the broad but shallow channel of the lower Niger while cold rain dripped through the roof of the small trading launch, *Zaria*. The rain, and an attack of toothache, did not improve his temper. He felt very seedy and wrapped himself up in a Jaeger rug, fuming over the discovery that the whisky had been left behind. He did not know how he was to raise a force of 2,000 men in an almost unexplored part of Africa, without any staff to help.

His friend and second-in-command, Lieutenant James Willcocks, had no such worries. He was captivated by the sight of the great river. It was Willcocks's first experience of Africa and he felt, he wrote later, 'like a child with a new toy'. A hippo grunted and vanished in a swirl of muddy foam. Parrots whistled overhead 'like showers of loose silver'.[29] At night the rush of a tropical storm through the leaves of the huge fern-clad trees sounded like the bursting of a dam. Lugard found Willcocks a perfect 'trump'. He would have to put him in charge of the troops in the field – the column advancing to challenge the French – while he stayed behind to sort out the chaos of the new base camp, Jebba, on the river. There was something alarmingly trusting and simple about Willcocks, to Lugard's mind. No doubt he would be able to control his own men, but would he be able to cope with those black 'fiends', the French-led Senegalese, who would use every trick to try and put him in the wrong?

Unfortunately Goldie, despite all his assurances, had failed to 'work the press and Parliament'[30] against Chamberlain's chessboard scheme. Lugard guessed this from the absence of any new orders. So he had to make the best of things, and pray to heaven Chamberlain was right, and the French were bluffing.

Willcocks left Jebba at the end of April with 300 soldiers, mainly fresh Hausa recruits, and a long caravan of porters. He began his march to Borgu through more or less uninhabited mimosa scrub. Two days from the river, he met the first sign of the French, a large tricolour flying over the village of Kiama, the capital of the region. Willcocks defiantly hoisted the Union Jack at Kanikoko, two miles away. Soon there were menacing messages from the French. On 5 May a French *sous officier* appeared, borne in a scarlet hammock, and escorted by twelve Senegalese carrying a tricolour. Willcocks's own khaki was already worn and stained. The Frenchman was wearing a dazzling white jacket with a medal, blue *zouave* trousers, brown gaiters and a white Marine helmet. Willcocks went into his tent to pull down the strap of his khaki helmet. Then the two Europeans saluted their respective flags. '*Mon colonel.*'

What did the African onlookers make of this confrontation? The 'King' of Kiama was one of those hospitable African chiefs whom Lugard, four years earlier, had persuaded to sign a treaty with the Niger Company. Now he expressed his bewilderment. He had made friends, he said, with a 'great white man' who had been to his country, made promises, and then left; and he had heard no more of him. That same year the French had taken over his town and made him swear allegiance to them. Willcocks explained, somewhat lamely, that he was the emissary of that great white man.

The *sous officier* angrily interposed. 'You have insulted our flag ... the history of Borgu shows how England has over-ridden all treaties.' When Willcocks replied, 'The history of Borgu has yet to be written,'[31] the Frenchman solemnly produced a French two-volume history of the state. Neither officer could keep a straight face any longer. The dangerous confrontation ended in peals of laughter. Both men's sense of the absurd, as well as a sense of European solidarity, was too strong. They shook hands and drank toasts to each other's flags.

Throughout the next weeks the dangerous farce continued, as Willcocks proceeded to hoist the Union Jack wherever it could provoke a protest from the tricolour: at Kishi, Bode, Okuta, Gbasora, Termanji and Borgasi, then back to Kiama. By now the rains had begun and the tracks through the thorny bush had turned to mud. Willcocks found himself delighted with his Hausa recruits, whose cheerfulness in these trying conditions amazed him. The pattern of events followed the first day at Kiama: protests from the French, defiance from the English. One day the French threatened to use bayonets, and the British were pursued by a mob of Africans, spitting and cursing at them. Yet often the stormy scenes dissolved in laughter and hand-shakes. However, on 17 May a crisis began which Willcocks was sure would lead to war in West Africa – 'and where else it was not for me to say'.

A week earlier Willcocks's men had hoisted the Union Jack at Betikuta, a small village teeming with sheep and cattle, about two miles from Kiama. That night a French sergeant impertinently crept up and hoisted the tricolour within 400 yards. Willcocks warned the French commandant that unless it was removed within forty-eight hours, he would, as a reprisal, hoist the Union Jack 400 yards from the main gate of Kiama. But that, said the Frenchman, would lead to war.

The tension was becoming unbearable for both sides. According to Willcocks, everyone, African soldiers and European officers, himself included, longed to stop this unsoldierly nonsense and try the 'appeal to the sword'.[32] However, the crisis was postponed for a week, to give both commanders time to refer to higher authority. Willcocks raced back from the bush to see Lugard at Jebba. Lugard endorsed what Willcocks had done, though, unlike Willcocks, he was desperately anxious to avoid a war.

The outbreak seemed set for 30 May. On that day an armed party of the West African Frontier Force (WAFFs) marched boldly on the main gate at Kiama, and planted a Union Jack. Willcocks had built a palisade and dug a trench around his camp. Now he set up the Maxims, ready to repel a French attack. He paraded his reserve, then pretended to write in his notebook, waiting breathless for the sound of firing. But no sound came back through the bush. The crisis ended, once again, in a ludicrous anti-climax.

The French commandant had decided not to notice the Union Jack after all. His good sense was confirmed a few hours later by an urgent telegram from the Governor of Dahomey, which he immediately showed the astounded Willcocks.

The Havas Press Agency reported that the Niger talks in Paris were on the verge of reaching a conclusion, and the French would surrender Borgu to the English.

*   *   *

Chamberlain's gamble had paid off. At the risk of his own career, he had steam-rollered everyone – the Prime Minister, the Cabinet, Goldie, Lugard. It had seemed utter folly to risk a great war in Europe for the sake of Borgu, an almost uninhabited strip of African bush.

Yet it turned out that Chamberlain was right. The French rifles might as well have been made of cardboard, and the tricolours props from *opéra bouffe*. In the war of the flags, the French officers, too, had been ordered not to fire first. Chamberlain had called the French bluff.

On 14 June 1898, a fortnight after Willcocks had ordered the Union Jack to be run up above the main gate of Kiama, Hanotaux finally signed the Niger Convention, 4,000 miles away in Paris. No doubt he breathed a sigh of relief. He had never seen the point of Borgu and the terms of the new Convention were a well-earned smack in the eye for Lebon and the Colonial Party. Goldie's Niger Company – shortly to be taken over by the British government – had won secure boundaries at last. In the north-west the British 'sphere' began at Ilo, above the rapids. It included Bussa, and most of Borgu. On the north, the far-flung empire of Sokoto, unconquered by either side, was confirmed to be British. All the French could show for the eight-year struggle since the Anglo-French Agreement of 1890 was a narrow triangle extending the eastern frontier of Dahomey 100 miles down-river from Say, and into western Borgu as far as Nikki. (This was a goal scored against Lugard, for it was his treaty, signed in November 1894 with the 'King' of Nikki, that had proved invalid.) Chamberlain had also grudgingly conceded the French commercial access, but without a corridor, to the navigable river below Bussa.

Salisbury breathed a sigh of relief. Strategy, not commerce, was his passion. Anyway, he was sceptical about the treasures of Borgu. ('There is no loot to get except in Goldie's dreams,'[33] he told Chamberlain.) Mercifully, they had at last disposed of those 'petty' squabbles over the Niger. They had troubles enough with the Nile. There would be no war – for the time being. But Salisbury predicted that there would be an even more dangerous crisis within a few months.

Already in June, British intelligence estimated that Captain Marchand was close to Fashoda, or perhaps already in occupation. By September, Kitchener should have smashed the Dervishes and captured Khartoum. His orders were then to steam up-river to call Marchand's bluff and force the French to withdraw. But were they bluffing on the Nile as they had bluffed on the Niger? Salisbury did not know. All that was certain was that on this issue Chamberlain had no need to browbeat the Cabinet. To save the southern Sudan, and so Egypt, *was* an issue over which it was worth risking a war with France.

It was true that Marchand and his tricolour might already have sunk into the swamps of the great Sudd. But there were other runners in the race for Fashoda. What about King Menelik and the two French expeditions supposed to be heading that way from the east? And what about King Leopold, whom Queen Victoria thought had taken leave of his senses when he threatened to snatch the southern Sudan from under the noses of Britain and France? Where on earth were King Leopold's men?

THE NIGER.

CHAPTER 29

The Race to the Middle of Nowhere

Brussels, the Congo, French West Africa, the Sudan and Ethiopia
5 May 1897–1 September 1898

> '... it has for a motive the task of reminding the
> country of its true greatness, of its mission in the
> world, begun nearly 20 centuries ago, the mission
> which we all have ... [to continue] on pain of being
> guilty of national cowardice.'
>
> *Capt. Marchand* on his mission to Fashoda, 1898

It was 5 May 1897, more than a year before the signing of the Anglo-French agreement on the Niger. Leopold basked in the mild spring sunshine that striped the towering rubber plants under the five great glass domes of the new Congo glasshouses at Laeken.

His wild dreams for Africa – to exploit the vast wealth of the Congo and then stretch out his hand to the Nile – seemed quite suddenly on the verge of fulfilment.

That week he would open the Industrial Exhibition in Brussels, and would play the part he played so well, now that his beard was as white as Santa Claus' – the benevolent king, father of his people, who had invested his private fortune in a great philanthropic venture in the wilds of Africa. The venture had flourished like the towering rubber plants, causing chagrin for all those 'Doubting Thomases', ranging from Van Eetvelde, his Congo adviser, to the masters of Europe, including Lord Salisbury and Gabriel Hanotaux.

The astonishing fact was that the Congo had just begun to make money, hand over fist. Unlike the rest of the new colonies in Africa founded in the Scramble, the Congo State no longer depended on a subsidy from Europe. It had turned out just as Leopold had foreseen in 1876, after he had read that first report in *The Times* describing the travels of Cameron. The Congo was a treasure house, teeming with tropical produce, in fact with wild rubber which was suddenly becoming a more important export than ivory. The world's appetite for rubber had become insatiable since 1888, when Dunlop had invented pneumatic tyres for bicycles. While a fall in palm-oil prices, caused by a world glut, threatened other colonies (palm oil was still the main export of the British and French colonies in West Africa), the price of rubber soared. So did the volume of Congo rubber exported: from under 250 tons in 1892 to over 1,200 tons in 1896. In 1897 it would exceed 1,500 tons. Obviously part of the profits of the rubber boom, however large, would be needed to underwrite the civilizing mission in Africa. With the surplus, however, the King planned to extend his benevolence from the Congo to Brussels. That year, 1897, he proposed to build a baroque palace at Tervuren to house a Congo Museum, linked to the city by an avenue of elm trees worthy of Versailles.

This bonanza in the Congo had occurred just in time to save the King from throwing in his hand. By early 1895 even Leopold's fund of optimism (and hard cash) had been exhausted. He had offered to hand over his rights as 'King-Sovereign' of the Congo State to Belgium. It was said he had poured 12 million francs (£500,000) of his personal fortune into the Congo since 1880, and the place had proved a bottomless pit. Of course, he insisted that he would be compensated.

The Belgian government had rallied to help the King out of this embarrassment. In January 1895 Leopold initialled a 'treaty of cession' drawn up between the Congo State and Belgium. Anxious to oblige, the Prime Minister, Jules de Burlet, persuaded his colleagues to approve the annexation. But would Parliament approve the acquisition of such a dubious asset? The Socialists were dead against diverting taxpayers' money from social improvements at home to adventures abroad. The Right shrank from the international complications. How would the French react? After all, since 1884 they had had a right of preemption. So the government would have to rely on middle-of-the-road Catholics, drawn mainly from the commercial and professional classes, and Jules de Burlet began to doubt if he could push annexation through Parliament.

Then in March 1895, before the matter could be tested, Leopold read the rubber sales figures and at last began to savour the sweet smell of success. Suddenly he repudiated his offer to part with the Congo, much to the relief of Burlet's government. They obliged the King by offering him a new loan of 6.5 million francs (£260,000) for the Congo, alarmed by his embarrassing claim (fictitious, it later emerged) that he had to pay off a five-million-franc loan borrowed from a Belgian banker.

Flush with an extra 6.5 million francs, the King had decided in 1895 that the time was right to send a new expedition, led by Baron Dhanis, to make an attempt on the Nile. His plan, astounding as it might seem, was for Dhanis to conquer the Sudan and add it to the Congo State, which already spanned half Africa. He would snatch the Sudan from under the noses of the two great Powers – Britain and France – already competing for the territory.

It will be recalled that Lord Salisbury had ridiculed any talk of Leopold acting as a neutral 'guardian' of the upper Nile. Nor would Hanotaux be likely to accept the plan, except possibly as a *fait accompli*. France and Britain might even combine to take reprisals against Leopold in Europe; the Congo's existence – and indeed Belgium's – depended on the goodwill of Belgium's powerful neighbours. So Leopold decided on a diplomatic stratagem to fool France and Britain.

He assured Hanotaux that the reports about Dhanis's great expedition, the largest ever launched in Central Africa, were ridiculous exaggerations. He said that all he wanted was to take over the Lado Enclave, the small corridor shaped like a leg of mutton, leased to him by Britain and supposed to link the Congo with the navigable Nile. This was all that remained of that earlier grandiose plan of the King's to bite off a chunk of the upper Nile and add it to the Congo. In 1894 the British had been prepared to lease him the whole mysterious Bahr al-Ghazal to keep it out of the hands of the French. The French had sabotaged this plan. The Lado Enclave included Rejaf, the strategic base below the rapids at Lado, and thus the terminus for steamers on the Nile, which was navigable to Khartoum and beyond. Of course, all this part of the river had been in the hands of the Mahdists for a decade ever since 1888 when Emin's Sudanese garrison had abandoned Equatoria and fled south. Therefore Dhanis's modest job was to drive the Mahdists out of the Lado Enclave and rebuild the station at Rejaf ready for the day, whenever that would be, when France or Britain took the Sudan and re-opened the Nile to trade.

This was the story Leopold told Hanotaux, and leaked to the international press. In fact, Dhanis, the hero of the Arab war, had been given secret orders to push on to Fashoda and from there to Khartoum. This was the task that Stanley had been offered and had declared impossible in 1890. It was in pursuit of a dream of becoming a modern Pharaoh that had haunted the King for more than forty years, ever since he had wandered among the ruins of Luxor on his honeymoon.

In 1896, Dhanis's expedition had left Stanleyville and vanished into the rainforest to the north-east – Dhanis, a handful of Belgian officers and an army of 3,000 Batetela and other raw tribesmen, many of whom were cannibals. To avoid being spotted by the French, Dhanis planned forced marches along the most forbidding of all the routes to the Nile, through the deadly Ituri forest – the route of Stanley's Emin Pasha expedition, and the graveyard of the rear column. Meanwhile, Leopold's commandant on the upper Uele, Chaltin, would take 700 other troops and advance in the open, following the well-trodden western route, heading straight for the Mahdists occupying Rejaf.

As an experienced gambler, both with borrowed money and other men's lives, the King had staked a lot on success. Stanley had warned him that the Mahdists might be too strong even for his own well-armed but ill-disciplined African troops. Yet Leopold was unprepared for the disaster that overtook Dhanis's expedition.

That day, 5 May 1897, as he basked in the Congo greenhouse at Laeken, Leopold received an extraordinary cable from the Congo. The Batetela in Baron Dhanis's advance guard had mutinied at Ndirfi in February, and killed their Belgian officers.

The Batetela proved to have been goaded into forced marches and starved long enough; and some of them had a personal score to settle against Dhanis for the judicial murder of their leader, Gongo Lutete, in 1893.

There was worse news to come. By the end of May, Leopold learnt that the Batetela mutiny had spread to the main army. Most of Dhanis's officers, including his brother, were hacked down or shot. Dhanis himself hid in the forest, then fled back to Stanleyville. There he cowered, the hero of the Arab war four years earlier, while his mutinous army rampaged across the whole north-east of the Congo State, killing anyone who tried to resist them. Stanleyville itself survived. But the administration of the province tumbled like a pack of cards, and for a time the small bands of Europeans, huddled in their tin-roofed huts all over the Congo, feared the mutiny would swallow everything.

A less stubborn man than the King would have lost his nerve. Leopold brushed aside Dhanis's disaster. The important thing was that in February Chaltin had expelled the Mahdists and occupied the Lado Enclave with amazing ease, considering his small force.

Leopold's next step was breathtaking. In the summer of 1897, he began negotiations with an Italian middleman to secure a lease of the Italian colony of Eritrea, by which he would share half the profits of the colony with the Italian government. When Lord Cromer was sounded, in September 1897, he commented drily, 'the King of the Belgians is very cunning'.[1] In fact, the idea was an absurdity. The colony was mostly scrub and desert. As for its potential as a corridor, the British had no intention of allowing Leopold, any more than the French, to grab this part of the Nile valley in order to link the Atlantic with the Red Sea.

By the spring of 1897 Congo State forces were digging in at the Nile, fortifying the new post at Rejaf. But Leopold had been forced to drop out of the race for Fashoda. It was the French, converging from both west and east, who were taking the lead.

* * *

On the high, green plateau of Ethiopia, the Big Rains usually start in June, and the mule tracks turn to mountain streams lubricated with yellow mud, making travel almost impossible. That year, 1897, the Big Rains came early. For forty-two days – from 17 May to 28 June – the small French expedition led by the Marquis de Bonchamps slipped and slithered westwards towards the Nile.

Bonchamps was the dashing young aristocrat who had served with Stairs's expedition to Katanga, a second-in-command who had found himself unexpectedly thrust to the head of the second French expedition. Marching west somewhere ahead of him, lost in those rain-drenched mountains, was the first expedition, led by Captain Clochette. They were both supposed to be advancing towards the Nile with a large Ethiopian army in support. At Fashoda nearby they would meet Captain Marchand. These were the orders that Lebon, the Minister for the Colonies, had given to Bonchamps's chief, Bonvalot, in Paris in December 1896. The hasty organization of the second expedition, a sudden afterthought, seemed likely to haunt Bonchamps. Clochette had been given 100,000 francs, Bonvalot only 55,000, to cover food and stores for an expedition expected to travel 3,000 kilometres from the Red Sea to the Nile and back. Paris was confident that Menelik would honour his offer of support; he had just signed a 'White Nile Convention' with France, giving him the east bank of the

White Nile, and seemed keen to push forward to protect his west flank against British expansion.

Paris had ordered Léonce Lagarde, the Governor of French Somaliland acting as the French Ambassador in Addis Ababa, to keep him up to the mark. But the further Bonchamps travelled, the more he was convinced that, for personal reasons of his own, Lagarde was sabotaging the second expedition.

Bonvalot, its original leader, had quarrelled violently with Lagarde at their first meeting, on the dusty track from Jibouti. In Addis Ababa, Bonvalot found that without Lagarde's backing he could get nowhere in Menelik's court. He threw in his hand and returned to France. Bonchamps was made of sterner stuff. He persuaded Menelik to let him have guides and a letter of introduction to the local Governor of Gore, on the upper Baro, the tributary that under the Sudanese name of the Sobat eventually flows into the White Nile near Fashoda. Then, snapping his fingers at the ordinary rules of Ethiopian travel, Bonchamps set off from Addis Ababa with three ardent French companions and an escort of 100 surly Ethiopians, just as the Big Rains began to beat down on the plateau.

For those forty-two days in May and June, Bonchamps and his men raced forward in the mud towards Gore, desperate to catch up with Clochette. There was no chance to dry their sodden clothes. There were few pack mules. To save cash, Bonvalot had bought camels in Somaliland, and these wretched beasts could not stand the mud and cold of the mountains. By now, most of them were dead or dying. The surly Ethiopians, forced to carry the six tons of stores, soon became mutinous. This was Galla country, and a green wasteland. Seven years earlier, Menelik's conquering army had swept through these green upland valleys, dotted with Galla villages and rich in grain and cattle. Now there was hardly a trace of huts, people or animals.

Bonchamps was told by an Ethiopian that one of Menelik's *Rases* had sent his cavalry to burn the villages in a wide circle around, killing the menfolk and enslaving the women and children. Then he would move his camp and repeat the process. Bonchamps was naturally shocked, his confidence in the benefits of European imperialism confirmed by the evidence of the African alternative. *Vae victis!* Yet these rough methods seemed to work. Unlike the European imperialists, Menelik made war a paying business. The Gallas had been taught a lesson in humility – those who survived. And the green valleys would not remain empty long. There would be settlers from the east, Menelik's Shoan soldiers, paid off with Galla land.

When the expedition finally staggered into Gore, after their forty-two-day march, Bonchamps found new evidence to damn Lagarde, his compatriot back in Addis Ababa. Apparently at Lagarde's request, Menelik had told the guides to take them on an interminable detour up and down the steepest mountains, instead of following the direct road like Captain Clochette. Competition with poor Clochette, however, was no longer a problem. The explorer was dying of an injury to the liver, inflicted by the kick from a horse months earlier. (He died within a few weeks.) Meanwhile, Bonchamps innocently presented the Emperor's letter of recommendation to the local Governor, Dejazmatch (Commander) Téssama, only to find his expedition immediately immobilized.

A more sophisticated traveller than Bonchamps would have spotted the ominous contradiction in the concluding sentences of Menelik's letter. After requesting the Governor to help Bonchamps by accompanying him to the frontier, it ended, 'But do you, come quickly, and we will speak of this when you are here.'[2] So Dejazmatch left for Addis Ababa, after impounding Bonchamps's few pack animals. Three weeks were spent sitting in sodden tents while rain deluged the valley. On 17 July, a courier arrived from the capital. They had His Majesty's full permission to go 'wherever they wished'. They set off again, brushing aside a mutiny by most of their escort, only to be stopped eighty kilometres further west, at Siba, by a force of 2,000 wild Ethiopian warriors, shouting war-cries and waving spears and rifles. The frontier was barred to them by the local chief, who insisted that he acted 'in the name of the Emperor'.[3]

How could Bonchamps convince these blockheads that the Emperor was the power behind their expedition? He saw nothing for it but to send two of his companions, Michel and Bartholin, all those terrible 400 kilometres back to the capital. They made it in three weeks, having ridden their last riding mules to death, and looking so tattered and torn that they were mistaken for Italian prisoners-of-war. It was 25 September, the eve of Maskal, the feast of the Finding of the Cross, normally a celebration to mark the end of the rainy season. But the capital, that wretched city of thatched huts without a single street, was no more cheerful than when they had left it, and the rain still beat down. However, good news was waiting for them up by the red roofs of the palace; they were expected at an audience with His Majesty. 'There has been a misunderstanding, that's for certain,' said M. Ilg, His Majesty's tactful Swiss counsellor. 'You will come and explain yourselves before the Emperor ... He is très désolé to hear of these events.'[4]

Soon after dawn on 27 September Michel and Bartholin were brought to the palace. As usual, the Emperor sat wrapped in a simple black cloak, squatting on the threshold of the audience chamber which opened on to a verandah. Michel and Bartholin had to face him, just as they were, on the lower steps, sitting or squatting – ('difficult positions to make dignified', wrote Michel later in his journal). But the great man was in high spirits. He asked about their route, looked at their maps, and chatted with them as though they were old friends. When Michel explained how they had been stopped at Siba by a crowd of 2,000 crazy warriors, there was a moment's silence. Then Menelik spoke: 'The people who stopped you are imbeciles. They have misunderstood things. I will arrange all this ... and give new orders.'[5]

Michel felt reassured. It was Lagarde, the French Ambassador, who had let them down. No wonder the Emperor had become confused when there were such ridiculous intrigues between the two official expeditions.

Menelik now ordered the embarrassed official who was standing beside him to make sure that the guilty were punished. It was Dejazmatch Tessama, the Governor of Gore, who had been such a thorn in their side:

Yes, they must be punished immediately ... As for me, I will arrange for all the letters you want, so that you can make a rapid departure: there's no time to lose! And the boats? Have you at last got the boats? If not, how can you follow the river [Baro/Sobat]? And you would need to have plenty of supplies and plenty of quinine; all the armies which have gone down to the plains have come back decimated by hunger and fever.[6]

Michel explained the wretched truth; they still had not received the all-important collapsible boat supposed to be sent from France. They had too few porters – and none they could rely on – no chance of fresh supplies and little money.

'What about the men of Clochette's mission?'
'We cannot give orders to them. M. Lagarde is their chief.'
'They should go with you [concluded the Emperor]. All that is very ill arranged ... Well, have a good rest after your exhausting travels. It's the first time anyone has crossed my country during the rainy season ...'[7]

Michel left the palace convinced that the Emperor would do all in his power to help them. Unfortunately he had no boat to lend. On 3 October Michel was confronted by the egregious Ambassador, Lagarde, who had marched back from the coast. The interview was a stormy one. It turned out that the collapsible boat had been despatched from France in July, three months earlier.

'You will be bringing it on to us, no doubt, M. le Ministre?'
'It's already arrived, in fact, at Jibouti, a *chaland*, collapsible, built of steel; *but I thought you were already at the Nile ... so I did not bring it on with me.*'

The news about the boat was shattering. They had been expecting it for eight months; it represented their only hope of success. It was still at Jibouti, and three months would pass before it could reach them. '*Perdus, tous nos efforts; vains, tous nos sacrifices,*'[8] wrote Michel in his journal.

Before they left Addis Ababa to return to Bonchamps, Michel and Bartholin made a last appeal to Lagarde's patriotism. He told them he had new orders from the Minister of Colonies in Paris; Lagarde was, after all, to take direct charge of their mission. But they had no men they could trust, no proper transport, little money. Would Lagarde send them extra supplies? Would he send the boat after them? If not, would he lend them twenty men from his escort of sixty-eight Sudanese soldiers? Michel got nothing out of him except the offer of a pair of camels.

By early November Michel and Bartholin were back with Bonchamps at Gore. At least they now had a proper letter, signed by the Emperor, confirming that they were to be given help to reach the White Nile. The Emperor had commissioned them to 'plant the Ethiopian flag and make the inhabitants submit in all the country as far as the White Nile'.[9] But without boat, money or disciplined escort, what chance had they of serving Menelik or of reaching Fashoda alive, except by a miracle?

For most of December Bonchamps's mission splashed miserably through the swamps of the eastern Sudan. Elephants charged them from the high grass, looming up suddenly like ships in the swamp. There was no escape by water, no canoes, only a narrow track along the river-bank, infested with elephants.

The new letter from Menelik meant that dozens of Gallas were forced to serve as escort. Many deserted. Others tried to desert but were recaptured and flogged with cowhide whips. Many died of fever or starvation in the swamps along the south bank of the river. As a final stroke Lagarde had told them to take the southerly route, rather than the direct one that followed the villages along the ivory trade route north of the river. The southerly route ended in a watery void inhabited only by elephants and crocodiles. On 30 December they turned back. Two of the Frenchmen were crippled by malaria. All of them were starving. And they were still 150 kilometres short of their goal.

The failure of Bonchamps's mission was reported to the palace in Addis Ababa many weeks later. The Emperor took the news calmly. In their innocence, Bonchamps and Michel had put all the blame on Lagarde for the 'misunderstandings'. But the Emperor had not misunderstood – nor had Dejazmatch Tessama. Menelik's aim was to give Bonchamps every help short of that actually needed for success.

Menelik's style of diplomacy was no less sophisticated than that of his European rivals. Unique among African rulers, he had the means to turn the Scramble to his own advantage. He had exploited the French to provide him with extra rifles. Without those precious European arms, smuggled in by camel across the desert from Jibouti despite the European arms embargo, he could never have crushed the Italians at Adowa in 1896. The French remained his chief suppliers of arms. He was also happy to grant a Franco-Ethiopian company the concession to build the railway across desert and mountain all the way to the capital, 300 miles inland and 8,000 feet above the Red Sea. That would take years to complete. Meanwhile, he had a strong diplomatic reason against helping the French reach Fashoda and joining forces with them there.

To protect western Ethiopia from British encroachment, the most effective allies would be the fanatical enemies of the British, not their jealous rivals – the Mahdists, not the French. For some time Menelik had been secretly intriguing with the Khalifa. It was a tribute to his broad-minded diplomacy. He had succeeded in courting a fanatical Muslim ruler, himself an upstart, but the leader of a people who had been the hereditary enemy of Ethiopia for hundreds of years. What is more, he had succeeded in concealing this intrigue from the Powers. In the summer of 1896, as Kitchener began to move up the Nile, the Emperor had offered the Khalifa co-operation against all Europeans in general and against 'the red English' in particular. As one of his most trusted advisers, Ras Mangasha, put it to the Khalifa, 'Your enemy is our enemy and our enemy is your enemy, and we should stand together as firm allies.'[10] At first the Khalifa was suspicious. But as the months passed and Kitchener crushed the *Ansar* like paper, their leader was in no position to rebuff Menelik's offer of arms and ammunition.

Early in 1898 Menelik sent some of his court officials on a mission to

Khartoum. They were warmly received. Special arrangements were made for their meat to be slaughtered according to Christian rules, for their tongues to be loosened and their hearts warmed, despite the Muslim prohibition of alcohol, with barrels of date wine. The task of Menelik's men was to flatter the Khalifa (His Majesty's 'superior, venerable, dear friend!')[11] and to pull the wool over his eyes. For Menelik was hungry to grab the eastern Sudan for his own empire; the best way seemed to be to help the Khalifa concentrate on beating the red English. For the time being he would play the good neighbour.

Under that guise Menelik was able to make a reconnaissance to the White Nile. Early in 1898, after reassuring the Khalifa that he only intended to protect himself against foreign encroachments, he ordered Dejazmatch Tessama to head for the White Nile. Tessama took an army of 10,000, and was persuaded to allow a Russian adventurer called Colonel Artamanov, and two of Bonchamps's recent companions – Maurice Potter and Faivre – to accompany him as observers.

At first the journey was a triumphant march through conquered Galla land. The soldiers pillaged the country for grain and meat. There followed a pestilential journey beyond the frontier: through that enormous malarial marsh, seemingly inhabited only by elephants, hippopotami and crocodiles. Many Ethiopians died. On 26 June a small advance party, most of them ill with fever, reached the Nile, after following the north bank of the Sobat. The two Frenchmen wanted to hoist the tricolour on an island in the Nile, if only they could cross that last 150 metres of crocodile-infested water. Faivre could not swim, Potter was stricken with fever. In the event it was a brave Yambo who dived into the Nile with the tricolour, followed by Colonel Artamanov shouting, 'Now it shall not be said that only a nigger dared plant the French flag.'[12]

The red, white and blue tricolour, so incongruously planted, soon melted into the broad, reed-fringed river. It was not visible seventeen days later when Captain Marchand and his *tirailleurs* sailed past on the last lap of their two-year-long journey from France to Fashoda.

*   *   *

The last lap of this astounding journey had begun at 10 a.m. on 4 June 1898, when Marchand launched a flotilla of small boats into the sandy river Sueh at Fort Desaix, a newly-built French mud fort in the country of the Dinkas, 500 kilometres to the west. This small column presented a fine contrast to Bonchamps's. There were seventy-five black *tirailleurs* recruited from the western Sudan (another small group of *tirailleurs* had gone ahead), and a party of Yakoma paddlers, under five French officers and NCOs, jammed shoulder to shoulder into four steel boats and a handful of dug-out canoes. The boats were heaped high with rolls of trade cloth, packets of scarlet or white beads for barter, quinine by the kilo, tents for the officers, mosquito nets for all, sacks of flour and dried elephant meat, as well as boxes and boxes of rifle ammunition for the Mousquiton-92.

For six months Marchand had been eating out his heart, waiting for this moment. The boats had been stuck at Fort Desaix while the men tortured themselves, measuring the level of the river. Even now, with only an extra metre of water since the start of the rainy season, the steel hulls of the boats scraped repeatedly against submerged sandbanks. But the wind blew fair for Fashoda, filling the grey canvas sails rigged on makeshift masts, so that the Yakoma paddlers, who had never seen a sailing boat, laughed like madmen, crying, '*Kaizoni pépé, bongo zoni mingui!*' ('Paddles no good, sails very good!'),[13] repeating the joke again and again.

Marchand himself was pale and haggard under his white tropical helmet. At first he had seemed indestructible, as expected of one of Archinard's favourites, a hero of the French marine infantry which had crushed the Tukolors of Ahmadu. But Dr Emily, the medical officer with the party, had become alarmed by his leader's habit of driving himself to the point of collapse. Emily himself was philosophical about their expedition. 'We don't know where we're going,' he wrote in his diary that day, 4 June, 'or at least we only know where we want to go. What difficulties we shall meet ... on our way ... Who will be there at Fashoda? ...'[14] But the long months of waiting had been like an illness for Marchand. He saw his mission in heroic terms; he was a standard-bearer for France, the heir to a centuries-old tradition of French patriotism, facing the 'hatred of Albion'. Writing to a friend before he set off, he explained how the capture of Fashoda was essential to the regeneration of the fatherland.

> At least don't go and think I believe I am carrying the world on my shoulders and that I'm exaggerating the role we're playing here. Certainly not... [but] an example ... is always an example. It is always respectable when it has for a motive the task of reminding this country of its true greatness, of its mission in the world, begun nearly 20 centuries ago, the mission which we all have the unavoidable obligation of continuing on pain of being guilty of national cowardice.[15]

As for their rivals, Marchand was not greatly upset by the news that disaster had overtaken the expeditions from the south: the Belgian expedition under Dhanis and the British one under MacDonald, both driven back by mutinies among their African troops. Rather, Marchand's anxiety centred on Kitchener and the Dervishes.

It had taken Marchand's force two years to struggle across from the Congo to launch this small column of *tirailleurs* on the Sueh, at the western extreme of the upper Nile. Was it possible that they would arrive at Fashoda too late – that is, a week or two after Kitchener? For Marchand knew that Kitchener was advancing from the north with a large Anglo-Egyptian army. He might already have taken Khartoum and then pushed on up the Nile. Khartoum was 1,100 kilometres north of Fashoda, yet the journey could be made in a mere fortnight by paddle steamer. Or Kitchener might have been repulsed by the Dervishes.

Was Marchand to pit one company of black *tirailleurs* against a whole army of fanatics? Originally, he had persuaded himself that the Dervishes would rush to his support against their common enemy, the British; hence the diminutive size of his column. But the Dervishes might well refuse his proffered hand. In 1898 he begged Paris for reinforcements. He also pinned his hopes on Clochette's mission, supported by Menelik's hordes, to protect him from both the Dervishes and Kitchener. Yet he had heard no word of this Franco-Ethiopian expedition and already was beginning to feel betrayed by Paris.

On 4 June, the day they sailed from Fort Desaix, Marchand had sent back a runner with a sharp telegram for Lebon, the Minister of Colonies: 'Present situation of indecision and uncertainty cannot be prolonged. Send means for occupation or order for evacuation.' He was furious that this opportunity was being thrown away by Paris out of sheer political funk. He felt 'sick and discouraged'. It was 'cowardice', he told a friend. 'I weep with rage.'[16]

Still, there was no more time to lose once the river Sueh rose high enough to take the flotilla of small boats. Marchand was too impatient to wait till the river could take his biggest boat, the *Faidherbe*. It was his insistence on dragging this eighty-foot-long steam launch (the postal launch commandeered from the upper Ubangi) across the Congo-Nile watershed that had made his expedition one of the most laborious ever attempted in Africa. The launch was not designed to be taken apart and carried on the backs of porters. An engineer had to hack it to pieces, bit by bit. Some sections, including the brass boilers, could not be cut up. They had to be dragged for 400 kilometres through the high grass between the end of the upper Congo and the beginning of the upper Nile. This ghastly ordeal took 200 Karari – slave labour provided by the local 'sultan' – months to accomplish. Now the *Faidherbe* had been miraculously reassembled, ready to follow the flotilla as soon as the rains permitted.

For the first few days the advance of Marchand's flotilla had a dream-like quality, what with the mad laughter of the Yakoma paddlers and the sight of white-painted Dinkas on the river-banks, naked, spectral and motionless, except for an occasional salute with the open palm of a right hand. There were flocks of small ducks, a pair of enormous elephants and inquisitive giraffes, most of which were shot for food. There was a moment's drama when a panic-stricken hippopotamus flung itself against the leading canoe, piloted by Marchand. But they covered the first 150 kilometres without injury to themselves.

On 12 June the Sueh lost itself in the fearsome Sudd, the vast weed-and-papyrus Sargasso that formed the gateway to the Bahr al-Ghazal. According to a reconnoitring party, it was fifty kilometres long and should take eight days to cross. It took thirteen days of torture, hacking a way along a channel so narrow that at times they lost themselves entirely; thirteen nights imprisoned on their small boats, the target for swarms of vampire-like mosquitoes. On 26 June they broke through the reeds into the Bahr al-Ghazal, the western branch of the upper Nile. Here they were rejoined by the small party sent in advance. Nine more days of pushing and paddling brought them to the junction with the Bahr al-Djebel, the true Nile, where the main river, flowing north from Lado and

Uganda, swings sharply east and takes the Arab name of Bahr al-Abiad, the White Nile.

Dr Emily savoured the moment. Here were the 'sacred springs, the cradle of civilization, constant object of our thoughts and our efforts for two years. For the first time since Saint Louis and since Bonaparte, the French colours float on the river of the Pharaohs and the Ptolemies.'[17] Another three days' rapid sailing brought them to the junction with the Sobat, the river from which Clochette and the Franco-Ethiopian expedition were supposed to emerge. They pressed on for another two days with a fair wind, under the sky so pale a blue that it reminded Dr Emily of his home in France. It was now 10 July 1898. That afternoon, at about 5.0 p.m., to the beat of drums in the Shillouk villages along the shore, blended with the mooing of cattle, the flotilla sailed round the bend and came at last to a cluster of maize fields and an Egyptian fort.

It was *res nullius*, no-man's-land. Marchand must have been reassured by the emptiness of this landscape of reeds, water and sky. This was Fashoda – a small island of maize fields in a great marsh. Its fort was still a ruin. There was no trace of newcomers, no sign of Kitchener's army – only line after line of crumbling mud walls, a jungle growth of grass and a tattered grove of date palms twelve foot above a creek in the river.

So they had got there first. That evening they toasted their victory in champagne, drinking to 'Greater France' as the *tirailleurs* and paddlers hurriedly began to rebuild the defences of the fort.

Two days later, to the edification of a large crowd of half-naked Shillouk tribesmen, Marchand formally took possession of Fashoda in the name of the French Republic. He and his fellow officers carried swords, as if on the parade ground at Dakar, and the Sudanese lined up in the yellow-and-black dress uniform of the *tirailleurs*. Fashoda would be the capital of a new French protectorate in the Bahr al-Ghazal. '*Portez armes! Présentez armes … Au drapeau.*' A large tricolour was being raised on a makeshift pole when the rope suddenly snapped. 'Bad omen,' said one of the officers, laughing. 'If we were Romans we would give up and go home!'[18] But soon the colours fluttered up again in the grey sky, saluted by a salvo of dynamite. (They had no artillery.)

But where were Kitchener's men? Where were their own friends and allies – Menelik's army and the French mission from Ethiopia? And where, for that matter, were their putative allies, the Dervishes? To all three questions the Shillouks were happy to supply contradictory answers. The English had been repulsed by the Dervishes at Metemma, 200 miles north of Omdurman; the English were advancing after a great victory. All that seemed clear was that Kitchener was still north of Omdurman. As for Clochette, he was said to be close at hand. Then a Dinka courier returned from the Sobat with the news that their 'brothers' had now turned back eastwards. A fortnight later they were told that a large expedition commanded by white men had recently planted French flags at the mouth of the Sobat. They were well furnished with horses and cattle, and their baggage was carried on elephants.

What was Marchand to make of such tales? The most disturbing news concerned the Dervishes. The Shillouk *Mek* (chief) who had allowed them to occupy Fashoda unopposed had himself been appointed *Mek* by the Dervishes. One of his councillors now revealed that the Dervishes would soon return and scatter the French 'like dust'.[19] Marchand did his best to reassure the *Mek*. The Dervishes were the enemy of the English, not the French. But the *Mek* and his people abandoned their huts and fled into the marsh. On 25 August, soon after dawn, a general alarm sounded. Two steamers – apparently old steamers of Gordon's – towing seven large rowing boats full of white-turbaned troops loomed into sight. Had they come to negotiate?

Just as the French hoisted the tricolour, puffs of smoke came from the steamers' cannons. So it was to be war. The contest must have seemed unequal. Marchand was facing at least 1,200 to 1,500 Dervishes armed with rifles and cannons. He had only ninety-nine *tirailleurs* and no artillery. But Marchand's men were disciplined and armed with the latest magazine rifles, well protected by trenches and hidden by the reeds. The Dervishes' rifles were out-ranged; their shells crashed into the soft ground without exploding. One of the steamers broke down, and then all the boats became sitting ducks. The Dervish attack proved a fiasco. That afternoon the attackers steamed back northwards into the heat haze, the steelwork of their boats punctured like colanders, and more than half the troops, so the Frenchmen were told later, lying dead or wounded in the bilges.

Dr Emily, who had no animus against the English (unlike Marchand and the other Marine officers), remarked that Gordon would have been surprised to know that it was Frenchmen who had avenged his death.

The repulse of the Dervish flotilla (in fact, Gordon's captured steamers, *Saphia* and *Tewfikieh*) did wonders for Marchand's standing among the Shillouk. So did the miraculous arrival of the *Faidherbe*, Marchand's long-lost steam launch, which puffed into the creek four days later, blowing its steam hooter triumphantly, after a twenty-four-day journey through the fearsome Sudd, to be greeted by a pandemonium of shouts and tears of joy. The *Faidherbe* was welcomed like a rescuer, its plume of black smoke a symbol of liberation. The *Mek* was all smiles, too, and consented to put his mark on a treaty giving France a formal protectorate over his possessions. They had nothing further to fear from the Dervishes, Marchand assured him. Then he was given the usual generous presents by which Europe bought its title deeds in Africa – obsolete rifles, three cavalry sabres, some rolls of cloth and some strings of beads.

Yet the Mahdists obviously planned to return, and how long would those ninety-nine *tirailleurs*, even with the forty reinforcements brought by the *Faidherbe*, hold out against the might of the Mahdist army? Marchand hoped the Mahdists would humble the English, but Dr Emily took the opposite view. An English victory would be a 'triumph for civilization and liberation against fanaticism'.[20] In the circumstances, Dr Emily's view was the more sensible. By 1 September it was clear that only one thing could now save the French at Fashoda from eventual destruction: Kitchener's victory over the Khalifa at Omdurman.

The same day, 1 September, soon after 1.0 p.m., a series of explosions shook the stone walls enclosing the inner quarter of Omdurman, the Khalifa's mud-walled capital, 700 miles north of Fashoda. A great pillar of yellow smoke and dust enveloped the most holy spot in the city – and indeed in the whole Sudan – the tomb of the Mahdi. When the smoke drifted away, the hundred-foot-high white dome was seen to be torn open in several places. In the great mosque nearby, the *mihrab*, the sacred niche facing Mecca, was smashed beyond recognition, its pulpit blown to pulp.

Charles Neufeld, a German arms dealer waiting for deliverance after twelve years as a prisoner of the Khalifa, heard the apocalyptic sounds from the city gaol. For months he had been shackled in leg irons. Now he was half-smothered in dust and stones. The explosion sounded to him and his fellow prisoners 'like the screeches of the damned let loose'. The gaolers climbed on to the roof and reported that the 'devils'[21] came from boats (in fact, they came from 5-inch howitzers) which had steamed up to Halfeya, a few miles north of the city. Later that afternoon, Neufeld was told that the bombardment had failed – just as it had failed in 1885, when the *Bordein* and *Talahaweh* sailed up the river to find Gordon dead and Khartoum taken. By the mercy of Allah, the boats of the infidel had been driven off once more and sunk. Neufeld collapsed into despair. But that night, he lay awake and heard an eerie sound – the pat-pat-pat of bare feet as thousands of men fled silently through the narrow streets to escape the English invaders.

Outside the low walls of Omdurman, facing the ruins of Khartoum across the river, the armies of the Khalifa Abdallahi were encamped that afternoon, ready to meet an attack. Despite the bombardment of the Mahdi's tomb, morale seemed excellent. The Khalifa's troops fired a volley of joy shots, as though to celebrate a victory. It was impossible to hide the scale of desertions; yet the great majority of the Khalifa's vast army stood firm. There must have been 50,000 white-robed *Ansar* there in the plain, banners flying, spears and swords flashing in the fierce sunlight.

A few weeks earlier, the Khalifa had made the decision to let the English advance the last stage unopposed. He put his faith in an old prophecy that the infidel would be destroyed at Karari, outside Omdurman. He had little choice, anyway. His generals had proved obstinate and incompetent. There was little food for his men in the north. All attempts to stem the advance of the English had failed – at Firket, Dongola, Berber and the Atbara – as though it was the wish of Allah that the infidel should come to Omdurman.

A great change had come over the Mahdist revolution in the thirteen years since it had passed into the Khalifa's capable hands. He did not now lead the people in prayer or attend the parades outside the mosque on Fridays. He remained withdrawn behind the great stone wall at the centre of Omdurman, more like an oriental monarch than the leader of a popular revolution. To his European prisoners he seemed the embodiment of cruelty as well as hypocrisy. This was the message of Rudolf Slatin's *Fire and Sword in the Sudan*, the best-selling account of the Khalifa's bloodstained reign, published with the help of

Kitchener's intelligence department after Slatin's escape to Europe in 1895.

But a less emotional look at the Khalifa would have credited him with more than a static tyranny, relieved with bouts of appalling cruelty. True, he had killed – often by treachery – a score of dangerous political rivals, and had condemned rebel cities to death by starvation or slavery. But when it suited his ambitions, he could be as conciliatory as anyone. During these thirteen years he had exploited the weakness of his rivals and forged an independent Islamic state like a personal kingdom. Independent it might have remained had he not been too proud – or too fearful – to seek allies.

Menelik, the nearest the Khalifa had to an ally, had shown that if an African ruler was to survive in the age of the Scramble, he must not be too proud to seek help from one European Power against another. Menelik was an infidel too, and the Khalifa shrank from this compromise. But what alternative had he to exploiting the rivalry among the infidel? To trust to the mercy of Allah and bury his head in the sand?

The key to political independence was the modern long-range quick-firing rifle. No one had proved this more clearly than Menelik. He had exploited the rivalry of four Great Powers – France, Italy, Britain, Russia – to buy 100,000 of the latest European rifles. Menelik had paid for these imports with gold looted from his neighbours, the unfortunate Kaffa and Galla on his southern borders. But the Mahdists had never been squeamish about the way they filled their treasury. Now that the British were advancing south, what was essential for the Khalifa was to arm and train the *Ansar* with modern weapons. Menelik was prepared to make common cause against the enemy or so he claimed. The French too longed to be the Khalifa's allies, and to arm his government against Britain, as they had armed Menelik covertly against the Italians.

For a time the Khalifa had been tempted. He had even considered flying a small French tricolour that the French Ambassador, Lagarde, had handed Menelik's emissary as a talisman for the Khalifa, a symbol of a Franco-Sudanese *entente* in the making. But his brother Yakob, less subtle than the Khalifa, was intensely suspicious. By September 1898 the die had been cast.

There was to be no compromise with the invaders from Europe. The army of the Khalifa was marshalled under its leaders on the plains of Karari. They had no effective artillery. Probably less than a fifth of the *Ansar* had rifles of any kind, and those they had were mostly obsolete Remingtons captured from the Egyptians years before, hopelessly out-ranged by the enemy's modern rifles. The *Ansar*'s main weapon was courage like wind from a furnace. Allah was great, and Abdullah Abdallahi was the Khalifa of the Mahdi, and Allah could make swords and spears prevail over the guns of the infidel.

CHAPTER 30

The Mahdi's Tomb

The Sudan, Paris and London
1 September 1898–May 1899

'Where our flag goes up, it does not quickly come
down. But what it meant to me, and I think to most
of us, was not that we had added so many thousand
square miles to the British Empire, but that we had
pledged ourselves to complete the work for which
Gordon died thirteen years ago, and to free this land
from brutality and tyranny.'

Captain Sir Henry Rawlinson, on the hoisting of the
British flag at Khartoum, 4 September 1898

The same day, 1 September, about 10.0 a.m., found a bumptious young soldier-reporter, who had wangled his way into the 21st Lancers, at the front of Kitchener's army, twenty-three-year-old Lieutenant Winston Churchill, staring through his binoculars like a racegoer at the moment when the horses come under starter's orders. What a spectacle, he wrote later, 'Never shall I see such a sight again ... I was in great awe'.[1]

There, only four miles away across the ribs of the sandy plain, lay the Khalifa's Omdurman, a low straggling line of mud walls, crowned by the white, egg-shaped dome of the Mahdi's tomb. On the left, the city was framed by the steel-grey Nile and a plump, palm-fringed island, Tuti Island, where the twin Niles, Blue and White, converged. Beyond the trees at the confluence you could catch a gleam of a white building, the ruins of Gordon's palace.

But it was not on Omdurman or on Khartoum that Churchill's binoculars were trained. In front of the mud walls, breasting a low ridge, like the Norman army marching into battle on the Bayeux Tapestry, the Khalifa's army was marching swiftly towards him. Perhaps there were 50,000 spearmen, swordsmen and riflemen concentrated on a front only four miles wide, under hundreds of wildly waving banners. 'The whole side of the hill seemed to move,' wrote Churchill later, 'and the sun, glinting on many hostile spear-points, spread a sparkling cloud.'[2]

Behind Jebel Surgham, the black hill at Churchill's back, and invisible to the Mahdists, rose the dust of 25,000 men, six brigades of Kitchener's British and Egyptian infantry, tramping like lead soldiers to confront the Khalifa. It was not merely the spectacle that held Churchill spellbound. It was the marvellous anachronism that struck him, from his godlike viewpoint on the black hill. Who would ever again see two great armies, two great worlds, marching into collision on a battlefield a few miles square: Kitchener's industrial world of the twelve-pounder and the Lee-Metford magazine rifle, against the Khalifa's medieval world of the spear, the banner, and the patched *jibbah*?

About 11.0 a.m. came the first shedding of blood. A salvo of shells crunched into the Khalifa's mud forts, fired from Kitchener's front line, the flotilla of eight white gunboats which had steamed up the Nile spouting black smoke ahead of the army. Churchill watched the shells kick the mud forts into clouds of red dust. Soon the gunners unloaded a five-inch howitzer battery beside Tuti Island, heavy guns with the range to crush the city itself. It was these high explosive shells that breached the great inner wall and crashed down into the Mahdi's tomb. Through his binoculars, Churchill saw the whole tomb vanish into red dust at the third howitzer shell, and when the dust cleared, the dome was shorn of its pointed crest.

All this time the Dervishes were still advancing across the desert, the south wind carrying the alarming sound of their horns and drums and – still more alarming – a deep-throated murmur from the *Ansar*. The cavalry CO, Colonel Broadwood, began to pull back the Lancers and the rest of the cavalry from the sandy plain. Someone must inform the Sirdar of the approach of the enemy. He grabbed a subaltern, who happened to be Winston Churchill, and told him to ride back four miles with an urgent report for the Sirdar, Kitchener. Churchill cantered off, wild with excitement, then slowed to a walk for a quarter of a mile when he spotted Kitchener's large red Egyptian flag. It was time for the stiff upper lip. However urgent the message, he was not going to look flustered when giving his report to the great man.

The Sirdar took the news of the Dervish advance with his usual impassivity. 'We want nothing better,' explained one of his HQ staff. 'Here is a good field of fire.' Then the staff invited Churchill for a bite of lunch, standing at a table spread in the wilderness, 'like a race lunch' (so Churchill wrote later), 'before the big event'.[3]

No event followed, nothing except anti-climax. It turned out that the Khalifa's army had halted in the plain. Kitchener did not attend the HQ lunch. He had schooled the architecture of his face – the large pale, *oeil-de-boeuf* eyes, the rusticated jowl, the moustache like a pediment – to present a profile of stone. But inside this stone casing, his emotions were liable to be volcanic. His impatience was understandable. This was more than the climax of the two-and-a-half-year struggle to re-conquer the Sudan, and the years of preparation before it. For him the war had begun thirteen years earlier, on 26 January 1885, that day of shame for Britain, when Khartoum fell and Gordon died. Now it was time for them to repay that debt and wipe the slate clean. So he had sternly reminded his men on 7 April that year, on the eve of the battle of Atbara.

The Sirdar is absolutely confident that every officer and every man will do his duty, he only wishes to impress upon them two words: 'Remember Gordon'. The enemy before them are Gordon's murderers.[4]

To avenge Gordon had become, over the years, an obsession of Kitchener's, as bitter-tasting as a blood feud. Now, within a few hours, so he hoped, that feud would be over. Either he would be granted a victory as swift and final as an execution, or he would fail – and pay the price in death or humiliation.

Kitchener did not expect to fail. To advance to Khartoum meant winning the battle of supply and transport, the battle fought against the desert itself, with the help of an army of camels, paddle steamers and trains. On these crucial technical questions, which had crucified Wolseley, the Sirdar, trained at Woolwich as an engineer, was in his element. He enjoyed nothing more than to drive a train without lights or brakes, shouting orders in colloquial Arabic to the terrified Egyptian officials, or to take an overloaded paddle steamer beam-end through the rapids – or, still more alarming, to hammer rivets into the hulls of the new gunboats. (His ADC had to mark the chief's rivets surreptitiously with chalk in order to be able to remove them later.) Kitchener made Wolseley seem a bungling amateur, Wolseley who had staked so much on wooden boats and Canadian *voyageurs*. Kitchener advanced with the deliberation of an elephant or a steamroller. He had one great advantage over Wolseley. With Gordon dead, he decided he had all the time in the world to reach Khartoum: years where Wolseley had months.

Kitchener had gone at his own pace, hustling the British government, but refusing to be hustled in turn by warnings that the French would reach Fashoda before him. Lord Salisbury had sent him a sealed packet of instructions to open *after* capturing Khartoum. It had taken him from April till September 1896 to pass the second and third cataracts and cover the first 200 miles to Dongola. There the advance halted for six months while he prepared the ground – both in the Cabinet room at 10 Downing Street and in the railway workshops of Wadi Halfa – for the next elephantine step. It took Kitchener till September 1897 to pass the next cataract and reach Berber, after forging a deadly new weapon, the Sudan Military Railway. This cut clean through the Nubian Desert, from Wadi Halfa to Abu Hamed, opened up a completely unexpected line of advance, and cut the troops' eighteen-day ordeal by camel and steamer to a single day and a night in a jolting cattle truck.

For two years Kitchener fought and won the battle with the desert, despite freak floods that washed away the rails and sleepers, despite epidemics of cholera and typhoid that marked his progress, all along the railway, with a neat line of graves. Then, in March 1898, he was brought to a halt by the Khalifa's obstinate young kinsman, Mahmud, who had been sent north to defend Berber but had insisted on digging in at the river Atbara. He had built a great *dem*, a camp fortified by a *zeriba* and with trenches cut into the banks of the river.

The thought of storming the *dem* made even Kitchener hesitate, and cable back to Cromer for advice. By now he had as many men as Mahmud, and his own were incomparably better fed and better armed. There were 14,000 troops: four British infantry battalions, five Egyptian and six Sudanese (including prisoners-of-war and slave troops conscripted into the Egyptian army). He had twenty-four pieces of artillery and twelve machine guns. All the British regulars carried the latest .303 Lee-Metford long-range magazine rifle, blessed with improvised dum-dum ammunition (General Gatacre had ordered his four battalions to file off the bullet tips to improve the .303's stopping power). But British casualties were politically dangerous. Was there any way to cut the butcher's bill? Cromer could offer no advice, and by Good Friday, 8 April 1898 Kitchener had decided to trust to courage and cold steel and storm the great *dem*.

In fifteen minutes the job was done, the trenches first 'leathered' by the artillery, then rushed by an incongruous line of battalions – kilted Camerons shouting 'Remember Gordon' above the skirl of the bagpipes; tarbooshed Egyptians who had fought for Arabi at Tel el-Kebir; wild ex-slaves from the Sudan, rushing forward with personal scores to settle – all hacking and stabbing like men in a slaughterhouse. At first the wounded were given no quarter. Mahmud, however, was found in a bloody *jibbah*, lying under the floor of a hut, and somehow a British officer managed to see that his life was spared. At the cost of 568 casualties (with only twenty-six killed and ninety-nine wounded in the British brigade) Kitchener flattened the great *dem* as if he had driven a train over it. The Mahdists' mangled corpses choked the trenches and the riverbed – at least three thousand of them. Many others must have died of wounds, as there was no medical aid to spare. Such was the stench on the battlefield that Henry Rawlinson, Kitchener's Deputy Assistant Adjutant General, said he was 'thankful to get away without being sick'.[5]

After this Good Friday's work – a very '*Good* Friday',[6] Kitchener agreed – the army halted for another three months. Although the enemy had fought with courage, nothing could redeem the idiocy of their commanders. Why on earth had the Khalifa divided his forces and let Mahmud wait patiently to be destroyed? But would the Dervishes learn in time how to fight? As one British staff officer put it, 'The fact he is a born fool in matters of strategy and tactics is so much to the good, but even born fools sometimes learn wisdom by experience.'[7] Kitchener decided to take no chances. He cabled Lord Salisbury for an extra brigade of British regulars, a British cavalry regiment and other reinforcements. Despite the extra expense, he still reckoned he could get the Sudan cheap: at a net cost of about £1 million. By the time the reinforcements arrived, the Nile flood would be ready to carry the steamers the last stage up the Nile.

In due course, Lord Salisbury and the Nile obliged. The August flood spirited the army to the gates of Omdurman: 25,000 men with forty-four guns, supported by a flock of gunboats, a force weaker in men but incomparably stronger in steel and cordite than their adversaries.

Kitchener might be a genius at improvising trains and ships, but he had little experience of fighting battles. By the evening of 1 September he had shelled Omdurman with howitzers, smashed the Mahdi's tomb, and built a *zeriba* five miles from Omdurman. But the Khalifa had halted his own army that afternoon.

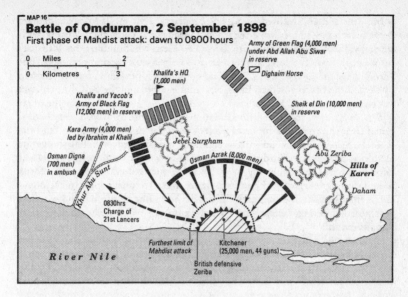

MAP 16

Battle of Omdurman, 2 September 1898
First phase of Mahdist attack: dawn to 0800 hours

0   Miles   2

0   Kilometres   3

Khalifa's HQ (1,000 men)

Army of Green Flag (4,000 men) under Abd Allah Abu Siwar in reserve

Dighaim Horse

Khalifa and Yacob's Army of Black Flag (12,000 men) in reserve

Sheik el Din (10,000 men) in reserve

Kara Army (4,000 men) led by Ibrahim al Khalil

Jebel Surgham

Abu Zeriba

Osman Digna (700 men) in ambush

Osman Azrak (8,000 men)

Khur Abu Sunt

Hills of Kareri

Daham

0830hrs Charge of 21st Lancers

Furthest limit of Mahdist attack

Kitchener (25,000 men, 44 guns)

British defensive Zeriba

River Nile

Had he finally realized that it would be folly to fight in the desert in daylight, at a time and place best suited for the British, who could exploit the extra range and overwhelming power of their weapons? Perhaps he would force the British to storm Omdurman itself, and gamble everything on the outcome of street fighting. Or perhaps the Khalifa would retreat in order to pursue what Kitchener most dreaded – a guerrilla war.

Fortunately for Kitchener, he and his Staff were right about the Khalifa. The man *was* a fool, though a gallant one. About an hour after dawn on 2 September, the cavalry patrols reported that the Dervish army was advancing straight towards the British camp. Within half an hour their flags and spears broke the skyline over the black hill to the south-west. Ahead of them the 21st Lancers and the rest of the cavalry scampered back to gain the cover of the *zeriba*. At 6.50 a.m. British field-guns began to knock holes in the advancing line, giving the cue to the Egyptian batteries, and the gunboats on the river to the east. Armageddon had begun.

The first phase of the battle was so unequal that it seemed more like an execution. Two divisions of the Khalifa's army (about 6,000 men under Osman Digna and 8,000 men under the Emir Osman Azrak) put their faith in Allah and charged straight at the British camp. They wore the holy uniform of the patched *jibbah* (plus, in some cases, chain mail). They advanced in an enormous crescent, brandishing their spears and their texts from the Koran, and chanting, like the *muezzin* from the minaret, '*La Illah illa'uah wa Muhammad rasul Allah*' ('There

543

is but one God and Muhammad is his Prophet').[8] The shells knocked holes in their lines, but the holes were soon filled. From 2,000 yards the British infantry started volley-firing with their smokeless Lee-Metfords. Still the Dervishes came on steadily, now running, now walking. The Maxims then joined in. At 800 yards' range the Egyptian and Sudanese battalions followed with their Martini-Henrys, firing black powder. There was pandemonium in the British camp, and the enemy was lost in the smoke.

Within a few years, the battle formations of Omdurman would seem hard to credit. British infantry were firing volleys shoulder to shoulder, with the front rank kneeling and the rear rank standing, just as redcoats had fought at Waterloo. But out in the open desert the Mahdists met a death that was modern enough. There they lay, as the smoke cleared, shot and mangled, 2,000 men at least in crumpled heaps. Thousands more were retreating, wounded. Not a single man had survived to reach the British firing line before the Sirdar's voice was heard shouting, 'Cease fire! Please! Cease fire. What a dreadful waste of ammunition!'[9]

If Kitchener had paid the Khalifa the compliment of making the Tommies dig trenches in front of the camp and letting them shoot lying down, he might have won this phase of the battle without losing a man. But no such orders had been issued in the British brigade. A hedge of camel-thorn made even kneeling difficult, but gave no defence against Mahdist bullets. Fortunately for the British brigade, only a minority of the *Ansar* were armed with rifles and most of these were obsolete Remingtons, better suited for bagging elephants than men. But a party of Dervish riflemen managed to find a lair behind some sandy ridges about 300 yards from the *zeriba*. They killed and wounded a number of British infantry before shrapnel from the field-guns flushed them into the open. The Egyptian and Sudanese infantry had improvised parapets and trenches; they hardly lost a man.

It was now about 8.30 a.m. and the battle seemed almost over. The attack on the camp had been repulsed with miraculous ease. Yet only about a quarter of the Khalifa's vast army had been fully engaged. The Army of the Green Flag, 20,000 men under Emir Wad el Sheikh and Ali Wad Helu, had vanished northwards. After a tussle with the cavalry and camel corps, they had slipped behind the Karari Hills, two miles north-west of the British camp. And where was the Army of the Black Flag: 17,000 men led by the Khalifa himself and his brother Yakob? Nothing had yet been heard of them. Were they lurking behind Jebel Surgam, the black hill? Kitchener did not apparently care. His only idea was to occupy Khartoum before the enemy returned there. He gave orders for the 21st Lancers to reconnoitre the plain, followed by the army, advancing in echelon of brigades from the left, as though today was a field day and this was Salisbury Plain.

To abandon the protection of gunboats, trenches and *zeriba*, and make a flank march exposing the final brigade to a pincer movement from the enemy, would not have won much praise from the umpires, even on a field day. But Kitchener's proverbial luck held fast.

The same could not be said for all his men. He had sent the 21st Lancers to reconnoitre. Their CO, Colonel Martin, insisted on a cavalry charge. The regiment had been mocked for having no battle honours, and now they got a bellyful. For a few extraordinary moments, Winston Churchill felt the stunning shock of the collision between 400 shouting horsemen and 2,000 yelling infantry:

> The whole scene flickered exactly like a cinematograph picture; and, besides, I remember no sound. The event seemed to pass in absolute silence. The yells .of the enemy, the shouts of the soldiers, the firing of many shots, the clashing of sword and spear, were unnoticed by the senses, unregistered by the brain.[10]

When his brain began to register, Churchill realized that war was no longer like a day at the races, but 'a dirty shoddy business, which only a fool would undertake'. The plain was suddenly full of men spouting blood:

> Men, clinging to their saddles, lurched helplessly about, covered with blood from perhaps a dozen wounds. Horses, streaming from tremendous gashes, limped and staggered with their riders. In 120 seconds five officers, 65 men and 119 horses out of less than 400 had been killed or wounded.[11]

Of course, the charge was magnificent. But it was an absurd anachronism for the British. What was the point of cold steel, the *arme blanche*, when the Lancers had excellent carbines, and behind them was an infantry brigade which could dislodge the enemy by firing from a safe distance? Indeed, it was worse than absurd. There was now no cavalry to reconnoitre. So Kitchener's two front brigades marched briskly off, vying with each other to be first into Omdurman, unaware that the rear brigade – the 1st Egyptian Brigade of Brigadier-General Hector MacDonald – was a mile behind the rest, and cut off by nearly 40,000 Dervishes.

If MacDonald had been as raw as Colonel Martin, that would probably have been the end of the brigade. But 'Fighting Mac' was a veteran of Majuba (where he was supposed to have knocked out a Boer with his bare fist). He was a square-jawed Scot, promoted from the ranks of the Gordons, a man who had spent three years drilling slave troops and fellahin and knew how to handle them. Now he rode out in front of the firing line, roaring abuse and knocking up the rifles of those who had lost their heads and were blazing away prematurely. In the meanwhile, he sent off a galloper, a messenger to tell the Sirdar about their predicament. The galloper got short change. 'Can't he see that we're marching on Omdurman?' was the Sirdar's reply. 'Tell him to follow on.'[12]

Fortunately, something made the great man change his mind. In a few minutes the two British brigades and the other Egyptian brigades wheeled away from Omdurman and swung west to protect MacDonald's left flank. Still more fortunately, the two surviving Mahdist armies – the Khalifa's and Yakob's of the Black Flag, and the twin armies of the Green Flag – were unable to co-ordinate their attacks. Even communication by galloper, the primitive method still used by the British, was beyond them. So MacDonald was able to parry each in turn. First he smashed down a charge from the west: a yelling line of white-robed figures, under a huge black banner, crumpled and mangled by the combined fire of Martini-Henrys, Maxims and field-guns firing case-shot. Then he smashed down a charge from the north, and drove the men of the Green Flag back to the shelter of Karari, pursued by Broadwood's Egyptian cavalry.

It was time to resume the march on Omdurman. At 11.30 a.m. Kitchener closed his glasses with a snap. The enemy, he remarked, had had a 'good dusting'.[13] The advance continued, led by the Sirdar with Yakob's captured Black Flag, escorted by only one battalion of Sudanese. Through the narrow streets and the breach in the great wall went the Sirdar and his Black Flag, and still there was no trouble from the enemy. Most of them were out in the plain, soon to turn black in the sun – 10,800 bodies were scattered there and at least 16,000 wounded, dependent on their friends, or left to their fate and trying to drag themselves down to the Nile. The main threat to Kitchener's troops came from their own side.

The men were told to shoot any tribesman still under arms (including the wounded, if they looked aggressive). Stray rifle shots ricocheted off the mud walls. A stray shell fired from a gunboat narrowly missed Kitchener and killed Hubert Howard, *The Times*'s correspondent. As darkness fell, the inner city bore the brunt of the confusion; released prisoners (including Charles Neufeld), mules, camels, men and generals, all converged simultaneously on the Mahdi's tomb.

It took Kitchener two hours after sunset to find his tent. Then he lay on his back dictating his despatches by the light of a candle. His victory was crushing, the cost trifling. He had lost only forty-eight officers and men killed, 382 wounded, out of 26,000 men. (The casualties of the 21st Lancers, more than half the dead on the British side, testified to Colonel Martin's folly.) He had destroyed the Khalifa's army and added a vast new territory to the British Empire, nominally in partnership with Egypt. Only one thing detracted from the completeness of his victory: taking a fresh camel, the Khalifa had escaped with a trusty band and sought refuge in the fastnesses of Kordofan. But all relics of the Mahdi were scattered to the winds.

Four days after the battle, Kitchener ordered the dome, cupola, plinth and every trace of the Mahdi's tomb to be razed to the ground, and his bones cast into the Nile. (The skull was recovered, it was claimed, for the Sirdar to use as an inkstand. But the Queen, was shocked to hear of this; the skull was decently buried at Wadi Halfa.)

With a less barbaric ceremony, Kitchener set the seal on the recovery of Khartoum. On 4 September the gunboats steamed across the river for a memorial service to be held in front of the ruins of Gordon's palace. The upper storey had crumbled away, and so had the famous staircase where Gordon died; the garden was choked with weeds and thorns; but the great tree by the river front survived. Twin flags, the Union Jack and the red flag of the Khedive, were solemnly hoisted on the broken wall and twin national anthems, 'God Save the Queen' and the Khedival anthem, crashed out across the river front. The service ended with Gordon's favourite hymn, 'Abide With Me', played by the 11th

Sudanese. And Kitchener, the man of stone, impervious to suffering or triumph, found he had no voice to dismiss the parade. Tears swelled the large pale-blue eyes, smudged the dust on his cheeks – tears of happiness and gratitude, he explained to his astonished staff.

'The sternness and harshness had dropped from him for a moment', wrote one of them later, 'and he was as gentle as a woman.' After thirteen years he had redeemed his country's honour. Gordon was avenged.

Three thousand miles away in Berlin, the Kaiser was writing to his grand-mother, Queen Victoria, to congratulate her on the British victory. She too was thinking of the place where 'poor Gordon met his cruel fate'.[14]

A week later, Kitchener ordered one hundred Cameron Highlanders and two battalions of Sudanese troops, with a gun battery, to board a flotilla of five gunboats and steam south for an undisclosed destination.

The crew of a captured Mahdist gunboat had told British intelligence that unknown 'foreigners' had attacked them at Fashoda; and by now Kitchener had opened the sealed packet sent by Lord Salisbury. He himself was to proceed up the White Nile with a small fighting force and to repudiate all rival claims. The entire upper Nile valley was now Egyptian – and British. The twin flags would fly over the Nile valley by right of conquest. If the French, or Abyssinians, were in occupation, they must be told to leave. Those were the orders, although privately Lord Salisbury warned Kitchener there were to be 'no corpses'.[15] On 10 September 1898 the flotilla vanished south into the heat haze, bound for Fashoda.

After their triumphant repulse of the Mahdists on 25 August, Marchand's band of ten Frenchmen and 140 blacks had continued to strengthen their grip on the sandy island with a handful of palm trees at Fashoda, in the great marsh 700 miles south of Khartoum. They dug trenches and built mud parapets, ready for anything. On 17 September, some terrified natives spread the alarm: a huge Dervish army – thousands of men in five gunboats – was on the warpath.

Before dawn next morning, when Marchand's men were already manning the trenches, they were astonished to be greeted by two handsome blacks, correctly dressed in the red tarbooshes and khaki drill uniforms of the Sirdar's army. They saluted with what one Frenchman called '*une raideur toute Britannique*', a stiffness, Kitchener-style. Then they handed Marchand a polite letter from the Sirdar. It was addressed to the 'Commander of the European Expedition at Fashoda', whoever that might be, and was written in French. After capturing Khartoum, the Sirdar was coming to reclaim the rest of the Khedive's empire. Marchand wrote a note back repudiating the claim, but welcoming Kitchener 'in the name of France'.[16]

The solemn meeting, a few hours later, between Marchand and Kitchener brought to the serious world of high politics a touch of '*opéra bouffe*', as Kitchener himself acknowledged.[17] Here was the climactic moment of Anglo-French rivalry, of the two hungry Powers that for twenty years had taken first place in the partition of Africa. Now they appeared ready to come to blows about a swamp in the middle of nowhere. But the absurd disproportion of forces made it seem as if no one in France had taken the idea of empire on the upper Nile seriously. Hence the dreamlike unreality of the meeting between Marchand and Kitchener.

At about 10.0 a.m. the *Dal*, Kitchener's flagship, and the other four boats of the flotilla steamed in line astern down the narrow channel with flags flying and 1,500 soldiers lining the decks. They anchored within 150 metres of the shore, training their guns on the French. Marchand and another officer were rowed across to the *Dal* in one of their whaleboats, carrying a huge tricolour. No one kept a full transcript of what followed, but there is enough evidence to reconstruct some of the frosty dialogue, spoken on Kitchener's part in his own brand of French:

Kitchener: 'My instructions are to regain possession of Fashoda in the name of the Sublime Porte and His Highness the Khedive.'

Marchand: 'My orders are to occupy Fashoda and other parts of the upper Nile abandoned by Egypt and therefore without a legal owner ...'

Kitchener: 'I cannot argue these points, but I would suggest you consider the preponderance of the force at my disposal ...'

Marchand: 'Until we receive orders to retire we shall not haul down our flag but are ready to die at our posts ...'

Kitchener: 'But this situation could lead to war ...'[18]

At which Marchand gave what his companion called *une profonde inclinaison de la tête*, to confirm that this was indeed so.

After this unpromising start, the frost melted. Both men agreed that the rights and wrongs of the case would have to be referred to Paris and London. In the meanwhile, Kitchener was prepared *not* to require Marchand to lower the tricolour or retire. For his part, Marchand was prepared *not* to object to Kitchener's hoisting the Khedive's flag, without the Union Jack, on a tree next to the fort. Perhaps each man was disoriented by the unexpected good sense of the other. At any rate, observers on the neighbouring gunboats, who had anticipated a shouting match, were now amazed to see some kind of celebration in progress. Through his field-glasses, Major Smith-Dorrien watched a trail of glasses and 'golden liquid' being carried to the upper deck, where the two great men were slapping each other on the back, swapping anecdotes about beating the Dervishes and clinking glasses of whisky and soda. (What a sacrifice for the French, Marchand later ruefully admitted, to have to drink '*cet affreux*' lukewarm whisky-and-soda.)

That afternoon the hospitality was repaid in sweet champagne, green vegetables and flowers. Then Kitchener deposited 600 black infantry on the crocodile-infested mud flat beside the fort, and steamed off to plant another British outpost fifty miles to the south, in the marsh where the Sobat joined the White Nile. There two robust flags, British and Egyptian, marked the scene of Colonel

Artamanov's gallant dip in the Nile three months earlier, and his forlorn attempt to fly the tricolour.

The next day Kitchener steamed back to Omdurman, from where he tele-graphed a report to London, saying that Marchand's position was 'as impossible as it is absurd'.[19]

Before he left Fashoda, Kitchener had extracted one interesting admission from Marchand's men. They were delighted to see the five gunboats were British, not Dervish. He then generously gave Marchand the latest French newspapers, sent by express from Cairo. The generosity was calculated. The renewed explosion of the Dreyfus Affair in 1898 had demolished the government and was threatening to tear France to pieces. Marchand said later, 'An hour after we opened the French papers the ten French officers were trembling and weeping ... and for thirty-six hours none of us was able to say anything ....'[20]

*   *   *

A copy of Kitchener's telegram to London, reporting that he had met Marchand, and that Marchand's position was 'impossible as it is absurd', exploded like a torpedo on Théophile Delcassé's desk in the Quai d'Orsay on 26 September, just as the Dreyfus Affair was moving to a climax.

Delcassé, the Foreign Minister who had replaced Gabriel Hanotaux at the Quai d'Orsay after the Dreyfus Affair had demolished Méline's government in June, was a forty-six-year-old ex-journalist in the south-west. He was a patriotic radical, a fervent colonialist, and a disciple of Gambetta and Ferry. Cartoonists found him a delight, for he was as squat and unprepossessing as a dwarf:

> The dwarf came into the Cabinet meetings [wrote Anatole France in his cruel satire, *The Island of Penguins*] with a briefcase bigger than himself and crammed with documents. He remained silent and answered no questions, even those put to him by the venerable President of the Republic. Soon afterwards he fell asleep, tired by his incessant work, until all that was visible above the green baize table was a small tuft of black hair.[21]

Of course, Delcassé did not really behave like this in a crisis. He was obsession-ally hard-working and also the most secretive of politicians, a man who hoped for nothing more from the new Prime Minister, Henri Brisson, and his Cabinet colleagues than to be able to run French foreign policy without their assistance. This, at least, was a redeeming feature of the tormenting Dreyfus Affair; it kept the Cabinet's gaze grimly fixed on home affairs. However, by late September, Henri Brisson's days were numbered – and so, perhaps, were those of the Third Republic itself.

The crisis had gathered momentum ever since Zola's sensational open letter to President Félix Faure, '*J'Accuse*', was printed in Clemenceau's *L'Aurore* in January 1898. Zola had been tried and condemned, and then fled to England. But there followed the downfall of Méline's government and the arrest and suicide of Major Henry, who had confessed to forging a crucial part of the evidence which had damned Captain Dreyfus as a traitor to France and a spy for the Germans. Had there been perjury on an astonishing scale, and then a cover-up in the highest places? The scandal spread like gangrene, first to the army itself, then to its anti-semitic allies in Church and state. Soon all France seemed divided into two festering camps. Mobs of Jew-baiters roamed the streets, abetted by the police. On 13 September, there was a strike of 20,000 building workers in Paris. The generals called out 60,000 troops and bivouacked them in the squares. Already people were talking of the '*Grande Peur*', as though a military *coup d'état* was imminent.

At the beginning Delcassé had been as convinced of Dreyfus's guilt as anyone. As Minister for the Colonies in 1894–5, he had been responsible for Devil's Island, the pestilential prison in French Guyana to which Dreyfus had been despatched. However, by 1898 he shared the misgivings of most radicals and was prepared to get at the truth, even if it meant rubbing the army's nose in it. After scandalous new revelations, most of the French electorate, too, seemed to be swinging that way. On 27 September, the day after Delcassé received that explosive telegram about Fashoda, Brisson and the majority of his Cabinet, including Delcassé, voted that Dreyfus's case should have a re-hearing.

It was poetic justice that the Minister of Foreign Affairs torpedoed by Fashoda should be Delcassé, for it was Delcassé who had launched the missile himself, five years earlier. As Minister for the Colonies, he had been the darling of the *Parti Colonial*, which fêted him as the first political master to put teeth into French colonial policy. The Pavillon de Flore was the symbol of Delcassé's magic. For it was he who had transformed the Colonies, that Cinderella of government departments imprisoned in an airless hovel under the Ministry of Commerce, into the independent Ministry of the Colonies housed in the Pavillon de Flore, an elegant wing of the Louvre overlooking the Tuileries.

Delcassé's policy was deliberately provocative. To expand the French Empire meant continually treading on England's toes. To his wife, he boasted that 'he was the man who insisted on not giving way to John Bull'.[22] Hence the series of deliberate confrontations with England – in Siam, West Africa and on the Nile – and in the French Cabinet with his more cautious colleagues. In 1893–4 Delcassé had insisted on sponsoring Monteil's mission from the Congo to the Nile in order to force England to re-open the Egyptian question, the same mission that Marchand took over the following year. Hanotaux had danced and wriggled in his vain efforts to keep Marchand from finding his way to the Nile.

Now the diplomatic boot was on the other foot. But four crucial shifts of position had transformed the diplomatic game in the two and a half years since Marchand had set off on his epic march. In Europe, the Kaiser's congratulations to Queen Victoria on recapturing Khartoum apparently signalled the start of an Anglo-German *rapprochement*. Russia, despite its erratic anglophobia, was not prepared to lift a finger to help France. In Africa, Menelik had made a fool of everyone. Worst of all, England had spent £1 million to recapture Khartoum, and suddenly the upper Nile was not merely a swamp in no-man's-land. It was one of the world's strategic steamer routes.

Strange to say, Delcassé had given little thought to this question. He had left a letter on the subject, written by the callow new Minister for the Colonies, Georges Trouillot, unanswered for two months. When he did reply, it was to express the hope, like Hanotaux before him, that Marchand would remain lost in the swamps. Marchand was only an explorer with a few rifles (so Delcassé assured the British Ambassador, Sir Edward Monson), just 'an emissary of civilization'.[23] He also tried to play down the expedition by claiming that Marchand was not really in command – a ridiculous fiction.

Now that Marchand had surfaced, Delcassé wondered how he could get rid of him without submitting his beloved France to abject humiliation. In a series of ominous interviews at the Quai, Monson made it clear that Lord Salisbury would not budge an inch. Monson generously gave Delcassé the choice between unconditional withdrawal and a 'rupture'[24] – which might mean war. Delcassé racked his brains for some face-saving concession to sweeten the taste of humble pie.

In early October he thought he had found the sweetener. He decided to send Baron de Courcel, the anglophile Ambassador who had just retired from his post in London, back on a special mission to Lord Salisbury. Courcel was to try to persuade the British Prime Minister to let the French keep a toe-hold, at least on paper, in the Bahr al-Ghazal as an outlet to the navigable Nile. It would be like that token concession made the previous spring of allowing France nominal access to the Niger. But would Lord Salisbury take the bait?

The awful truth was that as a great naval power France was a sham. Its navy could be sunk by the British within a fortnight. That was the forecast of many experts, and seemed to be shared by the French Chief of Naval Staff. Even in the unlikely event of the Russians agreeing to join hands, it was no match for the British. Anyway, the nearest Russian fleet would be ice-bound in the Baltic ports until the spring. The abject state of the French navy was a legacy of years of confusion in naval planning. Now there was only a *'flotte d'échantillons'* ('fleet of samples'), ships of dazzling variety but impossible to assimilate into a fighting force.

So Delcassé confessed to his diary that France did not have the option to fight England for it would be a 'naval war, which we are absolutely incapable of carrying on, even with Russian help'.[25] Courcel must find a sweetener. But perhaps Monson was bluffing. After all, Lord Salisbury had always despised jingoism and could pride himself that the twenty years of the Scramble, however undignified, had been conducted without a shot fired by one European Power against another.

*　　*　　*

Baron de Courcel found Salisbury polite but negative at their first meeting on 5 October in the Foreign Office. He managed to turn Salisbury's main legal argument – the right of conquest – against him. After all, if the legality of the

British claim to Omdurman was by right of defeating the Mahdists, this applied equally well to the French claim to Fashoda. Salisbury was forced to take the undignified position of claiming a *partial* right as heir of the Khedive, and a *partial* right as conqueror of the Mahdists. But these sophistries were neither here nor there. Salisbury's case rested on *power*. (As Delcassé put it, 'they have the troops ... we only have the arguments'.)[26] Marchand was in an impossible position. France had broken the unwritten rules of the Scramble by sending a secret expedition to try to steal what belonged to Britain and Egypt. Still, Courcel thought he detected a gleam of hope. Salisbury offered to consult his colleagues about an outlet in the Bahr al-Ghazal. A week later that hope had died. Courcel himself clumsily snuffed it out, by putting impossibly stiff terms on the table: the concession by Britain of the whole region between the Bahr al-Arab, the Bahr al-Ghazal and the Nile.

Events in England were now assuming a momentum of their own. On 10 October, Salisbury decided he would strengthen his hand by taking the British public into his confidence. He released a Blue Book on the negotiations in progress. It was an unusual course and, from Salisbury's point of view, almost too effective. Politicians came forward from every side, eager to denounce the French attempt at claim-jumping, and warned the government not to yield. The time had come for Britain to dig in its toes and defend the Nile valley, its vital interest in Africa; even at the risk of war. That was the message conveyed in speeches by both Lord Rosebery, the Liberal imperialist, and Sir William Harcourt, the Gladstonian Liberal. Moderate newspapers proved strangely intransigent. The jingo *Daily Mail* howled for war. By the third week of October the Reserve Fleet had been manned, and war orders drafted for the Home, Mediterranean and Channel fleets. Only the *Manchester Guardian* kept a cool head, and asked what the fuss was about. It was in this dangerous atmosphere that Lord Salisbury called a Cabinet meeting for 27 October, and refused to meet Courcel until after it had taken place.

If Salisbury had hoped to find a sop for Delcassé, this was now ruled out by the other members of the Cabinet. The sudden outburst of pugnacity seems hard to credit. But apparently Salisbury found himself struggling to hold back the hotheads from moving towards a preventive war. There is a story in the German archives that Chamberlain told a German informant in early November:

> I am afraid Lord Salisbury himself has not got the strength of mind to bring about the necessary crisis and choose the right moment to strike like Bismarck did at Ems. You may be certain, however, that all my colleagues, even Mr Arthur Balfour, are of the same opinion as I am, namely that Lord Salisbury's policy 'peace at any price' cannot go on any longer, and that England has to show to the whole world she *can act*.[27]

But the Prime Minister was not going to be hustled by Chamberlain. To his divided Cabinet he put the passionate convictions of their Queen: 'A war for so miserable and small an object is what I could hardly consent to.'[28] After bitter wrangling, the Cabinet agreed not to force the pace. The French would at least be given the chance to haul down their flag without an ultimatum. Once the tricolour had been lowered, the way might be open for negotiations on frontiers, but the Cabinet refused to make any promises in advance.

This was the cold comfort that Courcel had to cable back to the Quai after his delayed encounter with Lord Salisbury.

*   *   *

In the meantime, the agony in Paris had intensified. On 25 October the anti-Dreyfusards rioted and mobbed the government. Brisson fell, stabbed in the back by his colleagues, and seemed likely to bring Delcassé down with him. However, if Delcassé's time was numbered in hours he still hoped against hope to extricate France from the swamp.

He was aghast at the reports of British naval preparations. Who could now claim the English were bluffing when they talked of war? He grudgingly accepted the scrap thrown by Lord Salisbury. The sooner Marchand left Fashoda, the less the humiliation. And Delcassé groped for a new face-saver. The official reason for the withdrawal could be attributed to Marchand's own difficulties in keeping his head above water. After all, Kitchener had reported him to be in an 'impossible' position. Marchand's first garbled report did not confirm this story, but Delcassé counted on Baratier, Marchand's Number Two, to accommodate him. Baratier had been ordered hotfoot to Paris. So efficient was Kitchener's new steamer service that Baratier's train steamed into the capital only sixteen days after his ship had steamed out of Fashoda.

When Baratier came to the Quai to see Delcassé at 8.0 a.m. on 27 October, Delcassé raised his arms to heaven to indicate the harshness of fortune. Innocently, Baratier explained the strength of Marchand's position at Fashoda. Kitchener's telegram was a lie. The French fort had been resupplied from the steamer *Faidherbe*. Now they had enough ammunition to repel any number of Dervishes, and food to last for months. Their health and morale were excellent. This could hardly be said for the British garrison at Fashoda, whose black troops were on the verge of mutiny. (Marchand later claimed, 'All I need is ten minutes to wipe out Jackson's troops and his guns.')[29] M. le Ministre need have no fear, Baratier assured him. France would never suffer the disgrace of seeing the tricolour being hauled down at Fashoda.

'*Vous ne comprenez pas bien l'honneur de la France*,'[30] replied Delcassé. It took Baratier some time to realize that he and the Minister were at cross-purposes. Delcassé needed a witness to confirm that it would not be fair to ask Marchand to hold his impossible position any longer. All he got was a furious patriot who stormed out of the Quai, crying betrayal.

Shocked and outraged, Baratier set off to sabotage the plan for withdrawal. He found ready ears among Delcassé's own political intimates, Eugène Etienne, and the leaders of the *Parti Colonial*. Already the colonialist press was in an ugly mood. *La Dépêche Coloniale* called for war rather than humiliation.

Unfortunately for this campaign, Delcassé got wind of it immediately and ordered Baratier back to the Sudan. At the same time, Félix Faure, the President since 1895, assumed the role of *deus ex machina*.

Faure was a self-made – and self-indulgent – industrialist, known as '*Le Roi Soleil*' because of his pretentious style. In the 1880s he had served Gambetta and Ferry, and then played a leading part in the *Parti Colonial*. But he saw nothing to recommend a war over Fashoda. Apart from the fact that France would lose, his task was to unite a nation that had lost its government, and was being torn in half by the Dreyfus Affair. Fashoda would only add to those wounds. France, unlike Britain, could not agree that to defend a swamp in Central Africa was a vital national interest. On the contrary, the country was as divided on Fashoda, and on similar lines, as on the Affair. The Left condemned imperialism as roundly as it supported Dreyfus. The Right was jingo and it provided the driving force behind the anti-Dreyfusards. The no-nonsense businessmen of the towns and seaports were unconvinced that there was money in the upper Nile. For every patriot who identified national honour with the defence of the army and the refusal to climb down over Fashoda, there was another patriot who regarded the whole business of Fashoda as a red herring.

So Félix Faure, the industrialist, threw his weight behind Delcassé's realism and the colonialist challenge fizzled out. On 2 November, Charles Dupuy was able to piece together a new government, committed to the climb-down. Delcassé had been persuaded to swallow his pride and join it. On 4 November Lord Salisbury announced to rapturous applause at the Guildhall that the French would be leaving Fashoda. He had won this crucial game without conceding a point.

* * *

All over the world the Fashoda crisis and the French climb-down dominated the newspaper headlines. In Fashoda itself, where both sides were cut off from the telegraph line, the tension intensified. Across the half mile of rain-swept marsh, the men of each garrison exchanged presents – jam from the English, champagne from the French – but oiled their rifles and trained them on the other's camp.

Baratier had been called to Cairo on 10 October and nothing had been heard of him for weeks. (He had been recalled to Paris.) The strain was too much for Marchand. On the 25 October, without orders, he took a berth on one of Kitchener's paddle steamers, and vanished. The *Faidherbe* sailed off to visit one of the outposts, and one of the officers crossed the Nile to explore the marshes bordering Ethiopia. Everyone else's morale crumbled like the mud walls in the rain. It was not only the stifling heat, the fevers, and the mosquitoes that made life unendurable for the remains of the French garrison. It was the uncertainty, weeks with nothing to do except read English papers gloating about the Dreyfus Affair and brood on what news from Paris the next boat would bring. Civil war over the Affair? War with England? Relief – or betrayal?

The fourth of December 1898 was a Sunday, the feast of the Sainte-Barbe, and the wind blew fair from the north. Dr Emily felt calmer. In the last few days the atmosphere had been menacing, so much so that Emily was afraid the English commander, Jackson Bey, would pick a quarrel and then open fire. A month earlier Jackson had warned them, 'War's about to break out between France and England.'[31] Quite suddenly he apologized for his rudeness.

At 8.0 a.m. a paddle steamer came snorting into the anchorage. Good news from Paris at last? Dr Emily was handed a note for Captain Germain, who was busy with two miniature cannons and told Emily to read it. The text could hardly have been blunter: 'Commandant Marchand will arrive this evening on board the *Nasser* to proceed with the evacuation of the French troops.'[32]

That evening Marchand and Baratier were back with their comrades and confirmed the humiliation. They would have to leave Fashoda and haul down the tricolour. It was a cruel, unexpected blow. 'The crumbling walls which we have repaired, the ditches we have dug out, the bastions, the entrenchments, the fort which we have erected with our own hands, all this to be abandoned.'[33] At least the English responded without gloating. Jackson Bey threw a farewell banquet for his rivals and presented Marchand with a keepsake: the flag captured from the *Saphia*, the Mahdist ship repulsed by the French on 25 August. The chivalrous gesture went straight to Marchand's heart. He took the flag with tears in his eyes, as Jackson's black troops played '*La Marseillaise*'.

A week later '*La Marseillaise*' boomed out once again as the French steamed off in the *Faidherbe*, bound for the Sobat and the Baro. Marchand had refused to take the easy way home, by way of the Nile, which was now indisputably an English river. Paris agreed to let him return by way of Menelik's wild kingdom, and Jibouti, after crossing the whole continent.

Before weighing anchor, Dr Emily was put a question by the black *tirailleurs*, who had always accepted the white man's explanation for everything. Why did they have to leave Fashoda? For once Emily could not look them in the eye. 'The white man doesn't know.'[34] He could not begin to explain to these simple black souls the depth of the humiliation, or the bitter sense of betrayal.

*   *   *

In London, Lord Salisbury was not yet ready to let the French off the hook. Monson told him the French were in a blue funk, expecting that at any moment their fleet would be attacked by the British navy. Salisbury did not disabuse them. He wanted to win the match, not just a crucial game: to secure not only withdrawal from Fashoda but from the whole Nile valley, including Marchand's chain of thirty new posts in the Bahr al-Ghazal.

First he had matters to tidy up in the Sudan. There was the constitutional position to be arranged with the Khedive. In the event the Khedive proved most understanding. The polite fiction of the two flags, British and Egyptian – as though the Khedive and the Queen were equal partners – was to be extended, under the name of condominium, over the whole Sudan. Of course the Khedive had no more power than a rag doll. Britain now controlled Africa from Lake Victoria to the Mediterranean.

It was not until March 1899 that Lord Salisbury finally let the French off the hook. Meanwhile, they had been tormented by the latest twist of the Affair, including a right-wing *coup d'état* which had collapsed into farce, and the revelation that Félix Faure, the Roi Soleil, had died of over-exertion in the arms of his mistress. Delcassé swallowed the last of his pride by agreeing that France would leave its posts on the Bahr al-Ghazal, bag and baggage, and accept the Nile–Congo watershed as a frontier between their respective empires. On 21 March Delcassé signed a formal agreement, disguised, at his own request, as an annexe to the West African Convention of the previous year. When Marchand and his party returned to France in May 1899, Dupuy's government gave him a brief welcome as a hero, and then sent him off on leave, under police surveillance, to make sure he did not talk to politicians of the Right. The less said about that wretched marsh the better.

The same marsh had brought Lord Salisbury to the apogee of his long diplomatic career. Yet the Scramble was not yet over. A handful of African states still retained a fragile independence from the European Powers. Of these, by far the richest and most desirable was the Boer Republic of the Transvaal. Taking the Transvaal seemed child's play for Great Britain. Who could have guessed that it would demand a war of conquest, at the climax of the Scramble, that would cost more in blood and treasure and humiliation than all the preceding conquests in Africa?

CHAPTER 31

Milner's War

London and South Africa
8 September 1899–31 May 1902 and after

> 'I precipitated the crisis, which was inevitable, before
> it was too late ... It is not a very agreeable, and in
> many eyes, not very creditable piece of business to
> have been largely instrumental in bringing about a
> big war.'
>
> *Sir Alfred Milner* to Lord Roberts, 6 June 1900

It was 8 September 1899 and both the English summer and the Transvaal crisis had proved unexpectedly persistent. Outside Lord Salisbury's gilded room in the Foreign Office, the grass in St James's Park was burnt a glowing African brown. Inside, soon after midday, the hastily summoned Cabinet arrived in holiday clothes, but hardly holiday mood, to decide whether to risk a war by sending out troops to South Africa, followed by an ultimatum to President Kruger and the Boers.

Balfour, the deputy Prime Minister, looked as if he had taken the train straight from the Edinburgh golf links. He wore a blue serge suit and yellow shoes. Chamberlain, the Colonial Secretary, fresh from his garden at Highbury, Birmingham, sported an orchid grown in his greenhouse. Most of the other Cabinet members came hotfoot from covert or grouse moor: Hicks Beach, the Chancellor, from his 6,000 acres in Gloucestershire; Lansdowne, the War Minister, from his shooting lodge at Dereen, County Kerry, where the tree ferns grew like weeds and the Atlantic sparkled, for once, as blue as a kingfisher's wing. They took their places at the horseshoe table facing the Prime Minister, a sombre, bowed figure in a black frock coat.

The crisis had come at the worst moment for Salisbury. His health was failing; and he had torn himself away from Walmer, where his wife, the mainspring of his political life for forty-two years, was dying of cancer. But Salisbury, 'Old Sarum' to the cartoonists, was still in command.

Secret diplomacy – the subtle art of peaceful conquest in the conference room – he had always pursued with the passion of a connoisseur. He resented the crude, public way Chamberlain had handled the Transvaal crisis. He had no wish to be hustled into war by 'Pushful Joe' and his jingo supporters, including the British loyalists in South Africa. He would go at his own pace.

Chamberlain had forced the Transvaal on the Cabinet's attention in April 1899 by taking up the cause of the Uitlanders, the British immigrants to the Rand. Backed by some of the chief 'gold bugs' who had launched Jameson's Raid in

1895 (but not by Rhodes), the Uitlanders claimed they were oppressed by the Boers. It was six months since the government, impelled by Chamberlain, had outmanoeuvred the French and won a bloodless victory at Fashoda. Now it seemed a good time to outmanoeuvre Kruger.

The Colonial Secretary's objective was the same now as it had been four years earlier when he had tried to exploit Rhodes's plan for the Raid – and the same as Carnarvon's objective when Britain had annexed the Transvaal back in 1877. Chamberlain hoped to create a new British dominion by uniting the two British colonies, Cape Colony and Natal, in a federation with the two Boer republics. To unite all South Africa under the British flag would be Britain's crowning achievement in the Scramble, the culmination of the twenty-year struggle for mastery from Cairo to the Cape. But was Chamberlain going too fast? Could South African unity be achieved without a war – or, indeed, with one? The old guard in the Cabinet, including the Prime Minister, were predictably sceptical of the Colonial Secretary's optimism.

Both Chamberlain and Carnarvon, it must be stressed, shared the same imperial assumptions about South Africa, as did the rest of the Cabinet and most of the Liberals.

The independence of a Boer republic, bursting with gold and bristling with imported rifles, threatened Britain's status as 'paramount' power. British paramountcy (alias supremacy) was not a concept in international law. But most of the British thought it made practical sense – indeed was essential for good government in South Africa. Boer independence seemed worse than absurd; it was dangerous for world peace. These were the years of increasingly warm rivalry between the blocs of Great Powers, with Britain dangerously isolated. The solution seemed to be to wrap the whole of South Africa in the Union Jack, to make the whole country a British dominion, like Canada. Until then the government's aim must be to prevent the Transvaal defaulting on its obligations under the settlement made with Gladstone three years after Majuba, the London Convention of 1884. This gave the Boers of the Transvaal the title deeds for an ill-defined kind of independence, including self-government in home affairs. But the responsibility for the Transvaal's foreign affairs was left to Britain, the paramount power.

The need to confirm British paramountcy seemed all the more urgent because of the explosive effects of the gold rush that had begun two years after the signing of the London Convention. To the bankrupt farmers to whom Carnarvon had given £100,000 to bail out the Treasury, the Rand goldfields had seemed like the gifts of Midas. By 1899 the Transvaal, measured by its gold exports of £24 million a year, was much the most opulent state in Africa. This compounded the anomaly of Transvaal independence. Gold had transformed it into a modern military power, armed with the latest German rifles and French artillery. Yet Kruger had done nothing to redress the political grievances of the Uitlanders who had developed the Rand. These newcomers believed they now represented the majority of the white population. They were denied equal rights – especially the right to vote – and in March 1899 they made an appeal for Caesar, in the shape of Queen Victoria, to take up their cause.

From the first, Salisbury resented the provocative style with which Chamberlain had responded to the Uitlanders' appeal. In May, Chamberlain had sent the British High Commissioner, Sir Alfred Milner, to negotiate with Kruger, the Transvaal President, at Bloemfontein, capital of the Orange Free State, the Transvaal's sister republic. The Cabinet had accepted Milner's plan to pin down Kruger on the franchise issue. But Milner seemed to have scant respect for the old man's difficulties in dealing with the burghers' understandable fear of being swamped by the newcomers. Milner was polite but unyielding. He was determined to nail down Kruger to his plan for a five-year franchise; all male Uitlanders would be given the right to vote once they had been resident for five years in the Transvaal. When Kruger refused, he broke off negotiations. As the crisis deepened, Chamberlain published Milner's fire-eating private despatches to London ('The case for intervention is overwhelming ... The spectacle of thousands of British subjects kept permanently in the position of helots'[1]) in a series of incandescent Blue Books. It might have seemed an odd way to try to conciliate an opponent and end a century of conflict. But conciliation was not Chamberlain's objective. His aim was to stiffen public opinion among the British in both South Africa and at home, and use it to squeeze concessions out of Kruger. When dramatic concessions did come – a five-year franchise in return for a British commitment not to intervene further – Chamberlain only increased the pressure.

The climax of this provocative policy came on 28 August of that year when Chamberlain addressed his supporters, *urbi et orbi*, from his garden at Highbury. He appeared exasperated: 'Kruger ... dribbles out reforms like water from a squeezed sponge.'[2] This was the style of the new, open diplomacy. It was hardly a surprise that, after being compared to a sponge, Kruger became as obdurate as Milner. He withdrew his five-year offer and substituted an offer of a seven-year franchise, together with international arbitration. The stalemate resumed. It was now that Chamberlain had called for the Cabinet meeting of 8 September. He was determined to tighten the screw on Kruger. They should agree to send out reinforcements to Natal, and consider an ultimatum.

No formal record was taken of this crucial Cabinet meeting, but the arguments can be reconstructed from the papers that were circulated to the Cabinet. Chamberlain claimed that Kruger had proved immovable. Ever since March he had been given every opportunity to make terms. Now he should have one final chance. The issue was well understood by the British public. They saw it was no longer a technical dispute about the franchise for Uitlanders. What was at stake was Britain's right to be paramount power in South Africa. The Boers had challenged this, not only by their obstinacy in negotiations, but by recklessly asking Britain to commit itself not to intervene in future in the affairs of the Transvaal.

Chamberlain then put the case, in two different forms, for 'pressing the button'[3] and rushing out 10,000 British troops to reinforce Natal. If the Boers were bluffing – and Milner, backed by the gold magnates, had repeatedly assured him they were – the despatch of these troops would call Kruger's bluff, and frighten him back to the conference table. If Kruger was mad enough to challenge Britain to a fight, the 10,000 troops would protect Natal from a Boer pre-emptive strike until Britain's invasion force – an army corps of 47,000 men led by Sir Redvers Buller – could be mobilized in Britain and the Empire.

Chamberlain's own opinion was that the Boers were bluffing – or at any rate the Boer army was a paper tiger. So there was perhaps a case for an ultimatum. However, even Chamberlain acknowledged that the legal grounds were extremely 'weak'[4] because of the vague wording of the London Convention negotiated by the Liberals. It was the moral case, he claimed, that was unas-sailable. Chamberlain's terms would tighten the screw with a vengeance. The ultimatum would demand 'equal rights' for the Uitlanders, meaning a one-year franchise, that would presumably give the British immediate political control of the country; a 'new deal' for the gold magnates, meaning lower mining costs and cheaper black labour; an agreement to reduce armaments; above all, the acceptance of a new Convention that would copper-bottom British para-mountcy; and, as an afterthought, a fair deal for Africans. They must not purchase a 'shameful peace' by leaving them as they were.

The Cabinet agreed to 'press the button' by sending the 10,000 troops to reinforce Natal. But until they arrived, which would take a month, they had been advised by the War Office experts that it would be rash to provoke Kruger with an ultimatum. Lord Wolseley and the other war experts had warned them that Natal would be extremely vulnerable for a month. Although profoundly sceptical of any forecasts made by the War Office (Salisbury said he never doubted the 'futility'[5] of that great institution), the Cabinet decided to put safety first. Instead of an ultimatum, they decided to stall. In due course, they would send an 'interim' despatch (a 'pen-ultimatum',[6] as the wits called it). The Cabinet broke up at 2.50 p.m., and its younger members cheerfully returned to their broken holidays.

It was left to the old guard to deplore the way they had been manoeuvred into this adventure. Hicks Beach, the Chancellor, was appalled at the military cost: £350,000 for mules and other transport animals for the first instalment, the 10,000 troops for Natal, and up to £10 million for the invasion force, if it was needed. Twenty years earlier, Hicks Beach had been a member of Disraeli's Cabinet which had sanctioned Frere's half-baked annexation of the Transvaal. 'Does not this remind you of all that happened to Sir Bartle Frere?'[7] he asked Salisbury grimly. The Prime Minister could not restrain his bitterness. His nimble diplomacy in the Scramble had redeemed Gladstone's blunders at minimal cost. He had parried the Germans, outwitted the French and given the lion's share of Africa to the British. Now he sensed the magnitude of the task ahead.

Salisbury did not share the general optimism that Kruger would surrender rather than fight. He was afraid that Britain faced the greatest war since the Crimea. Perhaps he hinted to his colleagues what he had privately told

Lansdowne a week earlier: Britain could not flinch from war – that would mean resigning all pretensions to supremacy in South Africa, the strategic key to the route to India. But it was cruel to be forced into war for such a negative object, 'All for people whom we despise and for territory which will bring no power to England.' He had grasped too late the power that Chamberlain – and Milner – had achieved by manipulating public opinion. 'His view [Milner's] is too heated … but it recks little to think of that now. What he has done cannot be effaced. We have to act upon a moral field prepared for us by him and his jingo supporters.'[8]

The Cabinet's decision to 'press the button' and send out 10,000 troops to Natal provoked a sigh of relief from the Commander-in-Chief at the Horse Guards, General Lord Wolseley, but not because he hoped it would call Kruger's bluff and avert war. Like most British officers, Wolseley felt sick of the shame of Majuba and Gladstone's 'peace-under-defeat'. A war with the Boers was the simplest way to wipe that off the slate. Besides, as a lifelong army reformer, he believed that a new war would be the making of the British army. It would also destroy his small-minded enemies at home, including his own chief, Lord Lansdowne, the War Minister.

A short walk across St James's Park from the Horse Guards, at the end of Pall Mall, were the antiquated buildings of the War Office, presided over by Lord Lansdowne. For three months Wolseley had laid siege to him in an effort to persuade him to turn the military screw on Kruger. Patience had never been one of Wolseley's failings, he was glad to think. 'Little Lansdowne … is an obstinate little fellow, very conceited … I spend my days struggling with my little gentleman.'[9] Wolseley proposed to mobilize Buller's army corps on Salisbury Plain to frighten Kruger into submission. He also wanted to reinforce Natal. He found Lansdowne's obstruction intolerable. The man was more than a personal enemy; he seemed to epitomize the small-mindedness of the War Office, and the defects of the system that still persisted, despite Wolseley's long struggle for army reform: the reckless budget-cutting, the red tape, the complacent belief in muddling through – and above all, the encroachment of a civilian War Minister and his officials in a field that should have been the preserve of Wolseley and his Ring.

To complicate this wrangle between the stuffed shirts of the War Office and the brass hats of the Horse Guards, there was a war between the generals themselves. There were two Rings in the British army: the 'Africans', led by Lord Wolseley ('our only general'); and the 'Indians' led by Lord Roberts (Lord 'Bobs', alias 'our only other general'). For twenty years Wolseley had dominated the army in Britain and had been entrusted with the small wars in Africa generated by the Scramble. Lord Roberts, a year his senior, had dominated the army in India. In 1895, when the royal Commander-in-Chief, the Duke of Cambridge (alias the 'Great German Sausage'), had finally been put on the shelf, Wolseley had tightened his hold on the Horse Guards. He succeeded the Duke; Roberts, back from India, was put out to grass as c-in-c in Ireland. Wolseley's heir apparent was the Number Two of the 'Africans', Sir Redvers Buller. Yet it was clear that Roberts had not given up the struggle. Lansdowne, ex-Viceroy of India, cordially admired Roberts. He now gave the 'Indians' the first bite of the cherry in South Africa. Most of the 10,000 reinforcements for Natal would be men from Roberts's old army, proceeding directly from India, and would be led by an Indian veteran, General Sir George White. Wolseley was furious. He had no confidence in White, who was sixty-seven and knew nothing about Africa; and he could never forget that it had been a cowardly Indian regiment – the 85th – that had got into a funk and lost England the battle of Majuba.

To make matters worse, Wolseley had also lost confidence in many of his own 'Africans'. In fact, since Colley's day, the magic had gone out of the Ring. General Butler, the Irish nationalist, had taken an eccentrically 'pro-Boer' line in politics. As acting High Commissioner in South Africa in 1898–9, he had accused the gold magnates of trying to stir up a war, and had got himself sent home for his pains. General Brackenbury had betrayed Wolseley by joining the 'Indians'. General Buller remained the heir apparent, yet there was little sympathy between him and his old chief. Wolseley could not forgive Buller for his disloyalty in 1895, when Rosebery's government had nominated Buller to succeed the old Duke of Cambridge and Buller had accepted. (Wolseley had been saved by Rosebery's fall.)

If there was to be a war with the Boers, what kind of war would it be? This was the overwhelming question. On Wolseley's threadbare Intelligence Department, starved of resources by Lansdowne, rested an enormous responsibility. It forecast that the Orange Free State would probably join hands with the Transvaal. On paper the combined Boer armies would then total 54,000. This compared with a total British force of 15,000 regulars after the reinforcements reached Natal. However, the Intelligence Department did not consider the Boers a serious military adversary. The Boers only knew about fighting 'Kaffirs'. Fighting against British regulars would be beyond them. Their generals would be out of their depth in handling artillery and deploying large bodies of men. So the British need only guard against mere 'raids' across the border by 2,000 to 3,000 men. These would be 'so deficient in discipline and organization' that they would break and run 'after the first serious defeat'.[10] In short, the modern Boer had gone soft, and would be inferior to the Boers who had beaten Colley at Majuba.

Wolseley was at daggers drawn with Lansdowne, Buller cold-shouldered by Wolseley, White isolated from both, and the Intelligence Department knew nothing of the enemy. Small wonder that when White sailed for Natal in mid-September, he had no inkling of what lay ahead, and stumbled straight into the strategic trap laid by the Boers.

In Cape Town news of the Cabinet's decision on 8 September to 'press the button' and send the reinforcements provoked a sigh of relief from Sir Alfred Milner, too, when the news was cabled to him the same afternoon.

At times during these months of wrangling, the High Commissioner at the

Cape had thought he might be thrown over by Salisbury and the Cabinet, just as Sir Bartle Frere had been thrown over by Disraeli. There was no danger of that now. Not that Milner, any more than Wolseley, hoped that sending out troops would avert war. Milner had been less than candid with Chamberlain and the Cabinet in claiming that a show of military strength would call Kruger's bluff. This was indeed the message that all the British gold magnates, including Cecil Rhodes, had passed on to the authorities in London. Rhodes was convinced that Kruger would bluff right 'up to the cannon's mouth'.[11] Milner's private view was quite the contrary. Unlike the War Office, he paid the Boers the compliment of regarding them as a formidable enemy. But he did not make the mistake of saying this to Chamberlain.

Milner expected the combined armies of both Boer republics to try a preemptive strike at the exposed northern areas of both British colonies. In Cape Colony they would strike at Kimberley and at Mafeking; in Natal they would attack the salient north of the Tugela river. His call for reinforcements was not to prevent these strikes, but to turn them to his own advantage. Milner's own brand of imperialism was far more radical than that of Chamberlain and the most aggressive of Salisbury's Cabinet. Chamberlain wanted to nail down Kruger and force him to the conference table in order to confirm British paramountcy, and peacefully create a new Anglo-Boer dominion. Milner wanted to break the mould altogether and Anglicize South Africa. As he said himself, his aim was to 'precipitate the crisis, which was inevitable, before it was too late'.[12] To put it bluntly, Chamberlain wanted peace and Milner needed war.

It was easy to underrate Milner. His adversaries generally did. He was a bachelor of forty-six and looked older, with his long, thin face and melancholy grey-brown eyes. There was a whiff of the Athenaeum and the British Museum about him. When he appeared in public he looked so awkward that he seemed like a man walking on stilts. He appeared to epitomize the dullest ideals of the civil service – hard work, patience, loyalty to political masters. Yet there was a passionate side to Milner that only his intimates knew. His father was an improvident, half-German medical student from Giessen. He himself had been reared in Germany as a child, brought up to hero-worship Bismarck and Frederick the Great. Inside Milner, repressed but not extinguished, was the spirit of his father, romantic, bohemian, restless – and reckless as well.

In 1897 Chamberlain had sent Milner to Cape Town to pick up the pieces after Jameson's Raid. The next year, when the Cabinet was up to its eyes in the Fashoda affair, he had returned to London to consult with his chief and stamp on his 'rose-coloured illusions'[13] about South Africa. Kruger had just been re-elected for a fourth term as President of the Transvaal, and Milner reported that time was not on Britain's side. The gold rush to the Transvaal had turned South Africa on its head: the new political centre was Johannesburg, not Cape Town. London must intervene on the side of the Uitlanders, who felt betrayed by the mother country. Otherwise the Boers could unite the whole of South Africa in a republic, and Britain would lose both Natal and the Cape. Chamberlain had refused imperial intervention – for the time being. It was left to Milner on his own to 'work up to a crisis' (his own phrase) by 'bucking up'[14] the Uitlanders, with the help of a secret alliance which he had forged with the two richest 'gold bugs' of the Rand.

There were good political reasons to be discreet about this alliance. The 'gold bugs' were Alfred Beit and Julius Wernher, the two chief paymasters of the Raid (their firm had paid £200,000, twice as much as Cecil Rhodes). Since that fiasco they had distanced themselves from Rhodes and thrown in their lot with the imperial government. Both men were naturalized British of German origin – which gave them a special link with Milner. Wernher-Beit, their partnership, was based on Mincing Lane in the City. Each man had a palace of his own in Mayfair. They were both eager to redeem themselves in the eyes of their adopted country, and privately Milner showed them how. In March 1899 Kruger's government offered a 'great deal' for all the Rand capitalists. By arrangement with Milner, Wernher-Beit's agent, Percy Fitzpatrick, scuttled the settlement. Wernher-Beit offered Milner discreet help in many other ways – which included adding their disingenuous voices to Rhodes's claim that Kruger was bluffing. They also paid for an anti-Kruger press campaign in Johannesburg under the guidance of Milner. Led by Fitzpatrick, the Uitlanders now projected a well-scrubbed image of loyalty to the imperial government.

There was nothing hypocritical about this loyalty, at least on the part of the two 'gold bugs'. Like Milner, they had come to despair of doing business with Kruger. By September 1899, Wernher-Beit's £17 million stake in the Rand was proving dangerously vulnerable. For months the crisis had caused panic among the Uitlanders. Refugees were beginning to pour from the gold-mines, flooding down to Cape Town. Behind them, the huge black mine wheels stopped turning and the sky became blue above the chimneys. Perhaps Wernher-Beit was losing £100,000 a day. So a very private message was passed to Milner, encouraging his belligerence. The financiers were 'quite prepared for war' and they insisted that 'the situation be terminated now'.[15]

*   *   *

The news that 10,000 British troops were being sent to Natal, cabled by the London news agencies, reached President Kruger in Government Buildings, Pretoria, the next morning, 9 September, and confirmed his worst fears about Chamberlain.

Like Milner, Kruger now believed war to be inevitable. Unlike Milner, he had never understood that Chamberlain was searching for a compromise. The Raid had poisoned his opinion of Chamberlain. So he had come to regard the meeting with Milner at Bloemfontein as a mere sham. It was a trap to humiliate the volk, his people, and divide them from their kith and kin, their fellow Boers of the Orange Free State and the Afrikaners of Cape Colony. It was their moral support which had helped the Transvaal in its first War of Independence, culminating in Majuba. Now they had more: a military alliance with the Boers of the Orange Free State. Together, the volk would stand shoulder to shoulder against the aggressors and put their faith in God.

Understandably, Kruger, the seventy-six-year-old warrior, saw a symmetry in his long life as hunter and hunted. 'It is our country you want,'[16] he had said at Bloemfontein, his eyes watery behind his steel-rimmed spectacles. Yet to the younger members of the Transvaal government, like Kruger's protégé, Jan Smuts, the brilliant twenty-nine-year-old State Attorney, educated at Cambridge, Chamberlain's belligerence seemed baffling. How could he hope to launch a war without a real *casus belli*? The Uitlanders' franchise would not give him one. Bare-faced aggression would only create more solidarity among the kith and kin in South Africa – provided the Transvaal did not lose its head. Ever since May, Smuts had been the ready channel by which their friends in the neighbouring states pressed the case for concessions. Hence the dramatic offer, during August, of the five-year franchise. But what folly it was, as their friends did not fail to point out, to link this with an impossible condition – that the British should agree not to meddle any more in the internal affairs of the Transvaal.

By 8 September, confusing Milner's aims with Chamberlain's, Smuts and Kruger had despaired. 'Humanly speaking,' said Smuts, 'a war between the Republics and England is certain.'[17] It was Smuts who now produced a dramatic plan for a *blitzkrieg* against Natal before the promised 10,000 British troops could land. With 40,000 Boers, they could brush aside the British garrisons, go straight for the sea, and capture Durban before the first troopship could dock there. This would precipitate a rising by the Cape Afrikaners, who would declare a 'third republic'. The British Empire would reel, and Britain's rivals, Germany and France, would rush to exploit the collapse. Unfortunately for Smuts, President Marthinus Steyn of the Orange Free State had not despaired of peace in early September. Plans for the *blitzkrieg* lapsed. Smuts was baffled.

Then, on 22 September, a British newspaper reported that the British government was to press the war button for the second time. They were sending the 47,000 men of the army corps to invade the Transvaal. In quick succession both republics mobilized, the Transvaal on 28 September, the Orange Free State on 2 October. By now the first British troopship had docked in Durban, followed by an endless stream of troopships with reinforcements (including contingents from as far afield as Canada, Australia and New Zealand).

The governments of the republics then co-ordinated a plan for invading the two British colonies on much the same lines as Milner had expected. Two Boer columns would converge on Natal in the exposed triangle north of the Tugela river. Other columns would strike at the strategic border towns in the Cape – Kimberley and Mafeking, north of the Orange river. But, true to the convention of civilized war, the two republics first had to declare war on Britain. The ultimatum, apparently drafted by Smuts, was uncompromising, the voice of David challenging Goliath. It accused Britain of breaking the London Convention of 1884 by taking up the Uitlanders' cause and massing troops on the border. It demanded assurances from the British government on four crucial

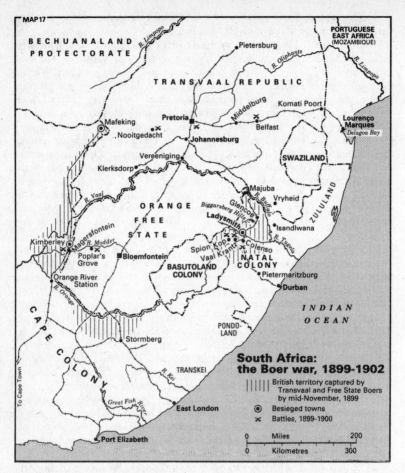

MAP 17

BECHUANALAND
PROTECTORATE

R. Limpopo

Pietersburg

PORTUGUESE
EAST AFRICA
(MOZAMBIQUE)

R. Oliphants

R. Limpopo

TRANSVAAL REPUBLIC

Mafeking
Nooitgedacht
Pretoria
Johannesburg

Middelburg
Belfast

Komati Poort

Lourenço
Marques
Delagoa Bay

Vereeniging
Klerksdorp

SWAZILAND

R. Vaal

ORANGE

FREE

STATE

Majuba
Glencoe
Biggarsberg Hills
Ladysmith

Vryheid
R. Buffalo

ZULULAND

Kimberley
Magersfontein
Poplar's
Grove
Bloemfontein
Orange River
Station

R. Modder

Spion Kop
Vaal Krantz
Colenso

Isandlwana

R. Tugela

NATAL
COLONY

Pietermaritzburg

Durban

BASUTOLAND
COLONY

R. Orange

INDIAN
OCEAN

PONDO-
LAND

C A P E

Stormberg

TRANSKEI

R. Kei

Great Fish River

East London

**South Africa:
the Boer war, 1899–1902**

||||| British territory captured by
Transvaal and Free State Boers
by mid-November, 1899

⊙ Besieged towns

✕ Battles, 1899–1900

To Cape Town

C O L O N Y

Port Elizabeth

| 0 | Miles | 200 |
| 0 | Kilometres | 300 |

issues. Britain must accept arbitration on all points of difference; withdraw all troops from the borders; recall recently-landed reinforcements; and agree not to land any further troops. Unless Her Majesty's Government complied with these demands within forty-eight hours, the government of the Transvaal would 'with great regret be compelled to regard the action as a formal declaration of war'.

Two hundred miles south of Pretoria, where the veld had begun to flush green in the spring rains, the Transvaal column, led by sixty-eight-year-old General Joubert, was poised to strike at Natal as soon as the ultimatum expired. Joubert was the general who had crushed General Colley and his 400 redcoats at Majuba eighteen years earlier. Could he deal the same blow to General White and his 'Khakis', now roughly 13,000 strong? Despite the British reinforcements, the Boers still had a useful advantage in numbers – about 15,000 Transvaalers and 6,000 Free Staters were poised on the border – and an incomparably better strategic position. Besides, they knew northern Natal better than the British. Natal, the Promised Land, stolen by the British from the voortrekkers in 1842, was theirs for the taking.

On Thursday, 12 October in the small hours, the Boers struck camp and rode across the frontier, in 'a weird opening to the great drama', according to young Leo Amery (*The Times*'s enterprising correspondent with the Boers). He saw 'an endless procession of silent misty figures, horsemen, artillery, and wagons, filing past in the dark, cold night along the winding road that led to where the black shoulder of Majuba stood up against the greyer sky'.[18]

*   *   *

The text of the ultimatum, amounting to a joint declaration of war by both republics, was received in London on Tuesday, 10 October with derision, delight, dismay – and indifference.

Derision was the keynote of the editorials in next day's papers. 'One is in doubt whether to laugh or to weep', proclaimed the *Daily Telegraph*. *The Times* called the ultimatum an 'infatuated step' by a 'petty republic'. Most papers agreed. 'Preposterous ... mountebank ... extravagant farce', were their kinder words. 'Of course there can only be one answer to this grotesque challenge ... Mr Kruger has asked for war and war he must have.'[19]

Inside the labyrinthine corridors of Whitehall the ultimatum sent a spasm of delight and relief. Kruger and Steyn had got them out of a political hole: the need to draft an ultimatum of their own. 'Accept my felicitations', scribbled Lansdowne to Chamberlain. 'I don't think Kruger could have played your cards better than he has.'[20] Chamberlain, too, was in ecstasies. 'They have done it!'[21] he exclaimed when woken by the Colonial Office messenger at the ungodly hour of 6.15 a.m. The joint declaration of war had given them both republics on a plate, for it was the Orange Free State, which was flat, not mountainous Natal, that gave the best line of advance on Pretoria. It had also pulled the rug from under the feet of the Liberals. Chamberlain had been racking his brains for a way to strengthen the *casus belli* when Parliament came to debate the £10-million estimate for Buller's invasion force. Now no further explanation was needed. They were sending out Buller to repel a Boer invasion.

By contrast, the *Manchester Guardian*, the *Daily News* and many Liberals were appalled. To throw away their moral position by this reckless act of aggression: what folly the ultimatum seemed to Campbell-Bannerman, who had taken over the Liberal leadership after that bed of nails had been vacated by Lord Rosebery. Campbell-Bannerman was a Liberal of the centre. Privately he felt sympathy for anyone, Kruger included, who had to face Chamberlain's bullying. But the issue was highly explosive for his own party, already torn apart by the Radicals and the Liberal Imperialists ('Limps'). There was a real risk that South Africa would be the reef that finally sank the Liberal boat. So Campbell-Bannerman had to swallow his words of protest and give the government a walk-over in the House.

It was the British people who took the news from South Africa with the least display of emotion. For most of the last twenty years the Scramble had seemed remote from the lives of most British families. Stanley, it is true, had made Africa a fashionable topic of conversation by discovering Livingstone and rescuing Emin; and Lugard had focused polite attention on the race for Uganda. But it was Britain's humiliations that had proved most memorable – when somebody had blundered and too little help was sent too late: when Chelmsford's men were cut down by the Zulus at Isandlwana, Colley's by the Boers at Majuba and Gordon by the Mahdi at Khartoum. There seemed no fear of that today.

Britain was despatching the largest force she had sent overseas since the Crimea. It would be in Pretoria by Christmas. The Boers would be squashed flat by Buller and his 'steamroller'. This is what the experts said.

Wednesday's *Times* said that Britain would be at war with the two republics 'at tea-time next day'.[22] People took up the phrase; this was to be the tea-time war. It was Newmarket week, and the Cesarewich coincided with the exact moment – 3.10 p.m. – when the ultimatum expired. No one could have guessed this from the behaviour of the crowds, which included the Duke of Devonshire. In the hot sunshine they watched Scintillant win by a short head from Ercildoune. The capital was half empty. Fashionable London was in the country, Parliament still on holiday. The smooth surface of Victorian life was not to be ruffled by a war – not a war at tea-time, a war in a tea cup.

Two days later a noisy, patriotic crowd gathered at Southampton to bid godspeed to General Sir Redvers Buller on his passage to South Africa. He was sailing on the *Dunottar Castle* with the first instalment of the invasion force (and an army of war correspondents, including twenty-six-year-old Winston Churchill). Buller was not a national hero like Wolseley. At Waterloo Station, people had hardly recognized the tall, burly figure in mufti, with a sprig of his own Devonshire violets in his button-hole. But here at Southampton people greeted him as if they had known him all his life. He made a gruff speech at the gangplank. He hoped he would not 'be away long'.[23] The crowd struck up 'For He's a Jolly Good Fellow'.

Few could have guessed Buller's feelings. He knew the Boers better than most Englishmen. He had fought side by side with them against the Zulus and admired their natural gift for fighting. That morning, when he had been seen off by the War Office staff at Waterloo, towering over both Wolseley and Lansdowne, he was overwhelmed apparently by forebodings. All through July and August he had warned the War Office, 'Do not go north of the Tugela'.[24] Lansdowne had ignored his advice. The latest War Office cables appalled Buller. Against all military principles, White had kept his force up in the dangerous northern triangle, and had now divided it, one part at Dundee, one part at Ladysmith. Despite Buller's protests, Lansdowne refused to order White back to safety.

The crowd in Southampton, led by Buller's wife, Lady Audrey, began to sing 'God Save the King'. There were cries of 'Bring back a piece of Kroojer's whiskers' and 'Remember Majuba'.[25] Buller stood on the navigation deck waving his felt hat as the *Dunottar Castle* steamed out into the fog. He seemed the very archetype of the British warrior – bronzed, heavily moustached, with a jowl like a bulldog. One thing gave him an air of supreme self-confidence. He did not try to hide his own emotion.

*　　*　　*

Pretoria, like London, was half deserted, but for different reasons. In August there had been a noisy war party in the Transvaal Parliament, the Raad, and a spasm of war fever. Many of the young Boers were spoiling for a fight. But now they had gone, sent off to one of the war fronts. For days the troop trains had been clanging through the station, most of them heading south to Natal. Several thousand Africans, too, had been commandeered and sent down in labour gangs, ready to dig trenches and do the rest of the menial work at the front. Forty miles away across the undulating veld, Johannesburg looked still more forlorn and deserted. The great exodus of British and black Uitlanders from the Rand had left half the shops boarded up. Only one or two iron mine wheels were still turning. The state had taken over several gold-mines for the duration, to pay for the war effort, using commandeered African labour.

Kruger worked late in Government Buildings and then retired to the *stoep* of his small house in Church Street, puffing his pipe and waiting in silence as he had waited on the night of the Raid. With his homely faith he epitomized the nation's defiance. When General Joubert telegraphed from the frontier that the commissariat was in chaos, Kruger told him sharply to put his faith in the Lord. It was the same when he made a speech to the final session of the Raad before its members left Pretoria to join their commandos. Whose hand had saved them at Majuba and during the Raid? 'The Lord will also protect you now, even if thousands of bullets fly around you.'

The day after the war began he was interviewed by a reporter from the *New York World*. What if Britain won? Then the price to be paid would 'stagger humanity'.

*　　*　　*

At Westminster, the government's motion for the £10 million invasion force steamed smoothly through the Commons. Chamberlain spoke for three hours, defending his South African policy from A to Z – or rather, from the Raid to the Ultimatum. His theme was that aggressive republicanism (in modern terms, militant Afrikaner nationalism) had made war inevitable. Apart from the Irish party, only a handful of opposition MPs dared to oppose. How the pendulum had swung. Less than four years earlier, the Boers had seemed ready to dig Chamberlain's grave. Now they gave him the triumph of his career.

*   *   *

It was eight weeks later, and the pendulum had swung back with a crash, deluging the government with mud from the veld, and humiliating Britain in the eyes of the whole world.

In all the conflicting forecasts made by Wolseley's warring generals, one nightmare had never been envisaged – that the Boers would fight the British, with both sides evenly matched in numbers, and the Boers would win. By the third week in December – 'Black Week' as it came to be called – that nightmare was a reality. Indeed, the reality was worse.

As Buller had forecast, the Boers had overrun the smooth veld of Cape Colony for a hundred miles south of the Orange river, and the rugged hills of Natal down to the Tugela and beyond. In the process they had cut off the three British garrisons at the strategic border towns: less than 1,000 regulars at Mafeking and Kimberley in Cape Colony, and 12,000 of White's field force at Ladysmith in Natal. By mid-November the tide of invasion had turned and the Boer invaders were thrown on the defensive. They had divided their forces, leaving one set of commandos to besiege each of the strategic towns, and sending other commandos south to block the advance of each of the relief columns. By mid-December Buller's army corps had landed, had been divided in three, and was marching to the relief of Kimberley and Ladysmith. On paper Buller now had a two to one advantage in numbers. The British forces in South Africa totalled over 60,000 regulars, supported by 150 field-guns. With such a weight of steel behind him, Buller was expected to teach a sharp lesson to the homely commandos. But it was the Boers who did the teaching in 'Black Week'.

The battle of Magersfontein on 11 December provided the first surprise by showing the futility of a frontal attack. Even when supported by artillery, and with a two to one superiority in numbers, the attackers could not break through a line of entrenched riflemen. Lieutenant-General Lord Methuen, a veteran of African campaigning to whom Buller had given two infantry brigades from the Army Corps, adopted the same bull-at-the-gate tactics that had served Wolseley well enough at Tel el-Kebir, and Kitchener at the Atbara. About half an hour before dawn, the Highland Brigade tried to storm the Magersfontein ridge, fifteen miles south of Kimberley, at the point of the bayonet. But what they met was not a rampart full of fellahin fuddled with sleep, like Arabi's line at Tel el-Kebir, nor a *zeriba* of 'Fuzzy-Wuzzies' armed with spears and elephant guns, like Mahmud's line at the Atbara. They met the Boers – or rather, they met Boer bullets. For the new smokeless, long-range, high-velocity rifle, fired from concealed trenches, made the Boers themselves invisible all day.

The battle of Stormberg on 10 December, if battle it was, confirmed the Boers' talent for tactical mobility and the British talent for tactical blunders. Lieutenant-General Sir William Gatacre, one of Kitchener's more energetic generals in the Sudan campaign (his men called him 'Back-acher'), took a small infantry column and tried to recapture the strategic railway junction of Stormberg, in the north of Cape Colony. Misled by a guide, the General lost his way in darkness. Next morning, a party of mounted Boers snapped up most of his column, killing or capturing nearly seven hundred.

The third battle, at Colenso in Natal on 15 December, dealt a sharp blow to Buller's own pride. After preliminary bombardment of the unseen enemy, he tried to break through General Botha's defence line on the Tugela, but found it too strong and tried to call off the attack. The Boers, firing from hidden trenches, gave a hiding to General Hart's Irish Brigade, and to the gunners of Colonel Long's batteries, both of whom were nailed down by rifle fire close to the river.

Together these three repulses, and the setbacks in Natal that had preceded them, cost the British 7,000 casualties in killed, wounded and captured. (The only light relief was provided by the escape of one enterprising prisoner, Winston Churchill, by hiding down a mine.) The chief military results were negative. Buller had failed to avert the threat to White and his 12,000 men. But no more territory was gained by the Boers.

In London, Black Week brought a shiver to the last month of the so-called 'British century'. Theatres emptied and (a gut reaction) restaurants, too. There was no hysteria, simply shock; this was a major war. But Queen Victoria spoke for most of her subjects when she told Arthur Balfour, 'Please understand that there is no one depressed in this house; we are not interested in the possibilities of defeat; they do not exist.'[26]

For the twenty years of the Scramble the English had made war on the cheap, measured in British lives and money. Ever since Isandlwana and Majuba, the price for Britain's taking the lion's share of Africa had been largely paid by Africans, whether victors or vanquished: Arabi's Egyptians, Gordon's and the Khalifa's Sudanese, Lobengula's Ndebele and his Shona vassals, the Wa-Ingleza and the Wa-Fransa in Uganda, the men of Nupe and Ilorin in Nigeria. Now the élite of the British army had been sent to conquer 50,000 farmers at a cost of £10 million, and they could make no headway at all.

Salisbury's government blamed Wolseley and the generals for the fiasco. This was understandable but hardly fair. The politicians had overridden their more percipient military advisers, like Buller, and had prepared for the struggle as if it was going to be a small war against black men.

What was to be done to save the three beleaguered garrisons – and the nation's face? Humiliation spurred the government to three expedients. The first was to throw economy to the winds and flood South Africa with reinforcements. Naturally Wolseley welcomed this. The 5th Division, largely reservists, was already being mobilized; a 6th and 7th Division would be sent after it. Canada,

Australia and New Zealand would be invited to send new contingents. The second expedient struck Wolseley as a stunt. Buller had cabled home emphasizing the need to raise volunteers who could ride and shoot like the Boers. The government decided to create and send out a new 'Imperial Yeomanry', 10,000 strong, drawn from the hunting and shooting classes in Britain and Ireland. The third expedient appalled Wolseley. Buller was to be superseded as C-in-C; he would have his work cut out left in charge of Natal. But instead of sending out sixty-seven-year-old Wolseley himself, the head of the 'Africans', Lansdowne had chosen sixty-eight-year-old Lord Roberts, head of the rival Ring, the 'Indians', who knew nothing at all about campaigning in Africa.

However, the government had anticipated this last objection. They sent out as Roberts's Chief of Staff Britain's youngest military hero, fifty-two-year-old Major-General Lord Kitchener, victor of Khartoum, avenger of Gordon and the man who was supposed to be immune to ordinary human weaknesses. Within a few days the Cabinet had wished the two men Godspeed for the Cape, and it was a poignant leave-taking. Roberts wore a black band on his right arm. His only son, Freddy, had fought with Buller's army at Colenso, and had been mortally wounded while trying to save the field-guns. Buller had recommended him for a VC.

Before Roberts could land at the Cape and take over command, Buller made a second attempt to batter his way through Botha's trench line on the Tugela and relieve White at Ladysmith. Before dawn on 24 January, Brigadier-General Woodgate, with about 2,000 men of the newly-arrived 5th Division, successfully seized Spion Kop, an undefended, precipitous hilltop about twenty miles from Ladysmith, that appeared to command the west flank of the enemy's lines. But Majuba, too, had commanded the Boers' line, and the pattern of Colley's disaster now began to repeat itself with uncanny precision.

It was young Winston Churchill, the soldier-journalist back on the British side of the lines after his daring escape from Pretoria, who provided the British public with the most startling insight into the new conditions of war. He took it upon himself to tell the Divisional General, Warren, the news of the collapse of the British positions. Like Colley at Majuba, Woodgate had been under-equipped but overconfident. He and Warren had failed to ensure that the men were safely entrenched on the summit of Spion Kop. They had brought up no artillery of their own, nor any means of signalling the British artillery to give support. The Boers courageously counter-attacked, and *they* were well served by artillery fired from higher ground. Early on, Woodgate was mortally wounded in the head and the battle soon lost all coherence. In the African sun, men became dazed: units muddled, officers missing, ammunition and water spent. Churchill gave a lucid description of the chaos:

> Men were staggering along alone, or supported by comrades, or crawling on hands or knees, or carried on stretchers. Corpses lay here and there ... The splinters and fragments had torn and mutilated [them] in the most ghastly manner. I passed about 200 while I was climbing up. There was, moreover,

a small but steady leakage of unwounded men of all corps. Some of these cursed and swore. Others were utterly exhausted and fell on the hillside in a stupor. Others again seemed drunk, though they had no liquor. Scores were sleeping heavily . . .[27]

On 5 February, Buller again tried to find the 'key' to the Tugela line – at Vaal Krantz – and again the key broke in the lock. But at his fourth attempt, beginning on 14 February, his luck changed. It turned out that the 'key' Buller was seeking was not so much a vulnerable point in the enemy's line as a method of attack, a new kind of infantry tactic. Despite his bovine appearance, and his difficulty in explaining himself to the British public (or his masters in London), Buller was an innovator. He recognized his own handicaps. As he had foreseen, the boulder-strewn ridges between the Tugela and Ladysmith were God-given for the defence. And the Boers were as nimble as centaurs. Although they fought dismounted, most of them kept a pony tethered behind the nearest hill. On the other hand, the arithmetic now favoured the British with a four to one superiority in fighting men, and a ten to one superiority in artillery. And Buller's men were as dogged as he was himself. The answer: Buller broke the rule book designed for one-day battles, arranged like three-act plays, with artillery, infantry and cavalry performing set roles in turn. He taught his men to use Boer tactics in the firing line – to advance in small rushes, covered by rifle fire from behind; to use the tactical support of artillery; and above all, to use the *ground*, making rock and earth work for them as it did for the enemy. It seemed a ponderous business, a ten-day battle to squeeze and hammer the enemy out of a series of stony ridges. But it worked, this painful prototype of modern warfare. On 28 February Buller's bronzed veterans marched into Ladysmith, to be given a cool handshake by White's pale-faced, typhoid-ridden garrison. White's men had spent four months in tents and shelters, dodging shells from long-range guns, caught between the hope of relief and the fear of being forced to surrender.

Meanwhile, 300 miles to the west, in the rolling veld of the Orange Free State, the expected walk-over was at last being fulfilled by Roberts. On 11 February, he launched his 'steamroller': 35,000 men (with about 5,000 African drivers) arranged in five divisions, including most of the mounted troops in South Africa. His first priority was to relieve Kimberley, where Cecil Rhodes was threatening to surrender; his second was to capture Bloemfontein. With his new weight of numbers, new mobility, and a terrain as green and level as a billiard table, these objectives were hardly in question. He had no need to go for Kimberley head-on, as Buller had gone for Ladysmith. He could go round. He left Methuen's infantry blocking Cronje's line at Magersfontein, while the Cavalry Division, led by Major-General French, trotted round the flank. Within four days French had relieved Kimberley with hardly a shot fired, and was welcomed by Cecil Rhodes with glasses of iced champagne.

Three days later Cronje, retreating eastwards, had dug his own grave at the river Modder. Caught off balance by the speed of Roberts's advance, he formed a wagon laager in the soft white river-bank of the Modder, as if he were surrounded by 'Kaffirs' armed with spears, not by 'Khakis' armed with fifteen-pounders. After a futile infantry attack on the laager, directed by Kitchener at the cost of nearly 1,000 casualties, Roberts let the fifteen-pounders do the job. On 27 February, Cronje raised the white flag and his men were marched off to the prisoner of war cages at the Cape. A fortnight later, on 13 March, after brushing aside the panic-struck enemy at Poplar's Grove (and nearly capturing both President Steyn and President Kruger, who were visiting the war front), Roberts rode straight through the streets of Bloemfontein, then hauled up a small, silk Union Jack, embroidered by his wife, on a flagpole outside President Steyn's house.

In London it all seemed too good to be true – and it was. Buller had relieved Ladysmith and rescued White. Roberts had relieved Kimberley and rescued Rhodes. Then Roberts had captured the Free State capital, with Cronje's surrender a bonus. But Roberts had not beaten the main enemy force in the field, either the Transvaalers or the Free Staters. The speed of his advance and the panic it created had led him to a fatal miscalculation. He relaxed his grip on the enemy and offered generous terms to all except the leaders. If they turned in their rifles, they could return home. As he told Queen Victoria from Bloemfontein, two days after its capture: 'It seems unlikely that the State will give much more trouble. The Transvaalers will probably hold out ... but I trust it will not be very long before the war will have been brought to a satisfactory conclusion ... We are obliged to rest here for a short time.'[28] As it turned out, Roberts dawdled for two months at Bloemfontein, handing out proclamations of amnesty, and wrestling with problems of transport and supply – problems partly of his own making. Meanwhile the Boer leaders, especially Christiaan De Wet, recovered their breath and resumed the initiative, intensifying Roberts's supply problems by capturing convoys and cutting the railway lines.

Back in December Wolseley had warned Lansdowne that Roberts and Kitchener might know a great deal about the Indian army and the Egyptian army respectively; they knew nothing about *his* army, the British army. Wolseley was jealous, and Lansdowne turned a deaf ear. Now, in April, Wolseley's words did not look so foolish. In the middle of a war, Roberts and Kitchener had tried to change the British army's system of transport and reorganize it on Indian army lines. There was an unholy mess, and the old system had to be restored. The price was paid by the 35,000 men who had made the daring flank march across the veld between the Modder and Bloemfontein. Rations were cut for men and horses; mule transport collapsed; there were pitifully few medical supplies; no one had been told to order more wagons and engines for the railway. The shortage of all supplies and the chaos in the medical department precipitated an epidemic of typhoid. Soon this war on the veld, in many respects the first modern war, had its traditional side, too. Typhoid and other preventable diseases struck down far more of Roberts's men in the safety of Bloemfontein than Boer bullets or shells had killed on the battlefield.

At long last, on 3 May, Roberts felt strong enough to relaunch his 'steamroller' across the veld. He co-ordinated his own advance with Buller's; he had left him and two divisions to perform the tricky job of turning the flank of the large Boer army dug in at the Biggarsberg and the hills of northern Natal. And he despatched a 1,100-strong flying column, led by Colonel Bryan Mahon, to relieve Mafeking. It was here, in the sandy outpost of Cape Colony on the edge of the Kalahari, that Baden-Powell had focused the attention of the British public for eight months, making himself the symbol of British pluck and endurance by his spirited (and well-advertised) defence. Everything went smoothly. Mahon's men were largely Uitlanders, including many of the Reformers once gaoled by Kruger, and many of them had ridden with Jameson on the Raid, launched from Mafeking five years earlier.

On 17 May they relieved the town after an uneventful eleven-day ride across the veld. ('Oh yes, I heard you were knocking about,' was all the welcome the first troopers received when they clattered into the market square in the moonlight.)[29] On 14 May Buller neatly outmanoeuvred Botha in the Biggarsberg. Meanwhile, in the Free State, Roberts's five divisions swatted at the enemy as if they had been flies, and on 27 May he rode unopposed across the Vaal river.

Back in Bloemfontein the annexation of the Free State was formally proclaimed the next day. On 31 May, Roberts captured Johannesburg and the Rand – with all 200 gold-mines intact. On 5 June he hoisted the small, silk Union Jack, embroidered by his wife, on a flagpole in Pretoria. Once again the speed of his advance threw the Boers into a panic, and once again Roberts misinterpreted what he saw. The war was 'practically over'.

By August, Roberts's five divisions had finally joined hands with Buller's three divisions from Natal. Their combined forces crushed the Boers at Bergendal on 27 August. The Boer retreat became a rout, and their army dissolved into fragments. Kruger took refuge in the Portuguese colony of Mozambique, and was brought to Europe on board the *Gelderland* ('the Gold Land'), a Dutch cruiser. Buller, his laurels much restored, returned in triumph to Southampton. Roberts handed over the reins to Kitchener and followed Buller back to England. He was promoted Earl and paid £100,000 as a reward for victory.

But this was premature. The war might be over: the war of regular battles, fought in lines on the battlefield. A new war – a guerrilla war – was just beginning.

*   *   *

In London the Unionist government celebrated what they believed was victory in the field with victory in the 'Khaki election'. Despite the blunders at the beginning of the war, and the well-publicized scandals of the military hospitals, they were returned to power with a majority increased from 130 to 134. However, the new administration itself seemed stale. Indeed, the reshuffle was more a concession of weakness than an assertion of strength. Lord Salisbury felt too old to continue to wear both his hats: as Prime Minister and Foreign Secretary. But the man he chose to replace him at the Foreign Office was Lord Lansdowne, the War Minister, who had won no laurels in that role. The 'Hotel Cecil', as the wags called the government, now included the Prime Minister's eldest son, Lord Cranborne, as well as his three nephews. Fortunately for them, there was no threat from the Liberals, who had their hands full fighting each other.

To prevent the Liberal Party breaking into three fragments – Liberal Imperialists, Moderates and Radicals – had taxed Campbell-Bannerman almost beyond endurance. Somehow he succeeded in making even David Lloyd George, the leading Radical, bite the bullet and accept the annexation of the two republics as a *fait accompli*. But the war in South Africa remained a torment for C-B, the Liberal leader. Criticizing the government was regarded as unpatriotic by most of the electorate, including most of his own party. To admit to his own sympathy for the Boers – and be labelled a 'pro-Boer' like Lloyd George – would have been suicide for him. The only hope was that the war would end quickly and allow normal politics to resume. Domestic issues could heal the party's wounds as efficiently as imperial issues tore them apart.

By January 1901, however, the guerrilla war had begun to intensify and make mockery of everyone's hopes – Kitchener's, Salisbury's, C-B's.

On 3 December 1900, a column of Boers led by Jan Smuts and General De La Rey, which had been lying low in the western Transvaal, pounced on a British convoy forty miles west of Pretoria. Ten days later, joining hands with a commando under General Beyers, they found the spoor of the bigger game – a camp of 1,200 British soldiers commanded by General Clements in a gorge at Nooitgedacht. Clements lost all his supplies and only cut his way out of the trap with difficulty. A week later, a mixed force led by General Kritzinger and Judge Herzog broke through Kitchener's cordons guarding the Orange river and launched a raid into Cape Colony to try to raise the Cape Afrikaners. Meanwhile Christiaan De Wet, the Free State general whose guerrilla column now included President Steyn, had humiliated Kitchener with a series of brilliant raids on the British supply lines. In February De Wet, too, broke across the Orange river, and for a time Kitchener's headquarters at Pretoria trembled at the prospect of a full-scale rising in the Cape.

However, the price of guerrillas' survival is often their own weakness. To raise the Cape meant co-ordinating strategy, and that was beyond the hundred or so fragmented commandos from both republics. In due course both Boer 'invasions' fizzled out. Kritzinger went to ground. De Wet was hunted back across the Orange river. Kitchener recovered the initiative, and resumed his 'drives' across the veld to flush out the enemy.

But how to bring them either to fight or to surrender? It was a problem that drove Kitchener to distraction. At first he had hopes of persuading the guerrillas to accept generous terms. He offered a ten-point settlement to General Botha at Middelburg; the talks proved abortive.

Kitchener next adopted the rough-and-ready policy of collective punishment

used by Lord Roberts the previous autumn. By burning the farms of combatant
Boers and stripping the veld of horses and cattle, a piece of territory could be
denied to the guerrillas, and the loyalty of other Boers, whose farms were left
intact, could (in theory) be confirmed. Kitchener also made his 'drives' more
systematic by improving the co-ordination of mobile columns. Yet the 'bag',[30]
as he called it, remained tantalizingly small – roughly 1,000 a month of an
enemy estimated by British intelligence at 20,000 men. (In the end it turned out
that there were over 25,000.) At this rate it would take several years to end the
war.

Like many of Kitchener's famous short cuts, farm-burning was crude and
counter-productive, as well as embarrassing for the government at home. In
practice, the farms of Boer collaborators got burnt too – burnt by mistake by
Tommies or in reprisal by the commandos. So Kitchener added a new twist to
farm-burning. He decided that his soldiers should not only strip the farms
of stock, but should take the families, too. Women and children would be
concentrated in 'camps of refuge'[31] along the railway line. In fact, these camps
consisted of two kinds of civilian: genuine refugees – that is, the families of Boers
who were helping the British, or at least keeping to their oath of neutrality – and
internees, the families of men who were still out on commando. The difference
was crucial, for at first there were two different scales of rations: little enough
in practice for the refugees, and a recklessly low scale for the internees.

But Kitchener was not interested in the life – or death – of civilians. He was
impatient to end the war, and by the summer of 1901 he thought he had found
the way.

The weakness of the policy of flushing out the enemy in 'drives' was that in
darkness most guerrillas could slip through the meshes of the human net. What
he needed was something solid at the end of the drive. Therefore he began to
divide both the ex-republics into a huge steel chequerboard made of barbed-
wire fence lines, guarded by concrete blockhouses. He also changed the ground
rules by employing 5,000 Africans armed with rifles to guard the blockhouse
lines. (The Boers usually shot the Africans they captured. So Kitchener had
armed them for their own safety.)

The first drive towards a blockhouse line proved encouraging to the British
headquarters in Pretoria and, with refinement, Kitchener's bag rose steadily.
But victory on the battlefield is not always enough. In London, Kitchener's
heavy-handed policies had finally created a problem of their own.

*　　*　　*

It was the 'pro-Boer' Liberal MPs who had first grasped Kitchener's blunder in
herding women and children into the so-called 'camps of refuge'. On 1 March
Lloyd George quoted a Reuters report that correctly described how there were
two ration scales in the camps. Other pro-Boer MPs – among them John Ellis
and C.P. Scott – then took up the attack, borrowing an ominous phrase,

'concentration camps',[32] from the notorious *reconcentrado* camps set up by the Spanish to deal with the Cuban guerrillas. How many lived in these camps, asked Ellis; indeed, how many had already died in them?

At first Brodrick, the new Minister of War, tried to brush aside the questions with a claim that the camp inmates had entered them voluntarily. When Lloyd George exposed this as humbug, Brodrick claimed that the camps had been set up on humanitarian grounds. How could they leave the women and children out on the veld to starve? Not till April and May did Brodrick reveal the first incomplete statistics for the inmates of the camps: there were 21,105 in the Transvaal, 19,680 in the Orange River Colony, and 2,524 in Natal. It was admitted that several hundred people had already died of disease. But it was claimed the death rate was now 'rapidly decreasing'.

In late May, however, the enormity of the tragedy in the camps first began to be grasped in England. A dumpy, forty-one-year-old English spinster, Emily Hobhouse, had toured the camps in both ex-republics from January to April on behalf of British sympathizers. Her eye-witness account shook not only radical Liberals, but the party leader himself, Campbell-Bannerman. He listened aghast: 'The wholesale burnings of farms ... the deportations ... the burnt out population brought in by hundreds in convoys ... deprived of clothes ... the semi-starvation in the camps ... the fever-stricken children lying ... upon the earth ... the appalling mortality.'[33] A few days later C-B abandoned his attempt to sit on the fence, and coined an explosive phrase to denounce the government's inhuman method of conducting the war. At a Liberal dinner at the Holborn Restaurant on 14 June, he said, half-concealing his own emotion behind the banter, 'A phrase often used is that "war is war". But when one comes to ask about it, one is told that no war is going on – that it is not war (Laughter). When is a war not a war? (Laughter) When it is carried on by methods of barbarism in South Africa. (Cheers)'[34]

Month by month the death rate from the camps proved that the pro-Boers had, if anything, understated the crisis. As Kitchener's columns intensified their drives, the population of the camps rose like water behind a dam. Typhoid, dysentery and (for children) measles – killers endemic to South Africa wherever people are concentrated – broke out and spread with frightening speed. But where were the doctors, the matrons, the nurses, the orderlies, the blankets, the medicines and the food for the invalids? Even the necessities for ordinary life on the veld were missing – a healthy diet, clean water, protection against the sun and frost.

Stung by the campaign against 'methods-of-barbarism', and the outcry pro-voked in France and Germany, the government sent out a Ladies Commission of investigation led by Dame Millicent Fawcett, feminist and Liberal Unionist. The Fawcett Report confirmed the grim forecasts of Emily Hobhouse. Incompetence and neglect at every level, from Kitchener down, had turned crisis to catastrophe. By October the populations of the camps had risen to 111,619 whites and 43,780 coloured people. In that single month, the mortality was 3,156 and 698 respectively; calculated as an annual rate, the October death rate for whites came to 34 per cent. The Fawcett Commission had no doubt the majority of deaths *were* preventable. The crisis had been caused by the failure to observe elementary rules of hygiene, the catastrophe by the failure to rush doctors and nurses out from England the moment the epidemics began.

Belatedly the government realized the enormity of its mistake in trusting Kitchener. They put Milner and the civilian authorities in control of the camps. By February the annualized death rate had fallen to 6 per cent, then to 2 per cent, less than that of Glasgow. But the damage had been done. As Lloyd George had forecast after listening to Emily Hobhouse, 'When children are being treated in this way and dying, it is simply ranging the deepest passions of the human heart against British rule in South Africa ... it will always be remembered that this is the way British rule started here ... the method by which it was brought about.'[35]

Meanwhile, Kitchener's new formula – blockhouses plus black troops – was demonstrably winning the guerrilla war. By April 1902, the main commando leaders, Botha, Smuts, De La Rey, De Wet and President Steyn, had come in from the veld under a flag of truce. Peace talks continued intermittently until the end of May, and the terms looked irresistible. With the exception of one clause, they were much the same as those offered Botha at Middelburg in 1901. Far from demanding war reparations (as Germany had exacted from France in 1871), Britain offered to compensate the enemy, who had lost horses and cattle during the war, and was prepared to offer £3 million for loans to help reconstruction. The new colonies would be given self-government, like the Cape and Natal, as soon as circumstances permitted. There was a crucial one-word change in the terms since Middelburg. This was a concession to the Boers' determination to refuse Africans the vote. When would 'Kaffirs' in the Transvaal and the Orange River Colony be given the same voting rights as their fellow Africans in the Cape? Not until representative government was granted, according to the Middelburg terms; not until *after* representative government was granted, according to the new terms. And 'after' meant quite simply, 'never', as the British government recognized. It was a concession that would echo and re-echo down the years ahead. Already it made a mockery of Chamberlain's warning that they must not 'purchase a shameful peace by leaving the Coloured population in the position they stood before the war.'[36]

The delegates from the commandos still out on the veld assembled in May in a great marquee at Vereeniging, near the Vaal, to debate the British terms. The volk were (and indeed are) a businesslike people. The arguments for acceptance were overwhelming. The war was ending in any case. 'Fight to the bitter end,' said De La Rey. 'Do you say that? But has the bitter end not come?' Botha declared that continuing the war was 'hopeless'.[37] Smuts, who had led a new 'invasion' of Cape Colony, admitted that nothing could be expected from the Afrikaners in the Cape. In the old republics the commandos were being hustled to death by Kitchener – starved of cattle, horses, ammunition. Some Boer families had now been abandoned on the veld. Ironically, Kitchener had recently begun to issue private orders for the columns *not* to bring in further women and children after a drive. This left the Boer families on the veld in a much worse plight than those in the camps, now that Milner had reformed them.

There was also new talk of 'black peril'. Africans were reported to be 'out of hand' in some areas, and a Zulu Impi had killed fifty-two Boers at Holkrantz, near Vryheid, in reprisal for a cattle raid by the Boers. Most serious of all, Kitchener had managed to recruit thousands of surrendered Boers to fight on the British side, including De Wet's brother, Piet. The struggle, always a civil war between Boers and British in South Africa, was now a civil war *within* the volk – between 21,000 'bitter-enders' fighting with the commandos, and 5,000 'hands-uppers' fighting for the British. In short, the war would soon end in disaster and humiliation. They must now win the peace.

When the votes were counted in the great marquee at Vereeniging on 31 May, all but a small minority voted for peace. The same evening, peace was formally signed in Pretoria, by Kitchener and Milner on behalf of the British, by Acting President Burger for the Transvaal and De Wet for the Free State. The Boers held their heads high, like men who had won a moral victory. It seemed a civilized way to end a quarrel that had bedevilled South Africa for a century. Kitchener was delighted with everything, including a viscountcy, and a grant of £50,000 as a token of the government's appreciation. (He immediately invested the money in South African gold shares.)

By contrast, Milner, the man who claimed he had precipitated the war, felt cheated of victory. In his heart, he had opposed the peace talks. His plan was to 'burst the mould'[38] and Anglicize the country. Better to leave the Boer political leaders to wither away out on the veld than to welcome them back to the fold with a promise of self-government 'as soon as possible'. When would this be? Milner shuddered. The arithmetic of democracy – an overall majority of Boers and Afrikaners in the four colonies combined – spelled disaster for his grand design. Apart from the British loyalists, who recognized him now as their champion, he had his private alliance with the 'gold bugs'.

Everything depended on the gold-mines. If they could cut the cost of producing gold – especially the cost of dynamite and transport, and the 'absurdly' high wages of African miners – there would be a new mining boom and a new gold-rush. Only by massive British immigration could a disaster be avoided. For only then would there be a majority of British voters in time for that dangerous moment when all four colonies were merged into a self-governing dominion like Canada.

*   *   *

The British public accepted the peace at Vereeniging without much display of emotion. They were relieved that it was over at last, this humiliating war, that had cost 20,000 British lives and £200 million. (It had cost the Boers relatively still more: 7,000 men killed in the war, and about 28,000 Boer women and children dead in the camps, as well as more than 14,000 blacks.)

There were no wild scenes in Trafalgar Square, as there had been on the night of the news that Mafeking had been relieved. How different things looked to the anxious Edwardian public of 1902. The war had exposed Britain to humiliation in the eyes of her European rivals, especially Germany and France. She still felt dangerously isolated. As for the end of the war, it had been forecast so often that when it finally came, it was bound to be an anti-climax. Not even the last phase of the Scramble provoked much public excitement. Except for special occasions, English people tended to take their Empire for granted. And no doubt there was one thing about the Transvaal and the Orange River Colony that many Empire-minded Englishmen would rather have forgotten: the methods by which the two colonies had been acquired.

Six weeks after the peace had been signed, Lord Salisbury finally succumbed to exhaustion and handed over his seals of office into the large, pudgy hands of the new King, Edward VII. Salisbury's elegant nephew, Arthur Balfour, then kissed hands on being appointed Prime Minister.

For sixteen years Salisbury had presided over the carve-up of the African cake. According to his official biographer, this was his greatest achievement in the conduct of British foreign affairs. He had certainly made sure that the lion's share of new colonies and protectorates – fifteen out of thirty – went to Britain. If his preoccupation had always been to give Britain the strategic advantage, it was fortunate for Britain that he also gave it most of Africa's most profitable territory: the gold-mines of the Transvaal, the teeming markets of the Niger, the tea and coffee of Uganda, the cotton of Egypt and the Sudan.

Carving up Africa without breaking the crockery in Europe; that was Lord Salisbury's achievement. But this did not mean keeping the peace in Africa. Most of Britain's fifteen new colonies and protectorates had been won by right of conquest, like the Transvaal, or extorted by threat of force, like Uganda. Théophile Delcassé's wry comment applied to Africans, too: 'They have the troops.... we only have the arguments.' The blank treaty forms meant little to an African, especially when looking down the barrel of an Englishman's gun.

The end of the Scramble was in sight, but it was not over yet. Three questions remained.

France was expected to take over Algeria's wayward neighbour, Morocco; it was already an unofficial French protectorate. Italy planned to prise two strips of desert – Tripoli and Cyrenaica – from the limp grasp of the Sultan at Constantinople. Would any of the Great Powers object?

Far more important, what was to be done with the Congo? It was still not the responsibility of any of the Powers. It remained unique among African colonies, the personal property of one self-styled philanthropist, King Leopold.

The third question concerned the African reaction to the Scramble. The powerful African states had resisted alien rule, and now they had been conquered. Little resistance had come from the thousands of scattered chiefdoms that comprised most of the continent. Empire on paper meant nothing to them.

How would they react when they experienced empire on the ground?

But how much thought had Lord Salisbury – or any of the Powers – given to the interests of the 110 million black and brown subjects they had just acquired? That Africans could hardly be worse off than under their own rulers had always been the optimistic assumption of Europeans, from Livingstone onwards. Now, as the Powers began to administer the thirty new colonies and protectorates, to inspect their strange slices of the cake – ranging from the claustrophobic jungles of the Congo, to the barren steppes of German West Africa – all that talk of 'commerce, Christianity and civilization' began to have a hollow ring.

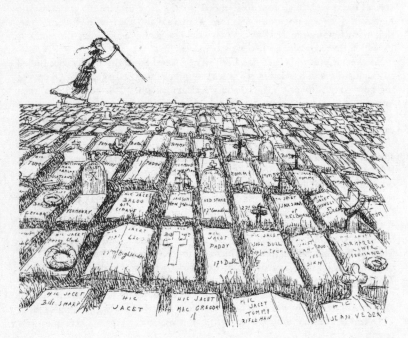

PART FOUR

RESISTANCE AND REFORM

IN THE RUBBER COILS.

CHAPTER 32

The Severed Hands

Brussels, London, Paris and the Congo
16 May 1902–February 1904

> 'Wild beasts – the leopards – killed some of us while
> we were working away in the forest and others got
> lost or died from exposure or starvation and we
> begged the white men to leave us alone, saying we
> could get no more rubber, but the white men and
> the soldiers said: Go. You are only beasts
> yourselves. You are only Nyama [meat].'
>
> Testimony of Congo villagers interviewed by Consul
> Casement, 1893

Early on the morning of 16 May 1902, a fortnight before the peace treaty between the British and the Boers was signed at Vereeniging, when stray shots from the veld still echoed through the columns of the European papers, the canister containing *The Times* arrived with its usual thump in the royal siding at Laeken, outside Brussels.

No doubt King Leopold read page eleven with attention, after enjoying his early morning ride round the park at Laeken, mounted on what he called '*mon animal*'[1] – a large new tricycle. That morning's *Times* devoted a half column to a protest meeting held in the Mansion House, London, the evening before, to condemn 'grievous wrongs' against the natives of the Congo. Two resolutions were solemnly adopted: to call on all the Powers which had signed the Berlin and Brussels Acts to 'co-operate in procuring the necessary reforms'; and to call on the British government to take the initiative.[2] But the hall at the Mansion House was half empty, and there seemed nothing to alarm the King.

The driving force behind this protest meeting was a couple of English do-gooders who had been yapping at the King's heels for many years – Richard Fox Bourne, secretary of the old-style emancipationist society, the Aborigines Protection Society, and Sir Charles Dilke, the Radical MP for the Forest of Dean. Clearly their aim was to poison international opinion against Leopold, but their efforts were only sporadically successful. Neither of these self-styled humanitarians was the man to turn Congo agitation into a movement – even in England. Fox Bourne enjoyed a wide circle of enemies, as he dutifully denounced European administration all over Africa. Dilke had been considered a pariah by many of his old friends ever since his appearance in Mrs Crawford's lurid divorce case, seventeen years before.

What was new was that these humanitarians had now joined hands with the men of commerce, God with Mammon. John Holt, Vice-President of the Liverpool Chamber of Commerce, claimed that he had a commercial grievance against the Congo Free State for breaking the rules of free trade laid down in the General Act of Berlin. Leopold seized upon this pact with Liverpool eagerly. For ten years Fox Bourne and Dilke had been shaking their fists at him and their motives had puzzled him. Had they been duped by disgruntled ex-employees of the Free State? It seemed clear to him now that their concern was a sham – a cloak beneath which the Liverpool merchants, jealous of his own commercial success, were trying to steal the Congo from him. (The King, so skilful at concealing his own motives, was all the more ready to detect the same talent in others.)

Leopold, however, did not have to muddy his hands exposing the plot against him. He left that to his official diplomatic network, and to the hidden ring of admirers he continued to recruit in Europe and America. The Free State delegates he sent to the Mansion House meeting in London (of which the organizers had forewarned him) had been instructed to be bland and reassuring. Let the evidence of wrongdoing, if such evidence existed, be conveyed to the government of the Free State. In other words, the world could trust the King-Sovereign. He would see justice was done.

It was this majestic self-confidence that had kept the shine on Leopold's armour throughout the last, dangerous phase of the Scramble. Only once, in 1895–6, had the armour shown a conspicuous dent. There was the unfortunate business of the British trader, Charlie Stokes, who had insisted on selling Congolese ivory to German East Africa, and German guns to the Congolese. (Stokes was the ex-missionary and ivory trader who had played the crucial part in supplying arms to Lugard in Uganda.) In January 1895 he was caught gun-running in the Congo, then tried and hanged by a Belgian officer, Captain Lothaire.

The story of the hanging had somehow slipped into the English newspapers, and there had been a fine hullabaloo. Salisbury's government protested about legal irregularities. As a result, Captain Lothaire had to endure three trials himself. He was conveniently acquitted, through lack of State evidence, and promoted director of the main concessionary company in the Congo. Leopold found the whole business distasteful. He had no wish to publicize the rough-and-ready way in which justice was dispensed on the Congo's eastern frontier, and he took steps to protect the good name of the Congo.

In 1896 Leopold appointed a six-man commission – the Native Protection Commission – to notify the judicial authorities of any 'acts of violence of which natives may be victims'.[3] Its members were all churchmen of unimpeachable rectitude: three Belgian Catholic priests, two British Baptist missionaries and one American Baptist. In the Congo their work never came to anything, of course. Their posts were too scattered for them to hold meetings, and they all lived far from the rubber-producing districts where the alleged atrocities took place. But in Europe the Commission worked wonders for Leopold. Who could now doubt his lofty motives – or deny that he was going to continue to put his personal fortune at the disposal of this great humanitarian venture in Africa to 'regenerate' the black man and make the Congo (as he put it) a 'model state'?[4]

This was the height of his ambition, Leopold repeated with arresting sincerity to the influential British visitors he counted on recruiting as admirers, after they enjoyed his hospitality at Laeken. Among them were diplomats, like the obsequious British minister, Sir Constantine Phipps, and the earnest young Consul, Roger Casement (whom Leopold entertained twice before he left to serve in the Congo as British Consul in 1900); timid missionaries, like Grattan Guinness and A. H. Baynes, the heads of the Congo Bolobo Mission and the Baptist Missionary Society; pushy capitalists like Alfred Jones, whose world-wide shipping interests included control of the Elder Dempster Shipping Line, which enjoyed the lucrative monopoly of the shipping service between Antwerp and the Congo.

Despite the lingering after-taste of the Stokes affair, the Native Commission took the sting out of the sporadic reports of abuses by the Congo State. As the years passed, the yelps of the British humanitarians began to seem faintly absurd. At the same time, the King savoured the new sensation of being honoured in Belgium.

Few constitutional monarchs have despised their subjects more cordially, yet yearned so much to win their affection. Leopold had long been fascinated by town planning. It symbolized autocracy, and suited his acquisitive tastes. He bought up land wherever he could find it – in the sand dunes of Ostend, the green fields outside Brussels, and the slums within it. In 1900, with the help of a French architect, he began to create public monuments of Napoleonic grandeur. He sliced avenues through Brussels, threw up a triumphal arch to celebrate, belatedly, the fiftieth anniversary of the Belgian State, built a Congo museum at Tervuren, enlarged Laeken, and laid out public parks in Ostend. Then he astonished everyone by presenting these splendid monuments to his people, together with Laeken and other royal domains he had inherited, in the form of a *donation royale*. Naturally his subjects were flattered to be invited to garden fêtes in the newly-donated property, though the King continued to occupy the palaces just as before. The point was symbolic. The monarch was prepared to be loved by his subjects – and love him some of them did. Once, when he came to lay the foundation stone of a new building, he was left speechless and almost in tears, so rapturous was the applause.

Less well advertised to his people were Leopold's ardent feelings for a buxom young French girl called Blanche Delacroix. The affair began in Paris some time in 1900 when Blanche was about sixteen. Leopold was sixty-five. For years he had enjoyed discreet diversions in the back streets of Paris. He was estranged from the Queen, Marie-Henriette, and from his tiresome daughters who insisted on marrying beneath them, after the collapse of the dynastic marriages he had provided. In 1902 the unfortunate Queen died at Spa. Leopold celebrated his release by installing Blanche in a villa discreetly linked to Laeken by a footbridge.

The affair with 'Baronne de Vaughan' (a sham title conferred on the girl) had its ludicrous side. Who would have dreamt that this imperious old man, pedalling in the palace grounds at Laeken on a large tricycle, had a mistress of eighteen from whom he would meekly accept instructions? Sometimes he protested when Blanche ordered him around. Then she would laugh and light a cigar. It seemed that Leopold had finally discovered himself. Forgotten were the lonely years of childhood and the loveless years of marriage. Domestic happiness was a revelation. No matter that the liaison – and the two strapping boys, Lucien and Philippe, it was to produce in 1906 and 1907 – had to be discreetly managed, so that even his personal secretary never set eyes on the voluptuous baroness during Leopold's lifetime.

With his private fund of happiness came another source of pride for the King, no less intense and private. In the Congo he was making money hand over fist. In public the emphasis remained on the success of private Belgian companies and of the King's own philanthropy. He had enough trouble from busy-bodies like Dilke and Fox Bourne to wish to reveal his unusual skills as a financier. Part of his own profits came from the Congo State's 50 per cent holding in these private companies. At the same time, its trade statistics were doctored to suggest that, like successful colonies in other parts of Africa, the Congo balanced its books, imports against exports, expenditure against revenue.

The true figures, as far as they can be disinterred, prove that the Congo was not like any other colony. Of course, it was not a colony. It was a personal state, the property of one capitalist of genius, the King-Sovereign. Leopold had ridden the world's rubber boom like a man on a trapeze. Before the boom, the Congo's exports had consisted of a trickle of oil and ivory. By 1902, rubber sales had risen fifteen times in eight years, and constituted over 80 per cent of exports, worth over forty-one million francs (£1.64 million). The rubber grew wild and the Free State method of harvesting, if rough-and-ready, was cheap. So exports came to twice as much as imports, and the State secretly amassed a huge surplus of income over expenditure.

Should Leopold re-invest this profit in the Congo, according to the unwritten code practised in colonies elsewhere, to benefit both the natives and European investors? Leopold saw no reason why he should. He flouted convention when he found it convenient, and this was his own money, not the Belgian taxpayers' (if one ignored interest-free loans). His own patrimony, fifteen million francs (£600,000), had been lavished on the Congo in those grim years when everyone except Leopold thought the State would go bankrupt.

He had put his fortune in the Congo. Now he intended to reap the benefit, repaying himself and enjoying the profits. It was these secret profits from the Congo, many times the size of the original investment, that supported the King's lavish spending in Belgium – for the arches and avenues, the parks and the palaces, which made up the *donation royale* – as well as a private paradise at Cap Ferrat in the French Riviera, to which he would slip away with Blanche, whenever the cares of the Belgian state and of his own African empire allowed.

How strange to think that in 1895, seven years before, Leopold had almost thrown in the sponge and handed over the Congo voluntarily to Belgium. On paper, the danger of a Belgian takeover had persisted. In March 1901 came Belgium's chance to exercise her ten-year option over the Congo, acquired in exchange for an interest-free loan of twenty-five million francs. Fortunately for Leopold, the Belgian government and people proved to have even less appetite for the Congo State when financially sound than in 1895 when it appeared on the verge of bankruptcy. The option to make the Congo a Belgian colony was allowed to evaporate. Fortune smiled on Leopold in other ways. He made a bold investment in Chinese railways, which was to net him a profit of about a quarter of a million pounds. But the Congo remained the source of his golden profits, and of his golden name as a philanthropist.

It was natural for English admirers to be dazzled by his talk of Livingstone, of the '3 Cs', and of the sacred task of opening Africa to civilization. Of course, that was not the way His Majesty spoke to his Belgian associates who directed the concessionary companies and their business partner, the Congo State. The employer they knew talked like an absentee landlord, eager for profit and determined not to know too much about how it was made.

In the 1890s, it is true, he had seemed to suffer from periodic twinges of conscience. Did the system of forced labour to extract rubber lend itself to abuse? When foreign missionaries first complained to him, he had accepted that at least some of these stories were true. 'It is necessary to put down the horrible abuses,' he told Liebrechts, one of the senior officials of the Free State. 'These horrors must end or I will retire from the Congo. I will not allow myself to be splattered with blood or mud; it is necessary that these villainies cease.'[5] Liebrechts and the others did nothing to check the abuses. They knew that the King's mood would soon pass, and they were right.

By now, in 1902, Leopold had written off his English critics as humbugs, and he was no longer troubled by his conscience. All he was concerned with was profit; and he saw no reason to be alarmed by the yapping of cranks like Fox Bourne or perverts like Dilke.

He had not reckoned with the earnest young man, a twenty-eight-year-old ex-shipping clerk, called Edmond Morel, who was about to change the faltering agitation for reform into one of the greatest of British crusades.

*   *   *

Georges Edmond Pierre Achille Dene Morel de Ville, to give him his Anglo-French drum-roll of names, was born in a seedy suburb of Paris, the son of a brilliant, feckless, French civil servant and a shy, prim, proud Englishwoman of Quaker stock. His tall, aristocratic good looks came from his father; his temperament from his mother. His father died, almost penniless, when Edmond was four, leaving his mother to scrape a living as a music teacher in Paris. Edmond was sent to England, to Bedford Modern, a public school whose no-nonsense teaching and modest fees appealed to expatriate parents. He left school at fifteen, a confirmed outsider. He identified with England, but with the England of Bunyan and his Quaker ancestors, the men who had launched the movement to abolish slavery.

When he was seventeen, in 1890, his mother wangled him a job as a clerk at Elder Dempster, the Liverpool shipping line controlled by Leopold's admirer, Alfred Jones. Liverpool was the centre of the West African trade and its sinister traditions. Morel soon came under the spell of the mysterious port. 'To watch a steamer unload her cargo of palm oil,' he wrote later, 'bags of kernels, bags and casks of rubber, elephant tusks, huge mahogany logs and so on, always sent a shiver of excitement down my back.'[6] To eke out his wages, he began to study Blue Books and write freelance articles on West Africa. In his early twenties he was already an expert on this obscure subject. At first his views on imperialism were conventional. He was a naturalized Englishman; he knew the French, and he distrusted them. He admired Chamberlain's energy in pushing railways into the West African interior. His heroes were the men on the spot who were outwitting Britain's rivals: Goldie, Lugard, Rhodes.

For ten years Morel burnt the candle at both ends, working for Elder Dempster by day, and writing for newspapers by night. His work delighted both sets of employers. At this period (though he did not care to recall it later) he took a brisk line with the old-style humanitarians like Dilke and Fox Bourne who were denouncing the ill-treatment of natives in the Congo. He told the readers of the *Pall Mall Gazette* that he could give them the facts *as they were*, 'not as disappointed adventurers, needy place-hunters and misinformed philanthropists would have us believe'.[7] As for those stories of ill-treatment of natives, even if true, 'What European nation which has undertaken the heavy responsibility of introducing the blessings and vices of civilization into the Dark Continent can claim immunity for its representatives in this respect?'

Were the atrocity stories true? In 1899, after ten years, Morel, the leading British authority on West Africa, found it hard to say. He was prepared to admit that when the King talked of the 'blessings' of civilization in the Congo, he was thinking of his own profits. Morel's own work at Elder Dempster brought him into frequent contact with Free State officials in Brussels and Antwerp, and he had not been impressed by their business morality. Whatever it was, the Free State was not a philanthropic enterprise.

There were only a handful of Europeans who claimed to have witnessed atrocities (apart from the Belgian witnesses to the hanging of Stokes). One was Captain Sidney Hinde, the British army doctor who had published a sensational book on his service with Dhanis in the Arab war, including accounts of the atrocities practised by the cannibals fighting for the Free State. Was Hinde's testimony above suspicion? The other witnesses were more objective – a Swedish missionary, the Reverend Sjöblom, two American missionaries, J.B. Murphy and William Morrison, and an English explorer, Edward Glave. All four claimed that administrative abuses were sickening and widespread. But why were these reports not corroborated by other missionaries? There were something like 240 Catholic and 220 Protestant missionaries scattered all over the Congo. Why did they keep silent? In any case, most of these charges were by now many years out of date.

Morel's conclusion was that if outrages had occurred, they must have been the work of African soldiers who got out of hand, and the stories were exaggerated. As for the central government officials, he had eaten and drunk with these cheery Belgians on the quays of Antwerp, and found it hard to imagine them having a hand in atrocities. If things had gone wrong, it must be due to ignorance and inexperience. Even British administrators would have had their work cut out dealing with savages like the Congolese.

But by 1900, Morel was prepared to eat his words. He had been duped by Leopold, after all.

While labouring over the desiccated statistics of the Free State, he suddenly stumbled on an amazing discovery. He saw what the humanitarians had never guessed – that the King had had the trade figures doctored. Morel compared the official figures with the Elder Dempster shipping returns and the sale of rubber by the Free State and its concessionary companies on the Antwerp market. The real figure for exports must be much higher than the figure given – and much higher than the figure for imports. (The so-called 'trade' included quantities of European arms imported for the army of the State. Thousands of tons of tropical products, mainly rubber, were reaching Europe without any corresponding trade in exchange.) Clearly the Free State officials were not paying the natives to bring the rubber from the jungle, nor were the natives doing it for love. The officials must be using forced labour, beating and shooting the rubber out of them. This meant that, if anything, the humanitarians had underestimated the abuses. These were not haphazard, but *systematic*. In short, the King's philanthropy was founded on 'legalized robbery enforced by violence'. But who would ever believe this?

His discoveries left Morel 'giddy and appalled'. 'It must be bad enough', he wrote later, 'to stumble upon a murder. I had stumbled upon a secret society of murderers with a King for a croniman.'[8] As soon as he could obtain a hearing, Morel went along to warn his chief, Alfred Jones. He found Jones curiously uninterested. It was absurd, Jones said, to imagine that the King would tolerate systematic abuse of the natives. Morel should remember that the Free State was one of Elder Dempster's best customers and had appointed Jones Honorary Consul at Liverpool. He told Morel to put his confidence in the King.

Morel found this impossible. His old colleagues at Elder Dempster now seemed to him to inhabit an 'atmosphere of foul and filthy talk, of gross ideals and grosser methods'.[9] He launched a series of expert articles in *The Speaker*, exposing the 'Congo scandal'. Then he decided to abandon ship at Elder Dempster, and take up his pen as a full-time writer on West Africa, before Jones threw him overboard.

Morel's articles in *The Speaker* during the summer of 1900, though anonymous, caught the eye of Dilke and Fox Bourne. Soon he was advising them on how to run their campaign. The Mansion House meeting of 15 May 1902, though not well attended, was their first joint project to arouse public opinion.

It was not easy to proceed against the 'royal megalomaniac', as Morel called Leopold, and strip the mask from him; Leopold was equally adept at threats and flattery. His was the 'cleverest brain in Europe', and his arm had 'a long reach',[10] Morel recognized with a shiver. They might never persuade the British missionaries in the Congo to end their craven silence.

Go for Mammon, was Morel's blunt advice to Dilke and Fox Bourne. For ten years they had been campaigning on too narrow a ground. They had appealed to the brotherhood of man, the good name of Britain, and the moral responsibility of Empire. It was the damage to British trade that would prod the imperialist public and stir Parliament to action. They had forgotten commercial self-interest. Commerce was, after all, the first of Livingstone's '3 cs', and in the Congo economics were the crux of the matter. At a stroke Leopold had abolished not only the African's right to his own land but his right to trade with whom he pleased. He had also abolished the rights of free trade in the Congo, guaranteed to the international business community by the Berlin Act of 1885. In its place he had created an illegal monopoly for the State and its concessionary companies. The Congo Free State was robbing British merchants as well as African peasants.

At first Morel found that his argument had strangely little appeal for British businessmen. Some, like Alfred Jones, were dependent on a lucrative contract with the Congo; others did business with Belgians who were proud of the King's African work. Most British businessmen seemed more anxious to protect their existing markets than to expand them.

Then, in November 1901, a legal bombshell in the French colonial court at Libreville, capital of Gabon, and the administrative base for the French Congo, gave Morel the opportunity he needed to bully Mammon into joining his crusade.

The French Congo, despite the heady predictions of its founder, Brazza, had remained a fever-ridden backwater. It lacked most of the infrastructure needed for a viable colony, especially a railway to bypass the rapids and open up the interior. Brazza had tried to persuade Paris to assist. He had been recalled instead. Paris had been persuaded by some of Leopold's associates to adopt a much more profitable policy. Like Leopold's Congo State, the French Congo now gave concessions to private companies, and exploited the power (and guns) of the State to enforce a legal monopoly. It was the confirmation of the legality of this State monopoly, and the abolition of free trade, that constituted the legal bombshell at Libreville.

The spread of this economic plague – Leopold's monopolistic system – to the French Congo, and the eviction of British trading firms, rallied at least one large trader, John Holt, to Morel's side. Holt protested that he felt utterly unequal to the task. He loathed publicity and he loathed politics. But he was a genuine humanitarian, and Morel convinced him where his duty lay.

The first step, to fire British public opinion, by prodding the British press, proved successful. The Mansion House meeting the following May, even if ill attended, created a consensus among editors that something must be done about the Congo. Britain bore part of the responsibility for creating the Congo State at Berlin, based on free trade and philanthropy. Britain must now take the lead in persuading the Powers to institute reforms. This was the view of both imperial stalwarts, like the *Morning Post*, and Liberal free traders, like the *Daily News* and the *Manchester Guardian*. Already the press had been united by the failure of Belgium to end the anomaly by annexing the Congo in 1901, instead of allowing the option to lapse.

The second step, to persuade the Foreign Office to enforce both the free trade and the humanitarian provisions of the Berlin Act, was a flop. Vital to this plan were the business connections of John Holt, for he was Vice-President of the Liverpool Chamber of Commerce. Unfortunately, Alfred Jones, his rival, was the President. Holt and his supporters received sympathy and nothing else from the Foreign Office. Lord Lansdowne, Foreign Secretary since 1900, did not wish to advertise Britain's isolation in Europe and shrank from trying to involve France or Germany. The story of the Congo was lamentable, he was the first to admit, but even if it had been practical to reconvene the Powers who had signed the Berlin Act, it would re-open the whole question of the partition of Africa. He had already explained this to Dilke. It would not be 'desirable in our own interests'.[11]

So the reformers turned back to educating the British public. Again and again the terms of the equation were hammered home. Internal reform was impossible. State monopoly depended on a system of forced labour. This in turn made atrocities inevitable. If enough of the public grasped this equation, Parliament itself might force the hand of Lansdowne and the FO to enforce the Berlin Act. Early in 1903 Morel published *Affairs of West Africa*, with a chapter exposing the extortionate economics of the Congo. This was followed by Fox Bourne's *Civilisation in Congoland*, reworking the old revelations of the 1890s, including the story of Stokes's illegal hanging. Independently of the reformers, a British officer who had served with the Free State, Captain Guy Burrows, published *The Curse of Central Africa*, with lurid illustrations confirming the allegations that for some Belgian officials torture and murder were all in a day's work.

As press reviews of these sensational books generated further momentum for the campaign, the reformers organized public meetings and lobbied MPs to ask questions in the House. One firm obstacle remained: the failure to persuade the craven British missionaries to break silence. However, in April 1903, the Aborigines Protection Society was able to manoeuvre the Baptist Union into calling for a joint appeal to the Belgian government to institute an inquiry into the atrocities; and in May the American Presbyterian missionary, William Morrison, whose earlier revelations had been so influential, returned from the Congo with an up-dated report.

The King's answer was predictably underhand – and well-financed. Early in 1903 the Free State announced that Captain Guy Burrows would be sued in a British court for criminal libel against certain Free State officers. If Burrows were proved guilty, it would be a damaging blow for the reformers. Meanwhile, the allegations remained *sub judice*. At the same time the King, having lost the support of the Baptist Union, retained his hold over the other British Baptists by reducing their taxes in the Congo. A deputation from the Baptist Missionary Society was invited to meet the King in Brussels. They assured him how grateful they were for all his 'wise efforts to instruct and elevate the conditions of the natives' in the Congo. Later they expressed 'satisfaction' that the Burrows case would prove the real truth about the allegations against the Free State. By the end of March the affair had been turned into a propaganda coup for Leopold. Burrows failed to produce any witnesses from the Congo. The British judge assessed libel at £500 and ordered the book to be suppressed.

The King also launched a whispering campaign against Dilke. 'The air was full of poisonous rumours,' wrote Morel somewhat primly. 'A public trial in which Sir Charles Dilke had formerly figured was revived.'[12] And a Belgian official was sent to London to see what was Morel's price to call off the whole crusade.

This clumsy attempt to bribe him gave Morel some light relief in these harrowing weeks of the spring of 1903. The official, introduced by Alfred Jones, was politeness itself. He asked Morel if he expected to succeed against the power of His Majesty. 'What did I stand to gain? My health would break down. I had done a great deal ... Reforms would undoubtedly ensue. Serious reforms ... I was a young man, I had a family – yes? I was running serious risks.'[13] It was easy to tell this smiling Satan to get behind him, but harder to persuade the British public of the King's true character. Again and again, Morel met with the same baffled scepticism.

Then, on 20 May, the American missionary, William Morrison, gave grim details of atrocities to a meeting organized by the Aborigines Protection Society in London, including half a dozen MPs, and matters moved swiftly forward. A fortnight later the House of Commons debated the 'evils' of the Congo for the first time since a motion had been proposed by Dilke in 1897. To Morel's delight and astonishment, the Commons accepted, without a division, the burden of the reformers' case. The government was now committed to conferring with the other Powers which had signed the General Act of Berlin 'in order that measures may be adopted to abate the evils prevalent in that State'.[14]

Lansdowne appeared to play for time. He was reluctant to have a row with Leopold and he still hoped to persuade him to abandon his dream of grabbing extra territory on the Nile beyond Lado. The FO announced that before Britain approached the other Powers about Congo abuses, the British Consul in the Congo Free State, Roger Casement, would be sent to make a full report.

* * *

Lord Lansdowne had good reason for his reluctance to be drawn into the crusade against Leopold in the summer of 1903 – quite apart from the complications concerning Leopold's designs on the Nile. The FO itself had designs on Britain's other neighbour in Central Africa, France.

It was nearly three years since Lord Salisbury had been persuaded to promote Lansdowne from the War Office after winning the Khaki Election of 1900, and to hand him the glittering burden of the Foreign Office which he was too old to carry any longer himself. The promotion had raised many people's eyebrows. Lansdowne had proved feeble enough as War Minister. He had failed to prevent the war between the generals at the War Office which had crippled preparations to fight the Boers. He had failed to grasp that the Boers would prove a real enemy, able to exploit the power of modern weapons a good deal more successfully than the British.

Lansdowne's friends pointed to the reputation for prudence he had earned as a Viceroy, first in Canada and then in India. Despite his glamorous Whig background and armies of obsequious tenants spread over six counties of England and Scotland (with some less obsequious ones in Ireland), 'Clan' Lansdowne was as diligent and serious-minded – and as unimaginative – as any civil servant in Whitehall.

As Foreign Secretary under Salisbury he had proved predictably modest. Now, in the summer of 1903, with the encouragement of the new Prime Minister, Arthur Balfour, he was contemplating the uncharacteristically radical step of ending Britain's isolation in Europe, which 'splendid or otherwise' (in Rosebery's sarcastic phrase), had made Britain the Aunt Sally of Europe during the Boer War.

The FO's plan was for a *rapprochement* with France – for more, for an *entente cordiale*, a warm understanding. It would end, once and for all, those dangerous disputes about African territory which had bedevilled relations between the two countries ever since the British had taken Egypt in 1882. It would also help resolve the still more vital question of strategic defence. The British Admiralty were looking for a naval ally to help defend Britain and the Empire. France, Russia and Germany, in that order, were all pursuing Britain in a naval arms race. At first the hunt for an ally had been directed at Germany, leader of the Triple Alliance. But in August 1901 the Kaiser had mocked Britain's outstretched hand, offered by his uncle, Edward VII, the new King of England. In 1903 the royal hand was proffered again, this time to Paris – if the French were not too proud, after Fashoda, to grab it.

The chance came in mid-May, a week before the humanitarians' triumph in the Congo debate in the House of Commons. Edward VII made a state visit to Paris and delighted his hosts. The King was no diplomatist. (He had bungled his recent meeting with the Kaiser and by mistake handed over Lansdowne's private notes.) But he had always felt at home in France, putting money on French racehorses, tucking into gargantuan meals and losing his heart to French actresses. He captured Paris in his three-day state visit. The sour refrains of '*Vive Marchand!*' and '*Vive les Boers!*' changed to rapturous cries of '*Vive Edouard! Notre Bon Edouard!*'[15] When the state visit was returned by the French President in London in July, it was time for Lansdowne to get down to brass tacks with Delcassé. Would M. le Ministre be interested in a final settlement of the African account?

The bargaining began at the FO at 9.30 a.m. on 9 July. While President Loubet was preparing to review 15,000 troops at Aldershot, his Foreign Minister, Delcassé, the victim of Fashoda, was welcomed to Lansdowne's sumptuous room overlooking St James's Park. The two men grasped six colonial nettles, by far the most important of which were African nettles, Morocco and Egypt. The atmosphere was friendly. More surprisingly, progress was rapid. By lunchtime the two men had begun to discern the lines of a general settlement.

Apart from Ethiopia, Liberia, Tripoli and Cyrenaica, Morocco was the only independent African state to survive the Scramble. But the power of Abd-el-Haziz, the twenty-five-year-old Sultan of Morocco, was tottering. His downfall threatened the French colony of Algeria with trouble on its border – and also presented an interesting opportunity. Give us a free hand in Morocco, said Delcassé. Lansdowne agreed, on condition that Britain was given a free hand in Egypt. At heart, the deal was as simple as that.

The wrangling over the small print went on for months. By January 1904 there was stalemate. The British public would not tolerate a straight swap, Morocco for Egypt. After all, Egypt was already effectively a British protectorate, whereas the French still had to gain control of Morocco. Delcassé agreed; a straight swap would not work, but for the opposite reason. The English, he pointed out, had no formal share in the government of Morocco. In Egypt the French were partners in the Caisse and would be abandoning Napoleon's dream, sacred to every Frenchman. The answer was to throw in some French fishing rights off the coast of Newfoundland, and balance it with a border rectification in Nigeria. Delcassé resisted the temptation until the spring. By then a ferocious war, not in Africa but in the East, had threatened to involve Britain and France on opposite sides. If the *entente* was to be signed, it was now or never.

The war was between Russia, France's ally since 1892, and Japan, Britain's ally since 1901. At first it looked as though Japan, much the weaker (on paper) in ships and regiments, would ask Britain to send her own fleet to the rescue. But the Japanese army and navy were more competent, and the Russians less, than anyone had thought possible. The Japanese needed no allies. At the battle of Tsushima on 27 May 1905, the Japanese achieved the unthinkable against the unsinkable. The Russian navy, third most powerful in the world, was sent to the bottom and Manchuria snatched from the paws of the bear.

Hearing the approaching thunder over the eastern horizon, Britain and France kissed and made up, ending twenty years of squabbles in Africa.

The *entente* – including a secret understanding to allow the French to take over most of Morocco – was signed on 8 April 1904. At the time it seemed a triumph of prudence, one of the few achievements of Balfour's government, now enfeebled by the resignation of Joe Chamberlain, who had in May 1903 split the Unionists by launching a campaign for tariff reform. After two years the *entente* with France led to an *entente* with Russia. Cromer at last got his free hand in Egypt and the Caisse was abolished.

But the FO had misunderstood the deal with France. The *entente* did not appear so friendly to Germany. It threatened her with encirclement. Delcassé had always grasped this. Indeed, it was one of the main attractions for Frenchmen who (following Gambetta's instructions) thought constantly of Armageddon, and the sacred pledge to liberate Alsace and Lorraine. The *entente* led smoothly down the slope to 1914.

* * *

It was on 4 June 1903, the year before the *entente* was signed, that the FO telegrams caught up with Roger Casement, the British Consul, staying with a missionary at Matadi, the rocky harbour connecting the navigable lower Congo with the new railway to Leopoldville. Casement found two of the telegrams in unintelligible code. But he had the cipher for the third, and it made his blood race. The FO commanded him (so he recorded in his diary) to 'go to the interior' as soon as he could, to investigate Congo abuses. The Commons debate had proved a 'terrible attack' on the Congo. Here was his chance. He would be Britain's special investigator – a public 'avenger', [16] he called it. The next morning he started on the 200-mile train journey to Leopoldville.

Casement seemed somewhat innocent for a life in that seedy and brutal world hacked out by Bula Matari, the Breaker of Rocks. He was thirty-eight years old, with the arresting looks of a Spanish aristocrat – large poetic eyes contrasting with neatly-trimmed black beard. He wrote girlish poetry to express his feelings of alienation as an Irish Protestant from Northern Ireland, orphaned as a boy, and identifying with the oppressed Gaels. In the 1880s he had worked, like Morel, for the Elder Dempster Line, then knocked about the Congo, picking up jobs and going down with fever, giving Stanley a hand in 1884, enlisting with the Baptists, even taking ivory down to the coast on his own account. Sometimes he would disappear into the bush for weeks with only a stick for a weapon and only one Loanda and a couple of English bulldogs for company. In 1890, ten years before Conrad wrote *The Heart of Darkness*, he spent an instructive year in the Congo, and a fortnight with Casement was one of its pleasant features. Conrad found him 'most intelligent and very sympathetic', with a 'touch of the conquistadore' in him – and mysterious, too. 'He could tell you things!' he wrote of Casement (as though as he were speaking of Marlow, the narrator of *The Heart of Darkness*, who was searching for a moral centre in Africa). 'Things I have tried to forget, things I never did know.' [17] But would Casement ever find the moral centre, in his own muddled search?

Casement was a slave to conflicting emotions and appetites. He was an ardent Irish nationalist yearning for social recognition in England; a hermit, thirsty for exotic pleasures, including the taste (recorded in his diary) for handsome sailors and muscular young Africans; a dispassionate investigator, hungry for the punishment of injustice.

Now, in 1903, after eleven years as a member of HM Consular Service in various foetid, fever-ridden African ports, Casement found these wild emotions converging as he took over the investigation of 'the evils prevalent' in the Congo.

The main symptom, visible even in the lower Congo, was the growing depopulation of the country. Disease, especially sleeping sickness, was one of the causes. The other, he felt sure, was the system of forced labour imposed by the Free State. But he needed to get evidence that would stand up in the court of world opinion. He had already won the confidence of many individual missionaries, including members of the Baptist Missionary Society, whose committee in London was too frightened to co-operate with Morel. The missionaries knew the people and were the only independent witnesses of what they suffered; but they risked reprisals from the Congo government.

Fortunately, news of the debate in the British House of Commons in June 1903 followed him to the Congo and gave British subjects a new courage. Casement was determined to avoid being stifled by official channels. The American Baptists let him hire a small steam launch, the *Henry Reed*, and he stocked it with supplies – sugar, soup, custard and several cases of carrots. Under his own steam, he ascended 160 miles above Leopoldville and reached the edge of the rainforest, where the rubber zone began.

At Bolobo, a mission station which had once numbered 40,000 souls, Casement was told the population was now reduced to 1,000. There were reports of troops raiding villages nearby, to punish them for failing to pay the 'food tax' – in other words, to do forced labour to provide food for the State. At Impoko he met witnesses to atrocities. A BMS missionary, Scrivener, took him to meet some Basingili men forced to work as blacksmiths who said they were refugees from persecution by State officials. Casement was shocked. At first, he would hardly credit the refugees' account of the way rubber was collected in the *Domaine de la Couronne*, a concessionary area under Leopold's direct control 100 miles to the south. When he asked why they had abandoned their homes, and all they possessed, to work like slaves with a neighbouring tribe, the men and their womenfolk shouted back: on account of the 'rubber tax' levied by the government.

'How does the government impose the "tax"?'

'From our country each village had to take 20 loads of rubber. These loads were big; they were nearly as big as this ... [He produced an empty basket which came nearly up to the handle of Casement's walking stick.] We had to take these loads in 4 times a month.'

'How much pay do you get for this?'

[The entire audience]: 'We got no pay. We got nothing ... Our village got cloth and a little salt, but not the people who did the work ... It used to take 10 days to get the 20 baskets of rubber – we were always in the forest to find the rubber vines, to go without food, and our women had to give up cultivating the fields and gardens. Then we starved. Wild beasts – the leopards – killed some of us while we were working away in the forest and others got lost or died from exposure or starvation and we begged the white men to leave us alone, saying we could get no more rubber, but the white men and their soldiers said: Go. You are only beasts yourselves. You are only

Nyama [meat]. We tried, always going further into the forest, and when we failed and our rubber was short, the soldiers came to our towns and killed us. Many were shot, some had their ears cut off; others were tied up with ropes around their necks and bodies and taken away. The white men at the posts sometimes did not know of the bad things the soldiers did to us, but it was the white men who sent the soldiers to punish us for not bringing in enough rubber.'

Another native took up the story:

'We said to the white man: "We are not enough people now to do what you want of us. Our country has not many people in it and the people are dying fast. We are killed by the work you make us do, by the stoppage of our plantations and the breaking up of our homes." The white man looked at us and said: "There are lots of white men in Mputu [Europe] ... there must be a way, there must be many in the black man's country." '

An old man who lived nearby told Casement:

'We used to hunt elephants long ago and there were plenty in our forests, and we got much meat; but Bula Matari [the Congo State] killed the elephant hunters because they could not get rubber, and so we starved. We are sent out to get rubber, and when we come back with little rubber we are shot.'
'Who shot you?'
'The white men sent their soldiers out to kill us.'
'How do you know it was the white men sent the soldiers? It might only be the savage soldiers themselves?'
'No, no, sometimes we brought rubber into the white men's stations ... when it was not enough the white men would put some of us in lines, one behind the other, and would shoot through all our bodies. Sometimes he would shoot us like that with his own hand; sometimes his soldiers would do it.'[18]

Casement said he could hardly believe these tales told at Impoko, but later they were confirmed by one of the English missionaries, who visited the villages where the atrocities had occurred. Meanwhile, Casement steamed on up-river in the *Henry Reed*. At Lukokela he was taken by the local English missionary, the Reverend J. Whitehead, to meet more Basingili refugees. They had the same harrowing tale. 'Poor frail folk seeking vexed mortality,' Casement wrote poetically in his diary – incongruously close to a note about a temptingly well-endowed African boy. ('July 13. At State Beach photoed pier and Loanaga – about 9".')[19]

But the official dossier he kept was grim enough. Wherever he pulled in to the river-bank, the natives would flee in terror of 'Bula Matari'. Then, after the missionaries had reassured them, Casement was treated to stories of atrocities: children running into the bush as their mothers and sisters were shot down by the soldiers, and then perhaps eaten by cannibals; hundreds of families butchered, or burnt in their homes; village after village burnt and looted, the men taken off as slaves, the women and children hacked to death.

Most gruesome were the tales of severed hands. Soldiers collected them by the basketload, hacking them off their victims, dead or alive, to prove they had not wasted ammunition. One of the State officials admitted to Casement that this had been done 'in the awful past'. He claimed it no longer occurred. But the missionaries brought him much evidence to the contrary, and the natives assured him that the reign of terror continued.

As the *Henry Reed* steamed on into the sticky, claustrophobic heart of the rubber districts, Casement's official reports to the Foreign Office changed tone. At first it was the desolation that had shocked him. His tone was indignant but judicial:

> In the lake district things were pretty bad ... whole villages and districts I knew well and visited as flourishing communities in 1887 are today without a human being; others are reduced to a handful of sick or harassed creatures who say of the government: 'Are the white men never going home; is this to last forever?'[20]

But by September the thought of the atrocities filled him with rage. On 6 September he was taken to see a boy of about sixteen, Epondo, whose right hand had been severed at the wrist – apparently by a soldier. Casement had seen enough. He set off for Stanley Pool and the coast, determined to return to London by the first boat. He must not lose control of himself. 'Of all the shameful and infamous expedients', he wrote to the Foreign Office, 'whereby man has preyed upon man ... this vile thing [the rubber trade] dares to call itself commerce....'[21]

The *Ambrose* landed him at Liverpool at 10.0 p.m. on 30 November, and he travelled that night by train to London. By 12 December, his eighty-four-page report exposing the evils of Leopold's government was typed, ready for what he called 'the gang of stupidities' and 'pifflers'[22] at the Foreign Office.

*　　*　　*

The Foreign Office officials found Casement's report surprisingly judicious. It detailed the abuses, but was terse and understated. Lansdowne congratulated him. It was 'proof of the most painfully convincing kind'.[23] But would the government find it politic to publish it? Already Leopold's lobby, led by Alfred Jones, was protesting at the damage it would do to British commercial interests.

Two days before finishing the report, Casement had at last made the acquaintance of Edmond Morel, the leader of the reformers. They met in a house in Chester Square lent by a friend. The meeting of these two outsiders proved a revelation to each of them. Casement found Morel 'honest as the day'.[24] Morel never forgot the impression of Casement's 'long, lean, swarthy Van Dyck type of face, graven with power and ... great gentleness'. For hours Casement talked away in his soft, musical voice, telling 'the story of a vile conspiracy against

civilization, the difficulties he had had to overcome, the traps laid for him ...'.
As the 'monologue of horror' proceeded, Morel felt he could see those 'hunted
women clutching their children and flying panic-stricken to the bush; the blood
flowing from those quivering black bodies as the hippopotamus-hide whip
struck again and again; the savage soldiers rushing hither and thither, burning
villages; the ghastly tally of severed hands'.[25]

By February 1904 things looked hopeful for the reformers. At last one section
of the British Baptists would back them openly: the Congo Bolobo Mission
(though not the Baptist Missionary Society) threw its weight behind the movement. At the same time, Casement persuaded Morel that the campaign could
not be left to Fox Bourne and Dilke. Morel – 'Bulldog' Morel, Casement called
him – must lead it himself. Morel duly founded the Congo Reform Association,
backed by the money of Liverpool traders like John Holt.

In the same month Lansdowne decided to overrule the protests of Leopold's
lobby and publish Casement's report – after judiciously removing most of the
proper names. Casement was furious. Without the names of witnesses, his report
would go off like a damp squib. In fact it made a deafening bang in the British
press, a bang that was universally welcomed. Not since Stanley's day had
the Congo captured such headlines. Morel was exultant. Casement – 'Tiger'
Casement, Morel called him – was every man's hero.

But at first Morel's dependence on Holt and the Liverpool traders seemed
to have delivered him straight into the King's hands. Backed by his outraged
Belgian subjects, Leopold planned his counter-attack: a knee in Morel's and
Casement's stomachs.

Neither France nor Germany had the slightest interest in convening a new
conference on the Congo. France had sound economic reasons to be happy with
the present arrangement; rubber gathering by concessionary companies using
forced labour – the system borrowed from Leopold – was beginning to pay
dividends in the French Congo. Germany maintained Bismarck's old policy of
backing Leopold for fear he would hand over the Congo to France.

Anyway, Germany had more pressing troubles of her own in Africa. In
January that year, 1904, there were reports of a great Herero revolt in south-
west Africa which soon threatened to sweep the isolated German garrisons into
the sea.

CHAPTER 33

The Kaiser's First War

Berlin and German South-West Africa
18 January 1904 and after

> 'The missionary says that we are the children of God
> like our white brothers ... but just look at us. Dogs,
> slaves, worse than baboons on the rocks ... that is
> how you treat us.'

A Herero to a German settler

Each day that second week of January 1904 the telegrams from Windhoek, the capital of German South-West Africa, had brought blacker news to the baffled experts of the Kolonialabteilung in Berlin. They were Dr Oskar Stübel and the ten other officials who directed the German colonial empire from a small department inside the Foreign Office in the Wilhelmstrasse.

At first there were reports of cattle theft and insubordination towards white settlers. Such incidents had not been unusual during the twenty years since German settlers had begun to trickle into German South-West Africa. However, this time the authorities had taken no chances, and in early January had called up the reservists. More ominous was the report from the town of Okahandja on 10 January that the local Herero were buying up all the available horses, saddles, bridles and clothing, not caring what price they paid.

The rebellion itself then exploded without any other warning on 12 January, smack in the strategic centre of German settlement, along the new railway line between the port of Swapokmund and Windhoek. Outlying farms were attacked and it was feared that white men had been murdered. Within days the reservists and regular troops posted in the main German towns of the central district – Okahandja, Omaruru and Windhoek itself – were under siege by well-armed Herero.

It was not easy to assess the threat to the 5,000-odd Germans of this unfortunate colony, whose assets comprised a wealth of rock and sand, and whose liabilities annually cost the German taxpayer a subsidy of nine million marks (£425,000). Dr Stübel could only report that the German garrisons were 'desperately assailed'.[1] The telegraph line had been cut in the first days of the rising, and nothing had been heard from Windhoek since 14 January. The rebellion had caught the experienced Governor, Colonel Theodor von Leutwein, completely off his guard. He had left only one company of German troops in the capital and surrounding districts when he had marched off with two other companies the previous autumn to put down a revolt of one of the southern Nama (Hottentot)

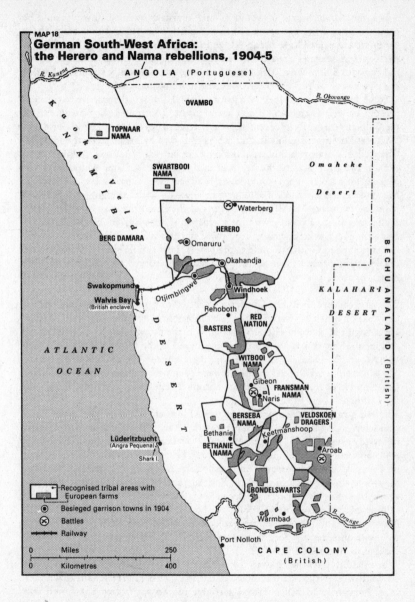

MAP 18

German South-West Africa: the Herero and Nama rebellions, 1904-5

R. Kunene

A N G O L A (Portuguese)

R. Okovango

OVAMBO

K a o k o V e l d

TOPNAAR NAMA

SWARTBOOI NAMA

Omaheke

Desert

⊗• Waterberg

HERERO

BERG DAMARA

•⊗ Omaruru

Okahandja ⊗

Swakopmund

Otjimbingwe

Windhoek

Walvis Bay
(British enclave)

Rehoboth

BASTERS

RED NATION

K A L A H A R I

D E S E R T

B E C H U A N A L A N D (British)

A T L A N T I C

O C E A N

D
E
S
E
R
T

WITBOOI NAMA

Gibeon
⊗
Naris

FRANSMAN NAMA

VELDSKOEN DRAGERS

BERSEBA NAMA

Bethanie

Keetmanshoop

Aroab
⊗

BETHANIE NAMA

Lüderitzbucht
(Angra Pequena)

Shark I.

BONDELSWARTS

R. Orange

Warmbad

Recognised tribal areas with
European farms

⊙ Besieged garrison towns in 1904

⊗ Battles

Railway

| 0 | Miles | 250 |

| 0 | Kilometres | 400 |

Port Nolloth

C A P E   C O L O N Y
(British)

tribes, the Bondelswarts. It would be mid-February before Leutwein could be expected back from the south. The only outside help that could reach those fortunate enough to have found refuge in the garrison towns was from eighty-five German Marines aboard the *Habicht*, a German gunboat which patrolled the coast of South-West Africa and had been providentially summoned when the alarm was raised, just before the telegraph line was cut.

By 18 January, the prospect of a great colonial disaster, destructive to German prestige as well as costly in blood and treasure, confronted the bureaucrats at the Wilhelmstrasse. Reinforcements would have to be rushed out from Germany. This was Dr Stübel's opinion, and it was endorsed by his masters, the Imperial Chancellor, Count von Bülow, and the Kaiser himself. That day, Bülow rose to explain the grim facts to the deputies in the Reichstag. They would send 500 Marine volunteers who would disembark at Swapokmund by 8 February. Meanwhile, the garrisons would have to make do with the eighty-five Marines from the *Habicht*. The Reichstag approved the supplementary estimates – 2.8 million marks (£140,000) – without a whisper of dissent from August Bebel, the Socialist leader, who normally denounced imperialism in all its forms.

But no one in Germany could explain why these simple Herero tribesmen, as docile as their cattle for a decade, had suddenly turned on their masters like hungry wolves.

Theodor von Leutwein, the Governor of the colony, could offer no satisfactory explanation when he wrote his own memoirs several years after the disaster. He recognized that the Herero had chosen their opportunity well, when he and most of his troops were otherwise engaged in the south. But why did they want to rebel? There was no reason, he claimed – apart from 'misplaced *Rassengegenfätzen*' (race-hatred).[2] Indeed, Samuel Maherero, the Paramount Chief, had been the keenest advocate and chief beneficiary of co-operation with the Germans.

It was strange that Leutwein, who prided himself on his insight into African character, with his romantic respect for Iron Age culture, and his own honest, not to say cynical, brand of realism about his fellow Germans, should have been so completely caught off his guard. He was a heavy-jawed soldier from Freiburg im Breisgau, stiff, professorial and bespectacled, a man of dogmatic opinions, though flexible enough in practice. For ten years he had laboured to keep the peace between his masters in Berlin and the settlers in the colony. Berlin shuddered at the cost of the colony to the Reich. The settlers were greedy for African land and labour, and prepared to force the pace, even at the risk of a war with the Herero. (Unfortunately for him, Lüderitz was drowned in the Orange river in 1886.)

In 1884 Bismarck had played the colonial card and made his famous pounce on south-west Africa. He was talked into it by Lüderitz, the merchant adventurer from Bremen, who had obtained a concession on the barren coast, and was impatient to exploit the unknown riches of the interior.

At that time the thin, brown grass of the central plateau was subject to a crippling territorial struggle between two semi-nomadic peoples: the Herero cattle-raisers of the arid central plateau and the Nama ('Hottentot') cattle-raisers – and cattle-raiders – of the still more arid steppes to the south. It was a war for cattle grazing – a grim sort of pastoral war – and it exhausted the resources of both African contestants, including the supply of guns and cartridges they bought from European traders. It also threatened, in the long term, the pockets of the traders themselves, some of whom were German, as well as the spiritual labours of the Rhenish Mission Society who had come to evangelize the Herero.

Backed by German traders and missionaries, Lüderitz persuaded Bismarck to fill the political vacuum and restore order. The Herero were duly informed of the takeover by Bismarck's Imperial Commissioner, Dr Nachtigal, who arrived loaded with blank treaty forms, offering 'protection'.[3] Old Samuel Maherero, father of the present Chief of the same name, hurried forward to put his cross on the treaty. Under this new flag – the black eagle of the Reich – the Herero would surely find relief from the crippling wars with the Nama.

But in the 1880s the German administrator, Dr Ernst Göring (father of Hermann, the Reichsmarshal), could afford only a handful of troops, and was too weak to help anyone. On the other hand, the Germans asked little of the Herero except for their signatures on the treaty forms. The Herero were allowed to keep their much-prized stock of modern rifles, bought from German trading companies (including one set up by the German missionaries). They continued their ancient pastoral life, and their ancient pastoral wars, secure in the knowledge that the treaty specifically confirmed their rights. As well as offering 'protection' to the chief and the tribe, the Germans had promised to respect native customs and abstain from any act that would be illegal in their own country. In return, the Herero had only ceded a nominal sovereignty – the right to control foreign affairs – as well as granting Germans the apparently harmless right to trade without let or hindrance, under the jurisdiction of the German authorities.

In 1892 the Nama-Herero war finally petered out, after the Chief of the Witbooi Nama, Hendrik Witbooi, appealed for national unity against German encroachment. But the Herero were then passing through a succession crisis and Samuel Maherero, the fourth son of the old Chief, saw his chance to exploit German intervention. He was not the nearest in line but he was a Christian and a candidate of the German missionaries. It was Maherero whom Theodor Leutwein, the newly-arrived German commander, backed against various rivals, including Nikodemus, his older half-brother who was first in succession. Meanwhile, Leutwein's predecessor, Captain von François, had invaded the camp of Hendrik Witbooi, the Witbooi Nama Chief, who still stubbornly refused to sign a treaty. German shelling killed about fifty women and children though Hendrik himself escaped.

Leutwein had only about 250 troops to fight the guerrilla war in progress when he arrived, so he offered what he considered generous terms to the Witboois. Like the Herero, they could retain their rifles, ammunition and traditional rights. But they must co-operate with the authorities and resign themselves to the end of cattle-raiding and tribal warfare. Hendrik Witbooi, a Christian convert like Samuel Maherero, anxiously seized on the peace terms. But he was shrewd enough to see that in the long run the conflict between Europeans and Africans would be impossible to reconcile. To succeed, a European colony demanded a revolution in African society. The Germans wanted land for settlement, cattle for export, gold and diamonds for mining – and Africans to work for long hours for little or no money. Neither Witboois nor Herero shared this vision. Their fathers had been nomads, worshipping their ancestors, living by cattle and the gun. This was the order of things, and they would, if desperate enough, give their lives to try and preserve it.

However, for a time the peace held. Hendrik Witbooi loyally sent a contingent to help the Germans against rebellious tribes. Samuel Maherero exploited German intervention so successfully that his two main rivals, including Nikodemus, were dealt with by a German firing squad. They had revolted against his own authority as paramount chief, and he insisted that the Germans make an example of them. Leutwein obliged, and gave Maherero part of the proceeds from confiscated cattle.

In the next decade the poverty and consequent military weakness of all three powers – German, Herero and Witbooi – gave Leutwein an opportunity to indulge his skill as a peacemaker. Like other colonial powers, the Germans needed peace to build up their strength. But in the 1890s the colony seemed irredeemably poor. In Berlin the Kaiser seriously discussed abandoning it to the British. (There was a secret memorandum, dated 1891, that the Director of the Colonial Department kept in a sealed envelope: 'The Emperor is prepared to give up South-West Africa if necessary, so that all energies may be focussed on East Africa.')[4] The climate could only be depended on to provide regular spells of drought and famine; otherwise nothing could be expected of German South-West. The glitter of diamonds, the vision which had haunted Lüderitz, seemed to have sunk with him the day in 1886 when his small boat overturned in the Orange river. These sun-blackened steppes produced the poorest of cattle, yet the Herero refused to trade in cattle, keeping part of the herd sacred to their ancestors.

Then, in 1897, disaster overtook the Herero nation. A wave of rinderpest, the cattle plague which had swept down from Central Africa in the mid-1890s, reached South-West Africa soon after it had engulfed the herds of Matabeleland. Within a year, the Herero were humbled and starving. Their herds withered like the grass. Once the cattle had numbered 250,000 head of stock. Now the Herero villages were almost empty. In desperation, individual Herero began to sell their land to German settlers to pay for vaccination, to buy new cattle, or simply to buy food and save their families from starvation. When the first census was taken a few years later, a few hundred German settlers owned 40,000 head of cattle, about the same number as belonged to the whole Herero people.

After the rinderpest came biblical plagues of malaria and typhoid (brought on by the shortage of milk) and an invasion of locusts, as though the Germans' god was determined to smite them. In the stricken villages the sense of doom must have been crushing. Those already baptized felt abandoned by God. Pagans, on the other hand, besieged the mission stations, begging for Christianity as well as food.

To Leutwein, the settlers and the missionaries, the disasters appeared indeed sent by heaven. Instead of precipitating a revolt, like similar disasters in Matabeleland and Mashonaland in 1896, the plagues smoothed the path of German colonial development. Leutwein reported to Berlin that the Herero were adapting to the new situation with admirable good sense. They now recognized their role as labourers on private farms or public works. The new railway running from Swapokmund to Windhoek, indispensable after the rinderpest had killed all the oxen, triumphantly opened in 1902. With a new railway, and a new telegraph beside it, the colony at last began to attract more immigrants, and more German capital. Many ex-soldiers and ex-civil servants became traders or farmers. The total number of Europeans rose sharply after the epidemics: from 2,000 in 1896 to 4,700 in 1903.

Yet the European community of German South-West Africa was still puny by any comparison. Across the border, in British Cape Colony, there were 700,000 Europeans. And within the borders of German South-West Africa there were perhaps 200,000 Africans, including the Ovambo who straddled the border with Angola, where the rains were good enough for mealies, and for malaria, too. (However, the Ovambo were still so warlike that no German dared to show his face in Ovamboland.)

By 1904 Leutwein was convinced that his peacemaking gamble had succeeded. He had tamed the Herero without a war – indeed without the means to fight one. Throughout the ten years of his governorship he had rejected the settlers' call to send out military reinforcements in order to disarm the Herero and break up the tribe. That would have provoked a war and been ruinously expensive – increasing still further the subsidies from Berlin. Instead, with the help of natural disasters, the Herero had come quietly to heel.

Leutwein had always treated their leader, Maherero, with studied politeness and preserved the fiction that the African was still a ruler rather than a subject. Of course, the ordinary Herero tribesmen were often treated less than politely by Leutwein's fellow Germans. Leutwein was the first to deplore what he privately called the 'barbarous'[5] conduct of the settlers – the brutal floggings and the reckless murders, many of which went unpunished, and the rape of Herero women, which was commonplace. (The settlers prevented any case ever being brought to justice.) At best, the Herero who worked for the Germans had to suffer systematic humiliation. They were called 'baboons' to their face. The settlers told the government in a petition that it was 'almost impossible to regard them as human beings'.[6] Leutwein deplored this, yet thought it unavoidable. After all, as he had told Berlin bluntly enough, German settlers were not risking their health in Africa to help the natives. They had come, like all colonizers, to help themselves – to African land and labour. It was self-deception for Socialist deputies, like Bebel, to talk in the Reichstag of 'humanitarian principles', borrowing the humbug from the British (and King Leopold). 'Colonization is always inhumane,' wrote Leutwein unflinchingly. The 'high-minded promises' given to the Herero by the Germans in order to get them to sign the blank treaty forms were simply a diplomatic ruse forced on the Germans 'by our weak strategic position at the time'.[7] Now that Germany was master of the whole territory, except for Ovamboland, Maherero would not, Leutwein believed, lightly take the decision to rebel. Indeed, it would be madness, for it would play straight into the hands of the more bloodthirsty settlers.

In one respect Leutwein was correct. Samuel Maherero had not lightly taken the decision to go to war. He himself would probably have voted against it. But the increasing desperation of his people, in the face of German provocation of every kind, coupled with the taunts of the younger tribesmen, left him no choice. It must have been a bitter decision. Maherero had none of the flair needed for the leader of a guerrilla war, the daring and the stoicism, qualities actually possessed by Hendrik Witbooi, the eighty-year-old veteran Chief of the Witbooi Nama. Maherero was a tall, handsome man, educated as a Christian by the Rhenish missionaries; he had a taste for white European suits, ranchers' hats and German brandy. Like all Herero he was devoted to his cattle and a patient negotiator – when he was sober.

His plan was simple to the point of naivety. Taking advantage of Leutwein's absence, the chiefs would co-ordinate attacks on all German settlements, and Maherero would persuade Hendrik Witbooi to raise his people in a simultaneous uprising.

A pact between hereditary enemies is not made in a day. But the crucial letters from Maherero to Hendrik Witbooi were not dispatched until immediately before the rising. They took the form of a national appeal, transcending the old tribal divisions:

> All our obedience and patience with the Germans is of little avail for each day they shoot someone dead for no reason at all. Hence I appeal to you, my Brother, not to hold aloof from the uprising, but to make your voice heard so that all Africa may take up arms against the Germans. Let us die fighting rather than die as a result of maltreatment, imprisonment or some other calamity. Tell all the Kapteins [chiefs] down there to rise and do battle.[8]

'All Africa ... let us die fighting.' It was a noble call to arms, but it fell on deaf ears – or worse. The Chief of a neighbouring people, the Rehoboth Nama, who had been asked to pass the letters on to Hendrik, handed them instead to the Germans. Still, had they reached Hendrik, they would hardly have changed his mind. True to his pact with Leutwein, Hendrik sent a contingent of one hundred Nama to fight with the Germans against his hereditary enemy, the Herero.

For less than a fortnight, from 12 January 1904 till 23 January, Maherero's united army had the field to itself. They had decided to get rid of the colony. So they killed every German man who could bear arms. By contrast, they spared the lives of German missionaries and German women and children, as well as all Europeans of other nationalities, including the English and Boers. The attacks on isolated farms presented no difficulty. Often the settlers were stabbed or hacked to death by the African servants they had trusted. Some were tortured in macabre rituals. Within a few days about one hundred German settlers had been killed, including some of the most hated traders.

Far more would have died if the reservists had not been recalled to the garrison towns just before the rising. The Herero, who could be as brave as lions in the stony veld, had no stomach for storming the sand-bagged walls of barracks, defended by mountain artillery and machine guns. The sporadic attacks on the garrison towns – Okahandja, Omaruru, Otjimbingwe and Wind-hoek itself – spent themselves like so many dust storms. One single company of German soldiers, commanded by Captain Franke, rode hell for leather from the south and relieved the beleaguered forts. By the end of January the initiative had passed once again to the Germans and by mid-February Leutwein was back at Swapokmund, ready to negotiate with Maherero.

* * *

Perhaps it was inevitable that in Berlin, 5,000 miles away, people should overreact to the news of the rebellion. It might be only a small war in an almost unknown corner of Africa, but it was the first war of Kaiser Wilhelm II's reign, and the first opportunity for nationalist Germany to show the power of its huge standing army, the largest in the world after the Tsar's, and second to none in efficiency. It was thirty-two years since the end of the Franco-Prussian war. Few of the officers and fewer still of the men had ever heard a shot fired in anger. Unlike its British counterpart, the Kaiser's army had had no outlet for its energies in the frontier wars of Asia or Africa. Apart from a belated (and ruthless) share in putting down the Boxer Rebellion in China in 1900–1, the army had earned no battle honours for a generation. Small wonder that thousands of soldiers now volunteered for the front as if some great Power threatened the Fatherland.

Inevitably, the man who overreacted most was the Kaiser. Wilhelm had always had a tendency to jump to conclusions. In this case he jumped to the same one as the settlers' lobby – that Leutwein and the colonial experts of the Wilhelmstrasse had precipitated the rebellion by their weakness in handling the Herero. Now, as Emperor, he had a constitutional right to deal with the rebellion himself. He removed the responsibility for the war from Dr Stübel and those old women in the Wilhelmstrasse, and delegated it to the Chief of the General Staff, Graf von Schlieffen. He also chose a single-minded soldier to supersede Leutwein as commander-in-chief (though not as Governor), General Lothar von Trotha, man enough not to let moral or political qualms cloud his judgement. His task was to crush the revolt, the Emperor told Trotha, by 'fair means or foul'.[9] But the pursuit of a military solution, without a thought of either the political price or the cost in African lives was to turn a small war into a great catastrophe.

General von Trotha did not sail from Germany until May. In the interval Leutwein had shot his bolt and failed. At Oviumbo, on 13 April, his counter-attack fizzled out when his small army was encircled by 3,000 Herero and only extricated itself by a humiliating retreat. Leutwein then decided to stay on the defensive until the arrival of Trotha and further reinforcements. His own nerve had been understandably shaken by the sudden explosion of rebellion, and the bloodthirsty reaction of the settlers, who celebrated their escape by taking reprisals on Africans. Under German law 'cattle thieves' could be sentenced to death after trial by jury. There were numerous executions of Africans that spring, which were barely distinguishable from lynchings. African suspects, unconnected with the rising, were caught by mobs of settlers, and then handed over to all-white juries, who invariably sentenced them to death. Leutwein, the legalist, deplored such abuse of the law. But how could he be expected to hold his own, he asked Berlin, against the prevailing hysteria?

With the arrival of Trotha, the Herero armies could be defeated, the barbarous settlers put in their place and peace restored. That was Leutwein's plan. Some kind of compromise would be necessary. The two most productive indigenous assets in the colony were the Herero and their cattle; to attempt to annihilate both would undo the work of twenty years and condemn the colony to bankruptcy. In short, a purely military solution would be political and economic madness – quite apart from practical difficulties and moral qualms. So Leutwein, as Governor, was ready to talk to Samuel Maherero. Berlin had insisted that the surrender should be unconditional. But, murderers excepted, he felt that the Herero could at least be offered their lives if they abandoned the struggle. After a decisive victory in the field, peace terms could be imposed.

General Lothar von Trotha landed at Swapokmund on 11 June and instantly brushed aside Leutwein's proposal. In the Boxer Rebellion he had made a reputation as a man of iron. Here, too, he would offer no compromise. He would simply gather his army and crush the rebellion. By August most of the Herero had concentrated themselves in a strategic dead-end, the Waterberg plateau, a stony upland on the western edge of the Omaheke sandveld, an out-rider of the great Kalahari desert. Trotha decided to throw a net around the rebels by sending six detachments to encircle the Waterberg.

One strange feature of his plan of attack shocked Leutwein, already smarting from his rebuff over peace terms. There appeared to be a hole in the net in the south-east, allowing access to the Omaheke sandveld. Was the General aware that the Herero might be driven out of the net into the desert? Leutwein protested violently, and so did one of his shrewdest commanders, Major von Estorff. But Trotha refused to explain himself, and would not budge.

The battle of Waterberg on 11–12 August was predictably indecisive. Attacked on all sides except one, the Herero fled through the hole in the net. Trotha then hustled the fleeing enemy to prevent them breaking back into Ovamboland and the fertile territory to the north. By 20 August he had driven them beyond the eastern lip of the plateau. He ordered the last waterhole to be sealed off. Then he erected a line of German guardposts, nailed down like a line of fence posts, to seal off the 250 kilometres of the desert border. Ahead of the Herero loomed the Omaheke sandveld, a waterless oven of sand, 200 miles wide, separating Bechuanaland from South-West Africa. Into this death trap, as though it was a refuge, fled the terrified Herero, perhaps 8,000 men, with twice that number of women and children, thirsty and starving, with the remnants of their cattle and horses.

*   *   *

It was many months before Trotha's plan to exterminate the Herero was publicly debated in Germany. By then the Socialist leader, August Bebel, had swung back to his self-appointed role as the conscience – and gadfly – of the Reich. In January 1904 even Socialists had been alarmed by the thought that German imperialists might have their throats cut. When Bülow launched a plan to put down the rebellion, Bebel's party had sheathed its sting and abstained from voting. But two months later they let fly by denouncing the 'Hunnish' character of German imperialism.

The settlers had provoked the rebellion by their reckless treatment of the natives: the rapes and murders that went unpunished, the abuse of the Herero as though they were animals. Now there were judicial lynchings by the settlers, and atrocities by the army. In March 1904, Bebel warned the Reichstag that apparently the army took no prisoners; German soldiers boasted of this to their families at home. In May, Leutwein had to admit that 'Deputy Bebel was this time correct in his judgement . . . .' Not a single prisoner had been taken. 'It is only natural, however, that after all that has happened our soldiers do not show excessive leniency.'[10] In effect, Leutwein admitted he had lost control of his own troops.

If Leutwein struggled, ineffectively, to modify the violence of his troops, this was not at all what Trotha had in mind. The Herero were trapped in the Omaheke. On 2 October 1904 he had issued a formal proclamation to them, to which there are few parallels in modern European history (outside the span of the Third Reich).

I, the Great General of the German soldiers, address this letter to the Herero people. The Herero are no longer considered German subjects. They have murdered, stolen, cut off ears and other parts from wounded soldiers, and now refuse to fight on, out of cowardice. I have this to say to them ... the Herero people will have to leave the country. Otherwise I shall force them to do so by means of guns. Within the German boundaries, every Herero, whether found armed or unarmed, with or without cattle, will be shot. I shall not accept any more women or children. I shall drive them back to their people – otherwise I shall order shots to be fired at them.

Signed: the Great General of the Mighty Kaiser, von Trotha.[11]

Drive them out – or wipe them out. The crudity of the great general's *Vernichtungsbefehl* (extermination order) was no surprise to Leutwein. But Leutwein's own policy had failed, and Trotha's must be tried. This was the army's and the Kaiser's verdict. Leutwein retired defeated, and Trotha stepped into his shoes as Governor. But by the end of October, even the Chief of the General Staff, Graf von Schlieffen, began to lose faith in his headstrong protégé. Trotha claimed that he had a method of eliminating the whole Herero people. 'While General von Trotha's intentions are commendable,' Schlieffen commented grimly, 'he is powerless to carry them out. He will have to stop on the western fringe of the Omaheke, unable to force the Herero to leave it ... We will have no choice, therefore, but to try to induce the Herero to surrender. This is complicated by General von Trotha's order to shoot each and every Herero.'[12]

To say that the *Vernichtungbefehl* complicated matters was to put it mildly. The Colonial Department in Berlin, and the Imperial Chancellor, Count von Bülow, were aghast when Trotha's order came to light. Bülow respectfully cabled the Kaiser, asking permission to have it cancelled. He gave four good reasons. First, the order would be a crime against humanity. Second, it was impractical. Third, it would damage the economy. ('If the rebellious natives were annihilated or expelled, this would seriously undermine the potential for development.') Fourth, it would be 'demeaning to our standing among the civilized nations of the world'.[13]

For five days the Kaiser hesitated. Then he agreed to give Bülow permission to direct Trotha to 'show mercy' to the Herero. Bülow insisted that the instructions to Trotha should be more explicit. This took another eight days. Then Trotha was formally told to cancel the *Vernichtungbefehl* and offer to accept the Herero's surrender – except for murderers and ringleaders. For this he was invited to use the 'good offices'[14] – a phrase calculated to enrage Trotha – of the very Germans he blamed for originally inciting the rebellion, the Rhenish missionaries.

Faced with Bülow's cable, Trotha reacted like a spoilt child deprived of a toy. For days he refused to co-operate. In fact, the need to pacify the Herero was now much more pressing. A day after he had issued his *Vernichtungbefehl* in October, the Witbooi Nama, led by Hendrik Witbooi, had belatedly responded to Samuel Maherero's call. The south of the colony was now on fire with revolt, and Trotha's troops were fully stretched trying to hunt down the elusive Nama guerrillas.

Hendrik's decision to join the rebellion seemed strange by military standards. It was too late to help the tens of thousands of Herero now dying of thirst in the Omaheke, and a handful of Nama riflemen could achieve little against the might of the German Empire. German troopships had been pouring men into Swapokmund ever since the spring. The army already totalled 10,000 men. Hendrik had barely 900 warriors to put into the field. Even with expected allies from three neighbouring Nama tribes – the Fransman Nama, the Red Nation and the Veldskoendragers – the total barely reached 1,500, less than half of whom were armed with modern rifles.

Yet Hendrik Witbooi had decided to go on the warpath (to 'put on the white feather', the Nama war emblem) with his eyes open. He was not persuaded to rebel, like Samuel Maherero, against his better judgement. Nor did a hope of saving the Herero, whom he had always loathed, enter into his calculations. But he had run out of patience with the Germans, and decided that it was time to end the alliance. Like the Boers who had invaded British colonies in 1899, he decided to put his faith in 'God and the Mauser'. In his own words to his fellow chiefs: 'I have now stopped walking submissively and will write a letter to the [German] Captain saying that I have put on the white feather and that the time is over when I will walk behind him ... The Saviour himself will now act and He will free us through His grace and compassion ....'[15]

In a sense the Nama revolt had a mystical origin. Hendrik Witbooi was eighty years old and a born-again Christian whose faith had grown more puritanical and more fanatical with the years. (He tried to have his daughter executed for having an illegitimate child.) But that year he had been swept off his feet by a self-styled prophet from the Cape, a Griqua called Stürmann, who claimed that God was coming to free Africa from the white man.

In another sense the Nama revolt shared its origins with the Herero revolt, despite the very different way the Germans had treated the two peoples. The Witbooi Nama were still proud and independent. They had not had to watch their menfolk called 'baboons', their wives raped, their sacred cattle slaughtered by traders. Yet the grim events of that year – the Herero rising and its murderous suppression, reported by some of the shocked Nama contingent fighting with the Germans – sent a shock wave down to the Orange river and the Cape frontier. This had snapped a vital link in Namaqualand: the personal loyalty connecting Hendrik with Germany. Leutwein, the German whom he had trusted, almost loved, had been humiliated and rebuffed. Trotha made no secret of his racist contempt for all Africans and of his plans to humble the Nama, and neither did the settlers. Trotha's success against the Herero thus encouraged Hendrik to revolt. Only by war, he believed, could he safeguard the liberties of his people, and with God's help, in the fastnesses of the south, save them from the terrible fate of the Herero.

Hendrik Witbooi, the shrewdest and most statesmanlike of all the African leaders of the region, had made a fatal miscalculation.

The Nama revolt that broke out on 3 October 1904 at first gave the Witboois full outlet for their genius at guerrilla war and the Germans plenty of scope for humiliation. Like the Herero revolt, the struggle began with a bloodthirsty massacre of unarmed civilians and helpless soldiers. About forty were killed in the first few days and the expected Nama allies, roughly half the various Nama tribes, rallied to Hendrik's standard. At first there were only 500 German troops in the district, but reinforcements rode hurriedly south and soon Trotha's troops regained the initiative. In December Hendrik's camp at Naris was surprised. He had to ride for his life, leaving fifty of his men dead on the field. In January 1905 he was driven out of the Aruob valley into the Kalahari. There the German offensive literally ran into the sand.

Small bodies of Witboois, adopting guerrilla tactics, retaliated by raiding the German supply line. Trotha's losses accumulated; hundreds of good men died from disease, especially typhus. Meanwhile, he was plagued by other equally elusive rebels: a cattle raider from the Cape called Morenga, and one of the Bethanie Nama tribe called Cornelius who had fought on the side of the Germans in the Herero war. Both Africans had a genius for raiding. In June 1905 Trotha softened his code of iron by sending his own son, a lieutenant, to parley in Cornelius's camp. The talks ended in disaster, as a German patrol inadvertently opened fire on the camp while Lieutenant von Trotha was chatting with Cornelius. The young lieutenant paid the price, shot by one of Cornelius's men. In August, Trotha tried to repeat his Waterberg tactics against the Witboois, and achieved nothing but humiliation. By the autumn of 1905 the stalemate seemed unbreakable. Perhaps 300 Nama riflemen, based in a maze of barren hills or the inaccessible fastnesses of the Kalahari, ran circles around 15,000 lumbering German troops. Berlin finally lost patience. Trotha was ordered home, to be replaced by a new partnership, a civilian Governor, Lindequist, and a military commander, Dame.

However, guerrilla war is always a contest in survival. The Nama were now at the end of their tether and fresh German troops flooded the country. On 29 October 1905, Hendrik Witbooi was mortally wounded in a raid on a German supply line. His last words were 'It is enough with me, it is all over. The children should now have rest.' Trotha made a sneering comment on the news, 'A beautiful message'.[16] Within a few weeks, the remnants of the Witboois, led by Hendrik's son Samuel, capitulated to the Germans. In return for their lives, they would surrender their horses and weapons and be settled in a camp near their old capital, Gibeon. The Bethanie Nama led by Cornelius accepted similar terms. By November 1905, when Trotha finally sailed for Germany, he could claim to have won the war after all – though Morenga, the Cape raider, with 400 men, was still a thorn in the flesh of Trotha's successors.

How close to total victory Trotha actually came was made clear by counting the emaciated survivors of the Herero and Nama in the forced labour camps.

Trotha had boasted of his policy – extermination. Berlin had tried to countermand it, but to a great extent it had remained his policy. Before the war, the Herero were estimated to be at least 80,000 strong. In August 1904 more than half the tribe had been driven into the Omaheke and the wells sealed behind them. No one will ever know how many died there of starvation and thirst. For months German patrols encountered the remnants trying to break back to the west, walking skeletons to be shot and bayoneted as a matter of course.

In a popular novel of the period, *Peter Moors Fahrt nach Südwest*, written to celebrate the success of the German army in South-West Africa, Gustav Frenssen described some of the scenes of the pursuit after the battle of Waterberg:

> The further we went into the burning sun ... the more disheartening became our journey. How deeply the wild, proud, sorrowful people had humbled themselves in the terror of death. There lay the wounded and old, women and children ... Others were lying alone, still living, with eyes and noses full of flies. Somebody sent out our black drivers, and I think they helped them to die. All this life lay scattered there, both men and beasts, broken in the knees, helpless, motionless: it looked as if it had all been thrown down out of the air. At noon we halted by the waterholes which were filled to the very brim with corpses.[17]

Only about 5,000 people, including Samuel Maherero, somehow broke through the Omaheke and found sanctuary in Bechuanaland or the Cape. The majority died in the sandveld, or crept back to the west where they were hunted down like game by Trotha's army. Many Herero surrendered and were sent to work in forced labour camps – a total of 9,000 by the summer of 1905. But many more must have died of starvation or been killed in the raids on Herero villages that continued until November 1905. After Trotha was recalled, a further 6,000 emaciated Herero and 2,000 Nama were taken prisoner.

For sick people to be sent to labour camps was a death sentence. Work was heavy (dragging railway trucks by hand), food meagre, medical supplies non-existent. By 1907 the Germans reported that *over half* the 15,000 Herero and 2,000 Nama prisoners had died in the camps. Worst of all were conditions on Shark Island, a windswept rock off Lüderitzbucht (Angra Pequena), where Hendrik Witbooi's gallant band and other Nama prisoners were sent in September 1906, in flagrant violation of the terms of their surrender. Within seven months, 1,032 out of 1,732 had died of cold and ill-treatment, including Cornelius, the Bethanie leader. Others were dying, and all but a tenth were crippled. When the census was taken in 1911, only half the Nama estimated a decade before (9,800 out of 20,000) and less than a quarter of the original number of Herero (15,000 out of 80,000) were found to have survived the war.

No doubt Trotha would have called this a 'beautiful message'. So perhaps would his employer. When Trotha returned to Germany in 1905, the Kaiser confounded Trotha's enemies by giving him the Order of Merit for his devotion to the Fatherland.

Yet even before the end of the rebellions in South-West Africa, costly and humiliating for the German army, catastrophic for the Herero and Nama, ordinary Germans had learnt a lesson. They suspected that something was fundamentally wrong in the government of the Reich overseas. Without political reforms, there would be more disasters. This suspicion was confirmed, eloquently enough, by a sudden uprising in German East Africa in July 1905.

CHAPTER 34

'Maji-Maji!'

German East Africa
July 1905 and after

'Hongo or the European, which is the stronger?'
'Hongo!'

Password during the Maji-Maji rebellion

One morning in late July 1905, some weeks after the end of the rains, when the hated cotton plants were ripening fast in the brilliant East African sun, two elders from Nandete, an impoverished village in the maze of Matumbi Hills, north-west of Kilwa, led a group of villagers up the stony path to the cotton plot. They could wait no longer. Cotton was a crop for export to Europe, a symbol of extortionate, alien rule. The men (or their wives, if the men could not be found) were forced to hoe for hours every week in the government plot, instead of cultivating their own gardens; the work gangs were paid only thirty-five cents a day, with a bonus of twenty-five strokes from the whip of the government agent, the Arab *akida*, if anyone stopped hoeing to straighten his back.

The two elders ritually uprooted three cotton plants and threw them on the ground. Then the war-drums tapped out the news to the next village across the steep, wooded hills. In Nandete they had uprooted the cotton. This was defiance – and more. It was a declaration of war on the Germans.

For months a spirit medium in Ngarambe – a village to the north, at a meeting place of many tracks – had laboured to unite people against the Germans. He was Kinjikitile Ngwale, an obscure immigrant suddenly possessed by a snake spirit, Hongo, who served in turn a famous spirit, Bokero, venerated in the main shrine of the region. Kinjikitile had built a spirit hut to which pilgrims flocked as though to a wedding. It was big enough for hundreds of worshippers who came to 'see' and talk with their ancestors. Like other spirit mediums – 'witch doctors' to the Germans – Kinjikitile distributed medicine to protect people and their crops. But Kinjikitile, or Bokero as he now began to call himself, was a prophet with a revolutionary message: unite and drive out the Germans.

The news spread like a fever. All they needed was *maji* ('water' in Swahili), with some castor oil and millet seeds. This was a 'war medicine'[1] strong enough to turn German bullets to water. The leaders of each clan flocked to Ngarambe to obtain the magic water and the magic seeds. The clan leaders came not only from the Matumbi, but from the Kichi to the north and the Ngindo to the south.

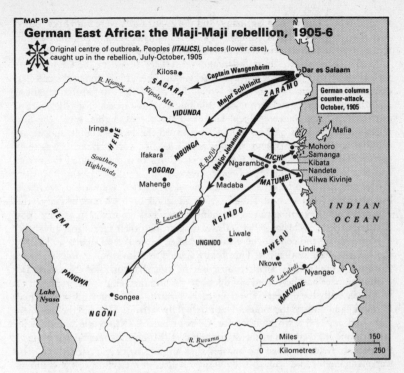

MAP 19

German East Africa: the Maji-Maji rebellion, 1905-6

Original centre of outbreak. Peoples *(ITALICS)*, places (lower case), caught up in the rebellion, July-October, 1905

The Germans heard about the snake cult, but thought Kinjikitile a harmless witch doctor. By the summer of 1905 the movement had spread more than a hundred miles west and south. But none of the men had modern rifles, only cap guns, spears and arrows. None of these peoples – Matumbi, Kichi or Ngindo – were trained as warriors under a great chief. They were poor and came from a region of diffuse clans, their chief strength a legacy of resentment against all authority, and a hatred of all invaders – Ngoni warriors from the south, Arab slavers and Germans.

For weeks, Kinjikitile hesitated. By late July 1905 the elders of Nandete had lost patience with their local *akida*. It was then that they climbed the stony path to the cotton plot and formally challenged the might of the German Reich by uprooting the three cotton plants.

From Dar-es-Salaam, the German capital, 120 miles to the north-east came a deafening silence. The German army was ignorant and over-stretched, with only 588 Askari and 458 native police for the whole south of the protectorate. Most of these African mercenaries were based in the coastal towns. In the interior there was only a handful of German NCOs in command of perhaps 200 Askari to rule an area bigger than Germany, and the guard-posts were mud huts roofed with thatch. Most of the south-east was still administered by Arabs and Swahili, the *akidas* and *jumbes* who had run it before the Abushiri revolt in 1888–9.

At first their job had been undemanding: to keep order for the Germans, as their predecessors had kept order for the Sultan. Then, to try to cut the colonial deficit, the Germans tightened the screw. The *akidas* had to enforce taxation, and organize commercial farming by fulfilling a quota of cash crops like cotton, grown with commandeered local labour. To accomplish this, given the low rainfall and the high quotas, would have taxed the most humane and incorruptible of civil servants, and the *akidas* and *jumbes* were neither. It was their corruption, compounding the German extortions, that precipitated the revolt and now sent them flying for refuge to the coast.

The first *akida* to feel the power of the *maji* directed against him was Sefu bin Amri, the local agent in Kibata. After an attack on his home, he fled to the coast and sent a warning to the Germans, which was ignored. On 31 July 1905 Matumbi rebels, wearing millet stalks strung around their foreheads, advanced to Samanga on the coast, where they uprooted more cotton plants and burnt the Asian trading settlement. This finally alerted the Governor, Adolf Graf von Götzen, of the need to send troops, but he still did not take the rising too seriously; there had been a good millet harvest and the people were reported to be awash with local beer. Then, in early August, a German officer reached Matumbi and noticed the 'unusual morale'[2] of the natives. They hid their women and children, and set ambushes for German patrols. Kinjikitile himself was arrested and taken down to the district office at Mohoro, where he was hanged for treason. Before he died, he boasted that his emissaries had carried the *maji* war medicine far and wide, all the way to Kilosa in the centre of the country, and to Mahenge, the main German garrison post in the southern Highlands.

It was not an empty boast. Day by day the fires of rebellion spread west and south. In Ungindo (the territory of the Ngindo) there were two centres of revolt, Madaba in the north, where the trading settlement was left in blackened ruins, and Liwale, where the thatched *boma* vanished in a shower of flaming arrows and the German garrison was burnt alive. On 14 August a Ngindo war party came up with some unfortunate German missionaries on safari. Their leader, Bishop Spiss, was the Catholic bishop of Dar-es-Salaam. He claimed that they were peaceful travellers, but to the Ngindo they were simply Germans. The bishop, two Benedictine monks and two Sisters of Mercy were all speared to death.

The news of the murder of the five missionaries, and the rapid spread of the rebellion, naturally caused a sensation in the capital, Dar-es-Salaam, 200 miles to the north-east, though few of the 180 European farmers in the country were threatened. Their commercial centre was much further north, in the cool highlands around Kilimanjaro, where coffee, sesame and sisal all flourished. But in the capital, the Europeans were quick to believe the worst. 'Fear bordering on panic', was the Governor's report to Berlin. Volunteers drilled each evening outside the railway station. Burning villages could be seen immediately south of the capital. Götzen cabled Berlin for 'immediate reinforcements'.[3] Berlin agreed to send 150 Marine infantry with several machine guns, together with perhaps fifty Marines from two small German cruisers then sailing in the China Sea and the Pacific. But would 200 Marines be enough to dowse the flames of the forest fire that was beginning to engulf the whole southern part of the colony, from the palm-fringed beaches at Kilwa to the rugged mountains around Lake Nyasa?

For the rebels, that first month, August, seemed to prove the miraculous truth of all that Kinjikitile had foretold. It was obvious to them that out of the German gun barrels came nothing but water. At a stroke, the Germans were driven from the land of all the peoples protected by the *maji* – the Matumbi, Ngindo and Kichi. Beyond Kichi territory to the north, in the flood plain close to the capital, the Zaramo of Kisangire had welcomed the self-styled *'hongos'* from Ngarambe. Their head man, Kibasila, had been recently imprisoned for refusing to grow cotton. Now he distributed *maji* in the area, recruiting professional elephant hunters and outlaws.

A hundred miles to the south, among the stateless Mwera, the *hongos* brought the same millennial message. The head man, Selemani Mamba of Nkowe, received it with gusto. 'This is not war,' he told his followers. 'We shall not die. We shall only kill.'[4] He was joined by another headman, *jumbe* Gabriel Mbuu of Rupota, and together they converged on the German Fathers who had built a mission post at Nyangao. They found the men had already fled into the bush. The mission servants were forced to reveal their hiding place. But then something occurred that left Selemani Mamba puzzled and silent as he rode back to the hills on a captured donkey, carrying the bell from the looted church. The missionaries had escaped to Lindi after first shooting dead the *hongos*. Those bullets had not turned to water. Why had the *maji* failed?

Meanwhile, *hongos* had brought bottles of *maji* for the politically weak peoples north-west of the Ngindo, the Pogoro and Mbunga. At first they, too, swept forward like a river in spate. They used the same revolutionary password: 'Hongo or the European, which is the stronger?' *'Hongo!'*[5] Few people refused to wear the insignia of millet stalks and castor seeds. If they did refuse (so it was said later) they were speared to death. On 16 August the Mbunga clans stormed the German outpost at Ifakara. In the battle all thirteen Askari were killed, and afterwards the black eagle of the German Reich was placed on the flagpole beside the blackened head of the German NCO. Then the Mbunga climbed the great escarpment that led south to Mahenge, the main German garrison post in the southern Highlands.

Fortunately for the garrison, and unfortunately for the rebels, the Ngindo and Pogoro did not co-ordinate their attack with the Mbunga. The Pogoro themselves were deeply divided about the power of the *maji*. In general, the highlanders were sceptical of this new war medicine. In the past, some of them had learnt a lesson from German Mausers. How could even the strongest medicine turn bullets to water? Some of the Mbunga chose not to wear, and could not be forced to wear, the sacred millet. A sub-chief, Kalmoto, fled to Mahenge and warned the German commander that the rebels were climbing the mountain and would kill him.

At first the commander, Captain Hassel, did not take the news too seriously. He blundered into a Mbunga ambush next day and was barely able to shoot his way out; after that he was inclined to agree with Kalmoto. He hastily fortified the *boma* at Mahenge and built a wooden tower, where he could retire with a machine gun, tins of food and several cases of wine. The *boma* offered shelter to some Benedictine priests and – a crucial stroke of fortune for Hassel – several hundred armed tribesmen from Ubena who had stayed loyal to the Germans. (Their cunning chief, Kiwanga, explained that he was keen to take the *maji* provided that the *hongos* survived a firing squad. They did not survive.)

Before the rebels attacked, Hassel gave orders for everyone suspected of disloyalty to be hanged from trees in the village. Then, soon after dawn on 30 August several columns of Pogoro and Ngindo, thousands of shouting men, marched straight for the *boma*, led by a *hongo* armed only with a millet stalk. A mission worker sadly described how faith in the *maji* carried the attackers right up to the barrels of the machine guns:

> Since they came to make an end of all of us, we had to defend ourselves and take part in the firing, which opened on the attackers at about 1,000 metres. Two machine guns, Europeans, and soldiers, rained death and destruction among the ranks of the advancing enemy. Although we saw the ranks thin, the survivors maintained order for about a quarter of an hour, marching closer amidst a hail of bullets. But then the ranks broke, and the men took cover behind numerous small rocks.... Then suddenly the cry broke out: 'New enemy on the Gambira [eastern] side!' Everybody looked in that direction, and there thick clouds of smoke were rising from our three schools and a second column of at least 1,200 men were advancing towards us ... As soon as they [appeared] within range they were met by deafening fire. The first attackers were only three paces from the firing line when they sank to the ground ... When no more enemy could be seen, the station commander climbed down from the top of the *boma* tower ... and distributed champagne.[6]

It was some weeks before Hassel could celebrate again. Next day the Mbunga closed in and laid siege to the *boma*. Hassel was trapped. Then, on 23 September, Captain Nigmann, the German commander from Iringa in the country of the Hehe (finally pacified after a rising in 1897–8), suddenly opened fire on the Mbunga's camp. Hassel was relieved, and African auxiliaries took a bloodthirsty revenge on the Mbunga.

The rebels' failure to capture Mahenge was decisive. If the tide had not yet turned, it was losing momentum. Yet the Germans still had plenty to worry about. Already the *maji* had spread south to the best-armed and best-organized people in the entire region, the Ngoni, whose chiefs were the aristocrats of a warrior people driven north during the Mfecane. Once they had been the terror of all the neighbouring tribes, for they had inherited from their Zulu cousins the puritanical discipline and the regimental system, along with the short stabbing spear perfected by the great Zulu King, Shaka. In 1897, they had watched the Hehe rising with sympathy, but had not followed suit. They were wary, then, of matching their spears against German Mausers. Now they had lost patience with the white men who forbade slave-raiding and imposed taxes that humiliated the aristocrats in the eyes of their subjects. In late August millennial rumours reached Songea, the Ngoni capital, brought by a mysterious *hongo*, Kinjala, dressed in a white loin cloth, who claimed to be possessed by a snake spirit like Kinjikitile's. By mid-October the *maji* had been distributed far and wide, and 5,000 Ngoni warriors were ready to wash their spears in the blood of the German garrison at Songea.

Perhaps it was to be expected that the sophisticated aristocrats of the Ngoni lacked the innocent faith of the peasants of Pogoro. At any rate, the Ngoni did not give the *maji* long to prove itself. At dawn on 21 October, the energetic Captain Nigmann, who had marched from Mahenge, attacked their camp with a pair of machine guns, and the whole Ngoni army threw away their *maji* bottles and took to their heels. 'The *maji* is a lie.'[7] The message of doom, spread through thicket and mountain, was carried by drums as fast as the original message of hope.

In the 1990s, forty years after independence won by constitutional methods, the name of Kinjikitile is honoured in modern Tanzania (the eventual heir to German East Africa). This may seem incongruous. He was not a true nationalist, or even a revolutionary. He had no positive programme. He preached only counter-revolution – to drive out the Germans and give people back the old order, in which power was safely dispensed by traditional chiefs. War seemed the only way to end the extortions of Arabs and Germans. Why Kinjikitile is honoured in the 1990s is because he gave the first taste of unity to the fragmented peoples of Tanganyika, from the peasant clans of Matumbi to the great warrior tribe of the Ngoni.

But now, by the end of 1905, it was once again each clan, each tribe for itself, as the rebels tried to disperse in the bush, and the Germans to close in for the kill.

Throughout the confusion of the last two and a half months, Count Götzen waited to launch his counter-attack. By mid-October, Berlin had at last sent the reinforcements, 200 Marines, little enough, but all that could be spared, in view of the Herero and Nama revolts in South-West Africa.

Götzen's plan was for a counter-attack, with three new columns fanning out from the capital. Captain Wangenheim struck west to atack the Sagara, then headed south to close with the Pogoro and Mbunga. Major Schleinitz swung south-west to crush the rebels in the Vidunda mountains. Major Johannes made for Songea, to attack the Ngoni, Bena and Pangwa. Meanwhile, the local garrison commanders continued to harass the rebels in their own districts, and tried to flush them out into the open.

Unlike General von Trotha, Governor von Götzen seemed ready to be lenient. Pardon for the rank and file of the rebels, provided they handed in their weapons and gave up the leaders and witch doctors – that was Götzen's first principle. His second was less humane. Only by creating a famine, he believed, could he flush out the more intransigent of the rebels. Captain Wangenheim agreed: 'Only hunger and want can bring about a final submission. Military actions alone will remain more or less a drop in the ocean.'[8] So Götzen combined leniency with terror. Tribe or clan, they would all have to be starved into submission.

The three columns rode through the south of the protectorate with fire and sword. Blackened villages and ruined crops marked their progress. When grain could not be removed (or given to loyal tribes), grain was burnt. Götzen's 'famine strategy' worked a great deal more efficiently than Trotha's extermination order. Major Johannes reached Songea on 29 November. By mid-January 1906 he had captured and hanged Mptua, Chief of the northern Ngoni. Chabruma, Chief of the southern Ngoni, fled to Mozambique, where he was murdered by his host. The Ngindo, Pogoro and Matumbi leaders took longer to round up. Eventually they, too, were shot or hanged or murdered by loyalists. By June 1906, almost all the 'Maji-Maji' districts were at peace again, but it was the peace of the wilderness.

Famine killed more than ten times the number that had ever taken up arms against the Germans – 250,000–300,000 according to the leading African historian of the revolt.[9] The worst suffering was in the Highlands, where the famine persisted longest. Perhaps half the Vidunda, more than half the Matumbi, and three-quarters of the Pangwa died in the rebellion or its aftermath. When the famine ended, the survivors returned to a country which was almost un-recognizable. Miambo forests had begun to take over the maize fields and cotton plots, and soon these forests gave sanctuary to rhino, buffalo and elephant. In due course the hills of Ungindo, once teeming with people, became the largest game park in the world.

*　　*　　*

To put down the 'Maji-Maji' rebels involved a mere 500 German troops and added a mere £2 million to the colonial deficit – a fraction of the 17,000 German troops and the £20 million which it took to crush the rebels in South-West Africa. But this rebellion, too, brought to light serious abuses of power. It also raised the fundamental question of how to govern the overseas Reich, a question which the opposition in the Reichstag could not fail to exploit.

1906 was the year when Bülow's colonial pigeons finally came home to roost, showering him with dirt. For six years he had served the Kaiser as Chancellor. He had left the Colonial Department to nonentities, mere technicians like Dr Stübel. Suddenly a series of colonial scandals in Africa bubbled to the surface, some contemporary, others showing signs of a long-standing cover-up, and for once they could not be lightly dismissed. The evidence implicated the highest officials in all four German colonies in Africa, in Cameroon and Togo as well as in German East Africa and German South-West Africa.

The most lurid scandal involved Jesco von Puttkamer, since 1895 the Governor of the West African colony of Cameroon, which had a long history of native disturbances. Von Puttkamer was an aristocratic rake, best known for the large sums he regularly borrowed and lost at cards. Berlin was warned of his 'frivolity' and 'vagabondism',[10] but von Puttkamer's father had been a famous Prussian Minister of the Interior, and his uncle was Bismarck. Young Jesco was sent out as Governor of Cameroon to keep him out of mischief. By 1906, a junior official in the Colonial Department, outraged by the cover-up in high places, finally let the cat out of the bag.

There were three well-documented charges against Puttkamer: atrocities against the natives, financial corruption and moral laxity. Excessive flogging, even flogging men to death, was quite commonplace. So was the crudest abuse of power by German officials. For example, the leaders of the judiciary – Councillor von Brauchisch and Supreme Judge Dr Meyer – forcibly bought two young native girls to use as concubines, although the girls were already betrothed.

Other German officials did not shrink from mutilation and murder. For example, the station officer at Jaune, Lieutenant Schenneman, who had taken a black mistress, heard rumours of her affairs with three Africans. He told his black servant to castrate the three men. The servant mistook his instructions, marched off with a party of soldiers and castrated the first three men he met in a nearby village. On another occasion, a Lieutenant Dominik was sent on an expedition to negotiate a treaty with the Bahoro. Instead, he shot down all the men and women in the village, and the fifty-four children that survived were put in baskets and drowned like kittens.

In 1902 the leading chiefs of Cameroon – King Acqua, Manga Bell and Ekwala Dido – took passage to Germany to protest against the 'excessive bad treatment' from Puttkamer. They were told they need have no fear; they would get redress. But on their return to Cameroon, King Acqua was thrown into prison by the Governor. In 1905 a formal petition from the chiefs and the people was sent over to the Reichstag. The Colonial Department sent it back for Puttkamer's comments. The result was that all thirty chiefs were put on trial in Cameroon for 'insubordination'[11] and were given long prison sentences; King Acqua received nine years. But now Puttkamer had gone too far.

When the junior official let the cat out of the bag, it emerged that Puttkamer had feathered his own nest by accepting shares in local commercial firms. He had also insulted the Imperial German navy – much worse offence in the eyes of officialdom – by inviting the captain of the *Habicht* to take the 'Baroness' in to dinner, meaning the German prostitute he had installed, complete with a false title on her passport, at his side at Government House.

As a result of the public outcry, King Acqua was released and brought to Germany to explain the petition. In due course Puttkamer was put on trial before a disciplinary court. He was reprimanded and fined 1,000 marks for certain breaches of discipline, including that of giving a false passport to his mistress. But neither he, nor the other officials, were punished for the reign of terror they had conducted against the Africans.

The scandal involving Valdemar Horn, Governor in Togoland since 1902, revealed an equally grim state of affairs in the nearby colony. In 1905, Governor Horn was tried in a colonial court – the High Court of Togoland and Cameroon – and fined 900 marks for cruelty towards an African boy. The boy had been found guilty of stealing a cash box. Horn had ordered him to be given twenty-five lashes and then left bound to a post, without food or water, for twenty-four hours, unless he revealed where the cash box was hidden. The young man died. Later Horn was sentenced by a disciplinary court in Germany and lost a third of his pension rights. Perhaps the Governor was made a scapegoat by his own officials, anxious to cover up their own abuses. These were directed not only at Africans, but at the German missionaries who tried to take their part.

Schmidt, a district director at Atakpamé, a hundred miles north of the capital, had flogged and raped a thirteen-year-old African girl called Adgaro, after locking her in his notorious harem, known as 'Schmidt's Rolle'.[12] The Catholic missionaries protested about this to the authorities, and were told to put the protest in writing. Early next morning the district judge, with nineteen armed soldiers, dragged all the missionaries from their beds and kept them imprisoned for three weeks, while the African witnesses in the case were being dealt with. In due course Schmidt was acquitted, owing to the absence of witnesses, and a missionary, Father Schmitz, was sentenced to fourteen days in prison for giving false testimony. (He was released on appeal.) Naturally there was an outcry when the story was published in Germany, but nobody succeeded in disciplining Schmidt. On the contrary, his black procuress, 'Jenusia' ('Queen'), was given a formal right to collect legal dues and decide minor cases of law.

The third colonial scandal involved Carl Peters, the founding father of German East Africa, the man who had talked Bismarck into giving his newly-created German Colonization Company the original charter for the colony, and had then been forced by the financial collapse of the Company to hand back the charter to the Reich. Peters was said to model himself on Nietzsche's *Superman*. He was certainly an apostle of *Rücklosigkeit* (ruthless imperialism). Not for him the usual euphemisms about the importance of 'firmness' and the regrettable need for 'vigorous measures'. He bragged to his readers about his 'exultation'[13] as he shot down any African bold enough to oppose him, and boasted of the trail of destruction he had left along the valley of the Tana, in what was soon to become British East Africa. (The Africans called him *Mkono-wa-damu*, the 'man-with-blood-stained-hands'.) Unfortunately, Peters was not only hyperactive but extremely quarrelsome.

In 1891 Peters was appointed Imperial Commissioner in German East Africa, but his fellow Germans, old friends like Count Pfeil, denounced his wayward behaviour. In the public outcry that followed, August Bebel and the German Socialists condemned Peters as a 'monster', the symbol of aggressive imperialism. In 1897 Peters was brought before a colonial court in Potsdam and accused of serious breaches of 'discipline' in Kilimanjaro district. He had illegally hanged his young African servant, Mabruk, nominally for stealing his cigars ('in order to maintain his authority', it was claimed). In fact, Mabruk was accused of having an affair with Peters's own mistress, a young girl called Jagodja. The wretched girl was flogged until her back was like 'chopped meat', and then she, too, was illegally hanged.

Peters was also accused of lying about the case in his report to the authorities. The colonial court found him guilty on all these charges and dismissed him from the Colonial Service without a pension. But his offence was 'indiscipline'.[14] No criminal prosecution followed, though two murders had been proved against him.

All this had taken place years before, and might have been long forgotten. But now, in 1906, the year of colonial scandals, the Social Democrats renewed the outcry against Carl Peters, and the skeleton fell out of the cupboard into Bülow's lap.

It turned out that Peters had friends in high places, including Dr Otto Arendt, the Conservative leader, who persuaded the Kaiser partiaily to rehabilitate Peters. He was restored to the title of Imperial Commissioner, though not to the pension that went with it. The Social Democrats then discovered that these friends of Peters's had forced Dr Hellwig, Peters's prosecutor, to resign from the Colonial Service. ('Listen, Herr Geheimrat' [privy councillor], hissed the Secretary of State, 'you have earned many enemies through the Peters case ... If I may advise you, ask for your pension.')[15]

There were extraordinary scenes in the Reichstag when this series of colonial scandals was made public. For days in December 1906, Bülow's government had to put up with the abuse of an incongruous alliance of Catholics of the Centre Party voting with the Socialists led by August Bebel. At first the Chancellor was anxious to appease his critics and talked of reform. Then, to everyone's surprise, he rounded on his accusers, and on 13 December formally dissolved the Reichstag. The pretext was the failure of the government to win a vote allocating 29,220,000 marks for the extra cost of mopping up in the final stages of the Herero and Nama wars. In fact, Bülow had seized his chance to denounce his enemies' lack of patriotism.

The ensuing election, equivalent to Britain's 'Khaki Election' in the first summer of the Boer War, came to be called the 'Hottentot Election'. The Kaiser's government certainly fought it with a good deal more finesse than they had fought the Hottentot war. As if he was the leader of a parliamentary party (rather than the nominee of a semi-autocratic sovereign) Bülow nimbly turned the colonial disasters to his own political advantage. For two years – ever since the Socialist gains in the election of 1905 – he had lived from hand to mouth in the

Reichstag. Now he was determined to rebuild a bloc of solidly pro-government parties, and break the power of his tormentors, the two strongest parties in the Reichstag, the Catholics at the centre and the Social Democrats. When they combined, these incongruous allies could bring the government to a halt.

The Centre was the strongest party in the Reichstag, but it was often split on colonial issues. Now it was trying to make common cause against these colonial scandals in the pursuit of political reform at home. Mathias Erzberger, the earnest thirty-year-old Catholic schoolmaster who led the hue and cry against Bülow in the Reichstag, was actually leader of the party's imperialist wing. Ever since 1903, Erzberger had protested against the incompetence and shiftiness of the Colonial Department, which fobbed off deputies with threadbare statistics and seven-year-old financial reports.

The Social Democrats led by August Bebel were even more split than the Centre. A majority, including Bebel, still stuck to the Marxist equation that imperialism equalled exploitation; and that the cure for colonies was abolition, not reform. But there was also the nagging voice of 'revisionists' who claimed that colonialism provided good jobs for German workers and might have a part to play in socialism after all.

Small wonder, then, that Bülow had no difficulty in pulling the colonial rug from under his enemies in the 'Hottentot Election' in 1907. The Social Democrats lost thirty-eight of their eighty-one seats. The Centre held firm. But the 'parties of order' – the Conservatives, National Liberals and Progressives – took 216 seats. At last Bülow had his solid majority, and could govern with a parliamentary consensus, like a British prime minister. The new Reichstag was dominated by the Right. (It now included hard-liners like General von Liebert, an ex-Governor of East Africa, who boasted of his admiration for Carl Peters.) Despite the humiliations of the Herero, Nama and '*Maji-Maji*' rebellions, and the sickening revelations of atrocities in Togo and Cameroon, Bülow's colonial policy seemed vindicated.

Still, Bülow had implicitly conceded the case of the colonial reformers five months before the election. He picked a new kind of Hercules to sweep out the Augean stables of the Colonial Department, not a grim Prussian bureaucrat, but a plump young banker with a light brown beard and smiling eyes, a man who smoked cigars and looked like a younger version of England's Edward VII. He was Bernhard Dernburg, son of a pro-British journalist of Jewish origin, who at forty-one was head of the Darmstadt Bank and one of the new men of German society.

It was Dernburg who was the hero of Bülow's election campaign. This cocky young expert stumped up and down the campaign trail handing out cigars like sweets with a swagger like Teddy Roosevelt's, and restoring to Germans their faith in their overseas empire. Dernburg's message was visionary, and apparently he believed it. Economic imperialism was his answer. The overseas empire could be run in a civilized fashion *and* be made to pay.

Germany's African colonies, he said, the Cinderellas of the Reich, would soon be the jewels in the Kaiser's crown. Where else could the Reich find such a cheap and secure source of raw materials – the oil, the cotton, the cocoa and the rubber, vital to its destiny as the world's greatest steel power after the United States? Of course, Dernburg could not effect the transformation of African pumpkins into German coaches simply by waving a wand. He proposed radical reforms of various kinds.

First, that creaking millstone, the Colonial Department, must be turned into a modern Colonial Ministry, with Dernburg as Secretary of State. Second, the state must train and recruit a professional Colonial Service on the lines pioneered by the British in India. Third, the state must take the plunge and splash out taxpayers' money. Only by digging deep foundations for an export-oriented economy – clearing the jungle for roads, dredging the sea for harbours, blasting the mountains to make railways – could the state pave the way for the success of private business.

There was only one flaw in Dernburg's visionary scheme. He knew nothing about Germany's colonies.

In July 1907 he sailed for German East Africa, the largest of the four colonies, where a reformist new Governor, Albrecht Freiherr von Rechenburg, had arranged a gruelling but instructive tour. Dernburg thundered up the amazing new British railway to Uganda, glided by German steamer down Lake Victoria, and then plodded on the back of a donkey all the 500 miles from Mwanza to the railhead at Morogoro. He returned to Germany in October wiser – and no doubt slimmer. He had begun to learn two conflicting lessons that would torment him in the embattled years he was to direct the new German Colonial Office.

The first lesson was economic. East Africa had little potential wealth to offer Europe. There was no gold or silver, not even copper. In most districts the soil was thin, the rainfall meagre, and investment in farming perilous. As a rule, African peasant agriculture could give the best – and safest – return. The second lesson was political. Lured by a few pockets of rich land in the north, a few thousand settlers had trickled into the country. There was now a settler lobby which could count on powerful political and emotional support in the Fatherland.

As Colonial Secretary, Dernburg was able to push through some long overdue reforms in the four colonies. He did his best to reduce the terrible abuses that had driven Africans to despair and precipitated the three rebellions – the forced labour, the flogging, the exploitation of Africans as though they were slaves or animals. But in the two colonies with a climate healthy enough for European settlement – in war-ravaged South-West Africa and German East Africa – his efforts were frustrated at every turn by the settlers. The discovery of a small pipe of diamonds in South-West Africa in 1908 – a bonus, but hardly the bonanza predicted by Lüderitz – only served to embitter the settlers against Dernburg. He wanted to use this unexpected bonus for the benefit of whites and blacks, including the surviving Herero and Nama. The settlers wanted the money all for themselves. In German East Africa, the struggle centred on choosing the best place to grow export crops such as sisal, coffee and tea. Could they be grown more economically in the European plantations of the north, which would necessitate an extra railway, as well as African forced labour? Or should they be grown on peasant small holdings spanning the existing central railway already paid for by the colony's taxes? The answer was obvious, but in the teeth of opposition from Dernburg and Governor Rechenburg, Berlin eventually surrendered to the settlers. Only in Togo, the smallest and poorest colony, did imperialism prove even marginally economic.

By 1910, Dernburg had made too many right-wing enemies in the Reichstag. He threw in his hand. His successor was Lindequist, an ex-Governor of South-West Africa, and a firm friend of the settlers. Meanwhile Bülow, too, had succumbed. A new Germany cast in the Kaiser's image – more isolated, more truculent, more reckless – was emerging in Europe. Once again German Africa slipped from the mind, as the Great Powers found themselves surging down the millrace.

But we must return to the Central Africa of 1906, to the French Congo, where the French government had just despatched the founding father, Savorgnan de Brazza, to report on the situation in the colony which seemed only too similar to the horrors of Leopold's Congo.

CHAPTER 35

Redeeming the French Congo

French Congo and Paris
29 April 1905 and after

Brazza 'saw the concessionary companies, rapacious
and cynical, trying to create a new form of
slavery ...'.

Félicien Challaye
Le Congo Francais, 1909

On 29 April 1905, Pierre de Brazza, dressed in the shining white uniform of a temporary Commissaire-Général, landed at Libreville, capital of Gabon and gateway to the French Congo, to be given a hero's welcome by the Africans.

Thirty-three years earlier, some of them had known him as a young ensign. Now a family of ex-slaves knelt at his feet. The old chief was back, the man who had liberated them. It was he who had taken the people's side against the French traders.

A few days later a steamer took him up the Ogowe, its tall funnel leaving a trail of sparks through the dark forest, and sending the beat of tom-toms rippling through the riverside villages. At Njole, an old man placed his black hand on Brazza's white tunic in ritual greeting. Brazza's sense of destiny began to return. It was high time that he came. Without him the Congo might be lost to France.

At fifty-three, Brazza looked like an old man, his hair almost white, his tall, bony frame bowed by repeated bouts of malaria and dysentery. For eight years from 1890 he had served as Commissaire-Général, the first governor of the empire he had given France, 'French Congo'. (It now stretched 1,400 miles to Lake Chad, and comprised four far-flung territories – Gabon, Congo, Ubangi and Chad – that would soon be known as French Equatorial Africa.) In 1898, Brazza had been thrown to the wolves.

As an ex-Italian, he had been something of a loner in French society, happier cracking jokes with a canoe-load of Africans than coping with fractious French colonials. He was not a success as an administrator. He was rarely to be found in Brazzaville, but preferred to spend his time out in the bush. He soon accumulated enemies. The veteran French missionary, Bishop Augouard, suspected him – with reason – of being a free-thinker and no friend to the spiritual work of the missions. The officers of the French Marine infantry, drafted from Senegal to the Congo, found him unresponsive. He stood by the principles of 'peaceful conquest' – never a popular standpoint for ambitious officers. He was reluctant to sanction forced labour, which entailed flogging, especially the flogging of half-starved villagers to make them serve as porters. His restraint earned him a reputation as a crank. After Marchand's humiliation at Fashoda in 1898, the officers of the French Marine infantry found their scapegoat in Brazza. It was said that this old woman had lost Marchand a vital six months by failing to press-gang 25,000 porters to carry his 750 tons of stores from the Atlantic to the navigable Congo. Similar charges of weakness were levelled at him by French – and Belgian – financiers.

These were the years of the great rubber boom. Why, they asked, did France not exploit the rubber of the French Congo along the lines of the admirable system adopted on King Leopold's side of the river Congo, by which all the rubber districts were declared a state monopoly to be exploited by concessionary companies?

So in 1898 Brazza was sacked, with the public relations campaign in the French press secretly orchestrated from the royal palace in Brussels. He was replaced by a more malleable colleague, Emile Gentil. Then the teeming jungle was parcelled up into forty huge blocks, each to be exploited by a European concessionary company as best it could, using native porters to carry most of the goods on their heads, in the absence of roads or railway.

Now, seven years later, in 1905, the French government was making amends to Brazza, though hardly in the way he would have preferred. Two French officers, Georges Toqué and Fernand Gaud, were to be tried in Brazzaville for murdering Africans in one of the remote concessionary districts of Shari-Ubangi, far to the north of the river Congo. The scandal had exploded in Paris like a small version of the Dreyfus affair. Was this an isolated incident? Or was it the inevitable result of the new concessionary system? It was with the answer to this question that Brazza, as the leader of a mission of inquiry, was supposed to return in six months to Paris.

In Paris, the French Minister for the Colonies, Etienne Clémentel, looked forward to Brazza's return without enthusiasm. The Toqué–Gaud trial in Brazzaville was going to be damaging enough; why let any more cats out of the bag – and give Brazza a chance of exposing the concessionary system that he was known to detest? The government had only agreed to launch Brazza's inquiry after strings had been gently pulled by a hand from the Elysée Palace. The new President, Emile Loubet, suggested that this was the best way to heal self-inflicted wounds. Brazza was outside politics, a political innocent, a firm champion of African rights; no one would be able to accuse the government of a cover-up. The government saw the point. Brazza was probably in too poor health to travel far from the beaten track. He would see what the Governor chose for him to see. They made no commitment that they would publish Brazza's report as the British government had published Casement's the year before.

Casement's inquiry had been confined to Leopold's side of the Congo; but in denouncing Leopold's system, Casement had implicitly denounced France for following the same path. The leader of the Congo Reform Association, E. D.

Morel, had already made this point explicit with his exposé, *The British Case in the French Congo*. In this book, published two years earlier, Morel showed how British traders like John Holt had been driven out of the French Congo by the new concessionary system modelled on Leopold's. Forced labour – and atrocities against Africans – were the inevitable result. Morel insisted that the French, too, should end the concessionary system and restore free trade, the sacred principle of the Berlin Act.

Fortunately for the French government, they had nothing to fear from either Casement or Morel. In 1905 there was still a honeymoon for Britain and France, the two Great Powers with the largest stakes in Africa; the *entente* had been signed only a year before. Lord Lansdowne, Britain's conscientious Foreign Secretary, had no desire to start a new row over the Congo. Nor did the Kaiser's government, its hands preoccupied with rebellions in two out of its four African colonies. True, the Kaiser felt increasingly suspicious about French policy now that the *entente* had been signed, and he was anxious to find a 'compensation' for France's apparent plan to grab Morocco. But the Congo was no place to attack Germany's rival. The alleged atrocities involved Leopold even more than they involved France and it was the Kaiser's policy – as it had been Bismarck's – to keep Leopold holding the balance in Central Africa.

Nothing must be done to disturb the concessionary system. Despite the despatch of Brazza's mission, this remained an axiom of French policy. At last, one of the poorest and most backward of France's new colonies seemed to have a chance of paying its way, thanks to the concessionary companies and the world's rubber boom. A quiet word was sent out from Paris to the Governor of the French Congo, Gentil: M. de Brazza should be given every assistance, of course, but M. Gentil was not to be alarmed. The mission did not threaten his administration 'on which we depend'. It was only to provide an 'outlet for [Brazza's] ardour which time seems to have increased without clearing his head'.[1]

If Brazza smelt a rat, he was too proud to admit it to the government, but he did make a few conditions. At an icy meeting in March he asked Clémentel to allocate him a dependable staff. Brazza was duly lent the prestigious Inspector of the Colonies, Hoarau-Desruisseaux, and a brilliant young civil servant, who was also to be writing for *Le Temps*, Félicien Challaye. There was also Brazza's young blue-eyed wife, Thérèse, an ardent Catholic with a lively mind, who had been educated in Washington DC, where her father was a French diplomat. Ten years before, she had set her cap at the great explorer and won his heart when he returned to Paris on sick leave. Marriage gave Brazza new strength, and his children gave him endless delight. However, Pierre's health was now precarious and the recent death of their eldest son, Jacques, from an attack of appendicitis had driven him alarmingly close to despair. So Thérèse insisted that she was allowed to accompany him on this dangerous mission.

In Gabon, in May 1905, Brazza found no atrocities but much to deplore. The old man who came to meet him at Njole, placing his black hands on Brazza's white tunic in ritual greeting, told him how harshly they were treated by the local concession companies. True, rubber was paid for, but the price was wretched, and the pay was in kind – European trade goods which Africans despised and were forced to exchange at a loss. Taxes were high and justice was arbitrary. Twenty strokes of the *chicotte* – a whip made of hippopotamus hide – were considered a handy way to keep Africans in their place.

When Brazza tried to follow up complaints of injustice, he found his path mysteriously blocked. Boats were delayed, documents lost, telegraph lines cut. By the time he arrived in a village, the facts were no longer to be found. Once or twice the authorities' mask slipped. It turned out that they had given orders for all prisoners in the chain gangs to be unshackled during M. de Brazza's visit. The order had somehow failed to reach one outpost, Sindara, many miles up-river, and the European passengers' luggage was unloaded on the river-bank by a sweating chain gang, exposed to the eyes of Brazza and his companions.

After a frustrating fortnight, Brazza decided to hurry on to the Congo itself, leaving Hoarau-Desruisseaux to deal with Gabon. This time he was able to travel to Brazzaville in speed and comfort. Seven years earlier, Leopold's first train had steamed triumphantly into Leopoldville, its smoke visible from Brazzaville across the brown waters of the Pool. It took Brazza's mission a mere day in the Belgian train to cover the 200 miles from the Free State port of Matadi. At about 3.0 p.m. on 15 May 1905, Brazza stepped down on to the sun-baked platform at Leopoldville.

His welcome was cool enough, from a veteran French missionary and two French subalterns who had taken the ferry across from Brazzaville. The veteran missionary was his old enemy, Bishop Prosper Augouard. Where was Gentil, Brazza's successor as Governor of the French Congo and the man perhaps responsible for the atrocities he had been sent to investigate?

The official banquet given next day set the tone for the whole visit. Gentil refused to wear his decorations, having already snubbed Brazza by rebuffing his attempt to talk with some friendly Bateke, as if it had been 'old times'. ('No,' Gentil replied, 'not like old times. Like today. The Bateke will come when I call for them!')[2] Now Gentil raised his champagne glass at the banquet to propose Brazza's health, his own face pale with emotion and his hand shaking. He said he expected that after Brazza's 'rather sudden departure' seven years earlier, his return must be a kind of 'revenge' for him and a 'legitimate source of satisfaction'. But he pointed out 'adroitly' (according to Bishop Augouard) that Brazza should never have accepted the mission to inquire into the proceedings of a colleague. 'For he should learn by experience that one often has thankless tasks to perform, tasks for which one receives more criticism than honours.'

There was a glacial silence. No one spoke, let alone applauded.

Bishop Augouard then seized his chance to deliver a eulogy on Gentil, designed to provoke his old enemy, Brazza. After dilating on Brazza's triumphs as an explorer, he went on to praise Gentil to the skies:

But it was reserved for our indefatigable Commissaire-Général of today to go forward with a giant's stride along the road traced by his illustrious predecessor and to give at last to our Congo the economic impulse for which it has been waiting so long ... The disciple has been worthy of the illustrious master who gave the Congo to France...[3]

Twenty years earlier Brazza had known how to handle provocative speeches at banquets. (Consider the masterful way he had dealt with Stanley's reckless attack in Paris.) But now he was too old and ill to damn Gentil – or the bishop – with conventional praise. He did not even rise to his feet. He mumbled a few words about his life as a *va-nu-pieds*, adding that the bishop by contrast had 'travelled under Stanley's aegis'. Predictably, this brought the bishop to his feet in protest. Brazza's words were a 'calumny'.[4]

It must be said that the bishop, whose diary throws a vivid (and malicious) light on Brazza's difficulties, was no ordinary enemy. As the 'Bishop of the Cannibals', he had a hunger for territory and a patriotic pride every bit as stubborn as Brazza's. Ever since 1878 he had exercised a double mission, now symbolized by the cross and the tricolour floating above his cathedral in Brazzaville. He had brought God to Central Africa and Central Africa to France. Other men were cut down or crippled by malaria. At fifty-three, Augouard seemed to grow fat on the climate of the Congo. He had covered *seventeen* times on foot the grim, fever-ridden 380-kilometre track between Vivi and Brazzaville. How God seemed to have blessed these arduous journeys. Of course his first loyalty was to God, not to the state, at a time when the two were becoming increasingly alienated from each other in French society. Out of the jungle he had carved his own empire of mission schools and mission hospitals. This was the man – a touchy, pugnacious prince of the Church intent on defending his Congo empire from the jealous hand of the state – whom Brazza somehow had to win over to his side.

Far from reassuring the bishop that he would help protect the Church's temporal interests, Brazza allowed each meeting between them to degenerate into an explosive – and ridiculous – squabble.

The day after the disastrous banquet, he was invited to visit the mission school in Brazzaville. There he found a line of small black children drawn up to welcome him. They sang a cantata composed in his honour, to the tune of Santa Lucia:

> Fondateur des cités
> Paisible conquérant
> Franceville est crée
> > Par lui triomphant...[5]

> (Founder of cities,
> Peaceful conqueror,
> He in his triumph
> > Created Franceville.)

Brazza was delighted by the compliment. It should have been a happy occasion. The bishop glowered. Brazza failed to mention a word about God when he addressed the children. Soon the two grey-haired men were fighting like schoolboys – like 'alley cats' was Brazza's own phrase – over what had or had not been done twenty-five years before in the Congo. The bishop had never forgiven Brazza for humiliating him before Sergeant Malamine by failing to tell him to wear the white cock's feather. Now they wrangled over who had roughed it most in those pioneering days. Like a fool, Brazza reminded the bishop that the bishop had been so well supplied with wine that he had sent him two bottles when he had returned ill from the bush. But that was *altar* wine, replied the bishop, thunderstruck. He had sent Brazza two demi-johns and he could ill afford it. The argument turned to religion, and Brazza could not resist boasting that he was an atheist. When he reminded the bishop of the serious crimes that had passed unpunished in the Congo the bishop retorted, 'You can well see, M. de Brazza, why impartial justice is necessary in the other world, in order to punish the crimes which have not been expiated in this world.'[6] Brazza's only reply was, predictably, a sceptical smile.

Fortunately for the mission of inquiry, Thérèse de Brazza attended seven o'clock Mass twice at Brazzaville and proved a far better diplomat than Pierre. The bishop was somewhat mollified. He was prepared to concede that, under the benevolent influence of Thérèse, Brazza might not after all try to grab the Church schools.

Gentil's ideas, on the other hand, still seemed to the bishop more practical than Brazza's, and he thought the government would take the same view when Gentil asked for thirty million francs in subsidies. The struggle between Gentil and Brazza was still unresolved. But if Gentil had made: '... certain mistakes at the beginning, one has to recognize that he has given the Congo a shove forward that no one else has managed to give it up till now. Moreover, M. Gentil is an enemy of the Freemasons, and formally opposed to laicization. On both counts we must sustain him.'[7]

It came to this. Augouard was committed to help protect Gentil from the prying eyes of the inquiry; the interests of the Church demanded it. In return, Gentil would continue to protect the Church against the hostile designs of the state.

The bishop was as good as his word. After Brazza had left for a two-month tour of the Shari-Ubangi far to the north, the bishop wrote private letters to Paris that helped save Gentil from exposure and hammered an extra nail into Brazza's coffin.

To penetrate as far as the upper Shari, the scene of the worst atrocities reported, involved a round trip of 2,800 kilometres through wild country by boat, canoe and on horseback. For a healthy young man it would have been an ordeal. For Brazza it seemed like suicide.

At first, however, they travelled in style, by double-decker steamer, the *Dolizie*, equipped with such luxuries as an ice-making machine. In places the

Congo was more like a sea than a river. The huge trees on the river-banks receded into the heat haze or were hidden by islands. The water was light brown, the colour of tea with a dash of milk. Brazza's spirits rose as he pointed out the scene of one of his early triumphs – the place where, half-dead with thirst, after struggling for days through the thorn scrub, he had first set eyes on the great, silent river glittering in the moonlight. 'Sublime, super-human,' he told the party, 'the joy of a dream fulfilled.'[8]

At Bolobo, on the Free State bank of the river, they met the celebrated British missionary and explorer, George Grenfell. It was Grenfell who had discovered in 1886, quite by accident, the mouth of the Congo's vast tributary, the Ubangi, a river the length of the Danube. It now served as France's main highway to the north, for it was navigable for 1,000 kilometres, all the way to the rim of low hills that divided the Congo basin from the Shari and Lake Chad. Grenfell ran a Protestant mission at Bolobo, serving 400 African children. He climbed aboard the *Dolizie* and was invited to dinner by Brazza. Like Augouard, the man was a prodigy: in perfect health after thirty years in the Congo. Brazza inquired how the natives were treated at Bolobo. Grenfell's reply was cheerful but ominous. 'They aren't treated badly here. There's no rubber.'[9]

Three hundred and fifty kilometres east of Leopoldville, the *Dolizie* swung north into the Ubangi and the water changed colour. Here it was more like milk with a dash of tea. The river-banks changed, too; they were more silent, more monotonously green, with fewer birds or animals, merely an occasional hippo or crocodile, and fewer villages along the banks. As Grenfell had warned them, many natives had left their homes and fled into the jungle. For this was the rubber zone, dominated by French and Belgian rubber companies.

At the village of Bétou, they were told that the local Bondjos were in a state of rebellion, and they were warned not to approach. 'You will go out and get yourselves eaten.'[10] But Brazza and his party insisted on going unarmed into the village, led by Thérèse de Brazza carrying a black child in her arms. The gesture was not lost on the Africans. The mission spent happy hours buying mementos from the women in exchange for small bags of salt: bangles made of iron, bracelets of snakeskin, necklaces of pearls, rings for noses, fetishes of every kind. But Bétou was an exception. At Lobaye nearby, the Bondjos had just rebelled against the tyranny of the concession company, whose black traders stole their womenfolk and forced them to harvest wild rubber. Twenty-seven black traders had been killed and eaten. The colonial authorities had sent in Senegalese troops, and a jungle war was in prospect, for which the Bondjos were well prepared, as the concession company had made a profitable trade in selling them guns and gunpowder.

A still more gruesome tale greeted Brazza's party at Bangui, beyond the first rapids, where they had to change to a smaller boat. They were shown a hut where, during the previous year, sixty-eight women and children had been held hostage by the local administrator in order to force their menfolk to pay their taxes in kind – wild rubber. Forty-seven of these wretched captives had died of starvation or suffocation before a young doctor discovered their plight. The scandal could not be hushed up, and protests were made to higher authority. But the only punishment given the French administrator responsible was to transfer him to Brazzaville – a much more desirable post than Bangui.

It took Brazza and his companions till early July to reach Fort Crampel, the regional HQ, riding ten days on horseback across the sandy watershed between the Ubangi and the Shari. They found this border region, which Brazza had first known as a place of fertile plantations of maize, reduced to a wilderness. No food could be bought now, except for an occasional chicken. Most of the villagers had fled, to avoid being kidnapped by agents of the government and forced to serve as porters. Brazza was stunned by the disastrous change in the landscape and its people. Day and night, exhausted though he was, he slaved away interviewing Africans about the concessionary system. Challaye, the young civil servant, was bewitched by his chief's unusual methods. At a stroke he saw the secret of Brazza's policy of peaceful conquest. He had the knack of mixing 'diplomatic realism' with a 'semi-mystical apostolate'. He tried to know these 'savages' as people, to understand their basic needs, their preoccupation with health, food, shelter, safety from their enemies. He was also determined to inspire them with his own imperialist ideals, 'impartiality, generosity, respect'.[11]

The irony was that here, at Fort Crampel, two fellow-Frenchmen, Toqué and Gaud, had sunk to the level of the most bestial Africans. Brazza was tormented by the thought. As Challaye put it:

An immense sadness added to the weight of all this physical and intellectual exhaustion. M. de Brazza had a passionate love for this Congo which he had explored and given to France, then governed and organized. He suffered misery to find it in such a fearful state. He saw a tyrannical and greedy administration establish an ill-conceived and damaging system of taxes, and enforce it by proceedings that were often brutal, terrifying the natives, and driving them from the government posts instead of drawing the people to them by the offer of effective protection. He saw the concessionary companies, rapacious and cynical, trying to create a new form of slavery ... instead of trying to win [the Africans'] loyalty by free trade. He learnt of frequent acts of brutality committed by Europeans, fallen to the level of the most barbarous Negro. He knew in all its details the ghastly story of the upper Chari: forced porterage, hostage camps, *razzias* and massacres.[12]

By now, Brazza's precarious health had given way. The 500 kilometres on horseback, the days in sodden uniform and the nights in sodden huts, the unhealthy food and, above all, the crushing discovery that the Congo, once teeming with Africans, was becoming a wilderness, picked clean by the concession companies, was all too much for his body and mind. In a sense, the shock he suffered was the same that Casement had felt when he had made his fact-finding tour of Leopold's Congo two years before. But Casement was not the founder of the state. He had not sought treaties with beads and bangles, and persuaded chiefs to trust his word and accept the protection of Europe.

In early August, as the *Dolizie* was steaming back down the Ubangi, Brazza developed a dangerous form of dysentery. The mission reached Brazzaville on 19 August, in time for the long-awaited murder trial of Georges Toqué and Fernand Gaud. But Brazza was already too ill to leave his room, and it was Challaye who kept him supplied with the grim news from the courtroom.

The Toqué–Gaud trial lasted six days and provoked a storm of indignation in the town of Brazzaville – against the verdict, not the evidence.

Each man was accused of several murders. The most sensational crime ascribed to Gaud was of celebrating Bastille Day, 14 July 1903, by ordering a prisoner called Papka to be blown up with a stick of dynamite. He was also accused of forcing another prisoner to drink soup made from human remains. The most serious charge against twenty-four-year-old Toqué was of ordering a chief called Ndagara to be thrown over a waterfall and drowned. But if these were unusual methods of keeping order in the upper Shari, the killings were clearly not isolated events. The trial showed that the young French administrators thought little more about shooting Africans than they would about shooting a dog. Porters, guides, labourers, taxes – all were taken by force and often by murder. The massacre of women and children, kidnapped to serve as hostages, was all part of a day's work. The only code of honour was to lie about what was being done.

It was all the stranger that two Europeans, a junior official called Chamarande and a doctor, were prepared to testify against Toqué and Gaud in open court, at the risk of their professional careers. The evidence of African regional guards could be lightly dismissed by the judges. The guards' stories were often legally full of holes, and they had blood on their own hands. But evidence from Europeans carried weight. Chamarande especially impressed the judges. He was Toqué's young subordinate, hardly more than a boy, plunged into a world of horror. At first he had been stupefied by the violence. But he stubbornly refused to join in the conspiracy of silence that had provided an effective cover-up for all the previous atrocities reported in the upper Shari.

At 6.0 p.m. on the evening of the sixth day the judges pronounced their verdict. Both men were cleared of most of the charges. But both men were found guilty of one case of unpremeditated killing: Toqué for drowning Ndagara, Gaud for blowing up Papka with dynamite. They were sentenced to five years in prison. 'Five years for killing some *sales nègres*.'[13] ('Dirty niggers'.) The unprecedented severity horrified most of the public who attended the trial. Toqué, in particular, was a popular fellow, and there had been heavy betting for his acquittal. People refused to shake hands with the judges – or even with those who sat down at table with them.

The verdict did not reassure Challaye. He understood the view of the small minority of Frenchmen who respected African rights, many of whom were army officers fresh from service in Chad. The harsh sentences would put a fitting end to that long list of unpunished crimes and scandalous acquittals. It would reassure the natives that French rule meant the rule of law, not the rule of torture and massacre, and it would deter the men of violence from further atrocities. But what left Challaye with a feeling of disquiet, almost of anguish, was this. He was uncertain who were the men principally responsible for these crimes. Were Toqué and Gaud scapegoats, or free agents, or trapped in a brutal system that made atrocities inevitable?

The more Challaye considered the trial, the stranger he thought the line of defence followed by the two men. They had not defended themselves by blaming the inhuman system by which they were supposed to provide porters on the upper Shari. Yet they had not invented the hostage camps, the summary executions, the massacres of women and children. Toqué, in contrast to Gaud, had impressed Challaye by his gentle character and by his surprising popularity with Africans. At twenty-two he had found himself in charge of the transport system across the watershed from the Ubangi to Chad. There was no money to pay porters – not that the natives would have willingly taken money for this appalling work. He should have resigned rather than commit atrocities; that would have been the action of a hero. But Toqué was anxious to make a success of his career. He did what was necessary and kept his mouth shut.

Toqué's and Gaud's demeanour in court seemed to Challaye to have only one explanation. Their silence must have been bought by Gentil. They had agreed to protect his administration from exposure, in return for a guarantee of a merely nominal sentence. Had the judges refused to play ball? Challaye did not know, though he had a dark suspicion – correct, as it turned out two years later – that both prisoners would be free men long before the five years were up.

Brazza's report damning Gentil was now beginning to take shape. His priority was to return to Paris and persuade the government to sack Gentil and abolish the concessionary system.

On 29 August, under a glowering sky (for the dry season was ending) Brazza took his farewell of the town to which he had given his name and so much else. The ferry to the station was a long way off, on the other side of the town. He ordered a litter, then insisted he would go on foot – tottering, like an old man, and leaning his weight on his umbrella. He hardly spoke and seemed not to see anything he passed. His face was the face of a dreamer. Challaye wondered if he was considering the past or the future: his triumphs as a young man, or the future grandeur of Brazzaville. Brazza crossed the whole town on foot, 'pale and grey, silent and proud'.

At first the doctors on board the *Ville-de-Macéio*, the ship carrying the mission back to France, kept discreetly quiet about the chief's condition. But day by day he grew weaker – and seemed prepared for the worst. At Libreville he handed over responsibility for the mission to Hoarau-Desruisseaux, the Inspector-General of the Colonies. The doctors decided he must be taken to the hospital at Dakar. He was now so weak that he could hardly speak, yet the Congo still occupied more of his thoughts than his own illness. He talked of the Mongala, the infamous concession company of Leopold's Congo. 'The

French Congo must not become a new Mongala.' He kept repeating those words, 'a new Mongala'.[14]

Four sailors carried Brazza off the boat at Dakar. By now he was clearly dying, his body stiff and emaciated, his eyes fixed and glassy, the bristles white on his shrunken cheeks. Challaye went to the stretcher and shook his hand for the last time. Many of the mission wept – and not merely for themselves. Africa, too, had lost a leader: one of the few imperialists revered by Africans, a man whose name would symbolize a new kind of chivalrous imperialism – so Challaye ventured to hope – the only kind compatible with a democracy like France, a real mission to civilize Africa and set it free.

*   *   *

The news of Brazza's death on 14 September at Dakar, closely followed by the arrival of his coffin in Paris, presented the government with an irresistible opportunity. To make amends for the years of official neglect they would give him a state funeral. Amid scenes of wild emotion, recalling the hero-worship he had received as a young explorer, Paris flocked to the triumphant farewell in the cemetery of Père Lachaise. Clémentel, the Minister for the Colonies, pronounced a eulogy over the martyr's grave. 'Brazza is not dead ... his passion lives ... If he is the chief no more, he is the example ... [which] bids one never despair of the eternal traditions of justice and humanity which are the glory of France.'[15]

Never despair, either, of the eternal traditions of humbug.

Brazza's burial was predictably followed within a few months by the burial of his report. There were too many disadvantages in allowing Brazza a posthumous crack at Gentil and his system. It would demoralize the French administration in the Congo and damage France's prestige in Europe; and, given the threat to their profits, the concession companies might turn sour and sue the government.

None of these arguments deterred Brazza's faithful disciple, Félicien Challaye, from exposing the cover-up in Le Temps. He made clear the gist of Brazza's missing report, that it was the concessionary system itself, not just the murderous acts of individuals and the corruption of Gentil's administration, which had to be stopped. All those atrocities brought to light in the Toqué–Gaud affair – the routine kidnappings and murders of women and children – would continue as long as the state handed over the Congo to be picked clean by the concession companies.

In a three-day debate in February 1906, the challenge to the government failed. By a vote of 345 to 167 the Chamber confirmed that Brazza's report should stay buried along with its heroic author. Clémentel offered a show of reform – a promise to keep a tight rein on the concession companies. But it would be many years before they were made to disgorge territory to the state.

Nineteen years later, in 1925, the celebrated novelist André Gide innocently set out on a tour of the French Congo on behalf of the Ministry of the Colonies.

Surprisingly, his report was later published by the Ministry. For it was, in a sense, more damning than Brazza's. The concession companies had now far less territory, but they had only handed over unprofitable territory. What they still exploited, they still exploited by terror. In Gide's words, 'The surprising thing is that this frightful regime, this shameless exploitation, still survives after its harmfulness is recognized, after it has been denounced many times by the governors of the colony....'[16]

Fundamentally, the answer was the same in 1925 as in 1905, the year of Brazza's death. Contrary to Brazza's claims, the French Congo was no tropical treasure house. Where were the gold, the diamonds, even the copper for European investors to exploit? Where, for that matter, was the rich red soil and the cool mountain air required for growing tea or coffee? The wealth of the Congo was the sodden wealth of the jungle – elephant tusks, wild rubber, mahogany. It was wealth thinly spread across hundreds of miles of marsh. To harvest these crops meant investing tens of millions of francs in roads and railways, with no prospect of any profit for decades.

No wonder the French government shrank from investing in the Congo, and preferred to leave it to the concession companies. By 1906, nine of the original forty companies had gone bankrupt and twenty-one had lost money, trying to exploit the riches Brazza had discovered for them. The vital railway from the Atlantic did not reach Brazzaville till 1934, twenty-nine years after his death. By then it had cost the French taxpayer 231 million francs (£9¼ million). It has also cost Africa an unprecedented toll in lives: 17,000 forced labourers who died of malnutrition and disease. Such was a small part of the butcher's bill for the peaceful conquest on which Brazza had embarked with such high hopes half a century before.

But let us turn back to the Britain of 1905, where a great crusade to reform the Congo of King Leopold was reaching its climax.

CHAPTER 36

Restoring Britain's 'Old Ideals'

Britain, the Transvaal, Natal and British East Africa
December 1905 and after

'... the chronic bloodshed which stains the West
African season is odious and disquieting. Moreover
the whole enterprise is liable to be misrepresented
by persons unacquainted with imperial terminology
as the murdering of natives and the stealing of their
lands.'

Minute by *Winston Churchill* as Under-Secretary for the
Colonies, 23 January 1906

By early December 1905 the incongruous alliance of humanitarians leading the Congo Reform Association in Britain – passionate young 'Bulldog' Morel, the veteran Liverpool trader John Holt, the disgraced Liberal MP Sir Charles Dilke, assisted unofficially by 'Tiger' Casement – saw at last some gleams of hope. Would next year be the year of abolition of what they called the 'new African slavery'?[1]

Leopold had set up in 1904 his own commission of inquiry into the Congo, led by a Belgian judge, Emile Janssens. From this the British reformers had expected nothing but a coat of royal whitewash. Its guarded criticisms, unsupported by evidence of witnesses, had finally been published in Brussels on 7 November 1905. Casement had written it off as a mass of 'half truths' and 'untruths'.[2]

But by December the Congo reformers discovered that they had misled themselves. The King's own commission had condemned the King's own system for exactly the same reason as they had condemned it themselves: systematic abuse of human rights. This was considered by the British press, and privately by the Foreign Office, to be a body-blow to Leopold – and to have completely vindicated Casement's report and the work of the Congo Reform Association.

Still more important, in early December the British press reported that Balfour and the Tories had finally come to the end of their tether.

For several years the Congo reformers' bandwagon had met a brick wall in Lansdowne's Foreign Office. He doesn't 'care a 2d. rush about the whole question'[3] was Morel's gloomy view. They could expect no help from him while his chief, Arthur Balfour, was tormented by the campaign for tariff reform conducted by that deserter from the Liberals, now turned Unionist mutineer, the ex-Colonial Secretary, Joe Chamberlain.

Then, on 4 December 1905, Balfour meekly resigned and left Downing Street. A week later the papers announced that the new Liberal Prime Minister would be Sir Henry Campbell-Bannerman, with Henry Asquith at the Treasury and Sir Edward Grey at the Foreign Office.

A general election would occupy the first few weeks of the new year. One question haunted everyone: would the Liberals win a majority over all-comers, including the Irish? To Morel and Casement it was a question of whether there would be a real Liberal government at last – strong enough to start to redeem the mistakes of the previous two decades, when the party was crippled by the agonizing split over Ireland, and the long divisive years of the Scramble.

Morel longed for what he called a 'strong' Foreign Secretary – one who would do what he was asked by Morel. In July 1905, under pressure from Harry Johnston, Salisbury's old protégé who had now left government service, the Congo Reform Association had adopted a new policy, the 'Belgian solution'. It meant pressing the Belgian state to take over the Congo from the King. If this was refused, the British government should then summon an international conference to settle the future of the Congo.

Morel felt hopeful that Grey would co-operate. After all, Grey came from good abolitionist stock. He was the great-great-nephew of the Earl Grey who had sponsored the bill that had abolished the slave trade in 1807. But Casement, the Irish nationalist, distrusted him. 'I am sorry Grey has gone to FO – he will be, more or less, a friend of Leopold I fear. These Imperialists are not to my heart!'[4]

Neither man had much insight into the mind of the new British Foreign Secretary.

Grey was a charmer and a romantic, reared among the woods and birds and huge skies of his beloved Fallodon, the family estate in Northumberland. He was equally adept at casting for trout in the river Itchen, and casting for votes in the Commons. He had idled away three undergraduate years in Jowett's Balliol, then stepped smoothly into the parliamentary shoes of his grandfather, Sir George Grey, a famous Liberal Home Secretary in Palmerston's day. But behind the aristocratic wit, and the grace with rod and line, Grey had an independence of mind, a love of solitude, and a moral sense quite as earnest as Morel's. He would prove a hard taskmaster for himself at the FO. He must safeguard the *entente* and help France block the Kaiser's 'Napoleonic' ambitions in Europe. But he must do this without sacrificing Britain's moral role as the champion of the weak and the oppressed in benighted places like the Congo.

The members of the new Cabinet began their work inauspiciously enough, on 11 December, groping their way through a London pea-souper. The brougham lost its way taking Grey back from Buckingham Palace where he had received his seal of office; and Grey stumbled off on foot. In the Foreign Office, gained at last, the officials were talking darkly of war in Europe – precipitated by a clash of interests over Morocco. Relations with Germany had cooled to ice since Britain had signed the *entente* with France. In April the Kaiser had sprung ashore from his yacht at Tangier and threatened a show-down in protest against England's agreement, without reference to Germany, to give France a free hand in Morocco. Lansdowne had promised diplomatic support to the French. He had also warned the German Ambassador that if Germany attacked France as a result of the *entente*, no British government could stand idly by. Grey's first task was to calm this storm – if it was a storm – over a strategic corner of Africa.

One hopeful sign was that both Germany and France had agreed to attend an international conference on Morocco, due to begin in Algeciras early in the new year, 1906. Meanwhile, the Liberals had to strain every nerve to win that overall majority in the general election. The issue here was not European peace, threatened by the Scramble for North Africa, but tariff reform and redeeming the Scramble for the South.

It was ironic that the Empire – the acid which had corroded the Liberal Party for twenty years – had now proved the undoing of the Tories, and helped, negatively at least, to provide the cement to bind the Liberals together. For tariff 'reform' meant imperial preference and the betrayal of free trade; Britain and the Empire would impose preferential tariffs against the rest of the world. Free trade remained a canon of faith for Liberals, hard and soft alike, for the 'Limps' (Liberal imperialists) like Grey and Asquith, as well as for the Gladstonians like Campbell-Bannerman, for the outsiders inside Parliament like Dilke, and for outsiders outside it like Morel.

Now that the Powers had taken over Africa – apart from Liberia, Ethiopia, Tripoli, Cyrenaica and the Congo – it was common ground for all Liberals that the Scramble had been sadly mismanaged by the Tories. The Tories' 'grab-and-brag' in Africa had culminated in those 'methods of barbarism' in the Boer War. As Campbell-Bannerman and Dilke both agreed, the Tories had brought shame on the British Empire. Bryce, the new Chief Secretary for Ireland, deplored the 'jingo whirlwind' which had obscured the 'old ideals'.[5]

Asquith, Haldane (the War Minister), and the other Limps in the Cabinet, did not see the Scramble in quite the same light. But they shared the distaste for the furtive alliance between Milner and the goldbugs, and the disgust for Chamberlain's belligerent diplomacy in the months leading up to the Boer War. Now, at long last, the moral element must be restored to imperialism. It was no good for Liberals to pretend, as 'Little Englanders' like Labouchère had once pretended, that they could do away with the Empire. Nor should they be ashamed of it. What they must do was reform it. As C-B (Campbell-Bannerman) put it, they must apply the principles of 'justice and liberty, not privilege and monopoly';[6] in other words, concentrate on the 3 Cs. They must also apply this humanitarian zeal beyond the frontiers of Britain's Empire to Leopold's Congo, the open sore of Africa, but prevent the diplomatic repercussions which could undermine the peace of Europe, by driving the Belgians into the arms of Germany.

In January 1906 the general election produced an avalanche of votes for C-B. Chamberlain's campaign for tariff reform had proved even more destructive for the Conservatives and Unionists than his campaign against Home Rule had proved destructive for the Liberals twenty years earlier. The Liberals straddled the Commons with 377 seats of their own, and 24 allies in the Labour Party, compared with 157 Conservatives and Liberal Unionists. Now there was no denying the Liberals a free hand in the Commons to redeem the mistakes of the Scramble, if redeem them they could.

The first priority for C-B, Grey and the Cabinet was to prevent an obscure squabble over Morocco plunging Europe into war. In January, Grey warned Count Metternich, the German Minister in London, that his own policy would be in step with that of his predecessor, Lansdowne. There was no military commitment to support France. But if Germany invaded its neighbour because of the *entente*, Grey believed the British government would have to send its small army and large navy (despite the naval arms race, the British navy was still much the strongest in the world) to the support of its new friend. These strong words seemed to bring the Kaiser to his senses. By March the German delegates at the Algeciras conference had been driven into a corner by those of Britain, France, Russia and Italy. Germany now accepted a face-saver. Their merchants would have a free hand to trade in Morocco. But the Kaiser accepted that France was to be paramount Power in north-west Africa.

Grey remained characteristically calm throughout the affair. But just when the crisis reached its peak, he himself was dealt a blow to his heart from which he would never fully recover. On 1 February, his secretary handed him a telegram. His wife Dorothy had been thrown from the carriage while driving near Fallodon. She died without recovering consciousness. The marriage had been childless and Dorothy had meant everything to him. She shared all his thoughts and interests – especially his gift for solitude. After the funeral at Fallodon, Grey plunged back into the maelstrom, trying to staunch the grief with the red boxes from the Foreign Office. But he was now, he said, truly 'alone'.

However, he was prepared to try harder than Lansdowne to cut Leopold down to size. Far from feeling any sympathy for Leopold (as Casement imagined), Grey regarded the Congo system as 'criminal' and detested the character of the man responsible for it. But it was difficult to attack Leopold without wounding the pride of his people and driving Belgium into the arms of the Kaiser. At the end of March, Grey's officials received a visit at the FO from a Belgian colonial expert, Professor Félicien Cattier, introduced by Henry Fox Bourne, Morel's partner in the Congo Reform Association. Cattier had just exploded a mine under Leopold by exposing in embarrassing detail the emptiness of his claim to be a philanthropist; the Congo Free State was 'not a colonial power; it is a business enterprise ... run only for the benefit of the King-Sovereign'. Now he proposed that the British government adopt the first of the two resolutions passed by the CRA in July of the previous year. The British government should persuade Belgium itself to annex the Congo.

Grey was impressed by Cattier's arguments, coming as they did from a Belgian. He knew of Leopold's unscrupulous allegation that John Bull, prompted by John Holt and Morel's other business allies in Liverpool, was trying to grab a slice of the eastern Congo for himself. The claim was laughable, not least because if Leopold did have to disgorge, the French would exercise their right of pre-emption. For the last few weeks Grey himself had inclined to the 'Belgian solution' as the only possible diplomatic way out of the impasse. He was now waiting for Leopold's answer to the report of the Janssens commission. But how could the people of Belgium be persuaded to take on a colony? The FO mandarins were sceptical. Belgium would have no appetite for annexation, as the Congo would lose money, once the abuses were ended; or if it became profitable again, once reformed, the King would have no reason to give it up.

Grey brushed aside these objections. On 5 July he politely informed the Commons for the first time that he favoured the 'Belgian solution' and added, 'We cannot wait forever.'[7] But nothing was made of Morel's idea of urging all the Powers to force Leopold to disgorge.

This did not satisfy Morel and the Congo reformers. They decided to press for the international conference with all their might. Meanwhile, Grey's colleagues in the Cabinet turned their attention to the embarrassing abuses in British Africa itself. Egypt and the Sudan apart, British Africa was ruled – or supervised – by the Colonial Office, not the Foreign Office. The CO's first priority must be to ensure that Britain was not vulnerable itself to the charges of exploitation and cruelty levied against the Congo State.

In other words, as Grey reminded his opposite number in the CO, the government must put its own house in order and make sure Britain was not a glasshouse before they started to throw stones at Leopold.

The new Secretary of State for the Colonies was not an imperialist, and a charmer, like Grey. Victor Bruce, 9th Earl of Elgin, was a Gladstonian Liberal to the hem of his frock coat and the bushy tip of his beard. Elgin was a man of high principles and low spirits; shy, thrifty, prudent, silent, and self-effacing to a fault. If only one of those epithets could have been applied to his Under-Secretary, the renegade member for Oldham, ex-soldier, ex-war correspondent, ex-Tory, ex-protectionist, the archetype of the bounder in politics, unreliable and unsquashable, thirty-one-year-old Winston Churchill. But if the pair looked incongruous, they were not ill-matched.

The Colonial Secretary was the grandson of the notorious 7th Earl, Ambassador to the Sublime Porte, who had stripped the Parthenon of its more interesting marble features and shipped them home to Scotland, then sold them cheap to the nation, losing £39,000 for himself in the process – enough to cripple the Elgin family fortunes for two generations. As a result, the current Lord Elgin had none of a great landowner's disdain for business. He was an expert in estate management, a director of the Royal Bank of Scotland and the North British Railway Company, a successful ex-Viceroy of India, as well as a pillar of the Scottish Liberals. He was also fair-minded enough to see that Churchill's virtues – enthusiasm, originality, magnetism – would complement his own. And if Churchill naturally talked in public as if he were running the Colonies, he was privately grateful to Elgin for taking his political education in hand.

When Liberals talked of restoring the 'old ideals' it was not mere rhetoric for the hustings. It meant reversing – or at least reforming – the Tories' policy in Africa. Honest free traders had nothing to fear. Financiers and monopolists would be cut down to size. There would be less imperial intervention, more colonial self-government – that is, political liberty. But there was a catch. To restore the old ideals meant creating a new balance of 'justice and liberty' – justice for Africans, liberty for British settlers. Could these ideals be reconciled?

This sombre question did not take the edge off Churchill's appetite for his first ministerial job, or lower Elgin's lofty sense of purpose as the two men called for the bundles of files at the CO, tied up with red tape and inscribed with the spidery minutes of Elgin's predecessors, Chamberlain and Lyttelton. The most pressing problems concerned the two Crown Colonies – the Transvaal and Orange River Colony – proclaimed in South Africa six years earlier. When could the CO safely restore self-government to these Boer ex-republics? An even more urgent task was to stop the exploitation of Chinese 'coolies' in the Transvaal, now being imported as sweated labour for the gold-mines of the Rand.

In the general election it was Chinese labour on the Rand, called 'Chinese slavery', that had brought the most violent abuse down on the heads of the Unionists, for it was they who had licensed the experiment. In 1904 the Liberals had denounced it as though it was a variant of the eighteenth-century Atlantic slave trade. Campbell-Bannerman called it 'the biggest scheme of human dumping since the Middle Passage was adopted'.[8]

Now that they were in power, the Liberals were pledged to save the Chinese from exploitation. The main objection was to the degrading conditions in which the indentured coolies were held. They were confined in compounds for three years without their families, forbidden to take skilled work, prevented from mixing with the rest of the population, and subject to harsh punishment if they tried to escape. Ending this scandal seemed a test case for Liberal principles. Here was a paradigm of the old imperialism of greed and humbug. The mine-owners paid wages too low to attract enough Africans to work in the mines, so they imported cheap labour from China and treated the immigrants like slaves. But nothing better could be expected of the South African mine-owners, Milner's furtive allies in the making of the Boer War. In fact, it was a sense of having been duped by the capitalists at the time of the Boer War that lay below the fury over 'Chinese slavery'. Herbert Paul, the Liberal politician and historian, wrote:

> What excited such intense indignation about Chinese labour in this country was the fact that it was the sign and symbol of that gigantic swindle, that colossal fraud, the policy of the late Government in South Africa. Five and a half years ago the people of this country were humbugged and deceived ... but their eyes were now open to the fact that the policy of the late government was engineered in South Africa by bloodthirsty money-grubbers ... [It was] a war for cheap labour.[9]

How could the Liberals now make amends for their failure to stand up to the Randlords in 1899? The trouble with saying boo to this goose was that it was the goose that laid the golden eggs on which all four South African colonies ultimately depended.

Tactically it made sense for the Liberals to leave the British (and Boer) voters of the new Transvaal – voting for their own government in due course – to extricate the mother country from all these embarrassments. Meanwhile, the government announced that the word 'slavery' was not the *mot juste*. (It was a 'terminological inexactitude',[10] in Churchill's famous phrase.) Somewhat sheepishly Downing Street recognized the political clout of the Randlords. How could it legally act to stop this flood of Chinese mineworkers increasing from 47,000 to 63,000, compared with 96,000 Africans? Perhaps it was fortunate for the Liberals that the Tories had already granted the extra licences. What about an offer of repatriation for 'coolies' who wished to return before their contracts let them? But the CO was warned that, given freedom to escape, a third of the coolies might take the boat back to China, which would cripple the Rand and bring disaster to South Africa. Elgin and Churchill backed down once more. The compounds continued to fill with bewildered Chinese, and the Liberal papers to fill with stories of their illegal treatment by the mine-owners.

What became the most celebrated example of abuse had already occurred before the Liberals came to power. Lord Milner, the Tories' knight in shining armour, and the Liberals' *bête noire*, was caught with a *jambok* in hand, so to speak. By some extraordinary 'blunder'[11] (the word was Balfour's), Milner, as High Commissioner, had given formal sanction in 1904 for illegal flogging of Chinese coolies. The grisly incident came to light a year later, and a censure motion was tabled against Milner in the Commons on 2 March 1906. Churchill had once been proud to exploit Milner's help to make his own name in the Boer War. He did not hesitate to kick his benefactor (calling him a 'guilty Parnell')[12] now that he was down. Even Churchill's admirers thought this was going too far. But the government's difficulty remained. How could Downing Street save Chinese labourers from being harshly disciplined in a South African colony where the right to flog blacks was taken for granted by most white employers?

In August 1906 Elgin made a new attempt to discipline the mine managers. He modified the rules. In future, for minor breaches of regulations, the Chinese were not to have their wages cut, or to suffer collective punishment, or to be tried in secret by mine inspectors. However, the deplorable compound system continued to lie heavy on Lord Elgin's conscience. Worst of all, the refusal of the mine-owners to allow the Chinese to enjoy a family life (or even to visit local prostitutes) had resulted in a practice of so horrible a kind that Lord Elgin shrank from naming it in the Lords. Churchill shrank from nothing, if it would shock the Commons. With impudent gusto, he pronounced that seismic word, 'sodomy'.[13]

Meanwhile, the Cabinet agreed there was only one way to escape from Chinese 'slavery' – or 'semi-slavery' as C-B had now renamed it. They must damn the risks and give immediate self-government to the Transvaal. (The

Orange River colony, the old Orange Free State, would have to wait its turn.) This meant changing the 'Lyttelton Constitution', the half-way house to self-government, voted but not put into effect by the Tories the previous year. The new constitution must be for 'responsible' self-government, the kind for dominions like Canada or Australia. It was vital in C-B's opinion for the Left of his Party to feel uncontaminated by the legacy of the past. It would also be desirable that the Boers should regard the restoration of self-government as a clear-cut act of magnanimity, a Liberal concession to the vanquished.

Concession or gesture? For practical reasons, the new constitution could not be ready to operate before the end of that year, 1906. But the Liberals assumed, like the Tories before them, that matters could be arranged to provide a pro-British majority in the new Transvaal Parliament.

*   *   *

At the end of March 1906 a different kind of crisis developed in the self-governing colony of Natal, the most 'British' of the four South African colonies and the one that had incorporated Zululand eighteen years after its capture by Lord Chelmsford's army in 1879.

In February there had been some kind of fracas between the Natal police and a party of Zulus, armed with assegais, who were refusing to pay the new poll tax. Two white policemen had been stabbed to death in the fracas. The Natal government had reacted swiftly. Martial law was declared on 9 February and two Zulus were executed after a drumhead court martial. By mid-March a further twelve Zulus were condemned to be executed for the same crime. It was then that the CO heard of the affair and was shocked by the severity of the punishment. Churchill drafted an unusually sharp telegram to the Governor of Natal, concluding, 'You should suspend executions until I have had the opportunity of considering your further observations.'[14]

The ministers in Natal found it outrageous for Downing Street to try to interfere in the affairs of a self-governing colony. A storm of abuse descended on the baffled experts in the CO from touchy white colonials (including Boers) all over South Africa. The ripples even spread to Australia and New Zealand. The entire government of Natal resigned in protest. The resignations were then withdrawn – but only after Elgin had explained (without any great conviction) that he had not tried to question the rights of Natal to punish its black subjects. All the CO had wanted was to be kept informed.

After this climb-down, Elgin had to watch, more or less helplessly, as the Natal government stamped out a series of uncoordinated risings with the iron heel of an army of white volunteers and black mercenaries. The revolt was led by a minor Zulu chief called Bambata. At least the CO could breathe a sigh of relief that there was no need for extra imperial troops. Bambata's rising was a pale shadow of the bloodthirsty revolts by Ndebele and Shona that had threatened the existence of Cecil Rhodes's infant colony ten years before. Only half a dozen white men – and no women or children – were murdered by the insurgents. The total white casualties in the risings were only twenty-six, including a number of deaths by accident. For their part, the Zulus learnt a bitter lesson about the realities of power. At least 3,000 pitifully ill-armed men were shot down by the colonial forces, most of them hunted down like animals in the Nkandla forests beside Cetshwayo's grave on the Zulu bank of the Tugela, or flushed out of their lairs in the scrubby hills on the Natal side of the river. Bambata was killed in June, and his head cut off by an army doctor – for purposes of identification, it was claimed.

The Liberals, too, had learnt a lesson – but it was embarrassing rather than bitter. Their claim to be regenerating the Empire sounded somewhat hollow as the London papers reprinted reports of the vengeful mood of the colonial troops and their black allies. The lash was applied to the backs of prisoners, officially and unofficially. There was widespread burning and looting of kraals. White-hall recognized its impotence. Elgin took the frustration calmly, while Churchill wrote caustic minutes in the co files. When the Governor of Natal proposed that Britain pay for an imperial medal to be struck for these colonial heroes, Churchill wrote:

> There were, I think, nearly a dozen casualties among these devoted men in the course of their prolonged operations and more than four or even five are dead on the field of honour ... A copper medal bearing Bambata's head, to be struck at the expense of the colony, seems to me the most appropriate memento of their sacrifices and their triumphs.[15]

In 1907 Elgin's attention was officially directed to the abuses of power committed by Europeans, and the sense of despair felt by Africans in some districts that had led to the risings. The report of the Natal Native Affairs Commission proved a polite indictment of the Natal government which had itself set up the Commission. The authorities had completely lost touch with their African subjects. Their proposed reforms were cautious; they included creating a better means for consulting African tribal opinion, and an attempt to give tribal Africans some limited form of self-government. Some of these reforms were adopted, but were soon overtaken by events. For, in the same year, 1907, the Natal government decided to strike with all its strength at the African leader who embodied more than anyone else the national pride and aspirations of the Zulus: Dinizulu, the son and heir of Cetshwayo.

Throughout the disturbances Dinizulu had sensibly resisted the temptation to lend his prestige to the uprising. Officially only a chief, he was the living symbol of the warrior state destroyed by Chelmsford's guns at Ulundi twenty-five years before. A word from him might have had momentous consequences. Not a word did he speak – at least in public. But the Natal government was determined to take no further chances. To depose him arbitrarily would have created an uproar. In 1907 the Natal ministers felt strong enough to arrest him on twenty-three charges of high treason.

Elgin and the co viewed the resulting prosecution with grave misgivings.

Most of the evidence was flawed; it had been extorted under martial law, and witnesses on both sides had testified in terror of their lives. The CO did at least succeed in arranging for Dinizulu to have a fair trial in open court. He was defended by the great South African advocate and ex-Prime Minister of Cape Colony, William Schreiner, whose fees were paid by Downing Street. The case attracted wide publicity in Britain, deeply embarrassing for the Liberals. In 1909, Dinizulu was found guilty on three charges of harbouring rebels. He was sentenced to four years in prison, and next year exiled to a small farm in the Transvaal. By this time both Elgin and Churchill had bade farewell to the Colonial Office. But both men had drawn the same conclusion from these painful events in Natal.

'Responsible' government had proved an unfortunate experiment in Natal. The white ruling class was too weak and insecure to be trusted with two million African subjects. Did this mean, as Fox Bourne and some humanitarians argued, that the CO should resume direct control over Zululand? On the contrary, the cure was to merge Natal with Cape Colony and the other South African states from which a more humane native policy could be expected.

*   *   *

Meanwhile in the early months of the year 1906, the Liberals were determined to see that the other pickings of the Scramble – protectorates such as Northern Nigeria, British East Africa (Kenya) and Uganda – were administered with justice and peace.

In many districts 'pacification' seemed a hollow euphemism. 'Butchery'[16] was Churchill's own phrase later, when he read one of the confidential reports. He now threw down a challenge to Sir Frederick Lugard, High Commissioner for the Protectorate of Northern Nigeria and the most articulate (and stubborn) of the great African proconsuls – apart from Lord Cromer himself. How could Lugard justify – either in moral or practical terms – a policy of 'pacification' which cost British taxpayers so much treasure and Nigerian tribesmen so much blood?

Understandably, Lugard did not take kindly to his motives being questioned.

In December 1899, in the deep shadow cast by Black Week in the Boer War, Lugard had sailed out to take over Goldie's huge, unexplored empire – 300,000 square miles and perhaps 24 million souls – after Chamberlain had forced Goldie to disgorge the Niger Company's 'sphere'. The Liberals had grumbled at the generosity of the deal, which had cost the Treasury £850,000 in compensation for Goldie and his company. Lugard had been given a grant-in-aid of £88,000 a year by the Treasury, and allowed by the CO a more or less free hand to spend it. With this he had to build a new state from zero. There was no tax revenue here in the great plains of the north, beyond the forests and the oil palms. The Treasury grant, plus customs, only paid for a makeshift government: a civilian staff of a mere hundred men by 1901, backed by only 200 officers and 2,000–3,000 black soldiers of the WAFF founded by Chamberlain.

In Goldie's time most of the 'sphere' in the north had been a sham. The Company did not have the means to occupy effectively more than a tenth of its empire. It controlled only a thin strip of pagan territory along the Niger and Benue, plus the half-subdued Muslim states of Bida and Ilorin. Lugard was determined to end this anomaly and make himself master of the whole Protectorate, as the only way to rescue the country from slavery and open it up to railways and legitimate trade. This meant breaking the independence of the Fulani states, the Muslim emirates to the north – successful exponents of trade yet corrupt and bloodthirsty too (in Lugard's eyes), for their wealth and power depended on raiding their pagan neighbours for slaves. He had no wish to destroy these states, only to redeem them and humble their rulers. He would impose the same sort of indirect rule as the British had pioneered in the princely states of India.

So Lugard had launched a series of lightning strikes in the windy plains of northern Nigeria and the narrow corridors of Whitehall. In 1902, when Chamberlain had his back turned (he was making speeches in the Transvaal), Lugard despatched a 700-man column to invade Kano. The CO was aghast when it tumbled to his plan. (In his own words: 'The government were in an insane funk re Kano ... censured me for going at it "without asking Mamma" as the *Pall Mall* puts it, and if we'd messed it, I should have been broke.')[17] In fact, his field-guns tore holes in the mud walls of the great city, sliced through the crenellated towers, and broke down the thirteen cowhide gates, as though they belonged to a child's fort. His Maxim guns sent the defenders running for their lives. Next, his column invaded Sokoto, the capital of the Fulani federation which dominated the north. As they were only armed with swords and spears, most of the defenders fled, and the city was surrendered intact.

Even the CO had to admit that Lugard's forward policy had brought success on the cheap. He lost only one man. The enemy's casualties – roughly 1,200 men at Kano, machine-gunned or smashed by artillery – were overlooked when Lugard's gift for choosing new emirs proved as successful as his battle plans. Within a few years he had subdued all the great Fulani emirates and there remained only one large pagan tribe, the Munshi, backward enough to defy him.

However, in the new moral climate created by Elgin and Churchill, Lugard's Maxim gun, and his drastic way of redeeming the heathen, seemed an embarrassing anachronism. Early in January 1906, Lugard tersely informed the CO that he intended to launch a 'strong military expedition'[18] against the Munshi, who had had the bad manners to burn the Niger Company's post at Abinsi, on the Benue, kill a number of Hausa, and close the river to international navigation. Elgin decided to put his foot down. There should be no punitive expeditions – not at least without the sanction of the CO. Churchill added a caustic minute: 'The chronic bloodshed which stains the West African seasons is odious and disquieting. Moreover the whole enterprise is liable to be misrepresented by persons unacquainted with imperial terminology as the murdering of natives and stealing of their lands.'[19] In short, the new government would not tolerate a forward policy. Lugard should advance only as far as was needed to protect Company property and clear the Benue for navigation.

Elgin was as pacific by nature as Churchill was pugnacious. But if they both thought a telegram from 'Mamma' would bring Lugard to heel, neither of them knew Lugard. He had 600 troops poised to strike at the Munshi, and he was damned if he would recall them. This was the best chance of breaking the tribe once and for all. If he shirked the challenge, there was a serious chance of a general rising in the south-east. While the CO still dithered, something occurred that forced Lugard himself to give the order for recall.

In the small village of Satiru, twelve miles from Sokoto and 500 miles away to the north-west, a self-styled Mahdi called Mallam Isa led a peasants' revolt against the British infidels. Two political Residents and a white officer, with the best part of seventy black mounted infantry, were hacked or stabbed to death with hoes, axes and spears. There were no other British troops within 200 miles. For the next six days Lugard waited grimly by the telegraph to hear whether the whole of his carefully constructed northern empire had been swept over like a line of skittles. But the British-appointed Sultan of Sokoto held firm to his oath of loyalty, sworn on the Koran. Mallam Isa was an upstart, and a traitor to Sokoto. A similar attitude was taken by the neighbouring Fulani emirs. By early March 1906 Lugard was able to send a 500-strong column hotfoot to the north to take revenge on the people of Satiru.

'Vae victis.' If revenge seems a strong word to apply to the policy of such a high-minded imperialist as Lugard, it was certainly the word on the lips of his own officers. Lugard left the details to them. But there was to be no negotiation, no attempt to separate guilty from innocent, or to save the women and children from the results of their menfolk's folly. Lugard insisted on 'annihilation'.[20] His avenging army, supported by the Sultan of Sokoto, emptied its magazines into the mob of peasants armed with hoes and hatchets, shooting them down as if they were vermin. Lugard later estimated that his men had killed 2,000 without loss to themselves. Prisoners were executed, their heads cut off and put on spikes. Then the village was razed to the ground, and the Sultan pronounced a curse on anyone who tried to rebuild Satiru or cultivate its fields.

When the news of the punitive expedition reached London, the reactions of the CO can well be imagined. As Churchill minuted:

> How does the extermination of an almost unarmed rabble ... compare with the execution of 12 kaffirs in Natal after trial? ... I confess I do not at all understand what our position is, or with what face we can put pressure on the government of Natal while these sort of things are done under our direct authority.[21]

Fortunately for the CO, Nigeria attracted little attention in Parliament, where South Africa and 'Chinese slavery' were still the main subjects of debate. But the gulf between the CO and Lugard continued to widen. In May, Flora Lugard

(who had married him in 1902) happened to be interviewing the Duke of
Marlborough at Blenheim. There she met the Duke's cousin, Winston Churchill – 'that bumptious young subaltern', as Lugard described him. Flora was
shocked by the immaturity of his ideas. 'Abolish the West African field force!'
she quoted him as saying. 'Give up the greater part of Nigeria, which is much
too big for us to hold! Put an end to the whole system of punitive expeditions
and be content with the peaceful administration of a small part of the whole.'
She warned her husband that Churchill was 'hopelessly ignorant' and so 'full
of personal activity that the damage he may do appears to be colossal'.[22] For
his part, Churchill grumbled in the CO minutes that Lugard fancied himself as
a Tsar with Nigeria his 'sultry Russia'.[23]

In the event, Lugard could not do without the Liberals, but the Liberals could
do without Lugard: his belligerence, his forward policy, his refusal to brook the
slightest criticism, betrayed a complete lack of sympathy between him and his
superiors. Lugard had also astonished the CO officials by applying for the right
to administer Northern Nigeria for six months every year from an office in
London. This bizarre scheme for absentee government, euphemistically styled
'continuous administration', had seized hold of his imagination as the way out
of his personal dilemma of how to reconcile service to the Empire with marriage
to Flora. It was Lugard's misfortune that Flora had decided her health was too
poor to allow her to live even part of the year in Nigeria.

In July 1905 he had floated the idea to Lyttelton at the CO and Lyttelton had
promised to help. But in March 1906, to the satisfaction of the CO officials,
Elgin had turned the scheme down flat. So Lugard resigned as Governor. Elgin
let him cool his heels in England for nearly a year, then tossed him a bone, the
governorship of Hong Kong. Somewhat crestfallen, Lugard – and Flora –
grabbed the bone. Hong Kong was a colonial backwater and a dead-end for an
empire-builder. But Nigeria had not seen the last of Lugard, whatever the
Liberals might think. Unique among the pioneers of the Scramble, he remained
to dominate the Colonial Service as a retired proconsul far into the 1930s, and
only died in 1945, within a decade of the era of independence.

The same summer, 1907, Winston Churchill set sail for a jaunt in British East
Africa, Uganda and the Sudan. He had Elgin's blessing to see for himself those
'great estates' (in Chamberlain's phrase) that Britain had 'pegged out' during
the Scramble. If Elgin and the CO officials looked forward to having Churchill
out of the way for four months, they had not reckoned with the exuberant
memoranda from Churchill which rained down on the CO with every post. They
were also dismayed to find the Under-Secretary had turned a harmless big-game
hunt into an 'official progress'.[24]

Churchill seized on the opportunity with gusto. He wallowed in his bath,
dictating ponderous reports to his unfortunate secretary, Eddie Marsh. He also
thrilled readers of the *Strand Magazine* with a series of boyish articles on his
adventures. He greeted them from Mombasa ('Be prepared to salute with feelings
of grateful delight these shores of vivid and exuberant green'). Then he whirled

them up the £5 million railway leading to Uganda, riding on the cowcatcher of the train. At the whistle stops the Minister was shrilly saluted by half-naked Africans ('There is a sleek grace about these active forms – bronze statues but for their frippery – which defeats all their own efforts to make themselves hideous').[25]

Between the Indian Ocean and Lake Victoria, Churchill descended from the cowcatcher and had himself photographed with various African celebrities he had encountered – and in some cases, shot, including two warthogs and a rhinoceros. The more testing part of the tour of British East Africa (modern Kenya) he did not confide to readers of the *Strand Magazine* (or of his exuberant travel book, *My African Journey*). A couple of thousand newly-arrived white settlers were defying – indeed, baiting – the governor of the protectorate. Their leaders, some of them old Etonians, others Boers from South Africa, swaggered around with guns and *jamboks*. Ewart Grogan, President of the Colonists Association and famous for his Cape-to-Cairo walk in 1899, was keen to show that Kenya was 'white man's country'. In March 1907, a few months before Churchill's arrival, Grogan had taken three Kikuyu servants and flogged them right in front of the courthouse at Nairobi. Their offence was that they had the 'impudence' to jolt a rickshaw, and the 'impertinence' to answer back to some white ladies. When the Governor reported the outrage to London, Elgin told him to be firm. These were 'flagrant acts of lawlessness and injustice'[26] and Grogan must be punished.

Just before he left England to see for himself, Churchill had penned his own trenchant minute on the Grogan affair:

> We must not let these first few ruffians steal our beautiful and promising protectorate away from us, after all we have spent upon it – under some shabby pretence of being a 'responsibly governed colony'. The House of Commons will never allow us to abdicate our duties towards the natives – as peaceful, industrious, law-abiding folk as can be found anywhere.[27]

But when he stood opposite the Nairobi courthouse where the outrage had occurred, Churchill's opinions became less confident. Race relations in East Africa was one of a 'herd of rhinoceros questions – awkward, thick-skinned and horned with a short sight and an evil temper, and a tendency to rush blindly upwind upon any alarm'.[28] It was not so much that he doubted the ability of the government to control the behaviour of the settlers. But he wondered whether this would ever be a white man's country. Could white men live and rear their families in these delicious highlands, with their 'cool and buoyant breezes, and temperate, unchanging climate', and would the terrible tropical diseases of cattle, horses and men ever be overcome?

Churchill met many white settlers who were not defiant but demoralized. He left for Uganda somewhat baffled. He was lucky to have come off so lightly. The following year in Nairobi, Governor Sadler was mobbed by the settlers led by Lord Delamere, demanding Sadler's head. The settlers wanted to be allowed to force natives to work for them. The CO resisted the demand, and for a time boldly considered trying to repatriate the more obstreperous white settlers – then let the chance slip.

Meanwhile, Churchill had swapped his seat on the cowcatcher for a seat on the boat to Uganda, and exchanged a so-called 'white man's country' for one which, he was glad to think, no one could deny was the black man's. The CO must often have felt grateful for those implacable diseases – malaria and sleeping sickness – that kept Uganda pure from white settlers. Churchill found Uganda a 'pearl'.[29] Here at last was one of the fruits of the Scramble that really seemed to live up to the hopes of its promoters. 'Disinterested' British officials helped develop the export economy, using the new railway. Churchill recommended that the railway should be rapidly extended. He was also delighted with the network of schools and hospitals run by British Protestant missionaries, and he was captivated by one of their pupils, the eleven-year-old Kabaka, Daudi Chewa, installed by the British instead of his father, Mwanga. At Namirembe, next to the stone-and-straw cathedral that Lugard had defended with his Maxim gun, the high school was now full of black schoolboys who sang English hymns in perfect tune.

Glowing with renewed faith in Britain's Empire – and his own star – Churchill bounded back to Elgin's side in January 1908. His egocentric travels confirmed his reputation as a bounder; and his theatrical tour had no effect on Colonial Office policy. Anyway, all eyes were now turning back to the Congo Free State, as the struggle to prise it from Leopold's grasp once again reached a climax.

Which of the great Powers would respond to Morel's appeal for international action? Surprisingly, the answer was President Roosevelt's America.

Even more surprisingly, Leopold lost his head at the prospect. Gone were the honeyed phrases, the talk of the civilizing mission, the hand on the heart, pledging reforms for the future. Gone the serene authority that had made him the master-diplomat of the Scramble. On 3 June 1906, he issued a 'royal letter' that read like a snarl of defiance. 'My rights over the Congo cannot be shared; they are the fruit of my labours and my expenditure ... It behoves me to proclaim these rights to the world.'[30]

After twenty-five years the mask had finally fallen. The Congo belonged to the King, and he challenged the world to take it from him.

CHAPTER 37

Leopold's Last Throw

Brussels, Washington, London and South Africa
3 June 1906 and after

> 'It is an extraordinary thing that the conscience of
> Europe which seventy years ago has put down the
> slave trade on humanitarian grounds tolerates the
> Congo State today. It is as if the moral clock had
> been put back ...'

Joseph Conrad to Roger Casement, December 1903

That year, 1906, the King had suffered a series of exasperating blows at home and abroad.

He was seventy-one, and he had put on thirty-five pounds in the last few years. His left leg, always weaker than the right, gave him continual pain. He could no longer take those long, tranquil walks in the greenhouses, or ride round the park on his stately tricycle. He spent much of the winter months on his delightful estate at Cap Ferrat, in the South of France, where his mistress, Blanche Delacroix, had just given birth to their first child, Lucien. Nothing pleased him about Laeken. Indeed, he seemed determined to pull the place to pieces. With 12.5 million francs (£500,000 sterling) from the *Fondation de la Couronne* – the trust fund he had established from the *Domaine de la Couronne* in the Congo – he had begun to rebuild it as a vast baroque palace. (Prince Albert, his heir: 'But Uncle, it will be a little Versailles!' King Leopold: 'Little?')[1] It was characteristic of the King's current mood that he was not afraid to batten on the Congo in order to feather his nest at Laeken, and feather it in public.

An ordinary millionaire would have disgorged the Congo long before, provided that he was compensated. Leopold was a Coburg millionaire, a constitutional monarch *malgré lui*, a throwback from the age of absolutism, with the brain of a Wall Street financier and the hide of an African rhinoceros. Years before he had given that chip from the Parthenon to his Finance Minister, Frère-Orban, inscribing it, '*Il faut à la Belgique une colonie*'.[2] Little Belgium needed a colony to bring it to maturity. He had found the colony, but now that little Belgium seemed almost prepared to accept it, the idea exasperated him. Hence that defiant outburst, in the extraordinary 'royal letter' of 3 June of that year, 1906: 'My rights over the Congo cannot be shared ...'. The defiance took everyone's breath away, especially the breath of the King's unfortunate Prime Minister, Smet de Naeyer.

As the leader of the conservative Catholics who comprised the governing party, Smet de Naeyer knew better than anyone how much damage had been done by the King's own commission under Emile Janssens, set up to investigate abuses in the Congo, whose report was published in 1905. Even the most ardent monarchists were beginning to find the King an embarrassment. The old lines of defence were crumbling fast. It could no longer be claimed that the campaign against the King's regime in the Congo was simply a plot by the perfidious English who wanted it for themselves, nor by the Protestant missionaries, trying to do down the Catholics, nor by the Socialists, who wanted to use the Congo to beat the government with.

The Janssens Report had confirmed Casement in principle, but also blamed the Catholic missionaries for keeping silent about the atrocities they had witnessed. Now, to defend themselves, the superiors of the Catholic missions revealed that they, too, had reported horrifying abuses, but privately to Congo State officials.

Janssens's polite condemnations were followed by the far more explosive arithmetic of Professor Félicien Cattier. His study revealed that the King had borrowed £5.2 million to pay for a Congo deficit of £1.08 million. Where had the rest of the money gone? Into the King's pocket? This was Cattier's sensational hypothesis: £0.73 million for property speculation in Brussels and Ostend alone, with plenty for buying the favours of the press, and millions more stowed away somewhere. Cattier's exposé gave a new handle to the attack of the Socialists, led by their leader, Emile Vandevelde. What damned Smet de Naeyer's government most was that Cattier's eloquent appeal for annexation – the 'Belgian solution' – found a welcome in the main opposing camps: among Vandevelde's socialists, hitherto hostile to all kinds of colonization; among the Liberals; and among the Young Right led by the ageing Auguste Beernaert, once the King's leading Congo collaborator, who had become sickened by the King's refusal to heed his advice.

Despite this dangerous new coalition against the governing party, Smet de Naeyer somehow avoided disaster in the general election of May 1906. He could still exploit one powerful line of defence, which appealed to the timidity of his electorate. Belgium lay exposed between an upper and a nether millstone: France and Germany. To take over the Congo might threaten Belgium's neutrality and produce dangerous complications abroad. Suddenly this line, too, failed. In July Sir Edward Grey came out in favour of annexation, the 'Belgian solution'. Then, on 3 November, just before the Belgian Parliament returned to the debate on the Congo, a British daily, *The Morning Post*, published news of a still more dangerous threat. A cloud the size of a man's hand – a severed hand – loomed far out across the Atlantic. The government of the United States of America was preparing to co-operate with the British government in forcing the King to disgorge. How could little Belgium now prevent the Great Powers intervening against her King? Only by becoming a colonial power herself.

*   *   *

The Morning Post was right. Astonishingly, the government of President Theodore Roosevelt had decided to break with tradition and open this European can of worms. Roosevelt's decision followed two years of furious lobbying from opposite sides – mostly in public by Morel's humanitarians, and in secret by the supporters of Leopold's regime. It was all the more astonishing because, left to himself, Roosevelt had no patience for the controversy, which he called 'tomfoolery . . . imbecile rather than noxious'.[3]

Two years earlier Morel had helped found the American Congo Reform Association after a barnstorming three-week tour of America. In New York, Lake Mohawk and Boston he told hushed audiences the horrors of Leopold's regime – the blackened ruins of villages, the mutilated corpses, the tally of severed hands. He extolled the courage of the American Protestant missionaries like William Morrison, the Mr-Valiant-for-Truths of the Congo, who had dared expose the atrocities, while their English counterparts (and the Belgian Catholic missionaries) had cravenly kept silent. At the Boston Peace Congress, Morel had to confront a conspiracy to prevent him being heard, organized by Leopold's admirers, including Cardinal Gibbons, the head of the Catholic hierarchy in the USA. So he assured John Holt in a letter describing his success, without false modesty. By sheer hard work he had outwitted his enemies and 'sowed the seeds which will give forth fruit' wherever he went.

In Washington he was cordially received by the Secretary of State, John Hay, and by President Roosevelt, who was 'most affable'.[4] (In fact, Roosevelt shared Hay's view that Morel's visit was a 'well-meant impertinence'.)[5]

The King's campaign to win hearts and minds in the US was certainly conducted with as much finesse as Morel's, and with far bigger financial resources. His director of propaganda was one of his ardent admirers, Baron Moncheur, the Belgian Ambassador in Washington. As usual, Leopold felt free to exploit Belgium's official diplomatic network as though it was the Congo's. He also hired a mysterious Californian lawyer, Colonel Harry Kowalsky, to work as an undercover lobbyist in Congress. He had sent over various envoys, including his own private secretary, Carton de Wiart, to square the politicians and the press. They claimed Morel had sold himself to Mammon. He was 'a paid agent of a syndicate of Liverpool merchants'[6] conspiring to divert the rubber trade from Antwerp. (In fact, the Congo Reform Association *was* chiefly financed by John Holt, the Liverpool merchant, and William Cadbury, the chocolate manufacturer from Birmingham, but for humanitarian not commercial reasons.)

In any case the American CRA, inspired by Morel, was dominated by impeccable American missionaries, some of whom could describe in only too ghastly detail what they had witnessed in the Congo. Morel's right-hand man, the Rev. John Harris, made an emotional tour of 200 American cities. Petitions converged on Washington from every corner of the Union. Church organizations provided a ready-made launching pad for a campaign directed at Senators and Congressmen who valued the Protestant vote.

At first the claims and counterclaims seemed to confuse the American public. Some notable writers and politicians, including Mark Twain and Senator Henry

Cabot Lodge, tended to favour Leopold. In February 1906, the new Secretary of State, Elihu Root, issued a statement which dashed the hopes of the American CRA. Root denied the validity of the CRA's appeal to the Berlin Act as a legal basis for international intervention. Anyway, the US government had never signed the Berlin Act (though they had signed the Brussels Act that followed). Worse, Root expressed sympathy for Leopold's difficulties. The Congo was five times as large and as populous as the Philippines; if America had tried to govern a country like that she, too, would have been criticized for her mistakes. Root's letter was music to the ears of Leopold, and helped him to orchestrate his propaganda campaign.

At the same time, Leopold, who denounced Morel for being the paid lackey of Liverpool, was making his own compact with American Mammon. In November 1906 he announced he was throwing the Congo open to the monopoly of four great international companies: Union Minière, a merger of British and Belgian interests; a Franco-Belgian railway-and-mining company; a mining-and-timber company owned jointly by American businessmen and the Congo State; and an American-Congo company formed by a syndicate of American millionaires led by Thomas Ryan and the Guggenheims. These tycoons were not mere fronts for the King. Indeed, they had powerful friends at Washington. It was no coincidence that Thomas Ryan was the man whom Elihu Root had served as attorney before he became Secretary of State. Would this stratagem have defeated the work of the American CRA? It will never be known. Within a month, the King's American lobby had shot itself in the foot.

It turned out that Colonel Henry Kowalsky, the mysterious Californian lawyer hired by the King as an undercover lobbyist, had been fired by the King for being 'only a Jew of ill repute'.[7] In revenge, Kowalsky sold his story, and the King's private correspondence, to the *New York American*. The scandal broke on 9 December. Americans woke up to discover that agents of a foreign power had been paid to corrupt their representatives in Congress – and had succeeded in bribing an official of the Senate Committee on Foreign Relations. The outcry played straight into the hands of the American CRA. By now, many of the American supporters of the King were changing sides, including Mark Twain and Senator Lodge. The latter now sponsored a resolution in the Senate to support the President who duly announced on 11 December that the US would co-operate with Britain in pressing for annexation of the Congo Free State by Belgium.

*   *   *

A fortnight earlier, the stormy debate on the Congo had begun to rattle the windows of the Belgian Parliament, and now it threatened to sink the government of Comte Smet de Naeyer. For once he saw no way to fudge the issue in the Chamber. The crisis followed from the King's defiant 'royal letter' of 3 June. The majority in the Chamber insisted on immediate annexation. The King would only agree on condition that he retained the revenues of the *Fondation de la Couronne* and the *Domaine Nationale*. In other words, he would give up the territory, but not the profits of the Congo. This was totally unacceptable to the majority of the Chamber. As Paul Hymans, the Liberal Leader, put it, Belgium would never accept sovereignty which was 'mutilated'[8] in this way.

No one expected Leopold to compromise, but on 14 December came astonishing news. Leopold seemed to be making a complete climb-down. Smet de Naeyer told the Chamber that the royal letter did not lay down 'conditions' for annexation, but only 'recommendations',[9] which were of no relevance. Belgium would be able to take over the Congo on its own terms. The government would act swiftly to agree to annexation and would draft a Colonial Bill to introduce a humane system for governing Belgium's first colony.

The news of President Roosevelt's intervention, cabled to Brussels on 13 December, forced the King to hatch a final stratagem. To appear to capitulate, while actually milking the Congo for all it was worth: that was the King's final throw. Early in the new year, he recovered his poise and proceeded to torment his own government with obstruction. In the US, he was pleased to hear, his Ambassador, Baron Moncheur, had so successfully lobbied the Senate that Senator Lodge's resolution had been emasculated. At home, Smet de Naeyer had lost all credibility. He depended on the King to keep him in power. The King refused to provide him with the financial information needed for drafting the new Colonial Bill. Even Smet de Naeyer's patience had its limits. In April 1907 he handed over his bed of nails, as Leopold's Prime Minister, to a colleague, Jules de Trooz, whose own health was as precarious as his majority in Parliament.

*   *   *

The recovery of the King's nerve, and his determination to sabotage the annexation, presented Sir Edward Grey with a dilemma when he faced the House of Commons in May 1907. He wondered how much pressure could be applied to the government of the unfortunate Jules de Trooz without knocking it flat. Anyway, it was against the grain of Grey's character to bully the weak; and he could not afford to lose sight of the part that Belgium was intended to play in his own European grand design. A new international agreement, to be signed in August, would pledge Britain's traditional enemy, Russia, to add her weight to the *entente* with France. If it came to a war with Germany, Belgium would stand in the front line. All this made Grey anxious to be firm without being threatening. But how to satisfy Morel and the CRA?

A year earlier the two men had met for the first time, face to face. Morel was convinced that Grey was 'straight',[10] and he begged him to speak out. He must issue a 'clear declaration'[11] to warn the Belgians that annexation would only be acceptable if it conformed to the principles of the Berlin Act. Grey refused to speak out. The more excitable members of the CRA were frankly disgusted by

Grey, finding his patience quite as exasperating as Leopold's obstructions. Holt exploded, 'What prevents him from acting? What crass timidity or weakness stops him ...?'[12] In the Lords, Lord Mayo called for a British gunboat to be let loose on the Congo. Morel tried to screw down the lid of the kettle. If they antagonized Grey, whom everyone respected, they would be throwing away their best asset, the unanimous support of all parties in Parliament. At least Morel had the satisfaction of telling Grey, 'Although it may appear strange to you, I am a moderating influence in the Councils of the CRA.'[13]

Then, in early December 1907, the lid blew off the kettle. The unfortunate de Trooz published the Treaty of Cession giving the proposed terms for the takeover from Leopold. There was a rambling eulogy of Leopold's regime and a passing reference to the allegations of abuses. Nothing was said about reform. All that was clear was that the new regime would take over the liabilities of the old, including a commitment to support the *Fondation de la Couronne*. In short, Belgium would take over everything in Leopold's Congo, except the revenues needed to run it. And still Grey kept as quiet as a mouse.

Fortunately for the unity of the CRA, there was an immediate outcry in Belgium. Outrageous, said Cattier and Vandevelde in unison. Of course the income from the *Fondation de la Couronne* must be kept in the Congo. Uniting against the treaty, Socialists, Liberals and Beernaert's Catholics decided to fight de Trooz. There was an appreciative cartoon in *La Dernière Heure* of the Belgian Cabinet prostrate before an enormous mound of skulls. De Trooz's majority evaporated. But he at least made good his escape. On 31 December, worn out by the King's intransigence, he collapsed and died.

*   *   *

Meanwhile, the American branch of the CRA had been bombarding the White House with requests that the American government intervene. It was now, in December 1907, that Secretary Root and the State Department were embarrassed to receive the official report of their own envoy to the Congo, Consul-General Smith. They had commissioned a report in the hope that it would provide an excuse for delay. But without a thought for his superiors, Smith's report sounded a clarion call for intervention. It might have been drafted by Casement himself. There was no 'shadow of doubt' that by abusing human rights the government of the Congo had 'openly violated the Berlin Act'. The Congo State did not civilize. It brutalized. It was not a real state at all, it was 'one tremendous commercial organization'.[14] With the American humanitarians baying at his heels, Secretary Root decided he could delay no longer. He told the American ambassador in Belgium to make a *démarche* with the new Belgian government. Belgium should annex the Congo. But that was not enough in itself. The new government must ensure that it would put an end to these abuses that made a mockery of both the Berlin and Brussels Acts.

No doubt the American Ambassador in Brussels found Secretary Root's instructions as embarrassing as Secretary Root had found Consul-General Smith's report. The Ambassador was H. I. Wilson, a naive apologist for Leopold, flattered, like many foreign ambassadors, to have the ear of the great man. Wilson was forced to confront the precarious new government of Franz Schollaert with the threat of dangerous consequences to Belgium if the annexation was not carried through on satisfactory terms. Wilson was kept up to the mark by the British Ambassador to Belgium, Arthur Hardinge, who had replaced Sir Constantine Phipps after Grey had diagnosed Phipps as a bad case of Congophilia.

The US and Britain made a joint *démarche* on 23 January 1908. They insisted that Schollaert's government recognize its predecessor's obligation under the Berlin and Brussels Acts to respect 'freedom of trade, rights of missionaries, and humane treatment of natives'.[15]

Franz Schollaert now had the task of bending the King to the will of two Great Powers – and of the opposition in Belgium. It seemed to Schollaert that the game was up. In Morel the King had at last met an opponent as tenacious as himself, and one better fitted to deal with the modern world. Morel had used the CRA to mobilize international opinion in an unstoppable crusade against the 'new slavery'. What humbug, Schollaert thought, but that was hardly to the point. Belgium was dangerously divided. Two Great Powers intended to impose their own terms on the King, and no one could say where this would lead Belgium, its monarchy and its constitution.

Within a week Schollaert had concocted an astonishing new deal which gave his own government a real chance of survival. The King agreed after all to abandon the *Fondation de la Couronne*. This was the key to the tropical treasure house that would have taken unlimited revenues from the Congo long after its annexation by Belgium. In return, Schollaert offered the King a few dollops of jam. Belgium would take over some of the liabilities of the *Fondation*, including payments to members of the royal family, and the government promised to compensate the King for his own 'sacrifices'. To round off Leopold's grandiose plans for embellishing Brussels and Ostend, forty-five million francs from the Congo (£1.8 million) would be spent on public works in Belgium. To mark their gratitude for the generosity of His Majesty, a further fifty million francs from the Congo (£2 million) would be paid to the Crown in fifteen annuities.

On these modest terms – that would cost the Africans of the Congo ninety-five million francs (£3.8 million) – the King agreed to hand over the whole Congo, lock, stock and barrel, to little Belgium.

No one will ever know what went through the King's mind in those days between the Anglo-American *démarche* and the deal with Schollaert. He had no political intimates now. He had broken with all his devoted collaborators of the last thirty years: Emile Banning, Lambermont, Thys, Beernaert. His private secretary, Carton de Wiart, cringed at his sudden outbursts of rage. Only in the company of Blanche Delacroix and his two fair-haired sons, Lucien and Philippe, did he recapture some of his vitality and Germanic humour.

In a sense, from the King's point of view, the joke was on Schollaert – and Belgium. They had shirked the responsibility of taking the colony, these petty-minded subjects of his. They had wriggled to try to avoid paying him a decent price.

The King had actually driven a much tougher bargain with Schollaert than anyone could know. He had been paid that extra fifty million francs (£2 million) to compensate him for his 'sacrifices'. He had always claimed that he had never personally profited from the fortune – about twenty million francs (£0.8 million) – that he had sunk in the Congo during its years of near bankruptcy before the rubber boom. The claim was fanciful: bluntly, a fraud. He had been repaid six-fold. He had put part of his Congo loot – forty-five million francs (£1.8 million) – into a secret trust, the Niederfullbach Foundation, based in Germany, in order to fool his legal heirs, as well as to fool the Belgian public.

By February 1908 Leopold seemed to be no longer a visible obstruction, like those mountains of granite that block the approach to the Congo; and although the Belgian Parliament seemed to be made of Congo rubber, it could not stretch out the matter indefinitely. After months of debate and frustration, the Bill ratifying the Treaty of Cession – with an additional Act to make sure that the colony would be truly subject to parliamentary sovereignty – passed through Parliament almost unscathed.

Leopold now imposed one last, exasperating condition on his long-suffering ministers. Everyone knew that Britain and the US would refuse to recognize the annexation if they were asked to do so by Belgium because the two Powers insisted on guarantees of reform. So why ask for recognition? In fact, Leopold did not trust Schollaert's government to honour the deal with himself, if Britain and the US had a chance of objecting to its terms. He defied the Powers to stop the annexation, Berlin Act or no Berlin Act.

So Belgium asked nothing of the Powers and told them nothing, except that on 20 October 1908 the *Moniteur Belge* had published a law approving the annexation in the name of the King of the Belgians. The King-Sovereign's Congo was dead. Long live the Congo of the King of the Belgians.

*   *   *

Grey must have been astonished when the Foreign Office brought him the news of this *fait accompli*. The issue of recognition had seemed an ace. The King had trumped it. Grey was genuinely shocked by the revelations of the atrocities in the Congo. He had checked the King's recent claim to have reformed the administration. It was a fraud. The FO had sounded its experts on the Congo – three vice-consuls and a consul – and they were unanimous that the system was unchanged. There was still no colonial administration in the proper sense, no schools or hospitals or other benefits for the natives, merely a huge commercial enterprise based on forced labour. But how to deal with the *fait accompli*?

Perhaps the Belgian solution was no solution, just a new sham created by the King.

It was Leopold's own corrupt officials, and his own concession companies, that would still dominate the Congo. Could Britain and the US trust the Belgian Parliament to introduce the radical reforms they had requested in January: 'Freedom of trade, rights of missionaries, and humane treatment of natives'? It was clear to Grey that Morel and the CRA were not going to give the new Congo the benefit of the doubt. Only a guarantee of reforms would convince them that the leopard had changed its spots. Then Grey would at last be able to get Morel off his back, escape from this sideshow in Africa, and return to his real task, his grand design for peace in Europe.

There was only one answer to the *fait accompli*, in defiance of the Berlin Act, and Grey seized on it. He would call on all the Powers, France, Germany and the rest, who had signed the Berlin Act. United, the crusade against evil would be irresistible. Grey called, but the Powers (like Owen Glendower's spirits in Shakespeare's *Henry IV*) did not come to him. France, the partner in the *entente*, was happy to offer recognition to Belgium as a price for tidying up frontiers and settling other minor issues. Germany, the enemy apparent, took the same unsentimental line. The lesser Powers could not understand what the fuss was about.

Grey ended the year 1908 increasingly baffled. Only Britain and the US firmly withheld recognition. But Belgium was firm too. Schollaert was afraid that Congo reform would mean subsidies from Belgium. So he withheld guarantees of reform. The impasse gathered again like London fog. How long would Morel be able to restrain his hot-headed supporters?

At first Grey was reassured by a pat on the back from the humanitarians. Two days before Christmas 1908, *The Times* published a letter expressing 'deep satisfaction'[16] with Grey's policy. It was organized by Morel. Other signatories included Cromer and Balfour, nineteen bishops, seventy-five MPs and other dignitaries. But soon Morel lost patience. By May 1909, he was talking of an ultimatum to the Belgian government. He told the FO that the rubber, ivory and other products of the Congo should be black-listed as the products of slavery. The British government should seal off the Nile outlet for Congo trade, and confiscate the cargo of Belgian ships carrying exports from the Congo, as the only way of bringing the Belgians to their senses. Morel warned the FO officials that he had the people of Britain behind him. Unless Grey responded, he would 'kick over the traces and raise a storm the like of which had never yet been seen'. The FO officials tapped their foreheads. 'Morel, though an honest fanatic, must be suffering from a swollen head.' Grey noted sarcastically that Morel was 'prepared for universal war'.[17]

The truth was that accepting Grey's policy – what Grey called 'benevolent expectancy' – had made the CRA look foolish. Morel the peacemaker now exchanged his role for Morel the goad in the side of the government. Yet Morel could not break the impasse by appealing over Grey's head to the British electorate. With its massive majority, the government was unassailable. The months drifted by with no word of concessions from Belgium, and the government's attention turned to another African problem – one that today, eighty-two years later, seems by far the most enduring, and disastrous, legacy of the Scramble.

✻   ✻   ✻

Five years after the end of the Boer War, which had cost the British £200 million and 20,000 lives, they had watched the Boers reconquer the Transvaal. That was the unexpected result of restoring self-government.

In 1907 Louis Botha was elected as the first Prime Minister of the self-governing colony of the Transvaal, under the new constitution granted by Lord Elgin. At the end of the war in 1902 Botha had been one of the leaders of the 'bitter-enders', one of the commando leaders who had grimly put their names to the Treaty of Vereeniging. Now he was Prime Minister, with another bitter-ender, Jan Smuts, as his second-in-command. The British Liberals were amazed at the results of their own 'magnanimity'.[18] They had confidently expected that the new Prime Minister of the Transvaal would be an English-speaking South African, head of a coalition of two parties, Het Volk, representing the Boers, and the Nationalists, representing a splinter group of English-speakers. In the event the British vote was more fatally divided, and the Boer vote more triumphantly disciplined, than expected. The Boer party, Het Volk, won an overall majority of seats: thirty-seven out of sixty-seven. But this was only the beginning for Botha and Jan Smuts.

In October 1908 the British government encouraged delegates from all four South African colonies – including the two ex-republics, the Transvaal and Orange River Colony, as well as the Cape and Natal – to hammer out a plan for forging a single new South African dominion. By the spring of 1909, the Convention had produced a draft constitution. Asquith's government in London now had to take it or leave it. Of course the Liberals were already committed to the principle of 'creative' withdrawal (recognized today as central to the idea of the Commonwealth), that had been established with the federations of Canada and Australia, and the self-governing colonies of New Zealand and South Africa. But would this withdrawal be creative or a betrayal?

The new constitution was for a South African *union*, not a federation, a union which would clearly be dominated by the Boers of the gold-rich Transvaal. Permeating the new constitution, like the taint in a suit of secondhand clothes, was the colour bar of the old republics. No 'native' would be able to serve in either House of the Union Parliament. No native would be able to vote in either the Transvaal province or that of the Orange Free State. In Natal there would remain next to no African or Indian voters. Even the Cape's precious tradition of freedom – its colour-blind, non-racial franchise – was under threat. Civilization, not race, had always been the test of fitness for voters. At present, a seventh of the men deemed fit to vote were Africans; and an educated African middle class was emerging, respectfully claiming a share of power and privilege. Under the new constitution their voting rights could be snuffed out by a simple two-thirds majority of both Houses of the Union Parliament.

There was a further danger. The draft constitution envisaged a hand-over of three black High Commission Territories – Bechuanaland, Basutoland and Swaziland – to the tender mercies of the Union.

How could Asquith and his government reconcile their liberal principles with this colour-tainted constitution? By July 1909, all three colonial Parliaments in South Africa, and the majority of Natal voters, had pledged themselves to the draft constitution. The British government could no longer shirk decisions. Two South African delegations now descended on London to plead opposite cases.

The first represented a million whites, so recently at each other's throats. It was led by Botha and Smuts from the Transvaal; Hofmeyr, Merriman and Dr Jameson (Rhodes's old henchman now rehabilitated as the Prime Minister) were the delegates from the Cape. All they asked for from the imperial government – 'Grandmama' – was the seal of assent. They were backed by Grandmama's representative in South Africa, the High Commissioner, Lord Selborne.

In mid-July they put their case to Lord Crewe, Elgin's successor as Colonial Secretary, and it was disarmingly simple. A century of disastrous conflict was over. The adversaries of the Great Trek – and the two Boer wars – had agreed to bury the hatchet. This miraculous reconciliation provided the long-awaited chance for a union. The terms of the union had been agreed by all the white communities in South Africa, including the Cape. (As a poor relation, the Cape did not dare defy the other three states' insistence on a colour bar.) The British government should seize its chance of creating a great new dominion, a jewel with a golden setting for the imperial crown.

The second delegation represented at least nine million black and brown people, the 'native' majority in South Africa. Their chief spokesman was actually white, William Schreiner, the crusading white lawyer (and ex-Prime Minister of the Cape) who had just returned from defending Dinizulu, Cetshwayo's son, at the treason trial in Natal. Schreiner, a convinced federalist, was appalled by the colour bar, the 'blot on the constitution'[19] of the new union. He came to London to try to get the blot removed. He found a warm welcome from Sir Charles Dilke and other veterans of the struggle to protect Africans from exploitation in the Scramble, including the leaders of the Aborigines Protection Society and the Anti-Slavery Society. But these men were generally thought of as cranks. Schreiner cut no ice with influential journalists and MPs, except the radicals on the *Manchester Guardian* and Labour MPs like Ramsay MacDonald, who had taken a strongly 'pro-Boer' line in the war. Schreiner pointed out how ironic it was that Morel's campaign for human rights in the Congo had stirred the conscience of the nation, Tory as well as Liberal, although the Congo was only indirectly a responsibility of Britain. Schreiner tried to warn the Liberal imperialists that the Union would be a betrayal. He found few listeners.

In mid-July he turned to Lord Crewe, and introduced the black and brown delegates. The Colonial Secretary offered his sympathy. He assured Schreiner that Bechuanaland, Basutoland and Swaziland would not be crudely parcelled up in a white-dominated union. But on the immediate issues – protecting the African franchise in the Cape, and opening the Union Parliament to black or brown MPs – Crewe gave no hope at all. Asquith's government was committed to union on the terms agreed to by the Convention. The Liberals called this 'magnanimous' – and Botha agreed. The miseries and humiliations felt by both sides in the Boer War seemed to have come to a miraculous, happy ending.

There was a high price to be paid for reconciling the warring white tribes of South Africa, and the price was paid by the blacks. Milner had not exaggerated when he gave Asquith some blunt advice ten years before: 'You have only to sacrifice "the nigger" and the game is easy.'

Lord Crewe's South Africa Bill was steered skilfully over the rapids in Parliament. Only a handful of Labour MPs made any attempt to block the measure. There was only one division on an amendment, and it was lost by a three to one majority. By 2 September 1909, the Bill had received the King's Assent. Next year, on 31 May 1910, the eighth anniversary of the Treaty of Vereeniging, Louis Botha would triumphantly take office as the first Prime Minister of the Union. As leader of what we would now call a Commonwealth power, Botha controlled three times the territory and more than four times the population of the republics that Kruger and Steyn had ruled before the Boer War.

* * *

Magnanimous or not, decolonization had already begun. Two years later, the Scramble was complete. By 1912, France had formally swallowed most of Morocco, leaving some scraps for Spain – Rio de Oro – Spain's desert protectorate since 1885, became Spanish West Africa. France silenced Germany's protests by giving it a large slice of the French Congo. At the same time Italy grabbed Tripoli and Cyrenaica, despite a small war with Turkey; they were nominally part of the Ottoman Empire. They were to be knocked together eventually as the new colony of Libya.

Only two African powers preserved their independence: Ethiopia, which had used the Scramble to double the size of its own empire; and Liberia, planted with black settlers (ex-slaves) from the United States, and a show-piece of poverty and mis-government in the golden age of imperialism.

* * *

But we must return to the Africa of 1909. Schreiner had failed in his campaign to obtain political rights for black and brown South Africans. No one had expected him to succeed; history had set too many obstacles in the path. As for Morel's campaign to obtain human rights for the Africans in the Congo, there seemed only one shadowy obstacle there – the King himself. Yet, shadow or not, he could still paralyse all reform. That was the wretched conclusion Morel had reached by the autumn of 1909.

In October the Belgian Parliament had finally announced its plans for reforming the Congo. Free trade would be introduced progressively: in the first half of the country by July 1910, in the second half phased over the two following years. In due course, the natives would be free to buy and sell their rubber as they chose. Morel denounced these reforms. Even if they were offered in good faith, the delays would be monstrous. But of course the reforms were shams. The King was still in secret control. Slavery was still the name of the game. In Morel's own words, 'There has been a change of name, but the old firm remains and is carrying on the old game of plunder and slavery.'[20]

In his frustration, Morel lashed out at Grey, accusing him of sacrificing the Congo for the demands of the *entente* and the secret military commitments which it was rumoured (perfectly correctly) were already being discussed with France. The attack on Grey began to alienate Morel's own supporters, especially imperialists like Lord Cromer. Gradually the unity of the CRA movement, which Morel had cherished for so long, began to dissolve in recrimination.

Then, two months after the news of the so-called reforms, Morel began to realize that he had won after all. The days of the old firm were numbered, and the King's final throw had failed.

*   *   *

Leopold was dying. He lay, wrapped in a dressing-gown, in a small outhouse, the Pavillon des Palmiers, beyond the glasshouses at Laeken. His stomach was distended by a blockage of the large intestine. At first the doctors were afraid to operate. The King asked for extreme unction, but this was refused because of his liaison with Blanche Delacroix. It is possible that his confessor then married the pair to put matters 'in order' (his own phrase), though this would have been illegal under civil law. Certainly Blanche remained with him to the end. His two daughters, Louise and Stephanie, came to Laeken in the hope of a deathbed reconciliation. He refused to admit them. His heir, Prince Albert, waited by his side. It was Albert who would personally supervise reform in the Congo.

On 14 December 1909 the doctors operated at last, but it was a forlorn hope. The King only survived the operation a few hours. Blanche had to be led away by force. Then someone read out the text of His Majesty's last wishes, bleak and not without poignancy: 'I wish to be buried in the early morning and without pomp. Apart from my nephew and those closest to me, I forbid anyone to follow my cortège.'

He lay in state for two days in the royal palace in Brussels. Then he was given a state funeral. Anything less, it was felt, might look like a deliberate insult from his seven million subjects in Belgium to whom he had given so much, including the care of sixteen million Africans.

Scrambling Out

Zimbabwe, Africa and Europe
18 April 1980, before and after

> For two or three generations we can show the Negro
> what we are: then we shall be asked to go away. Then
> we shall leave the land to those it belongs to, with
> the feeling that they have better business friends in
> us than in other white men.
>
> *Lord Lugard*

Up to the last moment it seemed too good to be true: that Rhodesia, Britain's fifteenth and final colony in Africa, the last fractious child of the Scramble still in the care of a European power, should peacefully graduate to independence.

Yet at midnight on 18 April 1980 the optimists were, for once in Africa, proved correct. In the Rufaro stadium at Salisbury, the independence ceremony passed off as smoothly as a graduation day. A Rhodesian Signal Corps band played 'God Save the Queen'. Prince Charles took the farewell salute, as his father, mother and other members of his family had taken the farewell salute on fourteen earlier independence days in Africa.

Veterans of these ceremonies were there to welcome the new graduate to the Commonwealth: Prime Minister Indira Gandhi (India, independent 1947); President Shagari (Nigeria, 1960); President Kenneth Kaunda (Zambia, 1964); President Seretse Khama (Botswana, 1966), as well as a representative of the old Commonwealth, Prime Minister Malcolm Fraser (Australia, 1901). There was polite clapping in the stadium from 35,000 Africans as the last British governor, Lord Soames, watched the Union Jack slither down the flagpole to be replaced by the red, black, green and gold flag of Zimbabwe, a new African nation.

After ninety years, Rhodesia was free – or rather Rhodesia was dead, the land which Rhodes and his men had grabbed from Lobengula. Long live Zimbabwe, the forty-third member of the British Commonwealth, and the forty-sixth European colony in Africa to win its freedom.

As a blue spotlight followed the new flag up to the top of the flagpole and a twenty-one-gun salute bombarded the veld, delight became delirium. (Nearby I saw some white Rhodesians in the VIP enclosure weep openly into their handkerchiefs, but it was only the police giving them, inadvertently, a dose of tear gas.) '*Pamberi, Comrade Mugabe!*' ('Forward with Comrade Mugabe!') In the stadium the ex-combatants – Rhodesian paramilitary police in khaki and

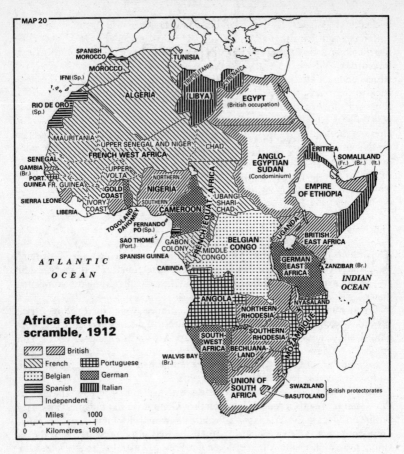

MAP 20

**Africa after the
scramble, 1912**

British
French
Belgian
Spanish
Independent

Portuguese
German
Italian

0   Miles   1000

0   Kilometres   1600

SPANISH
MOROCCO
MOROCCO
IFNI (Sp.)
TUNISIA
TRIPOLITANIA
CYRENAICA
RIO DE ORO
(Sp.)
ALGERIA
LIBYA
EGYPT
(British occupation)
MAURITANIA
UPPER SENEGAL AND NIGER
CHAD
ANGLO-
EGYPTIAN
SUDAN
(Condominium)
ERITREA
SOMALILAND
(Fr.) (Br.) (It.)
SENEGAL
FRENCH WEST AFRICA
GAMBIA
(Br.)
PORT.
GUINEA FR. GUINEA
UPPER
VOLTA
NORTHERN
GOLD
COAST
NIGERIA
EMPIRE
OF ETHIOPIA
SIERRA LEONE
IVORY
COAST
SOUTHERN
UBANGI
SHARI-
CHAD
LIBERIA
TOGOLAND
DAHOMEY
CAMEROON
FERNANDO
PO (Sp.)
SAO THOMÉ
(Port.)
SPANISH GUINEA
GABON
COLONY
MIDDLE
CONGO
FRENCH EQUAT. AFRICA
BELGIAN
CONGO
UGANDA
BRITISH
EAST AFRICA
ATLANTIC
OCEAN
CABINDA
GERMAN
EAST
AFRICA
ZANZIBAR (Br.)
INDIAN
OCEAN
ANGOLA
NORTHERN
RHODESIA
NYASALAND
SOUTHERN
RHODESIA
MOZAMBIQUE
SOUTH
WEST
AFRICA
BECHUANA-
LAND
WALVIS BAY
(Br.)
UNION OF
SOUTH
AFRICA
SWAZILAND
BASUTOLAND
British protectorates

Patriotic Front guerrillas in jungle fatigues – ran laps of honour like sportsmen.
It was a strangely innocent way to end a seven-year 'bush war' in which tens of
thousands had died and gruesome atrocities had been committed by both sides.

In 1966, unable to persuade London to allow Rhodesia to be decolonized as
a white-supremacist state (as the four colonies of South Africa had been decolonized in 1910), Ian Smith and the white minority had defied London by making
a unilateral declaration of independence. London counter-attacked with a half-
hearted trade boycott. But the white rebellion against Britain soon precipitated
a black rebellion against Salisbury. By the end of the 1970s there was a military
stalemate. Neither adversary – the white rebels sustained by South Africa, the
black rebels from Angola, Zambia and Mozambique, and split into two camps

backed by Russia and China – could bludgeon the other side into submission.

It was South Africa's will to sustain the war that cracked first. Alarmed by the ideological threat to their own heartland, the Afrikaners in South Africa forced their old white rivals in Rhodesia to throw in the sponge. A deal was struck, ending both colonial revolts. Ian Smith resigned. Britain turned the clock back to the 1960s, the decade of independence, and shook the dust out of the robes it had worn as an imperial power. Lord Soames was appointed colonial governor of Rhodesia – but only long enough to hold the first democratic election and legitimize the new Zimbabwe. There were short-term guarantees for the white minority. And the British government of Margaret Thatcher made no secret that they hoped the winner of the first free election would be Bishop Abel Muzorewa, a new black prime minister prepared to share power with the whites, not Comrade Mugabe, joint leader of the Zanu-Zapu pact, based on the rival guerrilla armies coming in from the bush.

In the event, what had embarrassed British governments often when the Union Jack was hauled down in the 1960s embarrassed the British in Rhodesia in 1980. The new African electorate paid no attention to their advice. Muzorewa, tainted by collaboration with Ian Smith, was hooted out of office, and his rival, Mugabe swept the polls. But Mugabe was not the Chinese-Red Marxist he had been painted. His creed was pragmatic African nationalism. On 18 April he told the new nation that the 'wrongs of the past must be forgiven and forgotten'.

Mugabe was a statesman in the making. And Zimbabwe had one all-important advantage over most of its predecessors on the road to independence. Its new African rulers were quite as well educated as the men they replaced.

✳   ✳   ✳

The Scramble *out* of Africa in the eleven years from 1957 to 1968 was pursued at the same undignified pace, taking the world as much by surprise, as the Scramble into Africa more than half a century earlier. *Torschlusspanik* (the 'door-closing-panic' of Bismarck's day) seized France, Belgium and even Britain. Of course imperial perspectives were now very different from those of the 1880s. For one thing, these countries perceived that the race was to get out through the door before they were kicked through it. For another, Germany was no longer in the race. The Kaiser's black and gold flag had been hauled down in the four German colonies forty years earlier.

It was the First World War that gave Britain the chance to reverse those unfortunate concessions that the 'bondage in Egypt' had induced Gladstone – and later Salisbury – to give Bismarck. At the Peace Conference in 1919 the victors divided the spoils, including the four German colonies, captured after heavy fighting, especially in East Africa. The British claimed and got the lion's share: German East (Tanganyika) for the home government, and German South West for the Dominion of South Africa. France and Britain divided the jungles of Togo and Cameroon between them. Belgium was thrown a picturesque bone:

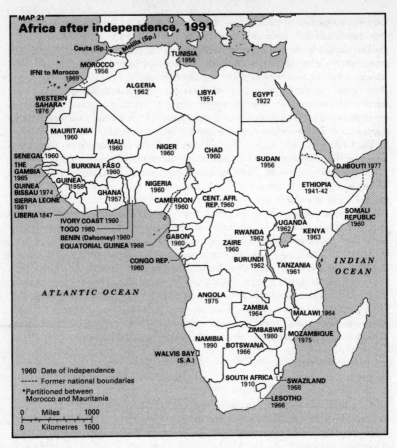

MAP 21

Africa after independence, 1991

Ceuta (Sp.) Melilla (Sp.)

TUNISIA 1956

MOROCCO 1956

IFNI to Morocco 1969

WESTERN SAHARA* 1976

ALGERIA 1962

LIBYA 1951

EGYPT 1922

MAURITANIA 1960

MALI 1960

NIGER 1960

CHAD 1960

SUDAN 1956

DJIBOUTI 1977

SENEGAL 1960

THE GAMBIA 1965

BURKINA FASO 1960

GUINEA BISSAU 1974

GUINEA 1958

GHANA 1957

NIGERIA 1960

CAMEROON 1960

CENT. AFR. REP. 1960

ETHIOPIA 1941-42

SIERRA LEONE 1961

LIBERIA 1847

IVORY COAST 1960

TOGO 1960

BENIN (Dahomey) 1960

EQUATORIAL GUINEA 1968

GABON 1960

ZAIRE 1960

UGANDA 1962

RWANDA 1962

KENYA 1963

SOMALI REPUBLIC 1960

CONGO REP. 1960

BURUNDI 1962

TANZANIA 1961

INDIAN OCEAN

ATLANTIC OCEAN

ANGOLA 1975

ZAMBIA 1964

MALAWI 1964

ZIMBABWE 1980

MOZAMBIQUE 1975

NAMIBIA 1990

BOTSWANA 1966

WALVIS BAY (S.A.)

SOUTH AFRICA 1910

SWAZILAND 1968

LESOTHO 1966

1960 Date of independence
----- Former national boundaries
*Partitioned between Morocco and Mauritania

0   Miles   1000

0   Kilometres   1600

Ruanda-Urundi, hidden away beside the Mountains of the Moon.

None of the Powers grew fat on the ex-German colonies. Apart from little Togo, the colonies had all needed large hand-outs from Berlin. Of course the changes seemed to make sense on the map. Cape-to-Cairo, the 'all-red' route across Africa, was now a reality. But the great trans-African railway, the stuff of Rhodes's Cape-to-Cairo dream, did not materialize. Africa was too poor for anything but a potholed motor track across its spine. Prestige apart, the chief benefit for Britain lay in improved security for her Empire. Bismarck had mischievously stuck his four German colonies like thorns into the side of four isolated British territories: the Gold Coast (later Ghana), Nigeria, South Africa and British East Africa (Kenya). After forty years, Britain's main setback in the Scramble had been redeemed.

The chief benefit for Africans, and the hope for those who aspired to self-government, were the title deeds of the 'mandates', as the ex-colonies were called. The peace conference of 1919, inspired by the idealism of President Woodrow Wilson, gave birth to the League of Nations and the League gave birth to the system of mandates for peoples 'not yet able to stand alone in the modern world'. It seemed that the ex-colonies would be given self-determination, like other small nations, when they were ready, whenever that should be.

Until after the Second World War, however, the mandate system proved a sham. Britain, France and Belgium ruled the mandates as arbitrarily as they ruled their other colonies. There was no supervision by the League, no progress towards self-government, very little education above primary level, abject poverty. The mandates, like the colonies, were selling their cocoa, coffee, palm-oil or sisal on a glutted market, prisoners of the world economy, which soon sank into the depression. (By contrast, the value of South African gold rose eight times in value.)

In 1935 the League of Nations ignominiously failed to prevent Mussolini from invading Ethiopia, the last independent African state (apart from Liberia) and itself a member of the League. Within a year Mussolini, the new Caesar, had driven the young Emperor, Haile Selassie, into exile in England and had united Ethiopia with Italy's earlier colonies, Eritrea and Somaliland. It was forty years since Menelik had crushed General Baratieri at Adowa and sent the Italians fleeing back into Eritrea, bringing down Crispi's government in Rome.

But Mussolini's Black Shirts had only three years to enjoy their revenge. The Second World War supervened. It turned out that ordinary Italians had no stomach for an imperial war in Africa and Mussolini's empire fell like a sandcastle. Ethiopia was liberated, establishing the new pattern of decolonization in Africa. Whether it made sense or not, the general rule for the next thirty years was to be: 'last in, first out.'

The campaign to liberate Ethiopia was completed in 1942. British, Nigerian and South African troops put Haile Selassie back on the throne of the King of Kings. But how to liberate Eritrea, claimed by Haile Selassie as part of his *own* empire, stolen from him by the Italians in 1885? It was an embarrassing question for the Allies. And what about the other captured Italian colonies, Somaliland and Libya? They would have to be administered until they were ready for self-government, whenever that might be. Did this mean a return to the cynical sham of the mandate system?

But an irreversible change had occurred in the world's attitude to colonies in the twenty-seven years since the end of the First World War. Gone was the empire-building alliance of God and Mammon that had helped to launch the Scramble. Now the imperialists were on the defensive. Both the men of God and the men of business had begun to see that formal empire was counter-productive. Colonies were becoming unfashionable. Even before the beginning of the Second World War, Britain had committed herself to grant India her independence on the model of the white dominions. This promise was redeemed in 1947, liberating 400 million British subjects at a stroke, three-quarters of the subject empire. Burma was set free soon afterwards. Other imperial powers followed suit in Asia, after bitterly contested rearguard actions, the Dutch in Indonesia, the French in Indo-China.

Ex-colonies in Asia crowded the plush seats of the Assembly of the United Nations, successor to the bankrupt League. Whatever their differences, and they had no shortage, the new states had not a good word to say for colonialism. Nor did the embattled Super-Powers, America and Russia, who bid for their favours in the UN and outside. It was the central irony of the Cold War, and the polar winds that chilled the world for the next forty-five years, that both Super-Powers were by origin aggressive settler states. They had expanded across rich, under-populated tracts of the world, conquering and exploiting indigenous peoples. This did not prevent them appearing on the world stage as the champions of anti-colonialism.

By the late 1940s it was obvious that self-government would come *one day* for Africa, too – at least for the black African colonies directly controlled by Britain and France. But when would that day be? The Powers were in no hurry to leave, their better educated subjects were too weak, despite a wide range of discontents, to make the Powers give any thought to a timetable. The UN was determined to give Libya, the ex-Italian colony, its independence in 1951. Otherwise there were no plans to haul flags down, and no one talked of the winds of change. Eager young Oxford and Cambridge graduates joined the British Colonial Service in Africa, expecting to find a good berth for life.

The wind changed in Africa in February 1948, more than a decade before Harold Macmillan made the metaphor famous, and was soon blowing a gale from the west. It started in the Gold Coast, a colony knocked together, like most of the colonies of the Scramble, from an incongruous ragbag of territories. There was the original coastal strip, there was King Prempeh's aggressive kingdom of Ashanti endowed with limited gold reserves, and a wilderness in the north. In the 1900s, no one had forecast a great future for the Gold Coast. But by the winter of 1947 cocoa was the new gold. The whole world seemed to want to eat chocolate in that first grim winter of the Cold War. And the colony's skilled African farmers supplied a third of the world's demands. Then one morning in February 1948 the British Governor awoke to find riots in Accra and his model colony tumbling about his ears. A crisis of expectations had built up unnoticed. Cocoa had brought new hope – especially to the British, in the throes of a sterling crisis – but not enough opportunities to satisfy Africans.

The chief beneficiary of the disaster, though not its instigator, was Kwame Nkrumah, the charismatic young general secretary of the Gold Coast's new Nationalist Party. Nkrumah was a black firebrand and would-be Messiah. He had also an earthy gift for machine politics. For twelve years he had drifted around Europe and the US, hob-nobbing with political enthusiasts of various shades of pink and red, including orthodox Communists and Trotskyites. People said he was an agent of the Kremlin, but his creed was more personal: populist nationalism and pan-Africanism. Since 1945 he had demanded 'complete and absolute independence' for the Gold Coast. The Governor's response to the riots was a plan for the first general election in the more advanced southern part of the colony and a gradual advance to self-government.

Nkrumah defied the Governor by launching an illegal general strike, and landed in prison. But his party won by a landslide in the election. His prison sentence did him no harm with the electorate when the Governor whisked him out of gaol so that he could lead the new government. He was the first of many African PMs to style himself a PG, 'prison graduate'. (He even had the initials PG embroidered in gold on a white cap and wore it regularly in Parliament.)

For six years Nkrumah and his party ruled the Gold Coast in partnership with the colonial Governor. Then, on 6 March 1957, 'Showboy' (his admirers' name for him) rolled up the Union Jack at last and hoisted the flag of his own country, the first black dominion, rechristened Ghana. He called this the 'turning point on the continent' and he was not boasting. Already Nkrumah's pan-African populist nationalism had sent a drum call for freedom echoing from village to village and from coast to coast. His drum call sounded loudest in the neighbouring colonies of Nigeria, Sierra Leone and Gambia, three British colonies which in opposite ways represented the artificiality of the Africa created by the Scramble.

Gambia was the *reductio ad absurdum*. It was as thin as a toothpick, a corridor of marshy land along the Gambia river, two hundred miles long but only about twenty miles wide, hemmed in on both sides by the French colony of Senegal. Twice the Colonial Office had tried to dump Gambia on the French by exchanging it for territory further south. But the toothpick was left as it was. Could independent Gambia ever stand on its own feet?

There were doubts, too, about the viability of Sierra Leone, isolated between French Guinea and Liberia. Like the Gold Coast it was an incongruous marriage between a coastal strip and a wild interior. With Nigeria the problem was almost the reverse. Was it too *big* to survive? The powerful appetites of Goldie and Lugard had created this African giant: a giant speaking two hundred languages, composed of 31 million people – a seventh of the population of the continent in 1953 (today it approaches 100 million). Would it hold together after independence or snap in two, like India?

It had been an axiom of the British that they would have decades to turn tropical colonies into nation states. After all, these haphazard blocks of scrub and desert, peppered with ill-matched tribes, had neither geographical nor political unity. Many had been kept divided, the better to rule them. Besides, there were nothing like enough Africans trained as an élite. Where were the tens of thousands of graduates needed for the civil service: teachers, engineers, businessmen – not to say politicians? Of course the colonial Power would control the pace of advance. Now the British found they had gravely miscalculated. In desperation Britain launched a crash programme in nation-building. Constitutions were borrowed from elsewhere or hammered out overnight, parliaments thrown up like theatre props (designed on the Westminster model down to the Speaker's wig), elections held, Prime Ministers lectured on the intricacies of British democracy.

The trickiest problem was to design the federal constitution of Nigeria. As a proconsul from 1897 till 1919 (apart from five years in Hong Kong), Lugard had encouraged the isolation of the north by imposing a system of indirect rule, using the Islamic emirs as the princes had been used in India. By contrast the originally pagan south had the bulk of the natural resources and had moved faster towards democratic politics. Disastrously, the new federal constitution was weighted heavily in favour of the north. However, no one forecast disaster at the time. Like everythin., the constitution was a desperate expedient. Euphoria seized all regions, as Nigeria stretched out a fumbling hand to take its freedom.

Meanwhile, as the British congratulated themselves on the timeliness of their exit, an Arab rebellion in the north of the continent was tearing France apart. In 1954, taking its cue from the newly-independent French mandates in the Near East and the French colonies in South-East Asia, the nationalist majority in Algeria rose against the French. Before the Second World War the nationalists' aim had been a modest programme of reform. In theory, France stood for the ideal of assimilation. Algeria had been declared an 'integral' part of France in 1848. Yet in this colony, the richest and most important in the French Empire, racial discrimination had been the rule from the beginning. One reason for the failure of assimilation was the counter-magnetism of Islam. The main reason was the power of the *colons*, the million French and other Europeans who dominated the life of the colony.

Barely a ninth of the population, they controlled most of the wine-growing and olive-bearing land, and nearly all the mines and factories. Few Arabs outside the cities could read or write. Half the rural population was officially classed 'destitute'. The rebellion soon assumed a ferocity that made the Accra riots look like a children's party. Paris threw 400,000 soldiers into the struggle, including the veterans of the French army in Indo-China, who hoped to repay with interest in Africa the humiliations they had suffered at Dien Bien Phu.

Overstretched in Algeria, the French tried to parry the Arab attack by dumping Morocco and Tunisia. They, too, were on the brink of rebellion, propelled by parallel waves of Arab nationalism. In Morocco, leadership of the national movement was contained within the conservative hands of the sultan, Muhammad V. It was his uncle, Mulay Yusuf, who had had to accept the French protectorate in 1912. In Tunisia there was no trace of the family of the unfortunate Bey who had been forced to sign the Treaty of Bardo in 1881. The national standard-bearer was Habib Bourguiba, an eloquent lawyer who had pleaded his country's case at the UN.

In 1956, the year of the fiasco of the Anglo-French invasion of Egypt, Morocco and Tunisia proceeded calmly to independence. Governments in Paris fell like packs of cards. But it seemed nothing would stop the bloodbath in Algeria.

It was General de Gaulle, the Cincinnatus from a country retreat at Colombey-les-Deux-Eglises, who was then restored to power by the forces of the Right. With majestic ambiguity he assured the Algerian *colons* he knew what they wanted: *'Je vous ai compris!'* But he had come to save France, not French Algeria, Africa – or indeed, the Fourth Republic. In a trice he had kicked the Fourth Republic into the grave, and cut France free from all her African colonies, as if they might choke her. True that, at first, he offered a choice to the twelve territories of French West Africa and French Equatorial Africa. Would they vote *oui* to join the *Communauté*, a kind of French Commonwealth? Or did they vote *non*, meaning complete independence?

Only one colony, Guinea, had the bad taste to vote *non*. But by 1960 all twelve colonies (and the two ex-mandates, Togo and Cameroon) for better or for worse, for richer or for poorer, were hustled into independence. Britain had made the gesture of preparing her colonies for the shock of leaving the nest. France simply gave them a push and told them to fly.

De Gaulle's tactics as a hustler reached a climax at the Evian agreement of 1962, when he negotiated an end to the Algerian war on terms the *colo* simply could not refuse: to be sent packing back to France. Six years later he was sent packing himself by the voters, back to his estate at Colombey-les-Deux-Eglises.

The Algerian war had a scale (and a horror) fortunately unmatched by anything the British experienced in Africa. The worst they suffered was the Mau-Mau revolt in Kenya of 1952–8, a shadowy civil war waged among the Kikuyu and against the British settlers, the imperial government and the Africans who collaborated with them. Even now the origins and character of Mau-Mau are disputed. Was it a Kikuyu war of independence? The Kikuyu's political leader was Jomo Kenyatta, a friend of Nkrumah's. Was he implicated in Mau-Mau? Or was it more atavistic than nationalistic, a return to the bloody rituals of pagan Africa?

The rebellion certainly exploited the burning resentments of the Kikuyu, the most politically conscious of Kenya's peoples. The British discriminated against them at every level: making them outsiders in their own country. But the grievance that touched them most widely was the land. More than half of Kenya is barren steppe and desert. The British settlers had reserved exclusively for themselves the best farmland, the cool, green 'White Highlands' on the railway to Uganda. For six years rebellion tormented the crown colony, and 20,000 Kikuyu were detained without trial. Hundreds were executed and thousands shot out of hand. Only one hundred white lives were lost. But to stamp out the flames cost the government in London £60 million, and inevitably London exacted its price.

By 1960 there was a new Conservative Colonial Secretary, Iain MacLeod, and he did not flinch. Both Kenya's pushy neighbours had their claims for independence settled: Uganda, Lugard's first love, helped by a guardian angel, the anopheles mosquito, to keep out white settlers; Tanganyika, Bismarck's old colony, now to be liberated under the aegis of the UN. Could Kenya be treated differently because 1 per cent of its people were white? In 1960 MacLeod horrified the white settlers by releasing the enigmatic Kenyatta from prison. And three years later Kenyatta led his country to freedom.

To call the bluff of the handful of white settlers in Kenya needed courage, but it worked. In Southern Rhodesia, the bluff worked the other way round. Cecil Rhodes's chartered colony had always been a political freak. Technically it was still a responsibility of London, but in practice it had been self-governing, and dedicated to white supremacy, South-African style, since the end of the First World War. How to transform it peacefully into a multi-racial state?

In 1953, London had tried to dilute the power of white racism in Southern Rhodesia by throwing it into a federation with Northern Rhodesia and Nyasaland, where the settlers were still under the thumb of the Colonial Office. Seen from London, the mixture looked more hopeful, at any rate less explosive. But this was not the view of African nationalists in either territory. After rioting by black miners on the Copperbelt, and violent demonstrations in Nyasaland, the federation fell apart. From the wreckage, London cut its crown colonies free, Northern Rhodesia as Zambia and Nyasaland as Malawi. With Rhodesia (no need now for 'Southern') the stalemate resumed. Any political rights for Africans seemed a pie in the sky.

In the Congo, the same year, 1960, the sky seemed to have fallen on the Belgians. It was fifty years since E. D. Morel and the Congo Reform Association had forced Leopold to disgorge the Congo to Belgium. Since then, the country had become even richer than the King had predicted. The world's factories hungered for copper and the Congo had plenty, together with diamonds, cobalt, gold, chrome and various other strategic minerals. The Congo became, by capitalist standards, a model state, with cheap, docile workers, and healthy profits for overseas companies, mainly based in Belgium.

Indeed, the Belgians believed their Congo was a model for other imperial powers. Africans were like children, they would explain, complacently enough. You must be fair but firm. And they firmly resisted the temptation to give higher education to more than a handful out of 20 million Africans. Nearly 100,000 Belgians monopolized most skilled jobs in the state. Neither white settlers nor black subjects had political rights. The key was not to let Africans be contaminated by dangerous ideas from Europe. (The story was told of a Congolese seaman who had jumped ship in Europe; the Belgians then forbade him to return home for the rest of his life.) The handful of Congolese allowed higher education were prevented from studying abroad.

But by 1959 the wind of change was blowing a gale from the west. It carried the germs of African nationalism, spread by Nkrumah and the pan-Africanists – Western ideals of the rights of man and the liberty of nations. There was no way Belgium could seal off the Congo from this wind. In 1959, after riots in Leopoldville, the Belgians suddenly lost their nerve. The prospect of an Algerian-type rebellion appalled them. They announced a date for a general election, to be followed by independence within eighteen months.

Unprepared for party politics, the country split along ethnic and regional fault lines. When the Belgians scuttled out of the Congo in July 1960, they had left the country well prepared for civil war and anarchy. The prospect of their departure from Ruanda-Urundi, though delayed for two years, had the same disastrous effect.

By 1968 the British had set free the last impoverished scraps of their empire south of the Zambezi: Basutoland (Lesotho), Bechuanaland (Botswana) and Swaziland. The Scramble out of Africa was complete, except for Portugal, the first European nation to go in. Portugal was now trapped up to the neck in Angola, Mozambique and Guiné. It was her policy, she claimed, to assimilate these ancient possessions. She had certainly exploited them systematically. After the Belgian Congo collapsed, Angola caught the prevailing fever, and soon ferocious guerrilla wars broke out in all three territories.

Unfortunately the Cold War only complicated, and perhaps prolonged, the conflict. At first America offered support to the nationalists in Angola, but backed down when Portugal threatened to leave NATO and take the Azores base with them. The nationalists turned to Russia and China for money and weapons, and to Cuba for experts of various kinds.

The three guerrilla wars were fought to a stalemate in Africa. But in Portugal people could no longer bear the strain, which was costing the government half of all its revenue. An army coup in 1974 disposed of the Portuguese dictatorship, and next year a new government liquidated the whole African empire. In effect the Portuguese colonies had liberated Portugal. And not merely Portugal. Once the Angolan and Mozambique wars were over, the bush war to free Rhodesia could begin. Which brings us back to that anachronistic ceremony on 18 April 1980, when Lord Soames watched the Union Jack slither down the flagpole to be replaced by the red, black, green and gold flag of Zimbabwe.

*　　　*　　　*

In the last ten years, Zimbabwe has continued to confound the croakers. Despite the inner strains of the Zanu-Zapu, Shona-Ndebele coalition, the links forged in the bush war have held. Disciplined by adversity, in prison or exile, the rulers of the new state have handled their minorities, white and black, with unpredicted restraint.

Most important, their statesmanship has helped break the deadlock in the struggle against the last bastion of white supremacy, South Africa. True, by themselves the 8 million Africans in Zimbabwe could do nothing to help their 24 million brother Africans to the south. But in 1988 came global warming – of the healthiest kind. The Cold War was over. With the end to the rivalry between the Super-Powers in Africa, everything began to fall into place.

In March 1990 Namibia became independent, the forty-seventh African colony to win its freedom. America and Russia had insisted that South Africa should disgorge Namibia, the ex-German mandate of South-West Africa given it by the League.

In South Africa itself political progress is astonishing. Despite a bloody feud between the Inkatha of the Zulus and the African National Congress, there is euphoria among the blacks. The dark age of apartheid is ending. The whites rub their eyes. The unthinkable is becoming unavoidable.

If only there was equally good news for the rest of the continent.

In 1963 the Organization of African Unity was formed as a bridge between the new African states. The members then took a sensible decision: to forgo the dream of unity, and to respect the divisive frontiers created by the Scramble. There is no doubt that this decision has helped to keep the peace between African states, protecting the weak from the strong.

Yet chaos there was in plenty. Twelve of the forty-seven new African states (including the Congo, Nigeria, Sudan and Ethiopia, that is, *all* the biggest states except Egypt and Algeria) have been crippled since independence by civil war. There have been forty military coups in the last thirty years, many of them involving the murder or execution of the head of state. In Uganda, a tenth of the population have been murdered in two successive reigns of terror.

Even the more civilized regimes have imposed one-party rule, abused human rights and suppressed civil liberties. Many governments are brazenly corrupt as well as absurdly inefficient. Poverty remains the common bond of too many African states, wealth of too many African rulers. The income per head in Zaire (Congo) is less than $200 a year. Its autocratic leader, President Mobutu, is said to be the fifth richest man in the world. He has certainly bled the Congo of its wealth far more efficiently than King Leopold.

By contrast with the uneven benefits that decolonization has brought Africa, it has well suited the interests of Europe. Missionaries have continued to offer Christianity and civilization to the needy. White businessmen have continued to make their fortunes in Africa. In the last thirty years, Africa's imports from the rest of the world have risen ten times. Lugard was right. In the post-colonial era, he predicted, Britain would still be Nigeria's best customer. Indeed, his forecast could have been applied to all the ex-imperial powers. Trade preceded the flag and has outlasted it. Giant European and North American companies continue to dominate the economies of fledgling African states. The new word for this is neo-colonialism. It is much the same as informal empire: the invisible empire of trade and influence that had preceded the Scramble.

Yet how many Africans would wish to turn the clock back to the 1880s? The steamers and airlines of the world now bring material benefits to the forty-seven new states of the continent on a scale undreamt of a century ago. Best of all, Europe has given Africa the aspirations for freedom and human dignity, the humanitarian ideals of Livingstone, even if Europe itself was seldom able to live up to them.

Chronology Pre-1870

Egypt, Sudan and N. Africa	Western Africa	Central Africa	Eastern Africa	Southern Africa	Europe and Rest of the World
1798 Napoleon takes Egypt, but French evacuate troops after British victory at Alexandria (1801)	1787 British settlers, including freed slaves, establish colony at Sierra Leone	1853–6 Livingstone's second expedition; crossing of Africa and discovery of Victoria Falls	1858–9 Burton and Speke discover Lake Tanganyika. Speke discovers Lake Victoria	1795–1803 British occupation of Cape Colony, captured from the Dutch East India Company	1807 Slave trade abolished throughout British Empire
1805–47 Muhammad Ali master of Egypt	1816 Gambia re-occupied by British after French withdrawal		1858–61 Livingstone's third expedition: discovery of Lake Nyasa	1806 Second British occupation begins	1834 Slavery abolished thoughout British Empire
1820–2 Muhammad Ali's troops conquer Sudan, in search of slaves and gold	1820 Al Haj Umar leaves Senegal to French		1860–3 Speke and Grant explore Lake Victoria and identify it as main source of White Nile	1814 British rule confirmed by Treaty of Paris	1848 Slavery abolished throughout French colonies
1823 Khartoum founded	1861 US recognises Liberia, founded for free slaves		1864 Baker discovers Lake Albert	1820 British settlers land in E. Cape	1865 Accession of Leopold II, King of the Belgians
1830 French capture Algiers	1861 British occupy Lagos		1866 Turkey grants Suakin and Massawa to Egypt	1820–34 The Mfecane (crushing) establishes Zulu kingdom as the leading African power in SA	1867 Britain gives Canada dominion status
1848–54 Abbas I Khedive of Egypt	1862 Al Haj Umar conquers Segu		1867–8 British expedition under Napier to rescue hostages taken by Ethiopian Emperor Theodore	1835 Beginning of Great Trek across Orange and Vaal rivers	1868 (29 Feb–2 Dec) Disraeli's first ministry
1854–63 Said Khedive of Egypt	1863 French declare protectorate over Porto Novo, on coast of Dahomey		1868 (April 11–13): Napier captures Magdala. Theodore commits suicide	1838 Dingane and Zulus kill Piet Retief and Voortrekkers in Natal	1868–74 Gladstone's first ministry
1854 Said grants Suez canal concession to Ferdinand de Lesseps	1864 Al Haj Umar killed at siege of Hamdallahi, succeeded by Sultan Ahmadu			1838 (16 Dec) Boers beat Dingane at Battle of Blood River	
1863–79 Ismael Khedive of Egypt	1866 French acquire posts on Guinea coast			1842 British take Natal (annexed 1845)	
1869 Inauguration of Suez Canal	1868 French protectorate treaties on Ivory Coast			1849–50 Livingstone's first expedition and discovery of Lake Ngami	independence of Orange Free State
				1852 Sand River Convention confirms Transvaal's independence	1867 Diamonds discovered at Hopetown, Cape Colony
				1854 Bloemfontein Convention confirms	1868 Britain annexes Basutoland at request of King Moshweshwe

1870–1879

Egypt, the Sudan and N. Africa	Western Africa	Central Africa	Eastern Africa	Southern Africa	Europe and Rest of the World
1871–3 Baker extends Egyptian power in Equatoria and negotiates with Kabaka Mtesa of Buganda	1874 British declare Gold Coast, transferred from Dutch control in 1868, a British colony 1874 British defeat Ashanti. Wolseley enters Kumasi (4 Feb) 1879 George Goldie founds United Africa Co. (later National Africa Co.)	1871 Livingstone discovers river Lualaba, believing it flows from the lost source of White Nile 1871 (10 Nov) Stanley meets Livingstone at Ujiji and re-supplies him	1870 Italian company takes over Assab on Red Sea 1872 Ras Kassa of Tigre crowned as Emperor Yohannes IV of Ethiopia 1873 Bartle Frere and John Kirk, consul at Zanzibar, persuade Sultan to abolish slave trade	1870 Lobengula succeeds Mzilikazi as King of Ndebele 1870 Diamond rush to Griqualand West 1871 Kimberley founded	1874 (18 April) Livingstone buried in Westminster Abbey 1874–80 Disraeli's second Ministry 1875 (Nov) Disraeli buys Khedive Ismael's 44 per cent holding of Suez Canal shares for Britain
1874–6 Gordon succeeds Baker as Governor of Equatoria and pushes Egyptian empire within sixty miles of Lake Victoria 1876–8 Egypt going bankrupt. 'Dual Control' of British and French controllers to supervise revenue		1873 (1 May) Livingstone dies at Chitambo's village, Ilala 1875 (6 Nov) Cameron reaches coast of Angola after crossing Africa	1875 (16 Nov) Yohannes defeats Egyptians at B. of Gundet 1876 (7 Mar) Yohannes wins decisive victory at B. of Gura 1877–8 British missionaries establish bases north and south of Lake Victoria	1871 (17 Oct) Britain annexes Griqualand West to Cape Colony despite protests of Orange Free State 1872 Britain gives Cape Colony responsible government 1873–5 Langalibalele affair and trial	1876 Abortive London conference on S A Federation 1876 (12–14 Sept) Leopold II sponsors geographical conference in Brussels 1876–7 Leopold founds International African Association
1878–9 Gordon's war against slavers when Governor General of Sudan 1879 (18 Feb) Nubar Pasha and Rivers Wilson mobbed in Cairo. Ismael sacks Nubar Pasha. (April) Ismael sacks Rivers Wilson: coup against Powers (June 25) At request of European Powers, Sultan deposes Khedive Ismael. Tewfik succeeds		1875 Stanley explores Buganda, and sends appeal for British missionaries 1875–8 Brazza explores river Ogowe and river Alima 1877 (17 Oct) Stanley reaches Boma after crossing Africa and discovering course of Congo 1879 (4 Aug) Stanley begins to open up Congo for Leopold	1879 Isandlwana but survive attack on Rorkes Drift (4 July) British win decisive victory over Zulus at Ulundi (28 Aug) Cetshwayo captured 1879 (28 Nov) Wolseley crushes Pedi and captures Sekhukhene	1876 Pedi war 1877–80 Frere bankrupts Transvaal 1877 (12 Mar) Britain annexes Walvis Bay to Cape Colony 1877 (12 April) Shepstone annexes Transvaal for Britain, despite Boer protests 1877–8 Frontier War with Gcalekas and Ngqikas 1878 (11 Dec) Frere sends ultimatum to Cetshwayo and Zulus 1879 (12 Jan) Outbreak of Zulu War (22 Jan) British beaten by Zulus at	1878 (13 June–13 July) Berlin Congress. Bismarck offers France the Tunisian 'pear' 1878–9 Leopold forms Comité d'Études du Haut Congo and enrols Stanley for five years' service 1879 Jules Grévy President of France (till 1887) 1879 (Nov) Gladstone denounces imperialism in Midlothian speeches

Egypt, Sudan and N. Africa	Western Africa	Central Africa	Eastern Africa	Southern Africa	Europe and Rest of the World
1881 (April) French army under Gen. Bréart invade Tunisia from Algeria (12 May) Treaty of Bardo by which French impose protectorate on Bey of Tunis (19 June) Muhammad Ahmad proclaims himself Mahdi in the Sudan (9 Sept) Nationalist coup in Egypt led by Arabi Pasha 1881 (June–July) Risings in south Tunisia 1882 (Jan) Arabi Pasha made War Minister. Anglo-French note sent to Khedive (10–12 June) Riots in Alexandria kill fifty Europeans. (11 July) British fleet bombards Alexandria. (13, 15 Sept) Wolseley's army defeats Arabi at Tel el-Kebir and occupies Cairo	1880 Gallieni negotiates Treaty of Nango with Ahmadu, Sultan of Tukolors (not ratified) 1880 Cameroon 'kings' appeal for British protection	1880 (10 Sep) Brazza signs treaty with King Makoko and founds Brazzaville (21 Nov) Brazza confronts Stanley on the Congo 1881–2 Stanley signs treaties with Congo chiefs and founds Leopoldville opposite Brazzaville 1882 (April) Stanley launches En Avant on Upper Congo 1882–3 Stanley and Brazza return to Congo with new expeditions	1881 French occupy Obock in Somaliland (acquired 1862) 1882 Italian government take over Assab	1880 (8–15 Dec) Transvaal Boers, under triumvirate led by Kruger, meet at Paardekraal and decide to hoist flag of republic and restore Transvaal's independence (20 Dec) Boers ambush 94th Regiment at Bronkhorst Spruit. British garrisons besieged in Transvaal 1881 Boers invade Natal and repulse Colley's relief column at Laing's Nek (28 Jan), Ingogo (7 Feb) and Majuba (27 Feb). Colley killed. Armistice and negotiated peace follow (3 Aug) Pretoria Convention. Britain restores independence to Transvaal subject to British 'suzerainty'	1880 (April) End of Disraeli's (Beaconsfield's) second and last Ministry. Start of Gladstone's second ministry (till 1885) (23 Sept) Start of Jules Ferry's first ministry 1881 Tunisian débâcle precipitates fall of Jules Ferry (5 Nov), succeeded by Gambetta (till Jan 1882) 1882 (Jan) Freycinet's ministry begins 1882 (6 May) Murders in Phoenix Park, Dublin 1882 (20 May) Triple Alliance (Germany, Austria, Italy) 1882 Egyptian débâcle precipitates fall of Freycinet 1882 Gladstone's government rejects appeal by Cameroon 'kings' 1882 (2 June) Brazza given hero's welcome on return to Paris (19 Oct) meets Stanley at Continental hotel, Paris (Nov) French Assembly ratifies Makoko Treaty

1883–1884

Egypt, Sudan and N. Africa	Western Africa	Central Africa	Eastern Africa	Southern Africa	Europe and Rest of the World
1883 (5 Nov) Mahdi annihilates Hicks Pasha and 10,000 Egyptian soldiers at B. of El Obeid (Shaykan) and seizes Kordofan	1883 (7 Feb) Borgnis-Desbordes lays foundation of fort at Bamako, first French foothold on Upper Niger		1884 (Nov and Dec) Carl Peters signs first treaties with chiefs on mainland opposite Zanzibar	1883 (16 April) After abolition of triumvirate, Kruger elected President of Transvaal for first time	1883 (21 Feb) Start of Ferry's second ministry (till 21 Mar 1885)
1884 (18 Feb) Gordon reaches Khartoum with orders to evacuate garrison.	(April) French repulse attack on Bamako fort by Fabou, brother of Samori, Malinka warlord		(Dec) Death of King Mtesa, Kabaka of Buganda. Mwanga, his erratic young son, succeeds	1884 (7 Aug) German protectorate declared over Angra Pequena. (Feb) Cetshwayo expelled from Zululand, then	1884 (26 May) Anglo-Portuguese treaty shuts mouth of Congo to Leopold and French. Treaty withdrawn after international protests
(12 Mar) Siege begins (Sept) Wolseley leaves Cairo with expedition to rescue Gordon and garrison of Khartoum	1883 French sign treaty with King Tofa re-establishing protectorate at Porto Novo adjoining Dahomey.			(May) Dinizulu, his son, crowned as king	1884 (22 April) USA formally recognises Leopold's Congo. French sign pre-emption treaty with Leopold
	Mattei fails to sign treaty for France with Brass chiefs but establishes factory at Nupe after help-ng Emir crush revolt			1884 (28 Aug) London Convention on Transvaal omits British suzerainty which had limited Transvaal independence	(July–Aug) Abortive London conference on Egyptian finance. Jules Ferry and Bismarck continue to frustrate British plans
	1884 (June) Hewett begins treaty-making trip to Oil Rivers			(Dec) To block Transvaal's advance to the sea, Britain annexes St Lucia Bay.	1884 (May) Gladstone's cabinet sends Consul Hewett to sign treaties with W. African chiefs
	1884 Nachtigal sent by Bismarck hoists German flag over Togo (5 July) and over Cameroon (14 July)				(June–July) British Protectorate over the Niger and Oil Rivers.
					(15 Nov) Berlin conference on W. Africa and Congo. With Bismarck's help, Leopold wins recognition of his claims to Congo

Egypt, Sudan and N. Africa	Western Africa	Central Africa	Eastern Africa	Southern Africa	Europe and Rest of the World
1885 (17 Jan) B. of Abu Klea (26 Jan) Mahdi takes Khartoum and massacres garrison including Gordon. (22 June) Death of Mahdi, succeeded by the Khalifa. Spain claims territory at Rio de Oro	1886 British gunboats mount punitive expedition against Brass villages along Niger after attacks on ships of Royal Niger Co.	1886 (Aug) Arab slave-traders attack Congo Free State garrison post at Stanley Falls	1885 (Feb) Egyptians evacuate Massawa and Italians take over. (7 Aug) German warships demonstrate at Zanzibar and force Sultan to accept loss of mainland empire (Nov) Boundary commission meets to decide frontier between German and British 'spheres'. (Nov) Bishop Hannington murdered at Buganda on orders of Mwanga. British occupy Berbera and Zeila 1886 (June) Christian converts, Protestant and Catholic, martyred in Buganda 1886 Junker reaches Mackay with SOS from Emin Pasha (Nov) Anglo-German agreement on 'spheres'	1886 (Sept) Gold rush to Transvaal begins. Johannesburg founded	1885 (17 Feb) Bismarck declares German protectorate over part of E. Africa to be administered by new charter company founded by Carl Peters (26 Feb) Conclusion of Berlin Conference with General Act of Berlin signed by the powers, including International Association. (31 Mar) Britain proclaims protectorate over Bechuanaland (April) Leopold proclaimed sovereign of Congo Free State (June) Humiliated by failure to save Gordon, Gladstone's government resigns. Salisbury's first ministry begins 1886 (Jan) Gladstone returns to power on a Home Rule ticket (to July) Goldie wins charter for Royal Niger Company (July) Defeated by Liberal split on Home Rule, Gladstone resigns. Salisbury's second ministry (till August 1892)

Egypt, Sudan and N. Africa	Western Africa	Central Africa	Eastern Africa	Southern Africa	Europe and Rest of the World
1887 Abortive convention with Turkey by which Britain made conditional agreement to withdraw from Egypt 1889 (May) Stanley and Emin leave Equatoria	1887 British deport King Jaja from Opobo for challenging monopoly exercised by Royal Niger Company 1889 (10 Jan) France declares protectorate over Ivory Coast	1887 (Feb) Stanley, sponsored by both Leopold and Mackinnon, leaves Zanzibar en route for river Congo to 'rescue' Emin Pasha 1888 (29 April) Stanley meets Emin Pasha at Lake Albert	1887 Mahdists attack Emperor Yohannes and burn Gondar. Yohannes's rival, King Menelik of Shoa, deposes Sultan of Harar and extends his kingdom further into Galla country 1888–9 Abushiri rebellion in German East Africa. French transfer Red Sea post from Obock to Jibouti. IBEA lease coastal strip from Sultan of Zanzibar and begin stations on mainland 1889 (12 Mar) Emperor Yohannes killed by Mahdists at B. of Metema (Gallabat). Menelik proclaims himself Emperor with Italian backing (2 May) Menelik signs Treaty of Wichale with Italians (6 Sept) Kabaka Mwanga deposed in Civil War (Dec) Stanley and Emin reach coast at Bagamoyo (Oct–Dec) Carl Peters eludes coastal blockade, crushes Masai, reaches Uganda (Feb 1890)	1887 British annex Zululand (to Natal 1897) 1888 Portuguese refuse transit for arms needed by British missionaries fighting slavers on Lake Nyasa. Portuguese advance into interior. Rhodes and Beit amalgamate diamond mines at Kimberley and form De Beers Consolidated (Oct) Rhodes obtains Rudd Concession from Lobengula giving him exclusive mining rights in Mashonaland and Matabeleland (29 Oct) Salisbury gives royal charter to Rhodes's BSA Company	1887 Sadi-Carnot succeeds Grévy as President (till 1894) (26 May) Salisbury gives royal charter to Mackinnon's IBEA Company 1888 Pope Leo XIII orders Cardinal Lavigerie to launch crusade against slavery. (15 June) Accession of Kaiser Wilhelm II 1889 Britain proclaims protectorate over Shire districts (and all Nyasaland in 1891)

Egypt, Sudan and N. Africa	Western Africa	Central Africa	Eastern Africa	Southern Africa	Europe and Rest of the World
	1890–1 Archinard captures Segu and other Tukolor towns. Bambara revolt 1890 (5 Aug) Anglo-French declaration on W. Africa, giving French territory from Mediterranean to Bight of Guinea, but securing N. frontier of Nigeria for Britain. Archinard attacks Samori's HQ at Kan Kan 1891–2 Humbert drives him eastwards 1892 (Sept) French crush King Behanzin of Dahomey and (Dec) extend protectorate	1891–2 Harry Johnston, sent to Nyasaland as first Commissioner, crushes slavers. Congo State sends four expeditions to Katanga including Stairs's expedition which kills Msiri at Bunkeya. Attack by Van Kerckhoven on ivory merchants 1892 (May) Murder of Hodister and five other agents of Congo State 1892 (23 Nov) Dhanis's force repulses Sefu's attack, and drives thousands of Sefu's men into Lomani	1890 (spring) Carl Peters reaches Uganda and signs treaty with Kabaka Mwanga (Dec) Lugard, sent to Uganda by IBEA Co., forces Mwanga to accept new treaty 1891 Lugard marches to Equatoria and enlists Sudanese left there by Emin Pasha 1891 Britain recognises Italian protectorate over Ethiopia. But Menelik denounces Italian claims 1891–3 Wahehe revolt in German East Africa 1891 (25 Dec) Lugard informed that IBEA Co. intend to evacuate Uganda 1892 (24 Jan) Lugard, with Maxim gun, helps pro-British Protestants defeat pro-French Catholics in Buganda civil war. Mwanga flees 1892 (Dec) Cabinet send out Portal to report on future of Uganda	1890 (17 July) Rhodes becomes Prime Minister at the Cape (July–Sept) Rhodes's pioneer column advances into Mashonaland and founds Salisbury (13 Sep) 1891 British government agrees that BSA Co. should extend operations to Barotseland (later northern Rhodesia). Portugal, near bankruptcy, accepts Mozambique frontier imposed by Britain 1892 (Sept) First train from Cape reaches Johannesburg and (Dec) Pretoria	1890 (18 Mar) Bismarck, dismissed by Kaiser Wilhelm II, replaced as chancellor by Caprivi (24 May) Mackinnon 'treaty' with Leopold gives IBEA Co. a corridor for missing link from Cape to Cairo (1 July) Anglo-German convention gives Germany Heligoland in return for Zanzibar, Uganda and Witu (2 July) The Brussels Act. Conclusion of conference on slave trade (3 July) Publication of Leopold's will leaving Congo Free State to Belgium. Belgium advances interest-free loan 1892 Gladstone defeats Salisbury in general election and (18 Aug) begins fourth and final ministry 1892 (28 Sep) Rosebery persuades cabinet to agree to postpone evacuation of Uganda 1892 (Oct) Lugard returns to England and helps orchestrate public opinion for retention of Uganda

Egypt, Sudan and N. Africa	Western Africa	Central Africa	Eastern Africa	Southern Africa	Europe and Rest of the World
1894 Italians capture Kassala from Mahdists	1893 (10 Mar) Formal establishment of Guinea and Ivory Coast as French colonies (Dec) French defeat Tuaregs and capture Timbuctu 1893–4 Third Ashanti war 1894 (Oct–Nov) Lugard signs treaties with frontier chiefs. Decoeur makes counter-claims 1895 (1 Jan) Niger Company claim protectorate covers Nikki and Bussa 1895 (29 Jan) Brassmen attack Akassa and kill and eat captives (Feb) Brassmen's revolt suppressed by British navy	1893 (4 Mar) Dhanis captures Nyangwe, massacres Arabs and burns town 1893 (22 April) Capture of Kasongo 1894 (12 April) Secret Congo treaty confirms Leopold's access to Bahr al-Ghazal, gives Britain a Cape-to-Cairo line. But after France and Germany protest, Britain loses corridor and Leopold is only allowed Lado enclave	1893 (10 Mar) IBEA Co. gives up responsibility for Uganda. Portal recommends retaining it for Britain 1894 (18 June) Rosebery formally makes Uganda a British protectorate 1895 (25 Mar) Italians begin invasion of Ethiopia from Eritrea (July) With collapse of IBEA Co., Rosebery creates British East African Protectorate. Menelik repulses Baratieri's advance guard at Amba Alagi (8 Dec)	1893 (22 April) Kruger elected for third term as Transvaal President (12 May) Natal given responsible government (Oct) After Ndebele raid on Fort Victoria, Dr Jameson invades Matabeleland, defeats Lobengula's Impis and captures Bulawayo (4 Nov) 1894 (Jan) Lobengula dies in hiding (Sept) To connect Cape and Natal, Britain annexes Pondoland 1895 (June) To seal off Transvaal from sea, Britain annexes Tongoland (July) Kruger ends isolation of Transvaal by opening railway from Pretoria and Johannesburg to Delagoa Bay in Mozambique	1894 (3 Mar) After Lords block second Home Rule Bill, Gladstone resigns. Rosebery takes over as PM (24 June) President Sadi-Carnot stabbed to death. Succeeded by Casimir-Perier (Oct) Caprivi replaced by Prince Hohenlohe (Dec) Dreyfus condemned and sent to Devil's Island 1895 (21 June) On collapse of Rosebery's government, Salisbury begins third and final ministry. Chamberlain is Colonial Secretary 1895 Félix Faure succeeds Casimir-Perier as President (till 1899) (Dec 29) Dr Jameson launches the Raid from bases in Cape and Bechuanaland

Egypt, Sudan and N. Africa	Western Africa	Central Africa	Eastern Africa	Southern Africa	Europe and Rest of the World
1896 (21 Sept) Kitchener and Anglo-Egyptian army start reconquest of Sudan by taking Dongola 1897 (8 Aug) Kitchener advances to Abu Hamed 1898 (8 April) Kitchener crushes Mahmud and Mahdists at B. of Atbara (10 July) Marchand reaches Fashoda, signs treaty with Dinka *mek*, and hoists French tricolour (2 Sept) Kitchener annihilates Khalifa's army at B. of Omdurman and recaptures Khartoum (19 Sept) Kitchener takes gunboats down Nile to confront Marchand at Fashoda	1896 (18 Jan) Fourth Ashanti War. British take Kumasi and impose protectorate 1898 (April–May) Lugard and WAFF contest French claims on western frontier of Nigeria. British and French close to blows (14 June) Salisbury negotiates Anglo-French agreement on W. Africa and ends Niger crisis (29 Sep) French capture Samori and exile him to Gabon	1897 (Feb) Congo Free State column under Chaltin seize Lado base on Upper Nile (Feb) Dhanis's army mutinies at Ndirfi and extinguishes Leopold's hopes of taking over southern Sudan Marchand's column drags *Faidherbe* in sections over Nile–Congo watershed	1896 (1 Mar) Menelik crushes Baratieri's invasion force at B. of Adowa and captures 4,000 prisoners (26 Oct) Italian treaty with Ethiopia. Menelik forces Italy to recognise Ethiopian independence in exchange for Italian prisoners, but agrees to let Italy keep Eritrea 1897 (20 Mar) French treaty with Ethiopia. Delcassé hopes to use it as a base for advance on Nile but two French expeditions fail to reach Fashoda via Ethiopia (14 May) British treaty with Ethiopia; Britain concedes part of Somaliland but gets nothing in return (July–Aug) Mwanga tries to regain Ugandan throne but is forced to flee (Sept) Mutiny of Sudanese troops in Uganda cripples MacDonald's force	1896 (2 Jan) Jameson and 500 Rhodesian police surrender to Transvaal burghers at Doornkop (6 Jan) Rhodes, implicated in the Raid, forced to resign as Prime Minister of Cape Colony (24 Mar) Withdrawal of Rhodesian police triggers rising in Matabeleland (June) Shona rising follows (Oct) Rhodes helps negotiate surrender with Ndebele indunas 1897 (Aug) Sir Alfred Milner appointed High Commissioner 1898 (Feb) Kruger elected President of the Transvaal for fourth term	1896 (3 Jan) Kaiser's telegram to Kruger, congratulating him on his defeat of Jameson (12 Mar) Salisbury's government decide to seize opportunity provided by Italian defeat at Adowa by beginning re-conquest of Sudan (May) Collapse of Anglo-French talks on Niger (June) Marchand's expedition leaves France with orders to advance to Nile–Congo watershed and beyond 1897 Crucial telegrams withheld from London enquiry into Raid, so Joseph Chamberlain cleared of collusion with Rhodes and Beit 1898 (Aug) Colonel Henry admits forging documents in Dreyfus Affair, and second Dreyfus crisis splits France (18 Sept–3 Nov) Acute phase of Fashoda crisis. Brisson's government in Paris collapses, replaced by Dupuy's. Unable to face a naval
war with Britain, French government agreed to climb down and order Marchand to evacuate Fashoda					

1899–1902

Egypt, Sudan and N. Africa	Western Africa	Central Africa	Eastern Africa	Southern Africa	Europe and Rest of the World
1899 (Jan) British and Egyptian governments create condominium over Sudan. (24 Nov) Wingate kills Khalifa at Mahdists' last stand in Kordofan 1902 Menelik accepts Anglo-Egyptian treaty by which he abandons claim to Upper Nile 1902–3 Sultan of Morocco unable to check growing disorder	1899 (21 Mar) Anglo-French agreement excludes the French from Bahr al-Ghazal and Darfur but leaves them free hand further west. (9 Aug) Chamberlain negotiates buy-out of Goldie's Niger Co. and replacement by British protectorate 1900 (Mar–Nov) Rising in Ashanti suppressed and besieged British garrison relieved. (May) French seize oases south of Morocco, formerly controlled by Sultan 1901 British annex Ashanti to Gold Coast	1899 French grant concessions to international rubber companies in French Congo	1899 (June) Mwanga and Kabarega both captured and exiled to Seychelles (from Sept) British and Italian Somaliland raided by self-proclaimed Mahdi ('Mad Mullah')	1899 (24 Mar) Transvaal Uitlanders send Queen Victoria petition for British intervention to redress political and economic grievances. (31 May–5 June) Abortive negotiations at Bloemfontein between Milner and Kruger. (11 Oct) Outbreak of war on expiry of Kruger's ultimatum. (14–16 Oct) Boers begin siege of Kekewich and Rhodes at Kimberley, and Baden-Powell at Mafeking. (30 Oct) 'Mournful Monday'. Nicholson's Nek and B. of Ladysmith. (2 Nov) Start of siege of Ladysmith	

Egypt, Sudan and N. Africa	Western Africa	Central Africa	Eastern Africa	Southern Africa	Europe and Rest of the World
				1899 (23 Nov) Boers abandon raid southwards as British begin attempt to relieve Kimberley and Ladysmith. (10–15 Dec) Black Week. Gatacre's mishap at Stormberg. Methuen's repulse at Magersfontein, Buller's first reverse: Colenso 1900 (24 Jan) Buller's second reverse: Spion Kop (11 Feb) Roberts launches great flank march (15 Feb) French relieves Kimberley (27 Feb) Surrender of Cronje at Paardeberg (14–27 Feb) Buller finally relieves Ladysmith. (13 Mar) Roberts takes Bloemfontein (17 May) Mahon and Plumer relieve Mafeking. (28 May) Roberts annexes Orange Free State. (31 May) Roberts captures Johannesburg and (June 5) Pretoria	1899 (16 Feb) Death of President Faure. Succeeded by Loubet (till 1906) (Oct) Hohenlohe resigns German chancellorship. Replaced by Bülow. 1900 (Aug–Sept) Salisbury wins 'Khaki Election'. War divides liberals, consolidates Unionist majority

1899–1902 (continued)

Egypt, Sudan and N. Africa	Western Africa	Central Africa	Eastern Africa	Southern Africa	Europe and Rest of the World
			1901 (Dec) First train on Uganda railway reaches Lake Victoria from Mombasa and opens up country for development 1902 (Feb) French government agrees to subsidise Jibouti-Addis Ababa railway 1902 Land grant of 500 square miles in highlands near Nairobi starts large-scale white settlement	1900 (27 Aug) Roberts's and Buller's armies join hands and win apparently decisive victory at Bergendal (19 Oct) Kruger sails for Europe (25 Oct) Annexation of Transvaal proclaimed at Pretoria (29 Nov) Kitchener succeeds Roberts as c in c but Boers launch guerrilla war 1901 (10–28 Feb) De Wet invades Cape Colony. (3 Sept) Smuts invades Cape Colony (26 Sept) Botha attacks forts in Natal 1902 (Feb–Nov) Successful anti-guerrilla drives in Orange River Colony and Transvaal. (6 May) Zulus attack Boers at Holkrantz (31 May) Final meeting at Vereeniging. Peace signed at Pretoria	1901 Belgium decides not to exercise option to take over Congo from Leopold. (22 Jan) Death of Queen Victoria. Edward VII succeeds 1902 (15 May) Protest meeting in Mansion House, London against Congo atrocities 1902 (July) Salisbury retires and Balfour takes over as Prime Minister

1903–1906

Egypt, Sudan and N. Africa	Western Africa	Central Africa	Eastern Africa	Southern Africa	Europe and Rest of the World
1905 (31 May) Offended by the *Entente*, Kaiser Wilhelm II lands at Tangier and precipitates first Moroccan crisis 1906 (Jan–April) Germans attend Algeciras conference, ending Moroccan crisis	1903 Lugard makes British masters of N. Nigeria by conquering Kano (3 Feb) and Sokoto (15 Mar) 1906 Lugard takes violent measures to put down Satiru rebellion in Sokoto	1903 (June) House of Commons debate Congo atrocities and government agrees to confer with signatories of Berlin Act to 'abate evils'. Consul Casement ordered to investigate situation in Congo 1904 (Feb) Casement report exposes atrocities by Congo state authorities 1905 (Nov) Janssens's report confirms Morel's claim that exploitation is systematic 1905 (29 April) Brazza arrives in Brazzaville to investigate reports of atrocities by officials in French Congo 1905 (Aug) French officials Toqué and Gaud sentenced to five years for atrocities 1906 (May) Leopold finally abandons claims to Bahr al-Ghazal 1906 (14 Sept) Brazza dies at Dakar. (Feb 1907) His report suppressed	1905 (July) Maji-Maji rising begins with attacks in Matumbi, then spreads to isolated German garrisons in Ungindo, Kichi and most of German East Africa south of Dar-es-Salaam. Murder of Bishop Spiss, two priests and two nuns (Aug 30) Germans repulse attack on Mahenge. Risings not coordinated. Governor Götzen suppresses rebellion by starving out rebels	1904 (12 Jan) Herero rising begins in German South-West Africa with attack on main garrisons 1904 Trotha issues 'extermination order' condemning 20,000 Herero – men, women and children – to death in the Omaheke sandveld (3 Oct) Outbreak of Nama rebellion 1905 (Oct) Hendrik Witbooi dies. End of Nama rebellion 1905–6 Boer ex-guerrillas agitate for restoration of self-government in Transvaal and the Orange Free State 1906 (10 Feb) Martial law declared in Zululand. Ruthless suppression of Zulu rebellion triggered by poll tax 1906 (Dec) Campbell-Bannerman and Liberals 'magnanimously' give Transvaal responsible government	1904 (8 April) *Entente Cordiale* between Britain and France ends twenty years' bitter rivalry; gives Britain free hand in Egypt and France free hand in Morocco 1906 Dernburg appointed Minister for Colonies. (Dec) Reichstag dissolved by Bülow. 'Hottentot Election' weakens Socialists (5 Dec) Balfour's government resigns. Campbell-Bannerman wins landslide victory for Liberals, with slogan 'no Chinese slavery for South Africa' 1906 (3 June) Leopold's 'royal letter' defying the Powers to take the Congo from him. President Loubet succeeded by Armand Fallières. (11 Dec) President Roosevelt announces us will help Britain persuade Belgium to take over Congo

1907–1912

Egypt, Sudan and N. Africa	Western Africa	Central Africa	Eastern Africa	Southern Africa	Europe and Rest of the World
1911 (2 May) The French enter Fez. The Italians invade Tripoli (1 July) German gunboat *Panther* reaches Agadir, precipitates second Moroccan crisis. (4 Nov) Franco-German Convention by which Germany gives France a free hand in Morocco in return for part of French Congo 1912 (30 Mar) Formal French protectorate imposed on Morocco, with Spanish Sahara for Spain. Italians invade Cyrenaica. Start of Senussi war (till 1931)	1910 Railway to Kano completed		1907–8 Churchill's E. African tour. Emperor Menelik paralysed by stroke 1908 Railway to Blantyre opened	1907 Campbell-Bannerman gives self-government to Orange River Colony 1908–9 (12 Oct–Feb) Constitutional Convention in Durban, then Cape Town 1909 (Sept) British Parliament passes South Africa Act, despite protests by Schreiner and other champions of African political rights 1910 (31 May) Union of South Africa (15 Sept) Boers and Afrikaners gain control in Union's first general election. Botha first Prime Minister	1907 (April) Leopold's obstruction over Congo leads to fall of Smet de Naeyer's government; de Trooz succeeds. (Dec) International outcry over too generous terms for Leopold when Congo transferred to Belgium. Death of de Trooz. Schollaert succeeds 1908 (8 April) Asquith succeeds Campbell-Bannerman as British PM 1908 (20 Oct) Annexation of Congo by Belgium officially gazetted 1909 Belgium publishes plan for Congo reform 1909 (14 July) Bülow resigns from German chancellorship 1909 (14 Dec) Death of Leopold II

Sources

Abbreviations

APR   Archives du Palais Royal, Brussels
BD   British Documents on the origins of the War, 1898–1918 (see Bibliography under Gooch and Temperley)
BL   British Library, Additional Manuscripts, London
C, Cd   Paper printed by command of Parliament
CO   Colonial Office papers in Public Record Office
DDF   Documents Diplomatiques Français (see Bibliography)
FO   Foreign Office papers in Public Record Office
PRO   Public Record Office, London
QVL   *Queen Victoria's Letters* (see Bibliography)
RHL   Rhodes House Library, Oxford
SOAS   School of Oriental and African Studies, London
JAH   *Journal of African History*
SPG   Society for the Propagation of the Gospel
NLI   National Library of Ireland
NLS   National Library of Scotland

Unpublished Sources

In United Kingdom
Official papers in:
    FO series (especially FO 84)
    CO series
Private papers of:
    Carnarvon, PRO
    Chamberlain, Birmingham University
    Dilke, BL
    Gladstone, BL
    Granville, BL
    Grant, NLS
    Mackinnon, SOAS
    Milner, Bodleian, Oxford
    Morel, London School of Economics and Political Science
    Rawlinson, Royal Asiatic Society, London
    Salisbury, Hatfield, Herts
    Stanley, BL (microfilm)
    Waller, RHL
    Wolseley, Hove Public Library, Sussex

SOURCES

In Ireland:
    Casement, NLI
In Brussels:
    APR, Fonds Congo
    Van Eetvelde, Archives Générales du Royaume
    Banning, as above
    Lambermont, Archives de la Ministère des Affaires Etrangères
    Strauch, as above and in the Musée de la Dynastie
In Paris:
    Archives de la Ministère des Affaires Etrangères

Published Sources

Newspapers and periodicals:
    Annual Register
    Black and White Budget
    Century Magazine
    Contemporary Review
    Correspondent
    Daily News
    Daily Telegraph
    Ethiopian Observer
    Figaro
    Globe
    Graphic
    L'Intransigent
    Illustrated London News
    Manchester Guardian
    Review of Reviews
    Standard
    The Times
    Westminster Gazette

Select Bibliography

Note: all books were published in London unless otherwise stated

Ajayi, J. F. A. and Crowder, M. (eds.), *History of West Africa*, II, 1974
Allen, B. M., *Gordon and the Sudan*, 1931
Amery, L. S. (ed.), *The Times History of the War in South Africa*, (7 vols.), 1900–1909
Andrew, C. M., *Théophile Delcassé and the making of the Entente Cordiale*, 1968
Anstey, R., *Britain and the Congo in the Nineteenth Century*, Oxford, 1962
Arnot, F., *Bihé and Garenganze* etc., 1893
Ascherson, N., *The King Incorporated: Leopold the Second in the Age of Trusts*, 1963
Ashe, Robert, *Two Kings of Uganda*, 1889
    Chronicles of Uganda, 1894
Autin, Jean, *Pierre Savorgnan de Brazza*, Paris, 1985
Axelson, E., *Portugal and the Scramble for Africa*, Johannesburg, 1967
Aydelotte, W. O., *Bismark and British Colonial Policy* etc., Philadelphia, 1937
Banning, E., *Mémoires Politiques et Diplomatiques*, Paris/Brussels, 1927
Baratier, A. F. A., *Souvenirs de la Mission Marchand:* (vol. 3) *Fashoda*, Paris, 1941
Baratieri, Oreste, *Mémoires d'Afrique*, (1892–96), Paris, 1899
Baring, E. (Earl of Cromer), *Modern Egypt*, (2 vols.), 1908
Bates, Darrell, *The Fashoda Incident 1898: Encounter on the Nile*, Oxford, 1984
Battaglia, R., *La Prima Guerra d'Africa*, Turin, 1958
Bayol, J., *Voyage en Senegambia*, Paris, 1888
Berkeley, George, *The Campaign of Adowa and the Rise of Menelik*, 1902
    Biographie Coloniale Belge, (6 vols.), Brussels, 1948–67
Blake, R., *Disraeli*, 1966
Bley, Helmut, *South-West Africa under German Rule 1894–1914*, (tr H. Ridley), 1971
Blunt, W. S., *My Diaries. Being a Personal Narrative of Events 1888–1914*, (2 vols.), 1919–20
Bontinck, *Aux origines de L'Etat Independant du Congo* etc., Louvain, 1966
Bovill, E. W., *The Golden Trade of the Moors* (2nd edn), revised R. Hallett, 1968
Brazza, Pierre Savorgnan de, *Conférences et Lettres*, Paris, 1887
Bridgman, J. M., *The Revolt of the Hereros*, Berkeley, 1981
Broadley, A. M., *The Last Punic War. Tunis. Past and Present*, etc., (2 vols.), 1882
Brunschwig, Henri, *Brazza Explorateur*, Paris, 1972
    Mythes et réalités de l'impérialisme colonial français, Paris, 1960. English trans: *French colonialism: myths and realities*, London, 1966
    L'Avènement de l'Afrique Noire du XIX Siècle à Nos Jours, Paris, 1963
    'Les Cahiers de Brazza' in *Les Traites Makoko, 1880–2, Cahiers d'Etudes Africaines* (1966)
Bülow, Prince, *Memoirs of Prince von Bülow* (4 vols.), 1931–2
Butler, J. (ed.), *Boston University Papers on African History*, (vol. 1), Boston, 1964
    The Liberal Party and the Jameson Raid, Oxford, 1968
Butler, Sir W. F., *The Campaign of the Cataracts*, etc., 1887
    The Life of Sir George Pomeroy-Colley, etc., 1899
    Sir William Butler: An Autobiography (ed.), Eileen Butler, 1911
Cameron, V. L., *Across Africa*, (2 vols.), 1877
Carter, T., *A Narrative of The Boer War*, 1883
Casement, Roger, (ed.) P. Singleton-Gates and M. Girodias, *The Black Diaries: an Account of Roger Casement's Life and Times, with a Collection of his Diaries*, etc., New York, 1959
Cecil, Lady Gwendolen, *Life of Robert, Marquis of Salisbury*, (4 vols.), 1921–32
Ceulemans, P., *La Question Arabe et Le Congo, 1883–1893*, Brussels, 1959
Challaye, Félicien, *Le Congo Français*, Paris, 1909
Chambrun, Gen de, *Brazza*, Paris, 1930
Chavannes, Ch. de, *Les origines de l'AEF: le Congo Français. Ma collaboration avec Brazza, 1886–1894. Nos Relations jusqu'à sa mort*, 1905, Paris, 1937

Churchill, W. S., *The River War*, (2 vols.), 1899
  London to Ladysmith via Pretoria, 1900
  My African Journey, 1908
Clarke, S., *Invasion of Zululand 1879 Anglo-Zulu War Experiences of Arthur Harness*, etc., Johannesburg, 1979
  Zululand at War. The Conduct of the Anglo-Zulu War, Johannesburg, 1984
Cline, Catherine, E. D. Morel. *1873–1924: The Strategies of Protest*, Belfast, 1980
Colenso, F. E. and Durnford, E., *History of the Zulu War and its Origin*, 1880
Collins, R. O., *The Southern Sudan 1883–1898: a Struggle for Control*, New Haven, 1962.
  King Leopold, England and the Upper Nile, 1899–1909, New Haven and London, 1968.
Colvile, Sir H. E., *History of the Sudan Campaign* (3 vols.), War Office, 1889
Colvin, Ian, *The Life of Jameson*, (2 vols.), 1922
Comaroff, J. L. (ed.), *The Boer War Diary of Sol T. Plaatje, an African at Mafeking*, 1973
(*La*) *Conférence de Géographie de 1876. Recueil d'études*, ARSOM, Brussels, 1976
Conrad, Joseph, *Heart of Darkness*, 1902
Cookey, S. J. S., *Britain and the Congo Question, 1885–1913*, London, 1968
  King Ja Ja of the Niger Delta, Nok, 1974
Cornet, R. J., *Katanga: le Katanga avant les Belges*, (3rd edn.), Brussels, 1946
  La bataille du rail: la construction du chemin de fer de Matadi au Stanley Pool, Brussels, 1947; (4th edn.), 1958
  Maniema: la lutte contre les Arabes esclavagistes au Congo, Brussels, 1952
Coupland, Sir R., *Livingstone's Last Journey*, 1945
  The Exploitation of East Africa 1856–1890: The Slave Trade and the Scramble, 1939 (2nd edn.), 1968
Crawford, Dan, *Thinking Black*, etc., 1912
Crowder, M. (ed.), *West African Resistance*, 1971
Crowe, S. E., *The Berlin West Africa Conference 1884–1885*, 1942
Curtin, P., Feierman, S., Thompson, L. and Vansina, J., *African History*
Dawson, E. C., *James Hannington … First Bishop of East Equatorial Africa*, etc., 1887
Daye, P., *Leopold II*, Brussels, 1934
De Kiewiet, C. W., *The Imperial Factor in South Africa: A Study in Politics and Economics*, Cambridge, 1930
De Wet, Christiaan, *Three Years War*, 1902
Debenham, F., *The Way to Ilala: David Livingstone's Pilgrimage*, 1955
Delbeque, J., *Vie de Général Marchand*, Paris, 1936
Delcommune, A., *Vingt Années de Vie Africaine*, (2 vols.), Brussels, 1922
Dike, K. O., *Trade and Politics in the Niger Delta 1830–1885*, Oxford, 1956
Documents Diplomatiques Français, (1871–1914), First Series, Paris, 1929
Drechsler, H., *Let us die fighting: the Struggle of the Herero and Nama against German Imperialism, 1884–1915*, 1980
Dugdale, E. (ed.), *German Diplomatic Documents, 1871–1914*, (4 vols.), 1928–31
Duminy, A. and Ballard, C., *The Anglo-Zulu War: New Perspectives*, Pietermaritzburg, 1981
Duponchel, A., *Le Chemin de Fer Trans-Saharien*, etc., Montpellier, 1878
Durnford, E., *A Soldier's Life and Work in South Africa 1872 to 1879: A Memoir of the late Colonel A. W. Durnford*, 1882
Elton, G., *General Gordon*, 1954
Emerson, B., *Leopold II of the Belgians: King of Colonialism*, 1979
Emery, F., *The Red Soldier: Letters from the Zulu War, 1879*, 1977
Emily, Dr J. M., *Mission Marchand. Journal de Route du Dr J. Emily*, Paris, 1913
Fage, J. D., *A History of Africa*, 1978
Farwell, Byron, *The Great Boer War*, 1977
Fieldhouse, D. K., *Economics and Empire*, 1973
Flint, J. E., *Sir George Goldie and the Making of Nigeria*, London, 1960
  Cecil Rhodes, 1976
  (ed.) *The Cambridge History of Africa*, Vol. 5 from c. 1790 to c. 1870, Cambridge, 1976
Fox-Bourne, H. R., *Civilization in Congoland: a Story of International Wrong-doing*, London, 1903
Fraser, M. and Jeeves, A. (eds.), *All that glittered: Selected Correspondence of Lionel Phillips, 1890–1924*, Cape Town, 1977
Freycinet, Charles de, *Souvenirs, 1878–1833*. Paris, 1913,
Fripp and Hillier, V. W., (ed.), *Gold and the Gospel in Mashonaland*, Johannesburg, 1949

Gabre-Sellassie, Zewde, *Yohannes IV of Ethiopia*, Oxford, 1975

Galbraith, J. S., *Mackinnon and East Africa, 1878–1895*, etc., Cambridge, 1972

    Crown and Charter: The Early Years of the British South Africa Company, Berkeley, 1974

Gallieni, J. S. *Voyage au Soudan Français 1879–1881*, Paris, 1885

Ganiage, J., *L'expansion coloniale de la France, 1871–1914*, Paris, 1968

    Les origines du protectorat français en Tunisie (1861–1881) (2nd edn.), Tunis, 1968

Gann, L. H. and Duignan, P., *The Rulers of German Africa, 1884–1914*, Stanford, 1977

    The Rulers of Belgian Africa 1884–1914. Princeton

    The Rulers of British Africa 1870–1914, 1978

    (eds.), *Colonialism in Africa 1870–1960*, Cambridge, 1969–75: I, The History and Politics of Colonialism, 1870–1914 (1969); II, The History and Politics of Colonialism, 1914–1960 (1970 – reprinted 1982); III, Profiles of Change: African Society and Colonial Rule, ed. V. Turner (1971); IV, The Economics of Colonialism (1975); V, A Bibliographical Guide to Colonialism in Africa (1973).

    (eds.) *African Proconsuls: European Governors in Africa*, New York, 1978.

Gardiner, A. G., *The Life of Sir William Harcourt*, (2 vols.), 1923

Garvin, J. L. and Amery, Julian: *The Life of Joseph Chamberlain*, (6 vols.), 1932–69

Gessi, R., trans., *Seven years in the Soudan*, 1892.

Gifford, P. and Louis, W. R. (ed.), *Britain and Germany in Africa. Imperial Rivalry and Colonial Rule*, Yale, 1967.

    France and Britain in Africa: Imperial Rivalry and Colonial Rule, Yale, 1971

Glass, S., *The Matabele War*, 1968

Gleichen, Count, *With the Camel Corps up the Nile*, 1888

Gooch, G. P., and Temperley, H. W., *British Documents on the Origins of the War, 1898–1914*, 1926–38

Goodfellow, C. F., *Great Britain and South African Confederation 1870–1881*, Cape Town, 1966

Gordon, C. G.,*Colonel Gordon in Central Africa 1874–1879*, from original letters and documents (ed.) G. B. Hill, 1881

    Letters of General C. G. Gordon to His Sister, M. A. Gordon, 1888

    The Journals of Major-General C. G. Gordon CB at Khartoum, (ed. A. Egmont Hake), 1885

Gordon, R. E., *Shepstone: The Role of the Family in the History of South Africa 1820–1900*, Cape Town, 1966

Götzen, A. von, *Deutsch Ostafrika im Aufstand 1905–6*, Berlin, 1909

Gray, R., *A History of the Southern Sudan 1839–1889*, Oxford, 1961

Grenville, J. A. S., *Lord Salisbury and Foreign Policy*, 1964

Grosse Politik der Europaische Kabinette, etc., 1871–1914 (40 vols.), Berlin, 1922–7

Guebre-Selassie, *Chronique du Règne de Menelik II*, etc., (ed.) M. de Coppet, Paris, 1930–1

Guy, J., *The Heretic, A Study of the Life of John William Colenso 1814–1883*, Johannesburg, 1983

    The Destruction of the Zulu Kingdom, London, 1979

Gwassa, G. C. K. and Iliffe, J. (eds.), *Records of the Maji-Maji Rising*, Dar-es-Salaam, 1968

Gwynn, S. and Tuckwell, G., *The Life of the Rt. Hon. Sir Charles Dilke, Bart, MP*, (2 vols.), 1917

Haggard, Sir H., *The Days of My Life: An Autobiography*, (2 vols.), 1926

Hall, Richard, *Stanley: An Adventurer Explored*, 1974

Hamilton, Sir Edward, (ed.) D. W. R. Bahlman, *The Diary of Sir Edward Walter Hamilton*, (2 vols.), Oxford, 1972

Hamilton, Sir Ian, *Listening for the Drums*, 1970

Hancock, W. K. and Van der Poel, J. (ed.), *Selections from the Smuts Papers, 1886–1919*, (4 vols.), Cambridge, 1966

Hanotaux, G., *Histoire des colonies françaises et de l'expansion de la France*, etc., (6 vols.), Paris, 1929–33

    Fashoda, Paris, 1909

Hardinge, Sir A. H., *The Life of Henry Howard Molyneaux Herbert, Fourth Earl of Carnavon (1831–1890)*, (3 vols.), 1925

Hargreaves, J. (ed.), *France and West Africa: An Anthology of Historical Documents*, 1969

    Prelude to the Partition of West Africa, 1966

    West Africa Partitioned, I: The Loaded Pause 1885–89, 1974; II: *The Elephants and the Grass*, 1984

Harlow, V. and Chilver, E. M. (eds.), *History of East Africa*, vol. II. , Oxford

Harrison, J., *A. M. Mackay* etc., by his sister, 1896

Headlam, Cecil, (ed.), *The Milner Papers: South Africa 1897–1899*, 1931

Heggay, Alfred, *The African Policies of Gabriel Hanotaux 1894–1898*, University of Georgia, 1972

Hertslet, Sir E., *The Map of Africa by Treaty*, (3rd edn., 3 vols.), 1909
Hicks Beach, Lady Victoria, *Life of Sir Michael Hicks Beach*, etc., (2 vols.), 1932
Hill, R. L., *Egypt in the Sudan, 1820–1881*, 1959
Hinde, Sidney, *The Fall of the Congo Arabs*, 1897
Hird, Frank, *H. M. Stanley: The Authorised Life*, 1935
Hobson, J. A., *The War in South Africa, Its Causes and Effects*, 1900
Hole, H. M., *The Making of Rhodesia*, 1926
 Old Rhodesian Days, 1928
Holland, Bernard, *The Life of Spencer Compton Eighth Duke of Devonshire*, (2 vols.), 1911
Holstein, F. von, (eds.) N. Rich and M. Fischer, *The Holstein Papers*, Vol. 2 (*Diaries*), Cambridge, 1957
Holt, P. M., *The Mahdist State in the Sudan 1881–1898: A Study of its Origins, Development and Overthrow*, (1st edn.), 1958, Nairobi, 1979 p'k
Hopkins, A. G., *An Economic History of West Africa*, 1973
Howard, G., *Splendid Isolation*, 1967
Hyam, Ronald, *Elgin and Churchill at the Colonial Office 1905–1908: the Watershed of the Empire–Commonwealth*, 1968
Iliffe, J., *Tanganyika under German Rule 1905–1912*, Cambridge, 1969
 A Modern History of Tanganyika, Cambridge, 1979
Jackson, F. W. D. 'Isandhlwana 1879 – The Sources Re-examined', *Journal of the Society for Army Historical Research*, 43, 1965
James, Robert Rhodes, *Rosebery*, etc., 1963
Jameson, Mrs J. S.: *The Story of the Rear Column*, 1890
Jeal, T., *Livingstone*, 1973
Jephson, A. J., (eds.) Middleton, D. and Jephson, M., *The Diary of A. J. Mounteney Jephson*, etc., Cambridge, 1969
 Emin Pasha and the Rebellion at the Equator, 1890; reprinted New York, 1969
Johnston, A., *The Life and Letters of Sir Henry Johnston*, 1929
Johnston, Sir H., *The Story of my Life*, 1923
Jones, Roger, *The Rescue of Emin Pasha*, 1972
Jorissen, E. J., *Transvaalse Herinneringen 1876–1896*, Amsterdam, 1897
Kanya-Forstner, A. S., *The Conquest of the Western Sudan*, etc., Cambridge, 1969
Kennedy, A. L., *Salisbury 1830–1903: Portrait of a Statesman*, 1953
Keppel–Jones, A. M., *Rhodes and Rhodesia* etc., Montreal, 1983
Kingsley, Mary, *Travels in West Africa*, etc., (1st edn., 1897) 4th edn., 1982
Kruger, S. J. P., *The Memoirs of Paul Kruger*, etc., 1902
Laband, J. P. C. and Thompson, P. S., *Field Guide to the War in Zululand and the Defence of Natal 1879*, Pietermaritzburg, 1983
Landes, D. S., *Bankers and Pashas*, London, 1958
Langer, W. L., *European Alliances and Alignments 1871–1890*, (2nd edn.), New York, 1956
 The Diplomacy of Imperialism, (2nd edn.), New York, 1951
Lee, Sir S., *King Edward VII: A Biography*, (2 vols.), 1925–7
Lehmann, J. H., *All Sir Garnet: A life of Field Marshal Lord Wolseley*, 1964
 The First Boer War, 1972
Leopold II et Beernaert d'après leur correspondance inédite de 1884 à 1894, (ed.), E. Van der Smissen, (2 vols.), Brussels, 1920
Le May, G. H. L., *British Supremacy in South Africa, 1899–1907*, Oxford, 1965
Leutwein, Theodor, *Elf Jahre Gouverneur in Deutsch Südwestafrika*, Berlin, 1906
Lewis, David Levering, *The Race to Fashoda* etc., New York, 1987.
de Lichtervelde, L., *Léopold II*, Brussels, 1926
Liebrechts, G., *Leopold II: Fondateur d'Empire*, Brussels, 1962
Livingstone, D., *Missionary Travels and Researches in South Africa*, etc., 1857
 Narrative of an expedition to the Zambesi, etc., 1865
 The Last Journals of David Livingstone in Central Africa, etc., (ed.), H. Waller (US edn.), New York, 1875
Lockhart, J. G. and Woodhouse, C. M., *Rhodes*, 1963
Longford, Elizabeth, *Victoria R.I.*, 1964
 Jameson's Raid (1st edn., 1960), 1980
Louis, W. R., 'Sir Percy Anderson's Grand African Strategy, 1883–1893', *Eng. Hist. Review*, 1966, 81, 319, 292–314

Louis, W. R. and Stengers, J., *E. D. Morel's History of the Congo Reform Movement*, Oxford, 1968
Low, D. A., *Buganda in Modern History*, Berkeley, 1971
  Lion Rampant: Essays in the Study of British Imperialism, 1973
Lugard, Lord, *The Rise of our East African Empire*, etc., (2 vols.), 1893
  The Diaries of Lord Lugard, etc., (ed.), Margery Perham and Mary Bull, (4 vols.), 1959–1963
Lyall, Sir A., *The Life of the Marquis of Dufferin and Ava*, etc., (2 vols.), 1905
McCalmont, Sir H., *The Memoirs of Major General Sir Hugh McCalmont*, (ed.), Sir C. E. Callwell, 1924
McLynn, Frank, *Stanley*, 1989
Mage, E., *Voyage*, etc., Paris, 1868
Maran, R., *Brazza et la Fondation de l'A.E.F.*, Paris, 1941
Marcus, H. G., *The Life and Times of Menelik II, Ethiopia 1844–1913*, Oxford, 1975
Marks, S., *Reluctant Rebellion: An Assessment of the 1906–8 Disturbances in Natal*, Oxford, 1970
Marks, S. and Atmore, A. (eds.), *Economy and Society in Pre-industrial South Africa*, 1980
Marlowe, J., *Mission to Khartoum*, etc., 1969
Marsden, A., *British Diplomacy and Tunis (1875–1902)*, New York, 1971
Martineau, J., *The Life and Correspondence of Sir Bartle Frere* (2 vols.), 1895
Mattei, A., *Bas Niger, Bénoué et Dahomey*, Grenoble, 1890
Maurice, Albert (ed.), *Unpublished Letters* (of Stanley), 1957
Maurice, Sir F., *The Life of General Lord Rawlinson of Trent*, etc., 1928
Maurice, Sir F. and Arthur, Sir G., *The Life of Lord Wolseley*, 1924
Méniaud, J., *Les pionniers du soudan: avant, avec et après Archinard*, (2 vols.), Paris, 1931
Michaux, O., *Carnet de Campagne*, Namur, 1913
Michel, C., *Mission de Bonchamps: vers Fashoda à la rencontre de la mission Marchand*, Paris, 1900
Michel, M., *La mission Marchand, 1895–1899*, Paris and The Hague, 1972
Michell, L., *The Life of the Rt. Hon. Cecil J. Rhodes*, (2 vols.), 1910–12
Moloney, J. A., *With Captain Stairs to Katanga*, 1893
Moneypenny, W. F. and Buckle, G. E., *The Life of Benjamin Disraeli: Earl of Beaconsfield*, (6 vols.), 1910–20
Morel, E. D., *The Affairs of West Africa*, (2nd edn.), 1968
  Great Britain and the Congo, 1909 (reprint), New York, 1969
Morris, D. R., *The Washing of the Spears: A History of the Rise of the Zulu Nation under Shaka and Its Fall in the Zulu War of 1879*, New York, 1965
Mouvement Géographique, Brussels, 1884–1924
Morris, J., Vol. I, *Pax Britannica: The Climax of an Empire*, 1968
  Vol. II, *Heaven's Command: An Imperial Progress*, 1973
  Vol. III, *Farewell the Trumpets: An Imperial Retreat*, 1978
Mungeam, G. H., *British Rule in Kenya 1895–1912*, Oxford, 1966
Neufeld, C., *A Prisoner of the Khaleefa*, etc., 1899
Newbury, C. W. and Kanya-Forstner, A. S., 'French Policy and the Origins of the Scramble for West Africa', *J. Afr. Hist.*, 1969, 10, 2, 253–76
  The Western Slave Coast and its Rulers, Oxford, 1961
Newton, Lord, *Lord Lansdowne: A Biography*, 1929
Norris Newman, C. L., *In Zululand with the British throughout the War of 1879*, 1880
Nwoye, Rosaline, *The Public Image of Pierre Savorgnan de Brazza and the Establishment of French Imperialism in the Congo, 1875–1885*, Aberdeen University, 1981
Oliver, R., *Sir Henry Johnston and the Scramble for Africa*, 1957
  The Missionary Factor in East Africa, 1952; (2nd edn.), 1965
Oliver, R. and Mathew, G. (eds.), *History of East Africa*, I, Oxford, 1963
Oliver, R. and Sanderson, G. N., (eds.), *Cambridge History of Africa*, Vol. 6 (from 1870 to c. 1905), Cambridge, 1985
Pakenham, Thomas, *The Boer War*, 1979
Parke, T. H., *My Personal Experiences*, etc., 1891
Penrose, E. F. (ed.), *European Imperialism and the Partition of Africa*, 1975
Perham, M., *Lugard*, I: *The Years of Adventure 1886–1898*; II: *The Years of Authority 1898–1945*, 1956, 1960
Person, Y. *Samori, Une Revolution Dyula*, (3 vols.), Dakar 1968–1975
Peters, Carl, *New Light on Darkest Africa: Being a narrative of the German Emin Pasha expedition*, 1891
  Die Gründung von Deutsche Ost-Afrika, etc., Berlin, 1906

Pietri, C., *Les Français au Niger*, Paris, 1885
Ponsonby, Arthur, *Henry Ponsonby*, etc., 1942
Ponsonby, F., (ed. C. Welsh), *Recollections of Three Reigns*, 1951
Porter, A. N., 'Lord Salisbury, Mr Chamberlain and South Africa, 1895–9', *J. Imp. C'wealth Hist.*, 1972, I, 1, 3–26
   The Origins of the South African War: Joseph Chamberlain and the Diplomacy of Imperialism, 1895–1899, Manchester, 1980
Porter, B., *Critics of Empire*, 1968
   The Lion's Share: a Short History of British Imperialism, 1850–1970, 1975
Prouty, Chris, *Empress Taytu and Menelik II*, etc., 1986
Queen Victoria, *Letters of Queen Victoria*, (ed.) G. E. Buckle (6 vols.: 2nd series, 1862–85, 3rd series 1866–1901), 1926–1932
Ramm, A. (ed.), *The Political Correspondence of Mr Gladstone and Lord Granville, 1876–1886*, (2 vols.), Oxford, 1962
Ranger, T. O., *Revolt in Southern Rhodesia 1896–7*, 1967
   (ed.), *Aspects of Central African History*, 1968
Ransford, O., *The Battle of Majuba Hill*, 1967
Repington, Charles à Court, *Vestigia*, 1919
Roberts, A. D., *Tanzania before 1900*, Nairobi, 1968
   A History of the Bemba: Political Growth and Change in North-Eastern Zambia before 1900, 1973
   A History of Zambia, 1976
   (ed.) *The Cambridge History of Africa Vol 7 from 1905 to 1940*, Cambridge 1986
Roberts, S. H., *A history of French colonial policy (1870–1905)*, (2nd edn.), 1963
Robinson, D., *Chiefs and Clerics*, etc., Oxford, 1975
Robinson, R. and Gallagher, J. with Denny, A., *Africa and the Victorians: The official mind of Imperialism*, London, 1961 (2nd edn., 1981)
Roeykens, A., *Les Débuts de l'oeuvre africaine de Léopold II*, Brussels, 1955
   Léopold et la Conférence géographique de Bruxelles (1876), 1958
Rolo, P. J. V., *Entente Cordiale* etc., 1969
Rotberg, Robert (ed.) and Mazrui, Ali, *Protest and Power in Black Africa*, New York, 1970
Rubenson, Sven, *The Survival of Ethiopian Independence*, 1976
Saint Martin, Y., *L'Empire Toucouleur 1848–1897*, Paris, 1970
Sanderson, G. M., *England, Europe and the Upper Nile, 1882–1899*, Edinburgh, 1965
Schreuder, D. M., *Gladstone and Kruger: Liberal Government and Colonial 'Home Rule', 1880–5*, 1969
   The Scramble for Southern Africa, 1877–1895, etc., Cambridge, 1980
Schweitzer, G., (English trans.) *Emin Pasha: His Life and Work*, 1898
Selous, F. C., *Sunshine and Storm in Rhodesia*, 1896
Simpson, D., *Dark Companions: The African Contribution to the European Exploration of East Africa*, 1975
Slade, Ruth, *English Speaking Missions in the Congo Independent State 1878–1908*, Brussels, 1959
   King Leopold's Congo, 1962
Slatin, Sir R., *Fire and Sword in the Sudan: A Personal Narrative of Fighting and Serving the Dervishes 1879–1895*, (1st edn. 1896) New edn., 1907
Smith, Iain R., *The Emin Pasha Relief Expedition*, (1886–1890) Oxford, 1972
Soleillet, P., *Avenir de la France en Afrique*, Paris, 1876
   Voyage à Segou etc., Paris, 1887
Spies, S. B., *The Origin of the Anglo-Boer War*, 1972
   Methods of Barbarism? Roberts and Kitchener and Civilians in the Boer Republics, January 1900–May 1902, Cape Town, 1977
Stanley, H. M., *How I Found Livingstone*, 1872
   Through the Dark Continent, etc. (2 vols.), 1878
   The Congo and the Founding of its Free State, etc. (2 vols.), 1885
   In Darkest Africa, etc. (2 vols.), New York, 1891
   The Story of Emin's Rescue, New York, (n.d.)
   The Exploration Diaries of H. M. Stanley, (eds.) R. Stanley and A. Neame, 1971
Dorothy Lady Stanley (ed.), *The Autobiography of Sir Henry Morton Stanley*, 1909
Stengers, J. (ed.), *Textes inédits d'Emile Banning*, Brussels, 1955
   Combien le Congo a-t-il coûté à la Belgique?, Brussels, 1957

'Leopold II et Brazza en 1882. Documents inédits', *Revue française d'histoire d'outremer*, 1976, 63, 105–36

Taylor, A. J. P., *Bismarck: The Man and the Statesman* (1st edn., 1955) 1961 edn.

Terrier, A. and Moury, C., *L'expansion Française*, etc., Paris, 1910

Thomson, R. S., *Fondation de L'Etat Independent du Congo*, etc., Brussels, 1933

Tilsley, E., *Dan Crawford, Missionary and Pioneer in Africa*, 1929

Townshend, M. E., *The Rise and Fall of German's Colonial Empire, 1886–1918*, New York, 1966

Van der Poel, Jean, *The Jameson Raid*, Cape Town, 1951

Van Zuylen, Baron P., *L'Echiquier Congolais ou le Secret du Roi*, Brussels, 1959

'Vindex', *Cecil Rhodes: His Political Life and Speeches*, 1900

Walker, E. A., *W. P. Schreiner: A South African*, 1937

Ward, H., *Five Years with the Congo Cannibals*, (2nd edn., 1890)

Warwick, P. (ed.), *The South African War: the Anglo–Boer War*, 1980
  Black People and the South African War, 1899–1902, Cambridge, 1983

West, Algernon, *Private Diaries of Sir Algernon West*, (ed.) H. G. Hutchinson, 1922

West, R., *Brazza of the Congo: European Exploration and Exploitation in French Equatorial Africa*, 1972

Whiteley, W. H. (trans.), *Maisha ya Hamed bin Mubammed el Murjebi Yanni Tippu Tip kwa maneno yake mwenyewe*, Nairobi, 1971

Willcocks, J., *From Kabul to Kumasi*, 1904

Wilson, Sir C., *From Korti to Khartoum: A Journal of the Desert March*, etc., 1885

Wilson, John, *CB: A Life of Sir Henry Campbell-Bannerman*, 1973

Wilson, M. and Thompson, L. M. (eds.), *The Oxford History of South Africa*, (2 vols.), Oxford, 1969

Wingate, F. R., *Mahdiism and the Egyptian Sudan*, (1st edn., 1891) 1968

Wingate, R., *Wingate of the Sudan*, 1955

Witte, Jehan de, *Monseigneur Augouard*, Paris, 1924

Wolseley, Lord, *The Letters of Lord and Lady Wolseley 1870–1911*, (ed. Sir G. Arthur), 1922
  In Relief of Gordon. Lord Wolseley's Campaign Journal of the Khartoum Relief Expedition 1884–5 (ed. A. Preston), 1967
  The South African Journal of Sir Garnet Wolseley, (ed. A. Preston), Balkema, 1973

Zetland, Marquess of, *Lord Cromer*, etc., 1932
  The Letters of Disraeli to Lady Bradford and Lady Chesterfield, (2 vols.), 1929

Notes

PROLOGUE: THE CROWNING ACHIEVEMENT
Head of Chapter: Livingstone, quoted Sir R.
Coupland, *Kirk on the Zambesi* (Oxford 1968),
185.
1 Cameron Papers in NLS with copy of
  Livingstone's letter to *The Times*, Nov 1870
  (Acc. 7513, microf, section 19).
2 Livingstone, *Last Journals*, 321–3, 25 Apr
  1873, 508.
3 Livingstone, *Last Journals*, 16–18 July 1871,
  386–7.
4 Livingstone to H. Waller, 2 Sep 1871 (and
  later), RHL Afr. S. 16/1, f180 foll.
5 Livingstone, *Last Journals*, 25 Apr 1873, 508.
6 Ibid., 7 Apr 1873, 501–2.
7 Ibid., 25 Mar and 27 Apr 1873, 498, 508.
8 Ibid., 511–12.
9 Waller notes on talks with Chuma and Susi in
  England in 1874, RHL Afr. S., 16/1.
10 Ibid.
11 Livingstone, *Last Journals*, 517.
12 Waller, loc cit.
13 Ibid.
14 Ibid.
15 V.L. Cameron, *Across Africa* I, 164–5
   (facsimile).
16 Livingstone, *Last Journals*, 16 Jun 1868, 245–
   6.

CHAPTER 1: LEOPOLD'S CRUSADE
Head of Chapter: Sir Bartle Frere to Lord
Northbrook, 22 Feb 1883, FO, 84/1803.
1 *The Times*, 11 Jan 1876.
2 Duke of Brabant to W. Frere-Orban, 27 Sep.
  1860. Archives Générales du Royaume
  Brussels Frere Papers no. 356. See paperweight
  in Tervuren Museum.
3 Carlus to Baron Lambermont, 6 May 1863,
  Lambermont Papers AMAE Brussels.
4 Cited J. Stengers, *Conférence Géographie*,
  313.
5 Ibid.
6 Leopold to Lambermont, 22 Aug 1875, AMAE
  Lambermont V, 9. Roeykens, *Débuts*, 95–6.
7 Devaux to Beyens, 28 Jun 1876, Beyens Papers,
  cited J. Stengers loc cit, 349.
8 Sir H. Rawlinson to Lady Rawlinson, 11 Sept
  1876, Rawlinson Papers, Royal Asiatic
  Society, London.
9 Vandewoude, *Conférence*, 434.
10 Ibid., 410.
11 Sir H. Rawlinson to Lady Rawlinson, loc cit,
   12 Sep 1876.
12 Vandewoude, *Conférence*, 313.

13 Sir H. Rawlinson to Lady Rawlinson, loc cit,
   14 Sep 1876.
14 Vandewoude, *Conférence*.
15 Leopold to Solvyns cited Roeykens, *Débuts*.

CHAPTER 2: THREE FLAGS ACROSS AFRICA
Head of Chapter: See note 16.
1 H. M. Stanley diary, 12 Sep 1876, *Exploration
  Diaries*, 130.
2 Stanley, *Autobiography*, 297–8. F. Hird,
  Stanley, 129–30.
3 Stanley, *Autobiography*, 295.
4 Ibid., 289.
5 Ibid.
6 Stanley, 24 Aug 1875, *Exploration Diaries*, 99.
7 Ibid., 96
8 Sir S. Baker to Col. J. Grant, 16 Nov 1875,
  Grant Papers NLS 17909, f28–29.
9 Stanley, *Dark Continent*, II, 92–3.
10 Ibid., II, 98.
11 Ibid. II, 119–20.
12 Ward, *Five Years*.
13 Stanley, *Dark Continent*, II, 140.
14 12 Jul 1874 quoted R. Hall, *Stanley*, 17–18.
15 Stanley to Alice Pike, 14 Aug 1876, quoted R.
   Hall, 61–2.
16 Stanley, *Dark Continent*, II, 152–3.
17 Ibid., II, 157.
18 Brazza, *Conférences*, 46.
19 Stanley, *Dark Continent*, II, 447–8.
20 Ibid., II, 462–3.
21 Stanley diary, 10 Jun 1876, *Exploration
   Diaries*, 195.
22 Leopold to Solvyns, 17 Nov 1877, APR Fonds
   Congo, 100/1.

CHAPTER 3: TWO STEPS FORWARD
1 C. 1776.
2 Sir B. Frere to Lord Carnarvon, 17 Apr 1877,
  Martineau, *Frere*, II, 164.
3 Martineau, II, 179.
4 Sir A. Hardinge, *Carnarvon*, II, 220
5 Carnarvon to Frere, 12 Dec 1876, PRO, 30/6/4.
  Goodfellow, *Confederation*, 117.
6 *Oxford History of South Africa*, II.
7 C 1025 no. 27 enc. 2, 5.
8 Bishop Colenso to Chesson, 24 Feb 1876,
  Colenso Papers, Killie Campbell Library,
  Durban. J. Guy, *Heretic*, 247.
9 Rees, *Colenso's Letters from Natal* 273, J.
  Guy, *Heretic*, 212.
10 Martineau, loc cit.

11 Sir T. Shepstone to Lord Carnarvon, 11 Dec 1877, PRO, 30/6/23. J. Guy, *Heretic*, 255.
12 See Duminy and Ballard, *Anglo-Zulu War*.
13 Col. Durnford to his mother quoted E. Durnford, *A Soldier's Life*, 184.
14 Ibid., 183
15 Ibid.
16 Ibid., 208, 214
17 D. Morris, *Washing of Spears*, 329–31.
18 Robertson to Macrorie, 23 Oct 1877, Wigram Papers, SPG, quoted N. Etherington in Duminy and Ballard (ed.), *The Anglo-Zulu War*, 43.

CHAPTER 4: THE CROUCHING LION
Head of Chapter: See note 20.
1 Lord Beaconsfield to Lady Bradford, 28 Sep 1878. Zetland, *Letters of Disraeli*, II, 189.
2 Quoted Lord Blake, *Disraeli*, 669.
3 Sir M. Hicks Beach to Lord Beaconsfield, 3 Nov 1878, Buckle, *Disraeli*, IV, (1910–20) 421.
4 Stanley's journal quoted Hird, *Stanley*, 171.
5 Hird, 173.
6 Ibid., 175–7. See also B. Emerson, *Leopold*, 285.
7 Dr J. Kirk to Lord Derby, 1 May 1878, FO, 84/1514. R. Hall, *Stanley*, 246.
8 Hicks Beach to Beaconsfield, 13 Jan 1879, Buckle, IV, 424.
9 Maj. C. Clery to Alison, 18 Mar 1879, Alison Papers, Brenthurst Library (Papers 6399). S. Clarke, *Invasion*, 64, *Zululand at War*, 122.
10 Maj C. Clery to Col. Harman, 17 Feb 1879, Alison Papers loc cit. Clarke *Zululand*, 83.
11 Clery's evidence at enquiry in C2260.
12 Clery to Alison, 28 Apr 1879, loc cit.
13 *The Times*, 22 Mar 1879 quoted H. Colenso, etc., *Zulu War*, 408.
14 E. Durnford, *A Soldier's Life*, 226.
15 Ibid.
16 Clery to Harman, 17 Feb 1879, loc cit.
17 Ibid.
18 E. Durnford, *A Soldier's Life*, 244.
19 Norris-Newman, *Zululand*, 57.
20 Clery to Alison, 18 Mar 1879, loc cit. Clarke *Zululand*, 122.
21 E. Durnford, *A Soldier's Life*, 228–9.
22 Lt. H. Smith-Dorrien in *Brecon County Times* quoted F. Emery, *The Red Soldier*, 88–90.
23 Clery to Harman, 17 Feb 1879, loc cit.
24 Ibid.
25 Beaconsfield to Lady Bradford, 12 Feb 1879, Zetland, *Disraeli's Letters*, II, 207.

CHAPTER 5: ISMAEL'S DREAM OF EMPIRE
Head of Chapter: Gordon, 11 Apr 1876, *Central Africa*, 163.
1 Consul Vivian to Lord Salisbury, 20 Feb 1879, FO, 407/iii/1/57.
2 Ibid.
3 Vivian to Salisbury, 20–22 Feb 1879, loc cit.

4 J. McCoan, *Egypt As It Is* (1878), 88–94.
5 Gordon's journal, 5 Mar 1879, Gordon, *Central Africa*, 339.
6 Ibid., 25 Apr 1879, Gordon, *Central Africa*, 352–3.
7 Ibid., 31 Aug 1877, Gordon, *Central Africa*, 271.
8 Ibid., 7 Jun 1877, Gordon, *Central Africa*, 235.
9 Ibid., 21 July 1879, Gordon, *Central Africa*, 397.
10 Ibid., 14 Feb 1874, Gordon, *Central Africa* I.
11 Ibid., 26 Feb 1874, Gordon, *Central Africa*, 5.
12 Ibid., 21 Jun 1875, Gordon, *Central Africa*, 65.
13 Ibid., 15 Jul 1875, Gordon, *Central Africa*, 93–4.
14 Ibid., 29 Oct 1876, Gordon, *Central Africa*, 197.
15 Ibid., 29 Nov 1876, Gordon, *Central Africa*, 200.
16 Gordon, *Central Africa*, 373
17 Gessi to Gordon, nd, Gordon, *Central Africa*, 380.
18 Gordon's journal, 27 May 1879, Gordon, *Central Africa*, 362.

CHAPTER 6: ONE STEP BACKWARD
Head of Chapter: Wolseley to Hicks Beach, 28 Oct 1879, quoted J. Lehmann, 71.
1 Col O. Lanyon to Sir G. Colley, 25 Oct 1880, W. F. Butler, *Colley*, 265–6.
2 Sir G. Wolseley, *SA Journal*, 303, 112, 124. Maurice and Arthur, *Life*, 122.
3 Wolseley, *Journal*, 138, 139, 240, 248, 254, 272–5.
4 Ibid., 173.
5 Ibid., 203.
6 Lanyon to Colley, 25 Oct 1880, Butler, *Colley*, loc cit.
7 E. J. P. Jorissen, *Transvaalse Herinneringen*, 60–9.
8 S. J. P. Kruger, *Memoirs*, I, 164.
9 W. Gladstone, *Speeches* (ed. T. Bisset, L. 1916), I, 63.
10 Jorissen, *Transvaalse Herinneringen*, loc cit.
11 Colley quoted *The Times*, 21 Dec 1880.
12 Lord Kimberley to Prime Minister, 25 Dec 1880, BL, 44225/265. D. Schreuder, *Gladstone*, 90.
13 Queen Victoria to Prime Minister, 26 Dec 1880, QVL II series III, 167.
14 E. Hamilton 29 Dec 1880, *Diary*, I, 94.
15 Ibid.
16 E. Hamilton, 10 Jan 1881 *Diary*, I, 99.
17 *The Times*, 7 Jan 1881. QVL II, III, 178–81.
18 E. Hamilton, 12 Jan 1881, *Diary*, I, 97.
19 Kimberley to Colley, 19 Feb 1881, C2837 10.
20 Colley to Kimberley, Kimberley to Colley, 19 Dec 1880, op cit, 13.
21 I. Hamilton, Oct 1881 quoted I. Hamilton, *Listening for the Drums*, 140. Douglas to Sir

G. White, 5 Apr 1881, White Papers quoted Lehmann, *First Boer War*, 239.

22 S. Roos (tr G. Tylden), *Journal of The Society for Army Historical Research*, XVII (1938), 9.

23 Lehmann, *First Boer War*, 240–1.

24 Roos, loc cit, 10.

25 Roos, loc cit, 11.

26 I. Hamilton, *Drums*, 135.

27 T. Carter, *History*, 276–7.

28 I. Hamilton, *Drums*, 136.

29 Carter, *History*, loc cit.

30 *The Times*, 2 Mar 1881.

CHAPTER 7: SAVING THE BEY
Head of Chapter: See note 10.

1 Baron Courcel, *Souvenirs Inedits* in G. Hanotaux, *Histoire des Colonies*, IV, 650–1.

2 Waddington to d'Harcourt, 21 Jul 1878, DDF, 1/2/330–2.

3 Salisbury quoted Ganiage, *L'expansion*, 50. Salisbury to Lyons, 24 Jul 1878, Salisbury Papers Hatfield quoted Marsden, *Tunis*, 55 (note 91).

4 Ganiage, *L'expansion*, 76.

5 Jauréquibery quoted C. W. Newbury and A. S. Kanya-Forstner, JAH, X, 2 (1969), 268.

6 Ibid.

7 Ganiage, *Origines*, (2nd edn. 1968), 512–13.

8 Roustan to Courcel, Feb 1881 quoted Ganiage, *L'expansion*, 513–14.

9 Noailles to Saint-Hilaire, 26 Jan 1881 DDF, III, 330.

10 Noailles to Saint-Hilaire loc cit.

11 Courcel in Hanotaux, *Colonies*, 650–1.

12 Saint-Hilaire to Roustan, 7 Apr 1881 quoted A. M. Broadley, *Last Punic War*, 216.

13 Broadley, 235.

14 Ibid., 237 (second sentence changed to direct speech).

15 Ibid., 242.

16 Bey of Tunis to Lord Granville, 25 Apr 1881 quoted Broadley 251–2.

17 Ibid., 265.

18 Ibid., 312.

19 Ibid., 313–19.

CHAPTER 8: SAVING THE KHEDIVE
Head of Chapter: Gladstone, *Nineteenth Century*, Aug 1877.

1 E. Hamilton, 31 Dec 1881, *Diary*, I, 207–8 (altered word order).

2 Gladstone, *Midlothian Speeches*, Leicester 1971), 93.

3 E. Hamilton, 3 Jan 1882, *Diary*, I, 209–10. W. Blunt, *Secret History of the English Occupation of Egypt* (L. 1907), 556–8.

4 Blunt, *Secret History*.

5 Cookson (enc Colvin), 10 Sep 1881, C 3161.

6 Blunt, *Secret History*, 189.

7 J. P. T. Bury, *Gambetta and the Making of the Third Republic*, (1973).

8 A Ramm *Gladstone Correspondence*, I, 337.

9 J. P. T. Bury, *Gambetta's Final Years*, (L. 1982) 311.

10 Ibid., 344.

11 Granville to Gladstone, 15 Dec 1881, BL 44173/249. A. Ramm, *Correspondence*, I, 320.

12 Hartington to Granville, 27 May 1882, PRO, 30/29/1320. Robinson, Gallagher etc., *Africa*, 105.

13 Bright cab min, 7 Jul 1882, PRO, 30/29/143. Robinson, Gallagher, 110.

14 Gladstone to Granville, 9 Jul 1882, PRO, 30/29/126. Robinson, Gallagher, 111.

15 Sir G. Wolseley to Lady Wolseley, 10 Sep 1882, Arthur Wolseley *Letters*, 76.

16 Wolseley to Lady Wolseley, (Sep 1882) Wolseley Papers Hove, Sussex WP, 11/17i/2.

17 McCalmont, *Memoirs*, 218–19.

18 Butler, *Autobiography*, 232.

19 Sir R. Buller to Lady Buller, 1882, Crediton Papers, Devon.

20 Butler, *Autobiography*, 235.

21 Ibid.

22 Ibid., 237.

23 Wolseley to Lady Wolseley, 15 Sep 1882, loc cit, WP, 11/19.

24 Wolseley to Lady Wolseley, 21 Sep 1882, loc cit, WP, 11/21i.

CHAPTER 9: THE RACE FOR THE POOL
Head of Chapter: See note 5.

1 R. Maran, *Brazza*, 181–2.

2 Brazza to Jauréguibery, n.d. (1879), Brazza *Conférences*, 414–15. R. Nwoye *Public Image*, 65–6.

3 R. West, 106, citing Brunschwig in *Cahiers d'Études Africaines* (1966), 187.

4 H. Brunschwig, *Makoko*, 22–3.

5 Ibid., 47–8. R. West, 110.

6 Maran, 170. R. West, 110.

7 H. Stanley, *Congo*, I, 231–4.

8 Leopold to Stanley, n.d., Maurice, *Unpublished Letters*.

9 Stanley to Leopold, 6 Feb 1880, *Unpublished Letters*, 34–5.

10 Stanley to Strauch, n.d. Maurice, ibid., 34–5.

11 Mgr. Augouard quoted R. West, 117.

12 Stanley, *Congo*, I, 292–3.

13 Stanley, *Congo*, I, 339–42.

14 Brazza to French ctte, Apr 1881, Brunschwig, *Makoko*, 183–4, 191. R. Nwoye, *Public Image*, 88–90.

15 Brazza to Jauréguibery, Aug 1882, Brunschwig, *Makoko*, 257–77. R. Nwoye, 100–1.

16 Jauréguibery to Duclerc, 26 Sep 1882, Brunschwig, *L'Avènement*, 152–3. R. Nwoye, 103.

17 Chambrun, *Brazza*, 110.

18 Stanley to Strauch, 11 May 1882, Maurice, *Unpublished Letters*

19 Stanley to Strauch, Sep 1882, Maurice, ibid., 148. R. West, 120.

20 Brazza, *Conférences*, 174. R. West, 120.
21 Leopold to Lesseps, 18 Sep 1882, cited Brunschwig, *L'Avènement*, 160. R. Nwoye, 104-5.
22 Leopold's minute for Solvyns, 8 Oct 1882, cited J. Stengers in P. Gifford and W. Louis, *France and Britain*, 138-9.
23 Leopold's minutes for Solvyns, 8 Oct 1882, ibid., 100.
24 Solvyns to Lambermont, 12 Oct 1882, cited J. Stengers, *France and Britain*, 139.
25 Leopold to Strauch, n.d. (1882), Maurice, *Unpublished Letters*, 151.
26 Chambrun, 120.
27 Maurice, *Unpublished Letters*, 153-50. *The Times* 20, 21 Oct 1882.
28 Ibid.
29 F. Hird, *Stanley*, 186.
30 Ibid., 190.

CHAPTER 10: HEAD IN THE CLOUDS
Head of Chapter: Col Borgnis-Desbordes 9 Apr 1881, Hargreaves, *France and West Africa*, 160.
1 Col Desbordes, 7 Feb 1881, Méniaud, *Pionniers*, I, 188.
2 Ibid., I, 189-90.
3 Ibid., I, 188.
4 Ibid., I, 190-1.
5 Soleillet, *Avenir de la France en Afrique* and Duponchel, *Le Chemin de Fer Trans-Saharien*, 218, both cited Kanya-Forstner, *Conquest*, 61.
6 Rouvier report, 10 Jun 1879, cited Kanya-Forstner, *Conquest*, 63.
7 Mage, *Voyage*, 67-8.
8 Muntaga to Desbordes, Méniaud, *Pionniers*, I, 177-8.
9 Gallieni, *Voyage*.
10 Archinard diary, 31 Mar – 1 Apr 1883, Méniaud, I, 220.
11 Ibid., 1 Apr 1883.
12 Archinard diary, 16 Apr 1883, Méniaud, I, 223.
13 Archinard diary, Apr 1883, Méniaud, I, 225.
14 Ferry speech, 3 Jul 1883, cited Kanya-Forstner, 108.

CHAPTER 11: HEWETT SHOWS THE FLAG
Head of Chapter: See note 1.
1 King Acqua etc. to Queen Victoria, 7 Aug 1879, PRO, 30/29/269 (FO 4824 no. 1).
2 Aberdare to Granville, 1 Jan 1883, FO, 84/1654/87-93.
3 Lister minute, FO, 84.
4 Derby quoted Meade to Lister, 4 Jun 1883, PRO, 30/29/269 (FO, 4825, no. 17).
5 Mary Kingsley, *Travels in West Africa*, 98.
6 King Ja-Ja to Granville, 26 May 1881, PRO, 30/29/269 (FO, 4824, no. 2).
7 Hewett report, 18 Nov 1882, PRO, 30/29/269 (FO, 4824, no. 40).
8 Mattei, *Bas Niger*, 3.

9 Brass chiefs to FO, 7 Jul 1876, FO, 84/1498. Flint, *Goldie*, 28.
10 Anderson memo, 11 Jun 1883, PRO, 30/29/269 (FO, 4824, no. 19).
11 E. Hamilton diary, 21, 24 Jun 1883, *Diary*, 451-2.

CHAPTER 12: WHY BISMARCK CHANGED HIS MIND
Head of Chapter: See note 24.
1 Bismarck quoted A. J. P. Taylor, *Bismarck*, 221.
2 Holstein diary, 5 May, 19 Sep 1884, *Holstein Papers*, II, 138, 161.
3 Holstein diary, 19 Sep 1884, loc cit, 161.
4 Ibid.
5 C 4265 no. 5. Aydelotte, *Colonial Policy*, 27 foll.
6 Bismarck quoted Turner in Gifford and Louis, *Britain and Germany*, 69, citing E. W. Pavenstedt in *Journal Modern History* (1934), 38.
7 Bismarck quoted Turner loc cit, citing Kusserow in *Deutsche Kolonialzeitung* (1898), 299.
8 Turner, loc cit, 70-1. Schreuder, *Scramble*, 124-5.
9 Turner, loc cit, 73. Fitzmaurice, *Life of Second Earl Granville* (L. 1905), II, 340.
10 Turner, loc cit, 75. Aydelotte, 60-1.
11 C 4190, 52-5.
12 Ibid., 56-7. Schreuder, *Scramble*, 127.
13 Gwynn & Tuckwell, *Dilke*.
14 C 4265 no. 6, 8. Schreuder, *Scramble*, 123.
15 Herbert Bismarck to Prince Bismarck, 17 Jun 1884, G.P. IV, 69.
16 Holstein diary, 27 Aug 1884, *Holstein Papers*, II, 157.
17 Bülow, *Memoirs*, 556.
18 Holstein diary, 30 Aug 1884, *Holstein Papers*, II, 160.
19 Gladstone to Granville, 5 Sep 1884, Ramm, *Political Correspondence*, II, 246.
20 Gladstone to Granville, 19 Sep 1884, Ramm, *Political Correspondence*, II, 260.
21 Chamberlain to Dilke, 18 Sep 1884, Gwynn and Tuckwell, II, 83.
22 Chamberlain to Dilke, 29 Dec 1884, Garvin, *Chamberlain*, I, 497.
23 Derby to Granville, 28 Dec 1884, PRO, 30/29/120.
24 Gladstone, 1 Sep, *The Times*, 2 Sep 1884.
25 Gladstone to Granville, Ramm, *Political Correspondence*, II, 260.
26 Derby to Granville, 28 Dec 1884, PRO, 30/29/120.

CHAPTER 13: TOO LATE?
Head of Chapter: See note 17.
1 Gordon diary, 26 Sep 1884, Gordon, *Journals*, 105.
2 Ibid., Gordon, *Journals*, 106.
3 Ibid., 1 Nov 1884, Gordon, *Journals*, 271.

4 Gordon, 8 Mar 1884, cited Allen, *Gordon*, 296.
5 Gordon to Dufferin, 11 Mar 1884, Lyall, *Life of Dufferin*, 346–70. Allen, 303.
6 Gordon to sister, 11 Mar 1884, Gordon, *Letters*, 381–2.
7 See Gordon, *Journals*, 254.
8 Gordon diary, 5 Nov 1884, Gordon, *Journals*, 287.
9 Gordon to Baring quoted Allen, 365.
10 Gordon diary, 5 Nov 1884, Gordon, *Journals*, 281.
11 Ibid., 24 Oct 1884, Gordon, *Journals*, 227.
12 Ibid., 9 Oct 1884, Gordon, *Journals*, 168–71.
13 Ibid., 12 Oct 1884, Gordon, *Journals*, 188.
14 Ibid., 24 Oct 1884, Gordon, *Journals*, 228–9.
15 Ibid., 12 Oct 1884, Gordon, *Journals*, 185.
16 Ibid., 15 Oct 1884, Gordon, *Journals*, 198–9.
17 Ibid., 22 Oct 1884, and Appendix U, Gordon, *Journals*, 220–1, 522–30.
18 Ibid., 23 Oct 1884, Gordon, *Journals*, 223–4.
19 Slatin, *Fire and Sword*, 185.
20 Ibid., 187.
21 Gordon diary, 20 Oct 1884, Gordon, *Journals*, 209.
22 Ibid., 10, 17 Oct 1884, Gordon, *Journals*, 200–2.
23 Ibid., 2 Nov 1884, Gordon, *Journals*, 271–2.
24 Wolseley, 20 Sep 1884, cited Allen, 400 (facsimile).
25 Gordon diary, 12 Nov 1884, Gordon, *Journals*, 317–8.
26 Ibid., 13 Oct 1884, Gordon, *Journals*, 191.
27 Wolseley to wife, 27 Sep 1884, Wolseley, *Letters*, 121.
28 Wolseley, *Journal* 27.
29 Report of McNeill, Buller and Butler quoted Colvile, *Sudan Campaign*, I, 39.
30 Wolseley diary, 31 Dec 1884.
31 Wolseley diary, 15 Jan 1885, Wolseley, *Letters*, 154–5.
32 Gordon to Wolseley, 4 Nov 1884 quoted Allen, 403.
33 Gordon, 14 Dec 1884 quoted Wolseley to wife 31 Dec 1884. Wolseley, *Letters* 137, (spelling 'Kartoum' restored).
34 Colvile, *Sudan*, I, 139. Allen, 414–15.
35 Wolseley to Wilson, C. Wilson, *Korti to Khartoum*.
36 C. Wilson, *Korti to Khartoum*, 28.
37 Gordon diary, 14 Dec 1884, Gordon, *Journals*, 395.

CHAPTER 14: WELCOME TO A
PHILANTHROPIST

1 Courcel to Ferry, 19 Jan 1885, DDF 1st series, 5, no. 528. W. Louis in Gifford and Louis, *Britain and France*, 193, footnote.
2 Anderson memo, 4 Oct 1884, FO, 84/1813. W. Louis, loc cit, 192.
3 Pauncefote minute, 30 Oct 1884, FO, 84/1814. W. Louis, ibid.

4 Lister minute, 19 Nov 1884, FO, 84/1815. W. Louis, loc cit, 193.
5 H. Johnston, *Life*, 147. Anstey, *Britain and the Congo*, 69.
6 Bontinck, *Origines*, 139.
7 Ibid., 144–5.
8 Ferry to Courcel, 16 Dec 1884, cited J. Stengers in Gifford and Louis, *Britain and France*, 156.
9 Stengers, loc cit, 155.
10 *The Times*, 28 Mar 1883, cited Stengers, loc cit, 144.
11 Bontinck, *Origines*. Stengers, *Le Flambeau* (1954), 383–5.
12 Leopold to Strauch, 26 Sep 1883, Strauch Papers, Musée de la Dynastie, Brussels.
13 Bontinck, *Origines*, 196.
14 Stengers in Gifford and Louis, *Britain and France*, 162.
15 Lister, 16 May 1884, PRO, 30/29/198. Louis in Gifford and Louis, *Britain and France*, 191.
16 P. Van Zuylen, *L'Echiquier*, 240.
17 Courcel's despatch, 30 Aug 1884, cited Stengers, loc cit, 163.
18 Malet to Granville, 19 Nov 1884, FO, 84/1815. Louis, loc cit, 202.
19 Malet to Granville, 1 Dec 1884, cited Louis, loc cit, 203.
20 P. Van Zuylen, loc cit.
21 Banning, *Mémoires*, 33.
22 Banning, 41. Thomson, *Fondation*, 261.
23 Banning, 41–2. Thomson, 262.
24 Bismarck, 26 Feb 1885, Parliamentary Paper, Africa no. 4 (1885), 300.
25 Bismarck, Ibid., 303.
26 *Standard*, 2 Mar 1885. Louis, loc cit, 220.
27 *Leeds Mercury*, 28 Feb 1886.

CHAPTER 15: GORDON'S HEAD
Head of Chapter: See note 18.

1 Wolseley to Hartington, 9.10 pm, 4 Feb 1885, C 4280, no. 7. Colvile, *Sudan*, II, 57–8.
2 E. Hamilton diary, 5 Feb 1884, *Diary*, II, 789.
3 A. Ponsonby, *Henry Ponsonby*, 231. Longford, *Queen Victoria*, 473.
4 Queen's journal, 5 Feb 1885, QVL, II, III, 597.
5 Queen to Gladstone etc., 5 Feb 1885. Ibid.
6 A. Ponsonby, 231–2.
7 Queen to Ponsonby, 5 Feb 1885, ibid., 598.
8 Queen to Ponsonby, 7 Feb 1885, A. Ponsonby, 232–3.
9 B. Holland, *Duke of Devonshire*, I, 69.
10 E. Hamilton diary 7 Jan 1885, *Diary*, II, 765.
11 Hartington to Louise Manchester, 3 Feb 1885.
12 E. Hamilton diary, 5 Feb 1885, *Diary*, II, 789.
13 E. Hamilton diary, 7 Feb 1885, *Diary*, II, 790.
14 Ibid.
15 The *World*, 11 Feb 1885.
16 E. Hamilton diary, 11 Feb 1885, *Diary*, II, 796.
17 E. Hamilton diary, 15 Feb 1885, ibid., 796.
18 Wolseley diary, 17 Feb 1885, Wolseley, *Journal*, 147.
19 Wolseley diary, 24 Feb 1885, ibid., 153.

20 Ibid.
21 Wolseley diary, 11 Feb 1885, ibid., 142.
22 Wolseley diary, 24 Feb 1885, ibid., 153.
23 Wolseley diary, 25 Feb 1885, ibid., 154-5.
24 Wolseley diary, 11 Feb 1885, ibid., 142.
25 Slatin, *Fire and Sword*, 206.
26 Wolseley diary, 11 Mar 1885, *Journal*, 164.
27 Ibid.
28 Wolseley diary, 14, 15 Apr 1885, ibid., 192-3.
29 Wolseley diary, 21, 24 Apr 1885, ibid., 196-8.
30 Wolseley diary, 4 Jun 1885, ibid., 222.
31 Queen to Ponsonby, 17 Feb 1885. QVL, II, III, 607-8.
32 Queen to Ponsonby, 1 Mar 1885. QVL, II, III, 616.
33 Queen to Gladstone, 17 Apr 1885, ibid., 638-9.
34 Queen to Hartington, 17 May 1885, ibid.
35 Slatin, *Fire and Sword*, 231.

CHAPTER 16: THE SULTAN'S FLAG
Head of Chapter: See note 14.
1 Salisbury 7 Jun, 1885, Lady Gwendolen Cecil, *Salisbury*, III, 133.
2 Queen to Gladstone, 11 Jun 1885, QVL, III, II, 662.
3 Lady Gwendolen Cecil III, 133.
4 Kennedy, *Salisbury*, 153.
5 FO to Kirk, 23, 24 Sep 1884, FO, 84/1676. R. Oliver, *Johnston*, 72.
6 S. Gwynn and Tuckwell, *Dilke*, II, 83-4.
7 R. Coupland, *East Africa*, 25.
8 Ibid., 52.
9 Kirk to FO, 5 Jul 1873, FO, 84/1374. Coupland, 209.
10 Kirk to Mackinnon, 13 Mar 1884, Box 23, Mackinnon Papers SOAS.
11 Kirk to Granville, 9 May 1885, FO, 403/93/70-1.
12 Salisbury to Kirk, 28 Jun 1885, Coupland, 418.
13 Kirk cited Coupland.
14 Gann and Duignan, *Rulers of German Africa*, 12.
15 C. Peters, *Gründung von Deutsch-Ostafrika*, 86.
16 Ibid., 87.
17 Ibid., 113.
18 Ibid., 115.

CHAPTER 17: CRIES FROM THE HEART
Head of Chapter: See note 4.
1 A. Mackay letter, 29 Sep 1885, *CMS Intelligencer*, Feb 1886. Ashe, *Two Kings*, 163-4.
2 Mackay, loc cit.
3 Ashe, 169.
4 Mackay, loc cit.
5 J. Harrison, *Mackay*, 106.
6 Ibid., 228.
7 Ibid., 42.
8 Ibid., 170.
9 Ibid., 164-5.

10 Ibid., 166.
11 Ibid., 183.
12 Ibid., 187.
13 Ashe, 178. Mackay, 10 Dec 1885, *CMS Intelligencer*, Jun 1886, 484 foll.
14 Hannington diary, 21-6 Oct 1885, E. Dawson, *Hannington*, 374-9.
15 Dawson, 333.
16 Jones quoted Dawson, 352, 4.
17 Hannington diary, 27-9 Oct 1885, Dawson, 380-2.
18 Dawson, 389.
19 Fr Lourdel quoted Dawson, 371.
20 Lourdel quoted *CMS Intelligencer*, 1886, 633-6.
21 Mackay, ibid.
22 Mackay, ibid., 495.
23 Mackay to Holmwood, 10 Aug 1887, FO, 84/1775. Smith, *Emin Pasha*, 42.
24 Ibid.
25 Mackay, 7 Apr 1886, Harrison, 275.
26 Ashe, 208.
27 Mackay, 26 Jun 1886, *CMS Intelligencer*, 1886, 888.
28 Mackay, 11 Jul 1886, Harrison, 280-1.
29 Holmwood to Iddesleigh, 23 Sep 1886, FO, 84/1775. Smith, 41.
30 Holmwood to Baring, 25 Sep 1886, FO, 78/3930. Smith, 43.
31 Leverson memo, 1 Oct 1886, Wolseley memo, 2 Oct 1886, cited Smith, 44.
32 Anderson memo, 18 Oct 1886, FO, 84/1775.
33 Salisbury, 19 Oct 1886, FO, 84/1775.
34 Kirk to Mackinnon, 17 Aug 1886, Mackinnon Papers, SOAS.
35 Kirk to Mackinnon, 30 Oct 1886, ibid., 94.
36 *The Times*, 15 Dec, 1 Nov, 15 Dec, 1886. Smith, 45-6.
37 Anderson memo, 30 Nov 1886, FO, 84/1794. Smith, 60.
38 *CMS Intelligencer*, 1886.

CHAPTER 18: DR EMIN, I PRESUME?
Head of Chapter: Stanley, *Autobiography*, 353
1 Hird, *Stanley*, 222-3.
2 Leopold to Stanley, n.d., Hird, 206.
3 Leopold to Stanley, n.d., Hird, 213.
4 Hird, 214.
5 Stanley to Dolly Tennant quoted R. Hall, *Stanley*, 283-4.
6 Stanley to Mackinnon, Sep 1886, Mackinnon Papers, SOAS, Box 55.
7 Hird, 222-3.
8 Emerson, *Leopold*, 19.
9 Jephson, *Diary*, 240.
10 Stanley, *Darkest Africa*, I, 367-8.
11 Smith, 181-5.
12 Stanley, *Darkest Africa*, I, 386.
13 Emin in *Berliner Tageblatt*, 2 Dec 1891, Smith, 158.
14 Jephson diary, 24 Apr, 26 Feb 1888, *Diary*, 248, 229.

15 Jephson diary, 26 May 1888, *Diary*, 255.
16 Jephson diary, 22 Jun 1888, *Diary*, 263.
17 Jephson diary, 16 Jul 1888, *Diary*, 271.
18 Jephson, *Rebellion*, 145–6.
19 Jephson diary, 6 Sep 1888, *Diary*, 286.
20 Jephson diary, 6 Sep, 7–8 Oct 1888, *Diary*, 286, 295, 291.
21 Jephson diary, 17 Oct 1888, *Diary*, 295.
22 Jephson diary, 5 Dec 1888, *Diary*, 309.
23 Jephson to Stanley, 7 Nov 1888, Stanley, *Story of Emin's Rescue*, 88.
24 Stanley, *Darkest Africa*, I, 493–4.
25 Ibid., 494.
26 Stanley to Jephson, 30 Aug 1888, Mrs Jameson, *Diary*, 365–6.
27 Parke, *Experiences*, 345.
28 Stanley footnote, *Darkest Africa*, II, 129.
29 Stanley to Jephson, 18 Jan 1889, Jephson, *Diary*, 325–7. Cf Stanley *Darkest Africa*, II, 127–8.
30 Jephson diary, 20 Apr 1889, *Diary*, 344.
31 Jephson diary, 13 Jun 1889, *Diary*, 362.
32 Jephson diary, 26 Apr 1889, *Diary*, 346–7.

CHAPTER 19: SALISBURY'S BARGAIN
Head of Chapter: Salisbury quoted by French ambassador in London, 3 Oct 1896, DDF, XII, no. 468.

1 H. Johnston, *The Story of My Life*, 217.
2 H. Johnston, *The Gay Dombeys* (L. 1919), 188–9.
3 H. Johnston, *The Story of My Life*, 221.
4 Ibid.
5 *The Times*, 2 Aug 1888.
6 Salisbury to Scot, 4 May 1887. Lady G. Cecil, *Salisbury*, IV, 43.
7 Ibid.
8 Ibid.
9 Salisbury to the Queen, 25 Aug 1888, QVL, III, I, 438.
10 Anderson note, Mar 1888, FO, 84/1917. Galbraith, *Mackinnon*, 138.
11 Kirk to Mackinnon, 17 Aug 1886, Mackinnon Papers, SOAS.
12 Kirk to Mackinnon, 17 Jan 1888, Mackinnon Papers, SOAS.
13 Johnston to Mackinnon, 26 Nov 1888, Mackinnon Papers, SOAS. Galbraith, *MacKinnon*, 120.
14 Jackson in Rotberg, *Protest and Power*, 50.
15 Ibid., 37–79.
16 Hemedi bin Abdallah, *Utenzi* (Dar-es-Salaam 1960), 67–9.
17 Dugdale, *German Diplomatic Documents*, II.
18 *Grosse Politik*, IV, 946, 949. Robinson and Gallagher, 295. Sanderson, EHR, 78.
19 Hatzfeld to Berlin, *Grosse Politik*, IV.
20 Peters, *New Light on Darkest Africa*, 32.
21 Ibid., 139–41.
22 Ibid.
23 Ibid., 324.
24 Ibid., 342.
25 H. Johnston, *Story*, 238. Oliver, *Johnston*, 154–5.
26 Dugdale, *German Diplomatic Documents*, II, 31.
27 Marschall to Hatzfeld, 17 May 1890, Dugdale, *German Diplomatic Documents*, II, 33–4.
28 Ibid., II, 37.
29 Queen to Salisbury, 12 Jun 1890, QVL, III, I, 615.

CHAPTER 20: AN INSUBORDINATE ARMY
Head of Chapter: Jules Ferry quoted H. Brunschwig, *Myths*, 82–4.

1 Waddington to Salisbury, 13 Aug 1890, Lady G. Cecil, *Salisbury*, IV, 324. Freycinet, *Souvenirs*, II, 452–3.
2 Quai d'Orsay, 13 Aug 1890, AEMD, Afrique, 129. Kanya-Forstner, *Conquest*, 162.
3 Etienne, 10 May 1890, JODPC (Journal Officiel Débat Parl. Chambre) cited Kanya-Forstner, *Conquest*, 164.
4 Report, 22 Jan 1890, cited Kanya-Forstner, *Conquest*, 172.
5 Gallieni to Etienne, 16 Jan 1888, cited Kanya-Forstner, *Conquest*, 144.
6 Gallieni to Archinard, 25 Sep, 17 Oct 1888, Archinard Papers cited Kanya-Forstner, *Conquest*, 175.
7 Méniaud, *Pionniers*, I, 438–44.
8 Méniaud, II, 107.
9 Etienne to Gov. Senegal, 14 Apr 1891, cited Kanya-Forstner, *Conquest*, 185.
10 Humbert to Gov. Senegal, 10, 12 Apr 1891, cited Kanya-Forstner, *Conquest*, 189.
11 Humbert to Gov. Senegal, 12 Jan 1892, cited Kanya-Forstner, *Conquest*, 187.
12 Archinard to Humbert, 8 Mar 1890, cited Kanya-Forstner, *Conquest*, 199.
13 *Le Siècle*, 20 May, 21 July 1891.
14 Delcassé to President, 21 Nov 1893, cited Kanya-Forstner, *Conquest*, 211.

CHAPTER 21: A NEW RAND?
Head of Chapter: Rhodes 23 July 1888, quoted D. Schreuder, *Scramble*, XI.

1 Colvin, *Life of Jameson*, I, 140.
2 Rhodes to Beit, Aug 1895, E. Longford, *Jameson Raid*.
3 Flint, *Rhodes*, 52–4.
4 Colvin, I, 50.
5 Lockhart and Wodehouse, *Rhodes*, 69–70.
6 Rhodes, quoted Schreuder, *Scramble*, 172. (Note original spelling: 'Grand Mamma.')
7 Vindex *Rhodes*, 16 Aug 1883, 62.
8 Vindex *Rhodes*, 62–4, 92–127.
9 C 5524, p. 14. Keppel-Jones, *Rhodesia*, 44.
10 L. Jameson to brother, Apr 1890, Colvin, I, 129–30.
11 Fripp and Hillier, *Gold and the Gospel*, (Jo'burg 1949), 219–20. Keppel-Jones, 78.
12 Helm to LMS, 29 Mar 1889, Fripp and Hillier. Blake, *Rhodesia*, 47. CO 879/30/369.
13 Galbraith, *Crown and Charter*, 56–7.

14 CO 417/28/422 pp 79–81. Keppel-Jones, 118.
15 CO 879/30/372 pp 24–5. Blake, 50.
16 Keppel-Jones, *Rhodesia*.
17 Johnston to Rhodes, 8 Oct 1893, Oliver, *Johnston*, 152–4.
18 Lobengula to Shippard, 10 Aug 1889, CO 879/30/372, pp 169–70.
19 Hole, *Rhodesia*, 114. Keppel-Jones, 141.
20 Keppel-Jones, 142.
21 Ibid., 145.
22 Hole, 136.
23 Keppel-Jones, 167.
24 Jameson to Harris, 1 Nov 1889, Keppel–Jones, 154.
25 Selous, *Travel and Adventure* (L. 1893), 310–11, 313–25.

CHAPTER 22: MSIRI'S MOCKING SMILE
Head of Chapter: A Delcommune, *Vingt Années*, II. 274.
1 Hird, *Stanley*, 272.
2 Stanley, *Autobiography*, 410.
3 Hird.
4 J. de Arteche, *Lavigerie*, 167. Slade, *Leopold*, 102–3.
5 Gifford and Louis, *Britain and Germany*, 87.
6 Kirk to Wilde, 14 May 1890, FO 84/2103. Gifford and Louis, *Britain and Germany*, 114.
7 Kirk to Mackinnon, 23 Jun 1890, Mackinnon Papers, Box 25, SOAS.
8 Slade, 120.
9 Ibid., 127.
10 Sanderson.
11 Arnot, *Bihé*, 61.
12 Ibid., 64.
13 Ibid., 59, 120.
14 Slade, *English Speaking Missions*, 119.
15 Cornet, *Katanga*, 149.
16 Delcommune, *Vingt Années*, 275.
17 Moloney, 28–9.
18 Ibid., 35.
19 Ibid., 148–9.
20 Moloney, 116.
21 Arnot, 122.
22 Moloney, 180. Slade citing Stairs diary, 133.
23 Moloney, 186.
24 Ibid.
25 Ibid., 193.
26 Ibid., 193–4.
27 Emerson, *Leopold*, 154.

CHAPTER 23: THE FLAG FOLLOWS THE CROSS
Head of Chapter: See note 7.
1 Perham, *Lugard*, I, 224.
2 Mackenzie to Lugard, 10 Aug 1891. Lugard's diary, 25 Dec 1891, *Diary*, II, 469–75.
3 Lugard's diary, 18 Dec 1891, *Diary*, II, 27–8.
4 Lugard's diary, 18–19 Dec 1891, *Diary*, II, 27–9.
5 Text of treaty in C 6555/16–17.
6 Ibid.
7 R. Walker, 1, 2 Feb 1891. CMS Papers cited Perham, *Lugard*, I, 232.

8 G. Leblond, *Le Père Auguste Achte* (Alger, 1912), 125. Perham, 233.
9 Ashe, *Chronicles*, 157.
10 Lugard diary, 13 Jan 1891, *Diary*, II, 115.
11 Lugard diary, 26 Feb 1891, *Diary*, II, 101.
12 Lugard diary, 8 Apr (31 Mar) 1891, *Diary*, II, 131.
13 Lugard diary, 17 Sep 1891, *Diary*, II, 332.
14 Lugard diary, 11 Sep ibid., 321.
15 Mackenzie to Lugard, 10 Aug 1891, *Diary*, II. 469–70.
16 Lugard diary, 25 Dec 1891, *Diary*, II, 475.
17 Ibid., 476.
18 Lugard, *East African Empire*, II, 290. Perham, 291.
19 Lugard, loc cit.
20 Lugard diary, 27 Jan 1892, *Diary*, III, 25.
21 Ibid., III, 26.
22 Lugard's report in C 6817.
23 Hirth, 14 Jul 1891, Lugard, *East African Empire*, II, 660–2.
24 Lugard to Hirth, Lugard, *East African Empire*, II, 332.
25 Perham, 298.
26 Lugard diary, 27 Jan, *Diary*, III, 31.
27 CMS *Intelligencer*, Jul 1892, p. 514.
28 Ibid.
29 Portal to Anderson, 12 Jun 1892, Portal Papers, RHL, cited Perham, 329.
30 Gladstone, 3 Mar 1892, *Parliamentary Debates*, (Hansard V, I, 1872).
31 Salisbury, 13 Jun 1892, *Parliamentary Debates*, IV, 5, 825.
32 C 6817.
33 Gladstone, *Gladstone to his Wife* (ed. T. Bassett, L. 1936), 257.
34 Algernon West, *Diaries*, 51.
35 Queen to Ponsonby, Ponsonby, *Autobiography*, 216.
36 Rhodes James, *Rosebery*, 250
37 Portal to Rosebery, 14 Sep 1892, QVL, III, II, 163–4.
38 Gardiner, *Harcourt*, II, 192.
39 West, 60–1.
40 Rhodes James, *Rosebery*, 266.
41 Ibid., 266.
42 Queen Victoria to Rosebery, 28 Sep 1982, QVL, III, II, 158.
43 Gladstone to Rosebery, 21 Sep 1892, BL 44549.
44 West, 60–1.
45 Rhodes James, *Rosebery*, 267.
46 *The Times*, 1 Oct 1892.
47 Harcourt to Gladstone, 3 Oct 1892, BL 44202.
48 Ibid.
49 Rosebery to Portal, 1, 9 Dec 1892. Portal Papers, RHL.

CHAPTER 24: AN IVORY WAR
Head of Chapter: Conrad, *Heart of Darkness*, 1902 (p'back edn 1989), 36.
1 Ceulemans, *La Question Arabe*, 330.
2 Biographie Belge Coloniale, I, 311–25.

3 *Mouvement Géographique*, 1892, p. 103. Ceulemans, 344.
4 Lippens to Tobback, 27 Nov 1891, Cornet, 156-7.
5 Cornet, 158-60.
6 Lippens to Dhanis, 6 Oct 1892, Cornet, 161.
7 Ceulemans, 351.
8 S. Hinde, *Fall of the Congo Arabs*, 120-1.
9 Ceulemans, 353.
10 Hinde quoted Cornet, 164-5.
11 Michaux, *Carnet de Campagne*, 176-8.
12 Ibid., 179-80.
13 Dhanis, 27 Oct 1892, Cornet, 166.
14 Ibid.
15 R. Jones, *Emin Pasha*, 393-4. R. Mohun, *Century Magazine*, Feb 1895, pp. 591-8.
16 Hinde, 147.
17 Slade, *Leopold's Congo*, 115, citing Lémery Papers, AMAA.
18 Michaux, 184-5.
19 Hinde, 184.
20 Portal's report, C 7303. Perham, *Lugard I*, 447-57.

CHAPTER 25: BLANK TREATY FORMS ON THE NIGER
Head of Chapter: See note 31.
1 A. Heggay, *The African Policies of Gabriel Hanotaux*.
2 Sanderson, *Upper Nile*, 188.
3 Hertslet, *Map of Africa by Treaty*, II, 229 (p. 738-9).
4 Phipps to Anderson, 8 Mar 1894, FO, 27/3184. Sanderson, *Upper Nile*, 196.
5 Ward in *L'Intransigéant*, 5 May 1893. Flint, *Goldie*, 176.
6 Ibid.
7 Phipps to Rosebery, 28 Jun 1893, FO, 27/3134. Flint, *Goldie*, 177.
8 Sanderson, *Upper Nile*, 143.
9 Monteil, *Souvenirs Vécus*, etc. (Paris 1924), 65-8. Sanderson, *Upper Nile*, 144.
10 Etienne, *Journal de Débats*, etc., 7 Jun 1894.
11 Footnote by Hanotaux, 12 July 1894, DDF, X, 1277. Sanderson, *Upper Nile*, 188-9.
12 Sanderson, *Upper Nile*, 192-4.
13 Phipps to Anderson, 6 Oct 1894, FO, 27/3188. Sanderson, *Upper Nile*, 197.
14 Anderson to Kimberley, 16 Oct 1894, FO, 27/3209. Sanderson, *Upper Nile*, 201.
15 Lugard diary, 27 Aug 1894, *Diary*, IV, 78.
16 Goldie to Lugard, 24 Apr 1894, Perham, *Lugard*, I, 490.
17 Lugard diary, 1 Sep 1894, *Diary*, IV, 83.
18 Goldie to Lugard, 24 Jul 1894, *Diary*, IV, 59.
19 Lugard diary, 3 Sep 1894, *Diary*, IV, 86.
20 Ibid., IV, 87.
21 Lugard diary, 5, 11 Sep 1894, *Diary*, IV, 89, 102.
22 Lugard diary, 11, 17, 19, Sep 1894, *Diary*, IV, 102, 205-6, 107.

23 Text in Lugard *Diary*, IV, 186.
24 Lugard diary, 21 Jan 1894, *Diary*, IV, 288.
25 Lugard diary, 23 Jan 1894, *Diary*, IV, 289.
26 Lugard diary, 25 Jan 1894, *Diary*, IV, 290.
27 Goldie to Hill, 1 Feb 1895, FO, 83/1374. Flint, *Goldie*, 204.
28 Macdonald to FO, 4 Feb 1895, FO, 2/83. Flint, *Goldie*, 203.
29 King Koko to Macdonald, 4 Feb 1895, FO, 2/83. Flint, *Goldie*, 201.
30 Goldie to Kimberley 8 Feb 1895, FO, 83/1374. Flint, *Goldie*, 204.
31 Koko and chiefs of Brass to Prince of Wales, 28 Jun 1895, FO, 83/1380. Flint, *Goldie*, 209.
32 Rosebery's speech.
33 Grey, 28 Mar 1895, *Hansard*, 4th series, XXXII, p. 406.
34 Marchand memo, 10 Nov 1895, DDF, XII, no. 192.
35 Salisbury to Cromer, 13 Mar 1896, Zetland, *Cromer*, 223.

CHAPTER 26: A LION'S SHARE
Head of Chapter: Michel, *Vers Fachoda*, 14.
1 C 4103. Gabre-Sellassie, *Yohannes IV of Ethiopia* (Oxford 1975), 135-9.
2 Marcus, *Menelik*, 114. Rubenson, *Ethiopian Independence*, 385-6. Hertslet, V, II (p. 454).
3 Keller, *Alfred Ilg: Sein Leben und Sein Wirken* (Leipzig 1918), 84. C. Prouty, *Taytu*, 133-4.
4 Prouty, 133-4.
5 R. Pankhurst in *Ethiopian Observer*, 1 Dec 1957, 347.
6 Crispi to Baratieri, 25 Dec 1896, Italian Green Books, XXIII (no. 260) cited Marcus, 170. Berkeley, *Adowa*, 256.
7 Berkeley, 258.
8 Ibid., 159.
9 Guebre-Selassie, *Chronique* II, 436-7.
10 Ibid, II, 440.
11 Ibid, II, 440.
12 Ibid, II, 441.
13 Baratieri, *Mémoires*.
14 Ibid.
15 Ibid.
16 Berkeley, 335.
17 Ibid., 339.
18 Baratieri.
19 Berkeley, 367-8.
20 Guebre-Selassie, Prouty, 157.
21 See Battaglia, *Prima Guerra*.

CHAPTER 27: RHODES, RAIDERS AND REBELS
Head of Chapter: See note 12.
1 Salisbury to Selborne, 30 June 1895, Box 5/31, Selborne Papers, Bodleian, Oxford.
2 Garvin, *Chamberlain*, III, 177-95.
3 Flora Lugard quoted Garvin, III, 11.
4 *Daily Chronicle*, 27 Nov 1895.
5 Mrs Chamberlain 15 Nov 1895, Garvin, III, 28.
6 Garvin, III, 89.

7 C7933 (no. 7) p. 4.
8 Luke, XIV, 31, quoted Colvin, *Jameson*, I, 259.
9 Jameson quoted Wrey, Colvin, I, 260.
10 Ripon minute 26 Aug 1895, CO, 417/99/15804. Keppel-Jones, *Rhodesia*, 248.
11 Glass, *Matabele War*, Ch. 20. Keppel-Jones, 279.
12 Interviews cited Keppel-Jones, 285.
13 O. Ransford, *Bulawayo*, 67–8. Keppel-Jones, 360.
14 Blake.
15 Marshall Hole, *Old Rhodesian Days*, 103.
16 Selous, *Sunshine and Storm*, 12.
17 Ibid., 24.
18 Ibid., 30.
19 T. Ranger, *Revolt*, 142–55. Keppel-Jones, 435–9.
20 Baden-Powell, 12, 98.
21 Garvin, III, 110. J. van der Poel, *Raid*, 30.
22 Garvin, III, 111. J. van der Poel, 49.

CHAPTER 28: CALLING HANOTAUX'S BLUFF
Head of Chapter: Chamberlain to Selborne, 29 Sep 1897, to Salisbury 1 Dec 1897, Garvin, III, 211–13.
1 Lee, *King Edward VII*, I, 726. Queen's Journal, 10 Jan 1896, QVL, III, III, 17–18.
2 Salisbury to the Queen, 12 Jan 1896, QVL, III, III, 20.
3 Queen to Salisbury, 14 Jan 1896, QVL, III, III, 20.
4 Chamberlain, 21 Jan 1896 in London quoting (and misquoting) George Foster's speech in the Canadian Commons, *The Times*, 22 Jan 1896. G. Howard, *Splendid Isolation* (1967), 14–15.
5 Salisbury to the Queen, 12 Jan 1896, QVL, III, III, 21.
6 Salisbury to Bigge, 5, 7 Dec 1895, QVL, III, II, 577–9.
7 The Queen to Bigge, 21 Jan 1896, QVL, III, III.
8 Salisbury to Queen, 11 Jan 1896, cited Hargreaves in *Cambridge Historical Journal* (1953), 69–74.
9 Chamberlain, 22 Aug 1895, Hansard 4th Series, XXX, VI, 641–2. Garvin, III, 19–21.
10 Salisbury to Bigge, 2 Sep 1896, QVL, III, III, 72–3.
11 G. Hanotaux, *Fachoda*, 64, foll.
12 Marchand, 10 Nov 1895, DDF, XII, no. 192. Sanderson *Upper Nile*, 273–4.
13 Marchand's and Liotard's instructions, 24 Feb 1896, DDF, XII, no. 312. Sanderson, *Upper Nile*, 278.
14 Liotard's instructions for Marchand, 23 Jun 1896, DDK, XII, no. 411. Hanotaux, 108–9.
15 Baratier, *Fachoda*, 133. Mangin, *Revue des Deux Mondes*, 1931, p. 277.
16 Interview with Shishkin, 14 Oct 1896, DDF, XII, no. 474. Sanderson, *Upper Nile*, 293.
17 Carter to Ripon, 24 Nov. 1894, FO, 83/1374. Flint, *Goldie*, 236.

18 FO, 83/1444. Flint, *Goldie*, 239.
19 Treaty with Nupe, 5 Feb 1897, FO, 2/167, no. 238. Flint, *Goldie*, 254–5.
20 Treaty with Ilorin, 18 Feb 1897, FO, 2/167, no. 239.
21 Bretonnet to *Goldie*, 23 Feb 1897, FO, 27/3368. Flint, *Goldie*, 257.
22 Note 16 Mar 1897, DDF, XIII, no. 16.
23 Chamberlain to Salisbury, 1 Dec 1897, Garvin, III, 213.
24 Chamberlain to Selborne, 1 Dec 1897, Garvin, III, 213.
25 Chamberlain to Salisbury, 22 Sep 1897, FO, 83/1533.
26 Lugard diary, 23 Oct 1897, Perham, *Lugard*, I, 620.
27 Lugard diary, 13 Mar 1898, *Diary*, IV, 332.
28 Lugard diary, ibid., IV, 353.
29 J. Willcocks, *From Kumasi*, 168.
30 Lugard diary, 14, 20 Apr 1898, *Diary*, IV, 382, 392.
31 Willcocks, 190–2.
32 Willcocks, 198.
33 Salisbury to Chamberlain, 3 Jun 1898, Garvin, III, 220.

CHAPTER 29: THE RACE TO THE MIDDLE OF NOWHERE
Head of Chapter: See note 15.
1 Ranieri, ARSC (1959) p. 105, cited Emerson, 197.
2 Michel, *Vers Fachoda*, 137.
3 Ibid., 162, 208.
4 Ibid., 237–8.
5 Ibid., 241.
6 Ibid., 242.
7 Ibid., 242.
8 Ibid., 244.
9 Menelik to Bonchamps, 12 Oct 1897, Michel, 251.
10 Menelik to Khalifa, 17 Jul 1896, cited Sanderson, *Upper Nile*, 297.
11 Menelik to Khalifa, Dec 1897, ibid.
12 Michel, 455.
13 Baratier, *Fachoda*.
14 Emily diary, 4 Jun 1898, *Mission Marchand*, 89.
15 Marchand to P. Bordarie, Mar 1898, Delbecque, *Marchand*, 113.
16 Emily, 89–110. Baratier, *Fachoda*, 43–54.
17 Emily, 123.
18 Ibid., 134.
19 Ibid., 144.
20 Ibid.
21 C. Neufeld, *A Prisoner of the Khaleefa*, 265.

CHAPTER 30: THE MAHDI'S TOMB
Head of Chapter: F. Maurice, *Rawlinson*, 42.
1 Churchill to Hamilton, 16 Sep 1898, R. Churchill, *Churchill*, (L. 1968), II, 416.
2 W. Churchill, *River War*, II, 87.
3 Ibid., II, 98.

4 F. Maurice, *Rawlinson*, 33.
5 Ibid., 5.
6 Repington, *Vestigia*, 166.
7 Ibid., 126.
8 Sandes, 262.
9 Ibid., 264.
10 W. Churchill, *River War*, II, 142.
11 Ibid., 143, 138.
12 Sandes, 268.
13 W. Churchill, *River War*, II, 162.
14 Repington, 170. Queen to Kitchener, 5 Sep 1898. QVL, III, III, 274.
15 Salisbury cited D. Bates, *Fashoda*, 140.
16 Delbecque, *Marchand*, 136–9 citing Baratier in *Correspondent*, 963.
17 Kitchener's report, 21 Sep 1898 in C 9055, p. 892–4.
18 Marchand to Forain in *Figaro*, 20 Nov 1898.
20 Ibid.
21 C. Andrew, *Delcassé*, 64, quoting A. France, *L'Isle de Pingouins* (Paris 1964), 385.
22 Delcassé to his wife, 27 July 1893, Delcassé Papers, quoted Andrew, 33.
23 Monson to Salisbury, 8 Sep 1898, FO, 78/5050. Sanderson, *Upper Nile*, 276.
24 Monson to Salisbury 27, 28 Sep 1898, BD, I, 169–71 (no. 196, 198).
25 Delcassé diary quoted Maurois, *King Edward* etc. (L 1933) p. 72.
26 Ibid., p. 88 (French edn).
27 Garvin, III, 232 translating *Grosse Politik* XIV, 2nd part, 388.
28 Queen Victoria to Salisbury, 30 Oct 1898, QVL, III, III, 305.
29 Marchand quoted Bates, 161.
30 Baratier, 206–13. Sanderson, 353.
31 Emily, 210.
32 Ibid., 222.
33 Ibid.

CHAPTER 31: MILNER'S WAR
Head of Chapter: Milner to Roberts, 6 Jun 1900, quoted T. Pakenham, *The Boer War*.
1 A. Milner to Chamberlain, C 3945. Headlam, *Milner Papers*, I, 349–53, Chamberlain, 26 Aug 1899.
2 Garvin, III, 438–9.
3 G. Wyndham to A. Balfour, 8 Aug 1899, Balfour Papers, BL, 49803.
4 Chamberlain to Milner, 2 Sep 1899, Garvin, III, 457.
5 Salisbury to Chamberlain, 16 Aug 1899, Chamberlain Papers, Birmingham University, JC/5/67/116.
6 Garvin, III, 465.
7 Hicks Beach, *Life*, 106.
8 Salisbury to Lansdowne, 30 Aug 1899, Newton, *Lansdowne*, 157.
9 Wolseley to his wife, 6 Sep, 13 Jul, 24 Jun 1899, Wolseley Papers, Hove, Sussex, 28/50, 40, 30.
10 *Military Notes on the Dutch Republics*

(confidential publication of War Office), 49–52. See Pakenham, *The Boer War*, 77.
11 Balfour, 2 Dec 1899, Balfour Papers BL, 49853/138–43. Margot Asquith, *Autobiography* (London 1962), 227.
12 Milner to Roberts, 6 Jun 1900, Roberts Papers, 45, National Army Museum.
13 Milner to Fiddes, 23 Dec 1898, Headlam, I, 299–300.
14 Milner to Fiddes, 3 Jan 1899, Milner Papers Bodleian, Oxford, Box 45 (SA 37).
15 Gell to Milner, 2 Jun (1899), Gell Papers Hopton Hall, Derbyshire, 532. See Pakenham, *Boer War*, 89, note 31.
16 Headlam, *Milner Papers*, I, 407, (presumably from Milner's notes; no ref. in C 9404).
17 Smuts Papers, I, 323.
18 Amery, *Times History of the War*, II, 142.
19 *The Times, Daily Telegraph, Globe*, 10 Oct 1899.
20 Lansdowne to Chamberlain, 10 Oct 1899, Chamberlain Papers, Birmingham University, JD/5/5.
21 Garvin, III, 471–2.
22 *The Times*, 9, 10 Oct 1899.
23 *The Times, Daily News*, 16 Oct 1899.
24 Buller to Sir A. Bigge, 4 Jan 1900, Bigge Papers (private collection).
25 See note 23. Information from Charles Monteith.
26 Cecil, *Salisbury*, IV, 191.
27 W. Churchill, *Ladysmith*, 308.
28 Roberts to Queen, 15 Mar 1900, Roberts Papers War Office Library, Home and Overseas Corr., I, 84.
29 Pakenham, *Boer War*, 415 (from tape of Mafeking veteran).
30 Ibid., 493, 537.
31 Ibid., 493/4.
32 *Hansard*, 1 Mar 1901, XC.
33 J. Wilson, CB (1973), 348.
34 *The Times*, 15 Jun 1900. J. Wilson, 349.
35 *Hansard*, 17 Jun 1901, XCV, 573–83.
36 Headlam, *Milner Papers*, II, 350–1. Pakenham, *Boer War*, 563–5.
37 De Wet, *Three Years War*, 426, 486–90. Pakenham, *Boer War*, 565–9.
38 Pakenham, *Boer War*, 118–19.

CHAPTER 32: THE SEVERED HANDS
Head of Chapter: See note 18.
1 Emerson, 270.
2 *The Times*, 16 May 1902.
3 Slade, *English Speaking Missions*, 247–9.
4 P. Van Zuylen *L'Echiquier Congolais* etc (Brussels 1959).
5 Leopold to Liebrechts, 17, 31 Jan 1899, Van Eetvelde Papers, Archives Générales du Royaume, Brussels.
6 Cline, *Morel*, 9, and K. D. Nwarah's intro to Morel's *Affairs of West Africa* (2nd edn 1968), IX–X.

7 *Pall Mall Gazette*, 19 Jul 1897. Cline, 24.
8 Louis and Stengers, *Congo Reform*, 42.
9 Morel to John Holt, 14 Aug 1906, Holt Papers, Box 18/3, RHL.
10 Louis and Stengers, *Congo Reform*.
11 Lansdowne to Dilke, 13 Mar 1902, Dilke Papers, BL, 43917.
12 Louis and Stengers, *Congo Reform*, 123.
13 Ibid., 129.
14 Hansard 4th series, CXXII, 20 May 1903.
15 F. Ponsonby, *Three Reigns*, 170. Rolo, *Entente*, 165–6.
16 Casement note in National Library of Ireland 5459, cited Reid, *The Lives of Roger Casement*, (L. 1976), 8.
17 Conrad quoted Reid, *Casement*, 14.
18 Casement report, Cd 1933, 60–2.
19 Casement diary, *Diary*, 149, 153.
20 Casement report, Cd 1933.
21 Casement to Lansdowne, Sep 1903, FO 10.
22 Reid, 51.
23 Casement, *Diary*, 183.
24 Ibid.
25 Louis and Stengers, *Congo Reform*, 160–1.

CHAPTER 33: THE KAISER'S FIRST WAR
Head of Chapter: H. Bley, *German South West Africa*.
1 Bülow in Reichstag 18 Jan 1904, *The Times*, 19 Jan 1904.
2 Leutwein, *Elf Jähre*, 30. Bley, *South-West Africa*, 73–145.
3 Drechsler, *Let us Die*, 27.
4 Ibid., 52.
5 Ibid., 168, note 13.
6 Petition to Colonial Dept., 21 Jul 1900, cited Bley, 97.
7 Leutwein, 4 Jul 1896 and Nov 1898 quoted Bley, 68–9.
8 Maharero to Witbooi, 11 Jan 1904 printed Drechsler, Ch. 3, notes 52, 53.
9 Drechsler.
10 Ibid., 151.
11 Bley, 163–4 quoting Rust, *Krieg and Frieden* (Berlin 1905), 385.
12 Schlieffen to Bülow, 23 Nov 1904, quoted Dreschler, 163.
13 Bülow to Wilhelm II, 24 Nov 1904, ibid., 164.
14 General Staff to Trotha, 12 Dec 1904, ibid., 164–5.
15 Bridgman, *The Revolt of the Hereros* (Berkeley 1968), 134–5.
16 Bridgman, 153.
17 G. Frenssen (M. Ward tr.) *Peter Moor* (L. 1914), 192.

CHAPTER 34: 'MAJI-MAJI!'
Head of Chapter: See note 5.
1 Götzen, *Aufstand*, 45–70. Iliffe, *Tanganyika*, 170.
2 Götzen, 54–6.

3 Götzen, 26 Aug 1905, quoted Iliffe. *Tanganyika*, 176. Götzen, *Aufstand*, 64–5.
4 P. M. Libaba cited Iliffe, *Tanganyika*, 174.
5 Gwassa and Iliffe, *Maji-Maji*.
6 Kwiro mission diary, 31 Aug 1905, Kwiro archives, quoted. Gwassa and Iliffe, *Maji-Maji*.
7 Kombo Ngalipa cited Iliffe, *Tanganyika*, 178.
8 Wangenheim to Götzen, 22 Oct 1905, Götzen, 149.
9 Gwassa, *Outbreak*, 389.
10 Lewin report on German administration of colonies, RCWS library (case A, 67).
11 Ibid., 84.
12 Ibid.
13 Peters, *New Light on Darkest Africa*, 139–41.
14 Lewin, loc cit.
15 Lewin, Appendix I, p. 11–12.

CHAPTER 35: REDEEMING THE FRENCH CONGO
Head of Chapter: See note 12.
1 Paris *Chef de Concessions* to Gentil, 25 Mar 1905, quoted J. Autin, *Brazza*, 242.
2 Witte, *Augouard*, 315. West, *Brazza*, 177.
3 Ibid., 315–16.
4 Ibid., 317–18.
5 Challaye, *Congo Français*, 35.
6 Witte, 344, 326.
7 Ibid., 338.
8 Challaye.
9 Ibid.
10 Ibid.
11 Ibid., 95–7.
12 Ibid., 146–7.
13 Ibid., 139.
14 Ibid.
15 Chavannes, *Congo Français*, 384–91.
16 A. Gide in *Revue de Paris*, 15 Oct 1927, quoted V. Thompson & R. Adloff, *The Emerging States of Equatorial Africa* (Stanford 1960), 17–18.

CHAPTER 36: RESTORING BRITAIN'S 'OLD IDEALS'
Head of Chapter: See note 19.
1 Headline in *West Africa Mail*, 25 May 1904.
2 Casement to Morel, 18 Nov 1905, quoted Louis and Stengers, *Congo Reform*, 187.
3 Morel to Dilke, 22 Jan 1903, quoted Cline, 53.
4 Casement to Morel, 14 Dec 1905, quoted Louis and Stengers, *Congo Reform*, 188.
5 Bryce to Smith, 12 Apr 1901, H. A. L. Fisher, *James Bryce*, (L. 1927), I, 317.
6 C–B, *Speeches*, 188, quoted Hyam, *Elgin*, 50.
7 Hansard, 4th series, CLX 5 Jul 1906.
8 See Hyam, 61–93.
9 Hansard 4th series, CL, II, 19 Feb 1906.
10 Churchill Hansard, CLIV 21 Mar 1906, quoted A. M. Gollin, *Proconsul in Politics*, (1964), 70–2.
11 Balfour quoted Hyam, 84–5.
12 Churchill, *Hansard*, CLIV, 21 Mar 1906.

13 See Hyam, 88.
14 Churchill quoted Hyam, 240–1.
15 Churchill quoted Marks *Rebellion*, 244.
16 Churchill quoted Hyam, 215.
17 Lugard to his brother Edward, 11 May 1903, quoted Perham, *Lugard II*, 104–5.
18 Lugard, 3 Jan 1906, Cd 3620.
19 Churchill minute, 23 Jan 1906, CO 446/52/2224, Hyam, 208.
20 Lugard to his wife, 9 Mar 1906, quoted Perham, *Lugard II*, 260.
21 Churchill minute, 14 Mar 1906, CO 446/53, quoted Perham, *Lugard II*, 271.
22 Flora Lugard to her husband, 6 May 1906, quoted Perham, *Lugard* II, 276–7.
23 Churchill, CO, 446.
24 Elgin quoted Hyam, 349.
25 Churchill, *My African Journey*, 2, 30.
26 Elgin, CO, 533/28/15409, quoted Hyam, 411.
27 Churchill quoted Hyam, 412.
28 Churchill, *My African Journey*, 61.
29 Ibid.
30 Leopold, 3 Jun 1906, quoted A. Stenmans, *La reprise du Congo par la Belgique* (Brussels 1949), p. 333.

CHAPTER 37: LEOPOLD'S LAST THROW
Head of Chapter: Conrad to Casement, 21 Dec 1903, *Casement Papers*, NLI.
1 Stinglhammer, G. and Dresse, P., *Leopold II au Travail* (Brussels 1945), 256.

2 Duke of Brabant to Frere-Orban, 27 Sep 1860, AGR, Frere-Orban Papers, no. 356.
3 T. Roosevelt, *Roosevelt Letters* (ed. E. E. Morrison, Harvard 1954), V, 439.
4 Morel to Holt (c. Oct 1904) Box 18/2, RHL.
5 T. Roosevelt, *Letters*.
6 Morel to Holt (c. Oct 1904) Box 18/2.
7 Moucheur to Favereau, 11 Dec 1906, quoted Cookey, *Congo*, 176.
8 P. Hymans reported *The Times*, 29 Nov 1906.
9 Smet de Naeyer quoted Cookey, *Congo*, 179.
10 Morel to Monkswell, 11 Jan 1907, RHL.
11 Morel to Grey (copy), 28 Dec 1906, Holt Papers Box 1813, RHL.
12 Holt to Morel, 27 May 1907, Morel Papers LSE, f 8.
13 See note 11.
14 Smith's report, Dec 1907, FO, 367/115 (copy).
15 Hardinge to Grey, 23 Jan 1908, FO, 367/115.
16 *The Times*, 23 Dec 1908.
17 Memo and Grey's minute, 21 May 1909, FO, 376/165.
18 J. C. Smuts, *Jan Christian Smuts* (L. 1952), 99.
19 E. Walker, *Schreiner*, 316–17.
20 Milner to Asquith, 18 Nov 1897, Asquith Papers, Dep. 9 (private collection).
21 Morel, *Great Britain and the Congo*, 6.
22 Lichtervelde, *Leopold II*, 360

Index

Now you can order superb titles directly from Abacus

☐ The Boer War	Thomas Pakenham	£12.99
☐ The Year of Liberty	Thomas Pakenham	£10.99
☐ Age of Extremes	Eric Hobsbawm	£12.99
☐ The Rise and Fall of the British Empire	Lawrence James	£12.99
☐ Long Walk to Freedom	Nelson Mandela	£12.99

Please allow for postage and packing: **Free UK delivery.**
Europe; add 25% of retail price; Rest of World; 45% of retail price.

To order any of the above or any other Abacus titles, please call our credit card orderline or fill in this coupon and send/fax it to:

Abacus, P.O. Box 121, Kettering, Northants NN14 4ZQ
Tel: 01832 737527   Fax: 01832 733076
Email: aspenhouse@FSBDial.co.uk

☐ I enclose a UK bank cheque made payable to Abacus for £ ....

☐ Please charge £.............. to my Access, Visa, Delta, Switch Card No.

☐☐☐☐☐☐☐☐☐☐☐☐☐☐☐☐☐☐☐

Expiry Date ☐☐☐☐   Switch Issue No. ☐☐

NAME (Block letters please) ....

ADDRESS ....

....

....

Postcode ....Telephone ....

Signature ....

Please allow 28 days for delivery within the UK. Offer subject to price and availability.

Please do not send any further mailings from companies carefully selected by Abacus ☐

THE BOER WAR

Thomas Pakenham

The war declared by the Boers on 11 October 1899 gave the British, as Kipling said, 'no end of a lesson'. It proved to be the longest, the costliest, the bloodiest and the most humiliating campaign that Britain fought between 1815 and 1914.

Thomas Pakenham has written the first full-scale history of the war since 1910. His narrative is based on first-hand and largely unpublished sources ranging from the private papers of the leading protagonists to the recollections of survivors from both sides. Out of this historical gold-mine, the author has constructed a narrative as vivid and fast-moving as a novel, and a history that in scholarship, breadth and impact will endure for many years.

'Not only a magnum opus, it is a conclusive work . . . Enjoyable as well as massively impressive'
C. P. Snow, Financial Times

'A consummate masterpiece'
Sunday Telegraph

'Hypnotically readable . . . A tremendous feat of research . . . This is grand-scale history with heroes and villains . . . a hot, impassioned work, and I recommend it wholeheartedly'
Newsweek

'Both a richly researched book and one that makes delightfully easy reading . . . deserves a huge success'
TLS